EXAMPLES & EXPLANATIONS

Family Law

EDITORIAL ADVISORS

EXAMPLES & EXPLANATIONS

Family Law

Fourth Edition

Robert E. Oliphant
Emeritus Professor of Law
William Mitchell College of Law

Nancy Ver Steegh
Associate Dean for Academic Programs
Justice Helen M. Meyer Professor of Child Protection Law
William Mitchell College of Law

Published by Wolters Kluwer Law & Business in New York.

Wolters Kluwer Law & Business serves customers worldwide with CCH, Aspen Publishers, and Kluwer Law International products. (www.wolterskluwerlb.com)

To contact Customer Service, e-mail customer.service@wolterskluwer.com, call 1-800-234-1660, fax 1-800-901-9075, or mail correspondence to:

Wolters Kluwer Law & Business
Attn: Order Department
PO Box 990
Frederick, MD 21705

Printed in the United States of America.

1 2 3 4 5 6 7 8 9 0

ISBN 978-1-4548-1552-5

Library of Congress Cataloging-in-Publication Data

Oliphant, Robert E., 1938-
Family law / Robert E. Oliphant, Emeritus Professor of Law, William Mitchell College of Law; Nancy Ver Steegh, Associate Professor of Law, William Mitchell College of Law. — Fourth edition.
pages cm
Includes bibliographical references and index.
ISBN 978-1-4548-1552-5 (perfectbound : alk. paper)
1. Domestic relations — United States — Outlines, syllabi, etc. I. Ver Steegh, Nancy, 1953- II. Title.

KF505.Z9O43 2013
346.7301'5 — dc23

2012047761

About Wolters Kluwer Law & Business

Wolters Kluwer Law & Business is a leading global provider of intelligent information and digital solutions for legal and business professionals in key specialty areas, and respected educational resources for professors and law students. Wolters Kluwer Law & Business connects legal and business professionals as well as those in the education market with timely, specialized authoritative content and information-enabled solutions to support success through productivity, accuracy and mobility.

Serving customers worldwide, Wolters Kluwer Law & Business products include those under the Aspen Publishers, CCH, Kluwer Law International, Loislaw, Best Case, ftwilliam.com and MediRegs family of products.

CCH products have been a trusted resource since 1913, and are highly regarded resources for legal, securities, antitrust and trade regulation, government contracting, banking, pension, payroll, employment and labor, and healthcare reimbursement and compliance professionals.

Aspen Publishers products provide essential information to attorneys, business professionals and law students. Written by preeminent authorities, the product line offers analytical and practical information in a range of specialty practice areas from securities law and intellectual property to mergers and acquisitions and pension/benefits. Aspen's trusted legal education resources provide professors and students with high-quality, up-to-date and effective resources for successful instruction and study in all areas of the law.

Kluwer Law International products provide the global business community with reliable international legal information in English. Legal practitioners, corporate counsel and business executives around the world rely on Kluwer Law journals, looseleafs, books, and electronic products for comprehensive information in many areas of international legal practice.

Loislaw is a comprehensive online legal research product providing legal content to law firm practitioners of various specializations. Loislaw provides attorneys with the ability to quickly and efficiently find the necessary legal information they need, when and where they need it, by facilitating access to primary law as well as state-specific law, records, forms and treatises.

Best Case Solutions is the leading bankruptcy software product to the bankruptcy industry. It provides software and workflow tools to flawlessly streamline petition preparation and the electronic filing process, while timely incorporating ever-changing court requirements.

ftwilliam.com offers employee benefits professionals the highest quality plan documents (retirement, welfare and non-qualified) and government forms (5500/PBGC, 1099 and IRS) software at highly competitive prices.

MediRegs products provide integrated health care compliance content and software solutions for professionals in healthcare, higher education and life sciences, including professionals in accounting, law and consulting.

Wolters Kluwer Law & Business, a division of Wolters Kluwer, is headquartered in New York. Wolters Kluwer is a market-leading global information services company focused on professionals.

Summary of Contents

Contents		*ix*
Preface		*xxix*
Acknowledgments		*xxxi*
Chapter 1	A History of Marriage and Divorce	1
Chapter 2	Marriage Contracts — Requirements and Restrictions	17
Chapter 3	Annulment of Marriage	93
Chapter 4	Who May Divorce? Restrictions and Requirements	129
Chapter 5	Child Custody and Parenting Plans	161
Chapter 6	Modifying Custody	189
Chapter 7	Interstate Custody Struggles: The Uniform Child Custody Jurisdiction Enforcement Act and the Parental Kidnapping Prevention Act — History, Restrictions, and Requirements	239
Chapter 8	Parenting Time and Visitation	273
Chapter 9	Establishing Child Support	295
Chapter 10	Child Support Modification and Enforcement	321
Chapter 11	Establishing Alimony	343
Chapter 12	Modification of Alimony	361
Chapter 13	Dividing the Marital Estate upon Divorce	377
Chapter 14	Premarital (Antenuptial or Prenuptial) Contracts — History, Requirements, and Restrictions	419
Chapter 15	Cohabitation and Contract Principles	457
Chapter 16	Determining Parentage	493
Chapter 17	Adoption	517
Chapter 18	Assisted Reproduction — History, Restrictions, and Requirements	541
Chapter 19	Domestic Violence	575
Chapter 20	Neglect, Dependency, Child Abuse, and Termination of Parental Rights	595

Chapter 21 Abortion 623
Chapter 22 Mediation, Collaborative Law, Parenting Coordination, and Arbitration 653
Chapter 23 Professional Responsibility 671
Chapter 24 Jurisdiction 683

Table of Cases 737
Index 767

Contents

Preface *xxix*
Acknowledgments *xxxi*

Chapter 1 A History of Marriage and Divorce **1**

1.1. Introduction 1
1.2. The Roman and Early English Views of Marriage 2
1.3. Reformation, Divorce, and Blackstone 3
1.4. Parliamentary Divorce 3
1.5. Colonial American Model of Marriage and Divorce 4
1.6. Nineteenth-Century Patriarchic Model of Marriage 6
1.7. The Family Law Revolution 10
1.8. The Changing Role of the Federal Government in Marriage 12
1.9. Same-Sex marriage 13
1.10. The Debate Concerning the Present Value of Marriage 14

Chapter 2 Marriage Contracts — Requirements and Restrictions **17**

2.1. Introduction 17
2.2. How Marriage Contracts Differ from Ordinary Contracts 18

Marriage Requirements 18

2.3. State of Mind to Marry: Capacity — Generally 18
2.4. Capacity — Guardian's Consent 19
2.5. Capacity — Age Restrictions 20
2.6. Form of Marriage — Ministerial Act 21
2.7. Marriage License 21
2.8. Solemnizing a Marriage 22
2.9. Void/Voidable Distinction 23
2.10. Premarital Medical Testing 28
2.11. Premarital Counseling and Education 30

Types of Marriage 31

2.12. Common Law Marriage 31

2.13. Putative Marriage Doctrine 35
Forms of Marriage 48
2.14. Proxy Marriage 48
2.15. Confidential Marriage 50
2.16. Tribal Marriages 51
2.17. Covenant Marriage 51
Historic Marriage Restrictions 52
2.18. Epilepsy 52
2.19. Anti-Miscegenation Statutes 53
2.20. Poverty 55
2.21. Prisoners 56
Existing Marriage Restrictions 58
2.22. Polygamy 58
2.23. Bigamy 59
2.24. Sham Marriages — Immigration Fraud 60
2.25. Consanguinity 61
2.26. Affinity 62
2.27. Adopted Children Marrying Each Other 62
2.28. Recognizing Another State's Marriage; *Lex Loci* and Full Faith and Credit 63
Same-Sex Relationships 72
2.29. Religious Perspectives 72
2.30. Federal Defense of Marriage Act (DOMA) 74
2.31. *Bowers v. Hardwick* and *Lawrence v. Texas* 76
2.32. Civil Unions/Domestic Partners 77
Domestic Partners 79
2.33. Connecticut, Massachusetts, Iowa, Vermont, New Hampshire, New York, Washington, and the District of Columbia Allow Same-Sex Marriage 82
2.34. Out-of-State Recognition of Same-Sex Marriage 84
Transsexual Relationships 85
2.35. Recognizing Transsexual Relationships 85

Chapter 3 Annulment of Marriage 93

3.1. Introduction 93
3.2. Void/Voidable Distinction 95
3.3. Time Limitations 96
3.4. Standing 98
Retroactivity 102
3.5. Relation Back — Generally 102
3.6. Relation Back — Alimony 103
3.7. Relation Back — Uniform Marriage and Divorce Act 106
3.8. Relation Back — Enoch Arden Statute 106

Capacity 107
3.9. Mental Capacity 107
3.10. Age 107
3.11. Under the Influence of Drugs or Alcohol 111
3.12. Marriage Made in Jest 111
Fraud 111
3.13. Fraud—General Rule 111
3.14. Immigration Fraud—Sham Marriage 115
3.15. Fraud—False Pregnancy Claims 116
3.16. Fraud—Broken Religious Promises 117
Other 118
3.17. Duress 118
3.18. Impotence or Sterility 119
3.19. Sexual Preference Issues 119
Defenses 120
3.20. Continued Cohabitation 120
Support and Property Distribution 120
3.21. Support 120
Procedure 121
3.22. *In Rem* Proceeding 121
3.23. Criminal Prosecutions—Bigamy, Incest, Adultery 121

Chapter 4 Who May Divorce? Restrictions and Requirements 129

4.1. Introduction 129
4.2. History 129
Grounds for Divorce 133
4.3. Fault 133
4.4. Common Law Grounds for Divorce 133
4.5. Common Defenses to Divorce Actions 139
4.6. The Modern Divorce Reform Movement 146
4.7. Limited Divorce 150
4.8. Right to Jury Trial in Divorce Actions 151
4.9. Covenant Marriage and Divorce 152
4.10. Recognizing Same-Sex Couple Marriages When They End in Divorce 153
4.11. Divisible Divorce 155

Chapter 5 Child Custody and Parenting Plans 161

5.1. Introduction 161
The Impact of Divorce and Parental Separation 161
5.2. Effects of Divorce and Separation on Children 161

5.3. Divorce, Separation, and Parenting 162
5.4. Parenting Education 163
Defining Custodial Relationships 163
5.5. Overview 163
5.6. Legal Custody 164
5.7. Physical Custody 164
5.8. Joint Legal and Physical Custody 164
5.9. Parenting Plans 165
Presumptions 168
5.10. Overview 168
5.11. Historical Paternal Presumption 168
5.12. Historical Maternal Presumption 169
5.13. Historical Primary Caretaker Presumption 169
5.14. Historical and Contemporary Natural Parent Presumption 171
5.15. Contemporary Joint Legal and Physical Custody Presumptions 171
Model Acts 176
5.16. Uniform Marriage and Divorce Act 176
5.17. American Law Institute 176
Standards for Determining the Best Interests of the Child 177
5.18. Race 177
5.19. Religion 178
5.20. Disability 178
5.21. Child's Preference 178
5.22. Separating Siblings 180
5.23. Parental Conduct Not Affecting the Child: The Nexus Test 181
5.24. Gay and Lesbian Parents 181
5.25. Cohabitation 181
5.26. Careers 182
5.27. Cooperative Parent Provisions 182
5.28. Intimate Partner Violence 183
Processes and Professionals 187
5.29. Child Custody Evaluators 187
5.30. Guardians *ad Litem* 188
5.31. Dispute Resolution Processes 188

Chapter 6 Modifying Custody 189

6.1. Introduction 189
6.2. The State as a Third Party 190
6.3. Stability Is the Goal 190
Barriers to Modification Actions 191

6.4. *Res Judicata*; Presumption; Change in Circumstances 191
6.5. Moratorium 193
Procedure 195
6.6. Initial Pleadings Must Demonstrate Necessity of Evidentiary Hearing 195
6.7. Two-Step Process 196
6.8. Illustrative State Modification Standards 197
Typical Claims Triggering Modification Demands 205
6.9. Unwarranted Denial of Visitation 205
6.10. Failure to Pay Child Support 206
6.11. Integration into Noncustodial Parent's Home 207
6.12. Custodial Parent's Alleged Immoral Conduct 207
6.13. Poor Parenting/Discipline 209
6.14. Smoking 210
6.15. Endangerment 211
6.16. Modifying Parenting Plans 212
The Role of a Child's Preference for Change 213
6.17. Maturity 213
Sole Custodian Relocating to another Jurisdiction 218
6.18. Relocation and Constitutional Right to Travel 218
6.19. The Social Science Relocation Debate 220
6.20. Relocation Trends 222
6.21. Relocation Standards 223
6.22. Natural Parent Presumption 227
6.23. Active Military Service 228
Model Relocation Drafting Efforts 229
6.24. American Law Institute (ALI) 229
6.25. American Academy of Matrimonial Lawyers (AAML) 230
Relocating where Parents Share Joint Physical Custody 230
6.26. Overview 230

Chapter 7 Interstate Custody Struggles: The Uniform Child Custody Jurisdiction Enforcement Act and the Parental Kidnapping Prevention Act — History, Restrictions, and Requirements 239

7.1. Introduction 239
7.2. History 240
7.3. The Status Theory of Jurisdiction 242
7.4. First Interstate Jurisdiction Model Act — UCCJA 244

7.5.	UCCJA Failure Triggers Congressional Action — Parental Kidnapping Prevention Act (PKPA)	245
7.6.	Second Interstate Model Child Custody Jurisdiction Act — UCCJEA	248
7.7.	Native Americans — PKPA	254
7.8.	International Application of UCCJEA and Related Laws	255
7.9.	Is Canada a State for UCCJEA Purposes?	256

Chapter 8 Parenting Time and Visitation **273**

8.1.	Introduction	273
Model Acts		274
8.2.	Uniform Marriage and Divorce Act (UMDA): Reasonable Visitation	274
8.3.	American Law Institute (ALI)	275
Standards for Denying or Limiting Parenting Time		276
8.4.	Denial or Suspension of Parenting Time	276
8.5.	Restrictions on Parenting Time	276
8.6.	Child Abuse and Intimate Partner Violence	277
8.7.	Alcohol and Substance Abuse	277
8.8.	Child Abduction	278
8.9.	Cohabitation	278
8.10.	Parent Who Is Gay or Lesbian	278
8.11.	Religious Differences	278
Enforcement of Parenting Time		281
8.12.	Contempt and Modification of Custody	281
8.13.	Compensatory Parenting Time	282
8.14.	Withholding Child Support	282
8.15.	Wishes of the Child	282
Modification of Parenting Time		284
8.16.	UMDA Provisions	284
Visitation by a Third-Party		285
8.17.	Grandparents and Third-Party Visitation Statutes	285
8.18.	*Troxel v. Granville*	285
8.19.	Visitation with Stepparents	289
8.20.	Visitation with a Nonbiological Gay or Lesbian Co-Parent	290
8.21.	Parents by Estoppel and De Facto Parents	291

Chapter 9 Establishing Child Support **295**

9.1.	Introduction	295
History		295
9.2.	Elizabethan Poor Laws	295

9.3. Common Law 296
9.4. The Changing Legal Landscape 297
Role of the Federal Government 297
9.5. Child Support Traditionally a State Issue 297
9.6. Child Support and Establishment of Paternity Act of 1974 297
9.7. State Guidelines Mandated 298
9.8. Omnibus Budget Reconciliation Act of 1993 298
9.9. Federal Enforcement Efforts 299
Income Deemed Available for Support 299
9.10. What Is Income? 299
9.11. Vested Stock Options 300
9.12. Employer's Contribution to Pension Plan 300
9.13. Lump-Sum Payments and Commissions 300
9.14. Seasonal Employment 301
9.15. Overtime 301
9.16. Military Retirement Pay and Allowances 301
9.17. Imputation of Income 302
Establishing Basic Child Support 305
9.18. Presumptive Guidelines 305
9.19. Income Shares Model 305
9.20. Percentage of Income Model 307
9.21. Joint Physical Custody and Parenting Time Offsets 308
9.22. Deviation from Child Support Guidelines 309
Additional Support 311
9.23. Medical Support 311
9.24. Child Care Costs 312
Duration of Child Support 313
9.25. General Duration of Child Support 313
9.26. Educational Support 313
9.27. Emancipation of Child 314
9.28. Obligor's Death 316
Other Support Considerations 317
9.29. Monitoring Support 317
9.30. Obligee Withholds Parenting Time 317
9.31. Federal Income Tax Treatment 318
9.32. Stepparent Liability 318

Chapter 10 Child Support Modification and Enforcement 321

10.1. Introduction 321
Standards for Modifying an Existing Award 321
10.2. Jurisdictional Context 321

10.3. Substantial Change in Circumstances 322
10.4. Cost-of-Living Adjustments 324
10.5. Obligor Employment Change 324
Retroactivity and Agreements by Parties 328
10.6. Retroactive Awards 328
10.7. Court Approval Required for Modification 329
10.8. Nonmodification Agreements 329
State Enforcement Efforts 330
10.9. Child Support Debt 330
10.10. Contempt of Court 330
10.11. Criminal Nonsupport 332
10.12. Interception of Tax Refunds 333
10.13. Garnishment 333
10.14. Credit Bureau Reporting 334
10.15. Driver's License Suspension 334
10.16. Recreational License Suspension 334
10.17. Publication of a "Most Wanted" List of "Deadbeat Obligors" 334
10.18. Occupational License Suspension 334
10.19. Passport Denial 335
10.20. Seizing Awards 335
10.21. Wage Assignment 335
10.22. Effect of Bankruptcy 336
Interstate Collection and Modification 336
10.23. Federal Partnership with States 336
10.24. Early Efforts: URESA and RURESA 336
10.25. Uniform Interstate Family Support Act (UIFSA) 337
10.26. Full Faith and Credit for Child Support Orders Act (FFCCSOA) 339
10.27. The Welfare Reform Act of 1996 340
10.28. Personal Responsibility and Work Opportunity Reconciliation Act of 1996 340
10.29. Federal Crime 340

Chapter 11 Establishing Alimony 343

11.1. Introduction 343
History of Alimony 344
11.2. Dowry 344
11.3. Unity Doctrine 344
11.4. Assignment of Fault 344
11.5. Fault Adopted by Secular Systems 345
11.6. Common Law Disabilities and Duties 345
11.7. Alimony and Gender 346

The Necessaries Doctrine 347
- 11.8. Husband's Common Law Duty 347
- 11.9. Gender-Neutral Application 347

Uniform Acts 348
- 11.10. The Uniform Marriage and Divorce Act (UMDA) Provisions 348
- 11.11. UMDA Two-Step Analysis 349
- 11.12. American Law Institute (ALI) Approach 350

Purposes and Duration of Alimony 351
- 11.13. Permanent Alimony 351
- 11.14. Incapacity Alimony 352
- 11.15. Rehabilitative Alimony 352
- 11.16. Reimbursement Alimony 353
- 11.17. Caregiver Alimony 354
- 11.18. Limited Durational Alimony 354
- 11.19. Fault-Related Alimony 354

State Limitations on Amount and Duration 357
- 11.20. Imputation of Income 357
- 11.21. Percentage Formulas 358
- 11.22. Alimony Guidelines 358
- 11.23. Statutory Limits on Duration of Alimony 359

Tax Treatment 359
- 11.24. Tax Treatment of Alimony 359
- 11.25. Alimony Distinguished from Property Division 360

Chapter 12 Modification of Alimony 361

- 12.1. Introduction 361

Standards for Modification of Alimony 361
- 12.2. UMDA's Unconscionability Standard 361
- 12.3. State Standards Vary 362
- 12.4. Change in Circumstances Must Be Subsequent and Unforeseeable 362

Procedural Considerations 363
- 12.5. Existing Order or Reservation of Jurisdiction 363
- 12.6. Burden of Proof 363
- 12.7. Retroactivity 363

Impact of Agreements on Subsequent Motions for Modification 364
- 12.8. Stipulations—Non-Modification Agreements 364

Obligor's Change in Circumstances 366
- 12.9. Obligor's Unanticipated Increased Income 366
- 12.10. Obligor's Retirement 366
- 12.11. Obligor's Change of Occupation 367
- 12.12. Death of an Obligor 368

Recipient's Change in Circumstances 370
12.13. Recipient Becomes Self-Sufficient 370
12.14. Recipient's Need Increases 371
12.15. Remarriage of a Recipient 371
12.16. Cohabitation by a Recipient 372
12.17. Death of a Recipient 373

Chapter 13 Dividing the Marital Estate upon Divorce 377

13.1. Introduction 377
Property Distribution Theories 378
13.2. Separate and Community Property Theories 378
13.3. Equitable Distribution Theory 380
13.4. Source of Funds Theory 382
13.5. The Transmutation Doctrine 383
13.6. Tracing Mingled Marital and Nonmarital Property 384
13.7. Formula for Calculating the Value of Nonmarital Assets (Home Example) 385
13.8. Active and Passive Appreciation 385
13.9. Fault 387
Model Acts 394
13.10. Uniform Marriage and Divorce Act (UMDA) 394
13.11. Income 395
13.12. American Law Institute (ALI) Recommendations 395
Pension and Retirement Benefits 396
13.13. Qualified Domestic Relations Order (QDRO) 396
13.14. Dividing Pension Benefits 398
13.15. Social Security 400
13.16. Military Retirement Benefits 402
Special Issues 402
13.17. Degrees and Professional Licenses 402
13.18. Workers' Compensation and Personal Injury Issues 405
13.19. Goodwill 409
Related Areas of Law 409
13.20. Premarital Contracts 409
13.21. Bankruptcy 409
13.22. Tax Treatment for Different-Sex Marriages versus Same-Sex Marriages 410

Chapter 14 Premarital (Antenuptial or Prenuptial) Contracts — History, Requirements, and Restrictions 419

14.1. Introduction 419
History 420

14.2. Ancient Origins 420
14.3. Overview of the Development of Premarital Contracts 421
Application 424
14.4. Uses Today 424
14.5. Difference Between Premarital and Commercial Contracts 425
14.6. Model Uniform Acts 425
14.7. Common Statutory Criteria 427
14.8. Special Duty to Disclose 428
14.9. Voluntarily Executed 430
14.10. Prior Understanding — Duress 432
14.11. Right to Consult with Counsel 433
Subject Matter of Agreements 435
14.12. Waiving Child Support and Custody 435
14.13. Waiving Alimony 436
14.14. Contracts Imposing Marital Duties and Obligations 440
Enforcing Premarital Contracts 440
14.15. Burden of Proof 440
14.16. Presumptions 443
14.17. Procedural Fairness When Executed 451
14.18. Unconscionable Contracts 452
14.19. The "Second Look" — "Change of Circumstances" Doctrine 453
14.20. Capacity 455

Chapter 15 Cohabitation and Contract Principles 457

15.1. Introduction 457
Changing Lifestyles 458
15.2. A Changing Social Perspective 458
Legal Redress for Cohabiting Couples 461
15.3. *Marvin v. Marvin* 461
15.4. Response to *Marvin* 463
15.5. Importance of Separating Illicit Relationship from Contract 467
15.6. Alimony 468
15.7. Model Acts and General Authorities 473
Application of Legal Theories 474
15.8. Overview of Legal Theories 474
15.9. Express Written Contracts 475
15.10. Legal Practice Issues 475
15.11. Express Oral Agreements 476
15.12. Implied Contracts 477

15.13. Quasi-Contracts 478
15.14. Resulting Trusts 479
15.15. Constructive Trusts 480
15.16. Statute of Wills 480
Other Claims 484
15.17. Wrongful Death Claims 484
15.18. Loss of Consortium Claims 485
15.19. Claiming State and Federal Statutory Benefits 486
15.20. Insurance Policy Coverage 486
15.21. Housing Discrimination 486
15.22. Statute of Limitations 488

Chapter 16 Determining Parentage 493

16.1. Introduction 493
Constitutional Protection for Nonmarital Children 494
16.2. Historic Disparate Treatment 494
16.3. Wrongful Death 495
16.4. Inheritance Rights 496
16.5. Social Security Benefits 497
Constitutional Rights of Putative Fathers? 499
16.6. Preponderance of Evidence Standard 499
16.7. Right to Counsel in Paternity Proceedings 500
16.8. Putative Father's Standing to Rebut Marital Presumption — The *Michael H.* Case 501
16.9. Putative Fathers and Consent to Adoption 502
Federal Legislation 504
16.10. Federal Focus 504
16.11. The Omnibus Budget Reconciliation Act of 1993 505
16.12. Personal Responsibility and Work Opportunity Reconciliation Act (PRWORA) of 1996 505
Uniform Parentage Act (UPA) 505
16.13. Overview 505
16.14. Establishing Paternity Under the UPA 506
16.15. Establishing Paternity through Presumption 506
16.16. Rebutting Presumptions of Paternity Under the UPA 507
16.17. Voluntary Acknowledgment 508
16.18. Genetic Testing Under the UPA 510
16.19. Statutes of Limitation 511
16.20. Registration to Receive Notice of Termination of Parental Rights 512
Equitable Theories 513
16.21. Equitable Parent Doctrine 513
16.22. Paternity by Estoppel 515

Establishing Maternity 516
16.23. Maternity Under the UPA 516
16.24. Same-Sex Partners 516

Chapter 17 Adoption 517

17.1. Introduction 517
Overview 517
17.2. History 517
17.3. Abrogation of Adoption 518
17.4. Legal Effect of Adoption 519
Forms of Adoption 520
17.5. Agency Adoptions 520
17.6. Independent Adoption 520
17.7. Stepparent Adoption 520
17.8. Near-Relative Adoption 521
17.9. Open Adoption 521
17.10. Subsidized Adoption 522
17.11. International Adoption 522
Procedures 524
17.12. Filing a Petition 524
17.13. Investigating Prospective Parents 524
17.14. Sealing Adoption Records 525
Qualifications of Potential Adoptive Parents 527
17.15. Race of Adoptive Parent and the Multiethnic Placement Act (MEPA) 527
17.16. Native American Status and the Indian Child Welfare Act (ICWA) 527
17.17. Sexual Orientation of Adoptive Parents 528
17.18. Age of Adoptive Parents 529
Who Must Consent to an Adoption? 530
17.19. Pre-Birth Consent of Mother 530
17.20. Putative Father's Consent 531
17.21. Putative Father Consents by Failing to Use Adoption Registry 533
17.22. Minor Child's Consent 534
17.23. Adults Adopting Adults 534
Uniform Acts 538
17.24. Uniform Adoption Act of 1994 538
Claims 538
17.25. Fraud 538
17.26. Negligent Misrepresentation 539

Chapter 18 Assisted Reproduction — History, Restrictions, and Requirements **541**

18.1. Introduction — History 541
Definitions 542
18.2. ART AID-AIH IVF, Defined and Explained 542
Model Acts 545
18.3. Uniform Parentage Act (UPA) 545
18.4. ABA Model Act Governing Assisted Reproductive Technology 546
18.5. Uniform Putative and Unknown Fathers Act; Uniform Status of Children of Assisted Conception Act 546
State AID and AIH Issues 547
18.6. Typical State Statutory Provisions 547
18.7. Husband's Consent 549
18.8. Application of Artificial Insemination Statutes to Same-Sex Couples? 550
18.9. Known Donors and Unmarried Recipients 551
Traditional Surrogacy 552
18.10. Surrogate Parent — Overview 552
18.11. Legislation Allowing and Banning Surrogacy 553
18.12. Baby M 554
Gestational Surrogacy 556
18.13. State Gestational Surrogacy Theories 556
18.14. Same-Sex Issues 558
18.15. Constitutional "Right" to Gestational Surrogacy? 559
Frozen Embryos 560
18.16. Disposition in the Event of Divorce 560
Liability Issues 562
18.17. Physician and Clinic Tort Liability to Parents 562
18.18. Wrongful Life 563
18.19. Wrongful Death 564
18.20. Liability When Genetic Material Mix-Up Occurs 564
Miscellaneous Issues 565
18.21. Insurance — Who Is Covered? 565
18.22. Posthumous Reproduction 566

Chapter 19 Domestic Violence **575**

19.1. Introduction 575
Understanding the Issue 575
19.2. Risk Factors 575
19.3. Importance of Context 576

19.4. Impact on Children 577
19.5. Screening Protocols 578
Domestic Abuse Statutes 579
19.6. History 579
19.7. Statutory Definitions of Domestic Violence 579
19.8. Who Is Covered? 581
19.9. What Relief Is Granted? 583
19.10. *Ex Parte* and "Permanent" Orders 583
19.11. Constitutional Challenges 585
19.12. Access to the Court 586
19.13. Issuance of Mutual Orders 587
19.14. Enforcement of Orders 588
19.15. Effectiveness of Orders 589
Related Areas of Law 591
19.16. Violence Against Women Act (VAWA) 591
19.17. Criminal Sanctions 592
19.18. Mandatory Arrest and No-Drop Policies 592
19.19. Tort Actions 593
19.20. Hague Convention 594

Chapter 20 Neglect, Dependency, Child Abuse, and Termination of Parental Rights 595

20.1. Introduction 595
20.2. Nature and Scope of the Problem 595
Standards for State Intervention 596
20.3. Parents' Right to Privacy — Liberty Interests 596
20.4. The Child Abuse Prevention and Treatment Act (CAPTA) 596
20.5. Indian Child Welfare Act (ICWA) 597
20.6. Defining Abuse, Neglect, and Dependency 597
Common Forms of Abuse and Neglect 598
20.7. Use of Unreasonable Force to Correct a Child 598
20.8. Spanking 599
20.9. Sexual Abuse 600
20.10. Neglect 600
20.11. Medical Treatment 601
20.12. Failure to Protect from Harm 602
20.13. Failure to Protect from Harm: Domestic Violence 602
20.14. Emotional or Mental Abuse 603
20.15. Prenatal Drug Abuse 603
Reporting Abuse and Neglect 609
20.16. Mandated Reporting 609
20.17. Central Registry of Reports 610

Adjudication and Disposition 610
20.18. Two-Stage Proceedings 610
20.19. Procedures When Child Is in Immediate Danger 611
20.20. Syndrome Testimony 611
20.21. Alternative Dispute Resolution 612
20.22. Prevention and Alternative Responses 613
Children in Foster Care 614
20.23. Foster Care: Safety and Accountability 614
20.24. Concurrent Planning 615
20.25. "Reasonable Efforts" to Reunify Families 615
20.26. "Active Efforts" Pursuant to the ICWA 616
20.27. Permanancy Planning 616
Involuntary Termination of Parental Rights 617
20.28. Specific Grounds for Termination 617
20.29. Legal Consequences of Termination 617
20.30. Standard of Proof 618
20.31. Parental Right to Counsel? 618

Chapter 21 Abortion 623

History and Background 623
21.1. Introduction 623
21.2. Twentieth Century 625
Constitutional Privacy 625
21.3. Roots of Privacy Theory 625
21.4. Statute Fails to Protect Fundamental Right to Privacy 627
21.5. *Roe v. Wade* 628
21.6. Expanding Personal Privacy 629
21.7. Second-Trimester Issues 630
21.8. Informed Consent, Reporting Requirement, Physician Duty to Inform, and Necessity of Second Physician Opinion 632
21.9. Wavering on *Roe* 633
21.10. A Further Departure from *Roe* 634
Deference to Physicians 635
21.11. Physician's Deference 635
21.12. Physician's Duty to Inform 636
Picketing 637
21.13. Buffer Zones 637
Partial-Birth Abortions 639
21.14. Partial-Birth Legislation: *Carhart* I and II 639
Parental Notification and Consent 641
21.15. Parental Notification of an Abortion 641
Abortion Funding 644
21.16. Medicaid Coverage 644

21.17. Selective Funding of Programs in the Public Interest 645
21.18. Barring Use of Public Facilities 645
21.19. State Constitutional Right to Privacy 646

Chapter 22 Mediation, Collaborative Law, Parenting Coordination, and Arbitration 653

22.1. Introduction 653
22.2. Use of Screening Protocols 653
22.3. Informed Decision Making About Participation in Dispute Resolution Processes 654
Mediation 655
22.4. Definition Under the Model Standards 655
22.5. Mediation as an Interest-Based Process 655
22.6. The Role of the Mediator 656
22.7. Legal Advice in Mediation 657
22.8. Mediator Qualifications 657
22.9. Mediation Settlement Rates 657
22.10. Court Approval of Agreements 658
22.11. Mediator Testimony 658
22.12. Mediation as Condition Precedent to Post-Decree Actions 659
22.13. Mandatory Mediation 659
22.14. Intimate Partner Violence 660
Collaborative Law 664
22.15. The Collaborative Process 664
22.16. Formal Opinion 07-447 665
22.17. Uniform Collaborative Law Rules (UCLR) and Uniform Collaborative Law Act (UCLA) 665
22.18. Cooperative Law Compared 666
Parenting Coordination 666
22.19. The Role of the Parenting Coordinator 666
22.20. Legislative Authorization in Some States 667
22.21. Common Practices 668
Arbitration 670
22.22. Use of Arbitration in Family Cases 670

Chapter 23 Professional Responsibility 671

23.1. Introduction 671
Conflicts of Interest 672
23.2. Prior Representation and Prospective Clients 672
23.3. Dual Representation 672
23.4. Sexual Relationships with Clients 673
Contingent Fees 676

23.5. Contingent Fee Arrangements 676
23.6. Exceptions 676
Communicating with Clients 677
23.7. Emotional Needs of Family Clients 677
23.8. Information and Consultation 677
Self-Represented Litigants 678
23.9. Self-Representation Becomes More Common 678
23.10. Attorney Conduct with Self-Represented Parties 679
23.11. Need for Pro Bono Representation (Rule 6.1) 679
Various Roles of Lawyers 680
23.12. Attorney as Conflict Resolver 680
23.13. Ethical Cautions for Lawyers Performing New Professional Roles 681
23.14. Collaborative Lawyers 681
23.15. Lawyer as Mediator or Arbitrator 682

Chapter 24 Jurisdiction 683

24.1. Introduction 683
Subject Matter Jurisdiction in Federal Court 684
24.2. Domestic Relations Exception 684
24.3. Probate Exception 687
24.4. Federal Court Review of State Court Domestic Relations Judgments 691
24.5. Procedural Issues — Liberty Interest 691
24.6. Abstention Doctrine 692
Subject Matter Jurisdiction in State Court 693
24.7. Challenges to Residency Requirements 693
24.8. Does Failure to Meet Residency Requirement Void a Divorce Decree? 695
24.9. Where May Subject Matter Jurisdiction Be Challenged? 696
Personal Jurisdiction in State Court 697
24.10. Jurisdiction to Grant Ex Parte Divorce — The Divisible Divorce Theory 697
24.11. State Long-Arm Statute Requirements 699
24.12. Due Process Barriers to Application of Long-Arm Statutes 703
24.13. Service Within State During Temporary Visit 704
24.14. Continuing Jurisdiction 704
24.15. Waiving Personal Jurisdiction Claim 705
Status as a Jurisdictional Theory 706
24.16. Overview of Status Theory 706
24.17. Restatement of Conflict of Laws — Status 709

Full Faith and Credit 716
24.18. State Recognition of Same-Sex Marriages (Defense of Marriage Act) 716
24.19. Full Faith and Credit for Child Support Orders Act 717
Special Situations 718
24.20. Overview of Indian Child Welfare Act (ICWA) 718
24.21. Overview of Soldiers and Sailors Civil Relief Act—Service Members Civil Relief Act 720
24.22. Child Custody Under SCRA 721
24.23. Uniform Interstate Family Support Act 722
24.24. Hague Convention 725

Table of Cases *737*
Index *767*

Preface

We are pleased to provide an updated and revised fourth edition of *Family Law: Examples & Explanations*. Each of the 24 chapters features recent developments in family law, and the book includes hundreds of hypothetical examples and explanations, most of which are based on fact patterns taken from actual cases. Because new developments in family law often reflect underlying societal changes in family structure and demographics, this volume incorporates empirical research and census data that are likely to be of interest to the reader. We also highlight ways that the practice of family law and the role of attorneys have been transformed through the use of processes such as mediation and collaborative law.

This book contains a balanced and in-depth analysis of family law. Because the tapestry of family law is complex, and because we believe that focus is an essential ingredient to learning, we have separated the subject of family law into specific topics that are organized as chapters. Each chapter is subdivided into discrete sections that often include hypothetical examples and illustrative explanations. We have based our analysis and the examples and explanations on nationally accepted legal principles. However, because family law is so often state specific, the text contains contrasting perspectives from various jurisdictions. To eliminate confusion and to assist with family law research, we have included hundreds of citations to relevant state decisions and legislation associated with the principles under consideration.

We believe that this book provides a clear, well-organized, and efficient learning platform that will assist readers in understanding and appreciating the subject of family law.

Robert E. Oliphant
Nancy Ver Steegh
January 2013

Acknowledgments

We are thankful for the hard work, assistance, and encouragement of the generous people who have helped us complete four editions of this book.

In addition to our Wolters Kluwer editors, William Mitchell College of Law and its administration have remained solid supporters of the project since its beginning. Faculty Publication Specialists Linda Thorstad and Cal Bonde helped with all of the editions and Jennifer Miller and Polly Saul contributed substantial proofreading assistance. For their commitment to the project, we say, "Thank you for all your efforts."

Our respective book widow and widower spouses, Susan Oliphant and Jack Ver Steegh, have been patient, tolerant, and supportive as we worked on the manuscripts for these editions. Thank you!

Robert E. Oliphant
Nancy Ver Steegh
January 2013

EXAMPLES & EXPLANATIONS

Family Law

CHAPTER 1

A History of Marriage and Divorce

1.1. Introduction

A detailed discussion of the history of family law would cover volumes and is well beyond the scope of this book. However, a skeleton historical overview of this topic provides necessary context for understanding the other topics covered in this book. Consequently, what follows is a brief historical sketch covering several hundred years of family law.

It probably understates the case to say that family law principles and practices have centuries of custom and tradition associated with them. This history may explain why changes in some areas of family law, such as allowing same-sex couples to marry, have generated such a strong emotional reaction in certain regions of the nation. Other less controversial but commonly accepted principles, such as those associated with consanguinity, can be traced to ancient Mosaic law, where a man was barred from marrying his mother, stepmother, sister, half-sister, granddaughter, or granddaughter-in-law. Even today Mosaic law may occasionally influence the outcome of an issue in a secular family courtroom. *See, e.g., Burns v. Burns*, 538 A.2d 438 (N.J. Super. Ct. 1987) (court ordering spouse to obtain a "get" so party could enter into a Jewish contract of marriage known as a "ketubbah").

The reliance by Americans on the Bible has, no doubt, played an influential role in the development of family law in the United States. It is said that the Bible was "nothing short of the underlying fabric upon which American society was founded" and helped form the earliest colonial laws. John W. Welch, *Biblical Law in America: Historical Perspectives and Potentials for Reform*, 2002 BYU L. Rev. 611, 619 (2002); Linda C. McClain, *The "Male Problematic" and the Problems of Family Law: A Response to Don Browning's "Critical Familism,"* 56 Emory L.J. 1407, 1427 (2007) ("For most of American history, . . . the law of marriage was consistent with and supported—if not created—by the views of dominant religious communities").

The theory adopted as an integral feature of early American family law that when a couple marry they become one, and that "one" is the husband, a custom most likely derived from the book of Genesis (Genesis 2:24). This passage of the Bible states that a husband must leave the home of his parents to be joined to his wife, and "they shall become one flesh." This Biblical view of marriage is repeated by Paul in his Epistle to the Ephesians (Ephesians 5:31). *See generally Wylly v. S.Z. Collins & Co.*, 9 Ga. 223, 1851 WL 1417 (1851) (observing that while the Bible may be the foundation of the common law view of husband and wife, Roman law viewed a husband and wife as distinct persons, with distinct property and distinct powers over that property); *Melvin v. Easley*, 52 N.C. 356, 1860 WL 1777 (1860) ("Ours is a Christian country, but Christianity is not established by law, and the genius of our free institutions requires that 'church' and 'State' should be kept separate. In England, religion is established by law. The head of the church is the head of the State").

1.2. The Roman and Early English Views of Marriage

Some believe that the concept of marriage began to evolve into a social institution as early as the period of Roman domination of Europe. *See* John Witte, Jr., *From Sacrament to Contract: Marriage, Religion, and Law in the Western Tradition* 3, 20-21 (1997). During that time in history, marriages were viewed as private rather than public matters, and there is little historical evidence suggesting that there was significant control by governmental authorities over them. Marriage was essentially a contract for the purchase of a wife—a purely private transaction. There was no "public license or registration; no authoritative intervention of priest or other public functionary." Mary Anne Case, *Marriage Licenses*, 89 Minn. L. Rev. 1758, 1766 (June 2005). A systematic theology of marriage is generally believed to have emerged in the fourth and fifth centuries as the Church of Rome provided a shape for it. Witte, Jr., *supra* at 19-21.

In the eleventh century, William the Conqueror http://www.historyonthenet.com/Chronology/timelinewilliami.htm (last visited July, 2012), separated the English ecclesiastical courts from lay courts and brought many of the Church's everyday functions under the authority of common law. However, the Church continued to claim exclusive jurisdiction over what pertained to one's soul, salvation, and sanctification, and those views were incorporated into the canon law and then applied to marriage, divorce, annulment, and probate by the ecclesiastical courts. The Church's legal authority over family matters appears to have been solidified in England by the thirteenth century.

1.3. Reformation, Divorce, and Blackstone

The Protestant Reformation was probably the greatest event of the sixteenth century. http://www.historyguide.org/earlymod/lecture3c.html (last visited May, 2012). The Reformation forced people to make a choice to be either Catholic or Protestant and in the context of the religious wars of the sixteenth and seventeenth centuries, they lived or died based on those choices.

The Reformers rejected the Church's view that marriage was a holy sacrament. They advocated the possibility of divorce under certain circumstances. Shaakirrah R. Sanders, *The Cyclical Nature of Divorce in the Western Legal Tradition*, 50 Loy. L. Rev. 407, 413 (Summer 2004). They also insisted that marriage and divorce be made public.

The Protestant view of divorce ran directly counter to Catholic teaching and canon law, which held that an absolute divorce was impossible. Under Catholic theology, the only "divorce" a person might obtain was a separation from bed and board, labeled a divorce *a mensa et thoro*. The decree of divorce *a mensa et thoro* did not sever the marital tie—the parties remained husband and wife. Should a divorce *a mensa et thoro* be granted, neither party could remarry during the lifetime of the other. Generally, the husband was required to provide his wife with permanent support.

The sixteenth-century feud between the Church and Henry VIII, over his view of annulments and when they could be used, plus his decision to replace the pope with himself as head of the Church of England is historically significant. However, as a practical matter, it had little influence on how marriage and divorce continued to be viewed in that country. *See generally* *http://www.royal.gov.uk/historyofthemonarchy/kingsandqueensofengland/thetudors/henryviii.aspx* (last visited March, 2012). During these early periods in history, most people could neither read nor write, divorces were rare, and marriage continued to be viewed, from a religious perspective by the Catholic Church and the Church of England after Henry took control of it, as a gracious symbol of the divine, a social unit of the earthly kingdom, and a solemn covenant with one's spouse. *See generally* Patrick McKinley, *Of Marriage and Monks, Community and Dialogue*, 48 Emory L.J. 689, 710 (1999). These early English views of marriage and divorce were transported to America by the colonists.

1.4. Parliamentary Divorce

By the late sixteenth century, England was the only Protestant country in Europe without some form of legalized divorce. At some point in the latter part of the sixteenth century, the idea that one could, by a private act of Parliament, obtain a divorce became a reality.

The path that a parliamentary divorce took began with an initial divorce petition being prepared and sent to the House of Lords. There, the petition was considered by a Committee of the Whole, and evidence was given by witnesses to support it. Divorce was granted by Parliament to husbands only for adultery although wives could initiate a divorce Bill if the adultery was compounded by life-threatening cruelty. *See generally*, *Head v. Head*, 2 Ga. 191, 202 (Ga. 1847) (Parliament had sovereign authority to grant divorces).

Historians estimate that between 1700 and 1857, there were 314 such Private Acts approved by the English parliament. Most of them were initiated by husbands. Because of the high costs associated with obtaining a Private Act, only the wealthy could afford this method of ending a marriage.

The example set by the English Parliament of allowing a legislative divorce was brought across the Atlantic and adopted by many colonial legislatures. The practice of granting divorce by legislative act persisted in this country well into the middle of the nineteenth century. The Supreme Court, for example, approved a legislative divorce issued by the Oregon Territorial Legislature in *Maynard v. Hill*, 125 U.S. 190 (1888).

It may be of interest that *Maynard v. Hill* involved a Seattle pioneer, "Doc" Maynard, who had left his wife, Lydia, and two children in Ohio. Although he had apparently promised to send them money and have them join him in the Oregon territory, he did neither. Instead, he convinced the 1852 Oregon territorial legislature to pass a Private Act declaring him divorced. He then remarried. Lydia, who remained in Ohio, received no notice of the legislation and was left divorced and penniless by the decision.

1.5. Colonial American Model of Marriage and Divorce

The early settlers imported a great many English customs, traditions, and law to this country. Most saw themselves as loyal British citizens. However, the residents of the various colonies differed in some respects in their views of marriage and divorce. Recall that marriage and divorce in England reflected canon law, and decisions about domestic matters fell exclusively within the jurisdiction of the ecclesiastical or church courts. 2 Pollock & Maitland, *History of English Law* (2d ed.) 366, 392-396. Because of a strong belief among many colonists in the separation of church and state, there were no ecclesiastical courts established in the colonies. During the early colonial period, because of an absence of clear provisions for a civil divorce, a request for such a determination, although extremely rare, was handled on an ad hoc basis. Herma Hill Kay, *From The Second Sex to the Joint Venture: An Overview of Women's Rights and Family Law in the United States During the Twentieth Century*, 88 Cal. L. Rev. 2017, 2025 (December 2000).

In general, most agree that the principal objectives of marriage during the American colonial period were "wealth, social position, and love—usually in that order." John C. Miller, *This New Man, The American* 414 (1974). Most parents considered marriage a matter too serious to be left to the individuals directly concerned. Consequently, it was not uncommon for a young man to seek permission from the parents of a single young woman before he dated her. *Id.* at 413. Legally, the father of the girl had the right to permit or deny consent to marry. Eric Foner & John A. Garraty, *The Reader's Companion to American History* 700 (1991). Unwanted suitors were often effectively discouraged when a daughter's father let it be known that he intended to withhold financial assistance should his daughter seek to marry an undesirable male.

For the most part, when one married in colonial America, the marriage was intended to last forever, and the law reflected this view by making it difficult for married couples to divorce or separate. Stuart A. Queen, Robert W. Habenstein, & Jill S. Quadagno, *The Family in Various Cultures* 214 (1985). For example, to keep marriages secure, husbands were penalized by expulsion from the Connecticut colony if they were estranged from their wives for more than three years. Jessica Kross et al., *American Eras, The Colonial Era* 278 (1998).

Slaves were not generally allowed to marry in most colonies. However, if they were permitted to marry, the ceremony had to be approved and performed by the slaveowner. Foner & Garraty, *supra* at 701. For couples who did marry under slavery, one of the horrors associated with these marriages is that they had no official recognition. Consequently, husbands and wives and children could be separated at any time at the whim of an owner. *See* http://www.npr.org/templates/story/story.php?storyId=123608207 (last visited March, 2012).

Racial intermarriage in most states was prohibited. For example, in Massachusetts in 1705, marriage between a white person and a black person or mulatto was prohibited, and a person who violated this law could be fined £50.

Post-revolution. Following the American Revolution, states had to decide the basis upon which a divorce could be obtained. Because the post-revolutionary courts of equity did not regard themselves as having inherent power over marriage and divorce, they "left to the legislatures either to grant special Acts of divorce, as the English Parliament had sometimes done, or to confer divorce jurisdiction upon the civil courts." Herma Hill Kay, *supra*.

Although England refused to allow an absolute divorce until 1857, 40 of the state legislatures granted jurisdiction to U.S. civil courts much earlier. *Ibid.* A total of 12 states and the Northwest Territories had adopted divorce statutes by 1799, and by 1860, "only South Carolina refused to permit absolute divorce." *Id.* at 2026. Legislative divorces, patterned by U.S. legislatures after the English parliamentary divorce, were slowly disappearing, with Delaware becoming the last state to end the practice in 1897.

1.6. Nineteenth-Century Patriarchic Model of Marriage

Marriage in the United States 150 years ago was driven by rigid customs and centuries of religious tradition. It was often viewed as a process to consolidate wealth and resources; occasionally, it was used to cement political alliances. Marriage provided men with legal authority over their wives and children and identified the husband's legal heirs. The husband was the legal head of the household, responsible for its support and its links to external society. The wife was the mistress of the home, responsible for the day-to-day management of its internal affairs and the care and education of children. Divorces were rare, as were paternity actions and adoptions. The family was viewed as a single unit consisting of the mother, the father, and the children, with each member playing a well-defined role.

Blackstone. William Blackstone viewed marriage as the unity of a man and a woman into a single unit. He observed that by marriage, "the husband and wife are one person in law: that is, the very being or legal existence is suspended during the marriage, or at least incorporated and consolidated into that of the husband." William Blackstone, *Commentaries on the Laws of England*, 442 (W. Lewis, ed., 1897).

Unity scheme. The common law scheme that made for unity in the marriage relations of husband and wife was extensive. *Palmer v. Turner*, 43 S.W.2d 1017, 1018 (Ky. App. 1931). To secure unity when a couple married, the "very legal being and existence of the woman was suspended during coverture, or entirely merged or incorporated in that of the husband." *Ibid.* Once married, a wife surrendered her property to her husband and was placed within his keeping, so far as her civil rights were concerned.

A wife could not earn money for herself, nor could she contract, sue, be contracted with, or be sued in her own right. While the wife's husband lost nothing by the marriage, the wife surrendered her property and lost her independence and identity in law. *See Robinson v. Trousdale County*, 516 S.W.2d 626, 628 (Tenn. 1974) (marriage conferred upon the husband the dominion of the wife's real estate; the rents and profits belonged to him and could be seized by his creditors). The husband was also in charge of disciplining the children and his wife. *Joyner v. Joyner*, 59 N.C. (6 Jones Eq.) 322, 325 (1862) ("It follows that the law gives the husband power to use such a degree of force as is necessary to make the wife behave herself and know her place").

Upon marriage, a husband became the owner absolutely of the wife's personal property. Her earnings, her personal property accruing to her during coverture, vested immediately in the husband. He was entitled to any rents arising from her land. *Dotson v. Dotson*, 189 S. W. 894 (Ky. 1916). He could sell, convey, or mortgage his land without her joining in the instrument with him. He had the right to select and fix her domicile, and it was her duty to accept it. When she died, he had the right to select her burial place or to change it. *Neighbors v. Neighbors*, 65 S. W. 607 (Ky. 1901); *see Babcock v. Adams*, 196 S.W. 1118 (Mo. 1917).

The common law also gave a husband/father a proprietary interest in the services of his wife and minor children. W. Prosser, *The Law of Torts* §124, at 916 (W. Keeton, 5th ed. 1984); *see also* Note, *Child's Right to Sue for Negligent Disruption of Parental Consortium*, 22 Washburn L.J. 78, 81-82 (1982) (a man's wife and children were perceived as chattels). When a wife or minor child was injured by the tort of a third party, the husband/father was entitled to recover from the tortfeasor for lost services. The action was viewed as involving a master who had lost the services of an injured servant. W. Prosser, *supra*, §125, at 931-935. Because a husband and wife, in legal fiction, are one person at common law, neither could maintain a civil action against the other based on a tort. *Carmichael v. Carmichael*, 187 S.E. 116 (Ga. App. 1936).

A primary purpose of marriage. Procreation was generally viewed as a primary purpose of a marriage relationship. *Chavias v. Chavias*, 184 N.Y.S. 761, 762 (N.Y. 1920). A wife's principal responsibility was to the home and children, and women were seldom allowed to enter any "man's profession." In 1872, for example, the Supreme Court upheld the constitutionality of a state law that denied women the right to practice law. The Court's ruling was based solely on the basis of gender. *Bradwell v. People of State of Illinois*, 83 U.S. 130 (1872). The Court in *Bradwell* observed the following:

> [T]he civil law, as well as nature herself, has always recognized a wide difference in the respective spheres and destinies of man and woman. Man is, or should be, woman's protector and defender. The natural and proper timidity and delicacy which belongs to the female sex evidently unfits it for many of the occupations of civil life. The constitution of the family organization, which is founded in the divine ordinance, as well as in the nature of things, indicates the domestic sphere as that which properly belongs to the domain and functions of womanhood. . . .

> The paramount destiny and mission of woman are to fulfill the noble and benign offices of wife and mother. This is the law of the Creator. And the rules of civil society must be adapted to the general constitution of things, and cannot be based upon exceptional cases.

Id. at 141-142. The *Bradwell* decision was used to support other actions denying women civil rights. *See, e.g., U.S. v. Anthony*, 24 F. Cas. 829 (N.D. N.Y. 1873) (The Fourteenth Amendment did not give a woman the right to vote, and the voting by Susan B. Anthony was unlawful); *Robinson's Case*, 131 Mass. 376 (1881) ("The conclusion that women cannot be admitted to the bar under the existing statutes of the Commonwealth is in accordance with judgments of the highest courts of the States of Illinois and Wisconsin").

Husband's duty. A husband had a common law duty to support his wife, which may have in part acted as a counterbalance to the legal disabilities imposed on her because of marriage and as compensation for his right to her earnings and services. *See, e.g.,* Orr v. Orr, 440 U.S. 268, 279 n. 9 (1979). If a husband refused to supply his wife with necessaries, she was authorized to purchase them on his credit, making him liable to the supplier for their costs. *See, e.g., Scott v. Carothers*, 47 N.E. 389, 390 (Ind. App. 1897) (husband owes the wife the duty of supporting and maintaining her, and she may enforce this duty in a proper case by pledging his credit to others to supply her with necessaries unless she has sufficient means of her own). She had a right to have her debts before marriage paid by the husband, and she secured a life interest in the one-third part of his estates of inheritance if she survived him.

Married Women's Acts. Passage of Married Women's Acts in many states around the close of the nineteenth century gave women new rights, including the right to sue for torts committed against them, engage in business, and make contracts. *See, e.g., Roberts v. Bailey*, 338 S.W.3d 540, 543 (Tenn. App. 2010) (the Married Women's Act of 1913 fully and effectively eradicated the common law disability of coverture); *Mathewson v. Mathewson*, 63 A. 285 (Conn. 1906) (reciting history of "the radical change in public policy introduced by the reform Act of 1877" that declared that equality in personal identity and in the ownership of property shall replace the unity of all rights in the husband as the legal status effected by intermarriage); *Boblitz v. Boblitz*, 462 A.2d 506, 507 (Md. App. 1983) ("As women's role in society changed, the burden of this imputation of inferiority became increasingly intolerable and led to an ever increasing storm of protest. This storm of protest, reaching hurricane proportions in the second half of the Nineteenth Century, caused the Legislatures of the several states to enact 'Married Women's Acts'").

In most versions of a Married Women's Act, a wife became competent to sue in her own name for injuries to herself and could retain the proceeds of those actions. Her injuries, for which she could recover judgment, included the loss of her capacity to render services in the home, as well as to earn money on the outside; the husband no longer had a claim for household help required because of his wife's disability.

Married Women's Property Acts were also passed; in effect, they abrogated a husband's common law dominance over the marital estate and placed a wife on a level of equality with him regarding the exercise of ownership over the whole estate. Usually, a state statute adopting some form of the Property Acts stated that the tenancy was still predicated upon the legal unity of husband and wife, but the Acts converted it into a unity of equals, not of unequals as at common law. *Sawada v. Endo*, 561 P.2d 1291, 1295 (Haw. 1977). No longer could the husband convey, lease, mortgage, or otherwise encumber the property without her consent.

The Married Women's Acts were often construed in a strained and grudging fashion. *See, e.g., Fernandez v. Fernandez*, 135 A.2d 886 (Md. 1957) ("The cases in Maryland have interpreted the [Married Women's] Act with such strictness and have given it such limited effect that we find ourselves unable to follow the authorities elsewhere without overruling our prior decision").

Miscegenation laws. A marriage between persons of different races was prohibited in a large number of states well into the twentieth century. These miscegenation laws arose as an incident of slavery and had been common in states since the colonial period. Miscegenation laws prohibited a "white person" marrying other than another "white person." They also prohibited officials from issuing marriage licenses until satisfied that the applicants' statements as to their race were correct. Certificates of "racial composition" were to be kept by both local and state registrars. The statutes were an obvious endorsement of the doctrine of white supremacy.

In 1883, the Supreme Court upheld a conviction under an Alabama statute forbidding adultery or fornication between a white person and a black person that imposed a greater penalty than that of a statute proscribing similar conduct by members of the same race. The Court reasoned that the statute did not discriminate against black persons because the punishment for each participant in the offense was the same. *Pace v. State of Alabama*, 106 U.S. 583 (1883).

The reasoning used by the *Pace* justices was rejected in 1964. *McLaughlin v. Florida*, 379 U.S. 184, 188 (1964). The Court stated that "Pace represents a limited view of the Equal Protection Clause which has not withstood analysis in the subsequent decisions of this Court." The Court said that the equal protection clause requires the consideration of whether the classifications drawn by any statute constitute an arbitrary and invidious discrimination. It also said that the clear and central purpose of the Fourteenth Amendment was to eliminate all official state sources of invidious racial discrimination in the States.

Finally, the Supreme Court abolished all remaining vestiges of miscegenation law in *Loving v. Virginia*, 388 U.S. 1 (1967); http://www.oyez.org/cases/1960-1969/1966/1966_395 (last visited July, 2012). The Lovings had been convicted of violating Virginia's ban on interracial marriage and sentenced to one year in jail. The trial court suspended the jail time for 25 years and commented that

> Almighty God created the races white, black, yellow, Malay, and red, and he placed them on separate continents. And but for the interference with his arrangement there would be no cause for such marriages. The fact that he separated the races shows that he did not intend for the races to mix.

The Virginia Court of Appeals upheld the conviction, endorsing the doctrine of white supremacy. *Id.* at 7 of 388 U.S. Among other matters, in reversing the conviction, the Supreme Court rejected the notion that the mere equal application of a statute containing racial classifications was sufficient to remove the classifications from the Fourteenth Amendment's proscription of all invidious racial discriminations.

The Pew Research organization reports a record 14.6 percent of all new marriages in the United States in 2008 were between spouses of a different race or ethnicity from one another. Jeffrey S. Passel, Wendy Wang, and Paul Taylor, *Marrying Out: One-in-Seven New U.S. Marriages Is Interracial or Interethnic* http://pewresearch.org/pubs/1616/american-marriage-interracial-interethnic (last visited July, 2012). This includes marriages between a Hispanic and non-Hispanic (Hispanics are an ethnic group, not a race), as well as marriages between spouses of different races—be they white, black, Asian, Native American, or those who identify as being of multiple races or "some other" race. *Ibid.*

1.7. The Family Law Revolution

By the middle of the twentieth century, marriage and divorce appeared firmly in the grasp of state and religious institutions. State marriage license laws provided a premarital fitness criterion and instituted waiting periods designed to prevent hasty marriages. Should a divorce occur, there was a waiting period of six months or more before either party could remarry. While common law marriages continued to exist in a handful of states, they were slowly being eliminated by legislatures who viewed them as frustrating state efforts to determine who could marry. Divorce laws were increasingly viewed as raising unnecessary, challenging barriers to unhappy couples seeking to terminate their relationship. However, any major change in a state's secular marriage and divorce law was generally opposed successfully by the clergy.

Most point to the 1960s as the period when American culture began its remarkable rebellion against rigid marriage and divorce laws, customs, and traditions. The changes dramatically altered the face of family law. These changes are reflected in an increased involvement of courts and legislatures into almost every facet of family life.

"Family" redefined. Few dispute that the definitions of what constitutes a "family" and a "parent" have been radically altered during the last few decades. During this period, divorce became progressively more available to unhappy couples, and a traditional marriage no longer necessarily symbolized a "family." State legislatures and state courts began to show an increasing willingness to recognize civil unions between cohabiting same-sex couples. Notably, at least seven jurisdictions now allow same-sex couples to marry legally.

Another factor influencing how "families" and "parents" are viewed today is the growing acceptance of cohabitation between couples who do not formally marry, but live together much as husband and wife. In jurisdictions where common law marriages are not recognized, legislation and court decisions have provided cohabiting unmarried couples with property rights, which was once thought to be impossible.

Children today may grow up in a traditional nuclear family consisting of two biological parents who share their children. However, it is increasingly common for children to grow up in households with only one parent present — usually, but not always, the biological mother. They may also grow up in households with each divorced adult bringing children from an earlier marriage to the new marriage. Or, they may reside in a household where the parents are of the same sex.

Volumes of data from a variety of sources reflect the changes that have occurred in America's family structure. For example, by the early 1990s, an estimated 15.5 million children were no longer living with two biological parents, and as many as 8 to 10 million children may have been born into families with a gay or lesbian parent. *See Alison D. v. Virginia M.*, 569 N.Y.S.2d 586, 589 (Judge Kay dissenting) (N.Y. App. 1991); Pew Social and Demographic Trends, *The Decline of Marriage and Rise of New Families* (November 2010); http://www.pewsocialtrends.org/2010/11/18/the-decline-of-marriage-and-rise-of-new-families/6/ (last visited July, 2012).

In December 2011, it was reported that "barely half of all adults in the United States — a record low — are currently married, and the median age at first marriage has never been higher for brides (26.5 years) and grooms (28.7)." D'Vera Cohn et al., *Barely Half of U.S. Adults Are Married — A Record Low*

New Marriages Down 5% from 2009 to 2010 (December 2011) http://www.pewsocialtrends.org/2011/12/14/barely-half-of-u-s-adults-are-married-a-record-low/ (last visited July, 2012); *see generally* Rose M. Kreider & Renee Ellis, Current Population Reports, *Number, Timing, and Duration of Marriages and Divorces:* 2009 (May 2011); http://www.census.gov/prod/2011pubs/p70-125.pdf (last visited July, 2012).

1.8. The Changing Role of the Federal Government in Marriage

As a broad generalization, family law remains primarily the province of state law. Furthermore, the Supreme Court has affirmed the state role in family matters, declaring that "the whole subject of domestic relations and husband and wife, parent and child, belongs to the laws of the States and not the laws of the United States." *Rose v. Rose*, 481 U.S. 619, 625 (1987), quoting *In re Burrus*, 136 U.S. 586, 693-694 (1890).

The Tenth Amendment's proviso that "the powers not delegated to the United States by the Constitution, nor prohibited by it to the States, are reserved to the States respectively, or to the people" was historically used to justify state exclusivity in the family law arena. *See Labine v. Cincent*, 401 U.S. 531 (1971). Despite this constitutional proviso, through application of the due process or equal protection clause of the Fourteenth Amendment, as well as the First Amendment, the Supreme Court has become involved in numerous areas of family law, including abortion, adoption, and termination of parental rights. *See generally* Linda D. Elrod, *The Federalization of Family Law*, 6-Sum Hum. Rts. 6 (Summer 2009).

Congress has also felt it necessary to legislate in several areas of family law. For example, when states could not agree on which of two jurisdictions should decide a fiercely contested interstate custody dispute, Congress stepped in to resolve the matter by enacting the Parental Kidnapping Prevention Act of 1980 (28 U.S.C. 1738A). In other areas, such as child support, Congress has enacted national legislation that affects how state courts arrive at support decisions. For example, in 1996, Congress passed the Personal Responsibility and Work Opportunity Act (42 U.S.C. §666). This Act required that states adopt a version of the Uniform Family Support Act by January 1, 1998 or face loss of federal funding for child support enforcement. Every state adopted some version of the Uniform Interstate Family Support Act (UIFSA), which limits the power of a state to modify another state's child support orders and addresses the enforcement of child support obligations within the United States. Congressional measures such as the Adoption and Safe Families Act (ASFA), which promotes the adoption of children with special needs, and the Adoption Assistance and Child

Welfare Act (AACWA), which provides incentives to move children from long-term foster care facilities to permanent homes, have been thought necessary. Another federal provision, the Child Abuse Prevention and Treatment Act (CAPTA), creates programs and procedures for states to address the prevention and treatment of child abuse and neglect. The Child Support Enforcement Act requires that states participate in the federal child support program. It also requires states to put in place procedures to establish paternity, obtain child support awards, and to enforce child support obligations.

These are a few examples of the many provisions passed into law by Congress that affect family law. Where states appear unwilling or incapable of solving a particular family law issue, one can anticipate continued involvement by Congress. In the process, states will continue to lose their claim that the whole subject of domestic relations belongs to the laws of the States and not the laws of the United States.

1.9. Same-Sex Marriage

Persons of the same-sex could not marry in any state of the United States until the beginning of the twenty-first century. In 2003, the Massachusetts Supreme Judicial Court opened the door for recognition of same-sex marriages. *See, e.g., Goodridge v. Department of Public Health*, 798 N.E.2d 941 (Mass. 2003) (holding that limitation of protections, benefits, and obligations of civil marriage to individuals of opposite sexes lacked rational basis and violated state constitutional equal protection principles). *Compare Andersen v. King County*, 138 P.3d 963 (2006) (rejecting constitutional right to marry) with *Kerrigan v. Commissioner of Public Health*, 957 A.2d 407 (Conn. 2008) (laws restricting civil marriage to heterosexual couples violated same-sex couples' state constitutional equal protection rights).

Early American sodomy criminal laws were not directed at homosexuals as such, but were intended to prohibit nonprocreative sexual activity more generally. *Lawrence v. Texas*, 539 U.S. 558, 559 (2003). The model sodomy 19th century indictments "addressed the predatory acts of an adult man against a minor girl or minor boy. Instead of targeting relations between consenting adults in private, 19th-century sodomy prosecutions typically involved relations between men and minor girls or minor boys, relations between adults involving force, relations between adults implicating disparity in status, or relations between men and animals." *Id.* at 569.

It is also of interest that in *Bower v. Hardwick*, 478 U.S. 186 (1986), the Supreme Court upheld the sodomy conviction of two consenting adults. In overruling that decision in *Lawrence v. Texas*, 539 U.S. 558 (2005), the Court noted that U.S. laws targeting same-sex couples did not develop until the last third of the 20th century. Even then, only nine states had singled out same-sex relations for criminal prosecution.

1.10. The Debate Concerning the Present Value of Marriage

Today, eminent scholars debate the question of the value of marriage to a society—a question to which an irrefutable answer appears somewhat elusive. Professor Lynn Wardle, for example, suggests that marriage "is the best, most promising foundation for lasting, growing, individual, and family happiness and security. It also is the very seedbed of democracy. Home is the place where we get our first ideas about ourselves, our attitudes toward other people, and our habits of approaching and solving problems." Lynn E. Wardle, *The Bonds of Matrimony and the Bonds of Constitutional Democracy*, 32 Hofstra L. Rev. 349, 371 (2003).

Maggie Gallagher, president of the Institute for Marriage and Public Policy, writes that "[m]arriage is an important social good, associated with an impressively broad array of positive outcomes for children and adults." 4 Ave Maria L.R. 409, 421 (Summer 2006).

However, Professor Martha Albertson Fineman suggests that "for all relevant and appropriate societal purposes, we do not need marriage, *per se*, at all. To state that we do not need marriage to accomplish many societal objectives is not the same thing as saying that we do not need a family to do so for some. However, family as a social category should not be dependent on having marriage as its core relationship. Nor is family synonymous with marriage." Martha Albertson Fineman, *Why Marriage?* 9 Va. J. Soc. Pol'y & L. 239, 245 (2001).

EXAMPLES

Examples

1. Assume that Lady Pamela and Lord Devlon were married in a sixteenth-century ceremony by the clergy in London, England. Unfortunately, the relationship broke down and each fell in love with another person and desperately wanted to marry the other person. With Lord Devlon's agreement, Lady Pamela sought the services of an ecclesiastical court to obtain a divorce. Would the court grant the couple a divorce?

2. Assume that Carl and Bertha married in Ohio in the nineteenth century. Before marriage, Bertha worked as a teacher and was paid a few hundred dollars a year. After they married, Carl began taking the money that Bertha continued to earn from teaching and got drunk on it. Bertha sought assistance from a common law court to prevent Carl from "boozing" and using up her salary. How successful will she be?

3. Assume that this is the nineteenth century, and that after Mary and Tom were married, Mary worked in a law office. Her employer considered her particularly gifted, and she actually did most of the work on the difficult

cases coming to the law office. She gained sufficient knowledge to apply to take the state bar examination, which she passed as the top student taking it. She then applied to be admitted to the state bar so that she could practice law. State law at the time permitted only men to be admitted to the bar. Mary challenged the state law on equal protection grounds. Will she be successful?

4. Assume that Lester, a World War II veteran who lost his legs on Iwo Jima, married Leona in 1945 in Alabama. Lester was white, Leona was black. The local prosecutor learned of the marriage and indicted them under Virginia's miscegenation statute. They were convicted and sentenced to three years in state prison. They challenge the Virginia law under which they were convicted on due process and equal protection grounds. How will a court rule on their challenge?

5. Assume that Professor Pinpot is interested in the origin of various principles applied in the past to family law by secular courts in the United States. He asks his students to explain the probable basis for the view held by common law family courts that when a couple married, they become one, and the one is the husband. Explain the possible origin of that concept.

EXPLANATIONS

Explanations

1. The ecclesiastical courts at this period in history would not grant an absolute divorce. The Church's view was that there existed a solemn covenant between the parties to marry, and this was carried into the canon law, which was applied by the ecclesiastical courts. The courts could not grant an absolute divorce, on any grounds. Note that Lady Pamela might attempt to seek an annulment of the marriage or ask for a decree of judicial separation, called divorce *a mensa et thoro* (divorce from bed and board). The decree of divorce *a mensa et thoro* did not sever the marital tie; the parties remained husband and wife. If granted by the ecclesiastical court, the parties could not remarry during the lifetime of their spouse, and the husband was normally required to provide his wife with permanent support. Lady Pamela might also seek an annulment on the basis of adultery. Annulments and divorce from bed and board are discussed in later chapters of this book.

2. Bertha will have a difficult time persuading a common law court to give her control of the rent funds. As a general rule, once married, a husband became the owner absolutely of the wife's personal property.

In addition, her earnings and her personal property accruing to her during coverture vested immediately in the husband. He was entitled to any rents arising from her land. *See Dotson v. Dotson*, 189 S. W. 894 (Ky. 1916); *Neighbors v. Neighbors*, 65 S. W. 607 (Ky. 1901); *Babcock v. Adams*, 196 S.W. 1118 (Mo. 1917).

3. Mary will fail in her attempt to persuade the court to allow her to practice law. In 1872, the Supreme Court upheld the constitutionality of a state law that denied women the right to practice law solely on grounds of sex. *Bradwell v. People of State of Illinois*, 83 U.S. 130 (1872).

4. It was not until 1967 that the Supreme Court in *Loving v. Virginia*, 388 U.S. 1 (1967), struck down state anti-miscegenation statutes.

5. The theory adopted as an integral feature of early American family law that, when a couple marry, they become one, and that "one" is the husband. This concept most likely is derived from the book of Genesis (Genesis 2:24). It states that a husband must leave the home of his parents to be joined to his wife, and "they shall become one flesh." This Biblical view of marriage is repeated by Paul in his Epistle to the Ephesians (Ephesians 5:31).

CHAPTER 2

Marriage Contracts — Requirements and Restrictions

2.1. Introduction

Historians and others report that the first recorded reference to a legal marriage can be traced to the Code of Hammurabi. Hammurabi was the ruler of the Kingdom of Babylon, 2125-2080 B.C. In the second year of his reign, he began reforms that resulted in the Hammurabi Code. It is said that he transformed a chaotic mass of customs into something like an orderly system of law, with dowries and bride prices as part of it. The Code provided that only those women who had once been married or had been seduced were free to marry the men of their choice. The others were given in marriage by their fathers who might accept or reject the suitors. Marriage was by contract; a marriage contract was drawn up, sealed, and witnessed. A Babylonian could have but one legal wife, though concubinage was permissible and common. *See In re Soeder's Estate*, 220 N.E.2d 547 (Ohio App. 1966) (discussing the ancient history of marriage).

Fast forward 4,000 years or so, and you have this chapter on marriage in this country. It reviews marriage customs, requirements, and restrictions from a general perspective found in most states of the United States. It examines many of the problems associated with the restrictions and requirements and considers constitutional rulings from state and federal courts that may affect marriage.

2.2. How Marriage Contracts Differ from Ordinary Contracts

A marriage contract is viewed in law as different from an ordinary civil contract. The distinction was recognized and discussed by the United States Supreme Court over 100 years ago in *Maynard v. Hill*, 125 U.S. 190 (1888). In *Maynard*, the Court explained that marriage is an institution of society, founded upon consent and contract of the parties. It stated that marriage contracts differed from ordinary contracts because the rights, duties, and obligations of the parties rested not upon their agreement but upon the general common or statutory law of the state, which defined and prescribed those rights, duties, and obligations. The Court observed that parties can neither modify nor change a marriage contract without state intervention and the contract binds them to a lifelong relationship. The Court emphasized that marriage contracts may not be terminated because of a simple agreement made solely between the two parties to it. According to the Court, the state always remains a third party and sets the grounds for ending the relationship.

A marriage contract can be created either by following criteria established by a state legislature by statute or, in a dwindling number of jurisdictions, by the parties' conduct. In the latter jurisdictions, the relationship creates what is referred to as a "common law marriage." Common law marriages are discussed in detail later in this chapter.

MARRIAGE REQUIREMENTS

2.3. State of Mind to Marry: Capacity — Generally

Capacity to marry may involve such diverse matters as mental or physical capacity, whether the marriage is incestuous, or whether the party is of sufficient age to marry. *See Matter of Estate of Hendrickson*, 805 P.2d 20, 21 (Kan. 1991). In general, capacity, except in states where same-sex marriages are allowed, requires that the parties be of different sex (male-female), not be married to someone else (bigamy), not be related to each other as defined by local statute, be of an age where state law permits them to marry, and be capable of understanding the nature of the act.

State of mind — mental capacity. As noted above, one must possess the mental capacity and state of mind to marry. In general, state of mind is said to consist of voluntarily entering into the relationship with the intent to marry at that time (not a sham). To determine mental capacity, a court asks whether a party is capable "of understanding the nature, effect, and consequences of the marriage." *Porter v. Ark. Dept. of Health & Human Servs.*, 286 S.W.3d 686, 696 (Ark. 2008). In *Matter of Estate of Hendrickson*, *supra*, the Arkansas court elaborated on the test for mental capacity:

> The test of mental capacity to contract is whether the person possesses sufficient mind to understand in a reasonable manner the nature and effect of the act in which he is engaged . . . . As related to the degree of mental capacity required to contract a marriage, there is a split of authority on whether the same degree of mental capacity necessary for entering into an ordinary contract is required or whether a lesser degree will suffice . . . . We adopt the test quoted in the [Annot., Mental Capacity to Marry, 82 A.L.R.2d 1040, 1044], which itself was taken from *Johnson v. Johnson*, 104 N.W.2d 8 (N.D. 1960), as follows:
>
> "'[T]he best accepted test as to whether there is a mental capacity sufficient to contract a valid marriage is whether there is a capacity to understand the nature of the contract and the duties and responsibilities which it creates.'"

The Uniform Marriage and Divorce Act, when considering capacity, states that a marriage is invalid if

> a party lacked capacity to consent to the marriage at the time the marriage was solemnized, either because of mental incapacity or infirmity or because of the influence of alcohol, drugs, or other incapacitating substances, or duress, or by fraud involving the essentials of marriage.

UMDA, §208(a)(1). Note that the issues of capacity and intent most commonly arise in the context of annulment actions.

2.4. Capacity — Guardian's Consent

In general, a guardian may consent to a marriage where the applicant is incompetent or is not of age to consent. *See Knight v. Radomski*, 414 A.2d 1211 (Me. 1980) (under the guardianship statutes, marriage of ward was not permitted without approval of the guardian, and thus marriage without consent of guardian should have been annulled); *Stiles v. Stiles*, 496 So. 2d 856 (Fla. App. 1986) (actions of guardian in attending and witnessing marriage of incompetent ward constituted consent to ward's marriage, despite his failure to sign consent form on marriage license). Depending on the language contained in a state statute, a guardian may petition to dissolve a marriage. *Ruvalcaba v. Ruvalcaba*, 850 P.2d 674 (Ariz. App. 1993) (guardian could petition for dissolution of marriage on behalf of incompetent adult ward); cf. *Samis v. Samis*, 22 A.3d 444 (Vt. 2011) (guardianship statute did not authorize guardian to file for divorce on behalf of wife).

2.5. Capacity — Age Restrictions

A state's interest in preventing unstable marriages is given as justification for allowing it to set a minimum age to marry. *Moe v. Dinkins*, 533 F. Supp. 623 (S.D. N.Y. 1981), judgment *aff'd*, 669 F.2d 67 (2d Cir. 1982). The justification rests on the theory that persons below a certain age lack the capacity to act in their own best interests.

The minimum legal age for marriage varies from jurisdiction to jurisdiction. However, in most states, a man and a woman 18 or older can marry without parental or judicial consent. In some states, with permission of the underage person's parents, guardian, or juvenile court, a person 15 years old who is pregnant or who is the father or putative father of a child may marry. *See, e.g.*, Indiana Code §31-11-1-6 (2012). However, most states set the minimum age to marry at 16.

The Uniform Marriage and Divorce Act (UMDA) §205, allows a judge, upon examination of the parties, to approve certain underage marriages. It declares that after a reasonable effort has been made to notify the parents or guardians of each underage party, the court may order the clerk to issue a marriage license and a marriage certificate form when a party is 16 or 17 and has no parent capable of consenting to marriage. Before a court can approve a marriage of an underage person, the judge must find that the underage person is capable of assuming the responsibilities of marriage and that marriage will serve the couple's best interests. Pregnancy alone does not necessarily establish that the best interest of the party will be served by allowing a marriage.

State statutory age barriers have withstood constitutional challenge, with courts applying the rational basis constitutional standard. *See, e.g.*, *Moe v. Dinkins*, 533 F. Supp. 623 (S.D. N.Y. 1981), *aff'd*, 669 F.2d 67 (2d Cir.), *cert. denied*, 459 U.S. 827 (1982). In *Moe v. Dinkins*, a New York law that required the consent of a parent before a minor between ages 14 to 18 could marry was upheld against a constitutional challenge. The court reasoned that the age restriction was rational because of the state's concern with unstable marriages and the inability of minors to make mature decisions. The court also explained that the statutory age restriction did not bar a marriage between the two applicants forever; rather, it delayed their marriage until they can marry without parental consent.

Note that in *State v. Gans*, 151 N.E.2d 709 (Ohio 1958), a child's parents consented to their daughter securing a marriage license by misrepresenting her age. They were found guilty of contributing to the delinquency of a minor because of their active participation in enabling the child to marry.

Note also *Stanton v. Stanton*, 421 U.S. 7 (1975), where the Supreme Court indicated that a difference in sex between children did not warrant a distinction in the Utah statute under which girls attained majority at 18 years of age, but boys did not attain majority until they were 21 years old. The Court observed that the statute could not, under any test, survive an attack based on an equal protection challenge.

2.6. Form of Marriage — Ministerial Act

Marriages are sometimes attacked by one of the parties, who claims there was a failure to comply with a particular rule or regulation. Because of the failure to comply, it is argued the marriage is void. For example, in *Application of Avery*, 445 N.Y.S.2d 672 (N.Y. Surr. 1981), the petitioner claimed that the marriage between the Petitioner and decedent was void because it occurred before the entry of the judgment of divorce. The court rejected the claim, stating that it was clear that the spouse of the Petitioner, before his marriage to the decedent, was granted a divorce, and all that remained was the entry of the decree of divorce. Under the facts, this was a ministerial act and did not form the basis to annul the second marriage. *See Poulos v. Poulos*, 737 A.2d 885 (Vt. 1999).

When courts refer to an action as "ministerial," they are generally describing a governmental decision involving little or no personal judgment by the public official as to the wisdom or manner of carrying out the project. *Hansen v. South Dakota DOT*, 584 N.W.2d 881 (S.D. 1998) (ministerial act is defined as absolute, certain, and imperative, involving merely the execution of a specific duty arising from fixed designated facts). However, judicial efforts to distinguish between discretionary and ministerial acts have produced an array of decisions with results that are difficult to harmonize. For example, in New York, requiring a clerk to ascertain if a party or the parties applicant are entitled to marry before issuing a license, is viewed as both discretionary and ministerial in nature. *Puffer v. City of Binghamton*, 301 N.Y.S.2d 274 (N.Y. Sup. 1969). In Illinois, issuance of marriage licenses and new birth certificates are considered ministerial acts that generally do not involve fact-finding. *See In re Marriage of Simmons*, 355 Ill. App. 949 (Ill. App. 2005); *see generally* John J. Dvorske, *Licenses — Issuance of license*, 55 C.J.S. Marriage §28 (May 2012).

2.7. Marriage License

Most state statutes impose a set of specific requirements on persons who intend to marry. For example, in all jurisdictions, a couple formally intending to marry must first obtain a state marriage license. This usually requires that one of the two persons seeking the license go to the office of a local official charged with issuing a license.

State statutes generally impose a short waiting period between the date the marriage license is obtained from the appropriate official and the date of the marriage ceremony. UMDA §204 suggests as a guideline that a marriage license become effective 3 days after it is issued and expire 180 days later. The 3-day waiting period may be waived or modified by a judge in an emergency or under extraordinary circumstances.

Strict compliance. States vary in terms of whether they will require strict or substantial compliance with their marriage license statutes. States that believe that strict compliance with marriage statutes is mandatory reason that they must guard against recognition of informal relationships. They also point to *specific language* contained in their marriage statutes that mandates compliance. *See, e.g.*, *Hall v. Maal*, 32 So. 3d 682 (Fla. App. 2010) (marital ceremony with marriage license obtained one year later and neither solemnized nor returned to clerk did not result in a legally cognizable marriage); *Yaghoubinejad v. Haghighi*, 894 A.2d 1173 (N.J. Super. 2006) (marriage without a license is void).

Substantial compliance. In a majority of jurisdictions, where the statutory language in marriage statutes is less specific, only substantial compliance is normally required for a valid marriage. These states reason that they should recognize the parties' reasonable expectations, even though there may be an imperfection in the marriage license or official application. *See, e.g.*, *McPeek v. McCardle*, 888 N.E.2d 171 (Ind. 2008) (marriage solemnized in Ohio without the benefit of an Ohio marriage license is defective but not void as against Ohio public policy); *Hames v. Hames*, 316 A.2d 379 (Conn. 1972) (mere signing of the marriage license by the priest while the defendant was present but during the absence of the plaintiff prevented solemnization — made marriage voidable rather than void); *Carabetta v. Carabetta*, 438 A.2d 109 (Conn. 1980) (where parties had gone through a duly solemnized marriage ceremony, although they had failed to obtain a marriage license, and thereafter lived together as husband and wife, raising a family of four children, all of whose birth certificates listed husband as their father, marriage of parties was not void); *Fryar v. Roberts*, 57 S.W.3d 727, 733 (Ark. 2001) ("Statutes requiring a marriage license shall not be regarded as mandatory in the absence of a clear legislative purpose that the statutes should be so construed").

Note that there is additional discussion about annulments and marriage license requirements in Chapter 3 of this book.

2.8. Solemnizing a Marriage

When a couple solemnizes their marriage, it is said to serve several purposes. For example, solemnization provides public notice of the impending marriage and creates a permanent public record of the event. It may also satisfy a religious tradition and act to impress on the couple the seriousness of the relationship. Courts are reluctant to void an improperly solemnized marriage. *Barbosa-Johnson v. Johnson*, 851 P.2d 866 (Ariz. App. 1993) (marriage was not invalid on grounds that it was solemnized by Puerto Rican pastor rather than duly licensed or ordained Arizona member of the clergy).

The UMDA suggests that "[a] marriage may be solemnized by a judge of a court of record, by a public official whose powers include solemnization of marriages, or in accordance with any mode of solemnization recognized by any religious denomination, Indian Nation or Tribe, or Native Group." UMDA §206(a).

Common law marriages, where recognized, raise an obvious issue about solemnization. However, the United States Supreme Court resolved that issue in *Meister v. Moore*, 96 U.S. 76 (1877), holding that common law marriages are valid, notwithstanding statutes that require ceremonial marriages to be solemnized by a minister or a magistrate, if no specific provision to the contrary exists. As the Court explained: "No doubt, a statute may take away a common law right; but there is always a presumption that the legislature has no such intention, unless it be plainly expressed." *Id.* at 79; *see J.M.H. v. Rouse*, 143 P.3d 1116 (Colo. App. 2006); *State v. Ward*, 28 S.E.2d 785 (S.C. 1944).

Note that Native American nations retain sovereign authority to regulate domestic relations laws, including marriage of their Indian subjects. *U.S. v. Jarvison*, 409 F.3d 1221 (10th Cir. 2005); *see Montana v. United States*, 450 U.S. 544, 564 (1981) ("Indian tribes retain their inherent power to determine tribal membership, to regulate domestic relations among members, and to prescribe rules of inheritance for members").

2.9. Void/Voidable Distinction

Although "void" and "voidable" as concepts are covered in detail in the following chapter, it is useful at this point to grasp their basic differences.

Void. In annulment actions, parties are seeking to void the relationship. When deciding these disputes, courts use the term "void" or "voidable," depending on the facts and the law in a particular jurisdiction. A *void* relationship is a nullity and is considered invalid from its inception, whether or not it has been so declared in a court of law. *See generally Black's Law Dictionary* 994-995, 1098 (8th ed. 2004).

A marriage that is ruled as "void" typically is one that offends a strong public policy. Examples of void marriages are those involving bigamy, polygamy, and incest. A void marriage normally does not require a judicial declaration or action to establish that it is not valid. However, a court order may be sought in order to provide certainty to a party to a void relationship and to establish a public record of its invalidity.

Voidable. In contrast to a void relationship, a *voidable* relationship is one that is recognized as valid for all purposes until it is judicially declared a nullity. As a rule, it may only be challenged by a party entitled by statute to assert its voidability. *In re Gregorson's Estate*, 160 Cal. 21 (1911); *Flaxman v. Flaxman*, 273 A.2d 567 (1971). Whether a court determines that a marriage is void or voidable may be of significant importance to the outcome of a particular dispute. *See, e.g.*, *Patey v. Peaslee*, 111 A.2d 194 (N.H. 1955) (marriage was voidable, not void; therefore, spouse not barred from intestate share of estate).

Note that even in the case of a voidable marriage, a court issuing a judgment of nullity will usually use language declaring that "no valid marriage ever existed." *Millar v. Millar*, 167 P. 394 (Cal. 1917). Unfortunately, this kind of language sometimes generates confusion in understanding the intended outcome of the dispute.

Examples

1. Assume that P married D when P was 83, D was 22, and the marriage took place less than a month before P's death from lung cancer. P left an estate valued at $10 million. At the time of the marriage, P was heavily medicated, undergoing chemotherapy, and required the daily assistance of an in-home nurse. P was also hooked up to an oxygen tank during the wedding. Following P's death, P's estate brings an action contesting the marriage, claiming it was void because P did not have the capacity to consent to the marriage. D asserts that the marriage is voidable at her option; that P's estate does not have standing to contest the marriage. How will a court most likely rule?
2. Lisa, who divorced Jack, married John. A few months following the marriage, Lisa sought to void the marriage on the ground that she lacked the capacity to marry. In support of her capacity claim, she testified that she is a Catholic and cannot remarry without the consent of the Catholic Church. She testified she did not obtain that consent; therefore, she lacked the capacity to go through with a civil marriage ceremony. How will a court rule on Lisa's effort to void (annul) the marriage?
3. Assume that P, age 15, who is pregnant, desires to marry X, age 50, who is the father of the child. P's mother consents to the marriage. P's father, D, objects and argued that the language of a statute in this jurisdiction

stating that a minor "between the ages of 16 and 18 may marry with the consent of one parent and district court authorization" prevents someone 15 from marrying. P and her mother challenge the age limitation in the statute as unconstitutional. Assume that common law marriages have been abolished in this jurisdiction. The trial court held without explanation that the statute limiting marriage by age was unconstitutional and permitted P, age 15, to marry. D challenged the constitutional ruling on appeal. How will an appellate court most likely rule?

4. Assume that a state statute established the age to marry without parental consent at 18 for women and 19 for men. P (a man), age 18, wants to marry D (a woman), age 18, but P's parents refuse to consent to the marriage. P challenges the state statute on gender grounds. Most likely, how will a court rule on P's challenge?

5. Assume that P and D desire to marry. P is 15, and D is 18. The jurisdiction where they intend to marry has abolished common law marriages and has enacted a statute that allows a minor age 15 to 17 to marry with either parent's consent or after a finding that the minor is capable of assuming the responsibilities of marriage and that the marriage would be in the minor's best interests. Both P's and D's parents are opposed to the marriage. Despite the opposition, P and D petition the juvenile court for permission to marry. At the juvenile court hearing, evidence is introduced that P is not pregnant; she loves D, lives with her parents, and is regularly attending high school as a sophomore. There was also evidence that D just graduated from high school and has a full-time job at a local fast food restaurant. He has his own apartment and owns an older-model car. He has no outstanding debts. He stated he wanted to get married because he loved P and he "can't live without her." Most likely, how will a court rule on the request by the couple to allow them to marry over both parents' objection?

6. Assume that Pam and Donald decide to marry and that Pam obtains a marriage license, which must be completed and returned to the county clerk's office within 60 days of the wedding ceremony so the court clerk can fill in information on the back of it. Then the license is filed. After obtaining the license, they go through with their marriage ceremony, which is presided over by a minister. The license is signed, but Pam puts the license in a drawer and forgets to return it to the local clerk's office for filing. Ten months later, the two break up. Donald seeks a divorce and Pam finds the marriage license in the drawer where she put it. She responds that there was never a marriage because the license was never properly filed with the county clerk and Donald is not entitled to use the state's divorce provisions. How will a court most likely rule on this question?

Explanations

1. A court will examine all the facts surrounding the alleged marriage. These cases will turn on the answer to the question of whether capacity is viewed in this jurisdiction as an action voidable only at the option of the surviving wife or void. The prevailing rule is that a void marriage may be annulled after the death of one of the parties in the absence of a statute to the contrary. *See*, *Estate of Davis*, 640 P.2d 692 (Or. App. 1982) ("A void marriage, . . . is invalid from the outset and may be challenged by third parties"); *Kuehmsted v. Turnwall*, 138 So. 775 (Fla. 1932) (holding wife was of unsound mind, insane, and wholly incompetent at time of marriage to husband nine days before her death; thus, marriage was void ab initio, and heirs of decedent permitted to bring annulment action after the wife's death); *Succession of Ricks*, 893 So. 2d 98 (La. App. 2004) (holding a child alleging deceased father lacked capacity to enter contract of marriage, acting as succession representative, is the proper plaintiff to bring action to have marriage annulled under statute giving succession representative authority to sue to enforce a right of the deceased, whether the action is personal, real, or mixed); *In re Canon's Estate*, 221 Wis. 322, 266 N.W. 918 (1936) (holding because a void marriage is an absolute nullity from its beginning and cannot be ratified, it may be questioned during the life of the parties to the marriage, and with some statutory exceptions, after the death of either or both, directly or collaterally); *In re Estate of Santolino*, 895 A.2d 506 (N.J. Super. 2005); *In re Estate of Crockett*, 728 N.E.2d 765 (Ill. App. 5 Dist. 2000). The answer rests solely with whether capacity in this jurisdiction is considered sufficient to void a marriage, or whether the marriage is only voidable. If void, the estate may proceed with its challenge.

2. Even if lack of permission from the Catholic Church prevented Lisa from marrying John within the church, it would not prevent her from entering into a civil or a common law marriage. A religious prohibition on remarriage is not a "legal impediment" to marriage and does not affect a person's legal capacity to marry. *In re Marriage of Seymour*, 2012 WL 309332 (Kan. App. 2012). (Note that annulment actions are discussed in detail later in this book.) On this evidence, a court will rule that Lisa has failed to prove she lacked capacity to enter into a marriage with John.

3. The law is well settled that states have the right and power to establish reasonable limitations on the age of a person to marry. This authority is justified as an exercise of police power, which confers upon the states the ability to enact laws to protect the safety, health, morals, and general

welfare of society. This general principle appears to collide with the United States Supreme Court view that parents have a fundamental liberty interest in the care, custody, and management of their children. However, the Court has made it clear that even though these parental rights are fundamental, they are not absolute; because of a state's interest in the welfare of children, it may limit parental authority. In this example, there exists a rational relation between the means chosen by the legislature and legitimate state interests in adopting and enforcing the age restriction. Considering the important state interest in promoting the welfare of children by preventing unstable marriages among those lacking the capacity to act in their own best interests, the restriction would most likely be upheld as constitutional (applying the rational basis theory) and the alleged marriage would be viewed as void.

4. There has been a longstanding gender difference in American jurisprudence between the age when men/boys and women/girls may marry. For example, the common law allowed girls age 12 and boys age 14 to marry. The gender distinction was carried from the common law and placed in an altered form into many early state marriage statutes. The Supreme Court in *Stanton v. Stanton*, 421 U.S. 7 (1975), ruled that a state statute was unconstitutional that specified for males a greater age of majority than it specified for females. It held the statute denied, in the context of a parent's obligation for support payments for his children, the equal protection of the laws guaranteed by the Fourteenth Amendment. In this hypothetical, there is no compelling state interest that justifies treating males and females of the same age differently for the purpose of determining their rights to a marriage license. There is likewise no rational basis for the distinction. In this example, the statute would most likely be struck down as unconstitutional because of the gender difference, and P would most likely be permitted by law to marry D. *See also Reed v. Reed*, 404 U.S. 71 (1971) (Idaho statute which provides that as between persons equally qualified to administer estates, males must be preferred to females, is based solely on a discrimination prohibited by and violative of the equal protection clause of the Fourteenth Amendment).

5. The court will consider whether both applicants understand and appreciate the duties and responsibilities of married life. Studies indicate teenage marriages have a high rate of instability, lead to decreased educational attainment for girls, and teen fathers earn less in early adulthood than males who delay parenting until after age 20. The court may consider the fact that P had proposed marriage to D, and to some extent, he may appear gallant in accepting the proposal. The opposition of both

families to the marriage, the fact that P is not pregnant, and D's current employment all suggest that granting a marriage at this time is not in P's best interests. Most likely, the court will not grant the marriage request.

6. A court will most likely rule that the failure to do a ministerial act, such as returning the marriage license to the county clerk within 60 days of its issuance, cannot render a marriage void and does not by itself defeat the existence of the alleged marriage. *See In Re Estate of Mirizzi*, 723 N.Y.S.2d 623 (N.Y. Surr. 2001) (entry of judgment of divorce was mere ministerial act); *Barbosa-Johnson v. Johnson*, 851 P.2d 866 (Ariz. App. 1993) (pastor who performed marriage ceremony in Puerto Rico failing to file marriage license in violation of Arizona statute, did not, alone, invalidate marriage under Arizona law); *Wright v. State*, 81 A.2d 602 (Md. 1951) (certified copy of an official record of a marriage is not the only means of establishing marriage); *In re Parson's Estate*, 59 A.2d 709 (Del. Super 1948) (parties participated in ceremony with witnesses and "the possibility of the existence of a license may be surmised," said the court, "for she described the production and signing of certain documents and we cannot absolutely assume that because no record of the marriage exists, our system of records is so perfect as to preclude the possibility of error in recording the issuance of a license"); *Fryar v. Roberts*, 57 S.W.3d 727 (Ark. 2001) (failure to do a ministerial act, such as returning the marriage license to the county clerk within 60 days of its issuance, cannot by itself render a marriage void). Even if a court were to rule the marriage void, the jurisdiction's putative spouse statute would provide protection for the innocent party.

2.10. Premarital Medical Testing

The nature and extent of medical testing a state may require of persons seeking to marry is relatively clear — states can require that a prospective bride and groom undertake certain premarital testing. *See, e.g., Jones v. Shaw*, 441 P.2d 990 (Okla. 1965) (premarital physical examination may be waived by the county judge only if there is medical testimony supporting such a decision).

The Supreme Court, in a decision made over 50 years ago, expressed its view of blood testing in *Breithaupt v. Abram*, 352 U.S. 432, 436, 448 (1957). In that decision, the Court observed:

> [t]he blood test procedure has become routine in our everyday life. It is a ritual for those going into the military service as well as those applying for marriage licenses. Many colleges require such tests before permitting entrance and

> literally millions of us have voluntarily gone through the same . . . routine in becoming blood donors.

The commentary to UMDA §203 suggests that premarital medical exams and tests are of little utility. According to the commentary,

> the traditional forms of premarital medical examination, now required by the marriage laws of most of the states, need not be preserved. The premarital medical examination requirement serves either to inform the prospective spouses of health hazards that may have an impact on their marriage, or to warn public health officials of the presence of venereal disease. For the latter purpose, the statutes have been proved to be both avoidable and highly inefficient.

The UMDA makes the requirement of a medical examination optional.

There is no doubt, however, that at various times, many states have required that a marriage license applicant file a health certificate of some sort with the licensing authority. The requirements have varied among the states, with some jurisdictions asking that applicants certify that they have submitted to a medical examination and do not have a venereal disease, or, if infected, that they are not in a communicable state. *Peterson v. Widule*, 147 N.W. 966 (Wis. 1914) (upon application for a marriage license, the male party to such marriage must, within 15 days prior to the application, be examined by a physician of designated qualifications with reference to the existence or nonexistence of any venereal disease); *see also* W.S.A. 765.13 ("The marriage license worksheet shall contain . . . any other information items that the department of health services determines are necessary . . ."). Some states have required tests for measles for female applicants. *See generally People v. Smith*, 23 Cal. Rptr. 5 (Cal. App. 1962); *Hall v. Hall*, 108 S.E.2d 487 (N.C. 1959).

In 1987, the Illinois legislature mandated that all marriage license applicants be tested for exposure to the AIDS virus. A year after its enactment, the number of marriage licenses issued in the state dropped by 25 percent, as many couples either went out of state to be married or simply declined to get married. Jana B. Singer, *The Privatization of Family Law*, 1992 Wis. L. Rev. 1443 n.115. "Of the 221,000 people married in Illinois during the first 18 months of the statute's operation, only 44 tested positive for HIV exposure. In June 1989, the legislature repealed the testing requirement." *Ibid; see generally* Michael Closen, Robert Gamrath, & Dem Hopkins, *Mandatory Premarital HIV Testing: Political Exploitation of the Aids Epidemic*, 69 Tul. L. Rev. 71 (November 1994) (strenuously taking issue with the idea that mandatory premarital HIV testing is necessary to serve the compelling HIV-AIDS related interests); Robert D. Goodman, *In Sickness or in Health: The Right to Marry and The Case of HIV Antibody Testing*, 38 DePaul L. Rev. 87 (Fall 1988). Louisiana mandated premarital AIDS testing for a brief period but repealed that requirement along with other medical testing requirements in 1988. *See* LA Rev. Stat. Ann. §9:230-31 (West Supp. 1988) (repealed 1988).

In *Matter of Kilpatrick*, 375 S.E.2d 794 (W. Va. 1988), a couple wishing to marry were ordained ministers of the Universal Life Church and challenged the constitutionality of a West Virginia statute requiring them to undergo serological tests. They claimed mandating the tests violated the free exercise clause of the United States Constitution and the state constitution because it required them to disobey the canon law of their church in order to marry. The state responded to their argument, saying that there were three compelling reasons for the test: (1) detection of a communicable disease (syphilis); (2) protection of the health interests of prenuptial couples; and (3) protection of the interests of the future children of the married couple. The court held that the free exercise clauses of the federal and state constitutions were not violated.

Note that a Utah statute prohibiting marriage by a person afflicted with AIDS was ruled invalid because it was in conflict with the Americans with Disabilities Act (ADA). *T.E.P. v. Leavitt*, 840 F. Supp. 110 (D. Utah 1993).

2.11. Premarital Counseling and Education

The serious nature of marriage makes adequate premarital counseling and education highly desirable. *See generally* Mayo Clinic, Premarital Counseling *http://www.mayoclinic.com/health/premarital-counseling/MY00951/DSECTION=why-its-done* (last visited March, 2012). Premarital counseling is viewed as one way to prevent unwise, hasty marriages. Some jurisdictions have proposed reducing marriage license fees for couples who receive premarital counseling. *See, e.g.*, U.C.A. 1953 §30-1-30 (policy of Utah to enhance the possibility of couples to achieve more stable, satisfying and enduring marital and family relationships by providing opportunities for and encouraging the use of premarital counseling prior to securing a marriage license by persons under 19 years of age and by persons who have been previously divorced); 43 Okl. St. Ann. §5.1 (2012) (reducing fee for marriage license to persons successfully completing premarital counseling program); Cal. Fam. Code §304 (2008) (court requires parties to prospective marriage of a minor to participate in premarital counseling concerning social, economic, and personal responsibilities incident to marriage, if the court considers the counseling to be necessary. The parties shall not be required, without their consent, to confer with counselors provided by religious organizations of any denomination).

Where premarital education legislation is in force, it normally specifies that the topics include a discussion of the seriousness of marriage, conflict management skills, and encouragement of counseling should the marriage fall into difficulty. The statutes usually allow the educational counseling to be provided by a member of the clergy, a person authorized by law to perform marriages, or a marriage and family therapist.

TYPES OF MARRIAGE

2.12. Common Law Marriage

Early common law view. It may be of some interest that the concept of parties engaging in a common law marriage was initially discouraged in colonial America. For example, the Colony of New Plymouth enacted legislation as early as 1636 to regulate the law of marriage and to discourage common law marriage. The General Assembly of New Hampshire passed legislation for the prevention of common law marriages in 1679. In 1684, the Colonial Assembly of New York passed an act requiring marriage to be solemnized formally. *In re Soeder's Estate*, 220 N.E.2d 547 (Ohio App. 1966) (discussing history of common law marriages). In England, it was declared in an 1844 decision of the House of Lords that informal marriages were never valid in that country. *Reg. v. Millis*, 10 Cl. & Fin. 534 (1844). However, a more accurate view of history is that the earlier English common law recognized informal marriages. *Dalrymple, v. Dalrymple*, 2 Hagg. Con. 54 (1811).

By 1753 "some of the the original colonies drafted legislation requiring marriage regulations while others adopted common law marriage under English common law." Sonya Garza, *Common Law Marriage: A Proposal for the Revival of a Dying Doctrine*, 40 New Eng. L. Rev. 541, 542 (Winter 2006). After the Revolution, many states adopted common law marriage and did so for a variety of reasons including the influence of a particular culture and/or the absence of clergy. *Ibid.*

By the end of the nineteenth century, common law marriages appered to be on the decline. It was recognized that a legislature had a right to abrogate common law marriage. However, states were slow in doing so. For example, by 1919, there were statutes in most, if not all jurisdictions, prescribing the formalities for the solemnization of marriages. However, the statutes did not have the effect of nullifying otherwise valid informal marriages, unless they expressly so provided. As a consequence, in most states during this period, common law marriages were still valid. Note *Marriage by Mail*, 32 Harv. L. Rev. 848, 849 (May 1919); *see generally State ex rel. Schneider v. Liggett*, 576 P.2d 221 (Kan. 1978). (Neither the Fourteenth Amendment to the United States Constitution nor the Kansas Bill of Rights prohibit the legislature from making changes in the law which affect a person's rights as they existed at common law.) Jurisdictions that recognized common law marriages came under increasing pressure to do away with them for a variety of reasons. *See P.N.C. Bank Corp. v. W.C.A.B. (Stamos)*, 831 A.2d 1269 (Pa. Commw. 2003) (discussing reasons for abrogating common law marriage in Pennsylvania); *see also* Cynthia Grant Bowman, *A Feminist Proposal to Bring Back Common Law Marriage*, 75 Or. L. Rev. 709 (Fall 1996) (exploring the origins of the institution of common law marriage and the impact upon women of its abolition).

As noted above, when states began to eliminate common law marriages, they justified their abolition on various grounds. It was observed that the pioneering conditions that had fostered common law marriages had disappeared and were not longer needed. There were concerns about the absence of public marriage records that would assist in verifying the property rights of spouses. There was a feeling in some quarters that recognition allowed spouses to avoid completely some of the state's objectives in enacting marriage statutes, such as obtaining medical examinations to prevent the spread of disease, collecting fee payments to finance recordkeeping, and requiring waiting periods to prevent impulsive unions. There was a practical difficulty of proving such marriages existed. Some criticized them as improperly sanctioning immorality and debasing formal marriage. Still others contended that the common law marriage concept encouraged perjury and fraud by unwed cohabitants hoping to gain the financial benefits of a "marriage" that never existed.

The Ohio Appellate Court in *In re Soeder's Estate*, *supra*, made the following observation:

> History has shown that at times, in years gone by, and still in some of the more remote parts of the United States, in order to get to a courthouse to obtain a marriage license, great hardships had to be undergone. In fact, in some of the southern states, years ago, a couple would marry by simply jumping over a gun lying on the ground, in the presence of witnesses. And when the traveling minister would make his monthly or semi-annual trips to that section, they would have a church ceremony. By the wildest stretch of one's imagination, such could not be the case . . . [today]. A fifteen minute ride would have brought [the parties to this action] to the courthouse for the license, and they were within the sound of the church bells from all directions when this alleged common-law marriage was entered into.

Id. at 562. Eventually, only a handful of jurisdictions retained the concept.

Limited recognition today. Today, only nine states (Alabama, Colorado, Kansas, Rhode Island, South Carolina, Iowa, Montana, Oklahoma, and Texas) and the District of Columbia recognize common law marriages contracted within their borders. National Conference of State Legislatures,

Common Law Marriage, http://www.ncsl.org/default.aspx?tabid=4265 (last visited October, 2011). Five states have "grandfathered" common law marriage (Georgia, Idaho, Ohio, Oklahoma, and Pennsylvania) and recognize common law marriages established before a certain date. New Hampshire recognizes common law marriage only for purposes of probate, and Utah recognizes common law marriages only if they have been validated by a court or administrative order. *Ibid.* Where recognized, a common law marriage provides an informal marriage relationship with legal standing.

Defined. A common law marriage is usually defined as a marriage created by the express agreement of the parties without ceremony, and often without a witness. It is an agreement in words — not *in futuro* or *in postea*, but *in praesenti*, uttered with a view and for the purpose of establishing the relationship of husband and wife. *See In re Wells' Estate*, 108 N.Y.S. 164, 166 (N.Y. 1908) (No specific form of words is needed, and all that is essential is proof of an agreement to enter into the legal relationship of marriage at the present time). Capacity and mutual consent are essential to a common law marriage. *Black's Law Dictionary* 277 (6th ed. 1990) (common law marriage requires "a positive mutual agreement, permanent and exclusive of all others, to enter into a marriage relationship, cohabitation sufficient to warrant a fulfillment of necessary relationship of man and wife, and an assumption of marital duties and obligations"); *Watson v. Bowden*, 38 S.3d 93 (Ala. App. 2009) (setting forth Alabama's criteria); *People v. Lucero*, 747 P.2d 660 (Colo. 1987).

Typical requirements. The elements of a common law marriage generally include (1) an agreement of marriage *in praesenti*, (2) made by parties competent to contract, (3) accompanied and followed by cohabitation as husband and wife, (4) subsequently holding oneself out as being married, and (5) gaining a reputation as being married. All five elements must usually be proven, although whether the proof must be clear and convincing or merely a preponderance varies among jurisdictions. *See, e.g., Nestor v. Nestor*, 472 N.E.2d 1091 (Ohio 1984) (clear and convincing); *Callen v. Callen*, 620 S.E.2d 59 (S.C. 2005) (preponderance); *Coleman v. U.S.*, 948 A.2d 534 (D.C. 2008) (the elements of common law marriage in this jurisdiction are cohabitation as husband and wife, following an express mutual agreement, which must be in words of the present tense; the existence of an agreement may be inferred from the character and duration of cohabitation); *Russell v. Russell*, 865 S.W.2d 929, 931 (Tex. 1993) (agreement to be married may be established by direct or circumstantial evidence). Although it is typically required that there be a holding out that the parties are married to those with whom they normally come in contact, a common law marriage will not necessarily be defeated if all persons in the community within which the parties reside are not aware of the marital arrangement.

When the parties are otherwise disabled from testifying regarding the creation of a common law contract *verba in praesenti*, or when there is a conflict in the evidence regarding the agreement, courts may apply a rebuttable presumption favoring the marriage if sufficient proof is presented of cohabitation and reputation of marriage. *Jeanes v. Jeanes*, 177 S.E.2d 537, 539-540 (S.C. 1970). This presumption may be overcome by "strong, cogent" evidence that the parties in fact never agreed to marry. *Id.* at 540.

Temporary absence from state. A few jurisdictions have concluded that residents of a state that prohibits common law marriages may temporarily leave the state without taking up a new residence and consummate a common law marriage elsewhere that will be recognized in the forum state. *See, e.g., Lieblein v. Charles Chips, Inc.*, 32 A.D.2d 1016, (N.Y. App. 1969), *affirmed* 271 N.E.2d 234 (N.Y. 1971) (one-week visit in Georgia sufficient for common law marriage in workers' compensation dispute). On the other hand, some jurisdictions have indicated they will not recognize common law marriages consummated where residents temporarily left the state and where the law of the forum state invalidates common law marriages. *See, e.g., Metropolitan Life Ins. Co. v. Chase*, 294 F.2d 500, 503 (3d Cir. 1961) (applying New Jersey law — temporary visit in District of Columbia insufficient to establish common law marriage); *Peirce v. Peirce*, 39 N.E.2d 990 (Ill. 1942); *Winn v. Wiggins*, 135 A.2d 673 (N.J. Super 1957). This is especially true, of course, if there is a statute in the forum state that expressly invalidates common law marriages entered into by residents while living temporarily in another state. *See In re Vetas' Estate*, 170 P.2d 183 (Utah 1946) (under Utah's statute in existence until 1989, persons domiciled in Utah could not go into another state, there contract a common law marriage, and, returning to Utah, have such marriage recognized as valid); Utah Code Ann. §30-1-4.5 (1989); *In re Van Schaick's Estate*, 40 N.W.2d 588 (Wisc. 1949) (woman living and cohabiting in Wisconsin with man to whom she was not formally married did not enter into common law marriage by living with him and holding herself out to public as his wife in Texas during their summer vacations in view of statute invalidating state residents' foreign marriages prohibited by state laws).

Mere cohabitation. Courts have consistently held that merely living together for a period of time does not support formation of a common law marriage relationship. *In re Thomas' Estate*, 367 N.Y.S.2d 182 (N.Y. Surr. 1975); *In re Marriage of Winegard*, 257 N.W.2d 609, 616 (Iowa 1977).

2.13. Putative Marriage Doctrine

Overview. Most jurisdictions have adopted by statute the "putative marriage doctrine." Under this doctrine, a spouse who believed in good faith that he or she was validly married, and who participated in a ceremonial marriage, is allowed to use a state's divorce provisions, even though the marriage is found to be void because of an impediment. The person is also allowed to participate as a surviving wife or husband in the deceased's estate *See* Christopher L. Blakesley, *The Putative Marriage Doctrine*, 60 Tul. L. Rev. 1, 6 (1985); *see, e.g.*, Neb. Rev. St. §42-378 (2012) ("When the court finds that a party entered into the contract of marriage in good faith supposing the other to be capable of contracting, and the marriage is declared a nullity, such fact shall be entered in the decree and the court may order such innocent party compensated as in the case of dissolution of marriage, including an award for costs and attorney fees"); Minn. Stat. §518.055 (1986) ("Any person who has cohabited with another to whom the person is not legally married in the good faith belief that the person was married to the other is a putative spouse until knowledge of the fact that the person is not legally married terminates the status and prevents acquisition of further rights.")

Rights acquired. Although provisions in various state statutes may vary, a putative spouse generally acquires the rights conferred upon a legal spouse, including the right to maintenance following termination of the status, whether or not the marriage is prohibited or declared a nullity. If there is a legal spouse or other putative spouses, rights acquired by a putative spouse do not supersede the rights of the legal spouse or those acquired by other putative spouses. In this case, the court will apportion property, maintenance, and support rights among the claimants as appropriate in the circumstances and in the interests of justice. The putative marriage doctrine is intended to protect a party who is ignorant of an impediment that makes the marriage either void or voidable.

Application. Putative spouses have received benefits as though the couple involved in the relationship were legally married in numerous cases. For example, putative spouses have received spousal benefits under the civil service retirement statute (5 U.S.C. §8341 (2000)), *Brown v. Devine*, 574 F. Supp. 790, 792 (N.D. Cal. 1983); the Longshoremen's and Harbor Workers' Compensation Act (33 U.S.C. §901 (1927) *et seq.*, *Powell v. Rogers* 496 F.2d 1248, 1250 (9th Cir. 1974), *cert. den.*, 419 U.S. 1032; and the Social Security Act (42 U.S.C. §416 (2004), *Aubrey v. Folsom* 151 F. Supp. 836, 840 (N.D. Cal. 1957). A putative spouse who was "dependent" on the decedent spouse had standing to bring a wrongful death action in California. *Kunakoff v. Woods*, 332 P2d 773, 775 (Cal. 1958). A putative spouse relationship legally terminates upon an innocent party's loss of a good-faith belief that he or she is married.

UMDA. The UMDA has suggested that states adopt the following language when enacting a putative spouse statute:

> [a]ny person who has cohabited with another to whom he is not legally married in the good faith belief that he was married to that person is a putative spouse until knowledge of the fact that he is not legally married terminates his status and prevents acquisition of further rights. A putative spouse acquires the rights conferred upon a legal spouse, including the right to maintenance following termination of his status, whether or not the marriage is prohibited or declared invalid. If there is a legal spouse or other putative spouses, rights acquired by a putative spouse do not supersede the rights of the legal spouse or those acquired by the other putative spouses, but the court shall apportion property, maintenance, and support rights among the claimants as appropriate in the circumstances and in the interests of justice.
>
> UMDA §209, 9A U.L.A. 192 (1998).

Community property states. Nine community property states recognize the putative spouse doctrine, although distribution and an award of divorce-like benefits may differ somewhat from that in states that don't recognize community property. For example, in a community property state such as California, as between a putative spouse and the other spouse, or as between the surviving putative spouse and the heirs of the decedent other than the decedent's surviving legal spouse, the putative spouse is entitled to share in the property accumulated by the partners during their void or voidable marriage. It is also settled that the share to which the putative spouse is entitled is the same share of the quasi-marital property as a spouse would receive as an actual and legal spouse if there had been a valid marriage; that is, the property is normally divided equally between the parties. *Estate of Leslie*, 689 P.2d 133 (Cal. 1984).

Objective standard. The term "good faith" found in the California statute providing for a declaration of putative spouse status for purposes of dividing community property requires a good-faith belief that void or voidable marriage was valid. This belief is tested by an objective standard. *In re Marriage of Xia Guo and Xiao Hua Sun*, 186 Cal. App. 4th 1491 (Cal. App. 2010).

EXAMPLES

Examples

7. Assume that Louis and Megan went through the motions of a ceremonial marriage but failed to obtain a marriage license. At the time, unknown to Megan, Louis was still married to Alice. Only after Louis died did Megan learn that he was still married to Alice. When Megan sought her intestate share of Louis's estate on the ground that she was his common law wife, Alice objected. The state where Louis and Megan reside recognizes such relationships. Alice argued that there could not be a common law marriage while Louis was still married to her (Alice). Most likely, how will a court rule on Alice's objection to Megan's effort to participate in his estate?

8. D and P decide to marry. D is 21 and has recently inherited a large sum of money and extensive real estate. P is 14. Both families approve of the marriage. The jurisdiction where they intend to marry has abolished common law marriages and has adopted a statute that allows a minor age 15 to 17 years to marry with either parent's consent or after a finding that the minor is capable of assuming the responsibilities of marriage and that the marriage would be in the minor's best interest. P lies about her age to obtain a marriage license, and P and D are married in a ceremony with the knowledge of their parents. On their honeymoon, they are involved in a serious automobile accident and D dies. P (age 14) now seeks her portion of D's estate as his widow. The administrator of the estate contends that she is not entitled to any of the estate because D and P were never legally married. How will a court most likely rule?

9. Assume that P and D prepare a detailed agreement that they believe contains the important provisions regarding their contemplated future "marriage." They call a group of friends together, then read the agreement and sign it as a part of their wedding ceremony. Although they do not obtain a license from the state to marry, clearly they fully intend the relationship to be that of husband and wife and the marriage agreement to act as proof of their formal relationship. When the relationship breaks down a few months after they have lived together as husband and wife, P brings an action to dissolve the marriage and seeks to use the state's divorce statutes. D responds by arguing that there is no marriage for two reasons: First, this state does not recognize common law marriages, which is true. Second, the parties failed to comply with any of the state's statutory marriage requirements, such as obtaining a marriage license, which are clear. P replies that the parties intended to marry, and that the marriage contract was complete when the last party exchanged vows. Because the marriage was properly solemnized, obtaining a

marriage license was not a mandated requirement. How will a court most likely rule?

10. Assume that P and D have decided to marry while D, the proposed groom, is very ill and confined to the hospital. The hospital chaplain, after checking with authorities, informs the couple that, in order to get married immediately, they are required to get a waiver of the three-day waiting period from a judge so that the license can be issued promptly. The parties decide to proceed with a ceremony that very day, despite the absence of a license. They intend to complete the paperwork following the ceremony. The parties are married by the hospital chaplain in an elaborate hospital ceremony; however, D dies one day following the ceremony. A marriage license is never obtained. Following D's death, P seeks an intestate share of D's estate. The relevant statute in this jurisdiction reads: "Previous to any marriage in this state, a license for that purpose shall be obtained from the officer authorized to issue the same, and no marriage hereafter contracted shall be recognized as valid unless the license has been previously obtained, and unless the marriage is solemnized by a person authorized by law to solemnize marriages." D's estate contends that no marriage existed because a license as required by state law was not obtained. P argues that the parties were married, as evidenced by the ceremony, and all that was needed was the license. She states that the witnesses at the marriage ceremony will testify that she and the deceased clearly intended to obtain a license a day or so after the ceremony. How will a court most likely rule on the validity of the marriage in a jurisdiction that does not recognize common law marriages?

11. Assume that before they marry, P and D obtain a marriage license form from the local court clerk that requires solemnization in state X. They do not have their marriage solemnized in that state. State X has a statute declaring that marriages solemnized in another state or country are invalid under X's law when parties residing in X intend to evade X's marriage laws by going to another state or country for solemnization. Before returning their completed license form to the local court clerk in state X, P and D fly to Puerto Rico for a vacation. In Puerto Rico, they have their marriage solemnized by a local pastor who signs the marriage license form. They then return to state X and file their completed marriage license form with the clerk of the court. Three years later, P files a petition to divorce D in state X. D replies to the divorce petition that P and D were never married under the laws of X because the marriage was solemnized outside that jurisdiction. D asks that the action be dismissed. Other than the testimony regarding the intent to vacation in Puerto Rico, there is no evidence suggesting an effort to evade X's marriage laws. How will a court most likely rule on the validity of the marriage?

12. Assume that P and P2 apply for a marriage license in state X. State X requires both to undergo a blood test to determine whether either has a venereal disease. P and P2 refuse to take the required test and challenge the requirement, arguing that this test violates the free exercise clause of the First Amendment to the U.S. Constitution. They contend that because the test requires the removal of blood from the body, which is a violation of a canon law of their church, the state is barred from applying the statute to them. How will a court most likely rule?

13. Assume that P and D reside in a jurisdiction that recognizes common law marriages. They never had a ceremonial marriage, do not live together on a regular basis, and generally keep the claimed relationship secret. They have occasionally told close friends that they were married and have had sexual relations. When D died, P sought his intestate share of her estate as her common law husband. P testifies that he and D agreed that they were common law husband and wife. Will P be successful on these facts in proving the existence of a common law marriage?

14. D and P reside in a jurisdiction that recognizes common law marriages. They have agreed that they are husband and wife, and their reputation in the community is that of husband and wife. However, they are concerned, that without a proper church ceremony, their relationship will not be legally recognized. They plan such a ceremony, but before it occurs, D dies. P now seeks her intestate share of D's estate as his wife. Will P be successful?

15. Assume that college students Pauline, age 19, and Don, age 21, roomed together as juniors in an apartment adjacent to the college for six months. They shared rent expenses, food, and were intimate. This jurisdiction recognizes common law marriages. When Don unexpectedly died in a motorcycle accident, Pauline sought her intestate share of Don's estate as his common law wife. Pauline testified at the probate hearing that they had agreed to be husband and wife and had been living together in Don's apartment for six months. One of Pauline's friends testified that Pauline told her once or twice that Pauline and Don were secretly married. The estate produced evidence that Pauline used her own name in school and publicly represented to her peers at school and at work that she was a single person. It also produced evidence that Pauline was never introduced to Don's family as his wife. In fact, it appeared Don was keeping the living arrangement secret from his family. How will a court most likely rule on the question of the existence of a common law marriage?

16. Assume the year is 1905, that Doris, age 41, and Paul, age 14, fall in love, and Paul moves in and begins living with Doris in state X. They

declare that they intend to be "married for the rest of our lives" and when asked by his parents to return home, Paul refuses. Under the common law, the couple would be viewed as husband and wife. Also assume that in 1904, state X enacted legislation that reads in part "that every male person who has attained the full age of eighteen years and every female who has attained the full age of fifteen years, is capable in law of contracting marriage if otherwise competent." The statute does not declare that, if a marriage is entered into when one or both of the parties are under the age limit prescribed, the marriage shall be void. Paul's father brings a writ of habeas corpus asking that Paul be returned to his home. Will a court recognize the marriage of Doris and Paul as legal in state X?

17. Assume that Patty and Duke reside in jurisdiction A that *does not recognize* that common law marriages can be consummated there. They are both receiving social security, Patty is 69, Duke is 70. They consider themselves husband and wife. They give each other wedding anniversary gifts, they live together, and Patty takes Duke's surname. Their friends are all told they are married and they have joint bank accounts. Their relationship continues for five years when Duke dies. Patty seeks her intestate share of Duke's estate as a surviving spouse.

    The evidence presented to the probate judge showed that the couple had visited another state (Y) on vacation annually for three weeks for 15 consecutive years. State Y recognizes common law marriages. During these visits, they lived together and held themselves out as a married couple to their families and friends. Will the court in state A recognize the out-of-state common law marriage in state Y as valid and allow Patty to recover a portion of the estate as a surviving spouse?

18. Assume that Pam and David lived together for five years in state X, which recognizes common law marriages. Pam and David did not hold themselves out as husband and wife; rather, they told their friends they were living with a "significant other." They moved to another state, and that state does not recognize common law marriages. When David died in an industrial accident two years after moving to the new state, Pam sought to claim workers' compensation benefits as a surviving spouse and seeks a declaratory judgment that she and David were married under the common law of state X, which would then make her eligible for coverage under the state act. Pam testifies that she and David had agreed to be husband and wife "but didn't make a big deal about it." A witness testifies for the state that Pam and David never used the same last name, did not have any joint savings or checking accounts, and did not jointly own any real or personal property. How will a court most likely rule on Pam's claim that they were married?

19. Assume that X, age 15, wants to marry Y, her 28-year-old high school civics teacher. Assume that X and Y cannot marry in state A, where they are living, because state A prohibits marriages on any basis of persons under age 17. After consulting a lawyer, X, Y, and X's mother drive to state B, where they establish a legal basis to obtain a marriage license. Also, assume that the relevant marriage statute in state B reads as follows: "A court is authorized to permit a marriage of a person less than 16 years old with consent of only one parent, in extraordinary circumstances in which marriage would serve best interests of minor." X's mother submits an affidavit in support of the marriage. It reads that she has "seen no other couple so right for each other," that they "have very real life plans at home, in the town in which we all reside," and that "their partnership and their talents will be most effectively utilized by this marriage." They obtain a court order, which allows them to marry if one parent agrees to the relationship. They are married with X's mother consent.

    When they return to their home state A, X's father, P, is outraged, and he seeks and obtains an ex parte temporary restraining order in the district court for the state of A that declares that "state A will not recognize this marriage." P also seeks a temporary court order awarding him legal and physical custody of his daughter. Four days later, however, the court rescinds its order because it finds that the daughter's marriage was valid under the law of state B. Because of this, the trial judge concludes that state A must recognize a marriage legal in state B, and that X was emancipated as a result of the marriage.

    P then brings an action in state B challenging the marriage. P argues that because the statute in that state allows a court to approve the marriage of a person under the age of 16 with the consent of only one parent, he has been deprived of his fundamental right under the Constitution to the parent-child relationship without a compelling reason. P also argues that his procedural due process rights under the Constitution were infringed because he was not provided with notice, an opportunity to be heard, or an opportunity to object to his daughter's marriage before the court authorized it.

    There are three issues in this example. First, did the trial judge in state A correctly rule that it must recognize the marriage that took place in state B? Second, was X emancipated by the marriage? Third, will a court in state B agree with P's constitutional challenge to the statute?

20. Assume that Paul and Doris begin living together at a time when Doris is still married to Maynard. Paul is aware of Doris's marital status. Paul and Doris continue to live together for several years. Doris dies without ever having obtained a divorce from Maynard. During the time that Paul and Doris lived together in this jurisdiction, which is one that recognizes

common law marriages, Paul and Doris held themselves out to the community as husband and wife. They used the same surname, jointly signed notes, opened joint bank accounts, and otherwise held themselves out as husband and wife. Paul asserts that Doris is his common law wife and he should be able to share in her estate. Paul also claims that if the court rejects his initial argument, then it should view him as a surviving spouse under the putative spouse doctrine.

EXPLANATIONS

Explanations

7. It appears that Megan and Louis entered into a relationship that would constitute a common law marriage if Louis had the capacity to marry; that is, if he were not married to Alice. Unfortunately, he was married and not divorced; therefore, courts will conclude that he did not have the capacity to marry. *See generally Sikes v. Guest*, 10 So. 2d 322 (Fla. App. 1964). Consequently, the common law relationship would be viewed as "void"; i.e., never existing. If the jurisdiction has a putative spouse statute, Megan may participate in the estate as a putative spouse. Whether she can participate depends on the specific language in the state's putative spouse statute. For example, Minnesota's putative spouse statute reads as follows: "Any person who has cohabited with another to whom the person is not legally married in the good faith belief that the person was married to the other is a putative spouse until knowledge of the fact that the person is not legally married terminates the status and prevents acquisition of further rights. A putative spouse acquires the rights conferred upon a legal spouse, including the right to maintenance following termination of the status, whether or not the marriage is prohibited or declared a nullity. If there is a legal spouse or other putative spouses, rights acquired by a putative spouse do not supersede the rights of the legal spouse or those acquired by other putative spouses, but the court shall apportion property, maintenance, and support rights among the claimants as appropriate in the circumstances and in the interests of justice." Minn. Stat. §518.055 (1986). In this hypothetical, Megan did not learn she was not Louis's spouse until after he had died; therefore, in a state like Minnesota, it appears she can claim putative spouse status.

8. The question for the court is whether the marriage is void or voidable. A court will most likely rule in favor of the administrator because the marriage is void. The reason that the marriage is void is that there is neither a statutory nor a common law basis upon which any marriage of a child age 14 could have occurred. The fact that the parents agreed to the marriage is irrelevant. If D had survived the car accident, it is

possible that he could face criminal sexual misconduct charges, including the possibility of statutory rape. P's family could also face neglect and dependency charges, or worse, from the local Child Protection Agency. The statute is very specific on the minimum age needed to marry. It was not met. Furthermore, there was no finding that the marriage was in the best interests of P and D.

9. If the specific language (we're assuming that D's assertion is correct) in the state statute is clear and mandates that a license be obtained before the state will recognize a marriage, a court will most likely rule that there never was a marriage. Here, there is only an agreement between the parties to which the state was never a party. Because the parties were never legally married, P cannot benefit from divorce statutes designed by the state to guide and protect the parties when a marital relationship breaks down. Note that if this state recognized common law marriages, P would have been considered married and would have been able to use the state's divorce statutes. *See, e.g.*, *Yaghoubinejad v. Haghighi*, 894 A.2d 1173 (N.J. Super. A.D. 2006). Note, however, the facts and ruling in *Carabetta v. Carabetta*, cited above.

10. A court that strictly relies on the statutory language cited in the hypothetical will most likely hold that there was not a legal marriage. *Nelson v. Marshall*, 869 S.W.2d 132, 135 (Mo. App. 1993) (no marriage where there was no license and groom died a day after the ceremony). Had D survived and later obtained and recorded a license, the court would have recognized the marriage. *But see*, *Yun v. Yun*, 908 S.W.2d 787 (Mo. App. 1995) (Kansas statutes do not specifically provide that a marriage ceremony conducted without a license is void). The most difficult obstacle that P has to overcome is the complete absence of a license (or even a belief that one existed).

11. A court will most likely take a practical approach to this problem and rule that the marriage is valid. From a judicial perspective, little is gained by ruling that the marriage was void after the parties lived together as husband and wife for three years. Moreover, there is nothing to suggest that the couple intentionally flew to Puerto Rico to evade the laws of X. *See McPeek v. McCardle*, 888 N.E.2d 171 (Ind. 2008) (where a couple complied with Indiana's statutory requirements regarding marriage licenses, certificates, and solemnization, such that the marriage would have been valid if solemnized in Indiana, Indiana will recognize the marriage as valid even if the marriage ceremony took place in another state and did not comply with that state's law or public policy). *See Barbosa-Johnson v. Johnson*, 851 P.2d 866 (Ariz. App. 1993) (marriage was not invalid on grounds that it was solemnized by Puerto Rican pastor rather than duly licensed or ordained Arizona clergyman).

12. Recall that the UMDA provided states with the option of requiring various tests. In his hypothetical, a state has decided to enact a testing provision. Most likely, the court will require that the parties take the test. Some jurisdictions have similar statutory provisions requiring tests for venereal disease, tuberculosis, mental incompetence, rubella immunity, or sickle cell anemia. *See* Homer H. Clark, *The Law of Domestic Relations in the United States* §2.11 (2d ed. 1987). These provisions have sustained constitutional attack. Courts have also found that compelling interests override religious free exercise in a number of other situations. *See, e.g.*, *State v. Meacham*, 612 P.2d 795 (Wash. 1980) (State has a compelling interest in requiring blood tests for putative fathers, under the Uniform Parentage Act, although providing blood was against the complaining parties' religious beliefs); *State ex rel. Holcomb*, 239 P.2d 545 (Wash. 1952) (State has a compelling interest in state university rule requiring an x-ray of all in-coming students for tuberculosis despite beliefs of a Christian Scientist student); *State v. Clifford*, 787 P.2d 571 (Wash. App. 1990), *review denied*, 792 P.2d 535 (Wash. 1990) (State has a compelling interest in requirement for a driver's license despite complaining party's religious belief that licensing requirement placed state on same level as God); *Matter of Paternity Petition of Com'r of Social Services of City of New York*, 466 N.Y.S.2d 194 (N.Y. Fam. 1983) (putative father opposed blood test stating that submitting to HLA composite blood grouping test was against his religious convictions because it was an integral part of his religion to follow his conscience as his convictions led him, court held his opposition to the test was merely based on his conscience and personal convictions; therefore, the court order that he submit to the test did not violate his right to free exercise of his religion); *see generally* *City of Canton v. Whitman*, 337 N.E.2d 766 (Ohio 1975) (regulations relating to control of venereal disease, blood tests for marriage licenses, sterilization, pasteurization of milk, chlorination of water and vaccination have all been held valid as based on police power exercised in regard to public health).

13. P will probably not be successful. Most jurisdictions require that to recognize a common law marriage there must be evidence that the parties agreed to be married, lived together after the agreement as husband and wife, and represented to others that they are married. P and D did not hold themselves out to the community as husband and wife and did not cohabit together on a regular basis. Isolated references to close friends that they were husband and wife, without more, will usually not persuade most courts that there was a common law marriage. While P's credibility will play a significant factor in the outcome his self-serving testimony is probably not sufficient to carry the burden

of showing that the marriage occurred. *Compare Matter of Estate of Giessel*, 734 S.W.2d 27 (Tex. App. 1987) (record is replete with evidence parties conduct and reputation — spoken words were not necessary to establish a "holding out") *with Gary v. Gary*, 490 S.W.2d 929 (Tex. App. 1973) (testimony of the purported wife conclusively proved that there was no agreement to be married).

14. Most likely, a court will recognize the relationship as a common law marriage. The hypothetical suggests that they had an agreement *in praesenti* to be husband and wife, lived together, and held themselves out to the community as such. There is no requirement that they go through a formal wedding ceremony before a court will recognize a common law marital relationship. P will most likely be successful in persuading a court that she is D's common law wife. *See Brooks v. Sanders*, 190 P.3d 357, 362 (Okla. App. 2008) (a common law marriage occurs upon the happening of three events: a declaration by the parties of an intent to marry, cohabitation, and a holding out of themselves to the community of being husband and wife); *In re Estate of Duval*, 777 N.W.2d 380 (S.D. 2010) (petitioner could not prove by clear and convincing evidence that the couple entered into a valid common law marriage while in Oklahoma).

15. In a case similar to these facts, the Supreme Court of Texas held that there was insufficient evidence to support a common law marriage. It found an absence of evidence indicating that the couple had ever moved into or occupied publicly a common residence or room. They did not have a reputation in the community as husband and wife, and P continued using her own name and publicly represented to those at her school and at her place of work that she was a single person. She did not establish that the couple lived together as man and wife or that they held themselves out to the public that they were man and wife. *Ex parte Threet*, 333 S.W.2d 361 (Tex. 1960).

16. Despite the statutory language, a court may well consider the parties married under the common law. The age of consent under the common law in most jurisdictions at this time in our history was set at 14 for a male and 12 for a female, so the ages of Paul and Doris pose no issue. Paul and Doris will argue that the statute fails to modify or abrogate the existing common law in the state clearly, therefore, common law marriages can continue. Those opposed to common law marriage will argue that the legislature intended to grandfather existing common law relationships but was intended to prevent future ones. Under this reading of the statute, Paul and Doris cannot marry under the common law. This question requires close scrutiny, however, because there is no language in the statute declaring that persons aged 12 (female) and 14 (male)

cannot consummate a common law marriage, a court may well recognize Paul and Doris as married under the common law. *See State v. Lowell*, 78 Minn. 166 (Minn. 1899); *State v. Ward*, 28 S.E.2d 785 (S.C. 1945) (trial judge erred in not allowing as a defense to statutory rape evidence that the couple aged 26 (male) and 13 (female) were married under the state's common law).

17. Patty will assert that her state should recognize that she and Duke were married under the common law in state Y. Duke's estate will claim that the decisions cited by Patty do not apply because all of them involved situations where a common law marriage was consummated while the parties were residents of the common law state. In this case, argues the estate, Patty and Duke were residents of the forum state at all times — the vacations did not change the fact that they were residents of state "A."

    A court may be persuaded to find for Patty by totaling the days the couple lived as husband and wife in state Y and conclude that the time spent in state Y is sufficient to justify finding a common law marriage. The evidence will have to be clear that they cohabited in state Y the entire time and continually held themselves out as husband and wife. The outcome will turn on the particular view of the forum jurisdiction toward short-term stays in common law jurisdictions as discussed in the section on common law marriages in this chapter. *See Mott v. Duncan Petroleum Trans.*, 434 N.Y.S.2d 155 (N.Y. App. 1980) (finding common law marriage where New York claimant traveled to Georgia on several occasions, staying there for weeks at a time with her daughter and while in Georgia she and decedent lived together as husband and wife and represented themselves to the local community as such — workers' compensation board erroneously assumed that a mere "visit" to Georgia could not result in a valid Georgia marriage); *Carpenter v. Carpenter*, 617 N.Y.S.2d 903 (N.Y. App. 1994) (parties' two brief periods of cohabitation in Pennsylvania established valid common law marriage under Pennsylvania law and, thus, marriage would be recognized in New York under principles of comity, in light of parties' conduct in New York by which they held themselves out to world as married — everyone who knew the parties-including their own children-regarded them as married).

18. Although the parties were apparently competent to make a common law marriage contract, the only evidence is Pam's testimony that such a contract was made *in praesenti*. Much of the evidence indicates they were living more like boyfriend and girlfriend than husband and wife. In particular, the complete separation of funds suggests they were not husband and wife and their statements that they were living with

a "significant other" weaken Pam's claim. Finally, it is conceded they did not hold themselves out to the community as husband and wife and were not treated and reputed in the community as husband and wife. Most likely, a court would find on these facts that a common law marriage did not exist. *See Smith v. Smith*, 966 A.2d 109 (R.I. 2009) (alleged wife failed to prove the existence of a common law marriage where majority of friends and family and those individuals that constituted their community did not believe they were married; none of alleged husband's family members testified they believed that alleged husband and alleged wife were married; and, other than in alleged wife's business, in which she used alleged husband's surname, public records and private accounts were in parties' own names as single persons).

19. First, the United States Constitution requires that every state accord "Full Faith and Credit" to the laws of its sister states. Consequently, a marriage that is validly contracted in a state where such marriages are legal will be valid even in states where such marriages cannot be contracted. This is generally true even if there is a strong policy in the form state (state A in our example) against such marriages. However, if there was a very strong policy specifically reflected in a state against recognition of a particular marriage formed in another state, the forum state (state A) most likely could refuse to enforce the out-of-state marriage. The lawyers will debate the strength of the limitation in the language of the state A statute regarding not allowing marriages of persons under 17. It is most likely that the court in state A will recognize the marriage in state B.

    Second, marriage is viewed as emancipating a minor by all jurisdictions. If the marriage in state B is valid, the daughter is emancipated.

    Third, when a somewhat similar problem came to the Nevada Supreme Court, it held that a statute that allowed a court to authorize the marriage of a person under 16 years old with the consent of only one parent, in extraordinary circumstances and where the marriage would serve the best interests of the minor, did not violate substantive or procedural due process rights of the father. *Kirkpatrick v. Eighth Judicial Dist. Court*, 64 P.3d 1056 (Nev. 2003). It said that there was no constitutional requirement that both parents be notified of the marriage. *See generally Hodgson v. Minnesota*, 497 U.S. 417 (U.S. 1990). The court said that even though the other parent may have an interest in the minor's decision, and full communication is desirable, "[t]he State has no more interest in requiring all family members to talk with one another than it has in requiring certain of them to live together."

    The Nevada court observed that states have the right and power to establish reasonable limitations on the right to marry. It said that this power is justified as an exercise of the police power, which confers upon the states the ability to enact laws in order to protect the safety, health, morals, and general welfare of society. It also said that there is "no one set of criteria that can be set forth as a litmus test to determine if a marriage will be successful. Neither is there a litmus test to determine whether a person is mature enough to enter a marriage. Age alone is an arbitrary factor. . . . The statute provides a safeguard against an erroneous marriage decision by the minor and the consenting parent, by giving the district court the discretion to withhold authorization if it finds that there are no extraordinary circumstances and/or the proposed marriage is not in the minor's best interest, regardless of parental consent. The statute strikes a balance between an arbitrary rule of age for marriage and accommodation of individual differences and circumstances." *Id.* at 1060-1061. Here, although it is somewhat questionable that there are extraordinary circumstances, a trial judge's decision allowing (or rejecting) the marriage would most likely not be overturned.

20. Doris has a preexisting impediment to a common law marriage (Doris was married to Maynard and never divorced), and Paul had knowledge of the impediment. Paul's argument that he was Doris's common law husband will fail. Paul will also fail in his second claim as Doris's putative spouse. Only if Paul did not have knowledge of the impediment and had lived with Doris in the good-faith belief that they were married under the state's common law doctrine, could Paul claim a share of Doris's estate as a putative spouse. Paul cannot claim a share of the estate under the putative spouse doctrine because he was aware of the impediment. A court will most likely reject both claims.

FORMS OF MARRIAGE

2.14. Proxy Marriage

Defined. A proxy marriage is defined as "[a] marriage contracted or celebrated through agents acting on behalf of one or both parties. A proxy marriage differs from the more conventional ceremony only in that one or both of the contracting parties are represented by an agent[,] all the other requirements having been met." *State v. Anderson*, 396 P.2d 558, 561 (Or. 1964). *Black's Law Dictionary*, 995 (8th ed. 2004), defines a proxy marriage as "[a] wedding in which someone stands in for an absent bride or groom, as when one party is stationed overseas in the military." *See generally* Andrea B. Carroll, *Reviving Proxy Marriage*, 6 Brook. L. Rev. 455, 459 (Winter 2011)

("The time has come to reassess our long-standing intolerance of proxy marriage").

History. The proxy marriage concept has an interesting history. *See* Adam Candeub & Mae Kuykendall, *Modernizing Marriage*, 44 U. Mich. J.L. Reform 735, 759 (Summer, 2011) (describing the present form of proxy marriages in the United States). The Catholic Church historically insisted that the parties to a marriage exchange consent face-to-face in the presence of the Church. However, there were exceptions, and the proxy marriage concept was one of them. It is thought that proxy marriage gained a foothold in Catholic theology when Pope Innocent III accepted the Roman view that marriage could be consented to by messenger. *See* Ernest G. Lorenzen, *Marriage by Proxy and the Conflict of Laws*, 32 Harv. L. Rev. 473, 474-475 (1919). Proxy marriages were recognized in the American colonies out of practical necessity. Colonists sent to establish a new settlement were men, and they left their future brides behind. Therefore, the colonists, similar to soldiers serving abroad, had a desire and a need for marriage by proxy. *Id.* at 482.

Proxy marriages became a modern issue during World War I. Some service members wanted to marry while they were stationed abroad, and because of this, various states revived marriage by proxy. Today, a few states extend proxy marriage to members of the armed services on active duty. "For example, California, Montana, and Texas extend the privilege of single proxy marriage to members of the armed services on active duty (California requires an armed conflict) without regard to their being a resident of the state. Montana permits double proxy marriage to be used, but only if one member of the couple is a resident of Montana or a member of the U.S. military on active duty." Candeub & Kuykendall, *supra*.

Validity. An interesting discussion regarding the validity of proxy marriages is found in *Barrons v. United States* 191 F.2d 92 (9th Cir. 1951). The dispute in the case was over who was entitled to the proceeds of a deceased service member's life insurance policy; his wife, whom he married in Nevada by proxy just one week before his death, or his father, who challenged the validity of the marriage. The widow was pregnant at the time the marriage was carried out with the help of the Red Cross. The various requirements of the Nevada marriage laws were complied with, and a proxy ceremony was duly celebrated before a regularly ordained minister authorized by law to perform ceremonies, the widow being personally present and the deceased being represented by a person designated by the Red Cross.

The court rejected the father's arguments that the Nevada marriage was invalid in Texas, the widow's residence, or that it was invalid in Nevada because it was not authorized under Nevada law. In ruling that the marriage was valid, the court observed that a "marriage relationship validly created by a proxy ceremony is in no way different from the same relationship created in the more usual manner." It said that a proxy marriage furthered the statutory objectives of the formal solemnization requirements to ensure "publicity and certainty." *Id.* at 95, 96. The "remote possibilities" of fraud and lack of consent were considered "not sufficiently substantial" to render proxy marriages, which in some cases may be the only way in which a desirable legal and social status can be achieved, "at variance with the Nevada marriage laws." *Id.* at 97.

UMDA. The UMDA permits proxy marriages. UMDA §206(b). The commentary to this section notes that the authors saw no reason to outlaw such marriages.

Final determination. The final determination of the validity of a proxy marriage in a particular jurisdiction rests with its legislature and its courts. *See In re Estate of Crockett*, 728 N.E.2d 765 (Ill. App. 2000). In New York, for example, there is a statutory requirement that the parties to a marriage make a declaration in the presence of an officiating person and at least one witness, Therefore, it initially appears that New York does not permit the solemnization of proxy marriages. However, because proxy marriages are not explicitly proscribed by statute, and are not regarded as repugnant to public policy or natural law, New York will at least recognize a proxy marriage that is valid in the jurisdiction where it was contracted. *See, e.g.*, *Ferraro v. Ferraro*, 77 N.Y.S.2d 246 (N.Y. City Dom. Rel. 1948), *affirmed sub nom. Fernandes v. Fernandes*, 275 A.D. 777 (N.Y. App. 1949); *In re Valente's Will*, 188 N.Y.S.2d 732 (N.Y. Surr. 1959). *But see*, N.H. Rev. Stat. §457:8 (2012) ("No magistrate or minister of religion shall solemnize any marriage by proxy").

Note that a marriage by proxy that is valid in the country in which marriage took place may be recognized in the United States. *U.S. v. Commissioner of immigration at Port of New York*, 298 F. 103 (S.D. N.Y. 1924); *see Chaiang v. Skeririk*, 582 F.3d 238 (1st Cir. 2009) (proxy marriages can sometimes be acceptable in immigration cases).

2.15. Confidential Marriage

California appears to be the only state that provides for a "confidential" or "secret" marriage. Under California law, the marriage is recorded but generally is not be open to the public for inspection. Cal. Fam. Code §511 (West 2006). The California confidential marriage statutes were apparently enacted to shield parties and their children, if any, from the publicity of a marriage recorded in the ordinary manner. It was thought that this would encourage unmarried persons who have been living together as man and wife to legalize their relationship. The statutes eliminate some of the procedural requirements such as filing a health certificate or obtaining a license. However, they do require a ceremony of solemnization. *See* Cal. Fam. Code §§500-536 (2003). "Living together as husband and wife," is required to obtain a confidential marriage, and this requires cohabiting in the same dwelling. *People v. Hassan*, 86 Cal. Rptr. 3d 314 (Cal. App. 2008).

2.16. Tribal Marriages

Historically, "Native American marriage practices were given deference by both the federal government and the states. Congress did not limit the types of tribal unions that the federal government would recognize. Similarly, states recognized Native American unions as long as they were valid under tribal customs and laws." Mark P. Strasser, *Tribal Marriages, Same-Sex Unions, and an Interstate Recognition Conundrum*, 30 B.C. Third World L.J. 207, 208 (Spring 2010). *See, e.g.*, Minn. Stat. §517.18, subd. 4 (2002) (marriages may be solemnized among American Indians according to the form and usage of their religion by an Indian Midé or holy person chosen by the parties to the marriage); *James v. Adams*, 155 P. 1121, 1122 (Okla. 1915) ("Marriages, contracted between tribal Indians according to the usages and customs of their tribe, at a time when the tribal government and relations are existing, will be upheld by the courts, in the absence of a federal law rendering invalid the laws and customs of the tribe"). Native American polygamous unions were recognized by the United States even though these unions would have been void had they been celebrated on non-tribal land. *See, e.g.*, *Kobogum v. Jackson Iron Co.*, 43 N.W. 602, 605 (Mich. 1889) (state laws do not have any force over Indians in their tribal relations); *Ortley v. Ross* 110 N.W. 982, 983 (Neb. 1907) (marriages valid under the customs of an Indian tribe, which were performed among members thereof while the tribal relation existed, are considered valid in Nebraska).

2.17. Covenant Marriage

Three states — Louisiana, Arizona, and Arkansas — have created a separate form of marriage termed "covenant marriage." Other states considered similar proposals but have yet to adopt them. *See generally* Lynne Marie Kohm, *A Comparative Study of Covenant Marriage Proposals in the United States*, 12 Regent U. L. Rev. 31 (1999). A covenant marriage is a purely elective status available only to different-sex couples that creates stringent requirements for both entry and exit. James L. Musselman, *What's Love Got to Do with It? A Proposal for Elevating the Status of Marriage by Narrowing Its Definition, While*

Universally Extending the Rights and Benefits Enjoyed by Married Couples, 16 Duke J. Gender L. & Pol'y 37, 39 (January 2009).

Louisiana was the first state to offer the option of entering into a covenant marriage contract. If a couple chooses a covenant marriage, they pledge to enter matrimony only after serious deliberation, including premarital counseling. They also agree to try to solve potential marriage conflicts through counseling, if either spouse requests it, before initiating divorce proceedings. There is either an agreed-upon two-year separation before a divorce will be granted or an agreement with a limited number of grounds such as adultery, abuse, imprisonment for a felony, or abandonment. The covenant provisions permit married couples to renew their vows and to recast their marriage under terms of the covenant.

In 2004, approximately 36,391 marriage licenses were issued in Louisiana, and 2 percent, or about 728, may have been covenant marriages. *See* Katherine Shaw Spaht, *Covenant Marriage Seven Years Later: Its as Yet Unfulfilled Promise*, 65 La. L. Rev. 605, 618 (2005) (only 2 percent to 3 percent of couples choose this option).

HISTORIC MARRIAGE RESTRICTIONS

2.18. Epilepsy

Throughout history, societies have restricted persons from marrying for a variety of reasons. These restrictions were often based on a faulty understanding or no understanding at all of science, or because of prejudice. For example, in the United States, persons suffering from epilepsy were barred from marrying in many states until the 1950s. In some instances, a marriage with a person suffering from epilepsy could result in a criminal conviction. *See, e.g.*, Section 6275 of the Connecticut General Statutes (1932), which provided as follows: "Every man and woman, either of whom is epileptic, imbecile or feebleminded, who shall intermarry, or live together as husband and wife, when the woman is under forty-five years of age, shall be imprisoned not more than three years." Minnesota's marriage law declared at one time that "No marriage shall be contracted while either of the parties has a husband or wife living; nor within six months after either has been divorced from a former spouse; nor between parties who are nearer of kin than second cousins, whether of the half or whole blood, computed by the rules of the civil law; nor between persons either of whom is epileptic, imbecile, feeble-minded or insane." Minn. Stat. §7090, G. S. (1915); *See generally Behsman v. Behsman*, 174 N.W. 611 (Minn. 1919). This marriage barrier has been removed in all jurisdictions.

2.19. Anti-Miscegenation Statutes

History. White supremacy was a hallmark of portions of the United States for centuries. For example, to keep the white race "pure," state laws barring whites from marrying blacks and other nonwhite persons were common. Of the 48 continental states, only six never enacted laws that prohibited black people from marrying white people. Those states were Connecticut, Minnesota, New Hampshire, New Jersey, Vermont, and Wisconsin. Harvey M. Appelbaum, *Miscegenation Statutes: A Constitutional and Social Problem*, 53 Geo. L.J. 49, 50 n.9 (1964). It was common for the state statutes barring these marriages to provide for felony convictions and substantial criminal sentences if they were violated.

In the main, repeal of these laws occurred in the northern states immediately before and after the Civil War. However, as of 1967, with only one exception, statutes criminalizing mixed-race marriages were upheld in an unbroken line of decisions by state courts when they were attacked as violating the Fourteenth Amendment to the federal constitution. *See, e.g., State v. Pass*, 121 P.2d 882 (Ariz. 1942) (a descendant of mixed Caucasian and Indian blood cannot marry a Caucasian or part Caucasian nor an Indian or part Indian); *Dodson v. State*, 31 S.W. 977 (Ark. 1895) (statute that bars marriages "between white persons and negroes is not in conflict with the provisions of either the state or federal constitution"); *Jackson v. Denver*, 124 P.2d 240 (Colo. 1942) ("cohabitation as husband and wife under an alleged common law marriage of a negro and a white woman, whose marriage was by statute made void, constituted 'vagrancy' within the meaning of city ordinance which defines a vagrant as any person who shall lead an immoral course of life'"); *Scott v. Georgia*, 39 Ga. 321 (Ga. 1869) ("The Code of Georgia, adopted by the new Constitution, forever prohibits the marriage relation between white persons and persons of African descent"); *State v. Jackson*, 80 Mo. 175, 1883 WL 9519 (Mo. 1883) (Mississippi bars "intermarriage of any person having one-eighth or more of negro blood with any white person"); *In Re Shun T. Takahashi's Estate*, 129 P.2d 217 (Mont. 1942) (marriage between a Japanese and a white woman void); *In Re Paquet's Estate*, 200 P. 911 (Or. 1921) (law prohibiting marriages "between white persons and Indians, Negroes, or Chinese, etc." is not unconstitutional as discriminating between the races).

In *Lonas v. State*, 3 Heiskell 287 (Tenn. 1871), the court provided the following bizarre justification for upholding Tennessee's discriminatory miscegenation laws:

> The Mosaic Law forbade the Jews to gender animals of a diverse kind together. Was there discrimination there between the horse and the ass? Would a law now against breeding mules be discrimination? If so, against which animal? Is a

> law against breeding mulattoes any more so? This is the substance of our law, to prevent the production of this hybrid race. To prevent violence and bloodshed which would arise from such cohabitation, distasteful to our people, and unfit to produce the human race in any of the types in which it was created.

The United States Supreme Court upheld the constitutionality of anti-miscegenation statutes in *Pace v. Alabama*, 106 U.S. 583 (1883). In that case, a black man, and a white woman were indicted under Alabama's criminal code for living together in a state of adultery or fornication. They were tried, convicted, and sentenced, each to two years' imprisonment in the state penitentiary. The Supreme Court rejected the challenge to the law, ruling that Alabama's anti-miscegenation statute did not violate the Fourteenth Amendment because the statute treated the races equally, insofar as both whites and blacks were punished in equal measure for breaking the law against interracial marriage and interracial sex. Sixty-one years later, the 10th Circuit Court of Appeals likewise upheld an Oklahoma constitutional anti-miscegenation statute. *Stevens v. U.S.*, 146 F.2d 120 (10th Cir. 1944) (Creek Indian barred from marrying person of African descent).

California became the first jurisdiction to strike down anti-miscegenation statutes when that State's Supreme Court ruled 4-3 that such limitations on marriage were unconstitutional. *Perez v. Lippold*, 198 P.2d 17 (Cal. 1948). The court held that in the absence of clear and present danger arising out of an emergency, a state cannot base a law impairing fundamental rights of individuals on general assumptions as to traits of racial groups.

Status in 1967. When *Loving v. Virginia*, 388 U.S. 1 (1967), came before the United States Supreme Court, it had decided *Brown v. Board of Education*, 347 U.S. 483 (1954), and many other cases mandating desegregation. The civil rights movement had resulted in enactment of the Civil Rights Act of 1964. However, there remained 17 states that punished interracial marriage with the prohibition spelled out in various state constitutions. There was also widespread popular support for the criminal ban on marriages between the races among white citizens. For example, a 1965 Gallup Poll found that 42 percent of northern whites supported bans on interracial marriage, as did 72 percent of southern whites.

The *Loving* case involved Richard Loving, a white male, and Mildred Jeter, a black female, who were married in Washington, D.C., in 1958 because their home state, Virginia, enforced anti-miscegenation laws. Once married, they returned to Virginia. In 1959, they were indicted and convicted of violating that state's anti-miscegenation law, which made it a crime to leave Virginia to evade its anti-miscegenation law and return to cohabit as husband and wife. They were each sentenced to 1 year in jail, with the sentence being suspended if they agreed to leave Virginia and not return for 25 years. Rather than serve time in the state penitentiary, the couple moved to Washington, D.C., where, in 1963, they initiated a suit challenging the constitutionality of the Virginia anti-miscegenation law. Their challenge was initially heard by the same trial judge who had suspended a 1-year jail sentence for 25 years on the condition that they leave Virginia. In denying the constitutional challenge, the judge made the following absurd comment justifying his ruling:

> Almighty God created the races white, black, yellow, Malay and red, and he placed them on separate continents. And but for the interference with his arrangement there would be no cause for such marriages. The fact that he separated the races shows that he did not intend for the races to mix

In March 1966, the Virginia Supreme Court of Appeals upheld the law, endorsing the doctrine of white supremacy in that state. *Loving v. Virginia*, 388 U.S. 1, 7 (1967). *See generally* Walter Wadlington, *The Loving Case: Virginia's Anti-Miscegenation Statute in Historical Perspective*, 52 Va. L. Rev. 1189 (1966).

The United States Supreme Court in a unanimous opinion struck down the conviction. http://www.law.cornell.edu/supct/html/historics/USSC_CR_0388_0001_ZO.html (last visited, September, 2011); http://www.npr.org/templates/story/story.php?storyId=10889047 (last visited September, 2011); http://www.nytimes.com/2008/05/14/opinion/14wed4.html (last visited July, 2012). It ruled that statutes barring marriage between the races violated the Fourteenth Amendment equal protection and due process clauses and constituted invidious discrimination. The equal protection ruling was based on restricting the freedom to marry solely because of racial classification. The due process ruling was based on the proposition that the right to marry is a fundamental right, and one could not suppress the right to marry based on racial classification. This case is recognized as establishing the principle that the right to marry is a constitutionally protected fundamental right. *See* oral arguments at http://www.oyez.org/cases/1960-1969/1966/1966_395 (last visited March, 2012).

2.20. Poverty

Can a state prevent a marriage under certain circumstances because an applicant for a marriage license is poor and behind in child support payments? That was essentially the question in *Zablocki v. Redhail*, 434 U.S. 374 (1978), http://supreme.justia.com/us/434/374/ (last visited September, 2011). In that decision, the Supreme Court held unconstitutional a Wisconsin statute that provided that members of a certain class of Wisconsin residents may not marry, within the state or elsewhere, without first obtaining a court order granting permission to marry. The class was defined by statute to include any "Wisconsin resident having minor issue not in his custody and which he is under obligation to support by any court order or judgment." The Court held that the statute violated the equal protection clause of the Fourteenth Amendment to the U.S. Constitution. The Court found the state interest in providing counseling before marriage and protecting a child's welfare legitimate and substantial. However, on close examination, the Court concluded that the statute did not require or provide counseling, and it barred an applicant from marrying without providing funds (child support) to the applicant's children. The Court believed that there were other reasonable avenues open to Wisconsin to obtain support for the children. In addition, the Court noted that the statute failed to consider the possibility that through a new marriage, the applicant might be better able to meet prior support obligations. *See* http://www.oyez.org/cases/1970-1979/1977/1977_76_879 (last visited March, 2012).

2.21. Prisoners

States have occasionally barred marriage of a person who is imprisoned for a crime. In the leading decision on this matter, *Turner v. Safely*, 482 U.S. 78 (1987), the Supreme Court held that a Missouri prison regulation barring prisoners from marriage absent a compelling reason to do so was unconstitutional. http://scholar.google.com/scholar_case?case=15686747716085264205&hl=en&as_sdt=2&as_vis=1&oi=scholarr (last visited September, 2011). The Court fashioned the following test to determine the regulation's constitutional fitness: "When a prison regulation impinges on inmates' constitutional rights, the regulation is valid if it is reasonably related to legitimate penological interests." *Id.* at 89. This test, which places the burden upon the prisoner, has been employed to determine the validity of various prison regulations. *See Overton v. Bazzetta*, 539 U.S. 126 (2003). In *Turner*, the Court affirmed *Butler v. Wilson*, 415 U.S. 953 (1974), which held that a marriage prohibition when an inmate has received a life sentence is constitutional.

The Supreme Court in *Turner* stated that "several factors are relevant in determining the reasonableness of a regulation including: (1) a valid, rational connection between the prison regulation and the legitimate governmental interest put forward to justify it, (2) whether there are alternative means of exercising the right that remain open to prison inmates, (3) the impact accommodation of the asserted constitutional right will have on guards and other inmates, and on the allocation of prison resources generally, and (4) the absence of ready alternatives." *See generally Kentucky Dep't of Corr. v. Thompson*, 490 U.S. 454, 461 (1989) (holding that prisoner has no due process right to particular visitors) http://supreme.justia.com/us/490/454/ (last visited September, 2011).

Justice O'Connor, writing for the Court in *Turner*, stated that prisoner marriages could be subjected to "substantial restrictions" (presumably referring to restrictions on conjugal visits), but cautioned that, "[m]any important attributes of marriage remain . . . after taking into account the limitations imposed by prison life. First, inmate marriages, like others, are expressions of emotional support and public commitment. These elements are an important and significant aspect of the marital relationship. In addition, many religions recognize marriage as having spiritual significance; for some inmates and their spouses, therefore, the commitment of marriage may be an exercise of religious faith as well as an expression of personal dedication. Third, most inmates eventually will be released by parole or commutation, and therefore most inmate marriages are formed in the expectation that they ultimately will be fully consummated. Finally, marital status often is a precondition to the receipt of government benefits . . . property rights . . . , and other, less tangible benefits . . . ." She concluded that "[t]hese incidents of marriage, like the religious and personal aspects of the marriage commitment, are unaffected by the fact of confinement or the pursuit of legitimate corrections goals." *Id.* at 96. *See generally Thornburgh v. Abbott*, 490 U.S. 401 (1989) (upholding a federal prison regulation that authorized prison wardens, following certain criteria, to prohibit prison inmates from receiving certain types of publications mailed to them); *Kentucky Department of Corrections v. Thompson*, 490 U.S. 454, (1989) (prisoner did not have a constitutional right to receive visitors following the taking of his liberty through the criminal process); *Overton v. Bazzetta*, 539 U.S. 126 (2003), (holding that (1) prison regulations that excluded, from family members with whom inmates were entitled to non-contact visits, any minor nieces and nephews and children as to whom parental rights had been terminated, that prohibited inmates from visiting with former inmates, that required children to be accompanied by family member or legal guardian, and that subjected inmates with two substance-abuse violations to ban of at least two years on future visitation, were rationally related to legitimate penological objectives and did not violate substantive due process or free association guarantee of the First Amendment; and (2) two-year ban on visitation for inmates with two substance-abuse violations did not violate Constitutional prohibition against cruel and unusual punishment); *Beard v. Banks*, 548 U.S. 521 (2006) (affirming a Pennsylvania Department of Corrections regulation restricting access to newspapers, magazines, and photographs by inmates placed in most restrictive level of prison's long-term segregation unit); *Salisbury v. List*, 501 F. Supp. 105 (D.C. Nevada 1980) (officials' inmate marriage procedure was unconstitutional).

EXISTING MARRIAGE RESTRICTIONS

2.22. Polygamy

Polygamous marriages have not been protected at any time by the laws of the United States and are considered void. *See Reynolds v. United States*, 98 U.S. 145 (1878) http://supreme.justia.com/us/98/145/ (last visited September, 2011); *State v. Holm*, 136 P.3d 726 (Utah 2006), *cert. denied*, 549 U.S. 1252, 127 (2007); see *generally* Shayna M. Sigman, *Everything Lawyers Know About Polygamy Is Wrong*, 16 Cornell J.L. & Pub. Pol'y 101 (Fall 2006) (providing the history of legal policy in the United States concerning the practice of polygamy and contrasts the rationale of the anti-polygamy movement and polygamy criminalization with the findings of the social science literature on the practice of polygamy); Maura I. Strassberg, *The Challenge of Post-Modern Polygamy: Considering Polyamory*, 31 Cap. U. L. Rev. 439 (2003) (distinguishing polyamory from traditional polygamy); *In re State ex rel. Black*, 238 P.2d 887 (Utah 1955). Because a polygamous relationship is viewed as a type of bigamy, such a relationship is punishable by imprisonment in most jurisdictions. Polyandry is likewise prohibited. *See generally Riepe v. Riepe*, 91 P.3d 312 (Az. App. 2005).

Religious examples. It may be of interest that "Polygamy has been a common theme found in Christianity, Judaism, Islam, and other religions." Michael G. Myer, *Polygamist Eye for the Monogamist Guy: Homosexual Sodomy . . . Gay Marriage . . . Is Polygamy Next?* 42 Hous. L. Rev. 1458-1459 (Spring 2006). In the Christian religion, there are Biblical examples of marriages that have apparently not followed the one man to one-woman implication of Genesis, which is often relied upon as a basis for supporting only monogamous relationships. For example, King Solomon is claimed to have had 700 wives. *See* 1 Kings 11:3. At his wife Sarai's insistence, Abram took a secondary wife (Genesis 16:3). Unlike his father before him, Isaac was monogamous, but two of Isaac's sons were polygamous. Esau married two women (Genesis 26:34) and then added a third wife (Genesis 28:9). Jacob, meanwhile, ended up married to both Leah and Rachel (Genesis 29:28-29), as well as to their two handmaids (Genesis 30). Following the period of the patriarchs, the judge, Gideon, had many wives (Judges 8:30-3 1). William B. Kessel, *Polygamy and the Patriots*, http://www.wlsessays.net/files/KesselPolygamy.pdf.

"There are other religions, including Islam and Hinduism, under which polygamy is merely an acceptable practice." Keith Jaasma, *The Religious Freedom Restoration Act: Responding to Smith; Reconsidering Reynolds*, 16 Whittier L. Rev. 211, 286 (1995) (citing Jeremy M. Miller, *A Critique of the Reynolds Decision*, 11 W. St. U. L. Rev. 165, 179 (1984)). Polygamous marriages are legally recognized in many African, Asian, and Muslim countries, although it is not the norm. Sondra Hale, *Gender and Economics; Islam and Polygamy — A Question of Causality*, 1 Feminist Econ. 67, 70 (1995).

Arguments used to justify polygamy. There are several arguments made in support of polygamy. For example, permitting polygamy is sometimes justified as being in a society's interests when a wife is infertile or unwell. The theory is that polygamy allows a husband to have children without divorcing his first wife or possibly leaving her when she is ill. It is claimed that polygamy prevents immorality such as prostitution, rape, fornication, adultery, and prevents a high divorce rate that destabilizes a society. Polygamy may protect widows and orphans and may respond to the excess of women over men in a society in time of war or other disasters. Polygamy may also offer women a viable solution to balance a career, motherhood, and marriage successfully. It may reduce the incidence of extramarital sex and children born out of wedlock without support from fathers.

2.23. Bigamy

The root of the bigamy prohibition in America can be traced at least to the Roman Catholic Council of Trent, which took a firm stand against polygamy in a statement issued November 11, 1563. William B. Kessel, *Polygamy and the Patriots*, http://www.wlsessays.net/files/KesselPolygamy.pdf. (last visited July, 2012).

Bigamy was not a felony in the early English common law; indeed, it was not a crime of which the ordinary common law tribunals took cognizance at all. Rather, the ecclesiastical courts were deemed the most appropriate forums for a bigamy charge because it was considered a "spiritual fault" and they received exclusive jurisdiction to try bigamy cases. In 1604, Parliament made bigamy a felony punishable by death. 2 Alexander's British Statutes, Coe's Ed., 580, 581. The statute, as later modified and amended, was copied in the American colonies and served as the basis for the bigamy statutes that were subsequently passed by the legislatures. For example, the state of Virginia's bigamy statute closely tracks the bigamy statute of King James I. *Cole v. Conn*, 712 S.E.2d 759, 762 (Va. App. 2011); *see generally Barber v. State*, 50 Md. 161 (Md. App. 1878).

Today, bigamy is a statutory crime found in all jurisdictions, although the degree of the punishment for the crime varies among the states. It is commonly defined as "the act of marrying one person while legally married to another." *Black's Law Dictionary* 172 (8th ed. 2004). *See also* http://www.merriam-webster.com/dictionary/bigamy (last visited September, 2011). The Utah Supreme Court has held that the term "marry" in that state's bigamy statute makes a married person guilty of bigamy when the person purports to marry another person. Furthermore, the concept of marriage in Utah is said to include both legally recognized marriages and those that are not state-sanctioned. *State v. Holm*, 136 P.3d 726 (Utah 2006) (defendant was legally married to one woman and illegally participated in religious marriage ceremony with others).

2.24. Sham Marriages — Immigration Fraud

A detailed analysis of immigration fraud cases related to marriage is beyond the scope of this book. In this section, we can only touch on a principle or two associated with a sham marriage. In general, sham marriages are those entered into without the intent to live together as a husband and wife. *Faustin v. Lewis*, 427 A.2d 1105 (N.J. 1981).

American immigration laws provide that the spouses of United States citizens and permanent resident aliens may gain entry to the country as permanent resident aliens. *See* 8 U.S.C.A. §§1151(a), 1151(b)(2), 1152(a)(4), 1153(a), 1154(a). They are given priority through the immigration laws. *See* Immigration Act of May 26, 1924, 43 Stat. 153 (1924); War Brides Act of Dec. 28, 1945, Pub.L. No. 271, ch. 591, 59 Stat. 659 (1945); Immigration and Nationality Act of June 27, 1952, Pub.L. No. 414, 616 Stat. 163(1952); Immigration and Nationality Act Amendments of October 3, 1965, Pub.L. 89–236, 79 Stat. 911 (1965).

Unfortunately, aliens occasionally use sham marriages to gain permanent residence in the United States. *See* 8 U.S.C. 1154, *Procedure for Granting Immigrant Status* http://www.law.cornell.edu/uscode/text/8/1154 (last visited December 2, 2012). *See generally* Kerry Abrams, *Immigration Law and the Regulation of Marriage*, 91 Minn. L. Rev. 1625 (June 2007). The Abrams' article compares immigration law's regulation of marriage with that of traditional family law in each of the four stages of marriage and considers how immigration law might tell us something important about how Americans — or at least lawmakers — envision marriage today. It provides a taxonomy of reasons why Congress regulates marriage through immigration law and suggests how courts and scholars might determine the legitimacy of congressional action in this area.

Out of concern with the potential use of sham marriages to circumvent immigration laws, Congress enacted the Marriage Fraud Amendments Act, 8 U.S.C. §1154(h), 1255(e) (1986). The Act made it a criminal offense for a person to knowingly enter into a marriage for the purpose of evading any provision of the immigration laws. 8 U.S.C.A. §1325(b) was redesignated to 8 U.S.C.A. §1325(c) without substantive change by Pub. L. 104–208, §105(a), 110 Stat. 3009–556 5. Section 1325(c) provides for both imprisonment and/or a fine upon a conviction under the section.

One of the features of the Marriage Fraud Amendments Act is found in Section 702 of the Act. That section permits an alien who marries during deportation proceedings to establish that the marriage was entered into in good faith, in accordance with law, not for the purpose of procuring the alien's entry as an immigrant, and that no fee or other consideration was given. The amendment applies to marriages entered into before, on, or after the date of enactment. *See generally* Comment, Marcel De Armas, *For Richer or Poorer or Any Other Reason: Adjudicating Immigration Marriage Fraud Cases Within the Scope of the Constitution*, 15 Am. U. J. Gender Soc. Pol'y & L. 743 (2007) (discussing the disagreement among federal circuit courts over the test to apply to determine fraudulent marriages).

2.25. Consanguinity

By the thirteenth century in England, marriage was under the firm control of the ecclesiastical courts and the canon law was the source of the rules declaring what classes of persons should be prohibited from marrying on account of a relationship by consanguinity or affinity. The ecclesiastical law originally followed the Jewish law as set out in the Old Testament, which prohibited to an equal degree the marriage of persons related by consanguinity or affinity. The historical basis for these statutes in America is rooted in English Canonical Law, which enforced what is considered a Biblical prohibition on incestuous relationships. *State v. Sharon H.*, 429 A.2d 1321, 1327 (Del. Super. 1981).

A medical reason advanced for the enactment of consanguinity statutes rests upon the generally accepted theory that genetic inbreeding by close blood relatives tends to increase the chances that offspring of the marriage will inherit certain unfavorable physical characteristics. *Ibid.* (a reason advanced for the enactment of incest and consanguinity statutes is a generally accepted theory that genetic inbreeding by close blood relatives tends to increase the chances that offspring of the marriage will inherit certain unfavorable physical characteristics).

Consanguinity restrictions bar marriages between persons related by blood within certain degrees of kinship, with the scope of the prohibition varying from state to state. All jurisdictions bar marriages within the immediate family; that is, between a parent and child or brother and sister. These relationships, if they occur, are void. Most states bar marriage between an aunt and nephew or an uncle and his niece. A majority of jurisdictions bar marriage between first cousins, although courts have on occasion waived the application of this prohibition. For example, in an Indiana case, two first cousins had married in Tennessee, where such marriages were legal. Later, after moving to Indiana, where such marriages are illegal, they sought a divorce. The Indiana court found that there was not a strong public policy against such marriages, so the marriage was given comity in Indiana and a divorce granted. *Mason v. Mason*, 725 N.E.2d 706 (Ind. App. 2002).

Consanguinity statutes that expressly prohibit marriages between brother and sister are applied to bar marriages or sexual relations between blood relatives, including relatives of the half-blood. *See State v. Skinner*, 43 A.2d 76 (Conn. 1945); *State v. Lamb*, 227 N.W. 830 (Iowa 1929); *State v. Smith*, 85 S.E. 958 (S.C. 1915).

2.26. Affinity

"Affinity" is defined, in part, as "[a]ny familial relation resulting from a marriage." *Black's Law Dictionary* 59 (7 ed. 1999). Courts have consistently defined "affinity" as "the relationship which arises by marriage." *See Chinn v. State*, 26 N.E. 986, 987 (1890). For example, a mother-in-law and son-in-law are related by affinity but not by blood. Affinity relationships are terminated upon divorce. *Hamilton v. Calvert*, 235 S.W.2d 453 (Tex. App. 1951).

The *Model Penal Code* explicitly rejects the criminalization of affinity relationships as incestuous. The *Code* criminalizes marriage, cohabitation, or sexual intercourse with "an ancestor or descendant, a brother or sister of the whole or half-blood [or an uncle, aunt, nephew or niece of the whole blood]." *Model Penal Code and Commentaries* §230.2 (1980). The *Code* adds that "The relationships referred to herein include blood relationships without regard to legitimacy, and relationship of parent and child by adoption." *Ibid.* The commentaries to the *Model Penal Code* make clear that the drafters carefully considered and rejected affinity-based incest (with the exception of the adoptive parent-child relationship). *Com. v. Rahim*, 805 N.E.2d 13 (Mass. 2004).

2.27. Adopted Children Marrying Each Other

Although all states prohibit marriage of relatives within certain degrees of kinship, most, but not all, do not prohibit marriage if the relationship is due to adoption. *See, e.g., State ex rel. Miesner v. Geile*, 747 S.W.2d 757 (Mo. App. 1988) (statutory prohibition against marriage between uncle and niece did not prohibit marriage between uncle and niece related by adoption); *Bagnardi v. Hartnett*, 366 N.Y.S.2d 89, 91 (N.Y. Sup. 1975) (marriage between adoptive father and adopted daughter legally permissible); *see also Israel v. Allen*, 577 P.2d 762 (Colo. 1978); *In re Enderle Marriage License*, 1 Pa. D & C Reports 2d 114 (Phila. Cy. 1954). In *Israel v. Allen*, the court held that the Colorado statute prohibiting marriage between a brother and sister related by adoption is unconstitutional. It stated that the statute violated the couple's equal protection rights because it failed to satisfy minimum rationality requirements and failed to further a legitimate state interest in family harmony. *Cf. Rhodes v. McAfee*, 457 S.W.2d 522, 524 (Tenn. 1970) (marriage of stepfather to stepdaughter after his divorce from her mother was void *ab initio* under the laws of Tennessee and Mississippi); *State v. Sharon H.*, 429 A.2d 1321 (Del. Super. 1981) (half-sister had been adopted, her marriage to half-brother was within scope of consanguinity statute; adoption statute eliminates only legal ties between adopted child and natural parents and does not impliedly amend consanguinity statute as to blood relationship).

2.28. Recognizing Another State's Marriage; *Lex Loci* and Full Faith and Credit

While states generally recognize valid marriages from other states, challenging questions arise when state law differs concerning validity of particular kinds of marriage. The full faith and credit clause of the Constitution and the *lex loci* doctrine are closely related. *Lex loci actus* is defined as "[t]he law of the place where the act was done." *Black's Law Dictionary* 911 (6th ed. 1990). For example, *lex loci* requires that a common law marriage legally created in one state be recognized outside that jurisdiction in a state where such relationships are prohibited. *Schofield v. Schofield*, 20 Pa. D. 805, 807-808 (Pa. Com. Pleas 1909) ("subsequent cases seem to have fixed in the law of New York the doctrine that the lex loci determines the validity of the marriage, even though it be contrary to a statute of the domicile determining a public policy with respect to maintenance of good morals, and although the parties went out of the state for the purpose of evading the statute of the domicile"); *Mission Ins. Co. v. Industrial Comm'n*, 559 P.2d 1085 (Ariz. 1976) (Arizona would recognize Kansas common law marriage if valid there); *Jennings v. Jennings*, 315 A.2d 816 (Md. 1974) (Maryland would recognize District of Columbia common law marriage); *Gallegos v. Wilkerson*, 445 P.2d 970 (N.M. 1968) (New Mexico would recognize valid Texas common law marriage). The United States Constitution also requires that every state accord "Full Faith and Credit" to the laws of its sister states. *See, e.g.*, *Kelderhaus v. Kelderhaus*, 467 S.E.2d 303 (1996) (a marriage's validity is to be determined by the law of the state where the marriage took place, unless the result would be repugnant to Virginia public policy); *Carpenter v. Carpenter*, 617 N.Y.S.2d 903 (N.Y. App. 1994); *Mott v. Duncan Petroleum Trans.*, 414 N.E.2d 657 (N.Y. 1980); *Netecke v. Louisiana*, 715 So. 2d 449 (La. App. 1998). The Constitutional provision must be followed even if there is a strong policy in the new state against, for example, common law marriage.

Note that concern about the possibility that the full faith and credit clause might require that state's recognize same-sex marriages triggered Congressional action that resulted in the Defense of Marriage Act of 1996 (DOMA). The Act, discussed later in this chapter, prohibits federal recognition of state domestic partnerships, civil unions, and same-sex marriages. 1 U.S.C. §7; 28 U.S.C. §1738C (1996). It provides states with the option of recognizing same-sex marriages but does not compel them to do so.

Examples

21. Assume that Darlene marries Maynard, joins the National Guard, and is dispatched for an eight-month assignment in Iraq. Darlene and Maynard agree to informally separate and formally divorce when Darlene returns from her tour of duty in Iraq. Darlene meets P, a corporal in another unit, and they marry. Darlene never informs P that she is still married to Maynard. P becomes suspicious when certain benefits due a spouse of a person in the military do not arrive, but he does nothing about it. While on leave, Darlene is killed while riding her motorcycle when the other driver ran a red light. P then discovers that Darlene is still married to Maynard. P seeks an intestate share of Darlene's estate as a putative spouse and wants to sue the driver of the car that ran the red light. Maynard claims P has no standing in either matter. Most likely, how will a court resolve these issues?

22. Social Security recipients Pam, 70, and David, 75, are married in California despite objections from David's children. The relationship deteriorated after a year, and they separated. David informed Pam that he had begun divorce proceedings. Pam subsequently signed a Marital Termination Agreement. However, shortly after signing the agreement, the couple decided to get back together. David allegedly lied to Pam that the divorce was never finalized, when in fact a default judgment and decree had been entered, divorcing them. They continued to live together for another year as husband and wife when David died, leaving a huge estate. David's children from a former marriage challenge any right of Pam to share in David's estate. They argue that she is lying about her ignorance of the divorce. Pam asserts she had no knowledge of the divorce decree. She claims regardless of the divorce, she is a putative spouse and should be allowed to take her widow's share of the estate. The relevant statute being considered by the family court judge reads as follows: "Whenever a determination is made that a marriage is void or voidable and the Court finds that either party or both parties believed in good faith that the marriage was valid, the Court shall declare such party or parties to have the status of a putative spouse." How will a court most likely treat the challenge by David's children?

23. Assume that Paul and Darlene were married at a time when Darlene suffered from an inoperable malignant brain tumor. The county clerk's office had issued Darlene and Paul a marriage license; however,

Darlene's physical condition prevented her from signing the application in the presence of either the county clerk or one of his deputies. Darlene never appeared before the county clerk. Both an appearance and a signature in the presence of the county clerk are required under state law. At the marriage ceremony, Darlene did not respond because of her brain tumor, and a third party was used as a proxy to acknowledge the marriage vows. Darlene died four days after the ceremony leaving a large estate. Paul seeks his intestate share of the estate as Darlene's widower. The estate challenges the marriage and the use of a proxy. How will a court most likely rule?

24. Assume that P and D marry in a jurisdiction that provides for a covenant marriage contract, and they execute such an agreement. After six months of marriage, the couple agrees that the relationship is not working. P files for a "no-fault" divorce, and D does not oppose the filing. The local court clerk, however, refuses to file the divorce action. P and D seek an order from the court requiring the clerk to file the divorce papers and place the matter on the divorce docket. Will a court in a covenant marriage jurisdiction grant P and D's request?

25. Assume that D and P married in 2000, and 12 years later, P sought a no-fault divorce. D produced a certified copy of their marriage certificate as proof of a valid Covenant Marriage and contended that the provisions of the state covenant marriage statute had to be complied with before the court could divorce the couple. In particular, she relied on what appeared to be the parties' signed statement stapled to the copy of the marriage certificate that stated: "We do hereby declare our intent to contract a Covenant Marriage and, accordingly, have executed a declaration of intent attached hereto." The declaration of intent was not to be found.

    P challenged the validity of the statement stapled to the marriage certificate. He called the minister who conducted their marriage to testify at a hearing on his challenge. The minister, age 88, testified that he did not specifically recall meeting with P and D, or even performing the ceremony. He was uncertain whether the parties signed a notarized form attesting that they had a discussion with him about the Covenant Marriage. He testified that he did not keep records of the "very few" Covenant Marriages that he had performed. He could not produce any informative pamphlets that he either read and/or provided to the parties when he allegedly met with them for the premarital counseling. He said that he could not be certain that he met with P for premarital counseling prior to the wedding date, in accordance with the Covenant Marriage Act. P testified the minister did not meet with him, and that the first time he met the minister was the night of the ceremony. He denied signing a Declaration of Intent to enter into a Covenant Marriage. D testified the minister met and counseled with both parties on at least two occasions before they were married. Most likely, how will a court rule on the challenge by P to the covenant marriage?

26. Assume that the year is 1953 and P, who is white and a Korean War veteran, and D, who is black, and an Army nurse, attempt to marry in Virginia. Under Virginia law, it is illegal for persons of different races to marry, and if they do, they will be sentenced to a minimum of one year in jail. They marry and shortly thereafter a neighbor alerts the local prosecutor about the relationship. P and D are indicted, convicted, and sentenced to one year in state prison. They challenge the anti-miscegenation statute in Virginia. Most likely, how will a court rule on their challenge?

27. Assume that state X is concerned about the increasing amount of unpaid child support, the high divorce rate, and the large percentage of children born out of wedlock. To assist the state in collecting support, a statute is enacted providing that, before a person can marry, he or she must complete a section on the marriage application form that asks whether there are any outstanding child support obligations. The applicant must state the total amount owed and suggest how it will be paid. If the section is not completed, a license will not be issued. If it is completed, a license will be issued. P, who owes several thousand dollars in child support, refuses to complete this area of the license application, and a marriage license is denied. P challenges the provision, arguing that it discriminates against persons who are indigent. How will a court most likely rule?

28. Assume that a state legislature is concerned about the state's high divorce rate and its impact on children. To discourage second marriages, it raised the marriage license fee to $500 for anyone seeking to marry in the state. P, who is indigent, is divorced and desires to remarry. P claims the statute is unconstitutional because he is indigent and without funds to pay the $500 filing fee. How will a court most likely rule?

29. Assume that P is convicted of a crime involving the use of prohibited drugs. The trial judge sentences P to a six-month rehabilitative drug program, which requires that P be incarcerated at a minimum security prison. While incarcerated, P decides to marry X and seeks to obtain a marriage license without a personal appearance before the clerk of court — a requirement under local law. The prison refuses to transport P to the clerk's office so he can obtain the license with his fiancée. P

brings an action against the clerk to require him to travel to the prison. P also contends that it is reasonable and feasible for the clerk or a representative to visit area prisons periodically for the purpose of issuing licenses. He claims that *Turner* requires the clerk to do so. How should a court rule?

30. Assume that Able marries Doris and Denise outside the United States. In the country where Able, Doris, and Denise are married, there is no barrier to a husband having two wives. Assume that Able migrates to the United States with Doris and Denise. Shortly after arriving in the United States, Doris begins divorce proceedings against Able. The clerk of court, John, discovers that Doris and Denise are both married to Able under the law of another country and refused to file the papers. What arguments might the lawyers for John and Doris make to the court when Doris challenges John's refusal to allow the filing of the divorce papers? How will a court most likely rule?

31. Assume that P and D are married in a state that allows marriage between first cousins. Following their marriage, they move to jurisdiction X that prohibits such marriages. When P brings an action in state X for divorce, D counters that there was never a marriage because the relationship was void. Most likely, how will a court rule?

Explanations

21. P should prevail as a putative spouse if the jurisdiction has adopted a typical putative spouse statute. P entered the marriage with Darlene in good faith and without any knowledge that Darlene was still married. As a putative spouse, P would normally be allowed to inherit from Darlene's estate. P most likely will not be given standing to sue as Darlene's husband unless there is a statute specifically allowing him to do so. Note that most of the putative spouse statutes limit recovery of the putative spouse to matters covering marriage and divorce.

22. The question of the credibility of the statements made by the parties and Pam will be decided by the trial judge. *Nahm v. Nahm*, 477 S.W.2d 713 (Mo. App. 1972) (due regard is given to the opportunity of the trial court to judge the credibility of the witnesses). The law the judge applies is found in the statute and most courts would interpret the language as allowing Pam to be considered a putative spouse. Here, if Pam's testimony is believed, she continued to live with David in good faith ignorance of a divorce and will most likely be deemed a putative

spouse. *In re Marriage of Monti*, 185 Cal. Rptr. 72 (Cal. 1982); *Manker v. Manker*, 644 N.W.2d 522 (Neb. 2002).

23. This is not a case involving a soldier or a war, and a court would obviously be concerned about a marriage being solemnized when only one party obtained the marriage license, only one party spoke or acknowledged the vows in any manner at the ceremony, and a representative spoke for the other party, with no evidence of a written proxy authorizing said representative. This is not a case analogous to proxy marriage during wartime, and it is not consistent with the requirements of the UMDA. A court will likely hold that there was never a valid marriage. *See In re Estate of Crockett*, 728 N.E.2d 765 (Ill. App. 2000); *Lopez v. Lopez*, 245 A.2d 771 (N.J. Super. 1968) (failure of the proxy marriage to comply with the statutory requirements, such as solemnization, renders it subject to annulment by either party); *Respole v. Respole*, 70 N.E.2d 465 (Ohio 1946) (proxy marriage invalid that did not comply with a statutory provision).

24. Given the current state of the statutory provisions regarding covenant marriage, the answer is most likely that a court will disallow the filing. Pursuant to their covenant, the parties would be required to engage in counseling and wait the appropriate amount of time that they specified in their agreement before seeking to dissolve their marital relationship. It is doubtful that a constitutional argument would result in a different outcome. *See generally Sosna v. Iowa*, 419 U.S. 393 (1975). Louisiana's covenant marriage statute illustrates the exemption for a covenant marriage. It reads in part: "Except in the case of a covenant marriage, a divorce shall be granted upon motion of a spouse when either spouse has filed a petition for divorce and upon proof that the requisite period of time . . . has elapsed from the service of the petition, or from the execution of written waiver of the service, and that the spouses have lived separate and apart continuously for at least the requisite period of time, in accordance with Article 103.1, prior to the filing of the rule to show cause." Louisiana Civil Code Article 102.

25. A declaration of intent to participate in a covenant marriage must be signed by the parties in a covenant marriage jurisdiction. It must contain (1) a detailed recitation of the elements of the Covenant Marriage contract; the parties' acknowledgment that they have received premarital counseling on the nature, purposes, and responsibilities of marriage; their acknowledgment that they have read the Covenant Marriage Act, and they understand that a covenant marriage is for life; and their commitment to each other. (2) An affidavit by the parties that they have received premarital counseling from certain entities, including a minister or clergyman of

any religious sect. (3) Premarital counseling, which includes a discussion of the seriousness of covenant marriage, communication of the fact that a covenant marriage is a commitment for life, a discussion of the obligation to seek marital counseling in times of marital difficulties, and a discussion of the exclusive grounds for legally terminating a covenant marriage by divorce or by divorce after a judgment of separation from bed and board. An attestation, signed by the counselor and attached to or included in the parties' affidavit, confirming that the parties were counseled as to the nature and purpose of the marriage. Here, the document cannot be found, and it was not filed with the local clerk of court.

Because of the lack of evidence, a court will most likely decide that there was not a covenant marriage. In doing so, the court will rely on the following: P's testimony denying signing the required declaration of intent, the total absence of such a document, and P's testimony that he never received the mandated premarital counseling required for a covenant marriage. The court will also rely on the minister's testimony that he was uncertain whether the parties signed a notarized form attesting that they had a discussion with him about a covenant marriage. *See Short v. Short*, 33 So. 3d 988 (La. App. 2010) (evidence insufficient to prove covenant marriage existed).

26. Clearly, the statute is unconstitutional. However, at this period in history, Virginia courts and most others would uphold such odious provisions. *See Naim v. Naim*, 87 S.E.2d 749 (Va. 1955). In *Naim*, the state court upheld Virginia's anti-miscegenation statute, which was obviously an endorsement of the doctrine of white supremacy. It also reasoned that marriage has traditionally been subject to state regulation without federal intervention, consequently the Tenth Amendment of the United States Constitution left the regulation of marriage to exclusive state control. Not until *Loving v. Virginia* did a provision that bars marriage between persons of different race or nationality be ruled to violate the Fourteenth Amendment's equal protection and due process provisions of the federal Constitution.

27. This provision is quite different from the one discussed in *Zablocki v. Redhail* because there is no actual barrier to the marriage, other than the requirement that an applicant complete the form. A court would most likely apply a rational basis test to the provision and conclude that the state's interest in obtaining information regarding child support obligations outweighs a citizen's interest in refusing to provide the information. This provision would most likely be upheld.

28. P will argue that the statute prevents a person from ever marrying if he or she cannot pay the filing fee. Because of the nature of the barrier, the court

will most likely subject it to strict constitutional scrutiny, which means the state will have to demonstrate a compelling interest in charging the fee. P has considerable authority to support his view, including *Loving*, *Zablocki*, and *Boddie v. Connecticut*, 401 U.S. 371 (1971) http://scholar.google.com/scholar_case?case=7056835094703499903&hl=en&as_sdt=2&as_vis=1&oi=scholarr (last visited September, 2011). In *Boddie*, the Supreme Court held that Connecticut could not deny access to divorce courts to those persons who could not afford to pay the required filing fee absent a countervailing state interest of overriding significance. *See also Crocker v. Finley*, 459 N.E.2d 1346 (Ill. 1984) http://scholar.google.com/scholar_case?case=17656304912517834678&hl=en&as_sdt=2&as_vis=1&oi=scholarr, and *Boynton v. Kusper*, 494 N.E.2d 135 (Ill. 1986). Here, there is no showing of an overriding interest by the state.

29. This is a close question. The issue not addressed by *Turner* is whether under the totality of all circumstances involved in operating a prison, a prisoner's fundamental right to marry can be enforced irrespective of the cost to the ancillary services, which have no statutory responsibility to ensure that the prisoner and his or her partner get to the marriage license bureau door. A court rejecting the prisoner's request would reason that the court clerk does not have a legal duty to ensure that a prisoner obtains a marriage license. It would say that for a court to direct the clerk to engage in an activity that would entail unknown expenditures of money, manpower, and security concerns and which would divert funds and resources beyond their statutory mandate is inappropriate. *In re Coates*, 849 A.2d 254 (Pa. Super. 2004). A court rejecting the prisoner's request would likely conclude that *Turner* never intended that its ruling be extrapolated to provide that prisoners must be accommodated regardless of cost or security problems in order to comply with the ministerial requirements of obtaining a marriage license.

    However, a court favoring the prisoner's argument would most likely view the matter as one where there are low-cost alternatives available to the clerk's office. For example, the clerk's office could schedule periodic trips to prisons within the county to conduct examinations and issue marriage licenses two or three times a year. Since the examinations would be performed at predetermined intervals rather than at the prisoners' request, the cost associated with this service would be minimal. Alternatively, the clerk could accept affidavits that were sworn, attested, and notarized at the prison and then mailed to the clerk's office.

30. Most likely, John will argue that the action should be dismissed because a polygamist relationship in every state in the United States is void, and

in most states, it is a crime punishable by imprisonment. Furthermore, he will correctly point out that the full faith and credit clause of the Constitution does not apply to the laws of a foreign government.

Doris will argue that because the marriage was valid where it was performed, it is valid everywhere. She will agree, as she must, that the full faith and credit clause does not apply to international marriages; however, she will argue that the forum state as a matter of comity should recognize the marriage. Doris will also argue that because she was married first, her marriage is valid, while the marriage to Denise is invalid.

Doris will also argue that there is no strong public policy against allowing her to divorce Able — just a policy against polygamous marriages. John will respond that, even though the rule of *lex loci* generally supports Doris's position, the rule should be tempered by the strong public policy in the forum state that bars bigamous marriages. Moreover, John will contend that the policy of the foreign government is contrary to that of the forum state, and a court should not, under these circumstances, parcel out the sequence of the marriage in order to allow a divorce (noting that, if the divorce is allowed to Doris, Denise apparently remains the wife of Able).

On these facts, the clerk's decision to reject the divorce petition will most likely be upheld — although some jurisdictions may agree with the divorce policy argument put forth by Doris. *Compare Earle v. Earle*, 126 N.Y.S. 317 (N.Y. App. 1910) ("no civilized Christian nation permits polygamy, and if the law of Italy did permit the marriage between parties, one of whom was already married and the bonds of matrimony in full force, the courts of this state would not be obliged to give effect to such law as between parties domiciled here at the time of the celebration of the marriage") with *In re Dalip Singh Bir's Estate*, 188 P.2d 499, 501-02 (Cal. App. 1948) (court recognized foreign polygamous second marriages for the purposes of succession, to avoid denying any inheritance to the second wife).

31. The marriage of first cousins was not forbidden at common law and is lawful, and not held to be incestuous, in most of the states of the United States. Note, however, that states may distinguish between first cousins of the half and whole blood. *In re Estate of Everhart*, 783 N.W.2d 1 (Neb. App. 2010) (Neb. Rev. Stat. §42-103(3) (Reissue 2008) provides that a marriage is void "when the parties are related to each other as parent and child, grandparent and grandchild, brother and sister of half as well as whole blood, first cousins when of whole blood, uncle and niece, and aunt and nephew." Paul and Arlene were first cousins of whole blood because Paul's father and Arlene's mother were siblings). Absent a strong

public policy against the marriage of first cousins, a court will most likely allow the marriage. It will reason that it should recognize marriages if valid where contracted, as valid in this jurisdiction. The court will most likely distinguish a marriage between first cousins and marriages contracted by more closely related collaterals, that is, uncle and niece, aunt and nephew, and siblings. *See Ghassemi v. Ghassemi*, 98 So. 2d 731, 743 (La. App. 2008) (a marriage between first cousins, if valid where contracted, is valid in Louisiana and is not a violation of a strong public policy) *See also Mason v. Mason*, 775 N.E.2d 706, 709 (Ind. App. 2002), trans. denied, 792 N.E.2d 34 (Ind. 2003) (Indiana court recognized marriage of first cousins contracted in Tennessee, noting that although Indiana prohibited such marriages, it had no statute stating that such marriages violated Indiana's public policy as it did regarding same-sex marriages); *Schofield v. Schofield*, 20 Pa. D. 805, 807 (Com. Pl. 1910) (court noted that Pennsylvania's prohibition against marriages between first cousins only applied to marriages contracted within Pennsylvania and that the Pennsylvania Legislature could have prohibited first-cousin marriages no matter where contracted, but had not done so).

SAME-SEX RELATIONSHIPS

2.29. Religious Perspectives

Although many religions recognize same-sex marriage, such as Buddhists, Quakers, Unitarians, Reform and Reconstructionist Jews, a majority of religious persons in the United States have generally opposed same-sex marriage. *Varnum v. Brien*, 763 N.W.2d 862 (Iowa 2009), n.31. A 2003 survey by the Pew Research Center reported that 59 percent of Americans opposed and 32 percent favored same-sex marriage, a ratio of less than 2-1. Note, Ben Schuman, *Gods & Gays: Analyzing the Same-Sex Marriage Debate from a Religious Perspective*, 96 Geo. L.J. 2103, 2108 (August 2008). "The ratio jumps to more than 6-1 (80 percent to 12 percent) for those 'with a high level of religious commitment.'" *Id. at* 2109. It is thought that the reason for the increase with high levels of religious commitment is that, as a general rule, religion views same-sex sexual activity as a sin and same-sex marriage as an unacceptable extension of that sin.

However, by October 2009, a majority of Americans (57 percent) favored allowing same-sex couples to enter into legal agreements with each other "that would give them many of the same rights as married couples, a status commonly known as civil unions. This finding marks a slight uptick in support for civil unions and appeared to continue a significant long-term trend since the question was first asked in Pew Research Center surveys in 2003, when support for civil unions stood at 45 percent." *Most Still Oppose Gay Marriage, But Support for Civil Unions Continues to Rise*, http://pewresearch.org/pubs/1375/gay-marriage-civil-unions-opinion (last visited September, 2011).

A Pew Research Center survey, released May 4, 2011, showed that opposition to same-sex marriage has continued to decline in the United States. The survey reported that 45 percent of those surveyed favored allowing same-sex couples to marry legally, while 46 percent were opposed. Two years earlier, in April 2009, 35 percent supported same-sex marriage, while 54 percent were opposed. Opposition to same-sex has fallen by 19 points (from 65 percent) since 1996. *Most Say Homosexuality Should Be Accepted by Society*, http://pewresearch.org/pubs/1994/poll-support-for-acceptance-of-homosexuality-gay-parenting-marriage (last visited March, 2012).

Biblical theory. Religious persons will often point to the Bible, which describes how woman was made from the rib of man, and states that "[f]or this reason a man will leave his father and mother and be united to his wife, and they will become one flesh." Genesis 2:24 (New International Version). This statement is said to imply that such unity, or marriage, shall be between one woman and one man. *See* Matthew 19:4-5. History, however, suggests that marriage has taken many different forms and has assumed varying degrees of importance in different cultures. *See* James L. Musselman, *What's Love Got to Do with It? A Proposal for Elevating the Status of Marriage by Narrowing Its Definition, While Universally Extending the Rights and Benefits Enjoyed by Married Couples*, 16 Duke J. Gender L. & Pol'y 37 (January 2009); Lynn D. Wardle, *The "Withering Away" of Marriage: Some Lessons from the Bolshevik Family Law Reforms in Russia, 1917-1926*, 2 Geo. J. L. & Pub. Pol'y 469 (2004), note 3 at 469; Mary Ann Glendon, *State, Law, and Family: Family Law in Transition in the United States and Western Europe* 7-14 (1977) (discussing alternative forms of marriage regulation and different meanings of marriage). Religious persons will also argue that sexual activity between same-sex persons is immoral and generally will base these views in part on passages from the Bible that promote opposite-sex relationships and apparently condemn homosexuality. *See, e.g.*, Genesis 2:18-24; Leviticus 20:7-16, 20:22-27; Romans 1:18-19, 1:22-32; and 1 Corinthians 6:1-3, 6:7-11.

Note that "[D]ata from a 2007 study show that states that do not include sexual orientation in their public discrimination laws have an average Evangelical Protestant population of around 33 percent, which is nearly twice the average percentage of Evangelical Protestants in states that do protect gay and lesbian individuals in public accommodations. A reported 64 percent of Evangelical Church members believe homosexuality should be discouraged by society — only the Church of Jesus Christ of Latter-Day Saints (the "Mormon Church") (68 percent) and Jehovah's Witnesses (76 percent) had a higher percentage of disapproving members." Note, Kelly Catherine Chapman, *Gay Rights, the Bible, and Public Accommodations: An Empirical Approach to Religious Exemptions for Holdout States*, 100 Geo. L.J. 1783, 1798 (June 2012). An inference that may be drawn from this data, assuming it is correct, is that "states that do not include sexual orientation in their public discrimination laws have, on average, a larger proportion of their populations that more often believe that homosexuality should be discouraged than do other religions." *Ibid.* This, of course, may also mean that more voters exist in these areas who might strike down any proposed gay rights ballot initiatives or not elect politicians who supported such legislation.

Separation of Church and State. Proponents of same-sex marriage contend that government regulation of marriage should not be based on religious doctrine because the Constitution requires the separation of church and state. *See, e.g.*, John G. Culhane, *Uprooting the Arguments Against Same-Sex Marriage*, 20 Cardozo L. Rev. 1119 (1999). They also argue that state restrictions on same-sex marriage has no effect, other than to lessen the status and human dignity of gays and lesbians, and to officially reclassify their relationships and families as inferior to those of opposite-sex couples. A Ninth Circuit panel appears to agree with the proponents. *Perry v. Brown*, 671 F.3d 1052, 1063 (9th Cir. 2012) (Proposition 8 was an enactment devoid of any rational relationship to a legitimate state interest and was unconstitutionally tainted by anti-gay animus).

2.30. Federal Defense of Marriage Act (DOMA)

The Defense of Marriage Act of 1996 (DOMA), was a direct legislative response to *Baehr v. Lewin*, 852 P.2d 44 Haw. 1993). In that decision, the Hawaii Supreme Court indicated that same-sex couples might be entitled to marry under the state's constitution. The decision raised the possibility, for the first time, that same-sex couples could begin to obtain state-sanctioned marriage licenses.

The House Judiciary Committee's Report on DOMA referenced the *Baehr* decision as the beginning of an "orchestrated legal assault being waged against traditional heterosexual marriage." It expressed concern that this development "threaten[ed] to have very real consequences . . . on federal law." Aff. of Gary D. Buseck, Ex. D, H.R.Rep. No. 104–664 at 2–3 (1996), reprinted in 1996 U.S.C.C.A.N. 2905, 2906–07 ("H. Rep."). Specifically, the Report warned that "a redefinition of marriage in Hawaii to include homosexual couples could make such couples eligible for a whole range of federal rights and benefits."

The Congressional Act prohibits federal recognition of state domestic partnerships, civil unions, and same-sex marriages. 1 U.S.C. §7; 28 U.S.C. §1738C (1996) http://thomas.loc.gov/cgi-bin/query/z?c104:H.R.3396.ENR: (last visited September, 2011). DOMA defines marriage as between a man and a woman and declares that states are not required to recognize any same-sex marriage or union formed in another state. DOMA also prevents same-sex couples from gaining access to federal laws providing certain benefits that are available to heterosexual married couples. *Comment*, Amanda Alquist, *The Migration of Same-Sex Marriage from Canada to the United States: An Incremental Approach*, 30 U. La Verne L. Rev. 200, 205 (November 2008). The benefits to heterosexual couples include favorable joint tax rates, filing for bankruptcy as a couple, social security spousal benefits, veteran benefits and pension rights. Nancy J. Knauer, *Same-Sex Marriage and Federalism*, 17 Temp. Pol. & Civ. Rts. L. Rev. 421, 425 (Spring 2008).

DOMA has received mixed reviews by federal courts. In *Golinski v. U.S. Office of Personnel Management*, 824 F. Supp. 2d 968 (N.D. Calif. 2012), the court found in favor of a federal same-sex employee who challenged DOMA. The employee was a lesbian married to someone of the same sex who brought action against the Office of Personnel Management (OPM). She sought a determination that DOMA, as applied to her, violated the Constitution by refusing to recognize lawful marriages for the purposes of application of the laws governing benefits for federal employees. The trial court agreed and granted her summary judgment. *See Windsor v. U.S.*, — F.2d — 2012 WL 4937310 (2d Cir. 2012) (DOMA violated equal protection as applied to lesbian couple); *Pederson v. Office of Personnel Management*, — F. Supp. 2d — 2012 WL 3113883 (D.C. Conn. 2012); *Gill v. Office of Personnel Management*, 699 F. Supp. 2d 374 (D.C. Mass. 2010) (DOMA violates core constitutional principles of equal protection); *Dragovich v. U.S. Dept. of Treasury*, 2012 WL 1909603 — F. Supp. 2d — (D.C. N.D. California 2012) (Section 3 of DOMA held unconstitutional barring the same-sex legal spouses and registered domestic partners of California public employees from enrollment in the California's long-term care plan, even though opposite-sex legal spouses are permitted to enroll).

However, in *In re Kandu*, 315 B.R. 123, 133 (Bankr. W.D. Wash. 2004), the court held that DOMA precluded same-sex couples from filing a joint bankruptcy petition. In *Massachusetts v. U.S. Dept. of Health and Human Services*, 698 F. Supp. 2d 234 (D.C. Mass. 2010), the court held that DOMA violates the Tenth Amendment of the Constitution, by intruding on areas of exclusive state authority, as well as the Spending Clause, by forcing the Commonwealth to engage in invidious discrimination against its own citizens in order to receive and retain federal funds in connection with two joint federal-state programs. The court in *Wilson v. Ake*, 354 F. Supp. 2d 1298 (M.D. Fla. 2005), found DOMA "constitutionally valid" where same-sex couple who married in Massachusetts challenged DOMA in Florida.

In *Smelt v. County of Orange*, 374 F. Supp. 2d 861, 880 (C.D. Cal. 2005), the court ruled that DOMA does not violate the equal protection or due process guarantees of the Fifth Amendment, *aff'd in part, rev'd in part*, 447 F.3d 673 (9th Cir. 2006). As of the date this manuscript is written, a constitutional challenge to DOMA has yet to reach the Supreme Court.

State DOMA. Currently, 44 states have either a mini-DOMA statute, state constitutional amendment, or some other legislation prohibiting same-sex marriage. Bryan K. Fair, *The Ultimate Association: Same-Sex Marriage and the Battle Against Jim Crow's Other Cousin*, 63 U. Miami L. Rev. 269, 277 (October 2008); http://www.ncsl.org/default.aspx?tabid=16430 (last visited February, 2012) (listing states with same-sex marriage, civil unions, and domestic partnerships). In May 2012, North Carolina became the 31st state to amend a constitution to define "marriage" as the union of one man and one woman.

2.31. *Bowers v. Hardwick* and *Lawrence v. Texas*

A major obstacle to same-sex marriages was the oft-criticized decision by the Supreme Court in *Bowers v. Hardwick*, 478 U.S. 186 (1986) (http://www.oyez.org/cases/1980-1989/1985/1985_85_140 (last visited March, 2012) (Oral arguments and case analysis). In that decision, the Supreme Court affirmed a lower court ruling that found constitutional a criminal statute punishing sex between same-sex consenting adults. The Court rejected the claim that the right to privacy ruling by the Court in *Griswald v. Connecticut*, 381 U.S. 479 (1965), protected consenting adults from prosecution under the state statute. http://www.oyez.org/cases/1960-1969/1964/1964_496 (last visited March, 2012) (oral arguments and case analysis). Subsequent to the Supreme Court's decision, the Georgia Supreme Court held that the statute considered in *Bowers* violated the due process rights of consenting adults under its state constitution. *Powell v. State*, 510 S.E.2d 18 (Ga. 1988).

Seven years after *Bowers* was decided, the Supreme Court reconsidered its ruling in *Lawrence v. Texas*, 539 U.S. 558 (2003). http://www.oyez.org/cases/2000-2009/2002/2002_02_102 (last visited March, 2012) (oral arguments and case analysis). *Lawrence* involved a Texas criminal statute that made it a crime for consenting adults to engage in anal intercourse. Justice Kennedy, writing for the Court, held that the criminal statute violated a liberty interest guaranteed by the due process clause of the Fourteenth Amendment and overruled *Bowers*. The Court reasoned that the liberty interest concerned behavior between two consenting adults, which is inherently private and should not be subject to government intervention. For Justice O'Connor, concurring, the Equal Protection Clause of the Fourteenth Amendment, rather than the Due Process Clause, should have been the basis on which the Texas law was declared unconstitutional.

Justice Scalia dissented and questioned whether homosexual sodomy is now a fundamental right, entitled to strict scrutiny, and speculated that the opinion opened the door to ending all moral legislation. He wrote: "This [opinion] effectively decrees the end of all morals legislation. State laws against bigamy, same-sex marriage, adult incest, prostitution, masturbation, adultery, fornication, bestiality, and obscenity are likewise sustainable only in light of *Bowers'* validation of laws based on moral choices. Every single one of these laws is called into question by today's decision." Decisions in several jurisdictions since *Lawrence* indicate that Justice Scalia was far from the mark in his speculation about the impact on the majority's decision.

It has been suggested that *Lawrence* "acutely calls DOMA's constitutionality into question." Roger Severino, *Or for Poorer? How Same-Sex Marriage Threatens Religious Liberty*, 30 Harv. J. L. & Pub. Pol'y 939, 956 (Summer 2007). Since the *Lawrence* ruling, several states have questioned the constitutionality of their adultery and fornication statutes. Because *Lawrence* held that individuals have a right to engage in private sexual behavior in their homes without government intrusion, and adultery and fornication statutes regulate similar private consensual behavior between adults, the statutes would not appear to survive scrutiny under *Lawrence. See, e.g., Martin v. Ziherl*, 607 S.E.2d 367, 370-371 (Va. 2005) (Virginia criminal fornication statute unconstitutional).

2.32. Civil Unions/Domestic Partners

In the following section is a list of states that have provided benefits to same-sex couples much as though they were married by enacting civil union legislation. The list is constantly changing.

Vermont. In *Baker v. State*, 744 A.2d 864 (Vt. 1999), the Vermont Supreme Court in a landmark ruling held that the limitation of state-recognized marriage to opposite-sex couples violated the common benefits clause of that state's constitution. It directed the Vermont legislature to fashion a remedy providing same-sex couples with the same benefits and security granted married couples. In response, the Vermont legislature passed a law extending the benefits and protections of marriage to same-sex couples through a system of civil unions. However, under the Vermont statute, "marriage" remains a union between a man and a woman.

However, Vermont's marriage equality law, effective September 1, 2009, discontinued the need for the separate status of "civil unions" in Vermont. Same-sex couples can now marry in that state. Civil unions entered into prior to September 1, 2009 will continue to be recognized as civil unions. Couples currently in a civil union who want to be married will need to go through the new marriage process. http://healthvermont.gov/research/records/cv_reciprocity.aspx (last visited February, 2012).

Connecticut legislative civil union. In 2005, Connecticut became the first state to promulgate legislation without a court order that provides same-sex couples with the opportunity to enter into a civil union. *Conn. Pub. Act* 05-10 (2005). The law extended to civil union partners "all the same benefits, protections and responsibilities under law . . . as are granted to spouses in a marriage." However, parties to a civil union under Connecticut law were not defined as spouses. However, Connecticut now allows same-sex marriage. On October 1, 2010, civil unions ceased to be provided and existing civil unions were automatically converted to marriages.

Delaware legislative civil union. Civil unions were approved by the Delaware legislature when, in April 2011 it recognized the legal relationship of civil union. Delaware law provides for the same rights, benefits, protections, and responsibilities as married persons under Delaware law. It does not require any religious institution to perform solemnizations of civil unions. The law takes effect January 1, 2012. http://www.ncsl.org/issues-research/human-services/civil-unions-and-domestic-partnership-statutes.aspx (last visited March, 2012).

Hawaii legislative civil union. The Hawaii legislature approved civil unions in February 2011. It made same-sex and opposite-sex couples eligible for civil union recognition beginning January 1, 2012. The law grants same-sex couples the same rights as married couples. http://www.ncsl.org/issues-research/human-services/civil-unions-and-domestic-partnership-statutes.aspx (last visited March, 2012). Civil unions, domestic partnerships, and same-sex marriages performed in other states will be recognized as civil unions in Hawaii.

Illinois legislative civil union. The Illinois General Assembly approved a bill labeled "SB 1716" in December 2010. The bill, referred to as the Illinois Religious Freedom Protection and Civil Union Act, allows same-sex and opposite-sex couples to enter into civil unions, giving them some of the same benefits available to married couples, including the right to visit a sick partner in the hospital, disposition of a deceased loved one's remains, and the right to make decisions about a loved one's medical care. http://www.ncsl.org/issues-research/human-services/civil-unions-and-domestic-partnership-statutes.aspx (last visited March, 2012).

New Hampshire legislative civil union. In 2007, the legislature passed a bill that created the legal status of civil unions. The New Hampshire legislature passed same-sex marriage legislation, HB 0436, in May 2009 that went into effect on January 1, 2010. All civil unions were merged into marriage no later than January 2011, unless otherwise annulled or dissolved.

http://www.ncsl.org/issues-research/human-services/civil-unions-and-domestic-partnership-statutes.aspx (last visited March, 2012).

New Jersey legislative civil union and domestic partnership. (Allows both civil unions and domestic partnerships). Same-sex couples in New Jersey were able to enter into civil unions beginning in February 2007. Civil unions offer same-sex couples state-level spousal rights and responsibilities, but none of the federal protections (such as Social Security survivor benefits), and there is no guarantee that the unions will be recognized by other states or the federal government. The domestic partnership law, Chapter 103, passed in 2004, is available only to opposite-sex couples over the age of 62. http://www.ncsl.org/issues-research/human-services/civil-unions-and-domestic-partnership-statutes.aspx (last visited March, 2012).

In February 2012, the New Jersey Assembly passed a same-sex marriage bill. The measure, approved by both houses, was vetoed by its Republican governor, who stated that "gay marriage was an issue for a referendum, not the legislature."

Rhode Island legislative civil union. The Rhode Island General Assembly passed legislation allowing civil unions in June 2011. The bill took effect July 1, 2011. Those who enter into a civil union are offered the same benefits as provided to married couples.

DOMESTIC PARTNERS

As a rule, parties to a civil union have all the same benefits, protections, and responsibilities under law as are granted to spouses in a marriage, which is defined as the union of one man and one woman. *Kerrigan v. Commissioner of Public Health*, 957 A.2d 407, 413 n. 8 (Conn. 2008). However, the rights, protections, and responsibilities for domestic partners vary widely from jurisdiction to jurisdiction. Generally, domestic partners are afforded only limited rights, protections, and responsibilities. *See, e.g., Irizarry v. Bd. of Edu. of Chicago*, 251 F.3d 604 (7th Cir. 2001) (spousal health benefits provided to domestic partners of school employees, but only if the partner was of the same sex as the employee, was rationally related to board's legitimate goals, and did not violate equal protection clause); *Slattery v. New York*, 266 A.D. 2d 24 (N.Y. App. 1999) (ordinance, which established registry for domestic partners and extended certain rights and benefits to domestic partners of city employees and city residents who become domestic partners, did not impermissibly legislate in the area of marriage). *But see Gerritsen v. City of Los Angeles*,

18 Trials Digest 13th 14, 2009 WL 6370933 (Cal. Super. 2009) (defendant was equitably estopped from denying plaintiff's status as the domestic partner of decedent for pension survivorship benefits under the Administrative Code).

California domestic partners. Three California laws provide rights and responsibilities to registered domestic partners (same-sex couples and opposite-sex couples over the age of 62 are eligible to register). Assembly Bill 26 passed in 1999 established the statewide domestic partner registry and conferred certain rights that included hospital visitation and the right of state and local employers the ability to offer health care coverage to the domestic partners of their employees. Assembly Bill 25 was passed in 2001 and extended the rights of domestic partners to include the right to make medical decisions, the right to inherit when partner dies without a will, the right to use state stepparent adoption procedures, the right to use sick leave to care for a domestic partner and the right to be appointed as administrator of estate. In 2003, Assembly Bill 205 was passed, which extended all of the state-level rights and responsibilities of marriage to domestic partners. The rights and responsibilities associated with Assembly Bill 205 went into effect on January 1, 2005.

Oregon domestic partners. As of January 1, 2008, same-sex couples in Oregon will be able to enter into domestic partnerships that provide the same rights, benefits, and responsibilities as marriage under state law, thanks to the Oregon Family Fairness Act, Public Law Number 99, Oregon HB 2007 (2007). Domestic partnerships will offer same-sex couples the benefits of marriage under state law, but none of the federal protections (such as Social Security survivor benefits), and there is no guarantee that the partnerships will be recognized by other states or the federal government. (Note: The law has not yet taken effect due to a federal court decision delaying implementation issued December 2007.) http://www.ncsl.org/issues-research/human-services/civil-unions-and-domestic-partnership-statutes.aspx (last visited March, 2012).

Washington domestic partners. With a 2009 expansion of the law (Chapter 26.60 RCW) originally passed in 2007, registered domestic partners were afforded nearly all statewide spousal rights. This expansion was challenged by a ballot measure to repeal the additional benefits, Referendum 71, which passed in November 2009. Washington's domestic partner law remains unchanged and provides a full scope of domestic partner benefits.

Maine domestic partners. The Maine legislature passed a same-sex marriage act in 2009. However, the law was challenged by a ballot measure, Initiative 1, which passed November 3, 2009, and the law was subsequently repealed.

Maine's domestic partnerships law allows registered domestic partners to be eligible for limited rights, including inheritance without a will, making funeral and burial arrangements, entitlement to be named a guardian or conservator if the partner becomes incapacitated or to be named a representative to administer a deceased partner's estate, entitlement to make organ and tissue donation, and explicit protection by the state's domestic violence laws. http://www.ncsl.org/issues-research/human-services/civil-unions-and-domestic-partnership-statutes.aspx (last visited March, 2012).

Hawaii domestic partners. In 1997, the Hawaii legislature passed a law that allows same-sex couples to enter into a reciprocal beneficiary relationship. "Couples secure the following benefits from a reciprocal beneficiary relationship: inheritance without a will, ability to sue for the wrongful death of their reciprocal beneficiary, hospital visitation and health care decisions, consent to postmortem exams, loan eligibility, property rights (including joint tenancy), tort liability and protection under Hawaii domestic violence laws."

Nevada domestic partners. In June 2009, the Nevada Assembly overrode the governor's veto establishing a statewide registry for domestic partners. The benefits are substantially comparable to the rights and responsibilities afforded in traditional marriage. One exception is that employers are not mandated to provide health care coverage for domestic partners. http://www.ncsl.org/issues-research/human-services/civil-unions-and-domestic-partnership-statutes.aspx (last visited March, 2012).

Wisconsin domestic partners. In June 2009, the Wisconsin legislature passed a law establishing a statewide domestic partnership registry. Registered domestic partners in Wisconsin are now afforded some of the spousal benefits of marriage, including: inheritance and survivor protections, family and medical leave, medical/hospital visitation rights, and exemption from the real estate transfer fee.

Wisconsin has a constitutional amendment defining marriage between one man and one woman. The amendment includes a clause that bans any legal status that is identical or substantially similar to marriage. Wisconsin was the first state with this type of constitutional amendment. At the time this manuscript was being prepared, the registry was being challenged in court. http://www.ncsl.org/issues-research/human-services/civil-unions-and-domestic-partnership-statutes.aspx (last visited March, 2012).

2.33. Connecticut, Massachusetts, Iowa, Vermont, New Hampshire, New York, Washington, and the District of Columbia Allow Same-Sex Marriage

Although the number of nontraditional families is increasing in the United States, and several jurisdictions have expanded the rights of same-sex couples, only seven jurisdictions and the District of Columbia have extended to same-sex couples the right to marry. Massachusetts was the first state to expand the marriage right when in a 4-3 opinion, *Goodridge v. Department of Public Health*, 798 N.E.2d 941 (Mass. 2003), it ruled that "barring an individual from the protections, benefits, and obligations of civil marriage solely because that person would marry a person of the same sex violated the Massachusetts Constitution." The court held that the state limitation of protections, benefits, and obligations of civil marriage to individuals of opposite sexes lacked a rational basis and violated the state constitutional equal protection principles. However, the majority stayed the entry of judgment for 180 days to allow the Massachusetts legislature to "take such action as it may deem appropriate in light of this opinion." When the legislature took no action, the court's ruling became law.

Connecticut technically became the third state — after Massachusetts and California — to legalize same-sex marriage. *Kerrigan and Mock v. Connecticut Department of Public Health*, 957 A.2d 407 (Conn. 2008) (California permitted them for about six months before voters approved a ban in November 2008). The court in Connecticut, in a 4-3 decision, held that laws restricting civil marriage to heterosexual couples violated same-sex couples' state constitutional equal protection rights. Because the ruling relied on the Connecticut state constitution, it cannot be appealed to the Supreme Court.

The Iowa Supreme Court overturned a ban on same-sex marriage in a unanimous, 69-page decision. *Varnum v. Brien*, 763 N.W.2d 862 (Iowa 2009). Justice Cady wrote, "We are firmly convinced the exclusion of gay and lesbian people from the institution of civil marriage does not substantially further any important governmental objective . . . . We have a constitutional duty to ensure equal protection of the law." Lawmakers in Vermont in April 2009 became the fourth state to legalize gay marriage and the first to do so by legislative enactment. The measure was approved over the governor's veto.

In May 2009, Maine became the fifth state to sanction same-sex marriage. Both the Maine House and Senate approved the measure, and the governor signed it into law the first week in May. However, opponents of the law mounted a successful veto process on the measure via a state referendum and the legislation was rescinded. New Hampshire became the sixth state in the nation to sanction same-sex marriages on June 2, 2009. The legislation signed by the governor allowed same-sex marriages to be performed in the state and provided that religious clergy and organizations and their employees will not be required to participate in the services or recognize the unions.

District of Columbia. In 1992, the District of Columbia City Council passed a law allowing unmarried couples to register as domestic partners. Since then, several rights have been added, including hospital visitation, the right to make medical decisions, the right to control the remains of a deceased partner, the right to take sick leave to take care of a partner and the right to sue for the wrongful death of a partner. Note that although DC's domestic partner registry was created in law in 1992, Congress prohibited DC from expending any public money on the registry. This ban was lifted in 2002. http://www.ncsl.org/issues-research/human-services/civil-unions-and-domestic-partnership-statutes.aspx (last visited March, 2012). At the end of 2009, the District of Columbia Council passed a resolution allowing same-sex marriage. Note that registered domestic partners may now marry and that marrying automatically converts the domestic partnership into a marriage.

California. In *Strauss v. Horton*, 207 P.3d 48 (Cal. 2009), the California Supreme Court rejected a challenge to Proposition 8, which amended the California constitution to define marriage as the union of a man and a woman. The court said that same-sex marriages that took place before Proposition 8 was enacted were still valid because the amendment could not apply retroactively. In describing the scope of Proposition 8, the court said that it would prohibit recognition of out-of-state same-sex marriages and prevent issuance of marriage licenses to same-sex couples in California. The United States Court of Appeals in San Francisco, in a 2-1 decision in February 2012, ruled that California voters could not deprive gay couples of the right to marry. http://www.ca9.uscourts.gov/datastore/opinions/2012/02/07/1016696com.pdf (last visited March, 2012). Proposition 8, which barred same-sex marriages after the California Supreme Court had legalized gay marriages, was described by the Ninth Circuit as having as its only purpose "to lessen the status and human dignity of gays and lesbians in California," which the United States Constitution doesn't allow, the court said.

Washington. In February 2012, Washington became the seventh state to legalize same-sex marriage. Opponents of the legislation said they would try to seek its repeal through a ballot measure. http://www.nytimes.com/2012/02/14/us/washington-gay-marriage-legalized.html (last visited February, 2012).

2.34. Out-of-State Recognition of Same-Sex Marriage

As noted earlier, the federal DOMA, 1 U.S.C. §7; 28 U.S.C. §1738C (1996), declares that states are not required to recognize any same-sex marriage or union formed in another state. However, it does not prevent them doing so. For example, the Supreme Court of Wyoming held in *Christiansen v. Christiansen*, 253 P.3d 153 (Wyo. 2011), that its courts had subject-matter jurisdiction to entertain a petition for divorce of a same-sex marriage validly solemnized in Canada. It found nothing in Wyoming statutes or policy that closed the doors of the district courts to them. It also found that respecting the law of Canada, for the limited purpose of accepting the existence of a condition precedent to granting a divorce, is not tantamount to state recognition of an ongoing same-sex marriage. The District of Columbia voted on May 5, 2009, to recognize same-sex marriages performed elsewhere. New York has ruled that a court in that state has equity jurisdiction to dissolve a civil union. *Dickerson v. Thompson*, 928 N.Y.S.2d 97 (N.Y. App. 2011).

The Maryland Court of Appeals ruled 7-0 in May 2012 that valid, out-of-state same-sex marriage was cognizable in the state pursuant to common law doctrine of comity, for purposes of application of the state's divorce law. *Port v. Cowan*, 44 A.3d 970 (Md. 2012). The court reasoned that under the doctrine of comity, long applied in that state, courts would give effect to laws and judicial decisions of another state or jurisdiction, not as a matter of obligation but out of deference and respect. It also reasoned that it had liberally recognized valid foreign marriages. Finally, it found nothing in the existing state statutes that prohibited as a matter of law allowing same-sex persons validly married in another jurisdiction access to Maryland's divorce courts.

Texas is an example of a state that refuses to recognize valid out-of-state same-sex marriages. For example, in the *Matter of the Marriage of J.B. and H.B.*, 326 S.W.3d 654 (Tex. App. 2010), the court held that Texas courts do not have subject-matter jurisdiction to adjudicate divorce petitions in the context of same-sex marriage. It reasoned that Section 6.204(c)(2) of that state's law forbids it from giving any effect to a "right or claim to any legal protection, benefit, or responsibility asserted as a result of a" same-sex marriage. Therefore, it could not give any legal effect even to a claim to a protection or benefit predicated on a same-sex marriage. *See Burns v. Burns*, 560 S.E.2d 47 (Ga. 2002) (in the context of a child visitation dispute, a Georgia court would not recognize a "civil union" entered into in Vermont as an act of marriage); *Langan v. State Farm Fire & Cas.*, 48 A.D.3d 76 (N.Y. App. 2007) (held that a domestic partner was not a worker's legal spouse under New York's Workers' Compensation Law by virtue of having entered into a civil union with the worker in Vermont. It also held that neither the doctrine of comity nor the equal protection clause of the Constitution require New York to recognize the relationship for compensation purposes).

Note that in *Cote-Whitacre v. Department of Public Health*, 844 N.E.2d 623 (Mass. 2006), the Supreme Judicial Court considered a challenge to a 1913 Massachusetts law, which barred nonresidents from marrying in that state if the marriage would be void if contracted in their home state. The Supreme Judicial Court upheld the law.

TRANSSEXUAL RELATIONSHIPS

2.35. Recognizing Transsexual Relationships

Courts and legislatures are not uniform in result when asked to recognize transsexual marriages. In M.T. *v.* J.T., 355 A.2d 204, 211 (N.J. App. Div. 1976), the petitioner underwent a sex change to become a woman and married. When the relationship broke down, she sought spousal support from her husband. He countered that the marriage was void because a man could not marry another man, even one who had had a sex change. He contended that the petitioner was born a male and did not possess the internal organs of a woman. The court rejected the argument, saying that when one has a sex change, for purposes of the state's marriage laws, that person is a woman and entitled to support. Sex reassignment surgery, under that view, merely harmonizes a person's physical characteristics with that identity. It said that the transsexual's gender and genitalia are no longer discordant; they have been harmonized through medical treatment. Plaintiff has become physically and psychologically unified and fully capable of sexual activity consistent with her reconciled sexual attributes of gender and anatomy.

In *Littleton v. Prange*, 9 S.W.3d 223 (Tex. App. 1999), the court of appeals held that a ceremonial marriage between a man and a transsexual born as a man, but surgically and chemically altered to have the physical characteristics of a woman, was not valid. *See In re Estate of Gardiner*, 42 P.3d 120 (Kan. 2002) (marriage between a postoperative male-to-female transsexual and a man is void as against public policy); *In re Ladrach*, 513 N.E.2d 828 (Ohio Prob. 1987) (postoperative male-to-female transsexual could not obtain marriage license to marry male). However, the Maryland Court of Appeals in *In re Heilig*, 816 A.2d 68 (Md. 2003), held that it would recognize a transsexual's new sexual identity.

s

.. Assume that P, age 50, and D, age 18, are married. P has a brother X, who adopted D when she was two months old. The family views D as P's niece. P dies unexpectedly shortly after the marriage, and D seeks her widow's share of P's large estate. P's children from a former marriage object citing a statute in effect in this jurisdiction that reads as follows: "All marriages between parents and children, including grandparents and grandchildren of every degree, between brothers and sisters of the half as well as the whole blood, between uncles and nieces, aunts and nephews, first cousins, and between persons who lack capacity to enter into a marriage contract, are presumptively void." Most likely, how will a court most likely rule on the objection?

33. Assume that P and D are brother and sister related by adoption and are not related by either half or whole blood. When both reach the age of majority, they attempt to marry. However, the clerk of court refuses to issue a license based on a provision in that jurisdiction's law that prohibits "[a] marriage between an ancestor and a descendant or between a brother and sister, whether the relationship is by the half or the whole blood or by adoption." P and D contend that the statute is unconstitutional. Most likely, how will a court rule?

34. Assume that P and D, a same-sex couple, are married in Massachusetts. They move to Minnesota, where the legislature had adopted a state DOMA. When their relationship breaks down, P seeks to use Minnesota's divorce statutes to obtain alimony and an equitable distribution of the couple's property. D contends that P cannot bring a divorce action in this jurisdiction because of its mini-DOMA. How will a court most likely rule?

35. Assume that the defendant is charged with inducing or enticing women to travel in interstate commerce to engage in prostitution. The defendant moves to dismiss the charges arguing that the United States Supreme Court's holding in *Lawrence v. Texas*, necessarily renders laws prohibiting prostitution unconstitutional. Most likely, how will a court rule?

36. Assume that a defendant is charged with receipt of obscene visual representations of the sexual abuse of children, possession of obscene visual representations of the sexual abuse of children, and mailing obscene matter. The defendant moves to dismiss the charges on the ground that the government can no longer rely on the advancement of a moral code as a legitimate state interest. The government asserts *Lawrence* merely held that the fact

that a particular practice has been traditionally viewed as immoral is not a sufficient reason to uphold a law prohibiting it. How will a court rule on the motion to dismiss?

37. Assume that Pam and Donald reside in a jurisdiction that has enacted a Domestic Partner Act. The act states that it "extends to registered domestic partners substantially all rights, benefits, and obligations of married persons under state law, with the exception of rights, benefits, and obligations accorded only to married persons by federal law, the State Constitution, or initiative statutes." Pam presented Donald with a partnership agreement required by the statute, and Donald completed it. Pam relied on Donald to complete the registration process by filing the document with the state after they had signed and had notarized it. However, Donald failed to do so, and the signed partnership agreement was found in the trunk of Donald's car after he died in an auto accident. Pam claims her right to property under the agreement as a putative spouse. Donald's estate opposes Pam, stating that the putative spouse doctrine is applicable only to heterosexual allegedly married husbands and wives — not domestic partners. The estate also asserts that the technical failure to register the domestic partner document properly means Pam must be treated as a single person. Most likely, how will a court rule?

38. Assume that Emily, age 15 and pregnant by Stanley, who is 19, decide to marry. Although they could marry in state X with parental consent, their parents refuse to give consent to the marriage. They drive to state Y, which will allow them to marry without parental consent because Emily is pregnant. After they marry in state Y, they immediately return to state X. The parents of Emily move to void the marriage. How will a court in state X rule on the effort of Emily's parents to void the marriage?

39. P, age 14, and D, age 30, decide to marry. P's parents agree to the marriage and permit P to lie on the marriage license about her age (she stated that she was 15). In state X, persons may marry when they are 18 without parental or judicial consent but can marry with parental or judicial consent if they are 15 and a court determines it is in their best interest to marry. In this case, a family court judge concluded it was in the best interest of the couple to marry. A state statute in X states that "A defendant is guilty of a class A felony if the defendant engages in a sexual act with a person who is 12, 13, or 14." The local prosecutor learns of the marriage and brings a criminal complaint against D and P's parents. D is charged with statutory rape and P's parents are charged with aiding and abetting D in the crime. They

defend on the basis that P and D were married at the time any sexual activity took place.

Explanations

32. While all states prohibit the marriage of relatives within certain degrees of kinship, not all prohibit that marriage if the relationship is due to adoption. The hypothetical statute used in the above example does not include the word "adoption." If the legislature intended to bar marriage between the parties to this action, it could have accomplished that by explicitly including the phrase "relatives by adoption" in the statute. For that reason, a court would most likely conclude that the marriage was not void and would allow the widow to pursue her action. *See State ex rel. Miesner v. Geile*, 747 S.W.2d 757, 758 (Mo. App. E.D. 1988) (there is no reference to relationship by adoption in the marriage statute); *but see U.S. v. Dedman*, 527 F.3d 577 (6th Cir. 2008), cert. denied, 129 S. Ct. 2379 (2009) (holding that the Arkansas marriage statute, which declares incestuous and absolutely void marriages between, inter alia, "grandparents and grandchildren of every degree," barred marriage between a grandfather and his adopted granddaughter); *In re Marriage of MEW*, 4 Pa. D. & C.3d 51, 1977 WL 321 (C.P. 1977) (holding that two persons who became brother and sister only through adoption could not obtain a marriage license); UMDA §207(a)(2) (prohibits a marriage between an ancestor and a descendant, or a marriage between a brother and a sister whether the relationship is by adoption).

33. At least one court considering this issue has found that marriage is a fundamental right and that no compelling state interest is furthered by prohibiting marriage between a brother and sister related only by adoption. The Colorado Supreme Court held such a provision unconstitutional as a denial of equal protection. *Israel v. Allen*, 577 P.2d 762 (Colo. 1978). In that case, the court adopted the following reasoning:

> According to the English law, relationship by affinity was an impediment to marriage to the same extent and in the same degree of consanguinity. While this principle, derived from the ecclesiastically administered canon law, still strongly persists in England, in the United States the statutory law governing the marriage relationship nowhere so sweepingly condemns the marriage of persons related only by affinity . . . . The objections that exist against consanguineous marriages are not present where the relationship is merely by affinity. The physical detriment to the offspring of persons

> related by blood is totally absent. The natural repugnance of people toward marriages of blood relatives that has resulted in well-nigh universal moral condemnation of such marriages is quite generally lacking in application to the union of those related only by affinity. It is difficult to construct any very logical case for the prohibition of marriage on grounds of affinity . . . 1 Vernier, American Family Laws 183.

Israel v. Allen, *supra at* 764 of 577 P.2. *See Miesner v. Geile*, 747 S.W.2d 757 (Mo. App. 1988) (statutory prohibition against marriage between uncle and niece did not prohibit marriage between uncle and niece related by adoption).

34. A court will most likely agree with D. Under the federal DOMA, Minnesota is not required to recognize the same-sex marriage, even though it is valid in Massachusetts. Therefore, there is no requirement that Minnesota give full faith and credit to the out-of-state marriage. Because Minnesota has its own state mini-DOMA, it has established a policy against recognition of same-sex marriages in other states. http://www.leg.state.mn.us/lrl/issues/issues.aspx?issue=gay (last visited March, 2012) (history and citations to Minnesota's mini-DOMA). Absent the state mini-DOMA, Minnesota might well recognize the same-sex marriage from Massachusetts.

35. A court will reject the motion to dismiss the charge based on *Lawrence v. Texas*. In *Lawrence*, the court noted the narrow scope of its ruling by stating that following:

> The present case [*Lawrence*] does not involve minors. It does not involve persons who might be injured or coerced or who are situated in relationships where consent might not easily be refused. It does not involve public conduct or prostitution. It does not involve whether the government must give formal recognition to any relationship that homosexual persons seek to enter. The case does involve two adults who, with full and mutual consent from each other, engaged in sexual practices common to a homosexual lifestyle. The petitioners are entitled to respect for their private lives. The State cannot demean their existence or control their destiny by making their private sexual conduct a crime. Their right to liberty under the due process clause gives them the full right to engage in their conduct without intervention of the government.

539 U.S. at 578.

The Court in *Lawrence* clearly excluded prostitution from its application. *See State v. Romano*, 155 P.3d 1102 (Hawaii 2007) (prostitution conviction affirmed); *U.S. v. Thompson*, 458 F. Supp. 2d 730 (N.D. Ind.

2006) (laws prohibiting commercial acts of prostitution did not violate the due process clause); *McDonald v. Com.*, 630 S.E.2d 754 (Va. App. 2006) (statute criminalizing sodomy did not violate due process rights of defendant who had been convicted of engaging in oral sodomy with a 16-year-old and a 17-year old minor).

36. A court will reject the motion to dismiss. Lawrence held that a Texas law prohibiting homosexual sodomy violated the due process clause of the Fifth and Fourteenth Amendments. Id. at 578-79. However, Lawrence solely addressed personal sexual relations in the privacy of an individual's home. *See U.S. v. Handley*, 564 F. Supp. 2d 996 (S.D. Iowa 2008); *see also State v. Oakley*, 605 S.E.2d 215 (N.C. App. 2004).

37. In a decision similar to the facts of the above example, a California Court of Appeals ruled that a person in Pam's position could pursue a claim as a putative domestic partner and seek whatever benefits allowed by the Domestic Partner Act. The court concluded that a person with a reasonable, good faith belief in the validity of his or her registered domestic partnership is entitled to protection as a putative registered domestic partner, even if the domestic partnership was not properly registered. *In re Domestic Partnership of Ellis*, 76 Cal. Rptr. 3d 401 (Cal. App. 2008).

38. Emily and Stanley will argue that the full faith and credit clause of the Constitution and the *lex loci* doctrine require state X to recognize their legal marriage in state Y. Recall that *Lex loci actus* is defined as "[t]he law of the place where the act was done." *Black's Law Dictionary* 911 (6th ed. 1990). Cases such as *Schofield v. Schofield*, 20 Pa. D. 805, 807-808 (Pa. Ct. Com. Pleas 1909), have established that X should recognize the validity of the marriage in state Y, even though it is contrary to the provisions of a statute in state X; a statute that reflects public policy with respect to maintenance of good morals. This is generally the case even though parties went out of the state for the purpose of evading the statute of the domicile. *See Mission Ins. Co. v. Industrial Comm'n*, 559 P.2d 1085 (Ariz. 1976) (Arizona would recognize Kansas common law marriage if valid there); *Jennings v. Jennings*, 315 A.2d 816 (Md. 1974) (Maryland would recognize District of Columbia common law marriage); *Gallegos v. Wilkerson*, 445 P.2d 970 (N.M. 1968) (New Mexico would recognize valid Texas common law marriage).

    Furthermore, the United States Constitution requires that every state accord "Full Faith and Credit" to the laws of its sister states. *See, e.g., Kelderhaus v. Kelderhaus*, 467 S.E.2d 303 (1996) (a marriage's validity is to be determined by the law of the state where the marriage took place, unless the result would be repugnant to Virginia public policy).

Is the marriage "repugnant" to state X's public policy? Probably not. The reason is that Emily and Stan could have been married in state X with parental consent. A family court judge would probably conclude that the public policy on these facts is not so strong as to grant Emily's parents motion to void the relationship. *See generally In re Estate of Everhart*, 783 N.W. 1 (Neb. 2010).

39. The defense will most likely fail. Here, state X does not have any provision that allows anyone to marry when they are younger than 15. The relationship is void. Furthermore, statutory rape is considered a strict liability crime. In adopting statutory rape statutes, state legislatures have decided to protect juveniles below a specified age from sexual intercourse. "The policy that underlies such a statute is a presumption that, because of their innocence and immaturity, juveniles are prevented from appreciating the full magnitude and consequences of their actions. The purpose of these statutes is to protect young children from illicit acts of sexual intercourse by making their consent legally impossible." Marie K. Pesando, *Statute protecting minors in a specified age range from rape or other sexual activity as applicable to defendant minor within protected age group*, 18 A.L.R.5th 856, 65 Am. Jur. 2d Rape §11 (May 2012). *Fleming v. State*, 323 S.W.3d 540 (Tex. App. 2010).

CHAPTER 3

Annulment of Marriage

3.1. Introduction

This chapter focuses exclusively on the legal problems associated with an annulment of a marriage, a concept that is already touched upon to some extent out of necessity in Chapter 2. It examines the history of annulments, discusses the differences between annulment actions that are considered void and those that are voidable, illustrates various issues associated with annulments through the use of state statutes, and provides examples and explanations intended to enhance your understanding of annulment law.

Differs from divorce. In general, annulment and divorce actions are significantly different from each other. For example, an annulment is granted when proof is presented that a marriage was invalid or void at the time it was performed. In theory, when a marriage is annulled, the relationship of husband and wife did not exist. In contrast, a divorce is granted when there was a valid marriage and the relationship between a husband and wife or same-sex couple is being terminated.

Biblical principles. The basic grounds for an annulment were established by the ecclesiastical courts hundreds of years ago based on Biblical principles. Today, all states have generated statutes that set forth the basis for an annulment but often reflect ancient Biblical roots.

Canon law. Annulment actions in the United States can trace their origin to the canon law as applied by the ecclesiastical courts in England. By the thirteenth century, these courts, which were controlled by the Catholic Church, had jurisdiction in all family matters. The Catholic Church's doctrinal view that a valid marriage entered into by two baptized Christians could not be dissolved by any human power was a fundamental principle applied by the ecclesiastical courts. They considered that marriage was a sacrament and once consummated through sexual intercourse, could be dissolved only by death.

However, the ecclesiastical courts provided two avenues of escape from an unhappy marriage. One was a divorce from bed and board, and the other was an annulment. The divorce from bed and board allowed the parties to live apart but did not divorce them. An annulment permanently severed a couple's marriage and was possible if you could prove that a Church-sanctioned impediment or defect existed from the outset of the relationship. For example, when Henry VIII decided to marry Anne Boleyn, an annulment to his marriage of Katherine of Aragon, on the grounds of affinity, was the only avenue available to him to achieve this goal. He argued that an annulment was proper because Katherine was his brother's widow. Therefore, the marriage between him and Katherine never really existed and could be annulled. However, according to Katherine, her marriage to Henry's brother Arthur had never been properly consummated, and so it was decided that Henry's argument had no basis. If Henry VIII had been successful in proving that such an impediment existed, the marriage would be annulled and viewed as never existing. In the end, although the pope denied King Henry VIII's annulment request, Henry defied the Church's authority, forming the Church of England, and then had his marriage to Katherine annulled by the Archbishop of Canterbury, Thomas Cranmer. *See generally* W. Scott, *Nullity of Marriage in Canon Law and English Law*, 2 U. Toronto L.J. 319 (1937-1938).

Annulments are rare. Annulment actions today are rare in U.S. family courts. To the extent they exist, they will usually be found in immigration, Social Security, and probate disputes. In these clashes, the outcome will usually determine whether a marriage qualifies or disqualifies an individual from eligibility for certain benefits. *See e.g.*, *Everetts v. Apfel*, 214 F.3d 990 (8th Cir. 2000) (annulment of claimant's first marriage, entered by state court after date of claimant's second marriage to wage earner, could not relate back and validate the second marriage; therefore, claimant never had valid marriage to wage earner for purposes of Social Security Act, and she did not qualify for widow's benefits).

Annulment theory. When a marriage is annulled, in theory it is considered to have never existed. Consequently, in theory, a judgment of nullity relates back and erases the marriage and all its implications. *Sefton v. Sefton*,

291 P.2d 439 (Cal. 1955). However, courts caution against a too literal application of the annulment theory in all cases. *Ibid*; *see also Berkely v. Berkely*, 75 Cal. Rptr. 294 (Cal. App. 1969); *Cecil v. Cecil*, 356 P.2d 279 (Utah 1960). Therefore, when analyzing a particular annulment dispute, it becomes important to distinguish between an action where a court has described it as "void" from one that has described it as "voidable." The term that is used makes a significant difference in the outcome of an annulment dispute. Note that in annulment disputes involving the rights of third parties, courts have been especially wary of a literal applicable of the "void" concept, lest the logical appeal of the annulment fiction of a "void" relationship obscures a fundamental problem and leads to an unjust or ill-advised result. These concepts will be discussed in detail in §3.2 later in this chapter.

Illustrative state annulment provision — Ohio. The following Ohio statute is fairly typical of many annulment provisions adopted by state courts in the nation. It declares that a marriage may be annulled for any of the following causes existing at the time of the marriage:

> (A) That the party in whose behalf it is sought to have the marriage annulled was under the age at which persons may be joined in marriage . . . unless after attaining such age such party cohabited with the other as husband or wife;
>
> (B) That the former husband or wife of either party was living and the marriage with such former husband or wife was then and still is in force;
>
> (C) That either party has been adjudicated to be mentally incompetent, unless such party after being restored to competency cohabited with the other as husband or wife;
>
> (D) That the consent of either party was obtained by fraud, unless such party afterwards, with full knowledge of the facts constituting the fraud, cohabited with the other as husband or wife;
>
> (E) That the consent to the marriage of either party was obtained by force, unless such party afterwards cohabited with the other as husband or wife;
>
> (F) That the marriage between the parties was never consummated although otherwise valid.

Ohio Revised Code §3105.31 (2011).

3.2. Void/Voidable Distinction

Void. As noted earlier in the chapter, annulment actions involve relationships that may be ruled void or voidable, depending on the facts and the law in a particular jurisdiction. Also as noted earlier, a void relationship is a nullity and is considered invalid from its inception, whether or not it has been so declared in a court of law. *See generally Black's Law Dictionary* 994-995, 1098 (8th ed. 2004).

A marriage that is void typically is one that offends a strong public policy. Examples of void marriages include relationships involving bigamy, polygamy, and incest. A void marriage normally does not require a judicial declaration or action to establish that it is not valid. However, a court order may be sought in order to provide a party to a void relationship with certainty and to establish a public record of its invalidity.

Voidable. In contrast to a void relationship, a voidable relationship is one that is recognized as valid for all purposes until it is judicially declared a nullity. As a rule, it may be challenged only by a party entitled by statute to assert its voidability. *In re Gregorson's Estate*, 160 Cal. 21 (Cal. 1911); *Flaxman v. Flaxman*, 273 A.2d 567 (1971). As already observed in this chapter, whether a court determines that a marriage is void or voidable may be of significant importance to the outcome of a particular dispute. *See, e.g., Patey v. Peaslee*, 111 A.2d 194 (N.H. 1955) (marriage was voidable, not void; therefore, spouse not barred from intestate share of estate).

Note that even in the case of a voidable marriage, a court issuing a judgment of nullity will usually use language declaring that "no valid marriage ever existed." *Millar v. Millar* 167 P. 394 (Cal. 1917). This may sometimes generate confusion in understanding the intended outcome of the dispute.

3.3. Time Limitations

Typically, most states have enacted statutes that place time limitations on bringing certain types of annulment actions. It is of interest to note that the time limitations appear to vary significantly from state to state.

Illustrative time limits — Idaho. Given the general preference of courts to preserve a marriage and avoid granting an annulment, it is surprising to discover jurisdictions, particularly some in the western United States, that provide extensive periods of time within which an annulment action may be brought. The Idaho statute set out below, for example, gives a person in some instances several years within which to seek an annulment. The relevant time Idaho limitation provision, with an italicized reference to the particular impediment taken from another section of the Idaho Code, reads as follows:

> An action to obtain a decree of nullity of marriage, for causes mentioned in the preceding section, must be commenced within the periods and by the parties as follows:

> 1. For causes mentioned in subdivision one [*underage*]; by the party to the marriage who was married under the age of legal consent, within four (4) years after arriving at the age of consent; or by a parent, guardian, or other person having charge of such nonaged male or female, at any time before such married minor has arrived at the age of legal consent;
>
> 2. For causes mentioned in subdivision two [*bigamy*]; by either party during the life of the other, or by such former husband or wife;
>
> 3. For causes mentioned in subdivision three [*unsound mind*]; by the party injured, or relative or guardian of the party of unsound mind, at any time before the death of either party;
>
> 4. For causes mentioned in subdivision four [*fraud*]; by the party injured, within four (4) years after the discovery of the facts constituting the fraud;
>
> 5. For causes mentioned in subdivision five [*marriage by force*]; by the injured party, within four (4) years after the marriage;
>
> 6. For causes mentioned in subdivision six [*incurable physical capacity*]; by the injured party, within four (4) years after the marriage.

Idaho Code Ann. §32-502 (2012).

Illustrative time limits — Minnesota. It is interesting to compare Idaho's long time periods associated with annulment actions with those enacted by a midwestern state such as Minnesota. The Minnesota annulment statute, in part and with inserted italicized explanations, reads as follows:

> An annulment may be sought by any of the following persons and must be commenced within the times specified, but in no event may an annulment be sought after the death of either party to the marriage:
>
> (a) for a reason set forth in section 518.02, clause (a), [*mental incapacity or infirmity, and the other party at the time the marriage was solemnized did not know of the incapacity; or because of the influence of alcohol, drugs, or other incapacitating substances; or because consent of either was obtained by force or fraud and there was no subsequent voluntary cohabitation of the parties*] by either party or by the legal representative of the party who lacked capacity to consent, no later than 90 days after the petitioner obtained knowledge of the described condition;
>
> (b) for the reason set forth in section 518.02, clause (b) [*party lacks the physical capacity to consummate the marriage by sexual intercourse and the other party at the time the marriage was solemnized did not know of the incapacity*], by either party no later than one year after the petitioner obtained knowledge of the described condition;
>
> (c) for the reason set forth in section 518.02, clause (c), [*party was under the age for marriage*] by the underaged party, the party's parent or guardian, before the time the underaged party reaches the age at which the party could have married without satisfying the omitted requirement.

Minn. Stat. §518.05 (1986).

3.4. Standing

Illustrative California standing statute: Generally, the question of who has standing to bring an annulment action will be found in a state statute. *See, e.g.*, Cal. Fam. Code §2211 (2012). To illustrate, the California Family Code, with italicized explanations inserted, provides for the time limits and standing to bring an annulment action as follows:

> A proceeding to obtain a judgment of nullity of marriage, for causes set forth in Section 2210, must be commenced within the periods and by the parties, as follows:
>
> (a) For causes mentioned in subdivision (a) of Section 2210 [*without the capability of consenting to the marriage or unless, after attaining the age of consent, the party for any time freely cohabited with the other as husband and wife*] by any of the following:
>
> (1) The party to the marriage who was married under the age of legal consent, within four years after arriving at the age of consent.
>
> (2) A parent, guardian, conservator, or other person having charge of the underaged male or female, at any time before the married minor has arrived at the age of legal consent.
>
> (b) For causes mentioned in subdivision (b) [*husband or wife of either party was living and the marriage with that husband or wife was then in force and that husband or wife (1) was absent and not known to the party commencing the proceeding to be living for a period of five successive years immediately preceding the subsequent marriage for which the judgment of nullity is sought; or (2) was generally reputed or believed by the party commencing the proceeding to be dead at the time the subsequent marriage was contracted*] of Section 2210, by either of the following:
>
> (1) Either party during the life of the other.
>
> (2) The former husband or wife.
>
> (c) For causes mentioned in subdivision (c) of Section 2210 [*Either party was of unsound mind, unless the party of unsound mind, after coming to reason, freely cohabited with the other as husband and wife*], by the party injured, or by a relative or conservator of the party of unsound mind, at any time before the death of either party.
>
> (d) For causes mentioned in subdivision (d) of Section 2210 [*consent of either party was obtained by fraud, unless the party whose consent was obtained by fraud afterward, with full knowledge of the facts constituting the fraud, freely cohabited with the other as husband or wife*], by the party whose consent was obtained by fraud, within four years after the discovery of the facts constituting the fraud.
>
> (e) For causes mentioned in subdivision (e) of Section 2210 [*consent of either party was obtained by force, unless the party whose consent was obtained by force afterward freely cohabited with the other as husband or wife*], by the party whose consent was obtained by force, within four years after the marriage.
>
> (f) For causes mentioned in subdivision (f) of Section 2210 [*Either party was, at the time of marriage, physically incapable of entering into the marriage state, and that*

> *incapacity continues, and appears to be incurable*], by the injured party, witl years after the marriage.

Cal. Fam. Code §2211 (2012).

In general, a disabled party or a third party to an alleged marriage may bring an annulment action to challenge its validity during the lifetime of the parties. However, unless the annulment action is seeking to void the marriage, actions in general are barred from being brought by third parties after the death of a party. For example, a legal representative of a decedent's estate may pursue an annulment action so long as it was commenced prior to the decedent's death. *See Hall v. Nelson*, 531 N.E.2d 929 (Ohio App. 1987). *See also In re Gregorson's Estate*, 160 Cal. 21 (Cal. 1911) ("If the parties who are alone recognized by the statutes as entitled to have the marriage annulled do not, during its existence, see fit to avoid it, a stranger to the marriage should not be permitted to question its validity in a collateral proceeding").

Obviously, an underage party has standing to seek an annulment of a marriage. However, a party who is of marriageable age and, therefore, not under a disability, may not attack the validity of the marriage to the underage person in most jurisdictions. The Uniform Marriage and Divorce Act (UMDA) states that "[a] declaration of invalidity . . . may be sought by the underage party, his parent or guardian." UMDA §208(b).

EXAMPLES

Examples

1. Assume that P married D with both parties having knowledge that P was still legally married to X, whom P had not seen in several years but believed was still alive. When the relationship between P and D broke down, D sought advice regarding an annulment action under the illustrative California statute set out earlier in this chapter. Under these circumstances, is an annulment initiated by a formal court necessary? Is the relationship "void" or "voidable?"

2. Assume that Patty marries Jeffrey. When their relationship breaks down, Patty moves out and, during a vacation in Nevada, marries Henry. A few days after marrying Henry, Patty realizes the marriage was a mistake and discusses obtaining a Nevada divorce from Henry. She is advised that the marriage to Henry is void because she is still married to Jeffrey. She does not seek a divorce from Henry, but two years later, she divorces Jeffrey. Following the divorce from Jeffrey, Patty marries Albert. When that marriage breaks down, Patty brings a divorce action. Albert moves to dismiss the divorce action on the ground that she never invalidated her marriage to Henry, and seeks an order annulling his marriage to Patty. How will a court rule?

3. Assume that D, age 20, and X, age 80, marry over the objection of X's children. X dies suddenly during the honeymoon, leaving a huge estate. P, who is one of X's children, is considering bringing an action in Minnesota or California, and asks the court to annul the marriage on the ground that X lacked the mental capacity to consent to the marriage when it was solemnized. P relies on Minn. Stat. §518.05 (1986) (set out earlier in the chapter) to support this annulment claim. How will a court that relies on that statute most likely rule in this case?

4. Assume that P is married to X and Y in a country outside the United States that permits polygamous marriages. P is X's second wife. P and X move to the United States. After living in the United States for five years, P brings an action to divorce X. X argues their marriage is void and the divorce action must be dismissed. The family court judge is considering the application of a provision of state law that reads as follows: "All marriages contracted outside this state that were valid at the time of the contract or subsequently validated by the laws of the place in which they were contracted or by the domicile of the parties are valid in this state." Most likely, how will the family court judge rule on P's divorce action?

5. Assume that P and D marry. This is a second marriage for both P and D. After D dies, it is discovered by D's son X that P and D were half-siblings. In other words, they had the same mother, but different fathers. Under Minnesota law, the marriage of two people with such a relationship is prohibited. Following this discovery, X immediately brings an annulment action in probate court which, if granted, will prevent P from sharing in D's estate. P argues that the annulment action should have been brought by X when D was alive and points to the language of Minn. Stat. §518.05 (1986) that reads in part: "in no event may an annulment be sought after the death of either party to a marriage." After reviewing the statute, what is the most probable outcome of this dispute?

Explanations

EXPLANATIONS

1. D will probably be advised that the relationship is void. Because it is void, a formal legal action annulling the relationship is not necessary. Section (b) of the illustrative California statute does not apply because of the knowledge possessed by the parties. However, a party may be so concerned about the implications of the relationship that an action to obtain a formal order that it is "void" may be brought. The advantage of such an action is the existence of a public record stating that the relationship is "void."

2. All courts will consider the second attempted marriage between Patty and Henry as "void *ab initio*" and bigamous. Most state bigamy statutes void attempted second marriages when the first has not yet been dissolved. Most courts will find that because a bigamous marriage is void from its inception, even if it has not been declared void by a court, no formal legal action was necessary to annul Patty's marriage to Henry. Therefore, she was free to divorce Jeffrey without obtaining a court order. The divorce from Jeffrey is legal, and then Patty was free to marry Albert.

3. Minnesota's annulment statute, 518.05, states that "in no event may an annulment be sought after the death of either party to the marriage." It appears pretty clear that P cannot bring an annulment action in Minnesota.

4. Even if a defendant's second marriage would have been valid in a nation in which one man could have multiple wives, bigamous marriage are absolutely void as against a strong public policy in the United States. *See People v. Ezeonu*, 588 N.Y.S.2d 116 (N.Y. Sup. 1992). *Compare Earle v. Earle*, 126 N.Y.S. 317 (N.Y. App. 1910) ("no civilized Christian nation permits polygamy, and if the law of Italy did permit the marriage between parties, one of whom was already married and the bonds of matrimony in full force, the courts of this state would not be obliged to give effect to such law as between parties domiciled here at the time of the celebration of the marriage") with *In re Dalip Singh Bir's Estate*, 188 P.2d 499, 501-02 (Cal. App. 1948) (court recognized foreign polygamous second marriages for the purposes of succession, to avoid denying any inheritance to the second wife). It would be pretty difficult to get around this strong policy as reflected in almost every state's civil and criminal code, but there is always a small chance of doing so, as illustrated by *Dalip Singh Bir's Estate*.

5. The trial judge must decide whether the marriage between P and D is void or voidable. Here, it appears that the marriage is void because the state "prohibits" such relationships. Consequently, there was no marital relationship between P and D. The language in Minn. Stat. §518.05 (1986) does not apply because P and D were never married. The most likely outcome is for the judge to rule the relationship void; therefore, P cannot share in the estate. Note that as a rule, courts allow third-party lawsuits seeking an annulment where the relationship is void, but they do not allow such lawsuits when the relationship is merely voidable. The Minnesota statute, as we interpret it in this problem, reflects this general rule.

RETROACTIVITY

3.5. Relation Back — Generally

When a court issues an order declaring that a marriage is annulled, a question remains regarding what date the order relates back to. Does the annulment order relate back to the date of the marriage, the date the party filed the annulment action, or the date the court entered its order? If the marriage is void because it is prohibited, common sense suggests that in most instances, an order relates back to the date of the claimed marriage.

However, when a marriage is voidable, courts will use different relation-back approaches, which appear to depend somewhat on the nature of the annulment claim and the jurisdiction where the action is brought. In other words, there does not appear to be a national consensus on this issue. For example, in *Seirafi-Pour v. Bagherinassab*, 197 P.3d 1097, 1102 (Okla. App. 2008), the court applied the theory that the relationship never existed. It annulled a marriage on the basis that the husband's Iranian wife fraudulently induced him to marry her. In granting the annulment, the court stated, "An annulment is said to 'relate back' and erase the marriage and all its implications from the outset." A California decision, *In re Marriage of Liu*, 242 Cal. Rptr. 649 (Cal. App. 1987), suggests that the California court follows the same theory as the Oklahoma court. It said that an annulment relates back and erases marriage and all its implications from outset; if marriage is annulled, there can be no community property.

By comparison, in *Levine v. Dumbra*, 604 N.Y.S.2d 207 (N.Y. App. 1993), the court ruled that a marriage is void from the date that a court enters its order of nullification if one of the parties was incapable of consenting to the marriage for want of understanding.

Note that various state statutes concerning property division and maintenance obligations must be read carefully, as they may be construed as not relating back to the time the marriage took place. *See, e.g.*, *Falk v. Falk*, 462 N.W.2d 547 (Wis. App. 1990) (Wisconsin statutes concerning property division and maintenance obligations do not reflect this relation-back theory; rather, under Wisconsin law, annulments and divorces have the same practical purpose and legal effect); *Hodges v. Hodges*, 578 P.2d 1001, 1003 (Ariz. App. 1978) (the legal fiction that an annulment decree relates back to destroy a marriage from the beginning is sometimes ignored "as the purposes of justice are deemed to require").

3.6. Relation Back — Alimony

The issue. There are occasional situations where a person marries, divorces, remarries another, and then annuls the second marriage. Typically, divorce statutes and judgments state that "if a person who is receiving alimony from the first marriage remarries, the alimony being paid from the first marriage ceases." How do such provisions found in a divorce judgment apply to annulments?

To illustrate the problem associated with relation back of an annulment, assume that Jack and Jill marry and divorce. Jack is ordered to "pay alimony to Jill for ten years or until Jill remarries, whichever occurs first." Jill weds Dick two years after her divorce from Jack. The alimony being paid to Jill by Jack terminated in accord with the judgment and decree. Then two years after her marriage to Dick (four years after her divorce from Jack), the marriage is annulled. She seeks reinstatement of Jack's alimony obligation. She argues that the word "remarries" in her divorce decree from Jack meant a valid "remarriage." She claims the marriage to Dick was invalid (void), therefore, she never "remarried." How will a court treat Jill's argument?

Unfortunately, there is not a clear answer to the question raised by our Jack and Jill hypothetical. At best, it can be said that it depends on the jurisdiction. The reason for this is that courts appear split as to how to classify the effect that Jill's remarriage and subsequent annulment has on Jack's preexisting periodic alimony obligation. When we look at the law in the United States, courts appear to have adopted one of the following three approaches: (1) the inflexible automatic termination approach, (2) the void/voidable approach, or (3) a case-by-case approach. *See generally*, Carla M. Venhoff, *Divorce or Death, Remarriage & Annulment: The Path Toward Reinstating Financial Obligations from a Previous Marriage*, 37 Brandeis L.J. 435 (1998) (advocating that courts should adopt the void/voidable approach).

Inflexible approach. Some jurisdictions have adopted an inflexible approach concluding that where by statute or divorce judgment an alimony obligation terminates upon remarriage, the obligation ends automatically, and a subsequent annulment (whether void or voidable) cannot revive the former obligation. *See, e.g., Fry v. Fry*, 85 Cal. Rptr. 126 (Cal. App. 1970) ("The former husband is entitled to rely upon his ex-wife's apparent material status after a new marriage ceremony and should thereafter be permitted to recommit assets previously chargeable to alimony obligations"); *Flaxman v. Flaxman*, 273 A.2d 567 (N.J. 1971) (Divorce decree was not revived by annulment of her second marriage on grounds that rendered it voidable); *In re Marriage of Kolb*, 425 N.E.2d 1301 (Ill. App. 1981) (annulment of wife's second marriage did not result in revival or reinstatement of her first husband's obligation to pay monthly installments on alimony in gross award pursuant to terms of divorce judgment that specifically provided for termination of such payments upon wife's remarriage, since use of term "remarriage" in divorce judgment referred to ceremony and not to maintaining relationship). *See Darling v. Darling*, 335 N.E.2d 708 (Conn. Super. 1975) (by entering into a second, valid, though voidable marriage to another, plaintiff voluntarily terminated her right to receive alimony from defendant, her first husband, under separation agreement, and after the second marriage was annulled by reason of non-consummation, the first husband should not be required to pay alimony).

The inflexible approach operates under the notion that the payee spouse (Jill), who entered into the subsequent marriage, should bear the risk that her subsequent marriage might be voided. *Glass v. Glass*, 546 S.W.2d 738 (Mo. App. 1977); *Shank v. Shank*, 691 P.2d 872 (Nev. 1984); *R.L.G. v. J.G.*, 387 A.2d 200 (Del. Fam. 1977); *Surabian v. Surabian*, 285 N.E.2d 909 (Mass. 1972) (divorce decree providing for termination of alimony upon remarriage intended that all matrimonial ties between the parties would be totally dissolved upon former wife's going through ceremony of marriage with another man and former wife was not entitled to alimony under the divorce decree, though her remarriage was later annulled); *Beebe v. Beebe*, 179 S.E.2d 758 (Ga. 1971) (first husband relieved of making further alimony payments when ex-wife entered into second ceremonial marriage, although such marriage was later annulled because second husband had a living spouse); *Chavez v. Chavez*, 485 P.2d 735 (N.M. 1971) (where alimony provision of divorce decree stated that in the event of her remarriage said payments shall cease, cessation of alimony did not turn on the status of the remarriage as being valid, but simply provided that in event of remarriage, alimony would cease, and when event occurred, alimony ceased, notwithstanding purported annulment of second marriage); *Dodd v. Dodd*, 499 P.2d 518 (Kan. 1972) (manifest intention or parties expressed therein was that husband's obligation to pay alimony should terminate upon her remarriage even though the remarriage was voidable, and obligation was not revived by subsequent annulment of the remarriage). Courts believe that the payor spouse should be able to rely on the expectation that payee spouse's subsequent marriage is not voided due to the actions of payee spouse's subsequent spouse. Jack, for example, should not be required to speculate that Jill might someday in the future annul the second marriage, leaving his alimony obligation never finally settled. *See Richards v. Richards*, 353 A.2d 141 (N.J. Super. 1976); *McConkey v. McConkey*, 215 S.E.2d 640 (Va. 1975).

Void/voidable approach. Some courts will approach the relation back issue by using the void/voidable distinction. They will decide whether the subsequent marriage was either *void ab initio* (void) or voidable. A subsequent marriage that is found *void ab initio* is deemed never to have existed. Thus, states that have adopted the void/voidable approach find that since a marriage never existed, the payor spouse is not relieved of his periodic alimony obligation, and alimony must be paid from the date the payor stopped such payment. *See Broadus v. Broadus*, 361 So. 2d 582, 585 (Ala. App. 1978) (wife's right to alimony under terms of original divorce is revived following annulment of wife's second marriage where second marriage is deemed to be void rather than voidable); *Reese v. Reese*, 192 So. 2d 1, 2 (Fla.1966) (bigamous marriage under Florida law is void and therefore ineffective to alter the legal rights of the parties involved in this controversy; second marriage failed to terminate wife's right to alimony under divorce decree); *Watts v. Watts*, 547 N.W.2d 466, 470 (Neb. 1996) (provision for termination of alimony upon remarriage of recipient requires valid remarriage, and void marriage, standing alone, does not terminate alimony obligations); *Johnston v. Johnston*, 592 P.2d 132 (Kan. App. 1979); *Brewer v. Miller*, 673 S.W.2d 530 (Tenn. App. 1984); 24A Am.Jur.2d *Divorce and Separation* §791 (1998).

Case-by-case approach. The third approach used by courts in resolving relation back of alimony is to consider each dispute on a case-by-case basis. Courts adopting this view believe that it allows them to achieve an equitable result in all cases. *See In re Marriage of Cargill*, 843 P.2d 1335 (Colo. 1993); *Peters v. Peters*, 214 N.W.2d 151 (Iowa 1974); Louanne S. Love, *The Way We Were: Reinstatement of Alimony After Annulment of Spouse's "Remarriage,"* 28 J. Fam. L. 289 (1990). The case-by-case approach does not require that a court adhere to a bright-line rule, and it permits the court to consider relevant factors such as the length of the second marriage, whether the payee spouse receives alimony from the annulled marriage, whether the payor spouse is prejudiced by the revival of alimony payments, whether the subsequent marriage was properly annulled, and any change in the spouses' personal and financial circumstances after the subsequent marriage is annulled. *See Cargill, supra. See also Peters, supra*, 214 N.W.2d *at* 151; *In re Marriage of Williams*, 677 P.2d 585 (Mont. 1984) (maintenance to former wife was not automatically reinstated upon issuance of decree of invalidity of former wife's second marriage).

It is further argued that just as family courts employ principles of equity in determining support and maintenance, equitable distribution, and child custody, it should also embrace these same principles in determining whether a payor spouse's periodic alimony obligation is revived after payee spouse's subsequent marriage is annulled. *Joye v. Yon*, 586 S.E.2d 131 (S.C. 2003).

The Utah Supreme Court appeared to apply a case-by-case approach in *Cecil v. Cecil*, 356 P.2d 279 (Utah 1960). In that case, it held that where a second marriage had been annulled because the wife was adjudged to have no mental capacity to enter into it, and the wife had a history of mental infirmity and had lived with her second husband but a few weeks before he separated from her, her first husband was not entitled to terminate alimony. It also held that he was not entitled to judgment for the alimony payments he made to his ex-wife before discovering the purported remarriage. The court reasoned that under such circumstances, it would be unjust to deprive the ex-wife of the support of her first husband, who, "after all, was obliged to support her, and her attempted marriage did not adversely alter or change his circumstances so that it would be inequitable to require him to continue his alimony payments." *Id. at* 281.

3.7. Relation Back — Uniform Marriage and Divorce Act

The National Conference of Commissioners on Uniform State Laws promulgated the Uniform Marriage and Divorce Act (UMDA). The UMDA, which serves as a model for state marriage laws, contains an annulment relation-back provision that has been followed by some states. The relation-back section of the UMDA states as follows:

> [U]nless the court finds, after a consideration of all relevant circumstances, including the effect of a retroactive decree on third parties, that the interests of justice would be served by making the decree not retroactive, it shall declare the marriage invalid as of the date of the marriage. The provisions of this Act relating to property rights of the spouses, maintenance, support, and custody of children on dissolution of marriage are applicable to non-retroactive decrees of invalidity.

UMDA §208(e).

3.8. Relation Back — Enoch Arden Statute

Enoch Arden statutes colloquially take their name from Alfred Lord Tennyson's 1864 poem, *Enoch Arden*. These statutes apply to situations where a person suddenly returns after a long absence from which he or she was not expected to return at all. *See, e.g.*, section (b) of the illustrative California statute set forth earlier in this chapter. In Tennyson's poem, Enoch married Annie, who was secretly loved by Phillip Ray, the miller's son. When Enoch did not return from a voyage, Annie and Phillip married, believing Enoch to be dead. Ten years after departing, Enoch returned.

Enoch Arden statutes provide a defense to bigamy when a spouse remarries with the good-faith belief that a former spouse is dead. However, the statutes do not necessarily validate the later marriage. For the later marriage to be upheld, some jurisdictions require an Enoch Arden divorce as a prerequisite to the later marriage. *See, e.g., Randolph v. Randolph*, 212 N.Y.S.2d 468 (N.Y. Sup. 1961). The effect of the Enoch Arden statute in some jurisdictions is to create an express statutory exception to the general rule that an annulment of marriage is retroactive. *Estate of Lemont*, 86 Cal. Rptr. 810 (Cal. App. 1970).

CAPACITY

3.9. Mental Capacity

A valid marriage requires that both parties possess sufficient mental capacity to understand the nature of the contract and the duties and responsibilities it creates. Generally, a party lacks the mental capacity to enter into a contract for marriage if that party is "incapable of understanding the nature, effect, and consequences of the marriage." 4 Am. Jur. 2d *Annulment of Marriage* §30. *See also Johnson v. Johnson*, 104 N.W.2d 8, 14 (N.D. 1960) ("[T]he best accepted test . . . is whether there is a capacity to understand the nature of the contract and the duties and responsibilities which it creates"). The relevant inquiry when an annulment of a marriage is sought on the ground of mental incapacity is to ask whether mental incapacity existed at the time the parties entered into the marriage. The mental capacity necessary to enter into marriage requires the ability to exercise "clear reason, discernment, and sound judgment." *Beddow v. Beddow*, 257 S.W.2d 45, 48 (Ky. 1953); *Guthery v. Ball*, 228 S.W. 887 (Mo. 1921) (there are "two things necessary for the making of a contract; one, mental consent, which cannot be had if a party is mentally incapacitated, and the other, physical assent to the agreement. The physical part might be manifested by word of mouth, writing, sign, or even in some negative manner on the part of a contracting party. One might have perfect mental capacity and desire to enter into a contract, but unless some physical assent is manifested there would be a total absence of any contract of any kind, either void or voidable").

3.10. Age

Common law. The common law allowed a girl age 12 and a boy age 14 to marry without the consent of parents or the approval and order of a court. Today, most jurisdictions set the age to marry legally by statute, and the minimum age is around 15 or 16 years with parental or court consent. The UMDA requires parental or judicial consent for persons 16 and 17.

If an underage person marries without consent of a parent or the court, the marriage is voidable (assuming that the marriage would have been recognized had the court or a parent given consent). If a person attempts a marriage where the law would not recognize the relationship under any circumstances, the marriage is void.

Standing. An annulment action may be maintained by the minor and usually by either parent of the minor or by a guardian of the minor's person. However, an annulment action is usually not allowed at the suit of a party who was of the age of legal consent when it was contracted or by a party who, for any time after he or she attained that age, freely cohabited with the other party as husband or wife.

EXAMPLES

Examples

6. Decedent D was P's first husband. They separated, and P never heard from D again and did not know whether he was alive or dead. Six years after the separation, and after her inquiries proved unavailing, P believed that D was dead, and P married X. However, D actually died ten years from the time that P and D had separated. When D died, P and X had been married for four years. P learned of D's death and that he had left behind a huge estate. P immediately secured an annulment order for her second marriage and then asserted a claim that she was D's widow and entitled to a portion of his estate. The Enoch Arden statute in this jurisdiction reads, in part, as follows:

   "A subsequent marriage contracted by any person during the life of a former husband or wife of such person, with any person other than such former husband or wife, is illegal and void from the beginning, when such former husband or wife is absent, and not known to such person to be living for the space of five successive years immediately preceding such subsequent marriage, or is generally reputed or believed by such person to be dead at the time such subsequent marriage was contracted. In either of which cases the subsequent marriage is valid until its nullity is adjudged by a competent tribunal."

   Given the language of the statute, may P make a claim as D's surviving widow that a court will recognize?

7. Assume that it is three months after P and D married and that P (the wife), with the help of her lawyer son who was the issue of a former marriage of P to X, and who was appointed guardian ad litem for P, brought an action to annul the marriage, claiming that P did not have sufficient mental capacity to understand the nature of the marriage ceremony. Experts called by P testified that she suffered from a severe and irreversible mental illness long before and at the time of her marriage and agree that based on their examinations, she was not capable of understanding the nature, consequences, and effect of marriage. D did not call any experts. However, D argued that P had waived her claim by delaying bringing the action for three months. D asserted that the only action available to P was one for divorce. How will a court most likely rule?

8. Assume that P is 23, and D is 16. D lies about her age, and the couple marries in a jurisdiction that requires consent of a parent or a court

order when a party is under 18 but over 15. D obtains neither. Three years later, D, who is now 19 and who is about to inherit a huge estate, continues to share an apartment with P. However, she decides to seek an annulment of the marriage on the ground that it was void when entered. P defends the annulment action by asserting that D waived whatever opportunity she might have had to obtain an annulment once she became an adult and continued cohabiting with P. How will a court applying the Idaho illustrative statute contained in this chapter most likely rule on the annulment request? How will a court applying the Minnesota illustrative statute contained in this chapter most likely rule on the annulment request? How would a state without either statute most likely rule?

9. Assume that P is 23 and D is 16. They marry in a jurisdiction that requires consent of a parent or a court order when a party is under 18 and older than 15. D obtains neither. A year later, P brings an action to annul the marriage. Most likely, how will a court rule on P's effort?

EXPLANATIONS

Explanations

6. P's claim will most likely not be recognized. Courts will take the view that the hypothetical statute requires that a claimant's status be determined as of the date of D's death, and as of that date, P's marriage to X remained valid. P's marriage to X could become invalid only as of the date of an annulment decree — necessarily at a time after her status in relation to the estate had been fixed. Courts will usually take the view that only if P had secured her annulment while D was still alive could she contend that her marriage to him had become revived so as to give her a widow's status. *See Estate of Lemont*, 86 Cal. Rptr. 810 (Cal. App. 1970); *Valleau v. Valleau*, 6 Paige (N.Y. 1836).

7. To obtain an annulment on the ground of lack of understanding, it must be shown that the party was incapable of understanding the nature, effect, and consequences of the marriage. Here, there is unrebutted expert evidence that the wife suffered from a severe and irreversible mental illness before and at the time of her marriage. The remaining question for the court is whether P waived her annulment claim by remaining in the relationship for three months before she initiated it. Absent a state statute guiding the outcome, the court will most likely

grant the annulment, reasoning that three months does not represent a long-term period of cohabitation of the kind that should bar an annulment. *See Levine v. Dumbra*, 604 N.Y.S.2d 207 (N.Y. App. 1993); *Faivre v. Faivre*, 128 A.2d 139 (Pa. Super. 1956); *but see Weinberg v. Weinberg*, 255 A.D. 366 (N.Y. App. 1938) (presumption of sanity in favor of the validity of a marriage celebrated in due form prevails unless it is overcome by proof clear and satisfactory that stands the test of most careful scrutiny).

8. The Idaho statute appears to allow an annulment action to be brought up to within four years after arriving at the age of consent. Idaho Code §32-501(1) (2012) provides the basis for an annulment. It reads: "A marriage may be annulled for any of the following causes, existing at the time of the marriage: 1. That the party in whose behalf it is sought to have the marriage annulled was under the age of legal consent, and such marriage was contracted without the consent of his or her parents or guardian, or persons having charge of him or her; unless, after attaining the age of consent, such party for any time freely cohabits with the other as husband or wife."

   Idaho Code §32-502 (2012) sets out the time limits on bringing an annulment action. This statute allows an annulment action such as that sketched out in our hypothetical to be heard. The reason is that this section of the Code states that "1. For causes mentioned in subdivision one; by the party to the marriage who was married under the age of legal consent, within four (4) years after arriving at the age of consent." Therefore, an action brought in Idaho for an annulment based on our hypothetical facts would be heard.

   However, Minnesota's statute appears quite different. The Minnesota statute requires that the action be brought before D reached age 18, which is the minimum age of consent to marry. Therefore, a Minnesota the couple could divorce but not obtain an annulment. Note that as a general rule, absent a specific state statute guiding a court in granting an annulment, a court would most likely deny the annulment request on the basis of waiver of the defect after the minor reached the age of consent and continued living with his or her married partner.

9. The court will most likely reject P's action, reasoning that P is not the party with the age disability. As a general rule, as reflected by the illustrative statutes of Idaho and Minnesota contained in this chapter, courts will not provide P, who is an adult, with standing to bring the annulment action. Therefore, P's only remedy is to seek a divorce.

3.11. Under the Influence of Drugs or Alcohol

General rule. Most jurisdictions have promulgated statutes providing that an annulment may be granted if a party lacked capacity to consent to the marriage at the time the marriage was solemnized, either because of mental incapacity or infirmity, or because of the influence of alcohol, drugs, or other incapacitating substances. *See, e.g.*, 13 Del. Code §1506(a)(1) (2009). An excessive use of intoxicants may render one incapable of contracting a marriage because of the inability to concentrate one's mental faculties or to understand the marital obligations. Absent a showing that the party ratified the marriage by continuing to voluntarily live with the other person following the ceremony, such a marriage may be annulled.

3.12. Marriage Made in Jest

As a general principle, when two people participate in a mock marriage ceremony as an act of jest, exuberance, hilarity, or dare and harbor no intention to be bound by it, most courts permit an annulment. *McClurg v. Terry*, 21 N.J. Eq. 225 (1870). Courts reason that mutual consent and bona fide agreement of the parties, freely given and with the intention of entering into a valid status of marriage, are fundamental and essential elements, and without them, the marriage is invalid. Courts also reason that the public interest would not be served by compelling the persons involved to accept the legal consequences of their imprudent conduct. *See Crouch v. Wartenberg*, 104 S.E. 117 (W. Va. 1920) (marriage in jest followed by no subsequent acts or conduct indicative of a purpose to enter into such relation, may be annulled in equity at the suit of either party).

FRAUD

3.13. Fraud — General Rule

Essence of relationship. Most state courts hold that a marriage may be annulled as a result of a fraud that goes to the "essence of the marriage." They reason that this particular type of fraud vitiates the parties' consent. Normally, the fraud must be of an extreme nature and go to present, not future, facts.

Consummation and burden. Once a marriage is consummated, courts require a greater quantum of proof before granting an annulment where fraud is alleged. When the injured party discovers the fraud, an annulment usually will not be granted unless he or she immediately and voluntarily ceases living with the other spouse as husband and wife. (Note, however, the illustrative Idaho statute found earlier in this chapter that sets forth various time limits in which to bring an annulment action, which may challenge this assertion.)

Lying, temper, idleness, fortune hunter. The mere fact of lying is generally not considered a sufficient basis for a court to grant an annulment. Lies that involve the concealment of incontinence, temper, idleness, extravagance, coldness, or fortune are not recognized as sufficient justification for annulling a marriage. For example, a shoe salesman's false representation to his bride-to-be that he owned his own shoe store fell short of fraud sufficient to annul a marriage in *Mayer v. Mayer*, 279 P. 783 (Cal. 1929). In another California dispute, a future husband's statement that he was a "man of means" when he was really "impecunious" was insufficient evidence on which to grant an annulment. *Marshall v. Marshall*, 300 P. 816 (Cal. 1931).

In Illinois, an annulment sought by a wife was rejected when the husband turned out to be, in her eyes, a lazy, unshaven disappointment with a drinking problem. She also produced evidence that her husband had falsely claimed that he was chaste prior to marriage, even though another woman was pregnant with his child. *Hull v. Hull*, 191 Ill. App. 307 (Ill. App. 1915). The Illinois court found that the claimed fraud did not impair the ability of the parties to live together and perform the obligations and duties of marriage.

EXAMPLES

Examples

10. P and D participated in a marriage ceremony in Nevada. P is now seeking to annul the marriage on the ground that he was under the influence of intoxicating liquor and so inebriated that he did not understand the nature of the ceremony or its legal effect.

    At trial, evidence was produced showing that two days after the marriage, when P claimed he was still suffering from the effects of intoxication, D advised P of the marriage. The next day, having fully recovered from his inebriation, P left the hotel room he shared with D and has not since cohabited with her.

    At trial, P testified he drank intoxicants for five hours prior to the marriage and for several hours after the ceremony was performed. A friend of P's, X, testified that he was with P before and after the marriage ceremony and P was "drunk" the entire time. X testified that P could hardly walk down the aisle and passed out for a minute or two during the wedding dinner. D testified that she felt that P was drinking "an awful lot before the ceremony, but we had talked about getting married for six months before the night we were married." D testified that P was "able to stand up during the ceremony" and was not "too strange." The trial court denied the annulment, stating in effect that it did not believe P or P's friend, X. The judge wrote in her order that she was "satisfied that there isn't any minister in the city or anywhere else that is ordained, who will marry a drunken person. Moreover, the couple had discussed getting married for several months." P appeals. How will an appellate court most likely rule?

11. Assume that P and D married, and P, who seeks an annulment, claims that he was intoxicated and can recall very little of the marriage ceremony. D concedes during her testimony that P's recollection of the marriage ceremony and his state of inebriation is probably correct. However, evidence shows that P continued to live with D as her husband for several months following the marriage. Furthermore, P contributed financially to D's support. How will a court most likely rule on P's request for an annulment?

12. P and D marry. Before they were married, D assured P that she was a virgin. A month after the marriage, P discovers that D had an affair only weeks before their wedding with his best friend. Based on this information, P seeks an annulment, arguing that D fraudulently concealed her moral character from him prior to the marriage. How will a court most likely rule?

13. After a 20-month marriage, P sought to have her marriage to D annulled on the ground that her consent had been obtained fraudulently. D agreed that the marriage should be terminated but requested a divorce. At the trial to determine whether the action should be one of divorce or annulment, P testified that she was not aware of D's severe drinking problem until after the marriage and that she was upset to discover this and disappointed in his refusal to seek help. P also testified that she knew before the nuptials that D was unemployed, but she did not realize he would refuse to work once they were married. P testified that her sex life with D after marriage was unsatisfactory and that D was dirty and unattractive. According to P, "D turned from a prince before marriage into a filthy frog after marriage." D testified to the contrary, but the trial court believed P. Is it likely that a court will grant an annulment on the basis that the marriage was obtained fraudulently?

Explanations

10. One who can prove participation in a marriage ceremony while under the influence of intoxicating beverages to such extent as to be of unsound mind and without knowledge of what is happening is entitled to an annulment of the marriage. *See* cases cited in 28 A.L.R. (1924) 648. Here, P's testimony was corroborated by X; however, the trial judge, who is the arbiter of credibility, concluded that both P and X were not telling the truth. The fact that P and D separated after three days and did not have further relations favors P. Most courts would consider the fact that the couple discussed marriage as not relevant to the specific issue, which is whether P was without knowledge of what was transpiring at the time of the ceremony. However, because of the credibility ruling by the trial judge, an appellate court would be reluctant to reverse the matter. If the appellate court decides to reverse the trial judge, it must do so on the basis that as a "matter of law, the facts support P's annulment action." *See Dobson v. Dobson*, 193 P.2d 794 (Cal. App. 1948). Most likely, the matter will be affirmed on appeal.

11. A court will most likely not grant an annulment. Although P was intoxicated to the degree that he cannot recall what happened at the time of the marriage, the facts are undisputed that P lived with D after the marriage ceremony and contributed financial support to the relationship when sober. Most courts will conclude that by this conduct, P effectively condoned the acts done while he was intoxicated as if they had been done when he was sober.

12. A majority of courts take the view that concealment of defects of character, morality, chastity, habits, and temper are not sufficient to justify an annulment unless there is also evidence of overreaching. Evidence of overreaching includes taking advantage of another because of disparity in age, experience, or knowledge. Here, it is unlikely that a court will grant an annulment. P's remedy is to seek a divorce.

13. A court will most likely not grant an annulment. Despite P's testimony, most courts will view D's behavior following marriage as mere character defects that do not go to the essence of the marriage. Another factor supporting the ruling is that P lived with D and his defects for 20 months. P's remedy is to seek a dissolution of the relationship.

3.14. Immigration Fraud — Sham Marriage

Immigration fraud involves a sham marriage. A *sham marriage* is a marriage where the parties entered into the relationship solely for the purpose of circumventing immigration laws. Annulment actions sometimes are used to sever a "sham" marriage.

Courts have said that a sham marriage may be annulled if an alien married a United States citizen merely for the purpose of gaining entry into the United States on a preferential basis, and the alien has no intention of living with the United States citizen as his or her spouse. *In re Marriage of Liu*, 242 Cal. Rptr. 649 (Cal. App. 1987); *S.B. v. P.B.*, 771 A.2d 978 (Del. Fam. 2000); *Pastore v. Pastore*, 100 N.Y.S.2d 552 (N.Y. Sup. 1950); *Ramshardt v. Ballardini*, 324 A.2d 69 (N.J. Ch. 1974) (marriage allegedly entered into so as to prevent deportation of defendant, which in no way was intended to be a valid "marital relationship," was void). *See also* Am. Jur. 2d, *Aliens & Citizens* §1524.

Federal Circuit debate. There is a debate among the Federal Circuit Courts of Appeal over the question of whether a finding of a sham marriage for federal immigration purposes also makes the marriage void under state law.

Seventh Circuit view. The Seventh Circuit has held that sham immigration marriages are void. *See United States v. Lutwak*, 195 F.2d 748, 753-54 (7th Cir.1952), *aff'd*, 344 U.S. 604 (1953). In *Lutwak*, several United States citizens entered into sham marriages with foreign citizens in France, for the purpose of allowing the foreign citizens to come to the United States. They were charged and convicted of violating federal immigration laws. On appeal from the convictions, the *Lutwak* court stated:

> A sham marriage, void under the law of this country as against public policy, can have no validity . . . . [A] marriage in jest is not a marriage at all . . . . [I]f the spouses agree to a marriage only for the sake of representing it as such to the outside world and with the understanding that they will put an end to it as soon as it has served its purpose to deceive, they have never really agreed to be married at all . . . . Furthermore a marriage void ab initio is void for all purposes and has no standing in court.

Ibid. The court also stated that "[u]nder Illinois law, and quite generally in this country, a sham marriage, one in jest, or one intended to be only a pretense is void."

Fifth Circuit view. In contrast, the Fifth Circuit has held that a finding that a marriage was a "sham" for immigration marriages does not mean that it is void for state law purposes. *See Ponce-Gonzalez v. Immigration & Naturalization Serv.*,

775 F.2d 1342, 1347 n. 7 (5th Cir.1985). The *Ponce-Gonzalez* court stated that "[u]nder Texas law, such a marriage would apparently be only voidable, and would remain valid until annulled." 775 F.2d at 1347 n. 7 (citing to relevant Texas statutory provisions).

In *In re Marriage of Kunz*, 136 P.3d 1278 (Utah 2006), the court concluded that the approach taken by the Fifth Circuit appeared to be most consistent with the Utah Code provision setting forth the specific types of marriages that "are prohibited and declared void" in that state. Utah Code Ann. §30-1-2 (1999). Although §30-1-2 of the Utah Code lists the specific types of marriages that are considered void in that state, a sham immigration marriage is not expressly included as one of them. The court in *Kunz* reasoned that because the legislature enumerated specific types of marriages that are void under Utah law and failed to include a sham immigration marriage among them, a decision by that a marriage was a sham for immigration purposes did not necessarily mean the marriage was void under Utah law.

3.15. Fraud — False Pregnancy Claims

Two categories. Cases involving misrepresentations of pregnancy fall into two general categories. As to the first category of cases, many courts have shown a reluctance to grant an annulment when a woman has claimed falsely that she is pregnant by her prospective husband to persuade him to marry her. Courts surmise that the false claim may have convinced the husband to marry the woman because he possessed honorable motives "to repair as far as possible wrongs inflicted or shared by him. Such conduct should be encouraged to the end that lesser wrongs be remedied instead of being followed by greater ones." *Mobley v. Mobley*, 16 So. 2d 5, 6-7 (Ala. 1943). They also reason that the false pregnancy claim fails to go to the essence of the marital relationship. For example, it does not prevent the future performance of the marital obligation to bear only the children of the husband. *See Hill v. Hill*, 398 N.E.2d 1048 (Ill. App. 1979) (woman's fraudulent representation of pregnancy that induces a man to marry her is not grounds for annulment); *Husband v. Wife*, 262 A.2d 656, 657-58 (Del. Super. 1970) (false pretension of pregnancy was not force or coercion); *Gondouin v. Gondouin*, 111 P. 756 (Cal. App. 1910) (intercourse by husband with wife prior to marriage who claimed she was pregnant but was not is not basis for annulment).

Minority view. At least two states, New York and Wisconsin, appear to have taken a minority view when a false pregnancy claim results in a marriage. *See Garfinkel v. Garfinkel*, 191 N.Y.S.2d 574, 575-76 (N.Y. App. 1959) ("our statute expressly provides that an action may be maintained for the annulment of a marriage on the ground 'that the consent of one of the parties thereto was obtained by fraud' subject to the limitation that it shall not be annulled for fraud 'if it appears that, at any time before the commencement thereof, the parties voluntarily cohabited as husband and wife, with a full knowledge of the facts constituting the fraud'"); *Masters v. Masters*, 108 N.W.2d 674 (Wis. 1961). In *Masters*, the trial court found that had the wife's fraudulent representations not been made, the husband would not have married her. The Wisconsin Supreme Court held that the character of such false representations were such as to be material as a matter of law, if they in fact caused the marriage to be entered into under circumstances that no marriage would have taken place absent such false representations. Therefore, the husband was entitled to a decree annulling the marriage. It reasoned as follows:

"The lone justification [for not granting an annulment] . . . is that [by not doing so] it might act as a future deterrent to unmarried persons engaging in illicit intercourse. If the thought of the unpleasant consequences, which are likely to befall the male participant should pregnancy result, or the fear of a criminal prosecution for fornication, are insufficient to deter him, we doubt very much that the example which would be afforded by denying an annulment . . . would be any more effective. On the other hand, to deny an annulment would reward the defendant for a palpable fraud and punish the plaintiff for being victimized thereby in an effort on his part to right a wrong, which he was induced by the fraud to think would result if he did not marry the defendant."

Pregnant by another. The other general category of cases consists of a true claim of an existing pregnancy coupled with a false representation that the prospective spouse is the child's father when, in fact, the father of the child is known or suspected to be another man. A majority of cases have held that such fraud goes to the essence of the marital relationship and vitiates the marriage contract. *Miller v. Miller*, 956 P.2d 887 (Okla. 1998). Relief has sometimes been denied on the theory of *inpari delicto;* that is, having engaged in premarital intercourse, the husband has created his own mess and should not expect the courts to clean it up. *Mobley v. Mobley*, 16 So. 2d 5 (Ala. 1943). There are usually aggravated situations where the doctrine of *in pari delicto* has been applied.

3.16. Fraud — Broken Religious Promises

Promises made before marriage about divorce or adopting a partner's particular religion have triggered annulment actions. The older annulment decisions suggest that courts were not overly enthusiastic about recognizing religious claims as the basis for annulment actions. *See Wells v. Talham*, 194 N.W. 36 (Wis. 1923); *Boehs v. Hanger*, 59 A. 904 (N.J. Eq. 1905). For example, in a decision made over 100 years ago, the court held that an annulment would not be granted even though a woman had falsely represented that she was a good, religious woman when in fact she was a prostitute. *Beckley v. Beckley*, 115 Ill. App. 27 (Ill. App. 1904).

However, in recent years, jurisdictions have taken a more liberal view toward granting annulments where religion forms the basis for the action. For example, in *Jordan v. Jordan*, 345 A.2d 168 (N.H. 1975), an annulment was granted on claims that the plaintiff, a Roman Catholic, was unaware of the defendant husband's prior marriage and divorce at the time she married him, that she would not have married him had she known, and that she could not live with the defendant because of her religious beliefs. Ten years earlier, the same court had denied an annulment request under similar circumstances. *See Fortin v. Fortin*, 208 A.2d 447 (N.H. 1965).

Today, most courts hold that misrepresentation of strong religious convictions goes to the essence of the marriage contract, particularly if the marriage has not been consummated. The rationale for this view is that religion has a significant impact on family life. *See Lamberti v. Lamberti*, 77 Cal. Rptr. 430 (Cal. App. 1969) (annulment granted where prospective spouse, to induce other to enter into a civil marriage, makes promise of a subsequent religious ceremony without intending to keep the promise, and there was no consummation by cohabitation).

OTHER

3.17. Duress

Duress is another ground that is occasionally used to seek an annulment of a marriage. Duress is broadly defined as "a threat of harm made to compel a person to do something against his or her will or judgment; esp., a wrongful threat made by one person to compel a manifestation of seeming assent by another person to a transaction without real volition." *Black's Law Dictionary* (8th ed. 2004). A marriage that is induced by duress is generally voidable. *Black's Law Dictionary* (8th ed. 2004). The duress must be of such a degree as to prevent the individual from acting as a free agent. A so-called shotgun wedding is evidence of duress.

Although physical duress is normally the evidence that a court looks for in a party seeking an annulment on this ground, some courts will accept evidence of mental stress. To have a marriage annulled on the grounds of coercion or duress, most courts will require clear and convincing evidence of the duress. *Fluharty v. Fluharty*, 193 A. 838 (Del. Super. 1937).

3.18. Impotence or Sterility

Impotence is defined as the want of power for copulation. *Dolan v. Dolan*, 259 A.2d 32 (Me. 1969); *Tannehill v. Tannehill*, 226 So. 2d 185 (La. App. 1969). If a person is impotent, it is not possible to have sexual intercourse.

Historically, there were two reasons why sex was considered to be an "essential of marriage": procreation and pleasure. Twila L. Perry, *The "Essentials of Marriage": Reconsidering the Duty of Support and Services*, 15 Yale J.L. & Feminism 1, 30 (2003). First, courts viewed procreation as a primary purpose of marriage. *Baker v. Nelson*, 191 N.W.2d 185, 186 (Minn. 1971), *appeal dismissed*, 409 U.S. 810 (1972). Second, sexual relations were valued for sexual pleasure within marriage. Perry, *supra*. The latter reason finds support by the fact that while historically, impotence was a ground for annulment, sterility was not a ground for annulment or divorce. *Ibid.*

Impotence has been held to render a marriage voidable if the condition was unknown to the parties, or at least to the party not under the disability, at the time of marriage. *Nakoneczna v. I & L Eisenberg*, 60 A.D.2d 403, 400 N.Y.S.2d 884 (N.Y.App. 1977) (marriage is voidable on the grounds of impotence, but is not void *ab initio*). To allow impotence to render the marriage invalid, the condition must be permanent and incurable and show that the other spouse was, at the time of marriage, and still is, incurably impotent. *See Manbeck v. Manbeck*, 489 A.2d 748 (Pa. Super. 1985); *see generally* Am. Jur. 2d, *Annulment of Marriage* §§27 *et seq.* Impotence "need not be purely physical or organic in nature but may be based on psychogenic causes, if the mental block or disturbance results in making the spouse physically incapable of performing sexual intercourse." *Ibid.*

The UMDA states that a court may annul a marriage entered into under circumstances where a party lacks the physical capacity to consummate the marriage by sexual intercourse, and at the time the marriage was solemnized the other party did not know of the incapacity. UMDA §208(a)(2).

3.19. Sexual Preference Issues

Issues involving the sexual preference of a husband or wife may on a rare occasion arise in the context of an annulment action. For example, in *Woy v. Woy*, 737 S.W.2d 769 (Mo. App. 1987), a husband sought an annulment, claiming that his wife had failed to disclose her same-sex relationship and drug use history before they married. The wife admitted she had sexual relations with a woman before and during her marriage to her husband. The court held that the wife's same-sex activities "had nothing to do with" the essential part of the marriage and denied the annulment. It reasoned that, the wife's "lesbian activities" did not interfere with her ability to engage in "normal" and "usual" sexual relations with her husband. Most courts would agree with this analysis. *See generally* Jay M. Zitter, *Homosexuality as Ground for Divorce*, 96 A.L.R.5th 83 (originally published in 2002).

DEFENSES

3.20. Continued Cohabitation

As noted earlier in this chapter, once the disability of a partner is discovered that would make the marriage voidable, and the parties continue to live together as husband and wife, courts are reluctant to grant an annulment. This rule reflects the strong public policy favoring marriage.

SUPPORT AND PROPERTY DISTRIBUTION

3.21. Support

At common law, an annulment resulted in the bastardization of any children born during the marriage. However, even older court decisions indicate that courts have exercised caution in granting an annulment that would in times past have bastardized a child. *See, e.g.*, *Wallace v. Wallace*, 145 S.E.2d 546 (Ga. 1965) (this court has striven vigorously to protect children of marriages where the parties sought an annulment that would, of course, bastardize the children, by denying that relief and leaving them to the only alternative remedy, divorce; and the legislature has done this by express language in the annulment statute). Where courts refused an annulment because of concern about children, this left the moving party with the option of staying married or seeking a divorce. *See Johnson v. Johnson*, 157 S.E. 689 (Ga. 1931); *Mackey v. Mackey*, 32 S.E.2d 764 (1945).

Statutes in all jurisdictions have removed the harsh common law view that an annulment results in an illegitimate child. *See, e.g.*, UMDA §207(c) (providing that children born to a void marriage are legitimate).

PROCEDURE

3.22. *In Rem* Proceeding

How should courts treat a situation where a party seeks to annul a marriage, but after a diligent search and inquiry, cannot locate the other party to serve an annulment petition on him or her? Courts are not in agreement on how courts should view the annulment petition.

Generally, if a court views an annulment action as similar to an action for a money judgment, it will probably be labeled an *in personam* proceeding. As a result, a judgment annulling a marriage solely upon constructive service would be void for lack of due process and not entitled to full faith and credit. On the other hand, if an annulment action is viewed as similar to a divisible divorce proceeding, and is considered an *in rem* or *quasi in rem* matter, a judgment of a court having jurisdiction of the subject matter, though rendered against a nonresident defendant upon constructive service only, is valid and entitled to full faith and credit.

One group of courts view an *in rem* annulment action as essentially the same as an *in rem* divorce. *See, e.g.*, *Shima v. Shima*, 130 F2d 809 (D.C. Cir. 1942); *Chapman v. Chapman* 11 Alaska 316 (D.C. 1947); *Bing Gee v. Chan Lai Young Gee*, 202 P2d 360 (Cal. App. 1949); *Buzzi v. Buzzi*, 205 P2d 1125 (Cal. App. 1949), *cert den* 338 US 894; *Rinaldi v. Rinaldi*, 118 A 685 (N.J. 1922); *Winter v. Winter*, 175 N.E. 533 (N.Y. 1931); *Piper v. Piper*, 91 P 189 (Wash. 1907).

A second group of courts view an *in rem* annulment action as basically an *in personam* action requiring personal jurisdiction over the defendant. *See, e.g.*, *Cale v. Davis*, 68 S.E. 1101 (Ga. 1910); *Gayle v. Gayle*, 192 S.W.2d 821 (Ky. 1946); *Cummington v. Belchertown*, 21 N.E. 435 (Mass. 1889); *Owen v. Owen*, 257 P2d 581 (Colo. 1953); *Pepper v. Shearer*, 26 SE 797 (S.C. 1897).

Realistically, it would appear that viewing an annulment action as similar to a divisible divorce makes the most sense. In such a proceeding, a court cannot impose personal obligations on the defaulting party. However, it can deal with the status of the citizen before it and change his or her status from married to single by annulling the relationship if proper grounds exist to do so.

3.23. Criminal Prosecutions — Bigamy, Incest, Adultery

Illustrative Mississippi bigamy statute. Certain relationships are considered so onerous, as a matter of public policy, that they are viewed as void in civil law and also subject to criminal prosecution. Bigamy, incest, and adultery generally reflect this strong public policy. While the punishment for being involved in one of these relationships varies from state to state, some jurisdictions have long-term imprisonment associated with them. For example, Mississippi's bigamy criminal statute provides as follows:

> Every person having a husband or wife living, who shall marry again, and every unmarried person who shall knowingly marry the husband or wife of another living, except in the cases hereinafter named, shall be guilty of bigamy, and imprisoned in the penitentiary not longer than ten years.

Miss. Code §97-29-13 (2011).

Illustrative New Jersey bigamy statute. New Jersey's bigamy statute is more comprehensive than Mississippi's and provides for a lesser penalty. It reads that:

> a. Bigamy. A married person is guilty of bigamy, a disorderly persons offense, if he contracts or purports to contract another marriage, unless at the time of the subsequent marriage:
>
> (1) The actor believes that the prior spouse is dead;
>
> (2) The actor and the prior spouse have been living apart for 5 consecutive years throughout which the prior spouse was not known by the actor to be alive;
>
> (3) A court has entered a judgment purporting to terminate or annul any prior disqualifying marriage, and the actor does not know that judgment to be invalid; or
>
> (4) The actor reasonably believes that he is legally eligible to remarry.
>
> b. Other party to bigamous marriage. A person is guilty of bigamy if he contracts or purports to contract marriage with another knowing that the other is thereby committing bigamy.
>
> A person who has been convicted of a disorderly persons offense under New Jersey law may be sentenced to imprisonment for a definite term which shall be fixed by the court and shall not exceed 6 months in the case of a disorderly persons offense.

N.J.Stat. Ann. §§2C:24-1, 43-8 (2012).

Note that in a proper case, a party's reasonable and honest belief that he was free to remarry may be a defense to a bigamy prosecution. *State v. De Meo*, 118 A.2d 1 (N.J. 1955).

Voidable bigamy provision. While most courts consider a bigamous marriage illegal and void from the beginning when the former marriage has not been dissolved or adjudged a nullity before the date of the subsequent marriage, there are exceptions. For example, in California, if the former husband or wife (a) is absent, and not known to the person contracting the subsequent marriage to be living for the period of five successive years immediately preceding the subsequent marriage, or (b) is generally reputed or believed by the person to be dead at the time the subsequent marriage was contracted, the subsequent marriage is merely voidable. Cal. Fam. Code §2201, subds. (a)(2) & (b) (1994). (Note the Enoch Arden discussion, *infra*.)

Incest. Incest is a statutory crime, without roots in common law. In the United States, its definition varies under different state statutory schemes. Joseph J. Bassano, *Incest*, 41 Am. Jur. 2d Incest §1 (2012). Statutes generally define incest as marriage or sexual intercourse between persons who are related within a particular degree of consanguinity or affinity prohibited by law, or between persons so closely related that a marriage between them would be void. The incest prohibition is intended to protect the integrity of the family and the welfare of minor children as well as to prevent genetic mutations which otherwise might purportedly occur in the issue of incestuous relationships. *Ibid.* It is one of the most common of all cultural taboos.

Scope of incest statutes. Incest statutes have been interpreted to include the relationship of parent and child by adoption and the relationship of stepparent and stepchild regardless of the existence of a blood relationship. *Raines v. Kentucky*, 2012 WL 246637—S.W.3d—(Ky. App. 2012). *See Edmonson v. State*, 464 S.E.2d 839 (Ga. App. 1995), *overruled on other grounds*, *Collins v. State*, 495 S.E.2d 59 (Ga. App. 1997). Courts have also reasoned that an incest statute protects the integrity of the family and that this protection extends not only to step-relationships, but also to relationships that are analogous to step-relationships. *Heikkila v. State*, 98 S.W.3d 805, 806 (Ark. 2003). Therefore, in *Heikkila*, the Arkansas court found that the incest statute prohibits sexual conduct between an uncle and a niece not related by blood.

Incest statutes relating to stepchildren generally limit the crime to victims who are minors. Therefore, an adult stepchild can in some jurisdictions consent to marrying a stepfather or stepmother. *State v. Johnson*, 670 N.W.2d 802 (Neb. App. 2003), *aff'd*, 695 N.W.2d 165 (Neb. 2005); cf. *State v. Collins*, 847 P.2d 528 Wash. App. 1993) (adult daughter could not consent to sexual intercourse with father).

Adultery. Adultery has ancient roots. Although not a crime at English common law, it was punishable under the canon law, which was administered by the ecclesiastical courts of England. *See United States v. Clapox*, 35 F. 575, 578 (D. Or. 1888); 2 Charles E. Torcia, *Wharton's Criminal Law* §210 (15th ed.1994). The ecclesiastical law regarded adultery as a sin arising out ıe marriage relation. As a violation of the marriage vow, adultery was ıidered equally great whether the offender was male or female. Adultery a ground for a divorce from bed and board.

The common law, brought to this country by the American colonists, not punish adultery unless the conduct was "open and notorious" as to amount to a "public nuisance," as defined by the English canon law. *See Cole v. State*, 94 A. 913, 914 (Md. 1915). The Puritans, however, made adultery with a married woman a capital offense, and from this Puritan legacy sprung state laws criminalizing adultery. *See* Jeremy D. Weinstein, Note *Adultery, Law, and the State: A History*, 38 Hastings L.J. 195, 225-26 (1986) cited in *Marcum v. McWhorter*, 308 F.3d 635 (6th Cir. 2002).

American common law concerned itself with the act of adultery only as it tended to expose an innocent husband to maintain another man's children, and having them succeed to his inheritance. Consequently, adultery was limited to sexual intercourse with a married woman. *Bashford v. Wells*, 96 P. 663 (Kan. 1908); *State v. Searle*, 56 Vt. 516 (Vt. 1884). Hence, the offense under canon law was broader than at common law.

Today, legislative treatment of adultery varies from state to state. Oklahoma criminal law states that "Any person guilty of the crime of adultery shall be guilty of a felony and punished by imprisonment in the State Penitentiary not exceeding five (5) years or by a fine not exceeding Five Hundred Dollars ($500.00), or by both such fine and imprisonment." 21 Okl. St. Ann. §872 (2012).

By contrast, in New York, a person is guilty of adultery, a class B misdemeanor, when he or she engages in sexual intercourse with another person at a time when he or she has a living spouse, or the other person has a living spouse. N.Y. Penal Law §255.17 (2012) (it is an affirmative defense to this crime that the defendant acted under a "reasonable belief" that both he and the other party to the sexual intercourse were unmarried). It is of interest that a New York commission that was asked to suggest revisions to that state's penal laws recommended eliminating adultery from the penal code. The Commission reasoned that adultery involved private rather than public morals, and "that its inclusion in a criminal code neither protects the public nor acts as a deterrent. It was further noted that proscribing conduct which is almost universally overlooked by law enforcement agencies tends to weaken the fabric of the whole penal law." William C. Donnino, *McKinney's Penal Law* §255.17 (2011).

Note that after *Lawrence v. Texas*, 539 U.S. 558 (2003) a strong argument that adultery is protected under the constitutional right of privacy can be made. In *Lawrence* the Court stated that "liberty gives substantial protection to adult persons in deciding how to conduct their private lives in matters pertaining to sex." *Id.* at 572. Whle *Lawrence* applied specifically to sodomy statutes, the majority suggested that any private, adult, consensual, sexual conduct should receive some protection under the constitutional right of privacy. *Id.* at 578-79. Adultery appears to be a type of conduct that would fall under the privacy right discussed in *Lawrence.* In his dissent, Justice Scalia specifically mentioned adultery laws as possibly no longer being enforceable. However, the Supreme Court has not yet specifically expanded the constitutional right to privacy to include adultery, and as observed above, many state adultery statutes remain.

Also note that the military continues to pursue adultery prosecutions of military personnel. *See* Comment, Katherine Annuschat, *An Affair to Remember: The State of the Crime of Adultery in the Military*, 47 San Diego L. Rev. 1161 (November-December 2010).

Examples

EXAMPLES

14. Assume that P knew that D was a deeply religious individual before they married. Once they were married, each went to his or her own church. After eight years of marriage, P filed suit for divorce on grounds of extreme and repeated mental cruelty. D was extremely upset by the divorce petition because D's religion, as P knew, did not approve of divorce. During discovery, P revealed for the first time that she had lied to D a few days before they were married about whether her former husband was alive or dead. She revealed that she told D before their marriage that her former husband was dead when in fact she had divorced him. She also stated that she believed that D "probably" would not have gone through with the marriage because of his religious conviction had she told him that she had divorced her former husband. "But he seemed to love me an awful lot," testified P. After P's revelation, D filed a counter-complaint for an annulment on the ground that D had been induced to marry P by P's fraudulent representation that her former husband was dead when in fact he was alive and she was divorced from him. During the hearing, D claimed that his strong religious beliefs would have prevented him from marrying P, a divorced woman, while her former husband was living. D also asserted that P's false representation was made to induce a marriage and constitutes fraud that goes to the essence of the marriage relationship. P argues that whatever basis D may have had for an annulment is barred by the length of their marriage. How will a court most likely rule on the annulment request?

15. Assume that after three months of marriage, P sought an annulment in a jurisdiction with a statute that declared that an annulment will be granted when there is "[i]ncurable physical impotency, or incapacity for copulation, at the suit of either party; if the party making the application was ignorant of such impotency or incapacity at the time of the marriage." Assume that at the annulment hearing, P's expert testified that D suffered from no physical defect of a sexually incapacitating nature; rather, it appeared that psychogenic cause was the reason for D's physical inability to copulate. The expert also testified that it was

probable that even with counseling, D would not overcome his inability to copulate with P. D's lawyer contends that the statute applies only to physical, not psychological, problems. She also contends that unless there is evidence that the condition is permanent, an annulment cannot be granted. P's lawyer argues that the statute should be construed broadly to include both physical and psychological causes and that P's expert testified that D's condition was most likely permanent. Will a court most likely grant P an annulment?

16. Assume that P petitions for an annulment in a common law court, claiming duress as the basis for relief. She testifies that she was forced to marry D because he threatened that if she didn't agree to the marriage, he would tell D's mother that the two had intercourse many times while they were dating. D admits that he made such threats but says they were made in jest. D's lawyer argues that the threats do not constitute duress, and even if they did, the fact the two lived together as husband and wife for two years following their marriage ceremony bars the annulment action. How will a court most likely rule?

17. Assume that the parties were married for four years when husband P sought an annulment of his marriage to D after she left the marital home to live with X, her new female partner. P learned that D had been involved in various "quiet" affairs during their marriage. P alleged that at the time of the marriage ceremony, he was unaware that D had engaged in a lesbian affair with another woman. P claimed that had he known of these facts at the time of the marriage, he would have refused to marry D. P's lawyer argued that the facts were material, touching upon vital aspects of the marital relationship, and that D, "in concealing these facts from P, acted in a fraudulent, malicious, and willful manner with the specific intent to deceive and defraud P."

Explanations

EXPLANATIONS

14. The parties were married a long time, and a statute in a particular state may bar the annulment claim. However, without a statutory barrier, and given the liberal trend in this area, a court might conclude that the false representations on these facts provide a sufficient basis upon which an annulment may be predicated. To one who is deeply religious, his or her faith is the foundation on which the person builds a life and conducts everyday affairs. In this hypothetical, D's religious commitment determines his attitudes and behavior toward others. When one partner has discovered that unwittingly he or she has been duped into a

violation of that person's religious beliefs, and that indeed the person has been living in a state of calamitous and grievous sin, that discovery may well make continuation of the relationship impossible. In such an instance, the fraud eliminates the innocent party's consent to the relationship and goes directly to the essence of the marriage relationship, which is not merely "flesh and bones," but heart and soul and mind as well. *Wolfe v. Wolfe*, 378 N.E.2d 1181, 1188 (Ill. 1978). Despite the length of the marriage, a court might award an annulment.

15. The court will most likely grant the annulment. The court will reason that it is not relevant that D's impotence resulted from psychological rather than physical causes. What is important to the determination is that D was and is impotent. *See Rickards v. Rickards*, 166 A.2d 425 (Del. 1960). In *Manbeck v. Manbeck*, 489 A.2d 748 (Pa. Super. 1985), the court concluded that the psychological or emotional disorder from which wife suffered, referred to by physicians as a sexual dysfunction and described as rendering her incapable of participating in normal sexual intercourse, was sufficient evidence on which to base a finding of "impotence" and to warrant an annulment of marriage given sufficient additional evidence to warrant an inference that this impotence was incurable.

16. A court will be troubled by P's petition on two bases. First, the testimony, at best, provides only weak support for P's claim of duress. This was not a "shotgun wedding." Second, because the two cohabited for two years following the marriage, this will act as ratification of it. The court will most likely rule that because of the cohabitation, the action should be dismissed. Of course, P may pursue a divorce action if she wishes.

17. A court will reject the annulment petition. D's same-sex activities have little, if anything, to do with the essential aspect of the marriage. Because the marriage was sufficiently consummated, the wife's lesbian activities did not interfere with her ability to engage in "normal" and "usual" sexual relations with her husband. Moreover, same-sex activities prior to marriage are similar to claims of unchastity, which a party need not disclose to another party prior to marriage. *Woy v. Woy*, 737 S.W.2d 769 (Mo. App. W.D. 1987).

CHAPTER 4

Who May Divorce? Restrictions and Requirements

4.1. Introduction

This chapter examines the history and development of the law of divorce. It traces the most important legal developments in this area of the law from ancient times to the present. Its focus is on issues related to changing the marital status of a couple. Issues related to child support, custody, property distribution, and other matters associated with a divorce are covered specifically in later chapters of this book.

Examples and explanations are included to clarify the application of legal principles to practical, real-life problems. To a certain extent, with the advent of no-fault divorce, a substantial portion of this chapter is arguably more historical than relevant to a divorce action today.

4.2. History

Ancient history. Divorce has existed in some form since ancient times. For example, under Athenian law, a divorce was occasioned when a Greek husband simply returned his wife to her paternal family. *The Journal of Hellenic Studies*, Vol. 115, pp. 1-14 (1995), http://www.jstor.org/pss/631640 (last visited March, 2012). A marriage in Roman times was usually an agreement between families. *See* http://www.pbs.org/empires/romans/empire/weddings.html (last visited August, 2012) (Weddings, Marriages, & Divorce). Typically, Roman men married in their mid-twenties, and women married in their early teens. Once a man or woman reached marrying age, parents consulted with friends to find suitable partners that could improve the family's wealth or class. A marriage carried no legal force of its own but was viewed as a personal agreement between the bride and groom. A wedding was a mere formality to prove that the couple intended to live together.

Roman divorce. Around 18 b.c., historians suggest that the Roman emperor Augustus turned his attention to husband-wife relationships out of concern that marriage was becoming increasingly infrequent among many upper-class Romans and they were failing to produce offspring. Augustus hoped to elevate both the morals and the numbers of the upper class in Rome and increase the population of native Italians in Italy. To accomplish his objectives, he enacted laws to encourage marriage and procreation of children (*Lex Julia de Maritandis Ordinibus*), and provisions establishing adultery as a crime. With the *Lex Julia de Adulteris*, divorce may have obtained a more formal structure. *Lex Julia de Adulteris* required that a divorcing couple execute a writing that renounced their marriage, making divorce something more than an informal dissociation. The *Lex Julia de Adulteris* also punished adultery with the possibility of banishment. The two guilty parties could be sent to different islands, and part of their property could be confiscated. The harsh law apparently allowed fathers to kill daughters and their partners caught in adultery. Husbands could kill their partners under certain circumstances and were required to divorce adulterous wives.

Catholic Church control. Christianity spread throughout Europe in the Early Middle Ages with the Catholic Church dominating official and proscribed religious beliefs. All aspects of existence were to a certain extent dominated by the Catholic Church. http://www.historylearningsite.co.uk/medieval_church.htm (last visited, March 2012). During this period, some historians estimate that 98% of the people were illiterate serfs and peasants with many no doubt believing that the only avenue of escape from their wretched existence rested not on Earth, but in the afterlife. The overriding factor of daily life was found in conformity to Church control of everyday matters.

The regulation of family matters by the Catholic Church was pervasive. By the twelfth century, it had gained complete legal control over marriage and divorce through its ecclesiastical courts in England and most of Europe. Among other matters, the ecclesiastical courts incorporated the Church's view that marriage was a sacrament and indissoluble except by death; not even the pope could break its bonds. Sexual indulgence outside marriage was a mortal sin. These beliefs were founded, at least in part, on the Gospels.

See, e.g., Matthew 19:5-6, 19:3-9; Luke 16:18; Ephesians 5:30-31; I Corinthians 7:10-11; and Romans 7:2-4.

Absolute divorce prohibited. Although the early Church forbade absolute divorce, when marriage vows were broken by adultery or acts of cruelty that rendered further cohabitation unsafe, the innocent spouse had two possible options. One was to seek an annulment, which has been discussed in Chapter 3. The other was to seek a judicial decree from an ecclesiastical court to live apart from the wrongdoer—a divorce *a mensa et thoro*.

***Divorce* a mensa et thoro.** A divorce *a mensa et thoro* provided relief by a decree of judicial separation, or a divorce from bed and board. A decree of divorce *a mensa et thoro* did not sever the marital ties; the parties remained husband and wife. They could not remarry while the other spouse was alive and the husband was normally required to provide his wife with permanent support. A *divorce a mensa et thoro* is defined in *Black's Law Dictionary* 515 (8th ed. 2004) as "[a] partial or qualified divorce by which the parties were separated and allowed or ordered to live apart, but remained technically married. This type of divorce was the forerunner of modern judicial separation."

Parliamentary divorce. By the end of the seventeenth century, the English parliament had concluded that it possessed power to divorce a warring couple by special legislation referred to as a "special act." A divorce by special act of Parliament provided the basis for an absolute divorce and was available on the basis of adultery. Special Act divorces were confined to the rich and were "largely the prerogative of men, only four being granted to wives during one hundred and fifty years. There are some indications that the virtual absence of practicable legal methods for terminating marriages led large segments of society to adopt non-legal methods for this purpose, i.e., to separate and contract subsequent marriages without benefit of divorce." Homer H. Clark, Jr. & Carol Glowinsky, *Domestic Relations*, note 117 at 6 (4th ed. 1990). *See Waite v. Waite*, 4 N.Y. 95 (N.Y. 1855) (discussing English parliamentary divorce). The English parliamentary divorce model was transported to the American colonies and adopted by many state and territorial legislatures. *See, e.g., Maynard v. Hill*, 125 U.S. 190 (1888).

Protestant Reformation. The sixteenth-century Protestant Reformation provided a different perspective on divorce than that held by Catholics. While the Catholic Church had the belief that once married, the relationship was a sacrament and could not be broken during the lifetime of the couple, the Protestant Reformers disagreed. They believed that marriage was not a sacrament in the Roman sense; rather, it was a natural and social institution. Therefore, marriage fell under the natural and civil law, not under Church law.

The conflicting Protestant and Catholic religious views were imported from England into this country, along with the concept of a parliamentary divorce. In states where the political power and religious views of the Catholic Church were strong, such as New York, divorces were extremely difficult to obtain well into the twenty-first century, except for adultery. It is no coincidence that the Catholic Church fought the no-fault divorce concept in New York right up to 2011, when it finally became law in that state. In areas where the political power and religious views of the Catholic Church was not so pervasive, divorces after the Revolutionary War were granted on grounds other than adultery.

Colonial divorce. The American colonies believed strongly in the separation of church and state and rejected the establishment of ecclesiastical courts. Although the colonies differed greatly in their specific approach to divorce, in general, they vested power in colonial legislatures or courts of equity to handle divorce matters. However, "since colonial times, divorce law has been a contested area of American culture," which has pitted "individualist liberalism" against "institutionalist conservatism." Jeanne Louise Carriere, *"It's Déjà Vu All Over Again" A1: The Covenant Marriage Act in Popular Cultural Perception and Legal Reality*, 72 Tul. L. Rev. 1701, 1732 (May 1998). Divorces were granted in some of the colonies, but not in others. *See generally* Barbara Dafoe Whitehead, *The Making of a Divorce Culture* 13 (Knopf) (1997). Courts and legislatures in New England occasionally granted divorces during colonial times; however, the South generally followed the English tradition during the early period of American history, and absolute divorces were not granted. Judicial separations were rare. *See* Ira M. Ellman, et al., *Family Law: Cases, Text, Problems* 162, note 17 (2d ed. 1991).

Divorce after the American Revolution. Following the American Revolution, statutory divorce was introduced in most states. Divorce actions were rare and were treated in a manner similar to other civil disputes; i.e., as a means of providing compensation to a person who had been wronged. For example, in most states, a divorced wife could recover the dowry that she brought to the marriage if she could prove to a jury that her husband was guilty of adultery. Furthermore, if she met her burden of proving she was wronged and her dowry did not provide for her adequately, her husband could be required to provide her with a limited means of support from his personal estate. *See Brown's Appeal*, 44 A. 22 (Conn. 1899).

GROUNDS FOR DIVORCE

4.3. Fault

Origin of fault. In the context of dissolving a marriage, fault has historically played a significant role. The use of "fault" can be traced to the early Church and the ecclesiastical courts' exercise of authority over domestic matters. As already pointed out, under the rules established by the ecclesiastical courts, a person could ask for permission to live apart from a spouse. However, to obtain permission, the person seeking the separation had to prove fault on the part of the other spouse. Generally, to determine fault, the court asked whether the erring spouse had committed one of the sins recognized by the Church. Adultery, physical cruelty, and unnatural sexual practices were recognized as valid reasons for parties to live apart, although they were not divorced permanently.

When the English parliament adopted the view that by private act a person could obtain a divorce, proof had to be submitted that the other party was at fault by committing adultery. As noted earlier in this chapter, the English view of fault was imported to this country by its earliest settlers and adopted by courts and legislatures.

Fault and support. Fault also played a role in determining whether support was to be ordered when a divorce *a mensa et thoro* was granted by the ecclesiastical courts. For example, if a wife committed adultery during the marriage, she was considered "at fault," and the ecclesiastical court was not obligated to require that her husband support her.

4.4. Common Law Grounds for Divorce

From the time the United States gained its independence from England, state courts and legislatures began to consider a variety of grounds for divorce. The type of fault-based grounds created by a legislature reflected the dominant culture of a particular state and the influence of religion on the law within that jurisdiction. The following is a list and brief explanation of the more common grounds developed by states, which if proved, provide the basis for a divorce.

Adultery. One of the oldest and most commonly accepted grounds for a divorce in the United States is to prove that someone is at fault because they committed adultery. Adultery statutes are justified on the basis that adultery has "serious and endangering social and psychological consequences."

Oliverson v. West Valley City, 875 F. Supp. 1465, 1484 (D.C. Utah 1995). Adultery is not only is a ground for divorce in a civil court; it is also a crime and punishable by imprisonment in many states. Early jurisdictions often limited the crime to commission by a single or married man with a married woman, and excluded a married man from commission of the crime if he had sex with a single woman. *See, e.g., Nelson v. Nelson*, 164 A.2d 234, 235 (Conn. Super. 1960) (husband's alleged adultery with an unmarried woman, such conduct was sufficient ground for divorce, notwithstanding fact that under criminal statute, adultery relates only to sexual intercourse between a man and a married woman).

Cruel and inhuman treatment. Another ground for divorce in many states is "cruel and inhuman treatment." To support a finding of cruel and inhuman treatment, the defendant's conduct must be serious and not merely an indication of incompatibility. *See Hessen v. Hessen*, 308 N.E.2d 891 (N.Y. App. 1974) (a high degree of proof is required to establish cruel and inhuman treatment) (superseded by statue as stated in *Brady v. Brady*, 486 N.Y.S.2d 891 (N.Y. App. 1985) that was amended to provide, in part, that either spouse could be required to pay alimony ("maintenance"), and to eliminate the rule that misconduct by a spouse precludes receiving an award of alimony or exclusive possession of the marital home).

In a few jurisdictions, a claim of cruel and inhuman conduct can be proven by producing evidence of emotional abuse; however, courts cautioned that the conduct must be something more than mere "unkindness, rudeness, or incompatibility." *Brooks v. Brooks*, 652 So. 2d 1113, 1124 (Miss. 1995). As a general rule, cruel and inhuman treatment is proven where the conduct is continuous; i.e., not based on one isolated incident.

Mental cruelty. Several jurisdictions established mental cruelty as a ground for divorce under the common law and subsequently incorporated the concept into their statutes. Generally, actual bodily harm or apprehension need not be shown. *Alfaro v. United States*, 859 A.2d 149 (D.C. App. 2004). The humiliation of another human by reducing him or her to tears is "cruel" in the commonly understood sense of the word. *Waltenberg v. Waltenberg*, 298 F. 842, 844 (D.C. App. 1924) (there must have been such treatment as to destroy the peace of mind and happiness of the injured party, and to endanger the health or utterly defeat the legitimate objects of the marriage). Mental cruelty can be inflicted by the use of words or acts, conduct that constitutes quarreling, or fault-finding that affects the health, well-being, or peace of mind of either of the parties. *Copeland v. McLean*, 763 N.E.2d 941 (Ill. App. 2002) (husband's actions toward terminally ill wife constituted mental cruelty as grounds for marital dissolution; husband treated wife badly, mocked her in front of others, shouted obscenities at her, and told her that he wished that she were dead); *Cochran v. Cochran*,

432 P.2d 752 (Colo. 1967). Incompatibility of temperament is not viewed as cruelty and a ground for divorce. *Neff v. Neff*, 192 P.2d 344, 345 (Wash. 1948). A drastic change in a partner because of a religious conversion may, depending on the facts, provide a basis for a mental cruelty claim. *Hybertson v. Hybertson*, 582 N.W.2d 402 (S.D. 1998) (husband following religious conversion would tell wife that she would not live in paradise on Earth if she was a nonbeliever and that she would "just lay in the dirt"; wife could no longer have a normal conversation with husband, as he continually stated he was there to teach her and the children and was quoting Bible verses to her constantly).

Desertion or abandonment. Desertion, sometimes labeled "abandonment," is a ground for divorce found in a majority of American jurisdictions. Matthew Butler, *Grounds for Divorce: A Survey*, 11 J. Contemp. Legal Issues 164, 170, 172 (2000). Desertion has been defined as (1) cessation from cohabitation, (2) an intention on the part of the absenting party not to resume it, (3) the absence of the other party's consent, and (4) the absence of justification. *McCurry v. McCurry*, 10 A.2d 365 (Conn. 1939). There must be intent to put an end to the marital condition and the intent to never renew it. *Tirrell v. Tirrell*, 45 A. 153, 154 (1900). Desertion consists of the cessation of cohabitation, coupled with a determination in the mind of the offending person not to renew it. Intent is the decisive characteristic, and the question of intent is a question of fact. *See Barnes v. Barnes*, 428 S.E.2d 294, 297 (1993); *Schubert v. Schubert*, 33 A.D.3d 1177 (N.Y. App. 2006) (to establish cause of action for divorce on ground of abandonment, plaintiff must demonstrate that defendant unjustifiably and without plaintiff's consent abandoned plaintiff for a period of one or more years and refused repeated requests to resume cohabitation or conjugal relations). *See Ballan v. Ballan*, 248 A.2d 871 (Md. App. 1975) ("the unjustifiable refusal of either a husband or wife to have sexual intercourse with the other may constitute desertion, the burden of proof is on the complaining spouse, whose testimony must be corroborated even though there be an admission by the other spouse, since such an admission is not regarded as conclusive").

Constructive desertion. Constructive desertion is a court-created cause of action and often has a specific period of time the parties must be apart to justify the desertion claim. The cause of action provides courts with a basis to grant relief on the ground of desertion to a spouse driven from the home by his or her partner. *Lynch v. Lynch*, 616 So. 2d 294 (Miss. 1993) (if either party, by reason of such conduct on the part of the other as would reasonably render the continuance of the marital relationship unendurable, or dangerous to life, health, or safety, is compelled to leave the home and seek safety, peace, and protection elsewhere, then the innocent one ordinarily will be justified in severing the marital relation and leaving the domicile of the other, so long as the conditions shall continue, and in such case as the one so leaving will not be guilty of desertion; and the one whose conduct caused the separation will be guilty of constructive desertion, and if the condition is persisted in for a period of more than one year, the other party will be entitled to a divorce); *Hartner v. Hartner*, 75 Pa. Super. 342 (Pa. 1921) (under Pennsylvania law, desertion must be "willful and malicious," and guilty intent is manifest when without cause or consent either party withdraws from the residence of the other, and the desertion is an actual abandonment of matrimonial cohabitation, with an intent to desert willfully and maliciously and persisted in for two years without cause).

Habitual drunkenness. Habitual drunkenness is a ground for divorce in several states. It has been defined as a fixed habit of frequently getting drunk; it does not necessarily imply continual drunkenness. *Rooney v. Rooney*, 131 S.E.2d 618 (S.C. 1963). One need not be an alcoholic to be guilty of habitual drunkenness. It is sufficient if the use or abuse of alcohol causes the breakdown of normal marital relations. *Ibid.* In *McVey v. McVey*, 289 A.2d 549 (N.J. Super. 1972), the court held that the evidence established the ground of "habitual drunkenness" for a divorce. The husband had progressed from a social drinker to an inebriate who was regularly drunk four or five times a week, both at home and in public. The condition existed for a period of 12 or more consecutive months subsequent to the marriage and preceding the filing of a complaint by the wife for divorce. *But see Kessel v. Kessel*, 46 S.E.2d 792 (W. Va. 1948) (proof that defendant occasionally became intoxicated from drinking intoxicating liquors does not establish the allegation of habitual drunkenness within the meaning of West Virginia law); *Whitehorn v. Whitehorn*, 36 P.2d 943 (Okla. 1934).

"Indignities." "Indignities" exists as a ground for divorce in some states. For a spouse to prevail, the evidence must show a course of behavior toward the spouse that is sufficiently humiliating and degrading as to render the condition of "any woman of ordinary sensibility and delicacy" intolerable and her life burdensome. *Steinke v. Steinke*, 357 A.2d 674, 676 et al. (Pa. Super. 1975) (husband who for several months was in a program leading up to anticipated sex change and who adopted clothing and physical appearance of a woman entitled wife to divorce on ground of indignities, in absence of showing of mental illness); *S.M.C. v. W.P.C.*, 44 A.3d 1181, 1188 et al. (Pa. Super. 2012) ("indignities" must consist of a course of conduct or continued treatment which renders the condition of the innocent party intolerable and his or her life burdensome, a course of conduct as is humiliating, degrading, and inconsistent with the position and relation as a spouse).

EXAMPLES

Examples

1. Assume that P and D are English citizens living in the fifteenth century, and P seeks a divorce claiming that D has committed adultery on numerous occasions. D admits his adulterous conduct. P files a request with an ecclesiastical court to grant an absolute divorce. The request, however, is denied. Was the denial appropriate under the existing law?
2. Assume that P and D are citizens of a jurisdiction that requires proof of adultery as the ground for divorce. P has discovered that D is visiting chat rooms on the Internet and has been carrying on an affair via the Internet with another woman, X. E-mail messages between D and X, copied from the family computer by P, are described by P as "intimate" and "embarrassing," including nude photographs of X. P testifies that D and X have apparently never met each other in person but have carried on an adulterous affair on the Internet. P seeks a divorce on the ground of adultery. D moves to dismiss the action. How would a jurisdiction that had adultery as its only basis for divorce most likely rule?
3. Assume that P (husband) and D (wife) were married ten years and had three children, and that P brought an action against D for divorce, alleging as the ground cruel and inhuman treatment. P's proof consisted of D's public statements, which P claimed disparaged and embarrassed him. P said that D would often make statements such as he was a "deadhead husband who cheated friends," a "lousy lover," and "couldn't balance a checkbook if it had two entries." These were uttered at different times before relatives, professional colleagues, and friends. P alleged he had a cold and indifferent personal and sexual relationship with D and that D's behavior had caused him to suffer depression. D conceded that she may have made such statements but explained that they were made in jest. P testified that their marital difficulties were attributable to P's problems with alcohol and the inability to live a family life with D and the children. As to P's claim of sexual problems, D denied a coldness or indifference and testified that their sexual problems stemmed from differing sexual appetites and drives. How will a judge mostly likely rule on P's petition for divorce where the only ground for the divorce is cruel and inhuman treatment?
4. Assume that P and D were married for five years before the relationship broke down. P sued D for divorce, claiming desertion under the common law, which in this jurisdiction permits a divorce if the desertion is excess of one year. At the trial, unchallenged evidence was presented by P that for the last year, D acted "more or less" as though the marriage was over. During this period, D slept "on the couch, in the garage attached to the house, or at his mother's house," despite P's repeated requests that he resume the marital relationship. D testified that he was happiest sleeping

in the garage or at his mother's home. By the time of trial, he testified he had moved in with his mother "for good." He said he intends to continue living with his mother unless "P changes her ways." P testified that she had never asked or forced D to leave their marital home. Does P have a sufficient basis to support a divorce on the ground of desertion?

EXPLANATIONS

Explanations

1. The early Church forbade absolute divorce; therefore, the request was appropriately denied. Note, however, that when the marriage vow was broken by adultery or acts of cruelty that rendered further cohabitation unsafe, the innocent spouse was permitted, by judicial decree, to live apart from the wrongdoer, and Church courts would afford the injured party relief by allowing a decree of divorce *a mensa et thoro*. Note that if the party possessed sufficient wealth, that a parliamentary divorce was a possibility — although it would be rare.

2. Most courts would likely dismiss the action because P has failed to produce sufficient evidence of sexual activity between D and X. "Typically, either under a statute or the common law adultery is committed whenever there is an intercourse from which spurious issue may arise. . . ." *State v. Wallace*, 9 N.H. 515, 517 (N.H. 1838). However, in a jurisdiction that considers adultery as a betrayal by a partner that can ruin the foundations of a marriage relationship, there is a possibility that a court might grant a divorce for adultery based on the facts in this hypothetical.

3. To prevail in most jurisdictions on a claim of cruel and inhuman treatment, P must produce evidence that demonstrates a course of conduct by D that is harmful to P's physical or mental health and that makes continued cohabitation unsafe or improper. Most courts would require that the conduct be serious and not just an indication of incompatibility. The proof of activities that are alleged to constitute cruel and inhuman treatment will be viewed in the scope of the entire marriage. Here, P and D were together some ten years and had three children before P moved to pursue a divorce. The marriage is of significant length, and the transgressions will be viewed in terms of the scope of the marriage, including the fact that it produced three children. The conflicting versions of alleged cruel and inhuman treatment rest entirely on the credibility of the parties. The length of the marriage and the weak nature of the evidence produced by P will probably result in the divorce being denied on this ground in a jurisdiction where fault is required. *Spence v. Spence*, 930 So. 2d 415 (Miss. App. 2005) (divorce on ground of habitual cruel and inhuman treatment

denied where the only evidence of bad circumstances in the marital home, which was corroborated, was that the spouses had arguments).

4. The evidence tends to support the conclusion that D's actions broke off marital cohabitation, and D apparently intends to remain apart from P permanently. The court will most likely rule that P has proven that D deserted her and grant the divorce petition. *See Skeens v. Skeens*, 2000 WL 1459867 (Va. App. 2000) (unpublished).

4.5. Common Defenses to Divorce Actions

Before the 1970s, almost all states had only fault-based divorce provisions. Fault grounds in these states varied, with some, such as New York, having very restrictive laws: "New York's only ground for divorce until 1967 was adultery, and South Carolina did not allow judicial divorce at all until 1949. Even where fault-based divorce was available, a spouse seeking one had to demonstrate that he or she was the innocent and injured spouse." Kerry Abrams, *Marriage Fraud*, 100 Cal. L. Rev. 1, 44 (February 2012).

The following section is a summary of many of the defenses to a divorce that were applied at various times in this country, both by common law courts without statutory guidance and courts with statutory guidance. Most of these defenses were related in one way or another to a party's "fault."

Unclean hands. This defense imposed a burden on the petitioning party to enter court without serious fault. It was sometimes used as a defense in mental cruelty or desertion cases when the petitioner's own acts were questionable. It is still in use in some jurisdictions. *See, e.g., Price v. Price*, 5 So. 3d 1151, 1157 (Miss. App. 2009) ("clean hands" doctrine provides a defense to civil contempt actions where provisions of marital dissolution agreements have been violated); *Hurston v. Hurston*, 635 S.E.2d 451 (N.C. App. 2006) (claim for the application of equity is barred by the doctrine of unclean hands). The defense resembles the defense of recrimination.

Recrimination. Recrimination as a defense to a divorce action under the common law meant that if the complaining party was guilty of an offense that would justify a divorce, then a court would not proceed to grant a divorce. *Courson v. Courson*, 117 A.2d 850 (Md. App. 1955) (where it appeared that husband had abandoned wife for 22 months prior to wife's alleged adultery, and that the abandonment had been deliberate, final, and beyond reasonable expectation of reconciliation, doctrine of recrimination barred husband from obtaining divorce). This defense is a variation on the clean hands defense. For example, if both parties were guilty of adultery, neither could obtain a divorce.

It should be noted, however, that in some jurisdictions, the guilt of both parties was weighed and had to be found equal in order to trigger the recrimination defense. For example, neither drunkenness nor cruelty would normally constitute a sufficient recriminatory defense when weighed against a charge of adultery. *Bast v. Bast*, 82 Ill. 584 (Ill. 1876) (desertion is not sufficient recriminatory defense to an action by a husband for divorce on the ground of adultery). *See also De Burgh v. De Burgh*, 250 P.2d 598 (Cal. 1952) (extensive discussion of history and application of the recrimination defense).

Condonation. Condonation as a defense represented forgiveness, usually conditional, based on a promise not to repeat the offense. *Owens v. Owens*, 31 S.E. 72 (Va. 1898) ("Condonation is defined to be the remission, by one of the married parties, of an offense which he knows the other has committed against the marriage, on the condition of being continually afterwards treated by the other with conjugal kindness"). The forgiveness could be either actually expressed or implied; in either case, the forgiver and the forgiven continued their married life as before. An offense that is condoned cannot later be used as grounds for a divorce. *Chastain v. Chastain*, 672 S.E.2d 108 (S.C. App. 2009) (husband commenced a divorce action on the grounds of adultery; however, family court dismissed the action based on condonation, finding husband and wife engaged in sexual relations before the divorce hearing); *Schubert v. Schubert*, 823 N.Y.S.2d 282 (N.Y. App. 2006) (wife testified that husband's conduct in having affairs caused her to suffer shingles and gain weight, such testimony was not supported by medical proof, and wife also testified that parties voluntarily cohabited subsequent to events in question); *see* Marvin M. Moore, *An Examination of the Condonation Doctrine*, 2 Akron L. Rev. 75 (1969).

Collusion. Collusion as a defense under the common law represented an agreement by the two parties to create a false-fact situation upon which a divorce could be granted when no ground existed. *See generally Nelson v. Nelson*, 24 N.W.2d 327 (S.D. 1946) (oral agreement to give wife half of all his property if wife went to California and obtained a divorce without asking for alimony, there being no agreement that husband would refrain from defending the action, was not collusive). For example, collusion occurred when the married partners, having decided that they would divorce, staged a fake adultery scene in an effort to create grounds for divorce. To carry out their scheme, the husband went to a hotel room, where a paid co-respondent joined him and partially undressed. While the two of them sat on the edge of the hotel bed, the wife, as prearranged, walked in with a detective and photographer. The photographs and testimony of the detective provided the evidence of adultery, and this formed the basis for the divorce action. Because the incident was rigged, the divorce proceeding would be viewed as collusive and as a fraud on the court. A divorce action based on this evidence would be dismissed.

Collusion vs. connivance. Connivance is sometimes confused with collusion; however, the two are quite different. Collusion occurs when the parties collaborate to impose on the court by fabricating a ground for the divorce. Connivance is consent to an offense that is actually committed. *Farwell v. Farwell*, 133 P. 958 (Mont. 1913) (connivance is the corrupt consent of one party to the commission of the acts of the other, constituting the cause of divorce).

Laches. Laches is an equitable defense that has been applied in cases where, from delay, loss of evidence, and death, a judgment would be "conjectural and difficult to do justice." *Williamson v. Shoults*, 423 So. 2d 874 (Ala. App. 1982) (action of foreclosure on mortgage was barred by husband's laches). It has also been applied where there has been such a neglect or omission to assert a right, when taken in conjunction with the lapse of time and other circumstances, causes the adverse party to be prejudiced. *Gover's Adm'r et al. v. Dunagan*, 184 S.W.2d 225, 226 (Ky. 1944); *Wooddy v. Wooddy*, 261 A.2d 486 (Md. 1970) (ex-wife who failed to file bill of review challenging divorce decree until some 26 months after she knew of decree and some 22 months after she discovered shortcomings of her original counsel was barred by laches from challenging divorce decree); *Pryor v. Pryor*, 213 A.2d 545 (Md. 1965) (laches barred wife's action, brought 13 years after the husband had obtained a divorce, to void divorce on the basis that he made false statement that he had been a resident of Maryland for 1 year prior to filing his bill of complaint); *Ross v. Ross*, 143 A.D.2d 429 (N.Y. App. 1988) (wife barred from amending divorce petition because of undue delay).

Insanity. Insanity as a defense to a divorce action was recognized by the common law under certain circumstances. *See Shaw v. Shaw*, 269 P. 804 (Wash. 1928) (record shows wife's conduct traceable to her mental condition and she is relieved from the imputation of fault—husband's divorce petition denied). For example, where the ground for a divorce was a claim of cruel and inhuman treatment, the action would fail if it was based on acts attributable to the insanity of the defending party. *Bosveld v. Bosveld*, 7 N.W.2d 782, 785 (Iowa 1943) (insanity is not a ground for divorce, and charge of "cruel and inhuman treatment" cannot be based on acts attributable to insanity). The common law view of this defense has been replaced in a majority of jurisdictions by statute. *See, e.g.*, Idaho Code §32-801 (2012) ("A divorce may be granted for the cause of permanent insanity of the spouse: provided, that no divorce shall be granted under the provisions of this chapter unless such insane person shall have been duly and regularly confined in an insane asylum of this state, or of a sister state or territory, or foreign country for at least three (3) years next preceding the commencement of the action for divorce, nor unless it shall appear to the court that such insanity is permanent and incurable").

Provocation. Provocation was also once a recognized defense to a divorce action in some jurisdictions. The theory was that one could not provoke physical retaliation on the part of his or her spouse and complain of such retaliation unless it was out of all proportion to the provocation. *Trenchard v. Trenchard*, 92 N.E. 243 (Ill. 1910) (there was no charge that certain acts were committed in anger, without justifiable provocation); *De La Hay v. De La Hay*, 21 Ill. 252, 254, (1859) (a single assault by a wife on her husband with a hammer, with no injury resulting and the evidence not showing whether there was provocation or justification, does not entitle the husband to a divorce, under a statute granting divorce for extreme and repeated cruelty); *Gress v. Gress*, 148 N.W.2d 166 (N.D. 1967) (when provocation is asserted as a defense, it is for the trial judge to determine whether sufficient provocation existed and whether the retaliatory action was out of proportion to the provocation).

Religious objections. A litigant who attempts to use his or her religious views as a defense to a divorce proceeding will fail. Three United States Supreme Court cases have settled the issue. First, in *Maynard v. Hill*, 125 U.S. 190, 210 (1888), the Court held that marriage was a social relationship governed by the laws of the individual states under their police powers. Second, in *Sherbert v. Verner*, 374 U.S. 398, 403 (1963), the Court reiterated the standard under which First Amendment infringements by state regulation are to be judged, stating that "any incidental burden on the free exercise of appellant's religion may be justified by a 'compelling state interest in the regulation of a subject within the State's constitutional power to regulate.'"

The third case, *Reynolds v. United States*, 98 U.S. 145 (1878), asked whether freedom of religion made a federal law prohibiting polygamy unconstitutional. In rejecting the challenge to the prohibition, the Supreme Court observed that "[m]arriage, while from its very nature a sacred obligation, is, nevertheless, in most civilized nations, a civil contract, and usually regulated by law. Upon it society may be said to be built, and out of its fruits spring social relations and social obligations and duties, with which government is necessarily required to deal." 98 U.S. at 165. The Court also observed that "[l]aws . . . cannot interfere with mere religious belief and opinions, they may with practices. . . . Can a man excuse his practices to the contrary because of his religious belief? To permit this would be to make the professed doctrines of religious belief superior to the law of the land, and in effect to permit every citizen to become a law unto himself. Government could exist only in name under such circumstances." 98 U.S. at 165-167.

Williams v. Williams, 543 P.2d 1401 (Okla. 1975), exemplifies the approach that courts will take to the religious issue. In *Williams*, the appellant complained that her constitutional right to the free exercise of religion was violated when a divorce was granted over her objection. The appellate court observed that the trial judge only dissolved the civil contract of marriage between the parties and that there was no attempt to dissolve it ecclesiastically. Consequently, there was no infringement of her constitutional right to freedom of religion. *See also Everson v. Board of Educ.*, 330 U.S. 1, 15 (1947) ("The establishment of religion clause of the First Amendment means at least this: Neither a state nor the Federal Government can set up a church. Neither can pass laws which aid one religion, aid all religions, or prefer one religion over another. Neither can force nor influence a person to go to or to remain away from church against his will or force him to profess a belief or disbelief in any religion"); *Sharma v. Sharma*, 667 P.2d 395, 396 (Kan. App. 1983) (order dissolving marriage did not violate the First Amendment rights of wife whose religion did not recognize divorce); *Martian v. Martian*, 328 N.W.2d 844 (N.D. 1983) (assumption of jurisdiction in divorce case did not constitute infringement of husband's religious freedom contrary to State and Federal Constitutions); *Trickey v. Trickey*, 642 S.W.2d 47 (Tex. App. 1982) (no-fault divorce provision was constitutional as applied to a Christian marriage performed in church by a minister).

Lord Mansfield's rule. Under Lord Mansfield's rule, a party seeking to divorce because of adultery might attempt to show that the wife had a child that was not her husband's. Application of Lord Mansfield's rule made this difficult because it presumed that a child of a married woman was that of her husband. *Goodright v. Moss*, 98 Eng. Rep. 1257 (Ct. ch. 1777). The rule was considered irrebutable.

However, the rule has been abolished in most, if not all jurisdictions. One may prove that the child is not that of the husband by showing through blood tests that this is the case; or by establishing that the husband is sterile or did not have access to the wife during the time of conception.

General failure to prove grounds. A 1971 decision by the Arizona Supreme court, *Acheson v. Acheson*, 485 P.2d 560 (Ariz. 1971), illustrates the importance of being able to provide a court with evidence to satisfy the grounds for a divorce even when a couple may jointly agree that their relationship is at an end. In *Acheson*, the couple jointly agreed to terminate their relationship and had executed a stipulation dissolving the marriage. They had both asserted as grounds for the breakup cruel and inhuman treatment. Their only disagreement at the trial level was over alimony.

When the wife appealed the trial judge's alimony award, the Arizona Supreme Court *sua sponte* reviewed the question of whether there was sufficient evidence supporting the allegation of cruel and inhuman treatment. It held that because of the lack of corroborating evidence to support the cruel and inhuman treatment claim, the parties failed to establish satisfactory legal grounds for divorce. "Under these circumstances," said the court, "the trial court was without jurisdiction to grant a divorce and the judgment entered by the trial court is therefore void."

EXAMPLES

Examples

5. Assume that P came before a nineteenth-century common law court asking for a divorce from D. D, who was serving a long prison sentence for a felony conviction, was properly served but failed to answer the divorce petition. At the required hearing where grounds for the divorce had to be proven, the court asked P several questions. The answers revealed that P had been living in a state of adultery during D's absence and had become the mother of an illegitimate child. When these facts were revealed, the court refused to grant P a divorce. Was the court most likely correct in its application of the common law?
6. Assume that P sued D seeking a divorce in a common law court and alleged as grounds that D committed adultery. D, while not denying the claim, asserted the defense of recrimination; i.e., that P had deserted D a year ago. In a jurisdiction that recognizes recrimination as a defense but weighs the various guilty acts of the parties, how will a court most likely rule?
7. Assume that in this common law jurisdiction, husband P learned of several adulterous affairs involving D, his wife. After a family fight, D left the family home to stay with her mother. P filed an action for divorce but dismissed it three days later at D's request. D then moved back into their home and they attempted to reconcile as husband and wife and were intimate on several occasions. However, the reconciliation lasted only a few weeks, after which P once again filed a petition alleging D's earlier adultery as the ground for the divorce. D answered and asserted the defense of condonation and asked the court to dismiss P's divorce action. Will a common law court be likely to recognize the defense of condonation on these facts.
8. Assume that P sues D for divorce in a jurisdiction that requires proof of misconduct, even if the matter goes by default. In her divorce petition, P alleges that D was an adulterer. D does not answer the petition, and a default hearing is set where P must prove that D committed adultery before the

divorce will be granted. At the hearing, only P appears. She produces a handwritten letter, allegedly written by D, in which he confesses to his adulterous behavior. Based on the letter and the testimony of P, who claims she was aware of D's behavior, will a common law court likely grant P a divorce from D?

9. Assume that P brings an action to divorce D in a no-fault jurisdiction. D challenges the action on the basis of his religious beliefs. He claims that his faith does not allow a divorce. D asserts that a divorce decree will violate his rights under the First Amendment to the United States Constitution. His sincerity in his position and his devotion to his faith are apparent to the trial judge. Assume that there is sufficient evidence produced by P to justify issuing the divorce decree; however, the court is concerned with the First Amendment argument made by D. How will a court most likely rule?

EXPLANATIONS

Explanations

5. Most divorce proceedings at common law were regarded as equitable in nature, and various defenses appropriate to courts of equity were available. One of them was the unclean hands defense. "Unclean hands, within the meaning of the maxim of equity, is a figurative description of a class of suitors to whom a court of equity as a court of conscience will not even listen, because the conduct of such suitors is itself unconscionable, i.e., morally reprehensible." *Pollino v. Pollino*, 121 A.2d 62 (N.J. Super. 1956) (held that where plaintiff had been guilty of bad faith, trickery, deception, and fraud with respect to marriage, the court would invoke doctrine of unclean hands and requested divorce would be denied). Here, although there was no opposition to the divorce, a common law court would most likely not permit the divorce action to proceed because of the petitioner's "unclean hands."

6. A common law court in these circumstances would most likely allow P's claim to proceed. It would weigh both claims and conclude that P's desertion cannot exonerate D from the more serious charge of adultery.

7. Condonation is the forgiveness of an antecedent matrimonial offense on the condition that it shall not be repeated, and that the offender shall thereafter treat the forgiving party with conjugal kindness. Under the common law, the condonation must be free, voluntary, not induced by duress or fraud, and not procured by unconscientious and fraudulent practices. Obviously, it cannot have

been obtained by force and violence. Here, P, with knowledge of D's repeated acts of adultery, dismissed the initial divorce action and allowed D to move back in with him, and they were intimate. A common law court would reason that the acts of intercourse by P with D, with knowledge that D had earlier been guilty of adultery, indicate that P condoned the earlier behavior. Because of this, a common law court would most likely dismiss P's divorce action. *See Tigert v. Tigert*, 595 P.2d 815 (Okla. App. 1979) (condonation of marital offense may be predicated upon an express condition, in which case the expressed condition must be fulfilled for condonation to be effective); *Panther v. Panther*, 295 P. 219, 221 (Okla. 1931) (wife's cohabitation with husband during his leave from penitentiary pending divorce action did not constitute "condonation" of cause for divorce, where accomplished by threats and duress of husband).

8. Common law courts would be concerned about the couple colluding to obtain a divorce. D's confession would be received in evidence. However, because of the potential for collusion, proceedings such as this were subject to close judicial scrutiny. In this hypothetical, a court would be suspicious of the evidence presented by P, and it would not be unusual for it to deny P a divorce. *See Grobin v. Grobin*, 55 N.Y.S.2d 32 (N.Y. Sup. 1945) (a divorce will not be granted on spouse's confession of adultery unsupported by any other evidence); *Zoske v. Zoske*, 64 N.Y.S.2d 819 (N.Y. Sup. 1946).
9. D will most likely fail in his constitutional argument. The court will view D's religious belief and practice as completely separate from the secular divorce proceeding. It finds support in this position from the Supreme Court cases discussed above.

4.6. The Modern Divorce Reform Movement

Statutes now dominate. The statutory grounds for a divorce in American jurisdictions have developed at varying speeds over the past two centuries. It is interesting to note, for example, that South Carolina did not have a provision for an absolute divorce until well into the twentieth century. *See, e.g., Poteet v. Poteet*, 114 P.2d 91, 92 (N.M. 1941) (South Carolina constitutionally prohibits absolute divorce). For many years, New York held to the view that the only ground for divorce in that state was adultery.

Some jurisdictions created statutes that provided for divorce on a variety of grounds, including desertion and habitual drunkenness. Cruel and inhuman treatment and mental cruelty were added as grounds for divorce in many jurisdictions in the twentieth century and became a commonly used basis for a divorce because they covered a multitude of marital sins.

UMDA — Liberal grounds for divorce. In August 1970, the National Conference of Commissioners on Uniform State Laws approved the Uniform Marriage and Divorce Act (UMDA). It was subsequently amended, and in 1974, the House of Delegates of the American Bar Association (ABA) approved the revised Act. *See* Harvey L. Zuckman, *The ABA Family Law Section v. The NCCUSI: Alienation, Separation and Forced Reconciliation over the UMDA*, 24 Cath. U. L. Rev. 61 (1974).

As a model for state legislatures, the UMDA encouraged major statutory change by its liberal view of grounds needed for a divorce. For example, section 305 established that a divorce could occur if there was an irretrievable breakdown of the marriage and both parties stated under oath or affirmed that this was the case. It also permitted a divorce to be granted when one party stated under oath that the marriage was irretrievably broken and the other failed to deny the claim. If one party raised a challenge to the claim that the marriage was irretrievably broken, a court was required to make specific findings that an irretrievable breakdown had occurred or continue the matter for 30 to 60 days with an eye toward recommending that the parties seek counseling.

The phrase "irretrievable breakdown" as a ground for divorce is general in nature. The phrase was the product of an intense debate and careful consideration by the commissioners toward accommodating a variety of contradictory interests. *See* Robert J. Levy, *Comments on Legislative History of Uniform Marriage & Divorce Act*, 7 Fam. L.Q. 405 (1973). The objective of the drafters of the model UMDA was to reduce the acrimony connected with divorce and the time devoted to divorce litigation in already overcrowded family court calendars.

Impact of UMDA — Emergence of no-fault divorce. Driven by changing societal values, various states became active participants in a nationwide family law revolution during the 1970s and 1980s. In response to these changes, states began adopting versions of the UMDA discussed above. *See* Lynn D. Wardle, *No-Fault Divorce and the Divorce Conundrum*, 1991 B.Y.U. L. Rev. 79, 82-97 (1991) (providing short history and reasons for move to no-fault). For most judges and family lawyers, no-fault divorce was viewed as a dramatic and welcome reform. Under the former system, couples seeking a divorce had to prove that one partner was guilty of fault. Often, when the parties arrived at court, they had already divided their property, lived apart for many years, and had little to dispute. Nevertheless, to prove that grounds for the divorce existed, they were required to produce witnesses to corroborate their in-court sworn testimony proving that the other party was at fault. This procedure was followed even when the other party failed to appear at the hearing. The result was that many divorce proceedings were a sham. In other cases in which fault dictated the amount of property to be divided, moral judgments about which party was right or wrong ignored the complexity of the underlying causes of the marital dispute. Before no-fault, the divorce process also made the eventual outcome of a divorce action speculative rather than reasonably certain. Too often, husbands and wives were combatants, with each of their lawyers arguing that responsibility for the marriage breakup belonged solely to the other spouse.

The advent of no-fault legislation dramatically altered the matrimonial landscape. Under no-fault statutes, divorces were granted when it was clear there were irreconcilable differences. The no-fault statutes eliminated fault as a substantive ground for a divorce. Typically, state statutes required consideration of the marriage as a whole and made the possibility of reconciliation an important issue. The changes were intended to induce a conciliatory and uncharged atmosphere, which might facilitate resolution of the other issues and perhaps effect reconciliation.

By the year 2012, every jurisdiction in the United States had adopted some form of no-fault divorce. A claim by either party that the relationship was irretrievably broken usually resulted in a divorce.

Note, however, that "in some jurisdictions the relevant statutes contain express provision precluding the consideration of fault in determining alimony, and in others they contain express provisions permitting or requiring the courts to consider the conduct of the parties. [I]n those jurisdictions where the statute is silent on the issue the courts have differed, some holding that fault should continue to be a factor in awarding alimony, and others holding that it should not." Russell L. Wald, *Abandonment of Marriage Without Cause — Defense in Alimony, Spousal Support, or Separate Maintenance Proceedings*, 27 Am. Jur. Proof of Facts 2d 737 (2012). *See also Monson v. Monson*, 2011 WL 4716320 (unpublished) (Conn. Super. 2011).

EXAMPLES

Examples

10. Assume that P seeks to dissolve the marriage between P and D in a typical no-fault jurisdiction. P and D have been married for 21 years. P is a self-employed trucker, and P's job requires him to do a lot of traveling and to spend long periods away from home. P has asked D to accompany him on the trips, but D has refused. P claims that D has refused to be P's "partner in life." P testifies that there has been an irretrievable breakdown of the marriage and that the marriage is at an end. D responds that the marriage is not irretrievably broken and that all P needs to do is to engage in "some marriage counseling." D testifies that the two should reconcile, even though D is aware that P is involved in a relationship with another woman. The no-fault statute in this jurisdiction reads as follows: "Dissolution of a marriage shall be granted by a county or district court when the court finds that there has been an irretrievable breakdown of the marriage relationship. A finding of irretrievable breakdown under this subdivision is a determination that there is no

reasonable prospect of reconciliation. The finding must be supported by evidence that there is serious marital discord adversely affecting the attitude of one or both of the parties toward the marriage. If after a hearing the court determines that there is a reasonable prospect of reconciliation between the parties, the court should continue the matter for at least 90 days and require the parties to attend marriage counseling."

How will a court most likely rule? Will it continue the matter for 90 days so the couple may obtain counseling?

11. Assume the existence of the same no-fault statute set out in Example 10 and the facts as stated in that example. In addition, assume that there was testimony that on various occasions, P asked D to accompany him on his trips so that they may attempt to reconcile, although she refused to do so. D also argues that P should have communicated in some way that their marriage was breaking down. How should a court rule? D asks for a 90-day delay to allow P to engage in counseling with D.

12. The marriage between P and D collapses, and D moves out of their home and begins living with another woman. Assume that P files a petition in a jurisdiction that provides alternative grounds for a divorce. In this jurisdiction, a divorce may be obtained on the basis of an irretrievable breakdown or adultery. P alleges in her complaint alternative grounds; i.e., that the marriage is irretrievably broken and that D has committed adultery. At the conclusion of the hearing, the trial court finds that there has been an irretrievable breakdown of the marriage and grants the divorce. P objects to the judge's decision and moves to withdraw the count in her petition regarding an irretrievable breakdown. P asserts that the court should have made a finding of adultery as the basis for the divorce. She believes it is important to show the final judgment to the world and "prove" that the dissolution of the marriage was not her fault. Is the trial judge likely to allow P to withdraw the count?

EXPLANATIONS

Explanations

10. Every marriage relationship is unique; therefore, the court will look at the facts of each individual case to determine whether the marriage is irretrievably broken, with no "reasonable prospect of reconciliation." Although it is commendable that D wishes to reconcile and is willing to forgive P for the adulterous affair, most courts will find that the marriage is irretrievably broken. They will take the position that a healthy marriage can be nurtured only by the love of both husband and wife. The fact that P stated he did not want to be married to D and demonstrated this desire through his romantic relationship with

another woman is sufficient evidence to persuade most courts that the marriage is irretrievably broken. The court will most likely not continue the matter for 90 days to allow the parties to engage in counseling.

11. These additional facts will normally not make a difference in the trial court's decision to grant P a divorce. When P filed the divorce petition alleging irretrievable breakdown of their marriage, D was put on notice that the marriage was in trouble. D was apparently aware of P's extramarital affair, and while D asserts that P had asked her to accompany him on trips in an attempt to reconcile, D did not join P on any of those trips. *See, e.g.*, *Mackey v. Mackey*, 545 A.2d 362 (Pa. Super. 1988) (a healthy marriage can exist only when nurtured by the love of both husband and wife and husband's testimony that he no longer desires to be married to his wife and has romantic relationships outside the marriage supports the trial court ruling to dissolve the marriage); *Liberto v. Liberto*, 520 A.2d 458, 461 (Pa. Super. 1987) (trial court was not required to order statutorily mandated marriage counseling requested by husband as prerequisite to granting divorce).

12. Most courts will not allow P to withdraw the irretrievable breakdown count and then enter a finding that D was an adulterer as the basis for the divorce. They will view the marriage as irretrievably broken when a husband moved out of the marital home to live with another woman. The policy of most courts is to make the law for legal dissolution of marriage effective for dealing with the realities of matrimonial experience and to give primary consideration to the welfare of the family, rather than the vindication of private rights or the punishment of matrimonial wrongs. To allow P to proceed would be tantamount to allowing P to invoke the power of the court to vindicate a private right. *See, e.g.*, *Rosenberg v. Rosenberg*, 39 Pa. D. & C.3d 549, 1984 WL 2628 (Pa. Com. Pl. 1984) (allowing withdrawal of one count would be tantamount to allowing plaintiff to invoke the power of the court to vindicate a private right).

4.7. Limited Divorce

It is of interest that under the common law in most states a court of equity did not have jurisdiction to issue a decree of separation or limited divorce. *Reisman v. Reisman*, 46 N.Y.S.2d 335 (N.Y. Sup. 1944). These alternatives to an absolute divorce were created by state legislatures. Persons who select this path when a relationship breaks down most likely do so because of religious reasons.

A modern legal separation is at least in part the residue of the divorce *a mensa et thoro* developed by the twelfth-century ecclesiastical courts. However, unlike the ancient divorce *a mensa et thoro*, a modern action for a legal separation in most jurisdictions does not expressly or necessarily authorize the parties to live apart from each other. *See generally Cregan v. Clark*, 658 S.W.2d 924 (Mo. App. 1983) (evidence sufficient to support decree of legal separation on ground that wife's behavior was such that husband could not reasonably be expected to live with her); P. H. Vartanian, *Jurisdiction of equity courts in the United States, without the aid of statute expressly conferring it, to entertain independent suit for alimony or separate maintenance without divorce or judicial separation*, 141 A.L.R. 399 (1942).

Depending on the jurisdiction, a legal separation may be referred to as "separate maintenance proceeding," a divorce from "bed and board," or a "limited divorce." *See, e.g., Lavino v. Lavino*, 130 A.2d 369 (N.J. 1957) (distinguishing an action for limited divorce from bed and board from one seeking separate maintenance). Although these limited proceedings are usually intended to provide only for the support of the wife and children, in some jurisdictions a court may determine child custody and property division, in addition to child support and alimony. *See, e.g., Anderson v. Anderson*, 382 N.W.2d 620, 621 (Neb. 1986) (in actions for legal separation, the adjustment of property and the award of support are matters initially entrusted to the sound discretion of the trial judge); *see generally* John Bourdeau, et al.; §3, *Divorce distinguished from a legal or judicial separation*, 27A C.J.S. Divorce §3 (May 2012).

4.8. Right to Jury Trial in Divorce Actions

During the nineteenth and early twentieth centuries, the question of whether a divorce should be granted was tried to a jury in most jurisdictions. *See, e.g., Gilpin v. Gilpin*, 21 P. 612 (Colo. 1889) (the issue for divorce was tried by a jury as required by statute). However, most, but not all, jurisdictions today view divorce actions as equitable in nature and have abolished applying the right to a jury trial to any aspect of a divorce proceeding. *See, e.g., Davis v. Spriggs*, 2010 WL 4881491 (unpublished) (Ohio App. 2010) (there is no right to a jury trial in a divorce proceeding in Ohio); *In re Marriage of Sigg*, 238 P.3d 331 (Kan. App. 2010) (because a divorce proceeding is equitable in nature, there is no right to a jury trial); *Gluck v. Gluck*, 435 A.2d 34 (Conn. 1980) (although a creature of statute, a divorce is essentially an equitable action, precluding right to jury trial). A very few jurisdictions, such as New York, Georgia, and Texas, continue to allow a jury trial in a divorce action. *See, e.g.*, McKinney's DRL §173 (2012) ("In an action for divorce [in New York], there is a right to trial by jury of the issues of the grounds for granting the divorce"). New York courts are divided on the question of whether the jury trial right in that state extends to no-fault divorce. *Tuper v. Tuper*, 2012 WL 2053770 n. 1, 98 A.D.3d 55 (N.Y. App. 2012) (legislature intended jury trial right to extend to no-fault); *cf Townes v. Coker*, 943 N.Y.S.2d 823 (N.Y. Sup. 2012) (no-fault divorce action in New York does not entitle parties to jury trial). *See also Curran v. Scharpf*, 726 S.E.2d 407 (Ga. 2012) (jury properly awarded husband his individual retirement account as his separate property); *Waits v. Waits*, 634 S.E.2d 799 (Ga. App. 2006) (jury's verdict awarded title and possession of the marital residence to Mrs. Waits); *Hausman v. Hausman*, 199 S.W.3d 38, 41 (Tex. App. 2006) (after trial judge's paternity decision, a jury trial was held with regard to custody).

4.9. Covenant Marriage and Divorce

As discussed in Chapter 2, a covenant marriage is a concept available in just three states: Arizona, Arkansas, and Louisiana. These states give couples the option of agreeing to a traditional marriage or a covenant marriage. The covenant marriage agreements generally provide a list of factors that must be followed should the couple decide to divorce.

For example, in general, a covenant marriage agreement will not permit the couple to divorce except under certain specific circumstances such as adultery, abandonment, or cruel and barbarous treatment. The agreement may also require a waiting time for a divorce corresponding to no-fault for up to two and a half years. In Louisiana, a covenant marriage may be terminated by divorce only upon one of the exclusive grounds enumerated in Louisiana Statute §9:307 (2011), which is set forth in part below:

> A. Notwithstanding any other law to the contrary and subsequent to the parties obtaining counseling, a spouse to a covenant marriage may obtain a judgment of divorce only upon proof of any of the following:
>
> (1) The other spouse has committed adultery.
>
> (2) The other spouse has committed a felony and has been sentenced to death or imprisonment at hard labor.
>
> (3) The other spouse has abandoned the matrimonial domicile for a period of one year and constantly refuses to return.
>
> (4) The other spouse has physically or sexually abused the spouse seeking the divorce or a child of one of the spouses.
>
> (5) The spouses have been living separate and apart continuously without reconciliation for a period of two years.
>
> (6)(a) The spouses have been living separate and apart continuously without reconciliation for a period of one year from the date the judgment of separation from bed and board was signed.
>
> (b) If there is a minor child or children of the marriage, the spouses have been living separate and apart continuously without reconciliation

> for a period of one year and six months from the date the judgment of separation from bed and board was signed; however, if abuse of a child of the marriage or a child of one of the spouses is the basis for which the judgment of separation from bed and board was obtained, then a judgment of divorce may be obtained if the spouses have been living separate and apart continuously without reconciliation for a period of one year from the date the judgment of separation from bed and board was signed.

La. Rev. Stat. §9:307 (A).

Covenant marriage proponents argue that restricting a divorce to the abovementioned grounds better reflects the sanctity of marriage. It is also seen as a way to protect children from the devastating effects of divorce. *See* Joel A. Nichols, *Louisiana's Covenant Marriage Law: A First Step Toward a More Robust Pluralism in Marriage and Divorce Law?* 47 Emory L.J. 929-931 (Summer 1998) ("Louisiana's covenant marriage statute encapsulates the increasing dissatisfaction with current marriage and divorce laws in America"). *But see* Robert M. Gordon, Note, *The Limits of Limits on Divorce*, 107 Yale L.J. 1435, 1437 (1998) (criticizing covenant marriage and arguing that restrictive divorce laws would be harmful for children). Proponents also argue covenant marriage provisions will not act as the revival of fault-based divorce actions. They point to Louisiana, which has never abandoned fault grounds in its divorce law but simply added a no-fault option. Elizabeth S. Scott, *Social Norms and the Legal Regulation of Marriage*, 86 Va. L. Rev. 1901, 1959 (November 2000).

Critics also argue that a covenant marriage involves unconstitutional state support of religion, entails too much state involvement in marriage, infringes on the right to marry, and is harmful to women and children. Additionally, it is argued that the intended benefits of covenant marriage laws may be spurious, with at least one commentator declaring that covenant marriage laws offer "nothing other than inconvenience as an obstacle to divorce." Jeanne Louise Carriere, *"It's Déjà Vu All Over Again": The Covenant Marriage Act in Popular Cultural Perception and Legal Reality*, 72 Tul. L. Rev. 1701, 1705-1717 (1998) (criticizing the Louisiana Covenant Marriage Act's mandatory counseling provisions as likely to be meaningless or even harmful to the parties involved). It is also thought that covenant marriage may resuscitate practices largely eliminated by the introduction of no-fault divorce, such as annulments, migratory divorces, or fabrication of an appropriate basis for divorce in court. *Id.* at note 103.

4.10. Recognizing Same-Sex Couple Marriages When They End in Divorce

With more and more states recognizing the right of same-sex persons to marry, a significant question remains about states that don't recognize same-sex marriages and their willingness to allow same-sex couples to use their divorce laws. The results so far are mixed. For example, in *Chambers v. Ormiston*, 935 A.2d 956 (R.I. 2007), Rhode Island refused to allow a couple married in Massachusetts to use Rhode Island divorce laws. The court reasoned that:

> In our judgment, when the General Assembly accorded the Family Court the power to grant divorces from "the bond of marriage," it had in mind only marriages between people of different sexes. Having said that, we remain mindful of the fact that, unlike a Constitutional Convention, the General Assembly meets every year. That body is free, if it so chooses, to enact divorce legislation that it might possibly deem more appropriate.

Id. at 966. *See generally* Barbara J. Cox, *Using an "Incidents of Marriage" Analysis When Considering Interstate Recognition of Same-Sex Couples' Marriages, Civil Unions, and Domestic Partnerships*, 13 Widener L.J. 699, 718-719 (2004) (using an "incidents of marriage" analysis when considering interstate recognition of same-sex relationships).

Texas joined Rhode Island in denying a same-sex couple the use of that state's divorce statutes. *In re Marriage of J.B. and H.B.*, 326 S.W.3d 654 (Tex. App. 2010). The Texas court reasoned that:

> [C]omity governs the recognition of out-of-state marriages only in the absence of "overriding legislation." . . . We have just such overriding legislation in Texas, where the constitution expressly limits "marriage" to opposite-sex couples, section 6.204(b) of the family code declares same-sex marriages to be contrary to public policy, and section 6.204(c) denies legal effect to same-sex marriages even if contracted in another jurisdiction.

Id. at 669.

On the other hand, in *Port v. Cowan*, 44 A.3d 970 (Md. App. 2012), the Maryland Court of Appeals held that an out-of-state same-sex marriage was cognizable in Maryland pursuant to the common law doctrine of comity for the purposes of applying that state's divorce law. The court stated that:

> Under the doctrine of comity, long applied in our State, Maryland courts "will give effect to laws and judicial decisions of another state or jurisdiction, not as a matter of obligation but out of deference and respect." . . . When considering a foreign marriage specifically, Maryland courts follow the choice-of-law rule of lex loci celebrationis, applying the substantive law of the place where the contract of marriage was formed.

Ibid.

New York has also recognized that a same-sex couple married under Massachusetts law could use New York's divorce statutes. *C.M. v. C.C.*, 867 N.Y.S.2d 884 (N.Y. Sup. 2008). The court reasoned that:

> The purpose of the full faith and credit provision of the constitution and the doctrine of comity is to accord parties, especially in today's mobile society, the ability to ensure that if they were married in another state, they can enforce the civil contract of marriage in New York. This Court's research and the cases cited by the parties provide no reason to carve out a unique exception for the parties here simply because they are of the same gender or because of their sexual orientation. As the Court of Appeals noted in *Gotlib v. Ratsutsky*, 635 N.E.2d 289 (N.Y. 1994), "[t]he comity doctrine is also pragmatically necessary to deal properly and fairly with the millions of relational and transactional decrees and determinations that would otherwise be put at risk, uncertainty and undoing in a world of different people, Nations and diverse views and policies."

Id. at 889.

4.11. Divisible Divorce

To a certain extent, we have already discussed some concepts associated with a divisible divorce in Chapter 3 — "*in rem* annulments." Divisible divorce is also discussed extensively in Chapter 24. Recall that a divisible divorce involves the situation where a party seeks to divorce his or her partner but the partner cannot be located, or if located, is residing outside the forum state and refuses to consent to jurisdiction in the forum state. Also recall that courts have uniformly described being married as a "status" and have ruled consistently that they may alter the status of a citizen or resident. However, while a state can change the status of a citizen or resident from "married" to "divorced," it cannot impose any personal obligations on the person who has not been found or is outside the state and refuses to consent to jurisdiction.

Adequate notice. The availability of an *ex parte* divorce decree or "divisible divorce" is limited by the Fourteenth Amendment, which provides that a person shall not be deprived of any interest in liberty or property without due process of law. *See Phelan v. Phelan*, 443 A.2d 1259 (R.I. 1982). This language has been interpreted to require adequate notice of the request for judicial relief and an opportunity to be heard concerning the merits of such relief.

Recognizing another state's divisible divorce. The law surrounding whether a state must recognize an *ex parte* divorce decree issued in another state begins with the full faith and credit clause of the United States Constitution, Article IV, §1. It states:

> Full faith and Credit shall be given in each State to the public Acts, Records, and judicial Proceedings of every other State. And the Congress may by general

> Laws prescribe the Manner in which such Acts, Records and Proceedings shall be proved, and the Effect thereof.

Reviewing domicile. The full faith and credit clause of the Constitution requires that a state recognize the decrees of a sister state, provided that the sister state had jurisdiction. The Supreme Court has held that the judicial power to grant an *ex parte* divorce exists when at least one of the spouses is legally domiciled in the divorce granting state. *Williams v. State of North Carolina (Williams I)*, 317 U.S. 287 (1942). The decree granting state, however, cannot foreclose the subsequent re-adjudication of the question of domicile by another state. *Williams v. State of North Carolina (Williams II)*, 325 U.S. 226 (1945).

Burden of proof. The burden of undermining an *ex parte* divorce decree "rests heavily upon the assailant." *Williams v. State of North Carolina (II), supra*, 325 U.S. at 233. Specifically, that burden is "to overthrow the apparent jurisdictional validity of the . . . divorce decree by disproving . . . intention to establish a domicile" in the granting state. *Ibid.*

Scope of divisible divorce theory. After the *Williams* cases, a question about the scope of an *ex parte* divorce proceeding remained. For example, could a valid *ex parte* divorce entered at the domicile of only one party to the marriage automatically terminate the other spouse's right to support? This question was settled via the theory of divisible divorce set forth in *Estin v. Estin*, 334 U.S. 541 (1948). There, the court held that an *ex parte* Nevada divorce procured by the husband did not terminate the wife's prior adjudicated right to separate maintenance. The result in *Estin* was to make the divorce divisible and give effect to the Nevada decree insofar as it affects marital status and to make it ineffective on the issue of alimony.

Finally, in *Vanderbilt v. Vanderbilt*, 354 U.S. 416 (1957), the court perfected the divisible divorce theory by holding that even when the wife's right to support had not been reduced to judgment before the *ex parte* divorce, that divorce could not affect her support rights. The due process clause forbids a divorce court from adjudicating an absent spouse's right to support. Consequently, a spouse cannot be deprived by that court of whatever rights of support the spouse had under the law of his or her domicile at the time of the divorce. An *ex parte* divorce may not impose child support obligations or set an amount of attorney fees to be paid by the absent spouse. To impose those personal obligations on the out-of-state absent spouse, the party obtaining the *ex parte* divorce must usually proceed to the state where the absent spouse is domiciled and bring a separate action that comports with the due process clause of the Constitution.

EXAMPLES

Examples

13. Assume that P and D marry and live together in state X. When their relationship breaks down, P travels to state Y and establishes residence there. P files for divorce in state Y on the ground of extreme mental cruelty. D receives notice of the action and retains counsel in state Y. D's lawyer denies the allegations in P's complaint and challenges the personal jurisdiction of the court in state Y to hear the matter. Despite the objections, the divorce is granted by the court in state Y. D does not appeal. P returns to state X, where she marries her high school sweetheart. D brings an action in state X alleging that the decree issued by the court in state Y is invalid; therefore, P's subsequent marriage is void and she is committing bigamy. How will a court in state X rule on D's challenge?

14. Assume that after ten years of marriage, P and D's relationship breaks down. P, a lawyer, has been having an affair with his secretary, and they decide that he should obtain an absolute divorce from D. P writes to a lawyer friend in state X, asking about the requirements for obtaining a divorce in that state. He is told that in order to obtain an *ex parte* divorce in state X, a petitioner must establish in good faith a domicile for a minimum of six weeks. P travels with his secretary to state X, where he rents a hotel room for the required six weeks. During this period, he continues to conduct business in state Y, where his home is located. He uses the telephone, fax, and Internet facilities located in his hotel room. He does not change the address on his driver's license or checking account or submit a postal change-of-address form. After obtaining an *ex parte* divorce from a court in state X, P returns to state Y, where his marriage to his secretary is announced. D begins an action in state Y claiming that the *ex parte* decree issued by the court in state X is not entitled to full faith and credit in state Y and, therefore, P and D are still married. D contends that P failed to establish a bona fide domicile in state X and that state Y is entitled to examine that issue. Is P's divorce decree entitled to full faith and credit in state Y?

15. Assume that P and D are married for five years and live in state X. When their relationship breaks down, D leaves P to live with her parents in state Y. P files a petition for divorce in state X based on the ground of desertion. However, P failed to have the divorce summons and petition served on D in state Y, even though he knows the mailing address of D's parents and believes that she is living with them. P also failed to provide D with a notice of the date on which the divorce petition is to be heard by the court in state X. As a consequence, and without D's knowledge, the court in state X enters an *ex parte* divorce decree. A few weeks after the

divorce decree is entered, P dies. D learns of the divorce when she attends P's funeral. She then seeks her intestate share of P's estate as his wife. Will she be successful?

16. Assume that W and H were married for 20 years before their marriage broke down. Five years before they were divorced, W discovered that H was having an affair. H did not want to break up his marriage, and H signed what is referred to as a "reconciliation agreement." It read in part: "I agree that if any of my indiscretions after the signing of this agreement lead to and/or are the cause of a separation or divorce between me and my wife, that I will accept full responsibility for my action. By doing so, I agree that I will do the following: If I carry on an affair with X."

    There followed a list of certain agreed-upon, generous provisions for division of property, support, and attorney fees should H break the agreement. Last year, H moved out of the family home and resumed his affair with X. In her divorce action, W insists the court should enforce the provisions of the reconciliation agreement. H contends that he does not remember signing the agreement, and anyway, this is a no-fault jurisdiction even as to property distribution and an alimony award. This agreement, argues H, is based on fault. However, H continues, fault cannot be used in dividing property, etc., even if it is included in such an agreement, because its use is contrary to the state's present no-fault divorce policy. Should the court enforce the terms of the reconciliation agreement?

Explanations

13. The court will most likely rule that the decree issued by the court in state Y is valid and comports with due process. In this case, D had his day in court in state Y, where, via his lawyers, he contested personal jurisdiction. Unlike the fact situation in *Williams* I, the finding of personal jurisdiction was made in a proceeding in state Y where D appeared and participated. Full faith and credit requires that state X recognize the decree rendered by the court in state Y, which gained personal jurisdiction over both parties. *Sherrer v. Sherrer*, 334 U.S. 343 (1948). (Note also that D did not appeal the decision of the court in state Y. This may be considered as another significant factor in barring further litigation about the divorce in state X.)

14. Based on the Supreme Court decisions of *Williams I* and *Williams II*, state Y is entitled to determine for itself the jurisdictional facts upon which the

decree issued by the court in state X was based. D never appeared in the state X proceeding, so the issue of personal jurisdiction over D was never litigated. D will contend that P was never domiciled in good faith in state X and that he never intended to abandon his domicile in state Y. D's evidence includes the following: P rented a hotel room (temporary residence); retained and continued working at his job in state Y through the use of e-mail, fax, and telephone; brought his secretary to live with him in a hotel room in state X; and never changed the location of his residence for his bank account or his home mailing address. This is substantial evidence that P never intended in good faith to establish a domicile in state X. *See Huntington v. Huntington*, 262 P.2d 104 (Cal. App. 1953). On these facts, D may well succeed in her challenge.

15. D will claim that she was denied due process because P knew her mailing address and should have provided her with notice of the divorce proceeding. D's argument most likely will be successful, and as a result, the *ex parte* divorce decree will be voided. *See Keating v. Keating*, 855 A.2d 80 (Pa. Super. 2004) (first wife was legal wife of husband at the time of his death, even though husband had obtained a divorce from first wife in Guam and had married second wife, where first wife had no notice or opportunity to be heard in the divorce proceeding in Guam); *Dalton v. Dalton*, 59 N.Y.S.2d 68 (N.Y. App. 1945) (In divorce suit, service by publication, if permissible by local law, satisfies requirement of due process, at least where reasonably calculated to give defendant notice and opportunity to be heard). In *Mullane v. Central Hanover Bank & Trust Co.*, 339 U.S.306, 313 (1950), the court stated that "An elementary and fundamental requirement of due process in any proceeding which is to be accorded finality is notice reasonably calculated, under all the circumstances, to apprise interested parties of the pendency of the action and afford them an opportunity to present their objections."

16. As with many issues in family law, courts appear to disagree over whether to enforce such contracts. Courts have historically prohibited enforcement of contracts between husbands and wives that address marital issues. This has been true even if the agreement was designed to remedy marital problems. One early case explains:

> Compensation for wrongs, under such circumstances, cannot be made in money. Their adjustment of differences must be conclusively presumed to have sprung from mutual affection, the interests of home and children, and their well-being in society, and not to have been induced by greed of worldly gain. *See Miller v. Miller*, 35 N.W. 464, 464 (Iowa 1887); *Miller v. Miller*, 182, 42 N.W. 641, 642 (Iowa 1889). Public policy forbids such inquiries, and the sacredness of the relation demands that conjugal

> consortium be kept without the domain of bargain and sale. The position that the courts should not inquire into matters of domestic discord was affirmed most legislatures when they erased any consideration of fault in dissolution matters.

Fisher v. Koontz, 80 N.W. 551, 553 (1899).

However, reconciliation agreements are enforceable according to some legal treatises.

> There is no reason why an agreement to resume marital relations where one of the parties has just cause for divorce should not be sustained, and it is generally held that a promise made in consideration of such resumption and of the dismissal or forbearance to bring justified proceedings for divorce, or in compromise of legal proceedings for non-support, is binding, unless its provisions violate public policy in some other manner. These so-called reconciliation agreements have become quite common, courts often applying the same rules to them as to premarital or antenuptial agreements.

7 Williston on Contracts §16:20, at 460–462 (4th ed. 1997).

Furthermore, courts from several states have enforced reconciliation agreements under somewhat similar facts. For example, in *Flansburg v. Flansburg*, 581 N.E.2d 430, 437 (Ind. App. 1991), the court enforced a postnuptial agreement that made certain financial provisions in the event of a divorce or dissolution. The court said that such agreements could be enforced so long as they were "entered into freely and without fraud or misrepresentation or is not otherwise unconscionable"); *See Crawford v. Crawford*, 392 S.E.2d 675, 676 (S.C. App. 1990) (parties lived together for three years following the signing of the agreement, and court held that "the property settlement agreement and reconciliation agreement preclude reapportionment of the property covered by them except to the extent such property has increased in value due to the joint efforts of the parties"); *Laudig v. Laudig*, 624 A.2d 651, 652–53 (Pa. Super. 1993) (lower court had committed no error at law or abuse of discretion in holding that a postnuptial agreement barred a wife's right to additional marital assets in a divorce proceeding); *Whalen v. Whalen*, 581 S.W.2d 578, 579 (Ky. App. 1979) (affirming trial court's enforcement of an agreement providing for distribution of property in the event a reconciliation failed).

However, in the case on which this hypothetical was created, *In re Marriage of Cooper*, 763 N.W.2d 276 (Iowa 2009), the Iowa Court of Appeals held that after considering *Miller v. Miller*, 42 N.W. 641 (Iowa 1889), and the statutory factors that the legislature has provided for dividing property, all of which exclude a fault component, it found the agreement in violation of the public policy in that it is triggered a finding of fault.

CHAPTER 5

Child Custody and Parenting Plans

5.1. Introduction

Providing for the safety and well-being of children is one of the most important functions of the family court system. Although there is widespread agreement concerning the fundamental nature of this goal, achieving it remains a work in progress. Consequently, the law of child custody and access has evolved significantly over the last century, and it continues to garner substantial judicial, legislative, and media attention today.

As a practical matter, only a small percentage of child custody disputes are resolved through a trial in a traditional court. Instead, the vast majority of cases are settled by the parties and submitted to a court for review and final approval. Agreements are often reached through negotiation or participation in dispute resolution processes such as those described in Chapter 22.

THE IMPACT OF DIVORCE AND PARENTAL SEPARATION

5.2. Effects of Divorce and Separation on Children

With nearly 50 percent of marriages ending in divorce, researchers estimate that 40 percent of children have experienced or will experience the divorce of their parents. *See* Stephen J. Bahr, *Social Science Research on Family Dissolution: What It Shows and How It Might Be of Interest to Family Law Reformers*, 4 J.L. & Fam. Stud. 5 (2002).

A frequently cited study concludes that children's adjustment following divorce is linked to factors such as the absence of the noncustodial parent, the adjustment of the custodial parent, the conflict between the parents, economic hardship, and stressful life changes associated with divorce. *See* Paul R. Amato, *Children's Adjustment to Divorce: Theories, Hypotheses, and Empirical Support*, 55 J. Marriage & Fam. 23 (1993). A child whose parents exhibit a continuing high degree of conflict before, during, and after divorce may experience more difficulty adjusting than one whose parents have a more cooperative relationship. *See* Irwin Sandler et al., *Effects of Father and Mother Parenting on Children's Mental Health in High- and Low-Conflict Divorces*, 46 Fam. Ct. Rev. 282 (2008); Joan B. Kelly & Robert E. Emery, *Children's Adjustment Following Divorce: Risk and Resilience Perspectives*, 52 Fam. Rel. 352 (2003); Joan B. Kelly, *Children's Adjustment in Conflicted Marriage and Divorce: A Decade Review of Research*, 39 J. Am. Acad. Child Adolescent Psychiatry 963 (2000).

In some families experiencing such problems as intimate partner violence, child abuse, substance abuse, or severe mental illness, the health and well-being of children may be endangered unless a court restricts a parent's access to the child. *See* Janet Johnston, Vivienne Roseby, & Kathryn Kuehnle, *In the Name of the Child: A Developmental Approach to Understanding and Helping Children of Conflicted and Violent Divorce*, 2d ed. (Springer Publishing Co., 2009).

5.3. Divorce, Separation, and Parenting

Although a marital or cohabiting relationship ends at divorce or separation, couples with children usually continue to deal with each other as parents. Consequently, they must give careful thought to structuring their parental relationship and renewing their commitment to the children at this critical time.

Divorce or the breakup of a relationship where the parties are not married is a stressful experience for parents as well as for children. Parents typically face their own emotional and financial pressures as they also cope with the heightened needs of their children. A parent's ability to put the needs of children first is an important indicator of that parent's ability to safeguard the well-being of the children into the future.

Researchers estimate that 25 percent of parents ease into a co-parenting relationship, half disengage for a period of time and then become more cooperative, and 25 percent remain at odds indefinitely. *See* Carla B. Garrity & Mitchell A. Baris, *Caught in the Middle: Protecting the Children of High-Conflict Divorce* 27 (Jossey-Bass, Inc., 1994). Parents in the latter group are often dealing with serious challenges such as child abuse, intimate partner violence, substance abuse, and serious mental illness, and courts and family law professionals struggle with how best to protect their children while also serving them.

5.4. Parenting Education

In an effort to reduce conflict and help parents develop strategies to work cooperatively, some jurisdictions offer, and in some cases require, that parents attend sessions addressing the impact of divorce on children, co-parenting after divorce, and conflict resolution. The purpose of such classes is to ease the children's adjustment to divorce, prevent long-term emotional difficulties, and avoid relitigation of custody and visitation issues. *See* Amanda Sigal et al., *Do Parent Education Programs Promote Healthy Postdivorce Parenting? Critical Distinctions and a Review of the Evidence*, 49 Fam. Ct. Rev. 120 (2011) (discussing research on effectiveness of programs); Brenda Bacon & Brad McKenzie, *Parent Education After Separation and Divorce*, 42 Fam. Ct. Rev. 85 (2004).

While helpful to many parents, those with a history of intimate partner violence should not attend general parent education courses because of safety issues and because messages about co-parenting and enhanced communication may be dangerous for them. Instead, when intimate partner violence is an isssue, specialized programs stressing safety planning and separate parenting should be provided. Geri S. W. Fuhrmann et al., *Parent Education's Second Generation: Integrating Violence Sensitivity*, 37 Fam. & Conciliation Cts. Rev. 24 (1999).

Some jurisdictions mandate attendance at educational sessions, and parents who fail to comply risk being held in contempt of court and other sanctions. Other states have implemented adult education programs but leave the issue of compulsory attendance to the discretion of the court. A few states make attendance entirely optional. *See* Solveig Erickson & Nancy Ver Steegh, *Mandatory Divorce Education Classes: What Do the Parents Say?* 28 W. Mitchell L. Rev. 889, 895 (2001).

DEFINING CUSTODIAL RELATIONSHIPS

5.5. Overview

Previously when a divorce was granted, one parent received sole custody of a child and the other parent was granted "reasonable" visitation. Visitation would typically occur on weekends and for a few weeks in the summer.

As a result of changing societal expectations related to parenting, a variety of custodial arrangements have emerged over the last 40 years. Although traditional child custody terminology remains in widespread use, focus on creation of workable day-to-day parenting schedules has worked to erode some of the emphasis on predefined labels. Some states, as well as the American Law Institute (ALI), have introduced terminology designed to discourage conflict over the relative legal status of parents.

5.6. Legal Custody

"Legal custody" is a technical term used by courts to describe a parent's authority to make major decisions on behalf of a child. Decisions that a legal custodian might make include those about the child's religion, education, and medical treatment. Legal custody can be given to one parent, an arrangement that courts refer to as "sole legal custody," or it can be shared by the parents, referred to as "joint legal custody." In contrast, the ALI conceives of legal custody as "decision making responsibility." ALI, *Principles of the Law of Family Dissolution: Analysis and Recommendations* §2.03(4) (2002).

5.7. Physical Custody

"Physical custody" is a technical term that describes a parent's right to have a child reside with him or her and the obligation of that parent to provide for the routine daily care and control of the child. Physical custody can be awarded to one parent, which courts refer to as "sole physical custody," or it can be shared, in what courts term a "joint physical custody" arrangement.

5.8. Joint Legal and Physical Custody

When parents share "joint legal custody," which is a technical term used by a court, they agree to work together to make major decisions affecting the child. For example, they plan to agree on where the child should attend school, whether the child should have a major medical procedure, and what (if any) religious training the child should receive. Under a typical joint legal custody arrangement, neither parent has a superior right to make such decisions. Consequently, a well-drawn joint legal custody agreement will include procedures for resolving conflicts (such as attending mediation) short of returning to court.

In contrast, when parents share "joint physical custody," also a technical term used by the court, a child maintains a residence in both homes. Joint physical custody does not require precise 50-50 time-sharing. In practice, it is sometimes difficult to distinguish a sole physical custody arrangement in which the noncustodial or nonresidential parent has liberal overnight parenting time from a joint physical custody arrangement.

Joint custody, as it is commonly practiced, encompasses a wide variety of parenting arrangements. Some couples share legal custody, even though one of the parents is the sole physical custodian. Other couples share both legal and physical custody.

5.9. Parenting Plans

Family law professionals encourage creation of detailed parenting agreements tailored to meet the needs of individual families. These parenting plans typically include parenting time schedules, decision-making protocols, expectations for parental cooperation and communication, dispute resolution options, and financial support arrangements. *See* Andrew Schepard, *Children, Courts, and Custody: Interdisciplinary Models for Divorcing Families* (Cambridge U. Press, 2004). Instead of using traditional custody labels, parents may create their own terms or use labels such as "on-duty" and "off-duty" parent or "residential" and "nonresidential" parent.

Consistent with this trend in terminology and perspective, the ALI replaced the terms "custody" and "visitation" with the concept of "custodial responsibility" in an effort to avoid the win-lose framework present in some custody disputes. ALI, *Principles of the Law of Family Dissolution: Analysis and Recommendations* §2.03(3), cmt. e (2002). The ALI encourages parents to allocate parenting responsibility and plan for dispute resolution through the use of detailed parenting plans. §2.05. However, an exception is made for couples with a history of child maltreatment, domestic violence, substance abuse, or interference with the child's relationship with the other parent.

Even when parents agree to provisions in a parenting plan, courts review them to ensure that they are in the best interests of the child. *See Vollet v.* Vollet, 202 S.W.3d 72 (Mo. App. 2006). Using a slightly different standard, the ALI proposes that courts reject agreed parenting plans only in cases where the agreement is not "knowing or voluntary," or if the plan would be harmful to the child. §2.06.

EXAMPLES

Examples

1. P and D reached an agreement concerning the care of their children after divorce. They agreed to discuss and reach consensus on matters such as the children's religion and schooling. During the school year, they agree that the children are to reside with P Monday through Friday and spend every weekend living with D. During the summer, the children are to reside with D Monday through Friday and live with P every weekend. What technical legal description(s) or term(s) will a court most likely assign to this arrangement?

2. P and D had one child, who was a preschooler at the time of their divorce. The parties resided 50 miles from each other, and both sought sole physical custody of the child. The court found that neither parent was an ideal custodian, and the evidence showed that their relationship was filled with strife and disagreement. On its own motion, and to the

surprise of the parents, the court ordered that primary physical custody of the child would alternate between them every year once the child started school. The court viewed this arrangement as a way for the child to have ongoing contact with both parents. P appealed the decision, believing that such an arrangement would not be in the child's best interest because the child would have to change schools every year. What is the likely result on appeal?

3. P (mother) resides in North Carolina, and D (father) lives in Pennsylvania. When the parties were unable to agree on custodial arrangements, a court ordered that they alternate physical custody every week. How is an appellate court likely to view this arrangement?

4. P and D are the divorced parents of one child. They have joint legal custody. The child lives primarily with D (mother). D would like the child to be home-schooled, primarily for religious reasons, and she initiated home-schooling over P's objection. D has asserted that the decision affects the fundamental right of a parent to make decisions on religious upbringing. P sought, and the trial court entered, an order compelling attendance at a public school. D appealed the decision. What is the most likely outcome of the appeal?

5. Assume that P and D have two children when they divorce, and both seek custody. Both parties agree that the other is a fit parent. P and D testify that they have a hard time communicating, and that when they were living together, D often left the home to avoid having disagreements in the presence of the children. The parents attempted to share physical custody on a temporary basis, but their minor son reported feeling as though he did not have a home. The trial court awards sole legal and physical custody to P. D appeals. What is the likely outcome on appeal?

Explanations

1. A court will consider the agreement as constituting joint legal custody because P and D will share the major policy-making decisions regarding the children. P may claim to have sole physical custody because the children will reside with P the majority of the time during the school year and 60 percent of the time on an annual basis. D may argue that this arrangement constitutes joint physical custody because joint physical custody does not necessitate equal time-sharing and, over the course of the year, the children will reside with D 40 percent of the time. A court would likely agree with D and consider these parents to have

joint legal and physical custody. However, P would be considered to have sole physical custody were it not for the fact that the children will reside substantially with D during the summer.

2. In *Headrick v. Headrick*, 916 So. 2d 610 (Ala. App. 2005), the appellate court was concerned about the annually alternating custody arrangement, as are most courts. The court stated, "[T]he alternation of residence and primary physical custody guarantees a recurring, yearly disruption in this young child's life for which we find no justification in the record." *Id.* at 614. One of the concerns with a joint physical custody arrangement is that the child may feel as if he or she doesn't have a primary home. Such feelings could be exacerbated by alternating physical custody on a yearly basis. In addition, in this example, the trial court was not in the position of approving a parenting plan agreed to by the parties. Rather, it created the alternating arrangement on its own, and without the agreement of the parents. Given the fact that the parents had a history of conflict, this unorthodox arrangement would likely not benefit the child.

   In *Bainbridge v. Pratt*, 68 So.3d 310 (Fla. App. 2011), in which the court considered similar facts, the appellate court found that although there was no presumption against rotating custody, there must still be evidence supporting such an arrangement, and a parent must request and argue for the plan. The court was concerned about the workability of an annually alternating custody arrangement, especially where neither parent nor the child expressed an interest in it. *But see Mundy v. Devon*, 2006 WL 902233 (Del. Supr. Apr. 6, 2006) (court approved yearly alternating primary placement). Because of the difficulty of anticipating the needs of the child into the future, P and D would be well advised to attend mediation before the child starts school.

3. Not surprisingly, in *Durning v. Balent/Kurdilla*, 19 A.3d 1125 (Pa. Super. 2011), the appellate court reversed an order awarding alternating-week physical custody. Because the parents did not live near each other, the appellate court found the arrangement to be "unreasonable" and expressed concern about how the child would deal with lack of continuity at home and in school.

4. In *In re Kurowski*, 20 A.3d 306 (N.H. 2011), on which the example is based, P and D had a joint right to determine the child's school placement. When they could not agree, the trial court determined that the best interests of the child were served by school attendance. The standard on appeal was whether the trial court abused its discretion; however, there was no abuse of discretion because the trial court heard testimony from the Guardian *ad Litem* and the order referred to statutory factors regarding the child's best interests.

5. Although both parties would be fit parents, the award of joint physical or legal custody must still be in the child's best interest. In *Klimek v. Klimek*, 775 N.W.2d 444 (Neb. App. 2009), P prevailed on appeal. Both parents testified that the other was fit, but they could not agree on joint custody. Where P had taken on most of the parenting responsibilities and there was evidence that joint physical custody would be problematic, the appellate court found the trial court's award of sole custody was not an abuse of discretion.

PRESUMPTIONS

5.10. Overview

Faced with the difficult task of making custody and access decisions, courts and legislatures have historically relied on various preferences and presumptions to lend predictability to decision making and give effect to societal beliefs about the nature of the family. Because presumptions limit the discretion of judges to intervene on behalf of children, they have largely, but not entirely, been replaced by individualized determinations concerning "the best interests of the child."

5.11. Historical Paternal Presumption

Under the English common law, fathers maintained nearly absolute control over their children. At marriage, a wife's legal identity merged with her husband's, and she had no right to property or to custody of children born during the marriage. The paternal presumption was seen to benefit the child because the mother often had no means of supporting the child in the father's absence. The father also had the right to appoint a guardian other than the mother in the event of his death. W. Blackstone, *Commentaries on the Laws of England* 446, 453 (9th ed. 1783). Only if the father engaged in highly immoral conduct might a mother be awarded custody.

The paternal presumption began to give way in 1873, when the English parliament granted women the right to have custody of children who were under the age of 16. Early American decisions initially adopted the common law view, but the paternal preference nevertheless began to wane by the end of the nineteenth century.

5.12. Historical Maternal Presumption

By the 1920s and 1930s, many American jurisdictions replaced the paternal preference with the "tender years" maternal presumption. Children of "tender years" included preschool children and sometimes children through the age of ten. These young children were seen as best cared for by mothers who would provide for their physical and emotional needs while the father worked outside the home. As was stated in *Freeland v. Freeland*, 159 P. 698, 699 (Wash. 1916), the presumption could be overcome by showing that the mother was unfit:

> Mother love is a dominant trait in even the weakest of women, and as a general thing surpasses the paternal affection for the common offspring, and, moreover, a child needs a mother's care even more than a father's. For these reasons courts are loathe to deprive the mother of the custody of her children and will not do so unless it be shown clearly that she is so far an unfit and improper person to be instructed with such custody as to endanger the welfare of the children.

In *Freeland*, the presumption operated in favor of the mother, even though she had been "indiscreet in her conduct with men." *See also Krieger v. Krieger*, 81 P.2d 1081 (Idaho 1938) (tender years presumption applied even over preference of eight-year-old child to live with father).

During the late 1960s and early 1970s, societal views shifted and fathers were viewed as having equal competence as mothers when it came to raising young children. As a result, courts and legislatures gradually became more concerned with the best interests of the child than with the sex of the parent seeking custody. In some jurisdictions, application of the tender years presumption was held to be unconstitutional. *Ex parte Devine*, 398 So. 2d 686 (Ala. 1981) (tender years presumption represents unconstitutional gender-based classification that discriminates between fathers and mothers in child custody proceedings solely on the basis of gender).

5.13. Historical Primary Caretaker Presumption

Although most states adopted the sex-neutral, "best interests of the child" standard during the 1970s, some states presumed that the interests of a young child are best served by placing him or her with the "primary caretaker." The primary caretaker was defined as the parent who performed the following types of tasks for the child:

1. preparing and planning meals;
2. bathing, grooming, and dressing;

3. purchasing, cleaning, and caring for clothes;
4. medical care, including nursing and trips to physicians;
5. arranging for social interaction among peers after school . . . ;
6. arranging alternative care, i.e., baby sitting, day-care, etc.;
7. putting the child to bed at night, attending to child in the middle of the night, waking the child in the morning;
8. disciplining, i.e., teaching general manners and toilet training;
9. educating, i.e., relgious, cultural, social, etc.; and
10. teaching elementary skills, i.e., reading, writing and arithmetic . . .

Pikula v. Pikula, 374 N.W.2d 705, 713 (Minn. 1985) (citing *Garska v. McCoy*, 278 S.E.2d 357 (W. Va. 1981)).

The primary caretaker presumption was based on the child's need for a stable and continuous relationship with a primary parent. Preference was given to the parent who was most experienced in caring for the child and who had the strongest history of meeting the child's daily needs.

Critics of the primary caretaker presumption contended that despite the sex-neutral language, the presumption favored women. In addition, courts sometimes had difficulty identifying a primary parent, and the preference had little application to older children such as teenagers.

States no longer use the primary caretaker preference as a presumption. However, some states use it as a factor to be considered among others in determining the best interest of the child. *See, e.g.*, *Gianvito v. Gianvito*, 975 A.2d 1164 (Pa. Super. 2009) (a trial court is to give positive consideration to the parent who has acted as their child's primary caretaker); *Sitts v. Sitts*, 74 A.D.3d 1722 (N.Y. App. 2010) (wife was primary caretaker).

The ALI incorporated the primary caretaker tasks into its definition of caretaking functions. *See* ALI, *Principles of the Law of Family Dissolution: Analysis and Recommendations* (2002). The ALI suggests that, in the absence of an agreed-upon parenting plan, post-divorce caretaking should mirror pre-divorce caretaking patterns. §2.03, cmt. g. In other words, caretaking should be allocated in a way that "approximates the proportion of time each parent spent performing caretaking functions" prior to separation. §2.08. If one parent performed the bulk of caretaking functions prior to divorce, the approximation standard would function similarly to the primary caretaker presumption. However, if caretaking tasks were shared more equally during the marriage, that past arrangement would be carried forward after the divorce. *See* Katharine T. Bartlett, *U.S. Custody Law and Trends in the Context of the ALI Principles of the Law of Family Dissolution*, 10 Va. J. Soc. Pol'y & L. 5, 18 (2002).

5.14. Historical and Contemporary Natural Parent Presumption

As against third parties, parents are entitled to custody of their children unless there is clear evidence of unfitness. *McDermott v. Dougherty*, 869 A.2d 751 (Md. 2005). Under the law, so-called third parties include stepparents and grandparents, as well as others. *See State of N.M. ex rel. CYFD v. Lisa A.*, 187 P.3d 189 (N.M. App. 2008); *Eifert v. Eifert*, 724 N.W.2d 109 (N.D. 2006); *Webb v. Webb*, 546 So. 2d 1062 (Fla. App. 1989) (trial court abused discretion in awarding custody to stepparent without clear and convincing evidence that mother was unfit); *Brewer v. Brewer*, 533 S.E.2d 541 (N.C. App. 2000) (presumed that fit parent will act in best interests of child). *But see Bennett v. Jeffreys*, 356 N.E.2d 277 (N.Y. App. 1976) (extraordinary circumstances required consideration of best interests of child).

The preference in favor of natural parents remains in effect today. However, courts have struggled with situations in which a parent seeking custody has had little or no contact with a child and the child has lived with a third party for an extended period. *See* Elizabeth Barker Brandt, *De Facto Custodians: A Response to the Needs of Informal Kin Caregivers?* 38 Fam. L.Q. 291 (2004).

The ALI deals with these situations by incorporating a broader definition of "parent," including parents by estoppel and *de facto* parents. ALI, *Principles of the Law of Family Dissolution: Analysis and Recommendations* §2.03(b), (c) (2002). A parent by estoppel is a person other than a legal parent who (1) is obligated to pay child support, (2) lived with the child and accepted parental responsibility for at least two years in the good-faith belief that he was the child's father, or (3) lived with the child since birth and acted as a parent pursuant to a parenting or co-parenting agreement.

A *de facto* parent is a person other than a legal parent or parent by estoppel who for at least two years (1) lived with the child and (2) performed the bulk of caretaking functions or as many caretaking functions as the parent with whom the child resided (3) either by agreement or due to the failure or inability of the legal parent to do so.

5.15. Contemporary Joint Legal and Physical Custody Presumptions

Some legislatures have created presumptions that joint legal custody and, to a lesser extent, joint physical custody are in the best interests of children. The presumptions vary considerably across states. For example, some state presumptions have limited application, such as when parents agree to share joint legal custody and/or joint physical custody, or when a parent requests a form of joint custody. In contrast, other states have adopted "preferences" for joint legal and/or physical custody or have decided that joint legal and physical custody decisions should be determined solely on the facts of each situation. A few states disfavor joint custody, particularly joint physical custody, and some states have presumptions against joint custody in cases involving intimate partner violence.

Careful reading of statutory language and relevant case law is necessary to determine the policy in any given state. This is especially true because there has been a good deal of recent legislative activity on the topic:

> As of 2011, forty-seven states and the District of Columbia have statutes that specifically authorize joint or shared custody. Eleven states and D.C. declare a general presumption in favor of joint custody. Seventeen states use a presumption in favor of joint custody if both parents agree to it. In the remaining states, joint custody is an explicit option without any presumptions. Two states require the consent of both parents without any presumptions.

Linda D. Elrod & Robert G. Spector, *A Review of the Year in Family Law: Numbers of Disputes Increase*, 45 Fam. L. Q. 443, 468 (2012).

The ALI, in the absence of a parenting plan, presumes that joint decision making (joint legal custody) will be in the best interests of a child if each parent has performed a reasonable share of parenting tasks and there has been no intimate partner violence or child abuse. ALI, *Principles of the Law of Family Dissolution: Analysis and Recommendations* §2.09 (2002).

Whether by presumption or otherwise, joint legal and physical custody arrangements have become more common. Researchers estimate that joint legal custody is the final disposition in nearly 80 percent of cases, whereas joint physical custody is the result in 20 percent of cases. *See* Eleanor E. Maccoby & Robert J. Mnookin, *Dividing the Child: Social and Legal Dilemmas of Custody* 108, 113 (1997). Viewed positively, this trend signifies an increasing commitment to cooperative parenting after divorce. *See* Isolina Ricci, *Mom's House, Dad's House: Making Two Homes for Your Child* (Simon & Schuster, 1997).

Nevertheless, experts caution that joint legal and/or physical custodial arrangements are not suitable for all families. In a lengthy decision holding that recent statutory amendments did not create a presumption of joint physical care, the Iowa Supreme Court analyzed research on joint legal and physical custody arrangements and identified four factors for determining whether joint physical care is in the best interests of a child: (1) stability and continuity of caregiving; (2) ability of parents to communicate and "show mutual respect"; (3) degree of parental conflict; and (4) parental agreement on approach to daily matters. *In re Marriage of Hansen*, 733 N.W.2d 683 (2007). In addition, the court relied on "growing support" for the assertion that in terms of benefit to the child, the quality of contact with a nonresidential parent may outweigh the quantity of contact. *See also* Christy M. Buchanan & Parissa L. Jahromi, *A Psychological Perspective on Shared Custody Arrangements*, 43 Wake Forest L. Rev. 419 (2008).

Research indicates that shared physical care is most viable for families with particular traits and characteristics:

> It [shared care] was a parenting arrangement that proved viable for a small and distinct group of families, who shared the following profile: electing a shared arrangement, as opposed to having legally enforceable orders to adopt such an arrangement; geographical proximity (within a moderate car trip); the ability of parents to get along sufficiently well; a business-like working relationship between parents; child-focused arrangements; a commitment by everyone to make shared care work; family-friendly work practices for both mothers and fathers; financial comfort (particularly for women); and shared confidence that the father is a competent parent.

Jennifer E. McIntosh, *Legislating for Shared Parenting: Exploring Some Underlying Assumptions*, 47 Fam. Ct. Rev. 389, 391 (2009). *See also* Jennifer McIntosh, et al., *Post-Separation Parenting Arrangements: Patterns and Developmental Outcomes for Infants and Children, Report to the Australian Government Attorney-General's Department* (2010) (successful shared physical care may involve older children and parents who live in proximity and value flexibility).

Experts agree that joint legal and physical custody arrangements are clearly inappropriate if parents have a history of intimate partner violence, high conflict, or other issues that have serious implications for parenting When underlying safety and parenting concerns are not accounted for and addressed, joint legal and physical custody arrangements exacerbate problems and may place children in danger. Janet R. Johnston, *A Child-Centered Approach to High Conflict and Domestic Families: Differential Assessment and Interventions*, 12 J. Fam. Stud. 15 (2006); Janet R. Johnston, *Building Multidisciplinary Professional Partnerships with the Court on Behalf of High-Conflict Divorcing Families and Their Children: Who Needs What Kind of Help?* 22 U. Ark. Little Rock L. Rev. 453 (2000).

EXAMPLES

Examples

6. Assume that P and D were married in 2007 and had one child, who was born in 2009. When P and D decided to divorce, they could not agree on a parenting arrangement, and the matter was set for trial. At the time of the custody hearing, the child was 28 months old. The court determined that both P and D were fit parents, even though the father (D) showed some immaturity and worked long hours and the mother (P) had some psychological problems. The court granted physical custody to P, taking "personal notice of the natural bond that develops between infants and a mother, especially when the mother breast-feeds the infant" and finding that "by the very nature of the age and gender of the minor child (28-month-old female)," placement with the father "would be a negative aspect in the

weighing of the positives and negatives." The father appealed, claiming that the court's reasoning amounted to an application of the historical tender years doctrine. The mother argued that this was a permissible consideration under the best-interests standard. What is the likely result of D's appeal?

7. P (father) sued D (mother) for divorce in 1986. They lived in a state that adopted the primary caretaker presumption. P and D had two children, who were two and five years old. D worked as an airline attendant and was consequently away from home overnight from Monday through Friday each week. She also worked one weekend per month. When she was at home, she helped care for the children by cooking meals, doing laundry, and entertaining them. P worked at home and was responsible for all the children's care while D was away from home. A year before the divorce, P went into treatment for an alcohol problem, and although he did not drink after his release, D was afraid that P would relapse while caring for the children. Both P and D sought custody of the children. Who would have been likely to prevail if the court applied the primary caretaker presumption to this dispute?

8. Assume that P (mother) and D (father) are the parents of one child, C. Because of severe alcohol dependency ultimately resulting in her incarceration, P was no longer involved with the child. D worked as a merchant seaman and was at sea for lengthy periods of time. Consequently, C's grandparents cared for C for the majority of a period of four years following his birth. The grandparents petitioned the court for custody of C, alleging that C needed stability and that it would be in C's best interest if custody were awarded to the grandparents. D promised to seek other employment and argued that he had acted responsibly in arranging for the child to be cared for in his absence. Without making a finding that D was an unfit parent, the court awarded custody of C to the grandparents, and D appealed. What will D argue, and what is the likely outcome?

Explanations

6. If this case had taken place in 1930, the mother of the young child would be the preferred custodian unless she was proved to be unfit. However, today the maternal presumption is no longer in effect, and courts do not award custody based on presumptions favoring either sex. Consequently, in *Greer v. Greer*, 624 S.E.2d 423 (N.C. App. 2006), on which this example is based, D prevailed on appeal. In that jurisdiction, the "tender years presumption" had been abolished by statute, and the appellate court agreed with D's argument that the trial court improperly applied it in

this case. It said that the best interests of the child is the appropriate test and is to be determined from the actual facts, without reference to any presumptions.

7. In a jurisdiction that applied the primary caretaker presumption, P would have prevailed as the primary caretaker of the couple's young children. He was the parent who spent more time feeding, disciplining, clothing, bathing, and generally caring for the children. D would probably argue that she performed these caretaking tasks when she was at home and that she should not be penalized for working long hours to meet the financial needs of the family. However, she would be unsuccessful because the primary caretaker presumption was intended to provide stability for the children, who in this case had been primarily cared for by their father. D would argue that because of his alcohol problem, P was not a fit parent and, consequently, the primary caretaker doctrine should not have applied. However, treatment for an alcohol problem would not be sufficient to show that D was not a fit parent. Here, no facts are presented showing that D was currently drinking or that his alcohol use was detrimental to the children. Although some states use "primary caretaker" as one factor in determining the best interests of the child, it is no longer used as a custodial presumption. Today, P and D would be encouraged to create a parenting plan that would allow both of them to have strong continuing relationships with the children.

8. D will argue that he is entitled to custody of C because he has not been found to be an unfit parent. Under the natural parent presumption, if D is fit, he is entitled to custody even if C might be "better raised" by the grandparents. In *McDermott v. Dougherty*, 869 A.2d 751 (Md. 2005), the court found that the father's employment at sea did not constitute an extraordinary circumstance sufficient to overcome the preference for the natural parent. The court stated:

> In the balancing of court-created or statutorily-created "standards," such as "the best interest of the child" test, with fundamental constitutional rights, in private custody actions involving private third-parties where the parents are fit, absent extraordinary (*i.e.*, exceptional) circumstances, the constitutional right is the ultimate determinative factor; and only if the parents are unfit or extraordinary circumstances exist is the "best interest of the child" test to be considered.

Id. at 808.

MODEL ACTS

5.16. Uniform Marriage and Divorce Act

A majority of the states have adopted statutes providing that custody should be awarded based on the best interests of the child. Many of these statutes are patterned on §402 of the Uniform Marriage and Divorce Act (UMDA), which states:

> The court shall determine custody in accordance with the best interest of the child. The court shall consider all relevant factors including:
>
> (1) the wishes of the child's parent or parents as to his custody;
>
> (2) the wishes of the child as to his custodian;
>
> (3) the interaction and interrelationship of the child with his parent or parents, his siblings, and any other person who may significantly affect the child's best interest;
>
> (4) the child's adjustment to his home, school, and community; and
>
> (5) the mental and physical health of all individuals involved.
>
> The court shall not consider conduct of a proposed custodian that does not affect his relationship to the child.

Some states have legislated additional factors to be considered in determining the best interests of the child. Examples include factors relating to the child's primary caretaker, the child's cultural background, the effect of domestic abuse on the child, and the propensity of each parent to encourage continuing contact between the child and the other parent.

Although widely used, the best interest standard has been criticized because of its indeterminate nature. Despite the enumerated factors, judges exercise substantial discretion in applying the standard, and this can lead to unpredictable and sometimes arbitrary results. Nevertheless the best interests standard remains popular because focuses attention on the particular needs of individual chidren involved in a custody determination.

5.17. American Law Institute

The ALI suggests an alternative definition of the best interests of the child that makes fairness between the parents clearly secondary to the child's interests. *See* ALI, *Principles of the Law of Family Dissolution: Analysis and Recommendations* (2002). Under §2.02, the child's best interests are served by parental planning and agreement, continuity in attachments, contact with both parents, caretaking by skilled and loving adults who place a priority on it, avoidance of conflict and violence, and "expeditious" decision making. The ALI favors the use of agreed parenting plans to achieve these goals. §2.05. But, if agreement is not reached, the ALI allocates custodial responsibility in a way that will "approximate" the proportion of caretaking done by each parent prior to the divorce. §2.08. Exceptions may be made to accommodate the wishes of some children, to avoid separating siblings, to avoid harm to a child, and for other reasons listed in §2.08(1). Joint decision-making responsibility is presumed to be in the child's best interest unless a contrary showing is made. §2.09.

STANDARDS FOR DETERMINING THE BEST INTERESTS OF THE CHILD

5.18. Race

The Supreme Court has held that courts cannot use race as the sole or decisive factor in awarding child custody. In *Palmore v. Sidoti*, 466 U.S. 429 (1984), the United States Supreme Court held that the lower court improperly failed to consider the relative qualifications of both parents and erred in depriving the mother of the custody of her child because she had entered into an interracial marriage.

Courts have consistently interpreted *Palmore* as stopping short of prohibiting the consideration of race in matters of child custody. Thus, so long as race is not the sole consideration for custody decisions, but only one of several factors, it is not an unconstitutional consideration. *See, e.g.*, J.H.H. v. *O'Hara*, 878 F.2d 240, 245 (8th Cir. 1989) (declining to read *Palmore* as "a broad proscription against the consideration of race in matters of child custody"); *Drummond v. Fulton County Department of Family & Children's Services*, 563 F.2d 1200, 1204-1206 (5th Cir. 1977) (*en banc*) (determining that use of race as merely one factor in making adoption decisions is constitutional), *cert. denied*, 437 U.S. 910 (1978); *Tallman v. Tabor*, 859 F. Supp. 1078 (E.D. Mich. 1994) (holding that race can be considered in determining custody so long as race is not the sole consideration); *In re Davis*, 465 A.2d 614, 621-629 (Pa. 1983) (holding that trial court should have considered race as a factor in making foster placement decision); *Farmer v. Farmer*, 439 N.Y.S.2d 584, 588 (1981) (stating that "the general rule appears to be that race is simply one factor among many others which should be considered in determining what is in the child's best interest"). The ALI prohibits court consideration of race or ethnicity. §2.12(1)(a).

5.19. Religion

If divorcing parents have religious differences, constitutional protections concerning the free exercise of religion may come into play and courts cannot favor one religious tradition over another. Neverthless, courts can consider the compatibility of a parent's religious behavior with the health and well-being of a child. As the Kansas Supreme Court recently ruled:

> Disapproval of mere *belief or nonbelief* cannot be a consideration in a custody determination — judges are not trained to mediate theological disputes. Yet consideration of religiously motivated *behavior* with an impact on a child's welfare cannot be ignored. It is one of the many relevant factors that must be part of the holistic custody calculus required under Kansas law.

Harrison v. Tauheed, 256 P.3d 851, 864 (Kan. 2011). *See also Hicks v. Cook*, 288 S.W.3d 244 (Ark. App. 2008) ("religious beliefs and practices are only material as they affect children's best interests"); *Sagar v. Sagar*, 781 N.E.2d 54 (Mass. App. 2003).

The ALI prohibits consideration of a parent's religious practices other than as necessary to protect the child from harm or to allow the child to continue to practice a religion that is significant to the child. ALI, *Principles of the Law of Family Dissolution: Analysis and Recommendations* §2.12(1)(c) (2002).

5.20. Disability

Under §102(5) of the UMDA, courts are instructed to consider the mental and physical health of all the parties. This does not give courts license to discriminate against parents with disabilities. Rather, this language has been interpreted to require the courts to make case-by-case determinations concerning the effect of the disability on the child. *See Arneson v. Arneson*, 670 N.W.2d 904 (S.D. 2003); *Schumm v. Schumm*, 510 N.W.2d 13 (Minn. App. 1993).

5.21. Child's Preference

Most courts will consider "the wishes of the child as to his custodians" as described in §402 of the UMDA. This broad language is tempered by the court's discretion to determine whether the child has sufficient maturity to express a meaningful preference. Although age is not the sole consideration in making this determination, teenagers are more often consulted than younger children. *See* Cal. Fam. Code §3042(c) (2011) (permitting children 14 and older to address the court); Randi L. Dulaney, *Children Should Be Seen AND Heard in Florida Custody Determinations*, 25 Nova L. Rev. 815 (2001) (discussing various state statutes regarding child preference). The ALI makes an exception to the "approximation" rule to accommodate the "firm and reasonable preference" of a child of a specific age. ALI, *Principles of the Law of Family Dissolution: Analysis and Recommendations* §208(1)(b) (2002).

When children are consulted, the judge will evaluate the reasons behind any views expressed by the child. For example, in *In re Marriage of Mehlmauer*, 131 Cal. Rptr. 325 (Cal. App. 1976), the court chose not to defer to the preference of a 14-year-old boy who preferred to live with his father because the father allowed him to wear his hair longer and stay out later. In contrast, in *McMillen v. McMillen*, 602 A.2d 845 (Pa. 1992), the court considered the preference of an 11-year-old child to live with his father where the two homes were equally suitable but the boy testified that his stepfather frightened and upset him and that he was left unattended by his mother and stepfather after school.

Procedure. If a judge decides to seek information concerning a child's perspective, §404 of the UMDA provides for two procedural alternatives: a judge can interview the child in chambers, on the record with the attorneys present; or a judge can "seek the advice" of a professional who will submit a written report to the court. In either event, care must be taken to avoid undue parental influence or coercion on the child being interviewed. *See Couch v. Couch*, 146 S.W.3d 923 (Ky. 2004) (mother entitled to access *in camera* interview tape). The Supreme Court of Wyoming recently elaborated on court discretion to design a suitable process for consulting a child:

> [T]he district court could have conducted the interview in chambers with counsel, recorded the interview, required the child to testify in court, appointed a neutral third party to speak with the child and report back to the parties and the court, or fashioned another suitable procedure for presenting the evidence. By not fashioning any procedure, not obtaining the evidence and consequently not considering the child's preference, the district court abused its discretion.

Holiday v. Holiday, 247 P.3d 29, 33 (Wy. 2011).

If a child is interviewed *in camera*, a court may encounter a variety of procedural decisions related to minimizing stress for the child, determining who will be present, deciding whether counsel may ask questions, and considering the extent to which and in what form parents should have access to the information. *See Ynclan v. Woodward*, 237 P.3d 145 (Okla. 2010).

A child's perspective may be communicated to the court through channels other than a direct conversation with the judge. For example, child custody evaluators (typically neutral mental health professionals) may be appointed to meet with children (and other family members) as part of an investigation in a contested child custody case.

Child's representative. Section 310 of the UMDA provides that the court may appoint an attorney to represent a child. However, this is relatively rare in most jurisdictions. In contrast, courts sometimes appoint a guardian *ad litem* who acts in the child's best interest as opposed to carrying out the child's wishes. *See* Andrew Schepard, *Children, Courts, and Custody* (Cambridge Univ. Press 2004); *see also* ALI, *Principles of the Law of Family Dissolution: Analysis and Recommendations* §2.13 (2002).

Alternative processes. When parents participate in alternative dispute resolution (ADR) processes such as mediation, children may have additional avenues for involvment. Jennifer McIntosh, et al., *Child-Focused and Child-Inclusive Divorce Mediation: Comparative Outcomes from a Prospective Study of Postseparation* Adjustment, 46 Fam. Ct. Rev. 105 (2008) (discussing method of child-inclusive mediation); Joan B. Kelly, *Psychological and Legal Interventions for Parents and Children in Custody and Access Disputes: Current Research and Practice*, 10 Va. J. Soc. Pol'y & L. 129 (2002) (discussing ramifications of excluding children from the process).

5.22. Separating Siblings

Courts avoid separating biological siblings when fashioning child custody arrangements. Unless there are compelling reasons to separate them, siblings are kept together to maintain stability and support their relationships. *See Johnson v. Johnson*, 66 So. 3d 784 (Ala. App. (2011) (separation of siblings must be shown to be in their best interest); *In re Marriage of Heath*, 18 Cal. Rptr. 3d 760 (Cal. App. 2004) (court improperly found detriment to one child based on sibling's disability). The ALI makes an exception to the "approximation" standard in order to keep siblings together. ALI, *Principles of the Law of Family Dissolution: Analysis and Recommendations* §2.08(1)(c) (2002).

Research suggests that children who are separated from siblings at divorce tend to be wider apart in age, exhibit behavior problems, have different parental preferences, or have needs best met by one parent. David M. Shumaker et al., *The Forgotten Bonds: The Assessment and Contemplation of Sibling Attachment in Divorce and Parental Separation*, 59 Fam. Ct. Rev. 46, 50 (2011).

5.23. Parental Conduct Not Affecting the Child: The Nexus Test

Many states have adopted statutory language contained in §402 of the UMDA preventing courts from considering parental conduct that does not affect the parent's relationship with the child. Under the nexus test, evidence concerning parental behavior is relevant to a child custody decision only if the parental behavior affects the parent's relationship with the child; in other words, there must be a nexus between the parental activity and harm to the child.

Whether parental conduct affects the child is a question of fact that the trial court must determine on a case-by-case basis. *See, e.g. Thompson v. Pafundi*, 8 A.3d 476 (Vt. 2010) (trial court judge appropriately considered mother's continued drug use and apparently routine decision to drive without a license, particularly as they concerned her ability to provide guidance to her young daughter); *Jarrett v. Jarrett*, 78 Ill.2d 337 (Ill. 2979) (statute does not penalize conduct which is essentially private and discreet); Minn. Stat. §518.17, subd. 1(b) (2006) (court may not consider conduct that does not affect the proposed custodian's relationship with the child).

5.24. Gay and Lesbian Parents

The nexus test has been used in cases where one parent is gay or lesbian. While some courts have hesitated to award custody to gay or lesbian parents, other courts have considered what, if any, effect the parent's sexual orientation has upon the child or children. *See Hollon v. Hollon*, 784 So. 2d 943 (Miss. 2001); *Massey-Holt v. Holt*, 255 S.W.3d 603 (Tenn. App. 2007). The nexus test view is consistent with the position taken by the American Psychological Association in passing a resolution stating that sexual orientation should not be the sole consideration in making custody decisions. The ALI specifically prohibits court consideration of the sexual orientation of the parent. ALI, *Principles of the Law of Family Dissolution: Analysis and Recommendations* §2.12(1)(d) (2002).

5.25. Cohabitation

In the past, a parent's cohabitation with a member of the opposite sex would typically result in loss of custody. *See Jarret v. Jarret*, 449 U.S. 927 (1980). However, under §402 of the UMDA, cohabitation is relevant only to the extent that the parent's sexual relationship adversely affects the child or children. Similarly, the ALI prohibits consideration of a parent's extramarital sexual behavior unless it harms the child. ALI, *Principles of the Law of Family Dissolution: Analysis and Recommendations* §2.12(1)(e) (2002). *See* Margaret F. Brinig, *Feminism and Child Custody Under Chapter Two of the American Law Institute's Principles of the Law of Family Dissolution*, 8 Duke J. Gender L. & Pol'y 301, 312 (2001).

5.26. Careers

Despite the gender-neutral language of the "best interests" test, working mothers sometimes fear that their careers could work against them in a custody dispute. This was the case in *Rowe v. Franklin*, 663 N.E.2d 955 (Ohio App. 1995), in which the trial court was found to have abused its discretion by focusing on a mother's behavior (including her enrollment in law school) rather than the best interests of the child. *See also Burchard v. Garay*, 724 P.2d 486 (Cal. 1986) (not permissible for court to award custody of child in day care based on economic advantage of father with new stay-at-home wife); *Linda R. v. Richard E.*, 162 A.D.2d 48 (N.Y. 1990) (mother who worked outside the home was not a "remote-control" mother). Fathers also sometimes fear that their employment, particularly if they work long hours or travel frequently, may hinder their chances of being awarded sole or joint physical custody of their children. The ALI prohibits consideration of the relative earning capacity of the parents. ALI, *Principles of the Law of Family Dissolution: Analysis and Recommendations* §2.12(1)(f) (2002).

5.27. Cooperative Parent Provisions

Most states encourage or require courts to consider the extent to which a proposed custodial parent is likely to encourage ongoing contact between the child and the other parent. These are known as "cooperative" or "friendly" parent provisions, and the idea behind them is to encourage awards of custody to the parent who is most likely to support the child's relationship with the noncustodial parent.

These provisions have come under attack when applied to situations involving intimate partner violence, serious substance abuse and other situations where the "uncooperative" parent is acting to protect children. Consequently, some states make this factor inapplicable if there is a history of family violence. Peter G. Jaffe et al., *Child Custody and Domestic Violence: A Call for Safety and Accountability* 68 (2003). *See also* ALI, *Principles of the Law of Family Dissolution: Analysis and Recommendations* §2.11(1)(d) (2002).

5.28. Intimate Partner Violence

Unfortunately, in approximately half of families experiencing intimate partner violence, children are also physically abused. In other cases, children are harmed by witnessing intimate partner violence. Jeffrey L. Edleson & Oliver J. Williams, "Involving Men Who Batter in Their Children's Lives," in *Parenting by Men Who Batter: New Directions for Assessment and Intervention* 12-15 (Jeffrey L. Edleson & Oliver J. Williams eds., 2007). *See also* Janis Wolak & David Finkelhor, "Children Exposed to Partner Violence," in *Partner Violence* 71-80 (Jana L. Jasinski et al. eds., 1998).

As states moved away from fault divorce and adopted provisions preventing courts from considering parental conduct that did not affect the child, some courts mistakenly viewed intimate partner violence as irrelevant to child custody determinations. But today, nearly every state requires courts to consider the presence of intimate partner violence when determining custody. *See Barry v. Barry*, 862 N.E. 2d 143, 146 (Ohio App. 2006) ("We cannot conceive how domestic violence by one spouse against another could not be relevant in a determination of an allocation of parental rights and responsibilities regarding their children."). Some states have created rebuttable presumptions against awards of custody to parents with a history of intimate partner violence. *See* Nancy K. D. Lemon, *Statutes Creating Rebuttable Presumptions Against Custody to Batterers: How Effective Are They?* 28 Wm. Mitchell L. Rev. 601 (2001); Nancy Ver Steegh, *Differentiating Types of Domestic Violence: Implications for Child Custody*, 65 La. L. Rev. 1379, 1422-1426 (2005).

The ALI requires special written findings before a parent who has engaged in intimate parnter violence is allowed to have custodial responsibility or decision-making responsibility for a child. The burden is placed on the parent who has committed intimate parnter violence to show that such contact will not endanger family members. ALI, *Principles of the Law of Family Dissolution: Analysis and Recommendations* §2.11(3) (2002).

Family courts and family law professionals continue to grapple with issues such as how to differentiate among families experiencing intimate partner violence, the development and use of effective screening protocols, the extent to which families can safely participate in court processes and services, ways to assure appropriate outcomes for children, and the repercussions of changing family court roles and diminishing resources. Nancy Ver Steegh & Clare Dalton, *Report from the Wingspread Conference on Domestic Violence and Family Courts*, 46 Fam. Ct. Rev. 454 (2008).

When intimate partner violence is an issue, special care must be taken in making child custody decisions and creating parenting plans. Researchers suggest that courts confronted with conflicting needs and multiple stakeholders implement the following priorities:

1. Protect children directly from violent, abusive, and neglectful environments.
2. Provide for the safety, support, and the well-being of parents who are victim-recipients of abuse (with the assumption that they will then be better able to protect their child).
3. Respect and empower victim parents to make their own decisions and direct their own lives (thereby recognizing the state's limitations in the role of *loco parentis*).
4. Hold perpetrators accountable for their past and future actions (in the context of family proceedings, have them acknowledge the problem and take measures to correct abusive behavior).
5. Allow and promote the least restrictive plan for parent-child access *that benefits the child*, along with parents' reciprocal rights.

If all five goals cannot be achieved simultaneously, the lower priorities (those with higher numbers on the list above) should be abandoned successively. Janet Johnston, et al., *In the Name of the Child: A Developmental Approach to Understanding and Helping Children of Conflicted and Violent Divorce* 326 (2009).

Examples

9. In the case of *Jones v. Jones*, 832 N.E.2d 1057 (Ind. App. 2005), P and D were the divorcing parents of one child. They both practiced Wicca, which is a form of paganism. The court awarded them joint legal custody and awarded D sole physical custody of their child. The judge directed the parents to "take such steps as are needed to shelter [the child] from involvement and observation of these non-mainstream religious beliefs and rituals." Both parents appealed the decision, alleging that the trial judge could not require that they shelter their child from thir non-mainstream religious beliefs and rituals. What was the most likely outcome of the appeal?

10. Assume that P and D have a child together. D (mother) is a chiropractor who believes in holistic medicine and who, for religious reasons, did not want the child to be vaccinated. She obtained an exemption for the child from the immunization requirement to attend public school. P (father) petitioned to grant him authority over health care, religion, and educational decisions. He wants the child to receive traditional medical care, including vaccinations. What will D argue, and what is the likely outcome?

11. Assume that P and D had a child together but did not marry. D (father) has three older children by a previous marriage and fathered

another child with a third woman, his now ex-girlfriend. Evidence was presented at the custody hearing showing that when the child is present, the ex-girlfriend spends the night at D's home. The mother, P, sought sole custody of their child and alleged that the overnight visits in the presence of the young child would constitute promiscuous behavior that should disqualify the father from having custody. How is a court likely to analyze the situation with respect to child custody?

12. P (mother) and D (father) are seeking a divorce. They separated in 2011, and they agreed that the couple's three children, ages four, six, and ten, would reside temporarily with D while the divorce was pending. D began cohabiting with C against the wishes of P, who strongly disapproves of cohabitation outside of marriage on moral grounds. P learns that C was twice convicted of shoplifting and that C drinks alcoholic beverages in the presence of the children. Assuming that D is otherwise a fit parent, will P be awarded physical custody based on D's cohabitation?

13. Assume that P and D live in a jurisdiction that has adopted UMDA (see Section 5.14 *supra*) and that the legislature has amended the Act to include the following additional factor: "(6) the disposition of each parent to encourage and permit frequent contact with the other parent by the child." Both P and D seek sole legal and physical custody of their child when P files for divorce. They are unable to agree on custodial arrangements and they have a history of conflict. The court awards P sole physical custody but, over P's objection, orders joint legal custody, stating that without such an order P would not "foster the relationship" between D and the child. Will P prevail on appeal?

14. Assume that P and D live in a jurisdiction that has adopted the UMDA (see §5.15 *supra*) and that the legislature amended the Act to add the following additional factors: "(6) the effect on the child of domestic abuse that has taken place between the parents; and (7) the disposition of each parent to encourage and permit frequent contact with the other parent by the child." D has been violent with P on several occasions, and D frequently uses tactics of intimidation to control P's behavior. When P files for divorce, P and D each seek custody of the two children. D has never physically harmed the children, but P claims that the children have witnessed the violence in the home and that D should not have custody of the children. How is a court likely to analyze the situation with respect to child custody?

EXPLANATIONS

Explanations

9. On appeal, the child's legal custodians (P and D jointly) were found to have the right to determine the child's religious upbringing. The appellate court found that there was no indication that the child would be endangered by Wiccan practice or that the parents disagreed about the choice of religion. Consequently, the appellate court held that the trial court lacked authority to limit the parents' direction with respect to religious practice. (The court did not reach the issue of the parents' constitutional right to control the religious training of the child.)

10. Courts may generally disfavor restrictions on exposing a child to the parents' religious beliefs; however, where there is a showing that religious practices may be harmful, the court will rule in favor of the best interests of the child. In *Winters v. Brown*, 51 So. 3d 656 (Fla. App. 2011), on which this example is based, the mother presented expert evidence that vaccination might be more harmful to a child than not vaccinating. The father presented testimony from two physicians who informed the court that vaccinations are very safe and that a schedule of vaccinations increases immunity from disease. The appellate court affirmed the trial court's decision in favor of the father.

11. The court is required to consider a number of factors in determining the best interests of the child. The court will exercise its discretion in determining which factors are most important in a given case. P will argue that the child is directly affected by the appearance of intimate or immoral relations because the child would have witnessed the sexual nature of D's arrangement. D will argue that D does not sleep with his ex-girlfriend and that the child has never witnessed inappropriate conduct.

    In *Reed v. Pieper*, 713 S.E.2d 309 (S.C. 2011), upon which this example is based, the court found that the trial court was in the best position to determine if the custodial parent's history of serial girlfriends and apparent cohabitation with a female friend was actually promiscuous under the circumstances. In the case, the lack of evidence that the child saw the ex-girlfriend unclothed or in sexual situations did not support a finding that the father's conduct was detrimental to the child. An order awarding the father primary custody was upheld.

12. D's cohabitation is relevant to the question of physical custody only if it adversely affects the children. P will argue that the shoplifting convictions and the drinking in front of the children show that C has poor moral character and will be a bad influence on the children. D will argue that P should not be awarded custody based on D's cohabitation with C unless P

can prove specific adverse consequences to the children. Because the children were not involved with the shoplifting charges (and may not even be aware of them), and there is no indication that C drinks to excess or has placed the children in danger while drinking, P is not likely to be awarded physical custody of the children based solely on D's cohabitation with C. However, if P can show specific adverse consequences to the children, via expert testimony or otherwise, the cohabitation could become a factor in the outcome of the case. This is an example of a situation where the parties might benefit from creating a mediated parenting plan addressing ground rules for parenting.

13. P is not likely to prevail on appeal because judges consider the proclivity of a proposed custodian to foster the child's relationship with the other parent when they award legal and physical custody. *Kay v. Ludwig*, 686 N.W.2d 619 (Neb. App. 2004). More typically, cooperative parent provisions are raised in connection with physical custody rather than legal custody awards. P and D may benefit from mediation addressing their decision-making process; otherwise, shared legal custody could result in an increased (rather than decreased) level of conflict.

14. Under the UMDA, the court is required to consider a number of factors in determining the best interests of the children. The court will exercise its discretion in determining which factors are most important in a given case. P will argue that the children are directly affected by the intimate partner violence because they have witnessed the physical abuse and intimidation. D will argue that D has never physically harmed the children and that if awarded custody, P will not be disposed to allowing D to have continuing contact with the children (P will not be a "cooperative" parent). Assuming that P has evidence of the abuse, a court is likely to award custody to P and carefully structure parenting time for D. If P lived in a jurisdiction that had adopted a rebuttable presumption against custody awards to perpetrators, P would be awarded custody if P could prove abuse of sufficient frequency and severity to trigger the presumption.

PROCESSES AND PROFESSIONALS

5.29. Child Custody Evaluators

In contested cases, courts may order a child custody evaluation, which are typically conducted by mental health professionsals, although in some jurisdictions, lawyers may be appointed. The investigation may be performed by a court agency, a state social services department, or a private practitioner. A report ordered by the court may be admitted into evidence. However, under §405 of the UMDA, any party can require the professional and those the professional has interviewed to testify.

Because courts frequently place substantial weight on the recommendations, commentators urge courts to scrutinize evaluator qualifications and report quality. *See* Andrew I. Schepard, *Children, Courts, and Custody* 152 (Cambridge U. Press) (2004). In response to concerns about accountability and variations in practice, groups such as the Association of Family and Conciliation Courts have published model professional standards for custody evaluators. *See* Task Force for Model Standards of Practice for Child Custody Evaluation, *Model Standards of Practice for Child Custody Evaluation*, 45 Fam. Ct. Rev. 70 (2007).

5.30. Guardians *ad Litem*

Under various state statutes and depending on the resources available, a guardian *ad litem* may be appointed to represent the interests of a child. The guardian *ad litem* investigates the child's situation, reports to the court, and advocates for the child's best interests. Although the guardian *ad litem* may be an attorney, this role differs from traditional attorney-client representation because the guardian *ad litem* formulates an opinion concerning the best interests of the child rather than acting as an advocate of the child's expressed preferences.

5.31. Dispute Resolution Processes

Various dispute resolution processes have been developed for use by families. Processes such as mediation, early neutral evaluation, collaborative law, parenting coordination, and arbitration are discussed in Chapter 22.

CHAPTER 6

Modifying Custody

6.1. Introduction

This chapter examines the legal problems associated with two reasonably discrete types of custody modification actions. The first type of custody modification action involves a request for a change of custody from one parent to the other where relocation of a minor child to another jurisdiction accompanied by one of the parents is not an issue. This request is typically made by a motion to modify custody after an initial order has been made by the family court judge and primary or sole physical (or residential) custody has been awarded to one of the parents. The noncustodial parent is typically asking in his or her motion that custody be altered because of a change in circumstances that makes the present arrangement not in the best interests of the child or children. The first half of this chapter focuses on this particular type of custody modification action.

The second type of custody modification action, discussed in the latter half of this chapter, involves a request by a custodial parent to move with a child from an existing location to a new one. This may involve a request to relocate from one city to another, from one state to another, or from the United States to a foreign country. These disputes are particularly difficult because usually there is not a question about the fitness of either parent. Rather, the dispute is over the potential loss of the child's relationship with the noncustodial parent because of the distance that a new location will place between the child and the noncustodial parent.

This chapter does not examine issues related solely to modifying parenting time and visitation, which are discussed in Chapter 8. It also does not examine the basis for jurisdiction in custody modification actions brought by parents who are living in different states. Interstate jurisdictional battles are explored in detail in Chapter 7 under the rubric of the Uniform Child Custody Jurisdiction Enforcement Act (UCCJEA). International jurisdictional issues involving where a child custody action may be brought are explored in the final chapter of this book.

6.2. The State as a Third Party

States uniformly agree that they have subject matter jurisdiction to initially decide custody and to later modify a custody order during the minority of the child or children if the modification request is made in the state where the original custody order was entered. This principle rests upon the well-accepted theory that the state always sits as a third party to divorce proceedings and carries the responsibility of ensuring that the best interest of a child is protected during minority. *See Troxel v. Granville*, 530 U.S. 57, 68-69 (2000) (so long as a parent adequately cares for his or her children, there will normally be no reason for the state to inject itself into the private realm of the family to question further the ability of that parent to make the best decisions concerning the rearing of that parent's children). *See also Opinion of the Justices to the Senate*, 691 N.E.2d 911, 916 (Mass. 1998) (as *parens patrie*, the state has a "compelling interest" in protecting children from domestic violence); *Glauber v. Glauber*, 600 N.Y.S.2d 740 (N.Y. App. 1993) (court rejected arbitration as an alternative method of dispute resolution in contested child custody cases, based on the prevailing policy that it is the court's duty to review the circumstances independently and determine the best interests of a child); *Roth v. Weston*, 789 A.2d 431 (Conn. 2002) (*parens patrie* interests of the state include authorizing emergency medical treatment where parent withholds consent, restricting child labor from certain occupations or workplaces, prohibiting parents from leaving child unsupervised in public accommodation or vehicle, and intruding upon a family's integrity in the face of allegations that parents are unfit).

6.3. Stability Is the Goal

Courts and legislatures repeatedly emphasize that the primary concern in determining custody or considering a modification action is the child's best interests, with the goal of assuring stability and continuity in the child's life. This is especially true when custody continues with one parent over a significant period of time. *In re Brittany*, 26 Cal. Rptr. 3d 487 (Cal. App. 2005);

Moeller-Prokosch v. Prokosch, 99 P.3d 531 (Alaska 2004) (stability may encompass a multitude of factors, including, but not limited to, the relationship with the custodial parent, the home provided by the custodial parent, the children's school, the community of friends and family, the cultural community, the children's relationship with the noncustodial parent, and stability of place); *Stoppler v. Stoppler*, 633 N.W.2d 142 (N.D. 2001) (court's analysis of length of time that the child lived in a stable satisfactory environment and desirability of maintaining continuity, and conclusion that this factor favored custody with husband); *see generally* Andrew S. Watson, *The Children of Armageddon: Problems of Custody Following Divorce*, 21 Syracuse L. Rev. 55 (1969)

UMDA. The Uniform Marriage and Divorce Act (UMDA), §409(b), which has influenced custody modification legislation in many jurisdictions, reflects a general concern about stability and continuity. For example, that section makes it clear that more than a mere change in circumstances must be shown before an existing custody decision is to be modified. It states that when sole physical custody is awarded to one parent, custody may be modified only upon a showing of changed circumstances. Changed circumstances are defined as (1) the present custodial parent agrees to the custody change; or (2) the child has been integrated into the petitioner's family with the consent of the custodial parent; or (3) the child's present environment seriously endangers his physical, mental, moral, or emotional health, and the harm likely to be caused by a change of environment is outweighed by its advantages. UMDA §409(b); 9A U.L.A. 628 (1987 & Supp. 1996).

BARRIERS TO MODIFICATION ACTIONS

6.4. *Res Judicata*; Presumption; Change in Circumstances

Res judicata plays an important role when a family court judge is asked to modify an existing custody order. *Black's Law Dictionary* (9th ed. 2009), defines *res judicata* in part as follows:

> An issue that has been definitively settled by judicial decision. . . . An affirmative defense barring the same parties from litigating a second lawsuit on the same claim, or any other claim arising from the same transaction or series of transactions and that could have been — but was not — raised in the first suit. The essential elements are (1) an earlier decision on the issue, (2) a

> final judgment on the merits, and (3) the involvement of the same parties, or parties in privity with the original parties. Restatement (Second) of Judgments §§17, 24 (1982).—Also termed *res judicata*; claim preclusion; doctrine of *res judicata*.

Once a family court custody order has been entered by a court with jurisdiction over the parties, that order is considered *res judicata* of the facts and circumstances existing at the time it became final. *Huish v. Munro*, 191 P.3d 1242, 1249 (Utah App. 2008) (*res judicata* applies to modification proceedings); *Sanchez v. Hernandez*, 45 So. 3d 57, 60 (Fla. App. 2010) ("There is a presumption in favor of the reasonableness of the original decree. Satisfaction of the 'substantial change' test is necessary to overcome the *res judicata* effect of the final judgment. To hold otherwise would render any rotating custody scheme in a final judgment inherently unstable"). Once the judgment is entered, a presumption arises that favors its reasonableness. The presumption serves the practical purpose of providing stability and continuity to the original action because subsequent modification actions attacking the original judgment are considered potentially highly disruptive to children. *See George v. Helliar*, 814 P.2d 238 (Wash. App. 1991).

While the presumption is rebuttable, a court will place a heavy burden on the moving party to provide a factual basis showing that changed circumstances exist that make consideration of a change necessary. *See Groves v. Groves*, 567 P.2d 459, 463 (Mont. 1977); *Wade v. Hirschman*, 903 So. 2d 928 (Fla. 2005); *Parish v. Spaulding*, 496 S.E.2d 91, 94 (Va. App. 1998) ("'Changed circumstances' is a broad concept and incorporates a broad range of positive and negative developments in the lives of the children. The purpose of the changed circumstances requirement is to avoid the bar on relitigation that would otherwise be imposed by *res judicata*").

The application of *res judicata* to modification proceedings is moderated by the equitable doctrine that allows courts to reopen custody determinations under certain circumstances. Some courts describe those circumstances as a finding that a material or substantial change in circumstances affecting the interest and welfare of the child or children has occurred since the custody order was entered. *Sanchez v. Hernandez*, *supra*. A change contemplated at the time of the initial decree or at the time of a prior modification is not a material change in circumstances. *Ebach v. Ebach*, 757 N.W.2d 34, 36 (N.D. 2008).

Family court judges are reluctant to modify custody and will almost always begin their analysis of a modification request by reviewing *res judicata* principles. Likewise, they will usually strictly apply the language found in modification statutes that provides the basis for a modification hearing. The reason for this somewhat rigid approach to custody modification actions is a perceived need to promote stability and continuity for the children and to discourage repeated litigation of the same issues by an unhappy noncustodial parent.

6.5. Moratorium

Two-year moratorium. As already observed, a paramount concern of courts and state legislatures is that children involved in family breakups should be provided as much continuity and stability as possible. To deal with this concern state statutes and model acts have erected time barriers that attempt to shield a custodial parent from unwarranted modification actions. *See generally* H. Joseph Gitlin, *The Standard for Changing Child Custody Within Two Years of a Final Order*, 87 Ill. B.J. 492 (September 1999). For example, absent a showing of consent, integration, or endangerment, the UMDA, §409(a), prohibits the filing of any motion to modify a custody decree for two years after the decree is entered. Section 409 states that:

> (a) No motion to modify a custody decree may be made earlier than 2 years after its date, unless the court permits it to be made on the basis of affidavits that there is reason to believe the child's present environment may endanger seriously his physical, mental, moral, or emotional health.

The Commission's notes following §409 explain the reason for a moratorium:

> This section is designed to maximize finality (and thus assure continuity for the child) without jeopardizing the child's interest. Because any emergency which poses an immediate threat to the child's physical safety usually can be handled by the juvenile court, subsection (a) prohibits modification petitions until at least two years have passed following the initial decree, with a "safety valve" for emergency situations. To discourage the noncustodial parent who tries to punish a former spouse by frequent motions to modify, the subsection includes a two-year waiting period following each modification decree. During that two-year period a contestant can get a hearing only if he can make an initial showing, by affidavit only, that there is some greater urgency for the change than that the child's "best interest" requires it. During the two-year period the judge should deny a motion to modify, without a hearing, unless the moving party carries the onerous burden of showing that the child's present environment may endanger his physical, mental, moral, or emotional health.

UMDA §409 Comment.

Several states have adopted some form of the UMDA's moratorium. *See, e.g., Pennington v. Marcum*, 266 S.W.3d 759 (Ky. 2008) (if a change in custody is sought within two years of the decree, then the court must apply the statutory standard requiring either serious endangerment or abandonment); *Molitor v. Molitor*, 718 N.W.2d 13 (N.D. 2006) (statute limiting modification of child custody orders where less than two years has passed since initial custody order was entered was enacted to provide a moratorium for the family during the two-year period following a custody determination, and spare children the painful, disruptive, and destabilizing effects of repeat custody litigation).

Some scholars assert that "the UMDA's two-year moratorium does little to insure the 'finality' of the custody decree even for the first twenty-four months of the decree's life." Joan G. Wexler, *Rethinking the Modification of Child Custody Decrees*, 94 Yale L.J. 757, 782 (March 1985). Professor Wexler argues that "the UMDA's waiting period seems to be something of a paper tiger. Its main practical effect may be to prevent consensual modification within the first two years of a custody award." *Ibid.*

Endangerment. The UMDA's two-year moratorium can be eclipsed when, on the basis of affidavits, a court believes a *prima facie* case has been established that there is reason to believe the child's present environment may seriously endanger the child's physical, mental, moral, or emotional health. *In re Marriage of Oehm*, 252 Ill. App.3d 311 (Ill. App. 1993). In general, to establish a *prima facie* case, the moving party, who has the initial burden in these proceedings, must establish four elements for an endangerment-based custody modification. They are (1) a change in circumstances since the prior custody order; (2) a showing that a modification would serve the child's best interests; (3) evidence that the child's present environment endangers his or her physical or emotional health; and (4) evidence that the harm to the child that likely would be caused by the change of environment is outweighed by the likely benefits of a change in custody. *See, e.g., Biagi v. Biagi*, 2003 WL 22015841 (unpublished) (Minn. App. 2003) (endangerment consisted of lack of supervision, permissive parenting style, allowing children to read pleadings in custody dispute, outbursts, using children to create abuse allegations, and children's frequent ill health).

Note that the language selected by a state legislature when putting in place a custody modification moratorium must be examined carefully because it can vary from state to state. For example, in Colorado, the first motion for custody modification following entry of the original decree or judgment can be filed at any time, assuming that appropriate grounds exist. In addition, a Colorado court is authorized to make or modify an order granting or denying parenting time rights whenever such an order or modification would serve the best interests of the child. *See In re F.A.G.*, 148 P.3d 375 (Colo. App. 2006); Frank L. McGuane, Jr. and Kathleen A. Hogan, *Post-Judgment Modification and Enforcement*, 20 Colo. Prac. Family Law & Practice §31:2 (2011).

Also note that most jurisdictions have not placed a moratorium on visitation modification motions. However, litigants will disagree on whether an action is one to change custody or merely one to alter visitation. *See, e.g., In re Marriage of Dorman*, 9 P.3d 329 (Ariz. App. 2000) (request that the court change the parties' access to the child from substantially equal time to a situation in which the child resides with father and has minimal visitation with mother or her current husband is a modification of the physical custody order and essentially a request for modification of physical custody — it is not a request for modification of visitation). Visitation modification motions also usually have a lower burden of proof associated with them. *See, e.g., In re Marriage of Brown*, 778 N.W.2d 47, 51-52 (Iowa 2009) (much less extensive change in circumstances is generally required in visitation cases; parent seeking to modify visitation must only establish "that there has been a material change in circumstances since the decree and that the requested change in visitation is in the best interests of the children).

One-year moratorium. Some jurisdictions have limited the ability to bring a motion to modify an existing custody decree to only one year after the judgment or decree was entered. An example of such a provision is found in Minnesota's custody modification statute. It reads in part:

> (a) Unless agreed to in writing by the parties, no motion to modify a custody order or parenting plan may be made earlier than one year after the date of the entry of a decree of dissolution or legal separation containing a provision dealing with custody, except in accordance with paragraph (c). . . .
>
> (c) The time limitations prescribed in paragraphs (a) . . . shall not prohibit a motion to modify a custody order or parenting plan if the court finds that there is persistent and willful denial or interference with parenting time, or has reason to believe that the child's present environment may endanger the child's physical or emotional health or impair the child's emotional development.

Minn. Stat. 518.18 (2010).

PROCEDURE

6.6. Initial Pleadings Must Demonstrate Necessity of Evidentiary Hearing

As observed earlier in this chapter, many jurisdictions require that a party seeking a modification hearing justify that such a hearing is needed in the initial moving papers. *See, e.g., In re Marriage of Tomsovic*, 74 P.3d 692 (Wash. 2003) (to establish that he or she is entitled to a full hearing on a petition to modify a residential schedule, the petitioner first must demonstrate that adequate cause exists). In these jurisdictions, the pleadings and accompanying affidavits must contain facts showing that changed circumstances exist and that given those changes, it may be inappropriate or unfair to continue the original custody order. Typically, courts will describe the burden on the moving party as a need to establish a *prima facie* case demonstrating the change and the need for a hearing. *See, e.g.*, *J.L.P. v. V.L.A.*, 30 P.3d 590, 595 (Alaska 2001) (court may deny custody modification without an evidentiary hearing if the facts alleged, even if proved, cannot warrant modification, or if the allegations are so general or conclusory, and so convincingly refuted by competent evidence, as to create no genuine issue of material fact requiring a hearing); *In re Weber*, 653 N.W.2d 804 (Minn. App. 2002) (*prima facie* case consists of a showing of (1) a change in the circumstances of the child or custodian, (2) that a modification would serve the best interests of the child, (3) that the child's present environment endangers his physical or emotional health or emotional development, and (4) that the harm to the child likely to be caused by the change of environment is outweighed by the advantage of change). *See generally* Robert Oliphant, *Redefining a Statute out of Existence: Minnesota's View of When a Custody Modification Hearing Can Be Held*, 26 Wm. Mitchell L. Rev. 711 (2000).

UMDA view. §410 of the UMDA suggests that the abovementioned affidavit process should be incorporated into a modification proceeding by a state. Under the UMDA, a parent seeking to modify an existing custody arrangement must submit an affidavit with the modification request that sets out facts in support of it. The opposing parent is given an opportunity to file affidavits, and the court then determines on the basis of all the affidavits filed by the parties whether adequate cause for a hearing is established. The purpose of this procedural requirement is to prevent a modification hearing absent a showing that substantial grounds exist that are supported by factual evidence.

When deciding whether a *prima facie* claim exists, most family courts will accept as true the allegations in the moving party's documents. They usually will not weigh conflicting allegations before a hearing is held and credibility of the parties and their witnesses can be tested. Once a *prima facie* case is established by the pleadings and any supporting affidavits, the matter is set for a full hearing.

6.7. Two-Step Process

It should be clear from the earlier material in this chapter that in a majority of jurisdictions, the test to determine whether to change an existing custody award is a two-step process. The first step is to decide whether, since the last judgment or order regarding custody, there has been a change in circumstances relevant to the capacity of one parent or both parents to care for the child. *Boldt and Boldt*, 176 P.3d 388 (Or. 2008), cert. den. 555 U.S. 814 (2008). If there has been such a change, then the second step is to determine whether a change of custody is in the child's best interests. *Ibid.*

Burden of proof. The party seeking the change in custody normally has the burden of proving both that there has been a qualifying change of circumstances since the original decision and that a change in custody is in the child's best interests. *Ibid.* The change must be based upon facts unknown to the court at the time of the original custody order or facts that have arisen since entry of the decree or plan. *Kelly v. Kelly*, 640 N.W.2d 38, 47 (N.D. 2002) (the doctrine of res judicata would make it inappropriate to rehash facts already tried or which could have been tried; *Boggs v. Boggs*, 383 N.E.2d 9 (Ill. App. 1978) (the wording of 610(b) is constructed in such a way as to indicate that evidence of both newly arisen facts and those previously unknown to the court can be considered not only on the question of the child's best interests but also on the change of circumstances requirement). *See also New York ex rel. Halvey v. Halvey*, 330 U.S. 610, 612 (1947) (stating Florida rule that court which originally awarded custody is within its jurisdiction to change custody where material facts were unknown to court when order entered originally; under Florida law the welfare of the child is the chief consideration in shaping the custody decree or in subsequently modifying or changing it).

In *Dunn v. Dunn*, 775 N.W.2d 486, 491-92 (N.D. 2009), the North Dakota court made the following helpful observation regarding the distinction between the burden of proof at an initial custody hearing and the burden of proof at a custody modification hearing:

> A court's analysis in considering whether to modify custody differs from its analysis when awarding original custody. For a determination of an original custody award, only the best interests of the child are considered. However, when a party is seeking to modify a custody arrangement, a court applies a two-step process. A trial court must determine: 1) Whether there has been a significant change of circumstances following the divorce and custody determination, and 2) Whether the changes of circumstances effect [sic] the child in such an adverse way that it compels or requires a change in the existing arrangement to further the best interests of the child.

6.8. Illustrative State Modification Standards

Lawyers are advised to check carefully the current custody modification statutes and court rulings in their state for the exact statutory language when a modification request is being considered. Some states, such as Minnesota, have created extensive criteria for modifying custody. Its modification statute, in part, reads as follows:

> (d) If the court has jurisdiction to determine child custody matters, the court shall not modify a prior custody order or a parenting plan provision which specifies the child's primary residence unless it finds, upon the basis of facts, including unwarranted denial of, or interference with, a duly established parenting time schedule, that have arisen since the prior order or that were unknown to the court at the time of the prior order, that a change has occurred in the circumstances of the child or the parties and that the modification is necessary to serve the best interests of the child. In applying these standards the court shall retain the custody arrangement or the parenting plan provision specifying the child's primary residence that was established by the prior order unless:
>
> (i) the court finds that a change in the custody arrangement or primary residence is in the best interests of the child and the parties previously agreed, in a writing approved by a court, to apply the best interests standard in section 518.17 or 257.025, as applicable; and, with respect to agreements approved by a court on or after April 28, 2000, both parties were represented by counsel when the agreement was approved or the court found the parties were fully informed, the agreement was voluntary, and the parties were aware of its implications;
>
> (ii) both parties agree to the modification;
>
> (iii) the child has been integrated into the family of the petitioner with the consent of the other party;
>
> (iv) the child's present environment endangers the child's physical or emotional health or impairs the child's emotional development and the harm likely to be caused by a change of environment is outweighed by the advantage of a change to the child; or
>
> (v) the court has denied a request of the primary custodial parent to move the residence of the child to another state, and the primary custodial parent has relocated to another state despite the court's order.

Minn. Stat. §518.18(d) (2006).

Note that where joint custody is involved, the parents may adopt modification provisions that do not necessarily follow of paragraph (d) of the above statute. Note also the provisions regarding a temporary order.

> (e) In deciding whether to modify a prior joint custody order, the court shall apply the standards set forth in paragraph (d) unless: (1) the parties agree in writing to the application of a different standard, or (2) the party seeking the modification is asking the court for permission to move the residence of the child to another state.
>
> (f) If a parent has been granted sole physical custody of a minor and the child subsequently lives with the other parent, and temporary sole physical

> custody has been approved by the court or by a court-appointed referee, the court may suspend the obligor's child support obligation pending the final custody determination. The court's order denying the suspension of child support must include a written explanation of the reasons why continuation of the child support obligation would be in the best interests of the child.

Minn. Stat. §§518.18 (e)(f) (2006).

The language used by courts and legislatures are not uniform. The examples selected below are intended to illustrate how states vary in the language that they use in guiding lawyers and judges in modification matters. One wonders, however, if the overarching best interests of the child concept make the language used by the states more consistent than inconsistent.

California — Significant change. California has articulated a best-interest standard, known as the "changed circumstance" rule, which is applied when a parent seeks to modify custody. *In re Marriage of Brown and Yana*, 127 P.3d 28 (Cal. 2006). Under California's approach, custody may be modified if a parent seeking modification demonstrates a significant change of circumstances indicating that a different custody arrangement would be in the child's best interests. *See generally In re Marriage of Lucio*, 74 Cal. Rptr. 3d 804 (Cal. App. 2008) (custody modification is appropriate only if the parent seeking modification demonstrates 'a significant change of circumstances,' indicating that a different custody arrangement would be in the child's best interest).

Note that in California, the changed circumstance rule does not apply to a modification request seeking a change in the parenting or visitation schedule. *Enrique M. v. Angelina V.*, 18 Cal. Rptr. 3d 306 (Cal. App. 2004).

Florida. Florida's approach is typical of most states. In *Wade v. Hirschman*, 903 So. 2d 928 (Fla. 2005), the Florida Supreme Court held that the substantial change test requires that the moving party prove "both that the circumstances have substantially, materially changed since the original custody determination and that the child's best interests justify changing custody." *Id.* at 931 n.2 (quoting *Cooper v. Gress*, 854 So. 2d 262, 265 (Fla. App. 2003)). In addition, "the substantial change must be one that was not reasonably contemplated at the time of the original judgment." *Id.* (quoting *Cooper*, 854 So. 2d at 265).

New York — Totality of circumstances. In New York, the legal standards for modifying custody and visitation are basically the same, although the extent and magnitude of the proposed modification have some bearing on the court's ultimate determination. *See Matter of Engwer v. Engwer*, 762 N.Y.S.2d

689 (N.Y. App. 2003). To modify an existing custody order, a petitioner must "demonstrate a change in circumstances warranting modification of the visitation or custody order to advance the best interest[s] of the children." *Matter of Reese v. Jones*, 671 N.Y.S.2d 170 (N.Y. App. 1998); *Matter of La Bier v. La Bier*, 738 N.Y.S.2d 132 (N.Y. App. 2002). A change-of-custody standard requires a clear demonstration of a significant change of circumstances, which, based on the *totality of circumstances*, warrants a modification of custody in the best interests of the children before moving them. *Renzulli v. McElrath*, 712 N.Y.S.2d 267 (N.Y. Sup. 2000).

Pennsylvania: Substantial change not required. In Pennsylvania, a custody order is subject to modification without proof of a substantial change in circumstances when it is shown that that change is in the best interests of the child. *Moore v. Moore*, 634 A.2d 163, 169 (Pa. 1993). Whenever a court is called upon to address the best interests of a child, traditional burdens or presumptions such as substantial change in circumstances, the fitness of one parent over another, or the tender years doctrine must all give way to the paramount concern: the best interests of the child. *Ibid*. In determining the best interests of a child, a court must consider all factors that legitimately affect the child's physical, intellectual, moral, and spiritual well-being. *Swope v. Swope*, 689 A.2d 264 (Pa. 1997).

Texas. To support modifying custody in Texas, a trial court must find that the modification would be in the best interest of the child and that the circumstances of the child have changed materially and substantially since the date of the original order. Tex. Rev. Family Code §156.101 (1) (2011). The party seeking modification has the burden to establish these elements by a preponderance of the evidence. *Agraz v. Carnley*, 143 S.W.3d 547, 552 (Tex. App. 2004). To prove that a material change in circumstances has occurred, the petitioner must demonstrate what material changes have occurred in the conditions existing at the time of the entry of the prior order compared to the circumstances existing at the time of the hearing on the motion to modify.

Examples

1. Assume that a child, Robert Jr., was born in January 2010. M (mother) and F (father) are listed on the birth certificate as the child's parents. Also assume that both parents were single and that F was in the military when the child was born. F was granted custody of the child by Minnesota family court with M's consent. However, while F completed his military service, the child remained in the care of M. Once F was discharged, M and F married. (The child was now a year old.) However, the marriage

lasted less than a year. When M and F divorced, a pa[illegible] included in the judgment that gave F sole legal and ph[illegible] the child. Despite the divorce, M and F continued to liv[illegible] next three years. At this point in the relationship, F left Minnesota with the child and moved to Kansas. M remained in Minnesota and raised no objection to F taking the child with him to Kansas. After 10 months in Kansas, the child was returned to Minnesota, where he has lived with M for the past 13 months.

F has informed M that he intends to move from Kansas to New York and take the child with him. Upon learning of F's decision, M has moved to modify the original custody order in Minnesota. M alleges in her affidavit seeking an evidentiary hearing that she agreed to F initially receiving custody when he was single so that he could gain an early release from the military. She alleges that she understood that she would have actual and permanent physical custody of the child. She further alleges that when they divorced, she agreed to the parenting plan because she was ill. She is now healthy. As a second basis for her claim, she alleges that the child was integrated into her family with the permission of F when F sent the child back to her in Minnesota.

In his response to M's affidavit, F submitted an affidavit in which he alleges that M is lying. F claims that M is an alcoholic and "has fallen off the wagon." He asserts that M has failed to meet her burden of establishing on a preliminary basis that a significant change of circumstances had occurred.

The trial judge is examining the provisions of the Minnesota statute set our earlier in this chapter and asks you, her clerk, whether you can find a reasonable basis in the language of the statute to grant an evidentiary hearing. What is your advice to the judge?

2. Assume that P and D divorce, and the trial judge awards sole physical and legal custody of X, age 13, to D, his mother. Six months after the judgment is entered (and no appeal was taken), P brings an action asking that the judgment be modified so that P is awarded sole legal and physical custody of X. In the moving papers, P asserts that X has told P that D is drinking heavily and has a boyfriend who was once convicted of drunk driving. In an affidavit submitted to the court in response to P's moving papers, D denies that she is drinking heavily, saying that X made up the story. She says that X is angry after being grounded for a month for bad behavior. D concedes that her boyfriend was convicted of drunken driving five years ago; however, affidavits are produced signed by him and his AA counselor stating that he has been "dry for two years."

Assume that this jurisdiction has adopted the UMDA and also requires a *prima facie* showing of endangerment before a modification hearing will be granted. The trial judge has two questions: Is the above action time-barred by a moratorium on bringing such actions? If it is not, has the party moving for modification made out a *prima facie* showing of endangerment? How will most courts answer these two questions?

3. Assume that the parties were divorced in 2009 and mother (M) received sole physical custody of two children, ages 6 and 10. Mother and father (F) shared joint legal custody. The parties' post-marital relationship was marred by intense acrimony, and M was later held in criminal contempt of a protective order that had been issued in favor of F. In May 2010, she was placed on probation for a period of three years. In late 2010, she violated the terms of her probation and was sentenced to 120 days in the county jail. Upon M's incarceration, M and F's two children came to live in F's home, along with F's fiancé and her three daughters. F thereafter sought sole legal and primary physical custody of the children. M, who was released from the county jail after serving 120 days, opposed the motion. At the time of the custody modification hearing, the children had been in F's custody for eight months. The court appointed a mental health expert to examine both parties. That expert concluded that M was either unable to appreciate, or was untruthful about, the self-destructive conduct in which she had engaged and the extent to which that conduct evidenced a failure to exercise good parental judgment. Using New York's approach to custody modification matters, how will a New York court most likely rule on the request for a change in custody?

4. Assume that this jurisdiction does not have a time-barrier moratorium for bringing modification actions similar to that found in the UMDA. Also assume that P and D were divorced and that D was awarded sole physical custody of child X. According to the findings made by the judge at the custody proceeding, she was concerned about P's abuse of drugs and alcohol. A year after the original custody decision, P sought to modify custody so that she would have sole physical custody of X. At the first custody hearing, the Department of Social Services had been involved because of concerns over P's fitness to care for X, age 10. The concerns were prompted in large part by P's history of drug abuse. At the modification proceeding, P called a social worker, who testified that P was having "great success in overcoming her alcohol and drug dependence" and that X "would be better nurtured by P." D's lawyer argued that there had not been a change in circumstances (the change alleged by M was anticipated at the original custody hearing), and even if there were, the change would not justify modifying custody. D testified that X was enrolled in school and was doing a good job (X's report cards supported D). D also testified that X had made friends in the neighborhood, that X attended church with D on a regular basis, and that X was on a Little

League baseball team. D testified that X appeared to enjoy the home setting. How will a court likely rule?

EXPLANATIONS

Explanations

1. The burden is on the moving party, M, to establish on a preliminary basis that a change of circumstances has occurred and that modification is necessary to serve the best interests of the child. To meet this test, the affidavits accompanying the motion for modification must allege sufficient facts to allow a court to reach the required findings. If they don't, the trial court should deny the motion and no evidentiary hearing is needed.

   In this case, M would most likely be granted a hearing. The affidavits demonstrate pretty clearly that a change of circumstances is being contemplated because F intends to move to New York with the child. Further, most judges would agree that M has made a preliminary showing under Minn. Stat. §518.18(d)(ii) that the child has been integrated into her family with F's consent. The child had lived with his mother for all but 10 months of his life at the time of the request for a hearing. Modification would provide continuity of care with M, who has been the child's primary caretaker. There is sufficient evidence to warrant providing M with an evidentiary hearing to decide whether modification may be in the child's best interests. *See Downey v. Zwigart*, 5378 N.W.2d 639 (Minn. App. 1985).

2. The answer to the "time-barred" question is found in the UMDA, which is applied in states that have adopted its language. Section 409 of the UMDA bars a change-of-custody hearing for two years following an initial custody decision absent a showing of endangerment, integration, or consent. Here, the original custody order was entered only six months ago. Therefore, the action is time-barred unless the moving party can establish a *prima facie* case of endangerment. More formally stated, the moving party must show that the child's present environment seriously endangers his or her physical, mental, or emotional health, and the harm likely to be caused by a change of environment is outweighed by its presumed advantages.

   Most courts will find that the noncustodial parent's evidence in support of his allegations falls short of establishing a *prima facie* case that justifies reopening the original order. The noncustodial parent would have a better chance of a favorable decision had he produced evidence in the form of affidavits from experts and disinterested non-expert third parties to support his claims. The custodial parent countered the drinking allegations with her responsive affidavit and the affidavits of her boyfriend and the AA counselor. Furthermore, the claimed evidence of drinking doesn't appear to be something new; therefore, a judge could reasonably assume that if such evidence existed, it should have been produced at the original custody hearing held only six months earlier.

3. A New York court will examine all of the circumstances. Father must show that there has been a sufficient change in circumstances such that modification will advance the best interests of the children. In making its decision, a family court will consider the quality of the respective home environments, the length of time that the present custody arrangement has been in place, and each parent's past performance, relative fitness, and ability to provide for and guide the child's intellectual and emotional development. The family court will also assess the credibility of the parties and their witnesses.

   Several factors will be considered. First, although the divorce decree provided for joint legal custody and primary physical custody with M, the children had already been subjected to an actual change of custody by reason of M's incarceration, which was the result of her volitional behavior. Therefore, a modification would actually maintain the existing custody arrangement that had been in place for approximately eight months at the time of the hearing.

   Second, the trial judge will have to decide who is a credible witness. It may well rely on M's mental health evaluation, which found that she was either unable to appreciate, or was untruthful about, the self-destructive conduct in which she had engaged and the extent to which that conduct evidenced a failure to exercise good parental judgment.

   Third, the court will seek throughout the hearing to answer the question of whether F was providing the children with an adequate and stable home environment in a school district where they had adjusted well.

   Fourth, the court will examine how M prepared the children for her incarceration and whether she is undergoing counseling to deal with her problems. In the case on which this hypothetical problem is modeled, the court transferred custody from M to F. It found, among other matters, that M did not engage in counseling and failed to prepare the children properly for her incarceration. Most likely, on these facts, a court would modify custody.

4. Jurisdictions will debate whether there has been a material change in circumstances since the initial custody order. Some courts may conclude there was a change, but it was not material. That is, it was foreseeable at the first hearing that P would eventually bring her drug problem under control. Other courts may take the view that there has been a material

change since the original hearing because P now apparently has her drug problem under control and it was not clearly foreseeable that she could gain control of her habit when custody was awarded to D. Foreseeability will usually turn on the particular facts and circumstances of the original hearing.

Because stability and continuity are so important in considering a modification request, and D has produced evidence demonstrating X's relationship to D's neighborhood and school, most courts will conclude that P's evidence has failed to overcome the presumption favoring the custodial parent. *See Ardizoni v. Raymond*, 667 N.E.2d 885 (Mass. App. 1996). Even without a presumption, it is doubtful that a court would change custody based on these facts even if it concludes there was a material change in circumstances.

TYPICAL CLAIMS TRIGGERING MODIFICATION DEMANDS

6.9. Unwarranted Denial of Visitation

Occasionally, a divorced couple may be unable to handle visitation issues amiably. When this occurs, it is not uncommon for the noncustodial parent to seek court intervention to either enforce the existing visitation schedule or ask that the custody order be modified.

As a general rule, it is rare that a court will modify custody based solely on a custodial parent's decision to deny visitation in defiance of the existing visitation order. This is the case even though a majority of jurisdictions have by statute stated that unwarranted denial of or interference with duly established visitation constitutes contempt of court and may be sufficient cause for reversal of a custody ruling. *See, e.g.*, Iowa Code §598.23(2)(b) (2006); New Hampshire Code Rev. §458:17, V(a)(2) (2004) (modification allowed if court finds repeated, intentional, and unwarranted interference by a custodial parent with the visitation or custodial rights of the noncustodial parent). Unwarranted denial of or interference with visitation is usually viewed as only one of several factors to be considered in contemplating modifying custody. *See, e.g., In re Marriage of Ciganovich*, 132 Cal. Rptr. 261 (Cal. App. 1976); *Slinkard v. Slinkard*, 589 S.W.2d 635 (Mo. App. 1979); *Lopez v. Lopez*, 639 P.2d 1186 (N.M. 1981); *Lemcke v. Lemcke*, 623 N.W.2d 916 (Minn. App. 2001). To warrant modification, the interference with visitation must be conspicuously bad or offensive. *See, e.g., Entwistle v. Entwistle*, 402 N.Y.S.2d 213 (N.Y. App. 1978) (custodial parent's interference with the other parent's visitation rights is so inconsistent with the child's best interests as to per se raise a strong probability that custodial parent is unfit); *Lindell v. Coen*, 896 S.W.2d 525 (Mo. App. 1995) (modification granted where father alleged that the custodial mother had refused to allow him to develop and maintain a father-child relationship with their child, refused to provide adequate clothing for the child during visitation, and regularly placed unreasonable restrictions on his visitation).

It should be obvious that a custodial parent's strict adherence to a visitation schedule is not a basis for considering changing custody. For example, in *Huffman v. Huffman*, 11 S.W.3d 883 (Mo. App. 2000), the court rejected a father's request for a change in custody. He had claimed that it was improper for the custodial mother to refuse visitation of any kind repeatedly beyond the dates specifically set out in the court's custody decree.

6.10. Failure to Pay Child Support

A noncustodial parent is often required by a court order or an agreement between the parties to make child support payments. When the noncustodial parent fails to make such payments, the custodial parent sometimes will resort to a self-help method of enforcement. The self-help may consist of withholding court-ordered visitation privileges from the noncustodial parent until that parent pays the outstanding child support arrearages. However, as a general rule, courts will not terminate visitation solely for reasons unrelated to the welfare of the child, and a failure to pay support is usually not included within the scope of this principle. *See Farmer v. Farmer*, 735 N.E.2d 285 (Ind. 2000) ("This court has held numerous times that a parent may not interfere with visitation when the noncustodial parent fails to pay support" — "parent may not withhold child support payments even though the other parent interferes with visitation rights"); *Pierpont v. Bond*, 744 So. 2d 843 (Miss. App. 1999) (while the coercive effect of withholding child support may be used to encourage the allowance of visitation when appropriate, its use is available only upon approval of the court); *Stewart v. Soda*, 642 N.Y.S.2d 105 (N.Y. App. 1996).

Courts also generally agree that a noncustodial parent may not withhold child support because of the custodial parent's actions, even if they are in defiance of a court order that the custodial parent is apparently violating. For example, in *Ewald v. Ewald*, 810 N.W.2d 396 (Mich. App. 2011), the noncustodial parent withheld child support because the custodial parent left the state without permission of the court. The Michigan Court of Appeals said that the defendant's remedy was to seek enforcement of his visitation rights, not to withhold his child support payments.

6.11. Integration into Noncustodial Parent's Home

Most jurisdictions recognize that custody may be modified when the child has been integrated into the noncustodial parent's family with the consent of the custodial parent. *See* UMDA §409, 9A U.L.A. 62829 (1987). The custodial parent's consent in these circumstances has been defined as "a voluntary acquiescence to surrender of legal custody." *In re Marriage of Timmons*, 617 P.2d 1032, 1037 (Wash. 1980). When the parties agree that a child has been integrated voluntarily into the noncustodian's family, there is no dispute and no litigation. However, when the parents disagree over whether integration has occurred, the family court will conduct a fact-specific inquiry before reaching a decision.

Most courts require something more than a mere claim of expanded visitation to support an integration claim. *In re Marriage of Chatten*, 967 P.2d 206 (Colo. App. 1998). Evidence showing integration should include the performance of normal parental duties such as washing clothes, providing meals, attending to medical needs, assisting with homework, and guiding the children physically, mentally, morally, socially, and emotionally. *See, e.g., In re Marriage of Wechselberger*, 450 N.E.2d 1385 (Ill. App. 1983). The time spent by the children with the proposed new custodial parent must be of sufficient duration that they have become settled into the home of that parent as though it were their primary home. *See In re Marriage of Paradis*, 689 P.2d 1263 (Mont. 1984); *In re Marriage of Pontius*, 761 P.2d 247 (Colo. App. 1988); *In re Marriage of DePalma*, 176 P.3d 829, 831 (Colo. App. 2007), *cert. denied*, 2008 WL 434613 (Colo. Feb. 19, 2008). Courts may also consider which residence the children themselves consider their true home. *In re Custody of Thompson*, 647 P.2d 1049 (Wash. App. 1982); *See generally Annot.*, 35 A.L.R. 4th 61 (1985).

Courts will be alert to situations where a noncustodial parent's conduct is used to manufacture a claim of integration into a household. For example, a noncustodial parent who violates an existing custody order by removing a child from the custodial parent's control, and the child remains with the noncustodial parent for a length of time, cannot later assert that the child has been integrated into the noncustodian's household. *George v. Helliar*, 814 P.2d. 238, 242 (Wash. App. 1991). If a court allowed such a claim, the result would shift the burden in a modification proceeding to the custodial parent named in the original decree to prove the fitness of the custodial home. This is contrary to the intent of the provisions enacted in this area of the law.

6.12. Custodial Parent's Alleged Immoral Conduct

Immoral conduct in general. Nineteenth-century courts considered that a parent's immorality made that person unfit to have custody of a minor child. That was particularly true in the case of a married woman who committed adultery. *Osterhoudt v. Osterhoudt*, 62 N. Y., Sup. 529 (N.Y. App. 1900); *Divorce — Adultery — Custody of Children — Osterhoudt v. Osterhoudt*, 9 Yale L. J. 275 (April 1900) ("Generally, a mother, guilty of adultery, is not a fit custodian for her children"). However, jurisdictions today do not consider immoral conduct a factor in custody disputes unless the conduct affects the child's relationship with a parent. To determine whether parental conduct affects the child's relationship with the parent is a question of fact that is determined on a case-by-case basis. *Thompson v. Pafundi*, 8 A.3d 476 (Vt. 2010) (conduct must affect the parent's relationship with the child); Minn. Stat. §518.17, subd. 1(b) (2006) (district court may not consider conduct that does not affect the proposed custodian's relationship with the child); *In re Custody of Farm*, 417 N.E.2d 240 (Ill. App. 1981); *Rowe v. Franklin*, 663 N.E.2d 955 (Ohio App. 1995) (mother's non-marital sexual conduct and lifestyle choices could be considered only to extent that they had a direct adverse impact on child's best interests); *A.W.C.*, 2010 WL 3064392 (Ohio App. 2010) (immoral conduct must be shown to have a direct or probable adverse impact on the welfare of the child in order to justify a change of custody).

UMDA §402 sets out as the standard for judicial consideration of immoral conduct the following:

> The court shall not consider conduct of a proposed custodian that does not affect his relationship to the child.

Cohabiting with unmarried partner. Historically, a parent's cohabitation outside marriage with a member of the same or opposite sex following a divorce would typically result in loss of child custody. Today, however, parental cohabitation with someone, regardless of that person's gender, is generally not used as a basis for denying custody or visitation absent evidence that the child was harmed by the conduct.

For example, the Virginia Supreme Court in *Brown v. Brown*, 37 S.E.2d 89 (Va. 1977), observed that the moral climate in which children are to be raised is an important consideration when determining custody, and adultery is a reflection of a mother's moral values. It said that exposing children to an illicit relationship cannot be condoned and should be given the most careful consideration in a custody proceeding. However, the Court rejected establishing a per se rule that would preclude an award of custody merely because a parent was cohabiting outside marriage following a divorce. Cf. *Alphin v. Alphin*, 219 S.W.3d 160 (Ark. 2005) (extramarital cohabitation in the presence of children "has never been condoned in Arkansas, is contrary to the public policy of promoting a stable environment for children, and may of itself constitute a material change of circumstances warranting a change of custody").

UMDA. As noted previously, UMDA §402 set as its standard that cohabitation outside marriage is relevant only to the extent that the parent's sexual relationship adversely affects the child or children.

American Law Institute. The American Law Institute (ALI) suggests that a trial court refrain from considering a parent's extramarital sexual behavior unless there is evidence that it harms the child. American Law Institute, *Principles of the Law of Family Dissolution: Analysis and Recommendations* §2.12(1)(e) (2002).

Example where immorality caused custodial change. A Delaware family court allowed a change in custody from mother to father where it considered that the mother's immoral conduct potentially endangered a minor child. Observed the court:

> Mother has used very poor judgment in rushing into intimate relationships, exposing her children to the relationships, not learning about the various individuals before exposing the children to the relationships, and only ending the relationships when she purportedly realized that the gentlemen were either total losers or the children did not like the gentlemen, probably because they were total losers, or . . . married. Mother has allowed [the children] to be exposed, not only to numerous individuals who may have put [the children] in danger or expose her to improper conduct, but also to an absolute lack of morality where [the children] is only learning from Mother's example that it is appropriate to engage in intimate relationships with numerous individuals over a relatively short time period.

Jefferson v. Jefferson, 980 A.2d 410, 415-416 (Del. Fam. 2008).

6.13. Poor Parenting/Discipline

Most courts will not consider evidence of "poor parenting" as a sufficient basis to justify modifying custody. For example, in *Stern v. Rey*, 616 So. 2d 145 (Fla. App. 1993), the court commented that evidence that a mother had been "somewhat less than a sterling parent" since the divorce was not sufficient to prove a substantial change of circumstances warranting custody modification.

However, a failure or inability to adequately discipline or properly control a child, following an award of custody, under some circumstances, may provide a basis for modification of an existing award. *See, e.g.*, *Lagrone v. Lagrone*, 311 So. 2d 290, 291 (La. App. 1975) (mother was unable to discipline her 12-year-old son, and son exhibited a marked improvement in attitude and schoolwork when he went to live with and was subjected to discipline from his father). Note that excessive physical discipline of a child may also form the basis of a modification motion. *See Vasquez-Williams v. Williams*, 821 N.Y.S.2d 226 (N.Y. App. 2006) (allegations that father imposed excessive and inappropriate discipline on children, including corporal punishment, was sufficient to warrant a hearing on mother's petition for modification of custody); *Breckner v.* Coble, 921 S.W.2d 624 (Mo. App. 1996) (modification denied where mother showed a consistent and appropriate pattern of discipline; the making and enforcing of rules for the children to follow; the encouragement and parental guidance for academic achievement of both children; and regular routines established for the children).

6.14. Smoking

When making custody awards, or considering a modification request, courts have shown increasing concern about parents smoking in the presence of a child. *See, e.g., Heagy v. Kean*, 864 N.E.2d 383 (Ind. App. 2007) (court ordered the mother to refrain from smoking in the child's presence and after alleged violations of the order, the father requested a modification of the custody arrangements); *Becker v. Becker*, 925 P.2d 162 (Or. App. 1996) (judgment of dissolution contained a provision prohibiting both parents and third parties from smoking cigarettes around the children).

In *Lizzio v. Jackson*, 226 A.D.2d 760 (N.Y. 1996), the child involved in the dispute was an asthmatic and had been diagnosed as being allergic to cigarette smoke. The New York appellate court rejected a lower court order modifying custody based on smoking alone. However, it required that both parents observe an order directing adherence to the instructions of their son's allergist regarding smoking in his presence. *See Breitung v. Trask*, 717 N.Y.S.2d 799 (N.Y. App. 2001) (other factors, aside from smoking, were inappropriate behavior and potentially dangerous situations); *Holden v. Tillotson*, 716 N.Y.S.2d 152 (N.Y. App. 2000) (other factors besides smoking included alcohol abuse and domestic violence); *Heagy v. Kean*, 864 N.E.2d 383 (Ind. App. 2007) (fact that child was exposed to dangers of secondhand smoke from mother's and maternal grandmother's smoking did not constitute substantial change in circumstances to warrant modification of custody); *Matter of Marriage of Heuberger*, 963 P.2d 153 (Or. App. 1998) (child's health problems, allegedly caused by former wife's smoking, did not constitute substantial change of circumstances). Note that medical research has shown that nonsmokers suffer many of the diseases of active smoking when they breathe secondhand smoke. This medical research may cause courts to become even more diligent in custody rulings where one or both parties are smokers. *See* University of Minnesota, Division of Periodontology, *Secondhand Smoke Facts*, http://www1.umn.edu/perio/tobacco/secondhandsmoke.html (last visited July, 2012).

6.15. Endangerment

While endangerment was discussed earlier in this chapter in the context of moratoriums, this section expands on the subject. As already observed, one of the more common grounds for seeking modification of custody, especially when a statutory bar of one or two years following the issuance of a custody order exists, is a claim that the present environment endangers a child's physical or emotional health or impairs a child's emotional development and that the advantages of the change in environment will outweigh the harm of change to the child. *See Goldman v. Greenwood*, 748 N.W.2d 279, 284 (Minn. 2008) (a party must demonstrate "a significant degree of danger" to satisfy the endangerment element in Minnesota law).

Burden of proof. If endangerment is asserted as a basis for changing custody, the burden of proof is normally placed on the person making the allegation. *Wolfe v. Wolfe*, 610 N.W.2d 222 (Wis. App. 2000); *Jines v. Jurich*, 783 N.E.2d 147 (Ill. App. 2002); *Jefferson v. Jefferson*, 980 A.2d 410 (Del. Fam. 2008). It is of interest that a majority of jurisdictions place a heightened pleading burden on the moving party and will require clear and convincing evidence rather than the lesser "preponderance of evidence" standard. *See, e.g., Doria v. Texas Dept. of Human Resources*, 747 S.W.2d 953, 959 (Tex. App. 1988).

Endangerment is often difficult to prove. For example, in *Molitor v. Molitor*, 718 N.W.2d 13 (N.D. 2006), the noncustodial father claimed endangerment following an incident in which the oldest child and his ex-wife's new husband's two children were "huffing" gasoline in the basement of her house. In rejecting the noncustodial father's modification claim, the court found that the incident was the result of the behavior of the child's sibling and step-siblings in the mother's home, and that the child was not in danger. *See Sharp v. Bilbro*, 614 N.W.2d 260, 263 (Minn. App. 2000), *review denied* (Minn. Sept. 26, 2000) (endangerment implies a significant degree of danger or likely harm to the child's physical or emotional state).

In a Texas case, *In re K.L.R.*, 162 S.W.3d 291 (Tex. App. 2005), the court found endangerment where (a) the custodial mother was about to move the child to a house of unknown quality and environment, (b) her physical condition was deteriorating, and (c) she had been arrested on two felony charges and subsequently spent time in jail. In addition, the noncustodial father feared that she might flee the jurisdiction with the child, and the child was thriving in his current environment with his father.

Note that if parties cannot cooperate following an initial custody decision, the noncooperation may be viewed by some courts as endangerment. If, for example, the noncooperation increases to a level of physical, mental, moral, or emotional endangerment, a court may consider modification. *See* Kansas Revised Statutes §403.340(3) (2010).

Poor school performance has on rare occasions been considered an indicator of endangered emotional health or impaired emotional development. *See Kimmel v. Kimmel*, 392 N.W.2d 904, 908-09 (Minn. App. 1986), *review denied* (Minn. Oct. 29, 1986) (modification allowed where there existed a history of physical abuse of child by his stepfather, child's poor school performance, behavioral problems, and lack of personal hygiene, as well as school records showing that the child had progressed significantly since placement with his father).

6.16. Modifying Parenting Plans

Jurisdictions are not uniform when it comes to a custody modification request where the parties had originally arrived at a joint parenting plan or stipulation. Generally, when an agreement is reached between the parties regarding child custody, several jurisdictions presume that the agreement is in the best interests of the child. *See, e.g., In re Marriage of Jennings*, 50 P.3d 506 (Kan. App. 2002). The presumption must be overcome when a modification motion is brought.

In a few states like Oregon, a party seeking modification of a parenting plan is not required to demonstrate that a substantial change of circumstances since the entry of the original dissolution judgment has occurred. *Cole v. Wyatt*, 116 P.3d 919, 921 (Or. App. 2005) ("[T]he modification of parenting time does not require a showing of a substantial change of circumstances"). Other jurisdictions treat a permanent custody order obtained by stipulation as little different from a permanent custody order obtained via litigation. *See, e.g., In re Marriage of Burgess*, 913 P.2d 473 (Cal. 1966). These jurisdictions apply the changed circumstance rule regardless of whether the initial determination of custody resulted from an agreement, default judgment, or litigation.

Note that some jurisdictions will give priority to the first determination of custody in the belief that the stability produced by this policy is in the child's best interests. *Eschbach v. Eschbach*, 451 N.Y.S.2d 658 (N.Y. 1982).

THE ROLE OF A CHILD'S PREFERENCE FOR CHANGE

6.17. Maturity

Whether a child's preferences and feelings regarding custody and visitation will be given weight by the trial judge in a custody dispute necessarily depends on all the facts, including the child's age and ability to form and express those preferences and feelings intelligently. *Azia v. DiLascia*, 780 A.2d 992 (Conn. App. 2001). In general, although the express wishes of the child are not controlling at a modification proceeding, they are entitled to great weight, particularly where the child's age and maturity would make his or her input particularly meaningful. *McMillian v. Rizzo*, 817 N.Y.S.2d 679 (N.Y. App. 2006).

Equally suitable households. In those situations where the households of both parents are equally suitable, a child's preference to live with one of the parents may well tip the evidentiary scale in favor of that parent at an initial custody hearing. *Bovard v. Baker*, 775 A.2d 835, 841 (Pa. Super. 2001). However, a court will probably not give the child's preference the same weight at a modification proceeding.

Parental influence. Obviously, when a child states a preference, a court will evaluate the opinion in light of a child's general susceptibility to influence, parental and otherwise. *See Clara L. v. Paul M.*, 673 N.Y.S.2d 657 (N.Y. App. 1998); *In re Leskovich*, 385 A.2d 373 (Pa. Super 1978) ("we are not unmindful of the fact that a parent in possession of young children can exert subtle persuasion on them to influence their parental preference in order to facilitate the parent's chances of gaining custody").

Older child. The predominant importance of the choice of an older child as to the parent with whom he or she desires to live is recognized in most jurisdictions. *See, e.g., State ex rel. Feeley v. Williams*, 222 N.W. 927, 928 (Minn. 1929) (preference of 12 1/2-year-old child given great weight in maintaining her custody with aunt and uncle); *David M. v. Margaret M.*, 385 S.E.2d 912, 920 (W. Va. 1989) (preference of child 14 years old or older is determinative); *Marcus v. Marcus*, 248 N.E.2d 800, 805 (Ill. App. 1969) (it was an error to award custody of 14-year-old to mother against his stated preference to remain with grandmother); *Patrick v. Patrick*, 212 So. 2d 145, 147 (La. App. 1968) (award of custody of 17- and 18-year-old children to father reversed when they expressed a preference to remain with mother;

from practical viewpoint, it would be a "vain and useless act" to order children who are approaching age of majority to live with parent with whom they do not wish to live).

Note that while some courts have placed particular emphasis on a teenager's preference, terming it "an overwhelming consideration," all courts agree that a teenager's preference will not necessarily be controlling, regardless of the strength of the conviction.

EXAMPLES

Examples

5. Assume that when M and F divorce, M is awarded sole physical and legal custody of X and that F is ordered to pay M $1,000 per month in child support. When F fails to make three consecutive child support payments, M refuses to allow F to visit with their minor child pursuant to the divorce decree. F reacts to M's withholding of visitation by bringing a motion to enforce the court-ordered visitation or, alternatively, to modify the custody decree and give F sole legal and physical custody of the child. M responds by asking the court to hold F in contempt because of his failure to pay child support and to deny F visitation on the ground that he has either forfeited his visitation rights or abandoned the child by failing to pay support. How will a court most likely rule on the motions by the parties?

6. Assume that upon the dissolution of F and M's marriage, sole physical and legal custody of their three children was awarded to M (mother). F (father) was ordered to pay child support. Six years after the original judgment was entered, F filed a motion asking that the judgment be modified so that he be awarded sole physical custody of the three children. The testimony at the modification hearing showed that when the dissolution decree was entered, F was granted visitation consisting of alternating weekends and Wednesday afternoons. However, shortly after the divorce became final, F remarried and requested additional visitation with the children. Because the children enjoyed the time they spent with F, M informally agreed to additional visitation, although the original visitation order was not amended. At the time that F filed the modification action, the evidence showed that the three children were spending about an equal amount of time with F and M. The children expressed no preference for living with either parent.

   F's wife submitted an affidavit stating that she was not working outside the home. She stated that the children loved her as their stepmother and that she could give them her undivided attention. She also stated that M was now working part-time for 10–15 hours a week at a local fast-food restaurant, and the outside work put a strain on M's ability to care for the three children.

In opposition to the motion, M presented evidence that since the divorce, she had continued to exercise daily control over the lives of the children, even when they stayed with F. She testified that she made the major decisions on their behalf and maintained other parenting duties, such as assisting with homework, attending parent-teacher conferences, transporting them to athletic activities and music lessons, assisting in their expenses, and providing love, support, and encouragement. F testified that he was working a great deal and found it difficult to attend many of the events and conferences involving his children, although his new wife attended many of them. M stated that her outside work, in her opinion, did not interfere with her ability to parent the children adequately. M testified that it was never her intention to expand visitation formally to constitute a change in her capacity as sole legal and physical custodian for the children. She testified that she had begun to reduce the amount of time that the children spent with F, and it was her opinion that F was bringing the modification motion in an attempt to reduce his child support obligation. F testified that "the fact is, the children have been integrated" into his home with M's permission. How will a court most likely rule on F's claim that the children have been integrated into his home and that the original custody order should be modified?

7. Mother (M) and Father (F) were married for ten years and had four children. When they divorced, mother received sole physical and legal custody. A year after the divorce, F brought a motion to modify custody that gave him sole physical custody of all four children. At a hearing on F's motion, M responded by asserting that F had sexually abused the youngest female child on one occasion. F denied the allegation and asserted that M was lying so that she would withhold his right to visitation with the children. A court-appointed psychiatrist was of the opinion that it was "not in the best interest of the children to remain living in the house with their mother as she is thoroughly incapable of supporting a relationship between the children and their father and has demonstrated this incapacity over the past year with consistent effort and diligence." M's expert stated that in his opinion, M was a fit parent for the children and custody should not be changed. M's expert admitted that his qualification to make a custody recommendation was limited because he had not seen both parents and he had not seen the children interact in the presence of both parents. There was no physical evidence that F had sexually abused the youngest child, and there was no statement from the child to this effect. How should a trial judge rule on F's motion to change custody?

8. Assume that F (father) and M (mother) divorced and that M was awarded sole physical custody of the two minor children of the marriage. Five years after the divorce, F began to suspect that M was having an affair. F hired private detectives to investigate M's behavior. After receiving various reports from the private detectives, who suggested that M was having an affair, F brought a motion to modify custody of the two minor children, then ages 16 and 17. F argued that the children were being raised in an immoral atmosphere by M and that he should have sole legal and physical custody of them. The evidence to substantiate the claim of the alleged immoral behavior was circumstantial and consisted of the testimony of the detectives, who had observed M enter a hotel on five occasions with a male and leave the hotel several hours later. The children appeared as witnesses and expressed their strong desire to remain with M. Despite their stated preference, the trial judge ordered that custody be changed to F. M appealed and raised a number of issues, one of which was that the trial judge had failed to give sufficient weight to the children's testimony. How will an appellate court most likely treat the issue of the children's preference?

Explanations

5. First, it is unlikely that a court will accept the abandonment argument because of the short period of time between the initial court order, M's decision to deny visitation; and F's motion. Second, courts will apply the general rule that proof of unwarranted denial of or interference with established visitation rights may be sufficient cause for reversal of custody. However, as noted earlier in this chapter, courts view a denial or interference with visitation as not necessarily controlling in a custody modification proceeding; it is considered along with all other factors. Here, there are no other factors suggesting a change in custody should occur. Finally, the court most likely will retain custody with the custodial parent and order visitation with the noncustodial parent to be resumed. It also will likely enter a civil contempt order in favor of M in an effort to force F to pay the ordered support.

6. A court will, of course, conduct a factual inquiry and most likely will conclude that there has been a change in circumstances; that is, the children are spending more time with F than was originally contemplated at the time of F and M's divorce. The test to apply is whether the agreed additional time that the children spent with F is merely a

change or a "material" or "substantial change" in circumstances. While definitions vary as to what constitutes a "material" or "substantial" change in circumstances, for the change to be considered by a court, it generally must be of a continuing nature. Here, the first part of the two-pronged analysis is most likely met; i.e., there has been a material or substantial change in circumstances since the original order because the time spent with both parents has changed. *See generally Cochran v. Cochran*, 5 So. 3d 1220 (Ala. 2008).

Regardless of the answer to the material/substantial change question, it appears that there was neither consent nor complete integration of the minor children into F's home. Moreover, it does not appear that F contests M's testimony that she has continued to make the major decisions and exercised control of the children. The evidence produced by F will be viewed by most courts as falling short of the kind of knowing integration that statutes and case law require to support a modification request. *See, e.g., In re Marriage of Pontius*, 761 P.2d 247 (Colo. App. 1988).

7. This hypothetical is based on the case of *Young v. Young*, 628 N.Y.S.2d 957 (N.Y. App. 1995). In that case, the trial judge retained custody with M despite the opinion of F's expert. However, the appellate court reversed and awarded custody to F. It found that repeated uncorroborated and unfounded allegations of sexual abuse brought by M against F cast serious doubt upon M's fitness to be the custodial parent. It also found that during the course of M's unrelenting campaign against F that she subjected the youngest child to numerous physical examinations, including the probing and photographing of her private parts. Furthermore, during an in-camera interview, the child told the court that her mother reminded her every night that her father hurt her and that her mother would not let her father have visitation "because then my mom said he would learn his lesson."

8. On these facts, an appellate court might not reach the issue of the children's preference because of a failure to show the kind of changed circumstances that most courts would recognize as significant. However, if the appellate court should consider the preferences of the children, it is difficult to believe that, given the ages of the children, anyone can practically contradict their choice, even if their opinions are shown to be misguided (and there is no such showing). Because of the apparent maturity of the children, after weighing their opinions, the appellate court most likely will reverse the lower court ruling. M will retain custody.

SOLE CUSTODIAN RELOCATING TO ANOTHER JURISDICTION

6.18. Relocation and Constitutional Right to Travel

Constitutional right to travel. How does the fundamental right of citizens to travel freely from state to state and to reside in the state of their choice affect the right of a custodial parent to relocate with a child in his or her custody? Unfortunately, jurisdictions do not appear to be uniform in their response to that question.

To begin with, the right to travel is not specifically articulated in the United States Constitution, and the Supreme Court has never definitively identified the exact source of the freedom to travel. *See Jones v. Helms*, 452 U.S. 412, 418 (1981). The Court has said that as a general rule, state action penalizing a citizen for leaving or entering a state violates the citizen's constitutional right to travel. *Jones*, 452 U.S. at 419. However, the Court has also said that a state may restrict a citizen's right to leave the jurisdiction when doing so is necessary to serve a compelling government interest. *Shapiro v. Thompson*, 394 U.S. 618, 634 (1969), *overruled on other grounds by Edelman v. Jordan*, 415 U.S. 651 (1974). The phrase "compelling government interest" has become the object of varying interpretation when applied to concrete situations where a custodial parent is seeking to relocate from one state to another.

Favoring the right to travel. Some states appear to favor the right of the custodial parent to travel with his or her child. For example in *Watt v. Watt*, 971 P.2d 608, 616 (Wyo. 1999), the court held that because of concern for the protection of the constitutional liberties of the citizens of Wyoming, an intrastate relocation by a custodial parent cannot by itself be considered a change in circumstances sufficiently substantial and material to justify reopening the question of custody. New Mexico, Oregon, and South Dakota generally appear to agree with Wyoming's perspective. *See, e.g., Jaramillo v. Jaramillo*, 823 P.2d 299, 304–05 (N.M. 1991) (placing burden on the relocating parent to show that relocation is in the best interests of the child and favoring the resisting parent, with a corresponding presumption that relocation is not in the child's best interests, unconstitutionally impairs the relocating parent's right to travel); *Matter of Marriage of Duckett*, 905 P.2d 1170, 1172 (Or. App. 1995); *Fossum v. Fossum*, 545 N.W.2d 828, 832–33 (S.D. 1996) (trial court placed undue weight on the desirability of father and daughter living near each other).

Child's best interests and compelling state interest. Some states view the child's best interests and a compelling state interest as trumping a parent's right to travel with the child. *See, e.g., LaChapelle v. Mitten*, 607 N.W.2d 151, 163-164 (Minn. App. 2000) (mother's argument that the award of sole physical custody conditioned on her return to Minnesota violated her fundamental right to travel rejected, with court saying that the conditional award did not restrict her right to remain out of state; the court only required her to return to Minnesota if she wished to maintain sole physical custody); *Ziegler v. Ziegler*, 691 P.2d 773, 780 (Idaho App. 1985) (restriction requiring the parties to seek a court order before changing the place of residence of the children was based upon a compelling state interest justifying interference with the constitutional right of free travel and by its terms was not arbitrary, capricious, or unduly restrictive); *Meadows v. Meadows*, 3 So. 3d 221 (Ala. App. 2008) (parent's fundamental right to travel can be overcome by the compelling state interest in the best interests of a child); *Carlson v. Carlson*, 661 P.2d 833 (Kan. App. 1983) (a modified custody decree awarding custody to the plaintiff "for so long as she resides in McPherson County, Kansas" is affirmed).

Relocation doesn't implicate the right to travel. Some courts have held that relocation does not implicate a parent's right to travel because relocation statutes do not outright prohibit a parent's traveling. Rather, the parent is merely prohibited from traveling to a new location with his or her child. *See, e.g., Lenz v. Lenz*, 40 S.W.3d 111, 118 n.3 (Tex. App. 2000), *rev'd on other grounds*, *Lenz v. Lenz*, 79 S.W.3d 10 (Tex. 2002).

Balancing travel with other interests. Some states balance the relocating parent's right to travel with two other important interests: the best interests of the child and the non-relocating parent's interest in the care and control of the child. For example, in *Baxendale v. Raich*, 878 N.E.2d 1252 (Ind. 2008), the mother argued that an Indiana statute allowing the noncustodial/non-relocating parent to object to the custodial parent's proposed relocation "without offering to take custody of the children," restricts the custodial/relocating parent's right to travel because the custodial/relocating parent is not given a choice to either relocate and lose custody of the children or keep custody by staying in the primary residence. The court provided the following analysis:

> We agree with those courts that . . . recogniz[e] that a chilling effect on travel can violate the federal Constitution, but also acknowledg[e] that other considerations may outweigh an individual's interest in travel. We think it clear that the child's interests are powerful countervailing considerations that cannot be swept aside as irrelevant in the face of a parent's claimed right to relocate. In addition, it is well established that the non-relocating parent's interest in

> parenting is itself of constitutional dimension . . . . In the custody context, Indiana statutes reflect these concerns by considering whether the relocation is indeed bona fide, and explicitly acknowledging the child's interests and the effect on nonrelocating persons including a nonrelocating parent.

Id. at 1259–60.

See In re Marriage of Ciesluk, 113 P.3d 135, 146 (Colo. 2005) (in relocation cases, the trial court is to balance custodial parent, child, and noncustodial parent concerns).

Qualified right. In *In re Marriage of Guffin*, 209 P.3d 225 (Mont. 2009), illustrates what some courts term a "qualified right" to relocate. In this case, the couple originally approved a joint parenting plan in which the mother was the primary custodian. When she decided to relocate about 700 miles away from the children's father, the trial court changed the plan so that the father was the primary custodian. In reversing the trial judge, whose expressed reason for changing custody was the mother's decision to move 700 miles across the state, the appellate court stated that the dispute implicated the constitutional issue of the right to travel. It observed that a custodial parent who bears the burdens and responsibilities of raising a child is entitled, to the greatest possible extent, to the same freedom to seek a better life for herself or himself and the children as the noncustodial parent enjoys. It said that a custodial parent has a fundamental, *although qualified*, constitutional right to migrate, resettle, find a new job, and start a new life, and the noncustodial parent bears a heavy burden to demonstrate a compelling interest on the part of a court to interfere with this right. *See Matter of Custody of D.M.G.*, 951 P.2d 1377 (Mont. 1998).

6.19. The Social Science Relocation Debate

Relocation cases have been recognized as presenting "some of the knottiest and most disturbing problems that courts are asked to resolve." *Tropea v. Tropea*, 665 N.E.2d 145, 148 (N.Y. 1996). The interests of the primary custodial parent in moving to a new location, where educational or work opportunities are better, are pitted against the parent who will be left behind and possesses a strong desire to maintain frequent and regular contact with the child or children. Cases involving the geographic relocation of the primary custodial parent following dissolution of a marriage are intensely emotional, and the issues are extensively litigated. Social scientists have been looked to by some courts to provide the best solution to this challenging issue. So far, they appear to disagree among themselves about the "best solution."

Family unit theory. There is an ongoing debate among experts over the impact relocation of a custodial parent with a minor child has on the child's psychological development. Some social science experts have suggested that the psychological welfare of a child depends more on the well-being of the family unit with whom the child primarily resides than on maintaining frequent and regular contact with the other parent. *See, e.g.*, Janet M. Bowermaster, *Sympathizing with Solomon: Choosing Between Parents in a Mobile Society*, 31 U. Louisville J. Fam. L. 791, 884 (1992) (custodial parents should be allowed to relocate with their child in good faith to pursue "their best opportunities"); Judith S. Wallerstein & Tony J. Tanke, *To Move or Not to Move: Psychological and Legal Considerations in the Relocation of Children Following Divorce*, 30 Fam. L.Q. 305, 311, 318 (1996) (social science research on custody does not support the presumption that frequent and continuing access to both parents is in the child's best interests; therefore, a parent with primary physical custody generally should be able to relocate with the child); William G. Austin, *Relocation, Research, and Forensic Evaluation, Part II: Research in Support of the Relocation Risk Assessment Model*, Fam. Ct. Rev. 46(2), 347, 359 (Apr. 2008) (relocation continues to be an area of ongoing controversy in the field of child custody). Austin finds "convincing evidence" that relocation significantly expands the level of risk for children of divorce, but cautions that the research should not be interpreted as a basis for a bias or legal presumption against relocation. William G. Austin, *Relocation and Forensic Evaluation: Relocation, Research, and Forensic Evaluation, Part I: Effects of Residential Mobility on Children of Divorce*, Fam. Ct. Rev. 46(1), 137, 139 (Jan. 2008).

Some states have viewed a divorce with sole physical custody of children awarded to one parent as the creation of a new family unit. Jurisdictions applying this theory have concluded that what is beneficial to the new family unit as a whole also benefits its individual members. *See, e.g.*, *In re Marriage of Harris*, 96 P.3d 141 (Cal. 2004) (final custody order creates a new family unit now commonly referred to as a single-parent family); *Rebsamen v. Rebsamen*, 107 S.W.3d 871 (Ark. 2003) (court should balance the needs of the noncustodial parent with that of the new family unit); *Rosenthal v. Maney*, 745 N.E.2d 350 (Mass. App. 2001); *Anderson v. Anderson*, 56 S.W.3d 5 (Tenn. App. 1999); *D'Onofrio v. D'Onofrio*, 365 A.2d 27, 29-30 (N.J. Super.), *aff'd*, 365 A.2d 716 (1976) (children belong to a different family unit after a divorce); Joan G. Wexler, *Rethinking the Modification of Child Custody Decrees*, 94 Yale L.J. 757, 808 (1985). The new family unit is entitled to a measure of constitutional protection against unwarranted governmental intrusion, which is similar to that accorded to an intact, two-parent family. *In re Marriage of Mentry*, 190 Cal. Rptr. 843, 848-849 (Cal. App. 1983).

In a "new family unit" jurisdiction, a court will take the view that a custodial parent should be permitted to make the significant, life-influencing decisions affecting a child so long as the parent remains fit to have custody, although the noncustodial parent's interests retain great importance. *Ascuitto v. Farricielli*, 711 A.2d 708 (Conn. 1998) (recognizing importance of familial relationship between noncustodial parent and child in context of parent-child immunity). The courts theorize that a child's interests can become so intricately interwoven with the well-being of the new family unit that the determination of the child's best interest also requires that the interests of the custodial parent be taken into account. *See, e.g.*, *Mize v. Mize*, 621 So. 2d 417, 419 (Fla. 1993) (it follows that what is good for custodial parent's well-being is good for child's well-being).

Frequent contact is better. Other social science research has suggested that children are better off if they have frequent contact and good relationships with both parents. *See, e.g.*, Marion Gindes, *The Psychological Effects of Relocation for Children of Divorce*, 10 J. Am. Acad. Matrimonial Law. 119, 132 (1998). Some experts believe that any move, even a relatively short one, is a stressful event for a child and can have a negative impact on the child's well-being. *See, e.g.*, Joan B. Kelly & Michael E. Lamb, *Using Child Development Research to Make Appropriate Custody and Access Decisions for Young Children*, 38 Fam. & Conciliation Cts. Rev. 297, 309 (2000) (regardless of who is the primary caretaker, a child benefits from extensive contact with both parents); David Wood et al., *Impact of Family Relocation on Children's Growth, Development, School Function, and Behavior*, 270 JAMA 1334, 1337 (1993) ("[a] family move disrupts the routines, relationships, and attachments that define the child's world"). This difference of opinion explains, at least in part, the sometimes disparate approaches among jurisdictions in considering relocation issues.

6.20. Relocation Trends

As Americans began divorcing in larger numbers beginning in the late 1960s, they also began to ask courts to allow them to relocate with their children to cities and states located far from the other parent. The initial judicial trend appeared to be one that imposed substantial restrictions on the ability of the primary parent to move with the child or children. *See* Arthur B. LaFrance, *Child Custody and Relocation: A Constitutional Perspective*, 34 U. Louisville J. Fam. L. 1 (1995-96). However, during the late 1990s, a number of jurisdictions began to articulate new, less-restrictive standards for relocation cases. *See* Carol S. Bruch & Janet M. Bowermaster, *The Relocation of Children and Custodial Parents: Public Policy, Past and Present*, 30 Fam. L.Q. 245 (Summer 1996).

The Oklahoma Supreme Court summarized its view of the status of relocation law among the states as follows in 2001:

> The majority of jurisdictions which have considered this subject have adopted approaches which favor the custodial parent's right to move away from the

> state with their child even though they do not have a presumptive right to relocate statute . . . . While the relevant statutory enactments which are placed at issue in those cases vary widely from state to state and some states have no applicable statutes, the decisions are generally based on judicial recognition of the post-divorce new family unit, and stability and continuity of the child's relationship with his primary custodian as the most important factor affecting the child's welfare. These courts also recognize that the well-being of the child is fundamentally interrelated with the well-being of the custodial parent, and that parent is the best person to make decisions affecting the child and the new family group, such as where they will reside. The courts therefore accord those childrearing decisions deference, and hold that judicial intervention in that decision making process should be limited to only the most extreme circumstances.

Kaiser v. Kaiser, 23 P.3d 278, 284-85 (Okla. 2001).

In a 2004 decision, the Rhode Island Supreme Court appeared to agree with Oklahoma and made the following observation regarding its view of the trend in relocation disputes:

> Although the several states have taken divergent approaches to the issue of relocation, it is clear that traditional policies that discouraged relocation are increasingly being replaced by a less restrictive view that favors the right of a parent exercising physical custody to relocate the child.

Dupre v. Dupre, 857 A.2d 242, 249 (R.I. 2004).

But see Theresa Glennon, *Divided Parents, Shared Children — Conflicting Approaches to Relocation Disputes in the USA*, 4 Utrecht L. Rev. 55, 57 (2008) (noting that relocation was favored in the 1990s and 2000s, but that the trend now is moving away from a presumptive right to relocate toward requiring the custodial parent to prove that a move is in the child's best interests). Texas appears to agree with Oklahoma and New Jersey. *Lenz v. Lenz*, 79 S.W.3d 10, 14-15 (Tex. 2002) ("Historically, courts have disfavored removing a child from the jurisdiction issuing the original custody decree . . . . Recently, however, courts have reassessed the standards for relocation, moving away from a relatively strict presumption against relocation and toward a more fluid balancing test that permits the trial court to take into account a greater number of relevant factors").

6.21. Relocation Standards

Diverse standards. It should be clear by now that the law applicable to interstate relocation of a child by a custodial parent is nationally diverse. Kenneth Waldron, *A Review of Social Science Research on Post Divorce Relocation*, 19 J. Am. Acad. Matrimonial L. 337, 338-39 (2005) (highlighting the inconsistency of courts and legislatures on the issue of relocation). Courts in various states do not necessarily agree with each other, and courts in the same jurisdiction are changing their positions on who has what burden in these disputes.

Presumptions. Traditional policies apparently disfavored relocation, and some courts imposed presumptions that favored the non-relocating parent. *See, e.g., Pollock v. Pollock*, 889 P.2d 633, 635, n. 1 (Ariz. App. 1995); *McAlister v. Patterson*, 299 S.E.2d 322, 323 (S.C. 1982) (in child custody cases, presumption is against removal of child from jurisdiction of state); *McAlister v. Patterson*, 299 S.E.2d 322 (S.C. 1982) (in situations where removal will benefit the child, removal has been allowed). In other states, the presumption against relocation was a matter of common law. *See, e.g.*, Ala. Code 1975 §30-3-169.4; Mo. Stat. Ann. §452.377 (2011); *Tremain v. Tremain*, 646 N.W.2d 661 (Neb. 2002) (child custody determinations are matters initially entrusted to the discretion of the trial court); *Parish v. Spaulding*, 496 S.E.2d 91 (Va. App. 1998), judgment *aff'd*, 513 S.E.2d 391 (1999).

Presumptive right to relocate. Some states appeared to create a presumptive right for a custodial parent to relocate. This was done by either by statute or decisional law. *See, e.g.*, Minn. Stat. §518.18(d) (2002) (presumption that court will retain the existing primary placement); Okla. Stat. Ann. tit. 10, §19 (West 1998) (in absence of a showing of prejudice to the rights or welfare of a child, a custodial parent has a presumptive right to change a child's residence); S.D. Codified Laws §25-5-13 (Michie 1999) (relocation should be permitted so long as it does not prejudice the rights or welfare of the child); Wis. Stat. Ann. §767.327(3)(a)2.a (West 2001) (rebuttable presumption that continuing the current custody arrangement is in the best interests of the child); *Jaramillo v. Jaramillo*, 823 P.2d 299, 303 (N.M. 1991) (rebuttable presumption that relocation with custodial parent is in best interest of child); *Mize v. Mize*, 621 So. 2d 417, 419 (Fla. 1993) (presuming that custodial parent's and child's best interests coincide, and that a good-faith desire to move ordinarily should be allowed); *Love v. Love*, 851 P.2d 1283, 1287 (Wyo. 1993) (good-faith decisions of custodial parent presumed to be in best interests of child).

In California, the custodial parent was given a presumptive right to relocate with the minor child, subject to the power of the court to restrain a change that would prejudice the rights or welfare of the child. *See, e.g., In re Marriage of LaMusga*, 88 P.3d 81, 98 (Cal. 2004); *In re Marriage of Burgess*, 913 P.2d 473, 482-483 (1996) (placing burden on noncustodial parent to show that move will be harmful to child); *Kaiser v. Kaiser*, 23 P.3d 278, 282 (Okla. 2001) (custodial parent has presumptive right under Oklahoma statute to move with the child). In Arkansas and Colorado, it is presumed that a parent's choice to move with the children should generally be allowed. *Hollandsworth v. Knyzewski*, 109 S.W.3d 653 (Ark. 2003); *In re Marriage of Francis*, 919 P.2d 776, 784 (Colo. 1996).

Burden-shifting approach. Some courts have adopted a burden-shifting approach for determining the outcome of a removal dispute when the primary physical custody seeks to relocate. Under this approach, the initial burden falls upon the relocating parent to demonstrate a legitimate or good-faith reason for the move. Once a *prima facie* case supporting relocation has been made by the custodial parent, the burden shifts to the non-relocating parent to show that the proposed move is not in the child's best interests. *See, e.g., Ireland v. Ireland*, 717 A.2d 676, 682 (Conn. 1998); *Baures v. Lewis*, 770 A.2d 214, 230-31 (N.J. 2001).

New York test. Historically, New York was considered one of the more restrictive relocation jurisdictions. It developed a policy requiring a three-step inquiry. Under this test, if it could be established that the proposed move would disrupt the non-relocating parent's "regular and meaningful access to and interaction with his or her children," the relocating parent had to demonstrate "exceptional circumstances" to justify the move, and "establish that the relocation is in the best interests of the child." *See, e.g., Lavane v. Lavane*, 608 N.Y.S.2d 475, 476 (N.Y. App. 1994) (quoting *Matter of Radford v. Propper*, 190 A.D.2d 93 (N.Y. App. 1993).

This test was rejected in *Tropea v. Tropea*, 665 N.E.2d 145, 150 (N.Y. 1996). In *Tropea* the court held that "each relocation request must be considered on its own merits with due consideration of all the relevant facts and circumstances and with predominant emphasis being placed on what outcome is most likely to serve the best interests of the child." The Tropea court identified various factors that the trial courts should consider including:

> each parent's reasons for seeking or opposing the move, the quality of the relationships between the child and [both] parents, the impact of the move on the quantity and quality of the child's future contact with the noncustodial parent, the degree to which the custodial parent's and child's life may be enhanced economically, emotionally and educationally by the move, and the feasibility of preserving the relationship between the noncustodial parent and child through suitable visitation arrangements.

Id. at 151.

No presumptive right to relocate; party seeking change has initial burden. In Oregon, the custodial parent does not enjoy a presumptive right to relocate with the child. *In re Marriage of Fedorov*, 206 P.3d 1124 (Or. App. 2009). In a relocation case in that state, the party seeking the change of custody "has the burden to show that there [has] been a substantial change of circumstances since the time of the original custody award"). The parent must also demonstrate that the change of custody is in the best interests of the child. *Colson and Peil*, 51 P.3d 607 (Or. App. 2002); *Hamilton-Waller and Waller*, 123 P.3d 310 (Or. App. 2005). Despite the 1993 *Mize* decision cited earlier, Florida now appears to follow an approach similar to Oregon. In Florida, the parent wishing to relocate has the burden of proving, by a preponderance of the evidence, that relocation is in the best interest of the child. If that burden is met, the non-relocating parent or other person must show by a preponderance of the evidence that the proposed relocation is not in the best interest of the child. West's Fla. Stat. Ann. §61.13001 (2006). In Connecticut, the custodial parent seeking permission to relocate bears the initial burden of demonstrating, by a preponderance of the evidence that the relocation is for a legitimate purpose and that the proposed relocation is reasonable in light of that purpose. Once the custodial parent has established a *prima facie* case, the burden shifts to the noncustodial parent to prove, by a preponderance of the evidence that the relocation would not be in the best interests of the child. *See, e.g.*, *Ireland v. Ireland*, 717 A.2d 676 (Conn. 1998) (limited to post-judgment relocation matters); *Ford v. Ford*, 789 A.2d 1104 (Conn. 2002).

Pennsylvania. Prior to 2011, a Pennsylvania court, on its own motion or upon the motion of either party, could review the existing custody order when a relocation request was received. *Gruber v. Gruber*, 583 A.2d 434, 440 (Pa. 1990). The custodial parent had the initial burden of showing that the move was likely to significantly improve the quality of life for that parent and the children. In addition, each parent had the burden of establishing the integrity of his or her motives in either desiring the move or seeking to prevent it.

However, the Pennsylvania Legislature recently adopted a Child Custody Act, which became effective on January 24, 2011. *See* 23 Pa. Con. Stat. Ann. §§5321–5340 (2011). "Relocation" is defined under the new Act as "[a] change in residence of the child which significantly impairs the ability of a non-relocating party to exercise custodial rights." The Act also provides that the relocating party carries the burden of proving that "relocation will serve the best interest of the child as shown under the factors set forth in subsection [h]." 23 Pa. Con. Stat. Ann. §5337(i)(1) (2011). Both parties have the burden of proving that their positions possess integrity. *Id.* at §5337(i)(2). In C.M.K. *v.* K.E.M., 45 A.3d 417 (Pa. Super. 2012), the court rejected a mother's relocation request where evidence indicated that the father of a child born out of wedlock had an active involvement in the child's sporting events, school activities, and medical appointments, and that the father had arranged his work schedule in order to attend many of the child's activities.

Two-part test. In *Baures v. Lewis*, 770 A.2d 214, 230 (N.J. 2001), New Jersey held that a custodial parent may move with the children so long as the move does not interfere with the best interests of the children or the visitation rights of the noncustodial parent. The court established essentially a two part test requiring a good-faith reason for the move and proof that the child will not suffer from it.

Note that in Texas, relocation disputes may be tried to a jury. For example, in *Lenz v. Lenz*, 79 S.W.3d 10 (Tex. 2002), the court held that a trial judge was not authorized to contravene a jury verdict allowing a mother to move to Germany with the custodial child by imposing additional geographical restrictions on her.

6.22. Natural Parent Presumption

How does the law view a modification request by a third party that custody of a child be modified when the child is currently in the custody of a parent? The answer is clear—the law in all jurisdictions provides the natural parent with substantial protection from such an eventuality, including a presumption that the child is best left in the protection and care of the natural parent as against a third party.

State custody standards generally reflect the view that the biological link between parents and their children should not be broken; the law gives a very clear preference for biological children to remain with their parents. *See* Laura Beresh Taylor, Note, *C.R.B.V.C.C. and B.C.: Protecting Children's Need for Stability in Custody Modification Disputes Between Biological Parents and Third Parties*, 32 Akron L. Rev. 371, 373 (1999). Although children today are no longer viewed as parental property, the view that biological parents retain a "natural right" to the custody of their children has endured. *Ibid.*

The preference for natural parents retaining custody of their children is justified as providing a measure of protection for the rights of the natural parent. *Allen v. Proksch*, 832 N.E.2d 1080, 1099 (Ind. App. 2005). It is also justified on the basis that it embodies innumerable social, psychological, cultural, and biological considerations that significantly benefit the child and serve the child's best interests. *Ibid.*

Only occasionally has the presumption associated with a natural parent's right to custody of a biological child been intellectually challenged. In one instance, the concurring judge in *Rowles v. Rowles*, 668 A.2d 126 (Pa. 1995), questioned application of the presumption. The judge observed that:

> [T]he underlying tenor of the presumption reflects an archaic concept that children are proprietary assets of parents. Serious questions may be posed with respect to the soundness of the apriorism that mere biological relationship assures solicitude, care, devotion, and love for one's offspring . . . . [W]here a third party better fulfills these needs, or where other circumstances indicate third party custody to be preferable, the courts, when exercising judgment as to a child's welfare, should not be restrained solely by a presumption.

Id. at 127 quoting *Ellerbe v. Hooks*, 416 A.2d 512, 516 (Pa. 1980) (Flaherty, J., concurring).

See Lawrence Schlam, *Third Party Custody Disputes in Minnesota: Overcoming the "Natural Rights" of Parents or Pursuing the "Best Interests" of Children?* 26 Wm. Mitchell L. Rev. 733, 738, n. 22 (2000) ("There is, however, little scientific basis for the presumption that a child's best interests are best served by being in the custody of natural parents").

Burden of proof. Before placing a child in the custody of a person other than the natural parent, most jurisdictions must be satisfied by clear and convincing evidence that the best interests of the child require such a placement. They must also be convinced that placement with a person other than the natural parent represents a substantial and significant advantage to the child. The presumption will not be overcome merely because a third party could provide the better things in life for the child.

6.23. Active Military Service

Because of the involvement of the United States in foreign wars over the past several years, many states have promulgated specific statutes to protect the military mother or father from unfair treatment when the custody of a child is at issue.

For example, California law provides that "[a] party's absence . . . shall not, by itself, be sufficient to justify a modification of a custody . . . order if the reason for the absence . . . is the party's activation to military service and deployment out of state." Cal. Fam. Code §3047 (West 2005). Arizona does not consider "military deployment of a custodial parent a change of circumstances that materially affects the welfare of the child if the custodial parent has filed a military family care plan and if the military deployment is less than six months." Ariz. Rev. Stat. Ann. §25-411B (2009). Kansas permits the parties to enter into a parenting plan in contemplation of military deployment and provides a presumption "that the agreement is in the best interests of the child." Kan. Stat. Ann. §60-1630(e) (2008).

In *Faucett v. Vasquez*, 984 A.2d 460 (N.J. Super 2009), a New Jersey court ruled that if legal or residential custody is contested, a parent's military deployment and absence from the home for a significant period of time is sufficient for the family court to order an investigation of the situation and search for a meaningful solution to serve the best interests of the child.

Indiana law states that a court may not consider a parent's absence or relocation due to active duty service as a factor in determining custody or permanently modifying a child custody order. Ind. Code 31–17–2–21.3 (2010). It protects a citizen-soldier from losing custody of their child based on their absence from their child's life while they are serving their country. However, once a soldier is no longer deployed or subject to deployment, the statute does not apply. *In re Paternity of C.S.*, 964 N.E.2d 879 (Ind. App. 2012).

MODEL RELOCATION DRAFTING EFFORTS

6.24. American Law Institute (ALI)

The American Law Institute (ALI) and the American Academy of Matrimonial Lawyers (AAML) have created model provisions for states to consider when drafting relocation legislation. The National Conference of Commissioners on Uniform State Laws has yet to create a model provision.

The ALI *Principles* reflect "the policy choice that a parent, like any other citizen, should be able to choose his or her place of residence, and that the job of rearing children after divorce should not be made too financially or emotionally burdensome to the parent who has the majority share of custodial responsibility." ALI, *Principles of the Law of Family Dissolution*, ch. 2, §2.17, cmt. d (2002).

Where physical custody is shared, the best-interest calculus pertaining to removal is appreciably different compared with those situations that involve sole physical custody. ALI, *Principles of the Law of Family Dissolution: Analysis and Recommendations*, §2.17(1), (4)(c) (2002). In such an instance, a parent with true joint physical custody proposing a move is required to prove that relocation is in the best interest of the child, and not merely desired by the moving parent. *See Mason v. Coleman*, 850 N.E.2d 513 (Mass. 2006) (discussing the difference between joint and sole physical custody standards under the ALI *Principles*).

6.25. American Academy of Matrimonial Lawyers (AAML)

The American Academy of Matrimonial Lawyers (AAML) proposed Model Act has 22 sections and covers notice, procedures for objection, and remedies. It "is meant to serve as a template for those jurisdictions desiring a statutory solution to the relocation quandary." *Perspectives on the Relocation of Children*, 15 J. Am. Acad. Matrimonial Law. 1, 2 (1998); AAML Proposed Model Relocation Act, http://www.aaml.org/library/publications/model-relocation-act-0 (last visited July, 2012).

Among its recommendations, the Model Act identifies nonexclusive factors that courts should consider in determining relocation issues, which include the following:

> (1) the nature, quality, and extent of involvement, and the duration of the child's relationship with the person proposing to relocate and with the non-relocating person, siblings, and other significant persons in the child's life; (2) the age, developmental stage, and needs of the child, and the likely impact the relocation will have on the child's physical, educational, and emotional development, taking into consideration any special needs of the child; (3) the feasibility of preserving the relationship between the nonrelocating person and the child through suitable [visitation] arrangements, considering the logistics and financial circumstances of the parties; (4) the child's preference, taking into consideration the age and maturity of the child; (5) whether there is an established pattern of conduct of the person seeking relocation, either to promote or to thwart the relationship between the child and the non-relocating person; (6) whether the relocation of the child will enhance the general quality of life for both the custodial party seeking the relocation and the child, including but not limited to financial or emotional benefit or educational opportunity; (7) the reasons of each person for seeking or opposing the relocation; and (8) any other factor affecting the best interests of the child.

15 J. Am. Acad. Matrimonial Law, §405 (1998).

RELOCATING WHERE PARENTS SHARE JOINT PHYSICAL CUSTODY

6.26. Overview

As discussed earlier in this chapter, when parties have joint or shared physical custody, courts will treat the burden of proof and standard for allowing relocation differently from situations where a custodial parent has received sole physical custody. It is clear from the decisions that when a court has decided that the parties should share joint physical custody of a child, it will most likely view the situation as one in which there is no noncustodial parent. Therefore, when a joint-custody parent opposes relocation, that parent is normally not saddled with an initial burden to come forward with evidence opposing the move. *In re Marriage of Seagondollar*, 43 Cal. Rptr. 3d 575 (Cal. App. 2006). Once the parent seeking relocation files a motion or petition, the burden of showing that the move is in the best interests of the child remains with that parent. *See, e.g., Mason v. Coleman*, 850 N.E.2d 513 (Mass. 2006); *In re Marriage of Burgess*, 913 P.2d 473, 483 n.12 (Cal. 1996) (when parents have shared joint physical custody, relocation of one of them justifies modification of custody under a best-interest test); *Ayers v. Ayers*, 508 N.W.2d 515, 519 (Minn. 1993) (in shared custody cases, relocation amounts to a modification of the custody award, and thus must be justified by the relocating parent); *cf. Jaramillo v. Jaramillo*, 823 P.2d 299, 309 (N.M. 1991) (when parties share custody equally, neither has the burden of proof in removal matter). The burden normally does not shift to the parent resisting the move to prove that the change would affect the child adversely. *See Stringer v. Vincent*, 411 N.W.2d 474 (Mich. App. 1987); Edwin J. Terry et al., *Relocation: Moving Forward, or Moving Backward?* 15 J. Am. Acad. Matrimonial L., 167, 212-213 (1998).

Examples

EXAMPLES

9. Assume that when P and D's marriage dissolved, the court awarded joint legal custody of their minor son to the parties but placed primary physical custody with P. The order allowed D to visit his son every other weekend, and D has exercised this right without missing a weekend. Assume that this jurisdiction has a relocation statute that provides that the custodial parent seeking permission to relocate bears the initial burden of demonstrating, by a preponderance of the evidence, that the relocation is for a legitimate purpose and that the proposed relocation is reasonable in light of that purpose. Once the custodial parent has established a *prima facie* case, the burden shifts to the noncustodial parent to prove, by a preponderance of the evidence, that relocating is not in the child's best interests. The jurisdiction has also accepted the "new family" theory in custody relocation disputes. At the time of the dissolution, P and D resided in state X. Three years after the divorce, P remarried. P's new husband is a computer consultant, and his major consulting contract ended when the company he was working with closed because of financial problems. He undertook a search for another job and secured a position in state Y. P informed D of her plan

to join her husband in state Y with their son, age 11, and moved to modify the existing custody order so that she could relocate there with the child. Is the court likely to grant P's request to relocate?

10. Assume that this dispute takes place in a jurisdiction that applies the "new family" theory discussed earlier. P and D dissolve their relationship. D (mother) is awarded sole legal and physical custody of their two children. Three months after the judgment is entered, D brings a motion to leave the forum state with the children, ages 4 and 7, and move to another state that is 1,000 miles away. D produces evidence that she has been accepted into law school in the distant state. She also produces a plan that outlines how the children will be cared for while she is in law school. D agrees that P may have extended visits with the children in the summer. P introduces evidence that since the divorce, P has exercised his visitation rights with the children on Saturday and Sunday of every other week and has seen them every Wednesday evening for two or three hours. The trial judge observes that P and D appear angry with each other over the divorce. P argues that D is seeking revenge because P just married his secretary, who is 15 years younger than he. Most likely, how will a court rule on D's request to relocate?

11. Assume that P and D have joint legal and physical custody of child C, with each parent sharing physical custody for half the week. C is 8 years old. Assume that three months after the divorce was final, P filed a motion asking for primary physical custody of C and for permission to relocate to another jurisdiction with C. In the motion to relocate, P maintained that as a result of her mother's recent death, she desires to return to her childhood home to be close to her siblings. P explained that she had inherited a substantial sum of money from her mother, as well as part ownership of her mother's house. Her siblings have agreed to permit her to live in the house, rent-free, while she finishes college and earns a teaching license. P explained that her mother's death not only resulted in closer contact with her siblings, but also renewed the importance of this contact. P also explained that she had exhausted her career opportunities as a secretary in the city where she currently lives. She stated that teaching would offer her a career, rather than a "job," and because her hours would mirror the minor child's school schedule, C would no longer need outside day care. D (father) opposed her motion, arguing that relocation offered no actual advantage to the child and would disturb the current, functioning joint custody arrangement. D asks the court to award him sole physical custody of the child. How will the court most likely rule on the relocation request?

12. Assume that a judgment of divorce was entered incorporating the terms of a stipulated agreement between the husband and wife. The judgment stated that "the parties agreed that P shall not remove the children outside the town of X until the youngest child shall have reached the age of eighteen (18) years." P was awarded sole legal and physical custody of the children.

Six months after the judgment was entered, P asked the court that she be allowed to move the children from the town of X to a large metropolitan city 200 miles away. P argued that as the custodial parent, she is allowed to make major decisions regarding the family, including moving to another location. In addition, she argued that she intended to marry Y, who was employed in a "good job" in the city. D opposed P's motion, arguing that P's right to move the children had been clearly addressed in the divorce action and that the court should honor the agreement. On these facts, should the court enforce the stipulation restricting movement that was contained in the judgment?

13. Assume that P and D had been married ten years before their relationship broke down. P was awarded sole legal and physical custody of the two male children, ages 1 and 8 at the time of the divorce. Five years after the divorce, P fell in love with X and decided to marry X and move with the children from Rhode Island to Texas. X was a colonel in the military stationed in Texas. An extensive hearing was held to determine whether P's request should be granted.

With respect to the importance of the children's maintaining contact with their father, P testified that she viewed it as "very important"; she stated that she "wanted them to continue a relationship with their father." She testified that her plans with respect to maintaining that relationship were that the children "would continue to have phone conversations with their father nightly or every other night." She added that "there is also Skype." P further stated that "there would also be extended summer vacations," as well as spring break and major holiday vacations; she also said that she would "welcome defendant to come down to Texas anytime he would like." P also testified that she had discussed the possibility of her "staying in Rhode Island with the children and trying to maintain a long-distance relationship"; however, she believed "that it wouldn't be beneficial to the children or her and her new husband as they tried to maintain a loving, nurturing relationship." P acknowledged that moving to Texas was going to reduce significantly the contact that D would have with his children.

P is currently a full-time public school teacher. She testified that when she and X are married, she would no longer have to work outside the home but could devote all of her efforts toward the children and her new spouse. Experts testified that the schools in Texas that the boys would attend were better performing than the schools in Rhode Island. Both children are doing well in Rhode Island schools, although the older son is undergoing counseling relative to the divorce. All of P and D's relatives are residents of Rhode Island.

D testified that during visitation, after their 12-year-old son learned of his mother's decision to move to Texas, he "broke down and started crying." He told his son "not to worry about moving to Texas;" he added that he had also told his older son that he would "do everything in his power to stop the children from going." D further testified that there was never a time when his older son did not cry when the move to Texas came up in a conversation.

With respect to his older son's activities with which he was involved, D testified that he coaches his soccer team and his baseball team; he added that he was previously a coach for his son's basketball team. He further testified that he was involved in his older son's Cub Scout activities and "various school activities," as well as church events. With respect to his involvement with his younger son's activities, D testified that he was the coach of his soccer team and that he was planning on coaching his T-ball team; he added that he formerly had taken him to swimming classes. D further elaborated that he attends all of his children's parent/teacher conferences; and, when asked whether he attends their sporting events on days on which he does not have visitation, he responded: "I have never missed." He also said that on days when he does not see the children, he almost always calls them for a brief chat.

With respect to the potential relocation to Texas, D stated as follows: "I just see a complete breakdown of my relationship with my children if this move is allowed." With respect to whether P would continue to foster a relationship between D and his children if they moved to Texas, D testified that, in his opinion, P was "not going to cooperate and she is going to do everything in her power to prohibit the boys from having contact with me." He also stated that it was his fear that "slowly but surely, all contact will end."

D also testified that P "was the primary contributor and person who assists their older son" on his school projects. When questioned as to the telephone contact he had with his sons when they visited Texas, D testified that he "did ask them to call each and every time they landed, and I am pretty sure that that request was allowed." With respect to an acceptable visitation schedule were his children to move to Texas, D stated: "There is no acceptable plan that I could foresee with my children being in Texas because it will completely prohibit me from everyday involvement with my children's lives."

D seeks sole legal and physical custody of the two boys if P is allowed to move to Texas. Most likely, how will a court rule?

Explanations

9. In this jurisdiction, P bears the initial burden of showing by a preponderance of the evidence that the relocation is for a legitimate purpose and that the proposed relocation is reasonable in light of that purpose. Given the fact that P's new husband lost his job and found a new one in state Y, a court would most likely rule that P has carried her burden. Once the custodial parent P establishes a *prima facie* case, the burden then shifts to the noncustodial parent to prove, by a preponderance of the evidence, that the relocation would not be in the best interests of the child. In this jurisdiction, which applies the "new family theory," significant weight will be given to the "new family," consisting of the custodial parent and child, and the custodian's decisions. As a result, the noncustodial parent will have a great deal of difficulty preventing the relocation; it most likely will be allowed. Note, however, that there appears to be a slight movement away from the "new family" theory toward one that gives greater weight to the relationship established by fathers such as D.

10. Obviously, one must carefully analyze the problem because of the varying standards that jurisdictions use to resolve this issue. However, a jurisdiction that applies the "new family" theory most likely will allow D to relocate to another state. The "new family" theory is, in reality, a presumption favoring the custodial parent. The party opposing relocation must offer reasonably strong evidence to establish that the relocation is not in the best interests of the child, or that the relocation is intended to interfere with visitation. A judge in this jurisdiction will most likely conclude that there is not enough "strong" evidence presented by P to prevent the relocation.

11. The court will not bar P from leaving the state, of course. However, it well may consider giving sole physical custody to D if P decides to relocate. It may reason that the best interests of C are to keep him in as stable an environment as possible—a familiar neighborhood and school system. This is a close issue, but one that P likely may lose.

12. Although various jurisdictions approach the issue from somewhat different perspectives, most courts will uphold the stipulation. They will reason that P knowingly entered into an agreement that contained

express and unmistakable relocation restrictions. Although P may be subject to financial and other advantages by moving to the big city, a court will most likely be unwilling to allow the change because of the stipulation made by the parties only a few months earlier. *See Zindulka v. Zindulka*, 726 N.Y.S.2d 173 (N.Y. App. 2001).

13. The judge will weigh the following factors in arriving at a decision: (1) P enjoys a good and loving relationship with her sons. With respect to the relationship between D and the children, that relationship was also a good and loving one. P's involvement with the children was centered on activities where structure and discipline are very important.

    (2) When P remarried, she would be able to be a stay-at-home mom and avoid any day-care costs; she would have additional time available to volunteer in her children's schools and be able to assist in their classes.

    (3) If P was not permitted to relocate with the children, it would be difficult for the children and X to build a relationship.

    (4) The parties' children are doing very well in school. The parties' older son had had some behavioral issues related to the divorce and he was currently undergoing counseling with respect to those issues.

    (5) D saw the children at their sporting events and practices and would usually speak with them by telephone on days when he did not see them in person. D testified that "his contact with the children will be greatly reduced if the children are allowed to move" and that "he will miss the opportunity to be a part of their everyday life." D had stated that he would gladly assume primary caretaking responsibilities for the children.

    (6) P wants to move in order to be with X, whom she planned to marry. X is required to live in Texas by the military at the present time; he could be required to move elsewhere.

    (7) P believes that relocating to Texas would result in a better quality of life for her and her children. D feels that life as he and his children have known it would never be the same if relocation is allowed.

    In the case on which this hypothetical is based, both children appeared to be well adjusted to their home, school, and community. The older child receives counseling for help in dealing with his parents' divorce and in dealing with his mother's remarriage. With respect to the stability of the children's home environment, both parties keep a safe home and environment for the children. There is nothing to indicate that either party is not morally fit to have custody of the children.

    The court, however, will probably refuse to allow the relocation. The court will reason that despite the fact that it may be in P's best interests to move to Texas, so that she can cultivate her relationship with her soon-to-be new husband, the long and continuous ties that the children have to their current environment and to their extended family that shares this environment tip the scale in favor of D. It appears that a move to Texas and the potential benefits of a lifestyle that may exist there does not outweigh the current lifestyle that the children enjoy, where they are doing well in their schools and have the benefit of their closeness to their extended families and to their father. Should P wish to relocate without the children, then the children may be placed with their father, D.

Interstate Custody Struggles: The Uniform Child Custody Jurisdiction Enforcement Act and the Parental Kidnapping Prevention Act — History, Restrictions, and Requirements

7.1. Introduction

This chapter focuses on the history, development, and reform efforts of the state and federal governments to provide a uniform set of jurisdictional rules and guidelines for national enforcement of child custody orders where the jurisdictional dispute is between two or more states. The reform efforts were a response to "a growing public concern over the fact that thousands of children are shifted from state to state and from one family to another every year while their parents or other persons battle over their custody in the courts of several states." National Conference of Commissioners on Uniform State Laws, Uniform Child Custody Jurisdiction Act (NCCUSL), *Prefatory Note* (1968). The federal and state legislation developed in this area of the law intends to prevent forum shopping and protect victims of domestic violence who may initially be perceived as forum shoppers, but in reality may be fleeing from one state to another to escape abuse. *See Felty v. Felty*, 882 N.Y.S.2d 504 (N.Y. App. 2009). The legislation is also intended to simplify the jurisdictional law applied to intra-state and interstate custody disputes; so, for example, the court making the original custody determination retains exclusive, continuing jurisdiction over the parents who continue to contest custody.

Before the decision by Congress in 1980 to enact the Parental Kidnapping Prevention Act (PKPA), and despite a first attempt to generate a model act by the Commissioners on Uniform State Laws, a parent who lost a custody battle in one state had every incentive to snatch the child and move to another state to re-litigate the custody issue. Often the snatcher would be rewarded with a favorable custody order, notwithstanding the existence of a conflicting custody decree from the original state where the issue had earlier been decided.

Congress found it necessary to step into the fray only after the states seemed hopelessly incapable of reaching uniform agreement on the jurisdictional issues associated with an interstate custody matter. It created the PKPA, which mandated that one state give full faith and credit to a child custody determination of another state and, by doing so, prevented the new state from acting inconsistently with the original custody determination. *See, e.g.*, *Miller-Jenkins v. Miller-Jenkins*, 912 A.2d 951 (Vt. 2006) (purpose of PKPA is to determine when one state must give full faith and credit to a child custody determination of another state, so the new state cannot thereafter act inconsistently with the original custody determination).

Once the PKPA was in place, the states began to enact legislation consistent with the federal statute. Furthermore, states were encouraged to enact uniform legislation on this issue when the Commissioners on Uniform State Laws announced a second model act called the Uniform Child Custody Jurisdiction Enforcement Act (UCCJEA). Much of the current litigation in state court focuses on the application of state statutes that have been modeled upon the UCCJEA and the PKPA.

7.2. History

Traditional view of "domicile." Before major efforts were launched at creating uniformity among the states when interstate custody jurisdiction was at issue, the traditional view of custody jurisdiction was that only a court of the state where a child was domiciled could issue a custody decree. *See, e.g.*, *Restatement, Conflict of Laws* §§1, 17 (1934); B. E. Witkin and Members of the Witkin Legal Institute, 2 Witkin, Cal. Proc. 5th, Jurisd, §77, p. 883 (2008). The domicile rule was based on the theory that only the child's domicile state possessed a sufficient relationship with the child to give it a legitimate interest in determining who should have custody.

The domicile rule was criticized by scholars as rigid and as failing to focus on the real issue in a custody dispute; that is, the best interests of the child. *See* George W. Strumburg, *The Status of Children in Conflicts of Laws*, 8 U. Chi. L. Rev. 42 (1940); Russell M. Coombs, *Interstate Child Custody: Jurisdiction, Recognition, and Enforcement*, 66 Minn. L. Rev. 711 (1982). Critics of the traditional rule said that it left states helpless to act when a child was in grave need of protection.

United States Supreme Court decisions breed uncertainty. Decisions by the Supreme Court over the past 60 years have failed to resolve effectively child custody jurisdictional disputes among litigants involved in interstate custody disputes. In fact, the Court's rulings may have increased jurisdictional unrest about them.

For example, in one of its earliest efforts to consider this issue, the Supreme Court held that the full faith and credit clause did not prevent modification of an existing custody decree by another state. *New York ex rel. Halvey v. Halvey*, 330 U.S. 610 (1947). The Court reasoned in *Halvey* that New York was free to modify a Florida custody decree because, under Florida law, custody decrees are not *res judicata* "except as to the facts before the court at the time of judgment." *Id.* at 613. *See* Stewart E. Sterk, *The Muddy Boundaries Between Res Judicata and Full Faith and Credit*, 58 Wash. & Lee L. Rev. 47, 79 (Winter 2001). In response to *Halvey*, state courts concluded that there was a custody exception to the full faith and credit mandate of the Constitution. *Id.* at 80. They began to exercise their custody modification power liberally, which may have encouraged forum shopping among warring parents. *See also Kovacs v. Brewer*, 356 U.S. 604 (1958) (the Court declined to rule that full faith and credit clause applied to custody disputes; state court could modify a custody decree issued in a sister state if the issuing state would not consider the decree *res judicata*).

May v. Anderson. The Supreme Court injected additional uncertainty into interstate custody disputes with its decision in *May v. Anderson*, 345 U.S. 528 (1953). In that case, when the mother failed to appear for a divorce and custody hearing in Wisconsin, the father obtained an *ex parte* Wisconsin divorce judgment that granted him custody of the couple's minor children. Subsequent to the decree, the mother refused to return the children to Wisconsin while they were visiting her in Ohio. The father's efforts to enforce the Wisconsin decree that gave him custody of the children in the state of Ohio were unsuccessful, and the matter came before the Supreme Court.

A plurality in *May* held that in an interstate custody dispute, personal service upon a nonresident defendant (Ohio mother) notifying her of a pending custody hearing in another state (Wisconsin), was not sufficient to confer *in personam* jurisdiction over her in Wisconsin insofar as custody of the minor children was concerned. Under these circumstances, Ohio was not bound to accord full faith and credit to the Wisconsin custody order, even though the domicile of the children at the time of the *ex parte* divorce was Wisconsin.

Critique of May v. Anderson. The decision in *May v. Anderson* has been the subject of considerable academic dialogue concerning its meaning and application. *See, e.g.*, Bridgette M. Bodenheimer & Janet Neeley-Kvarme, *Jurisdiction over Child Custody and Adoption After Shaffer and Kulko*, 12 U.C. Davis L. Rev. 229 (1979); Bridgette M. Bodenheimer, *The Uniform Child Custody Jurisdiction Act: A Legislative Remedy for Children Caught in the Conflict of Laws*, 22 Vand. L. Rev. 1207, 1232-1233 (1969).

Some scholars have argued that the better view of jurisdiction in interstate custody disputes is found in Justice Jackson's dissent in *May v. Anderson*. Justice Jackson argued that custody should be viewed not with the idea of adjudicating rights in the children, as if they were chattels, but rather with the idea of making the best disposition possible for the welfare of the children. He observed that personal jurisdiction of all parties to be affected by a custody proceeding is highly desirable. "But the assumption that it overrides all other considerations and in its absence a state is constitutionally impotent to resolve questions of custody flies in the face of our own cases." *May v. Anderson, supra at* 541.

Justice Frankfurter concurred in *May v. Anderson*, writing that although Ohio was not required to give full faith and credit to the Wisconsin order, the due process clause did not prohibit Ohio from recognizing it "as a matter of local law" or comity. *Id.* at 535-536. The *Restatement (Second) of Conflict of Laws* seems to agree with the Frankfurter interpretation of the law. "Under this view, a state may, as a matter of local law, recognize the custody disposition made by another state, regardless of lack of personal jurisdiction." Bodenheimer & Neeley-Kvarme, *supra* at 251.

Note that another explanation of the *May* decision given by some courts is that Wisconsin did not have language in its long-arm statute authorizing extraterritorial service of process over the mother who was served with process in Ohio. Therefore, Wisconsin did not have personal jurisdiction over her and could not render an enforceable custody ruling. *Mitchim v. Mitchim*, 518 S.W.2d 362, 365 (Tex. 1975). Note also that since *May* was decided, most states have enacted long-arm statutes containing specific language that makes them applicable to out-of-state custody disputes. *See generally, In re* M.L.W., 358 S.W.3d 772 (Tex. App. 2012).

7.3. The Status Theory of Jurisdiction

Federal law (i.e., PKPA) now governs state custody decisions, with most states having put in place some statutory version of the UCCJEA that is consistent with PKPA. However, in some situations where a state cannot obtain personal jurisdiction over one of the parents, a custody decision is made using what is referred to as the "status theory."

States adopting the status theory take the position that it allows a court to make a custody decision without jurisdiction over one of the parties (normally a parent) if the state where the custody proceeding is being held has the most significant connections with the child and the child's family at the time of the hearing. Authority for this theory is found in the UCCJA and the UCCJEA. *See, e.g., Burton v. Bishop*, 269 S.E.2d 417 (Ga. 1980) (under the UCCJA, effective in Ohio at the time of the original decree, Ohio decree which granted custody of children to father was entitled to recognition in Georgia, even though the

Ohio court did not have personal jurisdiction over the children's mother, where Ohio had been the home state of the children within six months before commencement of the proceeding and the children were absent from the state because they had been removed from the state by their mother, and where the children's father continued to live in Ohio); *Yearta v. Scroggins*, 268 S.E.2d 151, 153 (Ga. 1980) (public policy of Georgia is to recognize, under principles of comity, child custody decrees where there is no personal jurisdiction that would satisfy the full faith and credit clause of our federal Constitution; *McAtee v. McAtee*, 323 S.E.2d 611, 616-617 (W. Va. 1984) (West Virginia acquired jurisdiction to award child custody under the UCCJA and could make the custody determination, notwithstanding the fact that personal jurisdiction was not acquired over the wife, who was absent from the state). *Genoe v. Genoe*, 500 A.2d 3, 8 (N.J. Super. A.D. 1985) (custody status of a child or children may be decided *quasi in rem; in personam* jurisdiction is not required to entertain an application to modify an order for custody or visitation under the UCCJA, provided that notice and opportunity to be heard are given); *In re Marriage of O'Connor*, 690 P.2d 1095, 1097 (Or. App. 1984); *In re Marriage of Hudson*, 434 N.E.2d 107, 117-118 (Ind. App. 1982); *McArthur v. Superior Court*, 1 Cal. Rptr. 2d 296 (Cal. App. 1991).

The Tennessee Supreme Court wrote that "it is widely acknowledged that Mr. Justice Frankfurter's concurring opinion [in *May*] permitting states to recognize foreign custody decrees rendered without personal jurisdiction over an absent parent is the better rule of law." *Fernandez v. Fernandez*, No. 85-194-II, 1986 WL 7935, at 1-2 (Tenn. App. July 15, 1986); *see also Brown v. Brown*, 847 S.W.2d 496, 499 n.2 (Tenn. 1993) (noting that the Supreme Court decision in *May v. Anderson* has largely been ignored and that neither the UCCJA nor the PKPA requires personal jurisdiction over the respondent). The Tennessee Supreme Court has "abolished the distinctions between *in rem* and *in personam* jurisdiction," and "recognized that exceptions can be made to the 'minimum contacts' standard" in "status" cases, such as child custody decisions. The court in *Fernandez* wrote that a state "having the most significant connections with the child and his family will be permitted to make a custody adjudication even in the absence of personal jurisdiction over a parent who does not reside in the forum state." *Fernandez*, 1986 WL 7935, at 2. *See also Roderick v. Roderick*, 776 S.W.2d 533, 535-536 (Tenn. App. 1989) (noting that the UCCJA permits the courts of the state with the most significant contacts to make custody determinations even without personal jurisdiction over the nonresident parent).

A Texas court took essentially the same view as Tennessee and explained its reasoning as follows:

> [u]nlike adjudications of child support and visitation, custody determinations are status adjudications not dependent upon personal jurisdiction over the parents. Generally, a family relationship is among those matters in which

> the forum state has such a strong interest that its courts may reasonably make an adjudication affecting that relationship even though one of the parties to the relationship may have had no personal contacts with the forum state.

In re Interest of S.A.V., 837 S.W.2d 80, 84 (Tex. 1992).

See In re Marriage of Los, 593 N.E.2d 126, 129-130 (Ill. App. 1992) (status determinations do not require personal jurisdiction over the parents).

7.4. First Interstate Jurisdiction Model Act — UCCJA

This section and several of those that follow in this chapter will provide a more in-depth look at the efforts that were made to deal with interstate custody disputes. As discussed earlier in this chapter, because of the inability on the part of states to cooperate in interstate custody matters, an effort to encourage development of a uniform system to resolve these disputes was launched in 1968 by the National Conference of Commissioners on Uniform State Laws. It created a model act that it called the Uniform Child Custody Jurisdiction Act (UCCJA). http://www.law.upenn.edu/bll/archives/ulc/fnact99/1920_69/uccja68.htm (last visited August, 2012).

The model act had several purposes: First, it sought to avoid jurisdictional competition and conflict among courts of different states in matters of child custody and to promote cooperation among them in matters of child custody. Second, by promoting cooperation among the courts of different states, the Act sought to achieve a custody decree rendered in the state best suited to determine the best interests of a child. Third, the Act was aimed at deterring abductions and other unilateral removals of children undertaken by parents seeking to obtain favorable custody rulings.

The UCCJA was subsequently adopted by all 50 states; however, the versions were not uniform. Because of the dissimilarities, tension among the states developed over the goal of achieving stability of custody decrees and providing a system with sufficient flexibility to accommodate the best interests of a child. The Oregon Supreme Court critically characterized the UCCJA as "a schizophrenic attempt to bring about an orderly system of decision and at the same time to protect the best interests of the children who may be immediately before the court." *In re Marriage of Settle*, 556 P.2d 962, 968 (Or. 1976), *overruled*, *Matter of Custody of Russ*, 620 P.2d 353 (Or. 1981). It became clear after a number of years that the initial effort to achieve uniformity among the states had fallen far short of the mark.

7.5. UCCJA Failure Triggers Congressional Action — Parental Kidnapping Prevention Act (PKPA)

Overview. Frustrated by the failed efforts of the states to adopt uniform versions of the UCCJA, Congress enacted the Parental Kidnapping Prevention Act (PKPA) in 1980. 28 U.S.C. §1738A (1988) http://www.law.cornell.edu/uscode/text/28/1738A (last visited July, 2012). *See generally* Russell M. Coombs, *Progress Under the PKPA*, 6 J. Am. Acad. Matrimonial Law. 59 (1990). Despite its title, the Act is not limited to matters involving parental kidnapping but applies broadly to civil interstate custody disputes. *See* Anne B. Goldstein, *Tragedy of the Interstate Child: A Critical Reexamination of the Uniform Child Custody Jurisdiction Act and the Parental Kidnapping Prevention Act*, 25 U.C. Davis L. Rev. 845 (Summer 1992). The purpose of the PKPA is to determine when one state must give full faith and credit to a child custody determination of another state. It prevents the new state from acting inconsistently with the original custody determination. *Thompson v. Thompson*, 484 U.S. 174, 181 (1988) http://www.oyez.org/issues/judicial_power/standing_sue/private_or_implied cause_action (last visited July 2012). The Supreme Court stressed in *Thompson* that "[t]he sponsors and supporters of the [PKPA] continually indicated that the purpose of the PKPA was to provide for nationwide enforcement of custody orders made in accordance with [its terms]." 484 U.S. at 181. *See* Parental Kidnaping Prevention Act of 1980, Pub.L. No. 96–611, §77(c)(6) http://www.law.cornell.edu/uscode/text/28/1738A (last visited July, 2012) (One of the general purposes of the PKPA is to "deter interstate abductions and other unilateral removals of children undertaken to obtain custody and visitation awards"). The PKPA follows on, and includes many of the provisions of, the UCCJA.

The PKPA embodies preferences to leave jurisdiction in the state that rendered the original decree, to promote the best interests of the child and to discourage interstate abduction and other unilateral removals of children for the purpose of obtaining a favorable custody decree. *Michalik v. Michalik*, 494 N.W.2d 391, 398 (Wisc. 1993). Unlike the UCCJA, the PKPA prioritizes the bases of jurisdiction. It gives priority to the "home state" of the child. It also provides that once a state has exercised jurisdiction, the initial decree-granting state retains exclusive, continuing jurisdiction if it remains the residence of the children or any contestant.

State requirements. In order for a state court to exercise jurisdiction consistent with the PKPA, it must have jurisdiction under its own law (§1738A(c)(1)) (2000), and meet one of four conditions, which are set forth below as part of 28 U.S.C. §1738A(c)(2) (A-D) (2000):

> (c) A child custody or visitation determination made by a court of a State is consistent with the provisions of this section only if—

> (1) such court has jurisdiction under the law of such State; and
>
> (2) one of the following conditions is met:
>
> (A) such State (i) is the home State of the child on the date of the commencement of the proceeding, or (ii) had been the child's home State within six months before the date of the commencement of the proceeding and the child is absent from such State because of his removal or retention by a contestant or for other reasons, and a contestant continues to live in such State;
>
> (B) (i) it appears that no other State would have jurisdiction under subparagraph (A), and (ii) it is in the best interest of the child that a court of such State assume jurisdiction because (I) the child and his parents, or the child and at least one contestant, have a significant connection with such State other than mere physical presence in such State, and (II) there is available in such State substantial evidence concerning the child's present or future care, protection, training, and personal relationships;
>
> (C) the child is physically present in such State and (i) the child has been abandoned, or (ii) it is necessary in an emergency to protect the child because the child, a sibling, or parent of the child has been subjected to or threatened with mistreatment or abuse;
>
> (D) (i) it appears that no other State would have jurisdiction under subparagraph (A), (B), (C), or (E), or another State has declined to exercise jurisdiction on the ground that the State whose jurisdiction is in issue is the more appropriate forum to determine the custody or visitation of the child, and (ii) it is in the best interest of the child that such court assume jurisdiction; or
>
> (E) the court has continuing jurisdiction pursuant to subsection (d) of this section.

28 U.S.C. §1738A(c)(2)(A)-(D) (2000).

Effect. The effect of §§1738A(d) and 1738A(f) of the PKPA is to limit custody jurisdiction to the first state to enter a custody order properly, so long as two sets of requirements are met. 28 U.S.C. §1738A(d)(f) (1998). Those sections of PKPA declare that:

> (d) The jurisdiction of a court of a State which has made a child custody or visitation determination consistently with the provisions of this section continues as long as the requirement of subsection (c)(1) of this section continues to be met and such State remains the residence of the child or of any contestant. . . .
>
> (f) A court of a State may modify a determination of the custody of the same child made by a court of another State, if—

(1) it has jurisdiction to make such a child custody determination; and.

(2) the court of the other State no longer has jurisdiction, or it has declined to exercise such jurisdiction to modify such determination.

Exclusive, continuing jurisdiction. Exclusive, continuing jurisdiction under the PKPA protects an original decree state's jurisdiction to modify its own order. It gives the original home state exclusive, continuing jurisdiction to modify its own order to the exclusion of all other states, so long as at least one parent or the child continues to live there. All states, including a significant connection state, must grant full faith and credit to the home state's order. This includes a child's new home state.

Under the Act, when a court is asked to modify an existing custody order, it determines whether the rendering court has continuing jurisdiction under the law of the rendering state. *See Cann v. Howard*, 850 S.W.2d 57, 60 (Ky. App. 1993); *Pierce v. Pierce*, 640 P.2d 899, 903 (Mont. 1982).

Note that when determining continuing jurisdiction under §1738A(d) of PKPA, the Act does not mandate a home state preference. Therefore, once a state court acquires jurisdiction under the PKPA, whether it retains jurisdiction is wholly a matter of state law and the residence of one contestant. 28 U.S.C. §1738A(d). *See* §1738A(c)(2)(E) (determinations made by courts with continuing jurisdiction are consistent with PKPA and are entitled to interstate recognition and enforcement). The Act "does not affect the discretion of a state to limit its own continuing jurisdiction. The statute only curtails the freedom of another state to modify the decree for the period of time the rendering state's jurisdiction continues under its own law." Russell M. Coombs, *Interstate Child Custody: Jurisdiction, Recognition, and Enforcement*, 66 Minn. L. Rev. 711, 852 (1982).

The continuing jurisdiction theory discourages parties from relocating to reestablish a home state only for the purpose of modifying what is perceived as an unfavorable custody arrangement. In providing for continuing jurisdiction, the PKPA seeks to foster a stable home environment and family relationship for a child, promote "negotiated settlement of custody disputes, and facilitate visitation between a child and the other noncustodial parent." *Matthews v. Riley*, 649 A.2d 231, 239 (Vt. 1994).

Preemption. The PKPA preempts state law to the extent that only those foreign custody decrees made consistently with the provisions of the PKPA have the same effect and enforceability as custody determinations made by the forum court. *In re L.S.*, 257 P.3d 201 (Colo. 2011). Should a state UCCJEA provision conflict with PKPA, PKPA preempts the state law by virtue of the supremacy clause of the Constitution, http://www.law.cornell.edu/wex/Supremacy_Clause (last visited July, 2012); *Bowman v. Bowman*,

917 N.Y.S.2d 379 (N.Y. App. 2011); *In re Higera N.*, 2 A.3d 265 (Me. 2010) (PKPA preempts Maine UCCJEA).

As observed earlier, the Supreme Court held in *Thompson v. Thompson*, 484 U.S. 174 (1988) http://www.oyez.org/cases/1980-1989/1987/1987_86_964 (last visited July, 2012), that under the provisions of the PKPA, once a state properly exercises jurisdiction, other states must give full faith and credit to the determination and no other state may exercise concurrent jurisdiction, even if it would be entitled to under its own laws.

Note that the PKPA applies equally to a visitation determination, requiring states to enforce "any custody determination or visitation determination made consistently with the provisions of this section by a court of another State." 28 U.S.C. §1738A(a).

Private right of action. Prior to 1988, some state courts had concluded that the PKPA gave warring parents in different states an implied private cause of action in federal court, where, they contended, their custody contest could be resolved. *See, e.g., Meade v. Meade*, 812 F.2d 1473 (4th Cir. 1987). In *Thompson v. Thompson*, 484 U.S. 174 (1988), the Supreme Court held that the Act did not create an implied private right of relief. It reasoned that the language of PKPA and its legislative history indicated that Congress did not intend to create a new cause of action and did not intend federal courts to "play an enforcement role" in custody disputes. *Id.* at 184.

7.6. Second Interstate Model Child Custody Jurisdiction Act — UCCJEA

Overview. In 1997, 17 years after Congress enacted the PKPA, another effort to encourage a uniform approach among the states regarding interstate custody disputes was launched by the National Conference of Commissioners on Uniform State Laws with another model act, the Uniform Child Custody Jurisdiction Enforcement Act (UCCJEA), 9 U.L.A. (Part 1A) 649 (1997). The goal of the UCCJEA was to reconcile differences between the old UCCJA and the PKPA. This model act, like the UCCJA and the PKPA is based on Justice Frankfurter's concurrence in *May v. Anderson*, 345 U.S. 528 (1953). Since its release, some version of the UCCJEA has been adopted in all jurisdictions.

General objectives. The general objectives of the UCCJEA remained the same as those found in the earlier model act, the UCCJA. These include the goal of addressing problems associated with the growing number of custody disputes between geographically separated parents. *See Phillips v. Beaber*, 995 S.W.2d 655, 659 & n.2 (Tex. 1999). Like its predecessor, the UCCJEA is concerned with the refusal of some courts to give finality to custody decrees issued by other states, and it seeks to discourage the use of the interstate system for continuing controversies over child custody matters. It also is intended to deter the abduction of children. *Anthony H. v. Matthew G.*, 725 S.E.2d 132 (S.C. App. 2012) ("The UCCJEA's primary purpose is to provide uniformity of the law with respect to child custody decrees between courts in different states"); *In re Iliana M.*, 38 A.3d 130 (Conn. App. 2012) ("The purposes of the UCCJEA are to avoid jurisdictional competition and conflict with courts of other states in matters of child custody; promote cooperation with the courts of other states; discourage continuing controversies over child custody; deter abductions; avoid re-litigation of custody decisions; and to facilitate the enforcement of custody decrees of other states").

Scope of UCCJEA. In general, the UCCJEA applies to the following: custody, modification of custody, visitation disputes that arise in divorce and separation proceedings, domestic violence matters, and paternity disputes. It may also apply, depending on how a state legislature promulgates its version of the UCCJEA, to neglect, dependency, guardianship, termination of parental rights, and grandparental visitation. It has not been applied to adoption proceedings. *See generally* UCCJEA *prefatory note*, §4, 9 U.L.A. (Part 1A) 649 (1997).

Waiver of subject matter under UCCJEA. Adjudication under the UCCJEA requires that a court possess subject matter jurisdiction. Jurisdiction cannot be conferred by agreement, consent, estoppel, or waiver, and issues involving subject matter jurisdiction can be raised by the court at any time. *See, e.g.*, *Robertson v. Riplett*, 194 P.3d 382 (Alaska 2008); *Rosen v. Rosen*, 664 S.E.2d 743 (W. Va. App. 2008); *Rosen v. Celebrezze*, 883 N.E.2d 420 (Ohio 2008); *Harshberger v. Harshberger*, 724 N.W.2d 148 (N.D. 2006); *In re A.C.S.*, 157 S.W.3d 9 (Tex. App. 2004); *In re Marriage of Arnold and Cully*, 271 Cal. Rptr. 624 (Cal. App. 1990). The subject matter jurisdictional requirements of the UCCJEA must be satisfied whenever a court makes a custody determination and cannot be conferred or waived. *Fuller v. Fuller*, So. 3d, 2012 WL 1237758 (Ala. App. 2012) (Alabama lacked subject matter where Canada is child's home state).

Prioritization of jurisdiction: In §201, the UCCJEA prioritizes among the four bases of jurisdiction and follows the PKPA by giving priority to the child's home state. It also restricts the use of emergency jurisdiction to the issuance of temporary orders. The Act permits the exercise of emergency jurisdiction in §204 to protect a child, the child's siblings, or the child's parents. *See* Joan Zorza, *The UCCJEA: What Is It and How Does It Affect Battered Women in Child-Custody Disputes?* 27 Fordham Urb. L.J. 909, 917 (2000).

Exclusive, continuing jurisdiction. Continuing jurisdiction was not specifically addressed in the UCCJA. Its absence caused considerable confusion, particularly because the PKPA, in §1738(d), required states to give full faith and credit to custody determinations made by the original decree state, pursuant to the decree state's continuing jurisdiction, so long as that state has jurisdiction under its own law and remains the residence of the child or any contestant.

§2 of the UCCJEA provides the rules of continuing jurisdiction and establishes a jurisdictional hierarchy to provide guidance to courts deciding child custody and visitation cases. At the top of the hierarchy is the court that possesses exclusive, continuing jurisdiction. *See In re Isquierdo*, S.W., 2012 WL 2455074 (Tex. App. 2012) (under UCCJEA, generally, court that makes initial child custody determination retains exclusive, continuing jurisdiction over ongoing custody disputes). This is the most preferred jurisdictional basis, and it is applied if it is available, unless the court that has the preferred jurisdictional basis declines to exercise jurisdiction. *See generally Anthony H. v. Matthew G.*, 725 S.E.2d 132 (S.C. 2012) (South Carolina court lacked jurisdiction to hear the child custody dispute that terminated father's rights to child because Georgia still had exclusive, continuing jurisdiction under the PKPA and the UCCJEA).

Once a court makes an initial custody determination consistent with the UCCJEA, that court is viewed as retaining exclusive, continuing jurisdiction over the matter unless neither the child nor at least one parent or person acting as a parent has a significant connection with the state originally issuing the order and substantial evidence in that state is no longer available concerning the child. *See Highfill v. Moody*, WL 2075698 (Tenn. App. 2010).

In general, the state issuing the original decree continues to have jurisdiction to decide a custody dispute, regardless of the length of the absence of the child and the other parent from the jurisdiction.

If a court has entered a valid custody order and one of the parties or the child continues to live in the state, that court has the exclusive right to decide if the order should be modified. Courts of other states may not modify an order (assuming a parent or child continues to live in the state that issued an order) unless the court that issued the order gives permission to another state to decide the issue.

Losing exclusive continuing jurisdiction. A court continues with exclusive, continuing jurisdiction until any of the following occurs:

> A court of the state with exclusive jurisdiction determines that the child and one parent do not have, or the child and a person acting as a parent do not have a significant connection with the state and that substantial evidence is no longer available in the state concerning the child's care, protection, training, and personal relationships.

> A court of the state with exclusive jurisdiction or a court of another state determines that the child, the child's parents, and any person acting as a parent do not presently reside in the state that possessed exclusive continuing jurisdiction.

UCCJEA, §202 (a)(1)(2) (1997).

See In re Marriage of Trevino, 812 N.W.2d 726 (Iowa App. 2012).

A family court's jurisdiction does not end automatically once the parents and children moved out of state. *In re Lewin*, 149 S.W.3d 727, 736 (Tex. App. 2004) ("A court's exclusive continuing jurisdiction does not vanish immediately once all the parties leave the state."). As explained in §2 of the UCCJEA:

> Jurisdiction attaches at the commencement of a proceeding. If State A had jurisdiction under this section at the time a modification proceeding was commenced there, it would not be lost by all parties moving out of the State prior to the conclusion of proceeding. State B would not have jurisdiction to hear a modification unless State A decided that State B was more appropriate under §207.

UCCJEA, §202 Commentary (1997).

Inconvenient forum. A court that has jurisdiction pursuant to the UCCJEA may decline to exercise jurisdiction if it determines that it is an inconvenient forum and that a court of another state is a more appropriate forum. The declining court may consider the following factors:

> (1) Whether domestic violence has occurred and is likely to continue in the future and which state could best protect the parties and the child;
>
> (2) The length of time the child has resided out of the forum state;
>
> (3) The distance between the forum court and the court in the state that would assume jurisdiction;
>
> (4) The relative financial circumstances of the parties;
>
> (5) Any agreement of the parties as to which state should assume jurisdiction;
>
> (6) The nature and location of the evidence required to resolve the pending litigation, including testimony of the child;
>
> (7) The ability of the court of each state to decide the issue expeditiously and the procedures necessary to present the evidence; and
>
> (8) The familiarity of the court of each state with the facts and issues in the pending litigation.

UCCJEA, §207(b)(1-8) (1997).

Home state. Jurisdiction remains with the home state until the home state or another state determines that the exclusive, continuing jurisdiction of the home state has ended. *State of New Mexico ex rel. Children, Youth & Families Dep't v. Donna J.*, 129 P.3d 167, 171 (N.M. App. 2006) ("[T]he UCCJEA language specifically requires action by either the home or another state before exclusive, continuing jurisdiction in the home state ceases."). The Commentary to §202 of the UCCJEA explains in relevant part:

> If the child, the parents, and all persons acting as parents have all left the State which made the custody determination prior to the commencement of the modification proceeding, considerations of waste of resources dictate that a court in State B, as well as a court in State A, can decide that State A has lost exclusive, continuing jurisdiction.

UCCJEA, §202 (1997)

"Home state" is defined as the state where the child lived with a parent or a person acting as a parent for at least six consecutive months immediately before commencement of the proceeding. If the child is less than six months old, the home state is the state in which the child lived from birth. The definition of "home state" in the UCCJEA is identical to the definition found in the PKPA. UCCJEA §102(7) (1997); 28 U.S.C. §1738A(b)(4) (1994).

A court has jurisdiction to make an initial child custody determination if the state is the home state of the child on the date the proceeding is commenced. It also has such jurisdiction if the child no longer lives there, but the state was the home state of the child within six months before the proceeding commenced, and a parent or person acting as a parent continues to live in the state. A temporary absence from the forum state does not change the application of "home state" as found in the UCCJEA. In situations in which a parent has improperly removed a child from the home state, the home state may retain jurisdiction beyond six months.

No home state exists. If there is no home state, or the home state court declines to exercise jurisdiction, a court of another state may assume jurisdiction if it qualifies as one with "significant connections" to the action. UCCJEA §201(a)(2) (1997).

Emergency jurisdiction. A state court may assume temporary jurisdiction over a custody dispute if the child is present in the state and it is necessary to protect the child because he or she is subjected to or threatened with mistreatment or abuse. A trial court enjoys broad discretion in issuing orders for the immediate protection of a child. UCCJEA §204, cmt. 9 U.L.A. (Part 1A) 677 (1997) (states' duties to recognize, enforce, and not modify custody determinations of other states do not take precedence over the need to protect child); *see Garza v. Harney*, 726 S.W.2d 198, 202 (Tex. App. 1987). States have a *parens patriae* duty to children within their borders, and the possibility that allegations of immediate harm might be true is generally sufficient for a court to assume temporary emergency jurisdiction in the best interests of the child under the UCCJEA. *In re Nada R.*, 108 Cal. Rptr. 2d 493, 500 (Cal. App. 2001); *Hache v. Riley*, 451 A.2d 971, 975 (N.J. Super. 1982).

In *In re Marriage of Greenlaw*, 840 P.2d 223 (Wash. App. 1992), *rev'd* on other grounds, 869 P.2d 1024 (1994), the court held "that assumption of emergency jurisdiction under the UCCJA is to be undertaken only in extraordinary circumstances, such as where a child would be placed in imminent danger if jurisdiction were not exercised." *Ibid.*

Any order issued under emergency circumstances must be temporary in nature and specify a period that the court considers adequate to obtain an order from the state with jurisdiction. The temporary order remains in effect only until proper steps are taken in the original forum state to protect the children adequately, or until the specified period expires.

Emergency jurisdiction: communication with court making initial order. Once a court assumes temporary emergency jurisdiction, it has a duty to communicate with the other state that made the initial custody order. *In re Ruff*, 275 P.3d 1175, 1181 Wash. App. 2012). It should retain a record of those communications. This mandatory duty of cooperation between the courts of different states is a hallmark of the UCCJEA, and the cooperation is intended to lead to an informed decision on custody. One of the reasons for consulting with the other state's court is to determine the duration of the temporary order. *In re C.T.*, 121 Cal. Rptr. 2d 897, 906 (Cal. App. 2002). *See also* Patricia M. Hoff, *The ABC's of the UCCJEA: Interstate Child-Custody Practice Under the New Act*, 32 Fam. L.Q. 267, 284 (1998).

Temporary emergency jurisdiction is reserved for extraordinary circumstances, and the trial court's assumption of temporary emergency jurisdiction does not include jurisdiction to modify the original court's child custody determination. UCCJEA §204, cmt. 9 U.L.A. (Part 1A) 677 (1997). *See Abderholden v. Morizot*, 856 S.W.2d 829, 834 (Tex. App. 1993) (holding that exercise of emergency jurisdiction does not confer authority to make permanent custody disposition or modify custody decree of court with jurisdiction). Because a court's exercise of emergency jurisdiction is temporary in nature, it may not be used as a vehicle to attain modification jurisdiction for an ongoing, indefinite period.

Modification hearing: The UCCJEA is consistent with the PKPA in that §203 declares that a modification action can be brought only in the state that made the initial custody determination, so long as a child or parent involved in the original custody ruling remains in that state. Before a court may assume jurisdiction to modify an out-of-state custody order, it must communicate with issuing state pursuant to relevant provisions of UCCJEA and must conduct a hearing at which both sides are allowed to present evidence on any factual dispute as to the residency issue, with the burden of proof being on the parent petitioning for assumption of jurisdiction. *Brandt v. Brandt*, 268 P.3d 406 (Colo. 2012); *State of N.M. ex rel. CYFD v. Donna J.*, 129 P.3d 167, 171 (N.M. 2006) ("[a]n automatic loss of jurisdiction, without any factual determination, would add uncertainty, diminish oversight ability of the courts, and increase conflicts between the states"). In 2009, a California court emphasized the necessity for a probing examination of the jurisdictional question:

> The requirement of a judicial determination under the UCCJEA is more than a procedural technicality. It reflects a deliberate effort to provide a clear endpoint to the decree state's jurisdiction, to prevent courts from treading on one another's jurisdiction, and to ensure that custody orders will remain fully enforceable until a court determines they are not.

In re Marriage of Nurie, 98 Cal. Rptr. 3d 200, 221 (Cal. 2009).

7.7. Native Americans — PKPA

Courts are divided over whether the PKPA and similar full faith and credit legislation intend to treat Indian tribes the same as "states." Some jurisdictions have held that tribes should be treated as "states" under the PKPA and similar statutes. *See, e.g.*, *In re Larch*, 872 F.2d 66, 68 (4th Cir.1989) (holding that the Cherokee tribe is a "state" for purposes of the PKPA); *Martinez v. Superior Court*, 731 P.2d 1244, 1247 (Ariz. App. 1987) (holding that Indian reservations are "territories or possessions," and, therefore, are to be treated as "states" for purposes of Arizona's UCCJA). At least one tribal court has specifically held that the PKPA requires tribal courts to afford full faith and credit to state-court judgments. *See Eberhard v. Eberhard*, 24 Indian L. Rptr. 6059, 6060 (Cheyenne River Sioux Tribal Ct. App. 1997).

However, other courts have concluded that tribes should not be treated as "states" for the purpose of full faith and credit in a child-custody context. *See, e.g.*, *John v. Baker*, 982 P.2d 738, 762 (Alaska 1999) (concluding that "the PKPA does not accord full faith and credit to tribal judgments"); *Desjarlait v. Desjarlait*, 379 N.W.2d 139, 144 (Minn. App. 1985) (determining that Minnesota's UCCJA does not apply to jurisdictional disputes between state courts and tribal courts, and that the federal constitution's full faith and credit clause "expressly applies to matters between states, not to matters between tribal courts and states"); *Malaterre v. Malaterre*, 293 N.W.2d 139, 144 (N.D. 1980) (refusing to resolve a child-custody issue between a tribal court and a state court on the basis of the UCCJA, because the UCCJA "pertains to fact situations which involve jurisdictional disputes with sister states"). The New Mexico Supreme Court more recently held that the PKPA does not apply to tribes, and therefore, tribes are not bound to give full faith and credit, under the PKPA, to state-court judgments in state-court cases. *Garcia v. Gutierrez*, 1217 P.3d 591 (N.M. App. 2009).

7.8. International Application of UCCJEA and Related Laws

International abduction of children by parents is a serious problem, and the UCCJEA has attempted, at least in part, to deal with it. Under the UCCJEA, another country is treated as if it were a state of the United States for purposes of applying Articles 1 and 2 of the Act. The Act provides that custody determinations of other countries will be enforced if the facts of the case indicate that jurisdiction was in substantial compliance with the requirements of the act. However, at least one jurisdiction has said that certain provisions of the UCCJEA do not apply to international custody disputes. *See, e.g.*, *Temlock v. Temlock*, 898 A.2d 209 (Conn. 2006) (although Connecticut adopted the provisions set forth in §§105(b) and (c) of the Model Act that address foreign judgments, it chose not to treat foreign countries as states for purposes of other provisions, including its *forum non conveniens* provision, by excluding §105(a) of the Model Act).

Congress addressed international child abduction in 1993 when it promulgated the International Parental Kidnapping Act (IPKPA), 18 U.S.C. §1204 (2006). The Act imposes criminal penalties on parents who illegally abduct children. For example, the Act makes it a federal felony for a parent to wrongfully remove or retain a child outside the United States. Defenses to the criminal action include the following: (1) the defendant was granted custody or visitation pursuant to the UCCJEA; (2) the defendant is fleeing from domestic violence; or (3) the defendant was unable to return a child to the custodial parent because of circumstances beyond his or her control, and the defendant made reasonable attempts to notify the other parent.

Another area of law relevant to international child abduction is the Hague Convention on the Civil Aspects of International Abduction. The United States began implementing the Convention in 1980 when Congress promulgated the International Child Abduction Remedies Act (ICARA), 42 U.S.C. §§11601-11610 (2006). The Hague Convention is intended to secure the return of children who are wrongfully removed from or retained in a signatory state and to return them to the country of their habitual residence, which must be another contracting nation, where the merits of the custody dispute can be decided.

Courts have disagreed on various provisions of the Hague Convention, including the definition of "habitual residence." *See, e.g., Humphrey v. Humphrey*, 434 F.3d 243 (4th Cir. 2006) (father required to establish habitual residence by a preponderance); *Gitter v. Gitter*, 396 F.3d 124 (2d Cir. 2005) (courts must focus on parents' intent when deciding habitual residence).

7.9. Is Canada a State for UCCJEA Purposes?

Canada is a "state" for the purposes of the UCCJEA. To illustrate, Alabama Code, §30–3B–105 (2012), which tracks the model UCCJEA provision, governs the international application of the UCCJEA in that state and provides:

> (a) A court of this state shall treat a foreign country as if it were a state of the United States for the purpose of applying this article [§§30–3B–101 through 30–3B–112] and Article 2 [§§30–3B–201 through 3–3B–210].
>
> (b) Except as otherwise provided in subsection (c), a child custody determination made in a foreign country under factual circumstances in substantial conformity with the jurisdictional standards of this chapter [i.e., the UCCJEA] must be recognized and enforced under Article 3 [§§30–3B–301 through 30–3B–114].
>
> (c) A court of this state need not apply this chapter if the child custody law of a foreign country violates fundamental principles of human rights."

Fuller v. Fuller, — So. 3d —, 2012 WL 1237758 (Ala. App. 2012).

Canada, a signatory to the Hague Convention since 1988, has adopted specific and far-reaching legislation protecting the rights of noncustodial parents, including those who are not Canadian. *See generally Overview and Assessment of Approaches to Access Enforcement, Department of Justice, Canada*, (last visited August, 2012); *Toland v. Futagi*, 40 A.3d 1051 (Md. App. 2012) (appointment of grandmother as guardian pursuant to Japanese decree did not implicate fundamental principles of human rights); *Brausch v. Brausch*, 770 N.W.2d 77 (Mich. App. 2009); *Atchison v. Atchison*, 664 N.W.2d 249 (Mich. App. 2003).

EXAMPLES

Examples

1. Assume that M (mother) and F (father) divorced in state X and agreed they would share "joint care, custody, and control" of their only child, C. F would serve as C's residential custodian except during defined visitation periods with M. Two years after the divorce, the court in state X entered an order transferring physical custody during the school year to M, at which point M had relocated from state X to state Y.

One year after she obtained the order transferring physical custody to her during the school year, M filed a motion to modify custody and visitation in state Y. She sought to obtain sole physical and legal custody of C. M's petition stated that F had failed to remain in contact with C or to exercise visitation with C to the extent allowed by the order from the judge in state X. She also alleged that F was "believed to be using illegal substances, specifically methamphetamine." Thus, M sought an award of sole legal and physical custody of C in state Y.

The family court judge in state Y contacted the court in state X to determine which state at this point had jurisdiction to modify the existing custody order under the UCCJEA. During that communication, the parties were represented by attorneys in both states. The judge in state X said that it had continuing, exclusive jurisdiction over the child custody issue between the parties, pursuant to that state's enactment of the UCCJEA, The judge in state Y disagreed, stating that the mother and child were residents of state Y and clearly state Y was the home state of C. Which of the two family court judges was most likely correct in the application of the UCCJEA?

2. Assume that M (mother) and F (father) were married and lived in state X. After five years of marriage, the relationship broke down, and they separated but did not divorce. F left state X and established his domicile in state Y. The children remained with M in state X. One year after M and F separated, M brought a divorce action in state X. F ignored the matter and made no appearance in state X in response to a summons and dissolution petition served on him in state Y. M asked in her legal papers for sole physical and legal custody of the children. In its default judgment, state X's court awarded sole physical and legal custody of the parties' children to M, observing that the children are domiciled in that state with M. A few months later, after the children visited with F in state Y, F refuses to return them to M in state X. F then brings an action in state Y asking that he be granted sole legal and physical custody of the children. M argues that only state X may resolve this issue. How might the outcome of the action differ in state Y, depending on which of the various theories previously discussed in this chapter (domicile, long-arm statute, plurality view in *May v. Anderson*, status jurisdiction, UCCJEA, PKPA) the court may choose to apply?

3. Assume that M and F are divorced in state X at a time when state X has personal jurisdiction over both parties. M is awarded sole physical and legal custody of child C. Following the divorce, F moves to state Y, while M and C remain in state X. Assume that a year after the divorce, F becomes very concerned about the care and treatment afforded child C. During one of the periods that child C is visiting F in state Y, F brings an

action in a state Y family court seeking to modify the custody decree originally issued in state X. M responds to D's motion and asks the court to dismiss the action in state Y on the ground that only state X has jurisdiction in this matter. Most likely, how will a court rule?

4. Assume that M and F divorce in state X, and M is awarded sole legal and physical custody of their minor child. Following the divorce, M leaves state X with the child and has resided in state Y for one year. M brings an action in state Y to modify the order originally issued in state X and further restrict F's visitation with the minor child. F has never visited state Y. F argues that under the UCCJEA, the action can be brought only in state X, where F continues to reside. M argues that because she and the child are before the court in state Y, it can modify the original custody order. How will a judge most likely rule?

5. Assume that F has brought a petition in state X seeking a change in his visitation schedule with child C, who is in M's custody in state Y. When the couple divorced in state X eight years ago, the court awarded sole physical custody of C to M, with F receiving two weeks visitation in the summer and one week at Christmas and Easter. M relocated with C to state Y and has resided there since the divorce. After the relocation, the parties arranged informally for C to visit F for an extended period in state X over the summer and during some of the child's spring, winter, and other holiday vacations. This allowed C to visit with relatives of F and relatives of M, who reside in state X. In July of this year, M orally informed F that if he wanted to exercise any visitation with the child, now 16 years old, he would have to come to state Y and remain in that state to exercise said visitation. F has filed an action asking the court in state X to modify the former custody decree, giving F a greater amount of visitation with C and requiring M to allow the child to visit F in state X. M argues that state X should refer the matter to state Y because it does not have jurisdiction over M and C, as they are residents of state Y.

   Without conceding the jurisdictional issue, M has submitted an affidavit to the family court in state X alleging that C has an attitude when he returns from visiting F and that F and his family are a bad influence on C. M also alleges that she would no longer send the child to state X for visitation due to F's alcohol and marijuana abuse and because of her concerns regarding the child's safety during visits. M claims that F's family members and his current girlfriend were the source of her information. M asserts that the overwhelming evidence concerning the child's care, protection, training, and personal relationships are in state Y and that it would be very inconvenient for the child and M to litigate the matter in state X. Will a court in state X dismiss F's petition?

6. Assume that F and M divorced in state X, and the divorce judgment established M as the primary residential parent and acknowledged M's intent to relocate to state Y. F consented to M's relocation, and M relocated with the parties' three children to state Y, where she registered the divorce decree.

   Five months after the divorce, D, who continued to reside in state X, filed a motion in state X for a change of custody of the two oldest children claiming endangerment. M filed a motion to dismiss P's post-decree motion, asserting that the matter was within the jurisdiction of state Y because M resided in state Y with F's consent and M had registered the divorce decree in state Y. The trial judge in state X agreed and dismissed F's modification motion. F has appealed. Most likely, how will an appellate court rule on the issue of jurisdiction under the UCCJEA?

7. Assume that M (mother) and F (father) were married in state X and a child was born to them. When the child was approximately six months old, the two divorced in state X. The trial court, at the request of the parties, did not make a custody determination or issue a custody order. M moved to state Y to live with her mother and child until this year, when five months ago, she moved from Y to state Z with the child. F moved from state X to state A about four months ago, where he now resides. The child is almost 4 years old.

   Following their divorce, F had little contact with the child. However, in June of this year, the child visited F in state A for the first time for a three-week summer visit. F refused to return the child to M at the end of visitation. F commenced an action in state A asking for custody of the child. At the time the matter was commenced, F had been a resident of state A for four months, and the child had resided there for three weeks with F. F argued that because there was no "home state," that state "A" had jurisdiction to enter a custody order under the UCCJEA. F also argued that because there was no custody order, state A was not precluded by the UCCJEA from issuing an initial order.

   Assume that the UCCJEA, as adopted in state A by its legislature, provides a court in that state with jurisdiction to make child custody determination if:

   > A court of another state does not have jurisdiction, or a court of the home state of the child has declined to exercise jurisdiction on the ground that this state is the more appropriate forum because of inconvenient forum or "unjustifiable conduct" by the party seeking to invoke jurisdiction, and (a) the child and the child's parents, or the child and at least one parent . . . have a significant connection with this state other than mere physical presence, and (b) substantial evidence is available in this state

> concerning the child's care, protection, training, and personal relationships. (c) All courts having jurisdiction have declined to exercise jurisdiction on the ground that a court of this state is the more appropriate forum to determine the custody of the child because of inconvenient forum or unjustifiable conduct by the party seeking to invoke jurisdiction; or (d) No court of any other state would have jurisdiction.

Finally, assume that the trial court in state A issued a custody order giving F primary custody of the child and reasonable visitation to M. M appeals, challenging the jurisdiction of state A to make this decision. Most likely, how will an appellate court in state A rule?

8. Assume that in a paternity action, the state X trial judge awarded F (the father) custody of the minor child C, who was born to F and M. C resided with F at F's parents' home in state X. M made an unannounced visit to F's home and abducted C. F tried to locate M and the minor child, but he was unsuccessful.

   Several months after M abducted C, a state Y County Department of Social Services (DSS) filed a petition alleging C to be a neglected and dependent juvenile. The petition asserted that C was not receiving proper care, supervision, or discipline from M and that she lived in an environment injurious to C's welfare. Although the state Y trial judge knew of the state X order giving F custody, she made no effort to contact the state X court. At an adjudication hearing where F was not represented or notified, the court found C to be a neglected and dependent juvenile and placed her in DSS custody. F, who eventually learned of the proceeding, filed an appeal and argued that the trial court should have granted full faith and credit to the state X order and returned C to his custody. How will an appellate court most likely rule? Of what relevance are the UCCJEA's emergency provisions to the resolution of this issue, if any?

9. Assume that F and M divorced in state X, and a court there awarded sole legal and physical custody of child C to M. Both parents were before the court when it issued the order. F subsequently moved to state Y. Also, assume that about ten years following the entry of the divorce judgment, C called F from state X claiming that her new stepparent was abusing and mistreating her. F immediately sought an emergency order under the UCCJEA in state Y. F argued that state Y has jurisdiction to issue an emergency order, regardless of whether the child is present in the state. How will a court most likely rule?

10. Assume that mother (M) was granted sole physical custody of child in Montana. M moved to Washington State with the child. Father (F) followed M to the state of Washington and filed a motion for custody

of the minor child. M argues that the state of Washington lacks subject matter jurisdiction to hear F's custody motion. Both Washington and Montana have adopted the UCCJEA. Most likely, how will a court rule?

11. Assume that M (mother) and F (father) were divorced in Nevada in November 2008. They had three young children. The decree, which was stipulated, provided for joint legal and physical custody in M and F. The decree incorporated the parents' agreement that Nevada would have exclusive jurisdiction over future child custody disputes. It read: "The parties have agreed that the children's 'home state' shall always be considered to be Nevada, and jurisdiction over all issues pertaining to the custody of and each party's timeshare with the children shall be exclusively with this Court [i.e., the Family Court in Nevada]." The underlying settlement agreement amplified this provision and read in part: "Specifically, it is the parents' intent that no court other than the courts of the State of Nevada shall have jurisdiction over the parties or the subject matter to consider any issue pertaining to the custody and/or support of the parents' minor children, including, but not necessarily limited to, any motion or action that may be filed by either parent seeking a change of custody or a change in the parents' timeshare arrangement as set forth in this Agreement."

    Assume that in February 2010, both parties moved to California. The parents and children are now residents of California. In December 2011, M returned to Nevada family court to ask for an order awarding her primary physical custody of the children. F opposed M's motion and challenged the Nevada district court's jurisdiction to adjudicate the child custody dispute. F maintains that Nevada lacks subject matter jurisdiction. F has initiated competing custody proceedings in California.

    Assume that both Nevada and California have adopted the UCCJEA. Can the Nevada court proceed, or should it defer to California?

12. Assume that F (father) and M (mother) have been married ten years and are residents of state X. They have one child, C. Assume that F and C go to visit F's mother and father in state Y. After discussing marital difficulties with his parents, F decides to remain in state X with C. Four months after arriving in state X, F files a divorce action and asks for custody of C, claiming that the court in state X may decide custody on the basis of the significant connection between state X and F and C. F argues that a significant connection exists when a state has substantial evidence about a child as a result of the child's significant connections to that state. *See* UCCJEA 201(a)(2)(A)(B).

13. M (mother) and F (father) have moved on numerous occasions as F has sought a medical degree, internship, residency, and a medical job. After

five months at a medically related job in state X, F returned to work for a hospital in state Y. F, M, and their child had lived in state Y for four months before they moved to state X. There is evidence regarding care of C from day-care providers and pediatricians in both state X and Y.

F begins a divorce action in state Y and seeks custody of C. M simultaneously begins a custody action under the UCCJEA in state X. Which state most likely has jurisdiction to decide custody?

14. Assume that M and F are separated, but neither has filed for custody of C, their 7-year old child. They informally agree that C may reside with F, who is a pilot for a major airline. F lives in state X, while M lives in state Z. C spends the majority of her time with a nanny and a housekeeper because of her father's schedule. She spends one weekend each month with M, plus several holidays and two months in the summer.

    M is a programmer and often works late into the night for the software company by whom she is employed. As noted, she lives in state Z. Because of this, weekend visits with M are sometimes spent with friends in M's neighborhood or with a baby-sitter hired by M.

    F has an opportunity to move to city A in state Y, where the main facilities for his employer are located. In addition, C's grandparents live in city A. F moves to city A and files for sole legal and physical custody of C in a state Y court. In his papers seeking custody, he states that it is in the best interests of C to be in his custody because of M's working hours and the closeness of C's grandparents. F states that during the school year, C can be with his grandparents after school and on the days when F is out of town. M seeks joint legal and physical custody of C. Should the matter be heard in state X, Y, or Z?

15. M and F have been married for six years and they have two children. The have resided in state X for ten years. Following a domestic dispute with her husband, M takes their only child, C, and drives to state Y. Upon arrival in that state, she seeks out a domestic violence shelter.

    M then files for temporary custody of C under the UCCJEA's emergency jurisdiction provisions. F is served with the temporary custody motion in state X but does not respond to it. The court in state Y grants M temporary custody but stipulates that its order will become permanent after six months if no proceeding is commenced in state X, the child's home state. F commences a custody proceeding in state X shortly after he received notice of the entry of the order in state Y. M's attorney asks the court in state X to decline jurisdiction in favor state Y on the basis that state X is now an inconvenient forum. How should the court in state X rule?

16. Assume that P and D are married and living in state X. They have one child, C. Without any warning, F and C travel from X to state Y, where F

and C hide for a year. F then files a petition asking for custody of C in state Y. M receives notice of the action and files a motion to dismiss, claiming that F's conduct was not justified. How will a court in state Y rule?

Explanations

1. The question is whether the court in state Y lacked subject matter jurisdiction to modify permanently the court order issued in state X. Under the UCCJEA, a new state may not modify an out-of-state child custody order unless it properly finds that the issuing state has been divested of jurisdiction or declined to exercise it. Furthermore, the parent petitioning the new state to assume jurisdiction bears the burden of proving, not only that the new state would have jurisdiction to enter an initial child custody order, but that the issuing state has lost or declined to exercise jurisdiction as well. *Brandt v. Brandt*, 268 P.3d 406, 413 (Colo. 2012). Here, M has failed in meeting the burden placed on the moving party.

   Note that although state Y is the home of the child within six months before the proceeding commenced and a parent or person acting as a parent continues to live in state Y, that is not sufficient to confer subject matter jurisdiction on state "Y" to resolve this issue. Here is the reasoning:

   > First, there is no question but that state X made an initial custody determination, and X never determined that it no longer had exclusive, continuing jurisdiction.
   >
   > Second, although state Y may be a more convenient forum than state X, the UCCJEA specifies that the out-of-state court must make this determination, not state Y where P filed her action. State "X" has never made such a determination.

   In the absence of a determination by state X that it no longer had continuing, exclusive jurisdiction or a ruling by state X that state Y would be a more convenient forum, state Y could have subject matter jurisdiction to modify the order of state X only if either a court in state Y or the court in state X determined that "neither the child nor the child's parents or any person acting as a parent presently resides in state X." In this case, F was still residing in state X. State X continues to retain exclusive jurisdiction. *See Delgado v. Combs*, 724 S.E.2d 436 (Ga. App. 2012).

2. The purpose of this example is to generally review the theories on which courts over the past century or so have decided interstate custody

disputes. To begin with, if the court in state Y applies the traditional domicile rule, it most likely would find that the children take the father's domicile. Because the father is domiciled in state Y, that state would conclude that it has jurisdiction to decide custody and might well ignore the ex parte ruling of state X. Courts 100 years ago would not recognize a status theory associated with custody.

Second, there is an issue about whether state Y can obtain personal jurisdiction over M so that it can adjudicate a custody decision. There is nothing in the hypothetical to suggest that state Y has a long-arm statute covering domestic matters. Even if it has, it is clear that M does not have sufficient minimum contacts with state Y to satisfy constitutional requirements.

Third, in addition to the question about the existence of a long-arm statute and its language as discussed previously, a court will struggle with the meaning of the plurality view in *May v. Anderson*. If it applies the reasoning in that case by the plurality, it may refuse to enforce the state X ruling on the theory that state X lost personal jurisdiction over F before the divorce action was initiated when F became a citizen of state Y. (Note that F never appeared in the divorce hearing in state X and did not consent to the custody order.) It will reason that without personal jurisdiction over both parties, state X was without power to enter an enforceable judgment regarding custody outside its borders. Practically, this means that if F can obtain jurisdiction over M, it can proceed with a custody hearing.

Fourth, moving forward into the last three decades of family law, the court in state Y might recognize the newly emerged "status" theory. If it does, it may conclude that at the time of the default hearing in state X that the children were before the court and their status (i.e., custody) could be decided. Under this theory, a state may alter a child's custody status without having jurisdiction over both parties if at the time of the hearing it has the most significant connections with the child and the child's family. This theory suggests that "status" (custody) implies more than the state's concern with the relationship of the parties. It encompasses the right and obligation of the state in its *parens patriae* role to consider the welfare of the child subject to its jurisdiction and to make a determination that is in the best interests of the child. *In re Marriage of Leonard*, 175 Cal. Rptr. 903 (Cal. App. 1981). State Y may recognize the status theory and its application at the time of the default hearing and dismiss F's motion.

Finally, under the UCCJEA, it appears that the only jurisdiction where the modification issue could be brought is state X, absent a state X court waiving its right to adjudicate the matter in that state. If state Y has adopted the UCCJEA, it will refuse to entertain a custody motion involving F and the children because state X has already considered that issue. Moreover, state X is the home state of the children and F is not alleging an emergency.

3. This example should act as a quick review of a fundamental principle associated with PKPA and UCCJEA. A court will most likely rule in favor of M. Here, state X has retained jurisdiction under its own laws. State X possessed initial custody jurisdiction when it entered its first order at a time when it had personal jurisdiction over both parties. State X has remained the residence of C and P since the original custody order was entered. Under the PKPA and the UCCJEA, a custody modification action must be brought in state X unless state X declines to exercise jurisdiction, which in this hypothetical is highly unlikely. *See Matthews v. Riley*, 649 A.2d 231 (Vt. 1994).

4. This is another very straightforward example. A court applying the typical language found in the UCCJEA will take the view that no other jurisdiction, other than the issuing court in state X, may modify a custody determination. Only if an issuing court in state X determines that it no longer has exclusive, continuing jurisdiction may the matter be heard in state Y. Here, one of the parties, F, continues to live in state X, the state that issued the original custody order. State X does not appear to have lost jurisdiction or to be ready to give it up. It is unlikely that a court in state Y would ignore the PKPA and the UCCJEA and apply a status theory to resolve the dispute in state Y.

5. Although we added some facts suggesting that the problem is challenging, it is very straightforward. Under the UCCJEA, state X has exclusive, continuing jurisdiction unless a court in that state determines that neither the child, nor the child and one parent, have a significant connection with state X and that substantial evidence is no longer available in state X concerning the child's care, protection, training, and personal relationships. Before making a final decision, a judge in state X will consider that most, if not all, of the visitation between F and the child took place in state X. The child has an extended family in state X, and the primary witnesses regarding F's alleged alcohol abuse, use of marijuana, and any additional safety concerns (including any individual who may conduct a substance abuse evaluation), F's family members, and F's current girlfriend are located in state X. Basically, the most relevant information regarding the child's best interest and safety during visitation with F exists in state X. Because F still resides in state X and substantial evidence remains available in state X concerning the child's care, protection, and personal relationships during visitation, a court

will most likely rule that state X has exclusive, continuing jurisdiction to modify the original visitation schedule.

On the question of whether the matter should be heard in state Y rather than state X because state Y is a more convenient forum, it has already been noted that the evidence of alcohol and marijuana abuse involving F, if it exists, is located in state X. It also appears that the evidence that M intends to rely upon would include F's family members and F's current girlfriend. All those individuals are currently located in state X and most likely are not subject to the subpoena powers of state Y. State X would have a superior ability to compel, if necessary, the testimony of individuals having potentially relevant information regarding the child's safety.

Although M and the child have lived in state Y for eight years, a court in state X will not decline jurisdiction because Y is a more convenient forum. Practically, most of the evidence regarding M's allegations about F's behavior is located in state X, along with considerable other evidence as noted previously. This will probably cause a court in state X to conclude the length of time that the child and M lived in Y is not a compelling factor.

Other factors a court in X might consider in arriving at a decision are the distance that M and the child will have to travel from state Y to state X for a hearing, the costs associated with attending the hearing, such as hotels and meals, and M's loss of income if she is employed outside the home. However, because the child's best interests and safety during visitation are of paramount concern, a court probably would not rule that state X is an inconvenient forum.

6. Despite the fact that F originally agreed to allow M to relocate, an appellate court will most likely reverse the trial judge's ruling. The UCCJEA gives jurisdictional priority and exclusive, continuing jurisdiction to the home state, which is X. Under the UCCJEA, a court has home state jurisdiction if it is located in the child's home state (as of the date proceedings commenced) or if it is located in the state that was the child's home state within six months of the proceedings' commencement and the child's parent (or a person acting as his or her parent) continues to live in the state even after the child has been removed. This extended home state rule allows a left-behind parent to commence a custody proceeding within six months of a child's removal from the home state.

   Because the trial court properly exercised jurisdiction in the initial determination of the parties divorce and because F still resides in state X, and the home state of the children is X, state X retains jurisdiction over the matter. If both parents had relocated out of state X, then there might have been a question as to X's exclusive and continuing jurisdiction, but that is not the case here.

M's assertion that because she "registered" the decree in state Y upon moving to that state that Y has jurisdiction to determine the children's custody under the UCCJEA, finds no support in the language of the UCCJEA.

7. First, it is clear that state A is not the home state of the child for the purposes of jurisdiction as "home state" as defined by the UCCJEA. In this case, M and the child lived in state Y for substantially all of the child's life, until M's recent move to state Z. M lived in state Z for five months prior to commencement of the state A proceedings. The child had resided in state A only three weeks and in state Z less than six months prior to this action.

State X could not be the "home state" because the evidence shows that neither F, M, nor the child lived in state X at the time of the commencement of the custody proceeding. In addition, State Z could not be the "home state," as the evidence in this hypothetical shows that the child lived less than six months with M in that state and only three weeks with F in state A before F initiated the custody action.

Second, the language of the statute in this jurisdiction permits a court in state A to exercise jurisdiction only if (1) a court of another state does not have "home state" jurisdiction or has declined to exercise jurisdiction; and (2) the child has significant connections with state A; and (3) there is available in state A substantial evidence concerning the child's welfare. Here, there is little evidence to establish either the child's significant connection with state A beyond the child's limited presence during three weeks of this year, or the availability of substantial evidence concerning the child's past and future care, education, and safety. The child has, after all, lived with M in either state Y or state Z almost since birth.

Third, state A courts may exercise jurisdiction under the UCCJEA if no other state has jurisdiction. UCCJEA, §201, *comment*. Because neither state Y, state Z, nor state A could properly exercise "home state" jurisdiction, the trial court may have assumed jurisdiction under this default provision.

Fourth, the jurisdictional provisions of the UCCJEA seek to assure that litigation regarding custody of a child take place in the state with which the child and his family have the closest connection and where significant evidence concerning care and protection is readily available in order to provide a continuing stable environment for children. State A is not that state. While the trial court may not have erred in assuming jurisdiction, the spirit and intent of the UCCJEA is to protect the best interests of the child. It appears that F is left with a choice of state X or state Z in which to bring the custody action. *See Wood v. Redwine*, 33 P.3d 53 (Okla. App. 2001). State Z is the likely choice for F's modification action because M is residing there. State Y is most likely not available because it would be difficult to obtain personal jurisdiction over M in that state at this time.

8. This hypothetical, based on a real California case, seems to have a very clear answer. The trial court's decision will be reversed. Where interstate custody rulings are concerned, it does not matter whether they involve private parties or, as in this case, the state. Clearly, the order finding C to be a neglected and dependent juvenile and placing her in custody of the county department of social services violated the emergency jurisdiction provisions of UCCJEA. The reasoning is that the order does not appear to be temporary, and although the state Y judge knew about the prior state X custody decree, there was no effort to contact the state X court immediately to determine that court's willingness to assume jurisdiction.

9. A state Y court will most likely reject F's request. §204 of the UCCJEA codifies and clarifies several aspects of what has become common practice in emergency jurisdiction cases under the UCCJEA and PKPA. First, a court may take jurisdiction to protect a child even if it can claim neither home state nor significant connection jurisdiction. Second, the duties of states to recognize, enforce, and not modify a custody determination of another state do not take precedence over the need to enter a temporary emergency order to protect the child. However, §204 of the UCCJEA must be read in context with the federal PKPA. The PKPA states that a custody determination can be made by a state if it has jurisdiction under state law and the child is physically present in such state and if (1) the child has been abandoned or (2) it is necessary in an emergency to protect the child because he has been subjected to or threatened with mistreatment or abuse. 28 U.S.C. §1738A(c)(2)(C) (1994). This language is more explicit than the UCCJEA in defining that presence, as well as an additional emergency situation, is required. When the federal PKPA precludes exercise of UCCJEA jurisdiction, state courts "must give preemptive effect to the federal enactment." *See McLain v. McLain*, 569 N.W.2d 219, 224 (Minn. App. 1997). Because state Y meets none of the requirements for exercise of jurisdiction under either the PKPA, it is preempted from assuming jurisdiction. The action must be brought in state X.

10. Washington State courts lacks subject matter jurisdiction under the UCCJEA. Here, F still lives in Montana and seeks to modify a custody

determination initially made by Montana. However, Montana has never declined jurisdiction, and F cannot confer subject matter on the Washington court. Under the UCCJEA, a Washington court may modify Montana's initial child custody determination only if either Montana declines jurisdiction or all parties have left that state. RCW 26.27.221. See *In re Custody of A.C.*, 200 P.3d 689 (Wash. 2009).

11. Under the UCCJEA, California appears to have jurisdiction as the children's "home state," and Nevada cannot proceed unless California determines that Nevada is the more convenient forum. If asked to make an inconvenient/more appropriate forum determination, the California court could, under the UCCJEA, consider a number of factors, with the parties' agreement to litigate in Nevada being one of them. However, under the UCCJEA, the decision appears to rest with California's courts.

The child, the child's parents, and any person acting as a parent do not presently reside in Nevada. Because all parties, including the children, have become California residents, this suggests that Nevada would lose jurisdiction.

However, doesn't the parents' agreement and the language in the original divorce decree make Nevada the forum state and control where this dispute should be heard? Doesn't the agreement trump the UCCJEA?

Nobody disputes that Nevada had jurisdiction to make the initial child custody determination when it entered the divorce decree. Ordinarily, this would give Nevada "exclusive, continuing jurisdiction" under the UCCJEA. However, the UCCJEA provides that exclusive, continuing jurisdiction ceases when a Nevada court or a court of another state determines that the child, the child's parents, and any person acting as a parent do not presently reside in this state. Most would agree that the Nevada court made such a jurisdiction-ending determination in this case, when it found that the parties and their children are no longer residents of Nevada.

Once exclusive, continuing jurisdiction ceases, a court can modify its prior child custody determination "only if it has jurisdiction to make an initial child custody determination." *See* UCCJEA §202 cmt., 9/IA U.L.A. 673 (1997) ("[U]nless a modification proceeding has been commenced, when the child, the parents, and all persons acting as parents physically leave the State to live elsewhere, the exclusive, continuing jurisdiction ceases."). Under the UCCJEA, a Nevada court has jurisdiction to make an initial child custody determination only if Nevada "is the home state of the child on the date of the commencement of the proceeding," or "a court of the home state of the child has declined to exercise jurisdiction on the ground that this State is the more appropriate forum."

It is conceded that by December 2010, California had become the children's "home state" as defined by the UCCJEA ("home state" means "[t]he state in which a child lived with a parent or a person acting as a parent for at least 6 consecutive months . . . immediately before the commencement of a child custody proceeding"). This concession established that F's pending California proceeding as "a child custody proceeding commenced in a court in another state having jurisdiction substantially in accordance with the provisions of the UCCJEA."

Once this is clear, the Nevada court was required to stay its proceeding, communicate with the California court, and if the California court does not determine that the court in Nevada is a more appropriate forum, the Nevada court should dismiss the proceeding. *See Friedman v. County of Clark*, 264 P.3d 1161 (Nev. 2011).

12. The court in state X lacks jurisdiction and may not hear the motion unless state Y, the child's home state, declines jurisdiction in favor of Y. Note, however, than an argument can be made that if M fails to commence a custody proceeding in state Y within six months of C's removal, that state X becomes the child's home state, and that state may then exercise jurisdiction and decide custody.

13. Neither F nor M have lived in any state long enough for their child to have established a home state. Because of that, both X and Y arguably have significant connection jurisdiction. However, under the UCCJEA, only one of these states should exercise it. Under the UCCJEA, a court learns from the pleadings that a proceeding has been commenced in a sister state, that court must stay its proceeding and communicate with the other court to decide which proceeding should continue. If the courts cannot agree, the UCCJEA says that the court with the first-filed case may move forward and the other court should dismiss its proceeding. UCCJEA 206(a)(b) (1997).

14. Under the UCCJEA, initial jurisdiction exists when both the home state (X) and a significant connection state (Z) decline jurisdiction in favor of another, more appropriate state on the grounds of inconvenient forum or unjustifiable conduct. Given the facts of this hypothetical, the court in X (home state) and Z (significant connection state) might decline jurisdiction in favor of Y. Under the UCCJEA, a decision to decline jurisdiction in a case like this is discretionary and obviously depends on all the facts. Probably, the courts in X and Z would agree that the matter will he heard in state Y.

15. Under the UCCJEA, courts have temporary emergency jurisdiction when a child in the state has been abandoned or when emergency protection is necessary because a child was subjected to or is threatened with mistreatment or abuse. UCCJEA 204(A) (1997).

    A court may take jurisdiction to protect the child even though it can claim neither home state nor significant connection jurisdiction. Second, the duties of states to recognize, enforce, and not modify a custody determination of another state do not take precedence over the need to enter a temporary emergency order to protect the child. Third, a custody determination made under the emergency jurisdiction provisions of this section is a temporary order. The purpose of the order is to protect the child until the state that has jurisdiction under §§201-203 enters an order. *See Comment*, UCCJEA 204 (1997).

    The commentary to §304 notes that the UCCJEA narrows the definition of "emergency" by excluding neglect cases — thus bringing it into conformity with the PKPA — while expanding the definition to cover emergencies that put a child's parent or sibling at risk, such as those covered by the Violence Against Women Act. Note also that under the UCCJEA, courts may exercise emergency jurisdiction and make temporary orders even if a proceeding has been commenced in another state. Immediate judicial communication is mandatory to resolve the emergency, protect the safety of the parties and the child, and determine how long a temporary order should remain in effect.

    In this hypothetical, the state courts involved in this dispute would communicate with each other. If the court in state X finds that domestic violence has occurred and is likely to continue and that state Y can best protect the mother and child, it will grant M's motion and dismiss F's action. The only decision at this point is where the hearing on custody will be held.

    If state X agrees that state Y should hear the matter, there will be a hearing in that state on the merits. Only after such a hearing can the temporary order be made permanent.

16. At the outset, recall that if a parent takes the child from the home state and seeks an original custody determination elsewhere, the stay-at-home parent has six months to file a custody petition under the extended home state jurisdictional provision of §201. This will ensure that the case is retained in the home state. If a petitioner for a modification determination takes the child from the state that issued the original custody determination, another state cannot assume jurisdiction so long as the first state exercises exclusive, continuing jurisdiction. *Comment*, §208. Unfortunately for M, she did not take this action.

As to the issue in the example, §208, *Jurisdiction Declined by Reason of Conduct*, of the UCCJEA requires a court to decline jurisdiction if such jurisdiction was created because of the unjustifiable conduct of the party bringing the action. Furthermore, the Act requires the court to assess the wrongdoer necessary and reasonable expenses unless that party can prove that the assessment would be clearly inappropriate. UCCJEA 208(c). Although the UCCJEA does not define what constitutes "unjustifiable conduct," although most courts would agree that F's behavior was unjustified.

Most likely, the court in state Y will agree with M decline jurisdiction and dismiss F's petition. The UCCJEA also permits the court to order F pay the attorney's fees for M and investigative costs. Note that the only issue decided is which state may hear a custody dispute involving M and F.

M will most likely file a custody action in an X state court, which can exercise jurisdiction on significant connection grounds because Y, the home state, has declined its jurisdiction. Once state X issues its order, the UCCJEA and the PKPA require Y to enforce it.

CHAPTER 8

Parenting Time and Visitation

8.1. Introduction

When a divorce takes place or parents separate, children's relationships with caring adults also may change. Some relationships, such as those between parents and children, are legally protected and enforced. Other relationships, including those with grandparents and stepparents, may only be legally recognized under certain circumstances and conditions.

Continuing contact with both parents usually promotes a child's adjustment to a new family situation — that is, unless a child is likely to suffer from or be endangered by the contact. If parents share joint physical custody, they will spend considerable effort scheduling time for the child with each parent. Alternatively, if one parent has sole physical custody, the noncustodial or nonresidential parent is awarded "visitation rights" or "parenting time."

As awareness grew concerning the contribution of both parents to childrearing, family law professionals began to question the designation of one parent as a "noncustodial visitor" after divorce. Consequently, some jurisdictions no longer use the term *visitation* and have replaced it with the term *parenting time*. This term is sufficiently broad to encompass cases of joint physical custody (parents share roughly equal amounts of parenting time), as well as cases of sole physical custody (one parent exercises more parenting time).

Many children also benefit from relationships with adults other than their natural parents. Interested people such as grandparents and stepparents have consequently turned to the courts to assure that their relationships with children will continue. Legislatures and courts struggle to set policy in this area, recognizing some relationships but not others.

MODEL ACTS

8.2. Uniform Marriage and Divorce Act (UMDA): Reasonable Visitation

Section 407(a) of the Uniform Marriage and Divorce Act (UMDA) provides that a "parent not granted custody of the child is entitled to reasonable visitation rights unless the court finds, after a hearing, that visitation would endanger seriously the child's physical, mental, moral, or emotional health."

In practice, the "reasonable visitation" standard required parents to create their own parenting time arrangements following a divorce. Although some parents were able to reach amicable agreements, many found this to be a source of serious and ongoing conflict. These couples frequently sought post-decree assistance from the court in defining "reasonable" and "unreasonable." Consequently, courts and legislatures now require specific and detailed visitation or parenting time orders in most divorce decrees. In addition to scheduling hours for parenting time, final orders address issues such as transportation, holidays, and vacations.

In a situation in which one parent is given sole physical custody of children, the nonresidential parent typically exercises parenting time every other weekend, one evening during the week, alternating holidays, and several weeks during the summer.

Example

1. Assume that P and D divorced and agreed that D would have sole physical custody of the children because P traveled extensively for work — she was out of the country for six to eight weeks at a time and then returned home for two to four weeks. P was granted "reasonable" parenting time with the two children. One child, X, was 16 years old, and another child, Y, was 3 years old. The couple experienced continued difficulty working out a parenting time arrangement. P claimed that she was entitled to have the children stay with her during the two to four weeks that she was in the United States. D argued that such an arrangement would amount to joint physical custody and would undermine the court's decision granting D sole physical custody of the children. He also argued that long

blocks of parenting time would be disruptive to the children. If the couple does not reach an amicable agreement, what would a judge likely decide?

EXPLANATION

Explanation

1. The court is called on to interpret and enforce the divorce decree entitling P to reasonable parenting time. Because of P's unusual work schedule, she is not able to visit with the children every other weekend or have midweek face-to-face contact. The court will consider the best interests of the children when deciding what parenting time is reasonable under the circumstances However, this situation is complicated by the fact that one child is 3 and one child is 16. A very young child may particularly benefit from frequent physical contact with a nonresidential parent, whereas an older child might be able to supplement longer periods of face-to-face time with e-mail and phone conversations more easily than a younger one. Consequently, what is reasonable for one child may not be reasonable for the other. For example, the court might order that both children spend every weekend with P when she is in town and that the 3-year-old spend an additional overnight during the week with P.

8.3. American Law Institute (ALI)

The American Law Institute (ALI) replaces the traditional use of *custody* and *visitation* with the term *custodial responsibility*. American Law Institute, *Principles of the Law of Family Dissolution: Analysis and Recommendations* §2.03(3) (2002). Comment (e) to §2.03 explains,

> While any beneficial effects of this shift in terminology on people's perceptions of parenthood cannot be measured, it is assumed that the unified concept of custodial responsibility has some potential to strengthen the usual expectation that both parents have responsibility regardless of the proportion of time each spends with the child, and that neither parent is a mere "visitor."

§2.11 of the ALI *Principles* places limits on allocation of responsibility to parents who have abused, neglected, or abandoned a child; inflicted domestic violence; abused drugs and alcohol; and/or interfered with the other parent's access without cause. Limitations imposed can include reduction or limitation of custodial responsibility, supervision of custodial time, exchange of a child through an intermediary, restraints on communication and proximity, abstinence from prior drug and alcohol use, denial of overnight custodial responsibility, restrictions on persons present, requiring posting of bond, and completion of a treatment program.

STANDARDS FOR DENYING OR LIMITING PARENTING TIME

8.4. Denial or Suspension of Parenting Time

Because parents have a constitutional right to contact with their children, courts will deny parenting time only in the most extreme and egregious cases. *See Meyer v. Nebraska*, 262 U.S. 390 (1923); *Pierce v. Society of Sisters*, 268 U.S. 510 (1925). For example, in *Nelson v. Jones*, 781 P.2d 964 (Alaska 1989), supervised parenting time was denied to a father guilty of sexual abuse.

Incarceration. An incarcerated parent may be denied parenting time under some circumstances. In *Harmon v. Harmon*, 943 P.2d 599 (Okla. 1997), the court listed factors to be considered in deciding whether a father in a correctional facility should have parenting time. The factors included the age of the child, the distance to be traveled, the physical and emotional effect on the child, whether the parent had exhibited genuine interest in the child, past history of contact, and the nature of the crime committed. *See also Etter v. Rose*, 684 A.2d 1092 (Pa. Super. 1996) (rebuttable presumption that visitation with incarcerated parent is not in the best interests of the child); *Mark C. v. Patricia B.*, 42 A.D. 3d 1317 (N.Y. App. 2007) (by itself, incarceration does not make visitation inappropriate); Solangel Maldonado, *Recidivism and Paternal Engagement*, 40 Fam. L.Q. 191 (2006).

Burden. The burden is on the parent contesting parenting time to show that the child would be endangered seriously by contact with the other parent. *See Sterbling v. Sterbling*, 519 N.E.2d 673 (Ohio App. 1987).

8.5. Restrictions on Parenting Time

As noted previously, courts rarely deny a parent access to a child. More typically, with the proper showing, courts may place restrictions on the exercise of parenting time. For example, a parent might have contact with a child only in a supervised setting (either formally supervised by professional staff at a visitation center or supervised more informally by friends or family), or a parent may be denied overnight contact.

Under the UMDA, to place restrictions on a parent's right to parenting time, the court must find that "visitation would endanger seriously the child's physical, mental, moral, or emotional health." UMDA §407. Proof beyond mere allegations is required.

Research shows that when supervised parenting time is ordered to take place at a visitation center, it is usually in cases involving children who were severely traumatized. Typically, these children have been abused or neglected, have witnessed intimate partner violence, have lived with a mentally ill parent, or have been abducted. *See* Janet R. Johnston & Robert B. Straus, *Traumatized Children in Supervised Visitation: What Do They Need?* 37 Fam. & Conciliation Cts. Rev. 135 (1999). *See also* Elizabeth Barker Brandt, *Concerns at the Margins of Supervised Access to Children*, 9 J.L. & Fam. Stud. 201 (2007).

8.6. Child Abuse and Intimate Partner Violence

When a parent has committed child abuse or intimate partner violence, the other parent may be understandably frustrated by a court's insistence on allowing even limited parenting time. In such circumstances, if parenting time is going to occur, the parent and child are best protected if the court requires that the parenting time be formally supervised. *See In re M.M.M.*, 307 S.W.3d 846, 853 (Tex. App. 2010) (supervised visitation in case involving intimate partner violence); *Mallouf v. Saliba*, 766 N.E.2d 552 (Mass. App. 2002); *Hollingsworth v. Semerad*, 799 So. 2d 658 (La. App. 2001). *But see Sevland v. Sevland*, 646 N.W.2d 689 (N.D. 2002) (allowing unsupervised visitation in a case involving intimate partner violence).

Researchers have developed protocols for use in assessing when restrictions such as supervised exchange, supervised access, or suspended contact are appropriate. *See* Janet Johnston et al., *In the Name of the Child: A Developmental Approach to Understanding and Helping Children of Conflicted and Violent Divorce* (2009); Peter G. Jaffe et al., *Custody Disputes Involving Allegations of Domestic Violence: Toward a Differentiated Approach to Parenting Plans*, 46 Fam. Ct. Rev. 500 (2008).

8.7. Alcohol and Substance Abuse

Supervised parenting time may be required if the visiting parent's alcohol or drug use makes parenting time unsafe for the child. *See Allen v. Allen*, 787 So. 2d 215 (Fla. App. 2001) (requiring supervision because of the mother's alcohol use); *see also Pratt v. Pratt*, 56 So. 3d 638 (Ala. App. 2010) (supervised access due to mother's substance abuse); *White v. Nason*, 874 A.2d 891 (Me. 2005) (contempt action against father for violation of prohibition on substance use while children were in his care); *Fine v. Fine*, 626 N.W.2d 526 (Neb. 2001) (requiring supervised visitation because of the parent's mental illness, history of domestic violence, and substance abuse).

8.8. Child Abduction

If there is credible evidence that a parent with court-ordered parenting time will abduct or has previously abducted a child, parenting time is likely to be supervised to prevent abduction from occurring. For example, in *Chandler v. Chandler*, 409 S.E.2d 203 (Ga. 1991), the court ordered supervised parenting time after one parent took the child out of state without notice. However, in *Abouzahr v. Abouzahr-Matera*, 824 A.2d 268 (N.J. Super. 2003), a parent was allowed to exercise visitation in Lebanon, so long as the parent gave four weeks' advance notice.

8.9. Cohabitation

If the visiting parent cohabits with a person of the opposite sex, the other parent may petition to limit overnight visits with the child. However, such a restriction is not likely to be granted unless the cohabitation has a serious adverse impact on the child. *See Higgins v. Higgins*, 981 P.2d 134 (Ariz. App. 1999); *Harrington v. Harrington*, 648 So. 2d 543 (Miss. 1994). *But see Muller v. Muller*, 711 N.W.2d 329 (Mich. 2006) (upholding order that "neither party shall have an unrelated member of the opposite sex overnight while having parenting time with the minor children").

8.10. Parent Who Is Gay or Lesbian

Although courts take opposing views on the issue, the emerging view is that a parent who is gay or lesbian is entitled to overnight parenting time unless the parent opposing it can show specific endangerment to the child's physical or emotional health. *See Morris v. Hawk*, 907 N.E.2d 763 (Ohio App. 2009); *Miller-Jenkins v. Miller-Jenkins*, 661 S.E.2d 822 (Va. 2008); *Downey v. Muffley*, 767 N.E.2d 1014 (Ind. App. 2002); *T.B. v. L.R.M.*, 786 A.2d 913 (Pa. 2001); *In re Marriage of Dorworth*, 33 P.3d 1260 (Colo. App. 2001); *Boswell v. Boswell*, 701 A.2d 1153 (Md. App. 1997); and *Johnson v. Schlotman*, 502 N.W.2d 831 (N.D. 1993).

8.11. Religious Differences

A parent without legal custody can be restricted from imposing his or her religious views on a child during parenting time, and the nonresidential parent may be required to bring a child to religious services chosen by the legal custodian. *See Lange v. Lange*, 502 N.W.2d 143 (Wis. App. 1993) and

Zummo v. Zummo, 574 A.2d 1130 (Pa. Super. 1990). In extreme cases, limits may be placed on discussion of religious matters:

> Furthermore, in light of the evidence in the record that the father harmed the children by disobeying court orders and using religion to alienate them from the mother, we conclude that the court did not abuse its discretion by prohibiting the father from discussing religion with the children. Although "the court would be intruding on . . . [the] First Amendment rights [of the father] were it to enjoin [him] from discussing religion with his child[ren] absent a showing that the child[ren] will thereby be harmed," here, as noted, there was such a showing.

Mathews v. Mathews, 72 A.D.3d 1631, 1632 (N.Y. App. 2010).

See also Shepp v. Shepp, 906 A.2d 1165 (Pa. 2006) (a fundamentalist Mormon could not be prohibited from discussing polygamy with his minor daughter where such discussions did not jeopardize the child's health, safety, or pose a "grave threat" to the child).

Nevertheless, within limits, a nonresidential parent may take the child to religious services of his or her own choosing during parenting time. *See In re Nina R.*, 638 N.W.2d 393 (Wis. App. 2001); *In re Marriage of McSoud*, 131 P.3d 1208 (Colo. App. 2006); *Wood v. Dehan*, 571 N.W.2d 186 (Wis. App. 1997). In order to restrict this activity, the objecting parent may need to show that the child would be physically or emotionally harmed by it. *Zummo v. Zummo*, 574 A.2d 1130 (Pa. Super. 1990).

Examples

EXAMPLES

2. Assume that P (mother) and D (father) are divorcing. They have one child, X. D has been arrested several times for alcohol- and drug-related offenses, but he does not believe that he has a substance abuse problem. D argues that he neither drinks nor uses drugs in the presence of the child and that he should be entitled to spend unrestricted time with X. P asserts that D's drinking and drug use are out of control and that X would be in danger spending time alone with D. The trial court orders D to abstain entirely from alcohol and drug use at all times, whether he is with X or not. Will this restriction be upheld on appeal?

3. P (mother) was awarded legal and physical custody of X, and D (father) was awarded parenting time with X. As the sole legal custodian, P decided to raise X in a religion to which D objected. As a part of her faith tradition, P objected to D's giving gifts to X and to D's encouraging X to participate in various holiday activities. Because of ongoing conflict about the child's religious affiliation, the court entered an order

prohibiting D from interfering with X's religious training — D could not visit X on Christmas Eve or Christmas Day or allow X to participate in holiday activities, including gift-giving and trick-or-treating. D objected to the court order as an improper restriction on his parenting time. Will such an order be upheld on appeal?

4. Assume that P and D were divorced and agreed to a parenting plan that designated D (father) as the primary custodial parent and granted P (mother) substantial parenting time. P was living with her boyfriend at the time of the divorce, and the court inserted a provision that ordered P not to permit her boyfriend or any other person to whom she is not married but with whom she is romantically involved to spend the night during her exercise of residential time. D did not argue for the provision or present evidence that showed a negative effect on the children due to the mother's behavior. How is an appellate court likely to analyze the situation with respect to the "paramour" provision?

5. Assume that P (mother) and D (father) are getting divorced. Although there is no evidence that D has engaged in any inappropriate or sexual contact with the minor children, now ages 12 and 15, the children reported feeling uncomfortable when alone with D. At trial, D admitted he had sexual thoughts about children, including his own. An expert opined that D suffers from pedophilia. The trial court imposed strictly restricted parenting time to D. Would restricted visitation be upheld on appeal?

EXPLANATIONS

Explanations

2. Most likely, a court would order that parenting time with X take place in a supervised setting so that D is prevented from seeing the child if D is under the influence of drugs or alcohol. By complying with the order for supervised parenting time and consistently appearing for parenting time in a sober state, D can establish his trustworthiness and possibly petition the court in the future to be allowed to spend unsupervised time with X. This example, which is based on *Cohen v. Cohen*, 875 A.2d 814 (Md. App. 2005), found the court going a step further and ordering the father to stop drinking and using drugs outside the presence of the child as well. Although the court's order goes beyond ordering supervised parenting time, the appellate court upheld the trial judge who required the father to abstain completely from alcohol use.

3. As the sole legal custodian, P has the right to determine X's religious upbringing, even over the strong objection of D. In *A.G.R. ex rel. Conflenti v.*

Huff, 815 N.E.2d 120 (Ind. App. 2004), the court upheld a similar order because the custodial parent's right to determine religious training could be limited only by a showing that the child's physical health or emotional development would be "significantly impaired." In this example, D did not allege any harm to the child resulting from the religious practice. The appellate court found that the trial court's order did not unreasonably interfere with the nonresidential parent's right to parenting time because the father received the same amount of time with the child that he otherwise would.

4. Generally, a trial court's decision regarding a permanent parenting plan would be set aside only when it falls outside the range of rulings that result from an application of the correct legal standard. Where the trial court on its own motion has inserted a provision in a permanent parenting plan, there must be proof of actual or threatened harm to the children. The trial court's own notion of morality is not a substitute for a connection between the mother's living arrangement and the factors supporting a determination of the best interests of the child. In addition, the application of the paramour provision to only one party undercuts its application to the children. Accordingly, the insertion of the paramour provision would be found an abuse of discretion in the absence of proof of harm. See *Bargmann v. Bargmann*, 2011 WL 1026095 (Tenn. App. 2011). *See also Ward v. Ward*, 289 Ga. 250 (Ga. 2011) (holding that an order prohibiting "any overnight male guests" was overbroad and an abuse of discretion).

5. The court has ample reason to restrict access. In *Veronica S. v. Philip R.S.*, 70 A.D.3d 1459 (N.Y. App. 2010), the court found similar facts to be sufficient to sustain restricted parenting time. Even if the preferences of the children were not presented adequately to the court, the trial court had sufficient information to determine that the best interests of the children required restrictions on visitation.

ENFORCEMENT OF PARENTING TIME

8.12. Contempt and Modification of Custody

If parenting time arrangements are not carefully structured, parenting time can be an ongoing source of serious conflict. In such situations, the parties may negotiate or mediate their differences or return to court to seek enforcement of parenting time provisions.

If the parties cannot reach an agreement, a parent being denied parenting time may bring a contempt action to enforce a parenting time order. *See Ellis v. Ellis*, 840 So. 2d 806 (Miss. App. 2003). In extreme cases, the parent denying parenting time could lose custody. *See Miller-Jenkins v. Miller-Jenkins*, 12 A.3d 768 (Vt. 2010) (non-compliance with visitation order results in modification of custody); *Egle v. Egle*, 715 F.2d 999 (5th Cir. 1983).

8.13. Compensatory Parenting Time

If a parent has wrongfully been denied parenting time, that parent may be entitled to "makeup" or compensatory parenting time. *See* Mich. Comp. Laws Ann. §552.642 (2003) and Minn. Stat. §518.175 subd. (6)(b) (2002).

8.14. Withholding Child Support

In most states, a parent cannot deny parenting time because the non-residential parent has not paid child support. Similarly, a child support obligor must continue to pay child support even if parenting time is denied. *See Carter v. Carter*, 479 S.E.2d 681 (W. Va. 1996); *Seidel v. Seidel*, 10 S.W.3d 365 (Tex. App. 1999).

8.15. Wishes of the Child

Absent specific restrictions on parenting time, parents are expected to encourage and support a child's relationship with the other parent. Consequently, a parent cannot deny parenting time based on a child's desire not to visit. *Schutz v. Schutz*, 581 So. 2d 1290 (Fla. 1991). Nevertheless, parenting time is more difficult to enforce if teenagers are opposed to it. For example, in *Worley v. Whiddon*, 403 S.E.2d 799 (Ga. 1991), a 14-year-old's wishes were considered but were not dispositive.

In some cases, a child may resist having a relationship with a parent because that parent is abusive or seriously neglectful. Consequently, it is important that the concerns of children are taken seriously and appropriately assessed. *See* Barbara Jo Fidler & Nicholas Bala, *Children Resisting Postseparation Contact with a Parent: Concepts, Controversies, and Conundrums*, 48 Fam. Ct. Rev. 10 (2010); Peter G. Jaffe et al., *Early Identification and Prevention of Parent-Child Alienation: A Framework for Balancing Risks and Benefits of Intervention*, 48 Fam. Ct. Rev. 136 (2010).

EXAMPLES

Examples

6. P was awarded sole physical custody of the parties' two children, and D was awarded parenting time every other weekend, alternate Monday evenings, and on some holidays. Six months after the divorce, based on a motion to modify and an action for contempt, the court ordered that P could not schedule any activities for the children during D's parenting time periods unless D agreed ahead of time in writing. After some consultation with D, P enrolled the children in a religious education class 18 months later, which took place on one of D's parenting time evenings. D brought a contempt action against P and sought additional parenting time. The trial court found P in contempt and awarded D an additional ten hours per month of parenting time. If P appeals, what is the likely outcome?

7. Assume that when P (mother) and D (father) divorce, they have a 16-year-old son, X. Father and son have a difficult relationship, despite the fact that both have attended counseling. Because of their history and X's age, the judge orders that D's continuing contact with X be "contingent upon the contact being mutually requested." D appeals the order. What is the likely outcome?

EXPLANATIONS

Explanations

6. In an analogous case, *In re Kosek*, 871 A.2d 1 (N.H. 2005), the appellate court upheld the lower court's finding of civil contempt and the award of additional parenting time. The appellate court reasoned that the increase in parenting time was an appropriate sanction for civil contempt and that the new parenting time schedule was not contrary to the best interests of the child.

7. D will argue that the conditional order could have the effect of denying his right to parenting time and that parenting time cannot be restricted without a finding that visitation would endanger the child. P might argue that a 16-year-old should not and cannot be forced to spend time with a parent if the teenager is strongly opposed to doing so. In the final analysis, although a court may consider the child's wishes with respect to the scheduling of parenting time, courts do not generally allow children to choose whether or not to spend time with a nonresidential parent. *In re Marriage of Kimbrell*, 119 P.3d 684 (Kan. App. 2005). *See also Brown v. Erbstoesser*, 85 A.D.3d 1497 (N.Y. App. Div. 2011) (visitation continued, despite unwillingess of children, where no evidence of detriment presented).

MODIFICATION OF PARENTING TIME

8.16. UMDA Provisions

Like custody and child support, parenting time orders can be modified. Section 407 of the UMDA allows for modification in the best interests of the child, "but the court shall not restrict a parent's visitation rights unless it finds that the visitation would endanger seriously the child's physical, mental, moral, or emotional health." Typical restrictions are those discussed in prior sections. *See Baber v. Baber*, 2011 WL 478622 (Ark. 2011) (showing of material change in circumstances warranting visitation restriction). *But see Duva v. Duva*, 685 S.E.2d 842 (Va. App. 2009) (wife's alleged violation of oral agreement to provide children with therapy did not constitute a change in circumstances warranting modification, and modification was not in best interests of children).

EXAMPLE

Example

8. Assume that P (mother) and D (father) were divorced and that P was granted physical custody of their two children. A high level of conflict between P and D continued after the divorce, and they returned to court several times on post-decree motions. One summer, one of the children (age 11) wanted to participate in sports and a band program that conflicted with D's parenting time. Through her own attorney (hired by P), the 11-year-old filed a motion to modify parenting time in the parents' divorce. What is the likely result?

EXPLANATION

Explanation

8. Under similar facts in *In re Marriage of Osborn*, 135 P. 3d 199 (Kan. App. 2006), a father argued that no change in circumstances was shown and that, consequently, modification of the parenting time order was improper. He also argued that the child lacked standing to bring the modification action. The appellate court ultimately agreed with the father and held that the child lacked standing to file the motion to modify.

VISITATION BY A THIRD-PARTY

8.17. Grandparents and Third-Party Visitation Statutes

At common law, grandparents had no legally enforceable right to visit their grandchildren. However, as the number of living grandparents and the rate of divorce increased, more formal recognition was given to the grandparent-grandchild bond in hope of adding stability to the lives of children experiencing divorce. *See* Maegen E. Peek, *Grandparent Visitation Statutes: Do Legislatures Know the Way to Carry the Sleigh Through the Wide and Drifting Law?* 53 Fla. L. Rev. 321 (2001).

Thanks in large part to the efforts of organized grandparent groups, by 1994, every state had adopted a visitation statute incorporating grandparents and often addressing the rights of other third parties. The statutes vary widely in scope—some apply only if the parents divorce, die, or have their parental rights terminated, and other statutes apply regardless of the status of the child's immediate family unit.

8.18. *Troxel v. Granville*

State statutes providing for grandparent and other third-party visitation have been subject to reexamination since the United States Supreme Court decided *Troxel v. Granville*, 530 U.S. 57 (2000). In *Troxel*, the Court struck down a Washington statute allowing "any person" to petition for visitation rights "at any time" that "visitation may serve the best interests of the child."

The Court held that the statute as applied was an unconstitutional infringement on a fit parent's fundamental right to make decisions about the care and custody of minor children. The Court determined that some deference or "special weight" must be given to parental decisions because it is presumed that fit parents will act in their children's best interests. The court's decision rested in part on the breadth of the Washington statute, but the court stopped short of holding that specific types of statutes would violate due process.

The somewhat ambiguous nature of the decision spawned additional litigation as state courts considered the constitutionality of their visitation statutes in light of *Troxel*. Examining courts focused on the extent to which statutes deferred to the decisions of fit parents and the presence of statutory factors in addition to the "best interests of the child." Some state statutes have been found constitutional, whereas others have been held unconstitutional facially or as applied. For a discussion of the cases decided subsequent to *Troxel*, *see* Kristine L. Roberts, *State Supreme Court Applications of* Troxel v. Granville *and the Courts' Reluctance to Declare Grandparent Visitation Statutes Unconstitutional*, 41 Fam. Ct. Rev. 14 (2003). *See also* Elizabeth Williams, *Cause of Action by Grandparent to Obtain Visitation Rights to Grandchildren*, 17 Causes of Action 2d 331 (2008); George L. Blum, *Grandparents' Visitation Rights Where Child's Parents Are Living*, 71 A.L.R.5th 99 (1999); *Ex parte E.R.G. and D.W.G.*, 73 So. 3d 634 (Ala. 2011) (Grandparent Visitation Act that did not include a presumption in favor of parents violated due process).

EXAMPLES

Examples

9. P and D are married with two children. After years of a very contentious relationship with P's parents, P and D decided to end their contact with the grandparents of the children and moved to another state. The grandparents petitioned the court for grandparent visitation rights under the state statute in their home state. Assume that the state permits grandparent visitation when it is in the best interests of the children and would not interfere significantly with the parent-child relationship, or when the parents have denied the grandparents a reasonable opportunity to visit. The trial court ordered seven two-day visits each year, including an overnight each time. P and D appealed. What is the likely outcome?

10. Assume that P and D had a child but did not marry, and D died shortly after the child was born. P (mother) has plans to marry and wants the child to regard the stepfather as her only father figure. D's father brought a paternity action on his deceased son's behalf seeking visitation. He also contacted P with requests for visitation. The state permits grandparent visitation so long as it is in the child's best interests and does not interfere with the parent-child relationship. Trial courts are to also consider the amount of personal contact that the grandparent has had in the past. What will the parties argue with respect to visitation, and how will the court decide?

11. Assume that mother (M) and father (F) are married, and they live together with their two children. They reside in a jurisdiction with a statute allowing grandparents reasonable visitation of grandchildren if such visitation would be in the child's best interests and if a substantial relationship has been established between the child and the grandparent. The grandparents had ongoing contact with the grandchildren from their birth until recently, including regular phone contact, holiday visits, and overnight visits. However, since the grandmother mistakenly alleged that one of the children had been sexually abused, M and F have refused to

let the grandparents see the child. The grandparents sue for visitation with both children, over the objection of M and F. M and F argue that they are fit parents in a continuing nuclear family, and that it is their prerogative to deny visitation to the grandparents. The grandparents argue that the statute makes no distinction between intact families and those experiencing divorce or other disruption. What is the likely outcome?

12. Assume that P and D had a child but did not marry, and P (mother) was murdered less than a year after the child was born. At the time, she lived with Grandmother. Grandmother obtained an ex parte custody order after P's death. Three weeks later, D filed to establish paternity and custody. P had acknowledged D as the father and took steps to further his visitation rights before her untimely death. D and Grandmother have an unfriendly relationship, and once D established paternity and custody, he refused to allow Grandmother visitation. She petitioned for grandparent visitation rights. The trial court ordered visitation on a graduating scale so that she ultimately had the child every Tuesday and Thursday in the afternoon and every other weekend from Friday through Sunday. For his part, D had proposed one weekend per month of visitation from Saturday to Sunday. What arguments will the parties make on appeal?

13. Assume that P and D had a child but did not marry, and D died four years after the child was born. D died of a drug overdose, and D's mother has suggested that P may have been responsible for D's demise. D's mother brought a visitation action for the 4-year-old grandchild. Assume that the state has a statute that gives the grandparent of a deceased parent the right to visit. Courts in that state have ruled that there is a rebuttable presumption that a fit surviving parent's decisions regarding visitation are in the best interest of the children. P does not want to allow any visitation or contact with Grandmother. What will the parties argue with respect to visitation, and how will the court decide?

14. Assume that P and D had a child but did not marry, and D died one year after the child was born. During his paternity action, D had requested that his parents not be involved in the litigation. D died a short time later, having exercised his visitation rights on five or six occasions. The child's paternal grandparents saw the child a few more times before P declined their request for additional visitation. The grandparents sued for court-ordered grandparent visitation. Assume that the state standard is that a court is without authority to award such visitation unless clear and convincing evidence is presented to prove the statutory requirements. Among the requirements, a significant beneficial relationship must be demonstrated. What is the likely outcome?

Explanations

9. In *In re A.L.*, 781 N.W2d 482 (S.D. 2010), the South Dakota Supreme Court was faced with a similar situation, where the statute apparently permitted a court to order grandparent visitation when it had been denied by the parent, without linkage to whether the visitation would interfere with the parent-child relationship. However, the decision of the United States Supreme Court in *Troxel v. Granville*, 530 U.S. 57 (2000), compelled a ruling that the statute was applied unconstitutionally in the circumstances. As in the present example, the trial court did not find that the parents were unfit, or that any special circumstances existed that would override their *Troxel* liberty interest in childrearing and their right to make decisions that are presumed to be in the child's best interests. Generalities about the benefits of grandparent contact were not sufficient to establish special circumstances to justify governmental interference in the parent-child relationship. The grandparents' visitation rights were vacated and left to the decision of the parents.

10. The mother will assert that the grandfather had no existing relationship with the child, as required for the court to order visitation. She will also contend that as a fit parent, her decision not to allow contact is entitled to deference. The grandfather will argue that the natural connection was cut short when his son died and that he made reasonable contacts as time and distance permitted. In *R. F. V. M.M.*, 789 N.W.2d 723 (N.D. 2010), the North Dakota Supreme Court affirmed a trial court decision allowing grandparent visitation under similar facts. In that case, the trial court found that the mother resisted visitation and that the grandparent's visitation would not interfere with the parent-child relationship.

11. Because the mother and father are fit parents in a "continuing nuclear family," they argue that their decision not to allow visitation should be given absolute deference by the court. However, the grandparents argue that the statute makes no distinction between intact families and other families. In *Davis v. Heath*, 128 P.3d 434 (Kan. App. 2006), a court faced with this situation awarded visitation to the grandparents, holding that the language of the statute did not distinguish between intact and other families, that the parents' decision to terminate visitation was unreasonable, that the evidence showed that the grandmother and grandchild had a substantial relationship, and that visitation was in the child's best interests. *But see Santi v. Santi*, 633 N.W.2d 312 (Iowa 2001) (statute permitting visitation without circumstances such as divorce, death of parent, or adoption declared unconstitutional).

12. In the case that provides the basis for this example, a Minnesota court is permitted to award grandparent visitation if it does not interfere with the parent's relationship with the child. *In re C.D.G.D.*, 800 N.W.2d 652 (Minn. App. 2011). D will argue that the order interferes with his parent-child relationship. Grandmother will argue that she had significant prior personal contact with the child while her daughter lived with her. She would argue that the trial court referred to Grandmother as the primary caretaker with a substantial bond, and that the district court has substantial discretion in custody and visitation decisions. In *In re C.D.B.G.*, the appellate court reversed the visitation order, pointing out that, in effect, the grandmother was treated as a parent, and that was an abuse of discretion. The district court also did not give sufficient weight to the presumptively valid wishes of the natural parent. The appellate court ordered adoption of the father's plan without further hearings.

13. Grandmother will have to overcome the presumption concerning the decision-making authority of a surviving parent. She will need to establish that denial of grandparent visitation is not in the best interests of the child and that it would be detrimental to the child. P will assert her rights as a fit parent under *Troxel v. Granville*, 530 U.S. 57 (2000), and argue that the grandmother's open hostility to the parent-child relationship will be disruptive. In *Rich v. Thatcher*, 132 Cal. Rptr. 3d 897 (Cal. App. 2011), on which this example is based, the trial court decided that a grandparent must present clear and convincing evidence that denial of visitation would be detrimental to the child. In this case, the trial court expressly disbelieved the testimony of the grandmother and denied visitation. The appellate court affirmed.

14. In *Vratko v. Gibson*, 800 N.W.2d 676 (Neb. App. 2011), on which this example is based, the trial court found that the grandparents had seen the child on a limited number of occasions and that no significant beneficial relationship had been shown. The court of appeals pointed out that the fit natural parent's wishes were entitled to great weight, and there was no abuse of discretion in denying the grandparents visitation rights.

8.19. Visitation with Stepparents

Under the common law, stepparents have no protected right to ongoing contact with stepchildren at divorce or upon the death of the biological parent-spouse. *See Seyboth v. Seyboth*, 554 S.E.2d 378 (N.C. App. 2001) (visitation by stepparent was denied because there was no showing that the natural parent was unfit); *In re C.T.G.*, 179 P.3d 213 (Colo. App. 2007) (stepfather lacked standing to seek parenting time). Nevertheless, after a divorce, some stepparents seek visitation with their stepchildren, and in many cases, parties work out a voluntary arrangement that will allow the stepparent and stepchild to maintain their relationship.

When courts are asked to intervene, the outcomes vary by jurisdiction. In some states, visitation is denied; in others, courts may grant visitation under third-party visitation statutes or when a stepparent has acted *in loco parentis* prior to the divorce. *See Simmons v. Simmons*, 486 N.W.2d 788 (Minn. App. 1992); *Weinand v. Weinand*, 616 N.W.2d 1 (Neb. 2000); *In re Marriage of Riggs and Hem*, 129 P.3d 601 (Kan. App. 2006); *Visitation Rights of Persons Other than Natural Parents or Grandparents*, 1 A.L.R.4th 1270 (1980).

Comentators have expressed concern about the lack of unified public policy on the rights and roles of stepparents in light of the number of blended families:

> A review of our Nationwide Survey clearly reveals that the law with regard to stepparents' rights and obligations remains a patchwork quilt with little consistency with regard to the different categories we researched within a state, and a clear lack of uniformity between states. However, more jurisdictions are addressing the stepparent or third party question in their laws because of advocacy by the psychological and legal communities. More continued research is needed in both fields to determine the appropriate direction for stepfamily policies.

Susan L. Pollet, *Still a Patchwork Quilt: A Nationwide Survey of State Laws Regarding Stepparent Rights and Obligations*, 48 Fam. Ct. Rev. 528, 536 (2010).

Courts and policymakers face significant challenges as they seek to enforce the constitutional rights of objecting parents while also considering the enduring nature of some step-relationships.

8.20. Visitation with a Nonbiological Gay or Lesbian Co-Parent

Historically, courts have not granted visitation to unmarried lesbian or gay nonbiological co-parents (who have not formally adopted the child) after the relationship between the adult partners ends. For example, in *Nancy S. v. Michele G.*, 279 Cal. Rptr. 212 (Cal. App. 1991), the court refused to recognize the nonbiological mother as a parent under the Uniform Parentage Act or as a de facto parent. *See Behrens v. Rimland*, 32 A.D. 3d 929 (N.Y. 2006) (former same-sex partner lacked standing); *Stadter v. Siperko*, 661 S.E.2d 494

(Va. App. 2008) (former same-sex partner did not prove by clear and convincing evidence that denial of visitation would harm child); *Jones v. Barlow*, 154 P.3d 808 (Utah 2007) (common law doctrine of *in loco parentis* did not grant standing). *See also Alison D. v. Virginia M.*, 572 N.E.2d 27 (N.Y. 1991); and Robin Cheryl Miller, *Child Custody and Visitation Rights Arising from Same-Sex Relationships*, 80 A.L.R.5th 1 (2000).

More recently, some courts have ordered visitation in an exercise of the court's equitable power or based on the specific language of a third-party visitation statute. *See In re Custody of H.S.H.-K.*, 533 N.W.2d 419 (Wis. 1995); E.N.O. v. L.M.M., 711 N.E.2d 886 (Mass. 1999); *V.C. v. M.J.B.*, 748 A.2d 539 (N.J. 2000); *Laspina-Williams v. Laspina-Williams*, 742 A.2d 840 (Conn. Super. 1999) (same-sex partner had standing under visitation statute); *SooHoo v. Johnson*, 731 N.W.2d 815 (Minn. 2007) (former same-sex partner granted visition under third-party visitation statute). For example, the Arkansas Supreme Court reasoned as follows in a case involving a biological mother and her former same-sex partner (Jones):

> Considering the ample evidence about the relationship between Jones and E.B., we cannot say that the circuit court clearly erred in finding that she stood in loco parentis to the child. It was undisputed that she was the stay-at-home mom for over three years who took care of E.B. E.B. called her mommy. She thought of Jones's parents as her grandparents and spent holidays with Jones's family. The parties' intentions were always to co-parent, until Bethany unilaterally determined she no longer wanted to allow Jones to have visitation. Taking this all into consideration, we hold that the circuit court correctly determined that Jones was a parent figure to E.B. Having determined that Jones stood in loco parentis, the question then becomes whether it is in E.B.'s best interest for Jones to have visitation rights, as that is the polestar consideration.

Bethany v. Jones, 2011 Ark. 67, 11-12,—S.W.3d—(Ark. 2011). *See also* Deborah L. Forman, *Same-Sex Partners: Stranger, Third Parties, or Parents? The Changing Legal Landscape and the Struggle for Parental Equality*, 40 Fam. L.Q. 23 (2006); Jennifer L. Rosato, *Children of Same-Sex Parents Deserve the Security Blanket of the Parentage Presumption*, 44 Fam. Ct. Rev. 74 (2006).

8.21. Parents by Estoppel and De Facto Parents

Under the ALI's *Principles of the Law of Family Dissolution: Analysis and Recommendations* §2.18, individuals other than legal parents can be allocated parental responsibility, either as a parent by estoppel (§2.03(b)) or as a de facto parent (§2.03(c)). A parent by estoppel is a person other than a legal parent who (1) is obligated to pay child support; (2) lived with the child and accepted parental responsibility for at least two years in the good-faith belief that he was the child's father; or (3) lived with the child since birth and acted as a parent pursuant to a parenting or co-parenting agreement. A de facto parent is a person other than a legal parent or parent by estoppel who for at least two years (1) lived with the child and (2) performed the majority of caretaking functions, or as many caretaking functions as the parent with whom the child resided, (3) either by agreement or because of the failure or inability of the legal parent to do so.

Although a parent by estoppel has more rights than a de facto parent, both statuses require the adult in question to have functioned significantly as the child's parent which is theoretically consistent with acting *in loco parentis*. However, the ALI analysis appears to be broad enough to encompass petitions for parenting time by stepparents, lesbian and gay parents, and some grandparents.

EXAMPLES

Examples

15. Assume that after a father and mother divorce, the father has physical custody of their child, X. The father remarries, and X's new stepmother, S, functions as a parent to him. Approximately two years after the father's remarriage, he is killed in a car accident. Although X's biological mother assumes physical custody of X, the stepmother petitions for visitation with X. A state statute allows a person standing *in loco parentis* to a child to petition for visitation if it is in the child's best interests, and one of the legal parents is deceased. The statute defines *in loco parentis* as "a person who has been treated as a parent by the child and who has formed a meaningful parental relationship with the child for a substantial period of time." The biological mother opposes the visitation on the basis that X already has a biological and legal mother. The court agrees and denies the visitation on the grounds that the stepmother could not establish *in loco parentis* status unless she "stood in the place of either Father or Mother" before the father's death. What is the likely outcome on appeal?

16. Assume that P (legal mother) and D (same-sex partner) lived in a committed relationship for more than ten years. Because same-sex couples were not allowed to adopt children, the child was adopted by P individually. Both P and D were extensively involved in parenting the child, and they shared all major parenting decisions, including those related to education, religion, and medical care. After P and D part ways, D seeks visitation with the child under a statute allowing such a proceeding by a person "who has had physical care of a child for a period of six months or more." If P opposes D's request, what is the likely outcome?

17. D and P never married but had an off-and-on relationship over the years. D gave birth to two children, neither of which were P's biological children. P maintained relationships with the children and acted as a father to them in many respects. When D terminated P's contact with the chidren, P brought an action seeking visitation. D argues that she, as a fit parent, has the right to deny P access to the children. P argues that the children will be harmed by ending the relationship. What is the likely result?

EXPLANATIONS

Explanations

15. In *Riepe v. Riepe*, 91 P.3d. 312 (Ariz. App. 2004), the appellate court held that the statute did not require the stepmother to show that her relationship with the child was the same as or superior to the child's relationship with the biological parents in order to be awarded visitation. The case was remanded so that the stepmother could establish that she was treated as a parent by the child and that she had a meaningful relationship with the child for a substantial period of time as required under the statute. On remand in such a case, it is likely that the biological mother would argue that a two-year relationship did not amount to a substantial period of time and that the relationship was not a meaningful one. Note that if the parties lived in a state without an *in loco parentis* statute, the stepmother likely would not bc awarded visitation because under the common law, stepparents do not generally have an enforceable right to ongoing contact with a stepchild. *See Dodge v. Dodge*, 505 S.E.2d 344 (S.C. App. 1998) (where mother died, stepfather had no derivative right to visitation).

16. D will argue that she has cared for the child physically for more than six months as required by the statute, and she likely will succeed with this argument. In a similar case, *In re* E.L.M.C., 100 P.3d 546 (Colo. App. 2004), an adoptive legal mother, P, unsuccessfully argued that her former partner was required to establish a legal relationship with the child, that the visitation request must be incident to a dissolution proceeding, and that the legally recognized parent must have relinquished care of the child. Of course, D would have great difficulty obtaining parenting time over P's objection if D lived in a state that had not adopted a statute recognizing psychological parenthood.

17. In the similar case of *DiGiovanna v. St. George*, 12 A.3d 900 (Conn. 2011), the Supreme Court of Connecticut held that under existing case law, the former boyfriend could seek visitation over the objection of a parent

with a stringent showing. The non-parent seeking visitation would have to prove by clear and convincing evidence that there existed a parentlike relationship and that if the relationship ended, the children would be harmed to such an extent (akin to abuse or neglect) that the parent's consitutional interest could be overridden. In that case, the action of the former boyfriend was allowed to proceed. *But see Rohmiller v Hart*, 799 N.W.2d 612 (Minn. App. 2011) (denial of visitation to aunt).

CHAPTER 9

Establishing Child Support

9.1. Introduction

This chapter examines child support issues that arise at the time of divorce or between unmarried parents who do not live together. Issues related to the modification or enforcement of an existing child support award are considered in Chapter 10.

Child support is a court-ordered payment by one parent (often the noncustodial or nonresidential parent) to the other parent for the support of a common child. An order for child support transfers the income from one parent to the other so that the combined incomes of both parents are available to meet the child's needs.

A child support order is typically part of a divorce decree or parentage order and is usually payable on a monthly basis. Many states require that child support be paid by wage assignment (automatic deductions from the paycheck) when available because this procedure may reduce the need for subsequent enforcement actions.

HISTORY

9.2. Elizabethan Poor Laws

The Elizabethan Poor Laws, passed at the beginning of the seventeenth century, consituted one of the first efforts to establish a formal obligation to provide support for children. Passage of the Poor Laws was spurred by economic conditions that resulted in a large class of landless, often destitute laborers with children.

> The Poor Relief Act of 43 Eliz. Ch. 2 required the father and the mother, among other relatives, of every poor, old, blind, lame, and impotent person, or other poor person unable to work, to relieve and maintain such person at their own charges, if they were of sufficient ability to do so.

M. C. Dransfield, Annotation, *Parent's Obligation to Support Adult Child*, 1 A.L.R.2d 910, 935 (1948).

As a result of these laws, some moral duties of family members were transformed into legal obligations. They also provided the first public welfare program, funded through taxation, to assist needy members of the community when family support was unavailable.

9.3. Common Law

In the United States, the common law imposed the duty of supporting minor children on their parents. However, as a general rule, there was no obligation for a parent to support an adult child. M. C. Dransfield, *Parent's Obligation to Support Adult Child*, 1 A.L.R.2d 910, 914 (1948). The states eventually removed any doubt regarding parental responsibility for the support of children by enacting laws making it a criminal offense for a parent to desert or willfully neglect to provide support for a minor child.

Some common law courts hoped that "nature" would provide an adequate parental incentive to support children born during a marriage should a divorce occur. For example, in *Plaster v. Plaster*, 47 Ill. 290 (1868), the court observed that:

> [N]ature has implanted in all men a love for their offspring that is seldom so weak as to require the promptings of law, to compel them to discharge the duty of shielding and protecting them from injury, suffering and want, to the extent of their ability. Hence the courts are seldom called upon to enforce the duty of parents. The law of nature, the usages of society, as well as the laws of all civilized countries, impose the duty upon the parent of the support, nurture, and education of children.

Id. at 291.

Unfortunately, the hoped-for natural inclination of a parent to provide support for a child has not been entirely realized. Nevertheless, contemporary United States law reflects the view that the cost of raising children is primarily a private matter, with the parents as the responsible parties.

9.4. The Changing Legal Landscape

Today, extensive state and federal legislation drives a variety of programs intended to ensure that minor children receive financial support from their parents and, as a last resort, from the state. While child support orders are made and largely enforced on the state level, federal involvement has resulted in more uniform handling of cases.

ROLE OF THE FEDERAL GOVERNMENT

9.5. Child Support Traditionally a State Issue

Historically, the issue of child support was a matter of state law and judges exercised wide discretion in making child support determinations. The Uniform Marriage and Divorce Act (UMDA) was originally promulgated in 1970 by the National Conference of Commissioners on Uniform State Laws, and it acted as a model for many state legislatures. The UMDA provided that a parent or parents would pay a reasonable amount of child support based on their financial resources; the standard of living the child would have enjoyed; and the needs of the child. UMDA §309. Under this standard, awards were difficult to predict, and similarly situated children sometimes received different amounts. In an effort to promote uniformity and reduce public assistance expenditures, the federal government became increasingly involved in authoring national child support policy.

9.6. Child Support and Establishment of Paternity Act of 1974

The federal government initially began collecting national data regarding child support awards and payments because of concern about rising rates of unmarried parents and welfare dependence. Since this fledgling effort, a multitude of federal programs to deal with child support have been enacted.

The Child Support and Establishment of Paternity Act of 1974 was one of the first federal efforts. 42 U.S.C. §§651-655. The law was aimed at recipients of public assistance and required them to cooperate in locating potential obligors and establishing and enforcing support orders. The purposes of the act were to reduce public expenditures by obtaining child support from noncustodial parents, help families obtain support so that they could move off of public assistance, and stimulate state action to establish paternity and obtain support for children born outside marriage.

Under this early federal legislation, responsibility for administering the support program was left to individual states and local governments. Nevertheless, the federal government largely shaped the programs by linking funding to specific program features, assisting states in their attempts to locate absent parents, and providing technical assistance to state agencies.

9.7. State Guidelines Mandated

Under the UMDA, courts exercised wide discretion in setting child support amounts, and policymakers sought more predictability and fairness. As a result, in 1984 Congress mandated that states seeking federal funding for public assistance programs establish advisory child support guidelines. Child Support Enforcement Amendments of 1984, Pub. L. No. 98-378, 98 Stat. 1305. States that did not comply risked losing a large percentage of federal funding for their Aid to Families with Dependent Children (AFDC) program. *See* 42 U.S.C. §§651, 667(a)-(b) (1984). The legislation also required states to enact statutes authorizing expedited processes for obtaining and enforcing support orders.

Congress strengthened the guidelines in 1988 with the passage of the Family Support Act, which mandated that state guidelines be applied in all cases and that they operate as a rebuttable presumption of the correct support amount to be awarded in a divorce or parentage action. The Act also required that deviation from the presumptive amount be supported by specific findings, in writing or on the record. 42 U.S.C. §667(b)(2). *See also* Helen Donigan, *Calculating and Documenting Child Support Awards Under Washington Law*, 26 Gonz. L. Rev. 13 (1990-1991); Ira Mark Ellman & Tara O'Toole Ellman, *The Theory of Child Support*, 45 Harv. J. on Legis. (2008).

9.8. Omnibus Budget Reconciliation Act of 1993

The Omnibus Budget Reconciliation Act of 1993 mandated that states adopt in-hospital programs to facilitate voluntary acknowledgment of paternity in cases of children born outside of marriage. 42 U.S.C. §666. It also required states to create a rebuttable or conclusive presumption of paternity when genetic testing indicated that a man was the father of a child born outside of marriage. The Employee Retirement Income Security Act (ERISA), 29 U.S.C. §1132, as amended, requires that employers make group health care coverage available to the noncustodial children of their employees. This resulted in the implementation at the state level of Qualified Medical Child Support Orders (QMCSO), 29 U.S.C. §1144, which ordered an employer and insurance carrier to include the child in the employer's insurance program.

9.9. Federal Enforcement Efforts

The federal government has also taken an active role in promoting interstate enforcement of child support orders. Relevant legislation is discussed in Chapter 10.

INCOME DEEMED AVAILABLE FOR SUPPORT

9.10. What Is Income?

All jurisdictions have adopted provisions to provide general guidance to judges when determining what resources should be considered income for the purpose of calculating child support. The phrase "income from any source," used in most statutory child support guidelines, is broadly construed and normally includes all financial payments, whatever the source. The determination of income for child support purposes under statutory guidelines is not necessarily controlled by definitions of gross income used for federal or state income tax purposes.

The following are examples of resources that courts in many jurisdictions will consider as available income when calculating child support: (1) wage and salary income and other compensation for personal services (including commissions, overtime pay, tips, and bonuses); (2) interest, dividends, and royalty income; (3) self-employment income; (4) net rental income (defined as rent after deducting operating expenses and mortgage payments, but not including noncash items such as depreciation); and (5) other income actually being received, including severance pay, retirement benefits, pensions, trust income, annuities, capital gains, Social Security benefits, unemployment benefits, disability and workers' compensation benefits, interest income from notes regardless of the source, gifts and prizes, spousal maintenance, and alimony.

Neverthless, states differ to some extent concerning what constitutes income for the purpose of determining child support. Examples of resources that some states do not include in their calculation include return of principal or capital, accounts receivable, or benefits paid in accordance with public assistance programs.

In the final analysis, the duty to pay child support may extend not only to an obligor's ability to pay from earnings, but also to his or her ability to make payments from any and all sources that may be available. The following sections illustrate some of the issues that courts face when determining whether a particular resource is income available for the purpose of calculating child support.

9.11. Vested Stock Options

In *MacKinley v. Messerschmidt*, 814 A.2d 680 (Pa. Super. 2002), the court held that once vested, stock options constituted available income that had to be imputed to the parent holding them for the purposes of calculating the parent's child support obligation, regardless of whether the parent chose to exercise the options. When determining income available for child support, the court must consider all forms of income. *Blaisure v. Blaisure*, 577 A.2d 640, 642 (Pa. Super. 1990) (court must consider every aspect of parent's financial ability, including stocks). A stock option, typically a "form of compensation," is defined as "an option to buy or sell a specific quantity of stock at a designated price for a specified period regardless of shifts in market value during the period." *Black's Law Dictionary* 1431 (8th ed. 2004). An option is "vested" when all conditions attached to it have been satisfied and it may be exercised by the employee.

9.12. Employer's Contribution to Pension Plan

In *Portugal v. Portugal*, 798 A.2d 246, 253 (Pa. Super. 2002), the court held that an employer's contributions to a pension plan constitute income for purposes of support "if the employee could access his employer's contributions (regardless of penalties) at the time of the support calculation." The court reasoned that children should not be made to wait for support and that parents should not be permitted to defer income to which they are entitled until they choose to avail themselves of it. *But see Bruemmer v. Bruemmer*, 616 S.E.2d 740 (Va. App. 2005) (mandatory deductions excluded from income for child support purposes).

9.13. Lump-Sum Payments and Commissions

Regular commissions and lump-sum payments may be used to set the amount of child support. *See M.S. v. O.S.*, 97 Cal. Rptr. 3d 812 (Cal. App. 2009) (father's bonus from Indian tribe was considered available for purpose of calculating child support); *Strait v. Strait*, 224 P.3d 997 (Ariz. App. 2010) (deduction of remediation expenses from settlement from mold litigation). Lump-sum payments may also be withheld from an obligor for the purpose of paying past-due support or to pay future support if there is a history of willful nonpayment. *See In re Marriage of Heiner*, 39 Cal. Rptr. 3d 730 (Cal. App. 2006) (evaluating whether lump-sum personal injury award is income for the purpose of child support).

9.14. Seasonal Employment

Seasonally employed obligors are generally required to make equal monthly payments throughout the year. Because the expenses of raising a child are not seasonal, judges generally require equal monthly payments despite the seasonal nature of the income.

9.15. Overtime

The law in most jurisdictions does not impose an obligation on obligors to work overtime. However, if an obligor has a history of working overtime, the courts may conclude that overtime is a normal, regular source of income and consider it when setting support. Similarly, if the overtime is a condition of employment, it is normally considered an income. *See Welter v. Welter*, 711 N.W.2d 705 (Wis. App. 2006) (court could not apply a general policy excluding overtime pay).

9.16. Military Retirement Pay and Allowances

A military member's entire pay and allowances may be considered in the determination of child support amounts. *See Tamayo v. Arroyo*, 15 A.3d 1031 (R.I. 2011) (payments arising from service in the National Guard constituted income available for child support); *In re Marriage of Stanton*, 118 Cal. Rptr. 3d 249, 256 (Cal. App. 2010) ("The nontaxable status of military allowances does not suggest Congress had any preemptive intent with regard to either child or spousal support."); *Massey v. Evans*, 68 A.D.3d (N.Y. App. 2009) (military allowances for housing and subsistence fell within definition of income for purpose of calculating child support); *Alexander v. Armstrong*, 609 A.2d 183 (Pa. Super. 1992) (father's military allowances were included in his income for purposes of child support); *Hautala v. Hautala*, 417 N.W.2d 879 (S.D. 1988) (military allowances are a species of remuneration subject to child support payments); *Merkel v. Merkel*, 554 N.E.2d 1346 (Ohio App. 1988); *Jackson v. Jackson*, 403 N.W.2d 248 (Minn. App. 1987); *Peterson v. Peterson*, 652 P.2d 1195 (N.M. 1982).

Collection of child support through direct payment by the Defense Finance and Accounting Service is determined by individual military service rules, which differ among the branches of service. Involuntary attachment of child support payments is provided for under federal law but requires a court order.

9.17. Imputation of Income

The amount of child support paid is related to the income of the parent or parents supporting the child. In some cases, parents receive in-kind income such as lodging or food instead of wages, and in these situations, courts may view these benefits as income available for child support. *See Carolan v. Bell*, 916 A.2d 945 (Me. 2007).

In other situations, if a parent is unemployed or underemployed, courts will sometimes impute income to the parent and base the child support order on the imputed income. For example, income equivalent to the minimum wage may be imputed to a voluntarily unemployed obligor. Similarly, if a parent is voluntarily underemployed, the court may base the child support order on the net income that the obligor previously earned. *See Christofferson v. Giese*, 691 N.W.2d 195 (N.D. 2005) (imputation must be based on actual income over prior 12 months rather than an extrapolation). *See also Weinstein v. Weinstein*, 911 A.2d 1077 (Conn. 2007) (imputation of 2.96 percent rate of return on investment actually yielding 1.24 percent).

In the case of *Parnell v. Parnell*, 239 P.3d 216 (Okla. App. 2010), the court discussed factors relevant to imputation:

> In doing so, courts may consider a number of factors: (a) "whether a parent has been determined by the court to be willfully or voluntarily underemployed or unemployed," taking into consideration the impact of additional training or education; (b) "when there is no reliable evidence of income"; (c) a parent's "past and present employment"; (d) a parent's "education, training, and ability to work"; (e) a parent's lifestyle; (f) a parent's role as caretaker of a handicapped or seriously ill child or relative of the parent; or (g) any additional factors deemed relevant to the particular circumstances of the case.

Id. at 219. *See also In re Marriage of Connerton and Nevin*, 260 P.3d 62 (Colo. App. (2010) (applying factors to determine whether participation in educational program warrants imputation of income).

Decisions about imputation of income for the purpose of calculation of child support are highly dependent on the facts presented. *See Marriage of Applegate*, 801 N.W.2d 627 (Iowa App. 2011) (imputation in case involving voluntary decisions by payor); *Iliff v. Iliff*, 339 S.W.3d 74 (Tex. 2011) (intentional underemployment warrants imputation); *Metz v. Metz*, 711 S.E.2d 737 (N.C. App. 2011) (imputation where job lost as a result of sexual abuse by payor); *Sexton v. Seklak*, 946 N.E.2d 1177 (Ind. App. 2011) (job loss due to argument with boss). *But see Prisco v. Stroup*, 3 A.3d 316 (D.C. App. 2010) (patent attorney job loss was involuntary); *Shvetsova v. Paderno*, 84 A.D.3d 1095 (N.Y. App. 2011) (involuntary job loss).

EXAMPLES

Examples

1. P and D are divorcing, and they have two daughters who will be in the physical custody of P. D recently started a landscaping business, and due to business exigencies, he elected to defer some of his salary. D paid his living expenses out of his existing assets. D argues that child support should be established based on his actual take-home pay, but P believes that D's "deferred" income should be considered income for the purpose of calculating child support. What is a court likely to decide?

2. Assume that P and D are divorcing and the court is calculating child support for their child. P will have sole physical custody of the child, and D will pay child support to P. P claims that D earns $15,000 per year and receives $46,000 in gifts and loans from his parents. D argues that the gifts and loans should not be viewed as "net income" under the statute and thus not be available for child support purposes. P alleges that the loans and gifts are "net income" and should be included. What is the likely result?

3. Assume that during the marriage of the parties, P was employed as a builder earning approximately $100,000 per year. After the parties separated, P quit his job and lived on money that he made at weekend flea market sales. D seeks a divorce and asks the court to base the child support award on P's former income. What is the likely result?

4. M and F are divorced and have one minor child. F was ordered to pay $298 per month in child support as a part of the divorce settlement. Subsequently, F received a personal injury settlement in the amount of $250,275, and M sought additional child support. The trial court divided the amount of the settlement by the remaining number of months of child support (133 payments until the child reached majority) and determined that $1,882 was income available for the purpose of paying child support. F argues that he used the settlement to purchase a home and pay off debts and that the money is not available on an ongoing basis. What will a court decide with respect to availability of the settlement for the purpose of calculating child support?

5. F pays child support to M for the benefit of their child. F received a loan from his employer, and the employer subsequently released F from repayment. M argues that the amount of the forgiven loan is income for the purpose of paying child support. What is a court likely to decide?

6. F was offered a tenure-track faculty position at a state university, but he turned it down to start a summer camp for the performing arts called Camp Curtain Call. He had some additional income from a business, and

he performed at magic shows in the off-season. M asks the court to impute income to F. What is the likely result?

EXPLANATIONS

Explanations

1. In a similar case, *In re Marriage of Berger*, 88 Cal. Rptr. 3d 766 (Cal. App. 2009), the court held that D's deferred earnings should be regarded as income for the purpose of calculating child support. The court concluded that D could not avoid his duty to support his children by arranging his business affairs so that he lived off of his assets and deferred income.

2. One of the key determinations in calculating child support is the determination of net income. The payor is likely to claim various deductions in order to lower child support liability. The payee will seek to have questionable income included for purposes of calculating child support. In a case with similar facts, *In re Marriage of Rogers*, 280 Ill. Dec. 726 (Ill. App. 2003), the court held that the value of the gifts and loans could not be deducted from net income and that both were available for child support purposes. Given that D has more income from gifts and loans than from earnings, holding otherwise in this case would have substantially deprived the child of support.

   In a later case, *In re Tegeler*, 302 Ill. Dec. 173 (Ill. App. 2006), the court said that "We believe that, in general, loans should not be considered income . . . . [L]oans typically should not be counted as income because they usually do not directly increase an individual's wealth." *See also Gina P. v. Stephen S.*, 824 N.Y.S.2d 619 (N.Y. App. 2006) (magistrate improperly added to father's income $14,750 reported on his 2002 tax return, a sum that was a repayment of a loan that the father made, which was a nonrecurring payment that should not have been considered in calculating his support obligations).

3. Confronted with a similar situation, the court in *Bator v. Osborne*, 983 So. 2d 1198 (Fla. App. 2008), found that P was voluntarily underemployed and remanded the case so that income could be imputed to him based on his recent work history, occupational qualifications, and prevailing community earning levels.

4. In the case of *Dupray v. Dupay*, 782 N.W.2d 42 (N.D. 2010), the Supreme Court of North Dakota upheld the decision of the trial court, reasoning that F continued to benefit from having received the personal injury settlement and that in that sense, it had not "ceased."

5. The Supreme Court of New Hampshire considered such a situation in *In re Sullivan*, 982 A.2d 959 (N.H. 2009). The court decided that the loan

forgiveness was in the nature of a bonus and consequently was available for the purpose of paying child support.

6. In the case of *Armbrister v. Armbrister*, 2011 WL 5830466 (Tenn. App. 2010), the appellate court found under these facts that F was voluntarily underemployed, and it affirmed imputation of income to him for the purpose of paying child support.

ESTABLISHING BASIC CHILD SUPPORT

9.18. Presumptive Guidelines

States have adopted various models of child support guidelines in response to federal mandates. *See* 42 U.S.C. §§651-667 (1982 & 1984 Supp. II) and 45 C.F.R. §302.56 (1989). While the guidelines differ from state to state, two of the most common models, the "income shares" model and the "percentage of income" model are described in the following sections.

Although not discussed further in this chapter because it has not been as widely adopted, there is a third guidelines support model known as the "Melson formula." It is noteworthy in that it makes more explicit recognition of the obligor's need for self-support and it allows for higher levels of support for children with high-income parents. Pamela Foohey, *Child Support and (In)Ability to Pay: The Case for the Cost Shares Model*, 13 U.C. Davis J. Juv. L. & Pol'y 35, 53 (2009).

The state statutory guidelines amount is rebuttably presumed to be the correct child support award. Courts do, however, exercise considerable discretion with respect to issues such as determining available income, granting deviations from the guidelines, and sometimes imputing income to obligors.

9.19. Income Shares Model

The income shares model has been adopted by a majority of jurisdictions and operates on the theory that a child involved in a divorce or paternity determination should receive the same proportion of parental income as if the parents had lived or continued to live together. *See, e.g., Voishan v. Palmer*, 609 A.2d 319 (Md. 1992). State guidelines dictate a support amount based on the combined incomes of the parents, and that amount is prorated between the parents based on the percentage of combined income attributable to each.

The income shares model, in its simplest form, requires three steps to calculate a child support award. First, using a statutory formula, the net incomes of both parents are calculated, combined, and then prorated. For example, assume that the particular statutory formula resulted in a determination that parent A had a net income for child support purposes of $1,000, and the same formula resulted in a determination that parent B had a net child support income of $3,000. The parents would then be viewed as contributing 25 percent and 75 percent, respectively, to the support of a single child.

The second step is to apply the combined income to a guideline chart that suggests the amount of support that should be paid. For example, a state-mandated chart might suggest that with one child, when the combined net income is $4,000, the appropriate total amount of support is $1,000. Parent A would be required to pay 25 percent ($250), and parent B would pay 75 percent ($750). Thus, the parents are viewed as sharing equally in achieving the living standard for the child.

The final step in the application of this model allows a court to consider extraordinary medical expenses incurred by the child and a custodial parent's work-related child care expenses.

Example

7. Assume that P and D are divorcing in a state using the income shares method of child support calculation. They have one child. Assume that, for the purpose of calculating child support, P has a net income of $2,000 and that D has a net income of $4,000. Imagine that the amount of child support to be paid at a net income level of $6,000 is $2,000. How much child support will P and D pay?

Explanation

7. P has one-third of P and D's combined income, and D has two-thirds of their combined income. Consequently, P will pay one-third of $2,000 ($666.67) per month, and D will pay two-thirds of $2,000 ($1,333.33) per month. Rather than exchanging checks every month, D will probably just pay the difference ($666.66) to P each month.

9.20. Percentage of Income Model

The percentage of income model is sometimes viewed as the easiest of the various models to apply because of the limited need for calculation. Basically, the nonresidential parent pays a state-mandated percentage of his or her income for child support. When one parent is awarded sole physical and legal custody of a child, the model looks only at the noncustodial obligor's net income, although when joint physical custody (or shared custody) is ordered, this model considers both parents' incomes.

To begin the calculation, one takes an obligor's gross income and determines his or her net income by deducting those items allowed under the statute. The list of deductions is short and usually includes only items such as taxes, medical insurance, Social Security, and reasonable pension payments. An obligor is not allowed to deduct living expenses, or other items not on the statutory list, For example, assume that A is awarded sole legal and physical custody of child C. B, the noncustodial parent, has a gross income of $5,000 per month. To arrive at a net income figure for child support, B is allowed by statute to deduct state and federal taxes, Social Security payments, health care payments, and reasonable pension payments from the $5,000. Assume for the sake of simplicity that the allowed deductions reduce B's income to $4,000. Once net income is calculated, that figure is applied to a guideline formula, which takes into account the number of children to receive support. For example, assume that application of the formula to an obligor's gross income resulted in a net monthly income child support figure of $4,000. Also assume that there was one child born of the marriage. Using a typical guideline chart (see below), one would find the column headed by "1" (the number of children) and follow

Net Monthly Income of Obligor	Number of Children Percentage of Income 1	2	3	4	5	6	7 or more
$551-600	16%	19%	22%	25%	28%	30%	32%
$601-650	17%	21%	24%	27%	29%	32%	34%
$651-700	18%	22%	25%	28%	31%	34%	36%
$701-750	19%	23%	27%	30%	33%	36%	38%
$751-800	20%	24%	28%	31%	35%	38%	40%
$801-850	21%	25%	29%	33%	36%	40%	42%
$851-900	22%	27%	31%	34%	38%	41%	44%
$901-950	23%	28%	32%	36%	40%	43%	46%
$951-1,000	24%	29%	34%	38%	41%	45%	48%
$1,001-5,000	25%	30%	35%	39%	43%	47%	50%

it down to $4,000 net income. Where the column and the $4,000 intersect, one finds 25 percent. This means that in this jurisdiction, monthly child support is 25 percent of $4,000, or $1,000.

EXAMPLES

Examples

8. Assume that P and D divorce in a percentage of income jurisdiction, and they have two children. P is awarded sole legal and physical custody of the children, and D is ordered to pay child support in accordance with the following guidelines. After taking the deductions allowed by the statute, D's net income is $900 per month. Using the following table, calculate how much monthly child support D most likely will have to pay.

9. Assume that P and D live in a jurisdiction that calculates child support using the percentage of income method. Using the earlier chart, assume that P has sole legal and physical custody of the two children from P's marriage to D. D's net income after allowable statutory deductions is $3,000 per month, and P's net income after deductions is $4,000 per month. How much child support will each pay?

EXPLANATIONS

Explanations

8. D will most likely be required to pay $243 per month. D's net income is between $851 and $900 per month, and D is supporting two children. D will pay 27 percent of D's net income in child support ($900 × 0.27 = $243).

9. D will pay $900 per month to P ($3,000 × 0.30 = $900). However, even though P has the higher income, P will not pay any child support to D. P is the physical custodian of the two children, and P will be providing food, clothing, shelter, and such directly to the children. P's contribution was taken into consideration when the percentage of income chart was developed by the legislature.

9.21. Joint Physical Custody and Parenting Time Offsets

Because most child support guidelines were adopted by states before extended parenting time and joint physical custody arrangements became common, guidelines legislation typically did not address them. Consequently, courts and legislatures have had to reconsider how to calculate child support awards under these new circumstances.

Some states provide for an "offset" to the guidelines amount if both parents spend substantial time with a child. Other states allow courts to deviate from the child support guidelines in these cases. *See Hesse v. Hesse*, 778 N.W.2d 98 (Minn. App. 2009) (offset based on time awarded as opposed to time exercised); *In re Seay*, 746 N.W.2d 833 (Iowa 2008) (use of offset method to calculate child support in cases of joint physical care); *Rivero v. Rivero*, 195 P.3d 328 (Nev. 2008) (consideration of calculation of child support in joint custody arrangement with unequal time share); *Plymale v. Donnelly*, 157 P.3d 933 (Wyo. 2007) (50 percent abatement for summer months, when father had residential custody); *Cheverie v. Cheverie*, 898 So. 2d 1028 (Fla. App. 2005) (downward deviation from child support guidelines where parent has more than 40 percent of the overnight stays); Stephanie Giggetts, *Application of Child-Support Guidelines to Cases of Joint-, Split-, or Similar Shared-Custody Arrangements*, 57 A.L.R.5th 389 (2009).

EXAMPLE

Example

10. Assume that P and D divorce in a percentage of income state that uses the table shown in Section 9.20. They are awarded joint legal and joint physical custody of their only child. P's net monthly income after the statutorily allowed deductions is $4,000, and D's net monthly income after the statutorily allowed deductions is $1,000. Assuming that the child spends approximately equal time with each parent, how will child support be awarded using these guidelines?

EXPLANATION

Explanation

10. Each parent will pay the amount established by the guidelines for the period of time that he or she does *not* reside with the children. Another way to think of it is that D will pay $1,000 per month for half the year, for a total of $6,000 (when the child is with P), and P will pay $240 per month for half the year (when the child is with D), for a total of $1,440. ($4,000 × 0.25 × 6 = $6,000; $1,000 × 0.24 × 6 = $1,440.) P and D may regularize payments by having D pay P $380 per month for the entire year.

9.22. Deviation from Child Support Guidelines

Courts have limited discretion to deviate from the guidelines, although as a practical matter, few judges stray very far from them. In most jurisdictions, the guidelines are applied strictly. When courts deviate from the presumed guidelines, most states require specific findings explaining and supporting the deviation.

Extraordinary needs. Special circumstances, such as extraordinary medical expenses, special educational needs, unusual travel expenses incurred for parenting time, and sometimes the cost of basic living expenses for children from another relationship, can affect the amount of child support that is to be paid under the guidelines. *But see Scott v. Scott*, 879 A.2d 540 (Conn. App. 2005) (private boarding school was not "therapy," and parent was not required to pay additional cost); *Beck v. Beck*, 885 A.2d 887 (Md. App. 2005) ("Merely having two other children is not enough to rebut the presumption.").

High-earning obligors. States take different approaches to deviations in cases involving high-earning child support obligors where the other parent seeks child support beyond what guidelines provide. *See Maturo v. Maturo*, 995 A.2d 1 (Conn. 2010) (overturning payment of 20 percent of annual bonus in addition to guidelines support) *McKittrick v. McKittrick*, 732 N.W.2d 404 (S.D. 2007) (improper to extrapolate upward from guidelines without showing of actual need and standard of living); *In re Keon C.*, 800 N.E.2d 1257 (Ill. App. 2003) (court allowed upward deviation to an amount that exceeded the monthly expenses of the custodial parent's household). *See also Laughlin v. Laughlin*, 229 P.3d 1002 (Alaska 2010) (no deviation from guidelines support to establish a children's fund in lieu of support).

EXAMPLES

Examples

11. Assume that P and D divorce and that P is awarded sole legal and physical custody of the two children of the marriage. P does not work outside the home, and D's gross monthly income is $4,500. Assume that the guidelines set child support at $1,350 per month, leaving D with $3,150 net. D submits his monthly expenses and lists the following: $1,500 house payment, $500 car payment, $200 utilities, $300 attorney fees, $400 permanent maintenance, $500 on credit cards, and $200 miscellaneous (total $3,600). D argues for a downward deviation in child support because he cannot make the payments. How will a court most likely rule?

12. F sought a downward deviation from the child support guidelines based on his financial situation. F's wife (not the mother of the child for whom support was being calculated) developed a serious medical condition, and F incurred substantial debt related to medical expenses. F used a debt consolidation program, began paying only interest on his mortgage, refinanced his car, and took out loans. Will a court deviate from the child support guidelines?

13. F is ordered to pay child support according to guidelines and also to pay two-thirds of the children's expenses related to extracurricular activities. He objects that this constitutes an inappropriate deviation from the child support guidelines. What is the likely result?

Explanations

11. The court will most likely not grant a downward deviation. It is assumed that the plight of D and other similarly situated obligors was explored thoroughly by the legislature when the guidelines were enacted. The guidelines function as a presumption that can be overcome only in extraordinary circumstances. *But see Lozner v. Lozner*, 909 A.2d 728 (N.J. Super. 2006) (factors for consideration with respect to potential deviation based on student loans of payor).

12. In the similar case of *Linge v. Meyerink*, 806 N.W.2d 245 (S.D. 2011), the Supreme Court of South Dakota affirmed the trial court's decision to allow a downward modification. The relevant state statute made allowance for deviation in cases where adherence to child support guidelines would be "inequitable."

13. In a similar case, the Supreme Court of Georgia reasoned that part of the basic child support obligation under the guidelines is to cover the cost of extracurricular activities. Under state law, if special expenses exceed 7 percent of the basic support obligation, a special worksheet must be completed and written findings are required to deviate from state guidelines. The trial court was without authority to make a separate award because these procedures were not complied with. *Turner v. Turner*, 684 S.E.2d 596 (Ga. 2009).

ADDITIONAL SUPPORT

9.23. Medical Support

In 1988, the federal government mandated that the states enact provisions for "child[ren]'s health care needs, through health insurance coverage or other means." *See* 45 C.F.R. §302.56(c)(3)

State courts have found it within the trial court's discretion to require payment of uninsured medical expenses in addition to the child support award. *See generally Millette v. Millette*, 240 P.3d 1217 (Alaska 2010) (father required to pay portion of cost of nutritional supplements for autistic child); *Lulay v. Lulay*, 583 N.E.2d 171, 172 (Ind. App. 1991) (finding that the commentary to the Child Support Guidelines allows for apportionment of uninsured medical expenses because the guidelines do not mandate any specific treatment of these expenses); *Holdsworth v. Holdsworth*, 621 So. 2d 71, 78 and n.1 (La. App. 1993) (holding medical and dental expenses not covered by insurance were properly apportioned half to each party in addition to the child support award as determined under the guidelines); *Jamison v. Jamison*, 845 S.W.2d 133, 136-137 (Mo. App. 1993) (holding it was within the court's discretion to order the obligor to pay half the uninsured medical expenses, in addition to the child support award determined under the guidelines); *Lawrence v. Tise*, 419 S.E.2d 176, 183 (N.C. App. 1992) (holding ordinary medical expenses not covered by insurance are to be apportioned between the parties at the discretion of the trial court, in addition to the child support award as determined by the guidelines). *But see Hazuga v. Hazuga*, 648 N.E.2d 391, 395 n.1 (Ind. App. 1995) (noting that the guidelines had been amended and therefore declined to follow *Lulay v. Lulay*); *Family Services ex rel. J.L.M. by C.A.M. v. Buttram*, 924 S.W.2d 870, 871 (Mo. App. 1996) (ordering father to pay for medical insurance as well as 50 percent of all uncovered medical expenses was a deviation under the guidelines).

9.24. Child Care Costs

In addition to child support, costs associated with child care may be awarded to the parent with sole physical custody or the expense may be apportioned between the parents pursuant to a legislative formula.

Payment of child care expenses is a matter of continuing controversy. *See, e.g., Guard v. Guard*, 993 So. 2d 1086 (Fla. App. 2008) (specific findings required); *Mace v. Mace*, 610 N.W.2d 436 (Neb. App. 2000) (ex-wife entitled to modification of dissolution decree in order to require former husband to pay proportionate share of her work-related day care expenses); *Hoplamazian v. Hoplamazian*, 740 So. 2d 1100 (Ala. App. 1999) (court improperly added mother's work-related child care costs to father's basic child support obligation when mother was not seeking employment); *Cupstid v. Cupstid*, 724 So. 2d 238 (La. App. 1998) (ex-wife proved change in circumstances justifying increase in former husband's child support obligation when she returned to work and began incurring child care expenses); *Rosen v. Lantis*, 938 P.2d 729 (N.M. App. 1997) (court had authority under guidelines to adjust child support obligation in post-dissolution proceeding based on mother's testimony that she was incurring child care costs because of her employment); *Gal v. Gal*, 937 S.W.2d 391 (Mo. App. 1997) (day care costs incurred while mother attending nursing school full time could be included as an extraordinary expense in calculating father's child support obligation); *Sigg v. Sigg*, 905 P.2d 908 (Utah App. 1995) (court's decision requiring ex-wife to be solely responsible for one-third of day care costs, then splitting the remaining costs between ex-wife and ex-husband, was not based on fact and was an abuse of discretion).

DURATION OF CHILD SUPPORT

9.25. General Duration of Child Support

The duration of child support varies to some extent by state. All states require both parents to be financially responsible for their child during the child's minority. However, child support can be terminated in the event of the death of the child, if the child goes on active duty in the armed forces, or if the child becomes emancipated or self-supporting.

In many jurisdictions, a support order ends either when the child turns 18 or when the child completes secondary school (secondary school must be completed before the child reaches age 20). *See Draughn v. Draughn*, 707 S.E.2d 52 (Ga. 2011) (obligation not terminated where child reaches age 18 but is enrolled in online high school). However, support may continue indefinitely for a child incapable of self-support because of a physical or mental condition. *See* Sande L. Buhai, *Parental Support of Adult Children with Disabilities*, 91 Minn. L. Rev. 710 (2007).

9.26. Educational Support

Parents are not generally obligated to provide support for a child's college education although courts in some states have approved it. For example, under an Iowa statute, parents can be ordered to provide financial support for children attending college. Iowa Code §§598.21(5A), 598.1(8); *In re Marriage of Moore*, 702 N.W.2d 517 (Iowa App. 2005); *In re Marriage of Mullen-Funderburk and Funderburk*, 696 N.W.2d 607 (Iowa 2005). *See also* Ind. Code §31-16-6-2 (educational support order). In states without statutes authorizing contribution, settlement agreements related to college expenses may be enforced as contractual obligations. *See, e.g., Solomon v. Findley*, 808 P.2d 294 (Ariz. 1991) (parties' contract for post-majority support is enforceable in breach-of-contract action); *Nicoletti v. Nicoletti*, 901 So. 2d 290 (Fla. App. 2005); *Spalding v. Spalding*, 907 So. 2d 1270 (Fla. Dist. App. 2005).

Some commentators suggest that a parental obligation to pay college expenses be established or expanded. *See* Monica Hof Wallace, *A Federal Referendum: Extending Child Support for Higher Education*, 58 U. Kan. L. Rev. 665 (2010) ("To preserve equality for children of non-intact families, legislation is needed to mandate a parental obligation of support for higher education after the age of majority to capture the support that would have been realized had the relationship remained intact."). *See also* ALI, *Principles of the Law of Family Dissolution: Analysis and Recommendations* §3.12 (2002) (discusses provision of postsecondary education under "Providing for a Child's Life Opportunities").

9.27. Emancipation of Child

A child support obligation may end when the minor child is emancipated. Emancipation of a child occurs when the fundamental dependent relationship between parent and child is concluded, the parent relinquishes the right to custody and is relieved of the burden of support, and the child is no longer entitled to support. Emancipation may occur by reason of the child's marriage, by court order, or by the child attaining a certain age. Although in most states there is a presumption of emancipation at age 18, that presumption is rebuttable. *Filippone v. Lee*, 700 A.2d 384 (N.J. App. 1997). The emancipation issue is fact-specific, and the essential inquiry is whether the child has moved "beyond the sphere of influence and responsibility exercised by a parent and obtains an independent status of his or her own." *Bishop v. Bishop*, 671 A.2d 644 (N.J. Super. 1995). *See In re Marriage of Baumgartner*, 930 N.E.2d 1024 (Ill. 2010) (son's incarceration by itself inadquate to establish emancipation). Consent of the custodial parent, either express or implied, is a prerequisite to emancipation. *Vinson v. Vinson*, 628 S.W.2d 376 (Mo. App. 1982). The mere fact that a child is employed and retains her earnings does not by itself establish that parental control has been relinquished or that the obligation to support has been terminated. *Id.* at 377.

Constsructive emancipation. A state may recognize constructive emancipation under the common law. *See, e.g., In re Marriage of George*, 988 P.2d 251 (Kan. App. 1999). In *Harris v. Rattini*, 855 S.W.2d 410, 412 (Mo. App. 1993), the Missouri Court of Appeals for the Eastern District held that a child who drops out of school before his or her eighteenth birthday, takes a part-time job, and has no mental or physical incapacity is emancipated, and child support is no longer required. By way of contrast, in *Detwiler v. Detwiler*, 57 A.2d 426 (Pa. Super. 1948), the Superior Court of Pennsylvania found that a 17-year-old who dropped out of school and earned his own income, but lived at home, was not emancipated. The court found that the parents had not relinquished control over the child. In *In re Marriage of Clay*, 670 P.2d 31 (Colo. App. 1983), the Colorado Court of Appeals held that a 16-year-old daughter who was dependent on her mother for financial support, who had not established a residence away from both her parents, who was not married to the father of her child, and who did not receive support from her child's father was not emancipated and was entitled to support. *See also*

Dewitt v. Giampietro, 887 N.Y.S.2d 210 (N.Y. App. 2009) (insufficient evidence to establish constructive emancipation).

Parenthood. An otherwise unemancipated teenager who is dependent on parental support is not disqualified from receiving it because she has become pregnant and she elected to give birth to a child as an unmarried mother. Her own motherhood in these circumstances does not render her emancipated. *See, e.g., Filippone v. Lee, supra; In re Marriage of Clay*, 670 P.2d 31, 32 (Colo. App. 1983); *Doerrfeld v. Konz*, 524 So. 2d 1115, 1116-1117 (Fla. App. 1988); *Hicks v. Fulton County Dept. of Family and Children Services*, 270 S.E.2d 254, 255 (Ga. App. 1980); *French v. French*, 599 S.W.2d 40, 41 (Mo. App. 1980); *Wulff v. Wulff*, 500 N.W.2d 845, 851 (Neb. 1993); *Thompson v. Thompson*, 405 N.Y.S.2d 974, 975 (N.Y. Fam. Ct. 1978), *aff'd*, 419 N.Y.S.2d 239 (N.Y. App. 1979); *Griffin v. Griffin*, 558 A.2d 75, 80 (Pa. Super. 1989), *appeal denied*, 571 A.2d 383 (Pa. 1989).

Living separately. Residing apart from a minor's parents does not by itself result in the minor's emancipation. *Quinn v. Johnson*, 589 A.2d 1077 (N.J. Super. 1991). A troubled minor's removal from his parents' home to a public or private institutional alternative, or even to the home of friends or relatives, does not relieve the parents of their support obligation during minority, provided that the child is not entirely self-supporting. *See In re Marriage of Donahoe*, 448 N.E.2d 1030,1033 (Ill. App. 1983); *Quillen v. Quillen*, 659 N.E.2d 566, 576 (Ind. App. 1995), *vacated in part, adopted in part*, 671 N.E.2d 98 (Ind. 1996); *In re Marriage of Bordner*, 715 P.2d 436, 439 (Mont. 1986); *Hildebrand v. Hildebrand*, 477 N.W.2d. 1, 5 (Neb. 1991); *In re Owens*, 645 N.E.2d 130, 132 (Ohio App. 1994); *Trosky v. Mann*, 581 A.2d 177, 178 (Pa. Super. 1990); *In re Marriage of George*, 988 P.2d 251 (Kan. App. 1999).

Military service. Military service normally acts to emancipate a minor. However, in *Baker v. Baker*, 537 P.2d 171 (Kan. 1975), the father argued that when his son went into the Navy, he became emancipated, and that relieved the father of any further obligation of support. The court held that entry into the Navy was not grounds for automatically terminating child support, but it could be considered as a factor for reducing or terminating the support payments.

EXAMPLE

Example

14. Assume that P and D are divorced. They have one child, X, and D pays child support to P for the support of X. When X is 16, she marries Y, with the permission of P. However, X continues to live in P's home, and P continues to assist her financially. Seven months later, X's marriage is annulled on the ground of fraudulent inducement on the part of Y. D

stopped paying child support when X married Y, believing her to be emancipated. However, after the annulment, P again seeks child support from D, arguing that X was returned to her unemancipated status and consequently is entitled to support. How will a court likely rule?

Explanation

14. In *State ex rel. Dept. of Economic Sec. v. Demetz*, 130 P.3d 986 (Ariz. App. 2006), the court considered a similar situation. D argued that X's marriage was voidable, not void, and that the marriage consequently was valid when it occurred, thus emancipating X. The court disagreed, holding that once the annulment became final, the marriage was "deemed invalid from its inception." The court found that D's obligation to support X was revived when X's marriage was annulled. *See also Thomas v. Campbell*, 960 So. 2d 694 (Ala. App. 2006).

9.28. Obligor's Death

Statutory alteration of the common law. Under the common law, a father's death terminated his obligation of support for his minor children. However, by statute, states have altered that perspective. *See, e.g.*, Ariz. Rev. Stat. §25-327(c) ("Unless otherwise agreed in writing or expressly provided in the decree, provisions for the support of a minor child are not terminated by the death of a parent obligated to support the child. If a parent obligated to pay support dies, the amount of future support may be modified, revoked, or commuted to a lump sum payment").

The UMDA similarly repudiates the common law rule that an obligor's support obligation ends upon death by providing that a parent's child support obligation is terminated "by emancipation of the child but not by the death of a parent obligated to support the child. When a parent obligated to pay support dies, the amount of support may be modified, revoked, or commuted to a lump sum payment to the extent just and appropriate in the circumstances." UMDA §316(c).

Insurance. A child is no less dependent on a parent after the parent's death than before the parent died. In some cases, the surviving parent may be able to fully provide for the child's needs, but this is not always the case. In anticipation of such an event, a court may require the purchase or maintenance of insurance on the obligor's life for the benefit of the children. *Pittman v. Pittman*, 419 So. 2d 1376 (Ala. 1982); *Wolk v. Wolk*, 464 A.2d 780 (Conn. 1983); *Allen v. Allen*, 477

N.E.2d 104 (Ind. App. 1985); *Krueger v. Krueger*, 278 N.W.2d 514 (Mich. App. 1979); *Stein v. Sandow*, 468 N.Y.S.2d 910 (N.Y. App. 1983).

Post-death modification. The UMDA also states that the parties or the court may provide for the contingency of the premature death of the parent in the original decree. But even if no such provision is incorporated into the original decree, the act permits courts to modify the support provisions later, even after the death of the parent. In providing for the death of the parent, the act requires courts to use the criteria considered in the court's original order in modifying a child support order. The intent of these provisions is to encourage divorcing parents to provide support for their children during their entire minority. UMDA Commissioners' Note to §316(c). In the absence of the parents voluntarily making such provisions for their children, however, these provisions give the court the discretion and authority to *sua sponte* secure the children's support after the obligor's death.

OTHER SUPPORT CONSIDERATIONS

9.29. Monitoring Support

Courts do not generally allow a child support obligor to monitor support expenditures by the obligee. But in an extreme case where an obligee fails to meet the child's needs, a finding of neglect could be a basis for a change in custody.

9.30. Obligee Withholds Parenting Time

As a general rule, if an obligor fails to make child support payments, the obligee cannot on that basis interfere with parenting time between the obligor and the minor child. *See Ewald v. Ewald*, 810 N.W.2d 396 (Mich. App. 2011) (parenting time rights not enforced through modification of child support); *Engrassia v. Di Lullo*, 454 N.Y.S.2d 103 (N.Y. App. 1982) (failure of noncustodial parent to make child support payments, without other evidence, was insufficient basis upon which to deny visitation).

The child support obligation and the right to parenting time are viewed by most courts as separate issues. The reason for the distinction is that parenting time is ordered because it is in the best interest of most children to promote love and affection with both parents, residential and nonresidential. Child support is payment based on the financial needs of the child and the ability of both parents to provide for these needs; it is not viewed as directly related to the psychological needs of a minor child. *See Lindsay v.*

Lindsay, WL 197111 (Tenn. App. 2006) (father could not be ordered to pay an additional $50 in child support every time he missed visitation). When the parties cannot effectuate parenting time, the appropriate remedy is to seek the assistance of the court. *Pierpont v. Bond*, 744 So. 2d 843 (Miss. App. 1999).

9.31. Federal Income Tax Treatment

For federal income tax purposes, child support payments are not income to the obligee. The parent who makes the payments cannot deduct the amount as an expense on his or her federal tax return. *Maes v. U.S.*, 106 A.F.T.R.2d 2010-6752 (unpublished) (D. Mont. 2010) (child support is not taxable income; I.R.S. §71 (2009)).

9.32. Stepparent Liability

The common law did not impose a legal duty on a stepparent to provide support for a minor stepchild. *See Ulrich v. Cornell*, 484 N.W.2d 545, 548 (Wis. 1992). Courts reasoned that standing *in loco parentis* is voluntary and temporary and may be abrogated at will. Consequently, without a statute and absent an adoption or unusual circumstances, a stepparent is not responsible for providing support for a spouse's children.

Courts do not generally consider the income of a stepparent in calculating the presumptively correct child support amount for a child. *See Gina P. v. Stephen S.*, 33 A.D.3d 412 (N.Y. 2006). Courts hesitate to impose an ongoing support obligation on a stepparent who voluntarily supports a child, because stepparents might be discouraged from providing support for fear of becoming permanently obligated to do so.

Despite the general rule, a few states have adopted provisions requiring a stepparent to support stepchildren so long as the stepparent is married to the children's natural parent. *See, e.g.*, Wash. Rev. Code rule 205, which reads as follows:

> The expenses of the family and the education of the children, including stepchildren, are chargeable upon the property of both husband and wife, or either of them, and they may be sued jointly or separately. When a petition for dissolution of marriage or a petition for legal separation is filed, the court may, upon motion of the stepparent, terminate the obligation to support the stepchildren. The obligation to support stepchildren shall cease upon the entry of a decree of dissolution, decree of legal separation, or death.

See also Washington Statewide Org. of Stepparents v. Smith, 536 P.2d 1202 (Wash. 1975) (statute does not unconstitutionally impair marriage contracts or violate the equal protection clause because cohabitants are not held to the same standard).

Under North Dakota law, a stepparent may be liable for necessaries for a spouse's dependent children if they are "received into the stepparent's family . . . . [T]he stepparent is liable, to the extent of his or her ability, to support them during the marriage and so long thereafter as they remain in the stepparent's family." N.D. Stat. §14-09-09 (West 2005).

When stepparents divorce, most jurisdictions take the view that the support obligation, if any, ends. *See Bagwell v. Bagwell*, 698 So. 2d 746 (La. App. 1997) (no obligation after divorce). *But see Johnson v Johnson*, 617 N.W.2d 97 (N.D. 2000) (stepparent liable on equitable adoption theory).

EXAMPLES

Examples

15. Assume that P and D divorce and that P is awarded sole legal and physical custody of their child, C. D is awarded parenting time with C every other weekend and for four weeks during the summer. D is ordered to pay child support in the amount of $200 per month. D believes that P is using the child-support money to go out drinking and to attend concerts with friends rather than for the benefit of C. Consequently, D asks P for proof that the money is being spent on C, and when P refuses to provide an accounting, D stops paying child support. P tells D that P can barely make ends meet financially and that C has been unable to participate in some school activities because P cannot finance them without the child-support payments from D. In exasperation, P refuses to allow D to exercise parenting time with C until D resumes child support payments. D brings an action to enforce parenting time, and P brings an action for enforcement of the child support order. How will a court most likely rule?

16. Assume that P and D married in the state of Washington and that P brought two children from a former marriage into the relationship. Although the children regularly visited with their biological father, X, and received child support from him, D treated the children as though they were his biological children. During the last year of the marriage, X fell ill and died. About eight months later, P and D's marriage dissolved. P argues that under the Washington statute (Wash. Rev. Code §26.16.205 *supra*), D must continue to pay child support. How will the court most likely rule?

17. P (the biological mother of a child) was in a same-sex relationship with D, and they agreed that P would conceive a child via artificial insemination. When their relationship ended, P sought child support from D under the theory of equitable estoppel. What is the likely result?

EXPLANATIONS

Explanations

15. Sadly, both P and D could be held in contempt of court. In most states, the physical custodian is not required to provide an accounting concerning child-support expenditures, and D wrongfully violated the support order by unilaterally stopping payment. The right to parenting time is not conditioned on payment of support, so P could not prevent D from visiting with C, even though D's child support payments were in arrears. As described here, this is a situation where the parties might benefit from going to mediation to resolve the ongoing conflict between them.

16. The court will most likely reject P's claim. Although the statute mandates that D provide support to the children during D's marriage to P, there is no requirement that the support continue after the marriage. There is also no evidence presented that would equitably estop D from asserting that he is not the children's father. Therefore, he is not liable for their support.

17. This example is based on the case of H.M. v. E.T., 76 A.D.3d 528 (N.Y. App. 2010), where the appellate court held that the doctrine of "implied promise—equitable estoppel" could be used to hold D responsible for child-support payments. P and D chose to have a child, and P relied on D's implied promise of support.

CHAPTER 10

Child Support Modification and Enforcement

10.1. Introduction

Parents may return to court with a focus on child support in two circumstances. First, like child custody and parenting time decisions, court orders regarding child support may be modified as circumstances change. For example, if parents significantly alter their custodial arrangements, the issue of child support will be revisited. Similarly, if the obligor loses a job or has a substantial increase in income, the amount of child support is likely to be adjusted.

Second, parents may return to court in the unfortunate event that an obligor does not pay child support as ordered, Such an order may be enforced through a variety of legal measures.

STANDARDS FOR MODIFYING AN EXISTING AWARD

10.2. Jurisdictional Context

A modification action may occur in different jurisdictional contexts. First, a modification request may involve a dispute between citizens of the United States and a foreign country. States have passed special statutes to deal with these situations. *See, e.g.*, Utah Judical Code §78B-14-615, *Jurisdiction to modify child-support order of foreign country or political subdivision* (2008).

Second, a modification dispute may involve parents living in different states. All states have adopted some form of the Uniform Family Support Act (UIFSA), and criteria for modification under that act is discussed in section 10.26 of this chapter.

Third, a modification request may involve citizens of the same state, and the state law of that jurisdiction will apply. As discussed in subsequent sections, state statutes and standards regarding modification of child support vary considerably.

10.3. Substantial Change in Circumstances

Overview. Although the language used by state legislatures varies, in general, modification of a child support order may occur when a "substantial change in circumstances" has taken place since the issuance of the support order, a change that makes enforcement of the existing award unfair. For example, the relevant Maryland statute provides that "[t]he court may modify a child support award subsequent to the filing of a motion for modification and upon a showing of a material change of circumstance." MD Code, Famly Law, §12-104 (1988).

A substantial or material change in circumstances may take many forms. The change may concern an alteration in a parent's financial situation, such as loss of a job, receipt of a large inheritance, or winning a lottery. The change in circumstance could be the result of a new situation for the child, such as large unanticipated medical expenses, the need for special education, or other unexpected requirements. *But see Karagiannis v. Karagiannis*, 73 A.D.3d 1064 (N.Y. App. 2010) (obligor not entitled to modification because of illness where cancer is in remission).

Burden. The parent seeking to change the support obligation has the burden of proving that a modification is necessary.

Presumptions. Because courts seek to limit the number of post-decree filings, some jurisdictions have created rebuttable statutory presumptions for use in modification cases. These presumptions typically provide that modification is warranted if the parent seeking the change establishes that the child support order would be increased or decreased by more than 20 percent.

The following state statute incorporates various presumptions:

> **Subd. 2. Modification.** (a) The terms of an order respecting maintenance or support may be modified upon a showing of one or more of the following, any of which makes the terms unreasonable and unfair: (1) substantially increased

> or decreased gross income of an obligor or obligee; (2) substantially increased or decreased need of an obligor or obligee or the child or children that are the subject of these proceedings; (3) receipt of assistance under the AFDC program formerly codified under sections 256.72 to 256.87 or 256B.01 to 256B.40, or chapter 256J or 256K; (4) a change in the cost of living for either party as measured by the Federal Bureau of Labor Statistics; (5) extraordinary medical expenses of the child not provided for under section 518A.41; (6) a change in the availability of appropriate health care coverage or a substantial increase or decrease in health care coverage costs; (7) the addition of work-related or education-related child care expenses of the obligee or a substantial increase or decrease in existing work-related or education-related child care expenses; or (8) upon the emancipation of the child, as provided in subdivision 5.
>
> (b) It is presumed that there has been a substantial change in circumstances under paragraph (a) and the terms of a current support order shall be rebuttably presumed to be unreasonable and unfair if:
>
> (1) the application of the child support guidelines in section 518A.35, to the current circumstances of the parties results in a calculated court order that is at least 20 percent and at least $75 per month higher or lower than the current support order or, if the current support order is less than $75, it results in a calculated court order that is at least 20 percent per month higher or lower;
>
> (2) the medical support provisions of the order established under section 518A.41 are not enforceable by the public authority or the obligee;
>
> (3) health coverage ordered under section 518A.41 is not available to the child for whom the order is established by the parent ordered to provide;
>
> (4) the existing support obligation is in the form of a statement of percentage and not a specific dollar amount;
>
> (5) the gross income of an obligor or obligee has decreased by at least 20 percent through no fault or choice of the party; or
>
> (6) a deviation was granted based on the factor in section 518A.43, subdivision 1, clause (4), and the child no longer resides in a foreign country or the factor is otherwise no longer applicable.

Minn. Stat. §518A.39, subd. 2 (2012).

Courts strictly enforce presumptions requiring a 20 percent change in a resulting support order. For example, in *MacLafferty v. MacLafferty*, 829 N.W.2d 938 (Ind. 2005), the obligor sought to modify a child support order because of an increase in the physical custodian's income. The relevant statute provided that modification could be made only upon a showing that (1) the current order was unreasonable because of substantial changed circumstances, or (2) the support order had been in effect for more than one year and the modified guidelines payment would result in an increase or decrease of more than 20 percent. The modification was denied because the changed circumstance resulted in only a 14 percent difference in the child support order.

10.4. Cost-of-Living Adjustments

Most child support orders provide for a biennial adjustment in the amount to be paid based on a change in the cost of living. An order may direct that a trial court use a cost-of-living index published by the Department of Labor or provide for the use of a local index that more accurately reflects the economy in a particular area of the country. *See, e.g., Fronk v. Wilson*, 819 P.2d 1275 (Mont. 1991) (American Chamber of Commerce Researchers' Association Cost of Living Index obtained from the State of Montana's Census and Economic Information Center was admissible). *See McClenahan v. Warner*, 461 N.W.2d 509 (Minn. App. 1990) (trial court did not abuse its discretion or offend statutory standard in selecting Washington, D.C.'s cost of living index, even though it was not the most appropriate index; statute does not require that the court select the most appropriate index). In drafting final agreements in divorce actions, the parties may agree upon the appropriate cost of living index to be used. *See, e.g., Browne v. Browne*, 810 N.E.2d 1289 (unpublished) (Mass. App. 2004) (separation agreement required the father to provide child support that was linked to the cost of living index published by the Bureau of Labor Statistics).

The cost-of-living requirement may be waived if the court makes an express finding that the obligor's income or occupation does not provide for a cost-of-living increase. A cost-of-living provision providing for a biennial adjustment reflects an obligor's increase in income and the children's needs, which also are rising with inflation.

10.5. Obligor Employment Change

A parent ordinarily will not be relieved of a child support obligation if that parent is fired for misconduct or if the parent voluntarily leaves employment. Downward modifications are more often granted when changes in employment are involuntary and the parent is actively seeking employment, or employment commensurate with the prior position.

When seeking a reduction in child support payments because of a voluntary change in employment, the moving party must usually establish that the change was not made for the purpose of avoiding child support payments and that efforts have been made to mitigate income loss. Otherwise, for calculation of child support, the moving party will be considered to have an income equal to his or her earning capacity. *See Chen v. Warner*, 695 N.W.2d 758 (Wis. 2005) (mother's decision to forgo employment outside the home was "reasonable under the circumstances").

Courts have applied one of three tests to determine whether to modify a child support order when a parent voluntarily terminates employment. Each of the tests evidences its own strengths and weaknesses, and each reflects the public policy of its adopting jurisdiction.

The first of these tests, the good-faith test, considers the actual earnings of a party rather than his or her earning capacity, so long as he or she acted in good faith and not primarily for the purpose of avoiding a support obligation when terminating employment. *See Andrews* v. Andrews, 719 S.E.2d 128 (N.C. App. 2011 (engineer who left position to start church acted in bad faith). *See also In re Marriage of Horn*, 650 N.E.2d 1103, 1106 (Ill. App. 1995); *Giesner v. Giesner*, 319 N.W.2d 718, 720 (Minn. 1982); *Schuler v. Schuler*, 416 N.E.2d 197, 203 (Mass. 1981); *Fogel v. Fogel*, 168 N.W.2d 275, 277 (Neb. 1969); *Lambert v. Lambert*, 403 P.2d 664, 668 (Wash. 1965); *Nelson v. Nelson*, 357 P.2d 536, 538 (Or. 1960). *Compare Thomas v. Thomas*, 203 So. 2d 118, 123 (Ala. 1967) (good-faith test applied) *with Johnson v. Johnson*, 597 So. 2d 699 (Ala. App. 1991) (mother may not simply choose to ignore the current and continuing financial needs of her children merely because her preference is to pursue a law degree).

The good-faith test is criticized because it assumes that a divorced or separated party will continue to make decisions in the best overall interest of the family unit, when often, in fact, the party will not. The test is also criticized as focusing on the parent's motivation for leaving employment rather than on the parent's responsibility to his or her children and the effect of the parent's decision on the best interests of the children.

The second approach is the strict rule test, which disregards any income reduction produced by voluntary conduct and looks at the earning capacity of a party in fashioning a support obligation. Child support remains based solely on earning capacity. The strict rule test is viewed by some as too inflexible because it considers only one factor, the parent's earning capacity. *See Chastain v. Chastain*, 346 S.E.2d 33, 35 (S.C. App. 1986) (suggesting that South Carolina has adopted the strict rule test).

The third approach, which is referred to as the *intermediate balancing test*, balances various factors to determine whether to use actual income or earning capacity in making a support determination. The intermediate balancing test considers a number of factors and places the obligation to pay child support first and other financial obligations second. The court asks whether the parent's current educational level and physical capacity provide him or her with the ability to find suitable work in the marketplace. If so, the decision to leave employment is less reasonable. If the parent leaves employment to seek additional training, and if the additional training is likely to increase the parent's earning potential, the decision is more likely to be found reasonable. A court also will consider the length of the parent's proposed educational program because it matters whether the children are young enough to benefit from the parent's increased future income. *See Little v. Little*, 975 P.2d 108 (Ariz. 1999) (intermediate balancing test would be used to determine what effect former husband's decision to forgo employment and become full-time student had on his obligation to pay child support).

Examples

1. Assume that in a parentage action, D was determined to be the father of three children. At the time that the original child support order was entered, D was not employed, and the court imputed federal minimum-wage income to him and entered a child support order for $250 per month. D was later convicted of a federal crime and sent to prison. D moves for a reduction in child support, asserting that he lacks financial resources due to his incaceration. Will the support order be modified?

2. Assume that P and D are the unmarried parents of a child, X. When child support was determined, P had a weekly income of $450, and D, a professional basketball player, had a weekly income of $121,327. Under the child support guidelines, D was ordered to pay $760 per week in child support. Three years later, P brings an action to modify child support because D's annual income has increased from $6,309,004 to $9,061,875. The relevant statute provides that modification requires a showing that (1) the current order is unreasonable because of substantial changed circumstances or (2) the support order has been in effect for more than one year, and the modified guidelines payment would result in an increase or decrease of more than 20 percent. D argues (correctly) that under the child support guidelines, his increased income would result in only a 1 percent increase ($7.15 per week). P argues that X is entitled to live at the standard of living that X would have had if X resided with D, and that a deviation from the guidelines is warranted. What is the likely result?

3. Assume that the marriage between P and D dissolved and that D was ordered to pay $1,200 per month for child support. When the support was ordered, D was employed by the Air Force, earning an annual salary of $48,000, plus benefits. D also holds a master's degree in business administration. D terminated his employment with the Air Force and entered law school. He earns a monthly reserve pay from the Air Force of $308, and his ex-wife, a full-time student/caretaker, earns about $1,000 per month. D alleged a substantial and continuing change in circumstances in that his income was reduced because he terminated his position with the Air Force and entered law school. In his petition, appellant requested a reduction in child support payments from $1,200 to $200 per month. P contended that D could move to a nearby state where night law school is offered and be employed during the day. D's children at the time were ages 4 and 6.

Explanations

1. D will argue that his incarceration is a substantial change in circumstances sufficient to reduce his child support obligation. One difficulty D has in making this argument is that D's *income* (or lack thereof) did not change when he went to prison. However, D will argue that his *ability* to earn income changed substantially. In the similar case of *A.M.S. ex rel. Farthing v. Stoppleworth*, 694 N.W.2d 8 (N.D. 2005), the court held that the statutory support guideline amount could not be rebutted through a showing of incarceration because the obligor had brought the situation upon himself. The North Dakota court found that imprisonment was not a circumstance beyond the control of the obligor and consequently was not the type of change that warranted modification of the child support order. Some state courts have held as a matter of law that incarceration can never be a justification warranting the modification of child support. However, other courts have reasoned that incarceration is not a voluntary act and that the imprisoned, indigent child support obligor should be relieved of the support obligation during incarceration. The rationale underpinning this line of cases is that the child will not presently benefit from imposing on the parent a continuing support obligation that is beyond his or her ability to pay. Unlike the voluntarily unemployed parent, an incarcerated parent is not able to rectify the situation by obtaining employment. The obligor rarely will be able to pay the arrears upon release, and precious judicial resources and taxpayer funds will be expended in the attempt to collect. *See Commonwealth ex rel. Marshall v. Marshall*, 15 S.W.3d 396 (Ky. App. 2000).

2. This example is similar to the case of *Davis v. Knafel*, 837 N.E.2d 585 (Ind. App. 2005), in which the court denied the modification request. P failed to show that D's increased income would result in more than a 20 percent change in the guidelines support order. P also failed to establish substantial changed circumstances *occurring since the entry of the original support order* that would render the support order unreasonable. For example, the court was not persuaded that D's purchase of a $1,700,000 residence was a change in lifestyle, stating that P "fails to show how this is a change in lifestyle for a man who already owned two homes in two different states and who earns several million dollars per year." *Id.* at 589.

3. This is a close question and depends, at least in part, on the standard that the court uses when reviewing the facts. A court could allow the order to be reduced to the guidelines amount based on D's lower income. It is reasonable to believe that a law degree would enable D to embark on a career that could well result in enhanced economic fortunes, and the

increased income would inure to the benefit of his children, given their present ages. The suggestion that D attend night school in another state may be viewed as unreasonable because it would require relocation away from his children. The fact that D chose to stay in state near the children not only is reasonable but also shows D's desire to remain active in his children's upbringing, an important consideration to D and his children. However, in this example, P would have a difficult time supporting two children on a total income of $1,200 per month, and the first obligation of the court is to assure that the children are cared for financially. Consequently, a court is unlikely to approve a reduction in child support based on a voluntary action of the obligor that leaves the children in need.

RETROACTIVITY AND AGREEMENTS BY PARTIES

10.6. Retroactive Awards

Typically, a modification of support or maintenance may be made retroactive from the date of service of the motion for modification on the responding party. *Webber v. Webber*, 56 So. 3d 822 (Fl. App. 2011) (abuse of discretion to make modification retroactive to date prior to filing); *Kerby v. Kerby*, 164 P.3d 1049 (Okla. 2007) (date of motion is effective date of modification). However, the court has discretion to set the effective date of a support modification. *Borcherding v. Borcherding*, 566 N.W.2d 90, 93 (Minn. App. 1997) (court or administrative law judge has broad discretion to set effective date).

EXAMPLE

Example

4. Assume that P and D divorce and that D is ordered to pay $300 per month to P in child support. Five years later, P seeks to increase the child support award by $300 per month. The litigation and appeal concerning the increase last two years, from 2008 until 2010, as D unsuccessfully challenges the modification. When P wins on appeal, P believes that D owes P a lump-sum payment of $3,600 (the support increase over the two-year period). D argues that this is a windfall to P, and that the increase should begin from the date of the appellate court's decision. How will a court most likely treat this dispute?

EXPLANATION

Explanation

4. A court will most likely reject D's argument. P has been required to support the parties' child for nearly two years without receiving all the assistance that P was entitled to from D. For this reason, the back support now owed to P will not be considered a windfall, and the court will not abuse its discretion in making the modification retroactive to the time when D was served with the motion papers.

10.7. Court Approval Required for Modification

Child support modifications must be approved by a court to be enforceable. Consequently, if parents agree to increase or decrease support and the change is not formally approved by a judge, the agreement will not change the existing court order. *See Culver v. Culver*, 17 A.3d 1048 (Conn. App. 2011) (oral agreement that father would pay for private school in lieu of making child support payments was unenforceable); *Hunt v. Hunt*, 242 P.3d 682 (Or. App. 2010) (father failed to file and serve modification motion before the parties' daughter reached age 18; therefore, court had no authority to enforce the parties' oral agreement to reduce the support obligation to $200 per month).

10.8. Nonmodification Agreements

Ocassionally, parents will attempt to limit the ability of the court to modify child support orders. For example, in the case of *Fernandez v. Fernandez*, 222 P.3d 1031, 1033 (Nev. 2010), the parties attempted to "voluntarily waive any right they may have pursuant to Chapter 125B of the Nevada Revised Statutes to seek a modification to [father's] child support obligation to [mother]." The court disapproved the stipulation, stating as follows:

> Because a child support order affects the child's interests, as much or more than the parents', we are disinclined to find that a parent can waive the modification statutes' protections. We thus interpret the modification statutes to mean what they say, with no implied judicial exceptions. The purport of these statutes, as their unqualified language suggests, is that "the jurisdiction of the court never ends in a support matter, as long as the child is supposed to be getting support. If there is a significant change in circumstances in the parties' relative earning capacity, that can always be brought back to the court, and should be."

Id. at 1036. *But see* Conn. Gen. Stat. Ann. §46b-86 (2011) (decree may preclude modifcation); *In re Marriage of Matar*, 270 P.3d 257, 259 (Or.

App. 2011) ("enforcement of the agreement not to seek modification of child support, under the circumstances of this case, does not violate public policy").

STATE ENFORCEMENT EFFORTS

10.9. Child Support Debt

As of 2006, national child support debt exceeded $100 billion. The majority of obligors (57 percent) were less than $5,000 in arrears. However, very-low-income obligors accounted for 70 percent of arrears. U.S. Department of Health and Human Services, Administration for Children and Families, Office of Child Support Enforcement, *The Story Behind the Numbers* (May 2008), available at *http://www.acf.hhs.gov/programs/cse/pol/IM/2008/im-08-05a.pdf* (last visited July 6, 2012).

The following sections discuss the growing number of mechanisms for the enforcement of existing child support orders.

10.10. Contempt of Court

Civil contempt. Although family courts have many tools with which to enforce orders, one of the most powerful is the ability to hold an obligor in civil or criminal contempt. The purpose of civil contempt is to obtain compliance with the court order. In a civil contempt action, the person being held in contempt is said to hold the keys to the jailhouse door in his or her pocket—jail is conditioned on nonpayment, and the obligor is released when payment is made. *See Branum v. State*, 829 N.E.2d 622 (Ind. App. 2005) (in civil contempt case, court was required to ascertain that the obligor had the ability to pay and to advise that the obligor could obtain release from incarceration through compliance). The purpose of criminal contempt is to punish, and the obligor typically completes a determinate sentence. Despite the bright line between the two types of contempt, courts sometimes fail to distinguish between them in practice.

Criminal contempt. When criminal contempt is sought, the defendant-obligor is entitled to additional constitutional protections. In *Hicks v. Feiock*, 485 U.S. 624 (1988), the obligor failed to make child support payments, and the issue was whether the due process clause of the Fourteenth Amendment prohibited the state court from placing the burden on the obligor, rather than the state, to establish the obligor's inability to make payments. The Supreme Court held that shifting the burden to the defendant in a criminal case violated due process. However, if the proceeding had been civil in nature, the obligor would not have enjoyed this constitutional protection.

Counsel. Courts have historically split over the question of whether appointment of counsel is constitutionally required for an indigent civil contempt defendant. *See Rodriquez v. Eighth Judicial Dist. Court ex rel.*, 102 P.3d 41 (Nev. 2004) (Sixth Amendment right to counsel not applicable in civil contempt); *Price v. Turner*, 691 S.E.2d 470, 472 n.2 (S.C. 2010), *vacated*, 131 S. Ct. 2507 (2011) (noting that 11 states and 5 federal courts at the time of the decision had held that counsel is required for civil contemnors facing incarceration). *But see Pasqua v. Council*, 892 A.2d 663 (N.J. 2006) (civil contempt obligors entitled to counsel under due process clause and state constitution).

In *Turner v Rogers*, 131 S. Ct. 2507 (2011) the Supreme Court issued a narrow ruling denying the right to counsel in a case where the custodial parent, rather than the state, sought to enforce a support order through civil contempt:

> We consequently hold that the Due Process Clause does not automatically require the provision of counsel at civil contempt proceedings to an indigent individual who is subject to a child support order, even if that individual faces incarceration (for up to a year). In particular, that clause does not require the provision of counsel where the opposing parent or other custodian (to whom support funds are owed) is not represented by counsel and the State provides alternative procedural safeguards equivalent to those we have mentioned (Adequate notice of the importance of ability to pay, fair opportunity to present, and to dispute, relevant information and court findings).

Id. at 2520.

At least one commentator has noted that the "alternative procedural safeguards" contemplated by the Court are significant ones, including determination of ability to pay arrearages. Judith Resnik, *Fairness in Numbers: A Comment on AT&T v. Concepcion, Wal-Mart v. Dukes, and Turner v. Rogers*, 125 Harv. L. Rev. 78, 155-56 (2011).

Enforcement of property awards distinguished. Most states provide explicit statutory authority for courts to use during contempt proceedings to enforce maintenance and child support obligations. In contrast, property settlements are categorized as ordinary debts and are not subject to enforcement through contempt. In most jurisdictions, property settlements are enforced through execution of the judgment.

10.11. Criminal Nonsupport

All states have statutes that punish an obligor who willfully fails to pay child support. For example, Wisconsin law declares that

> [a]ny person who intentionally fails for 120 or more consecutive days to provide spousal, grandchild or child support which the person knows or reasonably should know the person is legally obligated to provide is guilty of a Class I felony. A prosecutor may charge a person with multiple counts for a violation under this subsection if each count covers a period of at least 120 consecutive days and there is no overlap between periods.

Wis. Stat. §948.22(2) (2012).

Such provisions have withstood constitutional attack from obligors who have claimed that being imprisoned for nonpayment of a debt is unconstitutional. In rejecting this argument, courts reason that unlike a debt arising from a contract, a child support obligation is based on a court order. *O'Connor v. O'Connor*, 180 N.W.2d 735, 738 (Wis. 1970). *See State v. Bren*, 704 N.W.2d 170 (Minn. App. 2005); *Cramer v. Petrie*, 637 N.E.2d 882 (Ohio 1994); *Lyons v. State*, 835 S.W.2d 715, 718 (Tex. App. 1992).

EXAMPLE

Example

5. Assume that the state of X charged D with criminal nonsupport. D and his ex-wife were divorced, there were three children born of the marriage, and D was ordered to pay child support in the amount of $150 per month. In a very brief jury trial, the ex-wife testified that from the date of the decree until the date of trial (two years), she had received no child support payments from D. D did not testify and was convicted of criminal nonsupport and sentenced to five years in prison. In this jurisdiction, the criminal nonsupport statute provides that "any person who intentionally fails, refuses, or neglects to provide proper support which he or she knows or reasonably should know he or she is legally obligated to provide to a spouse, minor child, minor stepchild, or other dependent commits criminal nonsupport."

   In her instructions to the jury, the trial judge stated, "Regarding criminal non-support, the elements of the State's case are: (1) The alleged crime occurred on or about a certain date. The alleged crime occurred in this County, and this state. (2) The defendant then and there failed to provide proper support for his minor children when he knew or reasonably should have known he was legally obligated to provide support pursuant to the Order of the Court." D argues that the conviction should be reversed because the words "intentionally fails, refuses, or neglects" were not included in the court's instruction. The state argues that D did not properly object to the court's instruction. The trial transcript shows that D's counsel objected to the court's instruction in the following manner: "[T]he defendant does object concerning the elements." How will a court most likely treat D's argument?

EXPLANATION

Explanation

5. The conviction most likely will be reversed. Although the objection could have been more specific, it was sufficient to inform the court of the claimed defect. Intent is an essential element of the crime of criminal nonsupport. In this hypothetical case, the court did not instruct the jury on all the essential elements of the crime charged. An instruction omitting an essential element is prejudicially erroneous. *State v. Noll*, 507 N.W.2d 44 (Neb. App. 1993). *See also State v. Nuzman*, 95 P.3d 252 (Or. App. 2004) (state had burden to show that nonpayment was without lawful excuse).

10.12. Interception of Tax Refunds

In 1981, the federal income tax refund offset program was enacted into law. Pub. L. No. 97-35, §2331, 95 Stat. 860-863 (1981). Initially, this program was restricted to public assistance cases and enforced delinquent child support obligations by intercepting part or all of the obligor's federal income tax refund. The program was expanded in 1984 to allow for its use in nonassistance cases.

The Debt Collection Improvement Act (DCIA) of 1996, Pub. L. No.104-134, was enacted into law on April 26, 1996. The primary purpose of the DCIA is to increase the collection of nontax debt owed to the federal government. The DCIA contains important provisions for use in the collection of past-due child support obligations.

The DCIA was strengthened further by Executive Order 13019 — *Supporting Families: Collecting Delinquent Child Support Obligations*, dated September 26, 1998. This order allows the Secretary of the Treasury, in consultation with the Secretary of Health and Human Services, to develop and implement the procedures necessary to collect child support debts by administrative offsets. *See* 31 C.F.R. §§285.1, 285.3.

10.13. Garnishment

The Child Support and Establishment of Paternity Act of 1974, 42 U.S.C. §659, made it possible for a federal employer to withhold child support and pay an obligor directly from the withheld funds.

10.14. Credit Bureau Reporting

In many jurisdictions, a report to a credit bureau may be triggered if a noncustodial parent owes $1,000 or more in past-due child support.

10.15. Driver's License Suspension

In a number of jurisdictions, when a noncustodial parent is behind in paying child support by a certain number of weeks or months, the obligor's license may be suspended. Before the suspension becomes effective, the obligor is entitled to due-process protections, including written notice and a reasonable period in which to rectify the arrearage. *See also Office of Child Support v. Stanzione*, 910 A.2d 882 (Vt. 2006) (suspension of license did not infringe free exercise of religion); *Wheeler v. Idaho Dept. of Health and Welfare*, 207 P.3d 988 (Idaho 2009) (driver's license not an exempt property interest).

10.16. Recreational License Suspension

Some jurisdictions suspend the hunting and fishing licenses of obligors who are behind in support payments for a certain period, usually six months.

10.17. Publication of a "Most Wanted" List of "Deadbeat Obligors"

When obligors generate substantial sums in arrears, some jurisdictions publish their names in a local newspaper or place their names and sometimes their photos on a government Web site.

10.18. Occupational License Suspension

Some states have provisions that permit license suspension for obligors working in occupations that require a license from the state, county, or municipal board or agency. Persons subject to suspension may include realtors, barbers, doctors, and lawyers. For example, Georgia's *Code of Professional Responsibility* for lawyers incorporates state law and provides that when a court makes a finding that a member of the bar has willfully failed to pay a child support obligation in a timely fashion, and such refusal continues for 30 days after the determination becomes final, the bar member "shall be deemed not to be in good standing and shall remain in such status until such time as the noncompliance is corrected." *See Matter of Carlson*, 489 S.E.2d 834 (Ga. 1997).

10.19. Passport Denial

Section 370 of the Personal Responsibility and Work Opportunity Reconciliation Act (PRWORA) of 1996 (Pub. L. No.104-193, 110 Stat. 2105) amended the Social Security Act by adding subsection 452(k). This subsection became effective October 1, 1997, and provides for the denial, revocation, and restriction of U.S. passports. A passport application may be denied when the noncustodial parent is $5,000 or more past due in a child support obligation. PRWORA §§312, 653(a). *See Dept. of Rev. v. Nesbitt*, 975 So. 2d 549 (Fla. App. 2008) (trial court lacked authority to lift federally mandated restrictions on basketball player's passport). Note that PRWORA, which is is discussed later in this chapter in section 10.29, also requires states to suspend licenses and notify consumer credit agencies about delinquent obligors.

10.20. Seizing Awards

Reemployment insurance, workers' compensation payments, and lottery winnings may be seized. *See Torres v. Kunze*, 945 A.2d 472 (Conn. App. 2008) (lottery winnings of delinquent parent will be reduced by amount of child support owed).

10.21. Wage Assignment

An obligee may seek to obtain an order that directs an employer to deduct the child support payment from the earnings of an employee-obligor parent and then make this payment directly to the obligee parent. Violation of a wage assignment order could result in the employer becoming responsible for such payment to the obligee parent. Assignment orders can be obtained through a relatively simple court procedure. Once obtained, the wage assignment order must be served on the employer of the obligor parent before it becomes effective. *See In re Marriage of Hopkins*, 92 Cal. Rptr. 3d 570 (Cal. App. 2009) (a wage assignment order required the Social Security Administration to withhold $750 per month for current and past-due child support from the benefits due the obligor); *Schultz v. Butterball*, 2012 Ark. 163 (Ark. 2012) (unsuccessful constitutional challenge of wage-withholding order).

Additional measures found in some states include the following: (1) Freezing bank accounts until support is paid. *See, e.g., Murry v. Watkins*,

2004 WL 2980357 (Ohio App. 2004). A bank is relieved from liability for damages, should it have acted inappropriately. Both the various state departments of revenue and the Internal Revenue Service (IRS) can also seize funds from these accounts. (2) Using traditional creditor's legal remedies, such as execution and garnishment, against any other property that the obligor may own. Some states will place liens on real estate owned by an obligor who is in arrears in child support payments. *See Les Realty Corp. v. Hogan*, 714 A.2d 366 (N.J. Super. 1998) (the Automated Child Support Enforcement System was enacted to help remedy the serious problem of unpaid child support by ensuring liens on real estate owned by the debtor).

10.22. Effect of Bankruptcy

Child support debt is not dischargeable in bankruptcy. See Janet Leach Richards, *A Guide to Spousal Support and Property Division Claims Under the Bankruptcy Abuse Prevention and Consumer Protection Act* of 2005, 41 Fam. L.Q. 227, 228 (2007); United State Government Accountability Office, "Bankruptcy and Child Support Enforcement" (2008).

INTERSTATE COLLECTION AND MODIFICATION

10.23. Federal Partnership with States

In 1974, Congress enacted Title IV-D of the Social Security Act, creating a federal-state partnership for the purpose of establishing and enforcing child support orders. 42 U.S.C. §651 *et seq*. Although originally available only to recipients of public assistance, enforcement services were later made available for the benefit of all children.

As national attention turned to the issue of child support, it became evident that establishment, enforcement, and modification of child support orders across state lines was problematic. Consequently, the federal government began to intercede by encouraging and mandating states to cooperate and pass uniform state laws.

10.24. Early Efforts: URESA and RURESA

Before the 1950s, a parent who wanted to secure support from a parent who lived in another state had to travel to the support debtor's state to take legal action. However, since that time, a uniform act has existed in one form or another allowing states that subscribe to it to enforce each other's support orders.

In 1950, the National Conference of Commissioners on Uniform State Laws (NCCUSL) prepared a model act that was eventually adopted in some form in all jurisdictions, which is called the Uniform Reciprocal Enforcement of Support Act (URESA). In 1968, URESA was amended, and the new act was called the Revised Uniform Reciprocal Enforcement of Support Act (RURESA). By 1992, all the states had enacted either RURESA or URESA. Even American Samoa, Puerto Rico, Guam, and the Virgin Islands have adopted a version of either URESA or RURESA.

The purpose of URESA, and as amended, RURESA, was to address "the problem of interstate enforcement of duties of support," given "the increasing mobility of the American population." *In re Marriage of Gerkin*, 74 Cal. Rptr. 3d 188, 192 (Cal. App. 2008). The greatest difficulty in enforcing support where the parties lived in different states was the expense of traveling the state to litigate and one of the purposes of RURESA was to reduce or obviate the need to do so. However, problems arose because some state legislatures adopted language in their individual RURESA statutes that was inconsistent with provisions suggested by the NCCUSL, and ultimately with the enactments of other states. In addition, it became evident that the process under RURESA was slow and involved a considerable amount of paperwork and administration.

10.25. Uniform Interstate Family Support Act (UIFSA)

With state efforts falling short, the federal government sponsored the revision of the uniform interstate support legislation, which resulted in the Uniform Interstate Family Support Act (UIFSA). In 1996, Congress enacted a law requiring all 50 states to adopt UIFSA by January 1, 1998. UIFSA was intended to replace URESA and RURESA provisions in the states.

An overiding goal of UIFSA is to establish a single valid court order governing support of a child and UIFSA requires state cooperation for this purpose. *See* John J. Sampson, *Uniform Interstate Family Support Act* (2001) *with Prefatory Note and Comments (with Still More Unofficial Annotations)*, 36 Fam. L. Q. 329 (2002). Jurisdiction under UIFSA rests on the concept of continuing, exclusive jurisdiction to establish and modify the levels of child support for a particular child. The state issuing a child support order retains continuing, exclusive jurisdiction so long as this state remains the residence of the obligor, the individual obligee, or the child for whose benefit the support order is issued. UIFSA requires that states recognize the continuing, exclusive jurisdiction of a tribunal of another state that issued a child support order.

UIFSA allows for only one enforceable order in a case by limiting jurisdiction to modify the original order. The trial court may modify the child support order (1) upon both parties' consent to the court assuming jurisdiction, section 205(a)(2), or (2) if, after registration of the order, the trial court determines that the child, the individual obligee, and the obligor do not reside in the issuing state. Thus, if the parties and their child no longer reside in the state that issued the original child support order, and a party seeks to modify an existing child support order, the action must be brought in the state where the nonmoving party resides, except for modification by agreement. But *see Sidell v. Sidell*, 18 A.3d 499 (R.I. 2011) (court has permissive continuing jurisdiction, even though none of the parties reside in the state).

NCCUSL proposed amendments to UIFSA in 2001, and in 2008, NCCUSL proposed additional amendments in response to the Hague Convention on the International Recovery of Child Support and Other Forms of Family Maintenance. *See* National Conference of Commissioners on United States Law, *Uniform Interstate Family Support Act (last amedned or revised in 2008) with Prefatory Note and Comments*, 43 Fam. L. Q. 75 (2009); Battle Rankin Robinson, *Integrating an International Convention into State Law: The UIFSA Experience*, 42 Fam. L. Q. 61 (2009).

EXAMPLES

Examples

6. Assume that P and D dissolve their marriage in Iowa, and that a trial judge with jurisdiction over both parties issues a child support order in 2008. P is the custodial parent or obligee, and D is the obligor. P and the minor child move to Texas in 2009, and D moves to New York in 2010. P seeks legal advice as to which state she should bring a modification of support action in under UIFSA. What advice will you give P?

7. Assume that P and D dissolve their marriage in Iowa, and that a trial judge with jurisdiction over both parties issues a child support order in 2009. P is the custodial parent or obligee, and D is the obligor. P and the minor child move to Texas in 2010, while D remains in Iowa. P seeks legal advice as to which state she should bring a modification of support action in under UIFSA. What advice will you give P?

8. Assume that P and D dissolve their marriage in Iowa, and that a trial judge with jurisdiction over both parties issues a child support order in 2009. P is the custodial parent or obligee, and D is the obligor. P and the minor child remain in Iowa when D moves to New York in 2010. P seeks legal advice as to which state she should bring a modification of support action in under UIFSA. What advice will you give P?

Explanations

6. Under UIFSA, Iowa lost jurisdiction to modify its own order when D moved to New York unless P and D consented in writing to Iowa retaining modification jurisdiction. Iowa retains jurisdiction to enforce any amount of arrears owed because of the Iowa order. However, P should be advised to bring her modification action in Texas. *See also In re Marriage of Amezquita & Archuleta*, 124 Cal. Rptr. 2d 887 (Cal. App. 2002).

7. Iowa retains modification jurisdiction so long as D is a resident, and Iowa has enforcement jurisdiction because it never lost it.

8. If D is the person who moved, but P and the child remained in Iowa, Iowa retains enforcement jurisdiction and modification jurisdiction because P and the child remained in that jurisdiction. Because D was originally a resident of Iowa at the time of the initial order, or consented to personal jurisdiction, Iowa retains the ability to modify this order, provided that at least one parent remains in that state.

10.26. Full Faith and Credit for Child Support Orders Act (FFCCSOA)

Congress enacted the Full Faith and Credit for Child Support Orders Act (FFCCSOA) in 1994 to establish national standards promoting the payment of child support, discourage interstate conflict over inconsistent orders, and avoid jurisdictional competition. FFCCSOA, codified at 28 U.S.C. §1738B, requires that state courts afford full faith and credit to child support orders issued in other states and refrain from modifying or issuing contrary orders except in limited circumstances. Under §1738B(e), a child support order may be modified by a sister state only if the rendering state has lost continuing, exclusive jurisdiction over the child support order, which in turn occurs only if (1) neither the child nor any of the parties continues to reside in the state, or (2) each of the parties has consented to the assumption of jurisdiction by another state. 28 U.S.C. §1738B(e)(2) (2003).

Under the supremacy clause of the United States Constitution, FFCCSOA is binding on all states and supersedes any inconsistent provisions of state law, including any inconsistent provisions of uniform state laws. *See Jackson v. Holiness*, 961 N.W.2d 48 (Ind. App. 2012); *Bowman v.* Bowman, 82 A.D.3d 144 (N.Y. App. 2011); *Spencer v. Spencer*, 882 N.E.2d 886, 889 (N.Y. 2008); *Superior Court v. Ricketts*, 836 A.2d 707 (Md. App. 2003).

10.27. The Welfare Reform Act of 1996

The Welfare Reform Act of 1996 mandated that states adopt a version of the UIFSA by January 1, 1998, and required that they develop expedited procedures that move away from complaint-driven approaches to collection of support and toward more efficient and faster administrative provisions. It also encouraged states to use liens, seizures of funds, license suspension, and administrative subpoenas to collect outstanding child support.

10.28. Personal Responsibility and Work Opportunity Reconciliation Act of 1996

The Personal Responsibility and Work Opportunity Reconciliation Act (PRWORA) of 1996 required each state desiring to receive block grants to develop a state directory of new hires that met federal requirements by either October 1, 1997, or October 1, 1998, depending upon whether a state had a new hire reporting law in effect before August 22, 1996. 42 U.S.C. §§601 *et seq*. The law required the Department of Health and Human Services to develop a national directory of new hires by October 1, 1997. States also were required to adopt laws that allowed for the automatic placement of liens on an obligor's property when the obligor was in arrears.

10.29. Federal Crime

The Child Support Recovery Act (CSRA) of 1992, 18 U.S.C. §228(a), made it a federal crime to willfully fail to pay a past-due support obligation, where the child was located in a state separate from that of the obligor. The purpose of the Act was to strengthen state enforcement of child support orders and improve chances of collecting billions of dollars in unpaid child support from interstate delinquent parents. 138 CONG. REC. at H7326 (daily ed. Aug. 4, 1992). Congress intended to take the incentive out of the delinquent parent's attempts to avoid the processes of state courts by moving out of the child's home state. *United States v. Gill*, 264 F.3d 929, 933 (9th Cir. 2001). The Act, when triggered and thereafter applied by federal courts, enhances state enforcement efforts by providing a greater or more efficient jurisdictional reach than possessed by the states. *Giordano v. Giordano*, 913 A.2d 146 (N.J. Super. 2007).

Past-due support is defined in the Act as either an amount determined by a state court that remains unpaid for longer than one year or one that exceeds $5,000. An obligor who violates the federal statute can be fined and imprisoned for not more than six months for the first offense, or two years maximum, and can be ordered to make restitution for subsequent offenses. Support must have been unpaid for at least a year and exceed $5,000. *But see U.S. v. Pillor*, 387 F. Supp. 2d 1053 (N.D. Cal. 2005); and *United States v. Morrow*, 368 F. Supp. 863 (C.D. Ill. 2005) (holding that the mandatory CSRA rebuttable presumption that the obligor has the ability to pay violates due process by shifting burden regarding willfulness).

In 1998 CSRA became the Deadbeat Parents Punishment Act (DPPA). *See United States v. Edelkind*, 525 F.3d 388 (5th Cir. 2008). Nearly all states criminalized the willful failure to pay child support and most utilized URESA to extradite interstate delinquent obligors and process interstate child support enforcement orders. Unfortunately, these methods proved slow and cumbersome, and Congress consequently passed the DPPA to help states collect past due support payments beyond their borders.

Two new federal felony categories were created by DPPA that carry a maximum sentence of of two years in prison, plus fines and restitution at the discretion of the court. Crossing state lines with the intent to evade child support payments is a felony for parents owing $5,000 or more, or for parents whose payments have remained unpaid for more than a year. Out-of-state parents owing $10,000 or more or who fail to pay for two years are also subject to felony charges.

The DPPA has been held constitutional by at least nine federal circuit courts of appeal. *United States v. Klinzing*, 315 F.3d 803 (7th Cir. 2003) (holding that DPPA does not violate the commerce clause, equal protection clause, or Sixth Amendment to the Constitution and listing the various circuit court decisions).

CHAPTER 11

Establishing Alimony

11.1. Introduction

Alimony is the obligation of a former (or soon-to-be-former) spouse to provide the other with support in the form of income. The terms *alimony*, *maintenance*, and *spousal support* all refer to the same obligation and can be used interchangeably. This chapter focuses on when and how alimony is awarded, and the next chapter concerns post-divorce modification of alimony.

Societal views about alimony have changed significantly over the years due to the changed legal and economic status of women. Consequently, legislatures and courts have struggled to shape relevant legal principles to meet modern-day needs. Although relatively little data exists, researchers estimate that some form of alimony is awarded in about 20 percent of divorces. *See* Thomas Oldham, *Changes in the Economic Consequences of Divorces, 1958-2008*, 42 Fam. L.Q. 419, 429 (2008); ALI, *Principles of the Law of Family Dissolution* §5.04 cmt. a (2001).

The current law with respect to alimony has deep historical roots stretching back for centuries. Three historical "customs" have particularly shaped modern doctrine, and the chapter begins with an explanation of these. The first is the custom of the bride's family providing dowry, gifts to a husband to protect the future wife upon marriage; the second is the Unity Doctrine; and the third is the need for finding fault before a legal support obligation is considered.

HISTORY OF ALIMONY

11.2. Dowry

The Anglo-Saxon custom of transferring a wife's property to her husband upon marriage probably began around A.D. 800. When a couple married, the bride's parents and relatives gave a husband all her property (her dowry) in return for his promise of care and protection. This early custom was apparently absorbed into the canon law and later found its way in part into English and United States common law.

11.3. Unity Doctrine

The Unity Doctrine arose from the early theological teachings that when a couple married, the wife's person was merged into that of the husband. The concept took many forms, and its effects were numerous. For example, because one could not sue oneself, neither married partner could sue the other, and a husband was responsible for defending his wife against any third-party actions involving her interests. It was not until the late 1800s, when Married Women's Acts were passed in most jurisdictions, that the law began to change.

11.4. Assignment of Fault

The concept of marital fault grew out of the early Church's teaching that marriage is indissoluble and divorce is a mortal sin. Although the Church banned absolute divorce, it created alternatives when faced with the practical problem of married couples who wanted to live apart. One option was to annul the marriage, a *divorce a vinculo*, thus avoiding a divorce and permitting remarriage. Another canonical option was a divorce from bed and board (*a mensa et thoro*). Under this early separation scheme, a couple could separate and live apart from each other without obtaining an absolute divorce. However, a separation was granted only if a wife could provide a good reason for living apart from her husband. The policy of the law, as administered by the English ecclesiastical courts, looked toward a reconciliation of the parties and preservation of the marriage relation; therefore, the allowance was for the reasonable support of the wife only. The courts sometimes sought to do justice by increasing the allowance in cases where the property originally came from the wife; however, the alimony remained based on the wife's reasonable support during the separation.

11.5. Fault Adopted by Secular Systems

The ancient ecclesiastical concept of fault was incorporated into the judicial thinking of most early secular family law in the United States. Divorce was a remedy available only to an innocent party who had been "wronged" by a guilty party. It was believed appropriate to punish a wife whose behavior constituted grounds for divorce by either denying alimony altogether or awarding a much smaller sum than she might otherwise receive. In effect, through her misconduct, she forfeited her claim to her husband's financial protection.

Conversely, a husband whose marital fault was serious may have had to pay additional alimony, either as compensation to the wife for the wrongs done to her or as a means of punishing the husband who was at fault. Alimony awards reflected the judiciary's perceptions of public morality, and the sanctions were considered appropriate when a citizen breached the community's acceptable moral standards.

11.6. Common Law Disabilities and Duties

At common law, a woman entering marriage faced severe legal disabilities. The husband and wife were considered one person, and that one person was the husband. Once married, all of a wife's personal property came under the husband's control, and she had no legal right to her husband's real property.

Under the common law, a husband was under a duty to maintain his wife in accordance with his means; however, there was no corresponding duty placed on a wife. *See Cruickshank-Wallace v. County Banking and Trust Co.*, 885 A.2d 403 (Md. App. 2005). A husband was obligated to provide a suitable home and necessaries such as food and clothing.

A wife was normally not entitled to alimony in a separate home, absent good reason to live apart from her husband. A husband did not have a duty to maintain his wife if she deserted the marriage, although the duty was revived if she returned. If she committed adultery that the husband did not condone or which had not been contrived, his duty of support normally ceased.

If a wife was living apart from her husband because of his desertion or misconduct, she was entitled to support, so long as she was free from misconduct herself. If a husband failed to provide for her, she could pledge his credit for necessaries that were suitable given their lifestyle prior to the separation. *See* Brenda M. Hoggett & David S. Pearl, *The Family Law and Society, Cases and Materials* 81 (Butterworths 1983).

During the nineteenth century, the common law in the United States in jurisdictions that permitted a divorce recognized the unfairness of leaving a wife in near poverty following a divorce or legal separation. Courts began to require that an ex-husband provide support — sometimes by returning all or a portion of the wife's dowry, and at other times by requiring that he provide her with a portion of his personal property. The common law reasoned that the award was supported by public policy, which declared that it was the duty of the husband to support his wife for life.

The common law limited a husband's support obligation and imposed no reciprocal support duty on the wife. While requiring the husband to support the ex-wife, that law did not necessarily require that he make periodic alimony payments or provide funds from his income. Divorces were, of course, rare and effectively discouraged by most religious institutions.

11.7. Alimony and Gender

At common law, a wife owed no reciprocal duty to support a husband, and this view continued until the Supreme Court decided *Orr v. Orr*, 440 U.S. 268 (1979). The Court invalidated an Alabama statute that imposed alimony obligations on husbands but not on wives. The Court observed that because the statute provided that different treatment be accorded persons on the basis of sex, it established a classification subject to strict scrutiny under the equal protection clause of the Fourteenth Amendment. To withstand such scrutiny, gender classifications must serve important governmental objectives and must be substantially related to achievement of those objectives. *Califano v. Webster*, 430 U.S. 313, 316-317 (1977).

Alabama argued that its interests included providing help for needy spouses and claimed that the statute used sex as a proxy for need. It also argued that the statute was intended to compensate women for past discrimination during marriage, which had left them unprepared to fend for themselves in the working world following divorce. These arguments did not persuade the Court. Though conceding that they were legitimate governmental objectives, the Court ruled that the statute was not "substantially" related to the achievement of those objectives. *Orr*, 440 U.S. at 286. It observed that even if gender were a reliable proxy for need, and even if the institution of marriage did discriminate against women, the state did not justify the salient features of the statutory scheme adequately.

The Court also observed that under the statute, individualized hearings at which the parties' relative financial circumstances are considered were already occurring, and therefore, no reason existed to use sex as a proxy for need. It reasoned that needy males could be helped along with needy females with little, if any, additional burden on the state. *But see In re Miltenberger Estate*, 737 N.W.2d 513 (Mich. App. 2007) (dower statutes were substantially related to an important governmental objective of cushioning the financial impact of spousal loss on the party disproportionately burdened by the loss and do not violate equal protection).

THE NECESSARIES DOCTRINE

11.8. Husband's Common Law Duty

At common law, it was the duty of the husband to provide for a wife's necessaries. In return, a wife was obliged to provide domestic services that pertained to the comfort, care, and well-being of her family and consortium to her husband. *See Ritchie v. White*, 35 S.E.2d 414, 416-417 (N.C. 1945).

As observed earlier, when a woman married, the common law took the view that she forfeited her legal existence and became the property of her husband, and her services and earnings belonged to him. *Cheshire Medical Center v. Holbrook*, 663 A.2d 1344 (N.H. 1995). Because the wife could not contract for food, clothing, or medical needs, her husband was obligated to provide her with such "necessaries," and if the husband failed to do so, the necessaries doctrine made him legally liable for essential goods or services provided to her by third parties. Most courts viewed the husband's duty as arising from the fact of the marriage, not from any express undertaking on his part. The duty also rested on a recognition of the traditional status of the husband as the financial provider of the family's needs.

Passage of Married Women's Acts around the close of the nineteenth century gave women additional rights, including that a married woman could carry on a trade or business and keep the earnings as her separate property. *Gaver v. Harrant*, 557 A.2d 210 (Md. 1989). The acts also provided that real and personal property brought into marriage by a woman remained her separate property after the marriage. The statutes were at first construed in a strained and grudging fashion. *See generally Condore v. Prince George's Co.*, 425 A.2d 1011 (Md. 1981).

11.9. Gender-Neutral Application

Most jurisdictions that have considered the issue of necessaries in the last three decades have held that the doctrine should be applied in a gender-neutral fashion. *See, e.g., Nicholson v. Hugh Chatham Memorial Hosp.*, 266 S.E.2d 818, 823 (N.C. 1980); *Jersey Shore Med. Ctr.–Fitkin Hosp. v. Baum's Estate*, 417 A.2d 1003, 1009 (N.J. 1980). Alternatively, some states have eliminated it altogether. *See, e.g., Condore v. Prince George's County*, 425 A.2d 1011, 1019 (Md. 1981).

All agree that the old notion that it is the man's primary responsibility to provide a home and its essentials is no longer justified. A female is also no longer destined solely for the home and the rearing of the family, and the male only for the marketplace and the world of ideas. *Orr, supra*; *Stanton v. Stanton*, 421 U.S. 7, 14-15 (1975). The traditional formulation of the necessaries doctrine, predicated on anachronistic assumptions about marital relations and female dependence, cannot withstand scrutiny under the compelling interest standard. *See Cheshire Med. Ctr. v. Holbrook*, 663 A.2d 1344 (N.H. 1995).

Example

1. Assume that the years are 1830 and 2012, and that a husband and wife live in a jurisdiction that recognizes the necessaries doctrine. Assume that the husband is admitted to the hospital and that the wife signs a form authorizing medical treatment for him. However, the wife refuses to sign a form that guarantees payment for the medical treatment. Assume that the husband recovers and that the hospital seeks payment of the expenses from the wife. The wife replies that the necessaries doctrine is limited to a husband providing for a wife. Furthermore, she claims that medical expenses are not encompassed within the doctrine. How would a court most likely rule in 1830? In 2012?

Explanation

1. Until recently, the wife's argument would have been sustained. Under the common law, the wife usually depended on her husband for financial support. However, a majority of jurisdictions have either abolished the doctrine or replaced it with one that makes both spouses equally liable for necessaries. Furthermore, medical expenses are viewed in most jurisdictions that retain the necessaries doctrine as encompassed within it. When both parties are viewed as liable for necessaries, in the absence of an agreement by a spouse to undertake a debt, the creditors may be required to seek initial redress from the spouse incurring the debt, and only if those assets are insufficient may the creditors then reach the other spouse's assets. In this example, therefore, the creditors would most likely be required to pursue their claim with the husband initially. If the husband failed to satisfy the debt, the wife would be liable.

UNIFORM ACTS

11.10. The Uniform Marriage and Divorce Act (UMDA) Provisions

During the 1970s, many states adopted all or a portion of the Uniform Marriage and Divorce Act (UMDA). The UMDA was originally ratified by the National Conference of Commissioners on Uniform State Laws in 1970, and after three additional drafts, the American Bar Association (ABA) endorsed it in 1974. *See* Brett R. Turner, *Rehabilitative Alimony Reconsidered: The "Second Wave" of Spousal Support Reform*, 10 Divorce Litigation 185 (October 1998) (article lists the year in which each individual state adopted various property division and spousal support reforms set forth above and graphically shows the influence of the UMDA in the timing of the reforms).

The UMDA was remarkable because it departed from awarding maintenance based on fault when a marriage relationship ended. For example, the commentary to section 308 of the Act reads in part, "Assuming that an award of maintenance is appropriate under subsection 308(a), the standards for setting the amount of the award are set forth in subsection 308(b). Here, as in Section 307, the court is expressly admonished not to consider the misconduct of a spouse during the marriage."

The UMDA also contained a provision regarding homemakers that has been adopted by statute in a majority of jurisdictions. The provision recognized the value of the contributions of a full-time homemaker to the marital partnership, and upon divorce, it entitled the homemaker to share equitably with the wage-earning spouse in the marital property.

11.11. UMDA Two-Step Analysis

The UMDA created a two-step process for determining whether alimony should be awarded and if so, its amount and duration. UMDA §308 provides:

> (a) In a proceeding for dissolution of marriage, legal separation, or maintenance following a decree of dissolution of the marriage by a court which lacked personal jurisdiction over the absent spouse, the court may grant a maintenance order for either spouse only if it finds that the spouse seeking maintence:
> (1) lacks sufficient property to provide for his reasonable needs; and
> (2) is unable to support himself through appropriate employment or is the custodian of a child whose condition or circumstances make it appropriate that the custodian not be required to seek employment outside the home.
>
> (b) The maintenance order shall be in amounts and for periods of time the court deems just, without regard to marital misconduct, and after considering all relevant factors, including:
> (1) the financial resources of the party seeking maintenance, including marital property apportioned to him, his ability to meet his needs independently, and the extent to which a provision for support of a child living with the party includes a sum for that party as custodian;
> (2) the time necessary to aquire sufficient education or training to enable the party seeking maintenance to find appropriate employment;
> (3) the standard of living established during the marriage;

(4) the duration of the marriage;
(5) the age and the physical and emotional condition of the spouse seeking maintenance; and
(6) the ability of the spouse from whom maintenance is sought to meet his needs while meeting those of the spouse seeking maintenance.

Thus, the first step of the analysis involves determination of need, and only if need exists does a court consider the factors relevant to setting an amount and duration of an award.

11.12. American Law Institute (ALI) Approach

Taking a different view of alimony, the American Law Institute (ALI) has proposed a "loss compensation" theory to use when alimony is to be considered. ALI, *Principles of the Law of Family Dissolution: Analysis and Recommendations* §5.05 (2002). Under this theory, one spouse makes compensatory spousal payments to the other spouse for certain losses experienced. Compensable losses include the loss of a standard of living and a loss incurred because the one spouse was primarily responsible for child care during the marriage. Under the ALI proposal, a spouse would be entitled at dissolution to compensation for the earning-capacity loss arising from his or her disproportionate share, during marriage, of the care of the marital children, or of the children of either spouse.

For example, assume that H and W were married for 20 years, and that during that time, their relationship was "traditional" in the sense that H worked at developing a business while W remained at home caring for their three children. If W proves that she provided a disproportionate share of the parental child care, the ALI proposal would create an inference that child care responsibilities adversely affected her earning capacity.

The ALI proposal provides that a presumption of entitlement to compensation is rebutted by evidence that the claimant did not provide a disproportionate share of the parental child care; however, "the inference that child-care responsibilities adversely affected the claimant's earning capacity is not rebuttable. The reasons are partly pragmatic, and arise from the difficulty of establishing what an individual's earning capacity would have been had the individual made different life choices years earlier." *Id.*

A spouse also would be entitled at dissolution to compensation for earning-capacity losses arising from the care provided during marriage to a sick, elderly, or disabled third party, in fulfillment of a moral obligation of the other spouse or of both spouses jointly. An award is allowed only to a claimant whose earning capacity at divorce is substantially less than that of the other spouse. ALI, *Principles of the Law of Family Dissolution: Analysis and*

Recommendations §5.11(1). For example, assume that H and W were married for 25 years before their marriage broke down. Also assume that H's mother M lived with H and W during the last five years of the marriage. In the twenty-first year of H and W's marriage, M was diagnosed with cancer but continued to live with H and W. W left her part-time employment to care for M at home. After a three-year struggle with cancer, M died. A year later, H and W filed to dissolve their marriage. The ALI would view the care for M as H's moral obligation and, during their marriage, the shared moral obligation of both H and W. As a consequence, W would be entitled to dissolution compensation for earning-capacity losses arising during her care of M.

PURPOSES AND DURATION OF ALIMONY

11.13. Permanent Alimony

Courts are most likely to award permanent alimony at the end of a long-term marriage, particularly where there will be a disparity in income after divorce. For example, in *Nuveen v. Nuveen*, 795 N.W.2d 308 (N.D. 2011) the Supreme Court of North Dakota upheld an award of permanent spousal support after a 16-year marriage where it would not have been possible for the wife, a long-term homemaker, to be rehabilitated to the point where her income would be "anywhere near" the husband's.

Marital duration. Most courts view the duration of the marriage as particularly important because it is often the major factor that creates the disparity in the parties' earning capacities. This is especially true in cases involving a homemaker spouse. Regardless of the spouses' respective roles, marital duration provides a benchmark for determining reasonable needs — the longer the marriage, the more precisely reasonable needs can be measured by the standard of living established during the marriage.

Unfortunately, there is no precise point at which a marriage is defined as long-term. In general, awards of permanent alimony may be made in marriages of more than 10 to 15 years. *See* Joan M. Krauskopf, *Rehabilitative Alimony: Uses and Abuses of Limited Duration* Alimony, 21 Fam. L. Q. 573, 579-580 (1988) (citing trend upholding permanent maintenance awards in cases involving marriages of 15 to 20 years); Marsha Garrison, *How Do Judges Decide Divorce Cases?* 74 N.C. L. Rev. 401, 467 (1996) (spousal income and marital duration as predictors of alimony awards); *Mobley v. Mobley*, 18 So. 3d 724, 727) (Fla. App. 2009) ("A ten-year marriage falls within the gray area in which there is neither a presumption for or against alimony.").

Rationales. There are two commonly expressed rationales for making an award of permanent alimony in traditional long-term marriages. The first is to compensate the recipient spouse for benefits conferred on the other spouse by being responsible for homemaking and child rearing. The primary benefit conferred on the other spouse is increased earning capacity because, while enjoying family life, he or she was free to devote all productive time to income activity outside the home.

The second rationale is to compensate for the lost opportunity costs associated with homemaking. Earning capacity may be reduced either by not being employed outside the home or by holding employment subject to the needs of the family. Courts recognize this lost opportunity cost when they refer to the fact that a claimant for alimony remained in the home in the traditional role of full-time homemaker during the marriage. *See In re Marriage of Olson*, 705 N.W.2d 312 (Iowa 2005) (long-term homemaker with health problems entitled to "traditional alimony" for life or as long as the homemaker is incapable of self-support). A transfer of earning power occurs during a traditional marriage, in which the homemaker spouse's efforts have increased the other's earning capacity at the expense of the homemaker. Alimony is an award formulated to compensate for that transfer by sufficiently meeting reasonable needs for support not otherwise met by property division and personal income. *See* Joan M. Krauskopf, *supra*.

11.14. Incapacity Alimony

Incapacity alimony is granted when a court finds a spouse to be physically or mentally incapacitated to the extent that the ability of the incapacitated spouse to support himself or herself is materially affected. *See Ferro v. Ferro*, 796 N.Y.2d 165 (N.Y. App. Div. 2005) (disability must prevent spouse from earning a living). Permanent awards are more likely in longer-term marriages where the recipient suffers from a disability or health concern. *See Brooks v. Brooks*, 257 S.W.3d 418 (Tex. App. 2008) (spousal maintenance award to wife of 30 years with "incapacitating" disability); *Stewart v. Stewart*, 152 P.3d 544 (Idaho 2007) (award to wife of 25 years with degenerative illness).

11.15. Rehabilitative Alimony

Rehabilitative alimony is commonly viewed as a short-term award, which is ordered to enable the former spouse to complete the preparation necessary for economic self-sufficiency. It usually ceases when the dependent spouse is in a position of self-support. *See Cox v. Cox*, 762 A.2d 1040 (N.J. 2000).

Rehabilitative alimony may be appropriate if, for example, a spouse gave up or postponed her own education to support the household during the marriage and requires a lump-sum or a short-term award to achieve economic self-sufficiency. Its purpose is to enhance and improve the earning capacity of the economically dependent spouse. Its focus is on the ability of a dependent spouse to engage in gainful employment, combined with the length of the marriage, the age of the parties, and the spouse's ability to regain a place in the workforce.

For example, in the case of *Hutchings v. Hutchings*, 250 P.3d 324 (Okla. 2011), the Supreme Court of Oklahoma reversed a trial court award of $250 per month and ordered payment of $1,500 per month for 36 months because the original award did not provide an adquate opportunity for "post-marital economic readjustment." *Id.* at 328. *See also Maiers v. Maiers*, 775 N.W.2d 666 (Minn. App. 2009) (based on finding that recipient would become self-supporting, award of temporary alimony with reservation of jurisdiction was upheld on appeal); *Mark v. Mark*, 223 P.3d 476 (Utah App. 2009) (alimony to "close the gap" during rehabilitative period).

11.16. Reimbursement Alimony

Reimbursement alimony is sometimes characterized as "not truly support but an equitable creation designed to eliminate injustice." Frank Louis, *Limited Duration Alimony*, 11 N.J. Fam. Law. 133, 137 (1991). It is intended to compensate a spouse who has made financial sacrifices, resulting in that spouse's reduced standard of living, in order to enable the other spouse to forgo gainful employment while securing an advanced degree or professional license to enhance the parties' future standard of living. *See Haugan v. Haugan*, 343 N.W.2d 796 (Wisc. 1984).

Reimbursement alimony is usually limited to monetary contributions made with the mutual and shared expectation that both parties to the marriage would derive increased income and material benefits. For example, in *In re Marriage of Harris*, 244 P.3d 801 (Or. 2010), the Supreme Court of Oregon upheld a compensatory alimony award of $2,000 per month for a period of ten years. In that case, the wife had worked full time to allow the husband to earn a dental degree. However, in the case of *Klimek v. Klimek*, 775 N.W.2d 444 (Neb. App. 2009), reimbursement alimony was denied when the wife failed to prove that not attending graduate school while attempting to start a family prevented her from being promoted.

11.17. Caregiver Alimony

Caregiver alimony is granted when a court finds that a spouse must forgo employment to care for a child with a physical or mental incapacity. *See Marriage of Snow v. England*, 862 N.E.2d 664 (Ind. 2007) (Indiana courts may order incapacity, caregiver, or rehabilitation maintenance only under conditions specified by statute).

11.18. Limited Durational Alimony

The focus of limited durational alimony is distinctly different from rehabilitative or reimbursement alimony. Limited durational alimony is not intended to facilitate the earning capacity of a dependent spouse or to make a sacrificing spouse whole. Instead, it is appropriate when an economic need for alimony is established, but the marriage was of short duration, and permanent alimony is therefore not appropriate. *See Gordon v. Rozenwald*, 880 A.2d 1157 (N.J. Super. A.D. 2005) (limited durational alimony appropriate for marriage of short duration). Such circumstances stand in sharp contrast to marriages of long duration in which economic need is also demonstrated. With respect to shorter marriages, limited durational alimony may provide an equitable solution and one that is sometimes circumscribed by statute.

An award of limited durational alimony should reflect the underlying policy considerations that distinguish it from rehabilitative and reimbursement alimony. Limited durational alimony is conceptually more closely related to permanent alimony than to rehabilitative or reimbursement alimony. The latter two types of alimony represent forms of limited spousal support for specified purposes; once the purpose is achieved, entitlement to that form of alimony ceases. Permanent and limited durational alimony, by contrast, reflect a policy of recognizing that marriage is an adaptive economic and social partnership, and an award of either validates that principle.

11.19. Fault-Related Alimony

Approximately half of jurisdictions may consider marital fault when awarding alimony. Linda D. Elrod & Robert Spector, *A Review of the Year in Family Law: Numbers of Disputes Increase*, 45 Fam. L.Q. 443, 492-93 (2012). Some states treat fault as one factor among several when considering whether to award alimony. *See Patterson v. Patterson*, 917 So. 2d 111 (Miss. App. 2005). Some preclude an award of alimony to a spouse who has been at fault. *See Brown v. Brown*, 665 S.E.2d 174 (S.C. App. 2008) (wife who committed adultery barred from receipt of alimony); *Washington v. Washington*, 846 So. 2d 895 (La. App. 2003);

Congdon v. Congdon, 578 S.E.2d 833 (Va. 2003) (whether denial of alimony would result in manifest injustice is based on the parties' economic circumstances and their fault). *But see Mani v. Mani*, 869 A.2d 904 (N.J. 2005) (fault relevant only if it has affected the parties' economic life, or where it "so violates societal norms that continuing the economic bonds between the parties would confound notions of simple justice").

A court in a jurisdiction that permits consideration of fault in awarding alimony is faced with the question of what type of conduct constitutes "fault." Although the standard varies, to constitute legal fault, misconduct generally must be of a serious nature and must be an independent contributory or proximate cause of the separation. Such acts are often viewed as synonymous with the fault grounds that previously entitled a spouse to a separation or divorce and may include adultery, conviction of a felony, habitual intemperance or excesses, cruel treatment or outrages, public defamation, abandonment, an attempt on the other's life, status as a fugitive, and intentional nonsupport. Mutual incompatibility and general unhappiness with the marital relationship are generally not viewed as lawful causes for leaving the family home. Lawful cause sufficient to justify a spouse's departure from the marital domicile is equivalent to grounds for alimony.

EXAMPLES

Examples

2. Assume that P and D were married for 30 years before their marriage ended in divorce. P is 50, and D is 48, and both are in good health. During the marriage, P managed the household and was the primary caretaker for the three children. The youngest of the three children was emancipated one year before the divorce action was initiated. Testimony at trial indicates that P is a high school graduate with limited employment prospects. An expert testified that P could earn from $18,000 to $24,000 annually. D has worked outside the home for the last 25 years as an assembly line worker in a car factory. D has gross annual income of approximately $58,000. P's lawyer has asked the trial judge to award P permanent alimony. D's lawyer argues that either D should pay nothing or that the court should award rehabilitative or durational alimony. What will P's lawyer argue, and how will a court most likely decide the alimony issue?

3. Assume that P and D live in a jurisdiction with a statute that allows an award of alimony, either rehabilitative or permanent, to a spouse where the court finds that (1) the spouse lacks sufficient income and/or property to provide for his or her reasonable needs and (2) the spouse is unable to support himself or herself through appropriate employment at the standard of living established during the marriage. The alimony must

be in the amount and for the duration the court deems just, based on the consideration of seven nonexclusive factors. Part of the purpose of the statute is to provide spousal support in relation to the standard of living established during the marriage. Another purpose is to recompense a homemaker for contributions made during the marriage.

Also assume that P and D had been married for ten years when their marriage ended. At the time of the divorce, there were no children. P is 55 years old, had back problems for which she received disability benefits, and has not worked outside the home for many years. During the marriage, P helped D obtain a college degree by doing secretarial work from home. At the time of the separation, P had an independent income of $670 per month, the bulk of which came from the disability payment. Despite receipt of disability benefits, P is capable of working and earning an income of approximately $800 per month. Her monthly living expenses are about $1,000 per month, including mortgage payments on her home. D's gross income from his work is $45,000 per year and is expected to increase in the future. D's monthly living expenses at the time of the divorce hearing were about $1,800 per month. What are the likely prospects of P being awarded permanent alimony?

4. Assume that P and D are divorcing after 18 years of marriage. D has been violent with P throughout the marriage, and D has been convicted of a domestic violence—related felony. Because of D's alcoholism and other personality problems, D is not self-supporting and would qualify for an alimony award under the alimony statute. However, the state where P and D reside also has a statute creating a rebuttable presumption against an award of spousal support to an abusive spouse. P claims that D is precluded from receiving alimony, but D argues that D will be destitute without it. What is the likely result?

EXPLANATIONS

Explanations

2. P's lawyer may concede that rehabilitative and limited durational maintenance awards are intended to assist a recipient spouse in becoming self-supporting, but she will contend that they are not appropriate in this case. P's lawyer may argue that this is a long-term marriage, and that alimony serves to compensate a homemaker for contributions to family well-being not otherwise recognized in the property distribution.

P's lawyer also may argue that the compensatory aspect of alimony reflects the reality that when one spouse stays home and raises the children, not only does that spouse lose future earning capacity by not being employed, but that spouse also increases the future earning capacity of the working spouse. In addition, the working spouse, while enjoying family life, is free to devote productive time to career enhancement. When determining the extent of the compensatory component of an alimony award, a court should give particular consideration to the role of the recipient spouse during the marriage and to the length of the marriage. It is likely that permanent alimony will be awarded to P.

3. In addition to the length of the marriage, the critical factors in determining the duration of an alimony award are the role that the recipient spouse played during the marriage and the income that that spouse is likely to achieve in relation to the standard of living established during the marriage. The latter factor, in turn, is closely related to the recipient spouse's age, health, child care duties, and access to income-producing assets. Although P is capable of employment, she is 55 years of age and has not worked outside the home for many years. Furthermore, she has a back problem for which she receives the disability payments. In addition, P was the homemaker, and she supported D's efforts to obtain a degree, which has allowed him to obtain the earning capacity that he now enjoys. A permanent alimony award is probably necessary to keep P in the standard of living established during the marriage.

4. This example is based on the somewhat similar case of *In re Marriage of Cauley*, 41 Cal. Rptr. 3d 902 (Cal. App. 2006), where the court considered the effect of such a rebuttable presumption statute and held that D was precluded from receiving alimony under it. *But see In re Peirano*, 930 A.2d 1165, 1173 (N.H. 2007) (alimony awarded to husband guilty of domestic violence where fault is only one factor in awarding alimony).

    As noted earlier, courts may consider marital fault in addition to whether one of the parties to the marriage has wasted community assets. The fact that a particular state statute may contain as many as ten "non-fault" factors, in addition to the fact that each factor on the list is considered nonexclusive, provide a court with broad discretion in making its ultimate determination.

STATE LIMITATIONS ON AMOUNT AND DURATION

11.20. Imputation of Income

The amount of alimony paid may be increased or decreased if a court decides to impute income to a party. This typically occurs if an obligor voluntarily reduces income to avoid payment. *See Pullen v. Pullen*, 222 P.3d 909 (Ariz. App.

2009) (husband's voluntary underemployment resulted in imputation of income to him for the purposes of paying alimony).

In some cases, income may be attributed to an obligee who has reduced income to create need. *See McGregor v. McGregor*, 334 S.W.3d 113 (Ky. App. 2011) (trial court could impute income to recipient based on work history and educational background); *Niederman v. Niederman*, 60 So. 3d 544 (Fl. App. 2011) (imputed income to wife based on annuities and individual retirement accounts that she received at divorce); *Shafer v. Shafer*, 45 So. 3d 494 (Fl. App. 2010) (discussing imputation of income to recipient who failed to pass the bar exam 16 years earlier). *But see Myland v. Myland*, 804 N.W.2d 124 (Mich. App. 2010) (error to impute income to recipient with progressive multiple sclerosis).

11.21. Percentage Formulas

In general, courts have not favored the use of formulas for determining alimony awards. *See, e.g., Kunkle v. Kunkle*, 554 N.E.2d 83, 89-90 (Ohio 1990) (citing cases in other jurisdictions). Particularly disfavored are awards requiring one spouse to pay a percentage of gross or net income to the other spouse. *See, e.g., McClung v. McClung*, 465 So. 2d 637, 638 (Fla. App. 1985) (reversing award requiring husband to pay 50 percent of combined net incomes of parties); *Bourassa v. Bourassa*, 481 N.W.2d 113, 115 (Minn. App. 1992) (disallowing award requiring husband to pay 40 percent of his gross monthly income to wife); *Kunkle*, 554 N.E.2d at 88-90 (overturning award requiring husband to pay wife one-third of his gross earned income). *See also Myland v. Myland*, 804 N.W.2d 124 (Mich. App. 2010) (error to use multiplier based on on difference in income). When percentage awards are allowed, the cases often involve unusual circumstances. *See, e.g., Hefty v. Hefty*, 493 N.W.2d 33, 36 (Wis. 1992) (considering fluctuation of husband's bonus income, court properly awarded wife fixed monthly sum plus 20 percent of any bonus pay).

11.22. Alimony Guidelines

Unlike child support, alimony awards are based in large part on court discretion. This makes awards difficult to predict and results in potentially different outcomes for similarly situated couples. Because of such concerns, a few jurisdictions have begun to experiment with adoption of alimony guidelines. *See* Twila B. Larkin, *Guidelines for Alimony: The New Mexico Experiment*, 38 Fam. L.Q. 29 (2004); *Boemio v.* Boemio, 994 A.2d 911 (Md. App. 2010); Cullum *v. Cullum*, 160 P.3d 231 (Ariz. App. 2007). *See also* J. Thomas Oldham, *Changes in the Economic Consequences of Divorces, 1958-2008*, 42 Fam. L. Q. 419 (2008) (critiquing spousal support guideline methodology).

11.23. Statutory Limits on Duration of Alimony

A few states have begun to impose limits on the duration of alimony awards. *See* 19-A M.R.S.A. §951-A (duration not to exceed half the length of 10- to 20-year marriage); 13 De. C. §1512(d) (duration not to exceed half the term of less than 20-year marriage); K.S.A. 60-1610 (b)(2) (limit of 121 months); U.C.A. 1953 §30-3-5(8)(h) (limit to number of years of marriage).

Example

5. Assume that the former husband (H) could increase his income if he retired from the university where he worked, started receiving retirement benefits, and then retured to work pursuant to a special early retirement program. His former wife (W) seeks to impute the difference in income to him for the purpose of paying alimony to her. What is the likely result?

Explanation

5. In the similar case of *In re Marriage of Kochan*, 122 Cal. Rptr. 3d 61 (Cal. App. 2011), the appellate court held that spousal support should not have been increased based on the obligor's "hypothetical" income if he retired. The court reasoned that "a spouse who continues working in a long-held position should not have his or her support obligation based on his or her earnings capacity measured by some alternative employment scenario." *Id.* at 70. Note that the result may have been different if there was indication that the husband acted in bad faith to avoid paying alimony.

TAX TREATMENT

11.24. Tax Treatment of Alimony

A payment to a spouse under a divorce or separation instrument is alimony if the spouses do not file a joint return and the payment meets both of two requirements. First, the payment must be based on the marital or family relationship; second, it must not be child support. In addition, the spouses must be separated and living apart for a payment under a separation agreement or court order to qualify as alimony.

For federal income tax purposes, alimony payments are included in the income of the payee and deductible from the income of the payor if, among other things, "there is no liability to make any such payment for any period after the death of the payee spouse and there is no liability to make any payment (in cash or property) as a substitute for such payments after the death of the payee spouse." 26 U.S.C.A. §§71(b)(1)(D), 215(b). As a result, in cases where a high-income payor pays alimony to a low-income recipient, the payor may enjoy some tax savings.

11.25. Alimony Distinguished from Property Division

Although alimony and property division are sometimes confused, alimony differs from property division in a variety of ways. First, alimony obligations cannot be discharged in bankruptcy, whereas some property obligations may be the object of discharge. Second, alimony is considered taxable income to the recipient and is deductible by the payor. Property settlements have no similar tax treatment. Third, alimony awards may be modified in the future, but property settlements are viewed as final. Fourth, alimony awards traditionally terminate upon the remarriage of the recipient, in contrast to property awards, which are not affected by remarriage. Finally, failure to pay alimony can be enforced by contempt proceedings, and enforcement of property awards generally occurs through traditional debtor-creditor remedies.

CHAPTER 12

Modification of Alimony

12.1. Introduction

This chapter examines the circumstances under which an existing alimony award may be modified. When a substantial change in circumstances occurs in the life of the obligor or the recipient, they may agree to a modification of an alimony award or a court may exercise its discretion to increase, decrease, or eliminate it. The issue of modification typically arises in cases where the obligor's income has increased, the recipient's income has decreased, the recipient has remarried, or one of the parties has died. Because a factual inquiry is central to determining whether modification is appropriate, a trial court's modification decision generally will not be overturned on appeal absent an abuse of discretion.

STANDARDS FOR MODIFICATION OF ALIMONY

12.2. UMDA's Unconscionability Standard

The Uniform Marriage and Divorce Act (UMDA) provides that an existing spousal support award can be modified only if a change in circumstances has occurred that is so substantial and continuing as to make the terms of the original agreement unconscionable. UMDA §316(b) (1974).

Unlike other provisions of the UMDA that have greatly influenced the development of the law in various areas, the UMDA standard for modification of alimony has not gained widespread acceptance among the states, most of which have adopted a less restrictive view.

12.3. State Standards Vary

Courts and legislatures use various legal standards for the purpose of modifying alimony awards. They specifically differ concerning how substantial a change in circumstances must be to warrant modification. *See Kamenski v. Kamenski*, 15 So. 3d 842 (Fla. App. 2009) (change is material, permanent, and involuntary); *Tsai v. Tien*, 832 N.E.2d 809 (Ohio App. 2005) (change need not be substantial or drastic, but it must be more than a nominal change); *Metz v. Metz*, 618 S.E.2d 477 (W. Va. 2005) (substantial change in circumstances); *Withers v. Withers*, 390 So. 2d 453 (Fla. Dist. Ct. App. 1980), *cert. denied*, 399 So. 2d 1147 (Fla. 1981) (substantial change not contemplated at time of judgment); *Zan v. Zan*, 820 N.E.2d 1284 (Ind. App. 2005) (change is so substantial and continuing that original terms are unreasonable); *Woodson v. Woodson*, 338 S.W.3d 261 (Ky. 2011) ("changed circumstances so substantial and continuing as to make the terms unconscionable"); *Beard v. Beard*, 751 N.Y.S.2d 304 (N.Y. App. 2002) (current order creates an "extreme hardship"). *But see Taylor v. Taylor*, 978 A.2d 538 (Conn. App. 2009) (where parties agreed that court would review alimony award at a certain point, with no change of circumstances required).

As the foregoing standards illustrate, it is important to consult the law of a particular state before initiating an action to modify an alimony award.

12.4. Change in Circumstances Must Be Subsequent and Unforeseeable

The relevant substantial change in circumstances must have occurred subsequent to the entry of the alimony award being modified. *See Metcalf v. Metcalf*, 769 N.W.2d 386 (Neb. 2009) (discussing time frame when there have been previous attempts to modify). Consequently, modification is not available to a party who regrets a settlement agreement or disagrees with a prior court determination. Similarly, as will be discussed in later sections of this chapter, if a change was foreseeable at the time of dissolution, courts will not consider it to be a substantial change in circumstances.

PROCEDURAL CONSIDERATIONS

12.5. Existing Order or Reservation of Jurisdiction

A court can modify an alimony award only if there is an order currently in effect, or if the court reserved subject matter jurisdiction over the issue at the time of the divorce. *See Midzak v. Midzak*, 697 N.W.2d 733 (S.D. 2005) (court expressly reserved jurisdiction); *Hartley v. Hartley*, 889 N.E.2d 1087 (Ohio App. 2008) (no "implied" reservation of jurisdiction). If a court did not award alimony in the original proceeding and failed to reserve jurisdiction, most courts hold that alimony cannot be awarded at a later date.

Similarly, once an alimony order has expired, it typically will not be reinstated or modified. *Cathey v. Cathey*, 707 S.E.2d 638 (N.C. App. 2011) (former wife unsuccessful in attempt to modify alimony after the award terminated).

12.6. Burden of Proof

The party seeking modification bears the burden of proving that a change in circumstances has occurred with respect to the needs of the recipient or the financial abilities of the obligor. *In re Marriage of Logston*, 469 N.E.2d 167, 176 (Ill. 1984); *Rice v. Rice*, 528 N.E.2d 14, 15 (Ill. App. 1988). For example, a former spouse's otherwise unsupported assertion that inflation had affected her ability to support herself was not sufficient to warrant modification of an existing alimony award. *Hillier v. Iglesias*, 901 So. 2d 947 (Fla. App. 2005). However, a showing of inability to obtain health insurance was a substantial change in circumstances for purposes of modification. *Metz v. Metz*, 618 S.E.2d 477 (W. Va. 2005).

12.7. Retroactivity

In most jurisdictions, orders modifying alimony agreements are potentially retroactive only to the date of filing a modification motion. However, the rule is not applied when the filing was delayed because of a misrepresentation by another party, so long as the motion is filed in a timely fashion after discovery of the misrepresentation. *See, e.g., Albert v. Albert*, 707 A.2d 234 (Pa. Super. Ct. 1998); *In re Marriage of Elenewski*, 828 N.E.2d 895 (Ill. App. 2005).

EXAMPLE

Example

1. Assume that P and D were divorced in 2007, and that D was ordered to pay alimony until November 30, 2011. D made the final alimony payment on October 15, 2011, approximately six weeks early. On October 30, 2011, P moved to modify the judgment, seeking a permanent alimony order. D moved for summary judgment on the grounds that the court no longer had jurisdiction over the issue of alimony because the order had been fully paid. P argued that D's voluntary early payment did not alter the due date and that the alimony order remained in effect because the final payment had not yet accrued. What is the likely result?

EXPLANATION

Explanation

1. This example is based on the situation in *In re Marriage of Harkins*, 115 P.3d 981 (Or. App. 2005), *review denied*, 136 P.3d 742 (2006). In that case, the court agreed with D and held that the court no longer had authority to modify the alimony award because payment had been made in full. Although some courts may take a different view, a wise practitioner will advise a client to petition for modification well in advance of the termination of the alimony order.

IMPACT OF AGREEMENTS ON SUBSEQUENT MOTIONS FOR MODIFICATION

12.8. Stipulations — Non-Modification Agreements

Purpose. Some potential obligors are reluctant to agree to pay time-limited alimony because of the possibility of later modification extending the payments or making them permanent. Consequently, in settlement negotiations, parties sometimes will agree that an alimony award cannot be modified, even in the event of a substantial change in circumstances. In essence, the recipient waives the right to seek subsequent modification of the award.

UMDA. Although courts have struggled with the issue of whether to enforce non-modification agreements, the UMDA strongly supports their approval and enforcement. §306(b) binds courts to agreements regarding alimony unless they are unconscionable. UMDA §306(f) states that "[e]xcept for terms concerning the support, custody, or visitation of children, the decree may expressly preclude or limit modification of terms set forth in the degree if the separation agreement so provides."

Enforcement. Courts usually enforce non-modification agreements, although they may review agreements for fraud, duress, or unconscionability. *See In re Marriage of Strieby*, 255 P.3d 34 (Kan. App. 2011) (pursuant to separation agreement, court could modify but not terminate alimony); *Maxwell v. Maxwell*, 650 S.E.2d 680 (S.C. App. 2007) (alimony "non-modifiable and shall continue until the death of the Husband"); *In re Marriage of Waldren*, 171 P.3d 1214 (Ariz. 2007) (statute providing for non-modification agreements prevents court from exercising jurisdiction); *In re Marriage of Hulscher*, 180 P.3d 199 (Wash. App. 2008) (non-modifiability provision valid and enforceable).

Agreement of parties. Absent an agreement by the parties, a court may not make alimony orders non-modifiable. *Blum v. Koster*, 919 N.E.2d 333, 346 (Ill. 2009) ("We agree with the appellate court that, absent the parties' express agreement, the Act does not permit a court to make a maintenance award non-modifiable and non-reviewable.").

EXAMPLE

Example

2. P and D divorced after 22 years of marriage. They owned a business, and to avoid liquidating it at the time of the divorce, they agreed that P would give up all interest in the business and that D would pay P $230,000 per year in alimony. The divorce judgment included the following: "It is the intention and understanding of the parties that the spousal support obligations of the defendant be non-modifiable regarding duration and amount . . . . This is the agreement of the parties, and it is the intention of the parties that regardless of any change in circumstances or in the lifestyles of plaintiff or defendant, this spousal support provision is to be non-modifiable." Due to financial improprieties of a manager, the business became insolvent and closed. D seeks modification of the alimony award. What is the likely result?

EXPLANATION

Explanation

2. In the case of *Rose v. Rose*, 289 N.W.2d 611 (Mich. App. 2010), on which this example is based, the appellate court enforced the non-modification agreement. Although sympathetic to the plight of D, the court was persuaded that valid non-modification agreements should be enforced. The court reviewed previous cases, concluding that enforcement of such agreements promotes public policy by allowing parties to structure their financial agreements, ensuring post-divorce predictability and achieving cost savings for parties and courts.

OBLIGOR'S CHANGE IN CIRCUMSTANCES

12.9. Obligor's Unanticipated Increased Income

An unanticipated large increase in the obligor's income may constitute a substantial, material change in circumstances. But if the increase does not make the original alimony award unfair, and the original award maintains the marital standard of living, most jurisdictions will not grant an increase in alimony.

For example, in the case of *Schwarz v. Schwarz*, 5 A.3d 548 (Conn. App. 2010), the former husband's gross income increased from $373,620 to $450,000 per year, and the appellate court determined that this increase was large enough to consititute a substantial change in circumstances. Examining the statutory factors with respect to the recipient's need and the obligor's ability to pay, the trial court did not abuse its discretion by increasing the alimony payment, particularly in light of the former wife's increased need.

12.10. Obligor's Retirement

Totality of circumstances. Retirement from the labor force does not necessarily consitute a substantial and material change in circumstances warranting modification of an alimony award. Courts examine the totality of the circumstances surrounding the retirement to determine whether it is objectively reasonable. In *Ebach v. Ebach*, 700 N.W.2d 684 (N.D. 2005), the court considered the following nonexclusive list of factors in determining the totality of the circumstances:

> A court may consider, for instance, the age gap between the parties; whether at the time of the initial [spousal support] award any attention was given by the parties to the possibility of future retirement; whether the particular retirement was mandatory or voluntary; whether the particular retirement occurred earlier than might have been anticipated at the time [spousal support] was awarded; and the financial impact of that retirement upon the respective financial positions of the parties. It should also assess the motivation which led to the decision to retire, i.e., was it reasonable under all the circumstances or motivated primarily by a desire to reduce the [spousal support] of a former spouse. A court may also wish to consider the degree of control retained by the parties over the disbursement of their retirement income, e.g., the ability to defer receipt of some or all. It may also wish to consider whether either spouse has transferred assets to others, thus reducing the amount available to meet their financial needs and obligations.

Id. at 689.

The burden of establishing that the retirement is objectively reasonable is on the party seeking modification of the award. *Seal v. Seal*, 802 S.W.2d 617, 620 (Tenn. App. 1990).

Foreseeability. When the retirement was foreseeable at the time of the divorce, a subseqent motion to reduce or terminate alimony payments may be denied. *See Wheeler v. Wheeler*, 548 N.W.2d 27 (N.D. 1996); *Leslie v. Leslie*, 827 S.W.2d 180, 183 (Mo. 1992); *Ellis v. Ellis*, 262 N.W.2d 265, 268 (Iowa 1978); *Deegan v. Deegan*, 603 A.2d 542 (N.J. App. 1992) (retirement should have been considered when parties originally divorced). Courts have held that at some point, parties must recognize that just as a married couple may expect a reduction in income because of retirement, a divorced spouse cannot expect to receive the same level of support after the supporting spouse retires. *See Pierce v. Pierce*, 916 N.E.2d 330 (Mass. 2009) (voluntary retirement warranted downward modification, but not termination of alimony); *Silvan v. Sylvan*, 632 A.2d 528 (N.J. Super. 1993) (concluding that a good-faith retirement at age 65 may warrant a finding of changed circumstances); *In re Marriage of Reynolds*, 71 Cal. Rptr. 2d 636, 640 (Cal. App. 1998).

12.11. Obligor's Change of Occupation

Involuntary reduction and mitigation. Courts may grant a temporary reduction or suspension in alimony payments when the obligor has suffered an involuntary reduction in income and is acting in good faith to return his or her income to its previous level.

Voluntary reduction and mitigation. A party ordinarily will not be relieved of part of or all an alimony obligation by voluntarily quitting work or accepting lower-paid employment. When seeking a reduction in alimony payments because of a change in employment, the obligor first must establish that the voluntary change in employment, which resulted in a reduction of income, was not made for the purpose of avoiding alimony payments and then establish that a reduction in alimony is warranted based on the party's efforts to mitigate income loss.

Bad faith. Courts have consistently ruled that obligors act in bad faith when they voluntarily change employment without alternate plans to generate income or when they are fired for misconduct. *See Curtis v. Curtis*, 442 N.W.2d 173, 177-178 (Minn. App. 1989) (holding that obligor acted in bad faith when he voluntarily left his employment of ten years without alternative employment plans); *Warwick v. Warwick*, 438 N.W.2d 673, 678 (Minn. App. 1989) (holding that obligor acted in bad faith by resigning from his job, unjustifiably limiting his income); *Juelfs v. Juelfs*, 359 N.W.2d 667, 670 (Minn. App. 1984) (holding that obligor acted in bad faith by voluntarily quitting long-time employment in favor of running a business that had little chance of producing similar income).

Imputation. Income commensurate with that previously earned may be imputed to an oblgor who incurs a reduction in income but who, as discussed above, is not relieved of an alimony obligation by the court. In such cases, a court may apply the earnings capacity standard. *See Pencovic v. Pencovic*, 287 P.2d 501 (Call. 1955) (the earning capacity standard is properly used when the paying parent willfully refuses to seek or accept gainful employment). A finding of good faith does not prevent application of the earning capacity standard. Although deliberate avoidance of family responsibilites is a significant factor in the decision to impute income, a trial court's consideration of earning capacity is not limited to cases in which a deliberate attempt to avoid support responsibilities is found. *See In re Marriage of Ilas*, 16 Cal. Rptr. 2d 345 (Cal. App. 1993).

12.12. Death of an Obligor

When an obligor dies, the maintenance obligation generally terminates unless stated otherwise in a court order. *See Findley v. Findley*, 629 S.E.2d 222 (Ga. 2006) (death of obligor terminates obligation to pay alimony); *Haville v. Haville*, 825 N.E.2d 375 (Ind. 2005) (order may continue spousal maintenance beyond the death of the obligor).

EXAMPLES

Examples

3. Assume that P and D divorced after a 20-year marriage. At the time of the divorce, they were both unemployed; however, D was receiving $3,000 each month from a trust. The court ordered that D pay P $500 per month in permanent alimony. A year after the divorce, D obtained a position that paid $5,000 a month. P remained unemployed and moved to increase alimony to $1,000 a month. How will a court most likely treat the motion?

4. Assume that P and D had been married for 25 years before they divorce. The court ordered that D pay P $1,500 a month permanent alimony. Following the divorce, P lived on the alimony payment plus a few hundred dollars that D took from an individual retirement account (IRA) each month. The IRA had a value of about $50,000. At the time of the divorce, D was earning about $5,000 a month. When he reached age 60, D voluntarily retired because he was offered a retirement package that would guarantee him $2,000 per month for life. D was also

suspicious of being laid off or fired, and D felt that coping with the boss was getting increasingly difficult. D now moves to reduce the alimony obligation. How will a court most likely treat D's motion?

5. Assume that P and D divorced and that D was ordered to pay alimony to P based on D's employment as a computer hardware specialist earning $111,000 per year. D lost his job because of a reduction in the workforce, and one month later, he took a position as a massage therapist earning $300 per week (approximately $15,000 per year). D petitioned to reduce the alimony payment, arguing that the order should be based on his present lower income given that his change of position was involuntary. P argues that the alimony payment should be calculated based on the prevailing wage for computer service technicians because D elected to pursue a less lucrative career. What is the likely result?

6. P and D's 15-year marriage was dissolved, and the court ordered D to pay $250 per month in alimony for 60 months. At the time of the dissolution, D was employed as a line technician earning about $24 per hour. He resigned from this position after about 18 years with the company. His resignation was precipitated by his failing a random drug test. A few months later, D also quit a second job because of a mutual disagreement with his employer. At D's request, the district court reduced his alimony obligation to $125 per month because he was now earning about half of what he had been earning at the time of the divorce. P appealed. How would an appellate court most likely treat the reduced alimony?

EXPLANATIONS

Explanations

3. P will argue that D's financial worth has increased substantially and that D can afford to pay additional alimony. P will explain that P cannot make ends meet on $500 per month and that P should be entitled to a standard of living more commensurate with that of the marriage. D will argue that P's needs haven't increased since the original alimony order was entered and that one of the purposes of divorce is to end the parties' financial interdependency. However, if P can establish her needs clearly, the court most likely will grant the request. *See Irwin v. Irwin*, 539 So. 2d 1177 (Fla. App. 1990).

4. D may have a difficult time obtaining a reduction, even though D acted in good faith. P will argue that P has relied on the alimony and that early retirement should have been addressed at the time of the divorce. A court may reduce the obligation if D has only the $2,000 to live on. Otherwise, the award well may stand. *See Deegan v. Deegan*, 603 A.2d 542 (N.J. App. 1992).

5. In the similar case of *Storey v. Storey*, 862 A.2d 551 (N.J. Super. 2004), the court imputed to D annual earnings of $60,000, the prevailing wage for a computer service technician. Although D's departure from his job was involuntary, the court held that because he had selected a less lucrative career, D had the burden of establishing that the resulting benefit to him substantially outweighed the disadvantages to P. The court found that D's decision was not reasonable under the circumstances.

6. As a general rule, a petition for modification will be denied if the change in financial condition is because of fault or voluntary wastage or dissipation of one's talents and assets. *See Grahovac v. Grahovac*, 680 N.W.2d 616 (Neb. App. 2004). It is undisputed that in this case, there has been a change in D's financial condition and that he is now earning approximately half as much as he once earned. However, the issue is whether the change was because of D's fault or voluntary wastage or dissipation of his talents and assets. Most courts would rule that the reduction in income was D's own fault and would not permit a modification on these facts. The appellate court most likely would reverse the trial court.

RECIPIENT'S CHANGE IN CIRCUMSTANCES

12.13. Recipient Becomes Self-Sufficient

Courts sometimes modify alimony awards based on an improvement in the financial circumstances of the recipient. If, for example, an unemployed recipient becomes employed, courts consider whether the employment was foreseeable at the time of the divorce and the extent to which the position provides funds sufficient to allow the recipient to live at the standard of living enjoyed during the marriage. The fact that the recipient's income has increased does not necessarily indicate that the recipient's long-term economic circumstances have improved to such an extent that alimony is no longer required or should be reduced.

In the case of *Daunhauer v. Daunhauer*, 295 S.W.3d 154 (Ky. App. 2009), the court terminated a 20-year alimony award that was rehabilitative in nature because the oblgee no longer depended on it and had the ability to meet her own needs. The court found the "change in the parties' circumstances so substantial and continuing as to render the continuation of the maintenance obligation unconscionable." *Id.* at 155.

In contrast, in *Block v. Block*, 717 N.Y.S.2d 24 (N.Y. App. Div. 2000), a court rejected a modification request when the ex-wife procured employment before the expiration of durational alimony. The alimony award was scheduled to expire when the parties' youngest child entered kindergarten. The court observed that although the original order awarding alimony stated that it would be "difficult" for the wife to return to work before the parties' youngest child entered kindergarten, "that possibility was not ruled out, and it certainly was not an unforeseeable event that could not have been taken into account in setting the original award." *Id.* at 87. *See Matter of Hermans v. Hermans*, 547 N.E.2d 87 (N.Y. 1989) (particularized showing of facts concerning the personal and financial circumstances of the parties, both at the time of the original divorce settlement and at the present time, is required, and changes in the prevailing social and legal climate that may have occurred since the parties were divorced do not satisfy this standard); *Wheeler v. Wheeler*, 230 A.D.2d 844 (N.Y. App. Div. 1996) (court erred in terminating maintenance when recipient's earning potential increased as a result of her receiving a nursing degree when there was a substantial increase in the obligor's income between the time of the parties' divorce and the modification hearing).

12.14. Recipient's Need Increases

A recipient's need for support may increase as a result of illness, disability, or inability to become employed as planned. Such events may constitute a substantial change in circumstances warranting an upward modification or a continuation of payments that are set to expire. However, courts typically examine changes with respect to foreseeability — if it is foreseeable at the time of divorce, modification will not be forthcoming.

12.15. Remarriage of a Recipient

Automatic termination. In many jurisdictions, alimony is terminated automatically on the remarriage of the recipient except for rare exceptions where the parties' agreement or the divorce decree expressly provides otherwise. *See Gibb v. Sepe*, 690 N.W.2d 230 (N.D. 2004) (express agreement that alimony would continue after remarriage enforced). The theory is that after remarriage, the recipient has formed a legal relationship with another who has assumed a joint legal duty of support. *See, e.g., Voyles v. Voyles*, 644 P.2d 847 (Alaska 1982); *Burr v. Burr*, 353 N.W.2d 644 (Minn. App. 1984), *Van Bloom v. Van Bloom*, 246 N.W.2d 588 (Neb. 1976).

Extraordinary circumstance. Some states do not provide for automatic termination of an alimony award on remarriage of the recipient spouse. Instead, the remarriage establishes a *prima facie* case for termination or reduction of the alimony payments. *See, e.g., Oman v. Oman*, 702 N.W.2d 11 (S.D. 2005); *Keller v. O'Brien*, 652 N.E.2d 589, 593 (Mass. 1995); *Marquardt v. Marquardt*, 396 N.W.2d 753, 754 (S.D. 1986). In these jurisdictions, the receiving spouse may continue to receive maintenance, but only in an extraordinary circumstance. *See, e.g., In re Marriage of Gillilland*, 487 N.W.2d 363, 366 (Iowa App. 1992) (extraordinary circumstance found when standard of living provided by new spouse with annual income of $30,000 would not meet standard of living during previous marriage to husband who earned $220,000 annually); *Bauer v. Bauer*, 356 N.W.2d 897, 898-899 (N.D. 1984) (extraordinary circumstance found when payor and recipient had large disparity in education and payor's unfulfilled agreement to pay for recipient's education was incorporated in original decree).

Change in circumstance analysis. In other states, remarriage is treated as any other potential change in circumstances, and courts consider the purpose of the alimony and examine the extent to which the need has been obviated by remarriage. For example, in *In re Marriage of Frost*, 260 P.3d 570 (Or. App. 2011), the court determined that the purpose of an alimony award was to remedy disparity in income and that the recipient's remarriage had done this. Consequently, the alimony award was terminated.

12.16. Cohabitation by a Recipient

Need analysis. In many states, when a recipient of alimony cohabits, the right to receive alimony is subject to modification or termination only to the extent that the recipient spouse's need for the support decreases as a result of the cohabitation. *See Schuchard v. Schuchard*, 292 S.W.3d 498 (Mo. App. 2009) (court failed to consider financial contribution of wife's new same-sex partner); *Miller v. Miller*, 892 A.2d 175 (Vt. 2005) (cohabitation must improve financial circumstances enough to reduce need for maintenance substantially); *Woodard v. Woodard*, 696 N.W.2d 221 (Wis. App. 2005) (recipient benefited from cohabitant's income); *Gayet v. Gayet*, 456 A.2d 102 (N.J. 1983). Thus, shared living arrangements, unaccompanied by evidence of a decrease in the actual financial needs of the recipient, generally are insufficient to warrant alimony modification. *See In re Marriage of Bross*, 845 P.2d 728, 731-732 (Mont. 1993); *Mitchell v. Mitchell*, 418 A.2d 1140, 1143 (Me. 1980) (cohabitant's benefit from a recipient's expenditures on heating fuel, which would have a similar cost absent the shared living arrangements, does not show a decreased need for alimony).

Presumption. Some states view cohabitation as a presumed substantial change in circumstances and they assess it as such. *See Wallace v. Wallace*,

12 So. 3d 572 (Miss. App. 2009) (proof of cohabitation creates presumption of material change in circumstances, shifting burden to the recipient spouse to prove lack of mutual support).

Termination. A few states liken cohabitiation to remarriage in that they authorize termination of alimony if a recipient cohabits. *See Underwood v. Underwood*, 717 S.E.2d 361 (N.C. 2011) (statute requires termination based on recipient cohabitation); *Myers v. Myers*, 231 P.3d 815 (Utah App. 2010) (analyzing statutory language). *See also Wallace v. Wallace*, 12 So. 3d 572 (Miss. App. 2009) (proof of cohabitation creates a presumption that a material change in circumstances has occurred).

Agreements. When a restriction regarding cohabitation is a part of a marital termination agreement, courts typically enforce the provision. *See Marshall v. Marshall*, 988 A.2d 314 (Conn. App. 2010); *Bell v. Bell*, 468 N.E.2d 849 (Mass. 1984).

Definition. Defining cohabitation has proved challenging in various fact situations. *See Remillard v. Remillard*, 999 A.2d 713 (Conn. 2010) (cohabition requires a sexual or romantic relationship); *Chopin v. Chopin*, 232 P.3d 583 (Ariz. App. 2010) (living together as an "indispensible factor" of cohabitation); *Biggins v. Burdette*, 708 S.E.2d 237 (S.C. App. 2011) (alleged cohabitants did not spend 90 consecutive nights together).

12.17. Death of a Recipient

Under UMDA §316(b), the recipient's death terminates ongoing alimony payments. Nevertheless, when a lump-sum alimony award has been ordered, it is viewed by some courts as vested in the recipient, and a spouse's estate may receive the payment. *See, e.g., Maxcy v. Estate of Maxcy*, 485 So. 2d 1077, 1078 (Miss. 1986) (installment payments resulting from division of assets remained payable after obligor's death).

Examples

7. When H and W divorced, the judgment required H to pay alimony to W. A subsequent modification (based on a stipulation by the parties) included the following: "Said maintenance obligation shall terminate only upon the death of Respondent or September 30, 2011, whichever occurs first." A statute provides that "[u]nless otherwise agreed in

writing or expressly provided in the judgment, the obligation to pay future statutory maintenance is terminated upon the death of either party or the remarriage of the party receiving maintenance." Under state law, it is rebuttably presumed that maintenance terminates under these conditions. When W remarries, H seeks to terminate the alimony payments. What is the likely result?

8. Assume that P and D divorce after a traditional 20-year marriage. P is required to pay D $1,000 per month permanent alimony. Six months after the divorce is final, D moves in with X. P brings a motion to eliminate the alimony award, arguing that it is unfair to require him to pay alimony when his ex-wife and another man are living together much like husband and wife. P argues that cohabiting is so similar to remarriage that it terminates spousal support. D responds that X is not supporting her and has no legal obligation to do so. P also notes that there is not a provision in the final divorce decree that eliminates alimony should she move in with another person following divorce. How will the court most likely rule?

9. At the time of divorce, P is awarded alimony "until P dies or remarries." Nine years after the divorce, P and her same-sex partner go through a marriage ceremony in a state that does not recognize same-sex marriages. D learns of the "marriage" and moves to terminate the alimony. What is the likely result?

10. When P and D divorce, D agrees to pay alimony to P. The divorce decree provides that alimony is to terminate "upon cohabitation of the Wife with an unrelated male." A year after the divorce, D moves to terminate alimony payments based on his assertion that D and their children were living in a "commune" with another family. What is the likely result?

11. P seeks to terminate his alimony payments to D, alleging that she is cohabiting with her boyfriend. According to D and her boyfriend, they had a relationship spanning 18 months, but there were periods of time when they did not see each other for a month or two. They stayed together for a couple of long weekends each month and went on a vacation together. The boyfriend dated other women and did not assume any of D's expenses. Based on information from the children and pictures of the boyfriend's car taken by P, he alleged that the boyfriend stayed over more frequently. What is the likely result?

Explanations

7. In this situation, the stipulation of the parties is at odds with state law. W will argue that the language in the stipulation and judgment rebuts the presumption. Nevertheless, in the case of *Maddick v. Deshon*, 296 S.W.3d 519 (Mo. App. 2009), the appellate court required an express statement that an alimony obligation would survive remarriage of the recipient — inference was not sufficient to rebut the presumption.

8. In ruling on P's request, the trial court may consider what effect, if any, D's cohabitation with another person has had on D's financial circumstances. If X makes financial or other tangible contributions toward the living expenses of D, D's ability to support herself may be enhanced, her needs may be reduced, and in some cases, the alimony award may be reduced accordingly; conversely, when the expenses of D are increased because of D's voluntary support of persons whom D is under no duty to support, a court may disregard those expenses to the extent that they are claimed by the recipient as evidence of increased "need." Here, a court would have to conduct an evidentiary hearing to make these determinations. Only then could it make a sound decision. *See Gilman v. Gilman*, 956 P.2d 761 (Nev. 1998).

9. D will argue that P is married and that under the terms of the divorce decree, his obligation to make alimony payments is over. P will argue that since the state will not recognize her "marriage" to her same-sex partner, she is not legally married for the purpose of terminating the alimony payments. Based on the similar case of *In re Marriage of Bureta*, 164 P.3d 534 (Wash. App. 2007), the court would find that P is not legally married and would require D to continue making the payments. However, D has the option of arguing that P's financial circumstances have changed as a result of the cohabitation.

10. In a case such as this, the court is called upon to determine what constitutes "cohabitation." In the similar case of *Clark v. Clark*, 827 N.Y.S.2d 159 (2006), the court found that sharing a house with another family was not sufficient to establish cohabitation under the divorce decree, especially because P had a certificate of occupancy for an "accessory apartment" and was paying rent to the owner. Courts are called on to make factual determinations about the definition of "cohabitation" with increasing frequency. *See Semken v. Semken*, 664 S.E.2d 493 (S.C. App. 2008) (statute defines continued "cohabitation" as residence for at least 90 consecutive days); *Graev v. Graev*, 898 N.E.2d 909 (N.Y. 2008) (reviewing multiple definitions of "cohabitation").

11. This example is based on the case of *Bishop v. Bishop*, 2010 WL 4151988 (Ala. App. 2010). The appellate court held that there was insufficient evidence that that D's relationship was of sufficient permanence to support a finding of cohabitation and consequent modification of alimony.

CHAPTER 13

Dividing the Marital Estate upon Divorce

13.1. Introduction

This chapter surveys the law and illustrates the application of the more common legal principles used by family courts to guide them in arriving at an appropriate distribution of marital and nonmarital property when a couple divorce. Note at the outset that an appropriate distribution may be equitable but not necessarily equal. *Hattaway v. Hattaway*, 2012 WL 1795090 (Tenn. App. 2012) (court has discretion to distribute property equitably — "An equitable distribution is not necessarily an equal one"); *Lurie v. Lurie*, 94 A.D.3d 1376 (N.Y. App. 2012) ("It is well established that equitable distribution of marital property does not necessarily mean equal, and [court] has substantial discretion in fashioning an award of equitable distribution"); *Chartier v. Chartier*, 815 N.W.2d 409 (Iowa App. 2012) (an equitable distribution of the parties' net worth should be a distribution that approximates an equal division but also takes into consideration the wife's health and that the husband still enjoys some earning capacity).

Family court tasks. When valuing and distributing marital property, most agree that the parties and a family court judge have three tasks. *See Alston v. Alston*, 629 A.2d 70 (Md. 1993); *Hanson v. Hanson*, 125 P.3d 299 (Alaska 2005). First, the parties gather and attempt to classify the couple's assets as martial property and nonmarital property. The nonmarital property usually will remain the separate property of each party.

Once the couple's property is classified, the second step is to place a reasonable value on those assets that are subject to distribution as marital assets. Finally, if the parties cannot agree, the family court judge makes a decision about what constitutes an equitable distribution of the martial assets. The distribution then is included in the final judgment ending the marriage. Note that in some jurisdictions, statutes allow judges to invade nonmarital assets under unusual circumstances. *See, e.g.*, Minn. Stat. §518.58, subd. 2 (1988) (allowing judges to award up to one-half of a spouse's nonmarital property to the other spouse if necessary to prevent unfair hardship).

PROPERTY DISTRIBUTION THEORIES

13.2. Separate and Community Property Theories

During the past century, courts have applied three general distribution theories when dividing marital property upon divorce. *See* Stephen J. Brake, *Equitable Distribution vs. Fixed Rules: Marital Property Reform and the Uniform Marital Property Act*, 23 B.C. L. Rev. 761, 762 (1982). The three distribution theories or "systems" are the now-outdated separate property system; the community property system, which is used today in about eight jurisdictions; and the equitable distribution system, which is used today by a majority of jurisdictions.

Separate property distribution theory. The now-disregarded separate property distribution theory was based on the view that each party was entitled to retain an asset to which that party had title. Should a couple divorce, the property was returned to the title-holding spouse.

The separate property distribution theory was criticized as unjust, especially in a traditional family setting where most of the marital property was titled in the husband's name. The separate property distribution system refused to recognize a homemaker's nonfinancial contributions to the marriage. Worse, if both spouses worked outside the home and the husband's income was placed into investments while the wife's earnings were devoted to family expenses, the husband usually received all the investments upon divorce.

Community property theory. Arizona, California, Idaho, Louisiana, New Mexico, Nevada, Texas, and Washington are currently recognized as community property states. Wisconsin closely aligned itself with the community property theory when it adopted the Uniform Marital Property Act.

The community property theory rests upon a system of co-ownership of assets between spouses during marriage. The concept came from continental Europe and found its way to the American territories governed by Spain and France. In general, all property, with the exception of that acquired by gift, devise, or descent, is community property and is owned equally by the spouses for purposes of division in the event of divorce or the death of one spouse. When a marital community no longer exists, there can be no community property because there is no longer any common enterprise to which each spouse is contributing. It should be noted that community property laws in the various states that have adopted this distribution theory are not necessarily uniform. *See generally* John G. Brant, *Colorado: Now A Community Property State?* Colo. Law., 55 (May 1996). *See also* Scott Greene, *Comparison of the Property Aspects of the Community Property and Common-Law Marital Property Systems and Their Relative Compatibility with the Current View of the Marriage Relationship and the Rights of Women*, 13 Creighton L. Rev. 71, 97 (1979); Harry M. Cross, *The Community Property Law*, 61 Wash. L. Rev. 13 (1986) (providing an excellent explanation of the mechanics of a community property system).

Acquisition point in community property jurisdictions. In general, in a community property jurisdiction, property acquired during the marriage is community property, and property acquired prior to marriage is separate property. A basic tenet of community property law is that property acquires its character as community or separate property depending upon the marriage status of its owner at the time of acquisition. *Lawson v. Ridgeway*, 233 P.2d 459 (Ariz. 1951) (lots acquired before marriage were husband's separate property). "Time of acquisition" refers to the time at which the right to obtain title occurs, not to the time when legal title actually is conveyed. *Hollingsworth v. Hicks*, 258 P.2d 724 (N.M. 1953) (property to which one spouse has acquired an equitable right before marriage is separate property, though such right is not perfected until after marriage). Once identified, the status of community or separate property becomes fixed and retains that character until changed by agreement of the parties or by operation of law. *Horton v. Horton*, 278 P. 370 (Ariz. 1929).

Marriage is a partnership. Community property jurisdictions accept the theory that a marriage is a partnership, and the partnership concept applies during the marriage as well as upon divorce. A divorce sometimes is analogized to the dissolution of a business partnership. "Regardless of the economic circumstances of business partners or of their moral conduct during the existence of the partnership, on dissolution the partners receive a portion of the assets commensurate with their respective partnership interests." *In re Marriage of Brigden*, 145 Cal. Rptr. 716, 723 (Cal. App. 1978).

As noted earlier in this chapter, in general, both spouses are vested in all the property acquired during the marriage, other than property that by statute is specifically excluded from the community, such as a gift to one partner but not the other or an inheritance to one partner but not the other. There are, of course, some limits on the application of the partnership theory in community property jurisdictions. For example, Arizona holds that a residence that is separate property does not change its character just because it is used as a family home and mortgage payments are made from community funds. *See Drahos v. Rens*, 717 P.2d 927, 928 (Ariz. App. 1985). However, because the community contributed capital to the separate property, it is entitled to compensation and has the right to an equitable lien against that property even though the property's character has not changed. *Ibid. But see Waldman v. Maini*, 195 P.3d 850 (Nev. 2008) (although life insurance policies were purchased with community funds, Nevada's Uniform Simultaneous Death Act precluded the division of life insurance proceeds as community property).

Community property presumptions. Community property states generally use presumptions. For example, in Texas, there is a presumption that property possessed by either spouse during a marriage is community property. If separate property and community property become so commingled as to defy resegregation and identification, the statutory presumption prevails. *Jones v. Jones*, 890 S.W.2d 471 (Tex. App. 1994). In *Smith v. Lanier*, 998 S.W.2d 324 (Tex. App. 1999), the court held that debts contracted during marriage are presumed to be on the credit of the community and are joint community obligations. The presumption is overcome if it is shown that the creditor agreed to look solely to the separate estate of the contracting spouse.

Partner's death. In a community property state, a spouse acquires a present vested undivided one-half interest in all property acquired during the existence of the marital relationship, regardless of the state of title. *Carpenter v. Carpenter*, 722 P.2d 230 (Ariz. 1986) (statutory death benefit was a community property interest, and ex-spouse entitled to one-half community share in the death benefit). When a spouse dies intestate, the survivor is viewed by law as owning one-half of the community property. The remaining issue involves the division of the deceased's one-half interest in the community property. In contrast, when a spouse dies intestate in a non–community property jurisdiction, intestacy laws may provide the survivor with a portion of or all of the deceased's estate.

13.3. Equitable Distribution Theory

Majority apply equitable distribution theory. The separate property distribution theory, discussed earlier in this chapter, has been rejected in all jurisdictions and replaced in a majority of states with the equitable distribution theory. The equitable distribution theory is a corollary of the principle that marriage is a joint enterprise whose vitality, success, and endurance depend on the conjunction of multiple components, only one of which is financial. *Mickey v. Mickey*, 974 A.2d 641 (Conn. 2009) (marriage is a shared enterprise or joint undertaking in the nature of a partnership to which both spouses contribute—directly and indirectly, financially and nonfinancially—the fruits of which are distributable at divorce); *Hall v. Hall*, 462 A.2d 1179 (Me. 1983) (contention that the property is entirely separate is inconsistent with the partnership theory). An equitable distribution jurisdiction views the nonremunerated efforts of raising children, making a home, performing a myriad of personal services, and providing physical and emotional support as important to a marriage and entitled to substantial recognition. Courts applying the equitable distribution theory recognize that a whole complex of financial and nonfinancial components measures the extent to which each party contributes to the marriage. When a marriage ends, each of the spouses, based on the totality of their contributions, has a right to a share of the marital assets because they represent the capital product of what was essentially a joint enterprise.

Nonmarital property. Legislatures in equitable distribution jurisdictions usually have excluded from the definition of marital property the following: (1) property acquired before the marriage, (2) property acquired by inheritance or gift from a third party during the marriage, (3) property excluded by valid agreement between the parties such as found in a premarital contract, or (4) property that is directly traceable to any of these sources.

Presumption of equal division. In several, but not all jurisdictions, a trial court initially will presume that all marital property is to be divided equally between the parties. *See Thompson v. Thompson*, 811 N.E.2d 888, 912 (Ind. App. 2004) (court presumes equal division of the marital property between the parties is just and reasonable—presumption may be rebutted by a party who presents relevant evidence that an equal division would not be just and reasonable). The presumption is applied regardless of how title is held—that is, regardless of whose name is on the legal document showing ownership of an asset. *But see Sfreddo v. Sfreddo*, 720 S.E.2d 145, 153 (Va. App. 2012) (Virginia equitable distribution law "does not establish a presumption of equal distribution of marital assets"); *Hess v. Hess*, 475 A.2d 796, 799 (Pa. Super. 1984) (equitable distribution does not presume an equal division of marital property, and "the goal of economic justice will often dictate otherwise").

Overcoming presumption. Parties can overcome the marital property presumptions found in most state statutes upon a proper showing that the property is nonmarital. For example, in most jurisdictions, if a party can show that a marital asset was acquired in exchange for nonmarital property, the presumption that the property was marital can be overcome. *See, e.g.*, *Kottke v. Kottke*, 353 N.W.2d 633, 636 (Minn. App. 1984), *pet. for rev. denied* (Minn. Dec. 20, 1984) (portion of homestead readily traceable to an earlier inheritance by wife was lawfully viewed as nonmarital property in dividing property of parties in dissolution proceeding, even though inherited funds were not placed in an account separate from joint account with husband). In several jurisdictions, the presumption also may be overcome by a finding that the property was acquired by one spouse and the purchase was not influenced directly or indirectly by the other spouse; that is, the other spouse contributed neither economically nor otherwise to the acquisition of the property. *See, e.g.*, *In re Marriage of Kunze*, 92 P.3d 100 (Or. 2004) (although the inquiry into the "just and proper" division necessarily includes consideration of the statutory factors, including the court's determination under the presumption of equal contribution, that inquiry also takes into account the social and financial objectives of the dissolution, as well as any other considerations that bear upon the question of what division of the marital property is equitable).

Conduct reducing value of property. Courts in some jurisdictions may consider a spouse's conduct that reduced the value of marital property as evidence in support of not applying the presumption that all marital property is to be divided equally between the parties. *See, e.g.*, *Somerville v. Somerville*, 369 S.E.2d 459, 460 (W. Va. 1988) (West Virginia statute permits court to consider the extent to which each party, during the marriage, may have conducted himself or herself so as to dissipate or depreciate the value of the marital property of the parties, but may not consider fault or unrelated marital misconduct).

13.4. Source of Funds Theory

Source of funds theory. The source of funds theory is in contradistinction to the old "inception of title" theory. Under this theory, if a spouse purchased a home prior to marriage with a cash down payment and a mortgage, and paid off the mortgage with money earned during the marriage, the purchasing spouse would own all the property of the home. However, under the source of funds theory, the spouse making the down payment would receive an amount directly proportional to the initial investment and the purchase price, but then divide the balance equally with his or her spouse. *See generally* Thomas P. Leff, *Developments in Maryland Law*, 1992-93, 53 Md. L. Rev. 881, n. 31 (1994). *But see Gordon v. Gordon*, 923 A.2d 149, 177 (Md. 2007) ("The Source of the Funds theory, to determine what part of a property is marital and what part is nonmarital, is not applicable to real estate held by tenants by the entireties; all real property owned by tenants by the entireties 'is' marital property").

Transmutation through commingling. Some jurisdictions have adopted the theory of "transmutation through commingling." For example, a jurisdiction may find that when the married couple improves nonmarital real property, that property is transmuted into marital property. Under that theory, the affirmative acts of augmenting separate property by commingling it with marital resources is viewed as indicative of an intent to transmute, or transform, the separate property to marital property. *See In re Marriage of Smith*, 427 N.E.2d 1239 (Ill. 1981) (failure of nonmarital property holder to segregate that property will give rise to rebuttable presumption that nonmarital property had been transmuted, regardless of status of title).

If a jurisdiction has not adopted the source of funds theory, a spouse who commingles separate property with marital property may be viewed as causing the separate property to lose its nonmarital character. Courts will then consider all of the commingled property as marital property and subject it to equitable distribution. *See, e.g., Smoot v. Smoot*, 357 S.E.2d 728 (Va. 1987) (Virginia's equitable distribution statute does not adopt source of funds doctrine and thus, when spouse fails to segregate and instead commingles separate property with marital property, chancellor must classify commingled property as marital property subject to equitable distribution).

13.5. The Transmutation Doctrine

Transmutation has already been discussed to some extent in this chapter in the previous "Source of Funds Theory" section. This section is intended to expand on the transmutation doctrine. Transmutation is a judicially created doctrine that generally is applied to prevent unfairness in the distribution of assets. When applied, property that once was classified as separate or nonmarital can be transmuted into marital property when a spouse with title to property represents to the other spouse that the property will be shared by the couple. *See Heustess v. Kelley-Heustess*, 158 P.3d 827 (Alaska 2007) (wife's house, which originally was separate, nonmarital property, transmuted into marital property through the husband's financial and personal contributions, as well as the intent of both parties to use the home as the marital residence). Transmutation allows a spouse to transform an item of nonmarital property into marital property by agreement, either express or implied, or by gift. For example, nonmarital property may be changed into marital property if a gift of nonmarital property is converted into co-tenancy with the other party. However, because technical application of the transmutation rule can result in unfair results, courts often will consider that equitable considerations take precedence over a mechanical application of the transmutation rule.

In most jurisdictions, nonmarital property does not transmute automatically into marital property solely because it may have become commingled with marital property. Rather, courts will examine carefully the owner's intent to convert the property to marital property in deciding how to characterize it. *See Ker v. Ker*, 776 S.W.2d 873, 877 (Mo. App. 1989) (holding that "[n]onmarital property may lose its character as such if there is evidence of an intention to contribute the property to the community"); *D.K.H. v. L.R.G.*, 102 S.W.3d 93, 100 (Mo. App. 2003) (wife proved by clear and convincing evidence that real property was her separate property); *Pirri v. Pirri*, 631 S.E.2d 279 (S.C. App. 2006) (wife failed to prove transmutation of husband's separate property); *Hanson v. Hanson*, 125 P.3d 299 (Alaska 2005) (nonmarital property cannot be transmuted to marital property based on evidence — oral, behavioral, or documentary — that is easily manipulated and unreliable); *In re Marriage of Benson*, 32 Cal. Rptr. 3d 471 (Cal. 2005) (purported transmutation of husband's retirement accounts to separate property was invalid for lack of "express declaration" in writing required by statute, and partial performance exception to the statute of frauds was not applicable to the transmutation agreement).

13.6. Tracing Mingled Marital and Nonmarital Property

In many jurisdictions, a spouse who owns nonmarital property is permitted to preserve its nonmarital status even if it changes in character or form during the marriage, so long as the spouse can trace the asset acquired during marriage directly to a nonmarital source. *Hoffmann v. Hoffmann*, 676 S.W.2d 817, 825 (Mo. 1984) (tracing theory of equitable distribution applied when there has been no joint titling after the marriage).

Generally, when a party claims that an asset is nonmarital, the burden of proof is placed on that party to trace the asset to its nonmarital source. *Kreilick v. Kreilick*, 831 N.E.2d 1046 (Ohio App. 2005) (party seeking to have certain property deemed separate for distribution in a divorce has the burden of proof by a preponderance of the evidence). When the original nonmarital asset is no longer owned, the nonmarital claimant must trace the previously owned asset to a presently owned specific asset. If the claimant is successful, the trial court assigns the asset, or an interest in it, to the claimant as his or her nonmarital property. *See In re Marriage of Wanstreet*, 847 N.E.2d 716 (Ill. App. 2006) (proponent, as the party claiming that property is nonmarital, must prove the elements of gift by the manifest weight of the evidence); *Terwilliger v. Terwilliger*, 64 S.W.3d 816 (Ky. 2002) (husband could not adequately trace $200,000 to a separate property source, and husband was an experienced businessman who was expected to have maintained detailed and accurate records of where the assets came from).

13.7. Formula for Calculating the Value of Nonmarital Assets (Home Example)

Courts face challenging issues when attempting to divide assets containing nonmarital and marital funds, particularly when the asset has increased (or decreased) in value. For example, one party may have purchased a house with nonmarital funds prior to the marriage. However, after the couple married, both may have made mortgage payments out of marital funds. Furthermore, by the time of the divorce, the house may have increased or decreased in value due to market forces. The question for the parties or a trial judge is: How should the increase or decrease in value be apportioned at the time of the divorce?

The answer to this question in an equitable distribution jurisdiction is usually stated as follows:

> The present value of a nonmarital asset used in the acquisition of marital property is the proportion the net equity or contribution at the time of acquisition bore to the value of the property at the time of purchase multiplied by the value of the property at the time of separation. The remainder of equity increase is characterized as marital property.

Baker v. Baker, 753 N.W.2d 644, 651 (Minn. 2008).

See Woosnam v. Woosnam, 587 S.W.2d 262 (Ky. App. 1979) (if either spouse owns property subject to indebtedness prior to the marriage, the net equity in that property shall be considered nonmarital property at the time of separation in the proportion that the net equity at the date of marriage bears to the value of the property at the date of marriage); *Keeling v. Keeling*, 624 S.E.2d 687 (Va. App. 2006) (trial court erred in failing to apply the *Brandenburg* formula, which would have apportioned the marital and nonmarital contributions of property in the same percentages as their respective contributions to the total equity in the property, to ascertain the current value of husband's separate contributions toward the purchase of the marital residence).

13.8. Active and Passive Appreciation

In an equitable distribution jurisdiction, courts apportion the increase (or decrease) in the value of an asset by combining marital and nonmarital property using the theory of active and passive appreciation. The increase in value of an asset attributable to the efforts of one or both of the parties is characterized as "active appreciation" and is treated as marital property. Active appreciation occurs when marital funds or marital efforts cause a spouse's separate property to increase in value during the marriage. The time and energy of both spouses during the marriage is considered in dividing marital property.

Active appreciation. The Alaska Supreme Court defined active appreciation by saying:

> Active appreciation occurs when marital funds or marital efforts cause a spouse's separate property to increase in value during the marriage. . . . [T]he time and energy of both spouses during the marriage is to be considered in dividing marital property. . . . A spouse should not be able to erase his or her contributions of time and energy from the marital estate by rolling them back into a business that he began before the marriage.

Hanson v. Hanson, 125 P.2d 299, 304 (Alaska, 2005).

Under this theory, "an asset's value at the inception of the marriage retains its separate character, but any subsequent increase in value is treated as marital property to the extent that it results from active marital conduct." *Harrower v. Harrower*, 71 P.3d 854, 858 (Alaska 2003). A finding of active appreciation requires application of a three-part test: First, the court must find that the separate property in question appreciated during the marriage. Second, it must find that the parties made marital contributions to the property. Finally, the court must find a causal connection between the marital contributions and at least part of the appreciation. *Ibid.*

Passive appreciation. Passive appreciation of an asset occurs without any significant contribution being made toward that increase in value by either spouse. *Odom v. Odom*, 141 P.3d 324, 335 (Alaska 2006). If an increase in value of an asset is attributable to inflationary forces, general economics, and market conditions beyond the spouse's control, the increase in value is considered "passive appreciation" and is treated as nonmarital property. *Middendorf v. Middendorf*, 696 N.E.2d 575, 578 (Ohio 1998) (if the evidence indicates that the appreciation of the separate property is not due to the input of either spouse's labor, money, or in-kind contributions, the increase in the value of the property is passive appreciation and remains separate property). Should the asset increase in value because of these forces, the entire increase is attributed to the partner holding the asset.

For example, if one party owns stock prior to the marriage and it increases in value during the marriage, a court will make a determination concerning whether the increase in value resulted from the active effort of one or both of the parties (marital property) or whether the increase in value was passive in nature (nonmarital property). *See, e.g., Uygur v. Urgy*, 2006 WL 1568845 (unpublished) (Mich. App. 2006) (appreciation during the marriage was wholly passive and unrelated to defendant's workplace duties because it was the result of stock splits and was not tied directly to defendant's compensation). If the party played no role in dealing with the stock during the marriage, any increase or decrease in value will be considered due to passive market forces. *See In re Marriage of Terhaar*, 14 P.3d 657 (Or. 2000) (increase in value was passive where husband proved that wife did not contribute directly to the appreciation of husband's stock gifted to him by his parents). Note that stock dividends usually are considered income and marital property. *See Mandell v. Mandell*, 310 S.W.3d 531 (Tex. App. 2010) (dividends from stock are treated like income); *Arneson v. Arneson*, 355 N.W.2d 16, 19 (Wis. App. 1984) (dividend income generated by husband's inherited stock was includable in marital estate in divorce proceeding).

Burden. If a spouse seeks to classify the appreciation of an asset as active, that spouse has the burden of proving the first two elements, that is, an increase in value and marital contribution. Usually, the burden of showing the absence of a causal link to the increase or decrease in value lies with the owning spouse. *See Mayhew v. Mayhew*, 519 S.E.2d 188 (W. Va. 1999) (court sets out a five-step process for conducting active and passive appreciation tests).

13.9. Fault

All jurisdictions have some form of no-fault grounds for a divorce. Because of this, a question is raised about whether the no-fault grounds for divorce impliedly signal to a court that it may not consider which party was at fault for the breakdown when dividing marital assets. The answer to the question is that a minority of jurisdictions continue to link fault for the breakup of the marriage to distribution of marital assets. A majority of them reject the direct link but will consider fault if there was an inappropriate economic dissipation of marital assets.

States such as Alabama and Texas continue to link who was at fault for the breakup of the marriage with the division of property. *See, e.g., Patterson v. Patterson*, 90 So. 3d 187, 190 (Ala. App. 2012) ("When dividing marital property, a trial court should consider several factors, including the length of the marriage; the age and health of the parties; the future prospects of the parties; the source, type, and value of the property; the standard of living to which the parties have become accustomed during the marriage; and the fault of the parties contributing to the breakup of the marriage"); *Ayala v. Ayala*, 2011 WL 2930311, S.W.3d (Tex. App. 2011) (a trial court may consider many factors when exercising its broad discretion to divide marital property, including who was at fault in breaking up the marriage).

A majority of states do not link the fault for the breakdown of the marriage directly with a decision on distributing marital property. *See, e.g., Cartee v. Cartee*, 239 P.3d 707 (Alaska 2010) (trial court must divide the marital property without regard to fault and may not consider a party's moral or legal marital failings that do not amount to economic misconduct); *Dusenberry v. Dusenberry*, 326 S.E.2d 65 (N.C. App. 1985) (finding an adulterous affair on the part of a wife was an irrelevant and inappropriate matter in determining equitable distribution of marital property). Occasionally, a jurisdiction seems to take conflicting views on the subject. *See, e.g., McCormick v. McCormick*, 2012 Ark. App. 318, S.W.3d (Ark. 2012) (fault or unclean hands are not among the factors listed for the court's consideration in dividing marital property unequally, but court has upheld unequal division of property based on fault considerations).

Several jurisdictions will consider economic misconduct on the part of one of the spouses when dividing marital property. *See, e.g., Washington v. Washington*, 770 N.W.2d 908 (Mich. App. 2009) (reckless spending justified in part an unequal property division). Where there is what some refer to as "egregious fault" by a party, courts will consider the conduct when dividing property. *See Alford v. Alford*, 478 N.Y.S.2d 717, 718 (N.Y. App. 1984) ("in the absence of egregious circumstances, marital fault is not a proper factor to be considered under equitable distribution").

Note that some jurisdictions refuse to consider fault when dividing marital property but will do so when awarding alimony. *See, e.g., Fisher v. Fisher*, 648 S.W.2d 244 (Tenn. 1983) (permitting consideration of fault when awarding alimony, but barring consideration of fault when dividing marital property); *Wilbur v. Wilbur*, 498 N.Y.S.2d 525 (N.Y. App. 1986) ("[M]arital fault is, generally, a proper consideration in awarding maintenance"). In *Charlton v. Charlton*, 413 S.E.2d 911, 915 (W.Va. 1991), the court observed that in enacting that state's equitable distribution statute, the legislature did not intend for fault to be considered as a factor in determining the division of marital property. However, said the court, the legislature did designate marital fault as a factor to consider when awarding alimony.

Examples

1. Assume that P sought to divorce D after 20 years of marriage in a jurisdiction that applied the separate property distribution theory of dividing marital assets. During the marriage, D worked inside the home caring for P and their five children. P worked outside the home. The marital assets consisted of a home, purchased a few years after the couple married with a down payment of $10,000 made by P and now valued at $200,000, and the family automobile, worth $10,000. The home and car were titled

in P's name. When D sought an equitable share of the home and car, how would a court in a separate property (title) jurisdiction most likely rule?

2. Assume that P and D were married in an equitable distribution jurisdiction. Before the marriage, D owned a home valued at $100,000, which did not have a mortgage on it. During the marriage, the couple lived in the home, and when they divorced, it was valued at $200,000. P argues that because this is an equitable distribution jurisdiction, P should receive an equitable interest in the home. P contends that the home is marital property, but D disagrees. How will a court most likely rule?

3. Assume that P and D divorce after 25 years of marriage in a jurisdiction that does not apply the source of funds theory. During the marriage, P received $20,000 cash as a gift from his mother. P placed the funds in P and D's joint bank account, which they use for household expenditures. When they divorce ten years after the money was placed into the account, P asserts that he is entitled to the $20,000 from the account as his non-marital property. How will a court in this jurisdiction most likely rule?

4. Assume that during their divorce hearing, stock acquired by P before and during his marriage to D was either shown to be a gift from his parents or purchased with nonmarital assets. However, the bank account through which P bought and sold stock and deposited dividends from the stock occasionally was used for marital purposes including household expenses and vacation trips. P argued that because this jurisdiction has adopted the source of funds theory, that the stock was his nonmarital property. D contended that once P used an account that occasionally was used for marital purposes, the stock was transmuted into marital property. How will a court most likely rule?

5. Assume that P and D married in a source of funds jurisdiction and that P brought $7,000 cash into the marriage. These funds and approximately $3,000 cash that D brought into the marriage were commingled in a joint account and used throughout the ten-year marriage for various expenses. When they divorce, P argues that she is entitled to the $7,000 as her nonmarital property. How will a court in a source of funds jurisdiction most likely rule?

6. Assume that P, an experienced businessperson, was injured in an accident prior to marriage to D. Because of the accident, P received a $50,000 cash settlement. Approximately one year after the parties married, P purchased a parcel of land with the title only in his name.

   The parties' marriage broke down after 20 years, and they were unable to agree on the division of property. The parcel of land purchased 19 years earlier was now valued at $500,000 and P asserted that it was his nonmarital property, and he was entitled to it. P testified that he used all of the $50,000 he received as compensation for injuries suffered in the accident he was involved in before his marriage to D to purchase the property. D disagreed. She testified that she recalled that some of the down payment on the land came from their joint bank account, estimating that it was as much as $15,000. She also testified that about $10,000 of the $50,000 came from an inheritance she had received when her father died. She also offered testimony that P purchased a new car for about $25,000, paying cash for it, in the first year of their marriage.

P produced a receipt at the hearing issued by the previous landowner, stating that P had paid $50,000. D's name was not on the receipt. The receipt also included a date showing that it was issued one year after P and D married. P produced a copy of the release of his injury claim, which indicated that the claim was settled for $50,000 prior to the marriage. During cross-examination, P testified that he had years of experience as a businessperson, juggling the assets and liabilities of a number of corporations and orchestrating complex business deals.

D produced a copy of a $10,000 check given to her as a part of her father's estate a year after they married, and a photograph of the car that P allegedly purchased just after they were married. No other evidence was introduced. Has P produced sufficient evidence to persuade a judge that the land is P's nonmarital property?

7. Assume that P and D were married in an equitable distribution jurisdiction. Before the marriage, D owned a home, which on the day of her marriage was valued at $100,000, with a $50,000 mortgage. During the marriage, the couple lived in the home, and D made all the house payments. At the time of their divorce, they had paid off the outstanding mortgage, and the home was valued at $200,000. P argues that because this is an equitable distribution jurisdiction, he should receive an interest in the home. D argues that because she owned the home before P and D married and made all the mortgage payments after they were married that she should receive 100 percent of the home; that is, the home, with a value of $200,000, free and clear of any claim to it by P. How will a court most likely resolve this dispute?

8. Assume that P and D were married in an equitable distribution jurisdiction. Also, assume that on the date of their marriage, P owned real estate then valued at $30,000, but subject to a $20,000 mortgage. A few months after they married, the couple, using marital funds and doing a lot of the work themselves, built an addition to the home and increased its value by $10,000—from $30,000 to $40,000. During the course of the marriage, the parties used marital funds to pay the mortgage balance down to $4,000. At the time of the divorce, the market value of the home was $100,000. P and D seek a determination of their marital and nonmarital interests in the $100,000. What will the court decide?

9. Assume that P and D divorce after ten years of marriage. How would a trial judge most likely characterize the following property, i.e., separate nonmarital or marital? (1) A farm that P inherited from her mother during the marriage? (2) An antique auto owned by D before the marriage? (3) A house that D inherited from his father before the marriage? (4) An antique auto purchased by D after the marriage with funds from an account that he set up before the marriage? (5) A car purchased by D during the marriage and paid for solely from income that he made during the marriage?

Explanations

1. The problem is used to illustrate the harsh realities of the literal application of the separate property theory to a divorce. Here, a court most likely would award P the home and the automobile, reasoning that title was only in P's name; therefore, it was P's separate property. Most likely, D would receive child support and possibly alimony.

2. Assuming that D can meet the burden of proving that the home was purchased and was free and clear of any mortgage before marriage, a court most likely will award the entire home to D. The home is exempt from consideration as marital property under most, if not all, equitable distribution statutes in the country. D is also entitled to the benefit of the increase in the value of the home because all the increase in the value is a result of market forces. D most likely will be awarded the home, worth $200,000, free and clear of any claim by P to a portion of it.

3. Note that most legislatures have adopted legislation that remedies the harsh effects of the strict application of the transmutation doctrine where the source of funds theory is not a part of the law. In this hypothetical, a court in a jurisdiction that has not adopted a source of funds theory most likely will rule that when P commingled separate property with marital property, the commingled property was transmuted and became marital property subject to equitable distribution. *See Smoot v. Smoot*, 357 S.E.2d 728, 731 (Va. 1987) (holding that Virginia's equitable distribution statute does not adopt the source of funds doctrine and thus, when spouse fails to segregate and instead commingles separate property with marital property, chancellor must classify commingled property as marital property subject to equitable distribution—*superseded* by statute as stated in *Catlett v. Catlett*, 2004 WL 1876377 (unpublished) (Va. App. 2004)). The court also may possibly view the evidence in this hypothetical as

P failing to prove that he considered his interest in the household account to be composed of discrete, segregated shares. The facts suggest that all P's funds were commingled with D's and were considered an integral part of the marital estate. *See also In re Marriage of Mayzner*, 144 Ill. App.3d 645 (Ill. App. 1986) (husband's $30,000 contribution to the parties' condominium, which was held in joint tenancy, was presumed to be a gift to the marital estate); Ill. Rev. Stat. 1983, ch. 40, par. 503(c).

4. A court most likely will rule in favor of P. A court will observe that transmutation is a matter of intent to be gleaned from the facts of each case, and the mere use of separate properties to support the marriage without some additional evidence of intent to treat it as marital property is not sufficient to establish transmutation. In general, the spouse claiming transmutation must produce objective evidence showing that during the marriage, the parties themselves regarded the property as the common property of the marriage. Nonmarital property is transmuted into marital property when it becomes so commingled as to be untraceable. However, the mere commingling of funds does not make them marital funds automatically. Here, the facts tend to support P. *See Wannamaker v. Wannamaker*, 406 S.E.2d 180 (S.C. App. 1991).

5. Although this is a source of funds jurisdiction, a court most likely will rule that the funds have lost their nonmarital character. The mere fact that the funds were placed in a joint account does not necessarily require that they be considered marital property. However, in many jurisdictions, a presumption arises that when deposits are made into a spousal joint bank account, the parties share a joint ownership in the funds on deposit. The presumption is rebuttable by either spouse if it can be shown that the account consists of his or her separate property only. Because everyone agrees that the premarital funds were contributed to a joint account, both parties used the account during the marriage, and there has been a significantly long passage of time since the deposit, a court most likely will rule that the funds were transmuted into marital property.

6. While a close question and the credibility of the witnesses will play a major factor in the outcome of the dispute, on the facts presented in this scenario, most courts would conclude that P has failed to meet his burden of tracing the asset to its nonmarital source. Because it appears that P is a skilled businessperson, with extensive recordkeeping experience, a court would be reluctant not to require that he comply with stringent tracing requirements. A court will find that it is reasonable to expect that P would keep detailed and accurate records and be able to produce them at the hearing to establish his nonmarital property claim. D's check and the car photograph, plus D's claim that some of the payment for the land came from their joint

bank account, raise unanswered questions that place the burden on P to answer. Note that case law suggests that while tracing to a mathematical certainty is not always possible, a precise requirement is more appropriate for skilled businesspersons who are expected to maintain comprehensive records of their financial affairs than it would be for persons with lesser business skills or persons who are imprecise in their recordkeeping abilities. *See Terwilliger v. Terwilliger*, 64 S.W.3d 816 (Ky. 2002).

7. A court will begin by recognizing that on the day the couple married, D had a 50 percent equitable interest in the home; that is, $50,000 is 50 percent of $100,000. During the marriage, the value of the home increased because of market forces. Consequently, D's equitable interest in the home because of her initial cash investment increased in value, and most courts believe that D should receive a fair return on the investment. A court will calculate that on divorce, D should receive $100,000 as her nonmarital interest in the homestead (50 percent of $200,000 is $100,000). A court then will divide the remaining $100,000 equitably between P and D, with each most likely receiving about $50,000. D most likely will receive a total of $150,000. Note that most courts will not consider the fact that D made all the mortgage payments during the marriage as altering the outcome of the final division of property because the payments, in the eyes of the court, were made with marital funds. (Analysis based on *Nardini v. Nardini*, 414 N.W.2d 184 (Minn. 1987) and *Schmitz v. Schmitz*, 309 N.W.2d 748 (Minn. 1981).)

8. The court will begin its analysis by recognizing that the home contains both marital and nonmarital interests. It will recognize that there are three types of "increases" involved in the example: (1) the increase in value attributable to the physical improvement of the property through application of marital funds and marital effort; (2) the increase in value attributable to the increase in equity by application of marital funds to reduce the mortgage indebtedness; and (3) the increase in value attributable to inflation and market forces. The hypothetical assumes an investment of cash and of property and services having a cash value in the total amount of $40,000. The amount that P invested in the property prior to the marriage, as valued on the date of the marriage, is P's nonmarital equity in the property. In this example, P's nonmarital equity was $10,000 (33 1/3 percent of the total value on the date of the marriage). During the marriage, the parties contributed marital funds and labor when they built an addition to the home. In this problem, the addition increased the value of the property by $10,000. The parties also undertook to pay off the $20,000 mortgage with marital funds, which at the time of the divorce reduced the unpaid mortgage balance to $4,000.

   The court will reason that the present value of P's nonmarital interest is the proportion of his net equity at the time of marriage ($10,000) bore to the aggregate of the value of the property on the date of the marriage ($30,000), plus the value of the addition on its completion ($10,000). The interests then will be apportioned as follows:

1. $10,000/$40,000 = 25 percent
2. $100,000 × 0.25 = $25,000 (P's nonmarital interest)
3. $100,000 – $25,000 = $75,000 (marital interest)

The net value of the property, however, is $96,000 ($100,000 –$4,000 mortgage balance).

Because the parties undertook payment of the mortgage debt with marital funds, reduction of the marital interests by the amount of the mortgage balance ($75,000 – $4,000 = $71,000) is appropriate. Thus, $71,000 is marital property, and $25,000 is P's nonmarital property. *See Nardini v. Nardini*, 414 N.W.2d 184, 193 (Minn. 1987). $71,000 will be equitably divided between P and D.

9. (1) The farm inherited from P's mother during the marriage normally would be considered her separate nonmarital property. (2) The antique auto owned by D before the marriage is D's separate nonmarital property. (3) The house inherited by D before the couple married is treated as D's separate nonmarital property. (4) Assuming that the jurisdiction allows D to trace the funds and D can persuade a judge that he removed the funds from a separate account that he set up before the marriage (i.e., there has been no commingling with marital funds), the antique auto remains D's separate nonmarital property. This is an example of property that is purchased during a marriage in exchange for separate property. (5) The car purchased by D and paid for by D solely from his salary during the marriage is considered marital property.

MODEL ACTS

13.10. Uniform Marriage and Divorce Act (UMDA)

The Uniform Marriage and Divorce Act (UMDA) contains provisions that address the disposition of property upon divorce. As originally drafted, §307(a) of the UMDA provided that the court "shall assign each spouse's property to him" and then divide the marital property in just proportions. The Act states that marital property does not include property acquired by gift, property acquired in exchange for property acquired by gift, or increase in value of property acquired before marriage. UMDA §307(b)(1), (2), (5).

According to the UMDA *Commissioners' Note* to §307, appreciation in the value of nonmarital property is not marital property.

In 1973, §307 of the UMDA was amended to provide two alternatives to dividing property upon divorce. Alternative "A" proceeds upon the principle that all property of the spouses, however acquired, should be regarded as assets of the married couple and be apportioned equitably between the spouses. Alternative "B" is intended for community property states; it allows courts to divide community property after considering certain criteria. It was added in response to complaints from community property jurisdictions that Alternative "A" did not allow them to distinguish adequately between separate and community property. Both of these alternatives recognize that the spouses have been partners in the marriage and require courts to look beyond title in deciding how much each spouse should share in the distribution of marital assets. *See* Elizabeth A. Cheadle, Comment, *The Development of Sharing Principles in Common Law Marital Property States*, 28 UCLA L. Rev. 1269, 1287 (1981).

13.11. Income

Courts in some jurisdictions adopting property distribution statutes primarily based upon the UMDA have held that income derived from nonmarital property during the marriage is marital property. *In re Marriage of Reed*, 427 N.E.2d 282, 285 (Ill. App. 1981) (interest earned during marriage on ex-husband's nonmarital property was marital property); *Sousley v. Sousley*, 614 S.W.2d 942, 944 (Ky. 1981) (income produced from nonmarital property is marital property—but holding called into doubt by statute in *Holman v. Holman*, 84 S.W.3d 903 (Ky. 2002)). The Uniform Marital Property Act (UMPA) provides that income received during the marriage is marital property, regardless of its source. *See* UMPA §4 cmt., 9A U.L.A. 110 (1987).

13.12. American Law Institute (ALI) Recommendations

The *Principles of the Law of Family Dissolution: Analysis and Recommendations* from the American Law Institute (ALI) is the result of 11 years of work. The following is a summary of several sections of the ALI *Principles* that are associated with dividing property upon divorce.

Section 4.03 contains the definition of marital and separate property, which follows standards used in community property and most equitable distribution jurisdictions. *See* David Westfall, *Unprincipled Family Dissolution: The American Law Institute's Recommendations for Spousal Support and Division of Property*, 27 Harv. J.L. & Pub. Pol'y 917 (2004). The section defines nonmarital property as property acquired either before marriage or as gifts (or inheritances) from third parties during marriage as the separate property of the acquiring spouse and hence not subject to division on divorce. §4.04 defines income and appreciation in the value of separate property as non-marital property unless its value has been enhanced by spousal labor or it is affected by §4.12, which provides for gradual recharacterization of non-marital property in marriages that last a minimum of five years. *Id.* at 947. §4.05(1) provides that a portion of any increase in the value of separate property is marital property whenever either spouse has devoted substantial time during marriage to the property's management or preservation.

Section 4.07 declares that occupational licenses and educational degrees should not be subject to division on divorce. §4.09(1) mandates an equal division of marital property and marital debts, but §4.09(2)(b) and §4.09(2)(c) allow a court under certain circumstances to order an unequal division of debts. §4.09(1) exceptions provide that a court may deviate from equal division if it determines that a spouse is entitled to alimony and chooses to provide for the alimony by means of a larger property settlement. It may also deviate if a party is guilty of misappropriating marital property by making substantial gifts to third parties within a specified time; by losing, expending, or destroying marital property by intentional misconduct within a specified time; or by negligently losing or destroying marital property after service of the dissolution petition. A court may deviate from equal division if marital debts exceed marital assets, and it is just and equitable to allocate unequally the excess debt because of financial capacity, participation in the decision to incur the debt, or the purpose of the debt. Finally, a court may deviate from equal division if an existing debt was incurred to finance a spouse's education.

Section 4.10 allows an unequal division of property when one of the spouses has committed some sort of financial misconduct. The misconduct may involve (1) certain gifts made without the other party's consent; (2) property lost, expended, or destroyed through intentional misconduct; and (3) property lost or destroyed through negligence after the service of the dissolution petition. The suggested time during which the conduct described is relevant is either six months — in the case of (1) or (2) — or a year prior to the service of the dissolution petition.

PENSION AND RETIREMENT BENEFITS

13.13. Qualified Domestic Relations Order (QDRO)

Defined. A Qualified Domestic Relations Order (QDRO) is a state court order in a domestic relations case that requires pension or retirement plan benefits to be used to provide alimony and/or child support, or to be divided as marital property upon a divorce. *See generally* Brett R. Turner, *Private Retirement Plans: Federal Law—Definition of a QDRO Under Federal Law*, 2 Equit. Distrib. of Property, 3d §6:19 (November 2011). The administrator of the pension plan that provides the benefits affected by an order is the individual (or entity) initially responsible for determining whether a domestic relations order is a QDRO.

History. QDROs were relatively ineffective until 1984 because of the anti-alienation provisions of the Employment Retirement Income Security Act (ERISA) of 1974. The early version of ERISA was primarily intended to protect the interests of employees who participated in employer-sponsored pension plans. It was not concerned about the financial consequences associated with distribution of a portion or all of a pension to a spouse upon divorce.

With the passage of the Retirement Equity Act (REA) of 1984, the concerns related to distributing pensions upon a divorce were addressed. In particular, this Act was intended to assure a greater and more equitable opportunity for women working as employees or homemakers to receive private pension income. REA focused on the division of pension benefits in marital dissolution or dependent support situations. Prior to this act, a spouse was denied a right to pension benefits upon divorce, regardless of how many years the spouse may have served as an economic partner to a married partner who was covered by a pension plan. Even in cases in which the state domestic relations court was willing to consider a pension as an asset of the marriage and award the ex-spouse a share of it, the ex-spouse's rights were thwarted. For example, pension plan trustees refused to honor state family court orders awarding pension benefits to an alternative payee (the ex-spouse), claiming that the orders constituted an impermissible assignment of benefits and were preempted by federal law as set out in ERISA.

The amendments to REA have made it clear that by honoring a legitimate state court order (a QDRO) awarding an ex-spouse all or some of a worker's entire pension does not violate the anti-alienation clause of ERISA. In addition, the legislation creates an exception from ERISA's broad preemption of state laws for QDROs. *See* 29 U.S.C.A. §§1056(d)(3)(A) (excepting QDROs from the prohibition against assignment or alienation).

State testamentary law. The REA did not resolve all of the federal-state conflicts over pension rights. One of the important issues concerned whether federal law preempts state testamentary law. That issue was addressed in *Boggs v. Boggs*, 520 U.S. 833 (1997), where the Supreme Court held that ERISA preempts a state community property law that allowed a nonparticipant spouse to transfer by testamentary instrument an interest in undistributed pension plan benefits. The ruling directly applies to California and the other eight community property jurisdictions. The Court rested its decision on the supremacy clause of Article 6 of the Constitution and the preemption provision of 29 U.S.C. §1144(a). The Court explained that the principal purpose of ERISA was "to protect plan participants and beneficiaries." *Id. at* 845. That purpose would be frustrated by testamentary transfers of pension benefits to third parties having no relation to the participant.

No limit on assignment. As noted above, a QDRO allows a state court to order a pension-plan administrator to distribute a portion of a pension to the other spouse who is referred to as the "alternate payee." It creates, recognizes, or assigns to an alternate payee the right to receive all or a portion of the benefits payable to a participant under a pension plan subject to ERISA. 26 U.S.C.A. §414(p)(1) and ERISA §206(d)(3)(B)(i); 29 U.S.C.A. §1056(d)(3)(A). "As a matter of federal law, there is nothing to preclude the assignment of 100 percent of the benefit to the alternate payee even where no portion of the benefit is marital property." Joanne Ross Wilder, *Chapter* 23. *Retirement Benefits and Qualified Domestic Relations Orders*, 17 West's Pa. Prac., Family Law §23:4 (7th ed.) (2011). The QDRO rules do not apply to any plan to which the assignment or alienation restrictions of ERISA do not apply.

Tax consequences. Generally, payments that are received by an alternate payee pursuant to a QDRO are treated as ordinary income for tax purposes. They are includable in the gross income of the alternate payee. 26 U.S.C.A. §§402(a)(9) and 72(m)(10) and the employee spouse is not taxed on those payments. Note that in the absence of a QDRO, it is the participant and not the alternate payee who must pay the taxes on the distributions. 26 U.S.C.A. §414(p)(1) and ERISA §206(d)(3)(B)(i); 29 U.S.C.A. §1056(d)(3)(A).

An alternative payee may "roll over" funds received via a QDRO into an eligible retirement plan, such as an individual retirement account (IRA), so as to preserve the funding of the alternative payee's retirement. 26 U.S.C. (1988 Ed.) §402(a)(6)(F). The rollover into a qualified account is done without tax consequences.

13.14. Dividing Pension Benefits

Pensions are an asset in the nature of deferred compensation and are subject to equitable division because they are presently earned, although not presently possessed. Pension benefits are considered marital property and often constitute a substantial percentage of the marital estate to be distributed by a family court. When considering the value of a pension, a court will initially have to determine whether it is vested or nonvested.

Vested pensions. A vested pension is one that is not subject to forfeiture, should the employee terminate employment or be terminated by an employer. The majority rule in the United States is that "vested" pension and retirement benefits are subject to division by a divorce court. *See* Charles C. Marvel, *Pension or Retirement Benefits as Subject to Award or Division by Court in Settlement of Property Rights Between Spouses*, 94 A.L.R.3d 176, 182; *Morlan v. Morlan*, 720 P.2d 497, 498 (Alaska 1986) ("pension rights should generally be awarded to the employee spouse if there is other marital property of appropriate worth which can be awarded to the non-employee spouse").

Nonvested pensions. A pension that is nonvested is subject to forfeiture should the employee quit or the employer terminate employment. Courts do not agree on whether nonvested pension rights should be included as a marital asset. However, the trend is to recognize them as a marital asset. *See, e.g.*, *Shaver v. Shaver*, 165 Cal. Rptr. 672 (Cal. App. 1982); *Shanks v. Treadway*, 110 S.W.3d 444 (Tex. 2003) (nonvested pension rights are a contingent interest in property, and to the extent that such rights derive from employment during coverture, they constitute a community asset subject to division in a dissolution proceeding); *Kendrick v. Kendrick*, 902 S.W.2d 918, 920 (Tenn. App. 1994) (nonvested pension rights accruing during a marriage are marital property subject to equitable division in divorce cases); *Swanson v. Swanson*, 583 N.W.2d 15 (Minn. App. 1998) (nonvested pensions are included within the definition of marital property); *Van Loan v. Van Loan*, 569 P.2d 214, 215–16 (Ariz. 1977); *In re Marriage of Gillmore*, 629 P.2d 1, 3 (Cal. 1981) (retirement benefits, whether vested or nonvested, matured or immature, earned by spouse during marriage are community property); *In re Marriage of Hunt*, 397 N.E.2d 511, 518 (Ill. App. 1979).

Those courts that refuse to recognize nonvested pension rights as property reason that they are a mere expectancy, and thus, not an asset subject to division upon dissolution of a marriage. However, the trend in this country appears to be toward holding that pension rights, vested or nonvested, are a property interest, and to the extent that such rights derive from employment during coverture, they constitute an asset subject to division in a dissolution proceeding. *See generally Ruggles v. Ruggles*, 860 P.2d 182 (N.M. 1993) (preferred method of dealing with community interests in retirement plans upon dissolution, regardless of whether they have vested or matured at time of dissolution, is to value, divide, and distribute them, or other assets of equivalent value, to the divorcing spouses in a lump sum at the time of dissolution, but where it is not possible or practicable to achieve this preferred method of distribution, other methods, including "reserve jurisdiction" or "pay as it comes in" method may be used). In *Ball v. Ball*, 445 S.E.2d 449 (S.C. 1994), the South Carolina Supreme Court held that a spouse's nonvested military pension was marital property subject to equitable distribution. The court provided the following explanation to support its decision:

> Whether vested or nonvested, pension plans are deferred compensation. . . . [T]o the extent that Wife participated in Husband's military career, she also contributed to the service for which he will be compensated in the future. We hold that Husband's participation in the pension plan was an actual right existing at the time of the divorce, even though the compensation, if received, is deferred.

Id. at 252-253.

See also Mullarkey v. Mullarkey, 723 S.E.2d 249 (S.C. App. 2012) (family court did not have authority to divide equitably military retirement benefits yet to be earned by husband at the time of the divorce, even if, at that time, any compensation that wife was entitled to was deferred by husband's decision to remain in the military).

13.15. Social Security

Courts have struggled with the issue of how Social Security benefits should be considered when a couple divorce. In *Hisquierdo v. Hisquierdo*, 439 U.S. 572 (1979), the Supreme Court held that Railroad Retirement Act benefits, which are analogous to Social Security benefits, may not offset an award of marital property to the other spouse in a community property state. Consequently, a wife did not have a community property interest in her husband's expectation of receiving railroad retirement benefits. The Court expressly pointed to the similarities between the railroad retirement benefits and benefits under the Social Security Act. *See also McCarty v. McCarty*, 453 U.S. 210, 232 (1981) (holding that military retirement pay was separate property because the federal military retirement scheme preempted state property laws).

Countermanding Hisquierdo and McCarty. Congress legislatively countermanded the holdings in *Hisquierdo* and *McCarty* by making railroad and military retirement benefits subject to community property law. *See* 45 U.S.C.A. §231m(b)(2) (West 1986); 10 U.S.C.A. §1408(c)(1) (West 1998). Congress has not passed similar legislation with respect to the division of Social Security benefits.

Offsetting Social Security benefits. Several courts have applied the *Hisquierdo* rationale to Social Security benefits, holding that transferring other assets to balance or offset expected Social Security benefits is not permitted. *See, e.g., Webster v. Webster*, 716 N.W.2d 47 (Neb. 2006) (federal Constitution and statutes prevent direct offset to adjust for disproportionate Social Security benefits in property division); *Johnson v. Johnson*, 726 So. 2d 393, 396 (Fla. App. 1999) (wife's future Social Security benefits would not be treated as an offset); *English v. English*, 879 P.2d 802, 808 (N.M. App. 1994) (trial court erred in considering wife's Social Security benefits as offset to retirement benefits paid to wife); *Stanley v. Stanley*, 956 A.2d 1 (Del. 2008) (trial court's order for former husband to pay part of his Social Security disability benefits to former wife violated federal law).

Social Security can be used to fashion an equitable award. However, a majority of jurisdictions have said that Social Security benefits may be considered as part of a trial court's fashioning of an equitable distribution of marital property while simultaneously not permitting them to be considered a marital asset. *See, e.g.*, *In re Marriage of Boyer*, 538 N.W.2d 293, 293-294, 296 (Iowa 1995) (trial court could make general adjustment in dividing marital property on the basis that one party was entitled to much greater Social Security benefits than the other); *In re Marriage of Brane*, 908 P.2d 625, 626, 628 (Kan. 1995) (although anti-assignment clause of Social Security Act precludes court from dividing Social Security income in divorce action, court may consider spouses' Social Security income when dividing marital property); *Pongonis v. Pongonis*, 606 A.2d 1055, 1058 (Me. 1992) (the deferred distribution value of anticipated Social Security retirement benefits was relevant factor in the division of marital property); *Mahoney v. Mahoney*, 681 N.E.2d 852, 856 (Mass. 1997) (judge could consider husband's anticipated Social Security benefits as a factor in making equitable distribution of distributable marital assets); *Litz v. Litz*, 288 S.W.3d 753 (Mo. App. 2009); *Dinges v. Dinges*, 743 N.W.2d 662, 671 (Neb. App. 2008) (wife's lump-sum Social Security award did not qualify as marital property; while an offset of a Social Security award is prohibited by the anti-assignment clause of the Social Security Act and the Supremacy Clause, a court may properly consider a spouse's Social Security award in equitably dividing the marital property); *Neville v. Neville*, 791 N.E.2d 434, 437 (Ohio 2003) (when making an equitable distribution of marital property in a divorce proceeding, a trial court may consider the parties' future Social Security benefits in relation to all marital assets); *Johnson v. Johnson*, 734 N.W.2d 801, 808 (S.D. 2007) (Social Security benefits may be considered as a factor, among others, when dividing marital property in a divorce action); *Olsen v. Olsen*, 169 P.3d 765, 772 (Utah App. 2007) (trial court in a divorce proceeding may consider reasonable likelihood that a spouse may receive or is receiving federal Social Security income in fashioning an equitable division of property); *In re Marriage of Zahm*, 978 P.2d 498, 502 (Wash. 1999) (when making equitable distribution of marital property, trial courts may consider Social Security benefits in determining the parties' relative economic circumstances at time of dissolution).

13.16. Military Retirement Benefits

As noted in the preceding section, in *McCarty v. McCarty*, *supra*, the Supreme Court held that military retirement benefits were the separate property of the retiree. The decision was subsequently overruled by the Uniform Services Former Spouses Protection Act (USFSPA), 10 U.S.C. §1408 (1982). The Act allows states to apply their own laws when determining the divisibility of military retirement benefits upon divorce.

SPECIAL ISSUES

13.17. Degrees and Professional Licenses

Courts throughout the United States take a variety of approaches when considering whether to place a property value on a degree or professional license earned while married. The valuation issue most commonly arises when one partner works outside the home during the marriage and financially supports the other partner who achieves the degree or professional license. When the marriage breaks down, the spouse who worked to support the other partner claims that the degree or license is marital property, its value should be established, and an award made based on its established value.

The leading minority view on placing a value on degrees and professional licenses earned while married is illustrated by New York case law. Courts in that state have construed its legislation as directing them to consider degrees and professional licenses as marital property. *O'Brien v. O'Brien*, 489 N.E.2d 712 (N.Y. 1985) (a professional license is "marital property" within the context of the governing New York statute); *McGowan v. McGowan*, 518 N.Y.S.2d 346 (N.Y. Sup. 1987) (a professional degree is marital property).

In *O'Brien v. O'Brien*, *supra*, the working wife supported the student husband through medical school, only to have the husband file for divorce two months after obtaining a medical license. The court concluded that New York's unique statutory scheme was broader than those of other states that had declined to consider degrees and licenses marital property, and that, unlike other states,

> our statute recognizes that spouses have an equitable claim to things of value arising out of the marital relationship and classifies them as subject to distribution by focusing on the marital status of the parties at the time of acquisition. . . .

489 N.E.2d. at 715.

The court stated that "the New York Legislature deliberately went beyond traditional concepts when it formulated the Equitable Distribution Law." *Ibid.* Under *O'Brien*, a court determines the present value of projected future earnings of the spouse holding the degree or license at the time of divorce.

Analogy to tort compensation. One of the difficulties with the *O'Brien* view is placing a present value on the enhanced earning capacity of a degree or professional license. The court in that case admitted that there were challenges but said that the problems are not insurmountable and are no more difficult than computing tort damages for wrongful death or diminished earning capacity resulting from injury. It said that fixing a value on a professional license differs only in degree from the problems presented when valuing a professional practice for purposes of a distributive award, something the courts have not hesitated to do. *See generally Procario v. Procario*, 623 N.Y.S.2d 971 (N.Y. Sup. 1994) (former husband's increased earning capacity as result of completion of surgical residence was marital property); *Parlow v. Parlow*, 548 N.Y.S.2d 373 (N.Y. Sup. 1989) (defendant's teaching license is marital property subject to equitable distribution); *Holterman v. Holterman*, 781 N.Y.S.2d 458 (N.Y. App. 2004) (awarding wife 35 percent of present value of husband's medical license as her marital portion of husband's enhanced earning capacity as a physician was not abuse of discretion).

Majority view. A majority of jurisdictions refuse to treat professional licenses and degrees obtained during marriage that represent one spouse's enhanced earning capacity as marital property. They provide a long list of reasons to support their position. They contend that a professional license is not property at all; rather, it represents a personal attainment in acquiring knowledge. It is also neither physically nor metaphysically property and does not have an exchange value or any objective transferable value on an open market. Moreover, an attempt to place a value on it is speculative. It is personal to the holder, terminates on the death of the holder, is not inheritable, and cannot be assigned, sold, transferred, conveyed, or pledged. They argue that an advanced degree is a cumulative product of many years of previous education, combined with diligence and hard work. Finally, it may not be acquired by the mere expenditure of money and it has none of the attributes of property in the usual sense of that term. *See Wilson v. Wilson*, 741 S.W.2d 640 (Ark. 1987) (medical degree, license, and increased earning capacity as an orthopedic surgeon were not marital property); *Hoak v. Hoak*, 370 S.E.2d 473 (W.Va. App. 1988) (professional degree or license earned during marriage is not marital property subject to equitable distribution upon divorce); *Nelson v. Nelson*, 736 P.2d 1145 (Alaska 1987) (most courts hold that a professional degree is not property subject to division); *Wisner v. Wisner*, 631 P.2d 115 (Ariz. App. 1981) (ex-husband's medical license, board certificate, and education value were not part of community property subject to property division); *Graham v. Graham*, 574 P.2d 75 (Colo. 1978) (husband's master's degree in business administration, which was obtained during marriage and while wife was providing approximately 70 percent of the spouses' income, was not "property" subject to division); *Simmons v. Simmons*, 708 A.2d 949 (Conn. 1998) (husband's medical degree was not property subject to equitable distribution); *Hughes v. Hughes*, 438 So. 2d 146 (Fla. App. 1983) (husband's educational degrees were not "property" subject to distribution as lump-sum alimony); *In re Marriage of Weinstein*, 470 N.E.2d 551 (Ill. App. 1984) (husband's osteopathy degree and his license to practice surgery were not marital property); *Drapek v. Drapek*, 503 N.E.2d 946 (Mass. 1987) (spouse's professional degree and enhanced earning capacity, acquired during marriage, were not marital assets); *Geer v. Geer*, 353 S.E.2d 427 (N.C. 1987) (professional license was separate property); *Ruben v. Ruben*, 461 A.2d 733 (N.H. 1983) (value of the husband's professional career was not a marital asset); *Hodge v. Hodge*, 520 A.2d 15 (Pa. Sup. Ct. 1986) (medical license was not marital property; doctor's increased future earning capacity cannot be considered for purposes of equitable distribution); *Wehrkamp v. Wehrkamp*, 357 N.W.2d 264 (S.D. 1984); *Petersen v. Petersen*, 737 P.2d 237 (Utah App. 1987) (medical degree not a marital asset).

Degrees — alternative solutions. Although a majority of jurisdictions reject treating a degree or professional license obtained during a marriage as marital property, they are not ignored. For example, some jurisdictions suggest that the future value of a degree acquired by one of the parties during the marriage, although not subject to division or transfer upon divorce, should be considered an element when reaching an equitable award of alimony. *See, e.g., Stevens v. Stevens*, 492 N.E.2d 131, 136-137 (Ohio 1986) (veterinary degree was not marital property; future value of veterinary degree was element to be considered in reaching alimony award); *Downs v. Downs*, 574 A.2d 156 (Vt. 1990) (future value of professional degree is relevant factor to be considered in reaching just and equitable maintenance award); *Mahoney v. Mahoney*, 453 A.2d 527 (N.J. 1982) (courts may not make any permanent distribution of value of professional degrees and licenses, whether based upon estimated worth or cost, but where a spouse receives from his or her partner financial contributions used in obtaining a professional degree or license, with expectation of deriving material benefits for both marriage partners, such spouse may be called upon to reimburse the supporting spouse for the amount of contributions received).

Cost-value theory. Rather than place a specific present value on a degree or license and treat it as a divisible asset, some courts will apply a cost-value theory to the parties' relationship. This theory recognizes the contributions that a supporting spouse made to the person who obtained the degree while that person was obtaining it. In a cost-value jurisdiction, a court calculates the value of the supporting spouse's contributions, not only in terms of expenditures of money for education and living expenses, but also in terms of personal services rendered during the marriage. *See, e.g., De La Rosa v. De La Rosa*, 309 N.W.2d 755 (Minn. 1981) (wife awarded restitution for financial contributions made to husband during his medical schooling).

Lost opportunity theory. Some courts may consider applying what is referred to as a "lost opportunity costs" theory to cases where one spouse supports the other spouse who attains a degree, license, or certificate. This theory considers the income that the supporting spouse and family may have sacrificed because the student spouse attended school rather than accepting employment. If, for example, the student spouse could have earned $50,000 a year at a job for eight years rather than enter school with the goal of obtaining a medical license, the loss of income to the family unit is considered a lost opportunity costs (roughly 8 years × $50,000).

Lost expectation theory. Another approach that might be used where the court is considering how to treat the present value of the student spouse's enhanced earning capacity is called the "lost expectation" theory. This theory recognizes the supporting spouse's lost expectation of sharing in the enhanced earning capacity of the partner. It provides the supporting spouse with a return on his or her investment in the student spouse, measured by the enhanced earning capacity of the student spouse. For example, assume that the estimated enhanced earning capacity of the husband after graduating from medical school and completing a residency program was estimated at $266,000. The figure is arrived at as "the product of multiplying the husband's after-tax annual enhanced earnings of $13,000 (the difference between the husband's annual salary as a physician and the mean salary for college-educated males in his age group) by 32.3 (estimated years remaining in the husband's expected working life) discounted to its present value." *Haugan v. Haugan*, 343 N.W.2d 796, 803 (Wis. 1984) (suggesting several possible approaches to problem of compensating supporting spouse for costs and opportunities forgone while student spouse was in school).

13.18. Workers' Compensation and Personal Injury Issues

Courts are not uniform in their treatment of workers' compensation and personal injury awards. Some courts appear to categorize them as benefits to the marital corpus, whereas others view them as a personal injury recovery and the separate property of the injured party. The various perspectives are summarized next.

Mechanistic approach. Some courts take a mechanistic approach when considering how workers' compensation and personal injury awards should be distributed between married couples who divorce. In a mechanistic jurisdiction, if a personal injury or workers' compensation award was acquired during the marriage, it is considered marital or community property and is divided as such, unless it falls within specific statutory exceptions. Arkansas, Colorado, Illinois, Iowa, Michigan, Pennsylvania, and South Carolina appear to have adopted this view. *See Liles v. Liles*, 711 S.W.2d 447 (Ark. 1986) (Jones Act settlement was marital property that was properly awarded equally); *In re Marriage of Fieldheim*, 676 P.2d 1234 (Colo. App. 1983) (settlement offer made by an insurer upon a claim for personal injuries arising from an automobile accident that occurred during the course of the marriage was "marital property" and should have been subjected to equitable disposition, even though it was only for wife's pain and suffering); *In re Marriage of McNerney*, 417 N.W.2d 205 (Iowa 1987) (proceeds of personal injury claim are "marital assets," to be divided according to the circumstances of each case); *In re Marriage of Dettore*, 408 N.E.2d 429 (Ill. App. 1980) (workers' compensation award received by husband for personal injuries sustained during their marital relationship was marital property); *Hagen v. Hagen*, 508 N.W.2d 196 (Mich. 1993) (division of payments on workers' compensation claim for injury that occurred during the marriage found proper); *Platek v. Platek*, 454 A.2d 1059 (Pa. Super. 1982) (in defining "marital property," the legislature did not intend to except the proceeds of the settlement of a personal injury claim); *Marsh v. Marsh*, 437 S.E.2d 34 (S.C. 1993) (proceeds of personal injury settlement acquired during marriage are marital property).

Analytical theory approach. A growing number of courts have adopted the analytical theory, which requires an analysis of the nature of a workers' compensation or personal injury damage award to determine whether the property is separate and belongs to the injured spouse or is marital property subject to distribution. Under this theory, the damage award is allocated along the following lines. First, a court identifies the separate property of the injured spouse, which includes the noneconomic compensatory damages for pain, suffering, disability, and loss of ability to lead a normal life. Separate property also includes the economic damages that occur subsequent to the termination of the marriage, including the amount of the award for loss of future wages and future medical expenses. Second, a court identifies the separate property of the noninjured spouse, which includes loss of consortium. Third, the court identifies the marital property subject to distribution, which includes the amount of the award for lost wages or lost earning capacity during the marriage of the parties and medical expenses paid out of marital funds during the marriage. *See Weisfeld v. Weisfeld*, 545 So. 2d 1341, 1344-1345 (Fla. 1989) (analytical, rather than the mechanistic or unitary, approach was to be used in deciding how to treat workers' compensation award upon dissolution); *Mistler v. Mistler*, 816 S.W.2d 241 (Mo. App. 1991) (in determining whether personal injury recovery awarded during marriage is marital or nonmarital property, "analytic" approach, which asks what award was intended to replace, was appropriate, rather than the "mechanistic" approach, which does not engage in replacement analysis); *Parde v. Parde*, 602 N.W.2d 657 (Neb. 1999) (compensation for an injury that a spouse has or will receive for pain, suffering, disfigurement, disability, or loss of post-divorce earning capacity should not equitably be included in the marital estate; however, compensation for past wages, medical expenses, and other items that compensate for the diminution of the marital estate should equitably be included in the marital estate, as they properly replace losses of property created by the marital partnership).

Although community property states originally followed the mechanistic approach and treated a personal injury award as part of a marital couple's community property, Texas was one of the first to alter its approach and adopt the analytical approach in *Graham v. Franco*, 488 S.W.2d 390 (Tex. 1972) (while recovery for injuries to the spouse should be separate, the rule is different for other elements of recovery). Most community property states have adopted the analytical theory. *See Jurek v. Jurek*, 606 P.2d 812 (Ariz. 1980) (if personal injury to spouse results in loss of wages and expenses for hospital and medical care, such losses and expenses are injuries to community, and recoveries for such items belongs to community; however, compensation for injuries to a spouse's personal well-being, as distinguished from compensation for loss of wages and for expenses, belong to the injured spouse); *Rogers v. Yellowstone Park Co.*, 97 539 P.2d 566 (Idaho 1974) (in a personal injury action by wife against husband, general damages for loss of future earnings that would be community property would be recoverable only in fraction of one-half as the separate property of the injured spouse, and general damages for pain and suffering and emotional distress would be fully recoverable as the injured spouse's separate property); *Placide v. Placide*, 408 So. 2d 330 (La. App. 1981) (where a husband's settlement monies, acquired after dissolution of the community, but based upon a pre-dissolution, accident-related cause of action, compensate for both pre-dissolution and post-dissolution losses, that portion of the settlement which compensates for post-dissolution losses falls into the separate estate of the husband); *Frederickson & Watson Constr. Co. v. Boyd*, 102 P.2d 627 (Nev. 1940) (statute providing that all property acquired after marriage by either husband or wife, with specified exceptions, shall be community property, the word "acquired" was not used in an all-comprehensive sense but in a more restricted sense, embracing wages, salaries, earnings, or other property acquired through the toil, talent, or other productive faculty of either spouse, and did not include compensation for injuries to the person arising from violation of right of personal security); *Luxton v. Luxton*, 648 P.2d 315 (N.M. 1982) (in personal injury case, award for pain and suffering is spouse's separate property; however, husband's civil service medical retirement benefits were community property).

A growing number of equitable distribution jurisdictions have also adopted the analytical theory: *See Campbell v. Campbell*, 339 S.E.2d 591 (Ga. 1986) (settlement of personal injury claim of husband, to the extent that it represented compensation for pain and suffering and loss of capacity, was not subject to equitable division as a marital asset; however, to the extent settlement represented compensation for medical expenses or lost wages during marriage, it could be considered asset of marriage, and any amount attributable to loss of consortium was not an asset of marriage, but an asset of the spouse who suffered loss of consortium); *Van de Loo v. Van de Loo*, 346 N.W.2d 173 (Minn. App. 1984) (although husband's personal injury recoveries may have been nonmarital property, it would have worked unfair hardship not to apportion assets purchased with those proceeds); *In re Marriage of Blankenship*, 682 P.2d 1354 (Mont. 1984) (court must ask the purpose of workers' compensation award — that is, was it made for lost earnings, loss of future earning capacity, or some other purpose?); *Rich v. Rich*, 483 N.Y.S.2d 150 (N.Y. Sup. 1984) (noneconomic loss is separate property, and economic loss is marital property); *Johnson v. Johnson*, 346 S.E.2d 430 (N.C. 1986) (proceeds representing settlement recovered by husband upon claim for his personal injuries sustained during marriage constituted marital property to extent recovery represented compensation for lost wages and medical expenses, and constituted separate property of husband to extent recovery represented husband's personal suffering and disability).

Claim not mature at time of divorce. Another issue, raised on rare occasions in family court, involves a divorce that is about to be finalized while an unsettled personal injury or workers' compensation claim is pending. Courts take two approaches when considering how to resolve these situations. Some view the existence of the uncertainty surrounding the question of whether a plaintiff spouse may win or lose the claim as speculative and not constituting marital property. However, a majority of courts view a pending claim as potentially constituting marital property, which is subject to later determination and possible distribution once the pending claim is resolved. In these jurisdictions, a divorce decree will include provisions allowing an examination of any proceeds later awarded from the unsettled claim to determine what portion is marital property.

13.19. Goodwill

In general, goodwill is an intangible asset of a marriage and may be valued and distributed upon divorce. Goodwill is defined as "the benefits that accrue to a business as a result of its location, reputation for dependability, skill or quality, and any other circumstances resulting in probable retention of old or acquisition of new patronage." Goodwill value is a transferable property right that is generally defined as the amount that a willing buyer would pay for a going concern above the book value of the assets.

When the future earning capacity of a business has been enhanced because of its reputation, this leads to probable future patronage from existing and potential clients, and goodwill may exist and have value. When that occurs, the resulting goodwill is property subject to equitable distribution. *Spayd v. Turner, Granzow & Hollenkamp*, 482 N.E.2d 1232 (Ohio 1985).

Essentially, goodwill in a dissolution context is a portion of the value of the business as a going concern. *In re Marriage of Rives*, 181 Cal. Rptr. 572 (Cal. App. 1982).

An in-depth discussion of the valuation of good will of a business is beyond the scope of this chapter. Because of the complexities presented, family-law lawyers often seek the assistance of valuation experts and may present expert testimony when judicial determination is required.

RELATED AREAS OF LAW

13.20. Premarital Contracts

Premarital contracts or settlements are treated in more depth in Chapter 14. In general, premarital contracts validly executed and in conformity with local statutes and common law of a particular jurisdiction may determine what rights each party has in the marital property should the couple divorce or legally separate, or one of them dies while married to the other. These contracts may bar a spouse's rights in the marital estate, which is normally protected by provisions in divorce and probate statutes. *See Gentry v. Gentry*, 798 S.W.2d 928 (Ky. 1990) (premarital agreement providing for disposition of property in event of divorce was valid). By entering into a premarital contract, a couple waives the right to have a court consider how to divide their marital property upon death or divorce.

13.21. Bankruptcy

Congress changed the bankruptcy law in 1994 and again in 2005 so that divorce-related property obligations are not always dischargeable.

For example, a debt owed to a spouse, former spouse, or child in connection with a court order is not dischargeable in bankruptcy. 11 U.S.C. §523(a)(5). This includes any liability that "is actually in the nature of alimony, maintenance, or support." 11 U.S.C. §523(a)(5)(B). *See generally In re Douglas*, 369 B.R. 462, 465 (Bankr. E.D. Ark. 2007); Janet Leach Richards, *A Guide to Spousal Support and Property Division Claims Under the Bankruptcy Abuse Prevention and Consumer Protection Act of 2005*, 41 Fam. L. Q. 227 (2007).

13.22. Tax Treatment for Different-Sex Marriages versus Same-Sex Marriages

Federal tax law does not treat legally married same-sex persons in the same fashion as it treats legally married different-sex persons. Consequently, same-sex couples who legally marry or enter into a civil union or domestic partnership in one of the states that permit such relationships are treated the same as married different-sex couples for state tax purposes. However, they are treated as "single" strangers for federal tax purposes.

For example, because of the Tax Reform Act of 1984, the recipient of property in a different-sex divorce takes the transferor's adjusted basis as the value attached to the property. Prior to the 1984 reform, when property was transferred from one spouse to another because of a divorce settlement, and the fair market value exceeded the asset basis, the Internal Revenue Service (IRS) considered this a taxable event, and taxes were due. If property that was transferred had lost value, this was also considered a taxable event. *United States v. Davis*, 370 U.S. 65 (1962). For an overview of tax policy and family law, *see* Patricia Cain, *Taxing Families Fairly*, 48 Santa Clara L. Rev. 805 (2008).

This differential tax treatment given different-sex couples by Congress was not an accident; rather, it was an act of intentional and purposeful discrimination against lesbians and gay men.

> The exclusion of same-sex couples from the marital provisions is intentional. As a result, there is nothing hidden or covert about the heterosexist bias of the tax code. There is no neutral principle at work. The rationale for the exclusion is not that same-sex couples do not pool their resources like opposite-sex married couples. Instead, the rationale for the exclusion is based on the beliefs that a same-sex couple is not a family, that no civilized society has ever countenanced such unions, and that our Judeo-Christian heritage forbids them.

Nancy J. Knauer, *Heteronormativity and Federal Tax Policy*, 101 W. Va. L. Rev. 129, 233 (1998).

See also Golinski v. U.S. Office of Personnel Management, 824 F. Supp. 2d 968 (D.C. N.D. Calif. 2012) (Defense of Marriage Act (DOMA) provision defining "marriage" as between a man and a woman unconstitutional); *Windsor v.*

U.S., 833 F. Supp. 2d 394 (S.D. N.Y. 2012) (challenged that a section of DOMA violated equal protection under rational basis review as applied to women).

However, unless a final decision by the Supreme Court removes the discrimination evident in the tax code, different-sex and same-sex married couples will continue to receive separate treatment by the IRS.

Examples

10. Assume that before she gets married, P opens an investment account with a small brokerage firm. She puts $25,000 into the account. She still has the account when she and D marry. During the marriage, she keeps the account and occasionally talks with her broker about what to do about the various investments in it. After ten years, P and D divorce, and the account has a value of $50,000. D argues that the increased value of the account during the marriage is marital property; P contends that it is her separate nonmarital property. Most likely, how will a court rule?

11. When P is single, he has a savings and checking account. Monthly, he deposits funds into the checking and savings account from his salary. When P marries D, they open a joint savings and checking account. However, P continues to retain the savings and checking accounts that he opened when he was single. After he marries, P places all but 10 percent of his paycheck into his checking account and then transfers about half of that to the couple's joint checking account to pay expenses. He also transfers half of the remaining 10 percent to the couple's savings account. After 20 years, the couple divorce. P claims that all the money in his separate savings and checking accounts is his. D contends the funds are marital. Most likely, how will a court sort this out?

12. Assume that P and D marry. Following the wedding ceremony, P's father calls her aside and, according to her, takes out a check for $50,000 and gives it to her. She claims he said that "this is my and your mother's gift to you. Use it wisely." P took the check and excitedly ran over to D and said, "Wow, look what Dad did for us." P later deposited the check in the couple's joint savings account. A year later, she withdrew the money and made a down payment on a $100,000 home, taking out a $50,000 mortgage. After ten years, P and D divorce, and the mortgage has been paid off. P's father died five years after P and D married. In his will, he gave his other three children, X, Y, and Z, $50,000. He did not leave anything in his will to P. P contends that the $50,000 was a gift solely to her. P also contends that because the gift was solely to her that the passive increase in value of

the home is hers. She asks the court to award her the home, free and clear of any interest D may have in it.

13. Assume that on the day of her marriage to P, D owned 300 shares of XYZ Company. On the date of marriage, the market value of the publicly traded, unencumbered shares was $25 per share, or $7,500. At the time of the divorce, D owned 800 shares of XYZ Company, which then had a market value of $40 per share or $32,000. The increase in the number of shares was the result of a 2-for-1 split during the marriage, which increased D's holdings from 300 to 600 shares. The additional 200 shares were acquired through the reinvestment by D of cash dividends paid during the marriage. D claims all 800 shares of XYZ Company as her nonmarital property. P argues that the increase in value of the shares during the marriage and the additional shares received during the marriage are marital property. How will a court most likely resolve the dispute?

14. Assume that X and Y live together as husband and wife for 30 years when Y dies. When Y's will is probated, it transfers all of her interest in X's undistributed pension plan benefits to their two children. X marries Z a year after Y's death. X dies three years after the marriage to Z. Z seeks a survivor annuity under X's pension plan. The two children from X and Y's earlier marriage, A and B, seek a portion of the surviving annuity based upon Y's testamentary transfer of Y's rights to them in Y's will under state law. How will a court most likely apportion the annuity among A, B, and Z?

15. Assume that P and D were married and that D immediately embarked on an accelerated medical school program to obtain a medical degree. P testified that while D attended medical school, she worked as a server five or six nights a week, earning between $30 and $40 a night. In the summers, P also was employed as a recreational assistant. Before the marriage, she had worked as a nurse's aide. The money P earned was used to support the family and, to some extent, D's medical school tuition and expenses. D received his medical degree after several years of study and notified P on graduation night that he wanted a separation. They separated for two years, and then P began divorce proceedings because D was living with a female doctor. P testified that during the separation, she had obtained a nursing certificate, and at the time of the divorce, she was earning about $50,000 a year. It was estimated that D was earning about $150,000 a year. Because the parties had not accumulated marital property of any significant value at the time of separation, P could not be reimbursed for her contributions to her husband's education through a distribution of

property. P also waived a request for alimony. An expert placed a present value on D's medical degree at $1 million, and P sought a one-third share of it. In a majority of jurisdictions, how will a court most likely treat P's argument?

16. Assume that P is injured in an industrial accident during his marriage to D, loses his right arm, and is out of work for six months. P and D divorce in a jurisdiction that applies the analytical approach to workers' compensation awards. Six months after the divorce settlement, P receives a lump-sum payment of $100,000. P argues that compensation for an injury resulting in the loss of his right arm is a benefit and not property acquired during the marriage to be considered for distribution as marital property. P also argues that as an individual, he brought his body into the marriage, and on dissolution of the marriage, he is entitled to take it with him. He contends that his body is his separate property, and compensation received for damage or loss to it is his separate property. P also argues that a spouse's health, life, limb, personal security, and so on can be viewed as property acquired prior to marriage and later exchanged for compensation. Finally, he argues that because the final award was speculative at the time of divorce, it cannot be considered as marital property now. How will a court most likely treat these arguments and distribute the property?

17. Assume that P purchased a home just before her marriage to D for $100,000. P made a $20,000 down payment and took out a $80,000 mortgage. Assume that during the marriage, P and D reduced the $80,000 mortgage by $30,000. At the time of the divorce, the home is valued at $200,000. The trial judge is asked to determine what portion of the home, if any, is P's nonmarital separate property. What is the most likely outcome in a jurisdiction applying the source of funds rule?

18. Assume that P and D divorce after ten years of marriage. During the marriage, P worked outside the home while D worked inside the home raising their two children. During the marriage, P has accumulated retirement benefits that will vest if he continues his employment for the next 15 years. P argues that the court may not consider his benefits as marital property because they are a mere expectancy; i.e., he will receive them only if he continues working for the next 15 years for his current employer. D argues that the pension has a present value that can be calculated. D also argues that even if the present value cannot be calculated, the court should reserve jurisdiction and split the pension equitably when it vests. How should a court resolve this issue?

Explanations

10. The court will have to decide whether the increase in value is due solely to market forces (passive) or the increase was due in part to P's active involvement. If P was an active investor during the marriage and was regularly involved in selecting stock or bonds for the account, it is possible that a court will rule that the increase in value is due to her marital labor and therefore marital property. The crucial issue will be how much marital work P put into running the account. Here, because the hypothetical suggests that she talked with her broker only "occasionally" about her investments, a court would most likely find the increase in value passive and award the increase to P as her nonmarital property.

11. First, the joint account contains marital property. Second, most courts will take the view that all income from whatever source is marital property. Therefore, the funds that P placed into his separate accounts during the marriage were marital property. Third, P will have the burden of somehow separating the marital income from the nonmarital income in his effort to claim a right to funds that were in the two separate accounts just before the couple married. Those funds have been comingled with marital funds, and the jurisdiction well may presume that they have been transmuted into marital property. P will have the burden of tracing out of the separate accounts the nonmarital funds. This could be challenging. *See generally* J. Thomas Oldham, *Tracing, Commingling, and Transmutation*, 23 Fam. L. Q. 219 (1989).

12. First, the court will have to decide whether the $50,000 was a gift to P or a gift to P and D. The evidence provided by the will suggests that P's father intended the $50,000 as an intestate gift to her. In his will, he provided $50,000 for his other three children and nothing for P. (Whether anything that P's father may have said is admitted will turn on the jurisdiction's rules of evidence.) P's statement that the gift may have been to both of them makes the outcome of this part of the lawsuit more challenging. Probably (and credibility will be an issue) P will prevail on her claim that the $50,000 was a gift solely to her.

    The increase in value of the home was due to passive forces. Therefore, all the increase is marital. The outcome may well be that P receives $75,000 from the home and D $25,000.

13. If the court applies the intent of the drafters of the UMDA, §307, *comment at* 204 (1970), a stock split is considered nonmarital property. The theory is that when stock splits, the value is determined by market forces and does not increase the shareholder's proportionate ownership

interest in the corporation. Therefore, its increased value is passive and not considered income generated actively by the parties. The 600 shares would be awarded to D.

A court will treat the remaining 200 shares as having been purchased with marital funds and, therefore, as being marital property. The 200 shares would be divided equally between P and D.

14. To the extent that a state law might provide A and B with a right to a portion of Z's survivor's annuity, it is preempted by ERISA. The annuity is a qualified joint and survivor annuity mandated by §1055 of ERISA, the object of which is to ensure a stream of income to surviving spouses. ERISA's solicitude for the economic security of such spouses would be undermined by allowing a predeceasing spouse's heirs and legatees to have a community property interest in the survivor's annuity. Even a plan participant cannot defeat a nonparticipant surviving spouse's statutory entitlement to such an annuity. See §1055(c)(2). Nothing in ERISA's language supports the conclusion that Congress decided to permit a predeceasing nonparticipant spouse to do so. Testamentary transfers such as the one at issue could reduce the annuity below the ERISA minimum. See §1055(d)(1). Perhaps even more troubling, the recipient of the transfer need not be a family member; for example, the annuity might be substantially reduced so that funds could be diverted to support an unrelated stranger. In the face of a direct clash between state law and ERISA's provisions and objectives, the state law cannot stand. *Boggs v. Boggs*, 520 U.S. 833 (1997); *See Gade v. National Solid Wastes Management Assn.*, 505 U.S. 88, 98 (1992). A court most likely will award the annuity to Z and nothing to A or B.

15. A court in a majority of jurisdictions will not place a value on the medical degree but will distribute it to P. It will recognize that shortly after the degree was received, the marriage failed, and P was unable to see any benefit for her years of sacrifice while D was able to pursue a professional medical degree and become a physician. Many courts will conclude that P should be compensated in some fashion for the financial support that she gave D while he was a student. Any one of the several theories discussed earlier in this section might be selected by the court. When the compensatory theory is selected and an award made, it will not be viewed as alimony. Rather, it will be considered compensation for P's contribution to attainment of the degree while they were married. *See Lehmicke v. Lehmicke*, 559, 489 A.2d 782 (Pa. Super. 1985); *Mahoney v. Mahoney*, 453 A.2d 527 (N.J. 1982). If alimony were awarded (P waived alimony), courts have a tendency to adjust the compensation to recognize the contributions made by the supporting spouse. A court

on the facts of the hypothetical is faced with a very challenging problem. One of the more favored theories is the cost-value approach, described earlier, and it might well be selected as an equitable method of resolving the dispute. *See, e.g., De La Rosa v. De La Rosa*, 309 N.W.2d 755 (Minn. 1981).

16. A court is likely to view the award as encompassing earnings lost both before and after the divorce and as involving individual pain and suffering. If a portion of the award is for income lost before divorce and while the couple was married, a court would hold that the pre-divorce portion is marital property subject to division. The post-divorce portion related to loss of income will likely be viewed as nonmarital property that belongs exclusively to P. *See Miller v. Miller*, 739 P.2d 163, 165 (Alaska 1987); *Queen v. Queen*, 521 A.2d 320, 324 (Md. 1987). The court would also consider that the noneconomic compensatory damages for pain, suffering, disability, and P's loss of ability to lead a normal life are P's nonmarital property and not subject to distribution.

17. First, it is clear that the $20,000 that P paid down on the home prior to her marriage to D is her separate nonmarital property. Second, $30,000 in marital funds was invested in the home. Third, the total equity in the home is the current market value ($200,000) minus the $30,000 that P and D reduced the mortgage by during their marriage. This leaves the total equity in the home at $170,000. Some courts will use the following calculation to arrive at the marital and nonmarital portion:

$$[30{,}000/\ (20{,}000 + 30{,}000)] \times 170{,}000 = 102{,}000 \text{ in marital property.}$$

$$[20{,}000/(20{,}000 + 30{,}000)] \times 170{,}000 = 68{,}000 \text{ in separate nonmarital property.}$$

See Holman v. Holman, 228 S.W.3d 628 (Mo. App. 2007) ("[t]he source of funds rule does not cause the entire increase in value of separate property accruing during a marriage to be marital property irrespective of the source of that increase"). Note that in several states, rental income from separate property remains separate nonmarital property. However, that is not the case in Missouri.

Also, note that some courts have held that where a mortgage is being paid down during a marriage that and both spouses contributed to its upkeep through labor, the entire $170,000 in this hypothetical will be considered marital property. *See, e.g., Kaaa v. Kaaa*, 58 So. 3d 867, 872-873 (Fla. 2010) ("when a marital home constitutes nonmarital real property, but is encumbered by a mortgage that marital funds service, the value of the passive, market-driven appreciation of the property that accrues during the course of the marriage is a marital asset"). *See generally* George L. Blum, *Divorce and Separation: Appreciation in Value of Separate Property During Marriage with Contribution by Either Spouse as Separate or Community Property (Doctrine of "Active Appreciation")*, 9 A.L.R. 6th 205 (originally published in 2008).

18. Most courts today will consider the unvested pension as marital property. The court then will consider two approaches. Either reserve jurisdiction and award the pension benefits equitably if and when the pension vests, or arrive at a present value for the unvested pension and award D offsetting assets.

If the judge reserves jurisdiction, this avoids placing the risk that the pension will never vest on P. The problem is that it continues a financial relationship for a long period after the divorce.

However, if the judge agrees to a present value of the unvested pension via an expert, and awards assets to D to offset that amount, P runs the entire risk of losing the pension because it fails to vest. Although courts will select either method, depending on the facts of each case, because of the long period before P's pension vests, the court in this hypothetical probably will seek to place a current value on the unvested pension and award offsetting assets to D. (One might argue that there is no good solution to the hypothetical—only a decision.)

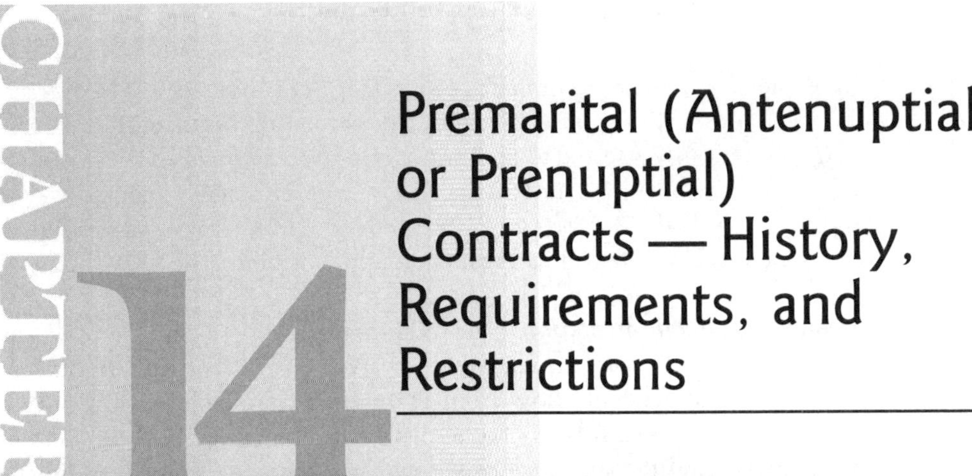

Chapter 14 Premarital (Antenuptial or Prenuptial) Contracts — History, Requirements, and Restrictions

14.1. Introduction

This chapter surveys the legal issues confronted by practicing lawyers, legislatures, and courts when dealing with a premarital contract. Unfortunately, as a leading scholar in this area has observed, it is fraught with jurisdictional inconsistencies and conflict:

> [S]ince 2000 the highest courts of four states have rendered conflicting decisions in cases with similar facts and issues. In two of these jurisdictions, the courts did so without seeming to recognize the conflicts. In two others, the courts offered unconvincing attempts to reconcile or distinguish the cases. Courts have also made elementary mistakes in interpretation, changed standards during the course of litigation, applied these standards without notice to the parties, and condoned results that offend established policy.

Judith T. Younger, *Lovers' Contracts in the Courts: Forsaking the Minimum Decencies*, 13 Wm. & Mary J. Women & L. 349, 412 (Winter 2007).

Despite the inconsistencies and conflict, this chapter endeavors to provide a general overview of premarital contracts, with an emphasis on the most common legal issues that courts are asked to resolve.

Jurisdictions variously label or refer to a premarital contract as a *premarital, antenuptial,* or *prenuptial* agreement or contract. *See, e.g., Ansin v. Craven-Ansin*, 929 N.E.2d 955, 958 n.1 (Mass. 2010) ("we adopt the term 'premarital' agreement for what is often termed a prenuptial or antenuptial agreement, and the term 'marital' agreement for what is often termed a postnuptial agreement"); *Lawrence v. Lawrence*, 687 S.E.2d 421 (Ga. 2009) (contracts between prospective spouses conditioned on the later occurrence of a marriage are variously referred to in statutes, case law, and treatises as "antenuptial," "prenuptial," "antemarital," or "premarital" contracts or agreements); *Black's Law Dictionary* 1220 (8th ed. 2004) (stating a prenuptial agreement is also referred to as an antenuptial or premarital agreement).

Limiting judicial discretion. A valid premarital contract permits the parties to agree before they marry to waive or limit certain "rights" or "benefits" that generally flow from the marital relationship via state law. A premarital contract may affect the distribution of property should either party die during the marriage or should they divorce. Depending on the jurisdiction, such a contract also may affect alimony. Premarital contracts modify or shrink the general discretion of a judge who is applying either probate or divorce law to a particular family law problem. Note that as a rule, a judge is not free to ignore the provisions of a premarital contract or render them ineffective. *Turchin v. Turchin*, 16 So. 3d 1042 (Fla. App. 2009).

Premarital contracts were traditionally used in the United States by individuals contemplating a second marriage who sought to protect from probate assets intended for children from a prior marriage. Much, however, has changed. Premarital contracts today have become increasingly used to condition marital rights upon death and divorce. This may be the result of the high divorce rate or greater numbers of second and third marriages, with the parties bringing to the relationship existing assets, liabilities, and children. It has been observed that "in a society of multiple marriages with all of the attendant property and debt acquisitions, family gifts and inheritances, a comprehensive premarital agreement may be one of the most important documents a couple will negotiate." Linda D. Elrod & the Honorable James P. Buchele, 1 *Kan. Law & Prac., Family Law* §2:1 (4th ed., Kansas Family Law (Current through the 2011 Update)).

HISTORY

14.2. Ancient Origins

Premarital agreements between parties contemplating marriage have existed in some form in almost every culture throughout the world for well over 2,000 years. Mary Lou Miller Wagstaff, *Drafting Marriage Contracts in Florida*, Chapter 2, The Florida Bar (10th ed. 2012). For example, Middle Eastern tribal families entered into dowry marriage contracts. The concept "traveled to ancient Greece and later established its roots in European history as the process whereby a woman's family negotiated with her intended husband's family to provide a certain amount of money, goods, animals, or land to the husband to be set aside so that the woman would not become impoverished in the event of a divorce or the husband's death." *Ibid.*

The ancient Jewish ketubah, entered into before the marriage, controlled the obligations of the parties to each other during the marriage, in addition to a provision for alimony in the event of divorce. *Ibid.* Sephardic Jewish women are said to have carried their dowry with them in the form of jewelry, which sometimes covered almost every visible inch of their bodies.

In some parts of the Arab world, a marriage contract requires that the husband give the wife sadaq, which is a material gift that becomes hers to keep in order to compensate for the fact that her husband can declare a divorce at any time. *See generally* C.M.A. McCauliff, *The Medieval Origin of the Doctrine of Estates in Land: Substantive Property Law, Family Considerations, and the Interests of Women*, 66 Tul. L. Rev. 919 (1992) (discussing twelfth- and thirteenth-century marriage "portions" in England (parents giving land to a betrothed couple in consideration of marriage)).

Premarital contracts, in somewhat the form we know them today, appeared in England as early as the sixteenth century. Both the chancery and law courts passed on their validity, and they were of sufficient importance to be included in the original Statute of Frauds of 1677. Judith T. Younger, *Perspectives on Antenuptial Contracts*, 40 Rutgers L. Rev. 1059, 1061, nn. 2, 5 (1988); W. Holdsworth, *A History of English Law* 310-312 Little Brown, and Company (3d ed. 1922). *See generally Wilson v. Wilson*, 185 N.W. 97 (Iowa 1921) (commenting on the Statute of Frauds).

14.3. Overview of the Development of Premarital Contracts

Limited use. Historically, in England and the United States, a premarital contract settled property rights at the time of the death of one of the parties to the relationship. As noted above, a contract was often executed when the parties were contemplating a second marriage, and one or both had substantial property and children from a first marriage to whom they wanted their property to go upon their death. Without a premarital contract, in most jurisdictions, a surviving spouse had the option of taking property under a will or taking a statutory share of the marital estate and ignoring the will.

Premarital contracts that were enforced upon death of a party were "favored by the law as promoting domestic happiness and adjusting property questions which would otherwise often be the source of fruitful litigation." *Buffington v. Buffington*, 51 N.E. 328, 329 (Ind. 1898). *See Williamson v.*

First Nat. Bank of Williamson, 164 S.E. 777 (W. Va. 1931) (premarital contracts tend to adjust family disputes).

Community property states. The Spanish system of community property was followed in some states in the west and southwest, such as Texas, as early as 1840. *See* W. Fred Cameron, Robert S. Hoffman, & Alan V. Ytterberg, *Marital and Premarital Agreements*, 39 Baylor L. Rev. 1095, 1099 (Fall 1987). At that time, both premarital and post-marital agreements were legally enforceable under the Spanish system of community property unless the contract resulted from undue influence on the part of the male. The Spanish system of community property treated a husband and wife as distinct and equal legal entities. Spanish laws were intended to apply only when the marriage partners had not voluntarily structured and ordered their own affairs. *Ibid.*

Use at common law. Common law and community property courts took the view that a premarital contract that contemplated and made provision for a divorce violated public policy, while one that only encompassed provision for property interests upon death did not. *See* 5 *Williston on Contracts* §11:8. They reasoned that the public's interest in the enforcement of a husband's duty of support should not be thwarted by a premarital provision that bore little or no reasonable relationship to the subsequent circumstances of the parties. A premarital contract that distributed property upon divorce was viewed as an instrument that would cause a marriage to lose its "dignity and sacredness," lead to endless, minor litigation, and encourage the property-owning spouse to desert the other spouse. Allison A. Marston, *Planning for Love: The Politics of Prenuptial Agreements*, 49 Stan. L. Rev. 887, 897 (April 1997). *See Cohn v. Cohn*, 121 A.2d 704 (Md. 1956) (rule is well established that a contract that provides for, facilitates, or tends to induce a separation or divorce of the parties after marriage is contrary to public policy and void); *Stratton v. Wilson*, 185 S.W. 522, 523 (Ky. 1916) (premarital agreements contemplating divorce and separation are void because they tended to promote, or at least predict, marital instability), *overruled by Gentry v. Genry*, 796 S.W.2d 928 (Ky. 1990). *See also In re Estate of Appleby*, 111 N.W. 305, 308 (Minn. 1907) (contracts that tend to induce a separation of husband and wife are, upon the same principle of public policy that discountenances contracts in restraint of marriage, utterly void and of no force or effect).

Common law barrier removed. By the 1970s, the public's perspective on marriage and divorce had markedly changed from years past. Doris Jonas Freed & Timothy B.Walker, *Family Law in the Fifty States: An Overview*, 19 Fam. L.Q. 331, 438 (1985-1986). The country was experiencing major cultural change, and views toward marriage and divorce were being radically altered. With the changes in societal norms, the traditional rule regarding the limitation on a premarital contract as available only upon the death of a party was being challenged.

The decision by the Florida Supreme Court in *Posner v. Posner*, 233 So. 2d 381 (Fla. 1970), marks a turning point in the use of premarital contracts upon divorce. When *Posner* was decided, the court took judicial notice of the fact that the ratio of marriages to divorces had:

> reached a disturbing rate in many states . . . . With divorce such a commonplace fact of life, it is fair to assume that many prospective marriage partners whose property and familial situation is such as to generate a valid premarital contract settling their property rights upon the death of either, might want to consider and discuss also — and agree upon, if possible — the disposition of their property and the alimony rights of the wife in the event their marriage, despite their best efforts, should fail.

Id. at 384.

After *Posner*, jurisdictions steadily retreated from the common law view that a premarital contract was limited to use only upon the death of a party. *See, e.g.*, *Rinvelt v. Rinvelt*, 475 N.W.2d 478 (Mich. App. 1991) (concluding that the outdated policy concerns that once led courts to refuse to enforce premarital agreements are no longer compelling); *Brooks v. Brooks*, 733 P.2d 1044 (Alaska 1987) (no-fault divorce laws and societal changes have given way to the more realistic view that premarital agreements for use upon divorce are not void *ab initio*).

Posner and the cases and legislation following that decision set out a general criterion that courts were to use when reviewing premarital agreements. In general, courts considered that a valid premarital agreement should usually contain a fair and reasonable provision for the non-monied, non-propertied spouse, often the wife. Absent such provision, there had to be a full and frank disclosure of each spouse's worth, or, absent such disclosure, at least a general and approximate knowledge of each spouse's prospective property. *Posner, supra* at 385 of 233 So. 2d. *citing Del Vecchio v. Del Vecchio*, 143 So. 2d 17 (Fla. 1962).

Minority view. A minority jurisdiction, Pennsylvania, has rejected the *Posner* criterion, which affords certain protections to the parties to a premarital contract. In *Simeone v. Simeone*, 581 A.2d 162 (Pa. 1990), the court decided that Pennsylvania would no longer inquire into whether the terms of the premarital agreement were fair or whether the parties had informed understandings of the rights that they were surrendering. The court concluded that challenges to premarital contracts would be the same as those available for conventional contract agreements; i.e., duress, unconscionability, and misrepresentation. In issuing its opinion, the court rejected earlier Pennsylvania decisions, such as *In re Estate of Geyer*, 533 A.2d 423 (Pa. 1987), that had said that premarital contracts would be approved only if they either "made an adequate provision for [a spouse]" or provided for "full and fair disclosure [of the] general financial pictures of the parties [and] the statutory rights [being relinquished]." *See* Howard Fink & June Carbon, *Between Private Ordering and Public Fiat: A New Paradigm for Family Law Decision-Making*, 5 J.L. & Fam. Stud. 1, 20-21 (2003).

The majority in *Simeone* reasoned that earlier Pennsylvania premarital contract opinions were based on the assumption that "spouses are of unequal status." Now, concluded the majority, spouses have equal bargaining status.

Note, however, that in *In re O'Brien*, 898 A.2d 1075 (Pa. Super. 2006), the court appeared to temper the views expressed in *Simeone* somewhat, stating that "in reorienting our standards for enforcing prenuptial agreements to the traditional principles of contract law, . . . we did not lose sight of the fact that parties to these agreements do not necessarily deal with each other at arm's length. Accordingly, we reaffirmed 'the longstanding principle that a full and fair disclosure of the financial positions of the parties is required.' " *Id.* at 1080.

APPLICATION

14.4. Uses Today

There are many provisions used in modern premarital contracts to limit recovery upon a spouse's death or divorce. A few of those include the following:

- To eliminate a widow's right to reject a will and take a statutory share of the estate upon the death of the advantaged partner.
- To protect each party's premarital separate property and post-marital inheritances from the other party. *Schmidt v. Schmidt*, 812 N.E.2d 1074, 1082 (Ind. App. 2004).
- To provide "family cooperation and harmony." *Gamache v. Smurro*, 904 A.2d 91, 98 (Vt. 2006).
- To protect the existing party's assets so that they will go to the children of a former marriage — usually where the former partner had died. *See Roth v. Roth*, 565 N.W.2d 782, 785 (S.D. 1997) (dominant purpose of the premarital agreement is clearly to protect the inheritance rights of the parties' respective children).

Objections to premarital contracts. There are several reasons given by opponents of these contracts to discourage their use. The most prominent of these is that the agreement may be unfair to the financially disadvantaged partner by placing too much emphasis on the good of the advantaged partner to the detriment of the disadvantaged partner. The agreement may also suggest a lack of trust in the other partner and have a dampening impact on the upcoming marriage.

There are also concerns about the drafting environment in which these contracts are signed. The environment is emotionally charged and the parties are generally described as "in love" and about to be married. Lawyers concerned with these contracts say that if there is a waiver of maintenance, the agreement is likely to be challenged in a subsequent divorce. Alternatively, they say that if the agreement waives rights under the Probate Act to disallow a will and take the statutory amount, it also likely will be challenged.

Some claim that premarital contracts overwhelmingly hurt women by virtue of their inferior bargaining position. A contrary argument is made that a premarital contract actually benefits women because women, who have traditionally possessed less power in the marriage relationship, may feel that their rights are better protected if they are formalized in a premarital contract. *See* Note, Alison J. Chen & Jonathan A. Sambur, *Are Consensual Relationship Agreements a Solution to Sexual Harassment in the Workplace?* 17 Hofstra Lab. & Emp. L.J. 165, 192 n. 224 (Fall 1999).

14.5. Difference Between Premarital and Commercial Contracts

Most agree that there are three basic differences between a premarital contract and an ordinary civil contract. First, the state has a greater interest in a premarital contract than in a commercial contract. Because of its interest, the state assumes the role of *parens patriae* with respect to protecting any children of the relationship and, in some cases, protecting against an unfair distribution of marital and nonmarital property and an improper waiver of alimony. Second, the relationship between the parties is different from that found in an ordinary business contract because at the time a premarital contract is signed, courts view the relationship between the parties as confidential, not as an arm's-length one. Furthermore, unlike most business contracts, the parties to a premarital contract may not be evenly matched in bargaining power. Finally, a premarital contract is to be performed in the future, in the context of a personal relationship that the parties have yet to experience. Judith T. Younger, *Perspectives on Antenuptial Contracts*, 40 Rutgers L. Rev. 1059, 1061 (1988).

14.6. Model Uniform Acts

The National Conference of Commissioners on Uniform State Laws (NCCUSL) and the American Law Institute (ALI) have both created model uniform premarital acts that they believe are worthy of state legislative consideration and adoption. This section highlights some of the provisions in these model acts.

NCCUSL. In 1983, the NCCUSL promulgated the Uniform Premarital Agreement Act (UPAA). The UPAA was written to provide state legislatures with a model statute to consider when drafting premarital contract provisions. The UPAA addresses the formalities for execution and enforcement of premarital contracts. The UPAA has been adopted in some form in more than 30 jurisdictions. *See* Richard A. Lord, *Agreements between husband and wife; premarital agreements*, 5 Williston on Contracts §11:8 (4th ed.) (May 2012).

The UPAA creates a presumption that premarital contracts are valid and enforceable and places on the party seeking to void the contract the burden of proving the contrary. A comment to the UPAA states that the marriage itself acts as consideration for a premarital contract. To invalidate a premarital contract, the party challenging it must prove that the contract was unconscionable, a somewhat amorphous concept. *See Coady v. Cross Country Bank*, 729 N.W.2d 732, 739 (Wisc. App. 2007) ("Unconscionability is an amorphous concept that evades precise definition. Indeed, it has been said that '[i]t is not possible to define unconscionability. It is not a concept but a determination to be made in light of a variety of factors not unifiable into a formula' ").

New effort. Since the UPAA has been adopted in some form in a majority of jurisdictions, it has brought some consistency to the legal treatment of premarital agreements. This is true where rights at the time a marriage is dissolved is concerned. However, as noted at the beginning of this chapter, the state of affairs regarding marital agreements has been unsettled and inconsistent. Some states have neither case law nor legislation, while the remaining states have created a wide range of approaches. In response to the inconsistency, in July of 2012 the National Conference of Commissioners on Uniform State Laws (NCCUSL) adopted the Uniform Premarital and Marital Agreements Act (UPMAA) at its 121st annual meeting in Nashville, Tennessee. According to a July 23, 2012, news release by the Uniform Law Commission:

> The general approach of this new Uniform Act is that parties should be free, within broad limits, to choose the financial terms of their marriage. The limits are those of due process in formation, on the one hand, and certain minimal standards of substantive fairness, on the other.

ALI. The ALI included provisions for drafting and evaluating premarital contracts in its *Principles of Family Dissolution: Analysis and Recommendations* (Tentative Draft No. 4 2000). The *Principles* contain procedural requirements that include provisions that a contract be signed and in writing, that there be full financial disclosure, and that consent not be obtained under duress. The *Principles* hold to the view that there is a presumption of informed consent and the absence of duress if the contract was executed at least 30 days before the parties' marriage and if the parties were advised to obtain legal counsel and had an opportunity to do so.

Burden. The ALI places the burden of proving the lack of duress and the presence of consent on the party who is trying to enforce the contract, which is intended to "caution" the stronger party against overreaching. Judith T. Younger, *Antenuptial Contracts*, 28 Wm. Mitchell L. Rev. 697, 718 (2000). Should one party fail to retain independent counsel, the informed-consent presumption will not go into effect unless the contract contains understandable language explaining the significance of its terms and the fact that the parties' interests may be adverse with respect to them. *Ibid.*

The ALI omits any requirement of substantive fairness at the time of execution. However, at the time that the contract is to be enforced, the *Principles* provide for "a wider substantive review of these contracts" than allowed under the UPAA. *Ibid.*

14.7. Common Statutory Criteria

Many jurisdictions have attempted to reduce the uncertainty surrounding the use of premarital contracts by promulgating statutes that replace the common law and set forth specific procedures that must be followed when drafting them. *See, e.g.*, N. J. Stat. §37:2-38 (2009) (enforcement of premarital or pre-civil union agreement, generally); Tenn. Code §36-3-501 (2009) (enforcement of premarital agreements); Minn. Stat. §519.11 (2005) (requirements for premarital and postnuptial contracts).

In a majority of states, a premarital contract relating to the property of the parties, and more specifically to the rights of the parties to that property upon the dissolution of the marriage, is generally enforceable where the following conditions are satisfied: (1) the contract was validly entered into; (2) its terms do not violate statute or public policy; and (3) the circumstances of the parties at the time that the marriage is dissolved are not so beyond the contemplation of the parties at the time that the contract was entered into as to cause its enforcement to work injustice. A contract must also be (4) fair, equitable, and reasonable in the view of all the surrounding facts and circumstances; (5) entered into voluntarily by both parties; with (6) each understanding his or her rights and the extent of the waiver of such rights. *See McHugh v. McHugh*, 436 A.2d 8, 11 (Conn. 1980).

Note that the fact that one party to the contract apparently made a bad bargain is not a sufficient ground, by itself, to vacate or modify a premarital contract. *Micale v. Micale*, 542 So. 2d 415, 417 (Fla. App. 1989) (while wife made a bad bargain for herself in entering into an agreement dividing various businesses between her and her husband, the evidence failed to support claim of fraud).

14.8. Special Duty to Disclose

Premarital contracts, unlike commercial contracts, are viewed in most jurisdictions as giving rise to a special duty of disclosure. It is common, for example, to find courts and statutes adhering to the principle that each person signing a premarital contract has an affirmative duty to disclose to the other the nature of his or her property interests so that the effect of the contract can be understandingly assessed and waived. Disclosure is important because it underscores that each party is exercising a meaningful choice when he or she agrees to give up certain rights to protect married persons should they divorce or should one of them die during the marriage. *See Ortel v. Gettig*, 116 A.2d 145 (Md. 1955) (refusing to uphold contract where there was no disclosure or discussion of the net worth of the parties); *Corbett v. Corbett*, 628 S.E.2d 585 (Ga. 2006) (upholding trial court's refusal to enforce premarital agreement based on finding that husband "failed to disclose his income" because "[h]usband's income was material to the premarital agreement"); *In re Benker's Estate*, 331 N.W.2d 193 (Mich. 1982) ("[i]n order for an antenuptial agreement to be valid, it must be fair, equitable, and reasonable in view of the surrounding facts and circumstances. It must be entered into voluntarily by both parties, with each understanding his or her rights and the extent of the waiver of such rights"); *Mabus v. Mabus*, 890 So. 2d 806 (Miss. 2003) (a duty to disclose is of paramount importance in a premarital agreement).

The requirement of disclosure is intimately connected to the concept of waiver. *See Burtoff v. Burtoff*, 418 A.2d 1085, 1089 (D.C. App. 1980) (prospective spouses may contractually define their rights in property and waive rights that otherwise would arise as a matter of law). The relationship is particularly important given the perspective of a majority of jurisdictions that consider the relationship as confidential; that is, not an arm's-length transaction. Courts reason that without full and truthful disclosure of the nature, extent, and worth of the real and personal property involved in the agreement, the party who contractually waives statutory protections cannot know what is in fact being waived. *See Newman v. Newman*, 653 P.2d 728, 732 (Colo. 1982) (if stringent tests of full disclosure and lack of fraud or overreaching are met, parties are free to agree to any arrangement for division of their property, including a waiver of any claim to the property of the other).

The full disclosure rule also helps level the bargaining field for the party who may be in the weaker bargaining position. *Kosik v. George*, 452 P.2d 560, 563 (Or. 1969) (invalid contract where decedent was a man of extensive business background, knowledge, and financial worth, and widow was a woman with high school education, very limited business experience, and limited financial worth; such wide disparity between decedent and widow invoked responsibility on decedent and his attorney to inform widow fully regarding consequences of executing premarital agreement, but the only advice given widow before she signed agreement was that purpose of agreement was to avoid dower and curtesy, and agreement instead acted as a bar to her right to claim property exempt from execution). Note that dower is generally defined as "a common-law right of a surviving widow to a life estate in one-third of the inheritable real estate owned by the husband during the coverture, which right, prior to the husband's decease, is said to be inchoate, and after his death it becomes consummate." *Silberman v. Jacobs*, 267 A.2d 209 (Md. App. 1970). *Curtesy* is generally defined as "When any man and his wife shall be seized in her right of any estate of inheritance in lands, the husband shall, on the death of his wife, hold the lands for his life as tenant thereof by the curtesy: Provided, that if the wife, at her death, shall leave issue by any former husband, to whom the estate might descend, such issue shall take the same, discharged from the right of the surviving husband to hold the same as tenant by the curtesy." *Tong v. Marvin*, 15 Mich. 60, 68 (Mich. 1866).

Meaning of "full disclosure." The meaning of what constitutes "full and fair" disclosure varies from case to case, and depends on a number of factors, which may include the parties' respective sophistication and experience in business affairs; their respective worth, ages, intelligence, and literacy; their prior family ties or commitments; the duration of their relationship prior to the execution of the contract; the time of the signing of the contract in relation to the time of the wedding; and their representation by, or opportunity to consult with, independent counsel. *See, e.g.*, *Randolph v. Randolph*, 937 S.W.2d 815 (Tenn. 1996) (former wife did not enter premarital agreement knowledgeably, even though she had lived with husband for about a year before marriage, was aware of nature of former husband's business but was not aware of nature or extent of his assets, had no prior business experience or knowledge, he was a shrewd businessperson, and she had no opportunity to study the agreement or to seek advice from her own attorney or others close to her); *Oldani v. Oldani*, 34 A.3d 407 (Conn. 2011) (although the husband may have provided a sufficient approximation of his property holdings and other financial obligations, he failed to provide the wife with sufficient information regarding his income prior to her signing the premarital agreement).

The nature and extent of disclosure turns on the language of a state's premarital statute (if it has one) or the common law of the state (if there is no statute). In general, under the common law, disclosure was usually not required to reveal precisely every asset owned by an individual spouse. *See Winchester v. McCue*, 882 A.2d 143 (Conn. App. 2005) (holding that parties' failure to disclose income not fatal to premarital agreement if parties had independent knowledge of each other's income). At a minimum, full and fair disclosure normally requires that each contracting party be given a clear idea of the nature, extent, and value of the other party's property and resources. *See, e.g., Pajak v. Pajak*, 385 S.E.2d 384, 388 (Va. 1989) (contract upheld where wife knew husband was a successful businessman and she was aware that he owned a number of businesses, had real estate holdings, and lived reasonably well; it is not necessary that parties execute a detailed, written financial statement such as is required by a bank before making a loan); *Hartz v. Hartz*, 234 A.2d 865, 871, n.3 (Md. 1967).

EXAMPLE

Example

1. Assume that P and D execute a premarital contract in 1890 containing a provision that limits the amount of marital property that D would receive should the couple divorce. In a typical common law jurisdiction, how is such a provision treated? In a twenty-first century jurisdiction that applies the *Posner* perspective, how would such a provision be treated?

EXPLANATION

Explanation

1. In a common law jurisdiction, the 1890 contract provision related to dividing marital property would not be enforced. Common law courts viewed a contract to distribute property upon divorce as contrary to public policy, on the theory that it encouraged a breakdown of the marriage relationship. In a jurisdiction that has adopted the *Posner* view of premarital contracts, courts would uphold the contract, assuming that it was arrived at fairly. *See Snedaker v. Snedaker*, 660 So. 2d 1070 (Fla. App. 1995) (provisions in premarital contract that neither spouse acquired any interest in property of other as a result of marriage, provisions that set the amount of the wife's support payments on escalating scale based on the length of marriage, and provisions that specifically waived a spouse's right to receive any further alimony, support, or maintenance payments were fair and reasonable to wife, given the circumstances of the spouses).

14.9. Voluntarily Executed

The UPAA, discussed earlier in this chapter and adopted in some form by several states, does not contain a section that defines the meaning of "voluntarily executed" in the context of premarital agreements. It has left it up to individual jurisdictions to decide voluntariness when considering specific disputes involving premarital contracts. As a starting point, the term *voluntarily* is defined in *Black's Law Dictionary* 1605 (8th ed. 2004) as "[i]ntentionally; without coercion."

California's Supreme Court engaged in a helpful discussion of the meaning of "voluntarily" in *In re Marriage of Bonds*, 5 P.3d 815 (Cal. 2000). The Court said that when considering voluntariness, and asking whether the evidence demonstrates coercion or lack of knowledge, the following factors should be considered:

- the coercion that may arise from the proximity of execution of the agreement to the wedding;
- or from surprise in the presentation of the agreement;
- the presence or absence of independent counsel or of an opportunity to consult independent counsel;
- inequality of bargaining power-in some cases indicated by the relative age and sophistication of the parties;
- whether there was full disclosure of assets; and
- the parties' understanding of the rights being waived under the agreement or at least their awareness of the intent of the agreement.

Id. at 824-25. *See Edwards v. Edwards*, 744 N.W.2d 243 (Neb. App. 2008) *citing In re Marriage of Bonds*, 5 P.3d 815 (Cal. (2000) (superseded by statute as stated in *In re Marriage of Cadwell–Faso and Faso*, 119 Cal. Rptr. 3d 818 (Cal. App. 2011)).

Other jurisdictions have followed California's view of "voluntarily." *See, e.g., Edwards v. Edwards*, 744 N.W.2d 243, 254 (Neb. App. 2008) (*quoting In re Marriage of Bonds*); *In re Marriage of Shanks*, 758 N.W.2d 506, 513-514 (Iowa 2008) (agreement voluntarily entered into would be enforced without regard to the apparent unfairness of its terms, so long as the objecting party knew or should have known of the other party's assets, or voluntarily had waived disclosure); *In re Marriage of Shirilla*, 89 P.3d 1, 4 (Mont. 2004) (agreement not voluntary where Russian wife relied on husband's promises and journeyed to Montana, where he presented her with a premarital contract, the terms of which she did not understand owing to her difficulty with the English language and the fact that the attorney provided to her did not speak Russian and any advice given was without the benefit of a translator); *Sheshunoff v. Sheshunoff*, 172 S.W.3d 686 (Tex. App. 2005) (citing *Bonds* for the proposition that it equated voluntariness with "procedural fairness," which takes account of such factors as coercion, duress, undue influence, and the parties' relative bargaining power and sophistication).

14.10. Prior Understanding — Duress

Lack of negotiations. Premarital agreements are sometimes challenged on the basis that they were executed under duress, which is a species of voluntariness. Generally, in order to prove duress in the execution of a contract, evidence must show that "(1) one party issues a wrongful or unlawful threat, and (2) the other party had no reasonable alternative to entering the contract." *In re Marriage of Schenkelberg*, 810 N.W.2d 532 (Iowa App. 2012).

On occasion, a spouse will claim that he or she was under duress to sign the contract because it was handed to the person suddenly and then signed with little opportunity to understand and negotiate its terms. In general, courts have held that the lack of negotiations prior to execution of an agreement, or insufficient notice about the desire of one party for an agreement, standing alone, is not enough to invalidate a premarital agreement. The outcome turns on the particular facts of each case. *See, e.g.*, *Moore v. Moore*, 2012 WL 2553565, S.W.3d (Tex. App. 2012) (parameters of involuntary execution of a premartial agreement may not be clear in every case and will tend to depend on the circumstances).

For example, in *Rose v. Rose*, 526 N.E.2d 231, 235-236 (Ind. App. 1988), the court upheld a premarital contract that was presented to the bride-to-be only two days before the wedding. The husband testified that he would not marry the bride if she did not sign the agreement. The court was swayed in its decision to enforce the agreement encompassing marital assets of $1million because it believed the husband's testimony that the two had discussed the necessity of a contract several times months before the marriage. *See Matter of the Marriage of Adams*, 729 P.2d 1151 (Kan. 1986) (contract enforced where husband approached wife the morning of wedding and asked her to sign the contract; the contract was identical to one that wife reviewed earlier with her attorney); *Taylor v. Taylor*, 832 P.2d 429, 431 (Okla. App. 1991) (agreement essentially upheld where wife knew prior to marriage that husband owned several businesses and had assisted husband in business in personal matters prior to marriage and had been conversant with general business practices and was in possession of the agreement for three months prior to its execution); *Shepherd v. Shepherd*, 876 P.2d 429, 432 (Utah App. 1994) (agreement upheld where parties discussed it for a period of four months prior to marriage, each party had opportunity to review and make changes to agreement, and husband, who was challenging validity of agreement, was a competent and able attorney who understood, or who should have understood, content and effect of agreement); *Lee v. Lee*, 816 S.W.2d 625 (Ark. App. 1991) (agreement enforced where there had been full disclosure of parties' financial conditions, wife had entered the agreement freely and voluntarily, and the provisions were fair and equitable, despite wife's contention that she had been rushed into signing an hour before wedding and had not read agreement or been aware of extent of husband's property).

Mere refusal to go through with the marriage unless the premarital contract is signed, by itself, is not sufficient standing to invalidate the agreement. For example, in *Liebelt v. Liebelt*, 801 P.2d 52 (Idaho App. 1990), the court stated that the threat of a refusal to marry if a premarital agreement is not signed is not wrongful in the eyes of the law. The court said that such a threat received from a proposed marriage partner should put the potential spouse on notice that the agreement was of a serious nature and should be dealt with in a serious manner. *But see Ryken v. Ryken*, 461 N.W.2d 122 (S.D. 1990) (agreement held invalid where presented to wife the night before the wedding, made no provision for the wife, and did not disclose the assets of either party).

14.11. Right to Consult with Counsel

As noted earlier, most jurisdictions view the presence of independent counsel as one factor among many in determining whether to enforce a premarital contract. They have said that the lack of representation alone is not sufficient to void a premarital contract. *See, e.g., In re Estate of Kinney*, 733 N.W.2d 118, 124 (Minn. 2007) (the opportunity to consult with independent counsel is not a requirement, but is one of several relevant factors that courts may consider when determining whether a premarital agreement is fair and equitable); *Panossian v. Panossian*, 569 N.Y.S.2d 182 (N.Y. App. 1991) (absence of independent counsel during the transaction does not, under the circumstances presented here, warrant setting aside the agreement); *Matter of Estate of Lutz*, 563 N.W.2d 90 (N.D. 1997) (absence of counsel not determinative of whether a party has entered into a premarital agreement voluntarily).

Hoag v. Dick, 799 A.2d 391 (Me. 2002), provides an interesting example of a court considering claims that the premarital contract was signed under duress and without the advice of counsel. To support the duress claim, the wife testified that she was initially threatened by her church with excommunication unless she stopped cohabiting with her future husband and married him. She also testified that before she married, there was an informal discussion about premarital agreements with her husband and his son, an attorney. When the discussion turned more specifically to drafting a premarital agreement, the son suggested that each party be represented by a separate attorney. The wife responded that she did not need separate counsel because she did not want anything from her husband-to-be. Her future husband insisted that he would marry her only if they executed a premarital agreement.

Ultimately, the lawyer-son drafted a premarital agreement, which was delivered to the parties on the date of the wedding. He made one modification at that time, and the bride-to-be said that she gave the agreement a cursory reading. There were no further discussions about obtaining the advice of independent counsel. The parties executed the document in the church parking lot immediately before the wedding ceremony.

When the marriage broke down, the wife successfully challenged the premarital agreement. The Maine Supreme Court found that the agreement all but eliminated the wife's rights to receive a share of the marital property and to recover any amount of spousal support. Pursuant to the agreement, she would recover only $6,000 in settlement of all claims, and as the party bringing the action, she would be responsible for all litigation costs. It found it important that the agreement was presented to her on the day of her wedding, thus depriving her of any opportunity to obtain advice from independent legal counsel regarding its terms. The court reasoned that without the advice of counsel or time for consideration of the document, she could not fully know and understand the rights that she relinquished. *See also In re Marriage of Norris*, 624 P.2d 636, 638-40 (Or. App. 1981) (holding agreement unenforceable when the husband presented a premarital agreement during the trip to the wedding without the wife's opportunity to seek legal counsel and without informing her of his financial holdings); *Bauer v. Bauer*, 464 P.2d 710, 711-12 (Or. App. 1970) (holding agreement unenforceable when the husband presented it the day the parties left to get married out of town, failed to disclose his assets, and failed to allow sufficient time for her to consult a lawyer independently); *Friedlander v. Friedlander*, 494 P.2d 208, 214 (Wash. 1972) (holding agreement unenforceable when wife lacked independent advice of counsel, did not freely and voluntarily sign the agreement with knowledge of the husband's property and worth, and was not fully aware of her rights); *Gant v. Gant*, 329 S.E.2d 106 (W. Va. 1985) (contract valid even though it was executed the day before parties were married, the wife was not represented by counsel, and it was not carefully prepared; contract fundamentally fair under the totality of the circumstances). In a later decision, *Ware v. Ware*, 687 S.E.2d 382 (W.Va. 2009), *Grant* was reversed in part with the court holding that where one party to a premarital agreement is represented by counsel while the other is not, the burden of establishing the validity of that agreement is on the party seeking its enforcement.

Some jurisdictions, such as California and Arkansas, have enacted statutory provisions to strengthen the independent counsel requirement. *See, e.g.*, Cal. Fam. Code §1615, which is reproduced in full in section 14.12 of this chapter, "Waiving Alimony." *See also In re Marriage of Howell*, 195 Cal. App. 4th 1062 (Cal. App. 2011) (statute precluding enforcement of premarital spousal support waivers without independent counsel is not retroactive).

Note that nothing in §6 of the UPAA makes the absence of assistance of independent legal counsel a condition for the unenforceability of a premarital agreement. However, the UPAA states that a lack of that assistance may well be a factor in determining whether the conditions stated in §6 may have existed. *See, e.g., Del Vecchio v. Del Vecchio*, 143 So. 2d 17 (Fla. 1962).

Also note that on July 23, 2012 the Commissioners on Uniform State Laws (NCCUSL) adopted the Uniform Premarital and Marital Agreement Act (UPMAA) at its 121st annual meeting in Nashville, Tennessee to include coverage of post-marital contracts. The UPMAA would treat premarital and post-marital agreements that waive benefits on divorce or death the same. "Both would be upheld as long as the parties observed safeguards in the formation and certain minimal standards at the time of enforcement." Linda D. Elrod, Robert G. Spector, *A Review of the Year in Family Law: Numbers of Disputes Increase*, 45 Fam. L.Q. 443, 454 (Winter, 2012).

Dual representation. Parties often ask whether a single lawyer may represent and advise them on a premarital contract. As a rule, an attorney may represent both parties to a premarital agreement only if each party to the agreement receives full disclosure of the potential problems inherent in such representation. If the circumstances are such that dual representation would be improper, an attorney for one party should not talk with or answer questions for the other party.

As observed earlier in this chapter, most courts take the view that the advice of independent counsel at the time that parties enter into a premarital agreement helps demonstrate that there has been no fraud, duress, or misrepresentation, and that the agreement was entered into knowledgeably and voluntarily. It may be the best evidence that a party has entered into an antenuptial agreement voluntarily and knowledgeably. *In re Estate of Smid*, 756 N.W.2d 1, 18 (S.D. 2008) ("Presence of independent counsel is the best indicator that the disadvantaged party understood the effect of the agreement").

In some circumstance, as in a divorce, "[t]he likelihood of prejudice is so great with dual representation so as to make adequate representation of both . . . [parties] impossible . . . ." *Walden v. Hoke*, 429 S.E.2d 504 (W.Va. 1993) (improper for attorneys for another party to file papers for guardian ad litem; or for plaintiff's lawyer to prepare answer for defendant in any divorce); *Ware v. Ware*, 687 S.E.2d 382 (W.Va. 2009) (one attorney may not represent, nor purport to counsel, both parties to a prenuptial agreement).

SUBJECT MATTER OF AGREEMENTS

14.12. Waiving Child Support and Custody

Although it is generally agreed that there is a strong public policy favoring individuals ordering and deciding their own interests through contractual arrangements, including premarital contracts, matters such as child support, custody, and visitation trump such interests. In the context of child support, custody, and visitation, a court will act as *parens patriae* and retain jurisdiction to act in the child's best interests. In all jurisdictions, a provision in a premarital contract establishing a party's child support obligation is void as being against public policy. *See, e.g.*, *Serio v. Serio*, 830 So. 2d 278 (Fla. App. 2002) (parents may not waive their children's right to support because that right belongs to the children).

When determining child custody, the best interest of the children is the court's paramount concern. Even if the premarital contract mandated joint custody should a couple divorce, this would not affect the trial court's authority and obligation to determine custody and parenting time in accordance with the best interests of the children. *See, e.g.*, *Edwardson v. Edwardson*, 798 S.W.2d 941, 946 (Ky. 1990) (holding that premarital agreements are ineffectual in determining child custody and visitation issues).

14.13. Waiving Alimony

Common law. Historically, common law courts assumed provisions regarding waiver of alimony were unenforceable and void as against public policy. The courts felt that if a husband were permitted to limit the amount of alimony that the wife could receive should the parties' divorce in the future, the provision might act as an economic incentive to obtain a divorce sometime in the future. Another concern was expressed that a man should not be able to contract before marriage against the liability to his wife that he would incur should he commit offenses against the wife during the marriage. Some courts were also concerned that such agreements tended to limit the rights of an unsophisticated prospective spouse.

Waiver under UPAA. Today, much of the common law policy barring spousal waiver of support in a premarital contract has disappeared. In a majority of jurisdictions, premarital waivers of alimony are authorized by statutes that adopt either all or substantially all the provisions of the UPAA. *See* UPAA subdivision (a)(4) (expressly allowing parties to a premarital agreement to contract with respect to modification or elimination of spousal support); *see also Uniform Premarital Agreement Act* (1983).

Public assistance under UPAA. *Note* that subdivision (b) of §6 of the UPAA provides that "If a provision of a premarital agreement modifies or eliminates spousal support and that modification or elimination causes one party to the agreement to be eligible for support under a program of public assistance at the time of separation or marital dissolution, a court, notwithstanding the terms of the agreement, may require the other party to provide support to the extent necessary to avoid that eligibility."

California view. Prior to 2001, California provided that a premarital agreement was not enforceable if the party against whom enforcement was pressed proved that (1) he or she did not execute the agreement voluntarily, or (2) the agreement was unconscionable when entered into, and the party did not have actual or constructive knowledge of the other party's assets and obligations, and did not waive disclosure of such assets and obligations. However, in 2000, California's Supreme Court decided *In re Marriage of Bonds*, 5 P.3d 815 (Calif. 2000). In that case, the fiancée of baseball player Barry Bonds, whose native language was Swedish, received a premarital agreement prepared by Bonds's attorney on the eve of their wedding. She signed the agreement without the benefit of independent counsel and later challenged the agreement when their marriage broke down. The Supreme Court ruled that the fact that the fiancée was not represented by independent counsel was one of several factors that courts must consider in deciding whether a premarital agreement was entered into voluntarily.

The statute in effect at the time of the *Bonds* decision did not define the term "voluntarily" and placed the burden on the party seeking to block enforcement to prove that he or she did not execute the agreement voluntarily. The legislature responded to the *Bonds* decision by amending Cal. Fam. Code §1615. It reads as follows:

> Unenforceable agreements; unconscionability; voluntariness
>
> (a) A premarital agreement is not enforceable if the party against whom enforcement is sought proves either of the following:
> (1) That party did not execute the agreement voluntarily.
> (2) The agreement was unconscionable when it was executed and, before execution of the agreement, all of the following applied to that party:
> (A) That party was not provided a fair, reasonable, and full disclosure of the property or financial obligations of the other party.
> (B) That party did not voluntarily and expressly waive, in writing, any right to disclosure of the property or financial obligations of the other party beyond the disclosure provided.
> (C) That party did not have, or reasonably could not have had, an adequate knowledge of the property or financial obligations of the other party.
>
> (b) An issue of unconscionability of a premarital agreement shall be decided by the court as a matter of law.

(c) For the purposes of subdivision (a), it shall be deemed that a premarital agreement was not executed voluntarily unless the court finds in writing or on the record all of the following:

(1) The party against whom enforcement is sought was represented by independent legal counsel at the time of signing the agreement or, after being advised to seek independent legal counsel, expressly waived, in a separate writing, representation by independent legal counsel.
(2) The party against whom enforcement is sought had not less than seven calendar days between the time that party was first presented with the agreement and advised to seek independent legal counsel and the time the agreement was signed.
(3) The party against whom enforcement is sought, if unrepresented by legal counsel, was fully informed of the terms and basic effect of the agreement as well as the rights and obligations he or she was giving up by signing the agreement, and was proficient in the language in which the explanation of the party's rights was conducted and in which the agreement was written. The explanation of the rights and obligations relinquished shall be memorialized in writing and delivered to the party prior to signing the agreement. The unrepresented party shall, on or before the signing of the premarital agreement, execute a document declaring that he or she received the information required by this paragraph and indicating who provided that information.
(4) The agreement and the writings executed pursuant to paragraphs (1) and (3) were not executed under duress, fraud, or undue influence, and the parties did not lack capacity to enter into the agreement.
(5) Any other factors the court deems relevant.

Note that a premarital agreement is not voluntarily executed unless a trial court makes all the five designated findings in (c) 1-5. With the five findings, the presumption of involuntary execution is overcome as a matter of law.

Also note that the statute provides that unless a court finds that the party against whom enforcement of a premarital agreement is sought had at least seven calendar days between the date that he or she was first presented with the agreement and advised to seek independent counsel, and the time that he or she signed the agreement, it is presumed that the agreement was not executed voluntarily unless the party against whom enforcement is sought was represented by counsel from the outset of the transaction. *In re Marriage of Cadwell–Faso and Faso*, 119 Cal. Rptr. 3d 818 (Cal. App. 2011).

Massachusetts view — fair and reasonable. The Massachusetts Supreme Judicial Court has ruled that it is permissible for parties contemplating marriage to enter into a premarital contract settling their alimony rights in the event their marriage should prove unsuccessful. *Osborne v. Osborne*, 428 N.E.2d 810 (Mass. 1981). The court in *Osborne* noted, however, that the freedom to limit or waive alimony in the event of divorce is not unrestricted, and it set forth guidelines to be used in determining the extent to which such agreements should be enforced. It also noted that the contract must be fair and reasonable at the time of entry of the divorce judgment, which obviously could obviate a waiver of alimony under certain circumstances.

Kentucky/Missouri view — unconscionable. The Kentucky Supreme Court uses an unconscionability test to determine whether a premarital contract should be upheld. It applied the test in *Lane v. Lane*, 202 S.W.3d 577 (Ky. 2006), concluding that the waiver of alimony provision was not enforceable. Factors leading to this conclusion included that the marriage was the first for both parties, they were in their twenties when they married, two children were born of the marriage, and the wife quit her job to care for children while her husband rapidly progressed in his career. Another factor was the significant disparity in the parties' incomes, which grew exponentially during the marriage because the husband was able to concentrate on his career while the wife stayed home to care for the children and home. Furthermore, during their marriage, the parties maintained an affluent lifestyle during marriage.

Missouri also applies an unconscionable test to determine whether to uphold alimony waivers in premarital contracts. *See, e.g.*, *In re Marriage of Thomas*, 199 S.W.3d 847 (Mo. App. 2006) (agreement was not unconscionable where wife waived maintenance, attorney fees, and any interest in corporation husband owned).

Waiving alimony disallowed. In some jurisdictions, the state legislature has acted to prevent alimony from being waived in a premarital contract. For example, Iowa has a statute stating that "[t]he right of a spouse or child to support shall not be adversely affected by a premarital agreement." Iowa Code §596.5(2) (1991). Therefore, the waiver of spousal support in a premarital agreement in Iowa is not binding. *In re Marriage of Regenmorter*, 587 N.W.2d 493, 495 n.3 (Iowa App. 1998). South Dakota's legislature has said that provisions in a premarital contract purporting to limit or waive spousal support are void and unenforceable because they are contrary to public policy. *See Sanford v. Sanford*, 694 N.W.2d 283 (S.D. 2005) (legislature did not enact those portions of UPAA that allowed parties to a premarital agreement to contract with respect to the modification or elimination of spousal support).

14.14. Contracts Imposing Marital Duties and Obligations

Occasionally, parties will incorporate provisions into a premarital contract that attempt to impose various marital duties and obligations on each other. Courts are generally reticent to enforce such provisions. The reason for the reticence begins with the principle that when a marriage occurs, it creates a status in which the state is vitally interested and under which certain rights and duties incident to the relationship come into being, irrespective of the wishes of the parties. *Graham v. Graham*, 33 F. Supp. 936 (D. Mich. 1940) (former husband's attempt to enforce agreement where wife would pay him $300 a month during marriage to adjust financial matters between them, so that in the future there would be no further arguments as to what money the husband would receive, was invalid). A private contract between persons about to be married that attempts to change the essential obligations of the marriage contract is contrary to public policy and unenforceable. *Michigan Trust Co. v. Chapin*, 64 N.W. 334 (Mich. 1895) (contract in which husband promised to pay his wife a specified sum per year for keeping house is contrary to public policy). *See Restatement of the Law of Contracts*, §587 (a bargain between married persons or persons contemplating marriage to change the essential incidents of marriage, such as to forgo sexual intercourse, is not enforceable).

A premarital contract that contains a provision stating that the parties will not live together after marriage is not enforceable, although practically, it seems useless. *See Mirizio v. Mirizio*, 150 N.E. 605 (N.Y. App. 1926) (finding premarital marriage agreement invalid where it declared that the marriage should not be consummated until a religious ceremony was performed); *cf. Franklin v. Franklin*, 28 N.E. 681 (Mass. 1891) (agreement that couple would not live together had no effect upon the marriage contract entered into in regular form in the presence of a magistrate or minister authorized to solemnize marriages — it is against the policy of the law that the validity of a contract of marriage or its effect upon the status of the parties should be in any way affected by their preliminary or collateral agreements).

Note that courts will not enforce provisions that control the sharing of expenses between spouses during the marriage because this would negate one spouse's statutory duty to support the other. Other matters, such as who does the cleaning and cooking or how often to have sex, are likewise unenforceable.

ENFORCING PREMARITAL CONTRACTS

14.15. Burden of Proof

Disagreement. Jurisdictions do not agree on which party carries the *initial* burden of proof in a premarital dispute. Does the spouse who allegedly waived his or her rights have the initial burden of proving the invalidity of the contract? Alternatively, does the party who relies on the contract and seeks to have it enforced have the initial burden of proving its validity? As noted earlier, the UPAA breaks from the common law in most jurisdictions by explicitly placing the burden of proof on the party seeking to avoid enforcement of the premarital agreement. *In re Estate of Martin*, 938 A.2d 812 (Me. 2008).

High burden. A party seeking to set aside a premarital agreement bears a very high burden of showing that it is manifestly unfair and that this unfairness was the result of overreaching on the part of the other party to the agreement. *Panossian v. Panossian*, 569 N.Y.S.2d 182 (N.Y. App. 1991).

Burden on those seeking to invalidate the contract. In the following list, courts and legislatures have usually placed the burden of proof on the attacking spouse to prove the invalidity of the contract. *See Linker v. Linker*, 470 P.2d 921 (Colo. App. 1970) (party contesting validity of premarital agreement has burden of proving fraud, concealment, or failure to disclose material information); *Christians v. Christians*, 44 N.W.2d 431 (Iowa 1950) (one assailing a premarital contract has burden of establishing its invalidity); *Howell v. Landry*, 386 S.E.2d 610 (N.C. App. 1989) (party claiming the invalidity of the agreement for reasons of undue influence, duress, fraud, unconscionability, or inadequate disclosure has the burden of proof—defenses of undue influence, duress, fraud, unconscionability, and inadequate disclosure are all affirmative in nature, they must be affirmatively pled); *In re Benker Estate*, 331 N.W.2d. 193 (Mich. 1982) (burden of proof is on the party who seeks to invalidate the premarital agreement on the basis of nondisclosure); Virginia Code §20–151(A)(2) (whether a premarital agreement is unconscionable is to be determined as of the time of its execution, and the party alleging unconscionability bears the burden of proof).

Shifting burden. In the following decisions, courts ordinarily would have placed the burden of proof on the attacking spouse. However, because of the unusual facts in each dispute, the burden of proof shifted to the proponent of the contract. *Del Vecchio v. Del Vecchio*, 143 So. 2d 17 (Fla. 1962) (ordinarily, burden of proving invalidity of a premarital agreement is on the wife alleging it, but if, on its face, the contract is unreasonable, a presumption of concealment arises, and the burden shifts, and it is incumbent upon husband to prove validity); *Matter of Greiff*, 703 N.E.2d 752, 755 (N.Y. 1998) (court should ask whether, based on all of the relevant evidence and standards, the nature of the relationship between the couple at the time that they executed their premarital agreements rose to the level of shifting the burden to the proponents of the agreements to prove freedom from fraud, deception, or undue influence); *Harbom v. Harbom*, 760 A.2d 272 (Md. App. 2000) (when there is neither full disclosure or actual knowledge and the allowance to the party waiving rights is unfairly disproportionate to the worth of the property involved, the party seeking to uphold the agreement must shoulder the burden to prove that it was entered into voluntarily, freely, and with full knowledge of its meaning and effect). *Also see In re Estate of Kinney*, 733 N.W.2d 118 (Minn. 2007) (common law placed burden of proof on proponent of an agreement when the parties stand in a confidential relationship and the agreement is not supported by adequate consideration; when the parties stand in a confidential relationship and the court finds that the premarital agreement is supported by adequate consideration, the burden is on the party challenging the agreement).

Burden on those seeking to enforce contract. Although not always entirely clear, it appears that in the following cases, courts have placed the *initial* burden on those relying on the contract to prove its validity: *In re Estate of Strickland*, 149 N.W.2d 344 (Neb. 1967) (burden on husband, or representatives, to show that premarital contract apparently unjust to wife was fairly procured).

The Georgia Supreme Court has stated that:

> the party seeking enforcement bears the burden of proof to demonstrate that: (1) the antenuptial agreement was not the result of fraud, duress, mistake, misrepresentation, or nondisclosure of material facts; (2) the agreement is not unconscionable; and (3) taking into account all relevant facts and circumstances, including changes beyond the parties' contemplation when the agreement was executed, enforcement of the antenuptial agreement would be neither unfair nor unreasonable.

Dove v. Dove, 680 S.E. 839, 842 (Ga. 2009). *See Lawson v. Loid*, 896 S.W.2d 1, 3 (Ky. 1995) ("[T]he burden of proof on the issue of full disclosure of assets at the time the agreement was signed in a premarital contract rests on the party relying on such agreement"); *Randolph v. Randolph*, 937 S.W.2d 815, 821 (Tenn. 1996) (the burden of proof is on the party seeking to enforce the premarital agreement to establish the necessary elements); *Ex parte Brown*, 26 S.3d 1222 (Ala. 2009) (proponent of an antenuptial agreement has the burden of showing that the consideration was adequate and that the entire transaction was fair, just, and equitable from the other party's point of view or that the agreement was freely and voluntarily entered into by the other party with competent independent advice and full knowledge of the other party's interest in the estate and its approximate value); *Seuss v. Schukat*, 192 N.E. 668 (Ill. 1934) (burden of proving premarital agreement rests on party alleging its existence). *See generally In re Estate of Harbers*, 449 P.2d 7 (Ariz. 1969) (after a will is admitted to probate, executor must defend and uphold it against subsequent attack; co-executors failed to prove by clear and convincing evidence that property division agreement was not fraudulent or coerced, or that it was not unfair or inequitable).

14.16. Presumptions

Presumption of legality. As a rule, a premarital agreement is valid and enforceable if it is in writing, subscribed to by the parties, and acknowledged or proved in a manner required to record a deed. A duly executed agreement is provided the same presumption of legality as any other contract. *Edmonds v. Edmonds*, 710 N.Y.S.2d 765 (N.Y. Sup. 2000); *Sabad v. Fessenden*, 825 A.2d 682 (Pa. Super. 2003).

Presumption of fraud. In some jurisdictions, a presumption of fraud may arise when an agreement contains inadequate consideration for the waiver of a spouse's rights. *See, e.g.*, *Seebecker v. Seebecker*, 368 N.W.2d 846 (Wis. App. 1985) (presumption of fraud may arise where prospective husband obtains from his intended wife waiver in consideration of marriage containing a manifestly inadequate pecuniary provision; here, wife failed to produce sufficient evidence to create presumption); *In re Mosier's Estate*, 133 N.E. 202 (Ohio 1954) (wife received $7,000 for giving up interest in estate worth $40,000, amount not so disproportionate as to give rise to presumption of fraud); *In re Neis' Estate*, 225 P.2d 110 (Kan. 1950) (in proceedings to enforce premarital contracts, it is only where fraud, deceit, or unreasonable inadequacy or disproportion appear that presumption of fraud is raised and burden put on husband, or those claiming under him, to show that wife was fully informed as to his property); *Davis v. Davis*, 116 S.W.2d 607 (Ark. 1938) (provision secured for wife by contract in event of husband's death is disproportionate to husband's means, presumption is that husband's means were designedly concealed, and persons claiming in husband's right have burden of proving full knowledge by wife of all that materially affected the contract).

Where fraud is presumed because of a disproportionate division of property, the burden of proving the absence of fraud normally shifts to the proponent of the contract to show that it was voluntarily entered with full and fair disclosure of the nature, extent, and value of the other spouse's property and knowledge of the rights that were being waived. *See In re Estate of Kinney*, 733 N.W.2d 118, 126 (Minn. 2007); *cf. In re Estate of Stephenson*, 503 N.W.2d 540, 546 (Neb. 1993) (the one alleging fraud must prove fraud; rejecting previous case law that held that if the contract is unjust and unreasonable to the prospective wife on its face, a presumption of fraud arises, the burden shifts, and it is incumbent on the husband to prove the validity of the contract).

Examples

2. Assume that P and his wife executed a premarital contract in 1900. A provision in the contract states that P would annually receive "an income of $10,000 from the estate of the wife if the parties were at the time of the death of the wife living together as husband and wife." Another provision declared that the $10,000 annual income should continue so long as the husband remained unmarried after the death of his wife. However, if his wife died and P remarried, P was to receive a lump-sum payment of $25,000, and the annual income from her estate would stop.

   P's wife was very wealthy; P was poor. When P's wife died suddenly, P challenged the provision that limited his income from the estate as a restraint on marriage. P argued that the provision encouraged separation of P with his wife or alternatively, it put a restraint on P remarrying after his wife died. Most likely, how will the court treat P's arguments?

3. Assume that P and D execute a premarital contract that provides that should a divorce occur, and children are born to the marriage of P and D, that P will receive sole legal and physical custody of them. After ten years, the couple divorce, and P seeks to enforce the terms of the contract over D's objection. At the hearing on the matter, both P and D admit that at the time that they signed the premarital contract, they completely understood its terms, including the provision regarding child custody. They also both agreed that they were represented by adequate counsel. How will a court most likely resolve the dispute?

4. Assume that P and D execute a premarital contract that provides that should a divorce occur, and children are born to the marriage, that D will be relieved of any child support responsibility. At the time that the couple signed the premarital contact, D was an airline pilot with a major airline, and P was a physician in a local clinic. After ten years, the couple divorce, and D, whose airline has undergone a merger and recently terminated D's employment, uses the terms of the contract to defend against a child support claim made by P. At the hearing on the matter, both P and D admit that at the time that they signed the premarital contract, they completely understood its terms, including the child support provision. How will a court most likely resolve the support issue?

5. Assume that P and D had been previously married with adult children from these marriages. P and D were 52 when they decided to marry. Five years later, their relationship broke down, and P filed for divorce. D, who was a multi-millionaire, submitted a premarital agreement that applied upon death or divorce to the court for review. P contested the agreement.

P testified at the hearing on the validity of the premarital contract that five days before the date of their marriage ceremony, she was surprised when D handed her some papers that he called a premarital agreement. He asked P to look the papers over and sign them. P became angry and threw the documents on the floor. D, who became upset, picked up the papers and said that if P would not sign the premarital agreement, he would not go through with the marriage. He then stormed out.

P testified that she felt under enormous pressure because she had planned a large wedding, the invitations were out, caterers hired, all her relatives were about to arrive, and the plans for the wedding were now cast "in cement." After thinking about D's threat for a few hours, she called D to apologize. In the conversation, D explained that he just wanted to be sure his children from his prior marriage were taken care of should he die unexpectedly or that P and D unfortunately divorce. D said he was very, very sorry, but he just could not go through with the marriage ceremony unless the premarital agreement was signed. D offered to get P a lawyer if she wanted one. P said that she felt pretty much in a box and, without consulting a lawyer, met with D the next day and signed the premarital agreement. She said that she read it the night before and it seemed fine to her. The agreement outlined in detail all of D's property, investments, and bank accounts. It provided that P waived any claim to future alimony or to any of D's present nonmarital property. It provided that should the couple divorce, D would provide P with annual support of $50,000 for ten years and that P would make no claim to any marital property. P now challenges the signing of the premarital agreement. D generally agreed with P's testimony.

P argues that the premarital agreement should not be enforced for two reasons: First, she was under duress and had no real choice but to sign the document. Second, she did not have the advice of a lawyer. How will a family court judge most likely rule?

6. Assume that this action is brought in a jurisdiction that recognizes the use of premarital contracts upon death or divorce. Assume that one day before their marriage, the parties entered into a contract prepared by P's lawyer. The contract provided, in part, that in the event of divorce or death, each party released all marital rights in the separate property of the other, and the division of marital property was to be based upon the amount of money that each party had invested in the property during the marriage. Also, assume that at the time the contract was signed, D owned no assets except personal belongings, while P, a successful businessperson, had substantial real estate holdings that were valued at approximately $8 million. In addition, assume that P had Certificates of Deposits (CDs) and cash of approximately $500,000.

   The marriage broke down after ten years, and P filed for divorce, asking that the premarital contract be enforced. At the hearing on the validity of the contract, D testified that she did not see the agreement until one day before the parties were to be married. At that time, she quickly reviewed the contract before signing it on the drive to P's attorney's office. She testified that P's attorney did not "really explain" the meaning of the document to her. She said that because she was responsible for a minor child and suffering from breast cancer at the time, her only choices were to sign the contract or be kicked out of the residence that she and her son had shared with P for the year prior to their marriage. On cross-examination, D conceded that P had told her about some of his property during the year they lived together before they were married. She insisted, however, that she was not aware of, nor did anyone disclose to her, the full extent and value of his assets and holdings.

Both parties agree that D was not represented by counsel when she signed the contract at P's lawyer's office. However, P's attorney testified that it is his normal practice to explain such contracts to both parties to ensure a mutual understanding of the terms. He could not specifically recall following that practice with D and acknowledged that he did not provide D with a copy of P's financial statement prior to execution of the contract. He testified that he probably discussed P's assets in general terms with D, a practice that he followed in every case where he drafted a premarital contract.

P testified that he never specifically advised D of his net worth prior to signing the contract, but he added that she must have been aware of it because they had lived together for more than one year before the contract was signed. He also testified that she had accompanied him to many of his properties to collect rent. He said that D also reviewed the contract before signing it and had made suggestions for changes, including a provision relating to a watch. Although D conceded that she read the provision regarding the watch before signing the contract, she denied that the provision was included at her suggestion. Will a court most likely uphold the contract on these facts?

7. Assume that P and D agree in a premarital contract that during their marriage, P will pay D $2,500 a month in return for D accompanying P on her business travels. D gives up his job in reliance on the written contract, which in part reads, "P hereby agrees to pay to D the sum of Two Thousand Five Hundred Dollars ($2,500.00) per month each and every month hereafter until the parties hereto no longer desire this arrangement to continue." After five years, P and D separate but do not divorce. When P stops making the monthly payment, D brings an action to enforce the contract. P responds that the contract is without consideration and cannot be enforced. P also contends that under its express provisions, the contract was to continue only until the parties no longer desired the arrangement to continue, and thus, it was

terminated when they separated. How will a court most likely treat this contract?

8. Assume that this is a common law jurisdiction and this case is brought in 1900. At this period of history, a court will apply an automatic presumption of fraud theory upon a finding that there has been a disproportionate division of property in a premarital contract. Also, assume that three weeks before P and D married, a premarital contract was executed at a time when P was 65 and without significant wealth; D was 68 and possessed substantial financial wealth. P agreed in the contract that both parties would make a will after their marriage, providing that should D die before P, P's marital property in the estate would be limited to $10,000 in cash. P also agreed to waive his right to an intestate share of the marital property. A list of D's property with an approximate value of $7 million was attached to the premarital contract. Following their marriage, both parties executed a wills incorporating the terms of the premarital contract.

   A year after the parties married, D died unexpectedly. P challenged the premarital agreement in probate court. She left an estate valued at more than $10 million.

   P testified that while there may have been a list of D's property attached to the premarital contract, it was not brought to his attention at the signing, and he did not read it. He also testified that D's father selected the attorney who drafted the premarital contract.

   The trial judge is asked to rule on the following: Was the consideration for the contract adequate? Is the premarital contract valid?

Explanations

2. As a general principle, contracts in restraint of marriage, or which tend to induce a separation of husband and wife, are on broad grounds of public policy utterly void. However, the terms in this hypothetical would not be viewed by most courts as a restraint on marriage. The provision constituted a limitation, not upon the right to remarry, but upon the continuance of the annuity that he was promised by his wife. There is no stipulation that P shall not remarry. He is perfectly free to form new relations in that respect; but if he does so, he relinquishes his annual income payment. Courts during this period in U.S. history will determine that there is nothing unreasonable in the condition attached to the premarital agreement. They will point out that P, the intended husband, was not a person with wealth at the time of the transaction. His intended wife

possessed the wealth and she was not under a legal or moral obligation to provide an income to use to support him and his new wife in comfort and luxury. He is at liberty to remarry, and in that event, he is entitled to receive $25,000 in lieu of the original income provided to him. *See In re Appleby's Estate*, 111 N.W. 305 (Minn. 1907), on which the example is based.

3. The court will not enforce the provision in the contract relating to custody of the children. The state has a very strong interest in protecting the children of a marriage and assumes the role of *parens patriae* with respect to them if a divorce action is brought. The state will not abrogate that responsibility, even if the couple clearly understood the terms contained in a premarital contract about how custody would be handled should a divorce occur. Here, the court will decide how the best interests of the child will be served, and the contract provision will be ignored.

4. The court will not enforce the provision in the contract relating to child support. As is the case in child custody matters, the state has a very strong interest in protecting the children of a marriage and assumes the role of *parens patriae* with respect to them in a divorce action. The state will not abrogate that responsibility, even if the couple clearly understood the terms contained in a premarital contract about how child support would be handled should a divorce occur. The court will protect the children at a support hearing from an earlier contract in which one parent agreed that the other did not have to pay child support should a divorce occur. The court will consider the financial circumstances of both parents. The fact that D lost a job with the airline and P is a physician will not cause a court to enforce a support provision in a premarital contract against the interests of the minor children. A court most likely will ignore the support provision in the premarital contract.

5. A court may turn to the Restatement of Contracts, which provides some guidance concerning the effect of duress on the enforceability of a contract. The Restatement declares that: "If a party's manifestation of assent is induced by an improper threat by the other party that leaves the victim no reasonable alternative, the contract is voidable by the victim." Restatement (Second) of Contracts §175(1), at 475 (1981).

   First, was there an improper threat? Probably not. Most courts will find that a threat must be wrongful or unlawful. Here, the threat is neither wrongful nor unlawful. *Liebelt v. Liebelt*, 801 P.2d 52, 55 (Idaho App. 1990) ("The threat of a refusal to marry is not wrongful in the eyes of the law"); *Lebeck v. Lebeck*, 881 P.2d 727, 734 (N.M. App. 1994) (husband's statement that he would not marry wife without premarital agreement was a lawful demand and would not support a claim of duress); *Gardner v. Gardner*, 527 N.W.2d 701, 706 (Wis. App. 1994) (insistence on a premarital agreement as a condition of marriage is not a "threat" and is not coercive); *see Howell v. Landry*, 386 S.E.2d 610, 617-18 N.C. App. 1989) (no duress even though husband-to-be threatened to cancel the wedding: "the cancellation of a proposed marriage would be a natural result of a failure of a party to execute a premarital agreement desired by the other party"); *Taylor v. Taylor*, 832 P.2d 429, 431(Ok. App. 1991) (duress not shown by proof that husband refused to marry wife unless she signed the agreement). Note the offer of D to obtain a lawyer for P, which P admits she turned down. A family court most likely will find that P has failed to show that she acted under duress in signing the premarital agreement. *See In re Marriage of Shanks*, 758 N.W.2d 506 (Iowa 2008).

Second, did P have a reasonable alternative to entering into the contract? Most courts would find that she did. She could have canceled the wedding. While it is true that she may have suffered embarrassment in cancelling the wedding, most courts will not consider the social embarrassment from the cancellation of wedding plans, even on the eve of the wedding, as rendering that choice unreasonable. *See, e.g., Howell v. Landry*, 386 S.E.2d 610, 618 (N.C. App. 1989) (holding there was no duress where wife was presented with premarital agreement on eve of wedding, noting that she was not obligated to go through with the ceremony).

Third, the right to counsel issue may sway the court one way or another. If the action is brought in California, the agreement will be tossed out because the waiver was not in writing. In other jurisdictions, given the $50,000 annual payment for ten years, it may be upheld. In this respect, it is dissimilar to the *Hoag* case discussed in section 14.10 in this chapter. In most jurisdictions without specific statutory direction such as that found in California, the absence of counsel is only one factor in determining whether to uphold a contract.

6. This is a close question; however, a court most likely will not uphold the contract for the following reasons. Although all agree that D resided with P for about a year before their marriage, P did not reveal the full extent or value of his holdings. It is clear that both parties agreed that D's knowledge of P's property was only general in nature, despite the fact that she accompanied D when he collected rent from some of his tenants. D's testimony regarding her general knowledge of P's holdings seemed to be corroborated by P and his attorney. Although specific appraisal values are not required to sustain the validity of a premarital contract, greater knowledge of the proponent spouse's overall net worth is usually necessary. In terms of the comparative sophistication and business experience of the parties, P was apparently a learned businessperson, whereas D possessed no prior business experience or knowledge. Moreover, the contract was executed only one day before the parties were

married, and D was presented with it on the way to P's attorney's office. Because of the short period between the presentation of the contract and the marriage, there was little time for D to study the contract or to contact her own attorney if she wanted one. As noted at the outset, a court most likely will not enforce the terms of this contract. *See Randolph v. Randolph*, 937 S.W.2d 815 (Tenn. 1996).

7. A court most likely will refuse to uphold this premarital contract. It will be viewed as altering by private contract the personal relationships and obligations assumed upon marriage. The court will reason that if P and D were permitted to regulate by private contract where they are to live and whether the husband is to work or be supported by his wife, there would seem to be no reason why they could not contract as to the allowance that the husband or wife may receive, the number of dresses that a wife may have, the places where they will spend their evenings and vacations, and innumerable other aspects of their personal relationships. Courts will also reason that if they recognized the existence of such a right, it would open an endless field for controversy and bickering and would destroy the element of flexibility needed in adjusting new conditions arising in marital life. A wife can pay her husband a monthly sum voluntarily, and the husband by mutual understanding can quit his job and travel with his wife. The objection to this agreement is that it put the husband's conduct into a binding contract, tying his hands in the future and inviting controversy and litigation between them. *See Graham v. Graham*, 33 F. Supp. 936 (D. Mich. 1940).

8. Common law courts took two views on the issue of the adequacy of consideration. Some viewed the marriage itself as sufficient consideration for the contract. Others reviewed the disparity in assets of the parties at the time the contract was signed, and if the disparity is sufficiently great, those courts would presume fraud. Here, if the latter view is applied, those courts likely will hold that the consideration was inadequate, and fraud will be presumed.

   Once fraud is presumed, the burden of proof shifts to the proponent of the contract, which in this hypothetical is the estate. To overcome the presumption, the proponent must prove that P knew the extent, character, and value of the property involved and the nature and extent of the rights being waived.

   At this point in history, most courts would find in favor of D's estate, concluding that it had overcome the presumption of fraud. They will reason that there is little evidence to suggest that P was placed under undue duress at the time the premarital contract was signed; that is, the signing was voluntary. The fact that P signed a will after the contract was executed that incorporated the terms of the premarital contract suggests that P was aware of the nature and extent of D's property and waived his marital rights to a share of it. The list that was attached to the contract is further evidence that D was not withholding information about his worth, even if P failed to read it. Although there is a question about legal representation, it seems reasonable to infer that the lawyer for D may have provided P with some legal advice. Furthermore, there is no evidence to suggest that P was prevented from obtaining council. Despite the apparent unfairness of the division of property upon D's death, given the disclosures and absence of duress, a common law court most likely will uphold the contract. *See, e.g., Estate of Serbus v. Serbus*, 324 N.W.2d 381 (Minn. 1982).

14.17. Procedural Fairness When Executed

This section, and the two that follow, describe the factors that courts use when holding a premarital contract procedurally unfair, substantively unfair, and unconscionable. The task has been challenging because courts may label a decision in this area as being "procedurally unconscionable," "procedurally and substantively unfair," and sometimes "procedurally and substantively unconscionable." When they use these terms, it is often not easy to distinguish one theory from another.

Procedural fairness might be interpreted as merely an examination by the court to determine whether statutorily mandated procedures have been followed, such as whether the appropriate number of witnesses signed a premarital contract. *See, e.g., Dove v. Dovc*, 285 Ga. 647 (Ga. 2009) (statute required agreement be attested by two witnesses). However, when discussing procedural fairness courts appear to go much further than just determining whether a number of witnesses were present. They usually consider the nature and extent of the disclosure of the parties' assets, whether the contract was voluntary, and whether the parties were represented by counsel. *Matter of Lutz*, 563 N.W.2d 90 (N.D. 1997) (procedural enforceability includes asking whether the contract was signed voluntarily); *In re Estate of Kinney*, 733 N.W.2d 118 (Minn. 2007) (agreement discussed in earlier case was "procedurally fair because there was adequate disclosure and because the party challenging the agreement had waived her right to 'unrestrained access to advice from independent counsel'"); *In re Marriage of Bernard*, 204 P.3d 907 (Wash. 2009) (agreement is procedurally fair if (1) spouses made a full disclosure of the amount, character, and value of the property involved and (2) agreement was freely entered into on independent advice from counsel, with full knowledge by both spouses of their rights); *see also In re Marriage of Gonzalez*, 561 N.W.2d 93 (Iowa 1997) (premarital agreements that are substantively unfair are still binding if they were executed in a procedurally fair manner).

14.18. Unconscionable Contracts

What are courts looking at when they describe their initial review of a premarital contract as unconscionable? Unfortunately, the meaning of the term *unconscionable* as used in various jurisdictions is far from clear. For example, in *Holler v. Holler*, 612 S.E.2d 469 (S.C. App. 2005), the court stated that under South Carolina law, unconscionability is the "absence of meaningful choice on the part of one party due to one-sided contract provisions, together with terms which are so oppressive that no reasonable person would make them and no fair and honest person would accept them." A New York court in *Clermont v. Clermont*, 603 N.Y.S.2d 923 (N.Y. App. 1933), defined unconscionable as involving a bargain "such as no [person] in his [or her] senses and not under delusion would make on the one hand, and as no honest and fair [person] would accept on the other."

The North Dakota Supreme Court held a contract unconscionable on the following facts: The wife was presented with the contract only three days before their wedding and she did not have independent legal advice before signing it. Her husband did not provide her with a fair and reasonable disclosure of his property and financial obligations. The trial judge found that the husband's representation of his income was not credible, and the wife did not waive her right to a fair and reasonable disclosure of husband's property or financial obligations. *Peters-Riemers v. Riemers*, 644 N.W.2d 197 (N.D. 2002).

The UPAA, which is found in the statutes of many jurisdictions, includes "unconscionability" as a reason for not enforcing these contracts. It states, in part:

> An agreement is not enforceable if the party against whom enforcement is sought proves that (a) he or she did not execute the agreement voluntarily or that (b) the agreement was unconscionable when it was executed and, before execution of the agreement, he or she (1) was not provided a fair and reasonable disclosure of the property or financial obligations of the other party, (2) did not voluntarily and expressly waive, in writing, any right to disclosure of the property or financial obligations of the other party beyond the disclosure provided, and (3) did not have, or reasonably could not have had, an adequate knowledge of the property and financial obligations of the other party.

Uniform Premarital Agreement Act, *Prefatory Note*. http://www.uniformlaws.org/shared/docs/premarital%20agreement/upaa_final_83.pdf (last visited July, 2012). In the commentary to §6 of the UPPA, it is stated that the test of "unconscionability" was drawn from §306 of the UMDA. It also states that "unconscionable" should be interpreted similarly to its use in commercial and contract law, "where its meaning includes protection against one-sidedness, oppression, or unfair surprise." *Ibid.* In addition, the term should be interpreted as it is used in the context of negotiations between spouses to include "protection against overreaching, concealment of assets, and sharp dealing not consistent with the obligations of marital partners to deal fairly with each other." Some states have adopted this standard. *See, e.g., In re Marriage of Thomas*, 199 S.W.3d 847 (Mo. App. 2006) (conscionability is the same standard employed in commercial law, meaning protection against one-sidedness, oppression, or unfair surprise).

Fair and reasonable distinguished from "unconscionability." Some jurisdictions have discussed the validity of a premarital contract when it was signed using a fair and reasonable test. This test is not perceived as identical to that for unconscionability. *Upham v. Upham*, 630 N.E.2d 307, 310-311 (Mass. App. 1994) (a "conscionability" standard is not the same as a "fair and reasonable" standard; although there may be substantial overlap between the standards, a standard of conscionability generally "requires a greater showing of inappropriateness"). *See also Ex parte Walters*, 580 So. 2d 1352, 1354 (Ala. 1991) (nothing to indicate that the agreement was not fair, just, and equitable); *Harbom v. Harbom*, 760 A.2d 272 (Md. 2000), quoting *Hartz v. Hartz*, 234 A.2d 865 (Md. 1967) (contract upheld if it was "fair and equitable under the circumstances"); *Matter of the Estate of Crawford*, 730 P.2d 675 (Wash. 1986) ("if the contract makes a fair and reasonable provision for the party not seeking its enforcement, the contract may be upheld").

14.19. The "Second Look" — "Change of Circumstances" Doctrine

Change of circumstances. Unlike commercial contracts, family courts in a few jurisdictions have adopted a contract theory that is unique to family law. This theory is sometimes referred to as the *second look doctrine*. In Michigan, the theory is labeled as one involving "a change of circumstances since the execution of the agreement [that] makes its enforcement unfair and unreasonable." *Woodington v. Shokoohi*, 792 N.W.2d 63, 73 (Mich. App. 2010). In that state, to determine whether a premarital agreement is unenforceable because of a change in circumstances, the focus is on whether the changed circumstances were reasonably foreseeable either before or during the signing of the premarital agreement. *Reed v. Reed*, 693 N.W.2d 825 (Mich. App. 2005).

The Wisconsin Supreme Court, in *Button v. Button*, 388 N.W.2d 546 (Wis. 1986), held that "if there are significantly changed circumstances after the execution of a contract and the contract as applied at divorce no longer comports with the reasonable expectations of the parties, a contract which is fair at execution may be unfair to the parties at divorce."

Conscionable. In some jurisdictions, courts will use the term "conscionable" when considering whether to enforce an agreement at the time of a divorce. In these jurisdictions, a judge will usually employ a two-step process. First, the court will determine whether the agreement was fair and reasonable at the time of execution. *See, e.g., DeMatteo v. DeMatteo*, 762 N.E.2d 797 (Mass. 2002). Second, if the court is satisfied that the agreement was fair and reasonable when executed, it will take a "second look." The court at this stage will ask whether the agreement, at the time of the divorce, is "conscionable." *DeMatteo v. DeMatteo, supra* at 797 of 762 N.E.2d.

Courts employing the "conscionable" approach will refuse to enforce the agreement if they find that the circumstances occurring during the course of the marriage would leave the contesting spouse "without sufficient property, maintenance, or appropriate employment to support" himself or herself. *Korff v. Korff*, 831 N.E.2d 385 (Mass. App. 2005). In *MacFarlane v. Rich*, 567 A.2d 585, 591 (N.H. 1989), the court concluded that a contract may become *unconscionable* when "provisions . . . lose their vitality by reason of changed circumstances so far beyond the contemplation of the parties at the time they entered the contract that its enforcement would work an unconscionable hardship." *See also Gentry v. Gentry*, 798 S.W.2d 928, 936 (Ky. 1990) ("An antenuptial agreement will not be enforced if facts and circumstances have changed so as to make its enforcement unconscionable").

Fair and reasonable, or unconscionable? Some jurisdictions employ an approach to premarital contracts that asks whether, under the present circumstances, the contract is fair and reasonable or unconscionable. *See, e.g., Gross v. Gross*, 464 N.E.2d 500 (Ohio 1984) (in light of substantial increase in husband's assets during marriage, provisions in the premarital agreement that wife was entitled to receive maximum maintenance of $200 per month for ten years was unconscionable).

Whether the courts that employ the second look doctrine claim that they are searching for "unconscionability," "unfairness and unreasonableness," "inequity," or something else, the judicial analysis appears remarkably similar in substance. *See McKee-Johnson v. Johnson*, 444 N.W.2d 259, 267-268 (Minn. 1989) (contract must be substantively fair at the time of enforcement).

Note that in Ohio, the issue of a premarital agreement's fairness at the time of the divorce appears to be limited to matters involving spousal support. *Gross v. Gross, supra.*

14.20. Capacity

Capacity. Like other contracts, the parties to a premarital contract must possess the capacity to enter into a contract. *Dexter v. Hall*, 82 U.S. 9, 20 (1873) ("The fundamental idea of a contract is that it requires the assent of two minds. But a lunatic or a person non compos mentis has nothing which the law recognizes as a mind, and it would seem, therefore, upon principle that he cannot make a contract which may have any efficacy as such.")

Abandoning a premarital contract. In some jurisdictions, a premarital contract may be abandoned by mutual consent of the parties without consideration. *McMullen v. McMullen*, 185 So. 2d 191 (Fla. App. 1966). The abandonment of a contract may be effected when the acts of one party are inconsistent with the existence of the contract and are acquiesced to by the other party. This is tantamount to a rescission of the contract by mutual assent.

Conflicts. When drafting a premarital agreement, lawyers are usually advised to include a provision regarding what state law will apply to it. *See, e.g.*, *Levin v. Carlton*, 213 P.3d 884 (Utah 2009) (Utah premarital agreement dispute; premarital contract provided that it was to be interpreted according to California law). Where there is no provision, courts may look to the *Restatement of Conflicts Second* to address conflict of law questions. *See, e.g.*, *Sabad v. Fessenden*, 825 A.2d 682 (Pa. Super. 2003) (applying New York law to Pennsylvania dispute).

Tax planning. Premarital contracts sometimes are related to the estate-planning wishes of either or both of the prospective spouses. Depending on the consideration being exchanged by the contract, there may be gift-tax or income tax consequences involved.

EXAMPLE

Example

9. Assume that P and D were employed outside the home and each represented by lawyers when they entered into a premarital contract that in part read as follows: "In the event that the Parties initiate dissolution of marriage proceedings, each Party waives and releases all rights and claims to receive alimony from the other Party." Also, assume that ten years into their marriage, D was in a life-shattering automobile accident that caused her permanent disability. She underwent a dozen reconstructive surgeries and is slated to have many more.

   A year after the accident, P filed a petition to dissolve the marriage. At the time that P filed the dissolution action, D had exhausted her insurance coverage and had only a few thousand dollars in assets. P was employed and had an annual gross income of about $180,000. D asked for an award of permanent alimony. How will a court treat the alimony request?

EXPLANATION

Explanation

9. The solution to the problem depends a great deal on the jurisdiction where the matter is litigated. In Hawaii, for example, that court has said that a support provision of a premarital agreement is unconscionable if at the time of the divorce, it appears in the best interest of the state that the financial well-being of the parties at the time of divorce be preserved by taking into consideration factors and circumstances arising throughout the marriage. *Prell v. Silverstein*, 162 P.3d 2 (Hawai'i 2007). It explained that

> the unconscionability of a spousal support provision can only be determined at the time of divorce by reviewing and considering all relevant factors and circumstances occurring after the execution of the premarital agreement. To enforce a spousal support provision of a premarital agreement because it was reasonable at the time of execution of the agreement can result in unforeseen economic hardship to a spouse that may shock the conscience of the court due to relevant changes in the circumstances of the marriage by the time of divorce. Public policy mandates against the enforcement of unconscionable support payments.

Id. at 13.

In Georgia, a court would take into account all relevant facts and circumstances, including changes beyond the parties' contemplation when the agreement was executed, to determine whether enforcement of the agreement would be either unfair or unreasonable. *Dove v. Dove*, 680 S.E.2d 839 (Ga. 2009). A Georgia court most likely would award alimony. *See also Sailer v. Sailer*, 788 N.W.2d 604 (N.D. 2010) (if a provision of a premarital agreement modifies or eliminates spousal support, North Dakota law authorizes a court to provide very limited relief to a party who otherwise would be eligible for public welfare); *Osborne v. Osborne*, 428 N.E.2d 810 (Mass. 1981); *Unander v. Unander*, 506 P.2d 719 (Or. 1973).

CHAPTER 15

Cohabitation and Contract Principles

15.1. Introduction

This chapter examines the legal issues that may give rise to disputes between unmarried partners who have lived together much as though they were married. The disputes occur when a partner dies or the relationship breaks up. As the chapter unfolds, it will become apparent that jurisdictions disagree about the nature and extent of legal redress available to a partner caught up in a cohabitation legal dispute.

There are three important matters that need to be explained at the outset. First, the contract principles discussed in this chapter often challenge century-old common law principles associated with these relationships. The common law took a dim view of enforcing agreements made between unmarried persons who were living together out of wedlock much like a husband and wife. If any part of an agreement, oral or written, rested upon the illicit relationship itself, the agreement would not be enforced. Common law courts objected to the parties' disregard of traditional moral values and were concerned that enforcement of such agreements might make meretricious relationships more attractive than marriage. The common law, it was said, should not allow a man to trade sexual services as consideration for contractual promises or make a woman's virtue an article of merchandise.

Second, the law in most jurisdictions has evolved away from the common law and now recognizes that cohabiting couples may acquire certain obligations to each other that survive the breakdown of the relationship. When considering whether to provide redress, courts rely upon the application of general contract principles. For example, a majority of jurisdictions will enforce express oral and written contracts made by cohabiting couples. A smaller number of jurisdictions have indicated that they will recognize and enforce implied contracts. Consequently, final resolution of a cohabitation dispute will rest on the contract philosophy of a jurisdiction's legislature and/or its courts.

Finally, cohabitation by unmarried partners, in both its rights and obligations, remains separate and legally distinct from marriage. For example, state statutory divorce provisions are not applicable to cohabitation disputes.

Note that specific issues involving the children of cohabitants are discussed in Chapter 5 (child custody and parenting plans), Chapter 8 (parenting time and visitation), Chapter 9 (child support), Chapter 10 (child support modification and enforcement), and Chapter 16 (parentage).

CHANGING LIFESTYLES

15.2. A Changing Social Perspective

During the last 50 years or so, a social and legal revolution has occurred in the United States regarding how unmarried cohabiting couples are viewed. As the number of persons living together like a married couple but without the benefit of marriage has increased, the social stigma associated with the view that such conduct is "shameful" or "illicit" has been waning. Many courts have followed in the wake of the social change by providing legal redress to partners where once none existed.

Why cohabit? A variety of reasons are given to explain why more couples than ever before are cohabiting but not formally marrying. Some think that a period of cohabitation provides a testing phase for the relationship; that is, it provides couples contemplating marriage time to evaluate the relationship before obtaining a marriage license from the state. The experience, they believe, may prevent an unwise marriage and avoid the financial and emotional consequences associated with divorce. Others say that cohabitation offers philosophical freedom from a marriage system dominated by traditional "outdated" societal values. It is also thought that a few cohabiting couples remain single because a formal marriage might end alimony payments from an earlier marriage or eliminate benefits provided by a public assistance program.

Cohabitation critics argue that there is little statistical evidence supporting the view that a "trial run" cohabitation relationship results in a greater chance of a successful marriage. Critics observe that when a relationship ends, partners should not be surprised to discover that courts are less than enthusiastic to assist them in sorting out property and support issues. Furthermore, critics say cohabitants should not be shocked by the fact that resolving cohabitation disputes can be as costly and challenging as resolving those associated with divorce. *See generally* Lynne Marie Kohm & Karen M. Groen, *Cohabitation and the Future of Marriage*, 17 Regent U. L. Rev. 261 (2005).

Cohabitation data. Data released by the Census Bureau shows married couples are no longer the majority in the United States. In the 2010 Census, married couples represented 48 percent of all households, which was down from 52 percent in the last Census. This was the first time that husband-wife families fell below 50 percent of all households in the United States since data on families were first tabulated in 1940. *Households and Families: 2010* http://www.census.gov/prod/cen2010/briefs/c2010br-14.pdf p. 5 (last visited May 2012). Opposite-sex unmarried partner households increased by 40 percent from 2000 to 2010, almost four times the national average. For same-sex households, the estimates for 2000 and 2010 showed an 80 percent increase in unmarried partner households.

The National Center for Family and Marriage Research (NCFMR) reports that the percentage of women ages 19–44 who have cohabited has increased by 75 percent over the past 20 years. In 1987, one-third of women had cohabited, and in 2006–2008, over half (58 percent) had cohabited. NCFMR Family Profiles http://ncfmr.bgsu.edu/pdf/family_profiles/file87411.pdf (last visited May 2012). NCFMR reports that "cohabitation is now the typical pathway into marriage, such that about two-thirds of women first married in the last decade cohabited prior to marriage." *Ibid.*

The Pew Research Center reported that 39 percent of Americans say they agree that marriage is becoming obsolete. However, in the same survey, most people who have never married said they would like to marry someday (including many who agree that marriage is becoming obsolete). Pew Social and Demographic Trends, December 14, 2011 http://www.pewsocialtrends.org/2011/12/14/marriage-rate-declines-and-marriage-age-rises/ (last visited May 2012).

Same-sex couples. According to revised estimates from the 2010 Census, there were 131,729 same-sex married couple households and 514,735 same-sex unmarried partner households in the United States. http://www.census.gov/newsroom/releases/archives/2010_census/cb11-cn181.html (last visited July 2012). However, same-sex partner households made up less than 1 percent of all households in both 2000 and 2010. *Ibid.*

Morality and criminality. Most states have, or had at one time, laws making it a criminal offense for unmarried persons to live together without benefit of marriage. These laws were originally intended to punish persons for sodomy, fornication, and cohabitation. However, a somewhat recent decision by the United States Supreme Court in *Lawrence v. Texas*, 539 U.S. 558 (2003), questions the continued validity of some of these laws.

In *Lawrence*, the Court held that a Texas statute making it a crime for two persons of the same sex to engage in intimate sexual conduct was unconstitutional, as applied to adult males who had engaged in consensual acts of sodomy in the privacy of their home. One may infer from the majority's opinion that some state criminal laws, such as those punishing fornication between consenting adults, are unconstitutional.

It is of interest to note that dissenting Associate Justice Antonin Scalia made the following moral doomsday prognostication in *Lawrence*:

> The Texas statute undeniably seeks to further the belief of its citizens that certain forms of sexual behavior are immoral and unacceptable — the same interest furthered by criminal laws against fornication, bigamy, adultery, adult incest, bestiality, and obscenity. Bowers held that this was a legitimate state interest. The Court today reaches the opposite conclusion. The Texas statute, it says, "furthers no legitimate state interest which can justify its intrusion into the personal and private life of the individual." The Court embraces instead Justice Stevens' declaration in his Bowers dissent, that " 'the fact that the governing majority in a State has traditionally viewed a particular practice as immoral is not a sufficient reason for upholding a law prohibiting the practice.' " This effectively decrees the end of all morals legislation. If, as the Court asserts, the promotion of majoritarian sexual morality is not even a legitimate state interest, none of the above-mentioned laws can survive rational-basis review.

Id. at 599 of 539 U.S.

However, based on what has transpired since the decision, Justice Scalia's forecast appears to have been well off the mark. *See, e.g., United States v. Thompson*, 458 F. Supp. 2d 730 (N.D. Ind. 2006) (holding that prostitution is not a protected activity under *Lawrence*); *Muth v. Frank*, 412 F.3d 808, 817-818 (7th Cir. 2005) (no protected privacy interest for incestuous relationship), cert. denied, 546 U.S. 988 (2005); *United States v. Orellana*, 62 M.J. 595, 601 (N.M. App. 2005) (adultery not constitutionally protected conduct under *Lawrence* where offense is service discrediting or prejudicial to good order and discipline), *rev. denied*, 63 M.J. 295 (C.A.A.F. 2006); *Cawood v. Haggard*, 327 F. Supp. 2d 863 (E.D. Tenn. 2004) (adulterous, sexual activities with client in the confines of lawyer's private office do not fall within a right of privacy that is constitutionally protected from government intrusion where client made criminal complaint to authorities about lawyer's behavior); *1568 Montgomery Highway, Inc. v. City of Hoover*, 45 So. 3d 319 (Ala. 2010) (public morality can still serve as a legitimate rational basis for regulating commercial sexual activity, which is not a private activity); *State v. Romano*,

155 P.3d 1102 (Haw. 2007) (application of prostitution statute to defendant did not violate her constitutional right to privacy); *State v. Oakley*, 605 S.E.2d 215 (N.C. App. 2004) (enforcing sodomy statutes in situations involving adults and minors).

LEGAL REDRESS FOR COHABITING COUPLES

15.3. *Marvin v. Marvin*

Marvin I. Legal recognition that partners in a cohabitating relationship may have enforceable rights is a byproduct of a phenomenon that began in the 1960s, when increasingly large numbers of adults began openly living together without a traditional marriage ceremony or state license. The legal movement was sparked, at least in part, by the publicity following a decision by the California Supreme Court in *Marvin v. Marvin*, 557 P.2d 106 (Cal. 1976).

In *Marvin*, a well-known Hollywood actor, Lee Marvin, was sued by Michelle Triola, his live-in girlfriend from 1965 to 1970. She had legally changed her surname to "Marvin." She alleged that she and Marvin had entered into an oral agreement that while they lived together, they would combine their efforts and earnings and share equally in any and all property accumulated as a result of their efforts, whether individual or combined. She also alleged they had agreed to hold themselves out to the general public as husband and wife and that she agreed to give up her career as an entertainer and singer in order to devote her full time to Marvin as his companion, homemaker, housekeeper, and cook. In return, she alleged that Marvin agreed to provide for all of her financial support and needs for the rest of her life. She alleged that after she had lived with Marvin for almost six years, he forced her to leave his household and refused to recognize her rights under the contract. She demanded declaratory relief, asking the court to determine her contractual and property rights and impose a constructive trust on half of the property acquired during the course of the relationship.

Marvin argued that the enforcement of the contract would violate public policy because it was related so closely to the "immoral" relationship of the parties. The trial judge agreed with this argument and granted Marvin's motion for judgment on the pleadings. The matter was appealed, and the California Supreme Court reversed the judgment.

The California Supreme Court stated that:

> [W]e base our opinion on the principle that adults who voluntarily live together and engage in sexual relations are nonetheless as competent as any

> other persons to contract respecting their earnings and property rights. Of course, they cannot lawfully contract to pay for the performance of sexual services, for such a contract is, in essence, an agreement for prostitution and unlawful for that reason. But they may agree to pool their earnings and to hold all property acquired during the relationship in accord with the law governing community property; conversely they may agree that each partner's earnings and the property acquired from those earnings remains the separate property of the earning partner. So long as the agreement does not rest upon illicit meretricious consideration, the parties may order their economic affairs as they choose, and no policy precludes the courts from enforcing such agreements.

Id. at 116.

When determining whether a cohabiters' agreement rests upon illicit meretricious consideration, the court said that it would be guided by the following principle:

> (A) contract between non-marital partners, even if expressly made in contemplation of a common living arrangement, is invalid only if sexual acts form an inseparable part of the consideration for the agreement. In sum, a court will not enforce a contract for the pooling of property and earnings if it is explicitly and inseparably based upon services as a paramour.

Id. at 114.

The court also said that:

> [t]he fact that a man and woman live together without marriage, and engage in a sexual relationship, does not in itself invalidate agreements between them relating to their earnings, property, or expenses. Neither is such an agreement invalid merely because the parties may have contemplated the creation or continuation of a nonmarital relationship when they entered into it. Agreements between nonmarital partners fail only to the extent that they rest upon a consideration of meretricious sexual services.

Id. at 113.

The court held that Triola had the same right to enforce contracts and to assert her equitable interest in property acquired through her efforts as does any other unmarried person. However, it refused to extend to her any rights that the California Family Law Act grants to a valid or putative spouse.

Marvin v. Marvin was the first major decision by a state court that clearly held that unmarried adults who live together are free under general principles of contract law to make agreements concerning their property and earnings. The case was remanded to the trial judge for further review.

Marvin II. On remand, the trial judge made a number of findings, including the following: (1) Marvin never had any obligation to pay Triola a reasonable sum as and for her maintenance. (2) Triola suffered no damage resulting from her relationship with Marvin, including its termination, and thus Marvin did not become monetarily liable to Triola at all. (3) Triola actually benefited economically and socially from the cohabitation of the parties, including payment by Marvin for goods and services for Triola's sole benefit in the approximate amount of $72,900. (4) There had been payments by Marvin of the living expenses of the two of them of approximately $221,400, and he made other substantial specified gifts. (5) A confidential and fiduciary relationship never existed between the parties with respect to property, and Marvin was never unjustly enriched as a result of the relationship of the parties or of the services performed by Triola for him or for them. (6) Marvin never acquired any property or money from Triola by any wrongful act.

The trial judge also found that the market value of Marvin's property at the time that the parties separated exceeded $1 million, that Triola at the time of the trial had been recently receiving unemployment insurance benefits, and that it was doubtful that she could return to the career she had enjoyed before the relationship of the parties commenced (namely, that of singer). The judge also found that Triola was in need of rehabilitation (i.e., to learn new employable skills), and that she should be able to accomplish such rehabilitation in two years.

In a controversial ruling, the judge awarded Triola $104,000, saying it was not only necessary for rehabilitation, but also for her living expenses (including her debts) during this period of rehabilitation. He found that Marvin had the ability to pay this sum "forthwith." *See Marvin v. Marvin*, 5 Fam. L. Rep. 3077 (1979).

Marvin III. The trial judge's controversial rehabilitative award was challenged on appeal. *Marvin v. Marvin*, 176 Cal. Rptr. 555 (Cal. App. 1981). The court ruled that an award to Triola of $104,000 for "occupational rehabilitation" was not a proper exercise of the trial court's power and reversed the judgment. *Id.* at 559 of 176 Cal. App.

The appellate court observed that the trial judge's findings in support of the challenged rehabilitative award merely established that Triola had a need for rehabilitation and that Marvin had the ability to respond to that need. "This is not enough," said the court. "The award, being nonconsensual in nature, must be supported by some recognized underlying obligation in law or in equity. A court of equity admittedly has broad powers, but it may not create totally new substantive rights under the guise of doing equity." *Ibid.*

15.4. Response to *Marvin*

There were mixed reactions by state legislatures and courts to *Marvin v. Marvin*. For example, states such as New Jersey and Minnesota appeared to accept and apply the various *Marvin* principles quite liberally. *See, e.g., Crowe v. De Gioia*, 495 A.2d 889 (N.J. Super. 1985) (so long as contract between unmarried cohabitants is not based on relationship proscribed by law, or on a promise to marry, agreements between cohabitants are enforceable); *Carlson v. Olson*, 256 N.W.2d 249, 255 (Minn. 1977) (courts should enforce express contracts between non-marital partners except to the extent that the contract is explicitly founded on the consideration of meretricious sexual services). In some other states, there was a cautious application of selected principles enunciated in *Marvin*. A few states rejected the doctrine completely.

Illinois minority view. The most influential state court ruling rejecting the *Marvin* doctrine is probably *Hewitt v. Hewitt*, 394 N.E.2d 1204 (Ill. 1979). In *Hewitt*, a woman cohabitant sought a one-half share in the property accumulated during the relationship. She and the defendant were students at Grinnell College in Iowa when she became pregnant. The defendant told her that they were already husband and wife and would live as such; therefore, no formal marriage ceremony or license was necessary. He also said that he would "share his life, his future, his earnings, and his property" with her. The parties immediately announced to their respective parents that they were married and for the next 15 years held themselves out as husband and wife. Three children were born to the relationship before it broke down.

At the trial court hearing, the woman testified that in reliance on the defendant's promises, she had devoted her efforts to his professional education and his establishment in the practice of pedodontia and obtained financial assistance from her parents for this purpose. She also assisted him in his career with her own special skills, and although she was given payroll checks for these services, she placed them in a common fund. She claimed that the defendant, who was without funds at the time of the marriage, as a result of her efforts, earned over $80,000 a year when their relationship ended and had accumulated large amounts of property, owned either jointly with her or separately. She also testified that she gave him every assistance that a wife and mother could give, including social activities designed to enhance his social and professional reputation.

The trial judge rejected her claims, reasoning that Illinois law and public policy require such claims to be based on a valid marriage. The dispute then went to the court of appeals, which reversed the trial judge, saying that because the parties had outwardly lived a conventional married life, the plaintiff's conduct had not "so affronted public policy that she should be denied any and all relief." It ruled that the plaintiff's complaint stated a cause of action on an express oral contract. The appellate court adopted the reasoning of the California Supreme Court in *Marvin v. Marvin*.

The matter was then reviewed by the Illinois Supreme Court. It rejected the woman's claim and the lower appeals' court analysis. It reasoned as follows:

> There are major public policy questions involved in determining whether, under what circumstances, and to what extent it is desirable to accord some type of legal status to claims arising from such relationships. Of substantially greater importance than the rights of the immediate parties is the impact of such recognition upon our society and the institution of marriage. Will the fact that legal rights closely resembling those arising from conventional marriages can be acquired by those who deliberately choose to enter into what have heretofore been commonly referred to as "illicit" or "meretricious" relationships encourage formation of such relationships and weaken marriage as the foundation of our family-based society? In the event of death shall the survivor have the status of a surviving spouse for purposes of inheritance, wrongful death actions, workmen's compensation, etc.? And still more importantly: what of the children born of such relationships? What are their support and inheritance rights and by what standards are custody questions resolved?
>
> What of the sociological and psychological effects upon them of that type of environment? Does not the recognition of legally enforceable property and custody rights emanating from non-marital cohabitation in practical effect equate with the legalization of common law marriage at least in the circumstances of this case?

Id. at 830-831.

The court concluded that:

> [the] plaintiff's claims are unenforceable for the reason that they contravene the public policy, implicit in the statutory scheme of the Illinois Marriage and Dissolution of Marriage Act, disfavoring the grant of mutually enforceable property rights to knowingly unmarried cohabitants.

Id. at 834. *See also Ayala v Fox*, 564 N.E.2d 920 (Ill. App. 1990). *See* Jan Skelton, *Hewitt to Ayala: A Wrong Turn for Cohabitants' Rights*, 82 Ill. B.J. 364 (July 1994).

The Wisconsin Supreme Court criticized the reasoning of the *Hewett* court in *Watts v. Watts*, 405 N.W.2d 303 (Wis. 1987). The court said:

> We agree with . . . commentators that the Hewitt court made an unsupportable inferential leap when it found that cohabitation agreements run contrary to statutory policy and that the Hewitt court's approach is patently inconsistent with the principle that public policy limits are to be narrowly and exactly applied.

Id. at 309.

Other jurisdictions that apparently accepted the *Hewitt* view, at least in part, include New Mexico, Mississippi, and New York. *See, e.g., Merrill v. Davis*, 673 P.2d 1285 (N.M. 1983) (expressly following *Hewitt*); *In re Estate of Alexander*, 445 So. 2d 836 (Miss. 1984) (rejecting placing equitable lien on home occupied by plaintiff and deceased partner for 30 years saying any change in common law rule should come from legislature rather than from courts).

New York view. New York courts have rejected the scope of *Marvin. See, e.g. Silver v. Starrett*, 674 N.Y.S.2d 915 (N.Y. Sup. 1998) ("fact of cohabitation without marriage would be no bar to carrying out an express agreement (but not an implied contract) within the normal rules of contract law"). *Id.* at 917. While rejecting *Marvin's* implied contract principles, New York courts have accepted the concept that an express agreement between unmarried persons living together is as enforceable as though they were not living together, provided only that illicit sexual relations were not part of the consideration of the contract. The theory is that while cohabitation without marriage does not give rise to the property and financial rights that normally attend the marital relation, neither does cohabitation disable the parties from making an agreement within the normal rules of contract law.

New York has made it clear in cases such as *Trimmer v. Van Bomel*, 434 N.Y.S.2d 82 (N.Y. Sup. 1980), that it will not enforce implied contracts based on cohabitant relationships. The dispute involved a nonsexual relationship between an unmarried couple, a wealthy elderly widow and a gentleman who acted as her steady (and well-subsidized) escort for at least five years. The court dismissed the gentleman's claim that an implied contract for support existed beyond breakup, declaring:

> The claims of friendship, like the claims of kinship, may be many and varied. To imply an obligation by a wealthy friend to compensate a less wealthy companion for being together, dining together, talking together and accepting tokens of regard stretches the bonds of friendship to the breaking point. The implied obligation to compensate arises from those things which, in normal society, we expect to pay for. An obligation to pay for friendship is not ordinarily to be implied — it is too crass. Friendship, like virtue, must be its own reward.

Id. at 85-86.

Minority view. A few courts apparently view cohabitation agreements under any circumstances as involving immoral consideration and unenforceable as against public policy. *Liles v. Still*, 335 S.E.2d 168 (Ga. App. 1985). In *Long v. Marino*, 441 S.E.2d 475, 476 (Ga. App. 1994), the court affirmed a view found in *Samples v. Monroe*, 358 S.E.2d 273 (Ga. App. 1987), where the court said that

> In Georgia, sexual intercourse outside of marriage is a criminal offense. It is well settled that neither a court of law nor a court of equity will lend its aid to either party to a contract founded upon an illegal or immoral consideration. Meretricious sexual relationships are by nature repugnant to social stability, and our courts have on sound public policy declined to reward them by allowing a money recovery therefor.

Id. at 274.

Same-sex couples. The general principles espoused in *Marvin v. Marvin* have been applied with equal force in some jurisdictions to agreements between same-sex partners. For example, in *Whorton v. Dillingham*, 202 Cal. App. 3d 447 (Cal. 1988), the court allowed one partner to seek recovery on a breach of express oral contract theory based on allegations that he provided the defendant with services as a chauffeur, bodyguard, secretary, and business partner. The court found that the oral agreement was supported by consideration independent of sexual services.

15.5. Importance of Separating Illicit Relationship from Contract

Majority view. A majority of jurisdictions distinguish contracts made by cohabiting couples that are explicitly and inseparably founded on sexual services and those that are not. Obviously, courts will not enforce contracts for the sexual services because that is akin to prostitution. *See, e.g., Cougler v. Fackler*, 510 S.W.2d 16 (Ky. 1974) (if agreement between the parties was founded on prostitution, no recovery of monies paid by plaintiff to defendant could be had, whereas if consideration was lawful, plaintiff could recover in restitution monies given to defendant); *Bergen v. Wood*, 18 Cal. Rptr. 2d 75 (Cal. App. 1993) (when parties did not live together, and services as companion were not severable from sexual services, no recovery on alleged promise of support could be had).

As a rule, a majority of courts consider a contract between cohabiting couples enforceable, so long as the agreement is (1) independent of the illicit relationship, (2) the illicit relationship is not part of the consideration bargained for, and (3) the relationship is not a condition of the agreement. *See, e.g., Wilcox v. Trautz*, 693 N.E.2d 141 (Mass. 1998) (unmarried cohabitants may lawfully contract concerning property, financial, and other matters relevant to their relationship, except to the extent that sexual services constitute only, or dominant, consideration for agreement, or that enforcement should be denied on some other public policy ground); *Jones v. Daly*, 176 Cal. Rptr. 130 (Cal. App. 1981) (court refused enforcement of alleged oral "cohabitors agreement" between two males where plaintiff's rendition of sexual services to decedent was an inseparable part of the consideration for the agreement).

A majority of courts believe that if they refused to enforce contract and property rights between unmarried cohabitants, the result would often leave one party with all or almost all the assets accumulated during the relationship, while the other party, who is no more or less "guilty," would be deprived of assets that he or she helped to accumulate. Such a result is viewed as unduly harsh and inequitable. *See generally* Richard A. Lord, 7 Williston on Contracts §16:23 (4th ed. 2012) *Immoral bargains; cohabitation agreements*.

Consideration. Courts appear to have little difficulty in finding consideration for most of these agreements. Although, as already observed above, they will not enforce an agreement if the sole consideration for it is "the contemplation of out-of-wedlock sexual relations," most are willing to sever the sexual aspects of the contract from the intimate relationship. *In re Estate of Eriksen*, 337 N.W.2d 671, 674 (Minn. 1983).

Services such as companionship, housekeeping, hostessing, and cooking may be sufficient consideration for a contract between cohabitants. For example, in *Chiba v. Greenwald*, 67 Cal. Rptr. 3d 86 (Cal. App. 2007), one partner promised the other to provide for her "financial needs and support for the rest of her life" in exchange for her domestic services as his "homemaker, housekeeper, cook, secretary, bookkeeper, and financial counselor," forgoing any independent career opportunities. The promise to perform these domestic services was held lawful and adequate consideration for a contract. *See Whorton v. Dillingham*, 248 Cal. Rptr. 405, 409-410 (1988) (holding that a same-sex, non-married cohabitant's alleged services as a chauffeur, bodyguard, secretary, and business partner were, if proven true, sufficient independent consideration for the formation of a contract); *cf., Zaremba v. Cliburn*, 949 S.W.2d 822 (Tex. App. 1997) (failure to comply with statute of frauds barred all causes of action in a cohabitation dispute).

15.6. Alimony

As pointed out at the beginning of this chapter, cohabitation does not trigger a right to future alimony. Alimony can be claimed only by a participant in a valid marriage, or possibly by a putative spouse. *See Combs v. Tibbitts*, 148 P.3d 430 (Colo. App. 2006) (right to maintenance can be claimed only by a participant in a valid marital relationship or by a putative spouse). However, it appears that there is a willingness among some courts in some cohabitation disputes to award financial support, which is arguably similar to alimony. In other words, courts in a few jurisdictions have not simply limited their rulings to the distribution of real and personal property.

For example, in *In re Estate of Roccamonte*, 808 A.2d 838 (N.J. 2002), the parties were married when they met, and after the defendant pursued the plaintiff, she left her husband and they began an affair that lasted the rest of the defendant's life. The parties lived together "intermittently" until she moved to California for the purpose of ending her relationship with Roccamonte, who had refused her requests that he divorce his wife and marry her. But, the defendant called the plaintiff repeatedly, promising that if she returned he would divorce his wife and support her for the rest of her life. The plaintiff returned and divorced her husband.

The parties lived together as man and wife in an apartment he leased; the defendant then purchased an interest in the apartment in the plaintiff's name, and they lived there together until his death. The defendant never divorced his wife, and told the plaintiff it was because a divorce would jeopardize his business. During their relationship, he repeatedly assured her that she had no cause for worry as he would see to it that she was provided for during her life.

The New Jersey Supreme Court said that:

> The principle we recognized and accepted is that the formation of a marital-type relationship between unmarried persons may, legitimately and enforceably, rest upon a promise by one to support the other. A marital-type relationship is no more exclusively dependent upon one partner's providing maid services than it is upon sexual accommodation. It is, rather, the undertaking of a way of life in which two people commit to each other, foregoing other liaisons and opportunities, doing for each other whatever each is capable of doing, providing companionship, and fulfilling each other's needs, financial, emotional, physical, and social, as best as they are able. And each couple defines its way of life and each partner's expected contribution to it in its own way. Whatever other consideration may be involved, the entry into such a relationship and then conducting oneself in accordance with its unique character is consideration to full measure. There is no doubt that plaintiff provided that consideration here until her obligation was discharged by Roccamonte's death.

Id. at 844. The Supreme Court determined that the defendant promised to support the plaintiff for life, as implied by his successful efforts to induce plaintiff's return when she moved to California. It found it was unlikely that the defendant intended to leave behind the plaintiff in an impoverished state. Furthermore, when the defendant died the plaintiff was seventy years old and relied upon him exclusively for support.

It should be noted that in 2009, New Jersey's legislature enacted a statute specifically intended to overrule *Roccamonte*. *See Botis v. Kudrick*, 22 A.3d 975, (N.J. Super. 2011) (amendment to statute of frauds, including palimony agreements among the types of agreements that must be in writing and signed by the parties in order to be enforceable, applied prospectively only); *McCullon v. McCullon*, 410 N.Y.S.2d 226 (N.Y. Sup. 1978) (woman's conduct in living with man for 28 years constituted implied promise to forbear employment and to provide household services for man in consideration for his implied conduct and promise to provide home and future support; on basis of such implied contract, alimony pendente lite, child support, and possession of parties' home would be awarded woman to avoid unjust enrichment).

Cohabiting, marrying, and divorcing. Courts are being asked in some jurisdictions to consider the amount of time that a couple cohabited prior to marriage in awarding alimony at the time they divorce. Georgia, Alaska, Oregon, and Wisconsin have held that it was proper to consider the premarital cohabitation period in awarding alimony. *See Sprouse v. Sprouse*, 678 S.E.2d 328 (Ga. 2009) (trial court when making alimony determination, did not abuse its discretion by considering the length of time the parties lived together before marriage); *Harrelson v. Harrelson*, 932 P.2d 247 (Alaska 1997) (court is free to consider the parties' entire relationship, including periods of premarital cohabitation, when deciding the amount of rehabilitative spousal support); *In re Marriage of Lind*, 139 P.3d 1032 (Or. App. 2006) (no reason to exclude length of the parties' premarital cohabitation when awarding alimony); *Meyer v. Meyer*, 620 N.W.2d 382 (Wis. 2000) (in awarding alimony, court did not abuse its discretion by considering the length of time the parties lived together before marriage).

Cohabitation following divorce. Cohabitation by an ex-spouse with a new partner following a divorce may be grounds to end alimony payments. *See, e.g., Linstroth v. Dorgan*, 2 So. 3d 305 (Fla. App. 2008) (terminating alimony upon showing of cohabitation); *Bird v. Bird*, 688 S.E.2d 420 (N.C. 2009) (under the current statute, if a dependent spouse engages in cohabitation, alimony shall terminate); *Black v. Black*, 199 P.3d 371 (Utah. App. 2008) (alimony terminated when former wife hid the fact that she was cohabitating with her boyfriend for five years); *Giltz v. Giltz*, 2012 WL 1378312 (Ohio App. 2012) (trial courts have the power to terminate or reduce an award of spousal support based on cohabitation but are not compelled to do so); *Reed v. Reed*, 2012 WL 1107888 (Tenn. App. 2012) (court allowed to terminate alimony obligation upon the finding that former spouse and her paramour were residing together and that the former spouse was paying all the expenses at the residence).

Connecticut's approach to cohabitation following divorce is similar to that of many other jurisdictions. Its relevant statute on this issue reads as follows:

> (b) In an action for divorce, dissolution of marriage, legal separation or annulment brought by a husband or wife, in which a final judgment has been entered providing for the payment of periodic alimony by one party to the other, the superior court may, in its discretion and upon notice and hearing,

> modify such judgment and suspend, reduce or terminate the p
> periodic alimony upon a showing that the party receiving the periodi
> is living with another person under circumstances which the court fir
> result in the modification, suspension, reduction or termination of alimony because the living arrangements cause such a change of circumstances as to alter the financial needs of that party.

Conn. Gen. Stat. §46b-86 (b) (2011).

Examples

1. Assume that D was arrested after he solicited an undercover police officer for oral sex in violation of State Code §18.2-361 (crimes against nature). The arresting officer testified that D walked into a men's restroom located in a department store, which is freely accessible to members of the public, including children. Once in the restroom, D approached a stall occupied by the undercover police officer, leaned forward, and "peered" into the stall through the crack in the stall door. The undercover police officer, who was in a state of undress, engaged in a conversation with D. During the conversation, D solicited the officer for oral sex, and the officer then arrested D. Based on the holding of the United States Supreme Court in *Lawrence v. Texas*, D contends that Code §18.2-361 is unconstitutional because as applied to him, it prohibits private acts of consensual sodomy. How will a court most likely rule on D's argument?

2. Assume that boyfriend P and girlfriend D agreed to share utilities and rent on an apartment while they were attending college. After three years of cohabiting, D purchased a small home in her name, paying $20,000 down and taking out a $150,000 mortgage. She also purchased insurance that would pay off her mortgage should she die prior to the final payment. While moving out of the apartment into the home, D suffered a sudden heart attack and died. The insurance company is ready to pay the $150,000 per the policy to the estate of D when P asserts that he has an interest in the home.

   At trial, D's estate produces all of the relevant real estate, loan, and insurance documents, and they contain only D's name and signature. The estate also produces evidence from D's bank showing that only D's name appears on the checking and savings accounts. P testifies that D expressly said the home was to be his should D die before P and introduces some checks showing that P, on occasion, purchased food for both P and D. P explains that he didn't want his name on any of the home purchase documents because he felt that home ownership might jeopardize his ability to obtain future student loans because he was intending to pursue a graduate degree. How will a court most likely rule on P's claim?

3. Assume that D, a wealthy businessman, and P, his unmarried personal assistant, became romantically involved and maintained a somewhat erratic romantic relationship for several years. The relationship continued even after D married X and they had two children. D unexpectedly suffered a serious stroke, and his financial affairs were taken over by his wife. She discovered that for the last 15 years, D had been providing P with a monthly financial supplement that ranged from $100 to $1,000. When she refused to continue making payments, P brought a legal action alleging that D had promised orally that in consideration for the emotional and social support that D received from P, that he would provide financial support to her for life. How will a court most likely decide P's claim?

Explanations

1. A careful review of *Lawrence*, which is discussed earlier in this chapter, shows that the issue in that case was whether the petitioners were free as adults to engage in the private conduct in the exercise of their liberty under the due process clause of the Fourteenth Amendment to the Constitution. *Lawrence* does not apply to this example because the restrooms are within stores open to the public and are not within the zone of privacy as contemplated by the United States Supreme Court. The trial judge most likely will reject a motion to dismiss. *See, e.g.*, *Singson v. Com.*, 621 S.E.2d 682 (Va. App. 2005) (Virginia's crimes against nature statute prohibiting oral sodomy did not violate due process as applied to defendant because he solicited oral sodomy in a public place).

2. There appears little to support a conclusion that there is consideration for an agreement awarding P a half interest or more in the home. P may argue that the intimate relationship of the couple provides the consideration for the contract. D's estate will counter that if contemplation of sexual relations was the sole consideration for the contract, that is insufficient consideration and should fail for public policy reasons.

   P may fail for other reasons as well. P has never alleged that he had any legal interest in the realty or that he contributed any money toward the purchase of the property. There is no allegation of unjust enrichment. At most, the pleading sets forth an unfulfilled expectation of P and nothing more. Compare the facts in this example with those in *In re Estate of Eriksen*, 337 N.W.2d 671 (Minn. 1983) (creation of constructive trust consisting of one-half interest in home was required to prevent unjust enrichment of estate). In *Eriksen*, evidence was produced that the surviving cohabitant and the deceased each contributed money equally toward the expenses of purchasing and maintaining the home, and each contributed equally to the premiums for the credit life insurance policy, which ultimately paid $48,334.63 on the mortgage when the other cohabitant died. The court felt that the surviving cohabitant's claim was similar to that of a joint venturer or partner. (Note that in some jurisdictions, the absence of an allegation of any written documentation that would satisfy the real property statute of frauds also would cause a court to dismiss P's complaint.)

3. Some courts will view the agreement between P and D as based entirely on a sexual, immoral relationship and dismiss P's claim outright. A few jurisdictions may take a more analytical approach, similar to that used by the court in *Levine v. Konvitz*, 890 A.2d 354 (N.J. Super. A.D. 2006). There, the court held that "[i]n order to establish a *prima facie* case for palimony, a plaintiff must present competent evidence showing (1) that the parties cohabitated; (2) in a marriage-type relationship; (3) that during this period of cohabitation, defendant promised plaintiff that he/she would support him/her for life; and (4) that this promise was made in exchange for valid consideration." *Id.* at 354. Note that the New Jersey legislature essentially abrogated *Levine* by statute in 2009. *See Botis v. Kudrick*, 22 A.3d 975 (N.J. Super. 2011).

   However, in this hypothetical, the parties did not live together or spend significant periods of time together, did not commingle property, did not hold themselves out in public as husband and wife, and the man remained married to and continued to live with his wife until he died. Most jurisdictions would reject the claim for lifetime support.

15.7. Model Acts and General Authorities

American Law Institute (ALI). The American Law Institute (ALI) approach to cohabitation issues is in contrast with the principles established in *Marvin v. Marvin*. Rather than relying on contract and equitable remedies discussed in *Marvin*, the ALI creates presumptive categories of "domestic partners" who are entitled to property and support in the same manner as legal spouses. Domestic partners are defined as two unmarried people (same- or opposite-sex) who "share a primary residence and a life together as a couple" for a significant period of time. ALI, *Principles of the Law of Family Dissolution: Analysis and Recommendations* §§6.01-6.06 (2002).

Restatement of Contracts. The Restatement (Third) of Restitution and Unjust Enrichment, note 1, §28, at 24 (Tent. Draft No. 3, 2004), appears to adopt the rule of *Marvin v. Marvin*, 557 P.2d 106 (Cal. 1976). The Restatement provides that if one former cohabitant "owns a specific asset to which the other has made substantial, uncompensated contributions in the form of property or services, the person making such contributions has a claim in restitution against the owner of the asset as necessary to prevent unjust enrichment." Emily Sherwin, *Love, Money, and Justice: Restitution Between Cohabitants*, 77 U. Colo. L. Rev. 711, 719 (2006).

Professor Sherwin disagrees with the Restatement's approach. She argues that "[a]lthough many cohabitant cases have strong appeal from the standpoint of fairness and decency, I believe that a remedy based on unjust enrichment represents a wrong turn in the law of restitution. To grant relief to disappointed cohabitants, courts must disregard the rules that traditionally have marked the boundaries of restitution and endorse an expansive reading of the unjust enrichment principle. This move is inconsistent with the premises of the new Restatement and jeopardizes the task of rationalizing and taming the field of restitution." *Ibid. See Featherston v. Steinhoff*, 575 N.W.2d 6 (Mich. App. 1997) (female cohabitant did not overcome presumption that she rendered services gratuitously, as required to establish implied in fact contract of support). *See also* Emily Sherwin, *Why "Omegas Group" Was Right: An Essay on the Legal Status of Equitable Rights, Conference on Restitution and Unjust Enrichment* (Boston University/American Law Institute, September 16-17, 2011); Richard A. Lord, 7 Williston on Contracts §16:23 (4th ed). *Immoral Bargains; Cohabitation Agreements*; 1 Williston on Contracts 4th *Forms* §16F:61 (4th ed).

APPLICATION OF LEGAL THEORIES

15.8. Overview of Legal Theories

It is obvious from the preceding material that American jurisdictions have utilized a variety of legal theories and approaches when cohabiting couples have sought enforcement of agreements made during their relationship. It is also obvious that a minority of jurisdictions have refused to provide any relief, viewing a cohabitant's relationship as immoral and illegal. However, most jurisdictions will enforce an express agreement between cohabiting couples. Still others will enforce either an express or an implied agreement based on the expectations of the parties. Some may allow a party to recover based on an unjust enrichment or *quantum meruit* contract principles. Some may apply gift law to avoid an inequitable result, and others may grant relief in the form of a constructive or resulting trust. A minority will consider the contract as similar to a commercial contract and reject application of equitable theories.

Burden of proof. Regardless of the legal theory selected, most jurisdictions agree that a party alleging the existence of an agreement bears the burden of producing evidence to support it. *See, e.g., Ball v. Smith*, 150 S.W.3d 889 (Tex. App. 2004) (plaintiff failed to produce more than "a scintilla of evidence" in support of claims for breach of contract and resulting trust).

15.9. Express Written Contracts

As noted above, courts are much more willing to enforce a written cohabitation contract than an oral one, assuming that the terms of the contract are independent of the parties' sexual relationship. A written contract defines the parties' expectations and understandings, and a signature on a written contract by both parties indicates their understanding and acceptance of the terms. It is generally agreed that although written contracts signed by both parties are seldom perfect, they are better than oral or implied contracts.

Statute of frauds. Note that in some states, only written agreements that comply with the state's statute of frauds will be enforced. Texas is one of those states. For example, in *Zaremba v. Cliburn*, 949 S.W.2d 822 (Tex. App. 1997), the court ruled that failure to comply with that state's statute of frauds provisions barred all causes of action in a cohabitation dispute. *Tompkins v. Jackson*, 880 N.Y.S.2d 876 (unpublished) (N.Y. Sup. 2009) (defendant argues that the alleged oral agreement violates the statute of frauds as it obligated defendant to support plaintiff for the rest of her life, and its terms cannot be performed within one year or before the end of a lifetime).

15.10. Legal Practice Issues

It has been suggested that an attorney should advise a client to never live together with a "romantic partner (or even a roommate) without a written cohabitation agreement." Elizabeth A. Pope, *Cohabitation: What to Do When Couples Cannot or Do Not Marry*, 20 DCBA Brief 22, 28 (Dec. 2007). Pope suggests that until a cohabitation agreement is effectuated for the client, an attorney should advise the client to never contribute money to an acquisition of a major asset, such as a house or car, which is held solely in the name of the other partner; never contribute money without keeping detailed records; and never put money into a joint account or hold title to other assets in joint names unless there is a written clear agreement of what is joint and what is separate. *Ibid.*

Confidentiality issues. Although cohabitation agreements are governed by contract rules, it can be argued that the same degree of confidentiality or fiduciary obligation exists between cohabiting couples as exists between those married or about to marry. Therefore, the same strict formalities in execution of a cohabitation agreement as one would follow in the execution of a premarital or post-marital agreement should be adhered to. *See, e.g.*, 1 Tex. Prac. Guide Family Law §2:216 (2011).

15.11. Express Oral Agreements

Few cohabitant disputes brought into family court involve an express written agreement. However, a large number involve alleged oral agreements. As observed earlier, New York will enforce an express oral contract between cohabitants unless it is based on an agreement to live together as man and wife. *See Tompkins v. Jackson*, 880 N.Y.S.2d 876 (unpublished) (N.Y. Sup. 2009).

Statute of frauds issues. The Court in *Marvin v. Marin*, 134 Cal. Rptr. 815, n. 9 (Cal. 1976), observed that most cohabitation agreements are oral, and that cases had expressly rejected defenses to such agreements grounded upon the statute of frauds. Because of *Marvin*'s endorsement of equitable remedies to protect the expectations of the parties to a nonmarital relationship, the court's observations on the enforcement of oral cohabitation agreements can be interpreted as an approval of the use of equitable estoppel by cohabitants in appropriate cases.

The Minnesota court in *In re Palmen*, 588 N.W.2d 493 (Minn. 1999), rejected application of the statute of frauds to an oral agreement reasoning that a claim by a cohabitant to recover, preserve, or protect his or her own property, which he or she acquired independent of any service contract related to cohabitation, is enforceable. In *In re Eriksen*, 337 N.W.2d 671, 674 (Minn.1983), the court explicitly held that the jurisdictional bar imposed by that state's statute of frauds applies only when the "sole consideration for a contract between cohabiting parties is their contemplation of sexual relations out of wedlock." *But see Williams v. Lynch*, 245 A.D.2d 715 (N.Y. App. 1997) (alleged oral contract between homeowner and his long-time cohabitant, under which homeowner purportedly promised to let cohabitant use home for rest of her life, could not by its terms be fully performed before end of cohabitant's lifetime; thus, statute of frauds barred breach of contract action that cohabitant brought against homeowner after they broke up).

Partial performance. Partial performance of an oral contract may remove the contract from the statute of frauds requirements. *See Sullivan v. Porter*, 861 A.2d 625, 630 (Me. 2004) (holding that the part performance doctrine is an exception to the statute of frauds); *Turon State Bank v. Estate of Frampton*, 845 P.2d

79 (Kan. App. 1993) (true basis for the application of the doctrine of partial performance is that it is grossly unjust and inequitable for one party of the oral contract to rely on the contract and partially perform his obligations thereunder while the other takes advantage of the partial performance and repudiates the contract by invoking the statute of frauds).

Wills. State statute of frauds provisions may bar cohabitation agreements, especially if they involve an attempt to enforce an agreement to make a will. For example, a majority of jurisdictions take the view that an oral agreement to execute a will in favor of a cohabitant who was living with a decedent is void under the statute of frauds. *In re Gorden's Estate*, 168 N.E.2d 239 (N.Y. 1960) (oral agreement to execute a will in favor of a woman who was living with decedent was void under the statute of frauds).

However, Massachusetts has ruled that an oral promise to leave a bequest to a cohabitant, although not binding under the statute of frauds, has been the basis for recovery in *quantum meruit* for the fair value of services rendered. *See Hastoupis v. Gargas*, 398 N.E.2d 745 (Mass. App. 1980) (although decedent's oral contract to bequeath to plaintiff one-half of his estate in return for plaintiff's performing services for him until his death was unenforceable by reason of statute of frauds, plaintiff, who fulfilled his part of the bargain, was entitled to recover in *quantum meruit* for fair and reasonable value of his services).

15.12. Implied Contracts

As already noted, some cohabitant disputes involve claims based on an implied contract theory. The formation of such a contract requires proof of the existence of an agreement, which is supported by consideration. The facts supporting the formation of an implied contract are found in the conduct of the parties rather than in express written or oral statements made by them.

For example, the New Jersey court held in *In re Estate of Roccamonte*, 808 A.2d 838 (N.J. 2002), that it would recognize implied palimony contracts. It reasoned that the existence of the terms of a contract between unmarried cohabitants is ordinarily not determinable by what was said. Rather, the terms are derived from the parties' actions and conduct in light of subject matter and surrounding circumstances. *Id.* at 843 of 808 A.2d. *See Herring v. Daniels*, 805 A.2d 718 (Conn. App. 2002) (where the parties have established an unmarried, cohabiting relationship, it is the specific conduct of the parties within that relationship that determines their respective rights and obligations, including the treatment of their individual property).

Some jurisdictions have adopted §589 of the Restatement of Contracts, which states that:

> while a bargain in whole or in part for or in consideration of illicit sexual intercourse or of a promise thereof is illegal, "such intercourse between parties to a bargain previously or subsequently formed does not invalidate it."

Restatement (First) Contracts §589 (1932).

In *Hudson v. DeLonjay*, 732 S.W.2d 922 (Mo. App. 1987). the court said that the relevant inquiry is whether there was an agreement, either express or implied in fact, between the parties which was supported by valid consideration. "This remains the test even though the parties' contemplation of cohabitation may have been the reason for their entering into such an agreement at the outset." *Id.* at 927. *See generally Cook v. Cook*, 691 P.2d 664 (Ariz. 1984) (the relevant question is whether the agreement was made for proper consideration).

The use of the implied contract theory is criticized as being conceptually amorphous. There are also concerns that because of the complex and varied relationships between men and women, once a relationship ends, one of the parties may be bitter and assert claims based on real or imaginary facts. Some courts surmise that personal service is often rendered by two people because they value each other's company or because they find it a convenient or rewarding thing to do—not as a contractual obligation. Without an express agreement, there is a substantially greater risk of emotion-laden afterthought and fraud when an effort is made to ascertain by implication what services, if any, were rendered gratuitously and what were rendered for compensation.

When the Mississippi Court of Appeals recently refused to allow an unjust enrichment claim by a cohabitant based on an implied contract, it justified its refusal as follows:

> The Mississippi Supreme Court has refused to circumvent the Mississippi Legislature's abolishment of common law marriage by extending implied contractual remedies to unmarried cohabitants. Similarly, this court is restrained from delving into policy issues of this nature and extending implied contractual remedies to unmarried cohabitants, whether opposite-sex or same-sex, when there is no express agreement for remuneration beyond cohabitation.

Cates v. Swain, 2012 WL 1292639, So. 3d (Miss. 2012).

15.13. Quasi-Contracts

Claims based on quasi-contract principles involving cohabitants have been recognized in several jurisdictions. *See, e.g., Suggs v. Norris*, 364 S.E.2d 159

(N.C. App. 1988) (agreements regarding finances and property of unmarried but cohabiting couple were enforceable under quasi-contractual theory on *quantum meruit*); *Jordan v. Mitchell*, 705 So. 2d 453 (Ala. App. 1997) (restitution in quasi-contract available but failed for proof); *Meyer v. Meyer*, 620 N.W.2d 382 (Wis. 2000) (Wisconsin law does not provide legal remedies for separating cohabitants except in the very narrow instance in which one party attempts to retain an unreasonable amount of property acquired during the relationship and the facts support application of a common law contract or quasi-contract theory); *Mason v. Rostad*, 476 A.2d 662 (D.C. App. 1984) (quasi-contractual claims for unjust enrichment allowable in cohabitation cases).

Quasi-contracts are viewed not as contracts based on the apparent intention of the parties to undertake the performance in question, but rather as contracts created by law for reasons of justice. An action for recovery based on a quasi-contract unjust enrichment claim is grounded on the moral principle that one who has received a benefit has a duty to make restitution when retaining such a benefit would be unjust. The remedy is based on the reasonable value of the benefit conferred by one party that enriched the other. The value of the benefit has two components: money expended and services or forbearance rendered.

Unlike express and implied contracts, the conduct of the parties is not critical to granting relief on a quasi-contract theory because no contract exists. Instead, a contract is imposed as a matter of law, not as a matter of fact. A party seeking to establish a quasi-contract must present evidence of the benefits conferred on the other party and services performed. In addition, the moving party must establish evidence of the reasonable value of those benefits and services. *See generally* Karen Moulding and National Lawyers Guild, Lesbian, Gay, Bisexual, and Transgender Committee, §4:31. *Division of property at termination of unrecognized cohabitation—Implied contracts and quantum meruit* (2012); John Bourdeau, 66 Am. Jur. 2d *Restitution and Implied Contracts* §67 (2012).

15.14. Resulting Trusts

One will find claims involving two types of implied trusts in some cohabitation disputes: resulting trusts and constructive trusts. A resulting trust is imposed to implement the parties' intent; a constructive trust is imposed to prevent the unjust enrichment of another. More specifically, a "resulting trust" has been defined as "[a] remedy imposed by equity when property is transferred under circumstances suggesting that the transferor did not intend for the transferee to have the beneficial interest in the property." *Black's Law Dictionary* 1551 (8th ed. 2004). "Because the transferee . . . is not entitled to the beneficial interest in question, and because that beneficial interest is not otherwise disposed of, it remains in and thus is said 'to result' (that is, it reverts) to the transferor or the transferor's estate or other successors in interest." *Restatement (Third) of Trusts*, §7, cmt. a. The transferee "is said to hold the property upon a resulting trust for the transferor," and so "the beneficial interest that is held in resulting trust is simply an equitable reversionary interest implied by law." *Ibid.*

15.15. Constructive Trusts

Like a resulting trust, a constructive trust is also an equitable remedy that is imposed to prevent the unjust enrichment of another. *See Black's Law Dictionary* 1547 (8th ed. 2004). A constructive trust arises by operation of law against one who, through any form of unconscionable conduct, holds legal title to property when equity and good conscience demands that he should not hold such title. *Henkle v. Henkle*, 600 N.E.2d 791, 795-796 (Ohio App. 1991). A constructive trust closely parallels the equitable remedy of *quantum meruit*, with the primary difference being that the trust transfers title, whereas the *quantum meruit* remedy is based on value, not title. The facts in a particular case may permit a plaintiff to choose which remedy is most appropriate.

Most courts view a constructive trust as compelling the restoration to another of property to which the holder thereof is not justly entitled. *Kraus v. Willow Park Public Golf Course*, 140 Cal. Rptr. 744 (Cal. 1977). One who gains a thing by fraud, accident, mistake, undue influence, the violation of a trust, or other wrongful act, is, unless he has some other and better right thereto, an involuntary trustee of the thing gained, for the benefit of the person who otherwise would have had it. Thus, a constructive trust may be imposed in practically any case where there is a wrongful acquisition or detention of property to which another is entitled. *Weiss v. Marcus*, 124 Cal. Rptr. 297 (Cal. App. 1975).

In *Evans v. Wall*, 542 So. 2d 1055 (Fla. 3d DCA 1989), the female cohabitant sought imposition of a constructive trust asking for recovery of the reasonable value of her capital, materials, and labor invested over a five-year period in the male cohabitant's residential and commercial property. She alleged that she contributed income and household services, worked in the male cohabitant's mango groves, assisted in construction of a new dwelling on the land, and contributed money and materials for construction of a barn. The court found in her favor, awarding her $8,000 as a constructive trust, which the court said was imposed to do equity between the unmarried cohabitants. *Id.* at 1056.

15.16. Statute of Wills

In most states, the doctrine of the Statute of Wills generally provides that a will shall not be valid, and no devise or bequest shall be valid, unless the will is in writing, signed, and attested to in the manner provided by the appropriate statute. A testamentary disposition is not valid unless the Statute of Wills is complied with. Therefore, generally an agreement to enforce a promise to execute a will generally is not enforceable under the statute of frauds. *See, e.g., Northrup v. Brigham*, 826 N.E.2d 239 (Mass. App. 2005). *See generally* John Bourdeau, Sonia Larsen, Karl Oakes, *Signature of party to be charged*, 37 C.J.S. Frauds, Statute of §144 (2012). However, while oral promises to leave a bequest to a cohabitant, although not binding under the Statute of Frauds, they may form the basis for recovery in quantum meruit for the fair value of services rendered. *Mangsen v. Costa*, 25 Mass. L. Rptr. 382 (Mass. Sup. 2009) (unreported) (where parties allegedly made promise to provide for one another upon other's death, plaintiff may not prevail on an oral promise to make a will under statute of frauds but may recover on quantum meruit claim for services rendered if evidence supports it).

EXAMPLES

Examples

4. Assume that D, a physician, and P, a nurse who works at the same hospital as D, developed a romantic relationship. When D decided to move her practice to another city, she wanted P to move with her. To induce P to quit her job, D made a number of requests and promises. She asked P to sell her home and reside with D "for the remainder of P's life to maintain and care for their home." D agreed that she would provide essentially all the support for the two, would make a will leaving her entire estate to P should she predecease P, and would "maintain bank accounts and other investments in P's name." The written agreement provided that P could cease residing with D if D failed to provide adequate support, if D brought a third person into the home for a period greater than four weeks without P's consent, or if D's abuse, harassment, or abnormal behavior made P's continued residence intolerable. D agreed to pay as liquidated damages the sum of $2,500 per month for the remainder of P's life, should one of the above contingencies occur.

   The agreement was drawn by a lawyer, properly witnessed, and P moved to the new city and set up housekeeping for P and D. Four years after the parties had moved to the new city, D announced that she had developed a new relationship and wanted to move her new friend into the house. When P rejected D's efforts to bring her new companion into the house, D moved out and took up residence with the other woman. P now seeks to enforce the agreement that D will pay her $2,500 per month for the remainder of P's life. How will a court most likely rule?

5. Assume that boyfriend P and girlfriend D live together in an apartment for four years while attending college. Upon graduation, P takes a job in another state. D, relying on *Marvin v. Marvin*, brings an action against P asking

that the court, in count one of the complaint, award D temporary alimony under the state dissolution statute of $200 per month for six months. In count two of the complaint, D seeks a $5,000 judgment against P, alleging that the couple orally agreed to share rent and utility living expenses equally for their apartment but that P fell far behind and now owes D $5,000. P brings a motion to dismiss the complaint on the ground that it fails to state a claim for relief. How will a court most likely rule?

6. Assume that P and D do not marry but have an ongoing romantic relationship for ten years preceding D's death. At the beginning of their relationship, D provided support to P in the form of apartment rental payments and occasional spending money. However, when P moved into D's home early in their relationship, the specific payments stopped. According to P, D asked P not to work outside the home, and he assured her that "This is our house, and most of what I have is going to be yours anyway. I will make sure the house is yours in my will." The couple shared D's home for seven years, with D paying for food, entertainment, utilities, etc. Even though D allegedly orally promised to create a will providing for P before he died, he failed to do so. P contends that a court should enforce D's promise and is seeking advice regarding any possible legal action that she may take to enforce the promise. What relief might P seek?

Explanations

4. The fact that the agreement is in writing, prepared by a lawyer, and witnessed makes it much more likely that a family court judge will enforce it. Some courts may view the $2,500 payment as a type of alimony and reject the effort to enforce the agreement on public policy grounds. However, a majority most likely will enforce the agreement. They will reason that there is no impediment to the parties agreeing between themselves to provide certain rights and obligations, including future financial support. *See Posik v. Layton*, 695 So. 2d 759 (Fla. App. 1997) (agreement for support between unmarried adults is valid unless agreement is inseparably based upon illicit consideration of sexual services). In *Marvin v. Marvin*, 557 P.2d 106 (Cal. 1976), the court observed that adults who voluntarily live together and engage in sexual relations are nonetheless as competent as any other persons to contract respecting their earnings and property rights, so long as the agreement does not rest upon illicit, meretricious consideration. Here, the parties, represented by counsel, took pains to assure that sexual services were not mentioned in the agreement.

Although the parties undoubtedly expected a sexual relationship, the agreement suggests that they contemplated much more. They contracted for a permanent sharing of, and participating in, one another's lives. The contract for permanent support is, therefore, much more likely enforceable in a majority of jurisdictions.

5. Most, if not all, jurisdictions would dismiss count one in the complaint asking for temporary alimony. *Marvin* and its progeny have made clear that cohabiting parties may not use state divorce statutes that provide for temporary or permanent alimony. The reasoning is that these provisions were specifically created for persons who were legally married and subsequently sought to dissolve their relationship.

   The simple express oral agreement between the parties to share living expenses is not *per se* an illegal or an immoral contract. The consideration for the agreement was the mutual exchange of promises to pay one-half of the rent and utilities. A majority of jurisdictions would recognize that the two can make an express contract to share the rent, so long as the contract is not explicitly and inseparably based upon services as a paramour.

   In a minority jurisdiction, a court might reason that the evidence supports a finding that the ultimate agreement as to sharing living expenses arose directly out of the parties' original agreement that they would find an apartment and live there together, the object being from the outset that the apartment to be rented would be the site of their meretricious rather than platonic relationship. *See, e.g., Wellmaker v. Roberts*, 101 S.E.2d 712 (Ga. 1958) (where a contract grows immediately out of, and is connected with, an illegal or immoral act, a court of justice will not lend its aid to enforce it). Consequently, a minority jurisdiction might not enforce any portion of the alleged contract; a majority of jurisdictions most likely would enforce the oral agreement to share rent and utilities.

6. First, regardless of the theory on which P proceeds, P will have to meet a high standard of proof.

   Second, if P seeks to enforce a promise to make a will, P will have difficulty doing to. For example, in *Estate of Spaulding*, 187 Ill. App.3d 1031 (Ill. App. 1989), the court said that while a contract to make a will supported by valid and adequate consideration is enforceable in a court of equity, in suit for specific performance of a contract, evidence of existence of the contract and its terms must be clear and explicit. The terms must be so convincing as to leave no doubt in mind of court; mere statements by the deceased of his intention to make will are not sufficient proof to warrant an inference that a contract of any kind was made.

   Third, the doctrine of the Statute of Wills in most jurisdictions makes an agreement to enforce a promise to execute a will not enforceable.

Fourth, P may well be more successful in pursuing other theories of relief such as enforcement of the express promise to transfer the house or a *quantum meruit* theory. P's testimony standing alone is probably not persuasive. However, evidence of her service to D over the past ten years will be given considerable weight by the court. A court also will consider the fact that P and D lived together in a single residence as further evidence supporting the existence of a contract. Here, it appears the elements of a contract exist, that is, offer, acceptance, and exchange of consideration and a meeting of minds. There appear to be sufficient facts to at least withstand summary judgment in some jurisdictions. *See, e.g., Devaney v. L'Esperance*, 949 A.2d 743 (N.J. 2008) (cohabitation was not an indispensable element of a palimony claim), which was specifically overruled by legislation in New Jersey in 2009. *Botis v. Kudrick*, 22 A.3d 975 (N.J. Super. 2011) (amendment to statute of frauds, including palimony agreements among the types of agreements that must be in writing and signed by the parties in order to be enforceable, applied prospectively only).

OTHER CLAIMS

15.17. Wrongful Death Claims

Because cohabitants are not legally married, they will have difficulty persuading courts that they should be considered "essentially married" and allowed to recover for wrongful death and other injury covered under standard insurance policies issued to married couples. For example, in *Cole v. State Farm Ins. Co.*, 128 P.3d 171 (Alaska 2006), a former husband's claim that he was entitled to medical and uninsured motorist coverage as the "spouse" of the insured (his former wife) while occupying her car. Following their divorce, the two reunited and the former husband was injured. The court reasoned that there was no coverage under the ex-wife's insurance policy because it unambiguously defined "spouse" as a currently, legally married husband or wife. *See Milberger v. KBHL, LLC*, 486 F. Supp. 1156 (D.C. Hawaii 2007) (legislature did not extend rights under the wrongful death statute to same-sex partners who are cohabiting but have not registered with the state). In *Ford v. American Original Corp.*, 475 F. Supp. 10 (E.D. Va. 1979), a cohabitant was held not entitled to any recovery as a beneficiary either under Death on the High Seas Act (DOHSA), the Jones Act, or Virginia's Wrongful Death Act where the cohabitant, a ship repair yard worker, was killed while performing repair work on a vessel. His female partner had lived with him for several years. *See Lawson v. United States*, 192 F.2d

479 (2d Cir.), *cert. denied*, 343 U.S. 904 (1951) (holding that a putative wife was not a "legal" wife and therefore could not recover for wrongful death of her putative husband under DOHSA); *Tetterton v. Arctic Tankers, Inc.*, 116 F. Supp. 429 (E.D. Pa. 1953) (declaring that even if a valid common law marriage had been perfected under the law of Florida, which recognized common law marriages, the claimant still did not become a legal wife and was at most a common law wife, and the congressional intent of DOHSA was to permit the recovery of wrongful death damages only by "legal" spouses).

However, the Washington Supreme Court has held that the law of committed intimate relationships, which exists in that jurisdiction, can be applied to divide assets between committed partners' estates where both partners are deceased. *Olver v. Fowler*, 168 P.3d 348 (Wash. 2007).

15.18. Loss of Consortium Claims

Spousal consortium is a right acquired through marriage, subject to forfeiture when the marriage is dissolved unless preserved in the dissolution decree. Courts generally recognize loss of consortium actions brought by spouses, parents, and children.

Most, if not all, jurisdictions have rejected allowing loss of consortium claims asserted by a cohabiting partner. *See, e.g.*, *Mega Life and Health Ins. Co. v. Superior Court*, 92 Cal. Rptr. 3d 399 (Cal. App. 2009) (a spouse may sue for loss of consortium deriving from the injury to his or her spouse, an unmarried cohabitant may not); *Charron v. Amaral*, 889 N.E.2d 946 (Mass. 2008) (loss of consortium cannot arise unless the family member has, *inter alia*, a legal relationship with the injured third party); *Biercevicz v. Liberty Mut. Ins. Co.*, 865 A.2d 1267 (Conn. Super. 2004) (fiancé was not "closely-related" to decedent so as to allow bystander emotional distress claim); *Tong v. Jocson*, 142 Cal. Rptr. 726 (Cal. 1977) (because at the time that the plaintiff and injured party were not married but engaged and living together and married after the accident, no action for loss of consortium arising from injured party's injuries could be maintained); *Sostock v. Reiss*, 415 N.E.2d 1094 (Ill. 1980) (husband could not recover loss of consortium damages as result of injuries to spouse when she fell off horse where accident occurred when they were engaged to be married); *Angelet v. Shivar*, 602 S.W.2d 185 (Ky. App. 1980) (husband's claim for loss of consortium could not be founded upon intentional injury inflicted upon wife before marriage); *Sawyer v. Bailey*, 413 A.2d 165 (Me. 1980) (cause of action for loss of consortium does not exist in favor of husband where injury to wife occurred before marriage while the couple was engaged to marry); *Milberger v. KBHL, LLC*, 486 F. Supp. 1156 (D.C. Hawaii 2007) (unmarried partner lacked standing to bring a common law loss of consortium claim based upon a severe injury to her partner).

15.19. Claiming State and Federal Statutory Benefits

Courts generally have been unwilling to award benefits that flow from various state and federal statutes to cohabiting partners absent statutory language that specifically recognizes the relationship. *See, e.g., Powell v. Rogers*, 496 F.2d 1248, 1250 (9th Cir. 1974), *cert. denied*, 419 U.S. 1032 (1974) (workers' compensation denied; federal law relied on state law defining whether claimant was married to decedent). *See Baldwin v. Sullivan*, 204 N.W. 420, 421-423 (Iowa 1925) (denying unmarried cohabitant's claim for workers' compensation).

Some states, such as Oregon, have provided for cohabitant compensation by statute. For example, in *Cato v. Alcoa-Reynolds Metals Co.*, 152 P.3d 981 (Or. App. 2007), a cohabitant sought to recover under that state's workers' compensation statute. While conceding that recovery was possible, the court denied it because the word *child* in its statute was construed as someone 18 years or younger, and the claimant's child was over the maximum age at the time of the accident.

15.20. Insurance Policy Coverage

Cohabitants will have difficulty persuading insurance carriers that they should be covered by a particular insurance policy where they are not specifically named in it. For example, in *Ortiz v. New York City Transit Authority*, 699 N.Y.S.2d 370 (N.Y. App. 1999), the court found that the named insured's same-sex, live-in partner was not entitled to underinsured motorist coverage under the supplementary uninsured motorist clause in the named insured's automobile policy. The court held that the partner was neither a "spouse" nor a "relative" of the named insured and was not covered by the policy. *See Hartford Ins. Co. v. Cline*, 139 P.3d 176 (N.M. 2006) (excluding domestic partners from the definition of family member in an automobile insurance policy is not invalid as contrary to public policy); *Cole v. State Farm Ins. Co.*, 128 P.3d 171 (Alaska 2006) (there was no coverage under policy which unambiguously defined *spouse* as currently, legally married husband or wife); *Hedlund v. Monumental Gen. Ins. Co.*, 404 N.W.2d 371, 373-374 (Minn. App. 1987) (*spouse* is commonly known to mean husband or wife; while many cohabitating relationships are permanent and analogous to marital relationships, they are not spousal relationships).

15.21. Housing Discrimination

The question of whether landlords may discriminate against cohabitants on the basis of the landlord's religious beliefs has been an issue in some jurisdictions. For example, the Supreme Court of California has held that the prohibition in California's Fair Employment and Housing Act (FEHA) against discrimination because of "marital status" prohibits landlords from refusing to rent to prospective tenants because they are not married. The court also ruled that FEHA's prohibition against discrimination based on marital status does not "substantially burden" a landlord's religious exercise under the state constitution's free exercise and enjoyment of religion clause. *Smith v. Fair Employment & Hous. Comm'n*, 913 P.2d 909 (Cal. 1996).

Michigan's Supreme court ruled in *McCready v. Hoffius*, 586 N.W.2d 723 (1999), that landlords could not violate the federal Civil Rights Act by refusing to rent apartments to them on the ground that couples were unmarried. It further ruled that requiring landlords to rent to cohabitants did not violate their religious freedom rights under the state or federal constitutions. However, it vacated that decision in part following a request for a rehearing in *McCready v. Hoffius*, 593 N.W.2d 545 (Mich. 1999). It later interpreted the *McCready* ruling as meaning that the unambiguous language of the Civil Rights Act protects only the consideration of a person's marital status. Adverse action against an individual for conduct, without regard to marital status, provides no basis for recourse under the act. *Veenstra v. Washtenaw Country Club*, 645 N.W.2d 643, 647-648 (Mich. 2002).

The dissent in *Veenstra* observed that "I cannot envision how an attorney could bring a discrimination claim on behalf of an unmarried couple denied housing on the basis of their marital status. Only if a landlord happened to expressly state that her refusal to rent was based on-and only on-their marital status would plaintiffs prevail." *Id.* at 652. *See Swanner v. Anchorage Equal Rights Comm.*, 874 P.2d 274, 278, n. 4 (Alaska 1994) (holding that a landlord "cannot reasonably claim that he does not rent or show property to cohabitating couples based on their conduct (living together outside of marriage) and not their marital status when their marital status (unmarried) is what makes their conduct immoral in [the landlord's] opinion").

Courts in Minnesota and Washington have sided with landlords where religious objections were raised to renting apartments to unmarried people. *See, e.g., State by Cooper v. French*, 460 N.W.2d 2, 5-6 (Minn. 1990) (landlord's refusal to rent house to a tenant because tenant intended to cohabitate with her fiancé prior to her marriage did not violate the Human Rights Act's prohibition of marital status discrimination, and the landlord's right to exercise his religion under Freedom of Conscience Provision of Minnesota Constitution outweighed any interest of tenant to cohabitate with her fiancé in rental property prior to her marriage); *McFadden v. Elma Country Club*, 613 P.2d 146, 150 (Wash. App. 1980) (holding that marital status discrimination as used in state statute, which makes it unfair practice for any person to refuse to engage in real estate transaction with another because of marital status, did not include discrimination against couples who chose to live together without being married, and country club's denial of woman's application for membership, because of her living with man without being married, did not constitute discrimination on basis of her marital status).

The Wisconsin Supreme Court declared a county ordinance similar to California's FEHA "invalid to the extent that it [sought] to protect 'cohabitants.'" *County of Dane v. Norman*, 497 N.W.2d 714, 716 (Wis. 1993). The court reasoned that the county had no power to enact statutes that were "inconsistent with the public policy of Wisconsin, which seeks to promote the stability of marriage and family." *Id.* at 720.

Rent control issues. Rent control issues involving cohabiting couples may come up in some jurisdictions such as New York. For example, in *390 West End Associates v. Wildfoerster*, 661 N.Y.S.2d 202 (N.Y. App. 1997), the court awarded possession of a rent-controlled apartment to the landlord, finding that there was an insufficient familial relationship between tenant and companion to allow for transfer of the apartment to the companion under rent-control regulations. The companion and the deceased tenant had a 20-year relationship, during which they lived together from 1976 to 1978 and again for more than two years prior to the tenant's death from AIDS in 1993. The court found that the relationship lacked the normal indicia of a familial relationship. It said that although the tenant's close friends testified, and the trial court found, that the tenant and respondent had a very close, loving relationship, this failed to establish sufficiently that the respondent was a family member within the meaning of the applicable rent control regulations.

15.22. Statute of Limitations

As a general rule, a *Marvin*-type agreement is breached when one of the partners ends the relationship. However, the limitations period is usually construed in light of the facts of a particular case. When no time for performance is specified, a person who has promised to do an act in the future and who has the ability to perform does not violate his or her agreement unless and until performance is demanded and refused. For example, if the parties have separated, but the obligor performs as required by the *Marvin* agreement, there has been no breach, no cause of action has accrued, and the statute of limitations has not begun to run. The statute of limitation begins to run only when the breach occurs. *See Cochran v. Cochran*, 66 Cal. Rptr. 2d 337 (Cal. App. 1997) (held that the two-year limitations period commenced to run when party charged with duty of support stopped making support payments, rather than when parties' romantic relationship ended nine years earlier).

Examples

7. P and D lived together for 14 years but never married. Three children were born of this union, and the entire household was supported by D. In the words of P, her "marriage" was legal "in the sight of God, yes; but in the sight of man, no." P and D lived together in a state that did not recognize common law marriages. The relevant state statute defined "wife" and "widow" as persons who were married under the laws of the states. When D died in an accident while working for the federal government, P sought death benefits as a surviving wife or widow under the applicable federal law. How will a court most likely treat P's claim?

8. Assume that P and D lived together in California for eight years without getting married. At some point in the relationship, D allegedly orally promised P that should their relationship ever end, D would pay P $400 a month for life because she had given up her job and moved to the country to live with D. When D marries X, P and D separate. D continues to pay P $400 a month for the next three years and then suddenly stops payment. P brings an action to enforce the agreement six months after D stopped payments but three years and six months after they separated. The statute of limitations for an action upon a contract not founded on a writing in California is two years. D asserts that the two-year statute of limitations on bringing contract actions has run because the breach of their contract occurred when they separated. How will a court most likely rule in this case?

9. Assume that D married C. However, after four years of marriage, D moved out and began living with his secretary, P, at an apartment D rented. D also substantially increased P's wages. P and D lived together for a year when D returned to his wife, C. P continued to work at her job with D. P sues D on an alleged oral contract that D made with her during their relationship. P claims that D agreed to provide her with financial support for the rest of her life should the relationship break down at a future date. D, who is a millionaire, testifies that he may have said something like that in jest, but he and P were merely having a fling. Will a court enforce the alleged oral promise?

EXPLANATIONS

Explanations

7. In cases like this, the federal law usually looks to state law to determine the status of the couple; that is, does the state that P and D lived in recognize P as a "surviving widow" on these facts? Unfortunately for P, if the jurisdiction fails to recognizes a common law marriage and adheres to the traditional definition of *wife* and *widow* found in the state statute, P will fail. She will not be recognized as D's lawful wife at the time of his death, and P will not be found eligible to receive any benefits.

8. A court most likely will rule that the statute of limitations began to run when the defendant stopped making the monthly $400 payments. Normally, a *Marvin*-type contract is said to have been breached when one partner terminates the relationship. *Estate of Fincher*, 119 Cal. App. 3d 343, 352 (1981) (cause of action on implied contract accrued when the widow left the decedent in 1971 and statute of limitations had clearly run by the time she asserted her claim in 1978). As noted in the example, the statute of limitations for an action upon a contract not founded on a writing in California is two years. (Code Civ. Proc. §339, subd. 1). This is a fairly typical state provision. The argument favoring P is that because D continued making payments for three years after separating from P, and P brought the action only a few months after D stopped making the payments, a breach in the contract did not occur until he stopped making the payments. Most courts will rule that P is well within the two-year limitation.

9. Most states would view the contract as too closely associated with alimony (sometimes referred to as "palimony"). They are reluctant to award palimony in cohabitant disputes reasoning that support of this nature is restricted to couples who divorce. Note that the term "palimony" has a meaning similar to alimony, except that the award, settlement, or agreement arises out of the nonmarital relationship of parties. *Black's Law Dictionary* 1110 (6th ed.1990).

In some jurisdictions, redress is not afforded on any basis to persons on these facts; therefore, the alleged contract would not be enforced. For example, the alleged contract would not be enforced in Rhode Island because that state does not recognize "palimony" as a cause of action. *Norton v. Hoyt*, 278 F. Supp. 2d 214, 226 (D. R.I. 2003); *see Davis v. Davis*, 643 So. 2d 931 (Miss. 1994) (endorsement of any form of "palimony" is a task for the legislature, and not this court); *Thomas v. LaRose*, 400 S.E.2d 809 (W.Va. 1990) (agreements, express or implied, made between adult, nonmarital partners for future support, even when such contracts are not explicitly and inseparably founded on sexual services, are not enforceable).

It is true that in a majority of jurisdictions, cohabiting parties may execute contracts that will be enforced so long as they are voluntary and not based on payment for sexual services. *Knauer v. Knauer*, 470 A.2d 553, 564 (Pa. Super. 1983) ("We are in accord with the majority of courts from other jurisdictions in that we hold that agreements between nonmarried cohabitors fail only to the extent that they involve payment for sexual services"). However, there is concern in this example about the nature of the consideration for the contract. In *Marvin v. Marvin, supra*, the California Supreme Court enforced an oral agreement between non-marital cohabiting parties, even though the alleged consideration was that the plaintiff "would further render her services as a companion, homemaker, housekeeper and cook to . . . defendant." 557 P.2d at 110. The court held that although the provision of sexual services would not support such an agreement, the provision of homemaking services would, and that such consideration was severable from the meretricious aspects of the arrangement. In this hypothetical, P did not give up her employment to provide homemaking services to D. Rather, she continued to work at her employment, and D provided an apartment for both of them. It is difficult to find consideration apart from the sexual relationship.

It is also doubtful that P can show an injury because of her reliance on the promise or make a showing that D was somehow financially unjustly enriched by her conduct. It is likely that most courts would refuse to enforce the agreement.

CHAPTER 16

Determining Parentage

16.1. Introduction

This chapter examines the legal relationships of parents and children when children are born outside of marriage or parentage is disputed. Although the chapter primarily focuses on establishment of paternity, issues concerning establishment of maternity are also discussed.

The percentage of children born outside of marriage has risen steadily and dramatically over the last 40 years:

> The percentage of births outside of marriage rose steeply from 1970 to 2009 for all age groups. Between 1970 and 2009, the percentage of all births that took place outside of marriage (the nonmarital birth ratio) increased from 11 to 41 percent. This increase occurred within every age category.

Elizabeth Wildsmith, et al., *Childbearing Outside of Marriage: Estimates and Trends in the United States*, Child Trends Research Brief (2011) located at http://www.childtrends.org/Files/Child_Trends-2011_11_01_RB_NonmaritalCB.pdf (last visited July 21, 2012). Consequently, it is likely that legal questions regarding parentage will occur more often.

There are many reasons why establishing parentage is important, some of which include the following: obtaining child support, establishing parenting time and custodial rights, creating peace of mind, determining grandparentage, establishing inheritance rights, establishing insurance claims, obtaining Social Security benefits, establishing Native American tribal rights, determining the likelihood of being a biological sibling, and helping a person seeking entry into the United States on the grounds that he or she is a biological relative of a citizen.

This topic cuts across other subjects discussed in this book. Consequently, it is useful to read this chapter in connection with Chapter 8, which examines visitation, Chapter 7, which concerns adoption, and Chapter 18, which explores alternative means of reproduction.

CONSTITUTIONAL PROTECTION FOR NONMARITAL CHILDREN

16.2. Historic Disparate Treatment

Historically, establishment of paternity was important because it fixed the line of succession. In England, primogeniture, which passed property to the first-born male, made the determination of an heir very important. Consequently, much of the early English law on this topic was inherited by the United States and initially was concerned with making a "legitimacy" determination. Note that courts today are more concerned with determining parentage than with issues of legitimacy.

The common law treated a child born during marriage and one born outside of marriage differently. If a child was born during a marriage, the common law was averse to declaring the child illegitimate — a result that could deprive the child of inheritance and succession and possibly make the child a ward of the state. It aided a child born during a marriage by applying a presumption that the child was the legitimate issue of the wife's husband. The presumption could be overcome only by evidence that the husband was incapable of procreation or had no access to his wife during the relevant period of conception.

Proof of illegitimacy was further complicated by the adoption in many jurisdictions of an evidentiary rule known as "Lord Mansfield's rule." The rule, developed in England and imported into the United States, provided that neither the husband nor the wife were permitted to "bastardize" the issue of the wife after marriage by testifying to the nonaccess of the husband. *See Egbert v. Greenwalt*, 6 N.W. 654 (1880). The rule was apparently applied in some jurisdictions until the mid-twentieth century, when legislatures and courts abandoned its use. *See People v. C.*, 85 N.Y.S.2d 751 (N.Y. Child. Ct. 1949).

For children born outside of marriage, the common law was harsh. It labeled these children "bastards" and considered them *filius nullius* — the children of no one and kin to nobody. In some jurisdictions, a child born outside of marriage remained illegitimate despite the subesquent marriage of the biological parents. Should a marriage be annulled, a child born during the relationship was considered illegitimate. Support for children born outside of marriage was almost nonexistent.

Discrimination against children born to unmarried parents was practiced in most jurisdictions in the United States until well into the 1960s. The United States Supreme Court, Congress, and the National Conference of Commissioners on Uniform State Laws (NCCUSL) all played a role in causing the states to abandon their unfair treatment of these children. One of the most important forces in changing society's views in this regard was the Supreme Court, which invalidated a host of state statutes that treated children born outside of marriage differently from those born during marriage.

EXAMPLE

Example

1. Assume that 200 years ago, P and D were married, and a child was born to them in a common law jurisdiction. D suspects that the child was conceived during an affair that his wife had with a neighbor, X, while P and D were separated for one year. D brings a legal action with the goal of proving that the child is the issue of X, or at least, not D's child. D is unable to produce any witnesses other than P and D. How would a common law court most likely rule on D's request that he be allowed to testify?

EXPLANATION

Explanation

1. The common law court most likely would reject the request, and the action would fail. In the common law jurisdiction that applied Lord Mansfield's rule, D would be barred from testifying to nonaccess.

16.3. Wrongful Death

Levy v. Louisiana, 391 U.S. 68 (1968) involved five children born outside of marriage who sued for damages as the result of the wrongful death of their mother. Under a Louisiana statute, the children did not have a legally recognizable interest in her death. Although not finding that "illegitimacy" was a suspect classification, the Supreme Court struck down the statute on equal protection grounds, holding that it was invidious to discriminate against the children "when no action, conduct, or demeanor of theirs was relevant to the harm that was done in the matter." *See also* Annot., *Discrimination on Basis of Illegitimacy as Denial of Constitutional Rights*, 38 A.L.R.3d 613 (1971).

In contrast, in *Parham v. Hughes*, 441 U.S. 347 (1979), the Supreme Court rejected a claim by a father who had not legally recognized his child and who sought to recover for the child's wrongful death. The relevant Georgia statute allowed a mother to bring a wrongful death action for the death of a child born outside of marriage and allowed the father, if he had legally recognized the child, to bring an action if there was no mother. The Court found that "unlike the illegitimate child for whom the status of illegitimacy is involuntary and immutable, the [father] here was responsible for fostering an illegitimate child and for failing to change its status." *Id.* at 441. The Court indicated concern about proving the paternity of nonmarital children and the related danger of spurious claims against intestate estates. It also evinced additional concern that if paternity has not been established before the commencement of a wrongful death action, a defendant might face lawsuits by multiple individuals, all claiming to be the father of the deceased child. Such uncertainty would make it difficult, if not impossible, for a defendant to settle a wrongful-death action because there would always be the risk of a subsequent suit by another person claiming to be the father.

16.4. Inheritance Rights

The Supreme Court has also aided children born outside of marriage in their efforts to inherit from their parents. For example, *Trimble v. Gordon*, 430 U.S. 762 (1977), involved Delta Mona Trimble, the nonmarital daughter of Jessie Trimble and the deceased biological father, Sherman Gordon. Gordon had provided support and had acknowledged the parent-child relationship; however, when he died without a will, Illinois probate law prohibited Delta Mona Trimble from collecting any portion of his estate. The statute declared that as a child born outside of marriage, she could inherit only if she had been "legitimized" by the subsequent marriage of her biological mother and father.

The Court held that a classification based on nonmarital parentage is not so suspect as to require strict scrutiny. However, using a mid-level or mid-tier analysis, the Court held that at a minimum, a statutory classification must bear some rational relationship to a legitimate state purpose. The Court explained that "in this context, the standard just stated is a minimum; the Court sometimes requires more. 'Though the latitude given state economic and social regulation is necessarily broad, when the state statutory classifications approach sensitive and fundamental personal rights, this Court exercises a stricter scrutiny.'" *Id.* at 767. The Court concluded that the statute bore only the most attenuated relationship to the asserted goal of family relationships and was unconstitutional.

In a subsequent decision, *Lalli v. Lalli*, 439 U.S. 259 (1978), the Court rejected a constitutional challenge to a New York intestacy statute that required nonmarital children seeking to inherit from their fathers to produce an order of affiliation made by a court of competent jurisdiction during the alleged father's lifetime. The Court observed that the statute was intended to soften the rigors of previous law, which permitted nonmarital children to inherit only from their mothers. It also believed that the statute provided for the just and orderly disposition of property at death and protected innocent adults, and those rightfully interested in their estates, from fraudulent claims of heirship and harassing litigation.

The Court distinguished *Trimble v. Gordon* on the grounds that the Illinois statute in *Trimble* was constitutionally unacceptable because it resulted in a total statutory disinheritance of children born out of wedlock who were not legitimated by the subsequent marriage of their parents. However, inheritance under the New York statute is barred only where there has been a failure to secure evidence of paternity during the father's lifetime. "This is not a requirement that inevitably disqualifies an unnecessarily large number of children born out of wedlock." *Id.* at 273. The Court concluded "that the requirement imposed by Section 4-1.2 on illegitimate children who would inherit from their fathers is substantially related to the important state interests the statute is intended to promote." *Id.* at 275.

Public policy debates concerning inheritance rights of children born to unmarried parents remain prevalent today. *See In re Estate of Farmer ex rel. Farmer*, 964 So. 2d 498 (Miss. 2007) (minor could inherit in case where deceased father had executed an acknowledgment of paternity); *In re Poldrugovaz*, 851 N.Y.S.2d 254 (N.Y. App. 2008) (posthumous genetic marker testing ordered if decedent "openly and notoriously acknowledged" child). *See also* Paula A. Monopoli, *Nonmarital Children and Post-Death Parentage: A Different Path for Inheritance Law?*, 48 Santa Clara L. Rev. 857 (2008).

16.5. Social Security Benefits

In *Mathews v. Lucas*, 427 U.S. 495 (1976), nonmarital children sought to obtain Social Security benefits after their biological father died. There was no dispute over the issue of the deceased being the biological father. The Social Security Act provided that a child of an individual who died fully insured under the act is entitled to surviving child's benefits if the child is under 18, or a student under 22, and was dependent at the time of the parent's death. A child is considered dependent if the insured parent was living with the child or the parent was contributing to the child's support at the time of death.

The Court upheld the statute, holding that it did not violate the equal protection clause of the Constitution, even though the statute treated children differently based at least in part on their parents' marital status. The Court said that the challenged statutory classifications are permissible because they are reasonably related to the likelihood of dependency at death. The Court concluded that although the act did not extend any presumption of dependency to nonmarital children as a group, it did not impermissibly discriminate against them when compared with children born during marriage or those nonmarital children who are statutorily deemed dependent.

EXAMPLES

Examples

2. Assume that P and D have a daughter, X, but they do not marry. D is not listed as the father on X's birth certificate, but D was found to be X's father in a paternity action and was ordered to pay monthly child support. D paid the child support as ordered but had little contact with X. X was not included in family gatherings, many of D's friends did not know of her existence, and D described her as an "$18,000 mistake." Prior to X's birth, D executed a will disposing of his estate. He did not change the will after X's birth, and she was not included in it. D dies, and X seeks a share of the estate as an omitted child. The state where the parties live has a statute providing that an nonmarital child born after the date that a will is executed can take an intestate share of the decedent's estate if the testator "recognized" the child during his lifetime. What is the likely result?

3. Assume that M and D are the biological parents of child P, who was born outside of marriage in state X. A month prior to P's birth, the biological father, D, was involved in an automobile accident. He remained in a coma for five months and died intestate. Under the law in state X, there are three means by which an nonmarital child may inherit from an intestate father: (1) the father may marry the mother and recognize the child as his own; (2) the father may legitimate the child by following the statutory procedure for legitimation by written declaration; or (3) a court may make a judicial determination of paternity during the father's lifetime. P argues that she was unable to qualify under any of these provisions because her biological father was fatally injured in an automobile accident that occurred before her birth and remained in a coma until his death some four months after her birth. P attacks the law in state X as unconstitutional. How will a court most likely rule?

EXPLANATIONS

Explanations

2. The other heirs will argue that D did not recognize X as his child because he did not treat her as his child or have a relationship with her. X will argue that if D had died intestate, she would have inherited from him based on the paternity judgment issued during D's lifetime. This example is based on the case of *In re Estate of Brewer*, 168 S.W.3d 135 (Mo. App. 2005), where the trial court found that X was not entitled to an intestate share of D's estate, but that decision was overturned on appeal. The appellate court reasoned that the paternity judgment constituted "recognition" within the meaning of the statute.

3. Obviously, after the accident, P's father could not have married her mother or acknowledged the child by written declaration. Nor did P have a meaningful opportunity to be legitimated through a paternity proceeding, which, under state X's law, must be maintained during the father's lifetime. As a practical matter, state X's intestacy scheme effectively denied P any means through which to become legitimated or qualify herself to inherit from her father's estate. On these facts, a court most likely will rule that the statute creates an insurmountable barrier and, as applied, is unconstitutional.

CONSTITUTIONAL RIGHTS OF PUTATIVE FATHERS?

16.6. Preponderance of Evidence Standard

In *Rivera v. Minnich*, 483 U.S. 574 (1987), the Supreme Court held that a paternity statute that provided proof by a preponderance of evidence did not violate the due process clause of the Fourteenth Amendment to the United States Constitution. It concluded that the clear and convincing standard of proof for terminating a parent-child relationship established in *Santosky v. Kramer*, 455 U.S. 745 (1982), was not applicable. The Court reasoned that the collective judgment of state legislatures adhering to a preponderance standard for paternity proceedings rests on legitmate and significant distinctions between termination and paternity proceedings. It distinguished ending an existing parent-child relationship from imposing legal obligations accompanying a biological relationship between parent and child.

16.7. Right to Counsel in Paternity Proceedings

The Supreme Court has not mandated that counsel be afforded to indigent defendants who have allegedly fathered a child outside of marriage. However, some state courts have required counsel either under the exercise of their supervisory power to ensure fairness or as a requirement of the state constitution. *Hepfel v. Bashaw*, 279 N.W.2d 342 (Minn. 1979) (supervisory power). In noncriminal cases in which a right to counsel has specifically been recognized (such as contempt or paternity cases), the court should exercise the same care in assuring the understanding of the right and voluntariness of the waiver, as in criminal cases.

Those jurisdictions that have determined that counsel should be provided reason that an adjudication of paternity can result in up to 18 years of child support payments and that paternity affects the distribution of defendant's estate, workers' compensation benefits, Social Security benefits, and insurance proceeds. A paternity adjudication may also reflect on the reputation of the defendant and have a deleterious effect on an already-established family of the defendant. The child's rights of support, inheritance, and custody are affected directly by a paternity proceeding, and a child's health interests are involved becasuse an accurate family medical history can be critical in the diagnosis and treatment of a child's injuries and illnesses. *See Reynolds v. Kimmons*, 569 P.2d 799, 803 (Alaska 1977) (under state constitution); *Artibee v. Cheboygan Circuit Judge*, 243 N.W.2d 248, 250 (Mich. 1976) (indigent defendant had right to appointed counsel); *Salas v. Cortez*, 593 P.2d 226, 234, *cert. denied*, 444 U.S. 900 (1979) (state constitution); *Wake Cty. ex rel. Carrington v. Townes*, 281 S.E.2d 765, 769 (N.C. App. 1981) (fourteenth Amendment and state constitution). *But see State ex rel. Hamilton v. Snodgrass*, 325 N.W.2d 740 (Iowa 1982) (no constitutional right to counsel); *Sheppard v. Mack*, 427 N.E.2d 522, 528 (Ohio App. 1980) (no due process or equal protection right to appointed counsel); *State ex rel. Adult and Family Serv. Div. v. Stoutt*, 644 P.2d 1232, 1137 (Or. App. 1982) (no due process right to appointed counsel under federal or state constitutions); *State v. Walker*, 553 P.2d 1093, 1095 (Wis. 1976) (no due process or equal protection right to appointed counsel).

There is contrary state authority regarding the right to counsel. *State ex rel. Hamilton v. Snodgrass*, 325 N.W.2d 740 (Iowa 1982); *Sheppard v. Mack*, 427 N.E.2d 522, 528 (Ohio App. 1980); *State ex rel. Adult and Family Serv. Div. v. Stoutt*, 644 P.2d 1232, 1137 (Or. App. 1982) (no due process right to appointed counsel under federal or state constitutions); *State v. Walker*, 553 P.2d 1093, 1095 (Wis. 1976) (no due process or equal protection right to appointed counsel).

16.8. Putative Father's Standing to Rebut Marital Presumption — The *Michael H.* Case

Marital presumption. The marital presumption of parentage applies when a child is born to married parents. The historic presumption of the "legitimacy" of a child born to a married woman was applied to avoid the serious disabilities associated with birth outside of marriage. It is universally recognized and considered one of the strongest presumptions known to the law. *See Presse v. Koenemann,* 554 So. 2d 403 (Ala. App. 1988) (man claiming to be father of child conceived and born during marriage of its mother to another man did not have standing under Uniform Parentage Act to initiate action to establish that he is the father).

Michael H. The dispute in *Michael H. v. Gerald D.*, 491 U.S. 110 (1988) involved a child fathered by the wife's lover during the marriage and born while she was cohabiting with her husband. The child was conclusively presumed by state statute to be a child of the marriage unless the husband was impotent or sterile. The husband's name was placed on the birth certificate, and he claimed the child as his daughter. Blood tests indicated, however, that the wife's lover, Michael H., was actually the child's biological father.

During the child's first three years, she and her mother intermittently lived with Michael, who consistently held himself out as her father. About 18 months after the child's birth, Michael filed a filiation action to establish his paternity and visitation rights, and during the course of this lawsuit, the constitutionality of the conclusive presumption was challenged.

The Court held that the biological father had no protected liberty interest in the parental relationship and that the state's interest in preserving the marital union was sufficient to support termination of his relationship with the child. The Court balanced the nonmarital father's rights against the rights of the married father. The plurality determined that the marital family and the marital father's rights are paramount and rested its holding on history and tradition. Five justices, however, refused to foreclose the possibility that the natural father might ever have a constitutionally protected interest in his relationship with a child, whose mother was married to and cohabiting with another man at the time of the child's conception and birth.

State decisions. Subsequent to *Michael H. v. Gerald D.*, various state courts have considered a putative father's standing to bring a paternity action. *See Slowinski v Sweeney*, 64 So. 3d 128 (Fl. App. 2011) (biological father could not maintain paternity action regarding child born during marriage); *Baker v. Kennedy*, 51 So. 3d 339 (Ala. App. 2010) (putative father lacked standing where husband "persisted" in status as presumed father); *Pearson v. Pearson*, 182 P.3d 353 (Utah 2008) (putative father denied standing based on public policy of preserving marital stability and protecting children); Barnes v. *Jeudevine*, 718 N.W.2d 311 (Mich. 2006) (biological father lacked standing to sue under state Paternity Act); *Numerick v. Krull*, 694 N.W.2d 552 (Mich. App. 2005) (paternity action barred by marriage of mother to another man); *Lisa I. v. Superior Court*, 34 Cal. Rptr. 3d 927 (Cal. App. 2005) (biological father with no existing relationship with child lacks standing); *J. K. v. R. S.*, 706 So. 2d 1262 (Ala. App. 1997) (alleged biological father was not a parent for purpose of standing to bring custody action involving child born to a married couple); *S. B. v. D. H.*, 736 So. 2d 766 (Fla. App. 1999) (putative biological father could not maintain a paternity action concerning a child conceived by a married woman over the objections of the woman and her husband); *In re Paternity of S. R. I.*, 602 N.E.2d 1014 (Ind. 1992) (interpreting the relevant statute to allow a putative father to establish paternity without regard to the mother's marital status).

Rebutting the marital presumption. While the marital presumption is among the strongest presumptions, many states have statutes or case law allowing rebuttal in some circumstances. *See J. A. S. v. Bushelman*, 342 S.W.3d 850, 864 (Ky. 2011) (discussing rebutting the marital presumption and holding that "a birth out of wedlock under KRS 406.180 occurs when a child is born to woman who, regardless of her marital status, was not lawfully married to the biological father at the time of the child's conception or at the time of the child's birth.") Historically, the presumption could be rebutted only through a showing that the husband was impotent or lacked access to the wife.

16.9. Putative Fathers and Consent to Adoption

The constitutional rights of putative fathers have been the subject of much controversy, particularly in the context of consent to adoption. Questions abound concerning when putative fathers are entitled to notice and an opportunity to be heard before parental rights are terminated prior to adoption of the child. This issue is discussed more fully in Chapter 17. *See Lehr v. Robertson*, 463 U.S. 248 (1983) (putative father who failed to establish a substantial relationship with a child did not have a right to notice and hearing prior to adoption).

Examples

4. Assume that P and D were married but had some relationship problems. They separated but did not divorce. During the separation, P had a sexual relationship with X, which resulted in the birth of a child. X's name appeared on the birth certificate as the father, and he provided some financial support for the child. X brings a paternity action. D objects to the proceeding, claiming that he is the legal father of the child because he is the husband of the child's mother, and the child was conceived and born while P and D were married. X contends that under state law, the presumption of legitimacy can be rebutted if its application is "outrageous to common sense and reason." What is the likely result?

5. Assume that M was married to F1 but that during the marriage, she had an affair with F2. When a child was conceived, all the parties believed that F1 was the father. However, routine hospital testing disclosed that F2 was the biological father of the child. F2 signed a support agreement, and F2's wife regularly cared for the child. F2 told family and friends that he was the father of the child. F2 brought an action to be declared the legal father of the child. F1 claimed to be the legal father of the child because he was M's husband at the time of conception and birth and was therefore the presumed father under state law. F1 claims that he is also a presumed father based on a state statute presuming paternity for a man who "receives the child into his home and openly holds out the child as his natural child." The state statute provides that "[i]f two or more presumptions conflict with each other, the presumption which on the facts is founded on the weightier considerations of policy and logic controls." What is the likely result?

6. M and F1 were married when twins were concieved and born in May 2009. F1 participated in their birth and actively parented them as a stay-at-home father. M was in the military, and while serving in Bahrain from May to October 2008, she had an affair with F2, who was also married at the time. When the twins were 10 months old, F2 sought to establish himself as their father. He claimed that while stationed in Bahrain, he sang to the twins in utero and brought M to prenatal care. F2 later attempted to have a relationship with the twins, but M prevented him from being involved. F2 seeks genetic testing to prove his paternity. What is the likely result?

EXPLANATIONS

Explanations

4. Historically, the presumption that a child born during a marriage was the child of the husband was a strong and an often-impossible presumption to overcome. Particularly when the married couple opposed the paternity action, a man in X's position would have lacked standing to file suit. With the advent of genetic testing and changing views of the family, some states provide that the traditional marital presumption can be rebutted under some circumstances. This example is based in part on the case of *Lander v. Smith*, 906 So. 2d 1130 (Fla. App. 2005), where the court found for X, holding that the presumption of legitimacy could be rebutted in a circumstance where "common sense and reason are outraged" by its rigid application. The court was swayed by the fact that X was eager to embrace the responsibilities of parenthood.

5. This example is based on the case of *Craig L. v. Sandy S.*, 125 Cal. App. 4th 36 (Cal. App. 2004), where the trial court's initial decision quashing F2's petition was reversed. The appellate court remanded the case for further consideration, giving the greatest weight to the well-being of the child. The court stated, "As we have indicated, in weighing the conflicting interests under [the statute] the trial court must in the end make a determination which gives the greatest weight to [the child's] well-being." *Id.* at 53. On remand, the court was instructed to consider the nature of F2's relationship with the child and the impact on the child of recognizing F2's paternity.

6. In the similar case of *Niel S. v. Mary L.*, 199 Cal. App. 4th 240 (Cal. App. 2011), the appellate court reasoned that F1 was the presumed marital father and that he had fully accepted the twins as his own. The appellate court gave significant weight to F1's "social" relationship to the children and held that under the state statutory scheme, F2 lacked standing to initiate a paternity contest. F2 was also unsuccessful in bringing a constitutional due process challenge.

FEDERAL LEGISLATION

16.10. Federal Focus

During the 1970s, Congress became concerned that more children were being born outside of marriage and that as a consequence, federal and state governments were providing support in the form of public assistance to some of them. Congress responded with legislation that reduced the government's financial burden by shifting it to the biological parents of the child, including unmarried fathers. To accomplish this objective, the federal government created a child support enforcement program that imposed requirements on states as a condition of receiving funding. The program, named after IV-D of the Social Security Act, requires that the states comply with various requirements, including establishment of paternity, or risk losing up to two-thirds of support payments provided by the government. 42 U.S.C.A. §654(4)(a).

Beginning in 1975, state and local IV-D agencies were required to establish the paternity of all children who were born to unmarried parents and who either received public assistance benefits or applied for IV-D services. In 1984, Congress required that each state permit a paternity action to be brought at any time before a child's 18th birthday, rather than allowing shorter statutes of limitations, which had been the practice in some states.

16.11. The Omnibus Budget Reconciliation Act of 1993

The Omnibus Budget Reconciliation Act of 1993, Pub. L. No. 103-66 (1993), required states to adopt an in-hospital, voluntary acknowledgment process as a condition of receiving federal IV-D funds. The Personal Responsibility and Work Opportunity Reconciliation Act (PRWORA) of 1996, Pub. L. No. 103-66 (1993), modified and expanded the required paternity acknowledgment procedures earlier established by Congress.

16.12. Personal Responsibility and Work Opportunity Reconciliation Act (PRWORA) of 1996

PRWORA mandates that states have laws requiring that genetic testing be ordered in any contested case. The party requesting the testing must execute a sworn statement that either alleges paternity, with a showing of a reasonable possibility of sexual contact between the parties, or denies paternity. The tribunal can then compel genetic testing of the child and all parties. *See State ex rel. Dept. of Justice and Division of Child Support*, 120 P.3d 1 (Or. App. 2005) (requiring parentage testing was a reasonable "search" under state and constitutions).

UNIFORM PARENTAGE ACT (UPA)

16.13. Overview

The Uniform Parentage Act (UPA) was originally approved in 1973 and most recently revised in 2002. The text of the Act can be found at http://

www.uniformlaws.org/Act.aspx?title=Parentage%20Act (last visited July 21, 2012). The 2002 revision has been adopted in nine states; however, earlier versions were adopted by a significant number of states or significantly influenced legislation in the area. *See* the Legislative Fact Sheet at http://www.uniformlaws.org/LegislativeFactSheet.aspx?title=Parentage% (last visited July 21, 2012).

The UPA declared that the law should treat children equally, regardless of the marital status of their parents. UPA §202 (2002). Consequently, the title "illegitimate" was replaced with the term "child with no presumed father."

16.14. Establishing Paternity Under the UPA

§201(b) of the UPA provides for establishment of paternity through six methods: an unrebutted presumption, voluntary acknowledgment, adjudication, adoption, consent to assisted reproduction, or a confirmed gestational agreement.

16.15. Establishing Paternity through Presumption

The UPA establishes five categories of presumed fathers, including the following: (1) the man is married to the mother and the child is born during the marriage; (2) the man is married to the mother and the child is born within 300 days of termination of the marriage; (3) the man and the mother attempted to marry and the child is born within 300 days of the termination of the relationship; (4) after the child is born, the man and the mother marry or attempt to marry, and the man voluntarily asserts paternity through methods set forth in the Act; and (5) the man resides with the child for the first two years of the child's life and holds himself out as the father. UPA §204.

An unrebutted presumption of paternity establishes a father-child relationship. UPA §201(b)(1). Such a presumption can be rebutted only through adjudication. UPA §204(b).

EXAMPLE

Example

7. M gave birth to a child outside of marriage. She named F1 as the father. F2 claimed to be the biological father, and the mother sought genetic testing of F1 and F2. The court denied testing to F2 because he was incarcerated at the time of conception. F2 brought a writ of mandamus asserting that the trial court erroneously decided that he had to be the biological father

in order to be considered a presumed father under the Alabama UPA. Could the claim of F2 be successful?

EXPLANATION

Explanation

7. In the case of *Ex parte T.J.*, 89 So. 3d 744 (Ala. 2012), the Supreme Court of Alabama decided that because the Alabama UPA creates a presumption of paternity when a man "receives the child into his home and openly holds the child out as his natural child . . . and establishes a significant parental relationship . . . ," a presumption of paternity could be established despite the fact that the putative father could not be the biological father.

16.16. Rebutting Presumptions of Paternity Under the UPA

The time limits and procedures for rebutting the presumptions of paternity are set forth in Article 6, *Proceeding to Adjudicate Parentage*. UPA §601 *et seq*. When the child has a presumed father, an action must generally be brought by the presumed father, the mother, or another individual within two years of the child's birth (unless the presumed father did not have sexual intercourse with the mother near the time of conception, and he never held the child out as his own). UPA §607. When there is a presumed father, his paternity can be rebutted only through genetic testing. UPA §631(1).

Challenging issues arise when more than one man is the presumed father of a child. The UPA previously provided that the presumption founded on "the weightier considerations of policy and logic" should control. Although this provision is no longer contained in the UPA, it does appear in some state statutes. *See Courtney v. Roggy*, 302 S.W.3d 141 (Mo. App. 2009).

EXAMPLE

Example

8. Assume that in a divorce action, the mother (M) of a child born during the marriage wants to assert that the husband (H) is not the father of the child. M wants H to submit to genetic testing. Arguing that he is the presumed father, H refuses to undergo genetic testing. What is the likely ruling by a court?

EXPLANATION

Explanation

8. This situation that was considered by the Court of Appeals of Georgia in the case of *Williamson v. Williamson*, 690 S.E.2d 257 (Ga. App. 2010). The appellate court decided that pursuant to state statute, a mother could seek to "delegitimate" her child, but that before genetic testing would be ordered, the mother would have to show that how delegitimizing the child was in the child's best interests. In *Williamson*, the mother failed to make such a showing, and her request for genetic testing was denied.

16.17. Voluntary Acknowledgment

Under the PRWORA, states are required to facilitate a man's ability to voluntarily acknowledge paternity. To this end, a valid acknowledgment of paternity is sufficient to establish the father-child relationship (assuming that there are no other presumed, acknowledged, or adjudicated fathers). UPA §§201(b)(2), 302(b). The UPA sets forth detailed procedures for acknowledgment and denial. UPA §300 *et seq.*

EXAMPLES

Examples

9. Assume that M gave birth to a child, and D executed a voluntary acknowledgment of paternity two days later. The acknowledgment form informed D of his right to genetic testing and the legal consequences of signature. When sued for child support, D claimed that he was not the father of the child. He provided DNA testing showing that there was a 0 percent chance that he was the child's father. The state where M and D live has a statute providing that a voluntary acknowledgment becomes conclusive if it is not rescinded in a timely fashion, which D's was not. In contrast, D argues that if the marital presumption of paternity applied in this case, it could be rebutted by clear and convincing evidence. Will a court allow D to rescind the acknowledgment?

10. M gave birth to a child outside of marriage, and F executed a valid voluntary acknowledgment of paternity. F had an ongoing relationship with the child and later sought custody based on M's drug use and criminal activity. M asserted that F was not the father of the child, and genetic testing indeed showed that he was not the biological father. M claims superior right to custody as the natural parent of the child. What is the likely outcome?

11. Assume that D had a sexual relationship with P, but they did not marry. One child, A, was born in 1999, and D signed a voluntary acknowledgment of paternity on the day that A was born. He did so based on assurances from P that he was the father of A. In 2000, D agreed to entry of a child support order, but several months later, he began to question whether he was actually A's father. After genetic tests were performed, it was determined that D was not A's biological father. In the state where P and D live, the statute addressing voluntary acknowledgment provides that an acknowledgment can be overturned if based on a material mistake of fact. D claims that his belief that he was the father of A, based on P's assertions, was a material mistake of fact and that he should be allowed to rescind the acknowledgment. P claims that the acknowledgment should be enforced, and she alleges that D's error was caused by his "neglect of legal duty" because he signed the acknowledgment without insisting on genetic testing. What is the likely result?

EXPLANATIONS

Explanations

9. This example is based on the case of *People ex rel. Dept. of Public Aid v. Smith*, 289 Ill. Dec. 1 (Ill. 2004), where the court found that the disparate treatment of the two groups of presumed fathers was logical and appropriate. The court reasoned that a man who signs an acknowledgment informing him of his rights and waiving them is in a very different position than a man assumed to be a father merely by virtue of his marital status. The court held that D could not rescind the voluntary acknowledgment of paternity.

10. The Supreme Court of Nebraska ruled on such as case in *Cesar C. v. Alicia L.*, 800 N.W.2d 249 (Neb. 2011). The court found that pursuant to the validly executed voluntary acknowledgment, F was the legal father of the child despite the results of the genetic testing. Consequently, the lower court erred in applying the parental preference doctrine in favor of the mother.

11. This example is based on *Department of Human Services v. Chisum*, 85 P.3d 860 (Okla. App. 2004), where the appellate court held that D had established a "material mistake of fact" as required under the statute. Consequently, he was allowed to rescind his prior acknowledgment of paternity. Note that the outcome likely would have been different were it not for the state statutory provision specifically providing for rescission of a voluntary acknowledgment based on a material mistake of fact.

16.18. Genetic Testing Under the UPA

The UPA sets forth procedures and guidelines to expedite and regulate the use of genetic testing in paternity cases. Scientific advances in the availability and accuracy of genetic testing have increased its importance in determining paternity. For example, a man may be "rebuttably identified" as the father of a child based on certain genetic testing results described in the Act. UPA §§501 *et seq.*; UPA §§621 *et seq.* In addition, where there is a presumed, acknowledged, or adjudicated father, paternity may be disproved only by genetic testing. UPA §631(1).

§608 of the UPA governs judicial authority to deny motions for genetic testing in adjudications involving presumed or acknowledged fathers. As a part of the analysis courts are instructed to consider the best interests of the child, and nine best interests factors are set forth for this purpose. UPA §608.

EXAMPLE

Example

12. M gave birth to a child born outside marriage, and F executed a paternity affidavit. A court entered an order granting custody to M and ordering F to pay child support. F developed a relationship with the child and had primary custody for some periods of time. About the time that the child completed eighth grade, F's wife noticed that the child didn't share many common traits with F, so they bought a DNA test kit at the drugstore and sought to use the negative results in court as evidence of fraud and mistake in the excution of the paternity affidavit. What is a court likely to decide?

EXPLANATION

Explanation

12. In the case of *Paternity of T.M.*, 953 N.E.2d 96 (Ind. App. 2011), the trial court held that the mail-in kit DNA test results were not sufficiently reliable to be admitted into evidence. The appellate court affirmed, noting that the mother's testimony that she was in an exclusive relationship with F at the time of conception was persuasive.

16.19. Statutes of Limitation

Constitutional challenges. States historically had statutes requiring that paternity actions be brought within a year or two of the birth of the child, and these short time frames proved problematic. For example, in *Mills v. Habluetzel*, 456 U.S. 91 (1982), the mother of an illegitimate child brought suit to establish paternity. The trial court dismissed the suit because the child was one year and seven months old when the suit was filed, and Texas law required a paternity action to be brought within one year of a child's birth. The Supreme Court held that the Texas statute effectively blocked legitimation by imposing such a short time limit on the initiation of paternity proceedings. The provision was unconstitutional under both the insurmountable barrier and the substantial relationship tests. The Court said that the statute denied equal protection to illegitimate children because a state that grants opportunity for legitimate children to obtain parental support also must grant that opportunity to illegitimate children, and this opportunity must be more than illusory.

In *Clark v. Jeter*, 486 U.S. 456 (1988), the mother of a child born out of wedlock waited ten years to seek support from the putative father. He claimed that Pennsylvania's six-year statute of limitations for bringing paternity actions barred the action to establish paternity. After reviewing *Mills v. Habluetzel*, 456 U.S. 91 (1982) (invalidating one-year statute of limitations) and *Pickett v. Brown*, 462 U.S. 1 (1983) (invalidating a two-year statute of limitations), the Court struck down the Pennsylvania limitation. The Court held that for a paternity limitation to pass intermediate scrutiny, the period must be sufficiently long to present a reasonable opportunity to be heard, and any limitation placed on that opportunity must be substantially related to the state's interest in avoiding litigation of stale or fraudulent claims.

State statutes. In response to these cases, and in order to retain federal subsidies for child support enforcement, states have extended their statutes of limitations for establishing paternity until the child reaches at least the age of 18. State statutes of limitation generally range from age 18 to age 23. While some states have no age limitation, other states have put some time limits in place. For example, in *In re Estate of Smith*, 685 So. 2d 1206 (Fla. 1996), the claim of a 60-year-old alleged daughter to the estate of her deceased father was denied on the basis that the Florida statute of limitations regarding adjudication of paternity had expired. *See also Roy v. Edmonds*, 261 P.3d 551 (Kan. App. 2011) (statute requiring that action to establish paternity be brought no later than three years after child reached age of majority did not violate public policy). *But see R. A. C. v. P. J. S.*, 880 A.2d 1179 (N.J. Super. 2005) (man declared father of 30-year-old child after 23-year statute of limitations equitably tolled).

UPA approach. The UPA analyzes time limits differently depending on the legal posture of the case. The UPA allows *a child with no presumed, acknowledged, or adjudicated father* to sue for determination of parentage at any time. UPA §606. In contrast, when *a child has a presumed father*, an action generally must be brought by the presumed father, the mother, or another individual within two years of the child's birth. Neverthless, an action to disprove the relationship with a presumed father may be brought at any time if the presumed father and mother did not cohabitate or have sexual intercourse with each other near the time of conception and if the presumed father never openly held the child out as his own. UPA §607.

EXAMPLE

Example

13. M and F1 had an "open" marriage at the time that a child (C) was conceived and born. More than two years later, M asserts that F2 is the father of C. The state in which the parties reside has a statute providing that disestablishment of paternity must occur within two years of birth, but that establishment of paternity can take place up until the child is two years over the age of majority. Which statute of limitations will a court apply?

EXPLANATION

Explanation

13. In the case of *In re G.M.*, 2012 IL. App. 2d 110370 (Ill. App. 2012), the appellate court considered a similar situation. The appellate court characterized the action as one to establish paternity on behalf of C, and consequently, the longer statute of limitation was applicable. Note that in a fact situation where the marital father was actively asserting parental rights and/or there was an unkown biological father, the result could be different.

16.20. Registration to Receive Notice of Termination of Parental Rights

The UPA provides for the use of parentage registries in order to expeditiously free children for adoption. A man who wants to receive notification of termination of parental rights and adoption proceedings concerning a child that he may have fathered must enter his name on the registry. Failure to do so can result in termination of parental rights without notice, if the child is under one year of age at the time of termination. UPA §404. Exception is made for situations where there is a presumed, acknowledged, or adjudicated father. UPA §402(b).

State activity. Approximately 33 states have enacted some form of a registry for putative fathers, with an estimated 27 remaining functional. Mary Joseph Beck, Wells Conference on Adoption Law, *A National Putative Father Registry*, 36 Cap. U. L. Rev. 295, 299-300 (2007).

Challenges. Registration statutes have been the subject of numerous unsuccessful challenges. In *Lehr v. Robertson*, 463 U.S. 248, 264-265 (1983), the United States Supreme Court found New York's paternity registry an appropriate means of accommodating and protecting the existing, yet undeveloped rights of putative fathers. The Court stated, "Sincc the New York statutes adequately protected [the putative father's] inchoate interest in establishing a relationship with [the child], we find no merit in the claim that his constitutional rights were offended because the family court strictly complied with the notice provisions of the statute." *Id.* at 265. *See In re C. M. D.*, 287 S.W.3d 510 (Tex. App. 2009) (no proof of injury); *A. S. B. v. Dep't of Children & Family Servs.*, 688 N.E.2d 1215, 1220-1225 (Ill. App. 1997) (no due process violation); *Heidbreder v. Carton*, 645 N.W.2d 355, 372-377 (Minn. 2002), *cert. denied*, 537 U.S. 1046 (2002) (no consitutional right); *Friehe v. Schaad*, 545 N.W.2d 740, 744-748 (Neb. 1996) (no equal protection or due process violation); *Robert O. v. Russell K.*, 604 N.E.2d 99, 101-105 (N.Y. 1992) (no consitutional violation); *In re Baby Boy K.*, 546 N.W.2d 86, 90-101 (S.D. 1996) (no constitional violation); *Beltran v. Allan*, 926 P.2d 892, 897-898 (Utah App. 1996) (no constitutional violation).

EQUITABLE THEORIES

16.21. Equitable Parent Doctrine

The "equitable parent" doctrine, which is recognized by some states, permits an individual to assume the rights and responsibilities of a natural parent through a judicial determination. *See, e.g., In re Nicholas H.*, 46 P.3d 932 (Cal. 2002) (biological relationship not determinative); *In re Marriage of Gallagher*, 539 N.W.2d 479 (Iowa 1995) (recognizing equitable parenthood); *Atkinson v. Atkinson*, 408 N.W.2d 516 (1987) (husband as equitable parent). It allows a court to find that a husband who is not the biological father of a child born or conceived during the marriage may be considered the natural father of that child when (1) the husband and the child mutually acknowledge a relationship as father and child, or the mother of the child has cooperated in the development of such a relationship over a period of time prior to the filing of a complaint for divorce; (2) the husband desires to have the rights afforded to a parent; and (3) the husband is willing to take on the responsibility of paying child support. This doctrine has not been extended beyond the context of marriage. *See Killingbeck v. Killingbeck*, 711 N.W.2d 759 (Mich. App. 2005) (child not conceived or born within marital relationship). Some states have rejected recognition of the doctrine. *See, e.g., Randy A. J. v. Norma I. J.*, 677 N.W.2d 630 (Wis. 2004) (no recognition of equitable parent doctrine).

Courts have refused to apply the doctrine to situations in which a child was not born or conceived during the marriage. *See Killingbeck v. Killingbeck*, 711 N.W.2d 759 (Mich. App. 2005); *People ex rel. J. A. U. v. R. L. C.*, 47 P.3d 327 (Colo. 2002) (man who waited 11 years before attacking a paternity judgment that he stipulated to without demanding genetic testing waited too long); *Huisman v. Miedema*, 644 N.W.2d 321 (Iowa 2002) (putative father's paternity action dismissed when it was brought seven years after child's birth, and mother and her husband raised child); *W. v. W.*, 779 A.2d 716 (Conn. 2001) (court estopped the husband from denying his paternity when he had treated the child as his for 12 years); *In re Paternity of Cheryl*, 746 N.E.2d 488 (Mass. 2001) (man waited five years after acknowledging paternity to have genetic tests that showed his nonpaternity was not relieved of support obligation); *Van v. Zahorik*, 597 N.W.2d 15 (Mich. 1999) (court refused to apply doctrine to putative unmarried father).

EXAMPLE

Example

14. Assume that P and D cohabited for five years but were never married. D claims that D and P continued their relationship for several years after they stopped living together, and P had two children in the course of this relationship. D alleges that P informed him that he was the father of the children, and he believes that he was named as the father on the birth certificates of both children. He also claims that he cared for and financially supported the children both during and after his relationship with P.

    When D started a relationship with another woman, P refused to allow him to see the children. D filed a petition to establish paternity, and he alleged that he believed and continues to believe he is the father of the two children. P argued that D was not the biological father of either child and could not be an "equitable parent" to them because D and P were never married. D conceded that blood testing showed that he was not the biological father but argued that he was an "equitable parent" and that P was equitably estopped from denying that he is the father. The trial court decided for P and indicated that its ruling turned on two factors: (1) D apparently was not the biological father of the children, and (2) D and P were never married. The court noted that the state's public policy favored marriage and concluded that the doctrines of equitable estoppel, equitable parenthood, and equitable adoption require marriage. On appeal, how will the court rule most likely?

EXPLANATION

Explanation

14. The appellate court most likely will reject D's claim because D is not the husband of P and the children were not even born while P and D were cohabiting. Courts have been generally reluctant to apply the equitable parent doctrine to situations similar to this hypothetical.

16.22. Paternity by Estoppel

Some courts have used the doctrine of paternity by estoppel to establish paternity. The Supreme Court of Pennsylvania, in *K. E. M. v. P. C. S.*, 38 A.3d 798 (Pa. 2012) recently reaffirmed the doctrine, quoting a prior decision in *Lynn v. Powell*, 809 A.2d 927. (Pa. Super. 2002):

> We do not allow a person to deny "parentage" of a child, regardless of biological status, if that person holds the child out as his own and provides support. When such circumstances exist, we will also not allow a child's mother to sue a third party for support based on biological status. Plainly, the law does not allow a person to challenge his role as a parent once he has accepted it, even with contrary DNA and blood tests.

K.E.M. at 802.

ESTABLISHING MATERNITY

16.23. Maternity Under the UPA

Traditionally, a woman who gives birth to a child is presumed to be the child's legal mother. However, societal changes and advances in reproductive technology, discussed more fully in Chapter 18, have made determination of maternity considerably more challenging. *See In re S. N. V.*, 2011 WL 6425562 (Col. App. 2011) (biological father's wife has standing to assert marital presumption to establish maternity over birth mother).

Under the UPA, the mother-child relationship is established when a woman gives birth, an adjudication of maternity is made, a woman adopts a child, or she is named as a parent under a validated or enforceable gestational agreement. UPA §201(a).

16.24. Same-Sex Partners

Questions of legal maternity sometimes arise when same-sex partners raise children together in states that do not recognize same-sex marriage or adoption. One partner may have legal rights to a child as the biological parent, but the other partner may not have traditional legal grounds for seeking custody or parenting time. *But see In re* M. C., 195 Cal. App. 4th 197 (Cal. App. 2011) (biological mother's ex-wife was presumed mother).

In such situations, courts have considered various theories for establishment of maternity. *See* Nancy D. Polikoff, *A Mother Should Not Have to Adopt Her Own Child: Parentage Laws for Children of Lesbian Couples in the Twenty-first Century*, 5 Stan. J. Civ. Rts. & Civ. Liberties 201 (2009). *See also Della Corte v. Ramirez*, 961 N.E.2d 601 (Mass. App. 2012) (former same-sex spouse of child's mother was the same as "husband" under statute); *Shineovich and Kemp*, 2009 WL 2032113 (Or. App. 2009) (statute granting legal parentage to husbands of women who conceived by artificial insemination extended to cover same-sex domestic partner); *Smith v. Gordon*, 968 A.2d 1 (Del. 2009) (same-sex partner deemed not to be a legal parent under Delaware UPA was found to be a de facto parent); *In re Parentage of L. B.*, 122 P.3d 161 (Wash. 2005) (same-sex partner recognized as a common law de facto parent). *But see Debra H. v. Janice R.*, 61 A.D.3d 460 (N.Y.A.D. 2009) (same-sex partner denied *in loco parentis* status despite the fact that the parties entered into a civil union in Vermont and registered as domestic partners in New York City).

CHAPTER 17

Adoption

17.1. Introduction

This chapter reviews the history, development, and application of the law involving various forms of adoption. In 2007 and 2008, approximately 136,000 children were adopted each year in the United States. Approximately 40 percent of adoptions were handled through publicly funded child welfare agencies, and nearly 14 percent were intercountry adoptions. The remainder were handled through other sources, such as private agencies or tribes. Child Welfare Information Gateway, *How Many Children Were Adopted in 2007 and 2008?* available at http://www.childwelfare.gov/pubs/adopted0708.pdf#Page=8&view=Fit (last visited August 19, 2012).

OVERVIEW

17.2. History

The law of adoption began to develop early in civilization. It apparently existed in Greece and Rome and in portions of continental Europe that received Roman law. It also existed in the Middle East, Asia, and in the tribal societies of Africa and Oceania.

Adoption was unknown to the common law. The first instance in which a state legislature authorized adoption can be traced to 1847, when the Massachusetts House of Representatives ordered that the Committee on the Judiciary consider a law for adoption of children. An adoption bill was passed in 1851, and within 25 years, most states followed the lead of Massachusetts and passed adoption legislation.

When states first established adoption laws, adoptive children were commonly not accorded the same legal rights as children born during marriage. For example, some states expressly provided that the relationship of parent and adopted child was to be without the right of inheritance.

During the early part of the twentieth century, states established laws requiring a pre-hearing investigation and a report by a local child welfare agency. They also required that adoption records be kept private and sealed. Secrecy was believed important because it assured anonymity, which protected the child from the stigma of illegitimacy and encouraged full integration of the child into the adoptive family.

During the 1970s, discussion in the adoption area focused on two issues: first, improving the policies and adoption practices so that special needs children could be placed in permanent homes; and second, determining the considerations under which certain persons would have access to adoption records. There emerged a movement during this period in which a small number of persons organized to provide support for others interested in searching for and meeting their biological parents. Two such organizations were the Adoptees Liberty Movement Association (ALMA) and the Concerned United Birthparents (CUB) group. The American Adoption Congress (AAC) was formed in 1980 to coordinate the efforts of those persons interested in legislative changes that would provide access to information that would lead to the discovery of biological parents. These organizations have been fairly successful in obtaining new legislation that permits adopted children, under limited circumstances, to locate their biological parents.

Adoption laws vary considerably among the states and it is common to find differences in terminology, organization, and procedure.

17.3. Abrogation of Adoption

In the past, many states allowed an adoption to be abrogated or annulled because the child was suffering from an undisclosed illness or disability. Some allowed the child to be returned to an orphanage because of the child's poor behavior. *See, e.g., In the Matter of the Abrogation of Anonymous*, 167 N.Y.S.2d 472 (N.Y. 1951) (adoptive parents abrogate adoption of 17-year-old emancipated boy whom they adopted when he was four years old). For example, in 1951, Minnesota passed a bill that gave parents of an adopted child five years from the time the child was adopted to annul the adoption if the child developed feeblemindedness, epilepsy, insanity, or venereal infection as a result of conditions existing prior to the adoption of which the adopting parent had no knowledge. The law was repealed in 1975.

Today, while some jurisdictions allow abrogation of an adoption on a limited basis such as in cases of fraud, annulment is rare and will usually not be granted unless it is in the best interest of the child. *See, e.g.*, *M.L.B. v. Department of Health and Rehabilitative Services*, 559 So. 2d 87 (Fla. App. 1990).

17.4. Legal Effect of Adoption

Adoption results in severing the ties of a child with the child's biological parents. The child's new adoptive parents are substituted for the biological parents and may exercise the same rights toward the child as a natural parent. The child has the same right to support as a biological child born to the adoptive parents and may inherit as would such a child. The adoptive parents may bar visitation or any other contact between the child and his or her biological parents.

Examples

1. Assume that M and D are a married couple who have three biological children. They farm land located in state X that has been in D's family for more than 100 years. They enjoy being parents, and they adopt another child, P. Unfortunately, P does not adjust well to the family and never adapts to rural living. P runs away from home repeatedly and does not develop close relationships with M, D, or the other children. M and D die suddenly in a plane crash without leaving a will. The biological children claim that, under the circumstances, P should not be allowed to inherit an interest in the family farm. Will P most likely inherit under the intestacy provisions of state X?

2. Assume that P is adopted by M and D. Three years after the adoption, P learns that her biological parents, X and Y, were killed in an automobile accident and have left a sizable estate. There is no will, and P seeks to inherit from her biological parents. What will be the likely outcome of P's effort to inherit from her biological parents?

Explanations

1. P most likely will be allowed to inherit under the provisions of state X because an adopted child is treated as a natural child of his adopted parent or parents. Just as with biological children, the quality of the adoptive parent-child relationship has no bearing on the right to inherit under intestacy provisions.

2. P will most likely be unsuccessful. The right to receive property by devise or descent is not a natural right but a privilege granted by the state, and absent a statutory provision allowing P to inherit from her biological

parents, her claim will be unsuccessful. *See Hall v. Vallandingham*, 540 A.2d 1162 (Md. App. 1988). Because the states will treat P as a natural issue of M and D for intestacy purposes, it will not allow her to inherit from both her adoptive and biological parents.

FORMS OF ADOPTION

17.5. Agency Adoptions

Agency adoptions involve the placement of a child with adoptive parents by a public agency, or by a private nonprofit agency licensed or regulated by the state. The agency acts as an intermediary between potential adoptive parents and the child's natural parent or parents. Adoption agencies generally place children who have become wards of the state or whose parents decide that it would be in the child's interest to be raised by others.

17.6. Independent Adoption

An independent or direct adoption usually involves newborn infants, often born to young parents. While the arrangements vary, sometimes there is a direct arrangement made between the birth parents and the adoptive parents. On other occasions, the arrangements are made through the use of an intermediary such as an attorney. A few states do not allow independent adoptions, and this form of adoption is carefully regulated in others.

Independent adoptions are used because the adoption can be accomplished faster than when working with an adoption agency. They are also viewed as advantageous to the natural parents of the child because they may participate in choosing the adoptive parents.

17.7. Stepparent Adoption

Stepparent adoption requires the consent of the spouse of the adopting stepparent (the child's mother or father) and the consent of or termination of the parental rights of the child's other legal parent. For example, if a couple with one child divorces and the mother remarries, the mother's new husband could not adopt the child unless the father consented or his parental rights were terminated. *See In re W. E. B.*, 980 So. 2d 123 (La. App. 2008) (father's failure to pay child support is not sufficient grounds to terminate parental rights); *In re R. M.*, 234 S.W.3d 619 (Mo. App. 2007) (stepfather's petition for adoption denied because of insufficient evidence to support termination of father's parental rights); *In re Adoption of T. H.*, 171 P.3d 480 (Utah App. 2007) (termination of father's parental rights not in child's best interest). However, if the other legal parent consents, stepparent adoption is generally less complicated than other agency or independent adoption procedures.

17.8. Near-Relative Adoption

The absence, inability, or incapacity of the natural parents to provide and care for their children may prompt other relatives to assume the benefits and responsibilities of that role. For example, grandparents may seek to adopt their grandchildren if the children's parents die while the children are minors. These adoptions are among the easiest to process.

While at one time judicial intervention was unnecessary, a body of common law developed according a custodial preference for near relatives. In most states, adoptive placement with a family member is presumptively in the best interests of a child, absent a showing of good cause to the contrary or detriment to the child. States may create a preference for near-relatives by statute. *See, e.g.*, Minn. Stat. §259.57, subd. 2 (2009) ("authorized child placing agency shall consider placement, consistent with the child's best interests and in the following order, with (1) a relative or relatives of the child, or (2) an important friend with whom the child has resided or had significant contact").

17.9. Open Adoption

As a general rule, adoptive parents may bar any contact between the minor child and the biological parents. In this sense, most adoptions are considered to be "closed." Nevertheless, in some situations, such as when the children being adopted are older, some contact may be permitted pursuant to an "open" adoption.

When there are no statutory provisions, the adoptive parents to an open adoption can prevent future contact between the child and the natural parents at will. However, several states have statutes that expressly address the issue of post-adoption contact between the adoptive and biological parents. *See* Cal. Fam. Code §8616.5 (West 2009) ("Post-Adoption Contact Agreements"); Mass. Gen. Laws Ann. ch. 210, §6C (West 2009) ("Agreement for Post-Adoption Contact or Communication"); Minn. Stat. Ann. §259.58

(West 2009) ("Communication or Contact Agreements"); Mont. Code Ann. §42-5-301 (2009) ("Visitation and Communication Agreements"); Neb. Rev. Stat. §43-162 (2009) ("Communication or contact agreement; authorized; approval"); Or. Rev. Stat. Ann. §109.305 (West 2009) ("Interpretation of adoption laws; agreement for continuing contact with birth relatives"). *See also* E. Gary Spitko, *Open Adoption, Inheritance, and the "Uncleing" Principle*, 48 Santa Clara L. Rev. 765 (2008) (proposing that adopted children who have "qualifying functional relationships" with birth parents be allowed to inherit from them).

17.10. Subsidized Adoption

Children with special needs waiting for adoptive families may be difficult to place because of the costs associated with caring for them. Consequently, some states provide financial help to parents who adopt these children. The two sources of funds used to support such programs come from the federal Title IV-E program under the Social Security Act and each state's individual program, which will vary from jurisdiction to jurisdiction.

17.11. International Adoption

The Hague Convention on Protection of Children and Co-operation in Respect of Intercountry Adoption (commonly referred to as the Hague Convention on Intercountry Adoption) was adopted and opened for signature at the conclusion of the Seventeenth Session of the Hague Conference on Private International Law on May 29, 1993. By 2012 more than 88 countries, including the United States, had become parties to the Convention. *See* Hague Conference on Private International Law, Status Table, at *http://www.hcch.net/index_en.php?act=conventions.status&cid=69* (last visited July 23, 2012); Elizabeth Bartholet, *International Adoption: Thoughts on the Human Rights Issues*, 13 Buffalo Human Rts. L. Rev. 151 (2007); David M. Smolin, *Child Laundering and the Hague Convention on Intercountry Adoption: The Future and Past of Intercountry Adoption*, 48 U. Louisville L. Rev. 441 (2010).

The Convention sets out norms and procedures to safeguard children involved in intercountry adoptions and to protect the interests of their birth and adoptive parents. These safeguards are designed to discourage trafficking in children and to ensure that intercountry adoptions are made in the best interest of the children involved. Cooperation between Contracting States is facilitated by the establishment in each Contracting State of a Central Authority with programmatic and case-specific functions. The Convention also provides for recognition of adoptions that fall within its scope in all other Contracting States. It leaves the details of its implementation up to each Contracting State.

The United States ratified the Convention in 2007, and it took effect in 2008. The Central Authority for the purpose of implementation in the United States is the Department of State's Office of Children's Issues. Implementing legislation, the Intercountry Adoption Act was passed in 2000, and final regulations have been issued. Trish Maskew, *The Failure of Promise: The U.S. Regulations on Intercountry Adoption Under the Hague Convention*, 60 Admin. L. Rev. 487 (2008).

In an international adoption, the new parents must satisfy the adoption requirements of both the foreign country and the parents' home state in the United States. The adoptive parents must apply for U.S. citizenship for the child because it is not granted automatically.

EXAMPLES

Examples

3. M and F were divorced and M had sole custody of the children. F was ordered to pay child support and was given parenting time every other weekend. F made child support payments sporadically, in that they were sometimes late and he failed to pay for a period of three months when he became incarcerated. M eventually married SF, and they file a petition for SF to adopt the children. F opposes the adoption. The state has a statute providing that a parent's consent to adoption is not required if during the prior year, the parent has willfully failed to comply substantially with a child support order. What is the likely result?

4. Assume that a child was born out of marriage to P. P meets with X and Y, who agree to adopt C, and the legal adoption becomes final when C is two months old. Prior to the adoption, the parties agree that P may visit with the child on occasion, but nothing is put in writing. P visits C several times each year. When C is five years old, X and Y overhear P using inappropriate language with C, and they hear P encouraging C to disobey household rules established by X and Y. X and Y conclude that P is upsetting the child, and they terminate the visits. P is shocked that X and Y would treat her this way after five years of contact with C, and P believes that X and Y are overreacting to innocent events. P consequently brings an action to enforce the oral visitation agreement. Will P be likely to succeed?

5. The state brings an action to terminate the parental rights of M and F. They agree to the termination and adoption of the child by the maternal grandparents. In the consent judgment, the grandparents were given permanent "care, custody, and control of the minor child . . . subject to reasonable, supervised visitation" by M and F. When problems develop, F seeks to enforce the visitation. What is the likely result?

EXPLANATIONS

Explanations

3. In the similar case of *In re Adoption of M. A. R.*, 229 P.3d 545 (Okla. App. 2009), the appellate court found that over the relevant period of time, F had either substantially complied with the child support order or that he had not willfully failed to do so. The appellate court was not persuaded by M's argument that by becoming incarcerated, F "intentionally incapaciated himself" to avoid paying support. Consequently, the stepparent adoption could not go forward.
4. X and Y will argue that as the legal parents of C, they have the obligation and prerogative to act in C's best interest, and a court would determine that X and Y are in the best position to know and understand C's needs. Especially in situations where there is no statute authorizing ongoing contact or a written agreement to that effect, P will not be able to enforce the oral agreement.
5. This example is based on the case of *State ex rel. C. S.*, 49 So. 3d 38 (La. App. 2010), where the appellate court found for the father. The appellate court deemed it significant that the consent judgment providing for visitation was "entered into simultaneously with the termination of his parental rights and prior to the adoption. . . ." The appellate court consequently ordered that the terms of the consent judgment be enforced.

PROCEDURES

17.12. Filing a Petition

In general, a petition for adoption is filed once consent is obtained from the child's natural parent or parents, or the adoption agency handling the matter. After a petition is filed, in most jurisdictions, the child is placed with the adoptive parents on a probationary basis. If the background checks, home study, and probationary period are satisfactory, a hearing is held in which the judge reviews the potential adoptive parents' qualifications. When the adoption is approved, a permanent decree of adoption is filed.

17.13. Investigating Prospective Parents

In most cases, a home study is conducted to determine the suitability of the potential adoptive parents' home. The adoptive parents' background is investigated, including a criminal background check. The purpose of the criminal records check is to safeguard the well-being of foster and adoptive children by ensuring that persons seeking to care for or adopt a foster child have not been arrested for or convicted of criminal charges that would place the child at risk. *See In re Adoption of Paul Y.*, 696 N.Y.S.2d 796 (N.Y. Fam. Ct. 1999).

17.14. Sealing Adoption Records

Since the 1940s, states have sealed adoption records from the public due to the stigma historically associated with bearing a child out of wedlock and concern that the biological parents would interfere with the adoptive parents if their names became known. To ensure privacy after the adoption, statutes typically provided for the issuance of a new birth certificate, which changed the adoptee's surname to that of the adoptive parents. The original birth certificate was then sealed.

Access to the sealed birth record is controlled by state statutes, which determine if, when, and how the information may be gained. *See* Shannon Clark Kief, *Restricting Access to Judicial Records of Concluded Adoption Proceedings*, 103 A.L.R.5th 255 (2002). While some state statutes provide adoptees with the opportunity to obtain the names of their biological parents from official records, a state may distinguish between a minor and an adult seeking access to the records, or may require an intermediary before access is allowed. *See In re J. N. H.*, 209 P.3d 1221 (Colo. App. 2009); *Mills v. Atlantic City Dept. of Vital Statistics*, 372 A.2d 646 (N.J. Super. 1977). The statutes reflect an effort to balance the privacy concerns of the parties originally involved in the adoption with the desire or need for later knowledge, which is usually sought by the adopted child.

Some states will grant access when certain conditions are met. For example, some states will allow an adopted child to gain access to birth information when the biological family and the adoptive parents agree to allow access. In contrast, a handful of states grant adult adoptees full access to birth records. Elizabeth J. Samuels, *The Idea of Adoption: An Inquiry into the History of Adult Adoptee Access to Birth Records*, 53 Rutgers L. Rev. 367, 371-372 (2001).

In *In re Adoption of S. J. D.*, 641 N.W.2d 794 (Iowa 2002), the adoptee's reasons for wanting adoption records unsealed, which included satisfaction of curiosity, thanking biological parents for what they did, and obtaining medical information, did not constitute sufficient good cause to entitle records to be unsealed, even though adoptee had been treated for manic depression. The adoptee presented no medical evidence that linked his manic depression to his status as an adopted child, and the adoptee was viewed as expressing more of a curiosity over whether manic depression was hereditary than any particular medical reason for wanting to know.

In *In re Long*, 745 A.2d 673 (Pa. Super. 2000), the adoptee sought disclosure of the identity of her biological parents and their medical histories. In support of her petition, she submitted a letter from her physician, who stressed the importance of obtaining a complete family medical history to diagnose and treat her recent complicated medical issues. She also asserted that she suffered from depression, panic attacks, and similar psychological afflictions because of her lack of identity. The court said that an adoptee had the burden of showing by clear and convincing evidence that there is good cause for unsealing, given the overriding privacy concerns of the adoption process and this statute. It warned that unsealing adoption records is not to be lightly undertaken, and a court must consider the ramifications to those specifically affected by that unsealing, including the adoptive and biological parents and their families, as well as the impact on the integrity of the adoption process in general. Only if the adoptee's need for the information clearly outweighs the considerations behind the statute may the records be unsealed. *See In re Baby Boy SS*, 276 A.D.2d 226 (N.Y.A.D. 2001) (statute providing for unsealing of adoption records for the purpose of addressing serious physical or mental illness does not require that party applying to unseal records must be the adoptive child or adoptive parents).

EXAMPLE

Example

6. P, now an adult, was adopted as a child, and he seeks information concerning his biological mother's health history. P provided physician affidavits indicating that the health information would be "very helpful" and "should assist" in diagnosis and provision of medical care for P and his children. The state statute requires a showing of good cause and medical certification that the information sought is "required to address a serious physical or mental illness." The trial court denied P's petition, and P appeals. What is the likely result?

EXPLANATION

Explanation

6. On similar facts, the appellate court in *In re Timonthy AA.*, 72 A.D.3d 1390 (N.Y. App. 2010) affirmed the trial court and denied access to the medical records. The appellate court reasoned that P failed to make the required showing of good cause.

QUALIFICATIONS OF POTENTIAL ADOPTIVE PARENTS

17.15. Race of Adoptive Parent and the Multiethnic Placement Act (MEPA)

Race may be considered legitimately as one factor in making an ultimate adoption placement decision. *See, e.g., J.H.H. v. O'Hara*, 878 F.2d 240, 244 (8th Cir. 1989). Race may not, of course, be used in an automatic fashion to prescribe the appropriate adoptive placement. *See Palmore v. Sidoti*, 466 U.S. 429, 434 (1984). Race also may not be used as the sole basis for making long-term foster care placements or in determining who may adopt a child. *See In re Moorehead*, 600 N.E.2d 778, 786 (Ohio App. 1991) ("The difficulties inherent in interracial adoption justify consideration of race as a relevant factor in adoption, but do not justify race as being the determinative factor."). *See* David D. Meyer, *Palmore Comes of Age: The Place of Race in the Placement of Children*, 18 U. Fla. J.L. & Pub. Pol'y 183 (2007) (urging case-by-case determination of whether race should be a factor in placement).

The Multiethnic Placement Act (MEPA), as amended, sets forth as part of the requirements for federal funding that a state plan for child welfare services provides "for the diligent recruitment of potential foster and adoptive families that reflect the ethnic and racial diversity of children in the State for whom foster and adoptive homes are needed." 42 U.S.C. §622(b)(7) (2011). The Act was amended in 1996 and made it illegal for a state to delay or deny an adoptive placement solely on the basis of race. Congress declared that no state or other entity receiving federal funds could deny to any individual the opportunity to become an adoptive or a foster parent on the basis of race, color, or national origin. 42 U.S.C. §1996b (West 2006). Native American children were exempted from the MEPA; therefore, adoptions involving these children continue to be controlled by the Indian Child Welfare Act (ICWA). 42 U.S.C. §1996b(3) (West 2006). *See also* Ralph Richard Banks, *The Multiethnic Placement Act and the Troubling Persistence of Race Matching*, 38 Cap. U. L. Rev. 271 (2009).

17.16. Native American Status and the Indian Child Welfare Act (ICWA)

The Indian Child Welfare Act (ICWA), 25 U.S.C. §§1901 *et seq.*, governs the placement of Native American children for adoption. The ICWA contains procedural and substantive provisions that apply to Native American children. The ICWA protects the best interests of Indian children by promoting the survival and stability of Indian families and tribes. It is aimed at preventing wholesale separation of Indian children from their families through state court proceedings. The ICWA applies to any child who is either a member of an Indian tribe, or eligible to be a member, and the biological child of a member of a tribe.

State courts must follow the jurisdictional requirements of the ICWA, and an adoption decree entered in violation of the Act can be invalidated by the tribe or custodian. *See* 25 U.S.C. §1914 (West 2006); *Mississippi Band of Choctaw Indians v. Holyfield*, 490 U.S. 30 (1989). (Note that there is additional discussion regarding this Act in Chapter 24 of this book.)

17.17. Sexual Orientation of Adoptive Parents

The issue of whether gay and lesbian partners can adopt a child has been a matter of controversy. *See* Lynn D. Wardle, *The "Inner Lives" of Children in Lesbigay Adoption: Narratives and Other Concerns*, 18 St. Thomas L. Rev. 511, 513-515 (2005) (reviewing the status of the legality of lesbigay adoption).

Several states allow gay men and lesbians to adopt where it is in the best interests of the child. *See Arkansas Department of Human Services v. Cole*, 2011 Ark. 145 (Ark. 2011) (Act 1 held unconstitutional under Arkansas Constitution); *In re Adoption of M. A.*, 930 A.2d 1088 (Me. Sup. 2007) (unmarried same-sex couple could petition for adoption despite statute authorizing married couples to adopt); *In re Infant Girl W.*, 845 N.E.2d 229 (Ind. App. 2006) (adoption granted to same-sex couple); *Sharon S. v. Superior Court*, 2 Cal. Rptr. 3d 699 (Cal. 2003) (second-parent adoption).

However, some states have legislated otherwise. *See* Ann K. Wooster, *Adoption of Child by Same-Sex Partners*, 61 A.L.R. 6th 1 (2011); Miss. Code Ann. §93-17-3 (West 2012) (prohibiting adoption by couples of the same gender); Conn. Gen. Stat. Ann. §45a-726A (West 2012) (child-placing agency may consider sexual orientation of adoptive or foster parent).

Florida and Oklahoma, in particular, have been the settings for lengthy court battles concerning adoption by gay and lesbian persons. For example, a 1977 Florida statute prohibiting adoption by gay or lesbian petitioners survived a constitutional challenge on equal protection grounds. *Lofton v. Sec'y of Dept. of Children and Family Services*, 358 F.3d 804 (11th Cir. 2004). Neverthless, the statute was subsequently held by a Florida court to violate equal protection and infringe on the Adoption and Safe Families Act of 1997. *In re Adoption of Doe*, 2008 WL 5006172 (Fla. App. 2008); *Florida Dept. of Children and Families v. Adoption of X. X. G.*, 45 So. 3d 79 (2010) (constitutional violation). *See also Embry v. Ryan*, 2009 WL 1311599 (Fla. App. 2009) (holding that full faith and credit must be given to an out-of-state adoption judgment involving same-sex parents).

The Oklahoma legislature passed a statute denying recognition of final adoption orders from states permitting adoption by same-sex couples. However, the Tenth Circuit Court of Appeals held the statute unconstitutional because it violated the full faith and credit clause. *Finstuen v. Crutcher*, 496 F.3d 1139 (10th Cir. 2007). *But see Adar v. Smith*, 639 F.3d 146 (5th Cir. 2011) (distinguishing *Finstuen*).

17.18. Age of Adoptive Parents

The age of a potential adoptive parent may play a role in some adoption matters:

> In approximately six States (Kentucky, Louisiana, Montana, New Jersey, Tennessee, and Washington), prospective parents must be 18 to be eligible to adopt; three States (Colorado, Delaware, and Oklahoma) and American Samoa set the age at 21; and Georgia and Idaho specify age 25. A few States allow minors to adopt under certain circumstances, such as when the minor is the spouse of an adult adoptive parent.
>
> In approximately six States (California, Georgia, Nevada, New Jersey, South Dakota, and Utah) and the Northern Mariana Islands, the adopting parents must be at least 10 years older than the person to be adopted. In Puerto Rico, the adopting parent must be at least 14 years older; in Idaho, the parent must be at least 15 years older.

Child Welfare Information Gateway, *Who May Adopt, Be Adopted, or Place a Child for Adoption?* 2 (2012), *available at http://www.childwelfare.gov/systemwide/laws_policies/statutes/parties.pdf#Page=2&view=Fit* (last visited July 23, 2012).

For example, California requires that a prospective adoptive parent be at least ten years older than the child, unless the adoption is by a stepparent, sister, brother, aunt, uncle, or first cousin, and the court is satisfied that adoption by the parent and by the parent's spouse (if applicable) is in the best interests of the parties and is in the public interest regardless of the ages of the child and the prospective adoptive parent. *See* Cal. Fam. Code §8601, subd. (a) (West 2012).

Being elderly does not absolutely bar adoption. In *Adoption of Michelle T.*, 117 Cal. Rptr. 856 (Cal. App. 1975), the court granted a petition to proposed parents, who were 71 and 55 years of age, who had a stable marriage, were financially secure, in good health, and had cared for the child for nine months prior to filing the petition. *See also In re T. S.*, 7 Cal. Rptr. 3d 173 (Cal. App. 2003) (grandparents aged 58 and 61 allowed to adopt despite objections that they were too old and had not passed physical examinations).

EXAMPLE

Example

7. Assume that P and D are members of an Indian tribe living on a reservation, and they conceive a child. They do not want the child born on the reservation, and they prefer that the child be adopted and raised by non-Indians. The child is born off reservation, and within two weeks, the child is adopted

by non-Indian parents. The child is healthy and thriving in the adoptive home. When the tribe learns of the adoption four months later, it moves to vacate the adoption decree, claiming that it had exclusive subject matter jurisdiction under the ICWA. How will a court most likely rule on the tribe's motion?

EXPLANATION

Explanation

7. Because the child's domicile is that of its mother, who apparently lives on the reservation, and there is no evidence the child was abandoned, a court most likely will vacate the judgment. Because of past abuses, one of the purposes of ICWA is to prevent Indian children from being adopted by non-Indians without the oversight of the tribe.

WHO MUST CONSENT TO AN ADOPTION?

17.19. Pre-Birth Consent of Mother

All states mandate that consent to adoption be obtained from the natural mother after the birth of the child unless her rights are involuntarily terminated. Most states mandate a waiting period following the birth of a child during which the natural mother may revoke her consent to the adoption. *See Sims v. Adoption Alliance*, 922 S.W.2d 213 (Tex. App. 1996) (legislation that required that a biological mother must wait 48 hours after the birth of the child before signing an affidavit of relinquishment is constitutional). This is to ensure that the consent is a fully deliberative act on the part of the biological parent and to provide a legal framework within which a future adoption can be undertaken with reasonable guarantees of permanence and with humane regard for the rights of the child, the natural mother, and the adoptive parents.

Occasionally, consent is obtained prior to the birth of the child, and the birth mother later seeks to void the adoption on the grounds that the pre-birth consent is void *ab initio*. Some courts that have examined this issue have concluded that in the case of a pre-birth consent, such consent is ratified by a post-birth act that sufficiently manifests a present intention to give the child up for adoption. *See, e.g.*,

Matter of Pima City Juvenile Action, 806 P.2d 892, 895 (Ariz. 1990). These courts have said that the statutory notice prerequisites and the mandate that consent must be executed after the birth of the child are aimed at safeguarding the rights and interests of the biological parents in adoption proceedings, rather than affording some kind of protection for the public at large. Under these statutes, the rights of a parent may be surrendered by a formally executed document. However, the purpose of the statute is to protect the parent's rights, and if this is done before birth and is after birth observed, recognized, and honored by all parties, the purpose of the law is fulfilled by the parent's ratification. *See In re Adoption of Krueger*, 448 P.2d 82 (Ariz. 1968); *Anonymous v. Anonymous*, 530 N.Y.S.2d 613, 617 (N.Y. App. 1988); *In re Adoption of Long*, 56 So. 2d 450 (Fla. 1952).

17.20. Putative Father's Consent

As the climate for children born outside of marriage has changed over the past 50 years, so has the treatment of unmarried biological fathers. Recognition of the biological fathers has provided them in some cases with a voice in adoption proceedings. In the leading case, *Stanley v. Illinois*, 405 U.S. 645 (1973), Stanley, an unwed father, lived with his children and their mother intermittently for 18 years prior to her death. When she died, under state law, the children automatically became wards of the state, and Stanley was presumed unfit to care for them. The statutory presumption applied even though there had not been a hearing regarding his fitness or proof of neglect on his part. Stanley sought custody of the children, arguing that he should be afforded a hearing on his fitness. When the Illinois Supreme Court refused to provide him with a hearing, the United States Supreme Court granted review.

The Court held that a putative father's interest in the companionship, care, custody, and management of his children was greater than the state's interest in the children, so long as the putative father was a fit parent. It ordered that a hearing be held to determine whether Stanley was in fact fit to have custody of the children. The Court did not, however, articulate the scope of the protection afforded an unwed father, especially when the state interests were more substantial. (On remand, the trial court found that Stanley was not a fit parent.)

Five years after *Stanley*, the Supreme Court clarified the principles articulated in *Stanley v. Illinois* in *Quilloin v. Walcott*, 434 U.S. 246 (1977), *reh', denied*, 435 U.S. 918 (1978). The Court held that a putative father who had little or no contact with his child did not have a constitutional right to veto the child's adoption. A unanimous Court rested its decision on the putative father's failure to seek actual or legal custody of the child and the fact he had played no part in the child's daily supervision, education, protection, or care. *Quilloin v. Walcott* established the principle that when there is no significant commitment on the part of the biological father to a child born out of wedlock, the state is not required to find anything more than that the adoption, and denial of legitimization, are in the best interests of the child.

In a third ruling, *Caban v. Mohammed*, 441 U.S. 380 (1979), both the mother and the putative father had emotionally and financially supported children born to them out of wedlock. When their relationship broke down, the mother married another man and then initiated proceedings asking the court to allow her new husband to adopt the children. The putative father filed a cross-petition in which he asked to adopt the children. Under New York law, a putative father could not adopt his children without the mother's consent. However, the mother could legally adopt the children without first obtaining the putative father's consent. The trial court permitted the mother and her new husband to adopt the children over their putative father's objection, and the Supreme Court granted review.

The Court reversed, holding that the New York statute had inappropriately created a gender-based distinction between unwed mothers and unwed fathers, which bore no substantial relation to any legitimate state interest. Because the putative father had demonstrated a substantial interest in his children, the Court said he had certain constitutionally protected rights that the state could not take from him.

In another significant decision, *Lehr v. Robertson*, 463 U.S. 248 (1983), the Court considered whether the due process and equal protection clauses of the Fourteenth Amendment provided a putative father with the right to notice and an opportunity to be heard before a child is adopted, although he had not established a substantial relationship with his biological child born outside of marriage. Lehr had never lived with his child or its mother, had never registered with the state putative-father registry as the child's father, and had failed to provide any financial support for the child following birth. When the child was eight months old, the mother married, and her husband adopted the child. The Court rejected Lehr's claim that he had a constitutional right to notice and a hearing before adoption. The Court reasoned that his rights had not been violated because he had failed to establish a substantial relationship with the child. The "mere existence of a biological link," wrote the court "does not merit equivalent constitutional protection."

The issue of consent by putative fathers remains a difficult one for courts seeking to balance the interests of the child, the adoptive parents, the putative father, and the mother. *See In re Adoption of Ethan S.*, 85 A.D.3d 1599 (N.Y. App. 2011) (father had no right to consent); *John Paul B. v. Dominica B.*, 909 N.Y.S.2d 753 (N.Y. App. 2010) (despite concealment of pregnancy putative father did not do all that he could to protect parental interest so his consent was not required); *Helen G. v. Mark J. H.*, 175 P.3d 914 (N.M. 2007) (consent was not required as an "acknowledged father" where putative father knew of pregnancy and did not register or file a timely paternity action); *In re Pedro Jason William M.*, 847 N.Y.S.2d 17 (N.Y.A.D. 2007) (putative father who did not provide financial support, visit monthly, or communicate regularly "never acquired a constitutionally protected interest in his children"); *In re Adoption of Arthur M.*, 57 Cal. Rptr. 3d (Cal. App. 2007) (putative father's consent not required when "he did not show that he promptly came forward and demonstrated as full a commitment to his parental responsibilities as the biological mother allowed and the circumstances permitted within a short time after he learned or reasonably should have learned that the biological mother was pregnant with his child"). *But see In re Adoption of Corbin J.*, 775 N.W.2d 404 (Neb. 2009) (consent required where putative father had "established a familial relationship"); *In re Heart Share Human Services of New York*, 906 N.Y.S.2d 472 (N.Y. Fam. 2010) (attained status as a "consent father"); and *In re Vanessa Ann G.-L.*, 856 N.Y.S.2d 657 (N.Y.A.D. 2008) (consent was required where father established paternity and paid child support).

17.21. Putative Father Consents by Failing to Use Adoption Registry

Some states have created a statutory adoption registry for the purpose of determining the identity and location of a putative father of a minor child who is, or who is expected to be, the subject of an adoption. The purpose of the registry is to provide notice to a putative father that a petition for adoption has been filed. States have adopted strict provisions regarding the registry. Some require that the putative fathers register within 30 days after the child's birth or the date the adoption petition is filed, whichever occurs later. If a father fails to do so, he is not entitled to notice of the child's adoption. *See* Child Welfare Information Gateway, *The Rights of Unmarried Fathers*, 3 (2010) *available at* http://www.childwelfare.gov/systemwide/laws_policies/statutes/putative.pdf#Page=1&view=Fit (last visited July 23, 2012) (24 states have paternity registries).

Implied consent. A putative father's failure to register not only waives his right to notice of the adoption but also irrevocably implies his consent. *See, e.g., In re Adoption of A. A. T.*, 196 P.3d 1180 (Kan. 2008); *In re J. D. C.*, 751 N.E.2d 747 (Ind. App. 2001) *Heart of Adoptions, Inc. v. J. A.*, 963 So. 2d 189 (Fla. 2007). Courts have held that a putative father was not entitled to notice of an adoption petition and that his consent was irrevocably implied when the biological mother did not disclose his identity or address and he failed to register with the putative father's registry until six months after the adoption petition was filed. *In re Paternity of Baby Doe*, 734 N.E.2d 281 (Ind. App. 2000). *See Robert O. v. Russell K.*, 604 N.E.2d 99 (N.Y. App. 1992) (putative father's notice or consent was not needed for the adoption when he failed to avail himself of the methods to qualify for notice until some ten months after the adoption became final); *Heidbreder v. Carton*, 645 N.W.2d 355 (Minn. 2002), *cert. denied*, 537 U.S. 1046 (2002) (requirement that putative father not otherwise entitled to notice of an adoption petition must register with the Minnesota Fathers' Adoption Registry no later than 30 days after birth of child to assert a claim to a child who is the subject of an adoption petition is not a statute of limitations that can be tolled by fraudulent concealment); *Petition of K. J. R.*, 687 N.E.2d 113 (Ill. App. 1997) (birth mother's misrepresentation that another man was child's father did not excuse putative father's failure to register, and provision of Adoption Act that operated to deprive putative father of right to proceed with parentage petition did not deprive him of equal protection of the laws or due process); *M. V. S. v. V. M. D.* 776 So. 2d 142 (Ala. Civ. App. 1999) (requirements and procedures of Putative Father Registry Act to establish parental rights did not violate due process or equal protection).

These statutes and court decisions reflect a strong interest in providing stable homes for children early in their lives and a belief that permanent placement of children with adoptive families is of the utmost importance. If a father fails to register within the specified amount of time allowed under the statute, the state's obligation to provide the child with a permanent, capable, and loving family becomes paramount.

UPA exceptions. Under the Uniform Parentage Act (UPA), discussed in Chapter 16, failure to register can result in termination of parental rights without notice if the child is under one year of age at the time of termination. UPA §404. An exception is made in situations where there is a presumed, acknowledged, or adjudicated father. UPA §402(b).

17.22. Minor Child's Consent

In some jurisdictions, the consent of a child over the age of 12 to the adoption is necessary. For example, in the case of *In re Adoption of J. E. H.*, 859 N.E.2d 388 (Ind. App. 2006), the trial court "lacked authority" to allow a stepmother to adopt a 14-year-old without his written consent.

17.23. Adults Adopting Adults

State policy with respect to adoption of adults varies considerably. The trend, however, is to allow adult adoption under limited circumstances. For example, in *In re Trust Created by Nixon*, 763 N.W.2d 404 (Neb. 2009), a California court's decree granting a trust beneficiary's petition to adopt an adult was not contrary to the public policy of Nebraska and was entitled to recognition, even though the adoption would not have been allowed under Nebraska statutes. In *In re Adoption of Holland*, 965 So. 2d 1213 (Fla. App. 2007), the court allowed a grandfather to adopt his adult grandson to make the grandson eligible for financial aid available to the children of disabled veterans. However, in *In re P. B. for Adoption of L. C.*, 920 A.2d 155 (N.J. Super. 2006), the petition of an adult couple to adopt a 52-year-old woman who resided with them was denied because the woman was not more than ten years younger than the proposed adoptive couple, and there was no "pre-existing parent-child relationship."

About half the states allow adoption irrespective of the age of the adoptee and others permit adoption of adults under certain conditions. Child Welfare Information Gateway, *Who May Adopt, Be Adopted, or Place a Child for Adoption?* 3-4 (2012) *available at* http://www.childwelfare.gov/systemwide/laws_policies/statutes/parties.pdf#Page=2&view=Fit (last visited July 23, 2012) (disabled adults, established parental relationship, age difference between adoptive parent and adult to be adopted).

EXAMPLES

Examples

8. P arranged with an adoption agency to place her child for adoption as soon as the child was born. The state statute requires that a birth mother's consent be obtained not sooner than 48 hours after the birth of a child. However, P signed adoption consent forms two weeks before the child was born, and once again on the day after the child was born. When the child is one month old, P changes her mind about the adoption and brings an action to void her consent. The adoptive parents argue that P waived the 48-hour requirement by giving consent both before and after the birth of the child. How will a court most likely rule?

9. P gave birth to a child, and two days after the birth, she consented in writing to the adoption of the child. Within a week, she attempted to revoke her consent to relinquish the child for adoption on the ground that it was involuntary. Prior to the birth of the child, P's boyfriend was killed in a car accident, her father died from cancer, and she lost her job and was unemployed. The child was the result of a rape. While in the hospital after the child's birth, a psychological evaluation was performed on the mother, and she was diagnosed with "significant adjustment disorder"; follow-up therapy, without medication, was recommended. P expressed confusion over the significance of the forms that she had signed. Would a court consider P's consent to be involuntary under these circumstances?

10. F and M dated while in college in Missouri and M became pregnant. M told F about the pregnancy and her plan to leave the state and give the child up for adoption. She refused to disclose her destination. F consulted an attorney and subsequently registered with the Missouri Putative Father Registry. M moved to Texas and had some communication with F but did not inform him of her location. An attorney representing a Texas adoption agency mailed F relinquishment of parental rights documents, but F refused to sign them, and he filed a parentage action and also registered with the Illinois and Texas Putative Father Registries. M moved to Arkansas and did not inform F of her relocation. M gave birth to the baby in Arkansas, and F filed a paternity action there and

registered with the Arkansas Putative Father Registry. The relevant Arkansas statute provides that consent is required in a circumstance like this one only if a putative father "proves a significant custodial, personal, or financial relationship existed with the minor before the petition for adoption is filed." Can F overturn the adoption?

11. F was 19 and M was 15 when she became pregnant. When F learned of the pregnancy he texted M saying "Go hay an abortion or sumthn get a life stop txtn me . . ." M gave birth to the baby and the baby was adopted without requiring the consent of F. F offered M $100 during the pregnancy (which she did not accept), and he attempted to see M and the baby shortly after birth but he was not admitted. The relevant state statute provides that consent is required if "the father paid a fair and reasonable sum, based on the father's financial ability, for the support of the child or for the expenses incurred in connection with the mother's pregancy or with the birth of the child, including, but not limited to, medical, hospital, and nursing expenses." F lived with his parents and worked repossessing cars making about $9 per hour. Will F be successful in overturning the adoption?

12. Assume that P and D have a casual sexual relationship, and P becomes pregnant and gives birth. D, the biological father, does not know of P's pregnancy or the birth of the child until the child is six months old and is in the process of being adopted. D resides in a jurisdiction with an adoption registry requiring that registration take place within 30 days of the birth of the child, but D has no idea what an adoption registry is or how to go about registering. He consequently fails to do so. How will a court most likely treat D's effort to block the adoption?

EXPLANATIONS

Explanations

8. Because of the intimate nature of the proceeding, and the unambiguous language in the statute, it is likely that a court will consider the consent invalid. This is particularly likely if a statute provides for a waiting period. In some jurisdictions, a mother may recover a child legally placed for adoption if there has not been an adoption decree entered, if she is fit, and if returning the child to the mother is in the child's best interests. *See also In re Adoption of* N.J.G., 891 N.E.2d 60 (Ind. App. 2008) (pre-birth consent void under statute providing that the "mother may not execute a consent to adoption before the birth of the child").

9. This fact situation is similar to that found in *McCann v. Doe*, 660 S.E.2d 500 (S.C. 2008), where the court considered whether under the totality of the circumstances, the signing of the consent was involuntary or done under duress or coercion and whether withdrawal of consent would be in the best interests of the child. After weighing conflicting evidence, the court determined that the mother was "incapable of giving a voluntary consent" and that relinquishment would be in the best interests of the child.

10. F will argue that he had no realistic opportunity to establish a significant relationship with the child prior to the filing of the adoption petition when the baby was nine days old. More specificially, F will argue that M thwarted his efforts to create a custodial, personal, or financial relationship with the child by keeping her location secret. In the similar case of *In re Adoption of Baby Boy B.*, 2012 Ark. 92 (Ark 2012), the Arkansas Supreme Court believed that F had done all he could to protect his paternal rights and held that the trial court erred in moving forward with the adoption without his consent. (Note that F's constitutional claim was not preserved for appeal, and the Arkansas Supreme Court did not rule on it.)

11. This example is based on the case of *Roe v. Reeves*, 708 S.E.2d 778 (S.C. 2011) where the Supreme Court of South Carolina ruled that the actions of F were insufficient efforts to assume parental responsibility. As the court explained, "a father's attempts to assert his parental rights are insufficient to protect his relationship with the minor child 'unless accompained by a *prompt, good-faith effort* to assume responsibility for either a financial contribution to the child's welfare or assitance in paying for the birth mother's pregnancy or childbirth expenses.' "

12. D most likely will not succeed. The adoption registry statute protects those putative fathers who have taken certain specified actions to preserve their rights. If the putative father has not so acted within the time limits provided by statute, the child's right to a stable environment and finality becomes paramount, and the putative father loses all right to intervene in adoption proceedings or to vacate a finalized adoption order. *See Lehr v. Robertson*, 463 U.S. 248 (1983). D's failure to register may well bar him from preventing the adoption. *See In re J. D. C.*, 751 N.E.2d 747 (Ind. App. 2001) (failure to register obviated need for notice).

UNIFORM ACTS

17.24. Uniform Adoption Act of 1994

The Uniform Adoption Act of 1994 was promulgated by the National Conference of Commissioners on Uniform State Laws (NCCUSL) as an attempt to codify and make uniform the current legal practice regarding adoption. It has been adopted in Vermont, and a half-dozen other states have adopted some provisions of the proposed uniform act. *See* Uniform Law Commission, Legislative Fact Sheet—Adoption Act (1994), http://www.uniformlaws.org/LegislativeFactSheet.aspx?title=Adoption%20Act%20(1994) (last visited July 23, 2012).

CLAIMS

17.25. Fraud

States have historically recognized a cause of action for fraud in the adoption setting. For example, the Supreme Judicial Court of Massachusetts held that one may annul an adoption decree based on fraud, even after death. *Tucker v. Fisk*, 28 N.E. 1051 (Mass. 1891). The same court later held that if a person dominates his wife to such an extent that it amounts to "undue influence," and he thereby forces her to bring a petition for adoption of his son, he commits a "gross fraud" upon both her and the court. In such a case, the decree of adoption should be set aside. *Phillips v. Chase*, 89 N.E. 1049, 1051-1052 (Mass. 1909). More recently, in *In re Lisa Diane G.*, 537 A.2d 131 (R.I. 1988), a court held that it possessed the authority to decide whether to vacate an adoption order based upon a claim of fraud or misrepresentation. In *Allen v. Allen*, 330 P.2d 151 (Or. 1958), Oregon recognized fraud as a cause of action in adoption matters while holding that the evidence was insufficient to support a determination that a decree of adoption was void by reason of fraud. Minnesota has ruled that if a party can demonstrate that an adoption decree was fraudulently obtained, the party is entitled to relief. *In re Welfare of Alle*, 230 N.W.2d 574, 577 (Minn. 1975).

The elements of a cause of action for fraudulent misrepresentation require that one must show (1) a false statement of material fact, (2) known or believed to be false by the party making it, (3) intent to induce the other party to act, (4) action by the other party in reliance on the truth of the statement, and (5) damage to the other party resulting from such reliance. The party must be justified in his reliance; he must have a right to rely. *See, e.g.*, *Roe v. Catholic Charities of the Diocese of Springfield*, 588 N.E.2d 354 (Ill. 1992).

17.26. Negligent Misrepresentation

Some states recognize claims against adoption agencies for negligent misrepresentation. The tort is based on the theory that an adoption placement agency owes prospective adoptive parents a duty of reasonable care to disclose information pertinent to the adoption. Courts find such a duty partly in a state's adoption statutes and partly in the existence of a "special relationship" between the agency and the prospective parents. Even if a state statute does not provide for such an action, the special relationship between adoption placement agencies and adopting parents may support recognition of a cause of action in tort. The purposes are not only to enable adoptive parents to obtain timely and appropriate medical care for the child, but also to enable them to make an intelligent and informed adoption decision. *See, e.g., Price v. State*, 57 P.3d 639 (Wash. App. 2002). The duty that emanates from the relationship of the potential adoptive parents and the agency is to exercise reasonable care in disclosing information pertinent to the adoption, thus enabling the adoptive parents to obtain timely and appropriate medical care for the child and make an intelligent and informed adoption decision. *See also Young v. Van Duyne*, 92 P.3d 1269 (N.M. App. 2004) (adoptive father whose wife was beaten to death by adoptive son could maintain wrongful death claim against agency regarding pre-adoption knowledge and conduct).

EXAMPLE

Example

13. Assume that P adopted a baby girl from Russia who was discovered to be carrying the hepatitis C virus when examined by a pediatrician in the United States. P adopted the child X in 1993. The contract between P and the adoption center, D, reads as follows: "P understands that D cannot guarantee the health of the child, but will make best efforts to ensure that the child's health is known to the parent(s) prior to placement. However, P understand[s] that it is very difficult to know all of the health issues involved."

    In addition to this contract language, P was made aware that even though D knew that her highest priority was adoption of a healthy baby, no baby available for adoption would have a clean medical record because Russian law at that time prohibited foreign adoption of healthy Russian babies. Further, Russian orphanages rarely supplied prospective foreign parents with complete medical histories of children available for adoption. A photograph and a medical excerpt (three pages long when translated into English) were the only documentation made available to P or D, as was the standard practice in Russian adoptions at the time.

The medical excerpt referenced one hospitalization for a respiratory infection, negative results on blood tests for HIV and hepatitis B, and some developmental delays, and a diagnosis that loosely translated as "encephalopathy."

When X was examined following the adoption in the United States, it was discovered that she contracted hepatitis C from blood transfusions when hospitalized in Russia, and also was suffering from fetal alcohol syndrome/fetal alcohol effect (FAS/FAE). P sued D for breach of contract, wrongful adoption/malpractice, and related counts. Given these facts, which are not in dispute, D moved for summary judgment. How will a court most likely rule?

EXPLANATION

Explanation

13. Because D was not aware of X's hepatitis C status or of her transfusions prior to her diagnosis in the United States, the motion for summary judgment most likely will be granted. It is undisputed that none of the defendants withheld any medical information made available to them. P also adopted X knowingly, in the face of incomplete information.

CHAPTER 18

Assisted Reproduction — History, Restrictions, and Requirements

18.1. Introduction — History

This chapter explores the controversial legal issues that have emerged in the last several years because of revolutionary biotechnological advances in assisted human reproduction. It also examines issues where only sperm are handled, which may involve intrauterine or artificial insemination. Among the legal issues considered are those related to identifying a child's father in third-party artificial insemination donor disputes, determining who is the legal parent in surrogate disputes, and resolving who owns frozen embryos when, for example, parties to a divorce both assert ownership of them. Overall, the chapter focuses on society's legal efforts to define the word *family* in the context of these scientific developments.

In general, when normal impregnation, for whatever reason, is undesirable or cannot be achieved, several alternative reproduction methods may result in parenthood. For example, a wife could bear a child conceived from a third-party donor's egg and her husband's sperm; or a surrogate could carry a child to birth that was implanted in her after the child was scientifically conceived using the wife's egg and her husband's sperm. A child also could be conceived using a husband's sperm and a surrogate's egg. Finally, a surrogate or a wife could carry a child to term who was conceived using a donated third-party egg and the husband's sperm.

Eighteenth-century. The use of artificial insemination of a wife by a husband (AIH) is said to have begun in the late eighteenth century. *See*

Susan Frelich Appleton & D. Kelly Weisberg, *Adoption and Assisted Reproduction: Families Under Construction*, 239 (Wolters Kluwer 2009). This procedure has engendered little legal difficulty because the child is the genetic issue of the donor and the donor's wife.

Third party donor — adultery. The process of a third-party donating semen (AID) to impregnate a woman probably arose during the late nineteenth century. *Ibid.* Unlike the situation where a wife was artificially inseminated with her husband's sperm, this process raised legal issues. For example, very early in its history, artificial insemination where a sperm came from a donor who was not the wife's husband was characterized by some as "adultery." *See Doornboos v. Doornboos*, No. 545.14981 (Ill. Super. 1954) (woman guilty of adultery although husband consented to her AID); *Orford v. Orford*, 49 O.L.R. 15, 20 (Ontario 1921) (denying alimony because the wife had committed adultery by AID), cited in Bridget R. Penick, Note, *Give the Child a Legal Father: A Plea for Iowa to Adopt a Statute Regulating Artificial Insemination by Anonymous Donor*, 83 Iowa L. Rev. 633, n.39 (March 1998); Gaia Bernstein, *The Socio-Legal Acceptance of New Technologies: A Close Look at Artificial Insemination*, 77 Wash. L. Rev. 1035 1058-1059 (October 2002). The court in *Orford v. Orford*, *supra*, reasoned that the essence of adultery was not in the moral turpitude of the act of sexual intercourse but in the voluntary surrender to another person of one's reproductive powers. *Ibid.*

This area of the law increased in complexity with the introduction of in vitro fertilization (IVF). The first "test-tube" baby was Louise Brown, born in July 1978 in Oldham, England. IVF involves removing a ripe egg from a woman's body and combining that egg with sperm in a petri dish, by a process called *laparoscopy* or *aspiration*. If fertilization occurs, the womb is implanted with the resulting embryo.

DEFINITIONS

18.2. ART AID-AIH IVF, Defined and Explained

How "ART" is used in this chapter. When the phrase *assisted reproductive technology (ART)* is used in this chapter, it is intended to include all fertility treatments in which both eggs and sperm are handled. "In general, ART procedures involve surgically removing eggs from a woman's ovaries, combining them with sperm in the laboratory, and returning them to the woman's body or donating them to another woman. They do NOT include treatments in which only sperm are handled (i.e., intrauterine — or artificial — insemination) or procedures in which a woman takes medicine only to stimulate egg production without the intention of having eggs retrieved." Centers for Disease Control and Prevention, Assisted Reproductive Technology (CDC), http://www.cdc.gov/art/ (last visited July 2012).

Artificial insemination — Homologous insemination defined. There are two types of artificial insemination. *Homologous insemination* is the process by which a wife is artificially impregnated with the semen of her husband (AIH). AIH creates no legal problems because the child born as a result of AIH is considered the natural child of the husband and wife. *See generally In re Baby Doe*, 353 S.E.2d 877, 878 (S.C. 1987) (defining artificial insemination terms).

Artificial insemination — Heterologous insemination defined. *Heterologous insemination* is the artificial insemination of a wife by the semen of a third-party donor (AID). *Ibid.* This procedure may be carried out with the consent of the husband or nonconsensual where the recipient is unmarried.

This process (AID) is apparently increasingly being used in the United States. One reason given to explain the increase is the lack of availability of adoptive children. *See In re Adoption of Anonymous*, 345 N.Y.S.2d 430, 431 (N.Y. Surr. 1973). Another reason given is a discovery that a husband's family has a history of hereditary disease, or RH incompatibility may lead to repeated stillbirths.

AID allows recipients to obtain semen from a variety of sources, including sperm banks. These "banks" often will provide profiles that summarize each donor's medical and family history, and include his short personal narrative. Some of these banks also will provide staff impressions of donors free of charge. *See, e.g.*, The Sperm Bank of California, http://www.thespermbankofca.org/ (last visited July 2012).

Self-insemination. Note that women can inseminate themselves with anonymous sperm, without medical assistance. It is thought that by using this process, a woman places custody of a child beyond the reach of government regulation and does not require that she share parental rights. Also note *Jhordan C. v. Mary K.*, 224 Cal. Rptr. 530 (Cal. App. 1986). In this case, although the mother had self-inseminated, the court declared that the sperm donor was the legal father of the child by construing California's law precluding recognition of a sperm donor as a putative father as applying only when a physician performs the procedure or otherwise provides the semen.

IVF, defined and explained. IVF is the fertilization of a human egg outside the human body in a laboratory. Children conceived in this way are often referred to as "test tube babies," because their actual conception may have occurred in a Petri dish. A majority of states do not have gestational surrogacy statutes.

The IVF procedure requires a woman to undergo a series of hormonal injections to stimulate the production of mature oocytes (egg cells or ova). The medication causes the ovaries to release multiple egg cells during a menstrual cycle rather than the single egg normally produced. The egg cells are retrieved from the woman's body and examined by a physician who evaluates their quality for fertilization. Egg cells ready for insemination are then combined with a sperm sample and allowed to incubate for approximately 12 to 18 hours. Successful fertilization results in a zygote that develops into a four- to eight-cell pre-embryo. At that stage, the pre-embryos are either returned to the woman's uterus for implantation or cryopreserved at a temperature of −196°C and stored for possible future use. *See generally Kass v. Kass*, 673 N.Y.S.2d 350 (N.Y. 1998) (describing this procedure).

In IVF programs, the embryo typically will be transferred to a uterus when it reaches the four, six-, or eight-cell stage, some 48 to 72 hours after conception. It is also at this stage that the embryo would be cryopreserved for later use. It is estimated that about one in ten pre-embryos initiates a successful pregnancy. Note that when cryopreservation is used, there is an estimated 70 percent rate of viability after having been frozen.

Gestational surrogacy. The phrase *gestational surrogacy* is used to describe the process in which one woman agrees to be impregnated with an embryo formed from another woman's fertilized egg. Among the technologies related to gestational surrogacy are IVF, embryo and gamete freezing and storage, gamete intra-fallopian transfer, and embryo transplantation. Gestational surrogacy is the result of two of these techniques: IVF and embryo transplantation.

Impact of ART in America. ART began in the United States around 1981. Women became pregnant, most commonly, through the transfer of fertilized human eggs into a woman's uterus (IVF). According to the Centers for Disease Control (CDC)'s 2010 *Preliminary Artificial Reproductive Technology Success Rates* report, 154,417 ART cycles were performed at 443 reporting clinics in the United States during 2010, resulting in 47,102 live births (deliveries of one or more living infants) and 61,561 infants. The CDC reports that the use of ART is still relatively rare compared to the potential demand; however, its use by women in America has doubled over the past decade. Today, over 1 percent of all infants born in the U.S. every year are conceived using ART. *Ibid.*

Oversight. There remains very little oversight or uniform regulation of ART in the United States. Jennifer L. Rosato, *The Children of ART (Assisted Reproduction Technology): Should the Law Protect Them from Harm?* 207 PLI/Crim 325, 340 (2006) ("There are a number of reasons to doubt whether the right to procreate extends far enough to encompass ART decisions.").

MODEL ACTS

18.3. Uniform Parentage Act (UPA)

The first version of the Uniform Parentage Act (UPA) was announced by the National Conference of Commissioners on Uniform State Laws (NCCUSL) in 1973. A second version emerged in 2000. The 2000 version was then revised in 2002. Each version has some sections that differ quite markedly from a previous rendition.

The UPA, as revised by the NCCUSL in 2002, has provisions that suggest how state legislatures should approach the issue of artificial insemination. *See* UPA, http://www.law.upenn.edu/bll/archives/ulc/upa/final2002.htm (last visited July 2012). For example, where artificial insemination is the process used to achieve pregnancy, the UPA recognizes the child's father as a

> man who provides sperm for, or consents to, assisted reproduction by a woman as provided in Section 704 with the intent to be the parent of her child, is a parent of the resulting child.

Section 703, UPA (2002).

The commentary to this section states that the provision reflects concern for the best interests of non-marital as well as marital children of assisted reproduction.

Section 704(a) of the UPA suggests that a process be incorporated into state law that will record the consent on the part of a man to the process. It states that a man, whether married or unmarried, who intends to be a parent of a child must consent in a record to all forms of assisted reproduction. It further provides that a man's failure to consent to assisted reproduction does not preclude his recognition as father, if the man and woman during the first two years of the child's life reside in the same household with the child and openly hold the child as their own.

UPA §§702, 704 (2000, amended 2002), 9B U.L.A. 355-356 (2001). The commentary to §702 states that:

> [I]f a married woman bears a child of assisted reproduction using a donor's sperm, the donor will not be the father in any event. Her husband will be the father unless and until the husband's lack of consent to the assisted reproduction is proven within two years of his learning of the birth, see §05, *infra*. This provides certainty of non-parentage for prospective donors.

UPA cmt. §702 (2002).

18.4. ABA Model Act Governing Assisted Reproductive Technology

The American Bar Association (ABA) approved a Model Act on Assisted Reproductive Technology in February 2008. *See* http://apps.americanbar.org/family/committees/artmodelact.pdf. *See* also Charles P. Kindregan, Jr., *Clarifyng the Law of ART: The New American Bar Association Model Act Governing Assisted Reproductive Technology*, http://claradoc.gpa.free.fr/doc/129.pdf, 42 Fam. L.Q. 203 (Summer 2008) (discussing the history of the Act and its provisions). The ABA Act is intended to provide model provisions that can be considered in whole or in part by legislative bodies in the states and territories. *Ibid.*

The Act encourages "intended parents" to enter into a written agreement prior to embryo creation and include the following in the agreement: (1) the intended use of the embryos; (2) disposition of embryos in the event of divorce, death, or incapacity; and (3) define and agree when the embryos will be deemed "abandoned." The Model Act clarifies which intended parent may control the embryos in the event of divorce, illness, or death. The Act suggests a mechanism to withdraw consent to the terms of the preembryo agreement to dispose of or transfer the embryos.

The Act includes a suggested default provision regarding abandonment of the frozen embryos, which is deemed to occur five years after the embryos are created. Where the parties cannot agree, the storage facility must obtain an order issued by a court of competent jurisdiction relating to disposition of the embryos. *See generally* Theresa M. Erickson & Megan T. Erickson, *What Happens to Embryos When a Marriage Dissolves? Embryo Disposition and Divorce*, 35 Wm. Mitchell L. Rev. 469, 470 (2009) ("It is through the debate of constitutional rights versus contract law, the debate over personhood versus property issues, and the use of the denial of the writ of certiorari in the case of *Roman v. Roman* that we can finally develop an enhanced legal landscape upon which the ART community and its patients can turn to without worrying about the legal implications of their actions in a world where having children is often their most important goal and desire.").

18.5. Uniform Putative and Unknown Fathers Act; Uniform Status of Children of Assisted Conception Act

Another model act drafted by the NCCUSL, the Uniform Putative and Unknown Fathers Act (UPUFA) §2(a), 9B U.L.A. 80 (1996) (approved 1988), is consistent with the UPA in that it excludes the semen donor in cases of artificial insemination from being a putative father. UPUFA https://

www.law.upenn.edu/library/archives/ulc/fnact99/upufa88.htm (last visited July 2012).

The Uniform Status of Children of Assisted Conception Act (USCACA) §4(a), 9B U.L.A. 191 (1966) (approved 1988), provides that a semen donor of a child conceived through assisted conception does not have parental status. USCACA, https://www.law.upenn.edu/library/archives/ulc/fnact99/uscaca88.htm (last visited July 2012). Because some of the commissioners believed that such agreements should be prohibited, while others believed that such agreements should be allowed, but regulated, USCACA offered two alternatives on the subject: either regulate such activities through a judicial review process or void such contracts. The only two states to enact USCACA selected opposite options: Virginia chose to regulate such agreements, while North Dakota opted to void them. Alterative "A" allows surrogacy contracts if they have received court approval. Alternative "B" states that surrogacy contracts are invalid and makes the surrogate parent the mother and her husband the father.

STATE AID AND AIH ISSUES

18.6. Typical State Statutory Provisions

The most commonly used alternative method of reproduction to achieve parenthood is artificial insemination, defined as the process where the sperm of a man is used to impregnate the egg of a woman artificially. *See generally* Browne Lewis, *Two Fathers, One Dad: Allocating the Paternal Obligations Between the Men Involved in the Artificial Insemination Process*, 13 Lewis & Clark L. Rev. 949, 956 (Winter 2009) ("the oldest and most commonly used form of assisted reproduction").

Because of its prevalence, most states have legislation directed at settling legal issues created by the process. The legislation typically eliminates claims of adultery and illegitimacy, while protecting the sperm donor from future child support obligations. The legislation usually provides that the husband of a woman who bears a child with donated sperm is automatically the legal father.

Purposes. Artificial insemination legislation serves several purposes: First, it allows married couples to have children, even though the husband is infertile, impotent, or ill. Second, it allows an unmarried woman to conceive and bear a child without sexual intercourse. Third, it resolves disputes about parental rights and responsibilities; that is, the mother's husband, if he consents, is the father of the child, and an unmarried mother is freed of any claims by the donor of parental rights. Fourth, it encourages men to donate semen while protecting them against claims by the mother or the child. *See, e.g., McIntyre v. Crouch*, 780 P.2d 239, 243 (Or. App. 1989) (statute barring donor of semen used in artificial insemination process from having rights or obligations with respect to resulting child applied even if, as alleged by donor, mother had agreed with him before he gave his semen that he would have such rights and responsibilities, and he acted in reliance on that agreement). Finally, it legitimizes the child that is born and gives it rights against the mother's husband if he consents to the insemination.

State-licensed physician requirement. Legislation often requires that the artificial insemination occur under the supervision of a licensed physician. For example, an Oregon statute states that

> Only physicians licensed under ORS chapter 677 and persons under their supervision may select artificial insemination donors and perform artificial insemination.

Or. Rev. Stat. §677.360 (2012).

The courts have indicated some reluctance to enforce this provision strictly. For example, in *In re Marriage of A.C.H. and D.R.H.*, 210 P.3d 929 (Or. App. 2009), the court required a husband to pay child support to a child born of AID, even though the procedure did not comply with Oregon's statute requiring that only physicians and persons under their supervision may select artificial insemination donors and perform artificial insemination. The court relied on a second related statute, O.R.S. §109.243, that established the parent-child relationship without following the procedure in O.R.S. §655.360 and did not require a writing. However, a few weeks after *A.C.H.* was handed down, the Court of Appeals in *Shineovich and Kemp*, 214 P.3d 29 (2009), held that O.R.S. §109.243 was unconstitutional. This apparently leaves O.R.S. §677.360 as a mandate in that state.

Arkansas and Oregon laws are similar. Arkansas law states that

> (a) Artificial insemination of a woman shall only be performed under the supervision of a physician licensed under the Arkansas Medical Practices Act, §17-95-201 et seq., §17-95-301 et seq., and §17-95-401 et seq.

Ark. Code Ann. §9-10-202 (2012).

Minnesota law contains a comprehensive provision regarding artificial insemination. Among other matters, it mandates the use of a licensed physician in the process. It reads that

> Subdivision 1. Husband treated as biological father. If, under the supervision of a licensed physician and with the consent of her husband, a wife is inseminated

> artificially with semen donated by a man not her husband, the husband is treated in law as if he were the biological father of a child thereby conceived. The husband's consent must be in writing and signed by him and his wife. The consent must be retained by the physician for at least four years after the confirmation of a pregnancy that occurs during the process of artificial insemination.
>
> All papers and records pertaining to the insemination, whether part of the permanent record of a court or of a file held by the supervising physician or elsewhere, are subject to inspection only upon an order of the court for good cause shown.
>
> Subd. 2. Donor not treated as biological father. The donor of semen provided to a licensed physician for use in artificial insemination of a married woman other than the donor's wife is treated in law as if he were not the biological father of a child thereby conceived.

Minn. Stat. §257.56 (2012).

Consent and certification. State statutes usually require that a husband's consent be in writing and require the physicians involved to certify the father's signature, the date of the insemination, and then file the husband's consent with the appropriate governmental authorities, where it remains confidential.

Donor privacy. Donor privacy is usually protected by state statutory provisions declaring that all papers and records pertaining to the insemination, whether part of the permanent record of a court or of a file held by the supervising physician or elsewhere, are subject to inspection only upon an order of the court for good cause shown. Good cause for invading the privacy of the donor papers and records may exist where the health and welfare of a child or children is at issue. *See, e.g., Johnson v. Superior Court*, 80 Cal. App. 1050 (2000) ("insemination records, including a sperm donor's identity and related information contained in those records, may be disclosed under certain circumstances, and moreover, enforcement under all circumstances of such a confidentiality provision would conflict with State's compelling interest in the health and welfare of children"). In *Johnson*, the court held that a court may compel the donor's deposition and production of documents in order to discover information relevant to their action against the sperm bank for selling sperm that they alleged transmitted autosomal dominant polycystic kidney disease (ADPKD) to the child. *See generally* Kevin Hopkins, *Blood, Sweat, and Tears: Toward a New Paradigm for Protecting Donor Privacy*, 7 Va. J. Soc. Pol'y & L. 141 (Winter 2000).

18.7. Husband's Consent

As noted earlier, artificial insemination statutes may require the written consent of the wife's husband before he will be determined to be the father of a child born of this procedure and required to provide financial support should the relationship break down. However, most courts agree that the best interests of children and society are served by recognizing that parental responsibility may be imposed based upon conduct evincing actual consent to the artificial insemination procedure. For example, in *Gursky v. Gursky*, 242 N.Y.S.2d 406 (N.Y. Sup. 1963), the husband's declaration and conduct respecting the artificial insemination of his wife by means of a third-party donor, including the husband's written consent to the procedure, was viewed by the court as an implied promise on the husband's part to furnish support for any offspring resulting from the insemination.

Other courts have followed New York. *See, e.g., K.S. v. G.S.*, 440 A.2d 64, 68-69 (N.J. Super. Ch. 1981) (oral consent of the husband to the artificial insemination process was effective at the time pregnancy occurs unless he can establish by clear and convincing evidence that consent was revoked or rescinded). In *In re Marriage of L.M.S.*, 312 N.W.2d 853, 855 (Wis. App. 1981), a husband who was sterile was required to support a child born during his marriage where he had suggested to his wife that she become pregnant by another man and promised that he would acknowledge the child as his own. *See generally In re Baby Doe*, 353 S.E.2d 877 (S.C. 1987) (husband's consent to artificial insemination may be express or implied from conduct); Donald T. Kramer, *Legal Rights of Children*, §4:3. *Obligation to support children artificially conceived*, 1 Leg. Rts. Child. Rev. 2D §4:3 (2011); Wadlington, *Artificial Conception: The Challenge for Family Law*, 69 Va. L. Rev. 465 (1983).

Same-sex couples. Note that in *T. F. v. B. L.*, 813 N.E.2d 1244 (Mass. 2004), the court declined to enforce an implied agreement between an unmarried same-sex couple that both individuals would be responsible for and parents of a child conceived through artificial insemination. The court relied on the absence of legislation recognizing such an agreement. *Ibid.* The court explained that "[t]he Legislature has identified those persons who are liable as parents to support their children," and cited, inter alia, G.L. c. 46, §4B. *Ibid.* It summarized c. 46, §4B, as establishing that "if the spouse of a woman who undergoes artificial insemination consents to the procedure, that spouse is considered the legitimate parent of a resulting child." *Ibid.* Also note the court's view that, for purposes of the artificial insemination statute, expressed consent to the procedure is enough to confer parental status.

18.8. Application of Artificial Insemination Statutes to Same-Sex Couples?

The question of whether artificial insemination statutes apply to same-sex female couples may arise when they dissolve their relationship. For example, in *Shineovich and Kemp*, 214 P.3d 29 (Or. App. 2009), the petitioner, a lesbian, separated from her former same-sex domestic partner who had given birth to two children after being artificially inseminated twice, with petitioner's consent, during the course of their ten-year relationship. She sought to be named a legal parent of the children and filed an action for declaratory relief against her former partner, challenging the constitutionality of two Oregon statutes under which a married man is, by operation of law, deemed to be the legal parent of children born to his wife, but excludes application to same-sex couples.

The Oregon Supreme Court ruled that the statute, which established legal parentage in the husband of a woman who gives birth to a child conceived by artificial insemination, without regard to the biological relationship of the husband and the child, improperly discriminates on the basis of sexual orientation. It stated that the constitutional infirmity of the statute would be remedied by extending the privilege to the same-sex domestic partner of a woman who gives birth to a child conceived by artificial insemination.

California also recognizes a dual same-sex parental relationship to children. For example, that state's Supreme Court held in *Elisa B. v. Superior Court*, 33 Cal. Rptr. 3d 46 (Cal. 2005), that under that state's version of the UPA, a child may have two parents, both of whom are women. It ruled that a former partner in a lesbian relationship was obliged to pay child support where she had agreed to raise the children, supported the birth mother's artificial insemination using an anonymous donor, and received the resulting twin children into her home and held them out as her own.

18.9. Known Donors and Unmarried Recipients

The issue of whether known sperm donors are afforded the same protection from subsequent paternity claims as those afforded anonymous donors is generally answered in the negative. For example, a Colorado court, in addressing this issue, ruled that a state statute that extinguishes the parental rights of unknown donors of semen to any child conceived by artificial insemination did not necessarily apply to known semen donors and unmarried recipients who agree the donor will be treated as the father of the child. *In Interest of R.C.*, 775 P.2d 27 (Colo. 1989).

The New Jersey court in C. M. *v.* C. C., 377 A.2d 821 (N.J. Super. 1977), considered the rights of a known donor who gave semen to an unmarried woman who then artificially inseminated herself without the aid of a licensed physician. The court held the donor was entitled to visitation rights with the resulting child. The court reasoned that the best interests of the child are served by recognizing the donor as its father, rather than by leaving the child with no father at all. The court found it significant that the woman and the donor had a longstanding dating relationship prior to her artificial insemination, that the child had "no one else who was in a position to assume the responsibilities of fatherhood when the child was conceived" because the woman was unmarried, and that the donor "fully intended to assume the responsibilities of parenthood" at the time of the insemination. *Id.* at 824. The New Jersey legislature subsequently enacted a statutory provision that provided that a donor of semen to someone other than his wife has no parental rights to a child conceived through artificial insemination unless the donor and the woman have entered into a written contract to the contrary. *See* N.J. Rev. Stat. §9:17-44(b) (2003).

Oregon considered the question of the rights of a known donor in *McIntyre v. Crouch*, 780 P.2d 239 (Or. App. 1989). The court ruled that the state statute excluding a semen donor from the rights or obligations of fatherhood with respect to the resulting child applied to the donor, even though the insemination process was not conducted by a doctor and the recipient knew the donor; and that the statute did not violate state constitutional provisions on its face. It also ruled that if the donor could establish that he and the mother agreed that he should have the rights and responsibilities of fatherhood and he donated his semen in reliance on this agreement, the statute as applied would violate the donor's federal constitutional due process rights. *Id.* at 244. *See In re Sullivan*, 157 S.W.3d 911 (Tex. App. 2005) (known donor had standing to adjudicate parentage).

TRADITIONAL SURROGACY

18.10. Surrogate Parent — Overview

Surrogacy is mentioned in the Old Testament. Abraham's wife Sara could not bear Abraham any children, so she gave her maidservant, Hagar, to him for this purpose, saying, "The Lord has kept me from bearing children. Have intercourse, then, with my maid; perhaps I shall have sons through her." Genesis 16:3. According to the Bible, a child, Ishmael, was born of this arrangement.

Today, in our modern world, surrogacy evokes a variety of responses:

> [M]any feminist and other commentators viewed it as representative of male control over reproduction, as exploitative of women and as wrongly treating reproductive capacity or, still worse, children as a commodity. However, though some compared it with prostitution or even slavery, others saw surrogacy as an acceptable means of reproduction and an expression of women's procreative autonomy. Today, while some disagreement regarding the ethics of surrogacy persists, it is fair to say the balance of views has gradually shifted

in a direction which is less hostile to surrogacy, with the practice becoming increasingly accepted in the UK.

Kirsty Horsey & Sally Sheldon, *Still Hazy After All These Years: The Law Regulating Surrogacy*, 20 Med. L. Rev. 67, 68 (Winter 2012).

Black's Law Dictionary 1145 (8th ed. 2006), defines a surrogate parent as "a person who carries out the role of a parent by court appointment or the voluntary assumption of parental responsibilities." It defines a surrogate mother as "a woman who carries out the gestational function and gives birth to a child for another; especially a woman who agrees to provide her uterus to carry an embryo throughout pregnancy, typically on behalf of an infertile couple, and who relinquishes any parental rights she may have upon the birth of a child." *Black's Law Dictionary* 1036 (8th ed. 2006). *See also* Williston on Contracts, 7 Williston on Contracts §16:22 (4th ed.) *Surrogacy Agreements.*

Some question the accuracy of the term *surrogate* when it is used to describe a woman who is in fact the actual biological mother of a child. One author expressed the opinion that "[t]he term 'surrogate' mother, coined by advocates of commercial surrogacy, is a misnomer. The woman who bears the child is an actual mother; she is a surrogate 'wife.' " Kathryn D. Katz, *The Public Policy Response to Surrogate Motherhood Agreements: Why They Should Be Illegal and Unenforceable*, N.Y. St. B. J. (May 1988).

18.11. Legislation Allowing and Banning Surrogacy

In contrast to artificial insemination where most states have statutes on the subject, only a handful of jurisdictions have legislation governing the subject of surrogacy. The result is a variety of contrary rulings among the states. For example, in *Doe v. Attorney General*, 487 N.W.2d 484 (1992), the Michigan Court of Appeals held that a surrogate parentage contract involving voluntary relinquishment after conception of a female's parental rights to a child, is void and unenforceable. The court reasoned that the state had a compelling interest in preventing children from becoming mere commodities, in promoting the best interests of the child (as distinct from the rights of parents promoted by a surrogacy agreement) and in preventing the exploitation of women which it viewed as both gender-based and economically based. As to the latter, the court said that "there is a danger of women being exploited by these surrogacy-for-profit arrangements, and the protection of women from that danger warrant government intrusion." *Ibid.* In contrast, in *J. F. v. D. B.*, 879 N.E.2d 740 (Ohio 2007), the court held that no public policy of Ohio is violated when a $20,000 gestational-surrogacy contract was made, even when one of the provisions of the contract prohibits the gestational surrogate from asserting parental rights regarding children she bears that are of another woman's artificially inseminated egg.

In *Surrogate Parenting Associates, Inc. v. Commonwealth ex rel. Armstrong*, 704 S.W.2d 209 (Ky. 1986), the court held that Kentucky's statute prohibiting the exchange of money for the transfer of children did not apply to a preconception agreement to bear a child for a fee so long as the mother retained the right to void the agreement after the birth of the child.

18.12. Baby M

In re Baby M, 537 A.2d 1227 (N.J. 1988), is a leading surrogacy decision. In that dispute, William Stern and a surrogate, Mary Beth Whitehead, entered into a surrogacy contract. The contract recited that Stern's wife, Elizabeth, was infertile, that they wanted a child, and that Whitehead was willing to provide that child as the mother with Stern as the father. The contract provided that through artificial insemination of Whitehead's ovum, using Stern's sperm, Whitehead would become pregnant, carry the child to term, bear it, deliver it to the Sterns, and thereafter do whatever was necessary to terminate her maternal rights so that Mrs. Stern could adopt the child. Whitehead's husband was also a party to the contract, although Mrs. Stern was not. Whitehead promised to do all acts necessary to rebut the presumption of paternity under New Jersey's version of the Uniform Parentage Act.

Following the birth of the child, Whitehead refused to relinquish her rights to the baby according to the terms of the contract, and the Sterns brought an action to enforce the contract. The trial court found that the surrogate contract was valid, ordered that Whitehead's parental rights be terminated and granted sole custody of child to Mr. Stern. The judge also authorized the adoption of the child by Mrs. Stern. Mary Beth Whitehead appealed, and the Supreme Court of New Jersey granted review.

In its review of the case, the New Jersey Supreme Court rejected the contract between Mr. Stern and the Whiteheads, finding that it was void. However, it concluded that the best interests of the child justified awarding custody to Mr. and Mrs. Stern, with Mary Beth Whitehead receiving visitation. The appellate court found that surrogacy contracts are directly contrary to the objectives of New Jersey's laws. It supported this conclusion by reasoning as follows: (1) They guarantee the separation of a child from its mother. (2) They allow adoption regardless of parental suitability. (3) They totally ignore the child and remove a child from the mother regardless of her wishes and her maternal fitness. (4) They accomplish their goals through the use of money.

Baby selling. The court seemed particularly concerned about the fact that money was involved in the contract between the Sterns and Whitehead. They said that money should not be used in a private adoption and suggested that in actuality, it was being paid to obtain an adoption and not for the personal services of Whitehead. It viewed the conduct as similar to baby selling, which is said was illegal, and perhaps criminal.

Coercion of contract. The court found that there is coercion of contract when the natural mother's irrevocable agreement is obtained prior to birth, even prior to conception, to surrender the child to the adoptive couple. It said that such agreements were totally unenforceable in private placement adoption. Furthermore, even where the adoption is through an approved agency, the formal agreement to surrender occurs only after birth.

Child's best interests. The court noted that surrogacy arrangements focus exclusively on the parents' desires and interests. Because of this, it felt that the parties to these types of contracts are apt to be insensitive to what would be in the child's best interests. It also was concerned that a child's best interests could not be protected because the child is placed without regard for whether the adoptive parents are suitable. Furthermore, it found that the natural mother receives no counseling and guidance, and the adoptive parents may not be fully informed of the natural parents' medical history.

Contrary to termination statute. The court also found that the agreement was contrary to New Jersey's termination statute. The statute required a showing of intentional abandonment or a very substantial neglect of parental duties without a reasonable expectation of a reversal of that conduct in the future before a court will order the rights of a natural parent to be terminated. None of these requirements are present in a surrogate contractual setting.

Women exploited. The court was also concerned that surrogacy arrangements may result in the exploitation of women. It suggested that surrogacy-for-profit arrangements may demean women by reducing them to the status of "breeding machines."

Emotionless machine. In addition to the arguments found against surrogate contracts in *Baby M*, it is argued by some that if surrogacy contracts were recognized, every surrogate mother would soon be cast in the role of an "unfeeling, emotionless machine whose purpose is to create a life and then disappear." *See* Steven M. Recht, "M" *Is for Money: Baby M and the Surrogate Motherhood Controversy*, 37 Am. U. L. Rev. 1013, 1022 (1988).

GESTATIONAL SURROGACY

18.13. State Gestational Surrogacy Theories

Husband's sperm, wife's egg, surrogate mother. *Johnson v. Calvert*, 851 P.2d 776 (Cal. 1993), is a leading case on gestational surrogacy. In contrast to *Baby M*, where the husband's sperm was used to fertilize the surrogate's egg, the married couple here supplied the egg and sperm, and a surrogate agreed to carry and deliver the child. The surrogate was not related to the genetic providers and was compensated for the surrogacy.

When the child was born, a dispute arose over the compensation that the surrogate was to be paid. She also asserted her claim as the legal parent of the child and refused to turn the child over to the gestational parents. The gestational parents filed an action asking that the child be turned over to them, and a California trial judge ruled in their favor. The surrogate, Anna Johnson, challenged the trial judge's ruling on appeal. The California Supreme Court affirmed the trial judge.

In its decision, the California Supreme Court observed that either the gestational surrogate or the genetic parents could be recognized as the natural and legal parents. It concluded, however, that recognition of the child's parents depended upon which party to the lawsuit intended to procreate and raise the child.

The court observed that when Anna Johnson agreed to bear the genetic child, both Johnson (the surrogate) and Crispina Calvert (the genetic mother) had equal claims to the child. However, because the child would not have existed but for the surrogacy agreement, the tie was broken in favor of Calvert, the "intended" mother under the contract. It reasoned that because the genetic mother intended to procreate, she was to be considered the natural parent. *See also* John Lawrence Hill, *What Does It Mean to Be a "Parent"? The Claims of Biology as the Basis for Parental Rights*, 66 N.Y.U. L. Rev. 353 (May, 1991).

Husband's sperm, anonymous egg donor, wife as surrogate. In *McDonald v. McDonald*, 608 N.Y.S.2d 477 (N.Y. App. 1994), the parties were divorcing, and the issue was whether the wife was the natural mother of the children born during the marriage for the purposes of resolving the issue of custody.

The eggs used in procreation were provided by an anonymous female donor, and the wife's husband provided the sperm. The sperm was mixed with the eggs, and the fertilized eggs were then implanted in the wife's uterus. The wife gave birth to the children, twin girls. When the relationship broke down, the husband challenged the right of his wife to consider the children her natural issue. The court rejected the claim, saying that in a true egg donation situation, where a woman gestates and gives birth to a child formed from the egg of another woman with the intent to raise the child as her own, the birth mother is the natural mother. *Id.* at 480.

Wife's eggs, husband's sperm, wife's sister as surrogate. In *Belsito v. Clark*, 644 N.E.2d 760 (Ohio Com. Pl. 1994), two fertilized eggs created through IVF by the use of the wife's eggs and the husband's sperm were transferred into the wife's sister's uterus by her physician. The surrogate was to receive no compensation for her role, and she agreed that she planned to be no more than an aunt to the child or children.

When a child was born from the process, the wife spoke with the hospital about the name to be placed on the birth certificate. She was told that the woman who gave birth to the child would be listed on the birth certificate as the child's mother. Furthermore, she was told that because the surrogate and the wife's husband are not married to each other, the child will be considered illegitimate. The husband and wife sought a declaratory judgment challenging the hospital's position.

The Court of Common Pleas, Probate Division, ruled that because the husband and wife provided the child with their genetics, they should be designated as the legal and natural parents. It stated that individuals who provide the genes of a child are the natural parents if the genetic providers have not waived their rights and have decided to raise the child. *See also In re Roberto d.B.*, 923 A.2d 115 (Md. 2007) (gestational carrier was not required to be listed as the mother on birth certificates).

Donated eggs, husband's sperm. The Tennessee Supreme Court was faced with the issue of whether a surrogate, with no genetic relationship to children born to her, could be considered her legal children. *In re C. K. G., C. A. G., & C. L. G*, 173 S.W.3d 714 (Tenn. 2005) (distinguished in *Coyle v. Erickson*, 2011 WL 3689157 (2011). Three children were born by obtaining eggs donated from an anonymous third-party female, fertilizing the eggs in vitro with the man's sperm, and implanting the fertilized eggs in the woman's uterus. The couple intended to rear the children together as father and mother. When the couple's relationship deteriorated, the woman filed a parentage action seeking custody and child support. In response, the man claimed that the woman had no standing as a parent because, lacking genetic connection to the children, she failed to qualify as a parent under Tennessee's parentage statutes.

The court ruled that the gestational carrier was the children's "legal mother," and this would confer standing upon her to bring parentage action against the father. It awarded joint custody of the children to both parties, with the legal mother designated as the primary custodial parent.

18.14. Same-Sex Issues

Florida view. Biological mother seeks relationship with child. Florida considered a parentage case where the biological mother of a child, who donated an egg to the birth mother and who was previously in an 11-year lesbian relationship with the birth mother of the child, requested a determination of parentage. The parties lived together with the child about two years before they broke up. The biological mother asked for a declaration that she was the biological mother and sought an order granting shared parental responsibility and child support. She also challenged the constitutionality of Florida's parentage statute. The trial judge granted the birth mother summary judgment and the biological mother appealed.

The Florida Court of Appeals ruled that application of the Florida statute that required an egg donor to relinquish all maternal rights to the resulting child violated a biological mother's constitutionally protected parental rights to the child. T. M. H. v. D. M. T., 79 So. 3d 787 (Fla. App. 2011). It also ruled that a form the biological mother had signed in the reproductive doctor's office did not act as a waiver of her parental rights.

California view. Biological mother seeks relationship with child. California considered a similar dispute in *K. M. v. E. G.*, 33 Cal. Rptr. 3d 61 (Cal. 2005). In that case, K. M. had donated her eggs so that her former lesbian partner, E. G., with whom she was registered in a domestic partnership, could bear a child through IVF. K. M. filed a petition to establish parental relationship with E. G.'s twin children after the relationship ended. The trial court dismissed K. M.'s petition, and she appealed.

The California Supreme Court observed that the couple in *Johnson v. Calvert* and the couple in this dispute intended to produce a child that would be raised in their own home. It also observed that in *Johnson*, it was clear that the married couple did not intend to "donate" their semen and ova to the surrogate mother, but rather permitted their semen and ova to be used to impregnate the surrogate mother in order to produce a child to be raised by them.

In this case, the couple lived together and intended to bring the children into their joint home. It concluded that K. M. did not intend to simply donate her ova to E. G., but rather K. M. provided her ova to E. G. so that E. G. could give birth to a child that would be raised in their joint home. It held that both lesbian partners were parents of the children and that the California statute providing that a sperm donor is treated as if he were not the natural father of a child so conceived did not apply to this situation.

New York view. Married same-sex partner seeks adoption of child born to surrogate partner. *In re Adoption of Sebastian*, 879 N.Y.S.2d 677 (N.Y. Surr. 2009), involved Ingrid and Mona, who were legally married in the

Netherlands. They desired to establish a family that would reflect their ethnic and racial diversity. Mona donated her ova, which were fertilized in vitro by an anonymous sperm donor chosen for his similarities to Ingrid's Dutch Italian ethnicity.

The fertilized ovum was successfully implanted in Ingrid's uterus, and she gave birth to Sebastian. A birth certificate named Ingrid alone as Sebastian's parent. Since then, Ingrid and Mona continued to live together and co-parent Sebastian, who they considered to be the child of each of them. Notwithstanding their marriage and Mona's unquestioned genetic relationship to Sebastian, Mona sought to adopt the child.

Ingrid and Mona's marriage in the Netherlands was recognized in New York, with the executive branch of government extending full protection to same-sex couples validly married in other jurisdictions. Therefore, adoption was arguably unnecessary and impermissibly duplicative. They argued, however, that while New York recognized the relationship, the same recognition and protection of Mona's parental rights does not currently exist in the rest of this country, or in most other nations in the world. For this reason, only an order of adoption would ensure the portability of Sebastian's parentage, and further ensure that the federal government and other states would recognize Mona as Sebastian's legal parent.

The court held that adoption was the sole means by which Mona could legally establish parentage of the child born to Ingrid and was the sole means by which the rights and obligations relative to the child could be fully protected. Mona's petition to adopt Sebastian was granted.

18.15. Constitutional "Right" to Gestational Surrogacy?

States do not approach gestational surrogacy uniformly. Some states have restricted the use of gestational surrogacy by statute or decision. Others have remained silent, without court rulings or legislation. When a question of gestational surrogacy constitutional protection is raised, some contend that gestational surrogacy is protected under the United States Constitution and should be restricted only upon a showing of a compelling state interest. *See* John A. Robertson, *Procreative Liberty and the Control of Conception, Pregnancy, and Childbirth*, 69 Va. L. Rev. 405, 427 (1983); John A. Robertson, *Embryos, Families, and Procreative Liberty: The Legal Structure of the New Reproduction*, 59 S. Cal. L. Rev. 939, 960 (1986). The theory is that procreation is protected by decisions of the United States Supreme Court that affirm the basic civil right to marry and raise children. Therefore, the right to procreate should extend to persons who cannot conceive or bear children. Note, however, that it is also suggested that a broad application of the constitutional right of privacy for all procreational techniques has been questioned by the Supreme Court in decisions such as *Michael H. v. Gerald D*, 491 U.S. 110 (1989).

FROZEN EMBRYOS

18.16. Disposition in the Event of Divorce

It is not uncommon for couples involved in a divorce to contest the disposition of frozen pre-embryos. In an attempt to resolve the issues raised by the divorcing couples, courts have used three types of analyses: the contractual approach, the contemporaneous mutual consent approach, and the balancing approach. Each of these approaches is discussed below.

Contractual approach. Some judges will search for a prior agreement made by the parties regarding the disposition of cryopreserved pre-embryos. *See, e.g., Kass v. Kass*, 696 N.E.2d 174 (N.Y. 1998); *Roman v. Roman*, 193 S.W.3d 40 (Tex. 2006); *In re Marriage of Dahl & Angle*, 194 P.3d 834, 841 (Or. App. 2008). In all three of these cases, the husband and wife signed a consent form where they agreed that in the event of death or divorce, any cryopreserved pre-embryos would be destroyed or donated to research. In each case, the court held that the agreement was enforceable and did not violate public policy.

However, Massachusetts does not necessarily agree with Texas, Oregon, or New York. *See A. Z. v. B. Z.*, 725 N.E.2d 1051 (Mass. 2000). In this case, before undergoing IVF, the married couple completed a portion of a consent form providing that should the parties "separate," the wife would attain possession of any cryopreserved pre-embryos. When they separated, the wife sought enforcement of the agreement so that she could have more children. Her ex-husband objected. After reviewing the evidence, the court found that the husband and wife never intended the agreement to be binding and further found that the consent form was ambiguous. *Id.* at 1056–7. It also opined in dictum that "even had the husband and the wife entered into an unambiguous agreement between themselves regarding the disposition of the frozen pre-embryos, [they] would not enforce an agreement that would compel one donor to become a parent against his or her will." *Id.* at 1057. Enforcement of such a contract against the will of one party, the Supreme Court concluded, would violate public policy. *Id.* at 1058. *But see In re Litowitz*, 48 P.3d 261, 271 (Wash. 2002) (enforcing parties' contract providing for disposition of pre-embryos after five years of storage).

Contemporaneous mutual consent model. The Supreme Court of Iowa applied the contemporaneous mutual consent approach when resolving a dispute over a consent form. In *In re Marriage of Witten*, 672 N.W.2d 768 (Iowa 2003), the informed consent agreement provided for the distribution of the pre-embryos only with the consent and agreement of both parties. At trial, the wife wanted custody of the pre-embryos for implantation in herself or a surrogate, while the husband wanted them donated to another couple. The Iowa court concluded that it violated public policy to enforce an "agreement between a couple regarding their future family and reproductive choices." *Id.* at 782. The Court then held that the best approach to resolve this dispute was to require the two parties to devise a new, contemporaneous agreement, with the party opposing destruction being responsible for storage fees. *Id.* at 783.

Balancing test. Some states approach resolution of disputes over pre-embryos by attempting to balance the interests of the parties. *Davis v. Davis*, 842 S.W.2d 588 (Tenn. 1992). In *Davis*, the husband and wife pursued fertility treatments for many years prior to the creation of the frozen pre-embryos at issue. When they divorced, they could not agree who controlled the pre-embryos. The wife wanted to donate them to another infertile individual for use, and the husband wanted to discard them. The Supreme Court of Tennessee weighed "the interests of each party to the dispute . . . in order to resolve that dispute in a fair and responsible manner." *Id.* at 591. The husband testified that he was "vehemently opposed to fathering a child that would not live with both parents" due to his own parents' history of divorce, and he opposed donating the pre-embryos to another couple whose marriage might end in divorce. *Id.* at 604.

The wife wanted to donate them to another couple because otherwise, she would have the "burden of knowing that the lengthy IVF procedures she underwent were futile." *Ibid.* The court concluded that the husband's interest outweighed the wife's observing that "[t]he case would be closer if [wife] were seeking to use the pre-embryos herself, but only if she could not achieve parenthood by any other reasonable means." *Ibid.*

New Jersey also appears to have applied the balancing test in *J. B. v. M. B.*, 170 N.J. 9, 783 A.2d 707 (N.J. 2001). In that case, the wife used IVF and gave birth during the course of the marriage. When the parties separated, the husband wanted control over the frozen pre-embryos for use by a surrogate, but the wife wanted the pre-embryos to be discarded. The court concluded that the wife's right not to procreate or be forced into parenthood outweighed the husband's right to procreate where the husband could still procreate without the wife's involvement (the fertility issues that led to the couple's use of IVF in the first place were due to issues associated with the wife). *Id.* at 717.

Pennsylvania applied the balancing test in *Reber v. Reiss*, 42 A.3d 1131 (Pa. Super 2012). In that case, neither party had signed the portion of the consent form related to the disposition of the pre-embryos in the event of divorce or the death of one party, nor could the parties reach a contemporaneous mutual agreement regarding the pre-embryos. The court awarded the pre-embryos to the wife observing that she had "compelling interests in using the pre-embryos [that] include the fact that these pre-embryos are the option that provides her with what is likely her only chance at genetic parenthood and her most reasonable chance for parenthood at all." *Id.* at 7. It rejected the husband's argument that it is against Pennsylvania public policy to force him to procreate, noting that "unless and until our legislature decides to tackle this issue, our courts must consider the individual circumstances of each case." *Id.* at 9.

Note that at least three states have enacted legislation addressing frozen embryos. *See, e.g.*, Fla. Stat. Ann. §742.17 (2012) (couples must execute written agreement providing for disposition in event of death, divorce, or other unforeseen circumstances); N.H. Rev. Stat. Ann. §§168-B:13-168-B:15, 168-B:18 (2012) (couples must undergo medical examinations and counseling; 14-day limit for maintenance of ex utero pre-zygotes); La. Rev. Stat. Ann. §§9:123 (2011) (in vitro fertilized human ovum exists as a juridical person until such time as the in vitro fertilized ovum is implanted in the womb; or at any other time when rights attach to an unborn child in accordance with law). *See also* Tex. Fam. Code Ann. §160.102(2) (2012) (defining assisted reproduction); *Roman v. Roman*, 193 S.W.3d 40 (Tex. App. 2006) (husband complied with §160.706(a) of the Texas Family Code, which allows him to seek parental rights to any child born from the embryos).

Also note that at least one commentator has suggested that the gamete donation process that both husband and wife experiences provide the consideration for an embryo contract. Marysol Rosado, *Sign on the Dotted Line: Enforceability of Signed Agreements, upon Divorce of the Married Couple, Concerning the Disposition of Their Frozen Pre-embryos*, 36 New Eng. L. Rev. 1041, 1069 (2002).

LIABILITY ISSUES

18.17. Physician and Clinic Tort Liability to Parents

Physicians or clinics involved in alternative reproduction may find themselves in court as defendants for a variety of reasons. For example, a doctor who counseled a childless couple about artificial insemination and agreed to perform the procedure on the wife using the husband's sperm was held subject to suit by the couple when he substituted his own sperm for that of the wife's husband. *James v. Jacobson*, 6 F.3d 233 (4th Cir. 1993); *United States v. Jacobson*, 785 F. Supp. 563 (E.D. Va. 1992) (mail fraud); *St. Paul Fire and Marine Ins. Co. v. Jacobson*, 826 F. Supp. 155, 158, n.3 (E.D. Va. 1993) (listing civil actions against physician for unauthorized use of physician's own semen).

A California clinic was sued by a child who claimed that its negligence had deprived the child of her legal parent because it failed to certify the signature of the mother's husband on a consent form used for artificial insemination. *Alexandria S. v. Pacific Fertility*, 64 Cal. Rptr. 2d 23 (Cal. App. 1997). The child claimed injury when the couple divorced, and a divorce court ruled that the husband did not have a legal obligation to support the child born of the procedure. The child, who was now technically fatherless, sued the clinic.

The court rejected the child's claim, reasoning that the failure to certify the signature was not the proximate cause of any injury to the child. It said the certification was not required to establish the husband's consent under the statute that treated a husband who consents to a wife being inseminated artificially by a donor as the natural father of the child conceived. *See Shin v. Kong*, 95 Cal. Rptr. 2d 304 (Cal. App. 2000) (husband could not recover against physician who had secretly artificially inseminated wife).

In *Harnicher v. University of Utah Medical Center*, 962 P.2d 67 (Utah 1998), the Utah Supreme Court upheld the dismissal of a couple's claim against a medical center that used sperm from a donor other than the one the couple selected for artificial insemination, resulting in the birth of triplets. The court found that the parents failed to raise a triable issue of fact that they had suffered bodily harm, and had failed to show that the medical center's alleged negligence was of the type that was likely to cause severe and unmanageable mental distress in a reasonable person. *See generally* Daniel J. Penofsky, *Sperm Bank Liability for Donor Semen Transmitted AIDS*, 25 Am. Jur. Proof of Facts 3d 1 (2012); Yaviv Heled, *The Regulation of Genetic Aspects of Donated Reproductive Tissue — The Need for Federal Regulation*, 11 Colum. Sci. & Tech. L. Rev. 243 (August 11, 2010).

18.18. Wrongful Life

In *D. D. v. Idant Laboratories*, 374 Fed. Appx. 319 (3d Cir. 2010), the court ruled that under New York law, a child did not have protected right to be born free of genetic defects. Therefore, it dismissed the allegation that a sperm bank caused injury to a child by providing sperm from a donor that carried a genetic disease. It observed that a cause of action may not be maintained on behalf of an infant plaintiff based on a claim of wrongful life.

18.19. Wrongful Death

In *Jeter v. Mayo Clinic Arizona*, 121 P.3d 1256 (Ariz. App. 2005), a couple alleged negligent destruction or loss of five of the couple's frozen pre-embryos that the clinic had agreed to cryopreserve and store. They brought claims for wrongful death, negligent loss of irreplaceable property, breach of fiduciary duty, and breach of bailment contract. The Arizona Court of Appeals held that cryopreserved, three-day-old, eight-cell pre-embryos were not persons for purposes of recovery under the wrongful death statute. However, it allowed the couple to proceed on claims of negligent loss or destruction of pre-embryos and for breach of bailment contract.

The Arkansas Supreme Court in *Aka v. Jefferson Hospital Association, Inc.*, 42 S.W.3d 508 (Ark. 2001), held that the term *person* in the Arkansas wrongful death statute includes an unborn viable fetus, overruling *Chatelain v. Kelley*, 910 S.W.2d 215 (Ark. 1995). In this case, the administrator of the estates of a mother and an unborn viable fetus brought wrongful death and medical malpractice actions against a hospital and physicians. The plaintiffs alleged medical negligence in unnecessarily inducing the mother's labor, failing to discontinue induction, failing to perform a cesarean section, failing to resuscitate her or the fetus, and failing to obtain informed consent, proximately causing the mother's and fetus's deaths. The trial court was reversed on appeal because it had granted summary judgment to defendants by concluding that a fetus was not a person for the purposes of a tort action. Cf. *In re Marriage of Witten*, 672 N.W.2d 768 (Iowa 2003) (frozen embryo is not a "child" for the purposes of Iowa's child custody laws).

18.20. Liability When Genetic Material Mix-Up Occurs

In *Robert B. v. Susan B.*, 135 Cal. Rptr. 2d 785 (Cal. App. 2003), a child, Daniel, was born to Susan B., a single woman, after a fertility clinic accidentally implanted embryos belonging to Robert and Denise B. into Susan. In an action to determine paternity, the trial court ruled that Susan was Daniel's mother, and Robert was his father. Denise was dismissed for lack of standing.

On appeal, the court held that the statute providing that the donor of semen for use in the artificial insemination of a woman who is not the donor's wife is treated as if the donor is not the natural father of the conceived child did not apply, and that the wife was not an interested person who had standing to bring action.

It is of interest that Robert and Denise B. had contracted with an anonymous ovum donor to obtain the donor's eggs for fertilization with Robert's sperm. The contract reflected the intent of the contracting parties that Robert and Denise would be the parents of any children produced from the resulting embryos. Susan went to the same fertility clinic with the intent of purchasing genetic material from "two strangers who would contractually sign away their rights" so that "there would be no paternity case against her, ever."

About 13 embryos were produced for Robert and Denise, and some of them were implanted in Denise's uterus. Through an apparent clinic error, Susan received three of these embryos. When she became pregnant, Susan believed that the child she was carrying was the result of the anonymous donation procedure for which she had contracted. In February, ten days apart, Susan gave birth to Daniel, and Denise gave birth to Daniel's genetic sister, Madeline.

In December 2001, the fertility physician informed Robert and Denise that a mistake had occurred, in that the clinic had inadvertently implanted some of Robert and Denise's embryos in Susan's uterus, resulting in Daniel's birth. Robert and Denise promptly sought contact with Daniel. Susan was initially receptive, but after the three adults and two children met, she refused to relinquish custody, and Robert and Denise brought a parentage action. The trial court determined that Robert had standing to bring a paternity action under California law and ordered genetic testing. After receiving the test results, the court declared Robert to be the father of Daniel.

In resolving the dispute, the appellate court held that a wife who is not biologically related to the child is not an "interested party" and has no standing to bring a parentage action. It also held that California's statute providing that the donor of semen for use in the artificial insemination of a woman who is not the donor's wife is treated as if the donor is not the natural father of the conceived child did not apply, and the genetic father was recognized as the child's father. *See Prato-Morrison v. Doe*, 126 Cal. Rptr. 2d 509 (Cal. App. 2002) (evidence insufficient to show that plaintiffs were the genetic parents of defendants' twin teenage daughters, based on the facts that plaintiffs and defendants were clients of the same fertility clinic when the twins were conceived, even though the clinic had been found guilty of misusing abandoned genetic material).

MISCELLANEOUS ISSUES

18.21. Insurance — Who Is Covered?

Dealing with infertility is often traumatic and can be costly and time consuming. The average cost of one IVF cycle in the United States (and it frequently takes multiple cycles in order to succeed) has been estimated at $24,500 to $32,000 at one Chicago clinic, and the cost is usually not covered by health insurance. *See Morrison v. Sadler*, 821 N.E.2d 15, 24 (Ind. App. 2005) (average cost of one IVF cycle in the United States is not covered by health insurance). In *Knight v. Hayward Unified School Dist.*, 33 Cal. Rptr. 3d 287 (Cal. App. 1 Dist. 2005), the provisions of a school district's health insurance were found to not include coverage of IVF treatment. The court rejected the argument that refusing IVF coverage constituted disability discrimination under the Fair Employment and Housing Act (FEHA) against the teacher and his wife. The couple was left to obtain IVF treatment at their own expense. *See Yeager v. Blue Cross of California*, 96 Cal. Rptr.3d 723 (Cal. App. 2009) (insurer had no statutory obligation to offer full coverage or coverage on the same terms and conditions as other medical conditions covered by the plan).

Some jurisdictions have statutorily required insurance carriers to provide coverage for diagnosing and treating infertility. *Goodridge v. Department of Public*, 798 N.E.2d 941, n. 31 (Mass. 2003). In *Ralston v. Connecticut General Life Ins. Co.*, 617 So. 2d 1379 (La. App. 1993), the court held that an IVF procedure to induce pregnancy was treatment for a "sickness" and covered by a health insurance policy.

18.22. Posthumous Reproduction

The law regarding the rights of posthumously conceived children is unsettled. Posthumous reproduction may occur if a man and woman arrange for sperm to be withdrawn from the husband for the purpose of artificially impregnating the woman, and the woman is impregnated with that sperm after the man has died.

Several reasons are given in support of this process. For example, there may be religious reasons, a tribute to a deceased partner, the survivor may be sterile, or it may allow a child to inherit from certain individuals. Benjamin C. Carpenter, *A Chip off the Old Iceblock: How Cryopreservation Has Changed Estate Law, Why Attempts to Address the Issue Have Fallen Short, And How To Fix It*, 21 Cornell J.L. & Pub. Pol'y 347, 358 (Winter 2011). It may cost significantly less to use the deceased partner's genetic material than to obtain gametes from a new donor and it may allow the child to inherit from certain individuals (including the decedent or other family members), to qualify as a beneficiary of certain trusts, or to receive Social Security or other survivor benefits. *Ibid. See* Kristine S. Knaplund, *Legal Issues of Maternity and Inheritance for the Biotech Child of the 21st Century*, 43 Real Prop. Tr. & Est. L.J. 393, 395 (2008).

Inheritance. In *Matter of Estate of Kolacy*, 753 A.2d 1257 (N.J. Super. 2000), the plaintiff sought a declaratory judgment to have her children, who were conceived after the death of her husband, declared the intestate heirs of her deceased husband in order to pursue the children's claims for survivor benefits with the Social Security Administration. A Superior Court judge held that, in circumstances in which the decedent left no estate and an adjudication of parentage did not unfairly intrude on the rights of others or cause "serious problems" with the orderly administration of estates, the children would be entitled to inherit under the state's intestacy law. *Id.* at 1257.

Woodward v. Commissioner of Social Sec., 760 N.E.2d 257 (Mass. 2002), involved a dispute where the husband was informed that he had leukemia when the couple was childless. Because the husband's leukemia treatment might leave him sterile, the couple arranged for a quantity of the husband's semen to be medically withdrawn and preserved, in a process commonly known as "sperm banking." The husband subsequently died from cancer, and the wife was appointed to administer his estate.

The wife later gave birth to twin girls who were conceived through artificial insemination using the husband's preserved semen. She then applied for Social Security survivor benefits for the children. The Social Security Administration denied such benefits, and the wife appealed. The United States District Court for the District of Massachusetts certified to the Supreme Judicial Court of Massachusetts the question of whether children enjoyed the inheritance rights of natural children under Massachusetts law of intestate succession.

The Massachusetts court held that children could inherit if the wife established their genetic relationship with the decedent, and that the decedent consented both to reproduce posthumously and support any resulting child. It stated that the question of recognition depends as a threshold matter upon a showing that the surviving parent or the child's other legal representative has a genetic relationship between the child and the decedent. Once that is shown, the survivor or representative must establish that the decedent affirmatively consented to posthumous conception and to the support of any resulting child. The court reasoned that because the parentage of such children can be neither acknowledged nor adjudicated prior to the decedent's death, under the state intestacy statute, posthumously conceived children first must obtain a judgment of paternity as a necessary prerequisite to seeking inheritance rights in the estate of the deceased genetic father. *But see Khabbaz v. Commissioner*, 930 A.2d 1180 (N.H. 2007) (child conceived via artificial insemination after father's death was not a "surviving issue" of father, and thus was not eligible to receive a portion of father's estate, with court noting that Massachusetts statutes relied on in *Woodward* differed from those in New Hampshire). *See generally* Allison Stewart Ellise, Comment, *Inheritance Rights of Posthumously Conceived Children in Texas*, 43 St. Mary's L.J. 413 (2012) (only 18 states have enacted laws recognizing posthumously conceived children).

Is sperm property? In *Hecht v. Superior Court*, 20 Cal. Rptr. 2d 275 (Cal. App. 1993), the California Court of Appeals considered whether a decedent's sperm was "property" that could be bequeathed to his girlfriend. It answered in the affirmative, noting that under the provisions of California's Probate Code, "it is unlikely that the estate would be subject to claims with respect to any such children" resulting from insemination of the girlfriend with the decedent's sperm. *Id.* at 290.

EXAMPLES

Examples

1. Alice, a married woman, and her husband, Pete, have difficulties conceiving a child. Without Pete's knowledge or consent, Alice is artificially inseminated with sperm from an anonymous donor. A child is born, and Pete believes that the child is the result of intercourse with Alice. When the child is three years old, Pete and Alice divorce. Pete discovers during the divorce process that Alice's pregnancy was the result of artificial insemination. Pete contends that the sperm donor is the father of the child; therefore, he must pay child support, not Pete. Most likely, how will a court rule under the 2002 version of the UPA?

2. Assume that pursuant to a typical state artificial insemination statute, wife P, with husband D's express written permission, is impregnated under the supervision of a physician using the sperm of third party Y. The sperm is obtained from a local sperm donor clinic. Following the birth of a child using this sperm, the local prosecutor decides to put the sperm donor clinic out of business by bringing criminal charges of adultery against sperm donors, as well as civil actions demanding that they pay child support for any children born to women who used their sperm. The prosecutor learns that Y was the sperm donor in the above matter and charges Y with adultery in criminal court and asks for a child support order in civil court. A motion to dismiss is brought in both courts by Y, the sperm donor. How will the criminal and civil courts most likely treat the motions?

3. Assume that D is a sperm donor in a jurisdiction that does not have an artificial insemination statute. The sperm is used to artificially inseminate X, a single woman, and a child is born. X discovers the identity of the sperm donor (D) and brings an action seeking support from him. How will a court most likely rule on the child support request?

4. Assume that P sues D, her former boyfriend, seeking to establish paternity and to impose support obligations for twin boys conceived through artificial insemination by an anonymous donor. They live in a jurisdiction that has a typical artificial insemination statute. At the trial, evidence was admitted showing that during their ten-year relationship, the parties discussed marriage, but D told P that he did not believe in

marriage. They also discussed P's desire to have children but it became apparent that D could not father children. P testified that D suggested that she be artificially inseminated by an anonymous donor as a means to have their child. P claims that D promised her that he would provide financial support for any child born by means of artificial insemination. According to P, with D's consent and active encouragement, she became pregnant through artificial insemination, and twin children were born.

There was also testimony at the hearing that D had provided financial assistance for the insemination procedure, accompanied P to the doctor's office for examinations, injected P with medication designed to enhance her fertility, and participated in selecting the donor so that the offspring would appear to be a product of their relationship. D also participated in selecting names for the children, although he did not allow his name to be placed on their birth certificates. For three years following their birth, D provided the children with monthly payments of cash and the purchase of food, clothing, furniture, toys, and play equipment. When the children were three years old, the relationship broke down, and P now wants to establish paternity and obtain child support. D states that he has no responsibility toward the children because they are not his genetic issue and he is not married to their mother. How will a court most likely rule?

5. Assume that wife P and husband D orally agree to have a child by artificial insemination because husband D is infertile. They live in a jurisdiction that will recognize a child born of this procedure as the child of P and D. The artificial insemination of P is successful. Two months before the child is born, husband D and wife P separate. Following the child's birth, husband D is listed as the father on the birth certificate. During divorce proceedings, D asks the court to declare that he is not the father of the child. P counterclaims, asking for child support. D argues that under the language of the state statute, his consent must have been in writing (it was not) and that he was not living with P when the child was born. How will a court most likely rule on P's and D's claims?

6. Assume that in this jurisdiction, no surrogate statute exists. Also assume that P and X are sisters and that P, for medical reasons, cannot carry a child to term. P and X agree in writing that X will be artificially inseminated with P's husband's sperm and that X will carry the child to term and turn it over to P at birth. Before going through with the procedure, P consults a lawyer to determine the potential legal roadblocks to such an agreement. What are some of the issues that a lawyer most likely would discuss with P?

7. Assume that surrogate X agrees to be inseminated with Y's sperm, bring the child to term, and turn the child over to Y and his wife when it is born. In return, X agrees to a $10,000 payment to be received if there is a successful birth. When a child is born, X turns the child over to Y and his wife. However, X challenges the $10,000 contract provision as unconscionable and argues that $50,000 is a reasonable sum. At the hearing on the matter, she testifies that $10,000 does not reflect the amount of work and physical risk involved in the surrogacy arrangement. What is the likely outcome of the dispute over the contract price?

8. Assume the same facts as set out in the problem above. Also assume that the birth mother challenges the surrogate agreement as deficient because the only advice that she received was from the lawyer hired by the company that arranges surrogacy contracts. Will a court void the agreement because of a lack of independent advice and counseling?

9. Assume that in this jurisdiction, there is no surrogate statute, that a birth certificate can be prepared up to five days after the birth of a child, and that the adoption statutes provide that in recognition of the emotional and physical changes that occur at birth, voluntary surrenders are not valid if made within 72 hours after the birth of the child. Assume further that X is the unmarried sister of P. P and P's husband, D, entered into a gestational surrogacy contract with X. X, without financial compensation, agrees to have embryos implanted into her uterus that were created from the sperm of D and the ova of her sister, P. The process is successful. Assume that a child is due to be born in about two weeks at the county hospital. P and D file an action to declare the maternity and paternity of unborn Baby A. They seek a pre-birth court order that establishes them as the legal mother and father of unborn Baby A and will allow the hospital to place their names on the child's birth certificate. They argue that a pre-birth order is appropriate in this situation. How will a court most likely treat P and D's request?

10. Assume that during their marriage, wife P had a dozen of her ova fertilized by husband D's sperm through the IVF process. They were cryopreserved by Clinic XYZ. When the couple divorced, the clinic was unable to locate an agreement in its files that the parties "thought" they had signed years earlier regarding the disposition of the fertilized ova. They could not recall the exact terms of the agreement. P sought custody of the frozen fertilized ova. At the hearing on the matter, D testified that he wanted them destroyed because he did not want children, and if children were born from the ova, that he did not have sufficient funds to provide support for them. P testified that she wished to donate them to her sister, who was having difficulty becoming pregnant. P admitted during cross-examination that she did not have any medical problems

that would prevent her from becoming pregnant, should she decide to do so. How will a court most likely resolve this issue?

11. Assume that P and D are married and D learns that he has a very serious heart problem and must undergo a difficult and dangerous surgical operation. Because they have no children, P and D agree that a quantity of D's semen will be medically withdrawn and preserved should D die during the surgery. P and D consult a lawyer regarding the most effective means of ensuring that any posthumous children will be D's legitimate children who are eligible for Social Security and other benefits. What legal advice should the lawyer give P and D?

EXPLANATIONS

Explanations

1. Under the UPA, the donor most likely will be protected from having to pay child support. In the commentary to §702 of the UPA, the commissioners stated that "[I]f a married woman bears a child of assisted reproduction using a donor's sperm, the donor will not be the father in any event. Her husband will be the father unless and until the husband's lack of consent to the assisted reproduction is proven within two years of his learning of the birth." This provides certainty of non-parentage for prospective donors. Pete may argue that the phrase in the commentary "within two years of his learning of the birth" means two years within learning that the child was born of artificial insemination. A court most likely will reject this argument. In another comment to §702, it states, "The donor can neither sue to establish parental rights, nor be sued and required to support the resulting child. In sum, donors are eliminated from the parental equation." *See generally In re Sullivan*, 157 S.W.3d 911 (Tex. App. 2005).

2. Although such claims have a possibility of success in a jurisdiction without a typical artificial insemination statute, they should have no possibility of success in a jurisdiction that has adopted one. Assuming that a typical artificial insemination statute is in place, the criminal charge should be dismissed, and Y relieved of any responsibility to pay child support. *See J. F. v. D. B.*, 848 N.E.2d 873 (Ohio App. 2006) (if a woman is the subject of a non-spousal artificial insemination, the donor shall not be treated in law or regarded as the natural father of a child conceived as a result of the artificial insemination, and a child so conceived shall not be treated in law or regarded as the natural child of the donor); *Levin v. Levin*, 645 N.E.2d 601, 604 (Ind. 1994)

(child conceived during marriage through artificial insemination by third-party donor was a "child of the marriage" — former husband stopped from denying obligation to support child).

3. The court may well grant the request for child support. Because the jurisdiction does not have a statute to guide the court in making a decision, there is little to help it distinguish between artificial and natural conception. A court may likely reason that because the child is the genetic issue of D, D will be required to provide the child with financial support.

4. The court may view D's conduct as evincing actual consent and a demonstration of a deliberate course of conduct with the goal of causing the birth of the children. It will reason that if an unmarried man who biologically causes conception through sexual relations without the premeditated intent of birth is legally obligated to support a child, the equivalent resulting birth of a child caused by the deliberate conduct of artificial insemination should receive the same treatment. Regardless of the method of conception, a child is born and needs support, and for a court to hold otherwise would deprive the children of financial support merely because of deception and a technical oversight. *See generally In re Parentage of M.J.*, 787 N.E.2d 144 (Ill. 2003) (held that failure to obtain written consent of putative father to insemination precluded claim for paternity under the Uniform Parentage Act as adopted by Illinois but did not prohibit mother's action based on common law theories of oral contract or promissory estoppel).

5. A court most likely will find that husband D is the father of the child and order the payment of child support. D's knowledge of and assistance with his wife's efforts to conceive through artificial insemination will be viewed as constituting implied consent on his part, rendering him the legal father. *See In re Baby Doe*, 353 S.E.2d 877, 878 (S.C. 1987). The fact that D was not living with P at the time of the child's birth most likely will be considered irrelevant.

6. The lawyer most likely will review all the concerns expressed by the court in *Baby M*. She will note that *Baby M* is distinguishable on at least two important bases. First, the court in this jurisdiction may view the close family relationship as important; that is, the surrogate X is the biological sister of P, the woman seeking parenthood. Second, it will recognize that no money is being exchanged between the parties. Consequently, the concerns about baby selling and female exploitation are significantly reduced, if not eliminated. However, many other obstacles remain, such as terminating X's parental rights, dealing with state

adoption requirements, and general considerations of the best interests of the child. While P may eventually achieve her goal, a lawyer could not provide such assurance with certainty.

7. The Supreme Court of New Jersey in *Baby M* did not address this issue because it had already found the surrogate contract unenforceable under state law. The issue turns on how a court will view the competency of the parties to the contract and the need to intervene to protect the surrogate. Without state legislation expressing public policy about these contracts, chances are the court will not agree with the surrogate's claim. Note that on appeal, Whitehead challenged a provision in the surrogate contract that denied her any payment in the event of miscarriage prior to the fifth month of pregnancy and providing for compensation of only $1,000 in the event of a miscarriage thereafter. She advanced the argument that the surrogacy agreement violated the state wage laws. However, because the court had declared the contract unenforceable on other grounds, it declined to address this issue.

8. The Supreme Court of New Jersey found merit in this issue, noting that there was "no counseling, independent or otherwise, of the natural mother, no evaluation, no warning." *In re Baby M*, 537 A.2d 1227, 1247 (N.J. 1988). The court noted that the "natural mother is irrevocably committed before she knows the strength of her bond with her child. She never makes a totally voluntary, informed decision, for quite clearly any decision prior to the baby's birth is, in the most important sense, uninformed, and any decision after that, compelled by a pre-existing contractual commitment, the threat of a lawsuit, and the inducement of a $10,000 payment, is less than totally voluntary." *Id.* at 1248 of 537 A.2d. It noted that the only legal advice given to the surrogate mother was that provided by an attorney to whom the commercial surrogacy agency referred surrogate candidates. The attorney's services consisted of spending one hour going through the contract with the Whiteheads, section by section, and answering their questions. Whitehead received no further legal advice prior to signing the contract with the Sterns.

9. The court most likely will reject the request for a pre-birth order primarily because it is contrary to the existing 72-hour statute. The gestational mother may surrender the child 72 hours after giving birth. This leaves 48 hours in which the birth certificate may be prepared. If X chooses to surrender the infant, and she certifies that she wishes to relinquish all rights, the original birth certificate can list the two biological parents, P and D, as the baby's parents. However, because of the statute expressing this jurisdiction's public policy, if X changes her mind about turning the child over to P and D once the child

is born, she most likely will have an opportunity to litigate to protect her parental rights to the child. *See generally A. H. W. v. G. H. B.*, 772 A.2d 948 (N.J. Super. Ch. 2000).

10. The trial judge most likely will look to the reasoning used in *Davis v. Davis, supra*. Because the prior agreement that the parties "thought" might resolve the dispute cannot be located, and the parties cannot recall the terms, the judge will treat the matter as though there was no prior agreement. She will weigh the relative interests of the parties in using or not using the fertilized ova. Under *Davis*, the party who wishes to avoid procreation should prevail if there is a dispute as to custody of the ova, assuming that the other party has a reasonable possibility of achieving parenthood by means other than use of the ova in question. P conceded at the hearing that she could achieve parenthood without the fertilized ova. Because P intends to donate the fertilized ova to her sister, D appears to have the greater interest and will most likely prevail.

11. The lawyer first will have to examine the jurisdiction's statutes to determine whether any of them address posthumously conceived children. Recall that states differ on the legal standing of posthumously conceived children depending on language in relevant statutes. Compare *Woodward v. Commissioner of Social Sec.*, 760 N.E.2d 257 (Mass. 2002) (children could inherit if wife established their genetic relationship with the decedent, and that the decedent consented both to reproduce posthumously and support any resulting child) with *Khabbaz v. Commissioner*, 930 A.2d 1180 (N.H. 2007) (statute that described the inheritance rights of children born to unwed parents did not deem the child eligible to inherit under New Hampshire intestacy laws).

    To give the couple the best chance of the state recognizing children conceived posthumously, the lawyer should advise the couple to draft a will setting out in detail the sperm donor's specific intention of supporting such children. The lawyer also should advise P and D to consider informing the sperm bank where the sperm will be stored in writing of the reason for banking D's sperm. The lawyer will explain that special care must be exercised to retain all records showing D's intent so that, should D die and children be born posthumously, establishing paternity may be possible. The language in the will and testimony of the witnesses to the will gives the couple the best chance of persuading a court that the children are D's issue and thereby establish their paternity. If the court is convinced and a state or federal statute does not specially bar this evidence from probate court, this should make the children eligible to receive Social Security benefits and provide inheritance rights similar to those available to children born before the death of a parent. A note of caution — recall that the outcome remains unsettled throughout the United States.

CHAPTER 19

Domestic Violence

19.1. Introduction

The existence of domestic violence has been traced as far back as ancient Rome and, as recently as the 1800s, an American husband could "chastise" his wife legally in the exercise of his property rights. Awareness of domestic violence has increased dramatically over the last half-century and it is no longer explicitly approved under the law. However, courts and legislatures struggle to make policy concerning when and how to intervene in family matters.

Statistics about domestic violence are sobering in that it is experienced by many families. Research in the context of mediation indicates more than half of divorcing couples report domestic violence. *See* Robin H. Ballard et al., *Detecting Intimate Partner Violence in Family and Divorce Mediation: A Randomized Trial of Intimate Partner Violence Screening*, 17 Psychol. Pub. Pol'y & L. 241 (2011).

UNDERSTANDING THE ISSUE

19.2. Risk Factors

Risk markers for domestic violence include growing up in a violent home, socioeconomic status, personality issues, substance abuse, biological factors, and situational dynamics. Rates of domestic violence may be higher when dating, in early marriage, during pregnancy, and at the time of divorce. Glenda Kaufman Kantor & Jana L. Jasinski, *Dynamics and Risk Factors in Partner Violence*, in *Partner Violence* 1, 41, 42 (Jana L. Jasinski et al., eds., 1998). Significant predictors of future male partner violence include past violence, past abuse, emotional dependency, relationship problems, mental health problems, control issues, and substance abuse. Desmond Ellis & Noreen Stuckless, *Domestic Violence, DOVE, and Divorce Mediation*, 44 Fam. Ct. Rev. 658 (2006).

19.3. Importance of Context

The impact and implications of domestic violence depend a great deal on the context in which it occurs. For example, consider three situations where partner A pushes partner B. In the first situation, there has been no prior history of violence or intimidation. In the second situation, there has been no previous physical violence, but partner A frequently threatens partner B and insists on knowing B's whereabouts at all times. In the third situation, partner A has a history of violence, including cutting B with a knife and breaking B's jaw. Although the physical act of partner A pushing B is the same in each hypothetical situation, the impact on B and the risk level to B is significantly different. Consequently, it is important to consider the context of the violence in addition to the physical acts. *See* Nancy Ver Steegh & Clare Dalton, *Report from the Wingspread Conference on Domestic Violence and Family Courts*, 46 Fam. Ct. Rev. 454 (2008).

Families experiencing domestic violence differ significantly from each other, and researchers, practitioners, and courts work to find appropriate and empirically valid ways to differentiate among them. Several prominent researchers suggest investigation of (a) the frequency, severity, and potential lethality of the violence; (b) the pattern of the violence, including dynamics of coercive control; and (c) whether there is a primary perpetrator of the violence. Peter G. Jaffe et al., *Custody Disputes Involving Allegations of Domestic Violence: Toward a Differentiated Approach to Parenting Plans*, 46 Fam. Ct. Rev. 500 (2008).

Preliminary research indicates that families experience different patterns of domestic violence. In cases of *coercive controlling violence* or *classic battering*, the perpetrator (usually male) uses violence to control the victim. Accompanying tactics of control include emotional abuse, psychological abuse, isolation of the victim, economic control, and manipulation of children. The use of controlling tactics escalates over time. In contrast, *conflict-instigated violence* occurs when partners have poor conflict resolution skills and a disagreement leads to a violent incident. Conflict-instigated violence is not part of a larger pattern of control, and it does not usually escalate. It may be initiated by either partner; however, the female partner is more likely to suffer negative consequences. Other potential patterns may include *separation-instigated violence* and *violence resulting from severe mental illness.* Consideration of patterns of domestic violence is useful for generating hypotheses to be investigated, but patterns are not diagnoses and should not be used by lawyers to label individual families. *See* Michael P. Johnson, *A Typology of Domestic Violence: Intimate Terrorism, Violent Resistance, and Situational Couple* Violence, (2008); Joan B. Kelly & Michael P. Johnson, *Differentiation Among Types of Intimate Partner Violence: Research Update and Implications for Interventions*, 46 Fam. Ct. Rev. 476 (2008).

Although courts and legislatures have historically viewed domestic violence through a one-size-fits-all lens, important distinctions among families have emerged. Consequently, it is important to tailor interventions such as parent education and dispute resolution processes to meet safety and other needs of family members. For some families, these services may be dangerous, and they should not participate, but for other families, participation in a modified process may be safe and helpful. In the final analysis, the specific needs of each individual family must be taken into account. *See* Nancy Ver Steegh et al., *Look Before You Leap: Court System Triage of Family Law Cases Involving Intimate Partner* Violence, 95 Marquette L. Rev. 955 (2012).

19.4. Impact on Children

Children who witness domestic abuse suffer a range of emotional and behavioral consequences. They are sometimes more fearful and inhibited, or they may act more aggressively than other children. Some children exhibit anxiety, depression, and trauma-related symptoms. Of course, the extent of the impact varies depending on the child's overall situation. Jeffrey L. Edleson, *Should Childhood Exposure to Adult Domestic Violence Be Defined as Child Maltreatment Under the Law?* in Protecting Children From Domestic Violence 8, 10 (Peter G. Jaffe et al., eds., 2004). Approximately half of the children who witness domestic violence are themselves physically abused. *See* Evan Stark & Anne Flitcraft, *Women at Risk* 76 (1996); Lundy Bancroft & Jay G. Silverman, *The Batterer as Parent* 42 (2002) (finding 40 to 70 percent concurrent child abuse).

Perpetrators of coercive-controlling violence frequently threaten and manipulate children in an effort to control and intimidate the victim-parent. Evan Stark, *Re-Presenting Woman Battering: From Battered Women Syndrome to Coercive Control*, 58 Albany L. Rev. 973, 40 (1995) (describing batterer's extension of coercive tactics to the children as "tangential spouse abuse"); Evan Stark, *Coercive Control: The Entrapment of Women in Personal Life* (2007). For example, the court in the case of *Krystyna W. v. Janusz W.*, 14 A.3d 483 (Conn. App. 2011) analyzed such a situation as follows:

> The plain language of §46b–15 clearly requires a continuous threat of present physical pain or physical injury before a court can grant a domestic violence

> restraining order. Immediately prior to the court's finding that such a threat had been established, the court indicated that the record reflected that the defendant had threatened to seek revenge on the children because they had hospitalized him, that he walked around the house with knives, that he had made a sharp and pointy object with a metal rod, that his threatening conduct occurred when he was intoxicated, that he did not remember his actions when sober, that he verbally abused the children and denied that he was doing so, that he had utilized carefully planned techniques to upset them, that he prevented the family from sleeping by purposely making loud noises, that he had asked their minor son to kill him with a hammer and knife, that he had threatened to kill himself because of his family's attempts to help him get treatment for his alcoholism, that he blamed their son for his alcoholism and his disruptive behavior, that the family had lived in fear for over a year and that he had threatened to burn the house down. As the court noted: "I don't know how close you can get to the statute [§46b–15] without actually burning the house down."

Id. at 486-87.

Special care must be taken when creating parenting plans and making child custody and access decisions in cases involving domestic violence. In order to keep children and other family members safe, supervised exchange, supervised access, or suspended contact may be necessary. *See* Janet Johnston et al., *In the Name of the Child: A Developmental Approach to Understanding and Helping Children of Conflicted and Violence Divorce* 307 (2009) (discussing the "5P" analysis of potency, pattern, primary perpetrator, parenting problems, and preferences and perspective of the child); Peter G. Jaffe et al., *Custody Disputes Involving Allegations of Domestic Violence: Toward a Differentiated Approach to Parenting Plans*, 46 Fam. Ct. Rev. 500 (2008).

19.5. Screening Protocols

Because the existence of domestic violence may dramatically alter how a case is handled and decided, lawyers and professionals working with families must follow a domestic violence screening protocol consistently. *See* Margaret Drew, *Lawyer Malpractice and Domestic Violence: Are We Revictimizing Our Clients?* 39 Fam. L.Q. 7 (2005) (exploring malpractice and ethical mistakes likely to occur when representing clients in cases involving domestic violence).

A screening protocol typically involves confidential, face-to-face interviews, use of screening instruments developed for various purposes, and ongoing monitoring and check-in throughout the case. Survivors of coercive-controlling abuse often risk retaliation and harm to children if they disclose its existence. Consequently, screening must occur over time and special care must be taken to identify coercive-controlling tactics such as emotional abuse, psychological abuse, isolation of the victim, economic control, and manipulation of children. Nancy Ver Steegh et al., *Look Before You Leap*, 972-979 (discussing best practices for screening and existing screening instruments).

Family law attorneys routinely assist domestic violence victims with safety planning and make appropriate referrals to community resources. These are key aspects of providing competent representation.

DOMESTIC ABUSE STATUTES

19.6. History

During the 1960s, awareness increased concerning the frequency and consequences of domestic violence, and more victims of domestic violence sought help. The need for safe shelter became immediately apparent, and volunteers cooperated to create safe homes and start shelters for survivors of abuse. It soon became apparent that legal remedies were needed to remove perpetrators from the home, establish child custody and support, and prevent future abuse. Civil domestic abuse acts were developed to meet these and other needs.

Between 1975 and 1980, 45 states passed some type of civil domestic abuse legislation. Currently, every state has a statute granting prospective civil relief to victims of domestic violence.

19.7. Statutory Definitions of Domestic Violence

Although domestic abuse statutes in each state define domestic violence somewhat differently, the definitions usually focus on physical (as opposed to emotional or psychological) abuse. §102 of the Model Code on Domestic and Family Violence defines domestic violence in the following way:

> Domestic or family violence means the occurrence of one or more of the following acts by a family or household member, but does not include acts of self defense:
>
> a. Attempting to cause or causing physical harm to another family or household member;
> b. Placing a family or household member in fear of physical harm; or
> c. Causing a family or household member to engage involuntarily in sexual activity by force, threat of force, or duress.

Typical acts of violence falling within this definition include pushing, slapping, choking, punching, use of weapons, use of household objects as weapons, and rape. Thus, definitions of domestic violence may encompass a continuum of behavior from verbal threats to homicide. *See* Jeffrey R. Baker,

Enjoining Coercion: Squaring Civil Protection Orders with the Reality of Domestic Violence, 11 J. L. & Fam. Stud. 35 (2008) (discussing challenges associated with capturing coercive-controlling dynamics in statutory defintions of domestic violence).

Examples

1. P and D decided to divorce. As they were separating, they had a heated argument about who should move out of the marital home. P heard D say that if he couldn't stay in the home, he would burn it down. P seeks an order for protection based on a statute allowing for an order of protection to be issued upon a showing of "actual or imminent domestic violence." D claims that he said that they should sell the house or burn it. The court issues an order for protection on P's behalf, and D appeals. What is the likely result?

2. Assume that P proves that D committed the following acts: (1) he shouted profanities at P, grabbed her hand, and pushed her against a bar; (2) he pushed a car door against P's arm; and (3) he yelled profanities at P's son. P alleges that she and her son are afraid of D. The domestic abuse act in P's state defines domestic and family violence as the occurrence of at least one of the following acts: (a) attempting to cause, threatening to cause, or causing physical harm to another family or household member; (b) placing a family or household member in fear of physical harm; (c) causing a family or household member to engage against his or her will in sexual activity by force, threat or force, or duress. D opposes entry of the order for protection, claiming that P's testimony is insufficient to establish that these events occurred. Is the evidence sufficient to issue an order for protection?

3. Assume that D attempted to isolate P from visitors, and he disrupted their Internet connection so that P could not communicate with family and friends. He cut off power to their home and attempted to control P's actions through intimidation. P testified that she lives in fear of D and that their child would not be safe if left alone with D, in part because D's conduct prevented the child from sleeping at night. D claims that no acts of physical abuse were alleged and that the trial court erred in issuing a protective order. Will a court issue a protective order?

4. P, who spoke little English, sought a protective order alleging that D threatened P if she did not have daily sex with D and that, after one such incident, D went outside to shoot targets and between shots would pretend to shoot at the house where P stood with her child. When driving, D would also deliberately "spin out" on dirt roads to scare P and the child. P moved out of state and several months later sought a protective order. Will a court issue the order?

Explanations

1. In a similar case, P obtained an order for protection from the trial court; however, that decision was overturned on appeal. In *Ficklin v. Ficklin*, 710 N.W.2d 387 (N.D. 2006), the court found that there was evidence that P was fearful that D would burn down the house; however, the court ruled that the evidence was not sufficient to establish that she was in fear of *imminent* harm. The appellate court noted that the trial court erroneously focused on eliminating the mere possibility of harm.
2. In *Aiken v. Stanley*, 816 N.E.2d 427 (Ind. App. 2004), the trial court issued the order for protection, and the court's decision was upheld on appeal. The appellate court found that the evidence outlined previously was sufficient to support issuance of the order for protection under the statute. The court noted that under the language of the statute, it was sufficient for P to show that she and her son were in fear of D. No particular threats or actions were specifically required, so long as this showing was made.
3. D's behavior shows a pattern of attempting to control, intimidate, and isolate P, and she is consequently afraid for herself and her child. In the similar case of *Cole v. Cole*, 940 A.2d 194 (Me. 2008), the appellate court upheld the issuance of a protective order finding that such behavior fell within the statutory definition of "compelling a person by force, threat of force, or intimidation to engage in conduct from which the person has a right or privilege to abstain or to abstain from conduct in which the person has a right to engage." Note that Maine's definition of domestic violence is different from that of most states, in that it specifically addresses intimidation and compulsion of someone to abstain from conduct.
4. In the case of *Ditmars v. Ditmars*, 788 N.W.2d 817 (Neb. App. 2010), the court held that P's allegations were insufficient to support a finding of "fear of imminent bodily injury" because the abuse occurred several months before and in another state. The court deemed the allegations "stale."

19.8. Who Is Covered?

State domestic abuse acts provide relief to spouses and former spouses of perpetrators. Most statutes extend coverage to children, other family members, household members, and unmarried parents of a common child. Many statutes include same-gender intimate partners and some include dating couples. *See Evans v. Braun*, 12 A.3d 395 (Pa. Super. 2010) (brief dating relationship sufficient to seek protective order); *Benjamin v. McKinnon*, 887 N.E.2d 14 (Ill.

App. 2008) ("because ex-wife had been married to applicant's son, ex-wife's father, and ex-wife's brother were applicant's relatives by collateral affinity" and were family members for purpose of seeking a protective order). *But see Smith v. Martin*, 2009 WL 2028403 (Ohio App. 2009) (unborn child falls outside statutory definition of "persons entitled to seek relief").

EXAMPLES

Examples

5. P was married to and lived with H and their 6-year-old child but had an "intermittent" intimate relationship with her "boyfriend," D. D hit P and threatened to kill P, H, and the child. P sought a protective order, but D challenges the action, asserting that the family court lacked jurisdiction under a statutory provision providing potential relief to those "who are or have been in an intimate relationship regardless of whether such persons have lived together at any time." How might a court rule?

6. P files for an order for protection after she is assaulted by her cohabiting boyfriend, D. The domestic violence statute in their state extends to "a person living as a spouse." The state has amended its constitution to include a Defense of Marriage Amendment (DOMA) stating the following, "Only a union between one man and one woman may be a marriage valid in or recognized by this state and its political subdivisions. This state and its political subdivisions shall not create or recognize a legal status for relationships of unmarried individuals that intends to approximate the design, qualities, significance, or effect of marriage." D asserts that applying the domestic violence statute to an unmarried couple violates the state constitution and that P is consequently not entitled to relief under the domestic violence statute. What is the likely result?

EXPLANATIONS

Explanations

5. In the case of *Jessica D. v. Jeremy H.*, 77 A.D.3d 87 (N.Y. App. 2010), the Supreme Court, Appellate Division, reversed a trial court that had previously denied P's petition. Pursuant to the statute, the lower court should have considered factors such as the nature of the relationship, frequency of contact, and the duration of the relationship because the purpose of the statute was to protect victims of domestic violence.

6. In *State v. Ward*, 849 N.E.2d 1076 (Ohio App. 2006), the court agreed with D and held that the domestic violence statute provision extending

protection to "a person living as a spouse" violated the state DOMA. However, due to a split among the Ohio courts, the Ohio Supreme Court considered the issue in *State v. Carswell*, 871 N.E.2d 547 (Ohio 2007), and held that the domestic violence statute did not conflict with the state DOMA. The court reasoned that the term "person living as a spouse" did not recognize or create a legal relationship but "merely identifie[d] a particular class of persons for the purposes of the domestic-violence statutes."

19.9. What Relief Is Granted?

The workhorse of domestic abuse legislation is an injunctive order, which may be referred to as an *order for protection, civil protective order, protective order,* or *restraining order.* The relief available varies by state but typically includes a prohibition against further abuse, no-contact orders, awards of exclusive possession of the residence, child custody and visitation arrangements, and/or support orders. *But see Harris v. Ross*, 2011 WL 825739 (Ohio. App. 2011) (protective order could not affect title to real property).

19.10. *Ex Parte* and "Permanent" Orders

Obtaining a protective order is usually a two-step process: first obtaining an *ex parte* order and then seeking a "permanent" order after notice and possibly a hearing. In many cases, the victim needs immediate relief, and giving notice to the perpetrator would result in additional harm. If the victim can demonstrate a substantial likelihood of abuse or an immediate and present danger of abuse, the victim can seek an *ex parte* order. In some jurisdictions, this can be done by affidavit, but in other jurisdictions, testimony is required. The relief available in an *ex parte* order is likely to be limited in scope.

In many jurisdictions, a full hearing is scheduled, and the respondent is served with the *ex parte* order and the hearing date. If the respondent is served but fails to appear at the hearing, the judge may issue a default order. In other jurisdictions, after the respondent is served, the respondent can request a hearing. If the respondent does not do so, the *ex parte* order becomes a permanent order. *See Hedgcock v. Hedgcock*, 221 P.3d 856 (Utah. App. 2009) (court determined hearing not required after telephone conference with parties); *Nakamura v. Parker*, 67 Cal. Rptr. 3d 286 (Cal. App. 2007) (abuse of discretion to deny "facially adequate" application for temporary restraining order without a hearing); *Connolly v. Connolly*, 892 A.2d 465 (Me. 2006) (court required to conduct an evidentiary hearing and make findings);

Wright v. Wright, 181 S.W.3d 49 (Ky. App. 2005) (court failed to hold evidentiary hearing as required by statute). Final or permanent orders typically remain in effect for a year, although some states issue them for shorter or longer periods of time.

EXAMPLES

Examples

7. Assume that P lives in a jurisdiction that authorizes temporary (*ex parte*) and permanent orders for protection. In order to obtain a temporary order for protection under the statute, P would be required to show "imminent danger." The statute authorizes issuance of a permanent order "If . . . the judge or magistrate is of the opinion that [a spouse] has committed acts constituting grounds for issuance of a civil protection order and that unless restrained will continue to commit such acts, the judge or magistrate shall order the temporary civil protection order to be made permanent or order a permanent civil protection order with different provisions from the temporary civil protection order." P seeks a permanent order, and after notice is given to D and a hearing is held, the court issues a permanent order without making a finding of imminent danger. D alleges that a finding of imminent danger was necessary, and D appeals on that basis. Will D succeed on appeal?
8. P and D reside in Illinois. Due to domestic violence, P leaves Illinois to stay with family members in New Jersey. She obtains an *ex parte* temporary restraining order against D from a New Jersey court. D has never been to New Jersey, and D claims that the New Jersey court lacked personal jurisdiction over him. What is the likely result?

EXPLANATIONS

Explanations

7. In a similar case, a court held that although a showing of imminent danger was required to obtain a temporary order, it was not statutorily required for issuance of a permanent order. The court reasoned that temporary orders are issued under urgent circumstances and often without notice to the respondent, whereas permanent orders are designed to prevent future harm. *In re Marriage of Fiffe*, 140 P.3d 160 (Colo. App. 2005).
8. In the similar case of *Shah v. Shah*, 875 A.2d 931 (N.J. 2005), the court held that it did not have personal jurisdiction over the defendant and that

it consequently could not issue a final restraining order requiring the defendant to perform affirmative acts. However, the court determined that a temporary restraining order issued by the New Jersey court was valid to the extent that it provided prohibitory relief. In addition, the court ruled that the temporary restraining order could remain in effect indefinitely.

19.11. Constitutional Challenges

Respondents have challenged state domestic abuse acts, alleging that issuance of *ex parte* orders of protection violate their due process rights. However, these challenges have not been successful. *See State ex rel. Williams v. Marsh*, 626 S.W.2d 223 (Mo. 1982); *Baker v. Baker*, 494 N.W.2d 282 (Minn. 1992) (upholding constitutionality of state domestic abuse statute). In analyzing constitutional claims, courts have used the balancing test set forth in *Mathews v. Eldridge*, 424 U.S. 319 (1976). Although the defendant has a property interest in the home and a liberty interest in the children, the government has a strong interest in preventing future violence. Furthermore, procedural safeguards exist, including requiring affidavits, taking testimony, having a judge or referee make the decision, giving notice of rights, and holding an immediate hearing.

Other aspects of civil domestic abuse statutes have also been subject to largely unsuccessful constitutional challenges. *See Crespo v. Crespo*, 972 A.2d 1169 (N.J. Super. 2009) (domestic violence act prohibition on possession of firearms did not violate Second Amendment); *Towner v. Ridgway*, 182 P.3d 347 (Utah 2008) (stalking injunction did not violate First Amendment rights); *Rew ex rel. T.C.B. v. Bergstrom*, 812 N.W.2d 832 (Minn. App. 2011) (extension of protective order for 50 years did not violate First Amendement or due process).

EXAMPLES

Examples

9. Assume that P and D have been married for five years. D is at work one day when he is served with an *ex parte* order of protection granting P exclusive possession of the residence, prohibiting D from contacting P, and barring D from seeing their children until after a hearing scheduled ten days later. In the petition, P accuses D of several acts of violence, which D denies, and P alleges that D has threatened to "kidnap" the children if P moves out of the marital home. D is outraged that he

cannot go home, cannot see his children, and that all of this can happen to him without his having a chance to tell his side of the story. He contacts an attorney for advice. Have D's due process rights been violated?

10. Assume that D assaults P, and P files for an order for protection. Under the state domestic abuse statute, before an order is issued, the court is required to make findings in an official record or in writing. In emergency situations, the court is required to examine the petitioner under oath and review a verified petition for relief. In this case, the court issued an order for protection but did not make findings or a record of testimony. D petitions to have the order overturned, arguing that significant provisions of the domestic abuse act were not followed. P argues that these were mere technicalities. What is the likely result?

EXPLANATIONS

Explanations

9. D's due process rights have not been violated. Although state action is involved and D clearly has a liberty interest in seeing the children and a property interest in the residence, this private interest is outweighed by the state's interest in preventing further abuse and possible parental kidnapping. D is protected by the requirement that P is required to file a verified affidavit and appear before a judge, who assessed P's credibility and most likely took testimony on the record. The deprivation is temporary because D has received notice and will have a full hearing shortly.

10. D is likely to have the order of protection overturned because D did not receive important procedural protections. In a similar case, *Hedrick-Koroll v. Bagley*, 816 N.E.2d 849 (Ill. App. 2004), the appellate court held that the trial court failed to comply with the Domestic Violence Act requirement of specific findings. The case was remanded for further proceedings.

19.12. Access to the Court

A victim of domestic violence who is not represented by counsel may have difficulty procuring a protective order and obtaining other necessary relief. Some statutes require clerks of court to assist unrepresented victims seeking to file petitions. Domestic violence advocates also provide information and support, and in some jurisdictions, their communications with the victim are privileged. *See People v. Turner*, 109 P.3d 639 (Colo. 2005). Nevertheless, legal representation for victims is a serious and ongoing problem. In an effort to make protection more readily available, a few courts provide for issuance of emergency orders outside of business hours. *See* Beverly Balos, *Domestic Violence Matters: The Case for Appointed Counsel in Protective Order Proceedings*, 15 Temple Pol. & Civ. Rts. L. Rev. 557 (2006).

19.13. Issuance of Mutual Orders

Sometimes respondents request that an order for protection be issued against the victim as well as the respondent. This practice is known as issuing *mutual* or *cross* orders of protection. In *Deacon v. Landers*, 587 N.E.2d 395 (Ohio App. 1990), the trial court granted mutual orders over the objection of the victim, without any presentation of evidence showing that she had been violent. The appellate court overruled the trial court and held that issuance of mutual orders violated the victim's right to due process. *See Cooper v. Cooper*, 144 P.3d 451 (Alaska 2006) (no independent basis for issuance of mutual order).

Unless clearly warranted by the evidence, issuance of mutual orders of protection can be dangerous. Such orders empower the perpetrator, put the victim and children at additional risk, and confuse police, who are trying to enforce the orders.

Example

11. P and D cohabited for a period of years but did not marry. During this time, D committed several severe acts of domestic violence against P, and D was imprisoned three times for these assaults. P sought a restraining order against D, and D appeared at the hearing where P was granted a three-year restraining order. About a week later, D filed a separate action for a domestic violence temporary restraining order against P, alleging that P harassed him while he was in prison by sending him letters, and that P later threatened to report him for stealing her ATM card. The court issued a temporary restraining order against P. The state where P and D reside has a statute stating that the court may not issue mutual restraining orders unless both parties personally appear in court to present evidence of abuse and the court makes detailed findings that both acted as primary aggressors and not in self-defense. P claims that mutual orders have been issued in violation of the statute. D claims that the requirements of the statute have been met because, with respect to

both orders, the petitioner appeared personally and the court made detailed findings. Does this situation describe mutual orders within the meaning of the statute?

EXPLANATION

Explanation

11. In the similar case of *Conness v. Satram*, 18 Cal. Rptr. 3d 577 (Cal. App. 2004), the appellate court found that the term "mutual order" meant a single order imposing parallel requirements on each party. The orders issued against P and D were deemed to be separate orders that included findings of credibility by the trial court. Consequently, according to the appellate court, the orders were not "mutual" under the state statute, and both orders could remain in effect.

19.14. Enforcement of Orders

Most domestic abuse statutes make violation of a protective order a criminal offense, typically a misdemeanor, although some violations may be charged as a felony. *See State v. Bunker*, 238 P.3d 487 (Wash. 2010) (statute criminalizes violation of no-contact orders). Despite such provisions, the Supreme Court has held that a domestic abuse victim who has obtained a restraining order does not have a constitutionally protected property interest in police enforcement of the order, even when there is probable cause to believe that the order was violated. *Town of Castle Rock, Colo. v. Gonzales*, 125 S. Ct. 2796 (2005).

In addition to being a criminal offense, violation of a protective order may constitute criminal contempt. Although both types of proceedings are useful, some commentators favor criminal contempt proceedings over prosecution because victims have more control over the process, and contempt actions may proceed more quickly than criminal prosecutions. *See* David M. Zlotnick, *Empowering the Battered Woman: The Use of Criminal Contempt Sanctions to Enforce Civil Protection Orders*, 56 Ohio St. L.J. 1153 (1995).

Special enforcement issues can arise if the parties decide to reconcile but do not petition the court to dissolve an existing protective order. For example, in *Cole v. Cole*, 556 N.Y.S.2d 217 (Fam. 1990), the couple reconciled after issuance of a protective order and then separated again. Subsequent to the separation, the husband broke into the residence, choked the wife, and threatened to kill her. The police refused to enforce the order because of the intervening reconciliation. The court ultimately found that the order remained in effect and held the husband in contempt of court. In so doing, the court noted that the husband could have returned to court to vacate the order and that reconciliation did not license the husband to commit further abuse. *See Com. v. Brumbaugh*, 932 A.2d 108 (Pa. Super. 2007) (defendant held in contempt for violation of protective order even though the victim invited him to attend party).

Example

12. P and D had a history of domestic violence. After 20 years of marriage, P initiated divorce proceedings against D and obtained a no-contact order. Six months later, after another incident, D pleaded *nolo contendere* to charges of domestic disorderly conduct and violation of the no-contact order. D's probation officer met with him to explain the terms of the order, but shortly after the meeting, D mailed two birthday cards to P. P claimed that D violated the no-contact order by sending the cards, but D claimed that the no-contact order did not specifically prohibit mailings. Did D violate the no-contact order?

Explanation

12. In the similar case of *State v. John*, 881 A.2d 920 (R.I. 2005), the court held that the order was reasonably clear and specific in restraining D from "any contact" with P. "Any contact" included sending mail to P. Consequently, D was in violation of the order. Although such a violation may sound trivial, coercive-controlling perpetrators commonly test the victim's resolve to enforce the protective order once it is obtained. Additionally, if there is a history of coercive control over the victim, gestures that seem innocent to an onlooker may actually have a threatening hidden meaning. *But see State v. Price*, 886 N.E.2d 852 (Ohio 2008) (court found implied exception to no-contact order to arrange visitation).

19.15. Effectiveness of Orders

Survivors of domestic violence frequently report that protective orders have been helpful and empowering. Nevertheless, researchers continue to investigate how and when protective orders are most effective in preventing further abuse. For example, one study found that 60 percent of temporary orders of protection were violated within a year. Victims who had been more seriously abused suffered more serious violations, and abusers who objected to entry of the order were more likely to violate it. Adele Harrell & Barbara E. Smith, *Effects of Restraining Orders on Domestic Violence Victims*, in *Do Arrests and Restraining Orders Work?* (Eve S. Buzawa & Carl G. Buzawa, eds., 1996). Protective orders *may* be less effective if the abuser has a past criminal history, the couple has minor children, and/or they have low incomes. *See* Eve S. Buzawa & Carl G. Buzawa, *Domestic Violence: The Criminal Justice Response* 242-245 (2003).

The decision about whether to obtain an order for protection must be made on a case-by-case basis. Survivors should be counseled concerning the availability of relief and the costs and benefits of seeking an order in light of the victim's particular circumstances. Survivors should be aware that jurisdictions vary in terms of the difficulty of obtaining an order and how seriously violations are viewed by police, prosecutors, and judges. *See* Sara R. Benson, *Failure to Arrest: A Pilot Study of Police Response to Domestic Violence in Rural Illinois*, 17 Am. U. J. Gender Soc. Pol'y & L. 685 (2009).

Example

13. Assume that P and D were married and that D was violent with P throughout the marriage. Most recently, D broke P's nose and threatened to kill her and take the children if she left him. P does not work outside the home and does not have relatives in the area. What factors should P be counseled about in deciding whether to obtain an order of protection?

Explanation

13. With respect to obtaining a protective order, P should be carefully counseled about the possibility that D might violate the order. P would probably have an accurate assessment of D's reaction to entry of the *ex parte* order — some respondents comply with orders, and others become more violent. Also, some police departments respond more quickly, and some jurisdictions prosecute violations more vigorously than others. P's safety is more important than staying in the house. Consequently, P should seriously consider making a temporary move to a shelter or having someone stay at the house with P and the children. In any event, P and the children should have a detailed safety plan.

RELATED AREAS OF LAW

19.16. Violence Against Women Act (VAWA)

The federal Violence Against Women Act (VAWA) was originally passed in 1994 and has been reauthorized several times. Among other provisions, the Act requires states to enforce protective orders from different states so long as the issuing court had jurisdiction and provided due process. In cases in which mutual orders of protection were issued, only the order issued on behalf of the petitioner is enforceable unless the respondent filed a counter-petition and the court made specific findings. 18 U.S.C. §2265 (2011). *See* Emily J. Sack, *Domestic Violence Across State Lines: The Full Faith and Credit Clause, Congressional Power, and Interstate Enforcement of Protection Orders*, 98 N.W. U. L. Rev. 827 (2004). The VAWA also includes criminal penalties for crossing state lines to injure an intimate partner or violate a protective order, and the Act criminalizes possession of a firearm by respondents subject to protective orders. *See* 18 U.S.C. §§922(g)(8)(9); Lisa D. May, *The Backfiring of the Domestic Violence Firearms Bans*, 14 Colum. J. Gender & L. 1 (2005).

EXAMPLE

Example

14. Assume that after a full hearing, an order for protection is issued against D in the state of X. D continues to contact P in spite of a "no contact" provision in the order. P no longer feels safe at the residence, so P goes to stay with a friend who lives an hour away in state Y. D tracks P down and goes to the house where P is staying with the friend. P calls the police when D arrives. Can the police in state Y enforce the order?

EXPLANATION

Explanation

14. Prior to passage of the VAWA, only a few states recognized protective orders from other states. However, the VAWA requires states to give full faith and credit to protective orders issued by other states, so long as due process was provided. Consequently, the police and the courts in state Y can enforce the order originally issued in state X.

19.17. Criminal Sanctions

Violence between intimate partners involves commission of crimes such as assault, battery, rape, and attempted murder. Police historically were trained not to arrest abusive partners, and domestic violence was, for the most part, not treated as a crime by prosecutors. This practice changed dramatically during the 1980s due to increased awareness of the issue, studies documenting the value of arrest as a deterrent, and lawsuits against police departments.

Arrest and criminal sanctions remain an important tool for victims of abuse — especially where police, prosecutors, and courts coordinate enforcement efforts. However, research indicates that arrest is less effective with some defendants than others. Eve S. Buzawa & Carl G. Buzawa, *Domestic Violence: The Criminal Justice Response* 104 (2003) (an excellent discussion of the history and effectiveness of arrest in cases of domestic violence). For example, arrest may not be as effective with unemployed defendants and may reduce violence only in the short run. Janell D. Schmidt & Lawrence W. Sherman, *Does Arrest Deter Domestic Violence?* in *Do Arrests and Restraining Orders Work?* (Eve S. Buzawa & Carl G. Buzawa eds., 1996).

If a victim does not testify at trial, prosecutors may seek to introduce statements made to police and medical personnel. However, under the Sixth Amendment, perpetrators facing criminal prosecution have the right to confront witnesses, and testimonial out-of-court statements cannot be admitted into evidence unless the witness is unavailable and the defendant had a prior opportunity to cross-examine. *Crawford v. Washington*, 541 U.S. 36 (2004). The United States Supreme Court held that a domestic abuse victim's statements to a 911 operator were not subject to the confrontation clause because they were not testimonial in nature. In contrast, a victim's written statements in an affidavit provided to police were testimonial and thus subject to the confrontation clause. *Davis v. Washington*, 126 S. Ct. 2266 (2006). *See* John M. Leventhal, *The Admission of Evidence in Domestic Violence Cases After Crawford v. Washington: A National Survey*, 11 Berkeley J. Crim. L. 77 (2006) (courts continue to admit victims' out-of-court statements).

19.18. Mandatory Arrest and No-Drop Policies

Some jurisdictions have adopted mandatory arrest (with probable cause) and/or no-drop policies so that the decision to press criminal charges is taken out of the hands of the victim. Such policies are designed to protect traumatized victims from pressure to drop charges by having the police and prosecutor bring the charges and subpoena the victim as a witness. Critics of these policies argue that they ignore the preferences of the victims and further disempower them. *See* David Hirschel et al., *Domestic Violence and Mandatory Arrest Laws: To What Extent Do They Influence Police Arrest Decisions*, 98 J. Crim. L. & Criminology 255 (2007) (preferred arrest policies increase arrest rates).

19.19. Tort Actions

Creative advocates have brought tort actions on behalf of battered spouses. Such actions may be based on torts such as assault and battery, wrongful death, false imprisonment, defamation, wiretapping, and intentional infliction of emotional distress. *See* Clare Dalton, *Domestic Violence, Domestic Torts, and Divorce: Constraints and Possibilities*, 31 New Eng. L. Rev. 319 (1997).

For example, in *Feltmeier v. Feltmeier*, 777 N.E.2d 1032 (Ill. App. 2002), *aff'd*, 798 N.E.2d 75 (Ill. 2003), the court upheld an action for intentional infliction of emotional distress based upon a finding of "extreme and outrageous" conduct. The husband unsuccessfully argued that a "reasonable wife" should have been able to endure 11 years of abuse. *See also Curtis v. Firth*, 850 P.2d 749 (Idaho 1993) (upholding damage award for intentional infliction of emotional distress); *Xiao Yang Chen v. Fischer*, 843 N.E.2d 723 (N.Y. 2005) (personal injury action for damages for physical and emotional abuse during marriage not barred by *res judicata*). *But see Hakkila v. Hakkila*, 812 P.2d 1320 (N.M. App. 1991) (husband's conduct did not meet "outrageousness" standard); *Pugliese v. Superior Court*, 53 Cal. Rptr. 3d 681 (Cal. App. 2007) (application of continuing tort doctrine in suit for damages for acts of domestic violence).

EXAMPLE

Example

15. In the case of *Graham v. Brown*, 26 A.3d 823 (Me. 2011), the petitioner alleged intentional infliction of emotional distress based on the following facts:

> Brown committed frequent acts of physical and emotional abuse against Graham. The acts committed included throwing her across a room so that she fell on her face and jaw, and nearly fell twelve feet into a basement; aggressively pulling Graham out of her truck, causing bruising on her arm; striking her hand with a drum stick, injuring her hand when he knew that she was studying to become a massage therapist and would need the use of her hands; refusing Graham assistance when she developed a uterine infection after an abortion, and telling her that she deserved to die; refusing her assistance after she had a miscarriage and telling her that she deserved the miscarriage and deserved to bleed to

> death; shoving Graham backwards into a cement step, resulting in injuries to her back and spine; on multiple occasions, hitting, slapping, or head-butting Graham during arguments; on several occasions, punishing her young son in front of her by covering his mouth so that he could not breathe; on several occasions, emptying onto the driveway potted plants that Brown knew were important to Graham; and throwing Graham's cat against a chimney because it annoyed him.

Id. at 825. She sought compensatory and punitive damages. What was the result?

EXPLANATION

Explanation

15. The trial court was affirmed on appeal with respect to an award of compensatory damages in the amount of $50,000 and an award of $5,000 in punitive damages. Graham was diagnosed with "post-traumatic stress disorder, anxiety disorder, depression, and insomnia, all resulting from Brown's action." *Id.* at 826.

19.20. Hague Convention

The Hague Convention on the Civil Aspects of International Child Abduction deals with international parental kidnapping. Unfortunately, recent research shows that some of these cases involve victims of domestic violence who cross international boundaries in an effort to escape abuse and protect children. *See* Jeffery L. Edleson et al., *Perspectives on Battered Mothers and Their Children Fleeing to the United States for Safety: A Study of Hague Convention Cases*, *available at* https://www.ncjrs.gov/pdffiles1/nij/grants/232624.pdf (last visited August 4, 2012). *See also* *Miltiadous v. Tetervak*, 686 F. Supp. 2d 544 (E.D. Penn. (2010) (analyzing grave risk defense); Karen Brown Williams, *Fleeing Domestic Violence: A Proposal to Change the Inadequacies of the Hague Convention on the Civil Aspects of International Child Abduction in Domestic Violence Cases*, 4 J. Marshall L.J. 39 (2011).

Neglect, Dependency, Child Abuse, and Termination of Parental Rights

20.1. Introduction

State intervention into the family unit historically has focused on strengthening and reuniting the family unit. In cases of substantiated child abuse and neglect, the state child protection agency may have worked with the family, sometimes for years, with the goal of returning the child to the home. This approach was questioned in the 1990s, as experts expressed concern that some children who might be made available for adoption instead were stranded in foster care without any realistic hope of reunification. Thus, in recent years, an emphasis has been placed on earlier termination of parental rights in order to free children in foster care for adoption.

20.2. Nature and Scope of the Problem

Of children experiencing maltreatment in 2010, most (78.3 percent) suffered neglect, 17.6 percent were abused physically, and 9.2 percent were abused sexually. Over 1,500 children died as a result of abuse, and 79.4 percent of the children who were killed were younger than four years of age. U.S. Dept. of Health and Human Services, Administration for Children and Families, *Child Maltreatment 2010*, http://www.acf.hhs.gov/programs/cb/pubs/cm10/cm10.pdf#page=9 (last visited July 18, 2012).

As of 2010, 408,425 children were in foster care, and the average age of a child in foster care was 9.4 years old. Of these children, 26 percent were placed in the home of a relative, but others lived in placements including non-relative foster family homes (48 percent), institutions (9 percent), and group homes (6 percent). The mean length of stay in foster care was 25.3 months. In about half the cases (51 percent) reunification was the stated case goal, and of children exiting foster care in 2010, 51 percent were reunited with their parent or primary caretaker. Adoption and Foster Care Analysis Reporting System (AFCARS) U.S. Department of Health and Human Services, Administration for Children and Families, Administration on Children, Youth and Families, Children's Bureau, http://www.acf.hhs.gov/programs/cb/stats_research/afcars/tar/report18.htm (last visited July 18, 2009).

STANDARDS FOR STATE INTERVENTION

20.3. Parents' Right to Privacy — Liberty Interests

The raising and disciplining of children has long been considered a private family matter, and this liberty interest receives constitutional protection. *Meyer v. Nebraska*, 262 U.S. 390 (1923); *Pierce v. Soc'y of Sisters*, 268 U.S. 510 (1925); *Troxel v. Granville*, 530 U.S. 57 (2000). However, parents' prerogatives are not without limits. As the Supreme Court stated in *Prince v. Massachusetts*, 321 U.S. 158, 166 (1944):

> And neither rights of religion nor rights of parenthood are beyond limitation. Acting to guard the general interest in youth's well being, the state as *parens patriae* may restrict the parent's control by requiring school attendance, regulating or prohibiting the child's labor, and in many other ways.

Consequently, if there is compelling justification, such as when a child is "at risk of harm," the state may intervene in the family. *In re Juvenile Appeal* (83-CD), 455 A.2d 1319 (Conn. 1983); *See In re Reese*, 227 P.3d 900 (2010). However, statutes prescribing when intervention may occur may not be vague or overly broad. *Roe v. Conn*, 417 F. Supp. 769, 778 (D.C. Ala. 1976) (standard that "the child is in such condition that its welfare requires" is unconstitutionally vague and infringes on fundamental rights); Scott A. Davidson, *When Is Parental Discipline Child Abuse? The Vagueness of Child Abuse Laws*, 34 U. Louisville J. Fam. L. 403, 409 (1996).

20.4. The Child Abuse Prevention and Treatment Act (CAPTA)

In 1974, Congress passed the Child Abuse Prevention and Treatment Act (CAPTA), which brought federal attention to the issues of child abuse and neglect. Pursuant to the Act, states adopted more uniform definitions, and in later years, CAPTA was amended to focus on sexual abuse, as well as preventive efforts. *See* Howard Davidson, *Federal Law and State Intervention When Parents Fail: Has National Guidance of Our Child Welfare System Been Successful?* 42 Fam. L.Q. 481 (2008).

20.5. Indian Child Welfare Act (ICWA)

Because of a history of disproportionate removal of Native American children from their homes, special protections are provided for these children under the Indian Child Welfare Act (ICWA). The Act requires clear and convincing evidence of serious emotional or physical harm before a child is removed from the home. 25 U.S.C. §1912(e). In addition, absent good cause to the contrary, if an Indian child is removed from the home, the Act requires that the child be placed in foster care with extended family, in a foster home approved by the tribe or a licensing authority, or in an institution approved of or operated by an Indian organization. 25 U.S.C. §1915(b). *But see People ex rel. South Dakota Dept. of Social Services*, 795 N.W.2d 39 (S.D. 2011) (clear and convincing evidence of good cause to deviate from placement preferences).

20.6. Defining Abuse, Neglect, and Dependency

State statutes define the circumstances under which states will intervene in the family. Historically, states have defined abuse, neglect, and dependency separately. Abuse typically involves excessive corporal punishment, sexual abuse, or serious psychological abuse. Neglect is associated with the failure to provide food or housing or to meet medical or educational needs. Dependency is similar to neglect, except that the lack of care occurs due to circumstances beyond the parent's control and without fault on the part of the parent.

Some states do not distinguish among abuse, neglect, and dependency, but instead use a definition that includes all three. For example, as shown here, the relevant California statute merges neglect and abuse into the definition of dependent child:

Cal. Welf. & Inst. Code §300 (West 2012). Children Subject to Jurisdiction . . .

Any child who comes within any of the following descriptions is within the jurisdiction of the juvenile court which may adjudge that person to be a dependent child of the court.

a. The child has suffered, or there is a substantial risk that the child will suffer, serious physical harm inflicted nonaccidentally upon the child by the child's parent or guardian. . . .

b. The child has suffered, or there is a substantial risk that the child will suffer, serious physical harm or illness, as a result of the failure or inability of his or her parent or guardian to adequately supervise or protect the child, or the willful or negligent failure of the child's parent or guardian to adequately supervise or protect the child from the conduct of the custodian with whom the child has been left, or by the willful or negligent failure of the parent or guardian to provide the child with adequate food, clothing, shelter, or medical treatment, or by the inability of the parent or guardian to provide regular care for the child due to the parent's or guardian's mental illness, developmental disability, or substance abuse. . . .

c. The child is suffering serious emotional damage, or is at substantial risk of suffering serious emotional damage, evidenced by severe anxiety, depression, withdrawal, or untoward aggressive behavior toward self or others, as a result of the conduct of the parent or guardian or who has no parent or guardian capable of providing appropriate care. . . .

d. The child has been sexually abused or there is substantial risk that the child will be sexually abused. . . .

e. The child is under the age of five and has suffered severe physical abuse by a parent, or by any person known by the parent, if the parent knew or reasonably should have known that the person was physically abusing the child. . . .

f. The child's parent or guardian caused the death of another child through abuse or neglect.

g. ***

h. ***

i. The child has been subjected to an act or acts of cruelty by the parent or guardian or a member of his or her household or the parent or guardian has failed to adequately protect the child from an act or acts of cruelty when the parent or guardian knew or reasonably should have known that the child was in danger of being subjected to an act or acts of cruelty.

j. The child's sibling has been abused or neglected. . . .

The following sections discuss how courts have interpreted and applied similar statutory provisions.

COMMON FORMS OF ABUSE AND NEGLECT

20.7. Use of Unreasonable Force to Correct a Child

Parents can legally use reasonable force to correct a child. *See South Carolina Dept. of Soc. Servs. v. Father and Mother*, 366 S.E.2d 40, 42 (S.C. App. 1988) (force or violence of discipline must be "reasonable in manner and moderate in degree"); *State v. Lefevre*, 117 P.3d 980 (N.M. App. 2005) (discipline involves controlling behavior and correcting misbehavior for the betterment and welfare of the child, and physical force cannot be cruel or excessive if it is to be justified).

The Restatement (Second) of Torts §147 provides that "[a] parent is privileged to apply such reasonable force or to impose such reasonable confinement upon his child as he reasonably believes to be necessary for its proper control, training, or education. . . ." §150 lists factors to be considered in determining whether the action was reasonable:

a. whether the actor is a parent;
b. the age, sex, and physical and mental condition of the child;
c. the nature of his offense and his apparent motive;
d. the influence of his example upon other children of the same family or group;
e. whether the force or confinement is reasonably necessary and appropriate to compel obedience to a proper command;
f. whether it is disproportionate to the offense, unnecessarily degrading, or likely to cause serious or permanent harm.

20.8. Spanking

Spanking children is a matter of some controversy, and judges may be called on to distinguish reasonable use of force from that which is excessive. For example, in *Raboin v. North Dakota Dept. of Human Servs*, 552 N.W.2d 329 (N.D. 1996), the court held that bruising on the buttocks resulting from the use of a wooden spoon, plastic spoon, or belt did not constitute child abuse. Nevertheless, the concurring judge frowned upon the use of corporal punishment, stating that it "can only diminish a child's sense of self-worth, and thereby unnecessarily limit the resources that child can bring to life's battles." *Id.* at 335. *See generally In re J.L.*, 891 N.E.2d 778 (Ohio App. 2008) (social worker testified that "developmentally, young children only understand that spanking means it's okay to hurt others").

In contrast, in *State v. Denzel B.*, 192 P.3d 260 (N.M. App. 2008), the appellate court stated that punishing a 16-year-old boy by beating him with a belt is not a reasonable use of force. It went on to say that where force is excessive or abusive, a child has a right to self-defense. *See State v. Lefevre*, 117 P.3d 980 (N.M. App. 2005). Similarly, the Georgia Supreme Court in *In re N.S.E.*, 666 S.E.2d 587 (Ga. App. 2008), upheld a trial court's ruling terminating a father's rights to his three children where he had disciplined them by spanking them with objects or slapping them, which resulted in bruises and marks on their bodies. He testified he was in charge of discipline and claimed that his mode of discipline was required by his religious beliefs. He asserted that "(a)ny sound spanking will leave a mark." He admitted that he began spanking one of the children at least one month prior to the child's death; that he had previously broken the child's femur due to slapping him; and that on the day the child was taken to the hospital, he had spanked and slapped the child, who he believed had exhibited "stubbornness."

Sweden, Norway, Denmark, Finland, and Austria have prohibited corporal punishment, and opponents of the practice have urged the United States to ratify the United Nations Convention on the Rights of the Child, which would prohibit its use. *See also* Alastair Nicholson, *Choose to Hug, Not Hit*, 46 Fam. Ct. Rev. 11 (2008); Benjamin Shmueli, *Who's Afraid of Banning Corporal Punishment? A Comparative View on Current and Desirable Models*, 26 Penn St. Int'l L. Rev. 57 (2007).

20.9. Sexual Abuse

Girls are more likely to be sexually abused than boys and about one-third of children who are sexually abused are abused by a biological parent. U.S. Dept. of Health & Human Services, Administration for Children and Families, *Fourth National Incidence Study of Child Abuse and Neglect, Report to Congress, Executive Summary* (NIS-4) (2010), http://www.acf.hhs.gov/programs/opre/abuse_neglect/natl_incid/reports/nis_execsumm/nis4_report_exec_summ_pdf_jan2010.pdf (last visited July 18, 2012).

Proving sexual abuse can be especially difficult because sexual abuse is rarely observed by a third party. Expert testimony is often required. *See State v. Waddell*, 504 S.E.2d 84 (N.C. App. 1998), *aff'd as modified*, 527 S.E.2d 644 (N.C. 2000) (discussion of issues related to child competency, hearsay, and use of anatomically correct dolls); *In re Jaclyn P.*, 179 A.D.2d 646 (N.Y. 1992), *aff'd*, 658 N.E.2d 1042 (N.Y. App. 1995). In cases of sexual abuse, some states specifically authorize the use of anatomically correct dolls to aid courtroom testimony. 42 Pa. C.S.A. §5987 (2009).

In *State v. J.Q.*, 617 A.2d 1196 (N.J. 1993), the court discussed behavioral indications of possible sexual abuse, known as the Child Sexual Abuse Accommodation Syndrome (CSAAS). These behaviors include overt or indirect disclosures, sexualized play, withdrawal, feelings of shame and guilt, falling grades, pseudo-mature personality development, sexual promiscuity, problems with peer relationships, attempted suicide, exhibiting positive relationship with the abuser, and being frightened or phobic.

20.10. Neglect

The term *neglect* refers to a variety of situations and conditions that may occur separately or concurrently. Common themes include lack of food, lack of appropriate housing, lack of medical care, lack of supervision, failure to thrive, and irregular school attendance. Not surprisingly, findings of neglect often are linked to poverty. *See* Elizabeth Bartholet, *Nobody's Children*, 33 (1999) (noting that children from families with incomes under $15,000 annually are 44 times more likely to be neglected than children from families with annual incomes over $30,000).

20.11. Medical Treatment

Medical neglect occurs when parents fail to obtain necessary medical care. For example, in *In re Seamus K.*, 33 A.D.3d 1030 (N.Y. App. 2006), the court found a father to have neglected a child by failing to obtain prompt medical care when his two-month-old child was "screaming, pale, acting strangely, vomiting, refusing to eat, and displaying seizure-like symptoms."

Difficult issues arise in both the civil and criminal context when parents withhold medical treatment for religious reasons. Some states have statutes addressing good-faith treatment by prayer, but if the child dies, a parent may be subject to criminal prosecution. For example, in the case of *Walker v. Superior Court*, 763 P.2d 852 (Cal. 1988), a parent was criminally prosecuted for failure to seek medical care for a child who died of meningitis after being treated through prayer.

The dispute in *In re Eli H.*, 871 N.Y.S.2d 846 (N.Y. Fam. Ct. 2008), involved an infant born with a hole between the lower chambers of his heart and a severe blockage between his right ventricle and his pulmonary artery. When the child's parents objected to the surgery to replace a shunt because the operation was against their religious beliefs, the Department of Social Services sought a court order finding the child neglected. The court found by a preponderance of the evidence that the child was in imminent danger because of the failure of his parents to exercise a minimum degree of care in supplying him with adequate medical care. It granted the petition reasoning that imminent risk to child's health justified the court's exercise of duty as *parens patriae* to order surgery without parents' consent. *See In re D.R.*, 20 P.3d 166, 169 (Ok. App. 2001) (court upheld finding of medical neglect when the parents refused medical treatment based upon their religious beliefs, saying that the "state has an interest in protecting the lives of its children, which may override parental decisions which threaten a child's life"); *In re McCauley*, 565 N.W.2d 411 (Mass. 1991) (court authorized blood transfusion over contrary religious beliefs of parents). *But see Marshall v. Sackett*, 907 S.W.2d 925 (Tex. App. 1995) (a parent or guardian is not considered negligent for failing to provide treatment based on legitimate religious practice but staff may request a court order to provide medical services if the child's health requires it); *In re E.G.*, 549 N.E.2d 322 (Ill. 1989) (minor whom court has determined to possess requisite degree of maturity has limited right to refuse life-sustaining medical treatment).

20.12. Failure to Protect from Harm

In addition to refraining from harming children, parents have a legal obligation to protect children from known or reasonably anticipated danger. Thus, a parent who fails to intercede to protect a child may be the focus of scrutiny by the child protection agency even though the parent did not affirmatively harm the child.

The case of *Raymond F. v. Arizona Dept. of Economic Sec.*, 231 P.3d 377 (Ariz. App. 2010) provides an extreme example of failure to protect from harm:

> The record supports the juvenile court's finding that Father is unable to discharge his parental responsibilities because of chronic drug abuse. First, Father is incapable of making appropriate decisions for his children, which has severely endangered them. Father failed to contact the police when he discovered A. F. had been sexually abused, and he allowed the children to remain in the home of the man who had abused A. F. Moreover, Father allowed Mother to reside with him after the court had granted him full custody and restricted Mother to supervised visitation with the children. During this time, Father allowed M. F.'s shoulder to be severely injured, which later resulted in a life-threatening infection. Father knew of M. F.'s injury, but he did not seek medical care for her. While Father had custody of the children, he permitted them to be driven by their grandfather who was intoxicated, which resulted in a head-on car accident.

Id. at 382.

In another example, in *People v. T. G.*, 578 N.W.2d 921 (S.D. 1998), a mother knew that the stepfather was sexually molesting her daughters but ignored and concealed the abuse. Sadly, the mother herself had been "sold" to adoptive parents and sexually abused as a child. Nevertheless, her parental rights were terminated because of her failure to protect her daughters.

20.13. Failure to Protect from Harm: Domestic Violence

Removal of children for failure to protect them from harm has been especially controversial in cases involving domestic violence. As discussed in Chapter 19, there are many reasons why a victim of domestic violence may remain in the home, including the fact that an abusive party may threaten to kill the victim and/or injure the children if the victim attempts to leave. Nevertheless, children growing up in violent homes suffer harm from witnessing abuse, and they are somewhat more likely to be physically abused too. Consequently, in some cases where a victim does not leave the home, the children may be removed by the state on the basis that the victim failed to protect them.

Neverthless, in a lawsuit regarding a New York policy, *Nicholson v. Scoppetta*, 820 N.E.2d 840 (N.Y. App. 2004), the court held that evidence that a caretaker allowed a child to witness domestic abuse was insufficient on its own to establish neglect. *See* Justine A. Dunlap, *Sometimes I Feel Like a Motherless Child: The Error of Pursuing Battered Mothers for Failure to Protect*, 50 Loy. L. Rev. 565 (2004); Beth A. Mandel, *The White Fist of the Child Welfare System: Racism, Patriarchy, and the Presumptive Removal of Children from Victims of Domestic Violence in* Nicholson v. Williams, 73 U. Cin. L. Rev. 1131 (2005); and Evan Stark, *A Failure to Protect: Unraveling the "Battered Mother's Dilemma,"* 27 W. St. U. L. Rev. 29 (1999-2000).

20.14. Emotional or Mental Abuse

Emotional abuse or neglect can be grounds for state intervention. Emotional abuse often accompanies physical abuse, but it can be more difficult to prove. Emotional abuse can also arise on its own. For example, in *In Interest of B. B.*, 500 N.W.2d 9 (Iowa 1993), a child suffered emotional harm when, because of his mother's obsession with his health, he was not allowed to attend school. Other examples of emotional abuse may include locking a child in barren rooms for extended periods of time, the existence of volatility and chaos in the home, or living with a parent who has a serious anger management issues. *See* Jean Dixon Weaver, *The Principle of Subsidiarity Applied: Reforming the Legal Framework to Capture the Psyshological Abuse of Children*, 18 Va. J. Soc. Pol'y & L. 247 (2011).

20.15. Prenatal Drug Abuse

Drug and alcohol use are frequently linked to child abuse and neglect, and unfortunately, some children are exposed to drugs and alcohol prior to birth. These children may have special needs and be difficult to parent, particularly if the parent's ability to cope is compromised by continued substance abuse. Because this is a dangerous combination of dynamics, child protection workers may attempt to intervene in such cases. *See* Elizabeth Bartholet, *Nobody's Children* (Beacon Press) 68-69 (1999).

However, intervention may be limited by the fact that some state courts hold that a fetus is not a "child" within the meaning of child protection statutes. *State ex rel. Angela M.W. v. Kruzicki*, 561 N.W.2d 729 (Wis. 1997). Policy makers also fear that prosecution of substance-abusing mothers could discourage them from seeking prenatal care and consequently bring more harm than benefit to unborn children. *Johnson v. State*, 602 So. 2d 1288 (Fla. 1992). *See also State of N.M. ex rel. CYFD v. Amanda H.*, 154 P.3d 674 (N.M. App. 2006) (no finding of neglect based on first-trimester drug use because child was born healthy and without signs of exposure to drugs).

In contrast, some state courts have held that the term *child* includes a viable fetus and that a mother can be criminally prosecuted for the death of a stillborn child related to drug use. *State v. McKnight*, 576 S.E.2d 168 (S.C. 2003). In addition, some state statutes include prenatal substance abuse in the definition of neglect. For example, Minn. Stat. §626.556(2)(f)(6) (2006) defines neglect, for the purpose of reporting, to include prenatal exposure to a controlled substance as evidenced by withdrawal symptoms, toxicological testing, medical effects, or developmental delays during the first year of life. *See also* M. Suzanne Kerney-Quillen, *Fetal Abuse: The Societal Impact of Drug-Exposed Infants and the State's Interest in Preventing Child Abuse and Neglect by Expectant Mothers*, 3 Appalachian J.L. 81 (2004); Ellen M. Weber, *Child Welfare Interventions for Drug-Dependent Pregnant Women: Limitations of a Non-Public Health Response*, 75 UMKC L. Rev. 789 (2006).

In Illinois, mothers who give birth to babies with a controlled substance in their blood, urine, or meconium are presumed unfit. If another child of the mother has been adjudicated as neglected based on "positive toxicology" at birth, the presumption is not rebuttable. *See* Ian Vandewalker, *Taking The Baby Before It's Born: Termination of the Parental Rights of Women Who Use Illegal Drugs While Pregnant*, 32 N.Y.U. Rev. L. & Soc. Change 423, 426 (2008). In Florida, the "use by the mother of a controlled substance or alcohol during pregnancy when the child, at birth, is demonstrably adversely affected by such usage" is "harm" and therefore constitutes child abuse if done willfully. *Id.* In Ohio, when a newborn child's toxicology screen yields a positive result for illegal drug due to prenatal maternal drug abuse, the newborn is, for the purposes of Ohio law, per se an abused child. *See In re Baby Boy Blackshear*, 736 N.E.2d 462 (Ohio 2000); R.C. 2151.031(D).

Examples

EXAMPLES

1. Assume that a 13-year-old girl, X, comes home at 2:00 a.m. from a party, even though she promised to be home by 11:00 p.m. Her father, D, is angry and frightened by X's failure to return home on time or call. He strikes the girl twice with his belt, leaving two large purple bruises, one on her thigh and the other on the back of her leg. D claims that X bruises easily and that he didn't use excessive force. X reports that D also struck her in the face with his hand, causing her ears to ring for the next 24 hours. D denies hitting X in the face and argues that X had no bruises

on her face and no witnesses to support her claim. Assume that the jurisdiction has a civil dependency statute identical to the statute presented in §20.6 above. Is it likely that a court would declare X to be neglected or dependent?

2. A mother, M, slapped her 15-year-old son on the face because when she confronted him about his inconsiderate behavior, he swore at her at some length. The son knocked her down, and M got up and hit the son in the face with the heel of her shoe. She immediately called the police to seek medical care for him. Would a court view this incident as involving unreasonable use of force?

3. Assume that a father was incarcerated and left his three children in the care of his longtime girlfriend. She did not have legal custody over them, and the children consequently were taken briefly by their drug-using biological mother. Neglect proceedings were filed, and the state argued that an incarcerated parent *ipso facto* could not care for children adequately. The father argued that he had arranged for someone else (his girlfriend) to care for the children, and that no nexus was shown between his unavailability and the condition of the children. What is the likely result?

4. Assume that a child protection worker visits the home of a child while investigating a complaint of neglect. The worker finds that the apartment reeks of cat feces and urine and is filled with garbage and overflowing ashtrays. Dirty dishes are stacked all over the kitchen, and the only food in the refrigerator is milk, eggs, and ketchup. Two litters of cats are living under the bed, and cats have defecated in the bathtub and on some of the child's clothing. Do these conditions constitute neglect? If so, should the child be placed in foster care?

5. A mother left the home for a few hours while her 6-year old child was asleep in bed. No other adult was present, but the mother had an electronic home security monitoring system in place. When she becomes subject to neglect proceedings, the mother asserts that the alarm company was monitoring the situation, and the company was staffed by adults versed in handling emergency situations. In addition, she correctly argues that no harm came to the child. Did the mother's actions constitute neglect?

6. A 16-year old child became the subject of a neglect proceeding because he was 5'3" tall but weighed 451 pounds. Although he had been overweight for most of his life, his parents never took him to a dietician. An examining physician determined that the child's medical condition was "life-threatening" and required hospitalization. The child subsequently was placed in foster care because it was believed that his mother would

not provide necessary help and support. The mother seeks return of the child to her care. What is the likely result?

7. A mother became the subject of a child protection proceeding based on her alleged failure to protect her children. The basis of the action was that the mother allowed the father, who was a level-three sex offender, to move home. There was no showing of actual harm to the children. What is the likely result of the proceeding?

8. Assume the same facts as in Example 1, except that M, X's mother, was present during the incident. M was extremely alarmed when X did not return home on time, and she began calling hospital emergency rooms, fearing that X had been in an accident. M feared that she was losing control of X, and she asked D, the father, to "lay down the law" to X. M saw D strike X multiple times with the belt and saw D hit X in the face. M told the child protection worker that D's use of force was appropriate and justified in order to "get X's attention." Assume that the statute found in §20.6 is in effect in this jurisdiction. Is M also likely to be the subject of the child protection investigation?

9. Assume that X is a 5-year-old child who attends kindergarten. His teacher is concerned that he is very anxious and withdrawn. X has never spoken, and he cries easily. He is sometimes observed pinching himself until he has black and blue marks on his body. The teacher contacts X's parents and asks them to attend a meeting about X. X's father comes to the meeting with X. At the meeting, he calls X a "dummy" and tells the teacher that X is "nothing but trouble." The teacher urges the father to accept help for X, but the father refuses to do so. After the meeting, the teacher reports the situation to child protection. Assume that this hypothetical situation takes place in a jurisdiction with a statute identical to that found in §20.6. Is this the sort of case in which child protection services should intervene?

10. Assume that a 12-year-old boy resides with his mother and father. He was awake in his bedroom when law enforcement officers executed a search warrant based on the alleged drug use of his parents. The officers found 1 gram of marijuana in a trash can and another gram loose on a coffee table. They uncovered residual amounts of cocaine in the kitchen and other drugs in the parents' bedroom. The police called child protection, and the trial court found that the child was abused, neglected, and at imminent risk of being further abused and neglected. The parents argued that no evidence was presented that the child had come in contact with the drugs or paraphernalia, and there was similarly no evidence that the child was denied food, clothing, or medical care. They appealed the decision. What is the likely outcome?

Explanations

1. The state child protection agency will argue that X falls under paragraph (a) of the dependency statute because X has suffered serious physical harm inflicted nonaccidentally by her parent. D will argue that the bruises on X's thigh and leg do not constitute serious physical harm because X has no broken bones and no permanent disfigurement, and that there is no evidence of a substantial risk that future serious harm will occur. Given that D struck X with a belt with enough force to leave physical marks, a court likely would rule that X is dependent under the statute. However, without more, the court will probably require that D participate in a parenting class or go to counseling, rather than placing X in foster care. *See South Carolina Dept. of Soc. Servs. v. Father and Mother*, 366 S.E.2d 40 (S.C. App. 1988).

2. M will argue that there was no other history of physical altercation and that this single instance was insufficient to support a finding of abuse or neglect. In the similar case of *In re Corey Mc.*, 67 A.D.3d 1015 (N.Y. App. 2009), the appellate reversed a lower court finding of neglect based on these facts. The court found it significant that the 15-year-old was 5 feet, 10 inches tall.

3. In *In re* T.T.C., 855 A.2d 1117 (D.C. 2004), the court agreed with the father that incarceration did not *ipso facto* constitute neglect. However, the court found that the father had put the children at risk by not granting his girlfriend (or someone else) legal authorization to care for the children and consequently had left them open to being taken by their unsuitable biological mother. The adjudication of neglect was affirmed.

4. This fact situation is based on *In Interest of* N.M.*W*., 461 N.W.2d 478, 479 (Iowa App. 1990), in which the appellate court upheld the finding of neglect. The dissenting judge agreed that the mother was "an extremely poor housekeeper," but argued that the child's interest would have been better served by having the house cleaned instead of placing the child in foster care. *Id.* at 482. She argued that a wealthier mother would have been able to hire someone to clean and that there was no evidence that "only people in clean houses were good parents." *Id.* at 483.

5. In the case of *T. J. v. Missouri Dept. of Social Services, Children's Div.*, 305 S.W.3d 469 (Mo. App. 2010), the appellate court affirmed the trial court's finding of neglect. The court was not persuaded that provision of a home alarm system constituted adequate supervision for a 6-year old.

6. The state will argue that the mother's inaction consitutes medical neglect. In the case of *In re D. K.*, 2002 WL 31968992 (Pa. Com. Pl. 2002), the court in a case involving similar facts refused to return the child to the mother's care until she was able to support his new eating habits and exercise program.

7. In the case of *In re Afton C.*, 71 A.D.3d 887 (N.Y. App. 2010), the appellate court found on similar facts that the mother's actions did not support a finding of failure to protect the children from harm. The court reasoned that there was insufficient evidence that the father "posed an imminent danger to the children." *Id.* at 888.

8. The child protection agency could argue that M falls within paragraph (i) of the dependency statute under the theory that M witnessed X being subjected to acts of cruelty by D and that M failed to protect X adequately. M will argue that D acted reasonably to discipline X and that X was not subjected to acts of cruelty under the statute. Furthermore, no other incidents of abuse are alleged. In many cases where failure to protect is alleged, there is an ongoing pattern of abuse such as sexual abuse. However, under the terms of the statute, failure to protect can be shown based on one incident. In a case somewhat similar to this hypothetical, the court found that M was guilty of neglect because she did not intervene or report the incident. *South Carolina Dept. of Soc. Servs. v. Father and Mother*, 366 S.E.2d 40 (S.C. App. 1988). *See also In re Craig* T., 744 A.2d 621 (N.H. 1999) (mother did not intervene to protect young child who was hit and shaken by father at shopping mall).

9. The child protection worker could argue that X falls under paragraph (c) of the statute because X is suffering serious emotional damage evidenced by severe anxiety and withdrawal as a result of the belittling conduct of the father. The father might argue that X is merely having trouble adjusting to kindergarten and that X's behavior has nothing to do with the father's parenting style. Paragraph (c) of the statute is carefully drafted to focus on the impact of alleged emotional abuse on the child. In this case, the teacher feels strongly that X is exhibiting behavior not normally seen in children adjusting to kindergarten. Although there is not a great deal of evidence linking the father's conduct to X's problems, the father's behavior at the meeting and his refusal to accept help for X would likely spur additional investigation by child protection.

10. In this case, the appellate court reasoned that exposing a child to controlled substances is harmful if it occurs during the mother's pregnancy

or when chronic drug use by a parent "demonstrably adversely" affects the child. The appellate court found that there was no evidence presented to support either assertion in this case. The court further reasoned that the child was not neglected because he was not deprived of food, clothing, shelter, etc., as defined under the statute. Finally the court found that the child was not in imminent danger of abuse or neglect because no nexus was shown between the parents' behavior and impending abuse or neglect of the child. *J. B., III v. Dept. of Children and Families*, 928 So. 2d 392 (Fla. App. 2006).

REPORTING ABUSE AND NEGLECT

20.16. Mandated Reporting

Professionals who come into frequent contact with children are required to make a report whenever the mandated reporter, in his or her professional capacity or within the scope of his or her employment, has knowledge of or observes a child whom the mandated reporter knows or reasonably suspects has been the victim of child abuse. Mandatory reporters typically include teachers, social workers, physicians, registered nurses, emergency medical technicians, and therapists, although clergy and attorneys may also be required to report. With respect to physical abuse occurring in 2010, 16.4 percent of incidents were reported by educators, 16.7 percent by law enforcement, and 11.1 percent by social services staff. U.S. Dept. of Health & Human Services, Administration for Children and Families, *Child Maltreatment* 2010, http://www.acf.hhs.gov/programs/cb/pubs/cm10/cm10.pdf#page=9 (last visited July 18, 2012).

States may grant immunity for good-faith mistakes in making reports that turn out to be unfounded. *Lieberman v. Scully*, 709 N.Y.S.2d 583 (N.Y. App. 2000) (evidence in action for intentional infliction of emotional distress and defamation based upon unfounded report of physical and sexual child abuse made against the plaintiffs raised fact issues for jury as to whether defendant who had reported the alleged abuse was a mandated reporter under Social Services law and, if so, whether presumption of good faith to which such a reporter is entitled under immunity statute was rebutted). *See also Ouellet v. Tillitski*, 604 S.E.2d 559 (Ga. App. 2004) (undisputed record showed that a mandated reporter had reasonable cause to believe that child abuse had occurred, and therefore could claim immunity, even if he had been negligent or exercised bad judgment). However, mandated reporters may be civilly or criminally liable for failing to report abuse and neglect. *See Landeros v. Flood*, 551 P.2d 389 (Cal. 1976).

20.17. Central Registry of Reports

Some states maintain a central registry of reports that can be used by some prospective employers. These have proved to be somewhat controversial. For example, in *In re* M. E., 15 A.3d 112 (Vt. 2010), the Vermont Supreme Court ruled that a parent could be listed on a child abuse and neglect registry, even though the Department for Children and Families did not file a petition alleging that the child was in need of care or supervision.

A New York reporting statute required health care workers, social workers, education employees, law enforcement agents, and judicial officers to report child maltreatment. After investigation, if there was "some credible evidence" of maltreatment, the name of the alleged perpetrator was placed on a central register made available to child care employers. Noting a high risk of possible error, the Second Circuit found that the alleged perpetrators' due process rights were violated by the statutory scheme. *Valmonte v. Bane*, 18 F.3d 992 (2d Cir. 1994). *See Humphries v. County of Los Angeles*, 554 F.3d 1170 (9th Cir. 2009) (listing on Child Abuse Central Index violated parents' procedural due process rights). *See also Division of Youth and Family Services v. D.F.*, 781 A.2d 699 (N.J. Super. A.D. 2005) (mother's name placed on registry even though no child protective action filed), and *DuBray v. S.D. Dept. of Social Services*, 690 N.W.2d 657 (S.D. 2004) (removed mother's name from registry after it had been placed there based on hearsay evidence).

ADJUDICATION AND DISPOSITION

20.18. Two-Stage Proceedings

Civil juvenile proceedings usually involve a two-stage procedure. First, a jurisdictional hearing is held to establish that the child falls within the relevant state statutory definition of a neglected, abused, or dependent child. *People ex rel. U.S.*, 121 P.3d 326 (Colo. App. 2005) (court did not have statutory authority over a mother where there was no adjudication of dependency or neglect by her). Second, a dispositional hearing is held to determine whether the child should remain with the parent subject to conditions, should be placed in foster care, or should be sent to an institution.

If a child is found to be neglected, abused, or dependent, a case plan is developed that typically involves provision of services for the family. However, if the child is removed from the home, the state agency will begin to plan concurrently for the reunification of the family and the possibility of terminating parental rights. *See In re Pedro Z., Jr.*, 117 Cal. Rptr. 3d 605 (Cal. App. 2010) (distinguishing family maintenance services from reunification services).

20.19. Procedures When Child Is in Immediate Danger

In emergency situations, when a child is in immediate danger, the state may assume temporary custody of children. For example, Kentucky Revised Statutes, set out here, provide as follows:

§620.060. Emergency Custody Orders

(1) The court for the county where the child is present may issue an *ex parte* emergency custody order when it appears to the court that removal is in the best interest of the child and that there are reasonable grounds to believe, as supported by affidavit or by recorded sworn testimony, that one (1) or more of the following conditions exist and that the parents or other person exercising custodial control or supervision are unable or unwilling to protect the child:

a. The child is in danger of imminent death or serious physical injury or is being sexually abused;

b. The parent has repeatedly inflicted or allowed to be inflicted by other than accidental means physical injury or emotional injury. This condition shall not include reasonable and ordinary discipline recognized in the community where the child lives, as long as reasonable and ordinary discipline does not result in abuse or neglect as defined in KRS 600.020(1); or

c. The child is in immediate danger due to the parent's failure or refusal to provide for the safety or needs of the child.

In Kentucky, a petition must be filed with the court within 72 hours of taking the child into custody. *See also Doe v. Kearney*, 329 F.3d 1286 (11th Cir. 2003) (upholding Florida statute permitting removal of children without court order when caseworker had probable cause to believe that children were in imminent danger of abuse). *See also* Mark R. Brown, *Rescuing Children from Abusive Parents: The Constitutional Value of Pre-Deprivation Process*, 65 Ohio St. L.J. 913 (2004).

20.20. Syndrome Testimony

During the 1960s, researchers labeled a cluster of symptoms as the "battered child syndrome." Battered child syndrome involves the infliction of multiple injuries over a period of time. When discovered, the injuries are in various stages of healing, and the parents' explanations of the injuries are inconsistent with the medical evidence. Expert knowledge is necessary to identify battered child syndrome. *Estelle v. McGuire*, 502 U.S. 62, 66 (1991) (battered child syndrome exists when "a child has sustained repeated and/or serious injuries by nonaccidental means"). *See also Commonwealth v. Rodgers*, 528 A.2d 610 (Pa. Super. 1987); *State v. Dumlao*, 491 A.2d 404 (Conn. App. 1985).

Significant controversy exists over the use of testimony concerning syndromes such as CSAAS, Battering Parent Syndrome (BPS), and Battered Child Syndrome (BCS). *See* Sarah J. Ramsey & Robert F. Kelly, *Social Science Knowledge in Family Law Cases: Judicial Gate-Keeping in the Daubert Era*, 59 U. Miami L. Rev. 1 (2004). However, the trend appears to be increasing acceptance of the syndrome by the courts.

The defendant in *In re E. C. L.*, 278 S.W.3d 510 (Tex. App. 2009), a juvenile, was convicted after a jury trial of engaging in delinquent conduct for fatally shooting his father. The appellate court reversed the conviction in part because the trial judge excluded expert testimony that the juvenile suffered from BCS and believed that his conduct was immediately necessary to avoid harm to himself or his brother.

Arizona recognized the syndrome in *State v. Hernandez*, 805 P.2d 1057, 1059-1060 (Az. App. 1990), where it upheld admission of expert testimony that a child's injuries most likely had been caused by violent shaking and were consistent with BCS. *See State v. Poehnelt*, 722 P.2d 304, 318 (App. 1985) (expert witnesses' use of term *battered child syndrome* in describing injuries not improper). *See Estelle v. McGuire*, 502 U.S. 62, 70 (1991) (testimony regarding BCS did not violate defendant's right to due process); *People v. Peterson*, 537 N.W.2d 857 (Mich. 1995) (limited use of CSAAS testimony); *State v. MacLennan*, 702 N.W.2d 219 (Minn. 2005) (admissibility of BCS determined under rules of evidence).

20.21. Alternative Dispute Resolution

In order to promote better communication and planning, an increasing number of states offer mediation or some form of alternative dispute resolution in child protection and termination of parental rights cases. Recent research indicates that in 60 to 80 percent of the cases, agreement is reached, and that the treatment plans developed in mediation are similar to those developed outside of mediation. However, visitation arrangements tend to be more specific, and there is some indication that agreements involve more visitation. In mediation, parents have more opportunity to be heard and to engage in finding solutions, and extended family members are more likely to participate. Compliance with agreements may also be higher in mediation. Nancy Thoennes, *What We Know Now: Findings from Dependency Mediation Research*, 47 Fam. Ct. Rev. 21 (2009). *See also* Bernie Mayer, *Reflections on the State of Consensus-Based Decision Making in Child Welfare*, 47 Fam. Ct. Rev. 10 (2009).

20.22. Prevention and Alternative Responses

Intervention of the state into the family system is inherently coercive in nature and can be upsetting to families in and of itself. Consequently, states are exploring innovative approaches aimed at establishing more positive relationships with struggling families. States such as Kentucky, Minnesota, Missouri, New Jersey, Oklahoma, and Wyoming authorize alternative approaches that are less confrontational and more assessment-oriented (and which may not require a formal finding of abuse or neglect) where children are at lower risk. Gila R. Shusterman et al., *Alternative Responses to Child Maltreatment: Findings from NCANDS*, http://aspe.hhs.gov/hsp/05/child-maltreat-resp/ (last visited August 13, 2009). *See also* U.S. Dept. of Health & Human Services, Administration for Children and Families, *Child Maltreatment* 2010, http://www.acf.hhs.gov/programs/cb/pubs/cm10/cm10.pdf#page=9 (last visited July 18, 2012) ("Forty-seven States reported approximately 3.4 million children received prevention services."); Clare Huntington, *Missing Parents*, 42 Fam. L.Q. 131 (2008) (urging focus on prevention).

EXAMPLE

Example

11. Assume that you are a judge in a jurisdiction with a statute identical to the Kentucky statute found in §20.19. On a Friday afternoon, you are presented with an affidavit stating that a teacher has reported a fourth-grade student who came to school that day with bruises and what appear to be cigarette burns on her arms. The child told the investigating caseworker who was called to the school by the teacher that the bruises resulted from an accidental fall down the stairs and that the other marks were bug bites. The experienced caseworker does not believe the child and asserts that the child will be in danger over the weekend. Will you issue an *ex parte* removal order?

EXPLANATION

Explanation

11. The statute allows issuance of an *ex parte* custody order if it is in the best interests of the child and there are reasonable grounds to believe that the child is in danger of serious physical injury or the child is in immediate danger because of a parent's failure to provide for the child's safety. This is the sort of case that is difficult to resolve without expert medical evidence. However, a judge is likely to give more credence to physical indications and the opinions of the teacher and caseworker than the protestations of a child who may be afraid to disclose the possible abuse. The judge probably has reasonable grounds to believe that the child is in immediate danger.

CHILDREN IN FOSTER CARE

20.23. Foster Care: Safety and Accountability

In the well-known case of *DeShaney v. Winnebago County Dept. of Soc. Servs.*, 489 U.S. 189 (1989), a boy was beaten and permanently injured by his father after repeated involvement with the department of social services. The Supreme Court held that there was no due process violation because there was no special relationship giving rise to a duty to protect. The Court reasoned that because the boy was in the physical care of his father, the state had no obligation to protect him from abuse.

After the Supreme Court decided *DeShaney*, several state courts have recognized due process violations where the state has established a special relationship with the child or if the state affirmatively places an individual in danger. *Waubanascum v. Shawano County*, 416 F.3d 658, 665 (7th Cir. 2005) (civil rights case). *See also Radke v. County of Freeborn*, 694 N.W.2d 788 (Minn. 2005) (wrongful death action against workers for negligent investigation of abuse reports).

When a child is placed in foster care, the state is viewed as having a special relationship with that child, and the state may have a consequent duty to protect the child while in foster care. *See Doe v. South Carolina Deparment of Social* Services, 597 F.3d 163 (4th Cir. 2010) (libility can be imposed where officials were "deliberately indifferent"); Lewis v. *Anderson*, 308 F.3d 768 (7th Cir. 2002) (state must know or suspect likely abuse); *Nicini v. Morra*, 212 F.3d 798 (3d Cir. 2000) (conduct did not "shock the conscience"); *Lintz v. Skipski*, 25 F.3d 304 (6th Cir. 1994) (insufficient evidence of deliberate indifference); *Braam ex rel. Braam v. State*, 81 P.3d 851 (Wash. 2003) (whether state conduct falls substantially short of the exercise of professional judgment, standards, or practices); *Weatherford ex rel. Michael L. v. State*, 81 P.3d 320 (Ariz. 2003) (whether workers acted with deliberate indifference); *Miller v. Martin*, 838 So. 2d 761 (La. 2003) (state vicariously liable for intentional abuse by foster parents); *Mosher-Simons v. County of Allegany*, 783 N.E.2d 509 (N.Y. 2002) (court ordered home study "cloaked in judicial immunity"). *See also* Joseph S. Jackson & Lauren G. Fasig, *The Parentless Child's Right to a Permanent Family*, 46 Wake Forest L. Rev. 1 (2011).

Experts believe that frequent visits from caseworkers are helpful in keeping children safe in foster care. As a result of lawsuits, consent decrees, and collaborations with child advocacy groups, 43 states have adopted standards calling for monthly caseworker visits to children in foster care. However, 27 states have been cited as needing improvement in this area. U.S. Dept. of Health & Human Services, Office of Inspector General, *State Standards and Capacity to Track Frequency of Caseworker Visits with Children in Foster Care* (2005), http://oig.hhs.gov/oei/reports/oei-04-03-00350.pdf (last visited July 18, 2012).

20.24. Concurrent Planning

In 1980, Congress passed the Adoption Assistance and Child Welfare Act (AACWA) as a result of concern about children languishing in foster care. The Act stressed reunification of the family but encouraged adoption in cases where reunification was not realistic. In order to receive matching funds, states were required to make "reasonable efforts" to prevent removal or reunify the family. States were also required to undertake "permanency planning" and make periodic case reviews. In *Suter v. Artist M.*, 503 U.S. 347 (1992), the Supreme Court held that there was no implied right of action to enforce the reasonable efforts language in AACWA.

20.25. "Reasonable Efforts" to Reunify Families

In 1997, Congress enacted the Adoption and Safe Families Act (ASFA) to limit the amount of time that children spend in foster care (known as *foster care drift*) and to speed adoption. Under ASFA, as under the AACWA, states are required to make "reasonable efforts" to prevent removal and reunify the family prior to terminating parental rights. *See In re Tiffany B.*, 228 S.W.3d 148 (Tenn. App. 2007) (factors to determine reasonableness of efforts include "(1) the reasons for separating the parents from their children, (2) the parents' physical and mental abilities, (3) the resources available to the parents, (4) the parents' efforts to remedy the conditions that required the removal of the children, (5) the resources available to the Department, (6) the duration and extent of the parents' efforts to address the problems that caused the children's removal, and (7) the closeness of the fit between the conditions that led to the initial removal of the children, the requirements of the permanency plan, and the Department's efforts").

However, under ASFA, reasonable efforts are not required when there are "aggravated circumstances" or parental rights to a sibling have been terminated. *See* Anne Kathleen S. Bean, *Reasonable Efforts: What State Courts Think*, 36 Tol. L. Rev. 321 (2005). *See also In re Jorden R.*, 979 A.2d 469 (Conn. 2009) (requiring reasonable efforts or a showing that parent is unwilling or unable to benefit from reunification efforts).

20.26. "Active Efforts" Pursuant to the ICWA

If termination proceedings involve a Native American child, the ICWA requires that "active efforts" be made to provide services designed to prevent removal of the child from the family, and this requirement is not overridden by AFSA. 25 U.S.C. §1912(d); *Yvonne L. v. Arizona Dept. of Economic Sec.*, 258 P.3d 233 (Ariz. App. 2011) (discussing active efforts); *In re I. B.*, 255 P.3d 56 (Mont. 2011) (substantial evidence of active efforts); *Pravat P. v State Dept. of Health & Social Services, Office of Children's Services*, 249 P.3d 264 (Alaska 2011); *People ex rel. J. S. B., Jr.*, 691 N.W.2d 611 (S.D. 2005). However, in *J. S. v. State*, 50 P.3d 388 (Alaska 2002), the father was convicted of sexual abuse, and, citing the aggravating circumstances language in ASFA, the court held that active efforts to reunify the family were not required under ICWA.

20.27. Permanency Planning

AFSA requires states to pursue termination of parental rights if children have been in foster care for 15 of the preceding 22 months. (This provision does not apply if the child has been placed with a relative, if termination is not believed to be in the best interests of the child, or if reunification services have not been provided.) Permanency hearings are to occur within a year, but "reasonable efforts" to reunify are not required where there are "aggravated circumstances" (such as sexual abuse) or parental rights to a sibling have been terminated. *See In re R. J. T.*, 9 A.3d 1179 (Penn. 2010) (affirming denial of permanency goal change); *In re Shirley B.*, 993 A.2d 675 (Md App. 2010) (affirming permanency goal change to adoption); Stephanie Jill Gendell, *In Search of Permanency: A Reflection on the First Three Years of the Adoption and Safe Families Act*, 39 Fam. & Conciliation Cts. Rev. 25 (2001); Kurtis A. Kemper, *Construction and Application by State Courts of the Federal Adoption and Safe Families Act and Its Implementing State Statutes*, 10 A.L.R.6th 173 (2006).

Critics of ASFA believe that inadequate resources and the Act's aggressive timelines have worked to the detriment of children and families. William Wesley Patton & Amy M. Pellman, *The Reality of Concurrent Planning: Juggling*

Multiple Family Plans Expeditiously Without Sufficient Resources, 9 U.C. Davis J. Juv. L. & Pol'y 171 (2005); Martin Guggenheim & Christine Gottliev, *Justice Denied: Delays in Resolving Child Protection Cases in New York*, 12 Va. J. Soc. Pol'y & L. 546 (2005); Catherine J. Ross, *The Tyranny of Time: Vulnerable Children, "Bad" Mothers, and Statutory Deadlines in Parental Termination Proceedings*, 11 Va. J. Soc. Pol'y & L. 176 (2004).

INVOLUNTARY TERMINATION OF PARENTAL RIGHTS

20.28. Specific Grounds for Termination

State statutes provide specific grounds and requirements for termination of parental rights. *See In re Adoption/Guardianship of Rashawn H.*, 937 A.2d 177 (Md. 2007) (clear and specific findings required for each statutory factor). Termination typically may be sought when there has been chronic abuse and neglect, abandonment, parental incapacity, abuse of a sibling, or termination of parental rights of a sibling. As discussed previously, with some exceptions, states may seek termination of parental rights pursuant to the ASFA if a child has been placed outside of the home for 15 of the preceding 22 months. *See In re Parental Rights as to D. R. H.*, 92 P.3d 1230 (Nev. 2004) (upholding termination where child placed outside the home for 14 of the last 20 months). Termination most often occurs after reasonable reunification efforts, as provided in the case plan, have failed and there is little likelihood of reuniting the family in the foreseeable future.

20.29. Legal Consequences of Termination

Termination of parental rights severs the parent-child relationship and makes the child available for adoption. The parent loses the right to see the child, and the child has no right to financial support from the parent or to inherit property upon the parent's death. *But see In re Stephen Tyler R.*, 584 S.E.2d 581 (W. Va. 2003) (under specially drafted statutory provision, terminated father ordered to pay child support), and Richard L. Brown, *Disinheriting the "Legal Orphan": Inheritance Rights of Children After Termination of Parental Rights*, 70 Mo. L. Rev. 125 (2005) (arguing for a change in the law to allow inheritance after termination). Because termination involves constitutional rights and is such a serious remedy, special procedural precautions are required.

In 2010, the parental rights to 64,000 children were terminated. *Trends in Foster Care and Adoption — FY 2002–FY 2010*, U.S. Dept. of Health & Human

Services, Administration for Children and Families, Children's Bureau, http://www.acf.hhs.gov/programs/cb/stats_research/afcars/trends.htm (last visited July 18, 2012).

20.30. Standard of Proof

Because termination of parental rights is such a drastic remedy, the standard of proof is "clear and convincing evidence." In *Santosky v. Kramer*, 455 U.S. 745 (1982), the Supreme Court held that a New York statute requiring only a "fair preponderance of the evidence" violated a parent's right to due process in termination of parental rights proceedings. The Court found that parents have a fundamental liberty interest in the care and upbringing of children and that the state had an advantage over parents with respect to proof and expertise.

The ICWA requires proof "beyond a reasonable doubt" when termination of parental rights is at issue. 25 U.S.C. §1912(f). *See Yvonne L. v. Arizona Dept. of Economic Sec.*, 258 P.3d 233 (Ariz. App. 2011).

20.31. Parental Right to Counsel?

In *Lassiter v. Department of Soc. Servs.*, 452 U.S. 18 (1981), the Supreme Court ruled that due process does not require the appointment of counsel for indigent parents in all termination actions. However, states typically have appointed counsel in termination cases pursuant to state statute or under state constitutional provisions. In *In re* C. M., 2012 WL 2479619 (N.H. 2012), the New Hampshire Supreme Court reaffirmed the right to counsel in termination of parental rights actions, but distinguished these from initial abuse and neglect proceedings where appointed counsel may not be required. *See Idaho Dept. of Health & Welfare v. Doe*, 249 P.3d 362 (Idaho 2011) (joint representation of parents not reversible error in termination case); *In re Dependency of MSR*, 271 P.3d 234 (Wash. 2012) (court has discretion regarding appointment of counsel for children in termination proceeding).

Once an attorney is appointed, the question of which standard states are to use when assessing the competency of representation is unsettled. *Compare In re R.E.S.* 978 A.2d 182 (D.C. 2009) (appointed counsel in a proceeding where the termination of the parent and child relationship is under consideration has the statutory duty to competently represent client) with *In re Elysa D.* 974 A.2d 834 (Conn. App. 2009) (a parent "is constitutionally entitled to the effective assistance of counsel only if he had a constitutional right to appointed counsel in the termination proceeding"). *See* Bruce A. Boyer, *Justice, Access to the Courts, and the Right to Free Counsel for Indigent Parents:*

The Continuing Scourge of Lassiter v. Department of Social Services of Durham, 15 Temp. Pol. & Civ. Rts. L. Rev. 635 (2006).

Examples

12. Assume that a four-year-old child, C, was placed in a foster home after her mother, D, developed cancer and was diagnosed with a schizoid personality disorder. At the time that C was placed in foster care, she was dirty and hungry, and her mother characterized her as a defiant child. C was formally evaluated by a team of experts and was diagnosed with reactive attachment disorder, Attention Deficit Hyperactivity Disorder (ADHD), and oppositional-defiant disorder. It was determined that she consequently needed a particularly high level of care. The child protection agency developed a case plan aimed at reunifying the family, and the plan was accepted by the court. The mother attended therapy sessions individually and with C in compliance with the treatment plan, but she failed to attend parenting classes, participate in a bonding study, or maintain regular contact with C. The therapist who saw C and her mother together issued a strong recommendation that parental rights be terminated. In contrast, the foster parents coped well with C. After C had been in foster care for two-and-a-half years, the state moved to terminate D's parental rights. In order to terminate, the state was required to show that reasonable efforts had been made to assist D in parenting and that there was little likelihood that the situation would change in the foreseeable future. D argued that, given her health and psychological problems, she had complied with as much of the treatment plan as she could and that she needed more assistance from child protection. At trial, one of the experts described the mother as "an eccentric person with a 'crusty demeanor' and a tendency to 'shut down' when she is feeling defensive," but he did note some improvement in her interpersonal skills. Is a court likely to terminate parental rights under these circumstances?

13. Assume that three minor children were placed in foster care because their mother, due to drug use, had failed to protect them and they suffered serious emotional damage. As a part of the treatment plan, the mother was required to stop using drugs. However, she continued to use methamphetamine and was in fact arrested for drug use while the children were in foster care. The mother repeatedly sought visitation with the children but was prevented from seeing them because she failed to pass a drug test, as required in the treatment plan. Pursuant to a statutory provision, after six months of no contact, the state ended reunification services and scheduled a permanency planning hearing likely to lead to termination of parental rights. The mother claimed that

the department had actively prevented her from visiting the children despite her requests and was now accusing her of not maintaining contact with the children. She asserted that she was entitled to a full year of reunification services before her parental rights could be terminated. What is the likely result?

14. Assume that a child, X, was placed in foster care based on his mother's inability to deal effectively with his health and behavioral problems. As part of the family treatment plan, the mother was required to maintain appropriate housing, which she had some difficulty affording, and to work on her parenting skills. She did not attend a parenting class because it was some distance away and she had transportation problems, but she did meet with a family support worker who assisted her with parenting. The worker testified that the mother had made improvements that were evident when the worker made home visits. The worker also observed that the mother had a warm and playful relationship with X. The child protection agency seeks termination of parental rights under a statutory provision allowing termination of parental rights if a child is in foster care for more than 15 of the most recent 22 months. The mother argues that she has made substantial progress with respect to her case plan and that the termination or parental rights is not in the best interests of the child. The family support worker testifies that the child would be harmed by the termination. However, the state argues that it is not in X's best interest to remain in foster care and that the mother has had sufficient time to make the required improvements. What is the likely outcome?

Explanations

12. This fact situation is based on the case of *State ex rel. Children, Youth, & Families Dept.*, 47 P.3d 859 (N.M. App. 2002), in which the court upheld termination of the mother's parental rights. The court considered the requirements of ASFA with respect to the state's obligation to make reasonable efforts to reunify the family and determined that the state had made reasonable, if not perfect, efforts to assist D. Because of the child's special needs and the mother's major parenting deficits, the court did not see any likelihood of change in the foreseeable future.

13. In the similar case of *Sara M. v. Superior Court*, 116 P.3d 550 (Cal. 2005), the court found that the department made reasonable efforts to reunify

the family. The appellate court upheld the trial court's finding that the mother was prevented appropriately from seeing the children while under the influence of drugs. Furthermore, the court held that under California law, reunification services could be terminated where clear and convincing evidence showed that a parent had not contacted the children for six months after the start of services. *But see In re O.S.*, 848 N.E.2d 130 (Ill. App. 2006) (termination reversed where department kept the true identity of mother a secret from her young son — she was introduced to the child as "Jenny" — but her parental rights were ultimately terminated in part because she had not established a parent child bond with the boy).

14. In *In re Interest of Aaron D.*, 691 N.W.2d 164 (Neb. 2005), the court held that, under the facts presented, termination based solely on the length of stay in foster care was not in the child's best interest. The court stated as follows:

> The 15-month condition set forth in [the statute] serves the purpose of providing a reasonable timetable for parents to rehabilitate themselves . . . [b]ut termination based on the ground that a child has been in out-of-home placement for 15 of the preceding 22 months is not in a child's best interests when the record demonstrates that a parent is making efforts toward reunification and has not been given a sufficient opportunity for compliance with a reunification plan. We do not mean to suggest that termination solely on the basis of [the statutory section] cannot be appropriate. Obviously, there will be cases in which clear and convincing evidence to that effect will be presented. But that may prove difficult in cases where the record is insufficient to prove any of the other statutory grounds, i.e., where the parent did not abandon the child, did not neglect to protect or provide for a child, was not unfit or unable to parent, did not fail to participate in necessary rehabilitation, and was not abusive.

Id. at 261.

CHAPTER 21

Abortion

HISTORY AND BACKGROUND

21.1. Introduction

The history of abortion dates back to ancient times, when unwanted pregnancies were terminated using such methods as the administration of abortifacient herbs, sharpened implements, the application of abdominal pressure, and other techniques.

> [A]t the time of the Persian Empire, abortifacients were known, and that criminal abortions were severely punished. We are also told, however, that abortion was practiced in Greek times as well as in the Roman Era, and that "it was resorted to without scruple." The Ephesian, Soranos, often described as the greatest of the ancient gynecologists, appears to have been generally opposed to Rome's prevailing free-abortion practices. He found it necessary to think first of the life of the mother, and he resorted to abortion when, upon this standard, he felt the procedure advisable. Greek and Roman law afforded little protection to the unborn. If abortion was prosecuted in some places, it seems to have been based on a concept of a violation of the father's right to his offspring. Ancient religion did not bar abortion.

Roe v. *Wade*, 410 U.S. 113, 130, nn. 8-11 (1973).

See also Wikipedia (describing the history of abortion), http://en.wikipedia.org/wiki/History_of_abortion (last visited July 2012).

From the 1700s into the early 1800s, most jurisdictions in the United States followed the British common law, which permitted an abortion before "quickening" but made abortion after "quickening" an offense. To "quicken" is generally defined as reaching the stage of pregnancy at which the child shows signs of life — when the initial motion of the fetus can be felt by the pregnant woman. This usually appears 16 to 20 weeks into pregnancy. *See McCarty v. State,*41 P.3d 981, 988 (Ok. App. 2002) ("Quickening" is generally used to denote the first motion of the fetus in the womb felt by the mother).

In 1800, no American jurisdictions had statutes on abortion. Most forms of abortion were not illegal, and those who wished to practice abortion did so.

England passed its first antiabortion law in 1803. In the United States, state statutory law slowly replaced the common law during the early part of the nineteenth century, and by 1840, at least eight states had statutes dealing with abortion.

The earliest abortion laws in the United States were often criminal in nature and targeted those who performed abortions, rather than the pregnant women who sought to have the procedure performed. The aim of these laws was to protect pregnant women and their fetuses from injury, not to prosecute them. At the time, abortion was an unsafe medical procedure for women. This was particularly true prior to the development of antisepsis.

After the Civil War, more legislation emerged from various state legislatures concerning an abortion. According to Professor William N. Eskridge, Jr., between the years 1850 and 1880, most states began adopting laws criminalizing abortion. He writes, "The federal Comstock Act of 1873 made it an obscenity crime to sell or distribute articles of contraception or abortion; to send such articles in the federal mail system; or to import such articles from abroad. By 1885, twenty-four states had enacted their own versions of the Comstock Act, many of which were more stringent than the federal law." William N. Eskridge Jr., *Some Effects of Identity-Based Social Movements on Constitutional Law in the Twentieth Century*, 100 Mich. L. Rev. 2062, 2117 (August 2002).

In 1868, at least 28 of the then 37 states and 8 territories had statutes banning or limiting abortion. James C. Mohr, *Abortion in America: The Origins and Evolution of National Policy*, 200 (Oxford University Press 1978). The legislation tended to provide severe penalties should an abortion occur after quickening but was more lenient with an abortion that occurred before quickening.

Most state statutes punished attempted abortions equally with completed abortions. Many early statutes included an exception for an abortion thought by one or more physicians to be necessary to save the mother's life. *See generally* Michael N. Giuliano, *Historial Background; Constitutional Rights Under Roe v. Wade*, 1 Ill. Law and Prac. Abortion and Birth Control §1 (February, 2012). *See also* Jared H. Jones, *Women's Reproductive Rights Concerning Abortion, and Government Regulation Thereof — Supreme Court Cases,*20 A.L.R.2d 1 (originally published in 2007).

21.2. Twentieth Century

By the turn of the nineteenth century, the quickening distinction had disappeared from the statutory law of most states, and the degree of the offense and the penalties were increased. By the end of 1950, a majority of the jurisdictions banned abortion, however and whenever performed, unless done to save or preserve the life of the mother. *Roe v. Wade*, 410 U.S. 113, 139 (1973). *See* Comment, *A Survey of the Present Statutory and Case Law on Abortion: The Contradictions and the Problems*, 1 U. Ill. L.F. 177, 179 (1972) (classifying the abortion statutes and listing 25 states as permitting abortion only if necessary to save or preserve the mother's life). The exceptions, Alabama and the District of Columbia, permitted an abortion to preserve the mother's health. *Roe v. Wade, supra*.

The widespread ban on abortions continued through the 1960s, although the Model Code of the American Law Institute (ALI) may have influenced several states to enact laws that allowed an abortion when it was necessary to save the life of the mother, in cases of rape or incest, if the fetus was deformed, or when continuation would impair a mother's mental or physical health (therapeutic abortion). ALI, Uniform Model Penal Code, §230.3 Abortion; *see also* discussion of ALI §230.3 in *Doe v. Bolton*, 410 U.S. 179, 182 (1973) (the ALI proposal has served as the model for recent legislation "in approximately one-fourth of our States").

Colorado broadened the circumstances under which a woman could obtain an abortion legally in 1967. *See Jacobs v. Theimer*, 519 S.W.2d 846 (Tex. 1975) (Colorado has permitted eugenic abortions since 1967). By 1970, 11 additional states had followed Colorado's lead by expanding the circumstances under which one could legally receive an abortion. In addition, New York, Washington, Hawaii, and Alaska had completely decriminalized abortion during the early stages of pregnancy. *See Reno v. D'Javid*, 379 N.Y.S.2d 290, 293-294 (N.Y. Sup. 1976).

A historic change in the legal landscape associated with abortion law occurred with the Supreme Court's decision in *Roe v. Wade*, 410 U.S. 113 (1973). Since the advent of *Roe*, state legislatures have encountered numerous constitutional limitations on how they may regulate abortion.

CONSTITUTIONAL PRIVACY

21.3. Roots of Privacy Theory

To understand current abortion law and how it has changed since *Roe*, it may be helpful to review the history of the treatment of family privacy by the Supreme Court. Although privacy is not mentioned in the Constitution, most agree that the roots of the privacy theory are found in *Meyer v. Nebraska*, 262 U.S. 390, 400 (1923) (reversing conviction of teacher based on teaching German language to a 10-year-old child). In that decision, with only two justices dissenting, the Court said that the liberty interest protected by the due process clause of the Fourteenth Amendment includes the right of parents to control the education of their own children. In *Pierce v. Soc'y of Sisters*, 268 U.S. 510, 534-535 (1925), the Court said that the liberty of parents and guardians includes the right "to direct the upbringing and education of children under their control."

The privacy theory made its way into bedrooms of married couples under the guise of a liberty interest in *Griswold v. Connecticut*, 381 U.S. 479 (1965). In that decision, with two justices dissenting, the Court held that the Constitution does not allow a state to forbid a married couple from using contraceptives. The majority asserted that "zones" of personal privacy are fundamental to the concept of liberty under the protected penumbra of specific guarantees of the Bill of Rights. The Court observed that although the word *liberty* is not defined in the Constitution, it includes at least the fundamental rights "retained by the people" under the Ninth Amendment. 381 U.S. at 484.

The right to privacy was not explicitly recognized by the Supreme Court until *Eisenstadt v. Baird*, 405 U.S. 438 (1972). In that case, the defendant was convicted under a criminal statute for exhibiting contraceptive articles in the course of delivering a lecture on contraception to a group of students at Boston University and for giving a young woman a package of vaginal foam at the close of his address. The defendant challenged the conviction, claiming there was a certain "right to privacy" protected by the Constitution that shielded him from prosecution.

The state argued that the legislative purpose of the criminal statute was to promote marital fidelity and discourage premarital sex. The Supreme Court invalidated the statute saying that contraceptives may be made available to married persons without regard to whether they are living with their spouses or the uses to which the contraceptives are to be put. The Court reasoned that the legislation had no deterrent effect on extramarital sexual relations and ruled that the Massachusetts statute permitting married persons to obtain contraceptives to prevent pregnancy but prohibiting distribution of contraceptives to single persons for that purpose violates the equal protection clause of the Constitution.

The *Eisenstadt* decision, authored by Justice Brennan, extended the "right of privacy" established in *Griswold v. Connecticut*, 381 U.S. 479 (1965), to all individuals regardless of marital status and explicitly recognized a constitutional right to privacy. *Eisenstadt* granted individuals the right "to be free from unwarranted governmental intrusion into matters so fundamentally affecting a person as the decision whether to bear or beget a child."

405 U.S. at 453. This decision is viewed by some as providing a specific theoretical foundation for the Court's subsequent decision in *Roe v. Wade*.

21.4. Statute Fails to Protect Fundamental Right to Privacy

A question about the scope of the right to privacy within the Fourteenth Amendment to the Constitution was raised in *Doe v. Bolton*, 410 U.S. 179 (1973). This case was a companion to *Roe v. Wade*. The Georgia statute being reviewed in *Doe* by the Court required that abortions be conducted in hospitals, or accredited hospitals; required the interposition of a hospital abortion committee; required confirmation by other physicians; and limited an abortion to Georgia residents.

The challenger contended in general that it would be physically and emotionally damaging for her to bring a child into her poor, "fatherless" family, and that advances in medicine and medical techniques had made it safer for a woman to have a medically induced abortion than for her to bear a child. This statute, she argued, essentially required her to carry an unwanted pregnancy to term.

She also contended that because her application for an abortion at a Georgia hospital was denied, she was being forced either to relinquish her right to decide when and how many children she will bear or to seek an abortion that was illegal under the statute. This, she contended, invaded her rights of privacy and liberty in matters related to family, marriage, and sex, and deprived her of the right to choose whether to bear children.

She challenged the provisions requiring that abortions be performed only in a hospital accredited by the Joint Commission on Accreditation of Hospitals, that the procedure be approved by the hospital staff abortion committee, and that the performing physician's judgment be confirmed by independent examinations of the patient by two other licensed physicians, as unduly restricting a woman's right of privacy. *Id.* at 192 of 410 U.S. She contended that by subjecting a doctor's individual medical judgment to committee approval and to confirming consultations, the statute was impermissibly restricting the physician's right to practice his profession and depriving him of due process.

The Supreme Court, with two dissenting justices, held that the requirement that the abortion be performed in an accredited hospital was invalid because accreditation was not legitimately related to the state's objective of protecting the woman's life. It also held that the requirement that a woman secure advance approval from a hospital committee for an abortion was unconstitutional because this would limit a woman's right to medical care and a physician's right to make medical decisions. Finally, the Court ruled that provisions that required consent from three physicians to justify the abortion and required that a woman be a citizen of Georgia in order to obtain an abortion were unconstitutional.

The Court emphasized that during the first trimester of pregnancy, a woman's decision as to the termination of pregnancy prevails untouchable and unquestionable, and that her free will cannot be subjected to any condition, not even if said condition is the prior medical determination that the abortion is necessary to preserve the health or life of the mother. *Id.* at 202 of 410 U.S. Overall, the Court made it clear that the Fourteenth Amendment's concept of personal liberty and restrictions upon state action contains a right of privacy that is broad enough to encompass a woman's decision whether or not to terminate her pregnancy.

21.5. *Roe v. Wade*

In *Roe v. Wade*, 410 U.S. 113 (1973), the Supreme Court was asked to review a Texas criminal abortion statute that made abortion illegal except for the purpose of saving a mother's life. The statute's challenger, Jane Roe, was an unmarried pregnant woman. She alleged she wanted to terminate her pregnancy by an abortion "performed by a competent, licensed physician, under safe, clinical conditions"; that she was unable to get a "legal" abortion in Texas because her life did not appear to be threatened by the continuation of her pregnancy; and that she could not afford to travel to another jurisdiction in order to secure a legal abortion under safe conditions. She also alleged that the Texas statutes were unconstitutionally vague and that they abridged her right of personal privacy, protected by the First, Fourth, Fifth, Ninth, and Fourteenth amendments.

Texas argued that the statute was constitutional and provided three reasons to support its view: First, the statute discouraged illicit sexual conduct outside marriage. Second, it protected a pregnant woman from the dangerous nature of an abortion. Third, it protected the state's interest in potential life.

The Court considered the competing views. It decided that the protection of a pregnant woman and the protection of potential life were compelling state interests, and it weighed those interests against a woman's right to privacy. Ultimately, it struck down the statute and created a trimester framework for reviewing abortion issues.

The Court held that no compelling state interest justified a sweeping prohibition of abortion and concluded that during the first trimester of the pregnancy, little or no regulation is permissible by a state. It said that even minor regulations on the abortion procedure may not interfere during the first trimester with physician-patient consultation or with the woman's choice between abortion and childbirth. The decision of whether to have an abortion is left with the woman, in conjunction with her physician.

The Court also ruled that after the first trimester and until viability — viability defined as the point when a fetus is capable of survival outside the womb (*Roe*, 410 U.S. at 160, 163) — the state may not place an outright ban on abortions. However, it may regulate the abortion procedure to protect the mother's health and safety.

During the third trimester, the state's interest in protecting potential life justifies regulating and banning abortions except when necessary for the preservation of the life or health of the mother.

In making its decision, the Court relied primarily on the Ninth Amendment to the United States Constitution, declaring, "the Ninth Amendment's reservation of rights to the people is broad enough to encompass a woman's decision whether or not to terminate her pregnancy." *Roe*, 410 U.S. at 153. It reasoned that from a practical perspective, modern medical techniques had reduced the medical risks of an abortion significantly, stating that prior to the end of the first trimester, abortion, although not without its risks, is now relatively safe. 410 U.S. at 149.

Associate Justice Byron White and Chief Justice William Rehnquist joined in dissent. Justice White wrote:

> I find nothing in the language or history of the Constitution to support the Court's judgment. The Court simply fashions and announces a new constitutional right for pregnant mothers and, with scarcely any reason or authority for its action, invests that right with sufficient substance to override most existing state abortion statutes. The upshot is that the people and the legislatures of the 50 States are constitutionally disentitled to weigh the relative importance of the continued existence and development of the fetus, on the one hand, against a spectrum of possible impacts on the mother, on the other hand.

410 U.S. at 221-222.

Roe v. Wade prompted the beginning of a national debate over abortion that continues to this very day. The debate encompasses such questions as whether and to what extent abortion should be legal, who should decide the legality of abortion, and what tests the Supreme Court should apply to various state statutes involving abortion. The decision has had a significant impact on national politics, splitting the nation into pro-*Roe* (mostly pro-choice) and anti-*Roe* (mostly pro-life) groups.

21.6. Expanding Personal Privacy

In *Whalen v. Roe*, 429 U.S. 589 (1977), the Supreme Court continued to expand the constitutional right to privacy. In *Whalen*, it held that the right to privacy extends to both "the individual interest in avoiding disclosure of personal matters, and . . . the interest in independence in making certain kinds of important decisions." 429 U.S. at 599. *Whalen* recognized that information contained in medical records, for example, is constitutionally protected under the confidentiality branch of the privacy right.

The Court also held that in conjunction with its police power to regulate the distribution of dangerous drugs, the state of New York could maintain a data bank of all prescription sales of such drugs against a claim that such a recording was an impermissible invasion of the right of privacy. The Court noted that the case did not involve the "affirmative, unannounced, narrowly focused intrusions into individual privacy" protected by the Fourth Amendment. *Id.* at 604 of 429 U.S. n.32. It stated that a state was not absolutely barred from collecting information that was reasonably related to the important public purpose in regulating dangerous drugs and was protected against disclosure. *Id.* at 605 of 429 U.S.

21.7. Second-Trimester Issues

In 1983, constitutional questions concerning an abortion ordinance enacted by the city of Akron, Ohio, that dealt primarily with second-trimester abortions, came before the Court. There was also a more subtle underlying political issue about whether *Roe v. Wade* might be overturned. *City of Akron v. Akron Center for Reproductive Health*, 462 U.S. 416 (1983).

The Akron, Ohio, ordinance, *inter alia*, (1) stipulated that all abortions performed after the first trimester of pregnancy had to be performed in a hospital; (2) prohibited a physician from performing an abortion on an unmarried minor under the age of 15 unless the physician obtained the consent of one of her parents or unless the minor obtained an order from a court having jurisdiction over her that the abortion be performed; (3) required that the attending physician inform the patient of the status of her pregnancy, the development of her fetus, the date of possible viability, the physical and emotional complications that may result from an abortion, and the availability of agencies to provide her with assistance and information with respect to birth control, adoption, and childbirth. The physician also was required to inform a patient of the particular risks associated with her pregnancy and the abortion technique to be employed. The ordinance prohibited a physician from performing an abortion until 24 hours after the pregnant woman signed a consent form and required physicians performing abortions to ensure that fetal remains were disposed of in a humane and sanitary manner. A violation of the ordinance was punishable as a misdemeanor. Here is how the Court resolved these issues.

First, the Court struck down as unconstitutional the provision requiring that all abortions be carried out in a hospital, saying it imposed a heavy and unnecessary burden on women's access to a relatively inexpensive, otherwise accessible, and safe abortion procedure.

Second, it also struck down a provision containing a blanket determination that all minors under the age of 15 are too immature to make an abortion decision or that an abortion never may be in the minor's best interests without parental approval.

Third, the Court said that the validity of an informed consent requirement rests on the state's interest in protecting the pregnant woman's health. However, this did not mean that a state has unreviewable authority to decide what information a woman must be given before she chooses to have an abortion. A state may not adopt regulations designed to influence the woman's informed choice between abortion and childbirth.

Fourth, the Court ruled that the requirement that the "attending physician" inform the woman of the specified information is unreasonable because there are nonphysicians who are competent to provide the information and counseling relevant to informed consent.

Fifth, it held that Akron had failed to demonstrate that any legitimate state interest is furthered by an arbitrary and inflexible waiting period. It said that there is no evidence that the abortion procedure will be performed more safely by requiring a 24-hour delay as a matter of course.

Sixth, it struck down a fetal disposal clause because its language was too vague to determine conduct that was subject to criminal prosecution.

Of possible significance to future constitutional abortion rulings by the Court was the dissent's position in *Akron* that the trimester approach, outlined in *Roe v. Wade* was unworkable. Justice O'Connor, writing for the three dissenters, stated that:

> [i]t is not difficult to see that despite the Court's purported adherence to the trimester approach adopted in *Roe*, the lines drawn in that decision have now been "blurred" because of what the Court accepts as technological advancement in the safety of abortion procedure. The State may no longer rely on a "bright line" that separates permissible from impermissible regulation, and it is no longer free to consider the second trimester as a unit.

462 U.S. at 452.

It is also of interest that the Solicitor General at the time was Rex Lee, appointed by President Ronald Reagan. In his *amicus curiae* brief, which supported the city of Akron, he argued that the Court should adopt the "unduly burdensome" standard when reviewing abortion regulations and in doing so, "accord heavy deference to the legislative judgment" in determining what constitutes an "undue burden." 410 U.S. at 465, n.10. While the majority rejected the application of the approach urged by the Solicitor General, this perspective on the trimester approach first appeared in *Roe* appears to be a precursor of future changes in the standard of review to be used in abortion cases by the Court.

It is important to note that nine years after *Akron*, the standard to determine the validity of laws restricting abortions, first urged by the Solicitor General in that case, was adopted. The new standard asked whether a state abortion regulation has the purpose or effect of imposing an "undue burden," which is defined as a "substantial obstacle in the path of a woman seeking an abortion before the fetus attains viability." *Planned Parenthood of Southeastern Pennsylvania v. Casey*, 505 U.S. 833, 837 (1992).

21.8. Informed Consent, Reporting Requirement, Physician Duty to Inform, and Necessity of Second Physician Opinion

In *Thornburgh v. American Coll. of Obst. & Gyn.*, 476 U.S. 747 (1986) (5-4 with Burger, White, Rehnquist, and O'Connor dissenting), the Supreme Court considered a challenge to a number of provisions of a Pennsylvania abortion statute. The Court held that the requirement that a physician inform women of the detrimental physical and psychological effects and of all particular medical risks was unconstitutional. The provision was viewed by the Court as the antithesis of informed consent because it intruded upon a physician's exercise of proper professional judgment.

The Court also held that the statutory reporting requirements of the Pennsylvania statute were unconstitutional. It said that the scope of information required by the reporting provisions found in the Abortion Control Act, and the availability of the information to the public, belied any assertion by the Commonwealth that it was advancing a legitimate interest. The requirements went "well beyond the health related interests" that may justify reporting requirements in some cases. 476 U.S. at 766. Among the defects noted by the Court was the fact that the statute required information "as to the woman's personal history." *Ibid.*

The Court also held that withholding a minor's name is not enough by itself to protect her anonymity where the publicly available information could identify the minor. 476 U.S. at 766-768. The Court reasoned that because the potentially identifying information is often so detailed, the absence of the minor's name will not protect her interests, and the use of a fictitious name does not protect a pregnant minor's confidences adequately. The Court felt that the reporting requirements raised the specter of public exposure and harassment of women who chose, with their physician, to exercise their personal, private right to end pregnancy.

Another provision that governed the degree of care for post-viability abortions was held facially invalid. The provision required that an abortion technique employed post-viability be one that provides the best opportunity for an unborn child to be aborted alive unless, in the physician's good-faith judgment, the technique would present a significantly greater medical risk to the life or health of the pregnant woman. The Court said this provision was unsusceptible to a construction that did not require the mother to bear an increased medical risk in order to save a viable fetus.

Finally, the Court ruled that a provision requiring the presence of a second physician during an abortion, when viability is possible, was unconstitutional because it failed to provide a medical-emergency exception for situations where the mother's health was endangered by a delay in the second physician's arrival. The Court said that this section chilled the performance of a late abortion, which, more than one performed at earlier dates, tends to occur under emergency conditions.

As you will find later in this chapter, *Thornburgh* was in part overruled by *Planned Parenthood of Southeastern Pennsylvania v. Casey*, 505 U.S. 833 (1992). In particular, the portions of the decision that addressed the issue of informed consent were reversed. However, the Supreme Court left *Thornburgh* intact to the extent that it relied upon *Roe's* approach to post-viability regulation of abortions.

21.9. Wavering on *Roe*

Three years before *Casey*, the Supreme Court in *Webster v. Reproductive Health Services*, 492 U.S. 490 (1989) (5-4, with Brennan, Marshall, Blackmun, and Stevens dissenting), seemed to cast doubt on the Court's decision in *Roe*. At issue was a Missouri statute that had been declared unconstitutional by the Eighth Circuit. The statute prohibited the use of public employees and facilities to perform or assist abortions not necessary to save the mother's life, and made it unlawful to use public funds, employees, or facilities for the purpose of "encouraging or counseling" a woman to have an abortion not necessary to save her life.

In its opinion, the Court upheld all the challenged provisions of the Missouri abortion law. The majority observed that the state's interest in protecting potential human life does not come into existence only at the point of viability but exists throughout pregnancy. The rigid trimester analysis set out by *Roe* was criticized as having "proved to be unsound in principle and unworkable in practice." 492 U.S. at 494. It was suggested that a less stringent standard of review be applied when reviewing state abortion statutes. 492 U.S. at 494. A plurality stated that there was no good reason for the rigid line allowing state regulation after viability, but prohibiting it before viability.

21.10. A Further Departure from *Roe*

In *Planned Parenthood of Southeastern Pennsylvania v. Casey*, 505 U.S. 833 (1992), the Supreme Court appeared to continue its retreat from application of the *Roe* standard of review. In the majority opinion, the court relegated the right to an abortion from a fundamental right established in *Roe* to one that involves a liberty interest. As noted earlier in this chapter, it also adopted the undue burden standard of review that had been suggested by the Solicitor General in his *amicus curiae* brief in *City of Akron*, *supra*. It rejected the trimester analysis used in *Roe*.

In *Casey*, the Pennsylvania provisions being challenged as unconstitutional included those that required that women seeking abortions sign a statement 24 hours before the procedure giving their consent and, except in special cases, that a parent must consent before a minor child could obtain an abortion. Another section of the statute required a wife to sign a statement that she had notified her husband that she intended to get an abortion. There were also sections providing for a medical emergency exception and a reporting requirement for abortion facilities.

Strict scrutiny and burden. The Court upheld all the statutory requirements except the spousal notification provision. Relying on the doctrine of *stare decisis*, the Court did not overrule the legality of abortions premised in *Roe v. Wade*. However, it said that in reviewing state statutes restricting abortions, that they were no longer *all* subject to review under the strict scrutiny standard. Rather, only those provisions in a statute that place an undue burden on a woman seeking an abortion would be reviewed under the strict scrutiny standard. 505 U.S. at 876.

Undue burden defined. The Court defined undue burden as "the conclusion that a state regulation has the purpose or effect of placing a substantial obstacle in the path of the woman." 505 U.S. at 877. According to the Court, neither the informed consent requirement nor the 24-hour provision found in the Pennsylvania statute created an undue burden for a woman seeking an abortion.

The Court stated that requiring a doctor to make certain information available to a woman in the first trimester is permissible, so long as the information is truthful and not misleading and was not an undue burden. This resulted in overruling *Akron I*, and *Thornburgh*, at least in part, where the Court had determined statutes that mandated that such information be provided by a physician were unconstitutional. The Court wrote that:

> Requiring that the woman be informed of the availability of information relating to the consequences to the fetus does not interfere with a constitutional right of privacy between a pregnant woman and her physician, since the

> doctor-patient relation is derivative of the woman's position, and does not underlie or override the abortion right. Moreover, the physician's First Amendment rights not to speak are implicated only as part of the practice of medicine, which is licensed and regulated by the State. There is no evidence here that requiring a doctor to give the required information would amount to a substantial obstacle to a woman seeking an abortion."

505 U.S. at 838.

The Court also abandoned *Roe*'s reliance on the trimester approach, stating that it did not consider "the trimester framework . . . to be part of the essential holding of *Roe*." 505 U.S. at 873. The Court explained that "[t]he trimester framework no doubt was erected to ensure that the woman's right to choose not become so subordinate to the State's interest in promoting fetal life that her choice exists in theory but not in fact. We do not agree, however, that the trimester approach is necessary to accomplish this objective." 505 U.S. at 872.

The Court continued:

> Even in the earliest stages of pregnancy, the State may enact rules and regulations designed to encourage her to know that there are philosophic and social arguments of great weight that can be brought to bear in favor of continuing the pregnancy to full term and that there are procedures and institutions to allow adoption of unwanted children as well as a certain degree of state assistance if the mother chooses to raise the child herself.

Ibid.

DEFERENCE TO PHYSICIANS

21.11. Physician's Deference

In this section and the next, we will describe the decisions that appear to affect the question of when, if ever, the Court will give deference to a physician's perspective in an abortion dispute. The first case discussed here is *Colautti v. Franklin*, 439 U.S. 379 (1979) (7-3, with Burger, White, and Rehnquist dissenting).

In *Colautti*, the majority held unconstitutionally vague a viability determination requirement in a Pennsylvania law that required that every person who performed or induced an abortion make a determination, "based on his experience, judgment, or professional competence," that the fetus was not viable; if such person determined that the fetus was viable, or if "there was sufficient reason to believe that the fetus may be viable," then the person had to adhere to a prescribed standard of care. *Id.* at 391 of 439 U.S.

The Court held that the viability determination requirement of the law was void for vagueness. It said it was not at all clear whether the statute contained a purely subjective standard or whether it imposed a mixed subjective and objective standard. *Ibid.* The Court emphasized that, while "viable" and "may be viable" presumably had different meanings, a physician could not know from the statute what they were. It said that the law provided no guidance and conditioned potential physician liability on "confusing and ambiguous criteria," and was, therefore, impermissibly vague. 439 U.S. at 394.

The Court also suggested that it favored providing broad discretion to physicians to make determinations as to "medical necessity" in the abortion context.

21.12. Physician's Duty to Inform

The approach of courts to defer to physicians may have reached its apex.in *City of Akron v. Akron Center for Reproductive Health, Inc*, 462 U.S. 416 (1983) (*Akron 1*) (7-3, with White, Rehnquist, and O'Connor dissenting), which was discussed in a somewhat different context earlier in this chapter. In *Akron*, a local city ordinance required that a physician inform a woman of the status of her pregnancy, the development of her fetus, the date of possible viability, the physical and emotional complications that may result from an abortion, and the availability of agencies to provide assistance and information. 462 U.S at 442. The physician was also required to advise the woman of the risks associated with the abortion technique to be employed and other information. *Ibid.*

The law was invalidated by the Court based on the physician's right to practice medicine in the way that he or she saw fit. According to the Court, "[i]t remains primarily the responsibility of the physician to ensure that appropriate information is conveyed to his patient, depending on her particular circumstances." 462 U.S at 443. The ordinance was viewed by the Court as an unwarranted "intrusion upon the discretion of the pregnant woman's physician." 462 U.S at 445. The Court believed that a physician subject to this ordinance was being placed in an "undesired and uncomfortable straitjacket." *Ibid.*

In *Planned Parenthood of Southeastern Pennsylvania v. Casey*, 505 U.S. 833 (1992), the Court rejected an argument that the Pennsylvania's informed consent law violated the constitutional right to privacy between the pregnant woman and her physician. The *Casey* Court said that *Akron* was wrongly decided on this point and that the doctor-patient relationship was only "entitled to the same solicitude it receives in other contexts." 505 U.S. at 884. The Court referred to the law's provision allowing doctors to exercise their best medical judgment by permitting them not to furnish the required advisories if they could demonstrate by a preponderance of the evidence that they reasonably believed that making the disclosures would result in a severely adverse effect on the health of the patient.

Since *Casey*, the federal circuits have considered various state physician-directed disclosure requirements. *See Planned Parenthood Minnesota, North Dakota, South Dakota v. Rounds*, 530 F.3d 724 (8th Cir. 2008) (abortion provider failed to demonstrate the requisite likelihood that disclosure which was statutorily required of physicians was untruthful or misleading); *Karlin v. Foust*, 188 F.3d 446 (7th Cir. 1999) (so long as a particular informed consent requirement is designed to further a legitimate state interest, whether it is protecting the life and health of the mother or the life of the fetus, it will not be considered a substantial obstacle to obtaining an abortion provided that the information that the state "requires to be made available to the woman is truthful and not misleading"; an informed consent provision that requires the distribution of false and misleading information places an unconstitutional burden on a woman's right to choose).

Note: *See Doe v. Bolton*, 410 U.S. 179 (1973), discussed earlier in the chapter, where a Georgia statute was held unconstitutional that required the interposition of a hospital abortion committee required confirmation by other physicians when a woman sought an abortion.

PICKETING

21.13. Buffer Zones

The question of the nature and extent of picketing outside abortion clinics has triggered a number of lawsuits. The issue came before the Supreme Court in *Madsen v. Women's Health Center*, 512 U.S. 753 (1994), where anti-abortion protesters threatened to picket and demonstrate around a Florida abortion clinic. A state trial court permanently enjoined the petitioners from blocking or interfering with public access to the clinic, and from physically abusing persons entering or leaving it.

Later, when the clinic operators sought to broaden the injunction, the trial court found that access to the clinic was still being impeded and that petitioners' activities were having deleterious physical effects on patients and discouraging some potential patients from entering the clinic. The trial court also found that doctors and clinic workers were being subjected to protests at their homes. In response to these findings, the trial judge issued an amended injunction, which applied to the antiabortion group and persons acting "in concert" with the group. The order excluded demonstrators from a 36-foot buffer zone around the clinic entrances and driveway and the private property to the north and west of the clinic. It also restricted excessive noisemaking within the earshot of the clinic, and the use of "images observable" by patients inside the clinic. It prohibited protesters within a 300-foot zone around the clinic from approaching patients and potential patients who do not consent to talking. It essentially created a 300-foot buffer zone around the residences of clinic staff.

The Florida Supreme Court upheld the amended injunction against antiabortion proponents' claim that it violated their First Amendment right to freedom of speech, and the Supreme Court granted review.

The Supreme Court upheld the injunction. It said that given the focus of the picketing on patients and clinic staff, the narrowness of the confines around the clinic, the fact that protesters could still be seen and heard from the clinic parking lots, and the failure of the first injunction to accomplish its purpose, the 36-foot buffer zone around the clinic entrances and driveway, on balance, burdens no more speech than necessary to accomplish the governmental interests in protecting access to the clinic and facilitating an orderly traffic flow on the street.

It held that the order under which the injunction was issued was content-neutral in terms of the time, place, and manner of regulation for First Amendment purposes. It also said that the injunction regulated only places where some speech could occur; applied equally to all demonstrators, regardless of viewpoint; and did not refer to content of speech. It concluded that the order issued as a part of the injunction provided the police with clear guidelines that were unrelated to the content of demonstrators' speech. The limited noise restrictions imposed by the injunction burdened no more speech than necessary to ensure the health and well-being of the clinic's patients.

However, the Court rejected the 300-foot buffer zone around staff residences as sweeping more broadly than is necessary to protect the tranquility and privacy of the home. The Court said that the record did not contain sufficient justification for so broad a ban on picketing. *See generally Hill v. Colorado*, 530 U.S. 703 (2000) (7-3, with Scalia, Kennedy, and Thomas dissenting) (the Supreme Court upheld a Colorado statute designed to restrict the activity of antiabortion protestors because it was a narrowly tailored time, place, and manner restriction). *See also Pro-Choice Schenck v. Pro-Choice Network of Western New York*, 519 U.S. 357 (1997) (Free-floating buffer zone instigated by District Court injunction ruled in violation of the First Amendment in lawsuit brought by abortion opponents).

PARTIAL-BIRTH ABORTIONS

21.14. Partial-Birth Legislation: *Carhart I* and *II*

In *Stenberg v. Carhart*, 530 U.S. 914 (2000) (*Carhart* I) (5-4, with Rehnquist, Scalia, Kennedy, and Thomas dissenting), a physician who performed abortions brought suit on behalf of himself and his patients challenging the constitutionality of a Nebraska statute banning a "partial-birth abortion." The statute prohibited any "partial birth abortion" unless that procedure was necessary to save the mother's life. The statute defined "partial birth abortion" as a procedure in which the doctor "partially delivers vaginally a living unborn child before killing the . . . child," and defined the latter phrase to mean "intentionally delivering into the vagina a living unborn child, or a substantial portion thereof, for the purpose of performing a procedure that the [abortionist] knows will kill the . . . child and does kill the . . . child." A violation of the law was a felony and provided for the automatic revocation of a convicted doctor's state license to practice medicine.

A majority of the Supreme Court held that the Nebraska statute violated the liberty protected by the due process clause of the Fourteenth Amendment in the U.S. Constitution. In the opinion, the Justices found it important to discuss the various procedures used by physicians conducting abortions during a pregnancy's second trimester (12-24 weeks).

The Court wrote that the most common abortion procedure is "dilation and evacuation" (D & E). 530 U.S. at 914-915. This procedure involves dilation of the cervix and removal of at least some fetal tissue using non-vacuum surgical instruments. After the 15th week, there is a potential need for instrumental dismemberment of the fetus or the collapse of fetal parts to facilitate evacuation from the uterus. When dismemberment is necessary, it typically occurs as the doctor pulls a portion of the fetus through the cervix into the birth canal. 530 U.S. at 915.

The risks of mortality and the complications that accompany D & E are significantly less than those accompanying induced-labor procedures (the next safest mid-second-trimester procedures). *Ibid.*

A variation of D & E, known as "intact D & E," is used after 16 weeks. "It involves removing the fetus from the uterus through the cervix 'intact,' i.e., in one pass rather than several passes. Intact D & E proceeds in one of two ways, depending on whether the fetus presents head first or feet first. The feet-first method is known as 'dilation and extraction' (D & X). D & X is ordinarily associated with the term 'partial birth abortion.' " *Ibid.*

The Nebraska federal district court concluded that clear and convincing evidence established that Dr. Carhart's D & X procedure is superior to, and safer than, the D & E and other abortion procedures used during the relevant gestational period in the 10 to 20 cases a year that he handled.

The Supreme Court held that the Nebraska statute imposed an undue burden on women. Without deciding the issue of whether a statute that outlawed only intact D & E would be unduly burdensome, the Court held that an abortion ban that failed to differentiate in its statutory language between intact D & E and non-intact D & E unquestionably constituted an undue burden, because it would prohibit most second-trimester abortions. 530 U.S. at 938-946. As part of its analysis, the *Stenberg* Court provided legislatures with guidance when drafting statutes that would distinguish adequately between the two forms of D & E.

The Court explained that a legislature should make clear that a statute intended to regulate only intact D & E applies only to that form of the procedure by using language that "track[s] the medical differences between" intact and non-intact D & E or by providing an express exception for the performance of non-intact D & E and other abortion procedures. 530 U.S. at 939. In her concurring opinion, Justice O'Connor emphasized how, by employing the above approach, a legislature could make it clear that a statute intended to regulate intact D & E was in fact narrowly tailored to reach only that form of the D & E procedure. 530 U.S. at 950. Citing three state statutes prohibiting intact D & E that had specifically excluded from their coverage other abortion methods, Justice O'Connor described the language each statute used, providing legislatures wishing to prohibit only intact D & E with a clear roadmap for how to avoid the problems regarding the scope of coverage that undid the Nebraska statute. *Ibid.*

Congressional action. Following the Court's decision in *Stenberg v. Carhart*, Congress passed the Partial-Birth Abortion Ban Act of 2003, 18 U.S.C. §1531 (2003), to proscribe a particular method of ending fetal life in the later stages of pregnancy. The Act does not regulate the most common abortion procedures used in the first trimester of pregnancy, when the vast majority of abortions take place. Congress obviously intended the new Act to be a response to *Carhart I*, and it was challenged almost immediately.

The Supreme Court, in a 5-4 ruling (Stevens, Souter, Ginsberg, and Breyer dissenting), upheld the Act. *Gonzales v. Carhart (Carhart II)*, 550 U.S. 124 (2007). It described the usual second-trimester procedure, "dilation and evacuation" (D & E), as the doctor dilating the cervix and inserting surgical instruments into the uterus and maneuvering them to grab the fetus and pull it back through the cervix and vagina. The fetus is usually ripped apart as it is removed, and the doctor may take 10 to 15 passes to remove it in its entirety.

The procedure that prompted the federal Act is a variation of the standard D & E, and is referred to as "intact D & E." The main difference between the two procedures is that in intact D & E, a doctor extracts the fetus intact or largely intact with only a few passes, pulling out its entire body instead of ripping it apart. In order to allow the head to pass through the cervix, the doctor typically pierces or crushes the skull.

The majority said that the congressional Act responded to *Stenberg* in two ways. First, Congress found that unlike the Supreme Court in *Stenberg*, it was not required to accept the district court's factual findings.

The Court also said that the Act's language differed from that of the Nebraska statute struck down in *Stenberg*. Among other things, the Act prohibits "knowingly perform[ing] a partial-birth abortion . . . that is [not] necessary to save the life of a mother," 18 U.S.C. §1531(a). It defined "partial-birth abortion," §1531(b)(1), as a procedure in which the doctor: "(A) deliberately and intentionally vaginally delivers a living fetus until, in the case of a head-first presentation, the entire fetal head is outside the [mother's] body . . . or, in the case of breech presentation, any part of the fetal trunk past the navel is outside the [mother's] body . . . for the purpose of performing an overt act that the person knows will kill the partially delivered living fetus"; and "(B) performs the overt act, other than completion of delivery, that kills the fetus."

The Court ruled that the lack of an exception in the Act for a woman's health was not fatal because medical uncertainty existed over whether the banned procedure was ever necessary to protect the health of the woman. Justice Thomas noted that although he joined the majority opinion, he believed that *Casey* and *Roe*, as well as the current abortion jurisprudence, are not rooted in the Constitution.

PARENTAL NOTIFICATION AND CONSENT

21.15. Parental Notification of an Abortion

Blanket consent. In *Planned Parenthood of Central Missouri v. Danforth*, 428 U.S. 52 (1976), a Missouri abortion statute required the written consent of a parent or person *in loco parentis* to an abortion of an unmarried woman under 18 during the first 12 weeks of pregnancy, unless a licensed physician certified that the abortion was necessary to preserve the mother's life. The Supreme Court held that such a provision was unconstitutional, at least insofar as it imposed a blanket parental consent requirement. Justice Blackmun wrote, "the State cannot 'delegate to a spouse a veto power which the [S]tate itself is absolutely and totally prohibited from exercising during the first trimester of pregnancy. . . .' "As stressed in *Roe*, "the abortion decision and its effectuation must be left to the medical judgment of the pregnant woman's attending physician." 424 U.S. at 53-54.

48-hour notification. In *Lambert v. Wicklund*, 520 U.S. 292 (1977), the constitutional challenge was to Montana's Parental Notice of Abortion Act. The Act prohibits a physician from performing an abortion on a minor unless the physician has notified one of the minor's parents or the minor's legal guardian 48 hours in advance. However, the Act provided that an "unemancipated" minor may petition the state youth court to waive the notification requirement, pursuant to the statute's "judicial bypass" provision. The provision gives the minor a right to court-appointed counsel and guarantees expeditious handling of the minor's petition (since the petition is automatically granted if the youth court fails to rule on the petition within 48 hours from the time it is filed). The minor's identity remains anonymous, and the proceedings and related documents are kept confidential.

The physicians and other medical personnel challenged the notification provision in the statute, alleging "the notification of a parent or guardian is not in the best interests of the minor."

The Supreme Court disagreed with the challengers. It held that a judicial bypass provision that allowed waiver of the notice requirement if notification was not in the minor's best interest was sufficient to protect a minor's right to abortion. Under the statute, a judge could waive the notice requirement if there was clear, convincing evidence that the minor was mature enough and well enough informed to make the abortion decision independently, and the minor establishes that the abortion would be in her best interests.

Mature minor exception. In *Bellotti v. Baird*, 443 U.S. 622 (1979), the Supreme Court, in separate opinions by Justice Powell and Justice Stevens, held that a Massachusetts statute that required a pregnant minor seeking an abortion to obtain the consent of her parents, or obtain judicial approval following notification to her parents, unconstitutionally burdened the right of the pregnant minor to seek an abortion. The Court stated that if a state decides to require that a pregnant minor obtain one parent's or both parents' consent to an abortion, it must also provide for an alternative procedure whereby authorization for the abortion can be obtained.

The Court also ruled that a pregnant minor is entitled to show either that she is mature enough and well enough informed to make her own abortion decision, in consultation with her physician, independently of her parents' wishes, or that even if she is not able to make this decision independently, the desired abortion would be in her best interests. Such a procedure must ensure that the provision requiring parental consent does not in fact amount to an impermissible, absolute, and possibly arbitrary veto.

Notifying both parents. In *Hodgson v. Minnesota*, 497 U.S. 417 (1990), the Supreme Court considered a provision in a Minnesota statute that regulated a minor's access to abortion. Women under 18 were denied access to an abortion until 48 hours after both their parents had been notified. The statute contained exceptions in the cases of medical emergencies and women who were victims of parental abuse. One provision allowed the courts to bypass the parental notification requirement judicially if the woman seeking an abortion could demonstrate maturely that notification would be unwise.

The Court struck down the provision that mandated that both parents be notified. It said such a requirement does not further any legitimate state interest reasonably. The Court also rejected as justification for the two-parent requirement the parents' concern for the child's welfare and the state's interest in protecting the parents' independent right to determine and strive for what they believe is best for their child. 497 U.S. at 452. Neither of these reasons, said the Court, can justify the two-parent notification requirement.

The Court recognized that the second parent may well have an interest in the minor's abortion decision, making full communication among all members of a family desirable in some cases, but the Court said that such communication may not be decreed by the state. The Court reasoned that the state has no more interest in requiring all family members to talk with one another than it has in requiring certain of them to live together. *Ibid.* The Court stated that to the extent that a parental consent or parental notification provision legitimately supports the parents' authority to act in the minor's best interest, and thus "assures that the minor's decision to terminate her pregnancy is knowing, intelligent, and deliberate," that interest is fully served by notice to one parent. 497 U.S. at 450.

The Court further held that the provision of the statute that requires 48-hour notification unless the pregnant minor obtains a judicial bypass was constitutional. *See Barnes v. State of Miss.*, 992 F.2d 1335 (5th Cir. 1993) (statute requiring consent of two parents but containing adequate judicial bypass mechanism is facially constitutional, and judicial bypass mechanism is constitutional).

Notifying one parent. In *Ohio v. Akron Center for Reproductive Health*, 497 U.S. 502 (1990) (*Akron II*), the Court observed that the statute under attack, which required a minor to notify one parent before having an abortion, contained a judicial bypass provision. The Court upheld the statute, concluding that its judicial bypass procedure complies with the Fourteenth Amendment; due process allowed the statute to require a minor to prove maturity or the minor's best interest by clear and convincing evidence when using the judicial bypass procedure; and the statute could require parental notice to be given by the physician performing the abortion. 497 U.S. at 508. The Court explicitly held that "the procedure must allow the minor to show that, even if she cannot make the abortion decision by herself, the desired abortion would be in her best interests." 497 U.S. at 511.

Necessary to preserve minor's health. *Ayotte v. Planned Parenthood of New England*, 546 U.S. 320 (2006), involved New Hampshire's Parental Notification Prior to Abortion Act, which prohibited physicians from performing an abortion on a minor until 48 hours following the delivery of written notice to the minor's parent or guardian. Although the Act did make an exception in cases where an abortion was necessary to preserve the life of the mother, it contained no corresponding health exception. The First Circuit invalidated the law in its entirety for want of the health exception. In a unanimous opinion, the Supreme Court held that because the parental notification law did not contain an exception allowing a minor to obtain an abortion without notice to her parent when necessary to preserve the minor's health, it was, as to that particular requirement, unconstitutional.

ABORTION FUNDING

21.16. Medicaid Coverage

In 1977, the Supreme Court decided three cases involving laws that permitted states to refuse Medicaid coverage for nontherapeutic abortions. *Beal v. Doe*, 432 U.S. 438 (1977); *Maher v. Roe*, 432 U.S. 464 (1977); *Poelker v. Doe*, 432 U.S. 519 (1977) (city not required to provide publicly financed hospital services for nontherapeutic abortions). In *Beal v. Doe*, the Court held that Title XIX of the Social Security Act does not require a state Medicaid program to fund elective (nontherapeutic) abortions, declaring that states have broad discretion to determine the extent of medical assistance that is "reasonable" and "consistent" with the objectives of the Act. 432 U.S. at 444. The Court explained that it was "not unsympathetic to the plight of an indigent woman who desires an abortion, but the Constitution does not provide judicial remedies for every social and economic ill."

A majority in *Maher v. Roe*, 432 U.S. 464 (1977), found no "unduly burdensome interference" with a woman's abortion decision and that the exclusion of elective abortions from Medicaid did not violate the equal protection clause. The Court treated the refusal to fund abortion as state inaction calling for the rational basis test rather than the strict scrutiny test applied in *Roe*. Because Connecticut encouraged childbirth over abortion, this was viewed as satisfying the application of the rational basis test.

In *Harris v. McRae*, 448 U.S. 297 (1980), an action was brought challenging the statutory and constitutional validity of the Hyde Amendment, which severely limits use of federal funds to reimburse the cost of abortions under the Medicaid program. The Supreme Court held that a state that participates in the Medicaid program is not obligated under Title XIX of the Social Security Act to continue to fund those medically necessary abortions for which federal reimbursement was unavailable under the Hyde Amendment. It also held that funding restrictions of the Hyde Amendment violated neither the Fifth Amendment nor the establishment clause of the First Amendment. The Court said that the language in the Medicaid statute prohibiting the use of federal funds to reimburse the cost of abortions "except where the life of the mother would be endangered if the fetus were carried to term" was facially constitutional under the equal protection clause.

21.17. Selective Funding of Programs in the Public Interest

In *Rust v. Sullivan*, 500 U.S. 173 (1991), recipients of family planning funds under Title X of the Public Health Service Act and doctors who supervised Title X funds brought two suits challenging regulations of the Department of Health and Human Services (HHS) that prohibit Title X projects from engaging in abortion counseling, referral, and activities advocating abortion as a method of family planning. The plaintiffs also challenged provisions of regulations requiring such projects to maintain an objective integrity and independence from prohibited abortion activities by the use of separate facilities, personnel, and accounting records.

The Supreme Court held that the regulations do not violate First Amendment free-speech rights of Title X fund recipients, their staffs, or their patients by impermissibly imposing viewpoint-discriminatory conditions on government subsidies.

The Court said that Congress may "selectively fund a program to encourage certain activities it believes to be in the public interest, without at the same time funding an alternative program which seeks to deal with the problem in another way." 500 U.S. at 193. In doing so, "the Government has not discriminated on the basis of viewpoint; it has merely chosen to fund one activity to the exclusion of the other." *Ibid. See also Maher v. Roe*, 432 U.S. 464, 475 (1977) ("There is a basic difference between direct state interference with a protected activity and state encouragement of an alternative activity consonant with legislative policy"). *Rust's* holding has been limited to situations in which the government is itself the speaker, or instances in which the government used private speakers to transmit its own message.

21.18. Barring Use of Public Facilities

In *Webster v. Reproductive Health Services*, 492 U.S. 490 (1989), Missouri legislation prohibited the use of public facilities for abortion and required that a physician rigorously examine a pregnant woman seeking an abortion if the physician believes the woman's pregnancy to be past 20 weeks. The medical tests were to determine "the gestational age, weight, and lung maturity of the unborn child." 493 U.S. at 512.

The legislation was successfully challenged in the United States District Court for the Western District of Missouri, which held the statute unconstitutional. The Eighth Circuit Court of Appeals upheld the lower court decision, and the Supreme Court granted review. Although the Solicitor General urged overturning *Roe v. Wade*, the Court did not do so. However, five of the nine justices agreed that restrictions such as Missouri's prohibition on the use of public facilities and funds for abortions and the state's required tests to determine viability do not burden procreational choice and are constitutional. In other words, the Court upheld a requirement that no public employees or facilities be used for nontherapeutic abortions.

21.19. State Constitutional Right to Privacy

Some believe that abortion rights are better protected by provisions found in state constitutions than under the federal Constitution. For example, in *American Academy of Pediatrics v. Lungren*, 940 P.2d 797 (Cal. 1997), a California statute required that health care providers secure parental consent or judicial authorization before performing an abortion on a minor. The statute applied to a pregnant minor who is willing to seek parental advice and consent and to "a pregnant minor [who] is too frightened or too embarrassed to disclose her condition to a parent or to a court." 940 P.2d at 800. The court held that the statute violated the minor's right of privacy guaranteed by Article I, Section 1 of the California Constitution. The court reasoned that "[t]he statute significantly intrudes upon autonomy privacy by denying a pregnant minor the ability to obtain a medically safe abortion on her own, and instead requiring her to secure parental consent or judicial authorization in order to obtain access to the medical care she needs to terminate her pregnancy safely. In this respect, the statute denies a pregnant minor, who believes it is in her best interest to terminate her pregnancy rather than have a child at such a young age, control over her own destiny." 940 P.2d at 817. The majority found that under the California Constitution, a minor has the same privacy interest as an adult woman in deciding whether to bear a child.

Other jurisdictions are turning to their state constitutional provisions in considering whether a particular state abortion provision is unconstitutional. *See generally Planned Parenthood League v. Attorney Gen.*, 677 N.E.2d 101, 103 (Mass. 1997) (held on state constitutional basis that statutory requirement that pregnant, unmarried minor obtain consent of both parents before obtaining abortion violated due process clause); *In re T. W.*, 551 So. 2d 1186, 1194 (Fla. 1989) (parental consent provision statute invalid under the Florida Constitution); *Planned Parenthood of Central N.J. v. Farmer*, 762 A.2d

620, 626, 631-639 (N.J. 2000) (Act that conditions minor's right to obtain abortion on parental notification unless judicial waiver is obtained, but imposes no corresponding limitation on minor who seeks medical and surgical care otherwise related to her pregnancy, violates state constitution's equal protection provision); *State v. Planned Parenthood of Alaska*, 35 P.3d 30 (Alaska 2001) (state constitution's provision guaranteeing right of privacy from unwarranted governmental intrusion is self-executing); *Committee to Defend Reprod. Rights v. Myers*, 625 P.2d 779 (Cal. 1981) (funding restrictions violated privacy, due process, and equal protection provisions of California Constitution); *Women of the State v. Gomez*, 542 N.W.2d 17, 19 (Minn. 1995) (using strict scrutiny to rule that "a pregnant woman . . . cannot be coerced into choosing childbirth over abortion by a legislated funding policy" under privacy sections of Minnesota Constitution); *Right to Choose v. Byrne*, 450 A.2d 925 (N.J. 1982) (ruling that restrictions violate fundamental right protected by equal protection provisions of New Jersey Constitution); *Planned Parenthood Ass'n, Inc. v. Department of Human Resources*, 663 P.2d 1247 (Or. App. 983) (violation of Equal Privileges and Immunities Clause of Oregon Constitution), *aff'd*, 687 P.2d 785 (Or. 1984); *Women's Health Ctr. of W. Va., Inc. v. Panepinto*, 446 S.E.2d 658 (W. Va. 1993) (relying on unique provisions of West Virginia Constitution to rule constitutional violation).

EXAMPLES

Examples

1. Assume that D, a druggist, stocks and sells contraceptives in direct violation of a state criminal statute that permits their sale only to married couples. D has regularly and knowingly provided contraceptives to unmarried adults. When the state brings criminal charges against D for selling contraceptives to unmarried couples, he defends on the basis that the criminal statute is unconstitutional. The state argues that the law is constitutional and that its purpose is to deter premarital sex and prevent unwanted out-of-wedlock pregnancies. Is it likely that D would be convicted under this statute after the decisions in *Griswold* and *Eisenstadt*?

2. Assume that a high school swim team coach, suspecting that a teenage team member was pregnant, required the young woman to take a pregnancy test. She and her mother filed a civil rights action against the coach claiming *inter alia* that the pregnancy test unconstitutionally interfered with the daughter's right to privacy regarding personal matters. Most likely, how will a court rule on the challenge?

3. Assume that state X is concerned that abortions should not threaten the life of the mother. To protect her health, state X promulgates a statute that allows abortions only in a state-accredited hospital, and only after two

doctors have concurred in the abortion decision. The statute is challenged on a constitutional basis. Will the challenge most likely succeed?

4. Assume that a state statute requires that before an abortion is performed on a married woman, she must obtain written permission from her husband for the procedure. P, a married woman, challenges the statute as unconstitutional. How will a court most likely rule?

5. Assume that state X passes an abortion statute providing that a woman's consent to an abortion is not voluntary or informed unless "the physician who is to perform the procedure, or the referring physician, has, at a minimum, orally, in person, informed the woman of described information." The XYZ Women's Center challenges the requirement on a constitutional basis. Both the center and a doctor handling abortions file affidavits in support of the challenge. The center's affidavit explains that first-trimester abortions, which compose the vast majority of its abortions, are done by two board-certified obstetrician/gynecologists three days each week. The information regarding the procedure, however, is given to the women primarily by counselors employed by the center. This is done during the first telephone call, which usually takes 10 to 15 minutes, but can last much longer. When a woman comes in for the abortion, she receives more extensive counseling and information from a counselor. It is not until after that counseling that the woman meets the physician, who ascertains whether the woman has any further questions. An affidavit from a doctor working at the clinic states, among other things, that requiring the physician performing the abortion to give all the informed consent information to women will "disrupt my practice, raise the cost of abortions, and burden women who seek to terminate a pregnancy." How will a court most likely treat the constitutional challenge?

6. Assume that state X enacts a statute that provides a two-step process to determine a minor's maturity to make an abortion decision. The statute mandates that the judge of the district court determine whether the minor is mature enough to make the abortion decision. If she is deemed mature, she is allowed to make the decision. In step 2, if the minor is not sufficiently mature to make the decision, the judge resolves the question of whether the abortion should occur. The challengers insist that undue burdens will result from the state's choice of the district court as the exclusive forum in which a minor may obtain judicial consent, arguing that the existence of a $250 filing fee in that court, the limited times during which it is in session, and the lack of easily utilized standard forms for such actions in fact will bar many minors from access to judicial consent. In response, the state asserts that there is a simple indigency form available to the minor that can be used in such a situation, and that

this form and an alternative one for nonindigents will provide immediate access to the court. How will a court most likely treat the challenge?

7. Assume that in 1972 P, age 17, underwent an abortion. D, the physician who performed the abortion, obtained an informed consent signed by P's mother but did not obtain P's formal consent to the abortion. Also, assume that the statute of limitations does not bar a civil action against D and that P sues D, alleging the physician was negligent in failing to consult with P prior to the abortion. In support of her claim, D responds that in 1972, D was not required to obtain the minor's consent. How will a court most likely rule on D's request that the lawsuit be dismissed?

8. Assume that state X enacted a statute that allows only one petition per pregnancy for minors seeking a judicial bypass of the parental-consent requirement. P challenges the statute on its face as placing an undue burden on a woman seeking an abortion. Most likely, how will a court rule on the challenge?

Explanations

1. It is unlikely that D would be convicted of a crime. Here, the statute provides dissimilar treatment for married and unmarried persons who are similarly situated. This would clearly be considered a violation of the equal protection clause.

   The statute also appears to be exactly the type of legislation that the Court in *Eisenstadt* ruled was unconstitutional. Recall that *Eisenstadt* extended the "right of privacy" to all individuals regardless of marital status and explicitly recognized a constitutional right to privacy.

2. The court in *Gruenke v. Seip*, 225 F.3d 290 (3d Cir. 2000), on which this example is based, held that the fact that the coach compelled the student to take the test, coupled with an alleged failure to take appropriate steps to keep the information confidential, infringed upon the young woman's right to privacy. Her claim fell squarely within the contours of the recognized right of a person to be free from disclosure of personal matters as outlined in *Whalen v. Roe*. *See Sterling v. Borough of Minersville*, 232 F.3d 190, 196 (3d Cir. 2000) ("It is difficult to imagine a more private matter than one's sexuality and a less likely probability that the government would have a legitimate interest in disclosure of sexual identity"); *U.S. v. Westinghouse Elec. Corp.*, 638 F.2d 570 (3d Cir. 1980) (information about one's body and state of health is a matter that the individual is ordinarily entitled to retain within the private enclave where he may lead a private life).

3. For the reasons outlined in *Doe v. Bolton* earlier in this chapter, the statute would be held unconstitutional. The Supreme Court in *Bolton* held that requiring two Georgia-licensed physicians to confirm the recommendation of a pregnant woman's own physician, a procedure that is not required in any other voluntary medical or surgical procedure, has no rational connection with the patient's needs and unduly infringes on the physician's right to practice. It also held that a statute similar to that in this example, requiring that abortions, unlike other surgical procedures, be done only in a hospital accredited by a private accreditation organization, is invalid because it is not based on differences reasonably related to the purposes of the Act in which it is found, in the absence of a showing that only Georgia-licensed hospitals aid the state's interest in fully protecting a patient.

4. A state may not require a spouse's prior written consent to an abortion. The Supreme Court has repeatedly invalidated both spousal notification and consent requirements. In *Planned Parenthood of Southeastern Pennsylvania v. Casey*, 505 U.S. 833, 837-838 (1992), the Court held that a husband notification provision in a state statute constitutes an undue burden on a woman seeking an abortion and is therefore invalid. It reasoned that a significant number of women likely would be prevented from obtaining an abortion by such a provision just as surely as if Pennsylvania had outlawed the procedure entirely. It observed that the fact that the provision may affect less than 1 percent of women seeking abortions does not save it from facial invalidity because the proper focus of constitutional inquiry is the group for whom the law is a restriction, not the group for whom it is irrelevant. The Court also observed that it cannot be claimed that the father's interest in the fetus's welfare is equal to the mother's protected liberty because it is an inescapable biological fact that state regulation with respect to the fetus will have a far greater impact on the pregnant woman's bodily integrity than it will on the father's. Such a provision requiring notification of a husband before a woman has an abortion embodies a view of marriage consonant with the common law status of married women but repugnant to the Court's present understanding of marriage and of the nature of the rights secured by the Constitution.

5. The court most likely will strike down the statute. The burden is on the state to demonstrate that this intrusion or restriction "serves a compelling state interest and accomplishes its goal through the use of the least intrusive means." Considering the fact that the state does not have a compelling interest in the health of a pregnant woman during the first trimester, or a fetus before it is viable, there is a substantial likelihood that the clinic will prevail. Even in the second trimester, where the state does have a compelling interest, this restriction will still have to meet the

"least intrusive" standard. *See State v. Presidential Women's Center*, 707 So. 2d 1145 (Fla. App. 1998).

6. The exclusive jurisdiction of the court could be troubling, but the availability of an indigency waiver form significantly reduces the possible burdensomeness of the filing fee. The provision for both immediate access to the court and a simple form for such actions make the possible obstacles far less substantial. It is doubtful that a court will find the process so burdensome as to deny due process of law to minors seeking to use it. *Planned Parenthood League of Massachusetts v. Bellotti*, 641 F.2d 1006 (1st Cir. 1981) (state-prescribed consent form, which a woman was required to sign as prerequisite to obtaining abortion in Massachusetts, was not in itself violative of due process).

7. D's motion will most likely be granted. Even if the trial court had *Roe v. Wade* before it, a case decided a year after the alleged negligence occurred in this hypothetical, *Roe* did not create a legal duty of a physician to obtain the consent of a minor patient before an abortion. Furthermore, at the time of the abortion, P was a minor who could not give effective consent. Given the purpose of requiring a physician to disclose information—that is, to help the person who will consent, or withhold consent, to make an informed decision—a physician was not required to make full disclosure to a minor because the minor could not give legally effective consent. Consent from the minor's mother is sufficient. *See Powers v. Floyd*, 904 S.W.2d 713 (Tex. App. 1995) (physician, who obtained patient's mother's written informed consent prior to performing the abortion, had no duty in 1974 to obtain patient's consent).

8. A state may regulate abortion before viability, so long as it does not impose an "undue burden" on a woman's right to terminate her pregnancy. An "undue burden" exists when "a state regulation has the purpose or effect of placing a substantial obstacle in the path of a woman seeking an abortion of a nonviable fetus."

The statute as written prevents women from seeking a judicial bypass for an abortion where changed circumstances may exist. The changed circumstances that affect abortion-seeking minors include increased maturity, increased medical knowledge about abortion, and discovery that the fetus has a medical anomaly such as gastroschisis. A court most likely will decide that a single-petition rule places an undue burden on a woman seeking an abortion and is facially unconstitutional. *See Cincinnati Women's Services, Inc. v. Taft*, 468 F.3d 361 (6th Cir. 2006) (provision limiting minors seeking a judicial bypass of statutory parental-consent requirement to one petition per pregnancy was an undue burden on the constitutional right to an abortion).

Mediation, Collaborative Law, Parenting Coordination, and Arbitration

22.1. Introduction

As a result of shifting societal values and expectations, the family court system and the process of divorce have changed remarkably over the last 40 years. Not surprisingly, the roles of family law professionals have been similarly transformed.

In light of research showing that ongoing parental conflict harms children, some parents began to seek divorce processes, such as mediation, designed to reduce conflict levels while also involving parents in the creation of parenting plans specific to the needs of their children. New societal norms about parenting were bolstered by research indicating that children often benefit from ongoing post-divorce contact with both parents. As a result of these trends, courts have embraced processes that help parents regularize their contact with each other for the purpose of parenting while keeping conflict to a minimum. Nancy Ver Steegh, *Family Court Reform and ADR: Shifting Values and Expectations Transform the Divorce Process*, 42 Fam. L.Q. 659 (2008). This chapter surveys several "alternative" processes and professional roles that have now become commonplace.

22.2. Use of Screening Protocols

For some families, such as those where parties have a history of intimate partner violence, substance abuse, mental illness, and other serious challenges, participation in alternative dispute resolution (ADR) processes may be unsafe or unproductive. Encouragement to co-parent or to participate in cooperative dispute resolution processes is likely to be harmful and inappropriate for these families. Thus, while the processes described in this chapter will benefit some families, they may work to the detriment of others.

Unfortunately, many families entering the divorce process have experienced intimate partner violence and other serious problems. Amy Holtzworth-Munroe et al., *The Mediator's Assessment of Safety Issues and Concerns (MASIC): A Screening Interview for Intimate Partner Violence and Abuse Available in the Public Domain*, 48 Fam. Ct. Rev. 646, 647 (2010) (studies show rates of 40 to 50 percent for couples entering mediation). Consequently, it is imperative that attorneys and providers of dispute resolution services adopt and use a screening protocol. *See* Nancy Ver Steegh et al., *Look Before You Leap: Court System Triage of Family Law Cases Involving Intimate Partner* Violence, 95 Marquette L. Rev. 955, 972-78 (2012) (discussing screening protocols and limitations of available instruments).

22.3. Informed Decision Making About Participation in Dispute Resolution Processes

Family law attorneys should be prepared to counsel clients concerning various services and processes to ensure that clients are able to make informed choices about whether to participate in various dispute resolution processes. Clients who elect to participate, or are ordered to do so, should be educated about how to participate effectively.

Because of the proliferation of new divorce processes and services, some courts have developed protocols for matching families with resources that might be helpful to them. Some courts use a "linear" or "tiered" system, in which families start in a less intrusive process such as mediation and progress through increasingly evaluative processes (potentially to trial) until the case is resolved. Other courts are experimenting with "triage" systems, in which families are screened and referred to what is believed to be the appropriate level of service for them. Peter Salem, *The Emergence of Triage in Family Court Services: The Beginning of the End for Mandatory Mediation?* 47 Fam. Ct. Rev. 371 (2009); Peter Salem, Debra Kulak, & Robin M. Deutsch, *Triaging Family Court Services: The Connecticut Judicial Branch's Family Intake Screen*, 27 Pace L. Rev. 741 (2007). *But see* Nancy Ver Steegh, et al., *Look Before You Leap* (favoring informed decision making by parties).

MEDIATION

22.4. Definition Under the Model Standards

The Model Standards of Practice for Family and Divorce Mediation define *mediation* as

> A process in which a mediator, an impartial third party, facilitates the resolution of family disputes by promoting the participants' voluntary agreement. The family mediator assists communication, encourages understanding and focuses the participants on their individual and common interests. The family mediator works with the participants to explore options, make decisions and reach their own agreements.

Andrew Schepard, *An Introduction to the Model Standards of Practice for Family and Divorce Mediation*, 35 Fam. L.Q. 1, 3 (2001).

The process of family mediation is designed to assist couples in communicating and determining their own post-divorce arrangements, while also reducing the emotional and financial costs of divorce. Mediation is not intended to supplant legal advice or therapy.

In practice, mediation programs differ significantly from each other. Some mediation takes place under the auspices of the court, and some mediation occurs in private practice settings. Other differences include the number of sessions offered, the qualifications of the mediator, and possible limitations on the issues considered. Mediators also adhere to different models of mediation. Consequently, processes referred to as mediation may differ in significant ways.

22.5. Mediation as an Interest-Based Process

The process of mediation focuses on the underlying needs and interests of family members. Most couples have some common interests, including the well-being of their children, and the mediation process encourages them to focus on working together to achieve common goals. Individual interests are also identified, and spouses examine the extent to which they can meet their own needs while taking into account the needs of the other party. For example, if one spouse wants to stay in the marital home and the other spouse is willing to move, the remaining spouse might agree to a division of assets that allocates liquid assets to the moving spouse for the purpose of making a down payment on a new residence. Couples are thus encouraged to look for ways to "enlarge the pie" and avoid adopting a win-lose, rights-based orientation. Although the past actions of the parties are seen as relevant for planning, couples are encouraged to look forward.

Mediation is a structured problem-solving process that is likely to include the following steps: (1) identifying issues to be mediated; (2) gathering and documenting facts related to the issues; (3) reaching consensus on standards of fairness for each issue; (4) brainstorming possible solutions and considering the ramifications of each; and (5) making decisions about the issues. *See* Stephen K. Erickson & Marilyn S. McKnight, *The Practitioner's Guide to Mediation* 63 (2001). For example, if a couple is considering how to divide assets, they might first make a list of their assets and document the existence and value of each one. Next, they would explore fair ways to divide the assets—for example, they might choose to divide their assets equally between themselves. With this information in mind, the couple is prepared to brainstorm about concrete plans for asset division, often with the use of a spreadsheet or more sophisticated software. After considering the pros and cons of each proposed plan, the couple might agree upon an option for dividing the assets.

22.6. The Role of the Mediator

The mediator functions as a neutral third party who facilitates the mediation process but generally does not express a point of view on the substantive issues. Instead, the mediator helps the participants reach their own decisions. This is quite different from the role of judges and arbitrators, who make final decisions for the parties.

The mediator actively controls the mediation process by setting the agenda, deciding who will speak and in what order, creating ground rules, and framing the discussion. Through modeling and discussion, the mediator teaches the couple effective conflict-resolution and problem-solving skills. In addition, the mediator watches for power imbalances and uses techniques such as verifying facts, meeting in separate caucuses, and asking probing questions to assist couples in making informed and voluntary decisions. Mediators carefully monitor the behavior of the participants and remain alert for lopsided agreements.

Research shows that mediation is most effective when the mediator actively structures the sessions, stays in "flexible control" of the process, "shapes" communication, and keeps the focus on problem solving and the parties' underlying interests. Joan B. Kelly, *A Decade of Divorce Mediation Research: Some Answers and Questions*, 34 Fam. & Conciliation Cts. Rev. 373, 382 (1996).

The mediator, if an attorney, does not represent either party in the mediation process. A mediator may draft a memorandum recording the agreements of the parties, but the mediator does not prepare legal documents for divorce or represent the parties in court.

22.7. Legal Advice in Mediation

Attorneys play different roles in mediation depending upon the model of mediation used. Sometimes lawyers attend mediation sessions with their clients and participate in the process. In other cases, the participants consult with their attorneys as needed between mediation sessions. Some parties in mediation seek legal advice only after the mediation has concluded, and others never consult an attorney. Most mediators prefer that participants consult separate attorneys as needed throughout the process, and also before a final divorce decree is entered in court. *See In re Approval of Application for Determination of Indigent Status Forms*, 910 So. 2d 194 (Fla. 2005) (mediators are not allowed to give legal advice); *Pappas v. Waggoner's Heating & Air, Inc.*, 108 P.3d 9 (Okla. App. 2004) (a mediator is not to "offer legal advice to parties").

22.8. Mediator Qualifications

The skill and experience of the mediator directly affect the quality of the mediation process. The Model Standards of Practice for Family and Divorce Mediation suggest that, at a minimum, family mediators should:

1. have knowledge of family law;
2. have knowledge of and training in the impact of family conflict on parents, children, and other participants, including knowledge of child development, domestic abuse, and child abuse and neglect;
3. have education and training specific to the process of mediation; and
4. be able to recognize the impact of culture and diversity.

Model Standards of Practice for Family and Divorce Mediation, Standard X (2001) *available at* http://www.afccnet.org/pdfs/modelstandards.pdf (last visited September 18, 2012).

Family mediation is a multidisciplinary practice, and mediators are likely to be psychologists, social workers, and/or lawyers. In part because mediators come from different professional backgrounds, regulation and quality control have been controversial issues, and mediators and commentators disagree about how to promote professional diversity and innovation while maintaining quality control. Nevertheless, some research shows that participants generally find that mediators are impartial, sensitive, and skilled. Joan B. Kelly, *A Decade of Divorce Mediation Research: Some Answers and Questions*, 34 Fam. & Conciliation Cts. Rev. 373, 378 (1996).

22.9. Mediation Settlement Rates

Mediation settlement rates vary by program. Overall, settlement rates range from 40 to 80 percent, with an average settlement rate of 60 percent. Robin

H. Ballard et al., *Factors Affecting the Outcome of Divorce and Paternity* Mediations, 49 Fam. Ct. Rev. 16, 21 (2011) (full agreement 59.8 percent, partial agreement 14.9 percent, no agreement 25.3 percent); Desmond Ellis & Noreen Stuckless, *Mediating and Negotiating Marital Conflicts* 103 (1996) (40 to 80 percent); Jeanne A. Clement & Andrew I. Schwebel, *A Research Agenda for Divorce Mediation: The Creation of Second-Order Knowledge to Inform Legal Policy*, 9 Ohio St. J. Disp. Resol. 95, 99 (1993) (40 to 75 percent); Jay Folberg, *Mediation of Child Custody Disputes*, 19 Colum. J. L. & Soc. Probs. 413, 422 (1985) (58 percent).

22.10. Court Approval of Agreements

A divorce is not final until the mediated agreement is approved and a decree is entered by the court. Thus, even when private mediation is used, the court oversees the process and may refuse to approve a mediated agreement for various reasons. For example, a court might refuse to adopt an agreement if the court believes that the parenting arrangements are not in the best interests of the children, or if the mediated agreement departs substantially from state law without good reason. *See Fletcher v. Fletcher*, 2011 WL 4447903 (Tenn. App. 2011) (court reviewed best interests even though there was a signed, mediated agreement by parents).

Courts are cautioned by the American Law Institute (ALI) to reject parenting plans agreed to by parents if the agreement is not "knowing or voluntary" or if the plan would harm the child. *See* ALI, *The Allocation of Custodial and Decisionmaking Responsibility for Children* §2.06 (2000).

22.11. Mediator Testimony

The confidential nature of mediation allows participants to brainstorm and speak candidly during mediation sessions. Consequently, most mediators resist being called as witnesses if mediation is unsuccessful and the parties return to court.

For example, in *Marchal v. Craig*, 681 N.E.2d 1160, 1161 (Ind. App. 1997), the parties failed to reach a mediated agreement but stipulated that the mediator could testify as a witness for both parties. The husband later changed his mind, but the lower court allowed the mediator to testify. *Id.* at 1162. The appellate court found that the testimony violated Indiana ADR Rule 2.12, providing that a "[m]ediator shall not be subject to process requiring the disclosure of any matter discussed during the mediation, but rather, such matter shall be considered confidential and privileged in nature." *Ibid. See Fackler v.* Powell, 891 N.E.2d 1091 (Ind. 2009) (parties may not waive confidentiality requirement). *But see Wilson v. Wilson*, 653

S.E.2d 702 (Ga. 2007) (mediator allowed to testify concerning husband's competency).

State laws vary concerning the extent to which mediation sessions are protected. For a discussion of confidentiality and privilege under the Uniform Mediation Act, *see* Scott H. Hughes, *The Uniform Mediation Act: To the Spoiled Go the Privileges*, 85 Marq. L. Rev. 9 (2001); Ellen Deason, *The Quest for Uniformity in Mediation Confidentiality: Foolish Consistency or Crucial Predictability?* 85 Marq. L. Rev. 79, 82 (2001) ("If a mediator can be converted into the opposing party's weapon in court, then her neutrality is only temporary and illusory."). *See also* ALI, *Principles of the Law of Family Dissolution: Analysis and Recommendations* §2.07(4), (5) (2000); *Lehr v. Afflitto*, 889 A.2d 462, 474-475 (N.J. Super. 2006) (courts should be especially wary of mediator testimony because "no matter how carefully presented, [it] will inevitably be characterized so as to favor one side or the other").

22.12. Mediation as Condition Precedent to Post-Decree Actions

If a final divorce decree requires the parties to mediate before filing post-decree motions in court, the provision is likely to be enforced by the court. For example, in *Gould v. Gould*, 523 S.E.2d 106, 107 (Ga. App. 1999), at the time of the divorce, the parties agreed to mediate conflicts prior to returning to court. Consequently, the court refused to hear a petition for modification and contempt until after mediation had taken place. *Id.* at 108. *See In re* Martin, 8 A.3d 60 (N.H. 2010) (no due process violaton to require assistance of neutral third party). *But see Maurer v. Maurer*, 872 A.2d 326 (Vt. 2005) (claim by father that mediation was condition precedent to litigation was rejected by the court because the father was the party who refused to attend mediation).

22.13. Mandatory Mediation

Because mediation is viewed as a cost-effective way to potentially reduce animosity, some states require divorcing couples to participate in mediation. For a state-by-state analysis, *see* Carrie-Anne Tondo et al., *Mediation Trends: A Survey of the States*, 39 Fam. Ct. Rev. 431 (2001). Proponents of mandatory mediation note high levels of satisfaction with the process and believe that most nonabusive couples can benefit from exposure to mediation. Andrew Schepard, *Children, Courts, and Custody: Interdisciplinary Models for the Twenty-first Century* (2004). *See also* Charles R. Stoner et al., *The Court, The Parent, and the Child: Mediator Perceptions of the Purpose and Impact of Mandated Mediation in Child Custody*

Cases, 13 J. L. & Fam. Stud. 151 (2011) (research regarding mandatory mediation in Illinois).

In contrast, the Model Standards of Practice for Family and Divorce Mediation endorse the notion of informed consent to participation in mediation. Standard III.C. provides that "[a] mediator should not agree to conduct the mediation if the mediator reasonably believes one or more of the participants is unable or unwilling to participate." Consequently, some mediators object to the idea of requiring participation in mediation. *See* Ann Milne & Jay Folberg, *The Theory and Practice of Divorce Mediation: An Overview*, in *Divorce Mediation: Theory and Practice* 19 (Jay Folberg & Ann Milne eds., 1988); René L. Rimelspach, *Mediating Family Disputes in a World with Domestic Violence: How to Devise a Safe and Effective Court-Connected Mediation Program*, 17 Ohio St. J. Disp. Resol. 95, 102 (2001); ALI, *The Allocation of Custodial and Decisionmaking Responsibility for Children* §2.07 (2000).

22.14. Intimate Partner Violence

Commentators express serious reservations about the use of mediation in some cases involving intimate violence. Concerns include the possibility of coercion and retribution by a perpetrator, as well as the likelihood of subjecting a victim and children to additional danger. There is also some indication in the research that cases involving intimate partner violence are less likely to settle in mediation. Robin H. Ballard et al., *Factors Affecting the Outcome of Divorce and Paternity* Mediations, 49 Fam. Ct. Rev. 16, 27 (2011).

As a result, even states that mandate mediation make exceptions or have special provisions for cases involving intimate partner violence. Other states are "victim choice" states in that they have followed the Model Code on Domestic and Family Violence (1994), which provides:

> Section 407. Duty of the mediator to screen for domestic violence during mediation referred or ordered by court.
>
> 1. A mediator who receives a referral or order from a court to conduct mediation shall screen for the occurrence of domestic violence between the parties.
> 2. A mediator shall not engage in mediation when it appears to the mediator or when either party asserts that domestic or family violence has occurred unless:
>   a. Mediation is requested by the victim of the alleged domestic or family violence;
>   b. Mediation is provided in a specialized manner that protects the safety of the victim by a certified mediator who is trained in domestic and family violence; and

c. The victim is permitted to have in attendance at mediation a supporting person of his or her choice, including but not limited to an attorney or advocate.

This approach allows victims of intimate partner violence to mediate if they choose to do so, but does not require them to engage in face-to-face negotiations with an abusive partner. See *Hendershott v. Westphal*, 253 P.3d 806 (Mont. 2011) (statutory bar to mediation where there is reason to suspect abuse). See *also* ALI, *Principles of the Law of Family Dissolution: Analysis and Recommendations* §2.07 (2000); *Rega v. L. S. R.*, 5 A.3d 666 (Me. 2010) (court properly exercised discretion not to order mediation in case involving intimate partner violence).

When there is a history of intimate partner violence, decision making about participation in mediation can be complex. Nancy Ver Steegh et al., *Look Before You Leap*. For a discussion of factors for consideration by victims of intimate partner violence in deciding whether to mediate their divorces and the special safety and procedural precautions that are needed, *see* Nancy Ver Steegh, *Yes, No, and Maybe: Informed Decision Making About Divorce Mediation in the Presence of Domestic Violence*, 9 Wm. & Mary J. Women & L. 145 (2003); Susan Landrum, *The Ongoing Debate About Mediation in the Context of Domestic Violence: A Call for Empirical Studies of Mediation Effectiveness*, 12 Cardozo J. Conflict Resol. 425 (2011). If mediation goes forward, experienced mediators institute special safety precautions and ground rules, and they substantially modify the mediation process.

All mediators should implement a screening protocol for intimate partner violence that includes carefully monitoring cases for signs of undisclosed intimate partner violence. *See also* Amy Holtzworth-Munroe et al., *The Mediator's Assessment of Safety Issues and Concerns (MASIC): A Screening Interview for Intimate Partner Violence and Abuse Available in the Public Domain*, 48 Fam. Ct. Rev. 646 (2010); Desmond Ellis & Noreen Stuckless, *Domestic Violence, DOVE, and Divorce Mediation*, 44 Fam. Ct. Rev. 658 (2006); Connie J. A. Beck & Chitra Raghavan, *Intimate Partner Abuse Screening in Custody Mediation: The Importance of Assessing Coercive Control*, 48 Fam. Ct. Rev. 555 (2010).

EXAMPLES

Examples

1. Assume that P and D, who plan to divorce, disagree about issues such as parenting time and child support. The court appoints an attorney to act as a guardian *ad litem*, which entails functioning as an independent fact finder and evaluator who reports to the court regarding the best interests of the child. In the same order, the judge appoints the same lawyer to mediate the economic aspects of the divorce. As a guardian *ad litem*, the attorney criticizes some of P's parenting practices, and P contends that the attorney is biased toward her and consequently not a suitable mediator of

economic issues. Was appointing the attorney to both roles in the same case improper?

2. P and D decided to divorce and were ordered by the court to attend mediation. After mediation concluded, the wife objected to the mediated agreement because during the mediation, the mediator (1) told the wife that she would lose in court on an issue; (2) threw papers on the table and announced "That's it—I give up"; (3) threatened to report to the court that mediation had failed because of the wife; (4) guessed about the value of assets; and (5) applied time pressure, saying that "you guys have five minutes to hurry up and get out of here" after eight hours of mediation. The mediator argued that P was represented by counsel and could have objected to the process, terminated the mediation, or simply not agreed to the terms. Will the wife be successful in having the mediated agreement overturned?

3. P and D mediate their divorce. Afterward, P claims that she was under duress because she had not slept during the 24 hours prior to the mediation, she was in pain from recent surgery, and she had a migraine headache. During the mediation, she took narcotic pain medication, an antidepressant, and a migraine-related injection. D presented evidence that (1) P was herself an experienced mediator who was represented by counsel at the mediation; (2) P appeared to understand what was transpiring; and (3) P did not seem confused or mentally incapacitated. Based on this evidence, the court ruled that P was not under duress. What is the likely result on appeal?

4. A and B attended divorce mediation pursuant to a court order that specifically provided that the mediation process was to be confidential and "nonevidential." After the mediation ended, the parties disagreed about whether they had actually reached a settlement. A calls the mediator to testify on that question. A asserts that an agreement was reached, and she argues that the mediator was present when the agreement was made and that the mediator is in an ideal position to testify objectively about what occurred. B asserts that no settlement was reached, and he argues that the under the court order, the mediation process was confidential and nonevidential and that mediator testimony would violate that order. Should the mediator be compelled to testify?

5. P and D, who are divorcing, have one child. They attended mediation sessions, where they entered into an agreement under which D was to have sole physical custody of the child, but P was not ordered to pay any child support. Instead, D paid P a reduced amount of alimony. D later objected to the agreement on the basis that, under state law, child support could not be waived. P argued that the arrangement did not affect the amount of money available for support of the child; it just prevented the

couple from exchanging unnecessary checks. Will a court adopt the mediated agreement?

6. Assume that P and D were divorced because during the marriage, P was physically abusive to D and was arrested and convicted of assault and domestic violence. P and D return to court to resolve an issue related to parenting time, and the court orders them to attend mediation before a hearing date will be set. The jurisdiction has a statute providing that "[a]ny court of record may, in its discretion, refer any case of mediation services or dispute resolution programs . . . except that the court shall not refer the case to mediation services or dispute resolution programs where one of the parties claims that it has been the victim of physical or psychological abuse by the other party and states that it is thereby unwilling to enter into mediation services or dispute resolution programs." D objects to the mediation. What is the court likely to do?

EXPLANATIONS

Explanations

1. In the similar case of *Isaacson v. Isaacson*, 792 A.2d 525 (N.J. Super. 2002), the court found that the two roles were indeed incompatible. In New Jersey, the guardian *ad litem* functions as an independent fact finder and evaluator who reports to the court. That role was inconsistent with that of the mediator, who operates as a neutral party in a confidential setting. The court stated that "[w]e are not persuaded that the language limiting the role of [the attorney] as mediator to mediate economic issues and her role as guardian *ad litem* to protect the best interests of the children presents a defining distinction allowing her to serve in both capacities. Despite the seemingly disparate nature of the roles, they were not so distinct as to avoid the necessary overlap generating the conflict." *Id.* at 534.

2. This mediator did not behave professionally during the mediation—the mediator should have remained neutral and should not have coerced the wife into agreeing to a settlement. A court will not adopt an agreement that is not made voluntarily and would not approve this one. *See Vitakis-Valchine v. Valchine*, 793 So. 2d 1094, 1099 (Fla. App. 2001).

3. In the similar case of *McMahan v. McMahan*, 2005 WL 3287475 (Tenn. App. 2005), the trial court found that P's testimony was "not persuasive." The appellate court did not overturn this finding on appeal and held that, based on the trial court's credibility finding, P's testimony did not rise to the level necessary to prove duress. *See also Ford v. Ford*, 68 P.3d 1258

(Alaska 2003) (agreement enforceable despite husband's poor health and desire to "get away from the intolerable stress of the mediation").

4. In a similar case, the court recognized that the ability to be open and honest during mediation is key to the success of the process and that parties would be less likely to speak candidly if their statements could later be used in court. The court concluded that there had been no express waiver of the confidentiality provision and that mediator testimony consequently was improper. *See Lehr v. Afflitto*, 889 A.2d 462 (N.J. Super. 2006); *In re Marriage of Kieturakis*, 41 Cal. Rptr. 3d 119 (Cal. App. 2006).

5. In the similar case of *Swanson v. Swanson*, 580 S.E.2d 526 (Ga. 2003), the court found that the right to child support belonged to the child and could not be waived by the parents in a mediated agreement. The court refused to incorporate the settlement agreement into a final decree, and the case consequently was reversed and remanded. *See also Esser v. Esser*, 586 S.E.2d 627 (Ga. 2003) (trial court not bound by an agreement regarding child support, nor is its obligation to determine whether the child support is sufficient simply by adopting the parties' agreement); *Hamilton v. Hamilton*, 976 A.2d 924 (Me. 2009) (Department of Health and Human Services (DHHS) had the right to seek child support from father, even though mother agreed at mediation that father would not have to pay any child support).

6. In most states, the court will not require D to mediate with P if she objects to the mediation based on the occurrence of domestic violence. The statute clearly states that the court "shall not" refer to mediation if one of the parties "claims" to be a victim of domestic violence. Here, P has been convicted of assault and domestic violence, and D is opposed to mediating. *See Pearson v. District Court*, 924 P.2d 512 (Colo. 1996).

COLLABORATIVE LAW

22.15. The Collaborative Process

Building on the success and popularity of interest-based processes such as mediation, collaborative lawyers use interest-based problem-solving negotiation techniques to assist parties in reaching a settlement. To participate in the collaborative law process, both parties must retain an identified collaborative law attorney and agree from the outset that the case will be resolved without going to court.

The parties and their lawyers typically engage in four-way meetings that sometimes involve other professionals such as child psychologists and financial planners. These professionals function as neutral advisors who assist the parties in better understanding their options going forward. Susan A. Hansen & Gregory M Hildebrand, *Collaborative Practice, in Innovations in Family Law Practice* 29 (Kelly Browe Olson & Nancy Ver Steegh, eds., 2008).

The disqualification agreement is a key distinguishing feature of the collaborative law process. To enhance commitment to the process and create a contained environment for negotiation, the parties agree that if the collaborative law process reaches an impasse and court activity begins, the collaborative lawyers will withdraw from representation and the parties will retain new litigation counsel. The disqualification agreement also reduces any financial incentive that a lawyer might have to boost fees by encouraging ongoing litigation. *See* Gary Voegele, Linda K. Wray, & Ron Ousky, *Collaborative Law: A Useful Tool for the Family Law Practitioner to Promote Better Outcomes*, 33 Wm. Mitchell L. Rev. 971 (2007).

Limited research is available concerning the collaborative law process, but one study indicates that practice varies considerably with respect to issues such as the extent of involvement by coaches and experts, whether attorneys meet with their clients outside of negotiation sessions, and how information disclosure is handled. Julie Macfarlane, *The Emerging Phenomenon of Collaborative Family Law (CFL): A Qualitative Study of CFL Cases* 13-14 (2005).

22.16. Formal Opinion 07-447

In 2007, the American Bar Association Standing Committee on Ethics and Professional Responsibility issued an ethical opinion approving the collaborative law process, so long as potential clients are advised of benefits and risks. American Bar Association Standing Committee on Ethics and Professional Responsibility, Ethical Considerations in Collaborative Law Practice, Formal Opinion 07-447 (August 9, 2007). The committee views collaborative law practice as a limited scope representation under Model Rule 1.2. It rejected an argument that a four-way agreement constitutes a non-waivable conflict of interest and concluded that the agreement to withdraw does not impair a lawyer's ability to represent a client. See Chapter 23 for additional discussion of ethical obligations of collaborative lawyers.

22.17. Uniform Collaborative Law Rules (UCLR) and Uniform Collaborative Law Act (UCLA)

The National Conference of Commissioners on Uniform State Laws (NCCUSL) has promulgated the Uniform Collaborative Law Rules

(UCLR) and Uniform Collaborative Law Act (UCLA) in an effort to establish best practices and bring uniformity to collaborative law practice. The final version (as of 2010) is available at http://www.law.upenn.edu/bll/archives/ulc/ucla/2010_final.htm (last visited July 25, 2012). The UCLR and the UCLA define relevant terms, set forth the contents of a valid collaborative law participation agreement, discuss the application of the disqualification agreement in various contexts, and create a privilege against disclosure of collaborative law communications.

Under the UCLR and the UCLA, collaborative law lawyers are required to "make reasonable inquiry" about the existence of domestic violence and special provisions apply in such cases. Nancy Ver Steegh, *The Uniform Collaborative Law Act and Intimate Partner Violence: A Roadmap for Collaborative (and Non-Collaborative) Lawyers*, 38 Hofstra L. Rev. 699 (2009).

Either the UCLR or the UCLA has been adopted in five jurisdictions and introduced for legislative consideration in three additional states. Uniform Law Commission, Legislative Fact Sheet, available at http://www.uniformlaws.org/LegislativeFactSheet.aspx?title=Collaborative%20Law%20Act (last visited July 25, 2012).

22.18. Cooperative Law Compared

In part because of controversy related to the disqualification agreement, some lawyers practice pursuant to a model called "cooperative law." These lawyers use a process very similar to that found in collaborative law, except that they do not enter into a disqualification agreement. Thus, if the parties decide to go to court for any reason, the cooperative lawyer does not withdraw from the case. Advocates of cooperative law believe that the model includes the benefits of collaborative law without potentially subjecting the parties to the added expense and delay that a change of counsel would entail. David A. Hoffman, *Cooperative Negotiation Agreements: Using Contracts to Make a Safe Place for a Difficult Conversation*, in *Innovations in Family Law Practice* 63 (Kelly Browe Olson & Nancy Ver Steegh, eds., 2008). *See also In re Mabray*, 355 S.W.3d 16 (Tex. App. 2010) (comparing collaborative law and cooperative law practice).

PARENTING COORDINATION

22.19. The Role of the Parenting Coordinator

A parenting coordinator functions much like a special master might in a federal civil case. In essence, the judge delegates limited decision-making authority regarding a specific family to a professional with expertise in family dynamics and family law. The idea is to provide high-conflict families with facilitation, additional oversight, and faster access to decision-making assistance.

Parenting coordination is defined as

> [A] child-focused alternative dispute resolution process in which a mental health or legal professional with mediation training and experience assists high conflict parents to implement their parenting plan by facilitating the resolution of their disputes in a timely manner, educating parents about children's needs, and with prior approval of the parties and/or the court, making decisions within the scope of the court order or appointment contract.

Association of Family and Conciliation Courts Task Force on Parenting Coordination, *Parenting Coordination: Implementation Issues*, 41 Fam. Ct. Rev. 533 (2003).

Parenting coordinators typically help families resolve day-to-day matters such as scheduling, transportation, and child care. In some cases, they facilitate communication between the parents; in others, they exercise limited decision-making authority. They are not empowered to make major decisions, such as those involved in modification of child custody or relocation. *See* Christine A. Coates et al., *Parenting Coordination for High-Conflict Families*, 42 Fam. Ct. Rev. 246 (2004); Matthew J. Sullivan, *Ethical, Legal, and Professional Practice Issues Involved in Acting as a Psychologist Parent Coordinator in Child Custody Cases*, 42 Fam. Ct. Rev. 576 (2004).

22.20. Legislative Authorization in Some States

Parenting coordination was initially conceptualized at a multidisciplinary meeting convened by the Family Law Section of the American Bar Association (ABA) in 2000. Conference Report and Action Plan, *High-Conflict Custody Cases: Reforming the System for Children, Wingspread Conference at Racine, Wisconsin*, September 8-10, 2000. Since then, parenting coordinators have been appointed in a variety of states, and at least eight states have gone so far as to formally authorize the role through legislation. Leta Parks et al., *Defining Parenting Coordination with State Laws*, 49 Fam. Ct. Rev. 629 630 (2011) (comparison of statutory provisions).

The Colorado statute governing appointment of a parenting coordinators is illustrative of similar provisions in other statutes and provides, in part, as follows:

> **§14-10-128.1. Appointment of parenting coordinator**
>
> (1) Pursuant to the provisions of this section, at any time after the entry of an order concerning parental responsibilities and upon notice to

the parties, the court may, on its own motion, a motion by either party, or an agreement of the parties, appoint a parenting coordinator as a neutral third party to assist in the resolution of disputes between the parties concerning parental responsibilities, including but not limited to implementation of the court-ordered parenting plan. The parenting coordinator shall be an individual with appropriate training and qualifications and a perspective acceptable to the court. . . .

(2)(a) Absent agreement of the parties, a court shall not appoint a parenting coordinator unless the court makes the following findings:

(I) That the parties have failed to adequately implement the parenting plan;

(II) That mediation has been determined by the court to be inappropriate, or, if not inappropriate, that mediation has been attempted and was unsuccessful; and

(III) That the appointment of a parenting coordinator is in the best interests of the child or children involved in the parenting plan. . . .

(3) A parenting coordinator shall assist the parties in implementing the terms of the parenting plan. Duties of a parenting coordinator include, but are not limited to, the following:

(a) Assisting the parties in creating an agreed-upon, structured guideline for implementation of the parenting plan;

(b) Developing guidelines for communication between the parties and suggesting appropriate resources to assist the parties in learning appropriate communication skills;

(c) Informing the parties about appropriate resources to assist them in developing improved parenting skills;

(d) Assisting the parties in realistically identifying the sources and causes of conflict between them, including but not limited to identifying each party's contribution to the conflict, when appropriate; and

(e) Assisting the parties in developing parenting strategies to minimize conflict.

C.R.S.A. §14-10-128.1.

See also In re Marriage of Rozzi, 190 P.3d 815 (Colo. App. 2008) (interpreting parenting coordination statute).

22.21. Common Practices

Despite the fact that parenting coordination is a new professional role, some practice trends are emerging. In a recent national survey of parenting coordinators researchers found that parenting coordinators are a multidisciplinary group of professionals including psychologists (44 percent), M.S.W. social workers (19 percent), LPC counselors (15 percent), B.A.-level practitioners (11 percent), and attorneys (11 percent). All the parenting coordinators surveyed work only by court order or under mutually signed consent decrees. Most use written parenting coordinator agreements that include the basis and scope of authority, advise that communications are not confidential, and clarify that the parenting coordinator will not provide therapy or give legal advice. Karl Kirkland & Matthew Sullivan, *Parenting Coordination (PC) Practice: A Survey of Experienced Professionals*, 46 Fam. Ct. Rev. 622 (2008).

Initial research indicates that use of a parenting coordinator may reduce post-divorce court filings. Wilma Henry et al., *Parening Coordination and Court Relitigation: A Case Study*, 47 Fam. Ct. Rev. 682, 690 (2011).

EXAMPLE

Example

7. During the divorce process, a mental health expert recommended that P and D work with a parenting coordinator. They consequently agreed to the entry of a court order appointing a parenting coordinator to assist with communications, resolve minor issues, monitor problems, and make recommendations about parenting time. The appointment was made pursuant to a state statute placing strict guidelines on the role. Despite having initially agreed, P later challenged the use of a parenting coordinator. She alleged that the parenting coordinator micromanaged the family and usurped her right to make decisions for her child. What is the likely result?

EXPLANATION

Explanation

7. In *Barnes v. Barnes*, 107 P.3d 560 (Okla. 2005), the court upheld the appointment of a parenting coordinator, noting that the role was a clearly limited one. The court held that the Oklahoma Parenting Coordinator Act did not violate equal protection and that P's substantive due process rights were not violated by the appointment.

ARBITRATION

22.22. Use of Arbitration in Family Cases

In arbitration, a neutral third party selected by the parties hears evidence and in most cases makes a binding decision. In recent years, some spouses have attempted to arbitrate issues related to divorce in an effort to reduce costs and speed the divorce process.

States differ concerning the use of arbitration in family cases. While agreements to arbitrate issues related to alimony will often be enforced, some courts hesitate to delegate issues related to children, which traditionally involve court determination of the children's best interests. Elizabeth A. Jenkins, *Validity and Construction of Provisions for Arbitration of Disputes as to Alimony or Support Payments or Child Visitation or Custody Matters*, 38 A.L.R.5th 69 (2009). *See Tuetken v. Tuetken*, 320 S.W.3d 262 (Tenn. 2010) (parenting issues not subject to binding arbitration); *Toiberman v. Tisera*, 998 So. 2d 4 (Fla. App. 2008) (interpreting arbitration statute, court held that prohibition of arbitration of child-related issues foreclosed arbitration of other issues in the case). *But see Fawzy v. Fawzy*, 973 A.2d 347 (N.J. 2009) (only threat of harm to child justifies infringement on right of parents to choose dispute resolution method); *Johnson v. Johnson*, 9 A.3d 1003 (N.J. 2010).

The Model Family Law Arbitration Act of the American Academy of Matrimonial Lawyers (AAML) provides for *de novo* judicial review of arbitration awards involving child custody and child support. Model Family Law Arbitration Act, *available at* http://www.aaml.org/go/library/publications/model-family-law-arbitration-act/ (last visited July 25, 2012). Several states have adopted statutes regarding matrimonial arbitration. Lynn P. Burleson, *Family Law Arbitration: Third-Party Alternative Dispute Resolution*, 30 Campbell L. Rev. 297 (2008) (noting that Colorado, Connecticut, Indiana, Michigan, New Hampshire, New Mexico, and North Carolina have matrimonial arbitration statutes).

CHAPTER 23

Professional Responsibility

23.1. Introduction

This chapter focuses on issues of professional responsibility, with particular relevance to practitioners of family law. Family law attorneys work closely with families as they navigate challenging transitions and make decisions that will affect the rest of their lives. As a result, they occupy a special position of trust, and their clients rely on them for candid, insightful advice delivered with clarity and compassion.

There is some indication that family lawyers are more subject to disciplinary complaints than other lawyers. This stems from a variety of causes, including poor practice, the emotional nature of family law representation, and unrealistic expectations on the part of some clients. *See* Barbara Glesner Fines & Cathy Madsen, *Caring Too Little, Caring Too Much: Competence and the Family Law Attorney*, 75 UMKC L. Rev. 965 (2007).

Of course, many clients are pleased with the representation they receive, and they report that their attorneys help them keep perspective, interpret legal proceedings, and provide emotional support. Connie J. A. Beck & Bruce D. Sales, *A Critical Reappraisal of Divorce Mediation Research and Policy*, 6 Psychol. Pub. Pol'y & L. 989, 1014 (2000); Marsha Kline Pruett & Tamara D. Jackson, *The Lawyer's Role During the Divorce Process: Perceptions of Parents, Their Young Children, and Their Attorneys*, 33 Fam. L. Q. 283, 294-295 (1999). In addition, lawyers serve an important function in protecting the interests of their clients.

CONFLICTS OF INTEREST

23.2. Prior Representation and Prospective Clients

According to Rule 1.9 of the Model Rules of Professional Conduct, "A lawyer who has formerly represented a client in a matter shall not thereafter represent another person in the same or a substantially related matter in which that person's interests are materially adverse to the interests of the former client unless the former client gives informed consent, confirmed in writing." Model Rules of Prof'l Conduct R. 1.9(a) (2012), *available at* http://www.americanbar.org/groups/professional_responsibility/publications/model_rules_of_professional_conduct/rule_1_9_duties_of_former_clients.html (last visited September 17, 2012).

Thus, if one party meets with an attorney to discuss representation in a divorce, that attorney may be prevented from representing the other spouse later in the action. *In re Marriage of Newton*, 353 Ill. Dec. 105 (Ill. App. 2011) (initial interview gave rise to presumption that confidential information had been imparted). *But see* Model Rules of Prof'l Conduct, R. 1.18 (2012) (discussing obligations to prospective clients); *Cargould v. Manning*, 2009 WL 3674669 (Ohio App. 2009) (alleged meeting with spouse did not bar representation of the other spouse).

23.3. Dual Representation

Sometimes parties ask an attorney to represent them simultaneously in a divorce action, often when they believe that they have reached full agreement. Unfortunately, once the lawyer starts to investigate, an issue or asset may come to light that the parties failed to consider or about which they disagree. Because parties may have conflicting legal interests, dual representation is generally ill-advised. *See In re Disciplinary Proceedings Against Gamino*, 314 Wis. 2d 544, 753 N.W.2d 521 (Wis. 2008) (dual representation of husband and wife in their divorce proceeding, absent obtaining any consent or waiver from husband or wife, violated rule of professional conduct for attorneys governing conflicts of interest).

The Supreme Court of Appeals of West Virginia reasoned as follows in a case involving dual representation concerning a prenuptial agreement:

> Like divorce actions, the nature of prenuptial agreements is such that the parties' interests are fundamentally antagonistic to one another. Indeed, the purpose of a prenuptial agreement is to preserve the property of one spouse, thereby preventing the other from obtaining that to which he or she might otherwise be legally entitled. In this circumstance, as in a divorce, "[t]he

> likelihood of prejudice is so great with dual representation so as to make adequate representation of both . . . [parties] impossible. . . ." Accordingly, the Court holds that one attorney may not represent, nor purport to counsel, both parties to a prenuptial agreement. [Citations omitted]

Ware v. Ware, 687 S.E.2d 382, 389 (W. Vir. 2009). *But see In re Disciplinary Proceedings Against Gamino*, 753 N.W.2d 521 (Wis. 2008) (dual representation may be allowed with voluntary consent and written waiver).

Rule 1.7(b)(3) of the Model Rules of Professional Conduct disapproves of representation that involves "the assertion of a claim by one client against another client represented by the lawyer in the same litigation or other proceeding before a tribunal." Model Rules of Prof'l Conduct R. 1.7(b)(3) (2012) *available at* http://www.americanbar.org/groups/professional_responsibility/publications/model_rules_of_professional_conduct/rule_1_7_conflict_of_interest_current_clients.html (last visited Sept. 17, 2012).

Comment [30] to Rule 1.7(b)(3) warns that the attorney-client privilege will not attach between commonly represented clients. If such representation proceeds and adverse interests surface, the attorney would have to withdraw from both representations, creating unnecessary hardship and expense for the clients. Comment [29] to Rule 1.7(b)(3).

23.4. Sexual Relationships with Clients

Although problematic in any case, sexual relationships with clients are especially detrimental in divorce cases. If the client is involved in a custody dispute, the existence of an affair or cohabitation may affect the outcome adversely. In fact, the lawyer may be called as a witness. At a minimum, the sexual relationship exacerbates an already emotionally charged situation, making resolution of the issues more difficult. Most people experiencing a divorce are more emotionally vulnerable than they normally would be, and exploitation is more likely to occur. *See Mann v. Saland*, 816 N.Y.S.2d 697 (N.Y. Sup. 2006) (in a dismantling marital relationship, the loss of love and intimacy, the bitter struggle over children, the marital home, and finances caused intense and conflicting feelings of anger, rejection, guilt, and vulnerability; litigants experienced a state of despair and isolation equaled only by the reaction to the death of a loved one); *Iowa Supreme Court Attorney Disciplinary Bd. v. Morrison*, 727 N.W.2d 115 (Iowa 2007) (attorney suspended for engaging in sexual relationship with client whom he was representing in a marriage dissolution proceeding); *Disciplinary Counsel v. Engler*, 851 N.E.2d 502 (Ohio 2006) (public reprimand was appropriate sanction for attorney's conduct in having two sexual encounters with client while representing her in divorce case).

The Model Rules of Professional Conduct provide that "[a] lawyer shall not have sexual relations with a client unless a consensual sexual relationship existed between them when the client-lawyer relationship commenced." Model Rules of Prof'l Conduct R. 1.8(j) (2012) *available at* http://www.americanbar.org/groups/professional_responsibility/publications/model_rules_of_professional_conduct/rule_1_8_current_clients_specific_rules.html (last visited September 17, 2012).

The comments following the rule explain the reasons for the prohibition of sexual relationships with clients. First, the attorney occupies a position of trust and has a fiduciary obligation to the client. The lawyer may not use this trust to disadvantage or exploit the client. Second, because of the nature of the relationship, the lawyer's independent professional judgment may be impaired. Third, it may be difficult to distinguish confidences protected by the attorney-client privilege from those that are not protected. Under these circumstances, the client is not considered able to give informed consent. *See In re Bash*, 880 N.E.2d 1182 (Ind. 2008) (attorney attempting to have sexual relations with client whom he represented in divorce action violated his ethical duty to client; failure to withdraw from representation following his sexual advances violated professional rules prohibiting lawyers from representing clients when such representation would be materially limited by a lawyer's self-interest, i.e., his desire to engage in a sexual relationship with client). *See also* Model Rules of Prof'l Conduct R. 1.8(j), R. 8.4(a)); Gregory G. Sarno, Annotation, *Sexual Misconduct as Ground for Disciplining Attorney or Judge*, 43 A.L.R.4th 1062 (1986).

Rule 1.8(j) creates an exception when the lawyer and client have a preexisting sexual relationship. Even in this circumstance, the comments direct the lawyer to consider whether the relationship would materially limit the lawyer's ability to represent the client.

EXAMPLES

Examples

1. A lawyer met briefly with a husband about pending divorce proceedings and an action for a restraining order. The husband did not retain the lawyer to represent him and instead hired other counsel. Some time later, the lawyer was contacted by the wife, met with her, and agreed to represent the wife in the divorce proceeding. Was this a conflict of interest?

2. A lawyer engages in a consensual sexual relationship with a client whom he is representing in a domestic relations matter, and she later files a disciplinary complaint against him. The attorney practices in a state with no specific rule prohibiting such a relationship, and he claims that he would not have engaged in the relationship if it were specifically barred. The attorney further argues that the former client has not presented any

evidence of impaired representation. Does the attorney nevertheless have a conflict of interest?

3. A lawyer has a sexual relationship with a woman, and while the relationship is ongoing, he undertakes the representation of her in her divorce. If the jurisdiction doesn't have a specific rule forbidding this behavior, what other rules might apply?

4. Attorney A was appointed to represent Client C in a divorce proceeding. C was incarcerated and never met in person with A. Nevertheless, A started a flirtatious letter-writing and telephone relationship with C. Did this behavior violate the prohibition on sexual relationships with clients?

Explanations

1. Under similar facts, in *In re Conduct of Knappendberger*, 108 P.3d 1161 (Or. 2005), the court found that the lawyer did have a conflict of interest. The court characterized the husband as a former client in a significantly related matter.

2. In a somewhat similar case, *In re Application for Disciplinary Action Against Chinquist*, 714 N.W.2d 469 (N.D. 2006), the court was not persuaded by either the absence of a "bright-line rule" prohibiting sexual relationships or the notion that evidence of impaired representation was necessary. The court found that the lawyer's relationship placed his interests above those of his client and was a conflict of interest.

3. This behavior may violate rules related to (1) competent and diligent representation, (2) attorney acting as an advocate and a potential witness, and (3) conduct prejudicial to the administration of justice. In the similar case of *State ex rel. Oklahoma Bar Assn. v. Downes*, 121 P.3d 1058 (Okla. 2005), the court noted that such behavior was adverse to the client's interest and added "even more hostility to an already acrimonious divorce."

4. In the similar case of *Lawyer Disciplinary Bd. v. Chittum*, 689 S.E.2d 811 (W.Va. App. 2010), the court found that while there was no physical sexual relationship, the relevant rule was violated because A's behavior constituted "an attempt to establish a sexual relationship" with C. Because of her incarceration, the court noted that C was in a vulnerable position and likely thought that she had to respond to the overtures to maintain pro bono representation in the divorce proceeding.

CONTINGENT FEES

23.5. Contingent Fee Arrangements

Sometimes potential clients are unable to pay hourly attorney fees and are interested in entering into a contingent fee arrangement. Under such an arrangement, the lawyer receives a percentage of the client's recovery in the action. Rule 1.5(d)(1) of the Model Rules of Professional Conduct forbids attorneys from charging or collecting "any fee in a domestic relations matter, the payment or amount of which is contingent upon the securing of a divorce or upon the amount of alimony or support, or property settlement in lieu thereof. . . ." Model Rules of Prof'l Conduct R. 1.5(d)(1) (2012) *available at* http://www.americanbar.org/groups/professional_responsibility/publications/model_rules_of_professional_conduct/rule_1_5_fees.html (last visited September 17, 2012).

Use of contingent fees in divorce cases goes against public policy because (1) the attorney would have a financial stake in the divorce proceeding and might promote divorce instead of encouraging reconciliation of the parties, and (2) a percentage fee might be unduly burdensome in the context of the work done and the financial circumstances of the parties. *See Maxwell Schuman & Co. v. Edwards*, 663 S.E.2d 329 (N.C. App. 2008) (contingent fee in child custody dispute was void).

23.6. Exceptions

Contingent fees are allowed in domestic relations cases involving collection of post-judgment amounts due "under support, alimony, or other financial orders." Comment [6] to Rule 1.5(d)(1) (these actions do not give rise to the same policy concerns). *See Burns v. Stewart*, 188 N.W.2d 760 (Minn. 1971).

EXAMPLE

Example

5. Assume that P and D are divorcing. D is unemployed and cannot afford to pay an attorney an hourly fee. However, in the divorce, D expects to be awarded a parcel of land located on a lake. D agrees that if the land is awarded to D, D will sell it and give half of the payment received to the attorney. D is very happy with this arrangement because otherwise, D will not be represented in the divorce. Is this an appropriate fee arrangement?

EXPLANATION

Explanation

5. This is the type of contingent fee prohibited under Rule 1.5(d)(1) because the arrangement gives the lawyer a financial interest in having D proceed with the divorce. The arrangement also gives the lawyer a vested stake in a certain outcome. If D decides to reconcile with P, or if D and P decide that P should have the lake property, the lawyer may have difficulty giving D objective advice because of the lawyer's own financial interest in the divorce.

COMMUNICATING WITH CLIENTS

23.7. Emotional Needs of Family Clients

A client in a family law case may experience serious emotional turmoil and is likely to have questions and want some emotional support as the case proceeds. Clients experiencing serious distress should be referred for counseling, but all clients are entitled to reasonable and regular communication with counsel. *See* Barbara Glesner Fines & Cathy Madsen, *Caring Too Little, Caring Too Much: Competence and the Family Law Attorney*, 75 UMKC L. Rev. 965 (2007) (discussing attorney competence in dealing with emotions).

23.8. Information and Consultation

Model Rule of Professional Conduct 1.4 provides as follows:

> a. A lawyer shall:
>
> 1. promptly inform the client of any decision or circumstance with respect to which the client's informed consent, as defined in Rule 1.0(e), is required by these Rules;
> 2. reasonably consult with the client about the means by which the client's objectives are to be accomplished;
> 3. keep the client reasonably informed about the status of the matter;
> 4. promptly comply with reasonable requests for information; and
> 5. consult with the client about any relevant limitation on the lawyer's conduct when the lawyer knows that the client expects assistance not permitted by the Rules of Professional Conduct or other law.
>
> b. A lawyer shall explain a matter to the extent reasonably necessary to permit the client to make informed decisions regarding the representation.

Model Rules of Prof'l Conduct R. 1.4 (2012) *available at* http://www.americanbar.org/groups/professional_responsibility/publications/model_rules_of_professional_conduct/rule_1_4_communications.html (last visited September 17, 2012).

Example

6. Lawyer L agreed to represent P in a divorce from D. P was shocked when D filed for divorce and was extremely upset by the entire proceeding. At first, P called L four or five times a week to "check on the case." Lawyer L became weary of the calls and stopped returning them. L continued to ignore P's calls and contacted P only when L had a particular need to talk to P. P didn't hear from L for a period of two months, and P became distraught when her calls were never returned. P finally filed a disciplinary complaint against L. Did L violate Rule 1.4?

Explanation

6. L should have referred P for counseling so that P could deal with the emotional aspects of the divorce more appropriately. L should also have had a conversation with P about the number of times that P was calling the office — P needed information about how P could stay informed about the case and under what circumstances P should call. L's decision not to return calls or contact P for two months was unreasonable and violates Rule 1.4.

SELF-REPRESENTED LITIGANTS

23.9. Self-Representation Becomes More Common

In recent years, the number of self-represented litigants in family cases has dramatically increased. For example, a 1990 American Bar Association (ABA) study conducted in Arizona found that at least one party was unrepresented in 88 percent of divorce cases. In contrast, a 1980 study found that at least one party was unrepresented in only 24 percent of cases. Steven K. Berenson, *A Family Law Residency Program? A Modest Proposal in Response to the Burdens Created by Self-Represented Litigants in Family Court*, 33 Rutgers L.J. 105, 109

(2001); Jim Hilbert, *Educational Workshops on Settlement and Dispute Resolution: Another Tool for Self-Represented Litigants in Family Court*, 43 Fam. L. Q. 545 (2009); Judith G. McMullan & Debra Oswald, *Why Do We Need a Lawyer? An Empirical Study of Divorce Cases*, 12 J. L. & Fam. Stud. 57 (2010).

23.10. Attorney Conduct with Self-Represented Parties

Attorneys dealing with self-represented parties have special obligations under Rule 4.3 of the Model Rules of Professional Conduct. Model Rules of Prof'l Conduct R. 4.3 (2012) *available at* http://www.americanbar.org/groups/professional_responsibility/publications/model_rules_of_professional_conduct/rule_4_3_dealing_with_unrepresented_person.html (last visited Sept. 17, 2012).

First, a lawyer cannot imply that he or she is disinterested. Second, a lawyer is required to make reasonable efforts to correct the self-represented party's misunderstandings of the lawyer's role. Third, the lawyer must not give legal advice to a self-represented litigant but should advise the person to obtain counsel if there is a reasonable possibility that the person's interest will conflict with the interests of the attorney's client. Within these guidelines, the Rule does not prohibit negotiating with an self-represented party or explaining the lawyer's view of the meaning of documents prepared by the lawyer. *See* Comment [2] to Rule 4.3.

23.11. Need for Pro Bono Representation (Rule 6.1)

All family law attorneys should provide pro bono representation to people who are unable to afford representation. Rule 6.1 of the Model Rules of Professional Conduct suggests that lawyers render at least 50 hours of pro bono representation each year. Model Rules of Prof'l Conduct R. 6.1 (2012) *available at* http://www.americanbar.org/groups/professional_responsibility/publications/model_rules_of_professional_conduct/rule_6_1_voluntary_pro_bono_publico_service.html (last visited September 17, 2012).

EXAMPLES

Examples

7. Attorney L represents P in a divorce against D, who is unrepresented. P and D live in a jurisdiction where the sole custodian of a child can move to another state, so long as the child is not endangered by the move. D is willing to agree to P having sole physical custody but does not want P to move from the state. D does not know that under state law, P could do so

easily if D agrees to the sole custody arrangement. Attorney L wants to wrap up the case and allows D to continue to think that P can't permanently leave the state without D's permission. Has L violated Rule 4.3?

8. Assume that as part of an organized clinic, lawyers provide limited advice to people who can't afford to retain an attorney. These lawyers occasionally assist in preparing documents for filing, but they do not appear in court or establish an ongoing professional relationship. Clients are informed of the limited nature of the representation and the fact that the attorneys will not make court appearances. Does this arrangement violate the rules of professional conduct?

EXPLANATIONS

Explanations

7. L has likely violated Rule 4.3. Even though L had no obligation under the rule to give D legal advice, L should have strongly encouraged D to retain a lawyer. Furthermore, L's client, P, is not well served by making an agreement based on a misunderstanding.

8. In Formal Opinion 2005-F-151 (2005), the Tennessee Supreme Court's ethics board concluded that such limited assistance was appropriate. Rule 1.2(c) allows lawyers to limit the scope of representation if reasonable under the circumstances. The board suggested that written client consent be sought and that documents drafted by the lawyers be labeled "Prepared with Assistance of Counsel." The board also cautioned lawyers to be mindful of potential conflicts of interest.

VARIOUS ROLES OF LAWYERS

23.12. Attorney as Conflict Resolver

A group of commentators suggest that family attorneys have an ethical obligation to seek to resolve family law cases in the following ways:

1. Counseling clients about the negative consequences of custody disputes and the availability of resources to reduce conflict;
2. Discussing alternatives to litigation, such as mediation;
3. Encouraging cooperation with custody and mental health evaluations;

4. Realistically evaluating cases and avoiding false expectations;
5. Seeking early intervention in high-conflict cases and making referrals;
6. Cooperating in narrowing the issues, procedures, and evidence needed to consider the best interests of the child;
7. Maintaining a civil demeanor and encouraging clients to do so;
8. Avoiding use of the media or protective services to exacerbate conflict;
9. Seeking training in child development, abuse and neglect, domestic violence, family dynamics, and alternative conflict resolution and becoming knowledgeable about community resources; and
10. Developing continuing legal education programs improving lawyers' ability to reduce conflict.

The Wingspread Report and Action Plan, *High-Conflict Custody Cases: Reforming the System for Children*, 39 Fam. Ct. Rev. 146, 150 (2001). See also Andrew Schepard, *Children, Courts, and Custody: Interdisciplinary Models for the Twenty-first Century* (Cambridge U. Press 2004).

23.13. Ethical Cautions for Lawyers Performing New Professional Roles

As discussed in Chapter 22, in addition to practicing in new forums, lawyers may decide to assume new professional roles such as that of mediator, arbitrator, or parenting coordinator. Attorneys also may adopt new models of practice such as collaborative law, cooperative law, and/or provision of unbundled legal services. *See* Forrest S. Mosten, *Unbundling Legal Services to Help Divorcing Families*, in *Innovations in Family Law Practice* 117 (Kelly Browe Olson & Nancy Ver Steegh, eds., 2008) (unbundling is a limited-scope representation wherein the client may contract for a specific aspect of representation such as drafting of documents, review of mediation agreement, and advice only).

As they take on different professional roles, lawyers must understand the boundaries and ethical obligations of each role thoroughly. In assuming new roles, lawyers may become subject to codes of ethics in addition to the Model Rules of Professional Conduct.

23.14. Collaborative Lawyers

As discussed in Chapter 22, collaborative lawyers use interest-based negotiation techniques to resolve family cases without going to court. If either party resorts to court action, the collaborative lawyers are disqualified and must withdraw from representation. The American Bar Assosication Standing Committee on Ethics and Professional Responsibility issued Formal Opinion 07-447, Ethical Considerations in Collaborative Law Practice, on August 9, 2007, *available at* http://www.collaborativelaw.us/articles/Ethics_Opinion_ABA.pdf (last visited September 17, 2012). The opinion approves the practice of collaborative law as limited scope representation pursuant to Model Rule 1.2 and sets out practices for obtaining informed consent from prospective collaborative law clients.

23.15. Lawyer as Mediator or Arbitrator

Sometimes rather than representing either party, a lawyer functions as a third-party neutral, such as a mediator or arbitrator. Under Model Rules of Professional Conduct 2.4, lawyers acting in these or other third-party neutral capacities are required to inform self-represented parties that they are not representing them. Model Rules of Prof'l Conduct R. 2.4 (2012) *available at* http://www.americanbar.org/groups/professional_responsibility/publications/model_rules_of_professional_conduct/rule_2_4_lawyer_serving_as_third_party_neutral.html (last visited September 17, 2012). Comment [2] explains that lawyer-neutrals may fall under the jurisdiction of additional codes of ethics, depending on the role being assumed.

Lawyers are also cautioned to avoid blurring roles by performing tasks (such as giving legal advice or filing papers in court) typically performed by lawyers representing clients. *See* ABA Section of Dispute Resolution Committee on Mediator Ethical Guidance, SODR-2010-1.

EXAMPLE

Example

9. A Texas lawyer is retained by a couple to mediate their divorce. Neither of the parties is represented by counsel. Mediation is successful, and the case is settled with respect to all issues. The parties ask the lawyer/mediator to draft the documents to be presented to the court. Should the lawyer/mediator agree to do so?

EXPLANATION

Explanation

9. In a similar situation, the Texas Bar Professional Ethics Committee, applying the Texas Disciplinary Rules of Professional Conduct, found that the lawyer/mediator could not draft the court documents to effectuate the divorce because the lawyer/mediator was prohibited from providing "both mediation and legal services" to the parties. *See* Texas State Bar Professional Ethics Comm., Op. 583, 9-08. *But see* Ohio Supreme Court Bd. of Commissioners on Grievances and Discipline, Op. 2009-4, 6-12-09, (lawyer/mediator may prepare legal documents on behalf of one party, with written consent of both parties).

CHAPTER 24

Jurisdiction

24.1. Introduction

This chapter focuses on the jurisdictional power of state and federal courts. Other chapters in this book cover some aspects of jurisdiction that are not covered in this chapter. For example, issues of jurisdiction under the Uniform Child Custody Jurisdiction Enforcement Act (UCCJEA) are considered in detail in Chapter 7.

Two fundamental issues. A family court judge must decide two fundamental jurisdictional issues when a case is placed on the court docket. The first issue involves a determination by the judge that the court has subject matter jurisdiction to hear the dispute. Absent subject matter jurisdiction, the judge does not possess the power to hear any portion of the dispute, and it must be dismissed. The subject matter determination is so fundamental that even if both parties agree to waive a subject matter defect, the judge must dismiss the case on his or her own motion.

Once a court is sure that it has subject matter to hear the dispute, the second issue is to determine whether it has personal jurisdiction over the parties. Without personal jurisdiction over both parties, a court with subject matter jurisdiction may well be limited in its ability to resolve all the issues in the case. For example, a court may possess subject matter jurisdiction so it can dissolve the relationship and issue a decree divorcing the couple even though it does not have personal jurisdiction over one of the parties. This type of divorce is sometimes referred to as a "divisible divorce." However, without personal jurisdiction over both parties, while a court may alter the status of the couple from married to single, it cannot impose personal obligations on the absent party without his or her consent, such as alimony, child support, or attorney fees.

SUBJECT MATTER JURISDICTION IN FEDERAL COURT

24.2. Domestic Relations Exception

Overview. In general, when it comes to jurisdiction, federal courts possess whatever subject matter jurisdiction is given to them by Congress in a federal statute. *See, e.g.*, 28 U.S.C. §1331 (federal question); 28 U.S.C. §1332(a)(1) (diversity actions between citizens of different states involving matters in controversy exceeding $75,000 exclusive of costs and interest). Examples of the limitations that Congress has placed on federal courts include the following:

- A federal court cannot hear a case between citizens of the same state where a federal question is not involved.
- A federal court cannot hear cases between citizens of different states where the amount in controversy fails to exceed a minimum amount set by Congress by statute.

In addition to the limitations expressed in congressional statutes, federal courts have carved out a domestic relations and probate exception to the exercise of subject matter jurisdiction. Neither exception is compelled by the text of the Constitution or federal statutes; rather, the exceptions are judicially created doctrines stemming in large measure from what has been described as "misty understandings of English legal history." *Marshall v. Marshall*, 547 U.S. 293, 299 (2006).

The domestic relations and probate exceptions to the exercise of federal jurisdiction bar a federal court from exercising jurisdiction over domestic disputes, probating wills, administering estates, or becoming involved in related actions that would interfere with a state court handling these matters. These exceptions are discussed in detail next.

Domestic relations exception. The decision that spawned the idea that federal courts do not have subject matter jurisdiction over actions involving divorce and alimony decrees, even though diversity of citizenship and the requisite jurisdictional amount are present, can be traced to 1859. That year, the Supreme Court announced in dicta—without citation or discussion—that federal courts lack jurisdiction over suits for divorce or alimony. *Barber v. Barber*, 62 U.S. 582, 584 (1858). The *Barber* majority did not expressly tie its announcement of a domestic relations exception to the text of the federal diversity statute, but the *Barber* dissenters made the connection.

Since *Barber*, the Court has indicated that it agreed with the *dicta* of the dissenters in *Barber* and has restated that the genesis of the exception is with the refusal of Congress to grant federal courts the statutory power to hear these disputes. *Ankenbrandt v. Richards*, 504 U.S. 689, 700 (1992). *See Ex Parte Burrus*, 136 U.S. 586, 593–94 (1890) ("[T]he whole subject of the domestic relations of husband and wife, parent and child, belongs to the laws of the States and not to the laws of the United States").

In addition, as a policy matter, federal courts recognize that they provide a difficult platform on which to adjudicate domestic disputes. *See Lloyd v. Loeffler*, 694 F.2d 489 (7th Cir. 1982). Federal courts reason that state courts have traditionally adjudicated marital and child custody disputes and have developed competence and expertise in adjudicating such matters, an expertise that federal courts lack. *See Mansell v. Mansell*, 490 U.S. 581, 587 (1989) ("[D]omestic relations are preeminently matters of state law"); *Moore v. Sims*, 442 U.S. 415, 435 (1979) ("Family relations are a traditional area of state concern").

State courts are also thought to be peculiarly suited to enforce state regulations and domestic relations decrees involving alimony and child custody because such decrees often demand substantial continuing judicial oversight. *See Firestone v. Cleveland Trust Co.*, 654 F.2d 1212, 1215 (6th Cir. 1981). Finally, state courts are believed to have closer connections to certain local agencies than do federal courts, and these agencies are often involved in resolving conflicts resulting from domestic decrees.

One of the leading United States Supreme Court domestic relations exception decisions is *Ankenbrandt v. Richards*,504 U.S. 689 (1992). In that decision, the Court held that federal courts are divested of the power to issue divorce decrees, alimony, and child custody orders. 504 U.S. at 703. It also held that while 28 U.S.C. §1332 does not contain explicit language excluding domestic relations matters from federal diversity jurisdiction, Congress's failure to alter the exception after more than 130 years demonstrated that "Congress 'adopted that interpretation' when it reenacted the diversity statute." *Id.* at 701 (quoting *Lorillard v. Pons*, 434 U.S. 575, 580 (1978)). The Court stated in *Ankenbrandt* that the exception is narrowly limited and that lawsuits affecting domestic relations are not within the exception unless the claim is one to obtain a divorce or establish alimony or child custody. This narrow construction led the Court to hold that the exception did not apply to the tort claims between the couple in *Ankenbrandt* despite their intimate connection to family affairs. 504 U.S. at 704.

Since *Ankenbrandt*, federal courts have shown great reluctance to become involved in domestic disputes. For example, in *Cassens v. Cassens*, 430 F. Supp.

2d 830 (S.D. Ill. 2006), the federal district court rejected hearing an action that had been removed from state to federal court. The wife claimed that a prenuptial agreement that she and her husband had signed was void because it was procured through fraud. Without reaching the merits of the claim, the court found that the relief was in the nature of a request for a decree regarding the division of marital property and alimony. It concluded that the domestic relations exception to diversity jurisdiction divested the court of subject matter jurisdiction to hear the dispute. *See generally Domestic Relations' Exception to Jurisdiction of Federal Courts under Diversity of Citizenship Provisions of* 28 *U.S.C.A.* §1332(*a*),100 A.L.R. Fed. 700.

Modification actions. Federal courts will not exercise subject matter jurisdiction when the goal of a lawsuit is to achieve modification of a divorce or alimony decree. *See, e.g., Rotolo v. Rotolo*, 682 F. Supp. 8 (D.C. Puerto Rico 1988) (modification of divorce decree sought that had incorporated property settlement agreement between parties); *Olsen v. Olsen*,580 F. Supp. 1569 (D.C. N.D. Ind. 1984) (wife sought award of support arrearage and entry of order holding former husband in contempt for his failure to pay support).

An example of a federal court retaining jurisdiction to hear a dispute that at first appears to be one to reject is a claim of intentional infliction of where the action arose during the marriage. In *Strasen v. Strasen*, 897 F. Supp. 1179, 1182 (E.D. Wis. 1995), the court concluded that it had jurisdiction to hear the claims against the plaintiff's former husband and his current wife for fraudulent conduct with regard to marital assets during pendency of state divorce proceedings. The court reasoned that since the plaintiff did not seek a decree of divorce, alimony, or child custody, her claim was not barred simply because it has some relation to a divorce proceeding. Moreover, one of the defendants had no marital relationship with the plaintiff whatsoever, and appeared to stand in the same position as any other opponent in a tort suit brought in federal court pursuant to diversity jurisdiction. *See Shelar v. Shelar*,910 F. Supp. 1307 (D.C. N.D. Ohio 1995) (emotional distress lawsuit was not within domestic relation exception to diversity jurisdiction).

Supremacy clause. Note that the Supreme Court, even in the limited application of federal law in the field of domestic relations, generally has not hesitated to protect, under the supremacy clause of the Constitution, the rights and expectancies established by federal law against the operation of state law, or to prevent the frustration and erosion of the congressional policy embodied in the federal rights. *See, e.g., McCarty v. McCarty*, 453 U.S. 210 (1981) (holding that military retirement pay is not subject to division under state community property laws — decision was effectively abrogated by the passage of the Federal Uniformed Services Former Spouses' Protection Act (FUSFSPA) (10 U.S.C.A. §1408)); *Hisquierdo v. Hisquierdo*, 439 U.S.

572 (1979) (federal court had jurisdiction to decide application of California's community property principles to Railroad Retirement Act benefits).

24.3. Probate Exception

In *Marshall v. Marshall*, 547 U.S. 293 (2006), the Supreme Court addressed the federal probate exception for the first time in over 60 years. Eight justices held that the probate exception doctrine was legitimate, but quite narrow.

The Court ruled that the probate exception was not applicable to deprive a bankruptcy court of jurisdiction over a widow's claim that her stepson tortiously interfered with her expectancy of inheritance or gift from her deceased husband. The Court said that a decision by a state probate court that it had exclusive subject matter jurisdiction over all of the widow's claims against her stepson did not deprive a federal district court of jurisdiction over the widow's tort claim against the stepson asserted in her bankruptcy proceeding. *See also Struck v. Cook County Public Guardian*, 508 F.3d 858 (7th Cir. 2007) (when state turned down guardianship challenge, son appealed to federal court, which rejected the appeal).

History of probate exception. The probate exception had been discussed in a number of decisions by the Supreme Court prior to the *Marshall* ruling. For example, in *Markham v. Allen*, 326 U.S. 490 (1946), the Court stated the general principle that "a federal court has no jurisdiction to probate a will or administer an estate, the reason being that the equity jurisdiction conferred by the Judiciary Act of 1789, 1 Stat. 73, and §24(1) of the Judicial Code, which is that of the English Court of Chancery in 1789, did not extend to probate matters." 326 U.S. at 494.

The probate exception applies to federal-question cases and diversity disputes. *Jones v. Brennan*, 465 F.3d 304 (7th Cir. 2006). *See generally Stern v Marshall*, 131 S.Ct. 2594 (2011) (the bankruptcy court had statutory authority to enter final judgment on widow's tortious interference counterclaim in which she asserted in bankruptcy court in response to her stepson's defamation claim against her bankruptcy estate, since counterclaim was a core proceeding, even though it did not arise under Title 11 of Bankruptcy Code).

EXAMPLES

Examples

1. Assume that P, acting on behalf of himself and his severely disabled son, brought suit in federal court against P's former wife and the son's mother, D, alleging various tort claims arising from the former wife's care of the son while the couple were separated but still married. The parties are of diverse citizenship, and the amount of damages sought

exceeds the minimum requirements set by Congress as contained in 28 U.S.C. §1332. D has moved to dismiss the action on the ground that this is a domestic matter and outside the jurisdiction of the federal court. How will a federal court most likely rule on D's motion?

2. Assume that P, who was not married at the time, began a relationship with D, who was married. P was employed as an elementary school teacher, a position she had held for some years. She resigned her teaching position, allegedly at D's urging. She claimed that she quit so that she could be free to spend more time with D and travel around the world with him. She also claimed that she quit her job in reliance on D's promises to provide for her and that he would eventually marry her. D provided P with an extravagant lifestyle because of the relationship. She traveled around the world with him, and he provided her with sundry material benefits and comforts. He paid the rent on homes they shared in two different states, purchased and maintained her automobiles, allowed her the use of his luxury yachts, presented her with lavish gifts, and told P he would support her for the rest of her life. P states that she trusted D and believed that he would support her forever. Occasionally, she and D discussed plans for their wedding. However, after ten years, D ended the relationship. P filed a palimony action in federal district court relying on the court's diversity subject matter jurisdiction (citizens of different states and claims exceeding $75,000) and asserted claims of intentional infliction of emotional distress and enforcement of the oral contract to support her for life. D moved to dismiss the claims on the ground that the court lacked subject matter jurisdiction. D argued that this was essentially a palimony case in which P was seeking distribution of property and support and a matter for state courts. How will the court most likely rule?

3. Assume that P filed a diversity action in federal district court against D, the administrator of her parents' estate. P alleged that D had breached his fiduciary duty by improperly paying inflated and fraudulent legal bills to the law firm that had represented the estate. D moved to dismiss the action on the ground the federal district court lacked subject matter jurisdiction. D contended that this was a probate matter within the exclusive jurisdiction of the state probate court. How will a court most likely resolve the issue?

4. Assume that P1 and P2 were the adoptive parents of child C. Assume that D, the State Department of Human Services, after an extensive investigation, brought an action in state court to terminate P1 and P2's parental rights to C. After a hearing, the state court judge issued an order terminating the rights of P1 and P2 to C. P1 and P2 then filed a civil rights action in federal district court against D alleging equal protection and due

process violations plus violations of the Federal Child Welfare Act of 1980 in connection with the termination. D has brought a motion to dismiss. How will a court most likely decide the motion?

5. Assume that state X enacts a statute that presumes that, on the death of an unmarried mother of a minor child, the father of the child is presumed to be unfit as the child's custodian. Under the statute, when the mother dies, the state, without conducting a hearing on the father's fitness, declares the child a ward of the state. In all other termination cases, the parties are provided with a pre-removal hearing. P, the father, challenges the statute in federal court as violating his due process rights by denying him a pre-removal hearing on the issue of his fitness. The state argues that P is challenging a termination proceeding; therefore, the federal court is without subject matter jurisdiction to hear the matter. How will a federal court most likely rule on P's challenge?

EXPLANATIONS

Explanations

1. The federal court most likely will find that it has subject matter jurisdiction to hear this case. While the action arises from the husband-wife relationship, it does not involve issuing a divorce decree, alimony, child support, or custody. *See Dunn v. Cometa*, 238 F.3d 38 (1st Cir. 2001). One court has explained the exception in the following terms:

> The domestic relations exception has a core and a penumbra. The core is occupied by cases in which the plaintiff is seeking in federal district court under the diversity jurisdiction one or more of the distinctive forms of relief associated with the domestic relations jurisdiction: the granting of a divorce or an annulment, an award of child custody, a decree of alimony or child support. . . . The penumbra of the exception consists of ancillary proceedings, such as a suit for the collection of unpaid alimony that state law would require be litigated as a tail to the original domestic relations proceeding. Thus, the test of whether claims come within the core of the domestic relations exception to diversity jurisdiction is whether they involve . . . distinctive forms of relief associated with the domestic relations jurisdiction.

Friedlander v. Friedlander, 149 F.3d 739 (7th Cir. 1998); *see Lloyd v. Loeffler*, 694 F.2d. 489, 492 (7th Cir. 1982).

Here, the claim does not clearly involve distinctive forms of relief associated with state-court domestic relations jurisdiction so as to fall within the core of the matters excluded from diversity jurisdiction by the domestic relations exception.

2. The court most likely will reject the claim that it lacks subject matter jurisdiction. Despite the breadth of the phrase "domestic relations exception" and the potential reach of the exception's aim, *Ankenbrandt* made clear that the exception is narrowly limited. In general, lawsuits affecting domestic relations are not within the exception unless the claim at issue is one to obtain, alter, or end a divorce, or to seek alimony, child custody, or child support. *Dunn v. Cometa*, 238 F.3d 38, 41 (1st Cir. 2001). Notwithstanding the fact that this hypothetical grows out of the breakdown of an intimate relationship, P's claims do not sound in family law, let alone the specific areas of divorce, alimony, child support, or child custody. Instead, P brought tort and contract claims. *See Norton v. McOsker*, 407 F.3d 501, n. 6 (1st Cir. 2005) (Rhode Island stated that it had never recognized a palimony claim — evincing lack of state interest — and Norton did not bring any claim related to a divorce, alimony, or a child custody decree).

3. Under the probate exception set forth by the Supreme Court in *Marshall v. Marshall*, 547 U.S. 293 (2006), 131 S.Ct. 2594 (2011), a federal court should decline subject matter jurisdiction only if a plaintiff seeks to achieve either administration or probate of an estate or a will, or to do any other purely probate matter. However, the probate exception should not bar P's claim in federal court against the executor of her parents' estate for breach of fiduciary duty. This claim is framed as an *in personam* tort action and does not directly implicate the *res* of the estate. It is not entirely intertwined with the issues of estate administration; consequently, the federal court most likely will accept jurisdiction and hear P's claim. *See Lefkowitz v. Bank of New York*, 528 F.3d 102 (2d. Cir. 2007).

4. Although the facts outlined in the example are sparse, the matter most likely will be dismissed by the federal court. In effect, P1 and P2 are seeking to collaterally attack the state agency and court proceedings that terminated their parental rights. In essence, a federal court is being asked to reverse a state court's termination determination. The rule applied by federal courts is that they may not decide federal issues that are raised in state proceedings and are "inextricably intertwined" with the state court's judgment. *Staley v. Ledbetter*, 837 F.2d 1016 (11th Cir. 1988). That would appear to be the case here, even though the plaintiffs have alleged violation of a federal statute. *See Anderson v. State of Colorado*, 793 F.2d 262, 263-265 (10th Cir. 1986) (lawsuit essentially sought to undo the custody decision of the Colorado state court and fits squarely within the parameters of the *Doe-Feldman* doctrine prohibiting federal district courts from reviewing state-court judgments).

5. The hypothetical is intended to contrast the outcome in Example 4. Here, unlike in Example 4, P most likely will prevail. P is not asking the court to evaluate the legitimacy of the state ends, i.e., termination of a father's right to a biological child born out of wedlock. Rather, P is asking the court to determine whether the means used by the state to terminate his rights without a hearing are constitutionally defensible. Under the statute, the state assumes custody of the children of married parents, divorced parents, and unmarried mothers only after a hearing and proof of neglect. The children of unmarried fathers, however, are declared dependent children without a hearing on parental fitness and without proof of neglect. The failure to afford P a hearing on his parental qualifications, while extending it to other parents, denied him equal protection of the law. Denying such a hearing to P and those like him while granting it to other parents is contrary to the equal protection clause. *Stanley v. Illinois*, 405 U.S. 645 (1972) (under the due process clause of the Fourteenth Amendment, unwed father was entitled to a hearing on his fitness as a parent before his children could be taken from him).

24.4. Federal Court Review of State Court Domestic Relations Judgments

There are occasional efforts made by unhappy litigants to persuade a federal court to hear an appeal from a state court domestic relations judgment. However, such requests are routinely rejected by the federal courts, which consistently hold that they lack subject matter jurisdiction to review judgments made by state tribunals. *See, e.g.*, *Exxon Mobil Corp. v. Saudi Basic Indus. Corp.*, 544 U.S. 280, 284 (2005); *Dist. of Columbia Court of Appeals v. Feldman*, 460 U.S. 462 (1983); *Staley v. Ledbetter*, 837 F.2d 1016, 1017-1018 (11th Cir. 1988) (district court lacked jurisdiction to hear a constitutional claim that essentially sought to reverse a state court's custody determination); *Sielck v. Sielck*, 202 Fed. Appx. 919 (7th Cir. 2006) (court rejected hearing claim that husband's misconduct throughout the divorce proceedings had resulted in a state court judgment that deprived her of "marital property" and custody of her children); *see also Rooker v. Fidelity Trust Co.*,263 U.S. 413 (1999).

24.5. Procedural Issues — Liberty Interest

Litigants involved in state domestic matters that are procedural may find relief in federal court. For example, in *Stanley v. Illinois*, 405 U.S. 645 (1972), the Court held that under the due process clause of the Fourteenth Amendment, an unwed father was entitled to a hearing on fitness as a parent before his children could be taken from him in a dependency proceeding instituted by the state. The Court made it clear that there is a protected liberty interest in familial relations. *But see Winston v. Children and Youth Servs. of Del. County*, 948 F.2d 1380 (3d Cir. 1991) (state-ordered visitation policies did not violate due process or free association rights in light of the procedures that the county had put in place for parents to request increased visitation).

24.6. Abstention Doctrine

In some situations, even though federal courts have subject matter jurisdiction and can hear a dispute, they may decide not to exercise their power and instead apply what is called the "abstention doctrine." The United States Supreme Court has suggested that abstention might be appropriate in a case involving elements of the domestic relationship even when the parties do not seek divorce, alimony, or child custody. It explained that the doctrine could, and most likely would, be applied when a case presents "difficult questions of state law bearing on policy problems of substantial public import whose importance transcends the result in the case then at bar." *Ankenbrandt*, 504 U.S. at 705 (quoting *Colorado River Water Conservation Dist. v. United States*, 424 U.S. 800, 814 (1976)).

One of the leading abstention doctrine decisions is *Younger v. Harris*, 401 U.S. 37 (1971). In that case, the Court suggested that a federal court apply the abstention doctrine when there is a pending state proceeding and there has not been a showing of great and immediate irreparable injury to the federal plaintiff. *Meyers v. Franklin Cnty. Court of Common Pleas*, 23 F. App'x 201, 204 (6th Cir. 2001) (quoting *Moore v. Sims*, 442 U.S. 415, 423 (1979)) (existence of pending state temporary custody commitment proceeding supported District Court's abstention under the *Younger* abstention doctrine). *See O'Neill v. Coughlan*, 511 F.3d 638, 643 (6th Cir. 2008) (federal court should abstain from granting injunctive or declaratory relief that would interfere with pending state judicial proceedings).

Criteria for abstaining. A federal court may abstain from hearing a case only when the following criteria are met: (1) the underlying proceedings constitute an ongoing state judicial proceeding; (2) the proceedings implicate important state interests; and (3) there is an adequate opportunity to raise constitutional challenges in the course of the underlying proceeding. *Danner v. Bd. of Prof'l Responsibility of the Tn. Sup. Ct.*, 277 F. App'x 575, 578 (6th Cir. 2008). For example, in *Middlesex County Ethics Comm. v. Garden State Bar Assn.*, 457 U.S. 423, 432 (1982), the Court applied the abstention doctrine to noncriminal judicial proceedings where it concluded that important state interests were involved. In *Pennzoil Co. v. Texaco, Inc.*, 481 U.S. 1 (1987), the Court held that "federal courts must abstain from hearing challenges to pending state proceedings where the state's interest is so important that exercising federal jurisdiction would disrupt the comity between federal and state courts." 481 U.S. at 17. *See DeMauro v. DeMauro*, 115 F.3d 94 (1st Cir. 1997) (abstention not automatic in RICO claim by wife involving husband's alleged efforts to conceal real property or cash during divorce).

SUBJECT MATTER JURISDICTION IN STATE COURT

24.7. Challenges to Residency Requirements

All states have statutes that provide some kind of residency requirement when a person seeks a divorce or separation. For example, North Dakota's residency statute, §14-05-17, requires the following:

> A separation or divorce may not be granted unless the plaintiff in good faith has been a resident of the state for six months next preceding commencement of the action. If the plaintiff has not been a resident of this state for the six months preceding commencement of the action, a separation or divorce may be granted if the plaintiff in good faith has been a resident of this state for the six months immediately preceding entry of the decree of separation or divorce.

Another example of a residency statute comes from Florida:

> To obtain a dissolution of marriage, one of the parties to the marriage must reside 6 months in the state before the filing of the petition.

West's F.S.A. §61.021.

The exact meaning of the word *residence* in various state statutes has raised some interesting issues. For example, in *Clark v. Clark*, 2012 WL 1089198 (unpublished) (Conn. 2012), the court stated that residence was to be construed under that state's law to require domicile plus substantially continuous physical residence in the state. It also said that jurisdiction, strictly speaking, is founded on domicile. *Domicile* implies a nexus between person and place of such permanence as to control the creation of legal relations and responsibilities of the utmost significance. The court concluded that a dissolution decree should be founded on domicile plus substantial continuance residence in Connecticut by one of the parties for the 12 months. *But see Jungnelius v. Jungnelius*, 35 A.3d 359 (Conn. App. 2011) ("For the purposes of filing a complaint for dissolution of marriage or for the granting of alimony or support pendente lite, residence of one party, without a showing of domicile, is sufficient to give the court subject-matter jurisdiction").

Military provisions. Most states have enacted special residency provisions for persons in the military. For example, North Carolina Gen. Stat. §50–18 declares that individuals who have resided or been stationed in North Carolina for at least six months in connection with the performance of their military duties satisfy the applicable residence requirement. However, the courts in that state have said that enactment of the statute did not eliminate the necessity for the military person seeking a divorce to satisfy the "intent to remain" requirement found in the statute. *Huston v. Huston*,713 S.E.2d 250 (N.C. App. 2011).

Residence in the context of divorce. The United States Supreme Court has examined state residency requirements in the context of constitutional challenges to them when a divorce is sought. For example, in *Sosna v. Iowa*, 419 U.S. 393 (1975), a challenge was brought in federal court to the constitutionality of Iowa's one-year residency requirement for a divorce, with the parties alleging that the durational residency requirement in the Iowa statute was unconstitutional because it was discriminatory.

The challenge was not successful. The Court rejected the argument that the statute established two classes of persons and discriminated against those who had recently exercised their right to travel to Iowa. It stated that the durational requirement was reasonably justified based on the state's interest in requiring those seeking a divorce from its courts to be genuinely attached to the state, and the state's desire to insulate its divorce decrees from the likelihood of successful collateral attack.

The Court also ruled that that the durational residency requirement did not violate the due process clause of the Fourteenth Amendment on the theory that it denied a litigant the opportunity to make an individualized showing of *bona fide* residence. It observed that there was not a total deprivation of access to divorce courts, only a delay in gaining access to them.

In *Kar v. Nanda*, 805 N.W.2d 609 (Mich. App. 2011), the Defendant maintained that the circuit court lacked subject-matter jurisdiction because, pursuant to Michigan law, a court "shall not" grant a judgment of divorce unless the complainant or defendant "has resided in Michigan for 180 days immediately preceding the filing of the complaint." According to the Defendant, neither party met this residency requirement.

The court found that that the Plaintiff and Defendant were both citizens of India and they married there in 2007. In 2009, while living in Atlanta, Georgia, plaintiff filed the complaint for divorce in Michigan. Plaintiff travels for work and does not live in any area of the country for long. Defendant lived in Ann Arbor when Plaintiff filed for divorce, but denied that she was a "resident" of Ann Arbor because she plans to return to India when she finishes graduate school at the University of Michigan. Defendant's temporary student visa expired on April 30, 2012.

The defendant maintained that Michigan law required a party not only to have been physically present in Michigan for 180 days but also to satisfy the legal definition of *residence*. According to the defendant, this required an intent to remain permanently or indefinitely in the state.

The court rejected the defendant's argument that the "intention to remain" language contained in the state statute required that a party intend to remain permanently or indefinitely in Michigan. MCL §552.9(1). The court found that although the plaintiff intended to leave Michigan once her studies are completed in 2012, she lived in Michigan for years before the divorce complaint was filed, far longer than the 180-day statutory requirement, and, when the action was filed, she intended to remain in the state for several more years. The court concluded that the plaintiff clearly "resided" in this state for the requisite period.

24.8. Does Failure to Meet Residency Requirement Void a Divorce Decree?

As observed previously, state legislatures have enacted statutes governing divorce proceedings that require the moving party to show a minimum period of residency before a court is authorized to hear the matter. Courts have generally approved such limitations. However, what happens when a divorce decree is entered by a court and it is discovered years later that the petitioner failed to meet a required statutory residency requirement at the outset of the proceeding.

When the defect is discovered, because the residency requirement was not met, the court was in theory without subject matter jurisdiction to hear the divorce, and the decree should be declared void. (Usually, the time for bringing an appeal has lapsed, so the issue cannot be raised directly before an appellate court.) The result of strict application of the theory could have startling consequences. For example, a person who divorced and remarried in reliance on the decree might find himself or herself accused of bigamy.

The theory is not, however, always applied strictly. In fact, courts appear reluctant to vacate a divorce decree because of a failure to meet residency requirements — especially after several months or years have passed since the divorce decree was entered. *See, e.g.*, *Waite v. Waite*, 959 So. 2d 610 (Ala. 2006) (court refusing to vacate divorce decree entered 46 years earlier); *Vaile v. Eighth Judicial Dist. Court ex rel. County of Clark*, 44 P.3d 506 (Nev. 2002) (procedural irregularity did not render the judgment void; it was merely voidable). *But see Lopez v. Lopzen*, 852 So. 2d 402 (Fla. App. 2003) (annulling marriage of 15 years because former divorce decree from Dominican Republic was not obtained when the party seeking it had failed to reside in that country for a period of six months as required by Florida).

In general, courts take two approaches to escape voiding a divorce where a defect is discovered years after the judgment was entered. In the first approach, a judge will thoroughly examine the language of the residency requirement in the appropriate section of the statute applicable at the time that a party first sought a divorce. The judge searches for language literally stating that a failure to meet the residency provision divests a court of subject matter jurisdiction. Without finding specific, literal language divesting the court of jurisdiction, a court most likely will refuse to vacate the judgment.

A second approach, where a court finds language that voids the marriage if applied literally, was used by the New York Court of Appeals in *Lacks v. Lacks*, 359 N.E.2d 384 (N.Y. 1976). In that case, the ex-wife asked the court to vacate a divorce judgment entered two years earlier on the basis that the court lacked subject matter jurisdiction because of a residence requirement defect. The court rejected the ex-wife's claim. It held that the residence requirements it found in the statute went only to the substance of the cause of action, not to the competence of the court to adjudicate the cause. 359 N.E.2d at 879. It said that even if the court, which granted the final judgment of divorce in the instant case, made an error of law or fact in determining the issue of residence, the error did not deprive it of jurisdiction to render the judgment.

24.9. Where May Subject Matter Jurisdiction Be Challenged?

Another issue related to residence requirements spawned two Supreme Court decisions involving North Carolina citizens: *Williams v. State of North Carolina*, 317 U.S. 287 (1942) (*Williams I*), and *Williams v. State of North Carolina* (*Williams II*), 325 U.S. 226 (1945), *reh. denied*, 325 U.S. 895 (1945). The dispute involved two married North Carolinians who traveled to Nevada to obtain a divorce from their spouses. Once there, they established themselves as residents of Nevada and filed a divorce action in a Nevada court. Neither of the two spouses who remained in North Carolina appeared or consented to the Nevada action. They were served by publication in Nevada.

Once divorced from their respective spouses, the couple married each other under Nevada law. They then returned to North Carolina, where they were charged and convicted of bigamous cohabitation under North Carolina's criminal code and sentenced to a term of years in the state prison.

The United States Supreme Court eventually reviewed the convictions. It held in *Williams I* that the unquestioned domicile in a state of one party to a divorce enabled that state to exercise its power over the marital relationship, and that an ex parte divorce granted in Nevada, for example, must be respected in all other states. The Court said that a state must recognize the out-of-state divorce even though the "other spouse" had neither appeared nor been served with process in the rendering state, and even though recognition of the divorce was contrary to the public policy of the other state.

Litigation continued following the Supreme Court's first *Williams* decision and the case found its way to the Supreme Court a second time. In *Williams* II, the Court explained that even though the petitioner obtained an ex parte divorce in Nevada, "[a] judgment in one State is conclusive upon the merits in every other State, but only if the court of the first State had power to pass on the merits — had jurisdiction, that is, to render the judgment." *Id.* at 229 of 325 U.S.

The Court went on to say that because the parties lived in North Carolina during the events in question (except for the six-week period in which the two spouses were in Nevada to meet Nevada residency requirements and obtain their divorces), "North Carolina was entitled to find, as she did, that they did not acquire domiciles in Nevada and that the Nevada court was therefore without power to liberate the petitioners from amenability to the laws of North Carolina governing domestic relations." *See Cook v. Cook*, 342 U.S. 126, 128 (1951) (if the defendant spouse had neither appeared nor been served in Florida, the Vermont court, under the ruling in *Williams v. State of North Carolina* (*Williams* II), could reopen the issue of domicile). *See generally* Lynn D. Wardle, *Williams v. North Carolina, Divorce Recognition, and Same-Sex Marriage Recognition*, 32 Creighton L. Rev. 187, 188 (October 1998).

PERSONAL JURISDICTION IN STATE COURT

24.10. Jurisdiction to Grant Ex Parte Divorce — The Divisible Divorce Theory

Occasionally, a person seeks a divorce and despite his or her best efforts, the other spouse cannot be found and personal service of the divorce summons and petition cannot be effectuated as in a normal civil dispute. Alternatively, a spouse is served while he or she is a resident of another state and refuses to consent to the forum state exercising jurisdiction over the dispute. Does this mean that it is impossible for the person seeking the divorce to obtain one? The answer is "No, it does not prevent a divorce." However, the ability of the state court where the divorce action is being pursued to resolve all the issues usually associated with a divorce is limited.

The theory supporting the view that a court may change a married couple's status from married to divorced is found in *Pennoyer v. Neff*, 95 U.S. 714 (1877). In that case, the Court stated that personal jurisdiction over a nonresident spouse is not necessary to dissolve a marriage because dissolution is a status determination. 95 U.S. at 735. The theory adopted by the Court rests on the proposition that a state possesses *in rem* jurisdiction over the *res*, or "thing," which is the marriage itself. The theory, when coupled with *in personam* jurisdiction over one of the spouses, provides a court with power to grant a valid ex parte divorce.

The status theory gives an ex parte divorce decree absolute and binding finality within the confines of the forum state's borders. Courts reason that every state possesses jurisdiction to determine the civil status and capacities of all its inhabitants and the authority to prescribe the conditions on which proceedings affecting them may be commenced and carried on within its territory. Consequently, a state is viewed as having an absolute right to prescribe the conditions upon which the marriage relation between its own citizens may be created, and the causes for which it may be dissolved.

Divisible divorce. Under the theory of "divisible divorce," issues other than the status of the divorcing parties are severed from the divorce action because the court does not have personal jurisdiction over one spouse. *Conlon by Conlon v. Heckler*, 719 F.2d 788, 795-796 (5th Cir. 1983) (a decree of divorce granted by a court that had no *in personam* jurisdiction over one spouse is not, however, conclusive as to all the accoutrements of marriage); *see also Vanderbilt v. Vanderbilt*, 354 U.S. 416, 418-419 (1957) (where wife was not subject to Nevada jurisdiction, Nevada court could not extinguish right to support in another state even though not reduced to judgment in the other state).

Application of the divisible divorce theory is illustrated by the United States Supreme Court decision in *Estin v. Estin*, 334 U.S. 541 (1948). In *Estin*, the husband and wife were married and lived in New York until their relationship broke down. The wife brought an action in New York for a legal separation, and the husband entered a general appearance. The New York court granted the legal separation and awarded the wife alimony. The husband then went to Nevada and instituted an action for divorce. The wife was notified of the action by constructive service but did not enter an appearance. The Nevada court granted the husband a divorce; however, a question remained about the power of the Nevada court to alter the existing New York alimony order.

The United States Supreme Court held that the Nevada court did not have personal jurisdiction over the wife living in New York because she was neither a resident of Nevada nor had she voluntarily submitted to the jurisdiction of the Nevada court in the divorce proceeding. The Court held that the absence of personal jurisdiction over the wife made the divorce "divisible"—accommodating the interest of both states but restricting each state to the matters of "dominant concern." 334 U.S. at 549. Based on this "divisible divorce" theory, the Court ruled that the Nevada decree was effective only in changing the parties' marital status. The Nevada order had no effect on alimony, which was earlier entered by a New York court with both parties before it.

In rem *procedures.* States have promulgated statutes allowing a divorce action to proceed without personal jurisdiction over an out-of-state party. The legal action is usually labeled *in rem* and requires compliance with provisions relating to service of process and proper notice, with publication in a legal newspaper often acting as a surrogate for personal service of the summons and complaint. As noted earlier, in personam jurisdiction is not necessary to the dissolution of a marriage because such a proceeding affects only the status of the marriage itself. Because the divorce action is *in rem*, a valid judgment requires only that the *res* or status be before the court on proper notice. *In re Marriage of Breen*, 560 S.W.2d 358, 361 (Mo. App. 1977); *see Black's Law Dictionary* (8th ed. 2004) (*res* is defined as "an object, interest or status as opposed to a person"). In addition to dissolving the marriage, a proper *in rem* action may in theory provide a court with the power to adjudicate interests in land located within the forum state, even though the person who claims an interest in it is not personally before the court.

24.11. State Long-Arm Statute Requirements

The traditional view of personal jurisdiction taken by early United States courts was that a plaintiff who could not find the defendant in his or her state had to go to the defendant's state and sue the defendant there. This approach was consistent with the idea that judicial process could not be served beyond the boundaries of the state or federal district.

Traditional view altered. In response to modern interstate travel, the traditional view has been altered to one that allows a state to make a nonresident amenable to a personal judgment in certain actions arising out of specified kinds of activities within the state. The constitutional test of amenability, developed by the Supreme Court, involves asking whether it is reasonable to try the particular action against the particular defendant in the forum state. *International Shoe Co. v. State of Washington etc.*, 326 U.S. 310, 316-317 (1945). *See also McGee v. International Life Ins. Co.*, 355 U.S. 220, 223 (1957) (because "modern transportation and communications have made it much less burdensome for a party sued to defend himself in a State where he engages in economic activity," it usually will not be unfair to subject him to the burdens of litigating in another forum for disputes relating to such activity); *Hanson v. Denckla*, 357 U.S. 235, 246 (1958) (the "minimum contacts" test of International Shoe is not susceptible of mechanical application; rather, the facts of each case must be weighed to determine whether the requisite "affiliating circumstances" are present).

The advent and growth of long-arm statutes represent attempts by states to provide a friendly litigation forum for the convenience of their own citizens at the expense of citizens of other states. Most agree that the use of such statutes is natural in a mobile, industrialized society that has effectively reduced the time and rigors of travel between states. *See generally* Annot., *Long-Arm Statutes: Obtaining Jurisdiction Over Nonresident Parent in Filiation or Support Proceeding*, 76 A.L.R.3d 708, 714-715 (1977).

Long-arm requirements. Today, all states have long-arm statutes with language intended to give them personal jurisdiction over a nonresident who does not intend to appear voluntarily at a court proceeding after a resident has asserted a claim against the nonresident. When considering these state statutes, two general requirements must be met: First, there must exist a long-arm statute with appropriate language that authorizes the state court to seek out and serve the nonresident and mandate that the nonresident appear and respond to the claim. Second, assuming that the language of a state long-arm statute applies to the nonresident, there must be sufficient contacts between the nonresident and the state seeking to compel the nonresident's appearance to satisfy the constitutional standard of "traditional notions of fair play and substantial justice." *Milliken v. Meyer*, 311 U.S. 457, 463 (1940).

Illustrative long-arm statute. The state generated long-arm statutes come in a number of varieties, with some specifically including domestic matters and others implicating but not necessarily specifically using language relating to domestic matters. For example, Wisconsin statute §801.05 sets out the grounds for a court exercising personal jurisdiction in that state without specifically containing language referring to domestic matters. It reads, in part, as follows:

> A court of this state having jurisdiction of the subject matter has jurisdiction over a person served in an action pursuant to s. 801.11 under any of the following circumstances:
>
> (1) Local presence or status. In any action whether arising within or without this state, against a defendant who when the action is commenced:
>
> (a) Is a natural person present within this state when served; or
>
> (b) Is a natural person domiciled within this state; or
>
> (c) Is a domestic corporation or limited liability company; or
>
> (d) Is engaged in substantial and not isolated activities within this state, whether such activities are wholly interstate, intrastate, or otherwise. . . .

Wash. Stat. Ann. §801.05 (2012).

Wisconsin's courts have said that the language in the long-arm statute provides a basis for personal jurisdiction over a respondent in a divorce action in which child support, maintenance, and attorney fees are sought, even though the action does not involve business-related or employment-related activities in the state. *Bushelman v. Bushelman*, 629 N.W.2d 795 (Wisc. 2001).

Purposeful availment. The conduct of a nonresident husband in sending child support payments to Wisconsin, sending letters to his children in Wisconsin, and making telephone calls to his wife and the children when they were in Wisconsin, was not "purposeful availment" of the privilege of conducting activities in Wisconsin. *Id.* at 807 of 629 N.W.2d. Therefore, such conduct could not act as a basis under the State's long-arm statute and under due-process minimum contacts for a court to exercise personal jurisdiction over the husband in a divorce action filed by the wife. *See also May v. Anderson*, 345 U.S. 528 (1953) (where the only service of process upon mother consisted of the delivery to her personally, in Ohio, of a copy of the Wisconsin summons and petition, such service was authorized by a Wisconsin statute for use in an action for a divorce, but statute made no mention of its availability in a proceeding for the custody of children). *See also Bebeau v. Berger*, 529 P.2d 234 (Ariz. App. 1974) (Arizona upheld Wisconsin paternity judgment on Arizona citizen where Wisconsin court had found that act of sexual intercourse occurred in Wisconsin, that minor child was conceived in Wisconsin, the child's birth occurred in Wisconsin, and the defendant was served properly in Arizona with process).

Awkward phrases. Courts have sometimes quite awkwardly applied commonly used phrases contained in long-arm statutes such as "transacting business" or "tortious conduct" to domestic disputes, even though such terms are generally understood as directed at personal injury claims or commercial activities. The Wisconsin statute discussed earlier in the chapter is one example. Another example is found in *Prybolsky v. Prybolsky*, 430 A.2d 804 (Del. Fam. 1981). In that case, the court held that it had acquired personal jurisdiction over a nonresident husband by means of the "doing business" provision of the Delaware long-arm statute. 430 A.2d at 807. The court reasoned that marriage is a contract and that support and other rights springing from a marriage contract have financial and business implications. (This decision was later overruled by statute. *See T.L. v. W.L.*, 820 A.2d 506 (Del. Fam. 2003).)

Child support theories. States have sometimes struggled with their long-arm statutes when searching for a theory to provide personal jurisdiction over nonresidents who owe child support to a resident. One approach has been to construe the phrase "a tortious act" found in a few state long-arm statutes as encompassing a failure on the part of the nonresident to support a child following birth. The failure to support is viewed as an injury. Some courts analogize the failure to pay child support to a typical tort injury and reason that the long-arm statute applies to a failure to pay child support, just as it would to an injured accident victim involved in a crash with a nonresident.

Other state courts have approached the jurisdictional issue by defining the phrase "tortious act" as including any act committed in the forum state that involves a breach of duty to another where the nonresident's act has resulted in ascertainable damages. *See Poindexter v. Willis*, 231 N.E.2d 1 (Ill. Ct. App. 1967); *accord In re Marriage of Highsmith*, 488 N.E.2d 1000, 1003 (1986); *Black v. Rasile*, 318 N.W.2d 475, 476 (Mich. App. 1982); *State ex rel. Nelson v. Nelson*, 216 N.W.2d 140, 143 (Minn. 1974); *In re Custody of Miller*, 548 P.2d 542, 546 (Wash. 1976).

Note that there is additional discussion regarding the application of state long-arm statutes in section 24-24 of this chapter. Section 201 of the Uniform Family Support Act (UIFSA) contains a long-arm provision that allows the broadest possible assertion of jurisdiction over nonresident child support obligors consistent with the Constitution. *See* UIFSA §201 cmt. 9 (pt. IB) ULA 275-277 1999). It contains eight bases for a court's exercise of personal jurisdiction over a nonresident individual in an action to establish, enforce, or modify a child support order.

Inconsistent language. Note that state long-arm statutes are inconsistent, with some drafted narrowly and others drafted expansively. For example, California's long-arm statute authorizes California courts to exercise jurisdiction on any basis not inconsistent with the Constitution of the United States or the Constitution of California. *Luberski, Inc. v. Oleficio F.LLI Amato S.R.L.*, 89 Cal. Rptr. 3d 774 (Cal. App. 2009). In *Luberski, Inc.*, an olive oil buyer brought action against foreign seller for breach of contract after promised oil shipment did not arrive. The court stated that court may exercise specific jurisdiction over a nonresident defendant if: (1) the defendant has purposefully availed himself or herself of forum benefits, (2) the controversy is related to or arises out of the defendant's contacts with the forum, and (3) the assertion of personal jurisdiction would comport with fair play and substantial justice. Here, the foreign olive oil seller purposefully availed itself of California forum such that court had specific personal jurisdiction over the seller in the buyer's breach of contract action because the negotiations were conducted and completed in both Italy and California, the contract negotiations were conducted via long distance communications with the implicit understanding that the goods were only useful to buyer if delivered to California, and the seller maintained responsibility for the goods until they arrived in California. Furthermore, the shipment order of $400,000 was substantial.

24.12. Due Process Barriers to Application of Long-Arm Statutes

This section was included to provide additional information and emphasis regarding the application of the due process clause of the federal Constitution to state long-arm statutes.

It is axiomatic that even though the language of a state long-arm statute applies to a domestic dispute, the Constitution may bar its application because the due process clause of the Fourteenth Amendment operates as a limitation on the jurisdiction of state courts to enter judgments affecting the rights or interests of nonresident defendants. *Kulko v. Superior Court of California*, 436 U.S. 84 (1978). Under *Kulko*, the existence of personal jurisdiction depends upon the presence of reasonable notice to the defendant that an action has been brought and a factual showing that there exists a sufficient connection between the defendant and the forum state to make it fair to require the defendant to defend the action in the forum state.

In *Kulko*, for example, after the couple formally separated, the husband remained in New York, the state of marital domicile, and the wife moved to California. They executed a separation agreement in New York providing that the parties' two children were to reside with Mr. Kulko in New York during the school year and with their mother during their Christmas, Easter, and summer vacations. Mr. Kulko also agreed to pay $3,000 a year in child support. The terms of this agreement were later incorporated into a Haitian divorce decree obtained by Mrs. Kulko.

Subsequently, the parties' daughter expressed a desire to live full-time with her mother. Mr. Kulko acquiesced and paid his daughter's airfare to California. A few years later, the couple's son expressed to his mother a desire to live with her. Without Mr. Kulko's knowledge, Mrs. Kulko sent the child a plane ticket, which he used to join his mother and sister in California.

With both children now living with her in California, Mrs. Kulko filed suit in that state seeking an increase in child support. Mr. Kulko was served with process under California's broad long-arm statute. He resisted the action on the ground that he did not have sufficient contacts to warrant the California court's assertion of personal jurisdiction over him. The California Supreme Court rejected this argument, reasoning that by his act of sending his daughter to reside permanently in California, Mr. Kulko had "purposely availed himself of the benefits and protections of the laws of California." 436 U.S. at 89.

The Supreme Court rejected the California court's analysis, reasoning that the mere fact that Mr. Kulko "acquiesced" in the desire of his daughter to live with her mother was not a sufficient contact with the state of California to warrant imposition of the unreasonable burden of having to litigate a child support action there. The Court observed that there was no other activity that would bring Mr. Kulko in contact with the state of California. The Court also said that Mrs. Kulko was not without a remedy because she could initiate a proceeding under the Uniform Reciprocal Enforcement of Support Act (URESA) and have the merits of her support request adjudicated in New York, where the ex-husband continued to reside, "without either party's having to leave his or her own State." 436 U.S. at 86.

24.13. Service Within State During Temporary Visit

It may come as a surprise to some that personal jurisdiction may be exercised over an individual by virtue of being served with legal process while he or she is only temporarily present within the forum state. This rule applies even if the person served is an out-of-state resident who comes into the forum state for almost any reason, or no reason at all. *Burnham v. Superior Court*, 495 U.S. 604 (1990). (Note that if the defendant is fraudulently induced into a state so he or she can be served, courts may as a matter of policy refuse to allow service to stand.) In *Burnham*, the wife brought a divorce action in California and served her husband with divorce papers when he visited their children in that state. The Supreme Court ruled that his physical presence within the state conferred personal jurisdiction over him — no additional "minimum contacts" were required. 495 U.S. at 619.

Justice Scalia, writing for a plurality of four in *Burnham*, stated, "jurisdiction based on physical presence alone constitutes due process because it is one of the continuing traditions of our legal system that define the due process standard of 'traditional notions of fair play and substantial justice.' " *Ibid.* Three other Justices joined in a concurring opinion filed by Justice Brennan. In the concurring view, tradition alone was not dispositive; they would judge the constitutionality of in-state service on a nonresident by examining contemporary notions of due process. 495 U.S. at 629-632 (Brennan, J., concurring). The justices ultimately concluded that "as a rule the exercise of personal jurisdiction over a defendant based on his voluntary presence in the forum will satisfy the requirements of due process." 495 U.S. at 639. They reasoned that by visiting the forum state, a defendant avails himself of significant benefits, such as the protection of his health and safety. 495 U.S. at 637-638. Justice Stevens joined neither Justice Scalia's nor Justice Brennan's opinion, but concurred in the judgment based on considerations of history, fairness, and common sense.

24.14. Continuing Jurisdiction

Most states take the view that they possess continuing jurisdiction over the parties to a dissolution if a court possessed personal jurisdiction over the parties at the time the divorce judgment was entered. Consequently, parties who move from a jurisdiction where a judgment was properly entered, and remain away for several years, cannot block modification or enforcement efforts on the ground the forum court lost personal jurisdiction because a party moved out of state. For example, in *Bjordahl v. Bjordahl*, 308 N.W.2d 817 (Minn. 1981), even though the husband had not resided in Minnesota for 22 years and the parties' children had reached the age of majority, the Minnesota Supreme Court ruled that its courts had continuing jurisdiction for modification and enforcement of the decree. *See Katz v. Katz*, 408 N.W.2d 835, 838 (Minn. 1987) (trial court's continuing jurisdiction extends to the modification or enforcement of the decree); *Angelos v. Angelos*, 367 N.W.2d 518, 519 (Minn. 1985) (domestic relationships, by their nature, continue under the jurisdiction of the court virtually throughout the lives of the parties); *Kenda v. Pleskovic*, 39 A.3d 1249 (D.C. App. 2012) (judicial estoppel applied to dispute by court issuing divorce decree where parties following issuance of decree had agreed to litigate custody issue in Indiana court and did so); *Craig v. Craig*, 721 S.E.2d 24 (Va. App. 2012) (trial court had continuing jurisdiction, after entry of divorce decree, to modify the Qualified Domestic Relations Order (QDRO)); *Busche v. Busche*, 272 P.3d 748 (Utah App. 2012); *Plumlee v. Plumlee*, 271 P.3d 807 (Okla. 2011) (divorce action is a special proceeding in which the district court retains continuing jurisdiction to modify some portions of its judgment and enter new orders in post-judgment proceedings).

24.15. Waiving Personal Jurisdiction Claim

Personal jurisdiction may be conferred upon a party by a state because the party has waived the defense. The waiver may occur when the defendant appears in court and fails to raise the jurisdictional issue properly at the first opportunity to do so. *Mesenbourg v. Mesenbourg*, 538 N.W.2d 489, 492-493 (Minn. App. 1995) (finding that the appellant waived his right to challenge personal jurisdiction when he failed to do so in the district court). For example, if a defendant appears in a divorce action in a state court and fails to challenge the court's exercise of personal jurisdiction at the first opportunity, she may not subsequently collaterally attack the divorce decree for lack of personal jurisdiction. *See Sherrer v. Sherrer*, 334 U.S. 343 (1948).

Counterclaims. Waiver of jurisdiction may or may not occur, depending on the jurisdiction and on whether the defendant has filed a permissive or compulsory counterclaim in response to a complaint. A permissive counterclaim may well be considered a waiver of jurisdiction. *Gates Learjet Corp. v. Jensen*, 743 F.2d 1325 (9th Cir. 1984) (recognizing federal court disagreement over whether permissive counterclaim waives personal jurisdiction defense, and holding that it does not); *Vanvelzor v. Vanvelzor*, 219 P.3d 184 (Alaska 2009) (wife, proceeding pro se, did not waive her personal jurisdiction defense to divorce action by filing a counterclaim for spousal support).

However, if the counterclaim is viewed as compulsory, a majority of jurisdictions will not treat the counterclaim as waiving a personal jurisdiction defense. *See, e.g., Arch Aluminum & Glass Co., Inc. v. Haney*, 964 So. 2d 228 (Fla. App. 2007). Courts reason that a compulsory counterclaim does not waive a personal jurisdiction defense because a compulsory counterclaim must be asserted in an answer or else it is waived. *Nelson v. World Wide Lease, Inc.*, 716 P.2d 513 (Idaho 1986) (the preferred rule is that a compulsory counterclaim does not waive jurisdictional defenses). *See generally* Charles Alan Wright, et al., §1397 *Waiver of Certain Defenses—Effect of Interposing a Claim for Relief*, 5C Fed. Prac. & Proc. Civ. §1397 (3d ed. 2012).

STATUS AS A JURISDICTIONAL THEORY

24.16. Overview of Status Theory

As observed earlier in this chapter, the application of the status theory in a divisible divorce is commonly accepted. The status theory originally sprang from actions where one spouse sought a divorce and the other spouse could not be found. Acceptance of the theory allowed courts to grant an *in rem* divorce to the spouse who was before the court, even though the other spouse could not be found or chose not to participate in the divorce action.

Expanding application of the theory. The status theory has been extended by some state courts to child custody disputes, which initially appears contrary to the Supreme Court's plurality view as expressed in *May v. Anderson*, 345 U.S. 528 (1953). Recall that in *May v. Anderson*, the Court held that a child custody decree of one state was not entitled to full faith and credit in another state when the decree was entered by a court that failed to possess personal jurisdiction over the nonresident parent.

Custody. Application of the *May* ruling has been challenged in subsequent child custody disputes by several courts for a variety of reasons. For example, Tennessee rejected *May v. Anderson* on the ground that subsequent Supreme Court decisions had abolished the distinctions between *in rem* and *in personam* jurisdiction, and "recognized that exceptions can be made to the 'minimum contacts' standard" in status cases, such as child custody decisions. *Fernandez v.*

Fernandez, 1986 WL 7935 (Tenn. App. 1986); *see also Brown v. Brown*, 847 S.W.2d 496, 499 n.2 (Tenn. 1993). The Tennessee court followed the rule that the courts of a state "having the most significant connections with the child and his family have jurisdiction to make a custody adjudication, even in the absence of personal jurisdiction over a parent who does not reside in the forum state." *Fernandez*, 1986 WL 7935, at 2. *See also Roderick v. Roderick*, 776 S.W.2d 533 (Tenn. App. 1989).

Texas is another state that has applied the status exception to custody disputes. It has justified its use of the exception by explaining that

> unlike adjudications of child support and visitation expense, custody determinations are status adjudications not dependent upon personal jurisdiction over the parents. Generally, a family relationship is among those matters in which the forum state has such a strong interest that its courts may reasonably make an adjudication affecting that relationship even though one of the parties to the relationship may have had no personal contacts with the forum state.

In re S. A. V., 837 S.W.2d 80, 84 (Tex. 1992).

See also In re R. W., 39 A.3d 682 (Vt. 2011) (source of statutory authority is not Vermont's general long-arm statute, which does not address jurisdiction based on status, but the Uniform Child Custody Jurisdiction Act (UCCJA), which contains specific provisions for determining which forum has jurisdiction to adjudicate matters related to child custody); *Rando v. Rando*, 722 So. 2d 1165, 1166 (La. App. 1999) (contrasting child support, which requires jurisdiction over the person, with child custody, which requires jurisdiction over the status).

Termination of parental rights. The status exception has been extended by a few courts to parental termination proceedings. *See In re Appeal in Maricopa County, Juvenile Action No. JS-734*, 543 P.2d 454, 459-460 (Ariz. App. 1975) (in termination proceeding, court did not err in denying motion to dismiss for lack of jurisdiction, notwithstanding lack of *in personam* jurisdiction over the mother); *In re Interest of M. L. K.*, 768 P.2d 316, 319-320 (Kan. App. 1989) (proceeding for termination of parental rights was exception to "minimum contacts" rule for personal jurisdiction, and thus personal jurisdiction over a parent who could not be located was not required to meet due process considerations); *In re Adoption of Copeland*, 43 S.W.3d 483, 487 (Tenn. App. 2000) (relying on status exception in parental rights termination proceeding against a father in prison); *Wenz v. Schwartze*, 598 P.2d 1086, 1091-1092 (Mont. 1979) (concluding personal jurisdiction over a parent is not necessary in order to terminate parental rights, without specifically discussing status exception), *cert. denied*, 444 U.S. 1071 (1980); *In re A. E. H.*, 468 N.W.2d 190, 198-200 (Wis. 1991) (focusing on child's contacts with the state in order to terminate parental rights), *cert. denied*, 502 U.S. 925 (1991).

Adoption proceeding. The Oklahoma Supreme Court applied the status rationale to an adoption proceeding in *In re Adoption of J. L. H.*, 737 P.2d 915 (Okla. 1987). In that case, the children's natural father and stepmother petitioned Oklahoma for the nonconsensual adoption of the father's children by the stepmother on the ground that their mother, a nonresident of Oklahoma, had willfully failed to pay child support. The adoption was allowed to proceed without the mother's consent or the court possessing personal jurisdiction over her. It relied upon *Williams v. State of North Carolina*, 317 U.S. 287 (1942), stating that "[a]ccording to *Williams*, judicial cognizance over personal status — be it one created by matrimony or by natural parentage — may be validly exercised by a court of the state in which only one party to the status is a *bona fide* domiciliary while the other party, whose bond is sought to be adversely affected by the litigation, is a resident of a foreign jurisdiction." 737 P.2d at 918-919.

Protective orders. In *Bartsch v. Bartsch*, 636 N.W.2d 3 (Iowa 2001), the court applied the status theory when a dispute arose over whether a wife could obtain what was essentially an ex parte protective order under Iowa's Domestic Abuse Act against her nonresident husband living in Colorado. The majority agreed that Iowa did not possess personal jurisdiction over him but ruled that the protective order could be issued without having such jurisdiction because of the wife's status in the state. It relied heavily on *Williams, supra*, to buttress its status theory and a decision from Minnesota.

Minnesota had ruled that there was no due process problem with a statute that allowed ex parte restraining orders in domestic abuse cases because of (1) a state's strong interest in preventing abuse, (2) the necessity for prompt action, and (3) the protection provided by judicial scrutiny. *Baker v. Baker*, 494 N.W.2d 282, 288 (Minn. 1992), *superseded in part by statute discussed in Burkstrand v. Burkstrand*, 632 N.W.2d 206 (Minn. 2001). The Iowa court reasoned that

> the order here does not attempt to impose a personal judgment against the defendant. . . . [I]t deals with jurisdiction to enforce liability arising from status rather than with determination of status. The district court merely ordered the defendant to "stay away from the protected party" and not assault or communicate with her, in furtherance of the State's strong interest in protecting Iowa residents from domestic abuse. If a court may constitutionally make orders affecting marriage, custody, and parental rights without personal jurisdiction of a defendant, it certainly should be able to do what the court did here — enter an order protecting a resident Iowa family from abuse.

636 N.W.2d at 10.

24.17. Restatement of Conflict of Laws — Status

The *Restatement of Conflict of Laws* discusses the traditional view of status but does not extend it beyond an ex parte divorce action. The *Restatement* uses the following illustration:

> Assume that A leaves his home in State X and goes to State Y, where he becomes domiciled and there obtains an ex parte divorce from B, his wife. Assuming that the requirements of proper notice and opportunity to be heard have been met, this divorce is valid and must be recognized in State X under full faith and credit even though B was not personally subject to the jurisdiction of the State Y court and at all times retained her domicile in State X.

Restatement (Second) of Conflict of Laws §71 cmt. a, illus. 1 (1971).

EXAMPLES

Examples

6. Assume that P filed an action in federal district court against state M and the family court judge who presided over the termination proceeding involving P's child. P alleges that he was unconstitutionally deprived of his right to a relationship with his son when the trial judge in state M terminated his parental rights.

   The record of the state proceeding shows that the state M judge held a full termination hearing at which P testified and was represented by counsel. The judge made findings at the conclusion of the hearing that P had willfully failed to contribute to the support of his child for one year and that it would be in the child's best interests to be adopted by his stepfather, with whom he had been living since his mother and stepfather's marriage five years earlier. In his federal court complaint, P does not attack state M's statute on termination of parental rights as unconstitutional, nor does he claim that his rights were terminated without a due process hearing. Rather, P contends that the court in state M did not have subject matter jurisdiction to terminate his parental rights because the custody of his child had previously been determined by a court in state Y. P also had made this argument before the court in state M and lost. The state and the judge seek dismissal of the federal action. How will a court most likely rule?

7. Assume that state X has a domestic violence statute that enables domestic violence victims to seek and obtain ex parte civil protection orders (CPOs) in a number of circumstances, including a divorce proceeding. The statute in state X states that a victim of domestic violence may "receive an ex parte CPO by filing a petition detailing (1) the nature

and extent of the domestic violence, (2) the relationship between the respondent, the petitioner, and the victim, and (3) the relief requested." The statute also requires that the petition allege the "immediate and present danger of domestic violence," which constitutes good cause.

D obtained an ex parte order during the course of the divorce proceedings between P and D, and the order granted D exclusive possession of their residence and household furniture. While the divorce matter was being litigated in state court, P filed an action in federal district court and sought injunctive relief pursuant to 42 U.S.C. §1983. P alleged that service and execution of the CPO denied him due process. The federal court applied the abstention doctrine, finding that the pending divorce proceedings implicated important state issues regarding the resolution of domestic disputes and that the state court provided P with an adequate opportunity to present his constitutional challenges. P has appealed. How will the federal appellate court most likely treat the lower court's decision to abstain from hearing the civil rights claim?

8. Assume that P and D divorce and the trial judge awards custody of their minor child to D. P files a complaint in federal court after the judgment is entered naming D, the trial judge, and D's lawyer as defendants. P argues that under 42 U.S.C. §1983, his civil rights were violated during the proceeding by these individuals. He also argues that at a minimum, he is entitled to a hearing in federal court on his claims and possibly a new divorce for violations of his due process and equal protection rights. The defendants have brought a joint motion in federal court to dismiss P's complaint. Should the court grant a hearing of their motion?

9. Assume that the marriage of P and D breaks down. P serves D with a petition to dissolve the marriage in state X, where both P and D have lived for four months. D does not appear, and the matter goes by default. Assume that the residency requirement for filing a divorce in this jurisdiction is six months. Furthermore, assume that two years following entry of the divorce decree, D moves to vacate it, alleging that the court lacked subject matter jurisdiction when it was entered because P had been a resident for only four months. D also has contacted the local prosecutor and has urged her to bring a criminal action against P, who has remarried, because she is committing bigamy and/or adultery under State X's criminal statutes. The trial judge has examined the subject matter statute in state X and it requires that a party filing for divorce must "reside in State X for six months prior to filing." Will a court most likely vacate the judgment?

10. Assume that P and D were married for ten years when their relationship broke down. They entered into a separation agreement in state X

providing that D was to pay P $750 per month for child support until their child reached age 18, plus $1,000 per month in alimony. The court in state X had subject matter and personal jurisdiction over the parties when it entered the order. Eight months later, D filed an action for divorce in state Y. P was served by constructive service. At the time, P was not a resident of state Y, was not served within state Y, and did not submit to the jurisdiction of state Y. The court in state Y granted a divorce, reduced D's child support to $250 a month, and eliminated any alimony payment. P challenges the decision from state Y in state X. How will a court in state X most likely treat the challenge?

11. Assume that P and D have been informally separated for six years. P decided that it was time to dissolve her marriage to D, and as a part of the divorce proceeding, she obtained title to the couple's home. D could not be located despite P's search for D at D's last place of employment and last known address. P checked the local telephone book and city directory, searched the Internet, and made inquiries of D's relatives without success in locating him. P's lawyer prepared a publication notice to be placed in a legal newspaper asking the state court to exercise *in rem* jurisdiction in the matter. The local statute states that service by publication notice for *in rem* civil actions shall include where appropriate:

    > A description of any property to be affected. When service is sought by means of constructive notice, strict compliance with the statute and rule allowing service by publication is required.

    Assume that a partial description of the property was included in the service by publication notice. The trial judge grants P an ex parte divorce and awards her all the interest in the home, which was in the name of P and D. P dies a year after the divorce. D suddenly appears and claims he was out of the country for the last two years and knew nothing of the divorce proceeding. D opposes providing P's heirs with any interest in the home, saying that he is still married to P and that notice was not sufficient. P's executor contends that the divorce action was legal and provided P with the real estate that once had been owned by P and D. The order eliminated any interest that D had in the property. How will a court most likely rule on the legality of the divorce and D's interest in the property?

12. Assume that P, a citizen of state X, alleges in a complaint filed in state X that she and D, a citizen of state Y, had a series of sexual encounters in state X that led to a pregnancy and the birth of a child. D denies that he is the father of the child. P seeks to establish the child's paternity and obtain

child support from D. The long-arm statute available in state X permits the exercise of jurisdiction over a nonresident "who transacts business in state X, causes tortious injury in it, or has an interest in real property there." When D is served in state Y via this statute, he challenges its application in state X to a domestic proceeding. In his motion to dismiss, he alleges that he dated P a half-dozen times in state X but had protected intercourse with her. He alleges that the child could not be his. How will a court most likely rule on D's challenge to the long-arm statute used by state X in an effort to gain personal jurisdiction over him?

Explanations

6. The federal court most likely will dismiss the lawsuit. It is true that the relationship between parent and child is constitutionally protected. As such, the state's power to legislate, adjudicate, and administer all aspects of family law, including determinations of custodial and visitation rights, is subject to scrutiny by the federal judiciary within the reach of the due process and/or equal protection clauses of the Fourteenth Amendment.

   It is clear, however, that the state has a compelling interest in the welfare of minor children and has authority to terminate parental rights under certain limited circumstances, so long as it makes that determination in the best interest of the child and after a hearing. *See Lassiter v. Dept. of Soc. Serv.*, 452 U.S. 18 (1981). Here, P appears to be relitigating issues identical to those raised in the state court. Under such circumstances, the federal court most likely will apply collateral estoppel to bar P's claim. *See Blair v. Supreme Court of State of Wyo.*, 671 F.2d 389 (10th Cir. 1982) (in proceeding for termination of parental rights, father raised jurisdictional claim in state trial court in Wyoming that custody of his child had previously been determined by a Colorado court, and because the jurisdictional claim was decided against him in Wyoming state trial court, he was precluded from re-litigating such issue in federal court).

7. The appellate court most likely will affirm the decision to abstain. In this hypothetical, it is undisputed that a divorce case was pending at the time that P filed his federal action. Therefore, the first element of *Younger* is satisfied.

   State X also has a strong state interest in regulating domestic violence. The challenged statute affects the underlying divorce and involves important state interests, thus satisfying the second *Younger* criterion. Note that in *Ankenbrandt*, the Supreme Court narrowed the scope of the traditional domestic relations exception, but it did not overrule its prior decisions holding that domestic relations is an area of traditional state concern.

Finally, P has failed to prove the inadequacy of the courts in state X. There is no reason to question their ability or willingness to address P's constitutional issue. Because state X courts provide an adequate forum for P's constitutional claim, the third criterion of *Younger* is satisfied. Thus, most federal courts will abstain from ruling on the constitutionality of the statute. *See Kelm v. Hyatt*, 44 F.3d 415 (6th Cir. 1995) (*Younger* abstention was warranted on claims for injunctive relief alleging that Ohio provisions denied due process to husband).

8. This appears to be a case where P is appealing a state court's final judgment. The *Rooker-Feldman* doctrine applies when a party bringing an action in federal district court "complain[s] of an injury caused by the state-court judgment and seek[s] review and rejection of that judgment." *Exxon Mobil*, *supra*, 544 U.S. at 291. "[T]he pertinent question in determining whether a federal district court is precluded under the *Rooker-Feldman* doctrine from exercising subject-matter jurisdiction over a claim is whether the 'source of the injury' upon which plaintiff bases his federal claim is the state court judgment." *In re Cook*, 551 F.3d at 548. "This is true regardless of whether the party challenges the validity of the state court judgment on constitutional grounds." *Ibid. See also Sturgis v. Hayes*, 283 F. App'x 309, 313 (6th Cir. 2008) ("[T]he *Rooker-Feldman* doctrine applies when a plaintiff asserts before a federal district court that a state court judgment itself was unconstitutional or in violation of federal law.") (internal quotations omitted). In this hypothetical, the federal court could dismiss the claim based on the *Rooker-Feldman* doctrine.

   It is also the case that federal courts have said that "in the field of domestic relations, it has been [its] consistent policy to refuse to exercise jurisdiction over claims which seek to collaterally attack a state court judgment." *Stephens v. Hayes*, 374 F. App'x 620, 623 (6th Cir. 2010). "Although this domestic relations exception to federal jurisdiction does not apply to a civil action that merely has domestic relations overtones . . . federal courts lack jurisdiction where the action is a mere pretense and the suit is actually concerned with domestic relations issues." *Danforth v. Celebrezze*, 76 F. App'x 615, 616–617 (6th Cir. 2003) (holding, pursuant to the domestic relations exception and the *Rooker-Feldman* doctrine, that the Court lacked jurisdiction over a §1983 action where the constitutional claims were conclusory and "a pretense to obtain federal review of domestic relations matters").

   Because P's claims against the judicial defendants seek the Court to review the state court decisions in his divorce and child custody proceedings, the court would most likely apply the *Rooker-Feldman* doctrine and dismiss the action.

9. A court will take at least two approaches. First, it will examine the residency language in its state statute. It will be looking for language that specifically states that if the residency requirement is not met, a divorce judgment otherwise valid from be ruled void. If it does not find this language, it will not void the divorce decree. In this hypothetical, the language of the statute is clear; i.e., a party must be a resident of State X for six months prior to filing the divorce petition. Therefore, it appears from a reading of the statute that the court was without subject matter jurisdiction, and the judgment is void.

   However, a court will not stop here. Even though it found language suggesting the judgment is void, it may rule that the statutory residence requirements for maintaining an action for divorce go only to the substance of the cause of action, not to the competence of the court to adjudicate the cause. Therefore, even if the court that granted the final judgment of divorce erred in determining the issue of residence, the error did not deprive it of subject matter jurisdiction to render the judgment, and the judgment was not subject to vacature on post-judgment motion made after the time for an appeal was exhausted.

   Because of the ruling in the civil matter, the prosecutor will not continue to pursue any criminal charges against P.

10. Based on *Estin v. Estin*, a separation order that is entered by a court in state X that had *in personam* jurisdiction over both parties, and that provided for alimony or child support, is not superseded by a subsequent divorce decree obtained in a foreign state where the foreign state did not have *in personam* jurisdiction over both parties. *See Burnett v. Burnett*, 542 S.E.2d 911 (W. Va. 2000) (West Virginia separation order, which directed former husband to pay former wife $750 per month for child support and alimony, was not superseded by later Arkansas divorce decree). The parties in this hypothetical are legally divorced, but the absence of personal jurisdiction over P means that the child support and alimony awards made in state X remain in effect. That portion of the judgment and decree regarding support and alimony made by the court in state Y is of no effect.

11. The divorce will be viewed as legal. It was not necessary to have personal jurisdiction over D in order to dissolve the marriage.

   Nevertheless, D appears to have a claim to his interest in the home. The reason for this is that the exact description of the property was not included in the service by publication notice. Because the service by publication requirement was not met, the court was without jurisdiction to enter a judgment relating to the property. The judgment divorcing the couple will remain untouched, but that portion of the judgment relating to the property most likely will be considered wholly void.

12. First, the court will ask whether the language of the long-arm statute applies to these facts. Second, even if the statute applies, a question remains whether the contacts between D and state X are sufficient to meet the minimal due process requirements of the Constitution.

    In this hypothetical, a court may rule that the language of the long-arm statute applies to these facts on the basis that a failure to support the child constitutes a tortious act. A "tortious act" is often defined as including any act committed in the state that involved a breach of duty to another and resulted in ascertainable damages. *See Poindexter v. Willis*, 231 N.E.2d 1 (Ill. App. 1967) (establishing the *Poindexter* rule); *Lozinski v. Lozinski*, 408 S.E.2d 310 (W. Va. 1991).

    However, some courts have refused to follow the *Poindexter* rule when the sexual intercourse occurred either within or outside the state, on the ground that the failure to support cannot be a tort until paternity, which gives rise to the duty to support, has been first established. These courts hold that even when the sexual intercourse occurs in the state, it is not a tort when it involves two consenting adults. *State ex rel. Garcia v. Dayton*, 695 P.2d 477 (N.M. 1985); *State ex rel. Larimore v. Snyder*, 291 N.W.2d 241 (Neb. 1980); *State ex rel. Carrington v. Schutts*, 535 P.2d 982 (Kan. 1975); *Barnhart v. Madvig*, 526 S.W.2d 106 (Tenn. 1975); *A.R.B. v. G.L.P.*, 507 P.2d 468 (Colo. 1973); *Anonymous v. Anonymous*, 268 N.Y.S.2d 710 (N.Y. Fam. 1966); *Taylor v. Texas Dept. of Public Welfare*, 549 S.W.2d 422 (Tex. App. 1977).

    It is not clear, therefore, what a court will rule in terms of the claim D committed a tortious act. It depends on the jurisdiction.

    P may also search in state X's statutes to determine whether it has adopted some form of the Uniform Interstate Family Support Act (UIFSA). In most jurisdictions where it has been adopted, the Act provides that a person who has sexual intercourse within a state submits to the jurisdiction of that state's courts with respect to a child who may have been conceived. However, even if state X has such a statute, application of the statute is always open to constitutional challenge.

    Assuming that a court applies its long-arm statute to these facts, the question of the constitutional minimum contacts requirement remains open. At least one court has held that sexual contact in the state constitutes minimum contacts such that an action maintained there does not offend "traditional notions of fair play and substantial justice." *Bell v. Arnold*, 279 S.E.2d 449 (Ga. 1981). In this example, the defendant admits being in state X and having intercourse with P. This is probably sufficient to meet the minimum contacts requirement of the Constitution.

FULL FAITH AND CREDIT

24.18. State Recognition of Same-Sex Marriages (Defense of Marriage Act)

Purpose. The purpose of the federal Defense of Marriage Act (DOMA) is to provide states with an opportunity to deny recognition of same-sex marriages originating in other states. It does not require that they do so. DOMA was enacted after the Supreme Court of Hawaii determined the state statute banning same-sex marriage fell under strict scrutiny, leading some to believe that constitutionalization of same-sex marriage was imminent.

The Federal DOMA declares that,

> No State . . . shall be required to give effect to any public act, record, or judicial proceeding of any other State . . . respecting a relationship between persons of the same sex that is treated as a marriage under the laws of such other State.

28 U.S.C. §1738C (Supp. 2000).

The statute provides each state with the power to determine the validity of same-sex marriage within its own borders. The statute is, in effect, an exception to the full faith and credit clause of the United States Constitution.

Recognizing same-sex marriages. As states have increasingly allowed same-sex couples to marry, the question is whether states that do not permit such relationships will recognize those made outside their borders. Some state courts, such as those in New York, have shown a willingness to recognize same-sex marriages from states where they were legally created. For example, in *Lewis v. New York State Dept. of Civil Service*, 60 A.D.3d 216 (N.Y. App. 2009), the court held that it would recognize the parties to a same-sex marriage as spouses if their marriage was valid in the jurisdiction where it was solemnized. The ruling allowed spouses of state employees access to the benefits provided under a state health insurance program. The relationships are also recognized in New York for purposes of insurance law, "including all provisions governing health insurance." *In re Donna S.*, 871 N.Y.S.2d 883 (N.Y. Fam. 2009). Note, however, that a New York trial court held in July 2009 that a woman who entered into a civil union in Vermont with her same-sex partner was not entitled to dissolution of the relationship as a marriage. The court explained that it could not treat the women's civil union as a marriage but had the authority to dissolve the civil union under its "general jurisdiction to hear and decide all equitable civil actions." It dismissed the marriage dissolution petition and advised the woman to return with a petition for dissolution of the civil union. *B.S. v. F.B.*, 883 N.Y.S.2d 458 (N.Y. Sup. 2009).

Rejecting recognition of same-sex marriages. Several state courts have indicated that they are unwilling to recognize a same-sex marriage validly created in another jurisdiction. *See, e.g., Ghassemi v. Ghassemi*, 998 So. 2d 731, 738 (La. App. 2008) (marriage between persons of the same sex violates a strong public policy of Louisiana, and such a marriage contracted in another state shall not be recognized in this state for any purpose, including the assertion of any right or claim as a result of the purported marriage); *Chambers v. Ormiston*, 935 A.2d 956 (R.I. 2007) (a court of limited statutory jurisdiction is without jurisdiction to entertain divorce petition involving same-sex couple who were married in Massachusetts); *O'Darling v. O'Darling*, 188 P.3d 137 (Okla. 2008) (divorce vacated when information received that parties seeking divorce were of same sex); *Rosengarten v. Downes*, 802 A.2d 170 (Conn. App. 2002) (affirming trial court's dismissal of an action to dissolve a Vermont civil union for lack of subject matter jurisdiction).

Note that Connecticut enacted a civil union statute in 2005, which gave couples the same rights and responsibilities as in marriage, but it included a provision limiting marriage to a man and a woman. The limitation on the sex of persons who could marry in the statute was challenged in *Kerrigan v. State*, 957 A.2d 407 (Conn. 2008), and was found to be unconstitutional. Connecticut now recognizes same-sex marriages.

24.19. Full Faith and Credit for Child Support Orders Act

Problems with uniform state enforcement of child support orders triggered federal legislation to deal with the issue in 1996. In that year, Congress enacted the Full Faith and Credit for Child Support Orders Act (FFCCSOA), 28 U.S.C.A. §1738(B) (1996). All interstate child support orders are now governed by FFCCSOA.

> Congress passed FFCCSOA because multiple and inconsistent child support orders, under statutory schemes like URESA, were contributing to: (1) excessive relitigation over existing orders; (2) a disregard of state child support orders "resulting in massive arrearages nationwide"; and (3) an epidemic of non-custodial parents failing to pay regularly scheduled child support for "extensive periods of time, resulting in substantial hardship for the children" and their custodians.

Wilson County ex rel. Egbert v. Egbert, 569 S.E.2d 727, 729 (N.C. App. 2002).

FFCCSOA established "national standards" to facilitate the payment of child support, discourage interstate conflict over inconsistent orders, and to avoid jurisdictional competition. *Ibid.*

FFCCSOA is binding on all states and supersedes inconsistent provisions of state law. *In re Marriage of Carrier*, 576 N.W.2d 97, 98 (Iowa 1998); *Kelly v. Otte*, 474 S.E.2d 131, 134 (N.C. App. 1996), *disc. review denied*, 479 S.E.2d 204 (1996). The Act ensures that only one child support order at a time is in effect, and it incorporates many of the concepts contained in the Uniform Interstate Family Support Act. For example, it requires that a state enforce a child support order made in another state at a time when that state had jurisdiction over both parties. The parties must be given reasonable notice and an opportunity to be heard. 28 U.S.C. §1738B(c)(2). The Act supersedes any inconsistent provisions of the Uniform Interstate Family Support Act (UIFSA) as adopted by a particular state. *Witowski v. Roosevelt*, 199 P.3d 1072 (Wyo. 2009) (under the supremacy clause, Wyoming was obligated to enforce a Virginia child support order, according to its terms, whether or not Virginia law differed from Wyoming law).

SPECIAL SITUATIONS

24.20. Overview of Indian Child Welfare Act (ICWA)

The Indian Child Welfare Act (ICWA), §§1901 and 1911, gives tribal courts exclusive jurisdiction over proceedings concerning a Native American child who resides or is domiciled on an Indian reservation. 25 U.S.C. §§1901, 1911 (1978). In the leading case of *Mississippi Band of Choctaw Indians v. Holyfield*, 490 U.S. 30 (1989), the Supreme Court held that custody and adoption decisions involving Native American children born off an Indian reservation to parents who were domiciled on the reservation at the time of birth gave the tribe to which the parents belonged exclusive jurisdiction to decide those issues. *Domicile* was defined as physical presence with the intent to remain on the reservation. Minors take the domicile of their parents because they are legally incapable of forming the requisite state of mind (intent) to create a domicile. The Court made it clear in *Holyfield* that parents could not defeat the intent of the ICWA absent changing their domicile.

A "child custody proceeding" is broadly defined by the ICWA as referring to any proceeding involving foster care placement, termination of parental rights, pre-adoptive placement, or adoptive placement. 25 U.S.C. §1903(1) (1978). The only two exceptions to that definition are awards of custody to one of the parents in divorce proceedings and delinquency proceeding placements. 25 U.S.C. §1903(1) (1978).

Defining an Indian child. The ICWA defines an "Indian child" as "any unmarried person who is under age eighteen and is either (a) a member of an Indian tribe or (b) is eligible for membership in an Indian tribe and is the biological child of a member of an Indian tribe." 25 U.S.C. §1903(4) (1978). *See In re Arianna R.G.*, 657 N.W.2d 363, 368 (Wis. 2003) (an "Indian child" [is defined as] "something more specific than merely having Native American ancestors").

Although the purpose of ICWA is to "protect the best interests of Indian children," its concomitant purpose is to "promote the stability and security of Indian tribes and families." 25 U.S.C. §1902. The North Dakota Supreme Court explained that the ICWA is not premised upon racial classifications—"[t]he different treatment of Indians and non-Indians under ICWA is based on the political status of the parents and children and the quasi-sovereign nature of the tribe." *In re A. B.*, 663 N.W.2d 625, 636 (N.D. 2003); *see also Rice v. Cayetano*, 528 U.S. 495, 519–20, (2000) (preference in hiring and promoting at the federal Bureau of Indian Affairs (BIA), which favored individuals who were one-fourth or more degree Indian blood and . . . member[s] of a federally recognized tribe was political rather than racial in nature).

Adopting an Indian child. In *Matter of Petition of Phillip A. C.*, 149 P.3d 51 (Nev. 2006), the court, in the context of an adoption dispute, considered the issue of the type of evidence that may be used to determine whether a child is a Native American child under the ICWA. The child, Z. R. K., was adopted by Phillip following a court hearing. The child was the son of Phillip's ex-stepdaughter, Tarah K. Phillip. Soon after the district court granted the order of adoption, Tarah contacted the Central Council of the Tlingit & Haida Indian Tribes of Alaska, seeking assistance in overturning the adoption. Tarah claimed that she had signed the adoption consent under extreme duress and that Phillip had prevented her from attending the subsequent adoption hearing through deception. The parties agreed that ethnically, Tarah is 7/16ths Native American and Z. R. K. is 7/32nds Native American. They disagreed, however, as to whether Z. R. K. is a Native American child under the ICWA.

An affidavit of the tribal enrollment officer was submitted in which the officer stated that (1) she had served as the tribal enrollment officer for 15 years; (2) Tarah had been an enrolled member of the Tlingit & Haida Indian Tribes since 1989; (3) Z. R. K. was eligible for enrollment at the time of her adoption by Phillip on June 8, 2004; and (4) Z. R. K. had been an enrolled member of the tribes since February 16, 2005. The court found that Z. R. K. was a Native American child to whom the ICWA applied and that the adoption proceedings had violated part of the ICWA, 25 U.S.C. §1913(a), because no judicial certification had been entered. However, it remanded the case to allow Phillip the opportunity to challenge the authority of the tribal enrollment officer to speak for the tribe. 149 P.3d at 1297.

24.21. Overview of Soldiers and Sailors Civil Relief Act — Service Members Civil Relief Act

The Soldiers and Sailors Civil Relief Act (SSCRA) of 1940 is essentially a reenactment of a 1918 statute, with a number of amendments. 50 U.S.C. app. §521. The statute was first amended in 1942, and again in 1991 because of the First Gulf War. In November 2002, Congress passed a law (the Veterans Benefits Act of 2002, Pub. L. No. 107-330 §305), which provides protection to National Guard members called to state active duty under Title 32 if the duty is because of a federal emergency, the request for active duty is made by the president or secretary of defense, and the member is activated for longer than 30 days. The statute was amended and given a new title in 2003. *See* 50 U.S.C. app. §501 (2003). It is now called the Servicemembers Civil Relief Act (SCRA).

SCRA protection. The SCRA states that a service member who is either the plaintiff or the defendant in a civil lawsuit may request a stay or postponement of a court proceeding in which he or she is a party and may request a stay at any point in the proceedings. *See In re A. R.*, 88 Cal. Rptr. 3d 448 (Cal. App. 2009) (SCRA stay provision overrides state requirement to complete dispositional hearing within six months).

SCRA protects service members by providing for "temporary suspension of judicial and administrative proceedings and transactions that may adversely affect the civil rights of service members during their military service." 50 U.S.C. app. §502(2). The purpose of this protection is to enable service members "to devote their entire energy to the defense needs of the Nation." 50 U.S.C. app. §502(1). SCRA also protects persons in military service from having default judgments entered against them without their knowledge. Judgments entered in violation of SCRA are merely voidable and not void. They remain valid until properly attacked under the Act's provisions, and the challenge must be timely under the statute. *See Wilson v. Butler*, 584 So. 2d 414, 416 (Miss. 1991) (paternity judgment upheld where defendant did not invoke SCRA until 13 months after final judgment); *see also Price v. McBeath*, 989 So. 2d 444 (Miss. App. 2008).

In general, courts take the view that the provisions of SCRA are to be liberally construed toward protecting the rights of men and women in the service who have been obliged to drop their own affairs to take up the burdens of the nation. *Reed v. Albaaj*, 723 N.W.2d 50, 54 (Minn. App. 2006) (quoting *Boone v. Lightner*, 319 U.S. 561, 564 (1943)); *see Omega Industry*,

Inc. v. Raffaele, 894 F. Supp. 1425 (D.C. Nev. 1995) (Servicemembers Civil Relief Act (SCRA) was intended to be liberally construed and applied in a broad spirit of gratitude toward service personnel); 50 U.S.C. app. §512(1). However, the Act does not empower a federal court to collaterally review, vacate, or impede the decisions of a state court. *See Scheidegg v. Dept. of Air Force*, 715 F. Supp. 11, 13-14 (D.C. N.H. 1989); *Sarfaty v. Sarfaty*, 534 F. Supp. 701, 704 n.4 (E.D. Pa. 1982). A judgment made in violation of the Act is subject to attack only in the court that rendered the judgment. *See* 50 U.S.C. app. §520(4).

Limits on SCRA — merchant marine. Members of the merchant marine are likely not covered by the SCRA. The express definition of "service members" in the SCRA makes the similarities between the merchant marines and branches of the armed services insufficient to grant a member of the merchant marines the protections of the Act. The "armed forces" are defined as the "Army, Navy, Air Force, Marine Corps, and Coast Guard." 10 U.S.C. §101(a)(4).

24.22. Child Custody Under SCRA

"Most states have a policy of providing for the best interests of the child when it comes to custody decisions. Reconciling the SCRA with state law, however, has produced a tremendous debate over which interests should take precedence: those of the child or those of the service member." Sara Estrin, *The Service Members Civil Relief Act: Why and How This Act Applies to Child Custody Proceedings*, 7 Law & Ineq. 211 (Winter 2009). It is believed that many individuals deployed in the United States armed forces often lose custody of their children, partially because of their deployments. Some contend that this is a result of the deficiencies of the SCRA. *See* Christopher Missick, *Comment, Child Custody Protections in the Service Members Civil Relief Act: Congress Acts to Protect Parents Serving in the Armed Forces*, 29 Whittier L. Rev. 857 (2008). Since 2005, at least 12 states have amended their child custody statutes in an attempt to accommodate both the best interests of the child and the legal rights of the service member parent. Estrin, *supra*, at 226. *See Lenser v. McGowan*, 191 S.W.3d 423 (Ark. 2004) (husband's request for a stay in divorce proceeding under SCRA did not deprive the trial court of jurisdiction to enter temporary custody order granting custody of child to wife).

In recognition that a national solution to the custody problem was needed when one spouse is in the military, Congress recently amended the SCRA and made it clear that the default judgment and stay provisions of SCRA are applicable in child custody proceedings involving active-duty service members. Pub. L. No. 110-181, §584, 122 Stat. 3, 128 (2008); Estrin, *supra*, at 238. However, because service members are being treated differently depending on their state of residence, it is suggested that a new federal law be enacted that balances the competing interests of minor children and service member parents. *Id.* at 239.

The federal amendment has been criticized, however, as failing to address the issue of whether the SCRA preempts state family law in child custody proceedings adequately. It is suggested that Congress enact legislation that explicitly deals with the problem of staying child custody actions pursuant to the SCRA. *Ibid.*

24.23. Uniform Interstate Family Support Act

As you are aware, states may enact a variety of specialized jurisdictional statutes in the area of family law that are based on models provided by outside interested groups. One of the model acts that is being enacted in whole or in part by the states is the Uniform Interstate Family Support Act (UIFSA). This model provision was originally drafted by the National Conference of Commissioners on Uniform State Laws (NCCUSL) in an effort to revise and replace the Uniform Reciprocal Enforcement Act (URESA) (as originally adopted in 1950 and amended in 1958) and its revised version, the Revised Uniform Reciprocal Enforcement Act of 1968 (RURESA). The UIFSA was approved by the NCCUSL in 1992, ratified by the American Bar Association (ABA) in February 1993, and amended in 1996. It governs a court's obligation to enforce and ability to modify a child support order of another state's court.

The primary purpose of the UIFSA was to eliminate multiple and inconsistent child support orders by establishing the principle of having only one controlling order in effect at any one time. This principle was implemented in UIFSA by a definitional concept called "continuing, exclusive jurisdiction," under which the state that issues the support order (the issuing state) retains exclusive jurisdiction over the order, until specified conditions occur that provide a basis for jurisdiction in another state.

Personal jurisdiction is required over an obligor before a child support order is enforceable because such an order involves the imposition of a personal obligation to pay money. Consequently, although the UIFSA grants states the jurisdiction to enforce child support orders issued by other states, it imposes limitations on the states' jurisdiction to modify such orders.

Continuing jurisdiction. At the core of the UIFSA is the concept that the state that issued the child support decree or order retains "continuing, exclusive jurisdiction" unless one of the delineated exceptions are met.

Long-arm provision. §201 of the UIFSA contains a long-arm provision that allows the broadest possible assertion of jurisdiction over nonresident child support obligors consistent with the Constitution. *See* UIFSA §201 cmt. 9 (pt. IB) ULA 275-277 1999). It contains eight bases for a court's exercise of personal jurisdiction over a nonresident individual in an action to establish, enforce, or modify a child support order. "The drafters caution that subsections (3) through (6), if applied too literally, could overreach due process, and should be applied 'on a case-by-case basis with an eye on procedural and substantive due process.'" Patricia W. Hatamyar, *Interstate Establishment, Enforcement, and Modification of Child Support Orders*, 25 Okla. City U. L. Rev. 511, 523 (Spring-Summer 2000).

Typically, a state UIFSA long-arm provision is similar to this section of Colorado's statutes, which provides that:

> (a) In a proceeding to establish or enforce a support order or to determine parentage, a tribunal of this state may exercise personal jurisdiction over a nonresident individual or the individual's guardian or conservator if: . . .
>
> (1) The individual is personally served with a summons within this state;
>
> (2) The individual submits to the jurisdiction of this state by consent, by entering a general appearance, or by filing a responsive document having the effect of waiving any contest to personal jurisdiction;
>
> (3) The individual resided with the child in this state;
>
> (4) The individual resided in this state and provided prenatal expenses or support for the child;
>
> (5) The child resides in this state as a result of the acts or directives of the individual;
>
> (6) The individual engaged in sexual intercourse in this state and the child may have been conceived by that act of intercourse; or
>
> (7) There is any other basis consistent with the constitutions of this state and the United States for the exercise of personal jurisdiction.

Colo. Rev. Stat. Ann. 14-5-201(5) (2004).

Other jurisdictions have interpreted the long-arm provision of UIFSA, reaching varying results depending on the particular facts and circumstances of each case. For example, in *McNabb v. McNabb*, 65 P.3d 1068 (Kan. App. 2003), the Kansas Court of Appeals refused to find personal jurisdiction over a nonresident father under UIFSA because the child involved in the dispute did not reside in Kansas as a result of the acts or directives of the father. The mother claimed that the father drank excessively, had abused her on one occasion a year before she and child moved to Kansas, and had dropped the child on one occasion several months before she and child moved to Kansas. 65 P.3d at 1070-1071. However, because the one physical incident between the father and mother occurred over a year before the mother fled and the father's drinking "did not cause [the mother] and the child to flee Virginia for Kansas," the court ruled that the father's "acts or directives" did not cause the mother and child to reside in Kansas. *Id.* at 1075. The court concluded that personal jurisdiction was not available under UIFSA. *Ibid.*

In *Windsor v. Windsor*, 700 N.E.2d 838 (Mass. App. 1998), the court found that personal jurisdiction over a nonresident father was inappropriate under UIFSA. In this case, the mother left the father in Florida in June 1977, gave birth to their son in Massachusetts in September 1977, and filed a complaint for divorce, including a demand for child support, nearly 20 years later, in June 1995. *Id.* at 839. In her complaint, the mother alleged that the father had been guilty of "cruel and abusive treatment" during the course of the marriage, but she did not offer any facts or testimony to support that claim. *Id.* at 841. The court found that "[n]o affidavit, testimony, or authenticated or verified document even intimates, . . . establishes, that the wife and her children were caused 'to flee' from Florida to Massachusetts as a result of any cruel and abusive acts of the husband or any 'directive' he made." Therefore, personal jurisdiction did not exist under UIFSA. *Id.* at 842.

However, in *Franklin v. Virginia*, 497 S.E.2d 881, 885-886 (Va. App. 1998), the court held that UIFSA's long-arm provision authorized jurisdiction over a husband who, "[a]fter several physical altercations, . . . ordered wife and the children from their home in Africa." In response to the husband's order, the wife and children fled to Virginia, which was the family's home prior to living in Africa, the point of entry for the family's return to the United States, and the location of the husband's employer's field office. *Id.* at 886.

The court rejected the husband's contention that because he did not specifically direct the wife and children to move to Virginia, the Virginia courts could not exercise jurisdiction. Instead, the court noted that "[t]o allow husband to escape his support obligations merely because he failed to dictate the specific destination when he ordered his family to leave the marital home would frustrate the purpose of the legislature in enacting [UIFSA]." *Ibid.* Because the court focused on the affirmative acts of the nonresident father that caused the wife and children to reside in Virginia, rather than the voluntary choices of the mother, it concluded that personal jurisdiction was appropriate under UIFSA.

Procedure. Procedurally, UIFSA enables an individual petitioner or a support enforcement agency to file a petition to issue, enforce, or modify a support order or determine parentage in an initiating tribunal to be forwarded to a tribunal in the state that has personal jurisdiction over the respondent, the responding tribunal. A tribunal is broadly defined as "a court, administrative agency, or quasi-judicial entity authorized to establish, enforce, or modify support orders or to determine parentage."

The UIFSA also allows the petition to be filed directly in the responding tribunal. UIFSA §301(b). The responding tribunal applies the procedural and substantive laws of its state to the proceedings. UIFSA §303(1). If a petition is filed in an initiating tribunal, that tribunal has the obligation to forward the petition and accompanying documents to the known responding tribunal or the support enforcement agency of the responding state. UIFSA §304(a)(1).

State to assist. Upon request, the support enforcement agency of the responding state must provide services to the petitioner to obtain jurisdiction over the respondent in the appropriate responding tribunal, obtain relevant information for the tribunal, request a setting, and communicate with the petitioner concerning court notices and jurisdiction.

Inconvenient forum. The UIFSA in most jurisdictions does not contain an inconvenient forum provision, unlike the UCCJEA. However, the state courts have the inherent power to utilize the doctrine of forum *non conveniens* to refuse to exercise jurisdiction over a cause of action. *See, e.g.*, *Zurick v. Inman*, 426 S.W.2d 767, 772 (Tenn. 1968). The doctrine addresses the discretionary power of a court to decline to exercise jurisdiction when it appears that there is another place where the case may be more suitably or conveniently tried. The doctrine is based on a court having both personal and subject matter jurisdiction and there being at least one other jurisdiction where the case could be brought. *Id.* at 771.

Foreign support order. Proper registration of a foreign child support order gives the court where the order is registered subject matter jurisdiction to enforce or to modify the order. *R.J.R. v. C.J.S.*, 72 So. 3d 643 (Ala. App. 2011); *Sidell v. Sidell*, 18 A.3d 499 (R.I. 2011) (family court's subject matter jurisdiction over child custody and support decisions is governed by the UCCJEA and the UIFSA).

24.24. Hague Convention

Custody. Sometimes parents seek to enforce child custody orders across international boundaries and the question is what country has jurisdiction to consider the dispute. The Hague Convention on the Civil Aspects of International Child Abduction was created to resolve these jurisdictional issues between nations. It reflects a universal concern about the harm done to children by parental kidnaping and a strong desire among the contracting states to implement an effective deterrent to such behavior.

Hague Convention, Preamble, 42 U.S.C. §11601(a)(1)-(4). It applies only when both countries are signatories to the convention. *U.S. v. Amer*, 110 F.3d 873 (2d Cir. 1997).

The preamble to the Hague Convention states that it has two main purposes: First, to ensure the prompt return of children to the state of their habitual residence when they have been wrongfully removed. Second, to ensure that rights of custody and of access under the law of one contracting state are effectively respected in other contracting states. *Hague Convention, preamble*.

In general, the Hague Convention is intended to preserve the *status quo* with respect to child custody and to deter feuding parents from crossing international boundaries in search of a more sympathetic custody court. *Miller v. Miller*, 240 F.3d 392, 398 (4th Cir. 2001); *Baxter v. Baxter*, 423 F.3d 363, 367 (3d Cir. 2005); *Clarke v. Clarke*, 2008 WL 2217608 (E.D. Pa. 2008) ("The Convention procedures are not designed to settle international custody disputes, but rather to restore the *status quo* prior to any wrongful removal or retention, and to deter parents from engaging in international forum shopping in custody"); *Hanley v. Roy*, 485 F.3d 641 (11th Cir. 2007) (court considering International Child Abduction Remedies Act (ICARA) petition may not decide the underlying custody dispute, but only has jurisdiction to decide the merits of the wrongful removal claim).

The Convention applies to pre- and-post decree wrongful removals of children under the age of 16. *See generally Litigating International Child Abduction Cases Under the Hague Convention* (prepared by Kilpatrick Stockton LLP 2007).

Congressional implementation. In order to implement the provisions of the convention, Congress enacted the International Child Abduction Remedies Act (ICARA), 42 U.S.C.A. §§11601 et seq. ICARA establishes procedures, defines, and allocates the burden of proof for various claims and defenses under it. *See* 42 U.S.C. §11601 *et seq*. For example, ICARA requires that a petitioner under the Hague Convention establish, by a preponderance of the evidence, that the child whose return is sought has been "wrongfully removed or retained within the meaning of the Convention." 42 U.S.C. §11603(e)(1)(A).

The distinction between a Hague Convention petition brought pursuant to ICARA and a petition to determine the legal custody of a minor is that a Hague Convention petition affects custody, but it is not a custody determination. *See* Hague Convention, art. 19. The Hague Convention states that courts "shall not decide on the merits of rights of custody until it has been determined that the child is not to be returned under this Convention." Hague Convention, art. 16. The intention and effect of the Hague Convention, then, is to "lend priority to the custody determination hailing from the child's state of habitual residence." *Miller*, 240 F.3d at 399. As a result, a state court of competent jurisdiction may proceed to determine legal custody only when that court or a federal district court first finds that the petitioner cannot prove wrongful removal or retention or when the respondent establishes one of the available affirmative defenses.

Habitual residence. Courts sometimes struggle with the definition of "habitual residence." In *Interest of J. J. L.-P.*, 256 S.W.3d 363, 372 (Tex. App. 2008), the court said that the habitual residence inquiry proceeds on a case-by-case basis, and focuses not upon a child's domicile or legal residence but where the child physically lived "for an amount of time sufficient for acclimatization and which has a degree of settled purpose from the child's perspective. The determination of whether any particular place satisfies this standard focuses "on the child, not the parents, and examine[s] past experience, not future intentions." *Humphrey v. Humphrey*, 434 F.3d 243 (4th Cir. 2006) (father required to establish habitual residence by a preponderance of evidence); *but see Gitter v. Gitter*, 396 F.3d 124 (2d Cir. 2005) (courts must focus on parental intent when deciding habitual residence).

Burden of proof. A petitioner, to be successful, must prove by a preponderance of the evidence (1) that the child was habitually resident in the foreign country at the time the child was retained by the other parent in the United States, (2) that the retention was in breach of the petitioner's custody rights under the laws of the foreign country, and (3) that the petitioner had been exercising those custody rights at the time of retention. *See Miller*, 240 F.3d at 398; Hague Convention, art. 3.

Defenses. The party opposing the return of a child to a country outside the United States may prevail if he or she establishes certain defenses designated by ICARA and available under the Convention. For example, an opposing party might prevail if it is established by clear and convincing evidence (1) that there is a grave risk that returning the child to the foreign country would expose the child to physical or psychological harm or otherwise place him or her in an intolerable situation (Hague Convention, art. 13b), or (2) that the return of the child would not be permitted by the fundamental principles of the United States "relating to the protection of human rights and fundamental freedoms" (Hague Convention, art. 20). The opponent might also prevail if it is established by a preponderance of the evidence that the petitioner "was not actually exercising the custody rights at the time of . . . retention" (Hague Convention, art. 13a) or if it is shown that "the child objects to being returned and has attained an age and degree of maturity at which it is appropriate to take account of [the child's] views." Hague Convention, Art. 13, §2.

Grave risk of harm. A grave risk of harm for the purposes of the convention can exist in at least two situations. First, there is a grave risk of harm when return of the child puts the child in imminent danger prior to the resolution of the custody dispute, e.g., returning the child to a zone of war, famine, or disease. Second, there is a grave risk of harm in cases of serious abuse or neglect, or extraordinary emotional dependence, when the court in the country of habitual residence, for whatever reason, may be incapable or unwilling to give the child adequate protection. *Friedrich v. Friedrich*, 78 F.3d 1060, 1067 (6th Cir. 2003).

Intimate partner violence. The Hague Convention on the Civil Aspects of International Child Abduction is particularly useful as a jurisdictional tool when there are allegations of parental kidnapping. Research shows that some of these cases involve victims of intimate partner violence who cross international borders to keep themselves and their children safe. *See* Jeffrey L. Edleson, et al., *Multiple Perspectives on Battered Mothers and Their Children Fleeing to the United States for Safety: A Study of Hague Convention Cases*, http://www.haguedv.org/reports/finalreport.pdf (last visited July 2012).

Judge or jury trial? Note that cases brought pursuant to ICARA and the Hague Convention are tried to a judge because neither ICARA nor the Hague Convention provides for trial by jury and the available remedy—return of the child—is considered equitable in nature. *See Silverman v. Silverman*, 338 F.3d 886 (8th Cir. 2003). A total of 44 countries (including the United States) have joined the Hague Convention on the Civil Aspects of International Child Abduction.

Felony. Removing a child from the United States, or retaining a child who has been in the United States outside the United States with intent to obstruct the lawful exercise of parental rights, is a federal felony punishable by up to three years in prison. 18 U.S.C. §1204.

Child support. In 2007, the United States became a signatory to the Hague Convention on the International Recovery of Child Support and Other Forms of Family Maintenance, and as a consequence, the NCCUSL amended the UIFSA. National Conference of Commissioners on United States Law, *Uniform Interstate Family Support Act (last amended or revised in 2008) with Prefatory Note and Comments* (UIFSA), 43 Fam. L. Q. 75 (2009). The purpose of the amendments to UIFSA was to promote "recognition and enforcement of support orders across national boundaries." Battle Rankin Robinson, *Integrating an International Convention into State Law: The UIFSA Experience*, 43 Fam. L. Q. 61, 62 (2009).

Additional articles that provide helpful legal information about the Hague Convention include the following: Carol S. Bruch & Margaret M. Durkin, *The Hague's Online Child Abduction Materials: A Trap for the Unwary*, 44

Fam. L. Q. 65 (2010); Linda Silberman, *Interpreting the Hague Abduction Convention: In Search of a Global Jurisprudence*, 38 U.C. Davis L. Rev. 1049, 1065-1066 (2005); Anastacia M. Greene, *Seen and Not Heard? Children's Objections Under The Hague Convention on International Child Abduction*, 13 U. Miami Int'l & Comp. L. Rev. 105 (2005); Veronica Torrez, Cheryl Coleman, & Tina Burleson, *The International Abduction of International Children: Conflicts of Laws Federal Statutes, and Judicial Interpretation of the Hague Convention on the Civil Aspects of International Child Abduction*, 5 Whittier J. Child & Fam. Advoc. 7 (2005).

Examples

13. Assume that P and D were married and lived in state X for five years. When P lost his part-time job at a local fast-food restaurant, he decided he needed more education. He applied and was accepted to graduate school in state Y. While D remained in state X because of her good job that helped pay for P's room, board, and tuition, P moved to state Y to attend the university. After seven months, D was served with a divorce petition begun by P in state Y. In it, P asked that the marriage to D be dissolved and that P be awarded alimony of $150 a month. D did not answer, and a decree of divorce was granted to P in state Y, with the court awarding P $150 per month in alimony. After graduation, P moved back to state X and sought to enforce the judgment. D countered by asking the state X court to declare P's state Y divorce decree void. Most likely, how will a state X court rule?

14. Assume that a statute in state X reads as follows:

> In a proceeding to establish, enforce, or modify a support order or to determine parentage, a tribunal of this state may exercise personal jurisdiction over a nonresident individual or the individual's guardian or conservator if the child resides in this State as a result of the acts or directives of the individual.

Assume that P, a citizen of state Y, was awarded custody of child C in a divorce five years ago in state Y. D, the child's mother, who was living in state X, did not appear in state Y but consented to the action. However, last month, P became angry with C, purchased a bus ticket, and sent C to live with D, who still lives in state X. Assume that D brought an action in state X asking for child support. P, who has never been to state X, challenges the court's exercise of personal jurisdiction over him on a constitutional basis. State X has a long-arm statute that extends personal jurisdiction over a non-resident as far as the Constitution will permit. How will a judge in state X most likely rule on the challenge?

15. Assume that P asserts that D is the father of a child born out of wedlock. P is a citizen of state X and D a citizen of state Y. P initiates a paternity action in state X. D is served with a summons and complaint when D's private airplane touched down at the state X airport to refuel. The process server handed the papers to D while D was on his way to the airport restroom. D promptly threw the papers on the floor and returned to the airplane, which took off immediately. D argues that state X does not have personal jurisdiction over him because a short stopover to refuel cannot meet the minimum contacts requirements of the due process clause. How will a court most likely rule on the constitutional challenge?

16. Assume that P and D divorced at a time when the court in state X had subject matter and personal jurisdiction over the parties. D left the jurisdiction and had been away for ten years when P brought an action against D in state X to enforce provisions in the original divorce decree. P alleges that D has ignored provisions in the original decree relating to a car that was to be delivered in new condition, but was delivered in used condition and five years late. P also asserts that certain insurance policies that D was required by the divorce decree to keep in effect have lapsed, and that alimony and child support totaling $17,175 remain unpaid. D argues that state X cannot gain personal jurisdiction over him for these claims because of his long absence from that jurisdiction. How would a court most likely rule on these hypothetical facts?

17. Assume that P and D's marriage broke down, and after several years of separation, P brought a divorce action in state X. D, who lives in state Y, appeared in state X through her lawyers. Following entry of the divorce decree, D believes that the court in state X did not have personal jurisdiction over her — that she never personally appeared; only her lawyers appeared on her behalf. The record of the divorce proceedings in state X show that D's lawyers contested the divorce in state X alleging that she was not a *bona fide* resident of the state, as required by a statute in state X. The trial judge in state X expressly found that P was a *bona fide* resident of state X and granted the divorce. That ruling was not appealed by D's lawyers. D now collaterally attacks enforcement of the divorce action in state Y, claiming that the court in state X lacked personal jurisdiction over her. How will a court in state Y most likely rule?

18. Assume that P and D divorced in state Y and that state Y had personal jurisdiction over both parties at the time. Neither was awarded alimony, and alimony was not reserved. Two years following entry of the divorce decree, D moves to state X and remarries. P goes to state X and brings an action seeking alimony. D contends that the state X court may not hear the alimony action. How will a court most likely rule?

19. Assume that P and D were divorced in state X. The court in state X ordered that P pay D $1,000 a month permanent maintenance and $600 a month child support. Shortly after the divorce, P moved to state Y, while D remained in state X. P had the original divorce judgment registered in state Y. A few months after registering the judgment, P lost his job and brought an action in state Y to modify the maintenance and child support ordered in the original judgment and decree. P stated at the modification hearing in state Y that he had discussed the matter with D, and she did not necessarily object to the court hearing P's request. While written consent was not filed with the court in state Y, and D did not appear at the modification hearing, the trial judge believed that D had waived any challenge to the modification hearing's going forward. The judge in state Y reduced the support payments to $200 a month and suspended further maintenance payments. D has appealed the reduction in support. How will the appellate court most likely view the action?

20. Assume P and D are married and enrolled members of the "Z" Indian tribe and residents and domiciliaries of the tribal reservation in Minnesota. For a variety of reasons, they decide that a child to be born to them in about two months should be put up for adoption. They move from the reservation to a town in state Y, where the infant is born. Six weeks later, non-Indians through a state Y court adopt the infant. Two months following the adoption, the tribe to which P and D belong bring an action in state Y to vacate the adoption decree on the ground that under the ICWA, exclusive jurisdiction was vested in the tribal court. The parents of the newly adopted infant respond that P and D waived the jurisdiction of the ICWA by word and act. They present a written waiver signed by P and D in which P and D state that their intention is to "waive any provisions of law under the ICWA that might prevent the adoption under state law." How should a court rule?

21. Assume that P and D married and that P joined the U.S. Army. P got into difficulty with the army and incarcerated because he went absent without leave (AWOL). While P was incarcerated, D filed a divorce action in state X. P asked for a delay in the divorce proceedings arguing that he was protected by the SCRA. D argues that he is not protected by SCRA because he was not on active duty as the law required. D provides the court with several sections of SCRA, including 10 U.S.C. §101(d)(1) (2000), which states that "active duty" means "full-time duty in the active military service of the United States. Such term includes full-time training duty, annual training duty, and attendance, while in the active military service, at a school designated as a service school by law or by the Secretary of the military department concerned." P also argues that he has been denied due process under the

Fifth Amendment to the Constitution by this provision. How will a court most likely resolve P's issues?

22. Assume that P and D divorce and P is awarded custody of their two minor children by a judge in state X, where D and D's lawyer appeared. D, who is upset with the ruling and who is in the military, files a petition in federal district court asking that it issue an order staying the enforcement of the child custody order pending the end of D's military service in Afghanistan. A motion to dismiss the action has been brought by P. How will a court most likely rule?

EXPLANATIONS

Explanations

13. Recall that in *Pennoyer v. Neff*, 95 U.S. 714 (1877), the Supreme Court stated that

> The jurisdiction which every State possesses to determine the *civil status* and capacities of all its inhabitants involves authority to prescribe the conditions on which proceedings affecting them may be commenced and carried on within its territory. The State, for example, has absolute right to prescribe the conditions upon which the marriage relation between its own citizens shall be created, and the causes for which it may be dissolved.

Id. at 734-735.

Therefore, so long as P has met the subject matter conditions that state Y established for granting a divorce, P and D are divorced, and all sister states will normally recognize that the relationship is dissolved. Consequently, D's action to have the divorce portion of the judgment in state Y voided normally would be dismissed, despite the fact that the divorcing court did not have personal jurisdiction over D.

However, the portion of the state Y judgment and decree dealing with the $150 monthly alimony payment will not be recognized in state X. This is a personal obligation, which is unrelated to the "status" of the couple's relationship. When the state Y court issued its decree, it did not have personal jurisdiction over D; therefore, it could not impose on D any personal obligations. Note that there is no suggestion in the example that D consented to or waived the personal jurisdiction defense.

14. This example is based on *Kulko v. Superior Court*, 436 U.S. 84 (1978). While the facts are not identical to those found in *Kulko*, they are not so dissimilar as to change the jurisdictional outcome. Here, regardless of the statutory language that provides the court with authority to bring a nonresident before it in a child support action, the due process clause of the Fourteenth Amendment will bar the application of the long-arm statute. P does not have sufficient minimum contacts with state X to satisfy the Constitution. D must seek to obtain child support under state X's UIFSA, or proceed to state Y and initiate a child support action in that state.

15. The state X court has personal jurisdiction over D because D was served within the boundaries of state X. There is no constitutional basis for D's argument. *See In re Gonzalez*, 993 S.W.2d 147 (Tex. App. 1999) (personal service effected on father while his plane touched down in state for refueling authorized exercise of personal jurisdiction).

16. It is quite likely a court will agree with P and reject D's defense. Here, state X was the original marital domicile. A due process argument can be made to support P as follows: The parties chose to resolve their marital dispute in state X, and thus D purposefully availed himself of the privilege of conducting activities within state X. At the time, it was foreseeable that a future breach of the agreement could lead to D being called into a court in state X.

    Furthermore, a court may reason that a finding that state X continues to have jurisdiction over the parties protects D from arbitrarily being sued in any other state. It may also reason that while D has not been a resident or transacted business in state X for ten years since the divorce decree, the obligations of that judgment have attached, and the obligations may constitute continuing contacts sufficient to satisfy due process.

17. A court in state Y will most likely dismiss D's challenge. Once parties participate in a proceeding in person or by their lawyers, even if it is later discovered that the court lacked personal jurisdiction, the issue cannot be successfully raised collaterally. The reason for this is that the party has made an appearance, and the party has been afforded an opportunity to be heard. *See Sherrer v. Sherrer*, *supra*, at 350-351 of 334 U.S. In this example, D's lawyers made an appearance and failed to challenge personal jurisdiction. Rather, they contested the provisions of a statute that they said did not apply to their client. They lost their argument and failed to appeal the trial judge's ruling. This is sufficient to constitute a waiver of a challenge to personal jurisdiction.

18. D will most likely be successful in preventing the court from hearing the action. D will contend that the action in state Y is *res judicata* and must be enforced under the full faith and credit clause of the federal Constitution, which reads as follows: "Full Faith and Credit shall be given in each state to the public acts, Records, and Judicial Proceedings of every other state." U.S. Const. art. 4, §1. When there is nothing in the judgment and decree dissolving a marriage that reserves for a future date the question of alimony, most, if not all, jurisdictions will take the view that alimony was permanently waived.

19. A literal application of the language in the FFCCSOA should result in a ruling that the court in one state did not have subject matter jurisdiction to modify the existing child support order. As a result, the lower court's judgment most likely will be vacated and the matter dismissed.

    The reason for the dismissal is that when the FFCCSOA became effective, it generally deprived courts in state Y of subject matter jurisdiction to modify an amount of child support of an order entered by another state and registered under URESA (now UIFSA). *See, e.g., Paton v. Brill*, 663 N.E.2d 421 (Ohio App. 1995) (Ohio court did not have jurisdiction to modify child support order pursuant to original Maryland divorce decree). The Act requires each state to enforce a child support order made by a court of another state.

    Pursuant to the statute, state courts are to refrain from modifying an existing order in another state unless the court of the other state no longer has continuing and exclusive jurisdiction of the child support order either because the child or any contestant is no longer a resident of the state, or each party has filed written consent in the original state, agreeing to permit the new state to modify the order. Here, D continues to reside in state X with the child, and neither party filed written consent in state X that the matter could be heard in state Y.

20. Despite the efforts of P and D, the court most likely will rule that the adoption is void and that subject matter jurisdiction rests with the Indian tribe. *Mississippi Band of Choctaw Indians v. Holyfield*, 490 U.S. 30 (1989). Recall that in *Holyfield*, the children were "domiciled" on the Indian reservation within the meaning of the Act's exclusive tribal jurisdiction provision, even though they were never physically present on the reservation themselves. Furthermore, the Court said that the state court lacked jurisdiction to enter an adoption decree, even though the children were "voluntarily surrendered" for adoption. In this hypothetical, the child was "domiciled" on the tribe's reservation within the meaning of the ICWA's exclusive tribal jurisdiction provision when it was born; therefore, the state court was without jurisdiction to enter the

adoption decree. A child under the ICWA takes the reservation domicile of its mother at birth — notwithstanding that the child was born off the reservation.

Note that Congress enacted the ICWA because of concerns going beyond the wishes of individual parents, finding that the removal of Indian children from their cultural setting seriously affects long-term tribal survival and has a damaging social and psychological impact on many individual Indian children. These concerns demonstrate that Congress could not have intended to enact a rule of domicile that would permit individual Indian parents to defeat the ICWA's jurisdictional scheme simply by giving birth and placing the child for adoption off the reservation.

21. Most courts have concluded that SCRA does not protect service members who are incarcerated in military prison or who are AWOL because such service members are not on active duty and are not absent from duty due to a lawful cause. *See, e.g.*, *United States v. Hampshire*, 95 F.3d 999, 1005 (10th Cir. 1996); *Mantz v. Mantz*, 69 N.E.2d 637, 639 (Ohio Com. Pl. 1946) (stating that the SCRA does not protect "those who through their voluntary aggressions and conduct remove themselves from the role of service members in active service or duty"); *Means v. Means*, 45 Pa. D. & C.2d 228, 231 (Pa. Com. Pl. 1968) (asking, "[c]an it be said in logic or reason that to permit [an AWOL service member's] wife to proceed with her divorce action prevents him from devoting his full energy to the defense needs of the Nation, or can it say that he has absented himself for any lawful cause?"). Because P was incarcerated in military prison for crimes that he committed while on active duty, he was not on active duty at the time of the dissolution proceeding and therefore was not entitled to the protections of the SCRA.

The court most likely also will reject the Fifth Amendment equal protection argument that the statute has created a class of service members who are unable to use the protections of the SCRA. His argument that, other than his confinement, there is no legitimate basis on which to differentiate P from nonconfined active duty personnel will be rejected. The court will reason that a service member who is serving time confined in a military prison for crimes committed while in military service is not situated similarly to service members not so confined. Therefore, P's confinement alone is not a legitimate basis to treat him differently from non-confined service members. The court most likely will conclude that because P has failed to show that he is being treated differently from similarly situated service members, his equal protection argument will fail. *See Reed v. Albaaj*, 723 N.W.2d 50 (Minn. App. 2006).

22. On these hypothetical facts, the federal court will most likely dismiss the request for injunctive relief. Note that under the Anti-Injunction Act, 28 U.S.C. §2283 (1948), a federal court may not stay a state court proceeding "except as expressly authorized by Act of Congress, or where necessary in aid of its jurisdiction, or to protect or effectuate its judgments." The SSCRA does not contain language that expressly authorizes the federal court to issue a stay against a state court proceeding.

Table of Cases

390 West End Associates v. Wildfoerster, 661 N.Y.S.2d 202 (N.Y. App. 1997), 488

A.G.R. ex rel. Conflenti v. Huff, 815 N.E.2d 120 (Ind. App. 2004), 280
A.H.W. v. G.H.B., 772 A.2d 948 (N.J. Super. Ch. 2000), 574
A.M.S. ex rel. Farthing v. Stopplewworth, 694 N.W.2d 8 (N.D. 2005), 327
A.R.B. v. G.L.P., 507 P.2d 468 (Colo. 1973), 715
A.S.B. v. Dep't of Children & Family Servs., 688 N.E.2d 1215, 1220-1225 (Ill. App. 1997), 513
A.Z. v. B.Z., 725 N.E.2d 1051, 1057 (2000), 560
Abderholden v. Morizot, 856 S.W.2d 829, 834 (Tex. App. 1993), 253
Abouzahr v. Abouzahr-Matera, 824 A.2d 268 (N.J. Super. 2003), 278
Adar v. Smith, 639 F.3rd 146 (5th Cir. 2011), 529
Adoption of Michelle T., 117 Cal. Rptr. 856 (Cal. App. 1975), 529
Agraz v. Carnley, 143 S.W.3d 547, 552 (Tex. App. 2004), 200
Aiken v. Stanley, 816 N.E.2d 427 (Ind. App. 2004), 581
Aka v. Jefferson Hospital Association, Inc., 42 S.W.3d 508 (Ark. 2001), 564
Akron v. Akron Center for Reproductive Health, 497 U.S. 502 (1990) (Akron II), 630, 636
Albert v. Albert, 707 A.2d 234 (Pa. Super. Ct. 1998), 363
Alexander v. Armstrong, 609 A.2d 183 (Pa. Super. 1992), 301
Alexandria S. v. Pacific Fertility, 64 Cal. Rptr. 2d 23 (Cal. App. 1997), 563
Alfaro v. U.S., 859 A.2d 149 (D.C. 2004), 134
Alford v. Alford, 478 N.Y.S.2d 717, 718 (N.Y. App. Div. 1984), 388
Alison D. v. Virginia M., 569 N.Y.S.2d 586, 589 (N.Y. App. 1991), 11
Alison D. v. Virginia M., 572 N.E.2d 27 (N.Y. 1991), 291
Allen v. Allen, 330 P.2d 151 (Or. 1958), 538
Allen v. Allen, 477 N.E.2d104 (Ind. App. 1985), 316-317
Allen v. Allen, 787 So. 2d 215 (Fla. App. 2001), 277
American Academy of Pediatrics v. Lungren, 940 P.2d 797 (Cal. 1997), 646
Anderson v. Anderson, 382 N.W.2d 620, 621 (Neb. 1986), 151
Anderson v. Anderson, 56 S.W.3d 5 (Tenn. App. 1999), 221
Anderson v. State of Colorado, 793 F.2d 262, 263-265 (10th Cir. 1986), 690
Angelet v. Shivar, 602 S.W.2d 185 (Ky. App. 1980), 485
Angelos v. Angelos, 367 N.W.2d 518, 519 (Minn. 1985), 705
Ankenbrandt v. Richards, 504 U.S. 689, 700 (1992), 685
Anonymous v. Anonymous, 268 N.Y.S.2d 710 (N.Y. Fam. 1966), 715
Anonymous v. Anonymous, 530 N.Y.S.2d 613, 617 (N.Y. App. Div. 3 Dept. 1988), 531
Anthony H. v. Matthew G., 725 S.E.2d 132 (S.C. App. 2012), 249
Arch Aluminum & Glass Co., Inc. v. Haney, 964 So.2d 228 (Fla. App. 2007), 706
Ardizoni v. Raymond, 667 N.E.2d 885 (Mass. App. 1996), 205
Arneson v. Arneson, 355 N.W.2d 16, 19 (Wis. App. 1984), 387
Arneson v. Arneson, 670 N.W.2d 904 (S.D. 2003), 178
Artibee v. Cheboygan Circuit Judge, 243 N.W.2d 248, 250 (Mich. 1976), 500
Ascuitto v. Farricielli, 711 A.2d 708 (Conn. 1998), 222
Atchison v. Atchison, 664 N.W.2d 249 (Mich. App. 2003), 256
Atkinson v. Atkinson, 408 N.W.2d 516 (1987), 513
Ayers v. Ayers, 508 N.W.2d 515, 519 (Minn. 1993), 231
Ayotte v. Planned Parenthood of New England, 546 U.S. 320 (2006), 644

Azia v. *DiLascia*, 780 A.2d 992 (Conn. App. 2001), 213

B.S. v. F.B., N.Y.S.2d 458 (N.Y. Sup. 2009), 717
Babcock v. *Adams*, 196 S.W. 1118 (Mo. 191), 7, 16
Bagnardi v. Hartnett, 366 N.Y.S.2d 89, 91 (N.Y. 1975), 62
Bagwell v. Bagwell, 698 So. 2d 746 (La. App. 1997), 319
Baker v. Baker, 753 N.W.2d 644, 651 (Minn. 2008), 385
Baker v. Baker, 494 N.W.2d 282, 288 (Minn. 1992), 585, 708
Baker v. Baker, 537 P.2d 171 (Kan. 1975), 315
Baker v. Nelson, 191 N.W.2d 185, 186 (Minn. 1971), 119
Baker v. State, 744 A.2d 864 (Vt. 1999), 77
Baldwin v. Sullivan, 204 N.W. 420, 421-423 (Iowa 1925), 486
Ball v. Ball, 445 S.E.2d 449 (S.C. 1994), 399
Ball v. Smith, 150 S.W.3d 889 (Tex. App. 2004), 475
Barber v. State, 50 Md. 161 (Md. App. 1878), 59
Barber v. Barber, 62 U.S. 582, 584 (1858), 685
Barbosa-Johnson v. Johnson, 851 P.2d 866 (Ariz. App. 1993), 23, 28, 43
Barnes v. Barnes, 107 P.3d 560 (Okla. 2005), 669
Barnes v. Barnes, 428 S.E.2d 294, 297 (1993), 135
Barnes v. Jeudevine, 718 N.W.2d 311 (Mich. 2006), 502
Barnes v. State of Miss., 992 F.2d 1335 (5th Cir. 1993), 643
Barnhart v. Madvig, 526 S.W.2d 106 (Tenn. 1975), 715
Barrons v. United States 191 F.2d 92 (9th Cir. 1951), 49
Barry v. Barry, 862 N.E. 2d 143, 146 (Ohio App. 2006), 183
Bartsch v. Bartsch, 636 N.W.2d 3 (Iowa 2001), 708
Bast v. Bast, 82 Ill. 584 (Ill. 1876), 140
Bator v. Osborne, 983 So.2d 1198 (Fla. App., 2008), 304
Bauer v. Bauer, 356 N.W.2d 897, 898-899 (N.D. 1984), 372
Bauer v. Bauer, 464 P.2d 710, 711-12 (Or. App. 1970), 434
Baures v. Lewis, 770 A.2d 214, 230-31 (N.J. 2001), 225, 227
Baxendale v. Raich, 878 N.E.2d 1252 (Ind. 2008), 219
Beal v. Doe, 432 U.S. 438 (1977), 644
Beard v. Banks, 548 U.S. 521(2006), 57
Beard v. Beard, 751 N.Y.S.2d 304 (App. Div. 2002), 362
Beckley v. Beckley, 115 Ill. App. 27 (1904), 118
Beddow v. Beddow, 257 S.W.2d 45 (Ky. 1953), 107
Behrens v. Rimland, 32 A.D. 3d 929 (N.Y. 2006), 290
Bell v. Arnold, 279 S.E.2d 449 (Ga. 1981), 715
Bell v. Bell, 468 N.E.2d 849 (Mass. 1984), 373
Bellotti v. Baird, 443 U.S. 622 (1979), 642
Belsito v. Clark, 644 N.E.2d 760 (Ohio Com. Pl. 1994), 557
Beltran v. Allan, 926 P.2d 892, 897-898 (Utah App. 1996), 513
Benjamin v. McKinnon, 887 N.E.2d 14 (Ill. App. 2008), 581
Bennett v. Jeffreys, 356 N.E.2d 277 (N.Y. App. 1976), 171
Berkely v. Berkely, 75 Cal. Rptr. 294 (Cal. App. 1969), 95
Bethany v. Jones, 2011 Ark. 67, 11-12,— S.W.3d—(Ark. 2011, 291
Biercevicz v. Liberty Mut. Ins. Co., 865 A.2d 1267 (Conn. Super. 2004), 485
Bishop v. Bishop, 2010 WL 4151988 (Ala. App. 2010), 375, 376
Bishop v. Bishop, 671 A.2d 644 (N.J. Super. 1995), 314
Bishop v. Bishop, 2010 WL 4151988 (Ala. App. 2010, 376
Bjordahl v. Bjordahl, 308 N.W.2d 817 (Minn. 1981), 705
Black v. Black, 199 P.3d 371 (Utah App. 2008), 470
Black v. Rasile, 318 N.W.2d 475, 476 (Mich. App. 1982), 702
Blair v. Supreme Court of State of *Wyo.*, 671 F.2d 389 (10th Cir. 1982), 712
Blaisure v. Blaisure, 577 A.2d 640, 642 (Pa. Super. 1990), 300
Block v. Block, 717 N.Y.S.2d 24 (N.Y. App. Div. 2000), 370
Boddie v. Connecticut, 401 U.S. 371 (1971), 70
Boehs v. Hanger, 59 A. 904 (N.J. Eq. 1905), 118
Boggs v. Boggs, 520 U.S. 833 (1997), 397, 415

Boggs v. Boggs, 383 N.E.2d 9 (Ill. App. 1978), 197
Borcherding v. Borcherding, 566 N.W.2d 90, 93 (Minn. App. 1997), 328
Bosveld v. Bosveld, 7 N.W.2d 782, 785 (Iowa 1943), 141
Boswell v. Boswell, 701 A.2d 1153 (Md. App. 1997), 278
Bourassa v. Bourassa, 481 N.W.2d 113, 115 (Minn. App. 1992), 358
Bovard v. Baker, 775 A.2d 835, 841 (Pa. Super. 2001), 213
Bowers v. Hardwick, 478 U.S. 186 (1986), 76
Boynton v. Kusper, 494 N.E.2d 135 (1986), 70
Braam ex rel. Braam v. State, 81 P.3d 851 (Wash. 2003), 614
Brandt v. Brandt, 268 P.3d 406 (Colo. 2012), 254
Branum v. State, 829 N.E.2d 622 (Ind. App. 2005), 330
Brausch v. Brausch, 770 N.W.2d 77 (Mich. App. 2009), 256
Breithaupt v. Abram, 352 U.S. 432, 436, 448 (1957), 28
Brewer v. Brewer, 533 S.E.2d 541 (N.C. App. 2000), 171
Brewer v. Miller, 673 S.W.2d 530 (Tenn. App. 1984), 105
Brooks v. Brooks, 257 S.W.3d 418 (Tex. App. 2008), 352
Brooks v. Brooks, 652 So. 2d 1113, 1124 (Miss. 1995), 134
Brooks v. Brooks, 733 P.2d 1044 (Alaska 1987), 423
Brooks v. Sanders, 190 P.3d 357, 362 (Okla. App. 2008), 45
Brown v. Brown, 665 S.E.2d 174 (S.C. App. 2008), 354
Brown v. Brown, 847 S.W.2d 496, 499 (Tenn. 1993), 243, 707
Brown v. Brown, 37 S.E.2d 89 (Va. 1977), 208
Brown v. Board of Education, 347 U.S. 483 (1954), 54
Brown v. Devine, 574 F. Supp. 790, 792 (N.D. Cal. 1983), 35
Brown v. Erbstoesser, 85 A.D.3d 1497 (N.Y. App. Div. 32011), 283
Brown's Appeal, 44 A. 22 (Conn. 1899), 132
Bruemmer v. Bruemmer, 616 S.E.2d 740 (Va. App. 2005), 300
Buffington v. Buffington, 51 N.E. 328, 329 (Ind. 1898), 421
Burchard v. Garay, 724 P.2d 486 (Cal. 1986), 182
Burkstrand v. Burkstrand, 632 N.W.2d 206 (Minn. 2001), 708
Burnett v. Burnett, 542 S.E.2d 911 (W. Va. 2000), 714
Burnham v. Superior Court, 495 U.S. 604 (1990), 704
Burns v. Burns, 538 A.2d 438 (N.J. Super. Ct. 1987), 1
Burns v. Burns, 560 S.E.2d 47 (Ga. 2002), 84
Burns v. Stewart, 188 N.W.2d 760 (Minn. 1971), 676
Burr v. Burr, 353 N.W.2d 644 (Minn. App. 1984), 371
Burtoff v. Burtoff, 418 A.2d 1085, 1089 (D.C. App. 1980), 428
Burton v. Bishop, 269 S.E.2d 417 (Ga. 1980), 242
Button v. Button, 388 N.W.2d 546 (Wis. 1986), 453

C.M. v. C.C., 967 N.Y.S.2d 884 (N.Y. Sup. 2008), 154
C.M. v. C.C., 377 A.2d 821 (N.J. Super 1977), 551
C.M.K. v. K.E.M., 45 A.3d 417 (Pa. Super. 2012), 226
Caban v. Mohammed, 441 U.S. 380 (1979), 532
Califano v. Webster, 430 U.S. 313, 316-317 (1977), 346
Callen v. Callen, 620 S.E.2d 59 (S.C. 2005), 33
Campbell v. Campbell, 339 S.E.2d 591 (Ga. 1986), 408
Cann v. Howard, 850 S.W.2d 57, 60 (Ky. App. 1993), 247
Carlson v. Carlson, 661 P.2d 833 (Kan. App. 1983), 219
Carlson v. Olson, 256 N.W.2d 249, 255 (Minn. 1977), 464
Carpenter v. Carpenter, 617 N.Y.S.2d 903 (1994), 46, 63
Carpenter v. Carpenter, 722 P.2d 230 (Ariz. 1986), 380
Carter v. Carter, 479 S.E.2d 681 (W. Va. 1996), 282
Cassens v. Cassens, 430 F. Supp. 2d 830 (S.D. Ill. 2006), 685
Cato v. Alcoa-Reynolds Metals Co., 152 P.3d 981 (Or. App. 2007), 486
Cawood v. Haggard, 327 F. Supp. 2d 863 (E.D. Tenn. 2004), 460

Chambers v. Ormiston, 935 A.2d 956 (R.I. 2007), 717
Chandler v. Chandler, 409 S.E.2d 203 (Ga. 1991), 278
Charlton v. Charlton, 413 S.E.2d 911, 915 (W. Va. 1991), 388
Charron v. Amaral, 889 N.E.2d 946 (Mass. 2008), 485
Chastain v. Chastain, 672 S.E.2d 108 (S. C. App. 2009), 140
Chastain v. Chastain, 346 S.E.2d 33, 35 (S. C. App. 1986), 325
Chen v. Warner, 695 N.W.2d 758 (Wis. 2005), 324
Cheshire Med. Ctr. v. Holbrook, 663 A.2d 1344 (N.H. 1995), 347, 348
Cheverie v. Cheverie, 898 So. 2d 1028 (Fla. App. 2005), 309
Chiba v. Greenwald, 67 Cal. Rptr. 3d 86 (Cal. App. 2007), 468
Chinn v. State, 26 N.E. 986, 987 (1890), 62
Christians v. Christians, 44 N.W.2d 431 (Iowa 1950), 441
Christofferson v. Giese, 691 N.W.2d 195 (N.D. 2005), 302
Cincinnati Women's Services, Inc. v. Taft, 468 F.3d 361 (6th Cir. 2006), 651
City of Akron v. Akron Center for Reproductive Health, Inc., 462 U.S. 416 (1983), 630, 636
Clara L. v. Paul M., 673 N.Y.S.2d 657 (N.Y. App. 1998), 213
Clark v. Clark, 2012 WL 1089198 (unpublished) (Conn. 2012), 693
Clark v. Clark, 827 N.Y.S.2d 159 (2006), 375
Clark v. Jeter, 486 U.S. 456 (1988), 511
Clermont v. Clermont, 603 N.Y.S.2d 923 (N.Y. App. 1933), 452
Cochran v. Cochran, 5 So.3d 1220 (Ala. 2008), 217
Cochran v. Cochran, 66 Cal. Rptr. 2d 337 (Cal. App. 1997), 488
Cochran v. Cochran, 432 P.2d 752 (Colo. 1967), 134
Cohen v. Cohen, 875 A.2d 814 (Md. App. 2005), 280
Cohn v. Cohn, 121 A.2d 704 (Md. 1956), 422
Colautti v. Franklin, 439 U.S. 379 (1979), 635
Cole v. Cole, 556 N.Y.S.2d 217 (Fam. 1990), 588
Cole v. Cole, 940 A.2d 194 (Me. 2008), 581
Cole v. Conn., 712 S.E.2d 759, 762 (Va. App. 2011), 59
Cole v. State, 94 A. 913, 914 (Md. 1915), 124
Cole v. State Farm Ins. Co., 128 P.3d 171 (Alaska 2006), 484, 486
Cole v. Wyatt, 116 P.3d 919, 921 (Or. App. 2005), 212
Colorado River Water Conservation Dist. v. United States, 626 U.S. 800, 814 (1976), 692
Colson and Peil, 51 P.3d 607 (Or. App. 2002), 33, 226
Com. v. Brumbaugh, 932 A.2d 108 (Pa. Super. 2007), 589
Com. v. Rahim, 805 N.E.2d 13 (Mass. 2004), 62
Combs v. Tibbitts, 148 P.3d 430 (Colo. App. 2006), 468
Committee to Defend Reprod. Rights v. Myers, 625 P.2d 779 (Cal. 1981), 647
Commonwealth ex rel. Marshall v. Marshall, 15 S.W.3d 396 (Ky. App. 2000), 327
Commonwealth v. Rodgers, 528 A.2d 610 (Pa. Super. 1987), 612
Condore v. Prince George's Co., 425 A.2d 1011, 1019 (Md. 1981), 347
Congdon v. Congdon, 578 S.E.2d 833 (Va. 2003), 355
Conlon by Conlon v. Heckler, 719 F.2d 788, 795-796 (5th Cir. 1983), 698
Conness v. Satram, 18 Cal. Rptr. 3d 577 (Cal. App. 2004), 588
Connolly v. Connolly, 892 A.2d 465 (Me. 2006), 583
Cook v. Cook, 691 P.2d 664 (Ariz. 1984), 478
Cook v. Cook, 342 U.S. 126 (1951), 697
Cooper v. Cooper, 144 P.3d 451 (Alaska 2006), 587
Cooper v. Gress, 854 So. 2d 262, 265 (Fla. App. 2003), 199
Copeland v. McLean, 763 N.E.2d 941 (Ill. App. 2002), 134
Cote-Whitacre v. Department of Public Health, 844 N.E.2d 623 (Mass. 2006), 85
Couch v. Couch, 146 S.W.3d 923 (Ky. 2004), 179
County of Dane v. Norman, 497 N.W.2d 714, 716 (Wis. 1993), 488
Courson v. Courson, 117 A.2d 850 (Md. App. 1955), 139
Coyle v. Erickson, 2011 WL 3689157 (2011), 557
Craig L. v. Sandy S., 125 Cal. App. 4th 36 (Cal. App. 2004), 504
Cramer v. Petrie, 637 N.E.2d 882 (Ohio 1994), 332

Crawford v. Crawford, 392 S.E.2d 675, 676 (S.C. App. 1990), 160
Crawford v. Washington, 541 U.S. 36 (2004), 592
Cregan v. Clark, 658 S.W.2d 924 (Mo. App. 1983), 151
Crespo v. Crespo, 972 A.2d 1169 (N.J. Super. 2009), 585
Crocker v. Finley, 459 N.E.2d 1346 (Ill. 1984), 70
Crouch v. Wartenberg, 104 S.E. 117 (W. Va. 1920), 111
Crowe v. De Gioia, 495 A.2d 889 (N.J. Super. 1985), 464
Cruickshank-Wallace v. County Banking and Trust Co., 885 A.2d 403 (Md. App 2005), 345
Cullum v. Cullum, 160 P.3d 231 (Ariz. App., 2007), 358
Cupstid v. Cupstid, 724 So. 2d 238 (La. App. 1998), 312
Curran v. Scharpf, 726 S.E.2d 407, 152
Curtis v. Curtis, 442 N.W.2d 173, 177-178 (Minn. App. 1989), 367
Curtis v. Firth, 850 P.2d 749 (Idaho 1993), 593

D.D. v. Idant Laboratories, 374 Fec. Appx. 319 (3d Cir. 2010), 563
D.K.H. v. L.R.G., 102 S.W.3d 93, 100 (Mo. App. 2003), 384
D'Onofrio v. D'Onofrio, 365 A.2d 27, 29-30 (N.J. Super. 1976), 221
Darling v. Darling, 335 N.E.2d 708 (Conn. Super. 1975), 104
David M. v. Margaret M., 385 S.E.2d 912, 920 (W. Va. 1989), 213
Davis v. Davis, 643 So.2d 931 (Miss. 1994), 490
Davis v. Davis, 116 S.W.2d 607 (Ark. 1938), 443
Davis v. Davis, 842 S.W.2d 588 (Tenn. 1992), 561
Davis v. Heath, 128 P.3d 434 (Kan. App. 2006), 288
Davis v. Knafel, 837 N.E.2d 585 (Ind. App. 2005), 327
Davis v. Spriggs, 2010 WL 4881491 (unpublished) (Ohio App. 2010), 151
Davis v. Washington, 126 S. Ct. 2266 (2006), 592
De Burgh v. De Burgh, 250 P.2d 598 (Cal. 1952), 140
De La Hay v. De La Hay, 21 Ill. 251, 254 (1859), 142
De La Rosa v. De La Rosa, 309 N.W.2d 755 (Minn. 1981), 405, 416
Deacon v. Landers, 587 N.E.2d 395 (Ohio App. 1990), 587
Debra H. v. Janice R., 61 A.D.3d 460 (N.Y.A.D. 2009), 516
Deegan v. Deegan, 603 A.2d 542 (N.J. App. 1992), 367, 369
Del Vecchio v. Del Vecchio, 143 So. 2d 17 (Fla. 1962), 423, 435, 441
DeMatteo v. DeMatteo, 762 N.E.2d 797 (Mass. 2002), 454
DeMauro v. DeMauro, 115 F.3d 94 (1st Cir. 1997), 693
Department of Human Services v. Chisum, 85 P.3d 860 (Okla. App. 2004), 509
Dept. of Rev. v. Nesbitt, 975 So.2d 549 (Fla. App. 2008), 335
DeShaney v. Winnebago County Dept. of Soc. Servs., 489 U.S. 189 (1989), 614
Detwiler v. Detwiler, 57 A.2d 426 (Pa. Super. 1948), 314
Devaney v. L'Esperance, 949 A.2d 743 (N.J. 2008), 484
Dinges v. Dinges, 743 N.W.2d 662, 671 (Neb. App. 2008), 401
Disciplinary Counsel v. Engler, 851 N.E.2d 502 (Ohio 2006), 673
Dist. of Columbia Court of Appeals v. Feldman, 460 U.S. 462 (1983), 691
Division of Youth and Family Services v. D.F., 781 A.2d 699 (N.J. Super. A.D. 2005), 610
Dobson v. Dobson, 193 P.2d 794 (Cal. App.1948), 114
Dodge v. Dodge, 505 S.E.2d 344 (S.C. App. 1998), 293
Doe v. Attorney General, 487 N.W.2d 484 (1992), 553
Doe v. Bolton, 410 U.S. 179 (1973), 625, 627, 637, 650
Doe v. Kearney, 329 F.3d 1286 (11th Cir. 2003), 611
Doe v. South Carolina Department of Social Services, 597 F.3d 1631 (4th Cir. 2010), 614
Doerrfeld v. Konz, 524 So. 2d 1115, 1116-1117 (Fla. App. 1988), 315
Dolan v. Dolan, 259 A.2d 32 (Me. 1969), 119
Downey v. Muffley, 767 N.E.2d 1014 (Ind. App. 2002), 278
Downey v. Zwigart, 5378 N.W.2d 639 (Minn. App. 1985), 203
Downs v. Downs, 574 A.2d 156 (Vt. 1990), 404
Drahos v. Rens, 717 P.2d 927, 928 (Ariz. App. 1985), 380

Drapek v. Drapek, 503 N.E.2d 946 (Mass. 1987), 404
Drummond v. Fulton County Department of Family & Children's Services, 563 F.2d 1200 (5th Cir. 1977), 177
DuBray v. S.D. Dept. of Social Services, 690 N.W.2d 657 (S.D. 2004), 610
Dunn v. Cometa, 238 F.3d 38 (1st Cir. 2001), 689, 690
Dunn v. Dunn, 775 N.W.2d 486, 491-92 (N.D. 2009), 197
Dusenberry v. Dusenberry, 326 S.E.2d 65 (N.C. App. 1985), 388

E.N.O. v. L.M.M., 711 N.E.2d 886 (Mass. 1999), 291
Ebach v. Ebach, 757 N.W.2d 34, 36 (N.D. 2008), 192
Ebach v. Ebach, 700 N.W.2d 684 (N.D. 2005), 366
Edwards v. Edwards, 744 N.W.2d 243 (Neb. App. 2008), 431
Edwardson v. Edwardson, 798 S.W.2d 941, 946 (Ky. 1990), 436
Egbert v. Egbert, 569 S.E.2d 727, 729 (N.C. App. 203), 717
Egbert v. Greenwalt, 6 N.W. 654 (1880), 494
Egle v. Egle, 715 F.2d 999 (5th Cir. 1983), 282
Eifert v. Eifert, 724 N.W.2d 109 (N.D. 2006), 171
Eisenstadt v. Baird, 405 U.S. 438 (1972), 626
Elisa B. v. Superior Court, 33 Cal. Rptr. 3d 46 (Cal. 2005), 551
Ellerbe v. Hooks, 416 A.2d 512 (Pa. 1980), 228
Ellis v. Ellis, 262 N.W.2d 265, 268 (Iowa 1978), 367
Ellis v. Ellis, 840 So. 2d 806 (Miss. App. 2003), 282
Embry v. Ryan, 2009 WL 1311599 (Fla. App. 2009), 528
English v. English, 879 P.2d 802, 808 (N.M. App. 1994), 401
Engrassia v. Di Lullo, 454 N.Y.S.2d 103 (N.Y. App. 1982), 317
Entwistle v. Entwistle, 402 N.Y.S.2d 213 (N.Y. App. 1978), 205
Eschbach v. Eschbach, 451 N.Y.S.2d 658 (N.Y. 1982), 212
Esser v. Esser, 586 S.E.2d 627 (Ga. 2003), 664
Estate of Lemont, 86 Cal. Rptr. 810 (Cal. App. 1970), 106, 109
Estate of Leslie, 689 P.2d 133 (Cal. 1984), 36
Estate of Serbus v. Serbus, 324 N.W.2d 381 (Minn. 1982), 451
Estelle v. McGuire, 502 U.S. 62, 66, 70 (1991), 612
Estin v. Estin, 334 U.S. 541 (1948), 156, 698, 714
Etter v. Rose, 684 A.2d 1092 (Pa. Super. 1996), 276
Evans v. Braun, 12 A.3d 395 (Pa. Super. 2010), 581
Evans v. Wall, 542 So. 2d 1055 (Fla. 3d DCA 1989), 480
Everetts v. Apfel, 214 F.3d 990 (8th Cir. 2000), 94
Everson v. Board of Educ., 330 U.S. 1, 15 (1947), 143
Ex parte Devine, 398 So. 2d 686 (Ala. 1981), 169
Ex parte Threet, 333 S.W.2d 361 (Tex. 1960), 45
Ex parte Walters, 580 So. 2d 1352, 1354 (Ala. 1991), 453
Exxon Mobil Corp. v. Saudi Basic Indus. Corp., 544 U.S. 280, 284 (2005), 691, 713

Faivre v. Faivre, 128 A.2d 139 (Pa. Super. 1956), 110
Falk v. Falk, 462 N.W.2d 547 (Wisc. App. 1990), 102
Family Services ex rel. J.L.M. by C.A.M. v. Buttram, 924 S.W.2d 870, 871 (Mo. App. 1996), 312
Farmer v. Farmer, 735 N.E.2d 285 (Ind. 2000), 206
Farmer v. Farmer, 439 N.Y.S.2d 584, 588 (1981), 177
Farwell v. Farwell, 133 P. 958 (Mont. 1913), 141
Faustin v. Lewis, 427 A.2d 1105 (N.J. 1981), 60
Fawzy v. Fawzy, 973 A.2d 347 (N.J. 2009), 670
Feltmeier v. Feltmeier, 777 N.E.2d 1032 (Ill. App. 2002), 593
Fernandez v. Fernandez, 222 P.3d 1031, 1033 (Nev. 2010), 329
Fernandez v. Fernandez, No. 85-194 II, 1986 WL 7935 (Tenn. App. 1986), 243
Fernandez v. Fernandez, 135 A.2d 886 (Md. 1967), 9
Ferro v. Ferro, 796 N.Y.2d 165 (N.Y. App. Div. 2005), 352

Ficklin v. Ficklin, 710 N.W.2d 387 (N.D. 2006), 581
Filippone v. Lee, 700 A.2d 384 (N.J. App. 1997), 314, 315
Findley v. Findley, 629 S.E.2d 222 (Ga. 2006), 368
Fine v. Fine, 626 N.W.2d 526 (Neb. 2001), 277
Finstuen v. Crutcher, 496 F.3d 1139 (10th Cir. 2007), 529
Firestone v. Cleveland Trust Co., 654 F.2d 1212, 1215 (6th Cir. 1981), 685
Fisher v. Fisher, 648 S.W.2d 244 (Tenn. 1983), 388
Fisher v. Koontz, 80 N.W. 551 (Iowa 1899), 160
Flaxman v. Flaxman, 273 A.2d 567 (1971), 24, 96, 103
Florida Dept. of Children & Families v. Adoption of X.X.G., 45 So. 3d 79 (2010), 528
Fluharty v. Fluharty, 193 A. 838 (Del. Super. 1937), 119
Fogel v. Fogel, 168 N.W.2d 275, 277 (Neb. 1969), 325
Ford v. American Original Corp., 475 F. Supp. 10 (E.D. Va. 1979), 484
Ford v. Ford, 68 P.3d 1258 (Alaska 2003), 663
Ford v. Ford, 789 A.2d 1104 (Conn. 2002), 226
Fortin v. Fortin, 208 A.2d 447 (N.H. 1965), 118
Franklin v. Franklin, 28 N.E. 681 (Mass. 1891), 440
Franklin v. Virginia, 497 S.E.2d 881, 885-886 (Va. App. 1998), 724
Frederickson & Watson Constr. Co. v. Boyd, 102 P.2d 627 (Nev. 1940), 407
Freeland v. Freeland, 159 P. 698, 699 (Wash. 1916), 169
French v. French, 599 S.W.2d 40, 41 (Mo. App. 1980), 315
Friedlander v. Friedlander, 149 F.3d 739 (7th Cir. 1998), 689
Friedlander v. Friedlander, 494 P.2d 208. 214 (Wash. 1972), 434
Friehe v. Schaad, 545 N.W.2d 740, 744-748 (Neb. 1996), 513
Fronk v. Wilson, 819 P.2d 1275 (Mont. 1991), 324
Fryar v. Roberts, 57 S.W.3d 727, 733 (Ark. 2001), 22, 28
Fuller v. Fuller, WL 1237758 (Ala. App. 2012), 249

Gade v. National Solid Wastes Management Assn., 505 U.S. 88, 98 (1992), 415
Gal v. Gal, 937 S.W.2d 391 (Mo. App. 1997), 312-313
Gallegos v. Wilkerson, 445 P.2d 970 (N.M. 1968), 63, 90
Gant v. Gant, 329 S.E.2d 106 (W. Va. 1985), 434
Garcia v. Dayton, 695 P.2d 477 (N.M. 1985), 715
Garcia v. Gutierrez, 1217 P.3d 591 (N.M. App. 2008), 255
Garska v. McCoy, 278 S.E.2d 357 (W. Va. 1981), 170
Garza v. Harney, 726 S.W.2d 198, 202 (Tex. App. 1987), 253
Gaver v. Harrant, 557 A.2d 210 (Md. 1989), 347
Gayet v. Gayet, 456 A.2d 102, 104 (N.J. 1983), 372
Geer v. Geer, 353 S.E.2d 427 (N.C. 1987), 404
Genoe v. Genoe, 500 A.2d 3, 8 (N.J. Super. A.D. 1985), 243
Gentry v. Gentry, 798 S.W.2d 928, 936 (Ky. 1990), 409, 454
Gerritzen v. City of Los Angeles, 2009 WL 6370933 (Cal. Super. 2009), 79, 80
George v. Helliar, 814 P.2d 238, 242 (Wash. App. 1991), 192, 207
Ghassemi v. Ghassemi, 998 So. 2d 731, 738 (La. App. 2008), 72, 717
Gianvito v. Gianvito, 975 A.2d 1164 (Pa. Super. 2009), 170
Gibb v. Sepe, 690 N.W.2d 230 (N.D. 2004), 371
Giesner v. Giesner, 319 N.W.2d 718, 720 (Minn. 1982), 325
Gilman v. Gilman, 956 P.2d 761 (Nev. 1998), 375
Gilpin v. Gilpin, 21 P. 612 (Colo. 1889), 151
Gina P. v. Stephen S., 824 N.Y.S.2d 619 (N.Y. App. 2006), 304
Gina P. v. Stephen S., 33 A.D.3d 412 (N.Y. 2006), 318
Giordano v. Giordano, 913 A.2d 146 (N.J. Super. 2007), 340
Gitter v. Gitter, 396 F.3d 124 (2d Cir. 2005), 256, 727
Goldman v. Greenwood, 748 N.W.2d 279, 284 (Minn. 2008), 211
Gondouin v. Gondouin, 111 P. 756 (Cal. 1910), 116
Gonzales v. Carhart (Carhart II), 550 U.S. 124 (2007), 640
Goodridge v. Department of Public Health, 798 N.E.2d 941 (Mass. 2003), 13, 82, 566

Gordon v. Gordon, 923 A.2d 149, 177 (Md. 2007), 382
Gordon v. Rozenwald, 880 A.2d 1157 (N.J. Super. A.D. 2005), 354
Gould v. Gould, 523 S.E.2d 106, 107 (Ga. App. 1999), 659
Gover's Adm'r et al. v. Dunagan, 184 S.W.2d 225, 226 (Ky. 1944), 141
Graev v. Graev, 898 N.E.2d 909 (N.Y., 2008), 375
Graham v. Brown, 26 A.3d 823 (Me. 2011), 593
Graham v. Franco, 488 S.W.2d 390 (Tex. 1972), 407
Graham v. Graham, 33 F. Supp. 936 (D. Mich. 1940), 440, 450
Graham v. Graham, 574 P.2d 75 (Colo. 1978), 404
Grahovac v. Grahovac, 680 N.W.2d 616 (Neb. App. 2004), 370
Greer v. Greer, 624 S.E.2d 423 (N.C. App. 2006), 174
Gress v. Gress, 148 N.W.2d 166 (N.D. 1967), 142
Griffin v. Griffin, 558 A.2d 75, 80 (Pa. Super. 1989), 315
Griswold v. Connecticut, 381 U.S. 479 (1965), 626
Grobin v. Grobin, 55 N.Y.S.2d 32 (N.Y. Sup. 1945), 146
Gross v. Gross, 464 N.E.2d 500 (Ohio 1984), 454
Groves v. Groves, 567 P.2d 459, 463 (Mont. 1977), 192
Gruber v. Gruber, 583 A.2d 434, 440 (Pa. 1990), 226
Gruenke v. Seip, 225 F.3d 290 (3d Cir. 2000), 649
Guard v. Guard, 993 So. 2d 1086 (Fla. App. 2008), 312
Gursky v. Gursky, 242 N.Y.S.2d 406 (N.Y. Sup. 1963), 550
Guthery v. Ball, 228 S.W. 887 (Mo. 1921), 107

Hache v. Riley, 451 A.2d 971, 975 (N.J. Super. 1982), 253
Hagen v. Hagen, 508 N.W.2d 196 (Mich. 1993), 406
Hakkila v. Hakkila, 812 P.2d 1320 (N.M. App. 1991), 593
Hall v. Hall, 108 S.E.2d 487 (N.C. 1959), 29
Hall v. Hall, 462 A.2d 1179 (Me. 1983), 381
Hall v. Maal, 32 So.3d 682 (Fla. App. 2010), 22
Hall v. Nelson, 534 N.E.2d 929 (Ohio App. 1987), 99
Hall v. Vallandingham, 540 A.2d 1162 (Md. App. 1988), 520
Hames v. Hames, 316 A.2d 379 (Conn. 1972), 22
Hamilton v. Calvert, 235 S.W.2d 453 (Tex. App. 1951), 62
Hamilton v. Hamilton, 976 A.2d 924 (Me. 2009), 664
Hamilton-Waller and Waller, 123 P.3d 310 (Or. App. 2005), 226
Hanson v. Denckla, 357 U.S. 325, 246 (1958), 699
Hanson v. Hanson, 125 P.3d 299 (Alaska 2005), 377, 384, 386
Harbom v. Harbom, 760 A.2d 272 (Md. App. 2000), 441, 453
Harmon v. Harmon, 943 P.2d 599 (Okla. 1997), 276
Harnicher v. University of Utah Medical Center, 962 P.2d 67 (Utah 1998), 563
Harrelson v. Harrelson, 932 P.2d 247 (Alaska 1997), 470
Harrington v. Harrington, 648 So. 2d 543 (Miss. 1994), 278
Harris v. McRae, 448 U.S. 297 (1980), 644
Harris v. Rattini, 855 S.W.2d 410, 412 (Mo. App. 1993), 314
Harris v. Ross, 2011 WL 825739 (Ohio App. 2011), 583
Harrower v. Harrower, 71 P.3d 854, 858 (Alaska 2003), 386
Hartford Ins. Co. v. Cline, 139 P.3d 176 (N.M. 2006), 486
Hartley v. Hartley, 889 N.E.2d 1087 (Ohio App. 2008), 363
Hartner v. Hartner, 75 Pa. Super. 342 (Pa. 1921), 136
Hartz v. Hartz, 234 A.2d 865 (Md. 1967), 430, 453
Hastoupis v. Gargas, 398 N.E.2d 745 (Mass. App. 1980), 477
Haugan v. Haugan, 343 N.W.2d 796, 803 (Wis. 1984), 353, 405
Hausman v. Hausman, 199 S.W.3d 38, 41 (Tex. App. 2006), 152
Hautala v. Hautala, 417 N.W.2d 879 (S.D. 1988), 301
Haville v. Haville, 825 N.E.2d 375 (Ind. 2005), 368
Hazuga v. Hazuga, 648 N.E.2d 391, 395 (Ind. App. 1995), 312
Headrick v. Headrick, 916 So. 2d 610 (Ala. App. 2005), 167

Heart of Adoptions, Inc. v. J.A., 963 So. 2d 189 (Fla. 2007), 533
Hecht v. Superior Court, 20 Cal. Rptr. 2d 275 (Cal. App. 1993), 567
Hedlund v. Monumental Gen. Ins. Co., 404 N.W.2d 371, 373-374 (Minn. App. 1987), 486
Hedrick-Koroll v. Bagley, 816 N.E.2d 849 (Ill. App. 2004), 586
Hefty v. Hefty, 493 N.W.2d 33, 36 (Wis. 1992), 358
Heidbreder v. Carton, 645 N.W.2d 355, 372-377 (Minn. 2002), 513, 533
Helen G. v. Mark J.H., 175 P.3d 914 (N.M. 2007), 532
Henkle v. Henkle, 600 N.E.2d 791, 795-796 (Ohio App. 1991), 480
Hepfel v. Bashaw, 279 N.W.2d 342 (Minn. 1979), 500
Herring v. Daniels, 805 A.2d 718 (Conn. App. 2002), 477
Hess v. Hess, 475 A.2d 796, 799 (Pa. Super. 1984), 381
Hessen v. Hessen, 308 N.E.2d 891 (N.Y. 1974), 134
Heustess v. Kelley-Heustess, 158 P.3d 827 (Alaska 2007), 383
Hicks v. Cook, 288 S.W.3d 244 (Ark. App. 2008), 178
Hicks v. Feiock, 485 U.S. 624 (1988), 330
Hicks v. Fulton County Dept. of Family and Children Services, 270 S.E.2d 254, 255 (Ga. App. 1980), 315
Higgins v. Higgins, 981 P.2d 134 (Ariz. App. 1999), 278
Hildebrand v. Hildebrand, 477 N.W.2d. 1, 5 (Neb. 1991), 315
Hill v. Colorado, 530 U.S. 703 (2000), 638
Hill v. Hill, 398 N.E.2d 1048 (Ill. App. 1979), 116
Hillier v. Iglesias, 901 So. 2d 947 (Fla. App. 2005), 363
Hisquierdo v. Hisquierdo, 439 U.S. 572 (1979), 400, 686
Hoag v. Dick, 799 A.2d 391 (Me. 2002), 433
Hodge v. Hodge, 520 A.2d 15 (Pa. Sup. Ct. 1986), 404
Hodges v. Hodges, 578 P.2d 1001, 1003 (Ariz. App. 1978), 102
Hodgson v. Minnesota, 497 U.S. 417 (1990), 47, 642
Hoffmann v. Hoffmann, 676 S.W.2d 817, 825 (Mo. 1984), 384
Holdsworth v. Holdsworth, 621 So. 2d 71, 78 (La. App. 1993), 312
Hollandsworth v. Knyzewski, 109 S.W.3d 653 (Ark. 2003), 225
Holler v. Holler, 612 S.E.2d 469 (S.C. App. 2005), 452
Hollingsworth v. Hicks, 258 P.2d 724 (N.M. 1953), 379
Hollingsworth v. Semerad, 799 So. 2d 658 (La. App. 2001), 277
Hollon v. Hollon, 784 So. 2d 943 (Miss. 2001), 181
Hoplamazian v. Hoplamazian, 740 So. 2d 1100 (Ala. App. 1999), 312
Horton v. Horton, 278 P. 370 (Ariz. 1929), 379
Howell v. Landry, 386 S.E.2d 610, 617-18 (N.C. App. 1989), 441, 449
Hughes v. Hughes, 438 So. 2d 146 (Fla. App. 1983), 404
Huisman v. Miedema, 644 N.W.2d 321 (Iowa 2002), 514
Hull v. Hull, 191 Ill. App. 307 (Ill. App. 1915), 112
Humphrey v. Humphrey, 434 F.3d 243 (4th Cir. 2006), 256, 727
Humphries v. County of Los Angeles, 554 F.3d 1170 (9th Cir. 2009), 610
Huntington v. Huntington, 262 P.2d 104 (Cal. App. 1953), 159
Hurston v. Hurston, 635 S.E.2d 451 (N.C. App. 2006), 139
Husband v. Wife, 262 A.2d 656, 657-658 (Del. Super. 1970), 116
Hybertson v. Hybertson, 582 N.W.2d 402 (S.D. 1998), 135

In Interest of B.B., 500 N.W.2d 9 (Iowa 1993), 603
In Interest of J.J.L.-P., 256 S.W.3d 363, 372 (Tex. App. 2008), 727
In Interest of N.M.W., 461 N.W.2d 478, 479 (Iowa App. 1990), 607
In Interest of R.C., 775 P.2d 27 (Colo. 1989), 551
In re A.B., 663 N.W.2d 625, 636 (N.D. 2003), 719
In re A.C.S., 157 S.W.3d 9 (Tex. App. 2004), 249
In re A.E.H., 468 N.W.2d 190, 198-200 (Wis. 1991), 707
In re A.L., 781 N.W.2d 482 (S.D. 2010), 288
In re A.R., 88 Cal. Rptr. 3d 448 (Cal. App. 2009), 720

In re *Adoption of A.A.T.*, 196 P.3d 1180 (Kan. 2008), 533
In re *Adoption of Anonymous*, 345 N.Y.S.2d 4320, 431 (N.Y. Surr. 1973), 543
In re *Adoption of Arthur M.*, 57 Cal. Rptr. 3d (Cal. App. 2007), 532-533
In re *Adoption of Baby Boy B.*, 2012 Ark. 92 (Ark. 2012), 537
In re *Adoption of Copeland*, 43 S.W.3d 483, 487 (Tenn. App. 2000), 707
In re *Adoption of Corbin J.*, 775 N.W.2d 404 (Neb. 2009), 533
In re *Adoption of Doe*, 2008 WL 5006172 (Fla. 2008), 528
In re *Adoption of Ethan S.*, 85 A.D.3d 1599 (N.Y. App. 2010), 532
In re *Adoption of Holland*, 965 So. 2d 1213 (Fla. App. 2007), 534
In re *Adoption of J.E.H.*, 859 N.E.2d 388 (Ind. App. 2006), 534
In re *Adoption of J.L.H.*, 737 P.2d 915 (Okla. 1987), 708
In re *Adoption of Krueger*, 448 P.2d 82 (Ariz. 1968), 531
In re *Adoption of Long*, 56 So. 2d 450 (Fla. 1952), 531
In re *Adoption of M.A.*, 930 A.2d 1088 (Me. Sup. 2007), 528
In re *Adoption of M.A.R.*, 229 P.3d 545 (Okla. App. 2009), 524
In re *Adoption of N.J.G.*, 891 N.E.2d 60 (Ind. App. 2008), 536
In re *Adoption of Paul Y.*, 696 N.Y.S.2d 796 (N.Y. Fam. Ct. 1999), 525
In re *Adoption of S.J.D.*, 641 N.W.2d 794 (Iowa 2002), 525
In re *Adoption of Sebastian*, 879 N.Y.S.2d 677 (N.Y. Sur. 2009), 558
In re *Adoption of T.H.*, 171 P.3d 480 (Utah App. 2007), 521
In re *Adoption/Guardianship of Rashawn H.*, 937 A.2d 177 (Md. 2007), 617
In re *Appeal in Maricopa County, Juvenile Action No. JS-734*, 543 P.2d 454, 459-460 (Ariz. App. 1975), 707
In re *Application for Disciplinary Action Against Chinquist*, 714 N.W.2d 469 (N.D. 2006), 675
In re *Approval of Application for Determination of Indigent Status Forms*, 910 So. 2d 194 (Fla. 2005), 657
In re *Baby Boy Blackshear*, 736 N.E.2d 462 (Ohio 2000), 604
In re *Baby Boy K.*, 546 N.W.2d 86, 90-101 (S.D. 1996), 513
In re *Baby Boy SS*, 276 A.D.2d 226 (N.Y.A.D. 2001), 526
In re *Baby Doe*, 353 S.E.2d 877 (S.C. 1987), 543, 550, 572
In re *Baby M.*, 537 A.2d 1227, 1247 (N.J. 1988), 554, 573
In re *Bash*, 880 N.E.2d 1182 (Ind. 2008), 674
In re *Benker Estate*, 331 N.W.2d 193 (Mich. 1982), 441
In re *Brittany*, 26 Cal. Rptr. 3d 487 (Cal. App. 2005), 190
In re *Burrus*, 136 U.S. 586, 693-94 (1890), 12
In re *C.D.G.D.*, 800 N.W.2d 652 (Minn. App. 2011), 289
In re *C.K.G., C.A.B., & C.L.G.*, 173 S.W.3d 714 (Tenn. 2005), 557
In re *C.M.*, 2012 WL 2479619 (N.H. 2012), 618
In re *C.M.D.*, 287 S.W.3d 510 (Tex. App 2009), 513
In re *C.T.*, 121 Cal. Rptr. 2d 897, 906 (Cal. App. 2002), 253
In re *C.T.G.*, 179 P.3d 213 (Colo. App. 2007), 290
In re *Canon's Estate*, 221 Wis. 322, 266 N.W. 918 (1936), 26
In re *Coates*, 849 A.2d 254 (Pa. Super. 2004), 70
In re *Conduct of Knappendberger*, 108 P.3d 1161 (Or. 2005), 675
In re *Corey Mc.*, 67 A.D.3d 1015 (N.Y. App. 2009), 607
In re *Craig T.*, 744 A.2d 621 (N.H. 1999), 608
In re *Custody of A.C.*, 200 P.3d 689 (Wash. 2009), 269
In re *Custody of Farm*, 417 N.E.2d 240 (Ill. App. 1981), 208
In re *Custody of H.S.H.-K.*, 533 N.W.2d 419 (Wis. 1995), 291
In re *Custody of Miller*, 548 P.2d 542, 546 (Wash. 1976), 702
In re *Custody of Thompson*, 647 P.2d 1049 (Wash. App. 1982), 207
In re *D.K.*, 2002 Wl 31968992 (Pa. Com. Pl. 2002), 608
In re *D.R.*, 20 P.3d 166, 169 (Ok. App. 2001), 601
In re *Dalip Singh Bir's Estate*, 188 P.2d 499, 501-02 (Cal. App. 1948), 71, 101
In re *Davis*, 465 A.2d 614, 621-629 (1983), 177

In *re Dependency of MSR*, 271 P.3d 234 (Wash. 2012), 618
In *re Disciplinary Proceedings Against Gamino*, 314 Wis. 2d 544, 753 N.W.2d 521 (Wis. 2008), 672, 673
In *re Domestic Partnership of Ellis*, 76 Cal. Rptr. 3d 401 (Cal. App. 2008), 90
In *re Donna S.*, 871 N.Y.S.2d 883 (N.Y. Fam. 2009), 716
In *re Douglas*, 369 B.R. 462, 465 (Bankr. E.D. Ark. 2007), 410
In *re E.C.L.*, 278 S.W.3d 510 (Tex. App. 2009), 612
In *re E.G.*, 549 N.E.2d 322 (Ill. 1989), 601
In *re E.L.M.C.*, 100 P.3d 546 (Colo. App. 2004), 293
In *re Eli H.*, 871 N.Y.S.2d 846 (N.Y. Fam .Ct. 2008), 601
In *re Elysa D.* 974 A.2d 834 (Conn. App. 2009), 618
In *re Enderle Marriage License*, 1 Pa. D & C Reports 2d 114 (Phila. Cy. 1954), 62
In *re Estate of Appleby*, 111 N.W. 305, 307 (Minn. 1907), 422, 488
In *re Estate of Alexander*, 445 So. 2d 836 (Miss. 1984), 466
In *re Estate of Brewer*, 168 S.W.3d 135 (Mo. App. 2005), 499
In *re Estate of Crockett*, 728 N.E.2d 765 (Ill. App. 2000), 26, 50, 68
In *re Estate of Duval*, 777 N.W.2d 830 (S.D. 2010), 45
In *re Estate of Eriksen*, 337 N.W.2d 671,674 (Minn. 1983), 468, 472
In *re Estate of Everhart*, 783 N.W.2d 1 (Neb. App. 2010), 71, 91
In *re Estate of Farmer ex rel. Farmer*, 964 So. 2d 498 (Miss. 2007), 497
In *re Estate of Gardiner*, 42 P.3d 120 (Kan. 2002), 85
In *re Estate of Geyer*, 533 A.2d (Pa. 1987), 423
In *re Estate of Harbers*, 449 P.2d 7 (Ariz. 1969), 442
In *re Estate of Kinney*, 733 N.W.2d 118, 124, 126 (Minn. 2007), 433, 442, 443, 451
In *re Estate of Martin*, 938 A.2d 812 (Me. 2008), 441
In *Re Estate of Mirizzi*, 723 N.Y.S.2d 623 (N.Y. Surr. 2001), 28
In *re Estate of Roccamonte*, 808 A.2d 838 (N.J. 2002), 469, 477
In *re Estate of Santolino*, 895 A.2d 506 (N.J. Super. 2005), 26
In *re Estate of Smid*, 756 N.W.2d 1, 18 (S.D. 2008), 435
In *re Estate of Smith*, 685 So. 2d 1206 (Fla. 1996), 511
In *re Estate of Stephenson*, 503 N.W.2d 540, 546 (Neb. 1993), 443
In *re Estate of Strickland*, 149 N.W.2d 344 (Neb. 1967), 442
In *re F.A.G.*, 148 P.3d 375 (Colo. App. 2006), 194
In *re G.M.*, 2012 Il. App. 2d 110370 (Ill. App. 2012), 512
In *re Gonzalez*, 993 S.W.2d 147 (Tex. App. 1999), 733
In *re Gorden's Estate*, 168 N.E.2d 239 (N.Y. 1960), 477
In *re Gregorson's Estate*, 160 Cal. 21 (Cal. 1911), 24, 96, 99
In *re Heart Share Human Services of New York*, 906 N.Y.S.2d 472 (N.Y. Fam. 2010), 533
In *re Heilig*, 816 A.2d 68 (Md. 2003), 85
In *re Higera N.*, 2 A.3d 265 (Me. 2010), 248
In *re I.B.*, 255 P.3d 56 (Mont. 2011), 616
In *re Iliana M.*, 38 A.3d 130 (Conn. App. 2012), 249
In *re Infant Girl W.*, 845 N.E.2d 229 (Ind. App. 2006), 528
In *re Interest of Aaron D.*, 691 N.W.2d 164 (Neb. 2005), 621
In *re Interest of M.L.K.*, 768 P.2d 316, 319-320 (Kan. App. 1989), 707
In *re Interest of S.A.V.*, 837 S.W.2d 80, 84 (Tex. 1992), 244
In *re Isquierdo*, S.W., 2012 WL 2455074 (Tex. App. 2012), 250
In *re J.D.C.*, 751 N.E.2d 747 (Ind. App. 2001), 533, 537
In *re J.L.*, 891 N.E.2d 778 Ohio App. 2008), 599
In *re J.N.H.*, 209 P.3d 1221 (Colo. App. 2009), 525
In *re Jaclyn P.*, 179 A.D.2d 646 (N.Y. 1992), 600
In *re Jorden R.*, 979 A.2d 469 (Conn. 2009), 616
In *re Juvenile Appeal* (83-CD), 455 A.2d 1319 (Conn. 1983), 596
In *re K.L.R.*, 162 S.W.3d 291 (Tex. App. 2005), 211
In *re Kandu*, 315 B.R. 123, 133 (Bankr. W.D. Wash. 2004), 75

In re Keon C., 800 N.E.2d 1257 (Ill. App. 2003), 310
In re Kosek, 871 A.2d 1 (N.H. 2005), 283
In re Kurowski, 20 A.3d 306 (N.H. 2011), 167
In re L.S., 257 P.3d 201 (Colo. 2011), 247
In re Ladrach, 513 N.E.2d 828 (Ohio Prob. 1987), 85
In re Larch, 872 F.2d 66, 68 (4th Cir. 1989), 254
In re Leskovich, 385 A.2d 373 (Pa. Super. 1978), 213
In re Lewin, 149 S.W. 3d 727, 736 (Tex. App.2004), 251
In re Lisa Diane G., 537 A.2d 131 (R.I. 1988), 538
In re Litowitz, 48 P.3d 261, 271 (Wash. 2002), 560
In re Long, 745 A.2d 673 (Pa. Super. 2000), 526
In re M.L.W., 358 S.W.3d 772 (Tex. App. 2012), 242
In re Marriage of A.C.H. and D.R.H., 210 P.3d 929 (Or. App. 2009), 548
In re Marriage of Amezquita & Archuleta, 124 Cal. Rptr. 2d 887 (Cal. App. 2002), 339
In re Marriage of Arnold and Cully, 222 Cal. App. 3d 499, 504 (1990), 249
In re Marriage of Benson, 32 Cal. Rptr. 3d 471 (Cal. 2005), 384
In re Marriage of Berger, 88 Cal. Rptr. 3d 766 (Cal. App. 2009), 304
In re Marriage of Blankenship, 682 P.2d 1354 (Mont. 1984), 408
In re Marriage of Bordner, 715 P.2d 436, 439 (Mont. 1986), 315
In re Marriage of Boyer, 538 N.W.2d 293, 293-294, 296 (Iowa 1995), 401
In re Marriage of Brane, 908 P.2d 625, 626, 628 (Kan. 1995), 401
In re Marriage of Breen, 560 S.W.2d 358, 361 (Mo. App. 1977), 699
In re Marriage of Brigden, 145 Cal. Rptr. 716. 723 (Cal. App. 1978), 379
In re Marriage of Bross, 845 P.2d 728, 731-732 (Mont. 1993), 372
In re Marriage of Brown, 778 N.W.2d 47, 51-52 (Iowa 2009), 195
In re Marriage of Brown and Yana, 127 P.3d 28 (Cal. 2006), 199
In re Marriage of Bureta, 164 P.3d 534 (Wash. App. 2007), 375
In re Marriage of Burgess, 913 P.2d 473 (Cal. 1966), 212, 224, 231
In re Marriage of Cadwell-Faso and Faso, 119 Cal. Rptr. 3d 818 (Cal. App. 2011), 431, 438
In re Marriage of Cargill, 842 P.2d 1335 (Colo. 1993), 105
In re Marriage of Carrier, 576 N.W.2d 97, 98 (Iowa 1998), 718
In re Marriage of Cauley, 41 Cal. Rptr. 3d 902 (Cal. App. 2006), 357
In re Marriage of Chatten, 967 P.2d 205 (Colo. App. 1998), 207
In re Marriage of Ciesluk, 113 P.3d 135, 146 (Colo. 2005), 220
In re Marriage of Ciganovich, 132 Cal. Rptr. 261 (Cal. App.1976), 205
In re Marriage of Clay, 670 P.2d 31 (Colo. App. 1983), 314, 315
In re Marriage of Connerton and Nevin, 290 P.3d 62 (Colo. App. 2010), 302
In re Marriage of Cooper, 763 N.W.2d 276 (Iowa 21009), 160
In re Marriage of Dahl and Angle, 572, 194 P.3d 834 (Or. App. 2008), 560
In re Marriage of DePalma, 176 P.3d 829, 831 (Colo. App. 2007), 207
In re Marriage of Dettore, 408 N.E.2d 429 (Ill. App. 1980), 406
In re Marriage of Donahoe, 448 N.E.2d1030,1033 (Ill. App. 1983), 315
In re Marriage of Dorman, 9 P.3d 329 (Ariz. App. 2000), 195
In re Marriage of Dorworth, 33 P.3d 1260 (Colo. App. 2001), 278
In re Marriage of Elenewski, 828 N.E.2d 895 (Ill. App. 2005), 363
In re Marriage of Fedorov, 206 P.3d 1124 (Or. App. 2009), 226
In re Marriage of Fieldheim, 676 P.2d 1234 (Colo. App. 1983), 406
In re Marriage of Fiffe, 140 P.3d 160 (Colo. App. 2005), 584
In re Marriage of Francis, 919 P.2d 776, 784 (Colo. 1996), 225
In re Marriage of Frost, 260 P.3d 570 (Or. App. 2011), 372
In re Marriage of Gallagher, 539 N.W.2d 479 (Iowa 1995), 513
In re Marriage of George, 988 P.2d 251 (Kan. App. 1999), 314, 315
In re Marriage of Gerkin, 74 Cal. Rptr. 3d 188, 192 (Cal. App. 2008), 337

In re Marriage of Gillilland, 487 N.W.2d 363, 366 (Iowa App. 1992), 372
In re Marriage Gillmore, 629 P.2d 1, 3 (Cal. 1981), 399
In re Marriage of Gonzalez, 561 N.W.2d 363, 366 (Iowa App. 1992), 451
In re Marriage of Greenlaw, 940 P.2d 223 (Wash. App. 1992), 253
In re Marriage of Guffin, 209 P.3d 225 (Mont. 2009), 220
In re Marriage of Hansen, 733 N.W.2d 683 (2007), 172
In re Marriage of Harkins, 115 P.3d 981 (Or. App. 2005), 364
In re Marriage of Harris, 244 P.3d 801 (Or. 2010), 353
In re Marriage of Harris, 96 P.3d 141 (Cal. 2004), 221
In re Marriage of Heath, 18 Cal. Rptr. 3d 760 (Cal. App. 2004), 180
In re Marriage of Heiner, 39 Cal. Rptr.3d 570 (Cal. App. 2006), 300
In re Marriage of Highsmith, 488 N.E.2d 1000, 1003 (1986), 702
In re Marriage of Hopkins, 92 Cal. Rptr. 3d 570 (Cal. App. 2009), 335
In re Marriage of Horn, 650 N.E.2d 1103, 1106 (Ill. App. 1995), 325
In re Marriage of Howell, 195 Cal. App. 4th 1062 (Cal. App. 2011), 434
In re Marriage of Hudson, 434 N.E.2d 107, 117-118 (Ind. App. 1982), 243
In re Marriage of Hulscher, 180 P.3d 199 (Wash. App. 2008), 365
In re Marriage of Hunt, 397 N.E. 2d 511, 518 (Ill. App. 1979), 399
In re Marriage of Ilas, 16 Cal. Rptr. 2d 345 (Cal. App. 1993), 368
In re Marriage of J.B. and H.B., 326 S.W.3d 654 (Tex. App. 2010), 84, 154
In re Marriage of Jennings, 50 P.3d 506 (Kan. App. 2002), 212
In re Marriage of Kieturakis, 41 Cal. Rptr. 3d 119 (Cal. App. 2006), 664
In re Marriage of Kimbrell, 119 P.3d 684 (Kan. App. 2005), 283
In re Marriage of Kochan, 122 Cal. Rptr.3d 61 (Cal. App. 2011), 359
In re Marriage of Kolb, 425 N.E.2d 1301 (Ill. App. 1981), 103
In re Marriage of Kunz, 136 P.3d 1278 (Utah 2006), 116
In re Marriage of Kunze, 92 P.3d 100 (Or. 2004), 382
In re Marriage of L.M.S., 312 N.W.2d 853, 855 (Wis. App. 1981), 550
In re Marriage of LaMusga, 88 P.3d 81, 98 (Cal. 2004), 224
In re Marriage of Leonard, 175 Cal. Rptr. 903 (Ct. App. 1981), 264
In re Marriage of Lind, 139 P.3d 1032 (Or. App. 2006), 470
In re Marriage of Liu, 242 Cal. Rptr. 649 (Cal. App. 1987), 102, 115
In re Marriage of Logston, 469 N.E.2d 167, 176 (Ill. 1984), 363
In re Marriage of Los, 593 N.E.2d 126, 129-130 (Ill. App. 1992), 244
In re Marriage of Lucio, 74 Cal. Rptr.3d 804 (Cal. App. 2008), 199
In re Marriage of MEW, 4 Pa. D. & C.3d 51, 1977 WL 321 (C.P. 197), 88
In re Marriage of Matar, 270 P.3d 257, 259 (Or. App. 2011), 329
In re Marriage of Mayzner, 144 Ill. App.3d 645 (Ill. App. 1986), 392
In re Marriage of McNerney, 417 N.W.2d 205 (Iowa 1987), 406
In re Marriage of McSoud, 131 P.3d 1208 (Colo. App. 2006), 279
In re Marriage of Mehlmauer, 131 Cal. Rptr. 325 (Ct. App. 1976), 179
In re Marriage of Mentry, 190 Cal. Rptr. 843, 848-849 (Cal. App. 1983), 221
In re Marriage of Monti, 185 Cal. Rptr. 72 (Cal. 1982), 68
In re Marriage of Moore, 702 N.W.2d 517 (Iowa App. 2005), 313
In re Marriage of Mullen-Funderburk and Funderburk, 696 N.W.2d 607 (Iowa 2005), 313
In re Marriage of Newton, 353 Ill. Dec. 105 (Ill. App. 2011), 672
In re Marriage of Norris, 624 P.2d 636, 638-640 (Or. App. 1981), 434
In re Marriage of Nurie, 98 Cal. Rptr.2d 200, 211 (Cal. 2009), 254
In re Marriage of O'Connor, 690 P.2d 1095, 1097 (Or. App. 1984), 243
In re Marriage of Oehm, 252 Ill. App.3d 311 (Ill. App. 1993), 194
In re Marriage of Olson, 705 N.W.2d 312 (Iowa 2005), 352
In re Marriage of Osborn, 135 P. 3d 199 (Kan. App. 2006), 284

In re Marriage of Paradis, 689 P.2d 1263 (Mont. 1984), 207
In re Marriage of Pontius, 761 P.2d 247 (Colo. App. 1988), 207, 217
In re Marriage of Reed, 427 N.E.2d 282, 285 (Ill. App. 1981), 395
In re Marriage of Regenmorter, 587 N.W.2d 493, 495 (Iowa App. 1998), 439
In re Marriage of Reynolds, 74 Cal. Rptr. 2d 636, 640 (Cal. App. 1998), 367
In re Marriage of Riggs and Hem, 129 P.3d 601 (Kan. App. 2006), 290
In re Marriage of Rives, 181 Cal. Rptr. 572 (Cal. App. 1982), 409
In re Marriage of Rogers, 280 Ill. Dec. 726 (Ill. App. 2003), 304
In re Marriage of Rozzi, 190 P.3d 815 (Colo. App. 2008), 668
In re Marriage of Schenkelberg, 810 N.W.2d 532 (Iowa App. 2012), 432
In re Marriage of Seagondollar, 43 Cal. Rptr. 3d 575 (Cal. App. 2006), 231
In re Marriage of Settle, 556 P.2d 962, 968 (Or. 1976), 244
In re Marriage of Seymour, 2012 WL 309332 (Kan. App. 2012), 26
In re Marriage of Shanks, 758 N.W.2d 506. 513-514 (Iowa 2008), 431, 449
In re Marriage of Shirilla, 89 P.3d 1, 4 (Mont. 2004), 431
In re Marriage of Sigg, 238 P.3d 331 (Kan. App. 2010), 151
In re Marriage of Simmons, 355 Ill. App. 949 (Ill. App. 2005), 21
In re Marriage of Smith, 427 N.E.2d 1239 (Ill. 1981), 383
In re Marriage of Stanton, 118 Cal. Rptr. 3d 249, 256 (Cal. App. 2010), 301
In re Marriage of Strieby, 255 P.3d 34 (Kan. App. 2011), 365
In re Marriage of Terhaar, 14 P.3d 657 (Or. 2000), 387
In re Marriage of Thomas, 199 S.W.3d 847 (Mo. App. 2006), 439, 453
In re Marriage of Timmons, 617 P.2d 1032, 1037 (Wash. 1980), 207
In re Marriage of Tomsovic, 74 P.3d 692 (Wash. 2003), 195
In re Marriage of Trevino, 812 N.W.2d 726 (Iowa App. 2012), 251
In re Marriage of Waldren, 171 P.3d 1214 (Ariz. 2007), 365
In re Marriage of Wanstreet, 847 N.E.2d 716 (Ill. App. 2006), 384
In re Marriage of Wechselberger, 450 N.E.2d 1385 (Ill. App. 1983), 207
In re Marriage of Weinstein, 470 N.E.2d 551 (Ill. App. 1984), 404
In re Marriage of Williams, 677 P.2d 585 (Mont. 1984), 105
In re Marriage of Winegard, 257 N.W.2d 609, 616 (Iowa 1997), 34
In re Marriage of Witten, 672 N.W.2d 768 (Iowa 2003), 561, 564
In re Marriage of Xia Guo and Xiao Hua Sun, 186 Cal. App. 4th 1491 (Cal. App. 2010), 36
In re Marriage of Zahm, 978 P.2d 498, 502 (Wash. 1999), 401
In re Matter of Baby M., 537 A.2d 1227, 1247 (N.J. 1988), 554, 572, 573
In re McCauley, 565 N.W.2d 411 (Mass. 1991), 601
In re Miltenberger Estate, 737 N.W.2d 513 (Mich. App. 2007), 346
In re Moorehead, 600 N.E.2d 778, 786 (Ohio App. 1991), 527
In re Mosier's Estate, 133 N.E. 202 (Ohio 1954), 443
In re N.S.E., 666 S.E.2d 587 (Ga. App. 2008), 599
In re Nada R., 108 Cal. Rptr. 2d 493, 500 (Cal. App. 2001), 253
In re Neis' Estate, 225 P.2d 110 (Kan. 1950), 443
In re Nicholas H., 46 P.3d 932 (Cal. 2002), 513
In re Nina R., 638 N.W.2d 393 (Wis. App. 2001), 279
In re O.S., 848 N.E.2d 130 (Ill. App. 2006), 621
In re O'Brien, 898 A.2d 1075 (Pa. Super. 2006), 424
In re Owens, 645 N.E.2d 130, 132 (Ohio App. 1994), 315
In re P.B. for Adoption of L.C., 920 A.2d 155 (N.J. Super. 2006), 535
In re Palmen, 588 N.W.2d 493 (Minn. 1999), 476
In re Paquet's Estate, 200 P.911 (Or. 1921), 53
In re Parentage of L.B., 122 P.3d 161 (Wash. 2005), 516
In re Parentage of M.J., 787 N.E.2d 144 (Ill. 2003), 572

In re Parental Rights as to D.R.H., 92 P.3d 1230 (Nev. 2004), 617
In re Parson's Estate, 59 A.2d 709 (Del. Super 1948), 28
In re Paternity of Baby Doe, 734 N.E.2d 281 (Ind. App. 2000), 533
In re Paternity of C.S., 964 N.E.2d 879 (Ind. App. 2012), 229
In re Paternity of Cheryl, 746 N.E.2d 488 (Mass. 2001), 514
In re Paternity of S.R.I., 602 N.E.2d 1014 (Ind. 1992), 502
In re Pedro Jason William M., 847 N.Y.S.2d 17 (N.Y.A.D. 2007), 532
In re Pedro Z., Jr., 117 Cal. Rptr. 3d 605 (Cal. App. 2010), 611
In re Peirano, 930 A.2d 1165, 1173 (N.H., 2007), 357
In re Poldrugovaz, 851 N.Y.S.2d 254 (N.Y. App. 2008), 497
In re R.J. T., 9 A.3d 1179 (Penn. 2010), 616
In re R.M., 234 S.W.3d 619 (Mo. App. 2007), 521
In re R.E.S., 978 A.2d 182 (D.C. 2009), 618
In re R.W., 39 A.3d 682 (Vt. 2011), 707
In re Reese, 227 P.3d 900 (2010), 596
In re Roberto d.B., 923 A.2d 115 (Md. 2007), 557
In re Ruff, 275 P.3d 1175, 1181 (Wash. App. 2012), 253
In re S.A.V., 837 S.W.2d 80, 84 (Tex. 1992), 707
In re Seamus K., 33 A.D.3d 1030 (N.Y. App. 2006), 601
In re Seay, 746 N.W.2d 833 (Iowa 2008), 309
In re Shirley B., 993 A.2d 675 (Md. App. 2010), 616
In re Shun T. Takahaski's Estate, 129 P.2d 217 (Mont. 1942), 53
In re S.N.V., 2011 WL 6425562 (Col. App. 2011), 516
In re Soeder's Estate, 200 N.E.2d 547 (Ohio App. 1966), 17, 31, 32
In re State ex rel. Black, 238 P.2d 887 (Utah 1955), 58
In re Stephen Tyler R., 584 S.E.2d 581 (W. Va. 2003), 617
In re Sullivan, 157 S.W.3d 911 (Tex. App. 2005), 552, 571
In re Sullivan, 982 A.2d 959 (N.H. 2009), 304
In re T.S., 7 Cal. Rptr. 3d 173 (Cal. App. 2003), 529
In re T.T.C., 855 A.2d 1117 (D.C. 2004), 607
In re T.W., 551 So. 2d 1186, 1194 (Fla. 1989), 646
In re Tegeler, 302 Ill. Dec. 173 (Ill. App. 2006), 304
In re Thomas' Estate, 367 N.Y.S.2d 182 (N.Y. Surr. 1975), 34
In re Tiffany B., 228 S.W.3d 148 (Tenn. App. 2007), 615
In re Timonthy AA. 72 A.D3d 1390 (N.Y. App. 2010), 526
In re Trust Created by Nixon, 763 N.W.2d 404 (Neb. 2009), 534
In re Valente's Will, 188 N.Y.S.2d 732 (N.Y. Surr. 1959), 50
In re Van Schaick's Estate, 40 N.W.2d 588 (Wisc. 1949), 34
In re Vanessa Ann G.-L., 856 N.Y.S.2d 657 (N.Y.A.D. 2008), 533
In re Vetas' Estate, 170 P.2d 183 (Utah 1946), 34
In re W.E.B., 980 So. 2d 123 (La. App. 2008), 521
In re Weber, 653 N.W.2d 804 (Minn. App. 2002), 196
In re Welfare of Alle, 230 N.W.2d 574, 577 (Minn. 1975), 538
In re Wells' Estate, 108 N.S.S. 164, 166 (N.Y. 1908), 33
In the Matter of the Abrogation of Anonymous, 167 N.Y.S.2d 472 (N.Y. 1951), 518
In the Matter of the Marriage of J.B. and H.B., 326 S.W.3d 654 (Tex. App. 2010), 84, 154
Interest of J.J.L.-P., 256 S.W.3d 363, 372 (Tex. App. 2008), 727
Iowa Supreme Court Attorney Disciplinary Bd. v. Morrison, 727 N.W.2d 115 (Iowa 2007), 673
Ireland v. Ireland, 717 A.2d 676, 682 (Conn. 1998), 225, 226
Irwin v. Irwin, 539 So. 2d 1177 (Fla. App. 1990), 369
Isaacson v. Isaacson, 792 A.2d 525 (N.J. Super. 2002), 663
Israel v. Allen, 577 P.2d 762 (Colo. 1978), 62, 88, 89

J. B., III v. Dept. of Children and Families, 928 So.2d 392 (Fla. App. 2006), 609
J.B. v. M.B., 170 N.J. 9, 783 A.2d 707 (N.J. 2001), 561
J.F. v. D.B., 848 N.E.2d 873 (Ohio App. 2006), 571

J.F. v. D.B., 879 N.E.2d 740 (Ohio 2007), 553
J.H.H. v. O'Hara, 878 F.2d 240, 244-245 (8th Cir. 1989), 177, 527
J.K. v. R.S., 706 So. 2d 1262 (Ala. App. 1997), 502
J.M.H. v. Rouse, 143 P.3d 1116 (Col. App. 2006), 23
J.S. v. State, 50 P.3d 388 (Alaska 2002), 616
Jackson v. Denver, 124 P.2d 240 (Colo. 1942), 53
Jackson v. Holiness, 961 N.W. 2d (In. App. 2012), 339
Jackson v. Jackson, 403 N.W.2d 248 (Minn. App. 1987), 301
James v. Adams, 155 P. 1121, 1122 (Okla. 1915), 51
James v. Jacobson, 6 F.3d 233 (4th Cir. 1993), 563
Jamison v. Jamison, 845 S.W.2d 133, 136-137 (Mo. App. 1993), 312
Jaramillo v. Jaramillo, 823 P.2d 299, 309 (N.M. 1991), 218, 224, 231
Jarret v. Jarret, 449 U.S. 927 (1980), 181
Jeanes v. Jeanes, 177 S.E.2d 537, 539-540 (S.C. 1970), 34
Jennings v. Jennings, 315 A.2d 816 (Md. 1974), 63, 90
Jersey Shore Med. Ctr.-Fitkin Hosp. v. Baum's Estate, 417 A.2d 1003, 1009 (N.J. 1980), 347
Jeter v. Mayo Clinic Arizona, 121 P.3d 1256 (Ariz. App. 2005), 564
Jhordan C. v. Mary K., 224 Cal. Rptr. 530 (Cal. App. 1986), 543
Johnson v. Calvert, 851 P.2d 776 (Cal. 1993), 556, 558
Johnson v. Johnson, 9A.3d 1003 (N.J. 2010), 670
Johnson v. Johnson, 66 So.3d 784 (Ala. App. 2011), 180
Johnson v. Johnson, 104 N.W.2d 8 (N.D. 1960), 19, 107
Johnson v. Johnson, 157 S.E. 689 (Ga. 1931), 120
Johnson v. Johnson, 346 S.E.2d 430 (N.C. 1986), 408
Johnson v. Johnson, 597 So.2d 699 (Ala. App. 1991), 325
Johnson v. Johnson, 617 N.W.2d 97 (N.D. 2000), 319
Johnson v. Johnson, 726 So. 2d 393, 396 (Fla. App. 1999), 401
Johnson v. Johnson, 734 N.W.2d 801, 808 (S.D. 2007), 401
Johnson v. Schlotman, 502 N.W.2d 831 (N.D. 1993), 278
Johnson v. State, 602 So. 2d 1288 (Fla. 1992), 604
Johnson v. Superior Court, 80 Cal. App. 1050 (2000), 549
Jones v. Barlow, 154 P. 3d 808 (Utah, 2007), 291
Jones v. Brennan, 465 F.3d 304 (7th Cir. 2006), 687
Jones v. Daly, 176 Cal. Rptr. 130 (Cal. App. 1981), 467
Jones v. Helms, 452 U.S. 412, 418 (1981), 218
Jones v. Jones, 832 N.E.2d 1057 (Ind. App. 2005), 184
Jones v. Jones, 890 S.W.2d 471 (Tex. App. 1994), 380
Jones v. Shaw, 441 P.2d 990 (Okla. 1965), 28
Jordan v. Jordan, 345 A.2d 168 (N.H. 1975), 118
Jordan v. Mitchell, 705 So.2d 453 (Ala. App. 1997), 479
Juelfs v. Juelfs, 359 N.W.2d 667, 670 (Minn. App. 1984), 367
Jurek v. Jurek, 606 P.2d 812 (Ariz. 1980), 407

K.M. v. E.G., 117 P.3d 673 (Cal. App. 2005), 558
K.S. v. G.S., 440 A.2d 64, 68-69 (N.J. Super. Ch. 1981), 550
Kaiser v. Kaiser, 23 P.3d 278, 282 (Okla. 2001), 223, 224
Kamenski v. Kamenski, 15 So.3d 842 (Fla. App. 2009), 362
Karlin v. Foust, 188 F.3d 446 (7th Cir. 1999), 637
Kass v. Kass, 673 N.Y.S.2d 350 (N.Y. 1998), 544
Kass v. Kass, 696 N.E.2d 174, 180 (N.Y. 1998), 560
Katz v. Katz, 408 N.W.2d 835, 838 (Minn. 1987), 705
Kay v. Ludwig, 686 N.W.2d 619 (Neb. App. 2004), 187
Keeling v. Keeling, 624 S.E.2d 687 (Va. App. 2006), 385
Kelderhaus v. Kelderhaus, 467 S.E.2d 303 (1996), 63, 90
Keller v. O'Brien, 652 N.E.2d 589, 593 (Mass. 1995), 372
Kelm v. Hyatt, 44 F.3d 415 (6th Cir. 1995), 713
Kendrick v. Kendrick, 902 S.W.2d 918, 920 (Tenn. App. 1994), 399
Kentucky Dep't of Corr. v. Thompson, 490 U.S. 454, 461 (1989), 56

Ker v. Ker, 776 S.W.2d 873, 877 (Mo. App. 1989), 384
Kerby v. Kerby, 164 P.3d 1049 (Okla. 2007), 328
Kerrigan and Mock v. Connecticut Department of Public Health, 957 A.2d 407 (Conn. 2008), 82
Kerrigan v. Commissioner of Public Health, 957 A.2d 407 (Conn. 2008), 13, 79
Kerrigan v. State, 957 A.2d 407 (Conn. 2008), 717
Kessel v. Kessel, 46 S.E.2d 792 (W. Va. 1948), 136
Killingbeck v. Killingbeck, 711 N.W.2d 759 (Mich. App. 2005), 514
Kirkpatrick v. Eighth Judicial Dist. Court, 64 P.3d 1056 (Nev. 2003), 47
Knight v. Hayward Unified School Dist., 33 Cal. Rptr. 3d 287 (Cal. App. 1 Dist. 2005), 566
Knight v. Radomski, 414 A.2d 1211 (Me. 1980), 19
Korff v. Korff, 831 N.E.2d 385 (Mass. App. 2005), 454
Kosik v. George, 452 P.2d 560, 563 (Or. 1969), 428
Kottke v. Kottke, 353 N.W.2d 633, 636 (Minn. App. 1984), 382
Kovacs v. Brewer, 356 U.S. 604 (1958), 241
Kraus v. Willow Park Public Golf Course, 140 Cal. Rptr. 744 (Cal. 1977), 480
Kreilick v. Kreilick, 831 N.E.2d 1046 (Ohio App. 2005), 384
Krieger v. Krieger, 81 P.2d 1081 (Idaho 1938), 169
Krueger v. Krueger, 278 N.W.2d 514 (Mich. App. 1979), 317
Kulko v. Superior Court of California, 436 U.S. 84 (1978), 703, 733
Kunkle v. Kunkle, 554 N.E.2d 83, 89-90 (Ohio 1990), 358

Labine v. Vincent, 401 U.S. 531 (1971), 12
LaChapelle v. Mitten, 607 N.W.2d 151, 163-164 (Minn. App. 2000), 219
Lacks v. Lacks, 359 N.E.2d 384 (N.Y. 1976), 696
Lalli v. Lalli, 439 U.S. 259 (1978), 497
Lambert v. Lambert, 403 P.2d 664, 668 (Wash. 1965), 325
Lambert v. Wicklund, 520 U.S. 292 (1977), 642
Lander v. Smith, 906 So. 2d 1130 (Fla. App. 2005), 504
Landeros v. Flood, 551 P.2d 389 (Cal. 1976), 610
Lane v. Lane, 202 S.W.3d 577 (Ky. 2006), 439
Langan v. State Farm Fire & Cas., 48 A.D.3d 76 (N.Y. App. 2007), 84
Lange v. Lange, 502 N.W.2d 143 (Wis. App. 1993), 278
Laspina-Williams v. Laspina-Williams, 742 A.2d 840 (Conn. Super. 1999), 291
Lassiter v. Dept. of Soc. Serv., 452 U.S. 18 (1981), 618, 619, 712
Lawrence v. Texas, 539 U.S. 558, 559 (2003), 13, 76, 86, 89, 124, 460, 471
Lawrence v. Tise, 419 S.E.2d 176, 183 (N.C. App. 1992), 312
Lawson v. Loid, 896 S.W.2d 1, 3 (Ky. 1995), 442
Lawson v. Ridgeway, 233 P.2d 459 (Ariz. 1951), 379
Lawson v. United States, 192 F.2d 479 (2d Cir.), cert. denied, 343 U.S. 904 (1951), 484
Lee v. Lee, 816 S.W.2d 625 (Ark. App. 1991), 432
Lefkowitz v. Bank of New York, 528 F.3d 102 (2d Cir. 2007), 690
Lehmicke v. Lehmicke, 559, 489 A.2d 782 (Pa. Super. 1985), 415
Lehr v. Afflitto, 889 A.2d 462 (N.J. Super. 2006), 659, 664
Lehr v. Robertson, 463 U.S. 248, 264-265 (1983), 502, 513, 532, 537
Lemcke v. Lemcke, 623 N.W.2d 916 (Minn. App. 2001), 205
Lenser v. McGowan, 191 S.W.3d 423 (Ark. 2004), 721
Lenz v. Lenz, 40 S.W.3d 111, 118 n.3 (Tex. App. 2000), 219
Lenz v. Lenz, 79 S.W.3d 10, 14-15 (Tex. 2002), 219, 223, 227
Les Realty Corp. v. Hogan, 714 A.2d 366 (N.J. Super. 1998), 336
Leslie v. Leslie, 827 S.W.2d 180, 183 (Mo. 1992), 367
Levin v. Carlton, 213 P.3d 884 (Utah 2009), 455
Levin v. Levin, 645 N.E.2d 601, 604 (Ind. 1994), 571
Levine v. Dumbra, 604 N.Y.S.2d 207 (N.Y. App. 1993), 102, 110
Levine v. Konvitz, 890 A.2d 354 (N.J. Super. A.D. 2006), 473
Levy v. Louisiana, 391 U.S. 68 (1968), 495
Lewis v. Anderson, 308 F.3d 768 (7th Cir. 2002), 614
Lewis v. New York State Dept. of Civil Service, 60 A.D.3d 216 (N.Y. App.. 2009), 716
Liberto v. Liberto, 520 A.2d 458, 461 (Pa. Super. 1987), 150

Liebelt v. Liebelt, 801 P.2d 52 (Idaho App. 1990), 433, 448
Lieberman v. Scully, 709 N.Y.S.2d 583 (N.Y. App. 2000), 609
Lieblein v. Charles Chips, Inc., 32 A.D.2d 1016 (N.Y. App. 1969), 34
Liles v. Liles, 711 S.W.2d 447 (Ark. 1986), 406
Liles v. Still, 335 S.E.2d 168 (Ga. App. 1985), 466
Linda R. v. Richard E., 162 A.D.2d 48 (N.Y. 1990), 182
Lindsay v. Lindsay, WL 197111 (Tenn. App. 2006), 317-318
Linker v. Linker, 470 P.2d 921 (Colo. App. 1970), 441
Lintz v. Skipski, 25 F.3d 304 (6th Cir. 1994), 614
Lisa I. v. Superior Court, 34 Cal. Rptr. 3d 927 (Cal. App. 2005), 502
Little v. Little, 969 P.2d 188 (Ariz. App. 1998), 325
Littleton v. Prange, 9 S.W.3d 223 (Tex. App. 1999), 85
Litz v. Litz, 288 S.W.3d 753 (Mo. App. 2009), 401
Lloyd v. Loeffler, 694 F.2d 489 (7th Cir. 1982), 685, 689
Lofton v. Sec'y of Dept. of Children and Family Services, 358 F.3d 804 (11th Cir. 2004), 528
Lopez v. Lopez, 245 A.2d 771 (N.J. Super. 1968), 68
Lopez v. Lopez, 639 P.2d 1186 (N.M. 1981), 205
Lopez v. Lopzen, 852 So.2d 402 (Fla. App. 2003), 695
Loving v. Virginia, 388 U.S. 1 (1967), 10, 16, 54, 55, 69
Lozinski v. Lozinski, 408 S.E.2d 310 (W.Va. 1991), 715
Lozner v. Lozner, 909 A.2d 728 (N.J. Super. 2006), 311
Luberski, Inc. v. Oleficio F.LLI Amato S.R.L., 89 Cal. Rptr. 3d 774 (Cal. App. 2009), 702
Lulay v. Lulay, 583 N.E.2d 171, 172 (Ind. App. 1991), 311
Lurie v. Lurie, 94 A.D.3d 1376 (N.Y. App. 2012), 377
Luxton v. Luxton, 648 P.2d 315 (N.M. 1982), 408
Lynch v. Lynch, 616 So.2d 294 (Miss. 1993), 135
Lyons v. State, 835 S.W.2d 715, 718 (Tex. App. 1992), 332

M.L.B. v. Department of Health and Rehabilitative Services, 559 So. 2d 87 (Fla. App. 1990), 519
M.T. v. J.T., 355 A.2d 204, 211 (N.J. App. Div. 1976), 85
M.V.S. v. V.M.D. 776 So. 2d 142 (Ala. Civ. App. 1999), 534
Mace v. Mace, 610 N.W.2d 436 (Neb. App. 2000), 312
MacFarlane v. Rich, 567 A.2d 585, 591 (N.H. 1989), 454
Mackey v. Mackey, 32 S.E.2d 764 (1945), 120
Mackey v. Mackey, 545 A.2d 362 (Pa. Super. 1988), 150
MacKinley v. Messerschmidt, 814 A.2d 680 (Pa. Super. 2002), 300
MacLafferty v. MacLafferty, 829 N.W.2d 938 (Ind. 2005), 323
Madsen v. Women's Health Center, 512 U.S. 753 (1994), 637
Maher v. Roe, 432 U.S. 464, 475 (1977), 644, 645
Mahoney v. Mahoney, 453 A.2d 527 (N.J. 1982), 404, 415
Mahoney v. Mahoney, 681 N.E.2d 852, 856 (Mass. 1997), 401
Mallouf v. Saliba, 766 N.E.2d 552 (Mass. App. 2002), 277
Manbeck v. Manbeck, 489 A.2d 748 (Pa. Super. 1985), 119, 127
Mani v. Mani, 869 A.2d 904 (N.J. 2005), 355
Manker v. Manker, 644 N.W.2d 522 (Neb. 2002), 68
Mann v. Saland, 816 N.Y.S.2d 697 (N.Y. Sup. 2006), 673
Mansell v. Mansell, 490 U.S. 581, 587 (1989), 685
Mantz v. Mantz, 69 N.E.2d 637, 639 (Ohio Com. Pl. 1946), 735
Marchal v. Craig, 681 N.E.2d 1160, 1161 (Ind. App. 1997), 658
Marcus v. Marcus, 248 N.E.2d 800, 805 (Ill. App. 1969), 213
Mark C. v. Patricia B., 42 A.D. 3d 1317 (N.Y. App. 2007), 276
Markham v. Allen, 326 U.S. 490 (1946), 687
Marquardt v. Marquardt, 396 N.W.2d 753, 754 (S.D. 1986), 372
Marriage of Snow v. England, 862 N.E.2d 664 (Ind. 2007), 354
Marshall v. Marshall, 300 P. 816 (Cal. 1931), 112
Marshall v. Marshall, 547 U.S. 293, 299 (2006), 684, 687, 690
Marshall v. Marshall, 988 A.2d 314 (Conn. App. 2010), 373

Marshall v. Sackett, 907 S.W.2d 925 (Tex. App. 1995), 601
Martian v. Martian, 328 N.W.2d 844 (N.D. 1983), 143
Martin v. Ziherl, 607 S.E.2d 367, 370-371 (Va. 2005), 77
Martinez v. Superior Court, 731 P.2d 1244, 1247 (Ariz. App. 1987), 254
Marvin v. Marvin, 557 P.2d 106 (Cal. 1976), 461, 462 467, 473, 474, 481, 482, 491
Marvin v. Marvin, 5 Fam. L. Rep. 2077 (1979), 463, 464
Marchal v. Craig, 681 N.E.2d 1160, 1161 (Ind. App. 1997), 658
Mason v. Coleman, 850 N.E.2d 513 (Mass. 2006), 229, 231
Mason v. Mason, 775 N.E.2d 706, 709 (Ind. App. 2002), 62, 72
Mason v. Rostad, 476 A.2d 662 (D.C. App. 1984), 479
Massey v. Evans, 68 A.D.3d (N.Y. App. 2009), 301
Massey-Holt v. Holt, 255 S.W. 3d 603 (Tenn. App. 2007), 181
Masters v. Masters, 108 N.W.2d 674 (Wis. 1961), 117
Mather v. Roe, 432 U.S. 464 (1977), 644, 645
Mathews v. Eldridge, 424 U.S. 319 (1976), 585
Mathews v. Lucas, 427 U.S. 495 (1976), 497
Mathews v. Mathews, 72 A.D.3d 1631, 1632 (N.Y. App. 2010), 279
Matter of Carlson, 489 S.E.2d 834 (Ga. 1997), 335
Matter of Custody of D.M.G., 951 P.2d 1377 (Mont. 1998), 220
Matter of Custody of Russ, 620 P.2d 353 (Or. 1981), 244
Matter of Engwer v. Engwer, 762 N.Y.S.2d 689 (N.Y. 2003), 199
Matter of Estate of Giessel, 734 S.W.2d 27 (Tex. App. 1987), 45
Matter of Estate of Hendrickson, 805 P.2d 20, 21 (Kan. 1991), 18, 19
Matter of Estate of Kolacy, 753 A.2d 1257 (N.J. Super. 2000), 566
Matter of Estate of Lutz, 563 N.W.21d 90 (N.D. 1997), 433
Matter of Greiff, 703 N.E.2d 752, 755 (N.Y. 1998), 441
Matter of Hermans v. Hermans, 547 N.E.2d 87 (N.Y. 1989), 371
Matter of Kilpatrick, 375 S.E.2d 794 (W. Va. 1988), 30
Matter of La Bier v. La Bier, 738 N.Y.S.2d 132 (N.Y. 2002), 200
Matter of Lutz, 563 N.W.2d 90 (N.D. 1997), 451
Matter of Paternity Petition of Com'r of Social Services of City of New York, 466 N.Y.S.2d 194 (N.Y. Fam. 1998), 44
Matter of Petition of Phillip A.C., 149 P.3d 51 (Nev. 2006), 719
Matter of Pima City Juvenile Action, 806 P.2d 892, 895 (Ariz. 1990), 531
Matter of Radford v. Propper, 190A.D.2d 93 (N.Y. App. 1993), 225
Matter of Reese v. Jones, 671 N.Y.S.2d 170 (N.Y. App. 1998), 220
Matter of the Estate of Crawford, 730 P.2d 675 (Wash. 1986), 453
Matter of the Marriage of Adams, 729 P.2d 1151 (Kan. 1986), 432
Matter of Tropea v. Tropea, 665 N.E.2d 145 (N.Y. 1996), 220, 225
Matthews v. Riley, 649 A.2d 231 (Vt. 1994), 247, 265
Maurer v. Maurer, 872 A.2d 326 (Vt. 2005), 659
Maxcy v. Estate of Maxcy, 485 So. 2d 1077, 1078 (Miss. 1986), 373
Maxwell Schuman & Co. v. Edwards, 663 S.E.2d 329 (N.C. App. 2008), 676
Maxwell v. Maxwell, 650 S.E.2d 680 (S.C. App. 2007), 365
May v. Anderson, 345 U.S. 528 (1953), 241, 242, 243, 248, 257, 264, 701, 706
Mayer v. Mayer, 279 P. 783 (Cal. 1929), 112
Mayhew v. Mayhew, 519 S.E.2d 188 (W. Va. 1999), 387
Maynard v. Hill, 125 U.S. 190 (1888), 4, 18, 131, 142
McAlister v. Patterson, 299 S.E.2d 322, 33 (S.C. 1982), 224
McArthur v. Superior Court, 1 Cal. Rptr. 2d 296 (Cal. App. 1991), 243
McAtee v. McAtee, 323 S.E.2d 611, 616-617 (W. Va. 1984), 243
McCann v. Doe, 660 S.E.2d 500 (S.C. 2008), 53
McCarty v. McCarty, 453 U.S. 210, 232 (1981), 400
McCarty v. State, 41 P.3d 981, 988 (Ok. App. 2002), 624
McClenahan v. Warner, 461 N.W.2d 509 (Minn. App. 1990), 324

McClung v. McClung, 465 So. 2d 637, 638 (Fla. App. 1985), 358
McClurg v. Terry, 21 N.J. Eq. 225 (1870), 111
McConkey v. McConkey, 215 S.E.2d 640 (Va. 1975), 104
McCready v. Hoffius, 586 N.W.2d 723 (Mich. 1999), 487
McCready v. Hoffius, 593 N.W.2d 545 (Mich. 1999), 487
McCullon v. McCullon, 410 N.Y.S.2d 226 (N.Y. Sup. 1978), 470
McCurry v. McCurry, 10 A.2d 365 (Conn. 1939), 135
McDermott v. Dougherty, 869 A.2d 751 (Md. 2005), 171, 75
McDonald v. Com., 630S.E.2d 754 (Va. App. 2006), 90
McDonald v. McDonald, 608 N.Y.S.2d 477 (N.Y. App. 1994), 566
McFadden v. Elma Country Club, 613 P.2d 146, 150 (Wash. App. 1980), 487
McGee v. International Life Ins. Co., 355 U.S. 220, 223 (1957), 699
McGowan v. McGowan, 518 N.Y.S.2d 346 (1987), 402
McGregory v. McGregor, 334 S.W.3d 113 (Ky. App. 2011), 358
McIntyre v. Crouch, 780 P.2d 239 (Or. App. 1989), 548, 552
McKee-Johnson v. Johnson, 444 N.W.2d 259, 267-268 (Minn. 1989), 454
McKittrick v. McKittrick, 732 N.W.2d 404 (S.D. 2007), 310
McLain v. McLain, 569 N.W.2d 219, 224 (Minn. App. 1997), 268
McLaughlin v. Florida, 379 U.S. 184, 188 (1964), 9
McMahan v. McMahan, 2005 WL 3287475 (Tenn. App. 2005), 663
McMillen v. McMillen, 602 A.2d 845 (Pa. 1992), 179
McMillian v. Rizzo, 817 N.Y.S.2d 679 (N.Y.A.D. 2006), 213
McMullen v. McMullen, 185 So. 2d 191 (Fla. App. 1966), 455
McPeek v. McCardle, 888 N.E.2d 171 (Ind. 2008), 22, 43
McVey v. McVey, 289 A.2d 549 (N.J. Super. 1972), 136
Meade v. Meade, 812 F.2d 1473 (4th Cir. 1987), 248
Means v. Means, 45 Pa. D. & C.2d 228, 231 (Pa. Com. Pl. 1968), 735
Mega Life and Health Ins. Co. v. Superior Court, 92 Cal. Rptr. 3d 399 (Cal. App. 2009), 485
Meister v. Moore, 96 U.S. 76 (1877), 23
Merkel v. Merkel, 554 N.E.2d 1346 (Ohio App. 1988), 301
Mesenbourg v. Mesenbourg, 538 N.W.2d 489, 492-493 (Minn. App.1995), 705
Metcalf v. Metcalf, 769 N.W.2d 386 (Neb. 2009), 362
Metropolitan Life Ins. Co. v. Chase, 294 F.2d 500, 503 (3d Cir. 1961), 34
Metz v. Metz, 618 S.E.2d 477 (W. Va. 2005), 362, 363
Metz v. Metz, 711 S.E.2d 737 (N.C. App. 2011), 302
Meyer v. Franklin Cnty. Court of Common Please, 23 F. App'x 201, 204 (6th Cir. 2001), 692
Meyer v. Meyer, 620 N.W.2d 382 (Wis. 2000), 470, 479
Meyer v. Nebraska, 262 U.S. 390 (1923), 276, 596, 626
Micale v. Micale, 542 So. 2d 415, 417 (Fla. App. 1989), 428
Michael H. v. Gerald D., 491 U.S. 110 (1989), 501, 560
Michigan Trust Co. v. Chapin, 64 N.W. 334 (Mich. 1895), 440
Mickey v. Mickey, 974 A.2d 641 (Conn. 2009), 381
Middendorf v. Middendorf, 696 N.E.2d 575, 578 (Ohio 1998), 386
Middlesex County Ethics Comm. v. Garden State Bar Assn., 457 U.S. 423, 432 (1982), 692
Midzak v. Midzak, 697 N.W.2d 733 (S.D. 2005), 363
Miller v. Martin, 838 So. 2d 761 (La. 2003), 615
Miller v. Miller, 35 N.W. 464, 464 (Iowa 1887), 159
Miller v. Miller, 42 N.W. 641, 642 (Iowa 1889), 159, 160
Miller v. Miller, 240 F.3d 392, 398 (4th Cir. 2001), 726
Miller v. Miller, 739 P.2d 163, 165 (Alaska 1987), 416
Miller v. Miller, 892 A.2d 175 (Vt. 2005), 372
Miller v. Miller, 956 P.2d 887 (Okla. 1998), 117
Miller-Jenkins v. Miller-Jenkins, 12 A.3d 768 (Vt. 2010), 282
Miller-Jenkins v. Miller-Jenkins, 661 S.E.2d 822 (Va. 2008), 278
Miller-Jenkins v. Miller-Jenkins, 912 A.2d 951 (Vt. 2006), 240

Milliken v. Meyer, 311 U.S. 457, 463 (1940), 700
Miltiadous v. Tetervak, 686 F. Supp. 2d 544 (E.D. Penn. 2010), 594
Mills v. Atlantic City Dept. of Vital Statistics, 372 A.2d 646 (N.J. Super. 1977), 525
Mills v. Habluetzel, 456 U.S. 91 (1982), 511
Mirizio v. Mirizio, 150 N.E. 605 (Mich. 1926), 440
Mission Ins. Co. v. Industrial Comm'n, 559 P.2d 1085 (Ariz. 1976), 63, 90
Mississippi Band of Choctaw Indians v. Holyfield, 490 U.S. 30 (1989), 528, 718, 734
Mitchell v. Mitchell, 418 A.2d 1140, 1143 (Me. 1980), 372
Mitchim v. Mitchim, 518 S.W.2d 362, 365 (Tex. 1975), 242
Mize v. Mize, 621 So. 2d 417, 419 (Fla. 1993), 222, 224
Mobley v. Mobley, 16 So.2d 5, 6-7 (Ala.1943), 116, 117
Mobley v. Mobley, 18 So.3d 724, 727 (Fla. App. 2009), 351
Moe v. Dinkins, 533 F. Supp. 623 (S.D. N.Y. 1981), 20
Molitor v. Molitor, 718 N.W.2d 13 (N.D. 2006), 193, 211
Monson v. Monson, 2011 WL 4716320 (Conn. Super. 2011), 148
Moore v. Moore, 2012 WL 2553565, S.W.3d (Tex. App. 2012), 432
Moore v. Moore, 634 A.2d 163, 169 (Pa. 1993), 200
Moore v. Sims, 442 U.S. 415, 435 (1979), 685, 692
Morris v. Hawk, 907 N.E.2d 763 (Ohio App. 2009), 278
Morrison v. Sadler, 821 N.E.2d 15 (Ind. App. 2005), 566
Mosher-Simons v. County of Allegany, 783 N.E.2d 509 (N.Y. 2002), 615
Mott v. Duncan Petroleum Trans., 414 N.E.2d 657 (1980), 46, 63
Muller v. Muller, 711 N.W.2d 329 (Mich. 2006), 278
Mundy v. Devon, 2006 WL 902233 (Del. Supr. Apr. 6, 2006), 167
Murry v. Watkins, 2004 WL 2980357 (Ohio App. 2004), 336
Muth v. Frank, 412 F.3d 808, 817-818 (7th Cir. 2005), 460

Nakamura v. Parker, 67 Cal. Rptr. 3d 286 (Cal. App. 2007), 583
Nakoneczna v. I & L Eisenberg, 60 A.D.2d 403, 400 N.Y.S.2d 884 (N.Y. App. 1977), 119
Nancy S. v. Michele G., 279 Cal. Rptr. 212 (Cal. App. 1991), 290
Nardini v. Nardini, 414 N.W.2d 184, 193 (Minn. 1987), 393, 394
Neff v. Neff, 192 P.2d 344, 345 (Wash. 1948), 135
Nelson v. Jones, 781 P.2d 964 (Alaska 1989), 276
Nelson v. Marshall, 869 S.W.2d 132, 135 (Mo. App. 1993), 43
Nelson v. Nelson, 24 N.W.2d 327 (S.D. 1946), 140
Nelson v. Nelson, 164 A.2d 234, 235 (Conn. Super. 1960), 134
Nelson v. Nelson, 215 N.W.2d 140, 143 (Minn. 1974), 702
Nelson v. Nelson, 357 P.2d 536, 538 (Or. 1960), 325
Nelson v. Nelson, 736 P.2d 1145 (Alaska 1987), 403
Nelson v. Wolrd Wide Lease, Inc., 716 P.2d 513 (Idaho 1986), 706
Nestor v. Nestor, 472 N.E.2d 1091 (Ohio 1984), 33
Netecke v. Louisiana, 715 So.2d 449 (La. App. 1998), 63
Neville v. Neville, 791 N.E.2d 434 (Ohio 2003), 401
New York ex rel. Halvey v. Halvey, 330 U.S. 610 (1947), 197, 241
Newman v. Newman, 653 P.2d 728, 732 (Colo. 1982), 428
Nicholson v. Hugh Chatham Memorial Hosp., 266 S.E.2d 818, 823 (N.C. 1980), 347
Nicholson v. Scoppetta, 820 N.E.2d 840 (N.Y. App. 2004), 603
Nicini v. Morra, 212 F.3d 798 (3d Cir. 2000), 614
Nicoletti v. Nicoletti, 901 So. 2d 290 (Fla. App. 2005), 313
Northrup v. Brigham, 826 N.E.2d 239 (Mass. App. 2005), 481
Norton v. Hoyt, 278 F.Supp. 214, 226 (D. R.I. 2003), 490
Norton v. McOsker, 407 F.3d 501 (1st Cir. 2005), 690
Numerick v. Krull, 694 N.W.2d 552 (Mich. App. 2005), 502

O'Brien v. O'Brien, 489 N.E.2d 712 (N.Y. 1985), 402, 403
O'Connor v. O'Connor, 180 N.W.2d 735, 738 (Wis. 1970), 332

O'Darling v. O'Darling, 188 P.3d 137 (Okla. 2008), 717
Odom v. Odom, 141 P.3d 324, 335 (Alaska 2006), 386
Office of Child Support v. Stanzione, 910 A.2d 882 (Vt. 2006), 334
Olsen v. Olsen, 169 P.3d 765, 772 (Utah App. 2007), 401
Olsen v. Olsen, 580 F.Supp. 1569 (D.C. N.D. Ind. 1984), 686
Olver v. Fowler, 168 P.3d 348 (Wash. 2007), 686
Oman v. Oman, 702 N.W.2d 11 (S.D. 2005), 372
Omega Industry, Inc. v. Raffaele, 894 F. Supp. 1425 (D.C. Nev. 1995), 720, 721
Orr v. Orr, 440 U.S. 268, 279 (1979), 8, 346
Ortel v. Gettig, 116 A.2d 145 (Md. 1955), 428
Ortiz v. New York City Transit Authority, 699 N.Y.S.2d 370 (N.Y. App. 1999), 486
Osborne v. Osborne, 428 N.E.2d 810 (Mass. 1981), 439, 456
Ouellet v. Tillitski, 604 S.E.2d 559 (Ga. App. 2004), 609
Owens v. Owens, 31 S.E. 72 (Va. 1898), 140

Pajak v. Pajak, 385 S.E.2d 384, 388 (Va. 1989), 430
Palmore v. Sidoti, 466 U.S. 429 (1984), 177, 527
Panossian v. Panossian, 569 N.Y.S.2d 182 (N.Y. App. 1991), 433, 441
Panther v. Panther, 295 P. 219, 221 (Okla. 1931), 146
Pappas v. Waggoner's Heating & Air, Inc., 108 P.3d 9 (Okla. App. 2004), 657
Parham v. Hughes, 441 U.S. 347 (1979), 496
Parlow v. Parlow, 548 N.Y.S.2d 373 (N.Y. Sup. 1989), 403
Pasqua v. Council, 892 A.2d 663 (N.J. 2006), 331
Patey v. Peaslee, 111 A.2d 194 (N.H. 1955), 24, 96
Paton v. Brill, 663 N.E.2d 421 (Ohio App. 1995), 734
Patrick v. Patrick, 212 So. 2d 145, 147 (La. App. 1968), 213
Patterson v. Patterson, 90 So.3d 187, 190 (Ala App. 2012), 387
Patterson v. Patterson, 917 So. 2d 111 (Miss. App. 2005), 354
Pearson v. District Court, 924 P.2d 512 (Colo. 1996), 664
Pearson v. Pearson, 182 P.3d 353 (Utah 2008), 502
Pencovic v. Pencovic, 287 P.2d 501 (Cal. 1955), 368
Pennington v. Marcum, 266 S.W.3d 759 (Ky. 2008), 193
Pennoyer v. Neff, 95 U.S. 714, 735 (1877), 697, 732
Pennzoil Co. v. Texaco, Inc., 481 U.S. 1 (1987), 693
People ex rel J.S.B., Jr., 691 N.W.2d 611 (S.D. 2005), 616
People ex rel. Dept. of Public Aid v. Smith, 289 Ill. Dec. 1 (Ill. 2004), 509
People ex rel. J.A.U. v. R.L.C., 47 P.3d 327 (Colo. 2002), 514
People ex rel. South Dakota Dept. of Social Services, 795 N.W.2d 39 (S.D. 2011), 597
People ex rel. U.S., 121 P.3d 326 (Col. App. 2005), 610
People v. C., 85 N.Y.S.2d 751 (N.Y. Child. Ct. 1949), 494
People v. Ezeonu, 588 N.Y.S.2d 116 (N.Y. Sup. 1992), 101
People v. Hassan, 86 Cal Rptr. 3d 314 (Cal. App. 2008), 51
People v. Lucero, 747 P.2d 660 (Colo. 1987), 33
People v. Peterson, 537 N.W.2d 857 (Mich. 1995), 612
People v. Smith, 23 Cal. Rptr. 5 (Cal. App. 1962), 29
People v. T.G., 578 N.W.2d 921 (S.D. 1998), 602
People v. Turner, 109 P.3d 639 (Colo. 2005), 587
Petersen v. Petersen, 737 P.2d 237 (Utah App., 1987), 404
Peterson v. Peterson, 652 P.2d 1195 (N.M. 1982), 301
Peterson v. Widule, 147 N.W. 966 (Wis. 1914), 29
Peters-Riemers v. Riemers, 644 N.W.2d 197 (N.D. 2002), 452
Petition of K.J.R., 687 N.E.2d 113 (Ill. App. 1 Dist. 1997), 534
Phillips v. Beaber, 995 S.W.2d 655, 659 (Tex. 1999), 248
Phillips v. Chase, 89 N.E. 1049, 1051-1052 (Mass. 1909), 538
Pickett v. Brown, 462 U.S. 1 (1983), 511
Pierce v. Pierce, 640 P.2d 899, 903 (Mont. 1982), 247
Pierce v. Pierce, 916 N.E.2d 330 (Mass. 2009), 367
Pierce v. Soc'y. of Sisters, 268 U.S. 510 (1925), 276, 596, 636

Pierpont v. Bond, 744 So. 2d 843 (Miss. App. 1999), 206, 318
Pikula v. Pikula, 374 N.W.2d 705, 713 (Minn. 1985), 170
Pirri v. Pirri, 631 S.E.2d 279 (S.C. App. 2006), 384
Pittman v. Pittman, 419 So. 2d 1376 (Ala. 1982), 316
Placide v. Placide, 408 So. 2d 330 (La. App. 1981), 407
Planned Parenthood Ass'n, Inc. v. Department of Human Resources, 663 P.2d 1247 (Or. App. 983), 647
Planned Parenthood League of Massachusetts v. Bellotti, 641 F.2d 1006 (1st Cir. 1981), 651
Planned Parenthood League v. Attorney Gen., 677 N.E.2d 101, 103 (Mass. 1997), 646
Planned Parenthood Minnesota, North Dakota, South Dakota v. Rounds, 530 F.3d 724 (8th Cir. 2008), 637
Planned Parenthood of Central Missouri v. Danforth, 428 U.S. 52 (1976), 641
Planned Parenthood of Central N.J. v. Farmer, 762 A.2d 620, 626, 631-639 (N.J. 2000), 646
Planned Parenthood of Southeastern Pennsylvania v. Casey, 505 U.S. 833, 837 (1992), 632, 633, 634, 636, 650
Plaster v. Plaster, 47 Ill. 290 (1868), 296
Platek v. Platek, 454 A.2d 1059 (Pa. Super. 1982), 406
Plymale v. Donnelly, 157 P.3d 933 (Wyo. 2007), 309
Poelker v. Doe, 432 U.S. 519 (1977), 644
Poindexter v. Willis, 231 N.E.2d 1 (Ill. App. 1967), 702, 715
Pollino v. Pollino, 121 A.2d 62 (N.J. Super. Ch. 1956), 145
Pollock v. Pollock, 889 P.2d 633 (Ariz. App. 1995), 224
Pongonis v. Pongonis, 606 A.2d 1055, 1058 (Me. 1992), 401
Portugal v. Portugal, 798 A.2d 246, 253 (Pa. Super. 2002), 300
Posik v. Layton, 695 So. 2d 759 (Fla. App. 1997), 482
Posner v. Posner, 233 So. 2d 381 (Fla. 1970), 423
Poteet v. Poteet, 114 P.2d 91, 92 (N.M. 1941), 146
Powell v. Rogers, 496 F.2d 1248, 1250 (9th Cir. 1974), 35, 486
Powell v. State, 510 S.E.2d 18 (Ga. 1988), 76
Powers v. Floyd, 904 S.W.2d 713 (Tex. App. 1995), 651
Prato-Morrison v. Doe, 126 Cal. Rptr. 2d 509 (Cal. App. 2002), 565
Price v. McBeath, 989 So. 2d 444 (Miss. App. 2008), 720
Price v. Price, 5 So. 3d 1151 (Miss. App. 2009), 139
Price v. State, 57 P.3d 639 (Wash. App. 2002), 539
Price v. Turner, 691 S.E.2d 470, 472 (S.C. 2010), 331
Prince v. Massachusetts, 321 U.S. 158, 166 (1944), 596
Procario v. Procario, 623 N.Y.S.2d 971 (N.Y. Sup. 1994), 403
Prybolsky v. Prybolsky, 430 A.2d 804 (Del. Fam. 1981), 701
Pryor v. Pryor, 213 A.2d 545 (Md. 1965), 141
Pugliese v. Superior Court, 53 Cal. Rptr. 3d 681 (Cal. App. 2007), 593

Queen v. Queen, 521 A.2d 320, 324 (Md. 1987), 416
Quillen v. Quillen, 659 N.E.2d 566, 576 (Ind. App. 1995), 315
Quilloin v. Walcott, 434 U.S. 246 (1977), reh', denied, 435 U.S. 918 (1978), 531
Quinn v. Johnson, 589 A.2d1077 (N.J. Super. 1991), 315

R.A.C. v. P.J. S., 880 A.2d 1179 (N.J. Super. 2005), 511
R.J.R. v. C.J.S., 72 So. 3d 643 (Ala. App. 2011), 725
Raboin v. North Dakota Dept. of Human Servs, 552 N.W.2d 329 (N.D. 1996), 599
Radke v. County of Freeborn, 694 N.W.2d 788 (Minn. 2005), 614
Ralston v. Connecticut General Life Ins. Co., 617 So. 2d 1379 (La. App. 1993), 566
Randolph v. Randolph, 212 N.Y.S.2d 468 (N.Y. Sup. 1961), 106
Randolph v. Randolph, 937 S.W.2d 815 (Tenn. 1996), 429, 442, 450
Randy A.J. v. Norma I.J., 677 N.W.2d 630 (Wis. 2004), 514
Rebsamen v. Rebsamen, 107 S.W.3d 871 (Ark. 2003), 221
Reed v. Albaaj, 723 N.W.2d 50 (Minn. App. 2006), 720, 735

Reed v. Pieper, 713 S.E.2d 309 (S.C. 2011), 186
Reed v. Reed, 404 U.S. 71 (1971), 27
Reed v. Reed, 2012 WL 1107888 (Tenn. App. 2012), 470
Reed v. Reed, 693 N.W.2d 825 (Mich. App. 2005), 453
Renzulli v. McElrath, 712 N.Y.S.2d 267 (N.Y. Sup. 2000), 200
Reynolds v. Kimmons, 569 P.2d 799, 803 (Alaska 1977), 500
Reynolds v. United States, 98 U.S. 145 (1878), 58, 142
Rice v. Cayetano, 528 U.S. 495, 519-20 (2000), 719
Rhodes v. McAfee, 457 S.W.2d 522, 524 (Tenn. 1970), 63
Rice v. Rice, 528 N.E.2d 14, 15 (Ill. App. 1988), 363
Rich v. Rich, 483 N.Y.S.2d 150 (N.Y. Sup. 1984), 408
Rich v. Thatcher, 132 Cal. Rptr. 3d 897 Cal. App. 2011), 289
Rickards v. Rickards, 166 A.2d 425 (Del. 1960), 160
Riepe v. Riepe, 91 P.3d 312 (Az. App. 2005), 58, 293
Right to Choose v. Byrne, 450 A.2d 925 (N.J. 1982), 647
Rinvelt v. Rinvelt, 475 N.W.2d 478 (Mich. App. 1991), 423
Ritchie v. White, 35 S.E.2d 414, 416-417 (N.C. 1945), 347
Rivera v. Minnich, 483 U.S. 574 (1987), 499
Rivero v. Rivero, 195 P.3d 328 (Nev. 2008), 309
Robert B. v. Susan B., 135 Cal. Rptr. 2d 785 (Cal. App. 2003), 564
Robert O. v. Russell K., 604 N.E.2d 99 (N.Y. App. 1992), 513, 533
Roderick v. Roderick, 776 S.W.2d 533 (Tenn. App. 1989), 243, 707
Rodriquez v. Eighth Judicial Dist. Court ex rel., 102 P.3d 41 (Nev. 2004), 331
Roe v. Catholic Charities of the Diocese of Springfield, 588 N.E.2d 354 (Ill. 1992), 538
Roe v. Conn, 417 F. Supp. 769, 778 (D.C. Ala. 1976), 596
Roe v. Reeves, 708 S.E.2d 778 (S.C. 2011), 537
Roe v. Wade, 410 U.S. 113 (1973), 623, 625, 627, 628, 629, 630, 631, 634, 646, 651
Rogers v. Yellowstone Park Co., 97 539 P.2d 566 (Idaho 1974), 407
Roman v. Roman, 193 S.W.3d 40 (Tex. App. 2006), 546, 560, 562
Rooker v. Fidelity Trust Co., 263 U.S. 413 (1999), 691
Rooney v. Rooney, 131 S.E.2d 618 (S.C. 1963), 136
Rose v. Rose, 526 N.E.2d 231, 235-236 (Ind. App. 1988), 432
Rose v. Rose, 481 U.S. 619, 625 (1987), 12
Rose v. Rose, 289 N.W.2d 611 (Mich. App. 2010), 365
Rosen v. Clebrezze, 883 N.E.2d 420 (Ohio 2008), 249
Rosen v. Lantis, 938 P.2d 729 (N.M. App. 1997), 312
Rosen v. Rosen, 664 S.E.2d 743 (W.Va. App. 208), 249
Rosenberg v. Rosenberg, 39 Pa. D. & C.3d 549 1984 WL 2628 (Pa. Com. Pl. 1984), 150
Rosengarten v. Downes, 802 A.2d 170 (Conn. App. 2002), 717
Rosenthal v. Maney, 745 N.E.2d 350 (Mass. App. 2001), 221
Ross v. Ross, 143 A.D.2d 429 (N.Y. App. 1988), 141
Roth v. Roth, 565 N.W.2d 782, 785 (S.D. 1997), 424
Roth v. Weston, 789 A.2d 431 (Conn. 2002), 190
Rotolo v. Rotolo, 682 F. Supp. 8 (D.C. Puerto Rico 1988), 686
Rowe v. Franklin, 663 N.E.2d 955 (Ohio App. 1995), 182, 208
Ruben v. Ruben, 461 A.2d 733 (N.H. 1983), 404
Rust v. Sullivan, 500 U.S. 173 (1991), 645
Ryken v. Ryken, 461 N.W.2d 122 (S.D. 1990), 433

S.B. v. D. H., 736 So. 2d 766 (Fla. App. 1999), 502
Sagar v. Sagar, 781 N.E.2d 54 (Mass. App. 2003), 178
Salas v. Cortez, 593 P.2d 226, 234, cert. denied, 444 U.S. 900 (1979), 500
Sanford v. Sanford, 694 N.W.2d 283 (S.D. 2005), 439
Santi v. Santi, 633 N.W.2d 312 (Iowa 2001), 288
Santosky v. Kramer, 455 U.S. 745 (1982), 499, 618
Sara M. v. Superior Court, 116 P.3d 550 (Cal. 2005), 620

Sarfaty v. Sarfaty, 534 F. Supp. 701 (E.D. Pa. 1982), 721
Sawyer v. Bailey, 413 A.2d 165 (Me. 1980), 485
Scheidegg v. Dept. of Air Force, 715 F. Supp. 11, 13-14 (D.C. N.H. 1989), 721
Schubert v. Schubert, 33 A.D.3d 1177 (N.Y.A.D. 3 Dept. 2006), 135
Schubert v. Schubert, 823 N.W.S.2d 282 (N.Y. App. 2006), 140
Schuler v. Schuler, 416 N.E.2d 197, 203 (Mass. 1981), 325
Schumm v. Schumm, 510 N.W.2d 13 (Minn. App. 1993), 178
Schutz v. Schutz, 581 So. 2d 1290 (Fla. 1991), 282
Scott v. Carothers, 47 N.E. 389, 390 (Ind. App. 1897), 8
Scott v. Georgia, 39 Ga. 321 (Ga. 1869), 53
Scott v. Scott, 879 A.2d 540 (Conn. App. 2005), 310
Seul v. Seul, 802 S.W.2d 617, 620 (Tenn. App. 1990), 367
Seebecker v. Seebecker, 368 N.W.2d 846 (Wis. App. 1985), 443
Sefton v. Sefton, 291 P.2d 439 (Cal. 1955), 94
Seidel v. Seidel, 10 S.W.3d 365 (Tex. App. 1999), 282
Seirafi-Pour v. Bagherinassab, 197 P.3d 1097, 1102 (Okla. App. 2008), 102
Semken v. Semken, 664 S.E.2d 493 (S.C. App. 2008), 375
Serio v. Serio, 830 So. 2d 278 (Fla. App. 2002), 436
Seuss v. Schukat, 192 N.E. 668 (Ill. 1934), 442
Sevland v. Sevland, 646 N.W.2d 689 (N.D. 2002), 277
Seyboth v. Seyboth, 554 S.E.2d 378 (N.C. App. 2001), 290
Shah v. Shah, 875 A.2d 931 (N.J. 2005), 584
Shanks v. Treadway, 110 S.W.3d 444 (Tex. 2003), 399
Shapiro v. Thompson, 394 U.S. 618, 634 (1969), 218
Sharma v. Sharma, 667 P.2d 395, 396 (Kan. App. 1983), 143
Sharon S. v. Superior Court, 2 Cal. Rptr. 3d 699 (Cal. 2003), 528
Sharp v. Bilbro, 614 N.W.2d 260, 263 (Minn. App. 2000), 211
Shaver v. Shaver, 165 Cal. Rptr. 672 (Cal. App. 1982), 399
Shaw v. Shaw, 269 P. 80 (Wash. 1928), 141
Shepherd v. Shepherd, 876 P.2d 429, 432 (Utah App. 1994), 432
Shepp v. Shepp, 906 A.2d 1165 (Pa. 2006), 279
Sheppard v. Mack, 427 N.E.2d 522, 528 (Ohio App. 1980), 500
Sherbert v. Verner, 374 U.S. 398, 403 (1963), 142
Sherrer v. Sherrer, 334 U.S. 343 (1948), 158, 705, 733
Shineovich and Kemp, 214 P.3d 29 (2009); 2009WL 2032113 (Or. App. 2009), 516, 548
Sielck v. Sielck, 202 Fed. Appx. 919 (7th Cir. 2006), 691
Sigg v. Sigg, 905 P.2d 908 (Utah. App. 1995), 313
Silvan v. Sylvan, 632 A.2d 528 (N.J. Super. 1993), 367
Silverman v. Silverman, 338 F.3d 886 (8th Cir. 2003), 728
Simeone v. Simeone, 581 A.2d 162 (Pa. 1990), 423
Simmons v. Simmons, 486 N.W.2d 788 (Minn. App. 1992), 290
Simmons v. Simmons, 708 A.2d 949 (Conn. 1998), 404
Sims v. Adoption Alliance, 922 S.W.2d 213 (Tex. App. 1996), 530
Singson v. Com., 621 S.E.2d 682 (Va. App. 2005), 472
Skeens v. Skeens, 2000 WL 1459867 (Va. App. 2000) (unpublished), 139
Slattery v. New York, 266 A.D.2d 24 (N.Y. App. 1999), 79
Slinkard v. Slinkard, 589 S.W.2d 635 (Mo. App. 1979), 205
Smelt v. County of Orange, 374 F. Supp. 2d 861, 880 (C.D. Cal. 2005), 76
Smith v. Fair Employment & Hous. Commn., 913 P.2d 909 (Cal. 1996), 487
Smith v. Gordon, 968 A.2d 1 (Del. 2009), 516
Smith v. Lanier, 998 S.W.2d 324 (Tex. App. 1999), 380
Smith v. Martin, 2009 WL 2028403 (Ohio App. 2009), 582
Smith v. Smith, 966 A.2d 109 (R.I. 2009), 47
Smoot v. Smoot, 357 S.E.2d 728 (Va. 1987), 383, 391
Snedaker v. Snedaker, 660 So. 2d 1070 (Fla. App. 1995), 430
Solomon v. Findley, 808 P.2d 294 (Ariz. 1991), 313

Somerville v. Somerville, 369 S.E.2d 459, 460 (W. Va. 1988), 382
Sosna v. Iowa, 419 U.S. 393 (1975), 68, 694
Sostock v. Reiss, 415 N.E.2d 1094 (Ill. 1980), 485
Sousley v. Sousley, 614 S.W.2d 942, 944 (Ky. 1981), 395
South Carolina Dept. of Soc. Servs. v. Father and Mother, 366 S.E.2d 40, 42 (S.C. App. 1988), 598, 607, 608
Spalding v. Spalding, 907 So. 2d 1270 (Fla. Dist. App. 2005), 313
Spayd v. Turner, Granzow & Hollenkamp, 482 N.E.2d 1232 (Ohio 1985), 409
Spence v. Spence, 930 So. 2d 415 (Miss. App. 2005), 138
Spencer v. Spencer, 882 N.E.2d 886, 889 (N.Y. 2008), 339
Sprouse v. Sprouse, 678 S.E.2d 328 (Ga. 2009), 470
St. Paul Fire and Marine Ins. Co. v. Jacobson, 826 F. Supp. 155, 158 (E.D. Va. 1993), 563
Stadter v. Siperko, 661 S.E. 2d 494 (Va. App. 2008), 290
Staley v. Ledbetter, 837 F.2d 1016, 1017-1018 (11th Cir. 1988), 690, 691
Stanley v. Illinois, 405 U.S. 645 (1972), 531, 691
Stanley v. Stanley, 956 A.2d 1 (Del. 2008), 401
Stanton v. Stanton, 421 U.S. 7 (1975), 20, 27, 347
State by Cooper v. French, 460 N.W.2d 2, 5-6 (Minn. 1990), 487
State ex rel. Adult and Family Serv. Div. v. Stoutt, 644 P.2d 1232, 1137 (Or. App. 1982), 500
State ex rel. Angela M.W. v. Kruzicki, 561 N.W.2d 729 (Wis. 1997), 603
State ex rel. C.S., 49 So. 3d 38 (La. App. 2010), 524
State ex rel. Carrington v. Schutts, 535 P.2d 982 (Kan. 1975), 715
State ex rel. Children, Youth & Families Dept., 47 P.3d 859 (N.M. App. 2002), 620
State ex rel. Dept. of Economic Sec. v. Demetz, 130 P.3d 986 (Ariz. App. 2006), 316
State ex rel. Dept. of Justice and Division of Child Support, 120 P.3d 1 (Ore. App. 2005), 505
State ex rel. Feeley v. Williams, 222 N.W. 927, 928 (Minn. 1929), 213
State ex rel. Garcia v. Dayton, 695 P.2d 477 (N.M. 1985), 715
State ex rel. Hamilton v. Snodgrass, 325 N.W.2d 740 (Iowa 1982), 500
State ex rel. Holcomb, 239 P.2d 545(Wash. 1952), 44
State ex rel. Larimore v. Snyder, 291 N.W.2d 241 (Neb. 1980), 715
State ex rel. Miesner v. Geile, 747 S.W.2d 757 (Mo. App. 1988), 66, 82
State ex rel. Nelson v. Nelson, 216 N.W.2d 140, 143 (Minn. 1974), 702
State ex rel. Oklahoma Bar Assn. v. Downes, 121 P.3d 1058 (Okla. 2005), 675
State ex rel. Schneider v. Liggett, 576 P.2d 221 (Kan. 1978), 31
State ex rel. Williams v. Marsh, 626 S.W.2d 223 (Mo. 1982), 585
State of N.M. ex rel. CYFD v. Amanda H., 154 P.3d 674 (N.M. App. 2006), 604
State of N.M. ex rel. CYFD v. Donna J., 129 P.3d 167, 171 (N.M. 2006), 254
State of N.M. ex rel. CYFD v. Lisa A., 187 P.3d 189 (N.M. App. 2008), 171
State v. Anderson, 396 P.2d 558, 561 (Or. 1964), 48
State v. Bren, 704 N.W.2d 170 (Minn. App. 2005), 332
State v. Bunker, 238 P.3d 487 (Wash. 2010), 588
State v. Carswell, 871 N.E.2d 547 (Ohio 2007), 583
State v. Clifford, 787 P.2d 571 (Wash. App. 1990), 44
State v. Collins, 847 P.2d 528 (Wash. App. 1993), 123
State v. DeMeo, 118 A.2d 1 (N.. 1955), 122
State v. Denzel B., 192 P.3d 260 (N.M. App. 2008), 599
State v. Dumlao, 491 A.2d 404 (Conn. App. 1985), 612
State v. Gans, 151 N.E.2d 709 (Ohio 1958), 20
State v. Hernandez, 805 P.2d 1057, 1059-1060 (Az. App. 1990), 612
State v. Holm, 136 P.3d 726 (Utah 2006), cert. denied, 549 U.S. 1252, 127 (2007), 58, 60
State v. J.Q., 617 A.2d 1196 (N.J. 1993), 600
State v. Jackson, 80 Mo. 175, 1883 WL 9519 (Mo. 1883), 53
State v. John, 881 A.2d 920 (R.I. 2005), 589
State v. Johnson, 670 N.W.2d 802 (Neb. App. 2003), 123
State v. Lamb, 227 N.W. 830 (Iowa 1929), 62
State v. Lefevre, 117 P.3d 980 (N.M. App. 2005), 599
State v. Lowell, 78 Minn. 166 (Minn. 1899), 46

State v. MacLennan, 702 N.W.2d 219 (Minn. 2005), 612
State v. McKnight, 576 S.E.2d 168 (S.C. 2003), 604
State v. Meacham, 612 P.2d 795 (Wash. 1980), 44
State v. Noll, 507 N.W.2d 44 (Neb. App. 1993), 333
State v. Nuzman, 95 P.3d 252 (Ore. App. 2004), 333
State v. Oakley, 605 S.E.2d 215 (N.C. App. 2004), 90, 461
State v. Pass, 121 P.2d 882 (Ariz. 1942), 53
State v. Planned Parenthood of Alaska, 35 P.3d 30 (Alaska 2001), 647
State v. Poehnelt, 722 P.2d 304, 318 (App. 1985), 612
State v. Presidential Women's Center, 707 So. 2d 1145 (Fla. App. 1998), 651
State v. Price, 886 N.E.2d 852 (Ohio 2008), 589
State v. Romano, 155 P.3d 1102 (Hawaii 2007), 89, 460
State v. Searle, 56 Vt. 516 (Vt. 1884), 121
State v. Sharon H., 429 A.2d 1321, 1326-28 (Del. Super. 1981), 61, 63
State v. Skinner, 43 A.2d 76 (Conn. 1945), 62
State v. Smith, 85 S.E. 958 (S.C. 1915), 62
State v. Waddell, 504 S.E.2d 84 (N.C. App. 1998), 60
State v. Walker, 553 P.2d 1093, 1095 (Wis. 1976), 500
State v. Wallace, 9 N.H. 515, 517 (N.H. 1838), 138
State v. Ward, 28 S.E.2d 785 (S.C. 1944), 23, 46
State v. Ward, 849 N.E.2d 1076 (Ohio App. 2006), 582
Stein v. Sandow, 468 N.Y.S.2d 910 (N.Y. App. 1983), 317
Steinke v. Steinke, 357 A.2d 674 (Pa. Super. 1975), 136
Stenberg v. Carhart, 530 U.S. 914 (2000) (Carhart I), 639, 640
Sterbling v. Sterbling, 519 N.E.2d 673 (Ohio App. 1987), 276
Sterling v. Borough of Minersville, 232 F.3d 190, 196 (3d Cir. 2000), 649
Stevens v. Stevens, 492 N.E.2d 131, 136-137 (Ohio 1986), 404
Stevens v. U.S., 146 F.2d 120 (10th Cir. 1944), 54
Stewart v. Soda, 226 A.D.2d 1102 (N.Y. 1996), 206
Stewart v. Stewart, 152 P.3d 544 (Idaho 2007), 352
Storey v. Storey, 862 A.2d 551 (N.J. Super. 2004), 370
Stratton v. Wilson, 185 S.W. 522, 523 (Ky. 1916), 422
Strauss v. Horton, 207 P.3d 48 (Cal. 2009), 83
Stringer v. Vincent, 411 N.W.2d 474 (Mich. App. 1987), 231
Sullivan v. Porter, 861 A.2d 625, 630 (Me. 2004), 476
Superior Court v. Ricketts, 836 A.2d 707 (Md. App. 2003), 339
Suter v. Artist M., 503 U.S. 347 (1992), 615
Swanson v. Swanson, 580 S.E.2d 526 (Ga. 2003), 664
Swanson v. Swanson, 583 N.W.2d 15 (Minn. App. 1998), 399
Swope v. Swope, 689 A.2d 264 (Pa. 1997), 200

T.B. v. L.R.M., 786 A.2d 913 (Pa. 2001), 278
T.E.P. v. Leavitt, 840 F. Supp. 110 (D. Utah 1993), 30
T.L. v. W.L., 820 A.2d 506 (Del. Fam. 2003), 701
T.M.H. v D.M.T., 79 So. 3d 787 (Fla. App. 2011), 558
Tallman v. Tabor, 859 F.Supp. 1078 (E.D. Mich. 1994), 177
Taylor v. Taylor, 832 P.2d 429, 431 (Okla. App. 1991), 432, 449
Taylor v. Taylor, 978 A.2d 538 (Conn. App. 2009), 362
Taylor v. Texas Dept. of Public Welfare, 549 S.W.2d 422 (Tex. App. 1977), 715
Temlock v. Temlock, 898 A.2d 209 (Conn. 2006), 255
Terwilliger v. Terwilliger, 64 S.W.3d 816 (Ky. 2002), 384, 393
Tetterton v. Arctic Tankers, Inc., 116 F. Supp. 429 (E.D. Pa. 1953), 485
Thomas v. Campbell, 960 So.2d 694 (Ala. App. 2006), 316
Thomas v. LaRose, 400 S.E.2d 809 (W.Va. 1990), 490
Thomas v. Thomas, 203 So. 2d 118, 123 (Ala. 1967), 325
Thompson v. Pafundi, 8 A.2d 476 (Vt. 2010), 181, 208
Thompson v. Thompson, 405 N.Y.S.2d 974, 975 (Fam. Ct. 1978), 315
Thompson v. Thompson, 484 U.S. 174 (1988), 245, 248
Thompson v. Thompson, 811 N.E.2d 888, 912 (Ind. App. 2004), 381

Thornburgh v. *Abbott*, 490 U.S. 401 (1989), 57
Thornburgh v. *American Coll. of Obst. & Gyn.*, 476 U.S. 747 (1986), 632
Tigert v. Tigert, 595 P.2d 815 (Okla. App. 1979), 146
Tirrell v. Tirrell, 45 A. 153, 154 (1900), 135
Toiberman v. Tisera, 998 So. 2d 4 (Fla. App. 2008), 670
Tong v. Jocson, 142 Cal. Rptr. 726 (Cal. 1977), 485
Tong v. Marvin, 15 Mich. 60, 68 (Mich. 1866), 429
Torres v. Kunze, 945 A.2d 472 Conn. App. 2008), 335
Town of Castle Rock, Colo. v. Gonzales, 125 S. Ct. 2796 (2005), 588
Towner v. Ridgway, 182 P.3d 347 (Utah 2008), 585
Tremain v. Tremain, 646 N.W.2d 661 (Neb. 2002), 224
Trenchard v. Trenchard, 92 N.E. 243 (Ill. 1910), 142
Trickey v. Trickey, 642 S.W.2d 47 (Tex. App. 1982), 143
Trimble v. Gordon, 430 U.S. 762 (1977), 496, 497
Trimmer v. *Van Bomel*, 434 N.Y.S.2d 82 (N.Y. Sup. 1980), 466
Tropea v. Tropea, 665 N.E.2d 145, 148 (N.Y. 1996), 220, 225
Trosky v. Mann, 581 A.2d 177, 178 (Pa. Super. 1990), 315
Troxel v. Granville, 530 U.S. 57, 68-69 (2000), 190, 285, 286, 288, 289, 596
Tsai v. Tien, 832 N.E.2d 809 (Ohio App. 2005), 362
Tucker v. Fisk, 28 N.E. 1051 (Mass. 1891), 538
Turner v. Rogers, 131 S. Ct. 2507 (2011), 331
Turner v. Safely, 482 U.S. 78 (1987), 56
Turner v. Turner, 684 S.E.2d 596 (Ga. 2009), 311
Turon State Bank v. Estate of Frampton, 845 P.2d 79 (Kan. App. 1993), 476

U.S. v. *Amer*, 110 F.3d 873 (2d Cir. 1997), 726
U.S. v. *Anthony*, 24 F. Cas. 829 (N.D. N.Y. 1873), 8
U.S. v. Commissioner of Immigration at Port of New York, 298 F. 103 (S.D. N.Y. 1924), 50
U.S. v. Dedman, 527 F.3d 577 (6th Cir. 2008), 88
U.S. v. Handley, 564 F. Supp. 2d 996 (S.D. Iowa 2008), 90
U.S. v. Jarvison, 409 F.3d 1221 (10th Cir. 2005), 23
U.S. v. Pillor, 387 F. Supp.2d 1053 (N.D. Cal. 2005), 341
U.S. v. Thompson, 458 F. Supp. 2d 730 (N.D. 2006), 89
U.S. v. *Westinghouse* Elec. Corp., 638 F.2d 570 (3d Cir. 1980), 649
Ulrich v. Cornell, 484 N.W.2d 545, 548 (Wis. 1992), 318
United States v. Clapox, 35 F. 575, 578 (D. Or. 1888), 123
United States v. Davis, 370 U.S. 65 (1962), 410
United States v. Edelkind, 525 F.3d 388 (5th Cir. 2008), 341
United States v. Gill, 264 F.3d 929, 933 (9th Cir. 2001), 340
United States v. Hampshire, 95 F.3d 999, 1005 (10th Cir. 1996), 735
United States v. Jacobson, 785 F. Supp. 563 (E.D. Va. 1992), 563
United States v. Klinzing, 315 F.3d 803 (7th Cir. 2003), 341
United States v. Lutwak, 195 F.2d 748, 753-54 (7th Cir. 1952), 115
United States v. Morrow, 368 F. Supp. 863 (C.D. Ill. 2005), 341
United States v. Orellana, 62 M.J. 595, 601 (N.M. App. 2005), 460
United States v. Thompson, 458 F. Supp. 2d 730 (N.D. Ind. 2006), 460
Upham v. Upham, 630 N.E.2d 307 (Mass. App. 1994), 453

V.C. v. M.J.B., 748 A.2d 539 (N.J. 2000), 291
Valleau v. Valleau, 6 Paige (N.Y. 1836), 109
Valmonte v. Bane, 18 F.3d 992 (2d Cir. 1994), 610
Van Bloom v. Van Bloom, 246 N.W.2d 588 (Neb. 1976), 371
Van de Loo v. Van de Loo, 346 N.W.2d 173 (Minn. App. 1984), 408
Van v. Zahorik, 597 N.W.2d 15 (Mich. 1999), 476
Vanderbilt v. Vanderbilt, 354 U.S. 416, 418-419 (1957), 156, 698
Varnum v. Brien, 763 N.W.2d 862 (Iowa 2009), 72, 82
Vitakis-Valchine v. Valchine, 793 So. 2d 1094, 1099 (Fla. App. 2001), 663
Voishan v. Palmer, 609 A.2d 319 (Md. 1992), 305
Voyles v. Voyles, 644 P.2d 847 (Alaska 1982), 371

W. v. W., 779 A.2d 716 (Conn. 2001), 514
Wade v. Hirschman, 903 So. 2d 928 (Fla. 2005), 192, 199
Waite v. *Waite*, 4 N.Y. 95 (N.Y. 1855), 131
Waite v. *Waite*, 959 So. 2d 610 (Ala. 2006), 695
Waits v. *Waits*, 634 S.E.2d 799 (Ga. App. 2006), 152
Wake Cty. ex rel. Carrington v. Townes, 281 S.E.2d 765, 769 (N.C. App. 1981), 500
Waldman v. Maini, 195 P.3d 850 (Nev. 2008), 380
Walker v. Superior Court, 763 P.2d 852 (Cal. 1988), 601
Wallace v. *Wallace*, 12 So.3d 572 (Miss. App. 2009), 372, 373
Wallace v. *Wallace*, 145 S.E. 2d 546 (Ga. 1965), 120
Waltenberg v. *Waltenberg*, 298 F. 842, 844 (D.C. App. 1924), 134
Wannamaker v. *Wannamaker*, 406 S.E.2d 180 (S.C. App. 1991), 392
Warwick v. *Warwick*, 438 N.W.2d 673, 678 (Minn. App. 1989), 367
Washington Statewide Org. of Stepparents v. Smith, 536 P.2d 1202 (Wash. 1975), 318
Washington v. *Washington*, 846 So. 2d 895 (La. App. 2003), 352
Washington v. *Washington*, 770 N.W.2d 908 (Mich. App. 2009), 388
Watt v. *Watt*, 971 P.2d 608, 616 (Wyo. 1999), 218
Waubanascum v. Shawano County, 416 F.3d 658, 665 (7th Cir. 2005), 614
Weatherford ex rel. Michael L. v. State, 81 P.3d 320 (Ariz. 2003), 615
Webb v. *Webb*, 546 So. 2d 1062 (Fla. App. 1989), 171
Webster v. Reproductive Health Services, 492 U.S. 490 (1989), 633, 645
Webster v. *Webster*, 716 N.W. 2d 471 (Neb. 2006), 400
Wehrkamp v. *Wehrkamp*, 357 N.W.2d 264 (S.D. 1984), 404
Weinand v. *Weinand*, 616 N.W.2d 1 (Neb. 2000), 290
Weinberg v. *Weinberg*, 255 A.D. 366 (N.Y. App. 1938), 110
Weinstein v. *Weinstein*, 911 A.2d 1077 (Conn., 2007), 302
Weiss v. Marcus, 124 Cal. Rptr. 297 (Cal. App. 1975), 480
Wellmaker v. Roberts, 101 S.E.2d 712 (Ga. 1958), 483
Wells v. Talham, 194 N.W. 36 (Wis. 1923), 118
Wenz v. Schwartze, 598 P.2d 1086, 1091-1092 (Mont. 1979), 707
Whalen v. Roe, 429 U.S. 589 (1977), 629, 649
Whalen v. *Whalen*, 581 S.W.2d 578, 579 (Ky. App. 1979), 160
Wheeler v. Idaho Dept. of Health and *Welfare*, 207 P.3d 988 (Idaho 2009), 334
Wheeler v. *Wheeler*, 230 A.D.2d 844 (N.Y. App. Div. 1996), 371
Wheeler v. *Wheeler*, 548 N.W.2d 27 (N.D. 1996), 367
White v. Nason, 874 A.2d 891 (Me. 2005), 277
Whitehorn v. *Whitehorn*, 332, 36 P.2d 943 (Okla. 1934), 136
Whorton v. Dillingham, 248 Cal. Rptr. 405, 409-410 (Cal. App 1998), 468
Whorton v. Dillingham, 202 Cal. App. 3d (Cal. 1988), 467
Wilbur v. *Wilbur*, 498 N.Y.S.2d 525 (N.Y. App. 1986), 388
Wilcox v. Trautz, 693 N.E.2d 141 (Mass. 1998), 467
Williams v. Lynch, 245 A.D.2d 715 (N.Y. App. 1997), 476
Williams v. State of North Carolina (*Williams* I), 317 U.S. 287 (1942), 156, 696, 708
Williams v. State of North Carolina (*Williams* II), 325 U.S. 226 (1945), 156, 696, 697
Williams v. *Williams*, 543 P.2d 1401 (Okla. 1975), 143
Williamson v. First Nat. Bank of *Williamson*, 164 S.E. 777 (W. Va. 1931), 421, 422
Williamson v. Shoults, 423 So. 2d 874 (Ala. App. 1982), 141
Williamson v. *Williamson*, 690 S.E.2d 25 7 (Ga. App. 2010), 508
Wilson v. Ake, 354 F. Supp. 2d 1298 (M.D. Fla. 2005), 75
Wilson v. Butler, 584 So. 2d 414, 416 (Miss. 1991), 720
Wilson County ex rel. Egbert v. Egbert, 569 S.E.2d 727 (N.C. App. 2002), 717
Wilson v. *Wilson*, 185 N.W. 97 (Iowa 1921), 421

Wilson v. *Wilson*, 653 S.E.2d 702 (Ga. 2007), 658
Wilson v. *Wilson*, 741 S.W.2d 640 (Ark. 1987), 403
Winn v. *Wiggins*, 135 A.2d 673 (N.J. Super 1957), 34
Winston v. *Children and Youth Servs. of Del. County*, 948 F.2d 1380 (3d Cir. 1991), 692
Wisner v. *Wisner*, 631 P.2d 115 (Ariz. App. 1981), 404
Withers v. *Withers*, 390 So. 2d 453 (Fla. Dist. Ct. App. 1980), 362
Witowski v. *Roosevelt*, 199 P.3d 1072 (Wyo. 2009), 718
Wolfe v. *Wolfe*, 378 N.E.2d 1181, 1188 (Ill. 1978), 127
Wolfe v. *Wolfe* 610 N.W.2d 222 (Wisc. App. 2000), 211
Wolk v. *Wolk*, 464 A.2d 780 (Conn. 1983), 316
Women of the State v. *Gomez*, 542 N.W.2d 17, 19 (Minn. 1995), 647
Women's Health Ctr. of W. Va., Inc. v. *Panepinto*, 446 S.E.2d 658 (W. Va. 1993), 647
Wood v. *Dehan*, 571 N.W.2d 186 (Wis. App. 1997), 279
Wood v. *Redwine*, 33 P.3d 53 (Okla. App. 2001), 268
Woodard v. *Woodard*, 696 N.W.2d 221 (Wis. App. 2005), 372
Wooddy v. *Wooddy*, 261 A.2d 486 (Md. 1970), 141
Woodward v. *Commissioner of Social Sec.*, 760 N.E.2d 257 (Mass. 2002), 567, 574
Woosnam v. *Woosnam*, 587 S.W.2d 262 (Ky. App. 1979), 385
Worley v. *Whiddon*, 403 S.E.2d 799 (Ga. 1991), 282
Woy v. *Woy*, 737 S.W.2d 769 (Mo. App. W.D. 1987), 119, 127
Wright v. *State*, 81 A.2d 602 (Md. 1951), 28
Wright v. *Wright*, 181 S.W.3d 49 (Ky. App. 2005), 584
Wulff v. *Wulff*, 500 N.W.2d 845, 851 (Neb. 1993), 315

Xiao Yang Chen v. *Fischer*, 843 N.E.2d 723 (N.Y. 2005), 593

Yaghoubinejad v. *Haghighi*, 894 A.2d 1173 (N.J. Super. 2006), 22, 43
Yearta v. *Scroggins*, 268 S.E.2d 151, 153 (Ga. 1980), 243
Young v. *Young*, 628 N.Y.S. 2d 957 (N.Y. App. 1995), 217
Young v. *Van Duyne*, 92 P.3d 1269 (N.M. App. 2004), 539
Younger v. *Harris*, 401 U.S. 37 (1971), 692
Yun v. *Yun*, 908 S.W.2d 787 (Mo. App. 1995), 43

Zablocki v. *Redhail*, 434 U.S. 374 (1978), 55, 69
Zan v. *Zan*, 820 N.E.2d 1284 (Ind. App. 2005), 362
Zaremba v. *Cliburn*, 949 S.W.2d 822 (Tex. App. 1997), 468, 475
Ziegler v. *Ziegler*, 691 P.2d 773, 780 (Idaho App. 1985), 219
Zindulka v. *Zindulka*, 726 N.Y.S.2d 173 (N.Y. App. 2001), 236
Zoske v. *Zoske*, 64 N.Y.S.2d 819 (N.Y. Sup. 1946), 146
Zummo v. *Zummo*, 574 A.2d 1130 (Pa. Super. 1990), 279
Zurick v. *Inman*, 426 S.W.2d 767 (Tenn. 1968), 725

Index

ABA (American Bar Association)
ethical opinion in re collaborative law process, 681
Model Act Governing Assisted Reproductive Technology, 546
Lawyer as mediator, 682
Parenting coordinator report, 667-668
Revised Uniform Reciprocal Enforcement Act, 722
self-representation, 678
Uniform Marriage and Divorce Act approved, 147, 348-49
Unrepresented litigants study, 678
Abortion
consent
informed, 631-633, 636-637
parental, 630, 641-644, 646
picketing, consent to talking, 638
statement giving consent, 634
three physicians, 628
deference to physicians, 635-636
history, 623-625
indigent abortions, 644
informed consent, 632-633
mature minor, 642
Medicaid coverage, 644-645
parental notification by minor, 641
blanket consent, 641
48-hour notification, 642
mature minor exception
notifying both parents, 642-643
notifying one parent, 643
written notice to parent, 644
partial birth legislation, 639-641
physician duty to inform, 636-637
picketing, 637-638
Planned Parenthood v. Casey, 632-637, 641
privacy theory discussed, 625-628
expanding privacy, 629-630
public facilities, 645-646
public funding, 645
Roe v. Wade, 628
second trimester issues, 630-632
state constitutional right to privacy provisions, 646-647
undue burden, 631-632, 634, 638, 647
viability determination, 629-630, 632-633, 635-636, 646, 651
waiting period, 631
Adoption
abrogation of, 518-519
Adoption and Safe Families Act, 528
Adoption Assistance and Child Welfare Act, 615
adoption registry, 533-534
adults adopting adults, 534-535
agency adoptions, 520
claims — generally
fraud, 538
negligent misrepresentation, 538-539
consent to adoption
birth mother's consent, 535
minor child's, 534
prebirth consent, 530-531
putative father's consent, 531-533
forms of
agency adoptions, 520
independent adoption, 520
international adoption, 522-523
near relative adoption, 521
open adoption, 521-522
stepparent adoption, 520-521
subsidized adoption, 522
history, 517-518
Indian Child Welfare Act (ICWA), 527-528
independent adoption, 520
legal effect of an adoption, 519
minor child's consent, 534
Multiethnic Placement Act (MEPA), 527
procedures for an adoption
filing a petition, 524
investigating prospective parents, 524-525
sealing adoption records, 525-526
waiting period, 530
negligent misrepresentation, 538-539
qualifications of potential adoptive parent
age, 529
race, 527
sexual orientation, 528
registry to determine putative father

failing to use adoption registry, 533
implied consent, 533-534
UPA exceptions, 534
subsidized adoption, 522
Uniform Adoption Act, 538
waiting period to adopt, 530
ALI (American Law Institute)
abortion, 625
alimony, 348-350
loss compensation theory, 350
best interests defined, 176-177
cohabitation, 473
custody
domestic violence, 275
extramarital sexual conduct, 209
relocation, model legislation, 229
shared, 229
parenting plans, 658
premarital contracts, 426-427
property definitions, 395-396
relocation, model legislation, 229
terminology created to reduce conflict, 164, 275
Alimony
ALI standards, 350-351
caregiver alimony, 354
distinguished from property division, 360
duration of award, 359
duration of marriage, 351
fault-related alimony, 354-355
ancient ecclesiastical concept of fault, 345
historic view, 344-345
forms and duration of alimony
caregiver, 354
incapacity, 352
limited durational, 354
permanent, 351
rehabilitative, 352-353
reimbursement, 353
gender, 346
guidelines discussed, 358
history
alimony for husbands, 346
ancient ecclesiastical concept of fault, 345
common law disabilities and duties, 345
dowry, 344
Ecclesiastical courts, 344-345
Fault, early view, 344-345
husband's common law duty, 347
unity doctrine, 344
imputation of income, 357-358
incapacity alimony, 352
limited durational, 354
modifying award. *See* modifying alimony
necessaries
common law duty to provide, 345, 347
percentage formulas, 358
permanent alimony, 351
rehabilitative alimony, 352-353
reimbursement alimony, 353
tax treatment, 359-360
Uniform Marriage and Divorce Act, 348-350
Alternative dispute resolution procedures. *See* Arbitration, Dispute Resolution processes, Mediation
Annulment
Adultery, 123-125
Biblical principles, 73, 93
California, standing statute, 98-99
bastardization of children, 120
bigamy as a crime, 121-122
canon law, 93-94
capacity
age, 107-108
influence of drugs or alcohol, 19, 97, 111
mental capacity, 107
cohabitation, 120
differs from divorce, 93
drugs, alcohol involved, 19, 97, 111
duress, 118-119
Enoch Arden statutes, 106
fraud
burden of proof, 111-112
essence of marriage, 111
fortune hunter, 112
lying, 112
misrepresentation, 116-117
pregnancy promises, 116-117
religious promises, 117-118
Idaho annulment time limits, 96-97
immigration fraud—sham marriage, 115-116
impotence, 119
incest criminal statutes, 123
in rem proceedings, 121
Minnesota annulment time limits, 97
mock marriage, 111
New Jersey bigamy statute, 122
Ohio annulment provision, 95
relation back
alimony, 103
Enoch Arden statutes, 106
generally, 102

three views described, 103-106
UMDA perspective, 106
sexual preference, 119-120
standing to bring action, 98, 108
sterile, 119
theory of annulment, 94-95
time limitations on bringing actions, 96-97
UMDA, 106
voidable relationship defined, 96
void relationship defined, 95-96
Antenuptial contracts. *See* Premarital contracts
Arbitration
arbitrator providing legal advice, 682
generally,, 670
Model Family Law Arbitration Act of AAML, 670
Artificial insemination. *See* Assisted reproduction
Assisted reproduction
ABA Model Act Governing Assisted Reproductive Technology, 546
artificial insemination
husband's consent, 548-549
husband's sperm, posthumous, 566-567
known donors and unmarried mothers, 551-552
baby selling, 554
child's best interests, 554
constitutional issues
definitions, 542-543
frozen embryos
balancing test, 561-562
contemporaneous consent, 561
disposition when divorced, 560
gestational surrogacy
constitutional right to, 559-560
defined, 544
donated eggs, husband's sperm, 557
husband's sperm, anonymous donor, 556
Johnson v. Calvert, 556
wife's eggs, husband's sperm, relative surrogate, 557
government oversight, 544
history, 541-542
third party donor—adultery, 542
husband's consent, 549-550
insurance, who is covered, 565-566
in vitro fertilization
history, 542-543
liability of physicians' generally, 562-563
genetic material mix-up, 564
wrongful death, 564
wrongful life, 563
known donors—unmarried recipients, 551-552
posthumous reproduction, 566-567
same-sex couples, 550-551, 558-559
sperm as property, 567-568
surrogacy
Baby M, 554-556
baby selling, 555
best interests, 555
coercion of contract, 555
women exploited, 555
legislation allow and banning, 553-554
overview, 552
Uniform Parentage Act, 545
Uniform Putative and Unknown Fathers Act, 546-547
Uniform Status of Children of Assisted Conception Act, 546-547
wrongful death, 564
wrongful life, 563

Battered child syndrome
generally, 611-612
Blood tests
general view, 28-29
HIV, 539
paternity, 44, 143, 501, 515

Child Abduction
general view,, 278
Child abuse
Adoption and Safe Families Act (ASFA), 12, 528, 615-616
Adoption Assistance and Child Welfare Act (AACWA), 12-13, 615
ADR (Alternative Dispute Resolution), 612-613, 657
battered child syndrome, 611-612
central registry of reports, 610
Child Abuse Prevention and Treatment Act, 13, 596-597
constitutional issues, vague and infringing fundamental rights, 596
defining, 597
emergency orders, 586, 611
UCCJEA, 268
failure to protect from harm, 602-603
force toward child, 598-599
forms of abuse and neglect
emotional or mental abuse, 593, 603

failure to protect from harm, 602
housing and housekeeping
medical treatment, 598, 601
neglect, 595
prenatal drug abuse, 603-604
reasonable force to correct a child, 599
sexual abuse, 600
spanking, 599-600
foster care, 614-617
ICWA, 597, 616
intimate partner violence, relation to child abuse, 162, 277
mandated reporting, 609
medical neglect, 190, 601-602
neglect, 600-601
parental duty to protect child from harm, 602
protocols for assessing, 277, 578-579
reasonable efforts to unify families, 615-616
supervised parenting time, 277
witnesses to domestic abuse, impact on, 577-578
Child custody. *See* Custody; Visitation; UCCJEA
Child support
child care costs, 312-313
duration of support, 313
education support, 313-314
emancipation of child, 314-315
enforcement by federal government. *See* chapter 10
guidelines
deviating from, 309-310
extraordinary needs, 310
high-earning obligors, 310
mandated, 298
presumptive guidelines, 305
history
common law, 296
Elizabethan poor laws, 295-296
income
defined, 299
employer's contribution to pension plan, 300
imputed income, 302
lump sum income payments and commissions, 300
military retirement income and allowances, 301
overtime income, 301
pensions, 300,
personal service income, 299
rental income, 299
seasonal employment income, 301
self-employment, 299
stepparent income, 318
vested stock options, 300
income shares model, 305-306
joint physical and parenting time offsets, 308-309
lump sum payments, 300
medical support, 311-312
monitoring how parental contribution to support is spent, 317
obligor's death, 316-317
Omnibus Budget Reconciliation Act of 1993, 298
pension plans, 300
percentage of income model, 307-308
state income models
income shares model, 305-306
percentage of income model, 307-308
stepparent liability, 318-319
stock options, 300
tax treatment, 318
withholding visitation (parenting time) for failure to pay support, 317-318
Child support enforcement
Bankruptcy, effect of, 336
Child Support Recovery Act of 1992, 340-341
contempt of court
civil contempt, 330
criminal contempt, 330-331
indigent right to counsel, 331
property awards, 331
credit bureau reporting, 334
criminal action
contempt, 330-331
debt, nonpayment of, 332
nonsupport, 332
driver's license suspension, 334
Full Faith and Credit Act for Child Support Orders Act, 339, 717-718
garnishment, 333
lottery winnings, 335
occupational license suspension, 334-335
passport denial, 335
Personal Responsibility and Work Opportunity Reconciliation Act, 340
publication as "deadbeat" obligor, 334
recreational license suspension, 334
tax return interception, 333
UIFSA, 12, 322, 337-338, 340, 702, 715, 718, 722-725, 728

URESA, 336-337
wage assignment, 335-336
Welfare Reform Act of 1996, 340
worker's compensation, 335
Child support and Establishment of Paternity Act of 1974
generally, 297
Child support modification. *See* Modifying child support
Child Support Recovery Act
generally, 340-341
Cohabitation without formal marriage
ALI (American Law Institute), 473
alimony, 468-471
benefits from state or federal government, 486
burden of proof, 475
contract theories
consideration, 468
constructive trusts, 480
express oral agreements, 458, 464, 467, 476-477
express written contracts, 475
implied in fact contracts, 474
quasi contracts, 478-479
resulting trusts, 479-480
confidentiality when drafting, 475-476
consideration, 468
constructive trusts, 480
data on cohabitation, 459-460
express oral contracts, 458, 464, 467, 476-477
express written contracts, 475
housing discrimination, 486-488
implied contracts, 477-478
insurance policy coverage, 486
loss of consortium claims, 485
Marvin Doctrine, 461-463
meretricious relationship doctrine, 457, 462, 464, 467, 491
minority view, 463-467
New York view, 466
partial performance, 476-477
prior to marriage, 470
quasi-contracts, 478-479
reasons people cohabit, 458
restatement of contracts, 473-474, 478
resulting trusts, 479-480
same-sex partners, 467
separating illicit relationship from contract, 467-468
statute of frauds, 475-476
statute of limitations, 488-489
statute of wills, 480-481
wills, 477
wrongful death claims, 484-485
Collaborative law
cooperative law compared, 666
collaborative lawyers, generally, 681-682
ethical opinion, 665
generally, 664-665
uniform collaborative law act, 665-666
Common law marriage. *See* Marriage
Contempt
alimony (maintenance), failure to pay, 360
child support, failure to pay, 686
civil contempt, 330
clean hands doctrine as defense to, 139
criminal contempt, 330-331
enforcement of property awards, 331
failing to attend mandatory divorce sessions, 163
indigent right to counsel, 331
paternity—right to council, 500
property settlements, 331
protective order—domestic violence, 588
Right to counsel, 331, 500, 587
substance abuse, 277
unwarranted denial of visitation, 205-206
violation of protective orders, 588
visitation order—enforcement, 205-206
Contingent fees
collection of post judgment arrearages, 676
exceptions, 676
explained, 676
model rules prohibit, 676
percentage agreements, 676
Cooperative law process
generally, 666
Covenant marriage
Generally, 51-52, 152-153
Custody of child
best interests considerations
careers, 182
child's preference, 178-179
cohabitation, 181
conduct not affecting child, 181
cooperative parenting agreement, 182
disability of parent, 178
domestic violence, 183
"friendly" parent provision, 182
gender of parents, 169, 182
race, 177
religion, 178

separating siblings, 180
cohabitation, 181-182
defining custodial relationships
joint legal and physical custody, 164
legal custody, 164
parenting plans, 165
physical custody, 163
domestic violence, 183
evaluators, 187-188
gay and lesbian parents, 181
guardian ad litem, 188
impact of divorce
effects of divorce on children, 161-162
effects on parenting, 162
legal custody, 164
joint legal custody, 171-173
maternal presumption, 169
mediation, 180
model acts
ALI, 176-177
UMDA, 176
natural parent presumption, 171
parental conduct, 181
paternal presumption, 168
parent education, 163
parenting plans, 165
physical custody, 164
primary parent presumption, 169-170
presumptions
joint legal and physical custody, 171-173
maternal, 169
natural parent, 171
paternal, 168
primary caretaker, 169-170
race of child, consideration, 177
religion of child, 178
right to representation, 180
separating siblings, 180
Custody modifying. *See* Modifying custody

Defense of Marriage Act (DOMA)
generally, 63-64, 74-75, 77, 84, 410-411, 716-717
state mini-DOMAs, 76
constitutional issues, 76
Dispute Resolution Processes
arbitration, 669-670
attorney's role, 657
collaborative process
disqualification agreement, 665
domestic violence, 665
ethical concerns, 665
generally, 664-665
condition precedent to post-decree action, 659
court approval of agreements, 658
defining, 655
domestic violence, 183-184, 653-654, 665
ethical concerns, 665
generally, 188
informed decision, 654
intimate partner violence, 660-661
interest-based process, 655
intimate partner violence, 660-661
legal advice, 657
mandatory mediation, 659-660
mediation as interest-based process, 655-656
mediation defined, 655
mediator
qualifications, 657
providing legal advice, 682
role of mediator, 656
testimony, 658-659
parenting coordinator, 666-669
screening protocols, 653
settlement rates, 657-658
testifying, 658-659
Uniform Collaborative Law Act, 665-666
Uniform Collaborative Law Rules, 665-666
Uniform Mediation Act, 659
Divorce — grounds and defenses
abandonment, 135
adultery, 133-134
constructive desertion, 135-136
covenant marriage and divorce, 152-153
cruel and inhuman treatment, 134
desertion, 135-137
divisible divorce, 155-157, 683-684, 697-699, 706
ex parte divorce. *See* divisible divorce
full faith and credit, 155-156
habitual drunkenness, 136
history
absolute divorce prohibited, 131
ancient history, 129-130
church control, 130
colonial divorce, 132
divorce after the American Revolution, 132
divorce *a mensa et thoro*, 131
jury trial, 151-152
parliamentary divorce, 131
protestant reformation, 131-132
Roman divorce, 130

irretrievable breakdown, 147
jury trial right, 151-152
legal separation, 151
limited divorce, 150-151
Lord Mansfield's rule, 143
mental cruelty, 134-135
same-sex divorce recognition, 153-154
recrimination, 139-140
religion as defense, 142-143
traditional defenses to divorce
collusion, 140
condonation, 140
connivance, 141
insanity, 141-142
laches, 141
provocation, 142
recrimination, 139-140
religious objections, 142-143
unclean hands, 139
traditional grounds for divorce
adultery, 133-134
constructive desertion, 135-136
cruel and inhuman treatment, 134
desertion, 135-137
habitual drunkenness, 136
indignities, 136
mental cruelty, 134-135
unclean hands, 139
Uniform Marriage and Divorce Act, 147-148
DNA testing
generally, 515
DOMA (Defense of Marriage Act)
generally, 63-64, 74-75, 77, 83, 410-411, 716-717
Domestic violence
access issues, 586-587
constitutional challenges, 585
co-operative parent provisions, 182
criminal sanctions, 592
defining by statute, 579-580
effectiveness of orders, 589-590
enforcement of orders, 588-589
ex parte and permanent orders, 583-584
Hague Convention, 594
history, 575, 579
impact on children, 577-588
intimate partner violence
co-operative parent provisions, 182
generally,, 162-163, 183-184
joint custody presumption, 172-173
mandatory arrest, 592-593
mutual restraining orders, 587
relief—who is covered, 581-582
relief that may be granted, 583
risk factors, 575-576
screening for domestic violence, 578-579
tort actions, 593
Violence Against Women Act, 591

Emancipation of minor
constructive, 314-315
criteria, 314
living separately, 315
military service, 315
UMDA, 316

Fault
origin of, 133

Grandparents
adoption, 521
ALI parenting time, 292
natural parent presumption vs third party, 171
parenting time—ALI standard
Troxel v. Granville, 285
visitation with grandchildren, 273, 285

Hague Convention
adoption, 522-523
burden of proof, 727
Canadian adoption of, 256
civil aspects of international abduction, 255, 593-594, 725-726
congressional implementation, 726-727
defenses, 727-728
habitual residence, 256, 727
jury trial, 728
recovery of child support, 338, 728-729

Incest
abortion, 625, 719-720
adopted children marrying each other, 62-63
affinity relationships
model penal code, 62
biblical prohibition, 61
crime, 62, 123
defined, 123
scope of typical statues,, 123, 460
void relationship, 23, 96
Indian Child Welfare Act (ICWA)
adoptions, 527-528
overview, 718-719

removal of child from home, 597
special protections afforded, 597
termination of parental rights, 616
burden of proof, 618
Intimate partner violence. *See also* Domestic violence
co-operative parent provisions, 182
generally,, 162-163, 183-184
joint custody presumption, 172-173
In vitro fertilization. *See* Assisted reproduction

Jurisdiction
abstention doctrine in federal court, criteria, 692-693
continuing jurisdiction by state court, 704-705
Defense of Marriage Act, 716
divisible divorce theory, 683-684, 697-699
domestic relations exception, 684-686
ex parte divorce, *see* divisible divorce
federal court reviewing state court judgments, 691
Full Faith and Credit for Child Support Orders Act, 717-718
full faith and credit given *ex parte* divorce
Hague Convention, 725-729
Indian Child Welfare Act, 718-720
in rem divorce, 699
liberty interest in familial relations, 691-692
long arm statutes, 699-702
due process issues, 703-704
personal jurisdiction in state court
continuing jurisdiction, 704-705
divisible divorce theory, 683-684, 697-699
due process considerations, 704, 707-708, 723
ex parte divorce, 155, 156, 696-697
generally, 683-684
in rem divorce, 699
long arm statutes, 699-702
waiving personal jurisdiction, 704-705
probate exception, 687
purposeful availment, 701
same-sex marriage, recognizing, 716-717
service of process within state, 704
Soldiers and Sailors Civil Relief Act, 720-722
status as a jurisdictional theory
adoption, 708
generally, 706
modifying custody, 706-707
protective orders, 708
restatement of conflict of laws, 709
termination of parental rights, 707
subject matter jurisdiction in federal court
abstention doctrine, 692-693
domestic relations exception, 684-686
federal question jurisdiction, 684
generally, 683
modification actions, 686
probate exception, 687
review of state court judgments, 691
subject matter jurisdiction in state court
challenging, 696-697
divisible divorce theory, 697-699
military provisions, 694
residency requirements, 693-695
voiding a decree, 695-696
supremacy clause, 686-687
Uniform Interstate Family Support Act (UIFSA), 722-725
waiving personal jurisdiction, 705-706

Maintenance. *See* Alimony
Marriage
capacity
age restrictions, 20-21, 107-108
guardian's consent, 19
state of mind, generally, 18-19
civil unions/domestic partners, 77-79
common law marriage
age to marry, 18
defined, 33
history, 31-32
limited recognition, 32-33
requirements, 33-34
temporary absence from state, 34
different from ordinary contracts, 18
domestic partners, 79-81
forms of marriage
confidential marriages, 50
covenant marriage, 51-52
ministerial act, 21
proxy marriage, 48-50
UMDA, 50
tribal marriages, 51
history, 17
lex loci doctrine, 63-64
license, 21-22
ministerial act, 21
parental consent, 20
premarital counseling, 30-31
premarital education, 30-31
premarital medical testing, 28-30

putative marriage doctrine, 35-36
community property states, 36
UMDA, 36, 50
restrictions removed
anti-miscegenation statutes, 53-55
child support owed, 55-56
epilepsy, 52-53
poverty, 55-56
prisoners, 56-57
race, 53-55
restrictions retained
adopted children marrying each other, 62-63
affinity, 62
bigamy, 59-60
consanguinity, 61-62
polygamy, 58-59
sham marriage — immigration fraud, 60-61
same-sex relationships
Biblical theory, 73-74
Bowers v. Hardwick, 76-77
civil unions, 77-79
Defense of Marriage Act, 74-75
Lawrence v. Texas, 76-78
outstate recognition of same-sex marriage, 84-85
religious perspectives, 72-74
same-sex marriage allowed, 82-83
separation of church and state, 74
state mini-DOMAs, 76
solemnizing a marriage, 22-23
transsexual relationships, 85
void/voidable relationships, 23-24, 85, 93, 95-96, 99, 102-127
UMDA, 19-20, 36, 50
Married Women's Acts
generally, 8-9, 344, 347
Mediation
arbitration, 669-670
attorney's role, 657
collaborative process
disqualification agreement, 665
domestic violence, 665
ethical concerns, 665
generally, 664-665
condition precedent to post decree action, 659
court approval of agreements, 658
defining, 655
domestic violence, 653-654, 665
ethical concerns, 665
informed decision, 654
interest-based process, 655
intimate partner violence, 660-661
legal advice, 657
mandatory mediation, 659-660
mediator
providing legal advice, 682
qualifications, 657
role of mediator, 656
parenting coordinator, 666-669
screening protocols, 653
settlement rates, 657-658
testifying, 658-659
Uniform Collaborative Law Act, 665-666
Uniform Collaborative Law Rules, 665-666
Uniform Mediation Act, 659
Modifying alimony
burden of proof, 363
change in circumstances
bad faith change, 367-368
change in occupation
voluntary change, 367
extraordinary circumstances, 371-372
generally, 362-363
obligor dies, 368
obligor retires, 366-367
obligor receives unanticipated income, 366
recipient becomes self-sufficient, 370-371
recipient cohabits after divorce, 372-373
recipient dies, 373
recipient remarries, 371-372
automatic termination, 371
recipient's needs increase, 371
cohabitation, 372-373
death of obligor, 368
death of recipient, 373
imputing income to obligor, 368
non-modification agreements
discretion of court to establish, 365
enforcement of, 365
UMDA, 364
reservation of jurisdiction, 363
retroactivity of award, 363
stipulations, 364
UMDA (Uniform Marriage and Divorce Act)
unconscionability test, 361-362
Modifying child support
bankruptcy, 336
Child Support Recovery Act of 1992, 340-341
cost-of-living adjustments, 324
court approval required, 329
criminal nonsupport, 332

duration of child support
emancipation of child, 322
employment changes, 324-325
enforcement efforts
child support debt, 330
contempt of court
civil contempt, 330
criminal contempt, 330
property awards, 331
right to counsel, 331
credit bureau reporting, 334
driver's license suspension, 334
federal crime, 340
garnishment, 333
lottery winnings, 335
occupational license suspension, 334-335
passport denial, 335
publication as "deadbeat,", 334
recreational license suspension, 334
tax return interception, 333
UIFSA, 337-338
wage assignment, 335-336
workers' compensation, 335
Full Faith and Credit for Child Support Orders Act, 339
non-modification agreements, 329-330
Personal Responsibility and Work Opportunity Reconciliation Act of 1966, 340
presumptions, 322-324
retroactive awards, 328
burden of proof, 322
overview, 322
presumptions, 322-324
Uniform Interstate Family Support Act, 337-338
Uniform Reciprocal Enforcement of Support Act, 336-337
voluntary unemployment
good faith test, 325
intermediate test, 325-326
strict rule test, 325
Welfare Reform Act of 1996, 340
Modifying custody — relocation
ALI, 209
burden of proof, 197
child's preference, 213-214
child support — failure to pay, 206
cohabiting with unmarried partner, 208
endangerment
burden of proof, 211
generally, 211
Minnesota, 195, 199
UMDA, 194
evidentiary hearing, necessity for, 195-196
immoral conduct, 207-209
integration into non-custodian's home, 207
modification standards — relocation not an issue
California, 199
Florida, 199
Minnesota, 195-198-199
New York, 199-200
Pennsylvania, 200
Texas, 200
moratorium on modification actions, 193
natural parent presumption, 227-228
new family theory, 221
parenting agreements, 212
poor parenting/lack of discipline, 209-210
preference, child's, 213-214
relocating to another state
AAML standard, 230
ALI standard, 229
Arkansas relocation standard, 225
California relocation standard, 199, 228-229
Colorado relocation standard, 225
constitutional right to travel, 218-220
debate over impact on child, 220-222
Florida relocation standard, 226
joint physical custody, 230-231
military service, 228-229
New Jersey relocation standard, 227
New York relocation standard, 225
no presumptive right to relocate, 226
Oklahoma relocation standard, 222-223
Oregon relocation standard, 226
Pennsylvania relocation standard, 226-227
Presumptions, 224-225
Texas relocation standard, 223
right to travel, 218-220
social science debate over impact of relocation on child, 220-222
trends among states on relocation, 222-223
res judicata, 191-193-194, 209
smoking, 210-211
state as third party to modification actions, 190
UCCJEA. *See* Uniform Child Custody Jurisdiction Enforcement Act
UMDA, 191, 193-194, 196
Visitation, unwarranted denial, 205-206
Multiethnic Placement Act (MEPA). *See* Adoption

Necessaries. *See* Alimony

Parental Kidnapping Prevention Act (PKPA)
- continuing jurisdiction, 247
- history, 239-240, 242, 245
- effect of, 246-247
- exclusive, continuing jurisdiction, 247, 250
- home state defined, 252
- international application, 255
- modification actions, 253-254
- Native Americans, 254-255
- preemption, 247-248
- prioritization, 249-250
- private right of action, 248
- state requirements, 245-246

Parenting Coordinator
- defined, 667
- legislative authorization, 667-668
- practice trends, 668-669
- role of, 666-667

Parenting time. *See* Visitation

Paternity (parentage)
- common law, 494
- discrimination, 495
- equitable parent doctrine, 513-514
- estoppel, 515
- genetic testing under UPA, 510
- history of disparate treatment, 494-495
- inheritance claims, 496-497
- marital presumption, 501
- Omnibus Budget Reconciliation Act of 1993, 505
- paternity by estoppel, 515
- Personal Responsibility and Work Opportunity Reconciliation Act of (PRWORA), 505
- presumptions of paternity—rebutting under UPA, 507, 515
- putative fathers consent to adoption, 502
- putative fathers rights, 499
- registration (termination notification), 512-513
- right to counsel, 500
- same-sex partners, 516
- social security benefits, 497-498
- standing to rebut marital presumption, 501-502
- Uniform Parentage Act (UPA), 505-507, 513
- voluntary acknowledgment of paternity, 508
- wrongful death claims, 495-496

Polygamy
- justification, 59
- Old Testament view, 58-59
- Religious examples where tolerated, 58
- Supreme Court view, 58, 142-143
- void marriage, 23, 96

Premarital contracts (antenuptial/prenuptial)
- abandoning a contract, 455
- alimony, waiving, 436-439
- ALI principles, 426-427
- Attorney—right to, 433-435
- burden of proof, 440-443
- capacity to sign contract, 455
- child support, waiving, 435-436
- common statutory criteria, 427-428
- consideration, 426, 442-443, 455
- differences between premarital and commercial agreements, 425
- divorce, use of when, 422-423
- duress, 432-433
- duty to disclose, 428-430
- fair and reasonable test when executed, 439
- history, 420-422
- imposing marital duties and obligations, 440
- limiting judicial discretion, 420
- marital duties and obligations imposed, 440
- Pennsylvania view (minority), 423-424
- presumptions, 443
- procedural fairness when executed, 451
- second look doctrine, 453-454
- strict contract principles applied, 423-424
- substantively fair when executed (unconscionable), 451, 454
- tax planning, 455
- Uniform Premarital Agreement Act, 426
- unconscionable contracts, 452-453
- uses today, 424-425
- voluntary executed, 430-431
- waiving alimony, 436-439
- waiving child and spousal support, 435-436
- waiving custody, 435-436

Professional responsibility
- arbitrator, lawyer acting as, 682
- attorney as conflict resolver, 680-681
- collaborative lawyers, 681-682
- collection of past due judgment, 676
- communicating with clients, 677
- conflicts of interest, 672
- contingent fees, 676
  - exceptions, 676
- dual representation, 672-673
- ethical caution for attorneys in mediation, etc., 681

informing client, 677-678
informed consent, 677
mediator, lawyer acting as, 682
new role for attorney
collaborative law, 681-682
conflict resolver, 680-681
ethical issues, 68
mediation, 682
prior representation, 672
pro bono representation, need for, 679
pro se litigants, 678-679
representing both parties, 672-673
self-represented clients, 678-679
attorney conduct with, 679
sexual relationships with clients
existing relationships exception, 674
generally, 673-674
Model Rules of Professional Conduct, 673-674
preexisting sexual relationship, 674
special concerns in family cases, 674
Property division
advanced degrees valued, 402-405
active appreciation defined, 385-386
ALI recommendations, 395-396
bankruptcy, 409
community property theories of property division
death of partner, 380
partnership theory, 379-380
separate property distribution theory, 378-380
equitable distribution theory
conduct reducing value of property, 382
marriage as a joint enterprise, 381
non-marital property exclusion, 381
overcoming marital presumption, 381-382
presumption of equal division, 381
source of funds theory, 382-383
source of funds theory not applied
transmutation theory, 383-384
fault linked to property distribution, 387-388
goodwill, 409
income from non-marital property, 395
military benefits, 402
passive appreciation defined, 386-387
pension benefits
generally, 398
non-vested, 398-399
vested, 398
personal injury awards, 300, 405-408
premarital agreements, 409
professional licenses and degrees
majority view, 403-405
minority view, 402-403
Qualified Domestic Relations Order (QDRO), 396-398
social security, 400
stock dividends, 387
tax treatment; same-sex marriages, 410-411
tracing mingled property, 384-385
transmutation, 383-384
Uniform Marital Property Act (UMPA), 395
Uniform Marriage and Divorce Act (UMDA), 394-395
valuing nonmarital assets (home), 385
workers' compensation awards, 405-408

Qualified Domestic Relations Order (QDRO). *See* Property division

Reproductive technology. *See* Assisted reproduction
Right to counsel
child's right in custody matters, 180
contempt proceedings, 331, 500, 587
indigent right to counsel (child support), 331
paternity — right to council, 500
premarital contracts (drafting), 433-435

Same-sex couples
adoption of child born to partner, 558-559
assisted reproduction, 550-551, 558-559
biological mother seek relationship with child, 558
Bowers v. Hardwick, 76-77
capacity to marry, 18-19
civil unions, 77-79
common benefits — civil unions, 77-79
Defense of Marriage Act (DOMA), 63-64, 74-75, 77, 83, 410-411, 716-717
divorce recognition, 153-154
domestic partners, 79-80
joint bankruptcy return, 75
Lawrence v. Texas, 13, 76-77, 124-125, 460-461
Massachusetts limits recognition, 13, 82
New York recognizes foreign marriage, 559
out-of-state recognition of, 84-85, 153-155, 716-717
rejecting legal recognition of legal marriage, 717
religious perspective, 72-74
states allowing, 82-83
tax treatment, 410-411

Termination of parental rights
- adjudication
  - right to counsel, 618-619
  - standard of proof—generally, 618
  - standard of proof, ICWA, 616
- foster home placement, 616-617
- grounds, 616
- Indian Child Welfare Act, 616
- legal consequences of termination, 617-618
- parental right to privacy, 596
- reasonable reunification efforts, 615-617
- right to counsel, 618-619
- standard of proof, 618

Transsexual relationships
- generally,, 85

Uniform Adoption Act
- generally, 538

Uniform Child Custody Jurisdiction Enforcement Act (UCCJEA)
- Canada, 256
- continuing exclusive jurisdiction, 250
- emergency jurisdiction, 252-253
- exclusive continuing jurisdiction, 250
- history, 240-242
- home state, 252
- inconvenient forum, 251
- international application of, 255-256
- losing exclusive continuing jurisdiction, 250-251
- modification hearing, 253-254
- Native Americans, PKPA, 254-255
- no home state, 252
- Parental Kidnapping Prevention Act (PKPA), 245-248
  - continuing jurisdiction theory, 250
  - private right of action, 248
- prioritization of jurisdiction, 249
- scope of, 249
- status theory of jurisdiction, 242-244
- Supreme Court breeds uncertainty, 240-241
- traditional view of custody jurisdiction, 240
- UCCJA, 244-245
- waiving subject matter, 249

Uniform Collaborative Law Act
- generally, 665-666

Uniform Marriage and Divorce Act (UMDA)
- adoption of states by, 348-349
- age to marry, 20, 107-108
- alimony (maintenance), 349
  - 2-step process to determine, 349
  - Death of recipient, 373
  - unconscionability standard, 361-362
- annulment (relation back), 106
- attorney representing child (custody), 180
- capacity to marry, 19, 119
- change in custody, 209
- child advocate (attorney), 180
- children born to void marriage, 120
- child preference for parent (custody), 178-179
  - procedures for obtaining, 179
- child support, 297
  - guidelines, 298
  - obligor's death, 316
  - post-death modification, 317
- cohabitation (custody), 181-182, 209
- court ordered report (custody), 188
- custody, 176, 191
- death of supporting parent, 316
- disabilities of parent (custody), 178
- effective date of marriage license, 21-22
- emancipation of minor, 316
- grounds for divorce, 147
- history
  - no-fault divorce, 147-148
- immoral conduct (custody), 208-209
- integration into home (custody), 207
- irretrievable breakdown of marriage theory, 148
- license to marry, 3-day waiting period, 21-22
- income received during marriage, 395
- medical exams, 29
- minimum age to marry, 20, 107-108
- modification of custody, 195-196
  - affidavit practice, 196
- moratorium (custody), 193-194
- no-fault divorce, 147-148
- non-modification agreements, 364
- property disposition upon divorce, 394
  - alternative approaches, 395
- proxy marriage, 50
- putative spouse statutes, 36
- restricting visitation, 276, 284
- solemnization, 23
- time barriers in re custody, 193-194
- unconscionable (premarital agreements), 452, 453
- visitation (parenting time), 274
  - restricting, 276, 284

Uniform Parentage Act (UPA)
- alimony, waiving, 439

genetic testing, 510
legal right to child, 516
maternity, establishing, 515
overview, 505-506
paternity, establishing, 506
presumptions, 506
rebuttal presumptions, 507
registration for notice of termination, 512, 534
time limits on determining parentage, 512-513
Uniform Premarital Agreement Act (UPAA)
burden of proof, 440-442
compared to ALI, 427
generally, 426
independent counsel, 424-425
unconscionability, 452-453
voluntarily executed, 430-431
waiving alimony, 436

Violence Against Women Act
generally, 240
Visitation and parenting time
ALI provisions, 275
burden on parent contesting, 276
child abuse, 277
enforcing visitation (parenting time)
compensatory parenting time, 282
contempt, 281-282
wishes of the child, 282
withholding child support, 282
grandparent visitation
history, 285
Troxel v. Granville, 285-286
incarceration, 276
lesbian and gay (biological) parent visitation, 290-291
modifying visitation or parenting time UMDA
parents by estoppel and de facto parents, 291-292
reasonable visitation, 274
restrictions on parenting time, 276-277
standards for denying or limiting visitation
alcohol and substance abuse, 277
child abduction, 278
child abuse and domestic violence, 277
cohabitation, 278
gay or lesbian parent, 278
religious differences, 278-279
stepparent visitation, 289-290
UMDA
modifying existing order, 284
reasonable visitation, 274

Welfare Reform Act of
generally, 340